DIPLOMAT IN BERLIN

1933-1939

Ambassador Lipski after presenting his credentials to Hitler, November, 1934

Papers and Memoirs of

Józef Lipski, Ambassador of Poland

DIPLOMAT

IN BERLIN

1933-1939

Edited by Wacław Jędrzejewicz

Columbia University Press 1968 *New York and London*

Wacław Jędrzejewicz, former Polish army officer, diplomat, and
cabinet member, is now Professor Emeritus
of Wellesley and Ripon colleges.

Preface

AMBASSADOR Józef Lipski's archives are on file in New York at the Józef Piłsudski Institute of America for Research in the Modern History of Poland. They consist of his reports (and also those of other Polish ambassadors); instructions received from Warsaw; various kinds of documents; notes; press clippings; texts of his articles, lectures, and speeches; correspondence; and a few photos.

Judging from the arrangement of these archives, as well as from remarks made to his family and closest friends, it is obvious that Lipski intended one day to publish these materials, possibly in the form of memoirs. His untimely death in Washington on November 1, 1958, forestalled this plan.

Mrs. Anna Maria Lipski, the Ambassador's widow, and I have undertaken to carry out the Ambassador's intentions. Through an orderly arrangement of his documents, we have presented the historical sequence of events between Poland and Germany during the years 1933–39 leading up to the outbreak of World War II.

This book is by no means intended to be a history of Polish-German relations. However, to those engaged in research in this period, it might well serve as another source for a definitive scholarly work. Lipski's reports, reminiscences, notes, and articles, as well as the instructions received by him, give the historian a rich reservoir of facts pertaining to Polish-German relations during the six years prior to the war, at the same time drawing a realistic picture of the man to whom the Polish government entrusted the responsible post of ambassador to Germany.

In our opinion, one of the major contributions of this publication is that it presents the day-to-day work and activities of a Polish diplomat at a key post. Lipski's archives thus represent a valuable contribution to the general history of diplomacy. They give his thoughts, intentions, and actions, and his communications with his government. These are all the more interesting since they were written, not *post factum* when events might easily be accommodated to fit final results, but rather in the *statu nascendi* of political moves often pregnant with fateful consequences. From his reports we can learn at firsthand what was known to the Polish Ambassador in Berlin, how he acted, what his intentions were, what conclusions he drew from the situation, and how he informed his government. In this respect, the material accumulated here might well serve a scholarly purpose for both present and future diplomats.

This book contains 163 selected documents. In addition, there are numerous handwritten notes, such as a detailed account of Lipski's conversation with Piłsudski on November 5, 1933. These notes are invaluable for a historian, since they illustrate the political climate connected with the events. There are also articles published in Polish in London during the years 1947–51. Unknown to many because of the language barrier, they are presented here for the first time in English translation. It seemed important to include these articles because in them the author repeatedly refers to his reminiscences, opinions, and comments on the trend of events, in which he often played a leading role. Some small stylistic alterations have been introduced; and when the author gave a résumé of his reports or of instructions received, this has been replaced by the full texts of the documents referred to, thus increasing the historical value of the articles.

In preparing the papers for publication, special care was taken to supply them with commentaries, indicating the special circumstances within which a particular event took place. It was assumed that the reader has some acquaintance with Polish-German relations. Thus, the commentaries are as concise as possible, containing the minimum of what must be known to understand the text of a particular document. The editor's commentaries are given in reduced type, to distinguish them from Ambassador Lipski's texts and from other documents.

In the selected bibliography, only basic works are cited, some of which were published after the author's death.

Lipski was an eminent diplomat of the Polish Foreign Service. He was very well educated, with a splendid command of foreign languages. With years of service in Polish legations in London and Paris, and with long service in the Ministry of Foreign Affairs in Warsaw as chief of the Western Department, he was especially well prepared and well qualified for the position of envoy and, later, ambassador in Berlin. With the easing of Polish-German relations in the middle of 1933, he envisaged for Poland a long-range policy of neighborliness with Germany, based on the nonaggression declaration of January 26, 1934, of which he was the main author and architect. He was deeply convinced that this declaration was the basis for continuing friendly Polish-German relations, mutually advantageous to both countries. He firmly supported the policy of the Polish government at that time: to side with neither the Germans against Soviet Russia within the framework of the Anti-Comintern Pact, nor with Russia against Germany. After the Munich Agreement in the autumn of 1938, when Ribbentrop pushed forward territorial claims against Poland, Lipski decided that his mission of maintaining good relations with Germany had failed and he presented his resignation to Foreign Minister Beck. It was refused. He tried again in the spring of 1939, and again it was refused. Thus, he remained at his post to the bitter end: September 1, 1939.

Lipski was a man of peace; he believed in peace and could see no profit for Germany in a war. However, to him as to nearly all of his contemporary statesmen, the character of the man with whom he had to negotiate—Adolf Hitler—remained a dark enigma until the spring of 1939.

Along with all other Western diplomats, Lipski believed that *pacta sunt servanda*. He believed that agreements concluded in good faith should be respected and that they should be altered only by the common consent of the states concerned. Hitler did not see things in this way, although this became fully apparent only on March 15, 1939, after the occupation of Prague. Correct evaluations of Hitler, unfortunately, began to appear only after the outbreak of the war.

Here are Hitler's words, as quoted by Hermann Rauschning:

"I am ready to underwrite and undersign anything. I will do whatever can render my politics easier. I am ready to guarantee all frontiers and to conclude—with whomever and whenever—nonaggression pacts and pacts of friendship. . . . Why should I not settle agreements today in good faith and break them tomorrow in cold blood—if the future of the German people is at stake."

Possibly the best characterization of Hitler was given by Sir Nevile Henderson, ambassador of Great Britain in Berlin, writing later during the war:

"In the midst of one of his tirades against the Poles in August, 1939, I interrupted Hitler to observe that he seemed to forget how useful the agreement with Piłsudski had been to him in 1934. Hitler's answer was that it had never been of any use whatsoever, and that it had merely made him unpopular with his own people. He had a phenomenal capacity for self-deception, and was able to forget everything which he had ever said or done in the past, if it no longer suited his present or future purpose to remember it. . . . Verbal or written engagements had absolutely no meaning for him once they ceased to contribute to the greater glory of Adolf Hitler and of Germany. They were merely provisional documents to be torn up whenever it suited him: whereupon he would then offer another agreement in exchange."

This was the man with whom Lipski had to deal—a man whose actions were often unpredictable and irrational. So, after six years of trying to maintain peace, when the first German bombs fell on Poland there was only one course of action left for the Polish Ambassador: to put on a soldier's uniform and join the ranks of the Polish forces.

And that is what Józef Lipski did.

Wacław Jędrzejewicz

Acknowledgments

THIS BOOK was intended to be written by my late husband, Ambassador Józef Lipski. Many diplomats and politicians had rendered controversial opinions concerning his mission in Berlin in the fateful years 1933–39, and he was preparing to give them an answer, utilizing the extensive material in his papers. Premature death frustrated this intention to write his memoirs. The urgent need for the publication of such a book, however, survived him. That book now finally appears thanks to the selflessly devoted and highly conscientious efforts of its editor, Professor Wacław Jędrzejewicz, who knew so well the two major figures of this book, Ambassador Józef Lipski and Foreign Minister Józef Beck.

The biographical sketch of Józef Lipski by Alexander Janta attempts to place in its true historical perspective the diplomatic career and professional skill of Poland's ambassador to the key diplomatic post of Berlin in the trying and fateful years preceding and up to the eve of World War II. Janta's biographical effort has been facilitated by recollections of three persons close to Józef Lipski at different stages of his life: Andrzej Lipski, Paweł Starzeński, and Henryk de Malhomme.

I am indebted to Andrew W. Cordier, dean of the School of International Affairs at Columbia University, for a grant to complete the translation and preparation of the manuscript. I also extend thanks to Professor Henry L. Roberts for his earlier encouragement. My gratitude goes to Professor Philip E. Mosely, of the European Institute at Columbia University, for his words of high esteem, reckoning Ambassador Józef Lipski as "truly one of the outstanding minds of the interwar period." Thanks are extended to Professor Zbigniew Brzezinski, director of the Research Institute on Communist Affairs at Columbia University, for his assistance, advice, and support in promoting this project, which in his opinion "will be a major and significant contribution to our understanding of the antecedents of World War II." Professor Joseph Rothschild, of the Department of Public Law and Government at Columbia University, is thanked for his advice and continuous assistance.

The Józef Piłsudski Institute of America for Research in the Modern History of Poland generously gave access to its archives and made a financial contribution.

To Bernard Gronert and William F. Bernhardt, of Columbia University Press, I express my appreciation for their efforts in the preparation of the manuscript for the printer. Thanks also are extended to Miss Pauline C. Ramsey, librarian and bibliographer, for her guidance and technical assistance and for compiling the bibliography; to Mrs. Maria de Görgey for rewriting the English translation of the manuscript, technically adjusting and copying; and to Mr. Henry Archacki, who has diligently and artistically prepared the photographs.

Mrs. Józef Lipski

Józef Lipski, a Biographical Note

WORLD WAR II exploded in his hands. This is no mere figure of speech in the case of Józef Lipski, the Polish ambassador to Hitler's Germany in the years preceding 1939, and through the days immediately before the German assault on that fateful September 1.

Yet the work of the man, whose difficult mission in Berlin ended in catastrophe, was sincerely and thoroughly dedicated to the preservation of peace.

In World War I he had escaped military obligation thanks to the fortunate, though skillfully engineered, coincidence of being then a student in neutral Switzerland. For young Poles from the Poznanian area, the overwhelming majority of whom wished victory for the Entente, the opportunity to avoid conscription, which German citizenship imposed on them, was a welcome one.

When World War I was over and Germany defeated, Lipski immediately joined the newly organized Polish Foreign Service, eventually to rise, thanks to his linguistic talents, his skill as negotiator, his personal affability, and a particularly keen knowledge of German problems, to one of the crucial positions of Polish diplomatic relations, that of ambassador in Berlin.

Now, on the eve of World War II, with the failure of Lipski's mission already certain, Göring, with whom the Polish Ambassador succeeded in developing a closer personal relationship than with the other associates of the German dictator, in a parting interview expressed regret at having to lead his Luftwaffe against Poland. This statement Lipski countered by saying that in such case he would join the Polish Army to shoot at the invading planes. In the light of the Polish Ambassador's known prowess in gunning flying birds, with which Göring, being more than once his host at official shooting parties, was well acquainted, the retort appears in its proper meaning.

In a small but significant way, Lipski's prediction was realized.

After a perilous journey through bombed and burning Poland, to give a last report to his government, he eventually made his way to France. Though forty-five years old and in a physical condition which would have gotten him easy exemption from military service, the now former Ambassador nevertheless enlisted as a volunteer, started his cadet schooling as a private, endured harsh training and highly uncomfortable quarters in the winter barracks of a Brittany boot camp, and at the earliest opportunity confronted the Germans, as promised a gun in hand. The machine-gun unit he commanded is credited with shooting down a German plane.

This phase was short-lived and ended in a new defeat that took place on the front line of the Polish Grenadier Division fighting a rear-guard action against overwhelming German forces in Lorraine and in the Vosges mountains. The time was June, 1940.

The rapid French collapse forced the Poles to disband their forces, or what remained of them, after fighting to the bitter end. Many, the author of this biographical note among them, fell into German hands. Sergeant Lipski, showing considerable stamina and good tactical judgment, managed to slip through German lines at the head of a group of three fellow soldiers, disguised as French civilians. He would have made a prize prisoner in German hands, and better than anybody he was aware of the asset his capture would have represented for the Goebbels propaganda circus.

He was therefore all the more strongly determined to deny the enemy so manifest an advantage. The supreme test came in Besançon, where he walked boldly into the office of the commanding German officer at the railway station and talked him into giving the group of fugitives Lipski headed a permit for free passage despite the restrictions of movement imposed by the German curfew.

In view of the fact that his face was often photographed in Germany over the previous years as Polish Ambassador in Berlin, hence presumably familiar, the achievement assumes its rightful place. Lipski himself would describe it later as possibly the most successful negotiation he ever conducted with the Germans, one that really worked.

It worked so well that shortly he was able to reach London, where a promotion to first lieutenant, the Cross of Valor with three clusters, and the Croix de Guerre from the Free French awaited him, together with an assignment as political counselor to the then Polish commander in chief and prime minister, General Sikorski.

Here again his German experience was of prime usefulness, and not only to the Poles.

In the growing literature of memoirs of foreign diplomats and observers of the Nazi power-play which led to World War II, the memoirs of Lipski, which should stand next to those of Sir Nevile Henderson, André François-Poncet, or Robert Coulondre, are alas missing. What remains, however, are his papers, a primary source to illuminate a tragic period of European history. They contain, by implication, the portrait of a man who carried the gruesome burden of what now seems to have been a hopeless mission in a Europe divided against itself and falling victim piecemeal to German cunning and German aggression.

The memoirs of another ambassador in Berlin at the outset of the Nazi period, André François-Poncet, show us Lipski as a man who was "silent, restrained, and aloof." Meetings of some foreign representatives, which the French Ambassador called "information clearings," used to take place in an elegant Berlin restaurant, Horcher, well known among the gourmets of the German capital. Lipski, on the verge of signing the nonaggression declaration with Hitler, refused to discuss this forthcoming development. Such were his instructions, and in addition he was well aware that Horcher was an easy and professionally manned listening post for the German secret service. Any indiscretion on his part would have immediately been known by the Germans, thus reducing the chances of success for the difficult arrangement in the making.

Conditions of a totalitarian system made the necessity of avoiding such type of diplomatic gatherings and contacts painfully clear.

Lipski preferred to remain aloof and, according to the nature of his assignment, though not of the nature of his outgoing, convivial disposition, to seek instead a way of coming close to the men responsible for Germany's future course. They in turn subjected his life, his mind, and his educational and professional preparation for the task he was given to perform to a very searching test. He had, indeed, a background made as if by order for the role that he was called to play in Berlin. He was born on June 5, 1894, in Breslau (the Polish, much older, name being Wrocław), the capital of Lower Silesia, a city of German pride and prosperity but still permeated with historically Polish roots. Young Lipski was the heir to a name and a family tradition of strong Polish resistance to the attempts at Germanization. In the nineteenth century this pressure for Germanization had assumed both cultural and economic forms against the Polish majority in German-annexed territories. Józef Lipski's great-grandfather, for instance, was a leader in the national and democratic people's uprising of 1848 and subsequently was for a time held prisoner in Berlin's Moabit. The father, in turn, a successful manager of the family estate in the province of Poznania, stood in the forefront of Polish resistance to the Kulturkampf initiated by Bismarck which aimed at undermining not only the cultural foundation of Polish life in the provinces taken by Prussia as a result of the eighteenth-century partitions but, principally, the roots of Polish economic strength. Stubborn resistance against the so-called colonization policy, which aimed at depriving Poles of the estates and farms they had cultivated for generations, was not only part of the Lipski family tradition but was also a hard school of political and economic practicality: survival, both individual and national, being at stake.

Portraits of distinguished forebears adorned the walls of the old manor at Lewków, which was the future ambassador's family place. Among them were Andrzej Lipski, bishop of Cracow and crown chancellor during the reign of Sigismund III in the early seventeenth century, and another historical personality, Cardinal Jan Alexander Lipski, who one hundred years later was Polish Primate in the time of the Saxon kings.

The high school which the boy attended had been founded by his great-grandfather to counteract German encroachments; by now, however, the teaching was all in German. In consequence, Polish language, literature, and history had to be not only taught, but lived, at home. The mother, from another Lipski family, prominent in the eastern borderlands of Poland, was as deeply religious as she was cultivated; as kind as demanding; speaking seven languages and managing the large household with a firm grip. She exercised a strong influence in the development of the two boys she raised—Józef and an elder brother Jan—tending with equal care the 400 beehives for which the family estate was famous.

The product of this system of education was multilingual, possessing equal fluency in Polish and in German, a solid foundation of Greek and Latin, an excellent command of French, and the beginnings of an initiation into the language of Shakespeare. But most important was to be his intimate knowledge of the two national worlds, that of Poland and that of Germany, historically intertwined, geographically overlapping, and yet, except for a few periods of enlightened liberalism, such as the first part of the nineteenth century, juxtaposed in perennial and at times cruel conflict.

One of the possibilities of countering German pressure lay in the cultivation by the Polish gentry and intelligentsia of a lively Frankophilic tradition, which dated from the seventeenth century when a Polish princess became queen of France while French princesses more than once were queens of Poland. Later and more particularly through the experience of the nineteenth-century emigration, centered in Paris, which provided visionary leadership to the subjugated nation, every educated Pole came to speak French and to hope to go "Ouest," eventually. This penchant also characterized Józef Lipski still in his teens.

The threat of an imminent war in which Poles living on all sides of the hostile camps could be forcibly involved prompted the decision to send the boy away for his higher education. In consequence, during the years of World War I, Lipski completed his studies of law and economics at the University of Lausanne in Switzerland. He graduated in social sciences and gained a broad international outlook on the problems and the place of his people in the now ravaged and rapidly changing Europe.

A new Poland emerged from the carnage thanks to the defeat of all three partitioning powers.

The Lausanne student, whose interest in political matters grew keen, was now ready to assume service in the foreign affairs of the newly founded state. In December, 1918, he was named secretary to the London mission of the Polish National Committee, whose headquarters during World War I had been in Paris. At the very outset of his diplomatic career Lipski was instrumental in preparing Paderewski's historical journey to Poland on board a British cruiser. The arrival of this man, who was a living legend among his people, became the spark provoking an uprising in the western German-held territories of Poland to bring about their joyous reunion with the rest of the newly liberated country.

After serving in London and Paris, with a brief interlude in the Polish Legation of Berlin, Józef Lipski at thirty-two became the head of the Western Department of the Foreign Office in Warsaw. This position kept him intimately acquainted with all aspects of European politics and brought him close to many leading personalities of the period.

When Mrs. Woodrow Wilson and Bernard Baruch came to Poland in 1928 for the unveiling of President Wilson's monument in Poznań, Józef Lipski accompanied them as official representative of the Polish government during their entire visit.

Already prior to his appointment in Warsaw, and later, in his capacity as the head of the Western Department, he played a conspicuous role in a number of international conferences, representing Poland at Locarno in 1925, The Hague in 1929 and 1930, and Lausanne in 1932. Signs of danger in the political development in Germany which he observed were the source of more than one alarm, especially in view of the lack of Western determination and solidarity to resist Hitler's campaign to undo the Versailles settlement. It was the recognition of this bitter reality which led to Poland's nonaggression declaration with Germany, signed on January 26, 1934. Lipski's role in negotiating this declaration brought about his selection by Marshal Piłsudski on November 1, 1934, to be in the future the first Polish ambassador in Berlin, and hence to be the man to deal directly with Hitler.

At the outset of his mission, Lipski's goal was a policy of long-range improvement in traditionally strained neighborly relations. He did his best to serve this interest, with the understanding that such was to the advantage of both partners.

This ultimately abortive mission must be viewed against the accumulating evidence, painfully clear to those responsible for Poland's foreign policy, that it was not possible to count on Western solidarity in case of German aggression. The Western alliance was not a reliable foundation on which Poland could base its security. Poland was left alone with two dynamic and potentially aggressive neighbors, and in case of a showdown, declarations to the contrary notwithstanding, it would have to face the brunt of German military power.

The moment that the chances for success of his essentially peaceful mission were shattered by the collision course on which Hitler had embarked, Lipski asked to be relieved of his Berlin post. Three times Warsaw rejected his resignation. Not that further illusions were harbored, but because even now in the gallop toward a European catastrophe, Poland saw no better man to represent its peaceful determination— but at the same time its firmness to resist—than Lipski.

It was an irony that in the year of the outbreak of war Lipski became dean of the Berlin diplomatic corps. He had endured longer than any of his foreign colleagues the unthankful, nerve-racking, and—toward the end—heartbreaking task of representing his country in the Nazi capital. Exposed more often than any foreign diplomat to direct personal contacts with Hitler, he found himself at the decisive moment in a situation in which the latter, already determined on war, deliberately avoided another confrontation with the Polish Ambassador.

Once the war erupted, Lipski continued to serve, as already shown, first as a soldier, later as political adviser to the Polish government-in-exile. In this capacity he accompanied General Sikorski, the prime minister and commander in chief, on his visit to the United States in 1942, renewing many contacts with prominent Americans whom he knew from his days of Warsaw and Berlin.

After the war, with the city of his birth back within the borders of Poland and his family estate nationalized by the Stalin-imposed government that received the recognition of the Western allies after Yalta, Lipski became the unofficial representative of Poles-in-exile at Washington, D.C. He established himself in the minds of a number of American political personalities, whom he contacted or who contacted him to discuss postwar developments in Europe, as a man of restrained wisdom and carefully measured judgment.

The former Polish Ambassador in Berlin passed away in Washington, D.C., on November 1, 1958. He was buried at the capital's Mount Olivet cemetery, the only inscription on the stone that marks his grave being, in addition to his name: Wrocław 1894 Washington 1958—a life span encompassing one of the most tragic periods of human history.

There is no finer tribute paid him than a passage in the book of Carl J. Burckhardt, a Swiss professor and diplomat, who as a former high commissioner of the League of Nations in the free city of Danzig was singularly well placed to observe and judge the behavior of those who were directly involved in the mounting drama of Hitler's attempt at conquering the world. In his book *Ma Mission à Danzig,* Burckhardt said:

"In the years preceding the war few men occupied a post more thorny than the ambassador of Poland in Berlin, Józef Lipski. In the framework of his instructions he acted with an admirable dignity and firmness; he was, without question, since 1933 the man of the German-Polish *détente,* one of the artisans of the agreement of January 26, 1934, an efficient negotiator in all the later attempts at a rapprochement between the two countries. . . . German he knew as well as his own language. He was certainly, as I have said before, one of the best-informed ambassadors in the Berlin of the epoch, nobody knowing as well as he did the always changing constellations of personalities directing the Third Reich.

"He went far in his concessions and his offers, he took account of the instability and the susceptibilities of the Führer, he flattered his immense pride, always restless, always seeking applause. . . . but when the sovereign rights of Poland and the honor of his country were at stake, he showed himself as firm as a rock, and at the end of his mission destined to failure, he acted in terms of one sovereign power toward another power, with an always measured and controlled rigor, as few knew how to do."

For those who knew Józef Lipski, no truer words have been spoken.

Alexander Janta

Contents

Illustrations follow p. 354

Analytical Table of Documents

DIPLOMAT IN BERLIN

1933–1939

Abbreviations

A.A.   Auswärtiges Amt

British Blue Book   Great Britain. Foreign Office. *Documents Concerning German-Polish Relations and the Outbreak of Hostilities between Great Britain and Germany on Sept. 3, 1939*

DGFP   Germany. Auswärtiges Amt. *Documents on German Foreign Policy, 1918–1945.* Series C: 1933–37. Series D: 1937–45

Diariusz   Szembek, *Diariusz i teki Jana Szembeka, 1935–1945.* Vol. I (1935), Vol. II (1936)

German White Book   Germany. Auswärtiges Amt. *Zweites Weisbuch der deutschen Regierung: Dokumente über die Entwickelung der deutsch-polnischen Beziehungen und die Ereignisse von 1933 bis zur Gegenwart*

Journal   Szembek, *Journal, 1933–1939*

Livre jaune   France. Ministère des Affaires Étrangères. *Documents diplomatiques, 1938–1939*

Polish White Book   Poland. Ministerstwo Spraw Zagranicznych. *Official Documents Concerning Polish-German and Polish-Soviet Relations, 1933–1939*

Shadow over the Polish-French Alliance[1]
1929

FOR CENTURIES, Poland and France were linked by a spontaneous and genuine friendship, deeply rooted in both countries. These mutual bonds of sentiment persisted, notwithstanding various (more or less successful) fluctuations of the political alliance. In its inaugural period, during Poincaré's premiership in France (1922–24), the alliance developed as a useful instrument for both partners, but difficulties set in with the initiation of the subsequent Franco-German rapprochement. Thus, Locarno [2] loosened the impact (that is, the automatic applicability) of the alliance; the Thoiry policy [3] smoothed the path for the Young Plan [4] and hence for the premature evacuation of the Rhineland,[5] which was decided upon during the First Hague Conference in August, 1929. Acting on the sidelines of this conference, the Polish government spared no efforts to restore the automatic applicability of the Franco-Polish alliance and avoid appellatory recourse to the League of Nations. From the time of the Locarno agreements, contradictory opinions had formed the basis for optional interpretations in this latter respect.

Despite increasing hostility toward Poland in Germany after the summer of 1930, and an upsurge of revisionist propaganda against the Polish frontiers, the West indulged in further concessions to Germany. German war indemnities were canceled at the Lausanne Conference in

[1] Published in *Bellona* (London), 1957, Nos. 1–2.

[2] The Locarno agreements were signed October 16, 1925.

[3] A conference between Briand and Stresemann was held at Thoiry, September 17, 1926, regarding the settlement of disagreements between France and Germany. Briand demanded an increase in war indemnities; Stresemann, the withdrawal of the Rhineland occupation and an earlier solution of the Saar question, where a plebiscite was to be held in 1935.

[4] The Young Plan was established at a conference of experts, held February 9–June 7, 1929, under the leadership of Owen D. Young. The Young Plan reduced reparations obligations of Germany, as compared with the Dawes Plan. It was approved at the First Hague Conference.

[5] In June, 1930, the Rhineland was finally evacuated by the French Army.

July, 1932, and in December of the same year the Great Powers conceded equality of armaments to Germany.

Poland was absent from all these conferences and meetings of the Western Great Powers, during which crucial decisions vital to its very existence were taken, and could but indirectly influence the trend of events.

After the signing of the Rhineland Pact,[6] with France constrained by the British guarantee, Paris became ever more closely bound to London, yielding to its influence and often to manifest pressure. For Great Britain, Europe's safety (alternatively Great Britain's safety) ended at the Rhine as far as Britain's direct engagements were concerned.

In the political constellation of that time, the Polish alliance was shifted to the background of French foreign policy and its role as an instrument of common action toward German problems became restricted.

For France this alliance still retained its value as a reinsurance factor in case of armed conflict with the Reich. A weakening of France's internal situation contributed to its gradual dependence on London's decisions. But public opinion in Poland, where the alliance with its Western confederate was firmly relied upon, was still ignorant of this fact. However, Polish diplomats were better informed and strove to cope with this new turn in the situation. From the moment Hitler came to power and the threat to Poland's interests began to grow, Piłsudski took more energetic steps (the case of the *Wicher* [7] and Westerplatte [8]) in

[6] The Rhineland guarantee pact was the main pact of the Locarno agreements, involving Germany, France, Great Britain, Italy, and Belgium.

[7] Poland had an agreement of *port d'attache* with Danzig which was to expire in 1932, since the Senate of Danzig refused Poland's demands for its extension. According to this agreement, a foreign navy entering the port of Danzig was to be greeted by one of the Polish Navy's warships. In June, 1932, a squadron of British warships was to visit Danzig. Owing to irregularities of the *port d'attache* question, the Polish government called the British government's attention to the untimely date of the visit, but the visit took place nevertheless. Under these circumstances, Marshal Piłsudski ordered the Polish destroyer *Wicher* to enter the Danzig harbor, salute the commander of the British squadron, and depart after an exchange of courtesy visits. The commander of the *Wicher* received an additional order: in case the Polish flag was insulted by Danzig, he was to open fire and bombard targets in the port of Danzig.

The *Wicher* executed the first part of the order and exchanged courtesy visits with the British squadron, thus stressing Polish rights in Danzig. The Danzig Senate lodged a protest, but no demonstration was staged. The *Wicher* case was widely commented upon in Europe and at the then current session of the League of Nations

[8] For Westerplatte, see pp. 53–59.

order to incite the West to common action with Poland. He also wanted to stress his determined attitude to Berlin.

The Polish-French alliance had been concluded during the journey to France of Józef Piłsudski, head of the Polish state, in February, 1921. He was accompanied by General Kazimierz Sosnkowski, minister of war, and Eustachy Sapieha, minister of foreign affairs. This visit took place in a friendly atmosphere of appreciation on the part of the French population and their leaders for the Polish armed victory that had so successfully stopped the Bolshevik invasion of Europe. In the eyes of the French people, Poland was a factor in the security of East Central Europe and a buffer state between Soviet Russia and Germany.

The help extended by France to Poland at the hour of danger contributed to an upsurge of friendship and confidence on the banks of the Vistula. Political motives were also favorable for the establishment of a firm basis of collaboration between the two nations.

The political treaty signed on February 19, 1921, by Sapieha and Briand was supplemented two days later (with reference to Article 3 of the agreement) by a secret military convention.[9] This article stated that, in case of unprovoked aggression against one of the signatory nations, the governments of both countries would be in touch in order to defend their territory and to protect their legitimate interests within the limits defined in the introduction to the agreement. This related to the maintenance of peace in Europe, to security and the defense of the territories of both countries, and to their mutual political and economic interests, through recognition of treaties mutually agreed to, as well as of treaties which might be recognized by both countries in the future.

Other clauses of the political agreement referred to conferences on foreign affairs in the spirit of the treaties and in accordance with the League of Nations Covenant, to mutual economic collaboration, and to consultations prior to entering into new agreements in Central and Eastern Europe.

The validity of the entire agreement, together with the military convention and a 4-million-franc French credit to purchase war material for Poland, was made dependent (according to final Article 5) on the signing of economic treaties, that is, a trade and oil agreement, as well as the

---

[9] For the text of the political agreement, see *Livre jaune,* p. 351. For the military convention, see Wandycz, pp. 394–95.

so-called bilateral agreement (*droits, biens, et intérêts*). The latter agreement was essential for the French concession companies in Poland established before 1914.

The coupling of political and economic matters, when the interests of private French enterprises were also involved, was by its nature hardly conducive to good relations, and often resulted in unnecessary friction.

Obligations under the military convention were far more explicit than under the political treaty. According to its text, if the situation in Germany became a menace—creating a danger of war against one of the countries, and especially in the event of German mobilization or the necessity for common action in order to fulfill the Versailles Treaty— both governments were to "reinforce their war preparedness to the extent of being in the position to give each other rapid assistance and act jointly." In case of German aggression, "both countries pledged to assist each other in accordance with the mutual understanding."

The military convention also contained resolutions in case Poland were threatened or invaded by Soviet Russia. French obligations in that event would be to check the Germans and secure for Poland a supply of war matériel by land and sea. It should be remembered that, at the time of the signing of the treaty, Polish-Soviet war entanglements seemed far more probable than aggression by a Germany defeated by the Allies.

Criticizing the too far-reaching obligations of France toward Poland, Ambassador Noël contended that originally Marshal Foch himself had been against making a military agreement with a country which, in his opinion, still had "ni frontières, ni gouvernement, ni armée." On the basis of clarifications obtained from General Weygand, Noël described the circumstances in which the decision on the alliance was made. This supposedly happened at a reception given at the Elysée Palace by President Millerand for Piłsudski and his entourage. After dinner the French President invited the Polish guests into his study. He was accompanied by Premier Briand and War Minister Barthou, but Marshal Foch and other high French military men were not invited to join in the negotiations at which the bases of the alliance were established.[10] In my opinion this version, taken from Noël's memoirs, calls for deeper scrutiny.

An alliance with a powerful France was of great importance for Poland, strengthening its international position and its position with regard to Germany and Soviet Russia.

[10] Noël, p. 100.

The year 1921 was a year of important achievements for Poland: the alliance with France, a peace treaty with Soviet Russia, and the restoration of a part of Upper Silesia.

However, already in April, 1922, the first clouds gathered on the horizon—forerunners of future dangers. In an atmosphere of total surprise to the participants of the Genoa Conference (April 16, 1922), Walter Rathenau and Chicherin signed the Russo-German friendship treaty at Rapallo.

Owing to difficulties encountered by the negotiation of the economic agreements, the settlement of the alliance with France dragged on for the whole year 1921. A more favorable turn came after the fall of Briand's cabinet—when Poincaré assumed the leadership of the government in January, 1922.

Since I was at that time transferred to our legation in Paris, after three years in London, I had an opportunity, to a certain extent, to observe French affairs at firsthand. I remember how, in his first conversation with Polish Envoy Count Maurycy Zamoyski, the new Prime Minister of France declared that he desired the negotiations to be terminated promptly and that he would give orders to this effect to his subordinates.

Zamoyski, the chief advocate of the Polish-French rapprochement ever since the time of the National Committee,[11] of which he was a member and representative to the French government, left the Quai d'Orsay in an optimistic mood on this occasion, feeling that things were at last moving. And indeed economic agreements were concluded soon afterward, and the alliance thus achieved binding power.

Poincaré was one of the last French statesmen who—following the path of inherited tradition—strove to carry on an independent policy on the continent. The period of his administration was marked by sharp friction with Germany over war indemnities, while London generally took a negative position toward French demands. But Germany was not the sole cause for Poincaré's disagreement with Great Britain; he also opposed Lloyd George's idea of drawing Soviet Russia into European collaboration, with the camouflaged concept of German participation in the economic restoration of the Soviet Union (Genoa Conference). In

[11] The Polish National Committee, formed in Paris in August, 1917, under the leadership of Roman Dmowski, was acknowledged by the Allied countries as representing Poland. In 1919 it represented Poland at the Versailles Peace Conference.

his political designs at that time, Poincaré realized the importance of Poland as an element of peace based upon the support of a powerful France. At the time when French troops occupied the Ruhr coal basin, Polish-French collaboration was developing successfully. During this period Warsaw rejected the secret suggestions of Soviet agents to let the Red Army pass through to Germany in case a revolution broke out in that country, in exchange for a free hand for Poland in East Prussia.

French elections in May, 1924, brought a total defeat of the national bloc in which Poincaré found his support. This closed one of the chapters in the history of independent French policy.

Poincaré, who was at the peak of his power in the international arena after the breakdown of passive resistance in Germany, was taken completely by surprise by the results of the elections. It was generally said that Poincaré was so deeply absorbed in foreign affairs that serious changes which occurred inside France escaped his attention. He was blamed for not having made essential changes in the posts of prefects— *faire valser les prefets,* as the French say—prior to the elections.

Shortly before the elections Poincaré paid a visit to the Polish Legation at 12 Rue Marignan to take part in the ceremony of decorating General Weygand with the Polish order of *Virtuti Militari.* In his conversation with the newly appointed envoy, Alfred Chłapowski, who replaced Maurycy Zamoyski, he seemed to be quite sure of the outcome of the voting. As an aside to this matter, I would like to note that I accompanied Chłapowski to Nancy on May 3, the Polish national holiday. Nancy was considered a fortress of "Poincarism." In his speech, the Polish Envoy referred to Poincaré as a great son of Lorraine. In the evening of the same day, when the Envoy went to a gala performance at the opera with the prefect of Nancy, the vice-prefect took me over to a local café, where by chance I quite unexpectedly became a witness to backstage election intrigues. Several friends and acquaintances of the vice-prefect came to our table asking him for information and guidance. In amazement, I listened to the then current election slogans of the *cartel des gauches,* such as the necessity of collaborating with the Soviets by entering into diplomatic relations with them. When I made a slightly puzzled remark, my host declared with a broad sweep of his arm: "If the boss wins—everything is all right; if he loses, I am covered from the other side." This was the first alarm bell.

The fall of Poincaré had its repercussions on Polish-French relations, which were wrongly accused of being right-wing. The defeat of the national bloc was used in propaganda hostile to Poland. Also, the overthrow of President Millerand by the newly elected parliament was connected with his pro-Polish attitude in 1921. Shortly afterward a manifesto appeared, signed by a number of French politicians of the left wing, against the so-called white terror in Poland—that is, persecutions of the minorities. It was later discovered that these politicians had been misled by "fellow travelers" very active at the time.

In March, 1924, soon after the change of government in France, General Stanisław Haller, chief of the Polish General Staff, came to Paris. During his stay there, Mr. Duca, the foreign minister of Rumania, was also in Paris holding conversations with the French government about the security pact. The chief of his cabinet, Mr. Constantinesco, informed me one day that Duca was receiving alarming news from Bucharest about the movements of Soviet troops on the Rumanian border, and inquired whether we had confirmation of these rumors. In the absence of the envoy, who was in Poland at the time, I arranged a meeting between General Haller and Minister Duca. Upon verification by Warsaw, these rumors proved to be exaggerated and caused by nervous tension on the frontier line. On this occasion I had a long talk with General Haller about his conversations with the [French] Army. He stated at that time that he felt the French military authorities were negatively disposed toward the obligations of the military convention with Poland in regard to the Soviets, and in his opinion no substantial aid could be expected in the event of trouble. The validity of the alliance was therefore limited to Germany only.

A new period in German foreign policy started from the time Stresemann took over the government and strove for closer understanding with the Western Powers. The British government, then represented in Berlin by Lord D'Abernon, a zealous supporter of an understanding with the Reich, played an intermediary role between Berlin and Paris. Financial problems were pushed to the foreground. The German economy, supported by American capital upon the introduction of the Dawes Plan, was making rapid progress. War indemnity payments in favor of France were carried out in accordance with the plan. From the financial field, conversations were shifted to political problems. Negotiations begun in February, 1925, reached the quite substantial form of the

Locarno treaties in October. Polish-French relations suffered a serious setback during these months. Difficulties with which Polish diplomacy had to contend were caused on the one side by the obstinate refusal of the Reich to abandon the idea of territorial revisions in the east, and on the other by the negative attitude of the British government to the extension of its guarantees beyond the Rhine line. The Rhineland Pact—a threat to the Polish-French alliance system—could easily jeopardize the security of Europe.

Count Aleksander Skrzyński, Poland's foreign minister, was at that time very skillfully active on the international chessboard. With remarkable energy and ability he defended the interests of Poland by remaining in constant touch with Paris, and also by dealing directly with London. Through his journey to the United States and his discussion with Chicherin when the latter passed through Warsaw (September 27, 1925), he tried to inject some vigor into Polish foreign policy.

War Minister General Władysław Sikorski, in his concern over the military convention with France, traveled to Paris to put pressure on French military and political authorities (April, 1925). In a letter addressed to the prime minister, Władysław Grabski, dated June 25, 1925, General Sikorski stated his conditions as follows:

1) Maintenance of a demilitarized zone in the Rhineland.

2) Readjustment of the military convention of 1921 to the new situation so as not to affect the *casus foederis*.

3) The conclusion of the Polish-German arbitration agreement simultaneously with the Rhineland Pact, taking territorial matters out of its jurisdiction and obtaining a French guarantee identical with the British guarantee in the West. The Polish-German conflict should therefore be taken to the League of Nations, in case of a breach of the treaty by Germany without armed action. If, however, the Reich should launch an attack, even in the form of an attack perpetrated by a civilian organization, sanctions should follow immediately.

4) Securing for Poland a place on the Council of the League of Nations.

Direct relations between Poland and Germany showed no sign of improvement during the period of talks between the Great Powers in the West. A short-term temporary economic agreement between Poland and Germany, concluded in January, 1925, expired in June of the same year, on the date of the expiration of the negotiated resolution to admit

Polish coal from Upper Silesia to the German market. Efforts made by the Polish government to extend the term of the temporary agreement were unsuccessful, and the import of coal was stopped. Thus a Polish-German tariff war began which was to last until March, 1934. The outflow of German capital from Polish banks was another blow to the financial situation of Poland, which at that time manifested ever more threatening signs of an approaching currency crisis.

The tariff war broke out at a time most undesirable for Poland's foreign policy, when the bulk of her efforts was concentrated on negotiations with the West.

The death of President Friedrich Ebert, in February, 1925, and the struggle for his succession absorbed the attention of the world for some time, focusing it on the internal situation of Germany.

I was in Berlin at the time and had an opportunity to observe from the windows of the British Embassy on the Wilhelmstrasse the funeral procession of the Socialist President of the Weimar Republic. There was no trace in that cortege of the prewar-style German drill-parades. The display was very modest. The late President was fondly remembered by members of the diplomatic corps.

Proffering Hindenburg's candidacy was a rather provocative step as far as the West was concerned. Skrzyński received incredulously my report with regard to the chances of a former commander of the Great World War to win the elections. After the plebiscite of April 26, 1925, international opinion quickly returned to normal and negotiations between Germany and the Great Powers went ahead.

In August, 1925, Skrzyński obtained affirmation from Briand and Austen Chamberlain that Poland would be admitted to the [Locarno] conference. Beneš, who at that time was not encumbered by quarrels with Germany, had an easy task, and he profited automatically from the achievements of his Polish colleague.

As head of the German section at the Polish Ministry of Foreign Affairs, I was present at the Locarno Conference, which led to the conclusion of several interconnected agreements, though the German government formally ignored guarantee pacts signed by France, Poland, and Czechoslovakia. The basis for the understanding was the Rhineland Pact.

Article 2, wherein exemptions from the prohibition of aggression and the launching of war were fixed between Germany, France, and Belgium, was of essential value for the working of the Polish-French alliance. Namely, power could be used

1) in case of defense of one's territory or of a flagrant breach of the provisions concerning the demilitarization of the Rhineland,

2) in the execution of Article 16 of the League of Nations Covenant,

3) in case of freedom of action for members of the League (provided by Article 15, par. 7, of the League of Nations Covenant) if the Council did not pass a unanimous decision (parties engaged in the disagreement being excluded) should armed conflict take place.[12]

Points 2 and 3 above were adjusted to the resolutions of the Covenant of the League of Nations, which in theory foresaw only these two cases of war.

In accordance with the Locarno resolutions, action under the Polish-French alliance was based on these very articles, which were adapted to the guarantee treaties signed by France, Poland, and Czechoslovakia.

Accordingly, allied assistance could immediately be applied in the Polish-French agreement in execution of Article 16 or by Article 15,

[12] Article 15, par. 7, of the Covenant of the League of Nations: "If the Council fails to reach a report which is unanimously agreed to by the members thereof, other than the Representatives of one or more of the parties to the dispute, the Members of the League reserve to themselves the right to take such action as they shall consider necessary for the maintenance of right and justice."

Article 16: "Should any Member of the League resort to war in disregard of its covenants under Articles 12, 13 or 15, it shall *ipso facto* be deemed to have committed an act of war against all other Members of the League, which hereby undertake immediately to subject it to the severance of all trade or financial relations, the prohibition of all intercourse between their nationals and the nationals of the Covenant-breaking State, and the prevention of all financial, commercial or personal intercourse between the nationals of the Covenant-breaking States and the nationals of any other State, whether a Member of the League or not.

"It shall be the duty of the Council in such case to recommend to the several Governments concerned what effective military, naval or air force the Members of the League shall severally contribute to the armed forces to be used to protect the covenants of the League.

"The Members of the League agree, further, that they will mutually support one another in the financial and economic measures which are taken under this Article, in order to minimize the loss and inconvenience resulting from the above measures, and that they will mutually support one another in resisting any special measures aimed at one of their number by the Covenant-breaking State, and that they will take the necessary steps to afford passage through their territory to the forces of any one of the Members of the League which are cooperating to protect the covenants of the League.

"Any Member of the League which has violated any covenant of the League may be declared to be no longer a Member of the League by a vote of the Council concurred in by the Representatives of all the other Members of the League represented thereon."

par. 7, in case of a breach by Germany of the Rhineland Pact's resolutions toward France and the arbitration treaty toward Poland, and in case of unprovoked German aggression against one of these countries.

This intricate legal system, as compared with the previous state of affairs, caused an obvious deterioration in the Polish situation.

In spite of the reference to previously concluded agreements, in the introduction to the Polish-French guarantee treaty, this was not sufficient to safeguard free operation of the military convention. French lawyers might in the future raise the question whether this convention was compatible with the [French] constitution and with the Covenant of the League. At any rate, the operation of the convention was restricted by the fact that the whole Locarno system was based on the Covenant of the League. From the moment Locarno was signed, there were doubts whether the act of assistance was to be dependent on a prior decision by the Council of the League.

In contrast to this dependence on the League, mutual British-French assistance (in accordance with Article 4 of the Rhineland Pact) was to be automatic in case of so-called *agression flagrante,* that is, unprovoked aggression such as crossing the frontier, starting war operations, or marching troops into the demilitarized zone.

Although, during the conference itself, discussion by Germany of territorial problems was avoided and Poland was able to maintain a common front with the West, the difference introduced at Locarno between the western and eastern frontiers of Germany threatened to become the heaviest burden for Poland in the future.

Upon his return to Warsaw, Skrzyński tried to interpret the Locarno agreements in a light most favorable for Poland. He made reference to his close collaboration with Briand and Chamberlain, as well as to the general spirit of understanding prevailing at the negotiations ("the spirit of Locarno").

However, the agreements met with criticism in the Polish Sejm, especially from the right-wing party, which tried to establish with documents that the Rhineland Pact weakened the alliance with France. For propaganda reasons Germany set the acceptance of the *status quo* in the west against the possibilities it envisaged in the east. Skrzyński therefore had to be on the defensive at home and abroad, and he sometimes went too far, creating the illusion that he was not sufficiently aware of the shortcomings of the treaties. It should be said, however, that Skrzyński—at a time so precarious for Poland—succeeded in skillfully adapting himself to the new situation in Western Europe. He moved closer to Great Britain, contributed to a large extent to the abolition of prejudice against Poland still rampant amidst leftists in France, and prepared the ground in Geneva for future attempts by Poland for a permanent place on the Council of the League.

In 1927 the French ambassador in Poland, Jules Laroche, approached the Ministry of Foreign Affairs with a proposition for the readjustment of the alliance agreements of 1921 (political and military) with the Locarno treaties. This project, presented by the French Ambassador in writing, was handed over to me, since I was at that time acting head of the Western Department. He stressed the principle that all agreements, and therefore also the military convention, had to be binding within the limits of the Covenant of the League of Nations, and that therefore the application of *casus foederis* was restricted to cases as foreseen by Article 16 and Article 15, par. 7, of the pact. The French Ambassador questioned the validity of the military convention, which, in his opinion, was not in accordance with the requirements of the French constitution and with the obligations of the League. I remember that Marshal Piłsudski decided that discussions on these subjects should not be undertaken with the French side.

Former French Minister of Foreign Affairs Bonnet wrote about this intervention of Laroche as follows:

"In 1927, on the initiative of our General Staff and under the pretext of bringing certain dispositions of our military convention up to date that had been overridden by events, an attempt was made to proceed toward its revision, with a double aim—to include it within the frame of the Locarno agreements, and to cancel the guarantee given by us to Poland vis-à-vis Russia. On Poland's side the negotiations showed no result." [13]

The mission of Marshal Franchet d'Esperey to Poland in November, 1927, which was connected with this proposition by Laroche, was also aimed at introducing changes in the military convention. In this case too the attitude of Piłsudski was unyielding.

General Kutrzeba [14] told me in London about the circumstances

[13] Bonnet, *Fin d'une Europe*, pp. 134–35.

[14] Gen. Tadeusz Kutrzeba (1886–1947), deputy chief of the General Staff, 1922–27. After 1928 he was commander of the War Academy. In the September campaign of 1939 he was commander of the army "Poznań."

under which he was sent by Marshal Piłsudski to Paris in the summer of 1928. Piłsudski instructed him to investigate the attitude of French military authorities toward the military convention with Poland. In his conversation with General Debeney, the chief of the French General Staff, General Kutrzeba declared in the name of the Marshal that, in case of German aggression against France, Poland would mobilize immediately and take military action. Further, General Kutrzeba asked what France would do in case of an attack on Poland. General Debeney replied evasively that in such circumstances the decision would fall to the political authorities. But he did add most significantly that the decision of the French government would depend in the first place on the attitude of London.

Attempts to tighten the alliance with France were undertaken by Poland during the discussions of the Western Powers with regard to the premature evacuation of the Rhineland. This problem arose in the fall of 1928 during the session of the League of Nations in Geneva. In conversations with the Great Powers, the German government obstinately insisted that, on the basis of the Dawes Plan and the Locarno resolutions, the Allied armies should leave German territory, in accordance with Article 431 of the Treaty of Versailles. The French government's point of view was that an early evacuation of the Rhineland could take place only by way of a special agreement in exchange for concessions in the field of indemnities and security measures. Belgium supported France, while British and Italian opinion was generally in accordance with the German point of view.

On September 16, 1928, a communiqué was issued at Geneva, signed by France, Germany, Great Britain, Italy, Belgium, and Japan, announcing the opening of official conversations on the evacuation of the Rhineland, as well as on the summoning of a commission of experts for the final settlement of war indemnities. Both of these problems were later the object of consultations at the Hague Conference in August, 1929. In Warsaw they were discussed from the Polish point of view. Since a premature evacuation could become a threat to Poland's security, the minister of foreign affairs, August Zaleski, tried to find adequate measures to balance the situation on the French sector. Discussions were held in government circles on a 2-billion-franc loan for Poland's armaments.

Simultaneously, various projects were considered in the Ministry of Foreign Affairs in Warsaw with the aim of safeguarding the alliance with France, over which some shadows were cast owing to the progressing German-French rapprochement. The concept of an agreement between Poland, France, and Germany was discussed. The result of these discussions was the selection of the so-called Pattern D of the Treaty of Mutual Assistance, elaborated on by the Committee of Arbitration and Security at Geneva and confirmed by the Assembly of the League of Nations. This type of agreement included three vital elements: nonaggression, peaceful settlement of disputes, and mutual assistance. If it were expanded to cover Poland, France, and Germany, it would in a certain way serve as an extension of the Rhineland Pact in the east, although it would be without the British guarantee and without the clause on the maintenance of the territorial *status quo*. Pattern D did not include such a clause, since it was felt that the resolutions of the League on this matter would be guarantee enough.

Personally, I had serious objections to this concept, since I feared a further watering-down of the Polish-French alliance. Besides, introducing Germany as a third partner into relations between Poland and France could seriously jeopardize the balance to Poland's disadvantage.

In my opinion the best course to follow would have been to strengthen Polish-French relations through a bilateral understanding. I was anxious to restore the automatic action of the alliance on the basis of an agreement containing a formula of *agression flagrante* styled on Article 4, par. 3, of the Rhineland Pact. The recently signed Kellogg Pact,[15] which condemned war and excluded it from international relations, went further than the Covenant of the League, thus creating a basis for a new treaty of alliance between Poland and France.

In the course of the Hague Conference, we worked out with Jan Mrozowski, president of the Supreme Court in Warsaw, and Włodzimierz Adamkiewicz, legal counselor of the Western Department in the Ministry of Foreign Affairs, a text on these principles which was approved by Mr. Zaleski and became the basis for negotiations with the French partners.

Prior to the opening of the Hague Conference, the Polish Embassy in

[15] The Kellogg-Briand Pact renouncing war was signed in Paris on August 28, 1928.

Paris presented an *aide-mémoire* to the Quai d'Orsay promoting several Polish motions aimed at strengthening the alliance with France. Referring to possible consequences of premature evacuation, the note expressed concern that this fact might contribute to the growth of a nationalistic atmosphere in the Reich.

At the First Hague Conference, which lasted from August 6 to August 31, 1929, Poland was represented by August Zaleski, minister of foreign affairs, and Jan Mrozowski as delegates of Poland, and by a group of political and economic experts. I took part in this conference in the capacity of secretary-general of the delegation. At the head of the secretariat of the conference was Lord Hankey, and secretaries of other delegations formed a team which remained in close mutual contact.

The work of the conference took place in two commissions: political and financial. Participation in the first was limited to the six inviting countries: France, Great Britain, Belgium, Italy, Germany, and Japan. The political commission worked on the early evacuation of the Rhineland. The Polish delegation had no access to it and could not even obtain minutes of its respective sessions.

On the margin of the conference, Polish-French talks were conducted and recorded by our secretariat. I am quoting the full text of this report, since it properly illustrates the course of the negotiations.

"1) During the first discussion, which took place at The Hague between Minister Zaleski and Prime Minister Briand, both ministers agreed that measures should be taken to strengthen Polish-French relations. Briand made a proposition that matters referred to in the *aide-mémoire* of the Embassy should definitely be settled in Paris in the interval of time between the end of the conference and the opening of the Assembly of the League. Briand considered commendable the suggestion of Minister Zaleski to profit by the presence of competent officials at The Hague and start talks on these matters without further delay, adding that Berthelot [16] would be at our disposal.

"2) Adam Tarnowski, head of the Eastern Department, had an informative talk with Massigli [17] based on previous exchanges of opinion between the Embassy in Paris and the Quai d'Orsay on the subject of

[16] Philippe Berthelot, secretary-general of the French Foreign Ministry, 1920–22, and 1925–32.
[17] René Massigli, political director of the French Foreign Ministry.

Pattern D of the pact between Poland, Germany, and France. M. Massigli declared that the Quai d'Orsay would not oppose such an agreement, although he doubted that the German side would agree to it.

"3) In his talk with Berthelot, Minister Zaleski, making reference to his and M. Briand's common desire to strengthen Polish-French relations, expressed the thought of introducing the formula of *agression flagrante* to the political agreement between France and Poland, as was done with the Rhineland Pact. Berthelot in general agreed with this concept, but with the reservation that it was necessary to investigate it from the legal point of view. At the same time he appointed M. Massigli to continue conversations on this subject with the Polish delegation.

"4) Two days later M. Massigli, upon meeting Mr. Zaleski at a session of the financial commission, mentioned that the *agression flagrante* formula met with legal difficulties owing to the text of Article 2 of the Rhineland Pact.

"5) Detailed talks with M. Massigli were started by the head of the Western Department, Mr. Lipski, who handed him an outline of the Polish-French agreement. At the same time he stated as follows: The Polish-French agreement of 1921 was already adapted to this general understanding in 1925, when the Locarno treaties were concluded. At present a new event had occurred in the field of security, namely, the conclusion of the Kellogg Pact, which was endowed with even deeper moral value by the fact that the United States belonged to it. This pact had already been tested in practice in the Chinese-Soviet conflict. A country which transgressed its clauses, resorting to war, would incur the unfavorable opinion of nearly the entire world.

"For the above general reasons we based the construction of our new Polish-French agreement on the Kellogg Pact.

"Besides, from the legal point of view, the Polish-French Locarno Pact provided for two alternatives in bringing armed assistance to the two nations, namely, in case of aggression under Article 16 of the Covenant of the League or in case of a legal war under Article 15, par. 7, of the same pact. The Kellogg Pact covered both of these eventualities by Article 1, excluding all war.

"Here it was pointed out to M. Massigli that the *agression flagrante* formula was mentioned in the *note introductive* of the works of the Committee of Arbitration and Security, presented to the IXth Assembly of the League of Nations as one possibly to be applied in the proposed regional treaties of mutual assistance.

"M. Massigli, who considered the idea of linking the new agreement with the Kellogg Pact interesting, stressed that he had to study the text. He had some doubts whether it could be reconciled with the Rhineland Pact. As to the question what our real intentions were, and if we were most interested in having a free hand—unhampered by the League—in case of aggression by Germany, M. Massigli received a positive answer, with the explanation that we were interested in having our *accords techniques* [18] develop freely. Questioned casually about the mobilization, M. Massigli declared firmly that we were free to mobilize. Further, M. Massigli asked whether we were abandoning Pattern D and whether we would not like to try to approach Germany on this matter. He received an evasive reply.

"6) At the next interview M. Massigli announced that, when the plan was presented to jurists (headed by Fromageot),[19] they declared that it could be interpreted as inconsistent with Article 2 of the Rhineland Pact.

"When questioned as to detailed legal objections, he explained that Article 2 of the Rhineland Pact foresaw the possibility of French troops marching across the zone under three circumstances:

"a) transgression by the Germans of declarations concerning the zone;

"b) a decision of the Council under Article 16 of the Covenant;

"c) in case of a legal war under Article 15, par. 7, of the Covenant.

"In his opinion two cases of war might occur in practice. Either it would be started by Germany as surprise aggression, in which case even France would have to mobilize prior to coming to our aid, and in the meantime a decision of the League would be taken, or the war would be preceded by a period of tension in diplomatic relations. In the latter case there would be no delay in coming to our aid. Therefore, from the practical point of view, M. Massigli did not consider the *agression flagrante* very meaningful, especially since the introduction of this provision could undermine the Rhineland Pact, which France considered very important.

[18] In respect to the military convention of 1921.
[19] Henri Fromageot was legal adviser of the French Foreign Ministry.

"Mr. Lipski remarked that our interpretation of Article 16 of the Covenant of the League made no reference to the *vote du conseil* that determined who the aggressor was. The aggressor reveals himself— 'l'agresseur se désigne lui-meme.' Therefore, paragraph 1 of Article 16 stated that a member of the League who undertook war steps would be considered *ipso facto* in a state of war with all the members of the League. As, under Article 2 of the Rhineland Pact, France could start war action against Germany in compliance with Article 16 of the Covenant of the League, the formula of *agression flagrante* could be applied.

"M. Massigli replied that such an interpretation could indeed give us a freedom of movement and could if necessary be utilized. However, it was contested. Therefore, treaty definitions to this effect could be regarded as incompatible with the Rhineland Pact. Questioned about the possible formula defining the matter of starting mobilization, M. Massigli replied that he would have to have it in writing, so that there would be time to think it over.

"He said that he would discuss this with M. Berthelot.

"7) In a conversation with Minister Zaleski on August 24, 1929, during the crisis of the conference, M. Briand stressed that he definitely wanted to begin talks with us without delay on the tightening of the alliance and that he would instruct M. Berthelot accordingly. He also remarked that M. Massigli had prepared certain formulas with regard to mobilization.

"8) On August 26 conversations took place between M. Berthelot, Minister Zaleski, and Mr. Lipski. When asked about the formulas prepared by M. Massigli on the instructions of M. Briand, M. Berthelot replied that M. Fromageot did not accept them, since he had doubts as to their compatibility with the Covenant. As to Pattern D, M. Berthelot volunteered the opinion that it would be difficult to apply to Germany and that there would be reason to fear that Germany would try to insert resolutions which could be awkward for French-Polish relations. Minister Zaleski asked M. Berthelot explicitly—since it was impossible for him to present the mobilization formula for fear that it might also not be in accordance with the Covenant—what would happen in case of German aggression. M. Berthelot replied that we had a military convention which would then be applied. Minister Zaleski then declared that Ambassador Laroche, when he brought up the plan to change this convention, had questioned its legal value. M. Berthelot tried to argue that

Laroche probably presented the matter in a false light, and that the convention was still valid.

"Coming back to the question of the formula introducing the *obligo* of mobilization, Lipski remarked that after his talks with Massigli he tried to work out a text with Polish jurists which would dispel all French doubts. He said that this text had evidently not yet won the approval of Polish military authorities, especially of Marshal Piłsudski. As M. Berthelot insisted that he would like to study this text, it was given to him for unofficial study. Mr. Lipski added some explanatory remarks to the text. M. Berthelot said that M. Massigli did not have any objections to a formula of this sort, but he could not make any statement without the jurists' opinion."

In this report it was not mentioned that in the course of his second talk with me M. Massigli said that in case of a conflict with Germany a consultation would take place between Paris and London and that in his opinion much would then depend on the attitude of Great Britain.

Upon my return to Warsaw I had a long talk with Ambassador Laroche on the subjects under discussion at The Hague. M. Laroche, who was a director at the Quai d'Orsay during the Locarno negotiations, argued that the French delegation was wrong when it contended that the operation of the guarantee pact between Poland and France required the decision of the League. Here he referred to the terms of the agreement which mentioned explicitly *immediate* assistance. He reported to his government in this vein, thus concluding the matter.

At The Hague Minister Zaleski conferred with the French delegation on the problem of loans. This matter was also discussed by treasury representatives of both countries present at the conference. They did not, however, go beyond a general exchange of opinions. At the close of the conference a Polish-French communiqué was issued, announcing collaboration of both countries in the field of financial operations. Out of these conversations came further negotiations in Paris that resulted in a loan for Poland to build a railway to transport coal from Silesia to Gdynia.

Early German Plans to Annex the Polish Seacoast[1]
1930

IN MARCH, 1930, there came to an end a period in Polish-German relations marked by endeavors of the Polish government to establish, by means of direct negotiations, some sort of normal coexistence between the two countries. This period had begun with a conversation between Foreign Minister Zaleski and Stresemann that took place at Geneva on March 7, 1927, during a session of the Council of the League of Nations. In February of that year the German government unexpectedly broke off trade negotiations with Poland that had been going on for two years in Berlin, giving as a reason the dismissal of four German directors from Polish Upper Silesia.[2] The meeting of the two ministers had as its aim the finding of a solution to a situation awkward for both parties. In the course of this exchange of opinion it was decided to seek an understanding through diplomatic channels, beginning with the most drastic question—the rights of physical and legal persons in the future Polish-German commercial treaty.

After several talks with the German minister in Warsaw, Ulrich Rauscher, that were carefully prepared by our lawyers under the expert leadership of Counselor Adamkiewicz, I set the text of a report on resettlement on July 21, 1927. This seemingly modest achievement, however, had deeper meaning for the future. It cleared the way for trade

---

[1] Published in *Sprawy Międzynarodowe* (London), 1947, Nos. 2–3.

[2] In January, 1927, four German citizens of the Schlesisch-Dabrowaer-Bahn-Exploitationsgesellschaft operating in Upper Silesia were, in accordance with the Polish law, deported from Poland. They received a notice of removal a year in advance, and their endeavors to obtain an extension of stay were refused by the Polish authorities owing to the unemployment among white-collar workers prevailing at that time. The Polish government's judgment under these circumstances was that foreign citizens should leave Poland in order to provide priority of employment to Polish citizens. This disposition was vehemently protested by the German government. See Krasuski, *Stosunki polsko-niemieckie, 1926–1932,* p. 85.

negotiations on a purely economic level. It also encouraged both negotiating parties to seek further solutions and overcome obstacles with regard to problems where there was a chance to reconcile Polish-German interests.

With considerable cooperation on the part of Minister Rauscher, who was not a professional diplomat and was therefore free from the anti-Polish complex so characteristic of Prussian bureaucrats, several agreements were concluded during the period from July, 1927, to March, 1930, in spite of the bitter opposition of German nationalistic circles, where the slightest tendency to normalize relations with Poland was furiously rejected.

At that time we signed a lumber agreement, which was financially profitable for Poland, an emigration agreement, which settled the difficult problem of agricultural workers who resided in Germany for a long time, an agreement on the nitrate fertilizer factory at Chorzów, an agreement dealing with deeds, and several others.

The most important was the liquidation agreement of October 31, 1929, signed after the First Hague Conference in execution of the provisions of the Young Plan. Connected with agreements signed by Poland during the Second Hague Conference in January, 1930, this treaty freed Poland from any German financial claims under the Peace Treaty. These claims were pending before international courts, namely, the Mixed Polish-German Arbitration Tribunal in Paris and the Permanent Court of International Justice at The Hague.

Negotiations on the trade treaty, which was to end the tariff war that had been dragging on between the two nations since June, 1925, were due to be concluded in the first days of March, 1930. The terms for the signing of the agreement were already fixed when news reached Warsaw that, upon acceptance of the Hague agreements by the Reichstag on March 12, the Reichspräsident excluded from ratification the liquidation agreement with Poland. The Polish government countered by witholding its signature from the trade agreement. This step was effective. After a few days, the German Envoy disclosed to the Polish Ministry of Foreign Affairs the text of a strictly confidential telegram from his government, informing him that the doubts which Hindenburg had with regard to the ratification of the liquidation agreement were clarified and that the Reichspräsident would soon sign the ratification document. It was later disclosed that Hindenburg had yielded to the pressure of German agrarians, who bargained with him in connection with the liquidation agreement on financial subsidies for their landed estates in East Prussia.

The trade treaty was signed in Warsaw on March 17, 1930. However, it remained a dead-letter pact. The Müller cabinet collapsed on March 27, before it could present the trade agreement with Poland to the Parliament for ratification.

From the moment the Western Powers decided to proceed with the premature evacuation of the Rhineland for the sake of relaxing the tension present in their relations with Germany, German nationalism reared its head. During the weak rule of Brüning, a struggle for power broke out in Germany. Anti-Polish feelings spread like wildfire. The question of revision of frontiers with Poland became the watchword. In August, 1930, public opinion in Poland was aroused by a speech delivered by Treviranus, a member of the Reich government, who, during a demonstration in front of the Reichstag in Berlin on the occasion of the evacuation of the Rhineland by the Allies, called for a drive eastward to recover territories lost to Poland.

From British diplomatic documents [3] it is obvious that at the same time—on July 3, 1930—Curtius, the Reich foreign minister, made it quite clear in his talk with the British ambassador that the Polish-German frontier must be changed, and declared that in response to Briand's memorandum on European federation the government of the Reich would unequivocally state its stand on this matter.

The tide of German revisionist propaganda grew faster and stronger in the following years, finding an outlet in the daily press, in all kinds of publications, in speeches of political party leaders, in various public demonstrations, in excursions to the "bleeding eastern frontier of the Reich." The Polish Corridor was the main target for attack. The most insignificant frontier incidents gave rise to diplomatic protests in Warsaw, supported by outbursts in the nationalistic German press. This propaganda was not destined solely for the home-market. Its chief aim was to persuade public opinion abroad that the territorial situation in the east could under no circumstances be maintained. German propaganda for revision of the Corridor problem gained considerable ground in America, in England, and also in France. The Corridor problem was becoming more and more of a handicap for Poland's international position.

[3] *Documents on British Foreign Policy, 1919–1939*, Series 2, Vol. I, No. 311.

What was behind this revisionist campaign undertaken at such an expenditure of energy and means?

So far as the real attempts of the Germans are concerned, some light was shed by one of the few documents pertaining to this period disclosed at the Nuremberg trials. It is a memorandum worked out by the staff of the German Navy that provided the historical background for the German war organization and its mobilization plan.[4]

The memorandum explained that, owing to the prohibition of mobilization preparations imposed by the Treaty of Versailles, the German General Staff was compelled to draw only a very restricted team of workers into these activities, and that work was done primarily only from the theoretical point of view. Beginning in 1930—"owing to the ever-growing tension in Polish-German relations"—the Reichswehr changed from theoretical planning to the elaboration of the mobilization plan *Verstaerkerungsplan*. This plan was to be adopted in case of a *local* conflict with Poland, that is, without the participation of other countries on the side of Poland. The plan was based on the strategic principle of a "blitz-annexation" of the Polish naval base at Gdynia. The period needed for carrying out the mobilization was fixed at 72 hours. It was also taken into consideration that the occupation of Gdynia might not be the final step in war operations.

This document, which does not fully explain the German plan, still throws some light on the leading idea of competent German Army circles, and at the same time also on the political leadership of Germany. It should be stressed that a practical mobilization plan existed only with regard to Poland, while German preparations against other countries remained theoretical. The operation was planned as a local confrontation with Poland based upon the problem of the Corridor, and it was founded on the premise that the West would not come to Poland's aid.

Germany probably expected that as a result of its propaganda activities it would obtain the agreement of the Western Powers to revise the Corridor problem at an internationally favorable moment. This concept was, to some extent, a prologue to the Munich agreements.

[4] *Trial of the Major War Criminals,* Vol. XXXIV, Document C-135.

From the Nomination of Wysocki as Envoy
Up to Westerplatte
January, 1931—March, 1933

DR. ALFRED WYSOCKI, undersecretary of state at the Ministry of Foreign Affairs, was nominated envoy to Berlin on January 10, 1931. Roman Knoll had been his precedessor at this post since July 1, 1928.

The years 1931 and 1932 marked a crucial period of discord in Polish-German relations. The tariff war, started in 1925, was still dragging on. Although negotiations led to the signing of the trade agreement (March 17, 1930) and its ratification by the Polish Sejm (March 11, 1931), the German Parliament postponed ratification indefinitely.

Chancellor Brüning's government was determined in its anti-Polish policy, pushing openly to the forefront the problem of revision of the Polish-German frontier. Foreign Minister Curtius made no bones about the matter; in his conversation with Great Britain's ambassador, Horace Rumbold, on July 3, 1930, he declared plainly that Germany could not be reconciled to its present frontier in the east.[1]

Soon afterward, on August 10, Reich Minister-without-portfolio Gottfried Treviranus delivered a speech in front of the Reichstag building in Berlin, in the course of which he said:

"In the depth of our souls we remember the torn land on the Vistula, the bleeding wound on the eastern border, this crippled split in the Reich's lungs. We think of what brutal pressure forced Wilson to an abnormal separation of East Prussia, to what equivocal fate Danzig was sentenced. The future of the Polish neighbor who, to a certain degree, owes his country to sacrifices of German blood can only be safe if Germany and Poland are not constantly in a state of alarm caused by an unjustly drawn frontier line. . . . Frontiers of injustice will not withstand the right of the nation and the national will to live." [2]

To a vehement protest by August Zaleski, Polish minister of foreign affairs, the German Legation in Warsaw responded that "the speech of the Reich Minister neither alters the bases of Polish-German relations nor is irreconcilable with the binding treaties. It is unthinkable that Minister

[1] *Documents on British Foreign Policy, 1919–1939*, Series 2, Vol. I, No. 311.
[2] Quoted from Krasuski, *Stosunki polsko-niemieckie, 1926–1932*, p. 297.

Treviranus would intend to evoke by his speech the impression that Germany plans to change the Polish-German frontier by force. Indeed, it is obvious that German foreign policy tends to revise the Polish-German frontier by peaceful methods; this point of view has been shared by all German governments, and has been clearly stated by them all." [3]

In March, 1931, Chancellor Brüning himself, in a speech delivered at Bytom, attacked Poland's frontiers.

Simultaneously, the German government was busy in the forum of the League of Nations, where it accused the Polish government of violating the rights of German minorities in Poland. In 1931 debates in the League on this matter lasted from January to September.

Józef Lipski was head of the Western Department at the Polish Ministry of Foreign Affairs during these years. In his office and under his direction, political instructions were prepared and forwarded to Mr. Wysocki in Berlin.

DOCUMENT 1   Lipski to Wysocki

Warsaw, February 23, 1931
Strictly Confidential

Thank you very much for the letters of February 16 and 21. In view of the considerable accumulation of problems to be discussed by the Ministry and the Legation which are not yet quite ready for basic instructions, I am taking the liberty of making a brief outline of certain problems of mutual interest in the range of Polish-German relations, and informing you on the subject of a number of current matters. I utilize, in doing so, the authorization contained in your letter, and I assume that information supplied in this way will save time and will facilitate the exchange of opinions between the Department and the Legation.

1. Development of Internal Relations in the German Reich

We are intensely absorbed in this problem, which, in my opinion, is becoming a sort of pivot in the development of international relations for the near future.

It is worth noting that the deprivation by Germany of its strongest political postwar personality—Stresemann—the rapid reaction of German nationalistic opinion to the accomplished evacuation of the Rhineland, and, finally, the outcome of the last elections to the Reichstag have

[3] *Ibid.,* p. 298.

all resulted in a temporary sobering effect in the West which is undoubtedly favorable to us. The impossibility of normal parliamentary governments in the Reich, Hitlerite subversive action, the upsurge of Communist votes, all these must have naturally caused a slowdown in the
tempo of collaboration with the Germans. Thus, in the eyes of well-
informed international observers, the importance of Poland as a peace-
contributing factor must have grown, situated as it is between a Germany in a state of political chaos and Bolshevik Russia.

In view of the above reasons, we are laying great stress upon the
necessity of observing closely a certain development of deeper significance which has been in the making for several months on the territory
of the Reich, an activity conducted by Chancellor Brüning (as far as we
can judge from here) with great consistency, and until now with some
degree of success, aimed at appeasing the German mentality: that of
forming a government which would inspire confidence beyond the frontiers of the Reich (as a matter of fact, a return of the Stresemann
system), considering of course the present altered position of Germany
and the changes in the international situation which have since occurred.
Evidently, such an attempt to restore a normal system of government in
the Reich must provide the Chancellor with far-reaching possibilities to
claim material and moral assistance from the West, bearing in mind the
tremendous interests of the Western Powers in Germany. We have to
consider this fact most seriously, since it results from the whole international constellation of our times. I should just like to mention the almost
panicky apprehension of French opinion to any kind of political or
financial convulsion. English opinion considers the normalization of relations with Germany as a factor of utmost importance to European
peace and a guarantee against too close contacts of the German right
wing with the Soviets. The role undertaken by the Chancellor is very
risky and difficult under the present circumstances, since he has to fight
on all fronts with Hitlerites, Communists, and even certain groups of the
center. Brüning's personal assets in this decisive contest are of the greatest importance for determining the probability of the final results of his
action. On many occasions, in my conversations with foreign representatives on the shortage of outstanding personalities in Germany, I was told
that Brüning is the man of vision. Already in the spring of last year
some well-informed American diplomats called my attention to Brüning.
I report here for your information several characteristic opinions about

him that I have recently noted. Mr. Poliakoff states that a final breach of the center by the Hitlerites will push Brüning on the track of a more peaceful policy, which might have an undesirable effect on Poland's interests in England.

From Stockholm I have the opinion of an eminent editor of Swedish journals with a thorough knowledge of the German situation who is personally acquainted with Chancellor Brüning. In his opinion, Brüning is the man who will accomplish a basic change in German policy. He is apparently far better educated than Stresemann and has plenty of arguments to support his thesis: "He has the appearance of a very refined and sophisticated Catholic Monsignor." This editor's thought is that Brüning will try to launch the idea of a rapprochement with France and has already recruited quite a number of adherents in Germany. In military circles which oppose this concept, Brüning is nevertheless respected as an officer with a distinguished record gained during the Great War.

Summing up the above information, the question arises what course Brüning will take in his foreign policy. Even before Geneva, especially when the Chancellor was touring the eastern provinces, the moderate tone of his speeches—devoid of provocative revisionistic allusions—was very significant. I should even say that the Chancellor's pronouncements were to a certain degree dissimilar in tone from the aggressive accent Curtius was obviously proffering to the right wing. Rumors have persistently circulated in Geneva about misunderstandings between Brüning and Curtius and the alleged secret intention of the Chancellor to take over the portfolio of the Minister of Foreign Affairs. Brüning—in my opinion—is striving in the first place to create an atmosphere of confidence for his government in the international field, and he is therefore avoiding too drastic anti-Polish or other stances. However, the success of his mission depends on the restoration of the unbalanced financial situation of the Reich by reinforced credit abroad. Hitlerism is, to a large extent, a product of the economic crisis. A mitigation of the crisis means appeasement of radical right- and left-wing elements.

I suppose that a further stage of the Chancellor's plans will be a revision of the Young Plan, which is closely connected with the attempts to revive Germany economically. In this respect, Hindenburg's statement on the reparations burdens, made on the occasion of the presentation of your letters of credence, seemed very characteristic, along with the well-known resolution of the Reichstag. It appears that the revision of the Young Plan has already become quite a pertinent question in the program of the German government for the near future.

I have taken the liberty of expanding more fully on the above problem, as we are presently quite absorbed in it here. Of course, it is difficult to have a complete grasp of these complicated matters from Warsaw and I would therefore very much appreciate your *mise au point* with regard to my suppositions, which might not be in accord with the actual situation.

2. Ratification of the Liquidation and Trade Agreements

The delay in the ratification of the liquidation agreement occurred when matters pertaining to foreign policy came up during a discussion at the Commission for Foreign Affairs and it consequently became necessary to await the return of Minister Zaleski from Geneva. Besides, there was a change of officials in charge of the agreement; Professor Krzyżanowski was replaced by Deputy Jeszke from Poznań. This fact was also a cause for the delay in ratification. As the matter stands now, the trade agreement with Germany will be discussed by the Commission for Foreign Affairs on Wednesday, February 25, and then both agreements will be presented simultaneously to the plenum. On this occasion Mr. Zaleski will deliver a speech dealing with the two agreements. At the Senate Mr. Wielowieyski was appointed to be in charge of the liquidation and trade agreements, and he has already prepared his report. Therefore it is to be expected that approximately within a fortnight the agreements will be ratified. . . .

4. Zechlin Case

For some time the German Legation in Warsaw has been circulating rumors that Herr Zechlin, at present German consul general at Petrograd, will replace Director Trautmann at the Auswärtiges Amt. The German Legation is, of course, trying to serve this bit of news in the most digestible form for the Ministry of Foreign Affairs, and ostensibly praises Herr Zechlin's accomplishments in the field of Polish-German collaboration. It was suggested that, in his capacity as the greatest expert on Polish-German relations, Herr Zechlin prepared the agreements to which Rauscher only put the final touches.

As a matter of fact, the truth about Herr Zechlin—who has a perfect knowledge of the situation in Poland, who worked in Poznań for a long time before the war, and who speaks fluent Polish—is that he has been one of the most rabid opponents of any sort of understanding with Poland. Mr. Schimitzek [4] is in a position to inform you fully on this. Only in 1927, upon direct negotiations with Stresemann, was the change of the official in charge of the Polish Desk at the A.A. effected, and Herr Zechlin was transferred to Russia.

His return to replace Trautmann, besides being a big promotion for him, could in my opinion be interpreted as a tendency of the A.A. to follow the line of continual disputes in its relations with Poland on the question of minorities. From the point of view of the general German policy, this is not impossible. The Germans are well aware that at the present time their claims for a revision of our frontiers have no practical chances for realization. Their ideas on this problem anticipate a number of stages, such as financial reinforcement (revision of the Young Plan), growth of military power (possible fiasco of the disarmament conference), and the revision of frontiers only at the third stage.

Nevertheless, especially since they are counting on such a long procedure, they try to keep the problem of Polish-German relations in a state of agitation, even if only for the benefit of their domestic and international public opinion. Reaction in Germany against the political aspects of our treaties was so strong because for international opinion this meant a stabilization of the *status quo*.

But to return to Zechlin.

It is obvious for us here that a reaction of the Legation in Berlin against this nomination is out of the question, since this could jeopardize the whole contact for the future. On the occasion of a talk I had with Geisenheimer, who knows Zechlin only too well (since Zechlin spoiled his chances of concluding the trade agreement, so important for coal interests in Silesia), I brought up the subject. Geisenheimer told me that there are two nominations under discussion for the post of Trautmann: Zechlin or von Grünau, former consul general at Katowice. Herr G. will at any rate try to give the word to Bülow. . . .

7. German Pacifists

German pacifists (in the person of Professor Foerster) have approached us for more substantial financial aid, finally claiming very considerable sums. The matter is under discussion at the Ministry of Foreign Affairs.

---

[4] Stanisław Schimitzek, counselor of the Polish Legation in Berlin since February, 1931.

The pacifists declare that, under the present conditions in Germany, their activities should be strongly backed. They stress that, in the general campaign of lies pervading the whole German press, their press organs alone are in a position to inject some portion of truth into German opinion with regard to the real situation in Poland and its attitude toward Germany.

Your confidential opinion as to the effectiveness of more substantial aid from us in support of this movement would be of great assistance to us.

8. Concrete Works in Polish-German Relations for the Future

In the field of Polish-German negotiations we have a series of projects in preparation. The next two weeks are to be devoted to pushing the liquidation and trade agreements through the chambers. You have probably already been informed that on February 16 the ratification documents of the valorization agreement were exchanged, together with annexes.

Future negotiations will deal with the liquidation of still pending incidents of the Graebe-Naumann [5] claim, cancellation of the Arbitration Tribunal in Paris, a complex of insurance problems which are of great importance and urgency, and, finally, a number of secondary matters of a legal-settlement nature (Prądzyński's negotiations).

We discussed with Schimitzek before his departure that it might be useful if some negotiations of a more general character, and with good prospects for finalization, were entrusted to the care of the Legation in Berlin in order to create an important contact with German offices on concrete matters. If you agree with this suggestion, please let me know, since I must set up a plan for these negotiations in the near future.

9. General Considerations

I am now turning to our general tactics toward Germany. It seems to me that they must develop basically as follows: We should make a further outward display of our good will. Putting agreements up for ratification has undoubtedly had a salutary effect abroad.

Even in Germany this achievement was favorably commented on by the leftist and the democratic press.

[5] Kurt Graebe and Eugene Naumann, of the German minority in Poland, lodged a claim with the League of Nations against the Polish government, accusing it of applying the land reform to the detriment of Polish citizens of German origin.

Here I pass to another point. We should endeavor to emphasize the principle of collaboration with elements in Germany which sincerely strive for the peaceful development of international coexistence. This principle, which the Germans themselves could hardly oppose, would give us a certain freedom of action; for example, in the field of economic relations in connection with the possibility of putting the trade agreement into practice. Additionally, this [principle] puts us on the same level as France and England. Referring further to my previous remarks about Brüning's policy, it is my opinion that French and English politicians will undoubtedly look for support to the so-called *elements raisonables* in Germany. An attempt to find bases for contact with these elements, although exceedingly difficult, is—in my view—the only possible direction for our action within the Reich.

The practical application of these principles in the fields where they would meet with the response of German public opinion (such as the question of our relations with German minorities in Silesia, the application of land reform, and many others) would, in my opinion, require more extensive investigation and coordination of the exact line of action.

We are conducting studies here on this.

Józef Lipski

DOCUMENT 2   Lipski to Wysocki

Warsaw, May 20, 1931

I would like to inform you, in strict confidence, about our intended policy toward Germany, which has been approved by Marshal Piłsudski in the course of his recent consultations with Minister Zaleski and Vice-Minister Beck.[6]

In view of the development of the international situation in connection with the recently created Austro-German union,[7] the Marshal feels

[6] Józef Beck had been undersecretary of state at the Ministry of Foreign Affairs since December 2, 1930; he became minister of foreign affairs on November 2, 1932, and held this post until 1939.

[7] A customs union between Austria and Germany was concluded on March 21, 1931. However, the Council of the League of Nations decided to submit to the Permanent Court of International Justice the question as to whether such a customs union could be established. On September 5, 1931, the Court decided

that the Polish government should at present avoid anything which might in the future restrict its freedom of action.

Bearing this in mind, the Marshal does not consider it advisable for us to enforce the trade agreement with the Reich for the time being.

In the light of these basic directions, I asked Minister Beck, when I discussed Polish-German relations with him, how we should deal with a number of concrete problems still pending between Poland and Germany which should now be finalized, such as: negotiations on insurance problems, Graebe-Naumann, cancellation of the Mixed Polish-German Arbitration Tribunal, etc. I drew Minister Beck's attention to a certain relaxation in secondary matters in Polish-German relations, which is confirmed by your reports. Consequently, this might be the right moment to try to finalize these concrete matters, taking advantage of the tension in which the Reich finds itself on the western and southern sectors.

Minister Beck fully agreed with my point of view, and felt that all matters of this kind should be concluded in the favorable moment of a better atmosphere. The Marshal is only concerned with the question of the trade agreement, which is of basic importance, and is to a certain extent binding.

I take the liberty of informing you of these matters confidentially in order to keep you abreast of these momentous events.

Obviously I am not disclosing to the Germans any change of tactics with regard to the trade agreement; I avoid conversations on this subject. At any rate, I abstain from taking any steps through interested parties, which would otherwise act to speed up the enforcement of the agreement by the German side.

I succeeded in delegating Lechnicki [8] to Geneva; he will provide information both to the Western Department and to the Legation in Berlin about the backstage rumors of Geneva. He is confidentially instructed on how to remain reserved toward the German delegation with regard to

---

that this union conflicted with the protocol signed with Austria on October 4, 1922, by England, France, Italy, and Czechoslovakia, and later by Belgium and Spain, calling upon them to "abstain from any negotiations or from any economic or financial engagement calculated directly or indirectly to compromise this independence" (see *DGFP*, Series D, I, 552).

[8] Tadeusz Lechnicki, deputy head of the Western Department at the Ministry of Foreign Affairs.

this basic economic problem, in case the Germans launch some tentative initiative in our direction.

I would like to take this opportunity to inform you that, according to news obtained from French circles, Ambassador Margerie is due to retire in the near future. Also, the fate of Ambassador Fleriau in London and of Count Clausel in Vienna is sealed. It will be a matter of some interest to see whom the French will send to Berlin. I think such a decision will not be taken before June 13, that is, the date when Laval's cabinet is due to resign. Besides, the question whether Briand will stay or retire from office, even if only for a time, is of utmost importance for us. For the moment, in case Briand resigns, I think Herriot will have the best chance, especially since he is labeled as a pacifist minister abroad. At the same time he does not appear to be a red scarecrow to the right wing, owing to his recent very firm public statements proclaiming respect for treaties and the security problem.

In the whole question of the last French elections, I am concerned by the fact that the leftists in France, who suffered an obvious defeat at the presidential election, will strive by all means possible to take revenge in the year 1932.

Józef Lipski

DOCUMENT 3   Wysocki to Lipski

Berlin, May 23, 1931

I am much obliged for the information contained in your letter of May 19,[9] all the more valuable since I was not aware of the subject of consultations recently held at the Belveder.[10] For my part I would like to add that for a long time now I have never mentioned the trade agreement in my conversations with official persons in Germany. Whenever I am asked for an opinion, I always refer to the changed situation due to the customs policy of Minister Schiele, which is depriving us of any benefit the agreement might otherwise bring us. Personally, I do not believe that the ratification of the agreement will be possible before the

[9] The exact date is May 20, 1931.
[10] The palace where Piłsudski lived.

Reichstag session in the fall if the government does not alter its attitude toward the right wing and the agrarian party.

In my last conversation with M. Margerie I tried to sound his chances of remaining in Berlin.

He was very depressed by Briand's possible resignation, evidently considering him as his protector. He was visibly upset because of plotting which in the last moment prevented his election. He declared that complete chaos prevails at present at the Quai d'Orsay, since nobody knows whether Briand will remain or retire and who will be his successor. They apparently plan to recall to active service an undersecretary of state, which—in Margerie's opinion—would be detrimental for the course of affairs.

If Margerie should leave Berlin, I would be one of those sincerely regretting his loss, as ours was a relation of true friendship, facilitating the arduous task of obtaining information.

In accordance with the Ministry's request I had two conversations with the Yugoslav envoy, Balugdzic. I shall report separately on the results.

Looking forward to the continuation of our correspondence, which is always of value and very useful to me, I remain . . .

Alfred Wysocki

DOCUMENT 4   Lipski to Wysocki

June 9, 1931

General attention is increasingly focused on two basic problems in the international arena, namely, the question of war indemnities and the future disarmament conference.

The conference at Chequers, about the results of which, outside of fragments of information from our Embassy, I do not yet possess full details, has undoubtedly made topical to a great extent the possibility of a revision of the Young Plan. The attitude taken by the United States will be a decisive factor, since the whole question of German payments is closely connected with the complex of inter-Allied debts. Stimson's and Mellon's trips to Europe should be given our closest attention, and we have today instructed the posts concerned accordingly. Filipowicz [11] informs us today of the possibility of certain American concessions in the financial field, provided their rearmament demands are properly satisfied.

In connection with these problems, it is essential for us to acquire the most complete analysis possible of the internal political and economic situation of the Reich. Germany outwardly plays the Stresemann card, pointing out that, if it does not obtain satisfaction with regard to reparations, a political upheaval will take place which Brüning will be unable to master, and then a Hitlerite government will come into power, proclaiming the abolition of obligations under the treaty. It is to be expected that the ghost of chaos in Germany has a somewhat haunting effect on the minds of the potentates of international finance. According to what Skirmunt [12] says, even Henderson thinks the situation in Germany is extremely tense. Consequently, it is important to understand what is to be considered tactics in the behavior of the responsible German elements and what is reality. In my opinion, from our point of view we should observe the situation in Germany from two angles: political and economic. Undoubtedly, some financial burdens in the Reich may politically serve as a brake to the active policy of aggression against Poland; on the other hand, a breakdown of the German market economically would result in deteriorating repercussions on the whole complex of Eastern Europe's economy, by which we would also suffer. So, in my opinion, the best situation from our point of view would be the state of a certain dependence of the German economy on the West through reparations payments, with the avoidance, however, of too strong shake-ups and disturbances on the international financial market with respect to economic development in this part of Europe.

I have taken the liberty of drafting these few loose thoughts for your information, making the observation that we here are preparing a very close consultation with regard to problems connected with the possible revision of the Young Plan. Therefore, any information pertaining to this question, and particularly with regard to the internal situation of the Reich, will be of utmost interest to us.

Józef Lipski

[11] Tytus Filipowicz, Polish minister in Washington.
[12] Konstanty Skirmunt, Polish ambassador in London.

DOCUMENT 5   Wysocki to Zaleski

NO. 2823/T   Berlin, July 9, 1931
                                            Confidential
                                            [Addressed *ad personam*]

German foreign policy has entered a phase of official visits. With Chequers already over, the next step will be Paris and then Rome. The governments of the above powers did not propose these visits; the initiative came from Germany. Italy alone, through its ambassador here, asked not to be overlooked at a moment when Germany is seeking personal contacts with other states. Also on his own initiative, but as a direct result of a skillful propaganda campaign, the American secretary of state, Stimson, will visit Berlin.

However, most significant of all these trips will be the departure of the Chancellor and the Minister of Foreign Affairs to Paris.

On the occasion of the realization of the Hoover Plan,[13] the Germans have become convinced once again how powerful France is financially, and in consequence also politically.

I had the opportunity of discussing this matter with several prominent Berlin bankers, who were unanimous in declaring that an understanding with France is an urgent necessity: "Our stock exchange will not calm down so long as the hostile attitude toward us prevails in Paris." Even financial potentates of the United States make the further flow of their capital dependent on the relaxation of tension in French public opinion and of French mistrust of Germany. Berlin is also well aware that the initial difficulties in Paris over the immediate approval of the Hoover Plan stem almost exclusively from the French opinion that this project is the first step of an action initiated by the Germans to abolish the Young Plan and free themselves from any burden of war obligations. It is now therefore very important that this mistrust be dispersed and disbelief turned into confidence.

German banking circles are behind this initiative and heavy industry is following in their footsteps. The German government, whose indulgence toward belligerent nationalism is rather alarming, agrees in principle with this necessity; Brüning's broadcast speech confirms this.

13 The Hoover Plan (1931) instituted a moratorium on war indemnities to relieve the Germans in their financial situation.

However, he is concerned about the forthcoming political discussion in Paris and about the obligations which perhaps will have to be accepted in order to appease France and regain its confidence. These obligations, if pushed too far, might topple him in the country, since the government of the Reich will then be obliged to suppress those German politicians whose activity is the very source of disturbances that make Europe resent Germany.

At any rate, the moment is near when something could be gained from Germany. Under threat of a repeated run on banks for foreign currency, and the withdrawal in panic of their own and foreign capital, the Germans are ready for a good many sacrifices. Would it not be advisable to take advantage of this moment?

After looking through informational material and reports of the Legation for the last several months, I have come to the conclusion that Germany's attitude toward Poland has not improved in the least.

In my conversations with German officials, primarily with President Hindenburg, they stressed the necessity of relaxing and improving our relations. These, however, were just empty words. The attitude of the government toward the trade agreement, which could easily be ratified by the Parliament when the Nationalists and the Hitlerites retire from it; the behavior of Luther, the president of the Reichsbank, who most vigorously vetoed our election to the council of the Basel Bank; the failure to extend the wheat agreement; the declaration that Germany will abstain from any agreement for export of grain if Poland takes part in it (my conversation with Soviet Ambassador Khinchuk); and, finally, the attempt to seduce Rumania, Hungary, and Yugoslavia with favorable terms for trade agreements with the goal of totally isolating Poland— here is the harvest of the last months. If we add to this the Stahlhelm demonstrations in Wrocław, the recent vindictive publications by eminent university professors, the speeches of high-ranking officials, and the tone of the press campaign, we shall then understand the irrefutable truth that, when the question of Poland arises, there is no difference between the opinion of the Reich government and that of General-Oberst von Seeckt, who says in his *Wege der deutschen Aussenpolitik* that "in all questions of German foreign policy *Poland should be treated as a basic enemy.*"

What is to be done? Should it not be ascertained if this is, indeed, the actual state of affairs? Should we not strive precisely now, during this period of constant visits and discussions, to draw Polish-German relations into the orbit of international interests, to strive for some personal direct exchange of opinion between the heads of the two countries and their ministers of foreign affairs?

I am taking the liberty of asking you to give some thought to this question and to inform me accordingly of your decision, so that I can if necessary undertake, first, preliminary, strictly confidential, and private investigations, and later discuss the question of a possible Polish-German meeting, not only with Minister Curtius, but particularly with Chancellor Brüning.

In view of the atmosphere prevailing here, I exclude *a priori* the possibility of an official visit in Warsaw or Berlin, but consider that a meeting on neutral ground could probably be arranged.

Awaiting your reply, on which will depend my inaugural talks and my endeavors to obtain an audience with Chancellor, which, in view of this constant traveling and heavy work-load, will not be an easy task, I remain . . .

Alfred Wysocki

DOCUMENT 6   Wysocki to Beck

Berlin, July 19, 1931

English and American visits are postponed either until the end of this month or until the beginning of August. In case you are not inclined to consider my suggestion to prepare the ground here for a direct understanding between the governments of Poland and Germany along the lines accepted by England and France, I would like to have your answer whether it would be possible for me to start, about August 1, a cure as prescribed by my doctor. . . .

Coming back to my idea, I am taking the liberty of drawing your attention to the fact that I see no reason why Poland should not discuss touchy matters with Germany, even the question of the revision of the frontiers and German political claims. The present state of silent subterranean strife in the economic, financial, and propaganda fields cannot last much longer. Particularly since Germany is determined, as soon as order is restored in its own finances, to settle the Young Plan and, after the disarmament conference, "the Polish question." Now, if we take up this problem, which is a main source of concern and lack of confidence toward Germany, as well as toward Poland, we will gain the support of a part of world opinion, and we will have the backing of a powerful France to face a weakened and isolated Germany. We have no guarantee that the present situation will not change for the worse. Even here in Berlin I can see how the questions of the revision of frontiers and of the Corridor are becoming more and more timely. There is an increasing number of foreign politicians and journalists who are of the opinion that Poland will inevitably have to give in under the pressure of public opinion. I am convinced of this from what I hear from Americans and Englishmen, who are genuinely surprised to hear my stereotyped arguments that I refuse so much as to discuss these matters for the simple reason that they just do not exist for me.

A frank, even slightly brutal, but basic exchange of opinions between the prime ministers of both countries and their foreign ministers would lead not only to the conclusion of the trade agreement but also to a considerable relaxation in the field of propaganda and in the policy of economically isolating Poland. In a few months Germany will again stand firmly on its feet, ready for further action, and again radical nationalistic elements will take over here. Would it then be worth while to argue with this kind of Germany?

Please let me have at least your opinion on this question.

Awaiting your reply, I remain . . .

Alfred Wysocki

DOCUMENT 7   Wysocki to Lipski

NO. 2994/T   Berlin, July 20, 1931

Yesterday was cold and dreary, and it was raining. So I went to the movies, since I was awaiting news from Paris at any moment and decided not to leave town. I must confess that, absorbed as I was in my thoughts about what was happening in Paris just then at the Brüning and Curtius conferences, I hardly paid attention to what was shown on the screen. Suddenly I was aroused out of my meditations by shouts: "Heil, Heil," and by sounds of a melody well known from the time of the war. On the screen, detachments of the Reichswehr were cavalcading on superb horses and in perfect war drill, followed by *Totenkopf* hussars, Bavarian uhlans, dragoons, etc. Finally, the picture changed, showing the General Staff reviewing the parade. In the forefront, clad in his characteristic black hussar uniform covered with decorations, stood Marshal Mackensen, next to him General von Einem, a general in active service of the Reichswehr, and Commander von Stülpnagel of the IVth Wehrkreis. Mackensen's entourage consisted of nearly one hundred military dignitaries of all branches, in smartly tailored prewar uniforms obviously just fresh from the tailor shops. Since this was a sound film, we were treated to some speeches as well. The old mayor of Dresden, Socialist Dr. Külz, talked as if he had never had anything in common with a party which often, when necessary, came out against militarism. He recalled the old saying of Derfflinger, "Aufgesessen und angetrabt" ["They mounted and rode on"], and repeated it twice with obvious delight.

The audience rose time after time with applause and shouts to salute the Army.

And all this was happening on July 19, 1931, on the second day of the Paris conference. . . .

N.B. There is something else I have on my mind. Germany constantly threatens that, if it is not granted a loan or this or that political concession, it will become a stage for Communist disturbances and a Bolshevik country. This argument can be heard here at every step. However, it is difficult to believe. Now, when the banks were closed the Communists had a unique opportunity to start disturbances. The population was stupefied, deprived of cash, and whipped into a panic by the press, which, by order of the Presseleitung, painted as black a picture of the situation as possible. And what did the Communists do? They issued a rather mild proclamation and avoided clashes with the police anywhere in Berlin; in the provinces, in two or three localities of the western industrial basins, they did shoot at the police, and the police shot back at the Communists, but it was all done so delicately that not a single man was killed or even injured. Does this not appear as a sort of insurance of the German rear by Bolshevik organizations, with the silent blessing of Moscow?

Alfred Wysocki

DOCUMENT 8   Lipski to Wysocki

NO. P·II. 5307/31   Warsaw, October 20, 1931
                                                      Confidential

Thank you very much for your letter of October 15, No. 4201/T. I can assure you that, together with Lechnicki and Fiedler, we are working very hard to establish a principal line of action toward Germany in connection with the possibility of discussions for a mutual relaxation of tensions. Presently we are still handicapped by the illness of Mr. Zaleski, who is bedridden and does not accept political reports, which is causing a delay in obtaining final decisions on these matters. However, I expect to secure them in a couple of days, and I am even considering a visit to Berlin by Lechnicki or myself in order to discuss these matters personally with you.

In the meantime I would like to share some conclusions with you, established here in our Department upon investigation of news signaled by our Berlin Legation with regard to indications that the Germans desire some sort of rapprochement with Poland.

Undoubtedly, in the minds of responsible German leaders there is a gradual recognition that, in view of Brüning's policy toward France and the approaching international settlements of great importance for Germany (reparations, disarmament), it has become a matter of urgency to clarify the Polish-German problems to the extent that they should not jeopardize German foreign policy.

It is also possible that the very nature of German internal affairs, owing to the acute economic crisis which threatens to become more serious with the oncoming winter season, combined with certain political disorders, is forcing the government of Chancellor Brüning, who as a representative of the center is in constant fear of Communism, to seek better relations with the immediate eastern neighbor of Germany.

From our point of view, however, it is most important to determine to what extent this German attempt at rapprochement is just a matter of strategy designed to evoke a desirable effect in the West, and to what extent we can count on some genuine effort to normalize relations with Poland. And also we should determine how far Germany is prepared to go in seeking an understanding with Poland.

We understand that it will be possible to answer this question only in the course of preliminary talks with our German partners, discussions for which we must have absolutely precise instructions.

I would like to call your attention to the fact that the first attempt at a Polish-German understanding on a larger scale was achieved during the period of the realization of the Young Plan. Then, as you recall, Germany found itself in a similar forced situation in relation to Poland and, realizing that it would be impossible for it to pass through the Hague Conference without an agreement with Poland, decided to conclude the liquidation agreement with us, completed later on by means of an economic understanding.

During these attempts at a rapprochement, we acted quite openly, using the apparatus of the press, winning over particular spheres of interest inside the Reich, and finally opening a broad discussion in the parliamentary forum. It then became obvious that German public opinion was not quite ripe for a rapprochement with Poland. The usefulness of the liquidation agreement was not canceled, since it had a completely realistic side, especially in the financial field. However, its political value, as a direct factor in Polish-German relations, decreased nearly to zero.

These past experiences compel us to use especially careful tactics if talks with Germany are to be undertaken once more.

As far as the formalities are concerned, in our opinion, this time such conversations should not be given press coverage for internal use. We have to bear in mind the difficulties with which Chancellor Brüning has to cope on the home front, which might greatly increase once he decides to take up the Polish question in earnest. As to the attitude we should adopt in face of the advances now made by the German side, which indicate an inclination on their part to begin talks, we think that too much zeal on our part would not help the cause.

For the time being, we should define our position as that of a state which in the last months has taken a number of steps that indicate our far-reaching good will toward our western neighbor.

And just to illustrate our efforts: the trade agreement was ratified, an objective stand was maintained in the face of the Austro-German union, a moderate reaction was displayed toward the Stahlhelm incident at Wrocław, the Young Plan was favorably received, the Polish press acknowledged with satisfaction the peaceful endeavors of the Reich Chancellor.

What was the German government's attitude at that time? The trade agreement was not ratified, the lumber and wheat agreements were not extended, aggressive action was taken against us on the territory of the Reich, our candidacy for the International Bank was opposed, etc.

Lipski

Years later Mr. Wysocki wrote about the 1931–32 period of his diplomatic service as follows:

In the long span of my service I have never lived days and months so personally enervating and disagreeable as those during the years 1931 and 1932. The atmosphere was becoming oppressive. At the Auswärtiges Amt I was received with haughty indifference as a representative of an illusory state, *ein Saisonstaat.* The prominent historian Professor Hoesch, president of the East European Institute, gave his students the following thesis to work on at a seminar on modern history: "Owing to what political and economic reasons can the Polish state not exist?" The daily press published accusation after accusation, putting the blame on Poland for instigating a war against the Reich and for persecuting German minorities, and circulated with relish any bit of news unfavorable to Poland. Journalists of Jewish origin played quite an important role in this campaign, clad in the long robes of defenders of "threatened Germania"; by attacking Poland they tried to safeguard their own position in the face of ever-growing nationalistic feelings. Not far from our Legation vulgar demonstrations took place regularly that illustrated the tragic fate of German victims of the brutal Polish soldiery. Also, we were boycotted socially, and we received invitations only for strictly official receptions at the Auswärtiges Amt. The tariff war ruined our economic balance, and each payment of German reparations was intentionally postponed indefinitely.

This situation can best be illustrated by a conversation I had in the summer of 1932 with an elderly lady whose garden adjoined that of the Legation. As we were both fond of flowers and plants, we often tended them with my wife. One day the lady approached the iron fence and expressed her surprise that we put so much work and expense into this garden. When I asked her why she was so surprised, she declared that after all we would soon be compelled to leave it all. It was my turn to express my astonishment, and I was informed that we would have to leave Berlin very soon, as the war with Poland would start at any moment. She added that her son said so, and he was in the Stahlhelm, where this was common talk.

Shortly afterward I received instructions [to which Mr. Lipski referred] that I should "investigate the attitude of the main political parties toward Poland."

I did not approach politicians of the stature of Hugenberg, at that time omnipotent leader of the nationalists, owner of several newspapers and a press agency, or Seldte, the chief of the Stahlhelm, or Treviranus, who just recently had said: "Give us back our territories and I will be the first to go to Warsaw and toast your health and peace between Poland and Germany." I confess, however, that I was counting to some extent on the cooperation of the Catholic Center Party, whose leader, Brüning, was the head of the government. I therefore called on Msgr. Kaas, director of the foreign department of the Center, and on von Papen, a very generous benefactor of this party, and a favorite of old President Hindenburg. However, they were both rather evasive and considered the settlement of the Corridor problem a condition *sine qua non* of normal Polish-German relations.

Hagemann was a man of confidence of the Center. He was the editor of the foreign department of *Germania.* In my interview with him he said that he considered that Germany's most urgent and essential demands were: total equality, settlement of the revision of the frontiers, and the annexation of Austria.

To my question as to what should be understood as the revision of frontiers, he replied that it meant recovery of all territories basically German and the removal of the anomaly, namely, the Corridor—a wedge thrust into the living body of the Reich. Hagemann further informed me, with a certain naïveté, that the Center was striving to achieve its demands not by war but by exclusively peaceful methods.

I then realized that the program of the Catholic Center in no way differed from that of the nationalists, retaliators, and Prussian Junkers; that the Center people only pretended that they wanted to reach these goals by peaceful methods, while the others openly called for war.

Only the Socialist Löbe, at that time president of the Reichstag, avoided aggressive accents in his speeches. He stressed the advantage of discontinuing mutual accusations and press attacks; he thought it advisable to appease public opinion and improve commercial relations, but he called the Corridor an anomaly difficult to accept, and declared that the Socialists disagreed with the ideology of the regime in Poland.[14]

[14] Alfred Wysocki, "Początek dramatu," *Tygodnik Powszechny* (Cracow), Feb. 15, 1959, No. 7 (525).

Westerplatte[1]
March, 1933

AFTER HITLER'S COMING TO POWER amidst general agitation, when unfettered Nazi forces, for long years fed on ultranationalistic catchwords, were exhilarating in the atmosphere of victory and their propaganda penetrated to the incendiary centers on the borders of the Reich, provoking ferment and many incidents, a dispute between Poland and Danzig occurred in connection with the problem of the harbor police in the Free City. This matter had serious consequences.

Polish-Danzig disputes had a long story behind them, reaching back to the resolutions of the Versailles Treaty, which were later developed and completed by the Paris Convention [2] and the Warsaw Agreement.[3] On these fundamental international acts were based later resolutions of the high commissioners of the League; decisions of the Council of the League of Nations; sometimes, in more intricate cases, even sentences of the International Tribunal at The Hague; and, finally, agreements and conciliatory understandings between parties.

The intricacy of Danzig law suits, as well as their complicated procedure, often obscured the very purport of the disputes, creating a false picture of the real intentions of the Danzig Senate, whose action was inspired by Berlin. The Free City of Danzig was an ideal springboard for German revisionism, which constituted the main goal of Germany's foreign policy toward Poland.

Through disputes and everlasting differences, which were shifted from

[1] Printed in *Bellona* (London), 1951, Nos. 1–2.
[2] The Paris Convention, concluded on January 9, 1920, dealt with the settlement of archives ceded by Germany to Poland in accordance with the Treaty of Versailles, repayments to families of soldiers mobilized by Germany, pensions and annuities for residents of territories ceded to Poland, the settlement of guarantee matters for the issuance of Polish marks during the occupation of the Polish Kingdom, and the obligation by Germany to conclude an agreement on financial matters according to Article 238 of the Versailles Treaty.
[3] A trade agreement signed in Warsaw on March 17, 1930.

Danzig to the international forum at Geneva, Germany attempted to mold international opinion, explaining that the situation on the Polish-German frontier created by the Treaty of Versailles was untenable.

The problem of the harbor police in Danzig began in the year 1921, when the Council of the Harbor and Water Communications, composed of delegates of Poland and the Free City, as well as a neutral representative, decided to have a security service of its own to control the vast territory of the harbor and its establishments, including the custom-free zone.

The High Commissioner of the League, by a resolution of June 6, 1923, agreed that the Harbor Council should be given police personnel by the Danzig authorities as requested. This decision at first met with a protest from both the Senate and the Polish government. The Free City did not want to have an independent police force at the harbor, while Poland—in order to safeguard its trade interests—wanted the harbor police, subject to the Council, to be composed of Polish functionaries.

In September, 1923, an agreement between Poland and Danzig was reached, both parties accepting as a basis for the understanding the above-mentioned resolution of the High Commissioner. This agreement was binding for two years, when each of the parties was entitled to "revise its standpoint." In the year 1925 the League of Nations based its decision on the Polish-Danzig agreement of September, 1923, confirming the rights of the Harbor Council to control the police and issue orders to them. This situation lasted until 1933. The Senate was ill-disposed toward these rights of the Council, and when, owing to several incidents at the time that Polish vessels docked in Danzig in the beginning of the year 1933, the Polish delegate at the Harbor Council demanded that directives for the security service be explicitly stated, his motions met with a protest of the Free City representative. This was not a good omen for the future.

By a note of February 15, 1933, addressed to the [Polish] commissioner-general, Kazimierz Papée, the Senate unexpectedly and without previous talks with the Polish government canceled the agreement of September, 1923, giving notice at the same time about instructions issued for the withdrawal of the security service controlled by the Harbor Council and introducing their own police instead. By such action the Senate created a *fait accompli* in a territory where the main interests of Poland's foreign trade were concentrated.

This action of the Senate gave Warsaw food for thought. The Ministry of Foreign Affairs was investigating this matter not only because of the threat to Polish interests in Danzig but, in the first place, in the light of Polish-German relations. These relations were in a state of crucial tension, caused by incidents with Polish minorities, mass offenses and acts of violence against Jewish citizens of Poland and their property, and chiefly by constant revisionist agitation on the Polish frontier. An interview with Hitler by the *Sunday Express* of February 12, 1933, complicated the drastic situation still further, in spite of later commentaries from Berlin that free alterations were made in the text of the Chancellor's declarations. Speaking of the Corridor, Hitler stressed that it was a great injustice for the German nation. A few days later the Polish Minister of Foreign Affairs, in his speech before the Commission for Foreign Affairs at the Diet, replied significantly that the Polish government would adopt the same attitude toward Germany and German problems as was taken by the Reich toward Poland.

After long deliberation the Polish government gave an answer to the Danzig action. On February 20, 1933, the Commissioner-General of Poland handed one note to the Senate of the Free City and another to the Council of the Harbor and Water Communications.

The first of these notes confirmed that the Senate had broken the agreement with Poland unilaterally and that it had withdrawn the police force controlled by the Harbor Council without a previous understanding. The note stressed that the Polish-Danzig agreement did not foresee any change of the existing status either *de jure* or *de facto* by way of one-sided action. This argument was presented in the claim of *action-directe* against the Free City presented by the Polish government to the High Commissioner of the League on March 7 (that is, the day after the reinforcement of the Westerplatte garrison).

In the meantime, Warsaw wanted to settle the matter locally, avoiding entanglement in League procedures, the effectiveness of which seemed rather doubtful. Standing by its objections to the illegal action of the Senate the Polish government nevertheless expressed its consent to the cancellation of the 1923 agreement, which, as the note stated, created a totally unsatisfactory situation as far as security at the harbor was concerned, since the police ceded by the Senate to the Harbor Council were unable to handle incidents that had repeatedly occurred on previous occasions when Polish vessels touched at the harbor. This evoked the concern of Polish public opinion, especially in economic circles. At the end of the note, the Polish government reserved the right to undertake necessary steps to safeguard the interests of its citizens in case the Council of the Harbor and Water Communications was not in a position to maintain order in the harbor territories, especially in the free zone included in its administration. These obligations imposed on the Council resulted from the Paris Agreement.

The note to the Council of the Harbor and Water Communications, more precise in its contents, explained the aims of the Polish government. It suggested that the Harbor Council, in accordance with its rights, should without further delay organize its own security service. This force could be subordinate to the commander of harbor pilots, since the tasks of the pilots and the police were closely connected. Since the pilot personnel was recruited exclusively from Danzig citizens, the Polish government was ready to place at the disposal of the Harbor Council an adequate number of trained policemen. Confirming that the situation resulting from the Danzig arrangements was illegal, the note requested the immediate withdrawal of the Free City police and stressed the extreme urgency of the matter.

In spite of urgent requests by the Polish government, this matter dragged on for nearly three weeks and the "exlex" situation persisted.

Meanwhile, serious events were taking place inside the Reich. Immediately upon coming to power Hitler disbanded the Reichstag and fixed the date of elections for March 5, 1933.

A brutal campaign with no holds barred was launched to destroy the opposition. In Hitler's government at that time, only two 100 percent Nazis were seated: Göring and Frick. Both, however, held key positions —Frick as minister of the interior of the Reich, Göring as minister president in Prussia. Both acted through the police apparatus supported by S.A. storm-detachments. Police methods, however, proved to be insufficient to destroy all opponents and to obtain a majority in the new parliament on such short notice.

So the new masters of Germany conceived a plot to capture the imagination of the German masses and direct their energy against "enemies of the nation and the state": to induce the old and ailing President Hindenburg to sign the decree suspending constitutional freedom in the name of the struggle against Communism.

The glare that swept the night's darkness over the Reichstag on February 27–28, 1933, was to accomplish this task. Nazi propaganda branded this act as "a crime of the Communist Van der Lübbe," a half-demented cretin.

I still recall the sensation this news provoked in Warsaw. It was the winter carnival season. That very evening the annual ball took place at the residence of Count and Countess Tyszkiewicz, at 5 Matejko Street, to which, as usual, several ambassadors and ministers were invited. At a certain moment, news was circulated by an employee of the Ministry of Foreign Affairs that the Polish Telegraph Agency had dispatched a message from Berlin about the Reichstag fire. Evidently this news was a sensation for the assembled guests. All eyes turned to Minister von Moltke, who quietly left the ball and hastened to his legation in order to put through a telephone call to Berlin. Since he was a self-possessed diplomat, he returned to the ball after some time, confirming the news by making scant comment. We were lost in conjecture, unable for the moment to grasp what was happening, while subconsciously we assumed that the burning Reichstag was a sort of symbolic torch kindled on the ruins of the abolished edifice of a Germany erected in the aftermath of Versailles.

Marshal Piłsudski keenly observed events inside Germany. Basic instructions with regard to Polish-German relations, as well as on more important foreign policy problems, were inspired by him or required his confirmation.

In the years 1931–32, in connection with increasing tension in the anti-Polish atmosphere in the Reich, Piłsudski recommended that Minister Wysocki probe the attitude of the main political parties toward Poland and orient himself as to the possibility of improving relations between the two countries. Wysocki executed this task by engaging in conversations with a number of leading German politicians, from Social Democrats down to German Nationals. In these talks certain differences could be noted. However, all parties inserted into their programs the revision of frontiers with Poland, if only by different methods. The most drastic approach was taken by the German Nationals. Their representative bluntly declared that he felt that any collaboration with Poland should depend upon the previous settlement of the problem of the Corridor and Upper Silesia in accordance with German demands.

Demagogic catchwords were of such importance at that time of chaos and struggle for power in Germany that none of the political parties could possibly afford to take a more conciliatory stand toward Poland. Consequently, Wysocki's talks hit a dead-end.

A memorandum of Wysocki from these times, dealing with one of his conversations with Piłsudski, has been preserved.[4]

This talk took place at a rather critical moment when, after the downfall of Brüning's cabinet, Hindenburg commissioned von Papen to form a new government. The Marshal wanted to be informed about the internal situation of Germany. One of the basic questions asked of Wysocki was: "Is the present political situation in Germany a cause for concern, and will its further development become a danger to us?" A detailed analysis presented by Wysocki led the Marshal to assume "that it is not to be expected that internal difficulties will decrease, but rather that they will increase, which will obviously weaken the aggressive impetus of that nation externally."

In the course of this conversation the problem of Hitler's coming to power was discussed, since this was the subject of the Marshal's direct question. Mr. Wysocki was of the opinion that "Hitler is neither a military genius nor an extraordinary personality" and that his success was to a great extent due to the fact that he managed to stir the German masses by purely demagogic catchwords, devoid of deeper meaning, while stirring their senses. Questioned by the Marshal, Mr. Wysocki gave the cautious reply that "everything seems to indicate that sooner or later Hitler will be faced with the necessity of taking over the government of the Reich," adding at the same time a comment most characteristic of the opinion of foreign observers in Berlin at that time: "Hitler will follow waiting tactics, since he is actually afraid of power, which would force him to fulfill all the promises he showered so profusely for so many years, and which in fact are impossible to realize. His coming to power may at the same time mark the beginning of his party's decay."

To the Marshal's question: "What is your opinion of the paramilitary organizations in Germany?" Wysocki replied: "There exists beyond any doubt a direct connection between them and the Ministry of the Reichswehr. They are an *ersatz* army, at least morally if not in fact. In the course of many centuries the Hohenzollern rulers implanted into the Germans a passion for militarism. As long as a German organization enables them to wear a uniform it will be very popular in Germany, until

---

[4] The text is in Józef Lipski's papers in the Piłsudski Historical Institute in New York (File 1).

compulsory conscription is again introduced in case of war. Anyhow, such assault-units of National Socialists who wear uniforms, take military pay, live in barracks, and drill often very strenuously and in purely military style may render invaluable service to the Army in time of emergency."

The Marshal did not concur in this opinion, saying: "It seems to me that you overestimate the importance of these organizations. There are a lot of appearances which are misleading, but they have not the real values of a true soldier. Leaders of such organizations and their officers often complain about the inadequate human material. The soldier who returned from the Great War ceased to be a good soldier. The postwar generation is often physically weak and unwilling to submit to the rigor of military discipline. Observers of the exercises and organization of these units repeatedly stated that, beyond *paraden marches,* roll-calls, and speeches, not much is happening there. And there is no question of comparing the value of such organizations with regular soldiers."

At the end of the conversation the Marshal asked about the chances for a monarchy in Germany, to which Wysocki replied that under the present circumstances this was out of the question.

When Jan Szembek, former minister of Poland to Bucharest, became undersecretary of state [November 5, 1932], Piłsudski sent him on a courtesy and information mission to Paris and London, instructing him to stop in Berlin on his way back. His visit in Berlin was chiefly designed for propaganda display. Following the Marshal's instructions, Szembek refrained from calling attention to the tension in Polish-German relations in his conversations at the Wilhelmstrasse, but expressed his conviction that, unless a reasonable *modus vivendi* were found, unforeseen consequences might follow.

Writing about this journey during the war, Szembek stated that the Marshal's guiding idea was to prod France into a more active policy toward its Polish ally. Strained Polish-German relations became an ever-increasing burden for Poland in the west. That is why Piłsudski took these measures, in order to maintain a certain balance on the political chessboard.[5]

In the late afternoon of March 5, 1933, I was unexpectedly summoned for a consultation to the Raczyński Palace, where the Foreign

[5] Letter of Szembek to Lipski from Lisbon dated August 31, 1942 (in Lipski's papers, File 3).

Minister resided at that time. I found several senior employees of the Ministry of Foreign Affairs already there, among them the head of the Danzig Desk. Directly on his return from the Belveder, Beck announced to us that Marshal Piłsudski had issued an order to reinforce the garrison which kept watch over the munitions stores at Westerplatte. A detachment of 120 armed soldiers was to board the cargo ship *Wilia,* which was to land the next day at dawn. Beck justified Piłsudski's decision by the threat to Polish interests in Danzig harbor and by circulated rumors of an intended assault of Hitlerite gangs on Westerplatte. He further explained to us that in deciding on this step the Marshal wanted first of all to test Germany's actual state of readiness; therefore the Minister asked me, as the head of the Western Department of the Ministry, to observe closely all possible reactions in Berlin. On the other hand, a determined attitude by Poland should be properly appreciated in Paris and London, rousing these countries to more energetic action in the face of the growing threat of Hitlerism.

To fill in the complete background of the situation, it is necessary to add that the whole West European press, alarmed by the drastic changes in the Reich, was at that time filled with sensational rumors about Hitler's schemes. In international circles and in the powerful Jewish organizations, anti-German feelings were growing fast. The same also occurred in America.

The Ministry of Foreign Affairs proclaimed a state of emergency and round-the-clock shifts were instituted at the Minister's cabinet, at the Danzig Desk, and at the Western Department. I therefore spent the night at the telephone, constantly receiving information from Berlin about the election results. Radio stations controlled by the National Socialists broadcast triumphant communiqués about Hitlerite victories at the polls for hours on end. From 196 mandates obtained in November, 1932, the National Socialists rose in strength to 288, thus receiving 43 percent of all the votes. In coalition with the German National Party, they were assured of a majority in the future parliament.

I realized that the news which would be reported from Danzig the next day would cause a serious shock at the chancellery of the Reich!

In the early morning hours of March 6 I was at the Ministry when news reached us that our detachment had landed at Westerplatte without incident. During the whole day reports streamed in from Danzig.

While Berlin was silent, protests were received, first from the High

Commissioner of the League of Nations in Danzig, followed by protests and warnings from representatives of France and Great Britain.

The Polish press published the following official communiqué:

"The Polish government has recently been informed that diversive elements in Danzig plan an assault on the peninsula of Westerplatte, where Polish stores of munitions and war matériel are located, guarded by a small detachment of Polish forces. In consequence, on March 6, a temporary reinforcement of this detachment was ordered. The Commissioner-General of the Polish Republic in Danzig informed the High Commissioner of the League of Nations about this order."

The *de facto* and *de jure* situation, as far as the Polish garrison at Westerplatte was concerned, was as follows:

The Poland-Danzig agreement of June 23, 1921, authorized Poland to keep a garrison on the peninsula to safeguard the munitions stores. On the basis of this agreement, the High Commissioner of the League of Nations was to be kept informed by the Polish side of the strength of the garrison. He was also entitled—upon agreement with the Polish government—to establish the number of the guarding detachment. The munitions stores were completed in the beginning of 1925 and the Polish government wrote a letter to High Commissioner McDonnell on April 18, 1925, for permission to send a detachment of two officers, 20 noncommissioned officers, and 60 soldiers. The League of Nations, by its decision of December 19, 1925, confirmed the Polish motion.

On the morning of March 6, 1933, the Commissioner-General of Poland informed High Commissioner Rosting about the reinforcement of the garrison. He explained that this step was precipitated by police measures taken by the Danzig Senate, as well as by the threat by ultra-nationalistic elements in Danzig to attack Polish munitions stores. The Commissioner-General of Poland was explicit in his assurances that the reinforcement of the garrison was only temporary and that, in accordance with the resolution of the League of Nations of December 19, 1925, the detachment would confine its functions strictly to guarding Westerplatte.

The High Commissioner of the League of Nations, who was unofficially advised by the Polish side on the previous day, could have availed himself of his rights to confirm the temporary reinforcement of the Polish garrison until the problem of the harbor police was settled and a calm atmosphere restored in Danzig. Mr. Rosting, formerly employed by the League's secretariat, by nature a man easily intimidated, took a purely formal stand; he expressed his protest and demanded the withdrawal of the detachment.

Only a few hours after this conversation, the Danzig Senate intervened at the office of the High Commissioner of the League. The intervention took the form of a letter which advised that from the ship *Wilia,* whose arrival at the harbor had been announced a few days before, a Polish crew of more than 100 men had landed armed with machine guns and other weapons. Aboard this ship were 40 cases of explosives weighing 1,720 kilograms.

The Senate inquired whether the reinforcement of the guard at Westerplatte had the consent of the High Commissioner, and if so, for what reasons?

The High Commissioner declared that it had occurred without his consent, thus compromising his stand in the conflict.

A rapid exchange of notes followed. The Senate demanded—according to Article 39 of the Paris Convention—the issuance of a declaration by the High Commissioner of the League imposing on Poland the obligation to return to the previous force of the garrison. It also lodged a claim of *action-directe,* that is, of a breach of the binding rules by one-sided action. The High Commisioner transferred the problem to the League of Nations. For its part, the Polish government accused the Senate of *action-directe* in introducing its own police force into the harbor.

In accordance with the rules of procedure, the High Commissioner, in his letter of March 7 addressed to the Commissioner-General of Poland, fixed a term of 48 hours for a reply by the Polish government, and 24 hours for a retort.

The Commissioner-General of Poland refused to give an answer until the deletion from the Danzig claim of a paragraph offensive to the Polish government. A dispute by letter was opened on this subject, which lasted until March 9. On this day Beck left for Geneva to attend the extraordinary session of the Council of the League. Before leaving Warsaw, he had no illusions about the attitude of Paris and London. The greater the tension in the West in connection with Hitler's behavior, the more cautious became the Great Powers' diplomacy (not to mention that of the smaller countries).

The Polish government's action was the cause of consternation at the

Wilhelmstrasse. This was obviously connected with apprehension that the Great Powers might interfere against Hitler. The step taken by Poland could therefore be regarded as a prelude to common action. Confirmation of these forebodings may to some extent be found in the conversation of the Chancellor with Mr. Wysocki on May 2, 1933.[6]

A report of the German Minister in Warsaw dated March 11, 1933, in the form of his account of conversations with representatives of the Great Powers at the Council of the League,[7] throws some interesting light on this matter.

According to von Moltke,[8] the majority of foreign diplomats in Warsaw defined the reinforcement of the Westerplatte garrison as "a violent reaction in the style of Beck." It resembled the *Wicher* case, with the difference that this time action was carried through with Marshal Piłsudski's consent (here Moltke was wrong; as is known, the *Wicher* case was personally directed by Piłsudski).[9] "I did not find among the diplomats here a single one who in more or less strong words would not criticize or negatively judge the Polish action," wrote Moltke. He added, however, that his collocutors called attention to the inopportune notice given by the Free City concerning the agreement on the harbor police. This step of the Senate was criticized, especially by the ambassador of Great Britain [Sir William Erskine], about whom Moltke complained that he usually showed bias in Polish-Danzig and Polish-German matters.

Reflecting on the motives that induced the Polish government to take such a step, von Moltke considered that the argument of threat alone was not convincing from the diplomatic point of view. Other secondary reasons probably existed as well. The step was possibly an answer to the elections in Germany. In all probability it was to serve as a warning to those who represented the idea of the revision of frontiers in Europe.

In his conclusions, von Moltke was obviously not far from the truth.

[6] Hitler then said: "The Germans will not acknowledge . . . any rights of Poland to Danzig which would overstep the frame of the existing treaties. They would also consider the occupation of Westerplatte by reinforced Polish garrisons illegal, and would have reason—Germany, not Poland—to get alarmed."

[7] *DGFP*, Series C, Vol. I, No. 74.

[8] After the death (on December 18, 1930) of Ulrich Rauscher, German envoy to Poland, his post was filled, on February 27, 1931, by Hans Adolf von Moltke, former director of the Eastern Division of the Auswärtiges Amt.

[9] "Zajazd O.R.P. 'Wicher' na Gdańsk", *Wiadomości* (London), No. 108, April 25, 1948, and T. Morgenstern, "Wejście O.R.P. "Wicher' do Gdańska w 1932 r.," *Bellona* (London), 1953, No. 1.

The epilogue of the Westerplatte incident took place at Geneva. The League of Nations avoided making a public display of quarrels and contentions as a matter of principle. Resolutions were agreed to between the parties involved even prior to their being placed on the agenda of the Council of the League. Thus, an apparent atmosphere of harmony and understanding was created among the delegates. Touchy issues were settled in backstage conversations or at secret sessions of the Council.

During the sessions at Geneva, the secretariat of the League played the role of chief stage manager. Its influence was far-reaching and deeply rooted. It had at its disposal an apparatus technically of the highest order; it was thoroughly acquainted with the background and arcana of every case; it knew perfectly the standpoint of particular delegations, paying most attention to the attitude taken by representatives of the Great Powers, thus adjusting its tactics to the prevailing international situation. Seeking solutions of compromise was the key problem of the secretariat. It also excelled in composing skillful formulas which often contributed to smoothing out difficulties.

Outsiders were lost in the labyrinth of Geneva proceedings. There were no secrets hidden from old-timers who had a master key to intricate resolutions and speeches of the delegates, in which the essence of their proposals was camouflaged by the sheer phraseology of the League.

In both Danzig matters turned over to the League of Nations (Westerplatte and the harbor police), the procedure did not deviate from the normal course.

The role of *rapporteur* was filled by Sir John Simon, the stiff and aloof spokesman of the British government.

In international matters Paris acted in full agreement with London, since the foreign policy of France was influenced by England. When the case of the Westerplatte garrison appeared in the forum of the League in the form of a claim against the Polish government concerning an *action-directe,* it became obvious that the French government was not inclined to collaborate more actively with Poland in view of the new situation in Germany and the growing danger of Nazism.

From the behavior of Germany in the face of the incident in Danzig, it was evident that Hitler did not yet have real strength at his disposal, and that his violent outbursts were to a great extent just sheer bluff. This, however, did not convince the Great Powers. The spontaneous reaction of the Polish government in Danzig was inconvenient for them in practice and highly disturbing, since these powers were also ready to apply a policy of appeasement toward Hitler.

Under these circumstances, the Polish delegation met with general criticism and strong pressure, backed up by threats of the *rapporteur* to place before the Council a report unfavorable to Poland. Therefore, the necessity for a compromise arose. It was reached on the eve of the session of the Council of the League, that is, on March 13, 1933. The compromise consisted in the restoration of the *de facto* situation in the case of the harbor police as it had existed on February 15, 1933, and in the obligation of the Polish government to reduce the garrison to its previous numbers.

At the session of the Council everything went in accordance with the set plan.

Sir John Simon informed those present that, in view of the announced declaration of the Polish Minister of Foreign Affairs, he would refrain from presenting his report.

Beck directed his opening question to the president of the Danzig Senate, asking whether the authorities of the Free City could guarantee that the rights of Poland on the Westerplatte peninsula would not be violated. President Ziehm replied affirmatively.

The delegate of Poland then declared that his government would withdraw the additional detachment at Westerplatte without delay, adding at the same time that the Polish move was of a temporary character and was not intended to create a precedent for the future.

Sir John Simon urged that the decision of the Polish government be put into life without delay, whereupon the Polish delegate expressed his readiness to fix immediately a precise date and hour for an understanding with the High Commissioner of the League. The *rapporteur* confirmed that the matter was settled, and, going over the contents of the agreement, he admonished both parties (Poland and Danzig) that neither of them had the right "to take the law into its own hands."

On behalf of the Free City, Ziehm stated that the agreement would remove the state of confusion which had prevailed in Danzig during the preceding few days.

The delegate of Germany, Herr von Keller, said, in part, that the attention of the whole world was focused on the Danzig incident and that the German nation followed the development of this problem with great anxiety and some concern.

The delegate of France—the "golden-tongued" Paul-Boncour—succeeded in sweetening the pill for the delegate of Poland by a well-rounded sentence. He praised the conciliatory stand taken by the Polish government to settle the dispute, and explained that the step taken by Poland in Danzig was dictated by the necessity of a prompt decision in view of the general tension in relations.

The delegate of Ireland, Lester, who later succeeded Rosting in Danzig and incurred the Nazis' disfavor by his protest against the *gleichschaltung* of the Free City, described the incident as unfortunate. He added, however, that the incident had had a happy ending, thanks to the sage behavior of the Polish government, which deserved appreciation. At the same session the report about the case of the harbor police was accepted, together with motions.

The Westerplatte case vanished from the agenda of the Geneva debates afterward. Its deeper meaning would only be appreciated many years later. The former ambassador of France in Berlin, André François-Poncet, referred to this incident in his memoirs, rightly stressing its weight and importance for the later decisions of the Polish government.[10]

R. Wendelin Keyserling [11] described his meeting with the Polish Foreign Minister in London in the spring of 1939, at the moment of tension in Polish-German relations. In the course of this conversation Beck allegedly referred to the Westerplatte case, explaining that its conclusion convinced Marshal Piłsudski about the necessity of entering into direct talks with Hitler.

[10] François-Poncet, p. 165.
[11] Keyserling, pp. 296–97.

The Four-Power Pact and Revisionism[1]
March, 1933

WHILE THE Westerplatte case was under discussion in Geneva, we received important news at Wierzbowa [2] about Italian-German relations from the Polish ambassador in London, Konstanty Skirmunt, usually well informed and a man who carefully weighed each word of his reports.

DOCUMENT 9   Skirmunt to Beck

Polish Embassy in London   March 9, 1933
NO. 18/conf./33   *Strictly Confidential*

In the course of the last weeks I received very confidential information about Italian politics from a most reliable source.

Since Hitler came to power in Germany, Ambassador Grandi,[3] in his conversations with friends (not in the Foreign Office), expressed concern about Mussolini's special support granted to the German government for all its activities, extending even to the field of the disarmament conference. Grandi was especially troubled, it seemed, by the news that, in order to ease internal difficulties for Hitler's government, Mussolini was prepared not only to agree to the *Anschluss* but to place this problem before the international forum on Italy's initiative. Under these circumstances, with the meeting of the Great Fascist Council close at hand, Grandi decided to leave for Rome to—as he said—fight it out with Mussolini.

Arriving in Rome on March 3, Grandi remained there for only one day and did not attend the Great Council, which was finally postponed.

[1] Printed in *Bellona* (London), 1951, No. 3.
[2] The Ministry of Foreign Affairs was located at Wierzbowa Street in Warsaw.
[3] Dino Grandi, former minister of foreign affairs (1929–32), at this time Italian ambassador in London.

He considers the result of this journey to be a fiasco. The sole advantage he succeeded in achieving was a promise that Mussolini, while supporting possible German plans for the *Anschluss* when they are presented, will not push the problem on his own. Besides this, Grandi failed to convince Mussolini on any other issue. Mussolini, in his opinion, is more than ever isolated from contact with the world and totally under the influence and orientation of the surrounding group of his closest collaborators and of General Balbo. Mussolini—as Grandi puts it— considers himself not only the chief of the Italian government but the pope of Fascism, and is primarily interested in the Hitlerite movement and its impact on Italian politics. As for Mussolini's possible trip to Geneva for a meeting with MacDonald and Daladier, for which Mac-Donald was pressing for real and prestige reasons, Grandi was convinced that under no circumstances would his chief go to Geneva and that he is putting pressure on Hitler to prevent him also from going to Geneva. Mussolini's goal seems to be to frustrate the chances of any way out of the impasse at the disarmament conference and to put up to ridicule any statesmen who would undertake this ungrateful task. Such a point of view is a source of deep concern for Grandi, who considers the present international situation to be genuinely dangerous and who is obviously most anxious to maintain very close relations with Great Britain. He adds that the expedition to Rome was connected with a certain risk for his personal position, and that in his opinion it really is endangered.

From another source I was informed that during the recent visit to Rome of Avenol, the secretary-general of the League of Nations, Mussolini stressed in his conversation with him the necessity of territorial concessions for Germany in the east and of a "partition of Czechoslovakia." The subject of this conversation was disclosed to the Czechs.

The information given above is known to the French government through its embassy here and possibly, if not to the full extent, also to the Foreign Office. When, on March 3, Undersecretary of State Vansittart summoned me to inform me about the planned trip of MacDonald and Simon to Geneva, we conversed at length about German and Italian politics. Vansittart stated clearly that the British government is concerned about the development of events in Germany, and he agreed with me when I called his attention to the constant support extended by Italy to Hitler's policy.

I gathered that Vansittart is definitely convinced about the possibility of Italy's promoting the *Anschluss* idea. On the other hand, he disagreed with my opinion as to a possible Fascist *coup d'état* in Vienna. However, the London press has openly been discussing this possibility for the past two days. News about the probability of the *Anschluss* also reached me from other sources and coincided with the possible planned visit of Hitler to Rome at the end of March. According to information in my possession, Mussolini and Hitler communicate with each other, completely bypassing diplomatic channels—at any rate, absolutely eliminating the Wilhelmstrasse. The Soviet ambassador here told me that he knows that Mussolini talks with Hitler by telephone every day. . . .

At the last moment I learned that the day before yesterday [March 8] a political gathering took place at Lady Londonderry's, at the so-called Arch Club, with the participation of MacDonald, Baldwin, Ambassador von Hoesch, and the Austrian and Swedish envoys. I heard from the last-named that at this gathering there was an unofficial discussion about the *Anschluss,* and the opinion was expressed that this was an immediate and unavoidable danger; the majority of those present thought that it might bring about a war. Polish-German matters were not discussed.

Grandi called on Simon just before the latter's departure. Rumors about this visit, which reached me indirectly from the Foreign Office, seem to point to the fact that Grandi was very open in his talk with Simon when he spoke about the error of his chief, even at the risk of his personal position, and that he impressed upon Simon the necessity of arranging a meeting for MacDonald with Mussolini as the only solution to influence the latter's policies. Simon, who is jealous of his personal influence—as I was told by the Foreign Office—let Grandi unburden himself of his feelings, and showed no reaction whatever in exchange.

K. Skirmunt

The news of Mussolini's alleged *volte-face* on the subject of the *Anschluss* was quite a surprise. The general opinion was that the Italian government was against any attempt at uniting Austria with Germany, for fear that Germany's expansion southward might become a threat to Italy's interests in the southern Tyrol.

Energetic objections by Rome concerning the initiative for the German-Austrian customs union at the time of Brüning and Curtius had confirmed us in our convictions. However, Skirmunt's information did not exclude the hypothesis that, in view of the planned visit of Mac-Donald and Simon to Rome, Grandi purposely gave an alarming report of Mussolini's readiness to offer all possible concessions to Hitler, in order to press the British statesmen to a more conciliatory attitude in their talks with the Italian side.

Such alternative probabilities notwithstanding, the very fact that competent London circles deliberated over the *Anschluss* question—moreover, with a certain undertone of resignation—was a characteristic sign of the then currently prevailing feeling toward German activities. The fact that the Hitlerite movement had originated in southern Germany and that Hitler, an Austrian by birth, had mastered the Reich focused all eyes on the Austrian problem, especially since, upon seizing power, the National Socialists started an energetic propaganda campaign both on the border and inside the territory of that country.

Mussolini's talk with the secretary-general of the League of Nations, Avenol, disclosed that the revisionist idea had made alarming progress in the mind of the chief of the Italian government against the background of ideological kinship with the Hitlerite Reich and that it might be expressed by the desire to shift German expansion eastward, in the direction least threatening for Italy. Mussolini's statement on the partition of Czechoslovakia was symptomatic of his hostile attitude toward the policies of the Little Entente and of his personal animosity toward Beneš.

At that time I had long conversations on these matters with Undersecretary of State Szembek, who asked for detailed information on the development of the German situation, owing to Marshal Piłsudski's very intense interest and his demands for a precise analysis of the situation. In the course of these conversations the idea was conceived for me to make a short trip to Germany in order to orient myself on the spot. I wrote to this effect to Mr. Wysocki, Polish minister in Berlin, on March 14, 1933, communicating for his information the contents of Skirmunt's report and announcing my arrival in Berlin after the return of Minister Beck from Geneva. This plan, however, was not realized. Shortly afterward news came streaming in about the Four-Power Pact, propagated by Mussolini during the visit of MacDonald and Simon in Rome [March

18]. The Italian plan would have created a sort of Power directorate for establishing common policy lines on all European problems and also on matters reaching beyond Europe's limits, as well as on colonial questions. In its original text, the document pressed openly for the revision of peace treaties in cases threatening to provoke conflict between countries, transferring the decision in matters of prime import for the disarmament conference from the League of Nations to direct understandings within the framework of the four powers. From confidential sources obtained by the Ministry of Foreign Affairs, it was evident that in his Rome talks Mussolini pointed bluntly to the Pomeranian Corridor as a problem requiring settlement within the framework of the planned political pact. . . .

News about the planned agreement evoked a serious commotion in Warsaw. An impulsive reaction showing the Polish government's dissatisfaction was the sudden recall of the newly appointed ambassador to the Quirinal, Jerzy Potocki,[4] the former aide-de-camp of Marshal Piłsudski. Potocki was to replace Stefan Przeździecki, who died when on leave in Warsaw. Ambassador Przeździecki held a high social position in Rome and enjoyed the personal confidence of high-ranking Italian elements.

The negative attitude of the Polish government toward the Four-Power Pact was not based solely upon purely prestige reasons, as was often erroneously remarked by the foreign press. The causes were far more important. According to the words of Mussolini—spoken on June 7, 1933, in Rome on the day when the Four-Power Pact was being prepared for initialing—this understanding was to become a further development and application of the Locarno agreements. Contrary to the democratic principle of equality for all states contained in the League of Nations Covenant, here a system based upon the hegemony of the Great Powers of Europe was being formed. In this system of powers, France could under certain circumstances be isolated, and its vote would not be sufficient to safeguard the vital interests of its eastern allies in the face of compromise solutions adopted by the Great Powers at their expense. In the very concept of the Four-Power Pact a serious danger was involved for the region of East Central Europe. The independence of smaller countries situated between Germany and Russia was threatened by the Hitlerite doctrine of *Lebensraum* and in the east by the still

[4] Potocki resigned on March 24, 1933, before even going to Rome.

lurking power of the Soviets, ever ready for further expansion in favorable circumstances.

In this situation, Warsaw's reaction was quite justified and correct. Already presaged were the haunting specters of Munich, Teheran, and Yalta.

Notwithstanding the changes introduced in the Italian text and French-British endeavors to conciliate the resolutions of the agreement with the principles and procedure of the League of Nations, the Polish government stood firm in its objections both to the text of the pact and, primarily, to the very principles on which it was based.

In an interview with the delegate of the Polish Telegraph Agency on June 8, 1933, that is, the day after the pact was initialed in Rome, the Polish Minister of Foreign Affairs thus defined the attitude of the Polish government toward the contracted agreement:

"First of all, it should be made clear that any resolutions whatsoever passed on the basis of this pact which would directly or indirectly concern the interests of the Polish state would in any event have no binding power for the Polish government. The Polish government did not accept any obligations concerning any kind of collaboration with the bloc of the four states as an international organ. The stand of the Polish government on this matter was clearly stated at the time."

As for the relation of the Four-Power Pact to the League of Nations, the Minister declared:

"Decisions and resolutions of the Council of the League and its organs can have binding power only if a strict observance of the letter and spirit of the Covenant of the League is respected. In case of any anomaly in the functions of the Council of the League, the Polish government would be forced to reserve to itself an absolutely free hand."

The Little Entente was also against the pact, considering itself, like Poland, threatened by it. However, the representatives of the Little Entente finally agreed with the principle of the pact when a number of alterations were introduced in the text of particular articles and a guarantee from the French government was obtained. In this respect, Poland's stand differed essentially from that of this group of three countries.

When news of the Italian plan of the Four-Power Pact was circulated, a journey by Beck to Paris, Prague, and Belgrade was planned in order to establish a common line of action with these governments. There was a moment of great tension at Wierzbowa as weighty decisions were taken at Belveder. Beck had some hopes then that a closer contact might be established between Warsaw and Prague in the face of a common threat; such contact would contribute to a broader consolidation of relations in East Central Europe based on good will and proper understanding of the situation of all countries concerned. This was an exceptionally favorable moment to demonstrate the solidarity of the smaller nations threatened by both totalitarian systems. Though Polish diplomatic posts were properly instructed in anticipation, and the visits were already announced, the journey did not take place. What was the cause of this change of decision?

In Beck's memoirs [5] we find some explanation of the circumstances which precluded the planned visit to Prague. Beck writes that, in connection with the Four-Power Pact, he envisaged the first opportunity in a long time to enter into a serious understanding with Czechoslovakia; abandoning the previous reserve toward that country, he proposed to the Czechoslovak government a friendly exchange of opinions. A meeting in Prague with Masaryk and Prime Minister Beneš was fixed for a common discussion of policies. However, even before the Polish Minister could reach the capital of Czechoslovakia, Prague was—as Beck writes— "already bowing before the Pact of the Four Powers and as could be expected in advance shunned any more pronounced attitude."

Describing this incident in more detail, Beck blames some of the smaller Central European countries for their ultrasubmissiveness to the Great Powers, which was an obstacle in forming a solid front.

Neither did the visit to Belgrade take place. On his way to Belgrade Beck also planned to stop in Budapest to demonstrate friendly Polish-Hungarian relations, in accordance with his policy. Owing to the inflamed state of Yugoslav-Hungarian relations at that time, the plan to visit the capital of Hungary brought a protest from the Yugoslav government, causing tension and finally resulting in a cancellation of the visit.

In our debates at the Ministry of Foreign Affairs on revisionist tactics practiced by the German authorities—even in the Weimar era—we came to the conclusion that, although revisionist action was carried out to exert immediate pressure on Poland and to weaken its international position, the Reich was pursuing a far-reaching goal in this policy.

[5] Beck, *Final Report*, pp. 38–39.

In my letter of February 23, 1931, to Mr. Wysocki in Berlin, I defined the role of Brüning as a successor to Stresemann.[6]

Such systematic revisionist action had far-reaching consequences, not only creating an impact on direct relations between Warsaw and Berlin but causing a serious setback for Poland in the international forum in the political and financial fields. Polish diplomatic representatives reported the progress of German propaganda for revision of the Corridor in the United States, in Great Britain, and in neutral countries. Alarming rumors also came out of France with regard to pacifist feelings spreading all over the country.

On January 29, 1933, that is, on the eve of Hitler's coming to power, the Polish Embassy in Paris reported rumors which had stubbornly circulated for some time about Poland's secret negotiations with Germany on the subject of Pomerania. The report stressed that, "while in right-wing circles news about secret Polish-German negotiations is causing some anxiety, the left wing accepts it with satisfaction as a possible prelude to Polish territorial concessions in favor of Germany without the necessity of any exterior pressure."

Almost simultaneously (January 15, 1933), Mr. Wysocki reported from Berlin that "revisionist tendencies are growing from day to day. The East Prussian Exhibition is in itself not a provocation, but it has become the arena for daily demonstrations, lectures, and speeches attended by schools, universities, and other institutions. This whole tide is streaming from the Auswärtiges Amt and the Reichspressestelle."

Sympathies enjoyed by the Germans in international circles suffered a serious setback when the Hitlerite government began to impose its undemocratic regime by violence. However, the growing distrust of the West toward the new German regime was accompanied by uneasiness and fear about the possibility of a conflict, which had to be avoided at any price. The chronic inflammable condition of Polish-German relations created the impression that the Corridor problem could be the very cause of the explosion.

A report of the former counselor of the Ministry of Foreign Affairs, Tomasz Bielski, sent to Mr. Babiński, the Polish minister at The Hague, and dated March 19, 1933, gives an interesting explanation of the atmosphere prevailing at that time. Mr. Bielski, who was married to a Dutch woman with important social connections, had access to high society

[6] See Document 1, p. 25.

and especially to financial circles. Since prior to his transfer to The
Hague he had worked for several years in the Western Department of
the Ministry of Foreign Affairs and was well acquainted with political
questions, he often shared his observations with headquarters.

Holland was at that time a center on the crossroads of various
currents, and the market of this neutral rich country was of great importance. I am quoting below some remarks by the author of the letter:

"Hitler's coming to power, the result of the last elections in Germany,
the speech delivered by the Chancellor at Königsberg, and, finally, the
Westerplatte incident brought the problem of the so-called Corridor to
the forefront and it became one of the topics under discussion here.
Although the local press did not give too much space to this problem,
and in spite of the fact that a number of articles were obviously friendly
to us, this matter is becoming a source of concern for public opinion,
which is growing more and more skeptical as far as the *status quo* is
concerned. This was very clear in my conversations here with representatives of financial and intellectual circles.

"Pro-German, pro-French, or pro-Polish sympathies notwithstanding, everyone is more or less agreed that the present state of tension in
Danzig and in Pomerania is impossible to maintain in the long run, and
that some change must be made if there is to be any relaxation in
European relations.

"Pro-German arguments are the least complicated. These are statements similar to those that may be heard in Berlin and Rome, London,
or even Paris. The Germans are considered to be absolutely right; Polish
arguments are unknown, treated lightly, or accused of exaggerations.
Polish policy is regarded as a sign of 'imperialistic' tendencies in Paris
that have driven Europe into ruin. The only remedy would be to give
satisfaction to 'justified' claims of the Germans. Then, as if by magic,
Europe would become a land flowing with milk and honey.

"Among the adherents of such concepts should be counted a considerable part—if not the majority—of the representatives of finance and
trade in Rotterdam and, to a lesser degree, in Amsterdam. These circles,
although recently disappointed and embittered by Germany's behavior
(customs duties, frozen credits, currency restrictions, etc.), are all more
inclined to accept the National Socialist movement in Germany than
Communism, assuming that Hitler as Chancellor will undoubtedly be
more moderate than Hitler the chief of the opposition, and that the

'Fascist order' installed in Germany offers a better chance of retrieving frozen credits than a possible Communist chaos. This standpoint is openly confirmed by quotations from the Amsterdam exchange.

"Since Hitler's earlier aggressive declarations against Poland are still remembered, and since the Chancellor's last speech at Königsberg— considered by many here as a declaration *sui generis* of war on Poland —has confirmed public opinion about the intentions of German policy in the east, Hitler's coming to power is synonymous with the increase of the possibility of disturbances on the eastern frontier of the Reich. The conclusion is simple. An unknown and faraway Poland should at last give in to Germany for the sake of European peace, instead of prolonging the atmosphere of tension.

"Pro-French arguments are different. They consider that, faced with a Hitlerite Germany, France was swept by genuine panic and helplessness instead of by a sound reaction, so that one can expect even further opportunism and pacifism from it, even to the point of defeatism. Under such conditions, a joint French-Polish action seems to be problematical, and the opinion prevails that in case of any armed conflict we should not count on France. No one here believes in a general European war caused by the Corridor problem. The possible conflict—according to these assumptions—would be localized and Poland would be forced to succumb to the overwhelming power of Germany in short order.

"It is difficult to judge at a distance what the real feelings in France are. According to news reaching me here from financial circles, it may be concluded that the atmosphere is really alarming, as far as the Paris exchange is concerned. Allegedly, in these circles the revision of the Corridor is considered a must, and it seems already a foregone conclusion. This information might be biased, and circulated on purpose by specific sources; however, it seems to be worthy of careful study. Also, I met with such opinions locally. For instance, Professor Siegfried, who visited here in the autumn, did not conceal his skeptical remarks as to the possibility of maintaining the Corridor. The former French minister here, M. Camere, told all the Dutchmen he came across that France does not attach much importance to its alliance with Poland, and that it would not risk any adventure with the Germans concerning the Corridor. I encountered similar more or less skeptical opinions among many Frenchmen residing here or traveling through Holland. It will also be worth noting that special thanks were extended to the director of the

Franco-Polish Bank in Paris at a shareholders' meeting for not engaging his bank during the current year in further financial operations in Poland."

Two weeks later, on April 5, Bielski, in a letter to the director of the Minister's cabinet, Mr. R. Dębicki, wrote:

"Anxieties about the Corridor in financial circles are increasing, and this psychological feeling might add to my difficulties in obtaining credits for Polish industrial undertakings. These fears have gone so far that bills of exchange endorsed by the Bank of Poland are not to be discounted."

The capital market was always most sensitive to all possible political entanglements in East Central Europe. In the years 1926–27, and during the following years when the Polish government was negotiating for the American stabilization loan and when attempts in general were made to attract foreign credits to Poland, I was often questioned in detail by American representatives in Warsaw about the development of Polish-German relations. I often discussed this subject with Mr. Charles Dewey, the American adviser of the Bank of Poland, who made all possible efforts to strengthen Polish credit in America.

The Wysocki–Hitler Conversation [1]
April—May, 1933

PIŁSUDSKI'S DECISION to establish contact with Hitler was probably made during the first days of April, when the Great Powers were negotiating the Four-Power Pact. This is confirmed by the fact that an instruction, signed by Beck, was dispatched to Polish Envoy Wysocki in Berlin on April 4, 1933.

This instruction was kept in strict secrecy even from senior officials of the Polish Ministry of Foreign Affairs. The various political sections of the Ministry had no knowledge of it, nor of the preparations leading to the meeting of the Polish Envoy with the German Chancellor.

The Marshal's intention at first was to send to Berlin Undersecretary of State Szembek, who, as stated in the above-mentioned instruction, was to undertake with Hitler, and "only with him in person, a conversation of the utmost importance" and to raise subjects of "primary concern." The condition that the meeting had to be with Hitler personally was due to the mistrust prevailing in Warsaw toward the Auswärtiges Amt, traditionally hostile to Poland.

German diplomacy had been bred on the cult of Bismarck. The Iron Chancellor, creator of a Germany united under the Prussian dynasty of the Hohenzollerns, had become for future generations of the German Foreign Service the ideal master-statesman. Thanks to his farsighted and skillful policy, and supported by military power, he had attained for his fatherland through numerous victorious campaigns the standing of a great power, and he had successfully consolidated its conquests. Bismarck's approach to the Polish problem was well known. He considered the creation of a Polish state a threat to Prussia, a vanguard of France on the Vistula. The downfall of the Hohenzollern monarchy after World War I and the introduction of a republican regime had produced no

[1] Published in *Bellona* (London), 1951, No. 3.

basic changes in the Wilhelmstrasse. The spirit of Prussia continued to permeate that office.

Although successive foreign ministers of the Weimar period belonged to various political parties, the caste of clerks remained within the same old framework. Only a few nonprofessional diplomats were admitted into their tight group; they were mainly recruited from those who, at the outbreak of the November Revolution of 1918, had joined the ranks of social democracy (the November Socialists).

Ulrich Rauscher was one of these November Socialists. He was the press chief of the Reich during the Kapp Putsch (March, 1920) and he was famous for publishing, after the departure of the president and the government to Dresden, under their signature but without their knowledge, an appeal to the German working classes calling for a general strike. This appeal had so decisive an impact that it led to a breakdown of the Kapp revolt.[2]

Later, as envoy in Warsaw, Rauscher participated in economic negotiations between the two governments (1927–30) and he made a positive contribution to the normalization of Polish-German relations.[3]

There were periods during which German governments found it expedient, for the sake of high-level government interests, to conclude agreements with Poland. This was especially true of the negotiations leading to the liquidation agreement of October, 1929, in connection with the Young Plan. At such times it was usually the old-guard bureaucracy that offered the most resistance and put the greatest difficulties in the way of settlement. Among the top officials of the Auswärtiges Amt there were also persons of greater vision, of course, who did not suffer from an anti-Polish complex and who understood the necessity of seeking solutions to intricate Polish-German problems. But they were not in a position to set policy.

Wysocki replied on April 6, after conducting a confidential investigation, that permission for a private conversation with Hitler had to be obtained from the German Foreign Office, and he asked for authorization to take this up with Neurath. He emphasized that Hitler might be embarrassed by such a meeting, from the point of view of internal politics, and that a refusal could be expected. He amplified on this in his

[2] Meissner, p. 87.
[3] Rauscher, named envoy to Poland on May 30, 1922, died December 18, 1930.

telegram of April 8, explaining that "Hitler, busy with the reconstruction of Germany, intent on filling all offices, and beset with struggles within the ranks of his own party and the government, might not be ready to make any declaration with regard to Poland, since this might put a weapon in the hands of right-wing elements and compromise him in the court of public opinion."

As can be seen from a letter written by Wysocki on April 9, he was doubtful whether, under these circumstances, the conversation would even be advisable. He thought Hitler was still too weak to "risk anything that might lower him in the estimation of Hugenberg and the Prussian nationalists, to whom even the slightest attempt to iron out Polish-German controversies is in itself a crime and treason of the state."

The Envoy feared that the Germans might use the meeting for propaganda purposes detrimental to Poland and he advised limiting the talks to a specific subject, namely, a declaration on the Danzig problem.

Nothing much happened until April 18, 1933, when Beck sent Wysocki the following instruction.

DOCUMENT 10   Beck to Wysocki

Warsaw, April 18, 1933

Pursuant to the instruction issued to you by letter of the 4th inst. and the information forwarded to me by telegrams 1, 2, and 3, and your letter dated April 9, this is to inform you that in view of the delay in Undersecretary Szembek's departure for a conversation with Chancellor Hitler I have decided completely to give up the idea of sending Mr. Szembek and to choose a more natural and appropriate form of communication with the Chancellor. I would like you to talk to the Chancellor and to limit your conversation to a single topic, namely, Danzig.

Please, therefore, take up with Chancellor Hitler the following:

Referring to your government's instructions, please tell the Chancellor that, in the opinion of some, he is held responsible, either as Chancellor of the Reich, or as chief of his party, for attempts to intervene in the internal affairs of Danzig, contrary to other rights and legal interests of Poland. We do not see the Chancellor personally making such attempts. However, we would like to inquire whether he would not consider it advisable publicly to denounce such action, thus putting an end to Polish suspicions. Continuation of the situation as it now exists would, in our opinion, unnecessarily create difficulties that would force us to draw dire conclusions.

As a minimum act of *démarche* I would consider the publication of a communiqué in the German and Polish press, stating therein that the Chancellor is against any action directed against Polish rights and legal interests in the Free City of Danzig.

A good way to resolve this problem would be a public declaration by Hitler, with no mention at all of your conversation with him.

The Marshal considers this conversation extremely important, in view of the necessity of establishing our policy on Danzig, which to a great extent would depend on the result of this exchange of ideas. I know, of course, that the outcome of this talk may be negative, or that the Germans may be purposely vague. The worst that could happen, in my opinion, would be an evasive reply, with no public declaration by Hitler.

I add that we are interested in a concrete solution for the present and for the near future, and not in a general discussion of principles on the Danzig problem.

Beck

Obviously the Marshal considered the moment a very critical one, for he simultaneously prepared a decree for issuance in case of war with Germany, a decree complete with the President's signature.[4] While striving to get an understanding with Hitler and a public declaration from him regarding Poland's rights in Danzig, the Marshal was also making preparations in case the talks failed at reaching a satisfactory conclusion.

It is difficult to determine exactly all the elements of Piłsudski's strategy at that time. Taking advantage of the chill in Soviet-German relations, he strengthened Poland's security in the east. In July, 1932, Poland signed a nonaggression pact with Moscow, bringing about a

[4] Maj. Mieczysław Lepecki's report in *Wiadomosci* (London), No. 26, June 26, 1949, states that on the same day, April 18, 1933, the Marshal had him type the original draft of the decree, calling into being, in case of war with Germany, a government of national defense and national unity and establishing new organs of military and civilian authorities. Below on the left-hand side was the notation: "I agree—I. Mościcki."

détente and a rapprochement with the Soviets. And in July, 1933, the Polish government, along with other neighbors of Soviet Russia, signed a convention clearly defining the term "aggression." This convention had first been proposed by Litvinov in the spring of 1933 during a session of the disarmament conference at Geneva.

To resist the Hitlerite threat Piłsudski's main hope lay in the possibility of French-Polish collaboration. He took steps to establish this through military channels rather than through normal diplomatic exchange; he had more confidence in the discretion of the military.

At that time tension in Belveder circles was such that a possible war of prevention was seriously under discussion. Rumors of this reached the Germans. Meissner, at that time undersecretary of state under Hindenburg, wrote that in the spring of 1933 Hitler learned from reports of the German Legation in Warsaw that the Polish government had proposed to France the taking of preventive action against Germany, and that the Chancellor feared such a suggestion might meet with favor in French right-wing circles.[5] At the same time former Chancellor Brüning was warned by the Reichswehr and the German Secretary of State that Piłsudski was investigating in Paris to see if France would be willing to join Poland in bringing military pressure to bear on Germany. Pressed by military and diplomatic circles, Brüning called Hitler's attention to the gravity of the situation.

Hitler was shocked to find out about the unfavorable reaction shown by the West toward the government he had formed. He deluded himself that, with time playing in his favor, international public opinion would accept events as they developed inside Germany. However, with Nazi ideology being violently crammed into everyday life, with war being proclaimed not only against Communists but also against democratic parties, professional unions, and above all against the Jewish population, the foreign press was aroused to sharp criticism and protests. Hitler was disturbed by all this, and when a clerk showed him such reports in the press he said that soon Paris, Warsaw, and Prague would write in a similarly contemptuous way about Germany and its government, but that when the German nation achieved power its neighbors would show more respect.

[5] Meissner, p. 335. See also W. Jedrzejewicz, "The Polish Plan for a 'Preventive War' against Germany in 1933," *The Polish Review* (New York), XI, No. 1 (1966), 62–91.

Hitler reiterated this at a cabinet meeting on March 15, 1933, persuading his ministers that Germany's reputation abroad had not deteriorated in the least.[6] This was also probably his answer to telegrams and reports sent in by chiefs of German diplomatic posts abroad, who were feeling the first impact of a cooling toward the Reich.

Right-wing nationalists were represented in the government and they were seriously concerned about the internal situation in Germany. Vice-Chancellor von Papen worked hard for a *modus vivendi* with the churches, and through personal contacts he tried to counteract anti-German propaganda in the United States (declaration of March 27, 1933, to the German-American Chamber of Commerce in New York). The Reichswehr and the Auswärtiges Amt recommended moderation in foreign policy, for fear of possible complications abroad.

Hitler was well aware that symptoms of distaste evoked by Nazi methods, as expressed by critical press commentators and public opinion abroad, did not of themselves constitute a serious threat to the Reich. His real worry was over those who wanted to take direct action. He felt that Piłsudski was one of these and that as a protective measure he had reinforced the Westerplatte garrison.

Thus, that which in the Marshal's tactics irritated the Western Powers and was labeled as rash impulsiveness in Polish policy was better interpreted and understood by perceptive government officials in Germany. Berlin closely followed every move made by the Belveder.

In spite of Warsaw's pressure for the earliest possible meeting (the Ministry of Foreign Affairs at first urged that it should take place as early as April 19), and in spite of personal intervention at the Wilhelmstrasse by the Polish Envoy, a decision on the date of the meeting was delayed for a number of days. Finally, on April 25, Director of Protocol Count Bassewitz informed Wysocki that the meeting was fixed for April 28. However, on the very next day he rescinded this by letter, regretfully advising that the Chancellor was obliged to postpone the meeting until May 2 at 12 o'clock noon, owing to unexpected changes in his official schedule. This change, one can guess, was due to the fact that on April 28 Hitler was to receive the Soviet ambassador. Four days earlier (on April 24) a serious incident had occurred in German-Soviet relations,

[6] *Trial of the Major War Criminals,* Vol. XXXI, Document PS-2962.

namely, the German police had raided the Soviet trade offices of DEROP (Deutsche Vertriebsgesellschaft für Russische Ölprodukte A.G., an organization for marketing Russian petroleum products). Breaking into the archives, they appropriated a number of documents.

In the early period of his regime, in spite of the struggle against Communism inside Germany, Hitler was reluctant to allow ideological conflict to influence relations between the two nations. He still felt too weak to take a positive stand against Soviet Russia. He placed great value on the continuation of economic relations with that country, and he stressed this point when he reported to President of the Reich Hindenburg.[7]

As for the Soviets, despite the blow they suffered when the German Communist Party was smashed, they had no desire to sever relations with Hitler's Reich. Their rapprochement with the Western Powers and the strengthening of ties with their smaller neighbors in Eastern Europe were aimed both at tightening their security and at obtaining trump cards to be used in negotiating with Berlin. Moscow was also worried about the Four-Power Pact.

Both parties therefore were seeking a *modus vivendi,* even though the atmosphere was one of mutual distrust.

As a result of Hiter's conversation with the Soviet ambassador there was an exchange of ratification documents on May 5 putting into effect the long-delayed conciliatory agreement of January 25, 1929, as well as the protocol of June 24, 1931, extending the Berlin Treaty. Thus, the understanding achieved sometime previously at Rapallo was further continued in force.

Foreign Minister of the Reich von Neurath was also present at the Wysocki-Hitler conference, which took place at noon on May 2, 1933, and lasted for forty minutes. However, the discourse was exclusively between the Polish Envoy and the Chancellor, and only at the end, when the matter of a communiqué was raised, did von Neurath speak out. In his report to Beck on May 2, 1933, Wysocki included instructions received from Warsaw, as well as additional information received orally from the chief of the Danzig Section of the Polish Ministry of Foreign Affairs who had made a special trip to Berlin.

[7] Meissner, pp. 341–42.

DOCUMENT 11   Wysocki to Beck

NO. N/49/6   Berlin, May 2, 1933
                                              Strictly Confidential

The main part of Envoy Wysocki's report of his conversation with Chancellor Hitler is published in *Polish White Book*, No. 1, p. 11. In that text, a statement made by Hitler, in the paragraph beginning with the words "The Chancellor is a pacifist . . . ," is omitted:

"The Treaty of Versailles was to bring happiness to Europe, but it actually brought misfortune. We would certainly talk in quite a different manner with a representative of Poland, the Chancellor said, turning directly to me, had the peace treaty assigned to Poland access to the sea further eastward from Danzig, instead of tearing up German territory. If not for that malicious and senseless act, Polish-German relations would undoubtedly adjust to the realities of the situation, and we would iron out as peaceful neighbors our political and economic problems. Continual concern and anxiety for the political morrow, etc. . . ." [8]

After the last sentence of Wysocki's report as printed in the *Polish White Book*, p. 13, the text of his report continues as given below; this material was omitted in the *Polish White Book:*

When I took leave of the Chancellor I was escorted to the door by Baron von Neurath, who asked me to wait for him in order to discuss the matter of the communiqué. I then gave him the previously prepared main paragraph of the draft of the communiqué, which I intended to draw up as follows:

". . . reckoning with the situation created by the negotiations, the Reich Chancellor is against such activity, which would be directed against the rights and just interests of Poland in the Free City of Danzig."

After a ten-minute wait in the Chancellor's drawing room, Minister von Neurath handed me the communiqué that he and the Chancellor had drafted, with the words: "The Chancellor is offering you much more than you requested."

Looking at the text of the Minister's draft, I realized that it reached beyond any instructions I had received, and that consequently I would have to telephone you for further instructions.

The draft read as follows:

[8] For Baron von Neurath's memorandum on this conversation, see *DGFP*, Series C, Vol. 1, No. 201.

"The Polish envoy, Mr. Wysocki, today paid a visit to the German Reich Chancellor. The conference dealt with current political questions regarding Germany's relations with Poland. The Reich Chancellor stressed the firm intention of the German government to keep its assumptions and proceedings strictly within the frame of the existing agreement. The Reich Chancellor expressed his wish that the two countries should dispassionately examine and handle their mutual interests bilaterally."

After a discussion with Secretary of State Bülow concerning the persecution of Polish citizens of the Mosaic faith living in Germany, I suggested to Minister von Neurath that a confirmation of the Chancellor's peaceful intentions toward Poland be printed in orders issued by him as chief of the National Socialist Party and sent to all units and organizations of that party.

Minister von Neurath not only promised to consider this but assured me in advance of compliance with my suggestion, for which, as he said, he found the ground well prepared and toward which the Chancellor was well disposed. However, quite unexpectedly he returned to the communiqué he had drafted at noon, declaring that he had serious misgivings about whether it could be published in the form of an official German communiqué. It would, in his opinion, give the impression of acknowledging some uncommitted wrongs, and this he could not go along with. He then proposed another text, which I forthwith turned down since it contained nothing but a series of empty statements.

Finally, after a lengthy discussion, the Minister stated that he would not object to the publication in the Polish press of the communiqué in its original wording, provided that the Minister of Foreign Affairs in Warsaw summoned the German envoy, who would then publish in the German press an identical communiqué with the sole difference that it would refer to the Polish Minister of Foreign Affairs and the Polish government.

This communiqué, according to von Neurath, would read as follows:

"After the German Reich Chancellor had received yesterday the Polish envoy, Dr. Alfred Wysocki, the Polish Minister of Foreign Affairs in Warsaw also invited the German envoy, von Moltke. The conference dealt with current political questions regarding Poland's relations with Germany. The Polish Minister of Foreign Affairs stressed the firm intention of the Polish government to keep its assumptions and proceedings strictly within the frame of the existing agreement. The Polish Minister of Foreign Affairs expressed his desire that both countries should dispassionately examine and handle their mutual interests bilaterally."

On reading this I made no effort to conceal my dissatisfaction. I declared that I was accepting this new proposition *ad referendum,* and I immediately began to talk about those Germans who, to further their careers, were trying to win favor with the National Socialist Party, or who, to save themselves because they had Jewish blood in their veins, were now in the vanguard of those strongly attacking Poland and who were against any attempts to bring about peaceful relations with it. I had in mind, of course, those clerks of the Auswärtiges Amt who had prevailed upon Minister von Neurath within the brief span of a few hours to change his mind about the communiqué he had previously drafted.

Dr. Alfred Wysocki

Minister Beck immediately informed Marshal Piłsudski of the contents of Wysocki's telegrams and the reports of his conversation with Hitler. On May 3, in the early hours of the morning, I was summoned by the Minister to discuss the communiqué, whereupon the following instruction was drawn up for Envoy Wysocki.

DOCUMENT 12　Beck to Wysocki

Telephone message to the Polish Legation in Berlin sent from the Minister's Office on May 3, 1933, at 2:10 A.M.

Please request a meeting with von Neurath and in accordance with your government's instructions inform him as follows:

The Chancellor's declaration handed to you and confirmed by the Chancellor in a communiqué was received by the Polish government with satisfaction and is duly appreciated. You must express firm exception to the changes which the Auswärtiges Amt has tried to make in the communiqué. Von Neurath's proposed changes have totally altered the desire expressed by the Chancellor for a *détente* in mutual relations. We must therefore stubbornly insist that the Chancellor's decision to have the Wolff Agency issue the communiqué in its original wording be carried out. Whereupon we are ready to receive Moltke and, after consultation with him, have the Polish Telegraph Agency issue a communiqué reading more or less as follows:

"Bearing in mind the contents of the conversation held on May 2 between the Chancellor of the Reich and the Envoy of the Polish Republic in Berlin, as published by the Wolff Agency, which conversation introduces a spirit of *détente* in Polish-German relations, Minister Beck received the German Envoy and emphasized that the Polish government, for its part, was firmly intent on keeping its posture and activities strictly within the framework of existing treaties. He further expressed his wish that both countries study their mutual interests and deal with them dispassionately."

If you encounter resistance, please make it known that we will be forced to report on the development of this whole problem to higher quarters.

DOCUMENT 13 Wysocki to Beck

Telephone Message from Envoy Wysocki in Berlin on May 3, 1933, at 18:50 [6:50 P.M.]

Envoy Wysocki communicates that he has executed the telephone instruction of this day. Von Neurath agreed that the Wolff Agency would publish a communiqué, the contents of which would conform strictly with that approved by the Chancellor, with the additional information that von Neurath had been present at the conversation. It was also agreed that after Minister Beck's conversation with Envoy von Moltke a communiqué would be issued by us to the Polish Telegraph Agency, in accordance with this same text.[9]

International public opinion was taken aback by the contents of the Wysocki-Hitler conversation. That Hitler would agree on a *détente* with Poland was most unexpected, and political circles kept speculating about the reasons for such action. Rumors were circulated at that time, thoroughly without foundation, that the Polish government, in exchange for this declaration, had agreed to close its eyes to the *Anschluss*. This

[9] *Ibid.*, No. 206.

same story was repeated again later, when the nonaggression declaration with Germany was concluded. Even during my wartime stay in London I had to deny these rumors.

On May 4 the Ministry of Foreign Affairs sent to its diplomatic posts abroad a statement explaining Poland's posture toward Germany. The statement made it clear that, because of the tension in Polish-German relations caused by German atrocities against Polish citizens and Polish minorities, and because of Hitlerite excesses in Danzig threatening Poland's rights and interests in the Free City, the Polish government had deemed it imperative to consult with high-level authorities of the Reich. The Polish government could not establish a policy toward Germany based on rumors and diversionary acts. After briefly reporting on the results of the Wysocki-Hitler meeting, the instruction pointed out that "the understanding reached as a result of our *démarche* in Berlin wipes out all rumors which the Germans have been circulating about our supposed intentions of waging a preventive war."

It was damaging to Poland to stand accused by peace-minded Western countries of inciting to war. Now was the time to silence such rumors.

On May 4 the Minister of Foreign Affairs informed the Ambassador of France about these recent developments. He then stated that, without any prejudice as to the real value of the Chancellor's declaration, he considered it a positive fact that "Hitler was backing away from an unpleasant confrontation with Poland." He also reminded M. Laroche that the same press which yesterday had printed rumors of a possible Polish-German war might today just as easily go to the opposite extreme and write about an alliance. He asked the Ambassador to use his influence with the French press and ask them to report only the known facts.[10]

The Ministry of Foreign Affairs asked the various embassies and legations to report foreign reaction to Hitler's declaration. Among others, the chargé d'affaires assigned to the Italian government, Mr. T. Romer, wrote:

"I can report that the *détente* brought about by our *démarche* in Polish-German relations came as a great surprise here and was received with genuine satisfaction. Some persons expressed the hope that this would contribute toward an easing of the Polish-Italian tensions engendered by the Four-Power Pact. Considerable propaganda advantage will

[10] Laroche, pp. 127–28.

be gained locally since this will dispel German-inspired rumors that we are intent on waging a preventive war with Germany because of its territorial claims. These rumors have been circulating rather subtly in Rome for some time now."

The Polish envoy in Budapest, Mr. S. Łepkowski, reported on May 10, 1933:

"The minister of foreign affairs, Mr. Kanya, expressed his satisfaction at the *détente* in Polish-German relations. However, I had the distinct impression, as far as he himself was concerned, that this satisfaction was neither enthusiastic nor heartfelt. Very pointedly he immediately began to talk about the *Anschluss,* and he seemed visibly disturbed by the conciliatory attitude of Hitler toward Poland, as well as toward Russia, and how this might fit in with Germany's designs on its neighbors to the southeast."

The envoy in Belgrade, Mr. Schwarzburg-Gunther, reported Yugoslav reaction as follows on May 10:

"With regard to reflections on the conversations of Minister Wysocki with Chancellor Hitler, public opinion here, as well as official opinion within the Ministry of Foreign Affairs, seems to be of two minds. On the one hand, there is genuine satisfaction, basically friendly toward Poland, that Poland's relations with its western neighbor have taken a turn for the better; though this turn might be only temporary, it is still a great advantage for Poland. On the other hand, there is a sort of anxiety that Poland's success on this most important front could put it into a position of such great advantage that it might become estranged from the Little Entente and might feel it no longer needed support from allies and friends."

The English press took a noncommittal attitude toward the Wolff Agency communiqué. The big newspapers, such as *The Times,* the *Daily Telegraph,* and the *Manchester Guardian,* printed the facts in just a few lines. Only the *Daily Express* published a short commentary by its Berlin correspondent, Delmar, adding that the meeting between the Envoy and the Chancellor would contribute to an easing of the serious tension between Germany and Poland. The Polish Telegraph Agency's correspondent in London attributed the comparative silence of the English press to a growing hostility toward Hitler.

On May 16 Ambassador Skirmunt telegraphed:

"Today, awaiting an interview with Simon, whom I shall see at the end of the week, I called on Undersecretary of State Vansittart, informing him about the recent developments in Polish-German relations. Vansittart showed some skepticism. He acknowledged that British opinion showed an extraordinary unanimity of negative feelings toward Hitler's government. He said that, in his opinion, Hitler's speech tomorrow, even if moderate and peaceful, should be looked upon with suspicion and should not have any influence on public opinion; the Germans had already done a lot of talking, and behavioristically the German mentality was such that it would now insist on direct action. He assured me that, for their part, the British had done everything possible to establish and develop an understanding with France and the United States. Generally speaking, I was confronted with a total about-face in the Foreign Office's attitude toward Germany."

This change was not, as a matter of fact, due exclusively to unfavorable British reaction to Hitlerite methods. First of all, it was not in line with Britain's interests that, at this very moment when the West was negotiating with Germany on difficult problems pertaining to the Four-Power Pact, the Reich should ease tension in the east by a sort of compromise with Poland and a sort of conciliation with the Soviets. It must be remembered that the Foreign Office in general, and Vansittart in particular, were far less favorably disposed toward the Hitler regime than most British political and government circles. Differences of opinion became drastically obvious in ensuing years, when Neville Chamberlain, as prime minister, tried for an understanding with Hitler, acting completely on his own and without Foreign Office approval.

Initial reaction of the French press was limited to a mere printing of the communiqué, making no effort to play it up as a news story. But French diplomacy, on the other hand, was aroused by this about-face shown by Berlin and Warsaw.

On May 6 M. Laroche called at the Western Department to get full information on German matters. We had a long, informative discussion with him.[11] M. Laroche evaluated the meeting of the Polish Envoy with Hitler as a step in the right direction toward introducing an element of calm into relations between the two countries. He was not quite sure, however, how long this conciliation would last, or what the practical results would be. Referring to economic ramifications, M. Laroche brought up the problem of the boycott of German goods in Poland.

[11] The full text of this conversation is available in Lipski's papers at the Piłsudski Institute in New York, File 3.

Even Moltke was complaining to him about this, stating that *Gazeta Polska* had taken an unfriendly stand toward Germany on this subject. I explained that this boycott had come about because of the persecution of Jews in Germany, and that the whole problem had a much wider scope, reaching beyond relations between just Warsaw and Berlin. Reactions to the boycott had come from numerous countries, most recently from Turkey and the Balkans. Governments had no influence in this area. Jewish merchants followed the advice of their international unions. As far as easing of tension was concerned, I pointed to a number of treaties agreed on two years ago and still not ratified by Berlin, to the necessity for prompt and efficient settlement of border incidents, thereby pacifying the people residing near the borders, and, finally, to the need for a strict observance of the Polish-German radio agreement.

When we talked about the internal situation in Germany, the Ambassador expressed the idea that the time might come when Hitler would have to take some drastic action in order to appease the masses. We talked about differences within the government itself, between Hitlerites and right-wing nationals. The Ambassador wondered about von Papen's chances of taking over the portfolio from von Neurath, in case some changes were made in that quarter. I told him that I was convinced that neither Hindenburg nor the Herrenclub should thank von Papen for bringing Hitler into the government, and that in this case the Vice-Chancellor's action had been ill-advised and was anything but a stroke of genius.

Since the removal from influence of conservative Prussian elements, the Wilhelmstrasse existed in a kind of dream world of political isolation. As proof of this I told him about our recent protestations of anti-Jewish atrocities; the Auswärtiges Amt offered us words of sympathy, but no action was forthcoming. This office could not even reply to our notes, lest it lay itself open to criticism by party officials.

Our deepest concern was Austria. M. Laroche expressed his fear that, if Hitler felt the need for a victory abroad, he could turn against Austria as a weak country that would offer no military opposition. Italy would not move to help Austria, neither would France, "at least, I presume not," Laroche added. So everything would end with a sharp diplomatic protest. When asked by the Ambassador about our point of view I replied that Dollfuss' trip to Rome was motivated by a fear that the Reich's ministers would gain Mussolini's support for the *Anchluss*. I said that a direct move by Germany should not be expected, but that, nevertheless, things were happening inside Austria. The entrance of large numbers of the Heimwehr into the Hitlerite S.A. was significant. In official agencies too the Nazi element was increasing. The provinces were ahead of Vienna in this respect, since in Vienna socialists abounded and there were strong international influences. Chancellor Dollfuss was defending himself against reactions throughout the country by applying the old law from the time of the world war, which enabled the government not to convoke parliament.

In agreement with our point of view that the danger consisted in the developing internal situation, the Ambassador mentioned in passing that some people said that Hitler's declaration was the result of Poland's conciliatory attitude toward the Reich's annexation of Austria. I branded this as one more rumor based upon sheer fantasy. When asked by the Ambassador about Poland's stand with regard to the *Anschluss* I stated that the *Anschluss* would certainly be a great catastrophe and would threaten our economic interests. When the government of Poland concluded a Treaty of Preference with Austria, we also had in mind the idea of obtaining some sort of security in the area of economic exchanges with that country.

M. Laroche informed me of his purely personal pessimistic conviction that the *Anschluss* was only a matter of time. He pondered on what would be the repercussion on German-Italian relations. He said that two contradictory opinions existed. While some people thought that the *Anschluss* would estrange Italy from Germany, others were of the opinion that a complete rapprochement would take place between the two nations, owing to the untenable situation in which Italy would then find itself. I thought at that time the *Anschluss* would be something of a burden for Italy in its relations with Germany.

In the course of this long conversation the Ambassador informed me that he had seen Ovsieyenko—the Soviet ambassador—who had expressed great satisfaction over his talk with Marshal Piłsudski. Ovsieyenko's attitude toward Hitler's Germany was supposed to be very unfavorable. He thought that Germany was beginning to feel isolated from the West. On the other hand, the Soviet Ambassador considered anti-German reaction in England to be minimal and feared the possibility of an anti-Soviet understanding between the Hitlerites and certain British circles. Speaking of this to Laroche, Ovsieyenko probably had in mind the announced visit of Rosenberg to London. According to Ambassador Skirmunt's report (May 4, 1933), the *Evening Standard,* in announcing the visit of the chief ideologist of the Hitlerite party, recommended him highly. In connection with the almost simultaneous removal of Easterman, the editor of the *Daily Express* (who went over to the *Daily Herald*), rumors spread in the world of journalism in London as to possible contacts and collaboration between Beaverbrook and Rosenberg.

A few days after the publication of the communiqués Envoy von Moltke left for Berlin to report to his government.

In the Western Department we were busy establishing the line of our further tactics toward Germany.

I made a full report thereof, first to Minister Szembek and later to Minister Beck, who issued detailed instructions, following closely the line fixed by Marshal Piłsudski.

In a detailed letter to Envoy Wysocki, dated May 16, 1933, I stressed the basic points of the instruction to serve as informative material for the Legation in Berlin.

DOCUMENT 14   Lipski to Wysocki

P.II. N.49/50/33.   May 16, 1933
                                                 Strictly Confidential

Sir: As a result of your conversation with Hitler on May 2, 1933, and the ensuing publication of communiqués in Berlin and Warsaw, we are faced with the problem of what of practical value should be drawn from this political fact and what our future tactics toward Germany should be.

Deliberating on this problem in the Department I decided that, first of all, we should define what your aim was when you approached Hitler. Was our idea primarily to investigate the real intentions toward Poland of the decisive factor in the Reich, without drawing far-reaching practical consequences from this step of ours, or do we intend, upon receiving a positive reply from the Chancellor, to undertake further action to normalize Polish-German relations?

I discussed this, in my opinion, rather basic question with the Vice-Minister and the Minister of Foreign Affairs.

Guidelines were established, directing the future activity of the Department, and I take the liberty to communicate them to you to serve as orientation material.

Addressing a question to the government of Hitler as to its intentions toward Poland, as you did to the Chancellor, was unavoidable in view of the growing conviction in public opinion of an ever-increasing tension in Polish-German relations, and of rumors about Poland's alleged intention to wage a war of prevention. Besides, this step was aimed to emphasize Poland's independence in her foreign policy on the international scene.

This action of ours resulted in a clarification of the situation, introducing a certain *détente* in Polish-German relations, and (on this point the Minister placed special emphasis) stressing Poland's importance as a factor to be respectfully considered by the dictator of Germany in formulating his policy.

On the international scene this step of ours did not hurt us in the least; on the contrary, it enhanced our prestige.

So your *démarche* has fulfilled its intentions. But, as to drawing other conclusions about a more lasting *détente* in Polish-German relations, utmost precaution must be observed.

I concede that this caution is due to the undetermined internal situation in Germany, to the ever-increasing hostile attitude of the West to the Hitler regime, and, finally, to the desire of keeping a free hand in the face of such international entanglements.

I now pass to specific Polish-German problems which require special handling as a result of the conversations of May 2 and 4, 1933.

I. The last Polish-German conversations, which evoked a strong repercussion in the press of both countries, undoubtedly brought about some clearance of the atmosphere. Both the government press and the national-democratic press in Poland welcomed the Berlin talks with satisfaction and a full realization of the reality of the situation. We cannot be held responsible for articles in the *Ilustrowany Kurier Codzienny* [*IKC,* a tabloid], banned from Germany and leading a furious campaign against the Hitler government, although the Ministry did everything in its power to soften the *IKC*'s tone. The Vice-Minister even had a personal talk with Deputy Dąbrowski to this effect. We also stopped some anti-Chancellor demonstrations, for example, on the stage, in window displays, etc., with one exception—when hostile anti-Hitler demonstrations came from or were performed by Jewish circles.

Similarly, if the German government were to launch a protest about the boycott of goods we would answer that, as long as the Reich's hostile attitude toward the Jews prevails, the Polish government can do practically nothing.

II. On the subject of the Jews, we have issued, as I have already advised you, instructions to our embassies and legations to act with considerable discretion in their propaganda action, not restraining it, however, in view of its importance in helping certain countries to ascertain and assume an attitude toward Germany.

We are also supporting fully, with due precaution, any claims made by the Jews to the League dealing with the persecution of Jews in Germany.

We do not plan to publish a White Book at this time, although we are continuing work on one.

In this connection the Minister considers it most important that the Polish Legation in Berlin and the consulates under its supervision continue to give assistance to Polish citizens of Jewish nationality living in the Reich, and that they should intervene, as they have been doing, at the central offices and with local authorities.

On the other hand, we do not consider it advisable to give special publicity to this assistance. We possess proof that our efforts to defend Jews in Germany meet with favor for the Polish government in international Jewish circles. This is communicated, among others, from Vienna, America, and England.

The Ministry of Foreign Affairs should certainly be informed without delay about all such steps taken by the Legation in Berlin and the consulates in Germany, in order to make them known to Jewish organizations.

III. The Minister has no restrictions as to the practical settlement of other basic Polish-German matters, namely:

a) ratification by Germany of conventions still pending

b) conclusion of an understanding in border incidents

c) strict observance of the radio agreement of March 31, 1931

In the last field an exchange of letters has already taken place between the Polish and German radio groups, and the German side has stated that it intends to comply with the provisions of the agreement. Copies of the letters will be forwarded to the Legation.

As to another problem, the Minister has some misgivings about whether it is advisable at present to bind ourselves with regard to the press, and he therefore asks you to postpone your discourse with Goebbels. In general, as far as eventual talks with other leaders of the National Socialist Party are concerned, the Minister has not yet committed himself.

Von Moltke returned from Berlin a few days ago. I thought he would discuss the *détente* in Polish-German relations, since I had inferred he would from information received indirectly. However, up until now he has not done so. I am dining with him on the 18th.

General Schindler [12] has made it known that he is very pleased with the way the Marshal received him; Piłsudski made a tremendous impression on him. Schindler, at this first encounter, appears to be a very skilled agent; he stresses his Bavarian origin and his Catholicism. Furthermore, he treats Polish-German differences lightly, even the territorial ones.

J. Lipski

I sent this instruction to Berlin on the eve of Hitler's speech in the Reichstag (May 17, 1933).

In his speech the Chancellor struck a conciliatory tone. He expressed his peaceful intentions and tried to reassure Poland and France that the Reich would respect their national feelings and the treaties in force.[13]

Here ends the article written by Jósef Lipski.

Thus, after a long period of difficulties in Polish-German relations, thanks to the initiative of Marshal Piłsudski many problems were now settled in the attempt to secure normal relations between the two neighboring states. Envoy Wysocki's mission in Berlin had been accomplished. In June, 1933, Marshal Piłsudski decided to recall Wysocki from Berlin and name him ambassador to Rome. To the Berlin post he appointed Lipski on July 3, 1933.

On July 13 Hitler received Envoy Wysocki at a farewell audience. In Wysocki's report to Beck on his conversation with Hitler (see *Polish White Book*, No. 4) were the following sentences which were omitted from the *White Book* (after the second paragraph):

"Hitler then repeated a sentence already familiar from his first talk with me on May 2 [1933]: 'If the so-called Corridor had been pushed further eastward, we would sit together today facing each other in peace and mutual understanding of our own interests! It happened otherwise, and now both nations carry the burden of that unreasonable solution.' "

[12] Gen. Max Joseph Schindler, military attaché to the German Legation in Warsaw. For the report by Schindler of his visit with Marshal Piłsudski, see *DGFP*, Series C, Vol. I, No. 221.

[13] *Polish White Book*, No. 3.

Order of the Reichswehr in Connection with the Withdrawal of Germany from the League of Nations[1]

October, 1933

WHEN HITLER came to power he fixed a period of five years in which to build up German military forces, that is, until April 1, 1938.

Starting from this date, the Reich's military power was to become a chief trump card in its international gamble. From 1933 basic changes were introduced by the Reichswehr into its previously existing foundations of strategy. In accordance with Hitler's orders, the auxiliary plan, formerly directed exclusively against Poland, was to be shifted, as of April 1, 1934, to a more extensive plan providing for a possible war on two fronts.

Work on the reorganization of the German Army could hardly keep pace with the dynamic policy of the dictator of the Third Reich. Hitler took risky decisions in his international policy, incommensurable with the state of the Reich's defenses. Warnings of the generals were not taken into consideration. Hitler's first risky step was walking out of the disarmament conference and withdrawing Germany from the League on October 14, 1933. Tactics applied by Hitler to the Western Powers, especially to France, with the concealed motive of breaking with the Geneva institution that restricted his actions in the field of armaments, were intended as a security measure for Germany against possible sanctions by the Western Powers. During this period Hitler displayed a far-reaching desire for an understanding when, on June 7, 1933, he concluded the Four-Power Pact; when, on May 5, 1933, he extended the Berlin Treaty of 1926 with Soviet Russia; and when, on July 20, 1933, he signed a concordat with the Vatican. In a series of talks carried on at that time with the French Ambassador, Hitler repeatedly expressed his

---

[1] Published in *Sprawy Międzynarodowe* (London), 1947, Nos. 2–3.

desire to reach an understanding with France, and made light of all revisionist intentions with regard to Alsace. Germany's top brain-trust was very much concerned with the idea of a preventive war.

François-Poncet, at that time French ambassador in Berlin, wrote about Hitler's attitude as follows:

"To straighten out external politics enough to regain independence, but not far enough to expose himself to a premature war, this is the program he has at present in mind and which he will force himself to follow. Are the Allied Powers able to understand to what extent his mind is obsessed by the fear of isolation and the dread of a preventive war in the first period of his domination? Even if they were fully conscious of it, the democratic nature of their institutions, the pacifism they are imbued with, the repugnance inspired in them and their people by the very idea of war, would prevent them from using the menace of which Hitler is most terrified. From episode to episode their passivity will enhance the audacity of the gambler, and when they wish to react it will be too late; the roles will be reversed, since Hitler will then menace them." [2]

The concept of a preventive war, conceived in the mind of Piłsudski during this time, did not meet with a warm reception in the capitals of the Western Powers. The reinforcement of the Westerplatte garrison on March 6, 1933, a striking symbol of Poland's decision to counteract Hitlerite aggressive attempts, met with firm opposition from French and British diplomacy. However, looking back retrospectively, there existed at that time all the means necessary to arrest Hitler's march and save Europe from so many disasters.

General Blomberg's order [3] issued on October 25, 1933, over a week after Hitler declared that Germany had withdrawn from the League of Nations, confirms to what extent Germany was unprepared to repel a joint French-Polish attack at that time.

A political analysis of this military order is reducible to the statement that the further development of the international situation brought about by Germany's withdrawal from the League of Nations and its walking out of the disarmament conference could lead to the application of sanctions against Germany. Blomberg stressed that, until a decision was made by the Council of the League, the possibility of France's admin-

[2] François-Poncet, p. 140.
[3] *Trial of the Major War Criminals*, XXXIV, 488.

istering sanctions and drawing Poland, Belgium, and Czechoslovakia into this action should be considered. Enumerating various possible moves of the enemy, the order stated that the government of the Reich was prepared to wage local military resistance, regardless of chances of military success. This last sentence is of particular significance.

The line of defense was to run westward along the rivers Roer and Rhine to the Black Forest; in the east from the river Hötzenplotz-Nischlitz and the river Oder, and along the river Ober, in conjunction with the defense of German Pomerania. Against Czechoslovakia defense was anticipated alongside the frontier. Against France and Poland resistance was to be maintained as long as possible, while to Czechoslovakia territory was to be ceded, but "inch by inch."

As compared with military directives of more recent years, the order of October 25, 1933, borders upon improvisation. This was due to a lack of proper military preparedness, as well as to the fact that the German command was taken by surprise by the possible international entanglements resulting from Germany's withdrawal from the League of Nations.

For an appraisal of Piłsudski's move toward Hitler on November 15, 1933, the above order is not without significance. Piłsudski was right in his estimation of the military potential of Germany when he directed me to use the argument of force in my interview with Hitler. Hitler understood: he proposed a nonaggression pact to Piłsudski. With this offer in hand, Piłsudski once more turned to France. He broke off further talks and left for Wilno. And once more Paris responded with no will to act.

On January 26, 1934, the Polish-German declaration of nonaggression was signed.

Declaration of Nonaggression

Autumn, 1933—January, 1934

THE UNDERSTANDING between Wysocki and Hitler led to a rapid relaxation of tension in Polish-German relations. After the elections in Danzig (May 28), when the Hitlerites came to power in the city (gaining 38 out of 72 mandates), Dr. Hermann Rauschning, president of the city, and Albert Forster, chief of the Nazi Party in Danzig, paid an official visit to Warsaw on July 3, 1933. The Polish-Danzig Agreement was concluded on August 5, liquidating many conflicts,[1] and on September 18 an implementing protocol was signed of which Poland tried to take advantage on the international scene.

On September 25 and 26 Minister Beck met in Geneva with Ministers von Neurath and Goebbels. They had a friendly conversation.[2]

Józef Lipski, the newly appointed Polish envoy in Germany, arrived in Berlin on October 2. On October 17 he had a talk with Minister von Neurath, and on October 18 he presented his credentials to President Hindenburg. In his speech Lipski emphasized that he would perform his mission along the lines of principles agreed to in the conversation of Envoy Wysocki with Chancellor Hitler on May 2, that is, the observance of treaties in force and a dispassionate investigation of mutual interests. Hindenburg stressed the need for a just and fair adjustment of mutual problems. Lipski observed that during the audience not a single Nazi was present in Hindenburg's entourage.

The following handwritten memorandum was found among the papers of Ambassador Lipski:

In the first days of November, 1933, I was summoned to Warsaw. At the Foreign Affairs Ministry I was told that Marshal Piłsudski wanted to see me. Before my departure for Berlin, I had been received by the President of the Polish Republic, but at that time Beck told me that the Marshal would probably be willing to receive me only at a later date.

On November 5 at 6 P.M. the Marshal received me at the Belveder, with Minister Beck also present. Piłsudski was sitting at a little round table in one of the smaller drawing rooms at the rear, on the right-hand

---

[1] *German White Book*, No. 179.
[2] *Polish White Book*, No. 5; *DGFP*, Series C, Vol. I, Nos. 449 and 451.

side of the entrance. Beck introduced me. Piłsudski stood up and extended his hand, which was small and narrow and impressed me as being very aristocratic. There was a moment of silence. I sat opposite Piłsudski, with Beck on his left.

Piłsudski began the conversation with a question: "You arrive, Mr. Envoy, from a very interesting country; how do you size up Hitler with regard to his regime's stability?"

I replied with a detailed analysis of the situation. First of all I stated that National Socialism was spreading like wildfire over all fields of German life.

However, I called attention to the fact that National Socialism, while a growing *dynamic* movement, showed no *static* features. Hence the difficulty to ascertain whether Hitlerism had constructive elements for durability.

This definition visibly arrested Piłsudski's attention. He remarked casually, "Obviously, it is easier to rule with a whip."

From my analysis of the situation in Germany I concluded that I saw no other person who could compete with Hitler. When I pointed to certain difficulties evident among German leftists (Communists), the Marshal asked what the attitude of the Prussian Junkers was. He remarked that people with such a long tradition for ruling would probably not be easily reconciled to the idea that power was slipping from their grasp. At this point I illustrated with numerous data and comments, pointing to the fact that so-called Prussian elements did not accept the fact that the reins were in Hitler's hands.

Piłsudski, turning to Beck and confirming what great weight he attached to this Prussian influence, said literally, "You see, this you underestimate."

When I finished the political analysis, Piłsudski inquired whether Hitler was not threatened from the economic side.

I gave an extensive factual explanation to the effect that, in spite of economic difficulties, I did not expect any convulsion from this side such as might turn the scale against the regime.

It was rather characteristic that, while Piłsudski followed my political review with great interest, asked questions, and discussed particular points of my statements, he listened rather passively to what I said about the economic situation.

When I finished, he simply said that he acknowledged my conclusions.

Then, addressing himself to Beck, Piłsudski said: "Well, then, *let us try.*"

Issuing detailed instructions for my conversation with Hitler, he was very precise, laid special stress on certain phrases, and repeated the instructions twice:

You will say to the Chancellor that you were summoned to Warsaw to report to Marshal Piłsudski. The Marshal received you in the presence of Minister of Foreign Affairs Beck and, upon listening to your report, recommended that you present to Chancellor Hitler the following trend of ideas on his behalf:

The coming to power in Germany of the National Socialist government caused a considerable uproar among international opinion at large. This event was linked with the possibility of serious military conflicts. Under these circumstances, it was expedient in Poland to consider measures necessary to safeguard national security. The Marshal, far from being impressed by the press and propaganda campaigns, had confidence in the Chancellor and his policies. He did not order any defense measures. The Marshal confirms with satisfaction that Polish-German relations have improved, owing to the Chancellor's personality, and so his expectations have been verified. Reflecting upon the present situation, the Marshal declares that Poland's security is based on two elements— namely, upon direct relations of Poland with other states (in this instance, on Polish-German relations), and upon the collaboration of states within the frame of the League of Nations. The Marshal describes this second element as a sort of reinsurance, ensuing from the fact that the states, as members of the League of Nations, are bound by obligations under the pact of the League of Nations, especially in case of conflict, etc.

Therefore the last decision of the Reich government, resulting in Germany's withdrawal from the League of Nations, deprived Poland of this second element of security. This decision of the Reich provoked a strong stir among international opinion and an agitation of minds.

All this compels the Marshal, as a person responsible for the security of the state, to review the situation.

He would not like to strain the atmosphere between the two states by reinforcing Poland's defense measures.

Prior to taking such a step, the Marshal desires to ask, quite loyally, a question of Chancellor Hitler: whether he is willing to compensate for this loss of a security factor in Polish-German relations.

"Upon your arrival in Berlin, you should immediately ask for an audience with Chancellor Hitler." Piłsudski laid special stress on the sentence about "the necessity of his taking steps to reinforce security," remarking: *"This you must tell him."*

Further, Piłsudski directed me to add on his behalf that security could not be guaranteed for the present only, "für die Gegenwart," as this would have just the opposite effect.

To my question—how to react if Hitler offered a nonaggression pact —Piłsudski replied that this should be seriously taken into consideration.

When I mentioned that I heard from the French side that at the Auswärtiges Amt they were allegedly thinking about a nonaggression pact with Poland, Piłsudski (rather incomprehensibly to me) replied in French: "C'est plutot une intrigue Tchèque."

From the Marshal's general statements I recall a sentence he said casually to Beck, talking about Poland's relations with Germany and Russia: *"Radek went the furthest, for he even wanted to give me the command of the two armies."* [3]

The Marshal also mentioned a certain statement which could be made in Berlin if the occasion arose, but then, looking at Beck, he said that to him (that is, to me) he would not say that, but that Beck would know himself how to do it.

When I asked Beck afterward what the Marshal had in mind, Beck

[3] The nonaggression pact between Poland and the USSR was signed on July 25, 1932. When Hitler seized power on January 30, 1933, Piłsudski tried to improve the rather cool atmosphere prevailing in Polish-Soviet relations by persuading Moscow of Poland's willingness to maintain the contracted pact and to establish friendly contacts as good neighbors. At the end of April, 1933, Mr. Bogusław Miedziński, the general editor of *Gazeta Polska,* a press organ which usually reflected the views of the Polish government, was sent on a special mission to Moscow. There he engaged in preliminary conversations with Karol Radek, editor of *Izvestiia.* He declared to him, on behalf of Piłsudski, that, contrary to what was thought in Russia, Poland was not a sally port to the invasion of Russia and that it would never, under any circumstances, join Germany against Russia (see Miedziński "Droga do Moskwy," *Kultura* [Paris], 1963, No. 188, p. 85).

Radek paid a return visit to Miedziński in Warsaw on July 6–22, 1933. During a number of conversations with Miedziński, he debated the possibilities of a further rapprochement between Poland and the USSR in the cultural, economic, and political fields (USSR *désintéressement* with regard to Lithuania). He also mentioned the possibility of armed conflict between Poland and Germany and Russia's readiness to come to Poland's rescue by supplying war matériel, munitions, and gasoline. He also suggested a possibility of contact between the general staffs of the two states (Miedziński, "Pakty Wilanowskie," *ibid.,* No. 189–90, p. 119).

The above words of Piłsudski probably refer to these conversations of Miedziński with Radek.

explained that Piłsudski had an idea for a certain revision of the Versailles Treaty with regard to the resolution depriving Germany of equality. According to his concept, signatories of the treaty should enter into a single agreement with Germany, revising some treaty clauses, instead of letting the Germans bargain concession after concession from them. All further German claims, as for instance under the territorial clause, would then be considered *casus belli*.

This concept, however, never saw the light of day.

At the end of the conversation, when I had already gotten up to take my leave, Piłsudski, with a gesture of his hand denoting some hesitation, said, looking at me: "If you succeed, well and good; if you fail, I shall not blame you for it."

N.B. The Marshal also mentioned during the conversation that, if I should succeed, then Beck would have a headache, but if my conversation with the Chancellor were a failure, then he [the Marshal] would be in trouble (as commander in chief).

The conversation lasted for an hour. Piłsudski was all the time in a very serious mood, and it was obvious that he had a weighty decision on his mind.

At Beck's request, he gave an order for a press communiqué to be published announcing that I had been received at the Belveder.

From the Belveder I left with Minister Beck for the Raczyński Palace, where we wrote down the Marshal's instructions.

On the same evening I left for Berlin.

The communiqué published in Warsaw on the evening of November 5 was telegraphed abroad.

At the station, when I was leaving Warsaw, Konrad Wrzos, a spry journalist smelling big news, was present. He even had a photographer with him, but I arrived at the last moment and the picture was not taken.

Immediately upon my arrival in Berlin, I took the necessary steps at the Auswärtiges Amt to obtain an audience with the Chancellor. I approached the director of protocol, Count von Bassewitz, on this matter.

However, a few days later Count Bassewitz advised me that Chancellor Hitler was busy with the election campaign, touring various cities, and would not be able to grant me an audience prior to the peoples referendum. In the meantime I was received by von Neurath. However I had strict orders from Warsaw that the Marshal's instructions were destined for Hitler only and were to be kept secret. I also had a visit from von Moltke at the Legation. He too was very anxious to learn something about the Marshal's message for Hitler. Von Moltke later told me that, being *au courant* of the situation, he was not mistaken in his suppositions as to what I was to present to the Chancellor.

Secrecy on our part was very appropriate, since the clerks of the Auswärtiges Amt still clung to their negative attitude toward Poland, and any indiscreet hint from me prior to my conversation with Hitler in person could easily be exploited by them to our disadvantage.

The conversation with Hitler took place on November 15 in the presence of Minister von Neurath, and Lipski informed Beck accordingly on the same day.

The text of Lipski's report is included in the *Polish White Book* (No. 6, p. 16). There are, however, two omissions. Lipski's opening words were:

"When the National Socialist government came to power in Germany, this evoked considerable commotion in international opinion, including even the possibility of poltical conflicts. Under these circumstances the necessity arose in Poland to administer measures to reinforce national security. The Marshal, far from being influenced by the atmosphere created by the press and propaganda, trusts the Chancellor and his policies. He has not taken any measures of a defensive character. The Marshal is satisfied to observe that Polish-German relations have improved since this time, owing to the Chancellor's personality, and that his expectations were realized."

At the end of the fifth paragraph, the following sentence of Hitler was omitted:

"Perhaps sometime in the future certain problems can be settled with Poland in a friendly atmosphere, for example, by compensation." (The Chancellor spoke of this as something very distant, never uttering the words "frontier" or "corridor.")

On the same day, November 15, the Wolff Agency issued a communiqué on Lipski's visit with Hitler; according to this communiqué, it was agreed that the Polish and German governments would "deal with the questions affecting both countries by way of direct negotiations, and further renounce all application of force in their mutual relations, with a view to strengthening European peace." [4]

After Lipski's visit with Hitler, a conference was held at the Belveder on November 20 among Piłsudski, Minister Beck, and Undersecretary of State Szembek. The German plan for a nonaggression declaration was not yet known to the Polish side.

Beck reported on the first international press comments about the Berlin visit, stressing that the Russian press took a very correct stand—more favorable than the French.

[4] *Polish White Book,* No. 7; *DGFP,* Series C, Vol. II, Nos. 69 and 70.

A note drawn up by Szembek immediately after the conference reads as follows:

"The Marshal is availing himself of this report. He thinks that the success achieved by us is not a 100 percent success. As a matter of fact, it does not give much. There is positive meaning not in what was done but in the moment when it was done, that is, after Germany left the League of Nations. What will follow next is not known. The Marshal is now interested in two problems: Russia and France. It is easier to come to an understanding with France; with Russia it is much more difficult. You have to be consistent and patient there, otherwise errors might occur which not we, but the Soviets, will profit by. . . . The Marshal says that he intends to summon the French military attaché, receive him in a military manner, and talk to him as one soldier to another. He will tell him *l'historique* of Lipski's conversation, from an angle not very favorable for the Germans, and he will tell him that we want to know what France really wants. *Further talks with the Germans will depend on the answer.* [Emphasis in the original.] The Marshal considers a 'plus' the sending of a chief of the French Second Bureau. This conversation will reach Daladier, probably through General Gamelin. It is rather doubtful whether via Laroche. The Marshal will tell him that this is strictly confidential, and 'si Monsieur Daladier est homme d'honneur' it will end there (these last words referred to keeping it secret from the press)." [5]

After the Lipski-Hitler conversation the Auswärtiges Amt promptly prepared a plan of the declaration, and on November 24 Envoy von Moltke received instructions in Warsaw to obtain an audience with Piłsudski to present him with the draft-declaration.[6]

On November 27 Lipski was summoned by von Neurath. The conversation and his critical remarks are described by Lipski in his report to Beck dated November 30, 1933.

DOCUMENT 15   Lipski to Beck

Berlin, November 30, 1933
Strictly Confidential

On November 27 I was unexpectedly summoned by Foreign Affairs Minister von Neurath, who stated to me as follows:

Minister von Moltke has been instructed to ask for an audience with Marshal Piłsudski. The audience was fixed for this afternoon. In this conversation, Moltke was to convey to the Marshal the greetings of

[5] The note is quoted in Szembek's letter to Raczyński of August 31, 1942 (Lipski's papers, File 3).

[6] *DGFP*, Series C, Vol. II, No. 84. See also Nos. 77, 79, and 81.

Chancellor Hitler and at the same time hand him the German draft of the declaration.

Neurath handed me a copy of the plan, stressing that he was doing this as a gesture of courtesy, *à titre d'information.* I noticed at the time that the plan bears the heading *Erklärung,* since nowadays the use of the word "pact" is too commonplace.

At Neurath's request I read the document in his presence but, for obvious reasons, I abstained from making any comment.

Minister von Neurath finally told me that he is awaiting a communiqué about the audience in Warsaw and asked for my assistance in case of any technical difficulties with the publication of the communiqué.

Following your instructions, forwarded to me by Mr. Dębicki, I kept the whole matter strictly secret. However, as I have on occasion for Warsaw, I am taking the liberty of sending you the following observations:

In his talk with me on November 15, Hitler assumed that the possibility of war would be excluded from Polish-German relations. He is ready to have this principle take the form of a treaty. I also stress that after this conversation, as I have already informed you, the Chancellor publicly declared that "there are no questions between the German Reich and Poland which might justify bloodshed" (interview for *Matin*).[7]

The Chancellor further developed the idea that an atmosphere of confidence should be created between the countries by means of relaxation in various fields. The problem of frontiers was not touched on by the Chancellor specifically in the conversation; he only hinted that these matters should be left for the future, in the hope that under favorable circumstances a solution might be found to satisfy both parties.

Let us now take into consideration the known plan;[8] even upon a perfunctory analysis we can discover therein the following points:

[7] In the part of the interview for *Matin* referring to the opinion that no contestable problem existed in Europe which would justify the outbreak of war, the Chancellor stressed: "Everything can be settled between national governments if they are conscious of honor and responsibility. There exist a patriotic Poland and a Germany devoted to their traditions. Between them there are contentions and frictions caused by a bad treaty, but there is nothing else which would be worthy of bloodshed, especially since on a battlefield the best usually perish. Therefore a good-neighborly understanding between Germany and Poland is fully possible." And polemizing on the statement that the present German government had aggressive intentions, the Chancellor expressed himself thus: "I have not the slightest intention of attacking my neighbors. Poland understands this. Situated further east than France, Poland knows us better."

[8] *DGFP,* Series C, Vol. II, No. 81.

The authors of the plan tried not to call the document a pact, limiting themselves to giving it the heading *Erklärung*. Neurath's explanation that this was done in order to avoid the commonplace term, that is, "pact," is not logical. It rather seems that a general definition was used instead of "pact excluding war" or else "pact" with some other adjective —for example, nonaggression—since this would not correspond with the real text of the plan. It was probably not the authors' intention to use a term conforming with the actual meaning of the word "plan."

The first paragraph, purely political in character, tries to shift Polish-German relations from the platform of the Treaty of Versailles to the ground of direct understanding. Hitherto, in German opinion, Poland existed only as a creation of the Treaty of Versailles.

In the second paragraph, attention is drawn to the assertion that maintaining and assuring a "just peace" between the two nations is an indispensable condition for a general peace in Europe. The idea of a just peace, however, might provoke different interpretations, and therefore should be accepted with reserve, especially since the word "justly" takes on a special meaning as it is used in further paragraphs.

The third paragraph ties in the planned declaration with the Polish-German arbitration agreement signed at Locarno and with the Kellogg Pact, and states that obligations ensuing from these agreements should be defined.

This definition follows immediately in the next [fourth] paragraph, when parties bind themselves to seek solutions for *all* contentions that arise between them in a conciliatory way or by arbitration. Such a broad concept of the matter reserves for the Germans the possibility of introducing on the platform of bilateral talks, and later submitting to arbitration, such problems as minorities and even territorial problems. The declaration of abstention from force, in conformity with the principles of the Kellogg Pact in this respect, makes no difference whatsoever here.

The fifth paragraph would in general correspond to the Chancellor's concept that "important problems" which divide the two countries because of a "bad" treaty should be left to a better atmosphere in the future. This semirestriction to settle these problems in the future might also be necessary to the Chancellor, bearing in mind the attitude of the Prussian elements definitely hostile to Hitler's policies toward Poland. However, attention is drawn here to the fact that the expression "schwebende Probleme" was used, which, if accepted, would consist of a mutual ascertainment that in these matters there is contention between the two states about "serious problems" demanding settlement. With the simultaneous acceptance of the principle of obligatory arbitration for all matters under dispute, this entails grave danger of the possibility for one party to raise any problem, even a territorial one, at a favorable moment, without any responsibility of guilt for provoking the conflict. This is of the utmost importance, as far as the *casus foederis* of Poland with its allies is concerned.

If we now compare the plan handed to us, which was probably technically elaborated on by the Auswärtiges Amt, with the contents of my conversation with Hitler on November 15, we can observe that this plan, though drawn along Hitler's lines, nevertheless at many points goes beyond and even changes this line, as it was presented to me by Hitler, to our disadvantage.

In comparison with the declaration of November 15, wherein the willingness of both governments not to resort to force in mutual relations was expressed, the plan imposes on both governments the obligation not to apply force, with the simultaneous formal commitment to submit to conciliation and arbitration all problems deriving from mutual relations, thus impairing guarantees resulting from Poland's membership in the League of Nations as well as from our direct defensive alliances.

When deliberating over this document, two suppositions come to mind which are difficult to confirm; nevertheless, I am taking the liberty of revealing them to you:

Chancellor Hitler, if this step is taken directly by him, wants to find out how far Poland would go to achieve a direct understanding with Germany, its relations with the League of Nations and the Western Powers notwithstanding.

As far as the Auswärtiges Amt is concerned, it is not impossible that this office, composed of persons utterly hostile toward any kind of understanding with Poland, could try, by sufficient editing of the plan, to render difficult the settlement of relations between the new masters of Germany and Poland. For it is quite possible that the Chancellor limited himself simply to tracing general directions, and the Office of Foreign Affairs elaborated on the text, introducing adequate encumbrances.

Józef Lipski

Moltke was received by Beck on November 25 [9] and by Marshal Piłsudski in Beck's presence on the 27th, when he handed over the German draft-declaration.[10]

Soon after the conversation with Moltke, Piłsudski received the French military attaché, General d'Arbonneau, with whom he discussed the problem of Polish-German relations, as one soldier to another.[11] Then Piłsudski left for Wilno, taking Moltke's plan with him and issuing no further decisions. He requested an explanation of several points. The long delay in Piłsudski's answer caused considerable trouble for Moltke.

Meanwhile the feelings of German circles toward the Polish Legation in Berlin underwent a radical change as compared with the period referred to by Envoy Wysocki in the article quoted above (see pp. 43–45). This is clear from the letter Lipski wrote to Roman Dębicki, director of Beck's cabinet.

DOCUMENT 16   Lipski to Dębicki

Berlin, December 3, 1933
Strictly Confidential

Events and moods develop so rapidly in this dynamic territory of ours that, although I was only in Warsaw on November 4, I already feel the necessity for contact with the Ministry.

As I have to continue my visits to other members of the cabinet, following the rule of protocol, good orientation is very advisable.

On Monday I shall call on Vice-Chancellor von Papen. I am still delaying the visit to Goebbels, since a discussion with him might be highly political in character. However, further delay is becoming embarrassing, and I am afraid of offending Goebbels, who is well disposed toward us.

Owing to my experience with Darré,[12] you will understand that I must take all precautions, since I am practically empty-handed. Ministers of the new regime are very fond of pursuing, so to say, their own

[9] For Moltke's report, see *ibid.*, No. 87.
[10] Moltke's report, *ibid.*, No. 90.
[11] Laroche, p. 141.
[12] Walter Darré became minister of food and agriculture after the resignation of Hugenberg in June, 1933. On November 25, the Polish-German rye agreement was signed; afterward Minister Lipski paid a visit to Minister Darré. As a result of this visit, the Ministry prepared a communiqué for the press quoting opinions of the Polish Envoy on internal German regulations concerning agriculture. Lipski, to whom the text of the communiqué was forwarded for confirmation, had to make a number of corrections.

policy, and at the present moment, seeing as their particular task the leading of Germany away from isolation, they try to be most active in international problems. As if by orders from the top, a change of front toward us is taking place all along the line. In Hitlerite spheres they talk about the new Polish-German friendship. Every activity of mine, even the most insignificant, such as the exchange of ratification documents with regard to the small frontier traffic, serves as an excuse for political enunciations by the press about the rapprochement. Everyone wants to be in contact with us. At a reception for our military attaché, the full brass of the Reichswehr appeared, including General Hammerstein, General Schaumburg, and Colonel von Reichenau, a thing which had never happened before. You can imagine the surprise of other military attachés, the French, etc. Yesterday, at the reception for the football team, the Brown Shirts and representatives of the Reichswehr created a most cordial atmosphere. Rumors are circulated that the Führer himself is interested in this match, and might possibly appear personally in the stands.

My initial response to these demonstrations was to instruct all our professional offices in the territory of the Reich, above all the consuls, to avail themselves of this disposition in order to settle matters hitherto impossible to arrange, and to establish contacts with the authorities to settle whatever is possible and what is definitely to our advantage.

However, as far as my diplomatic tactics are concerned, things are far more complicated, bearing in mind what I have mentioned before—that every step of the Legation is discounted on the outside, and that I do not know what our Ministry's directive is and whether a strong action in Berlin would not cause embarrassment in other territories. I therefore am maintaining a sort of reserve, at the same time being careful not to estrange people of the new regime and to keep them well disposed toward us.

Now if I am to speak of politics, I had the first echo of Moltke's conversation with the Marshal from Secretary of State Meissner, privy adviser of Hindenburg. Meissner told me that he read the report of Moltke, who sounds very enthusiastic about the reception the Marshal accorded him. This was also confirmed by the chief of the Eastern Department of the A.A., who told me that Moltke, who arrived here on Friday, was very much impressed by this conversation and by the Marshal's profound appraisal of Polish-German problems. Director Meyer stressed the fact that Moltke was so promptly received, and that the audience lasted nearly one hour and a half. He touched on the matter of the document, mentioning that he had not drawn it up himself. Stressing that he was only doing his best to accommodate us, he tried discreetly to sound out my point of view, but I kept aloof. Moltke, who called on me today before his departure, also asked about my opinion, but he received no reply. He emphasized that the document reflects ideas of the Chancellor, who practically dictated it. He added that he hopes there will not be too many cancellations on our side.

I think that you will agree with my tactics of absolute silence, which seems to me the only possible way of acting and perhaps to a certain degree also a useful one.

Moltke complained to me about the difficulties he encounters in Warsaw in trade negotiations. He stressed that I have here such a friendly relationship with the authorities, while he sometimes waits in vain for the promised answers of the Ministry of Industry on economic matters. He added that, in response to my request, the A.A. agreed to abolish the *junctim* between the rye agreement and other trade negotiations.

The situation here remains most intricate and it is exceedingly difficult to guess the real intentions of the government. No progress has hitherto been achieved on the French sector. The conversation of François-Poncet with the Chancellor, which has leaked to the press, was exaggeratedly blown up by the local press and presented as an overture for concrete talks. However, the Ambassador told me, and it was confirmed from other sources, that his conversation was only a vague exchange of opinions without any tangible results. The only concrete thing was the Chancellor's firm declaration that the Germans would in any case not return to a League of Nations based on the present principles. In the French Embassy I was told that the conversation of François-Poncet with Hitler is so distorted by both the German and the French press that it is always necessary to revert to the protocol of the conversation to avoid misinterpretations.

At the A.A. I had a talk on French-German relations with the acknowledged friend of Ambassador Wysocki, Köpke. Herr Köpke says that it will be a long time before French opinion changes basically on the subject of Germany. The flow of events in Germany is so dynamic that—in the words of Köpke—French opinion, composed of little people whose very logical minds react very slowly in the face of new international manifestations, simply cannot keep pace. This is causing confusion and consequently a critical approach to all happenings in Germany.

Herr Köpke gave me to understand that the A.A. counted on the fact that a *détente* with Poland would also appease France. However, the turn in Polish-German relations was possibly too rapid, and France had reacted unfavorably. Herr Köpke seems to persist in the assumption that an improvement in relations with Poland is necessary for a *détente* with France.

However, it should not be taken for granted that this opinion prevails here, for the present German foreign policy is far from being uniform, especially where tactics are concerned. A pronounced tendency can also be detected here to separate Poland from France, thus abolishing the so-called French hegemony in Europe. Finally, with regard to German-French relations, I must call your attention to the fact that from rather important official German personages who have certain contacts in Paris I heard quite anxious comments on possible serious conflicts with France resulting from the growth of right-wing forces in France and certain tendencies of the General Staff. On this occasion, statements were quoted even of such persons as Caillaux [13] to the effect that the situation is becoming intolerable. I am noting these loose comments here only to point out how the opinions circulated among the local community differ. Official spheres, however, seem to evaluate the French situation as fluid.

Some German diplomatic action may again be noted on the Italian sector. Mussolini's endeavors to reorganize the League of Nations are discussed, as well as his efforts to force the Four-Power Pact, or perhaps a Five-Power Pact, into the frame of the League. I have no more detailed information at present on this, but I presume that Ambassador Wysocki has probably already reported on this subject.

In conclusion, I would like to draw your attention to the report of the Legation concerning the latest internal German moves with regard to drawing Hess and Röhm into the cabinet. This step, taken at a moment of such international tension, regardless of reasons of a purely internal nature, deserves to be taken into consideration. It means, at any rate, a very important grouping of forces, and at this time of staggering tempo in the policy of the Chancellor it ought to be closely observed.

I am continually watching one point which is, so to say, crystal-clear

[13] Joseph Caillaux, French senator, former prime minister and finance minister.

in the foreign policy of Hitlerite Germany, namely, Austria. Concepts with regard to other international problems are still subject to rather serious fluctuations.

Józef Lipski

The Ministry of Foreign Affairs and the Legation in Berlin worked to clarify problems that appeared doubtful to Marshal Piłsudski, so that on December 16 Lipski was in a position to discuss them with Minister von Neurath.

DOCUMENT 17   Lipski to Beck

Berlin, December 16, 1933
Strictly Confidential

Following your instructions, I referred today during my conversation with the minister of foreign affairs, Baron von Neurath, to the question of the Oder Navigation Act and to the proposed declaration presented by Herr Moltke to Marshal Piłsudski on November 27.

When I told Herr Neurath that I would like to discuss the Oder question with him in a friendly way, he immediately answered that he was not sufficiently acquainted with this matter and would first have to consult his professional staff. I gave Herr Neurath the following explanation:

The Navigation Act for the river Oder was composed by the International Commission at Dresden on July 29, 1932. However, the Reich government neither signed nor acceded to it. All signatory states of the act have been notified by the government of the Reich as to the reason for its abstention; the Polish government received a note from the German government dated January 13, 1933. Owing to this stand taken by the German government, it was decided within the frame of the International Commission to transfer the dispute to the Hague Tribunal by way of compromise. As far as we are informed, some governments represented at the International Commission have already forwarded their propositions to the German government. The Polish government—in quite a friendly way and wishing to avoid any difficulties—would like, prior to taking any measures in connection with the note of the German government dated January 13, 1933, to be informed about the German government's opinion on this matter, especially since recently the Reich government has taken a special position toward the Hague Tribunal.

Herr von Neurath apparently fully understood our intention and thanked me very much for our friendly attitude. He stressed, however, that he would have to confer with experts on his staff before giving me an answer.

I then took up the question of the proposed document.

I declared that I had been to Warsaw recently and that the document presented to Marshal Piłsudski by Herr Moltke and brought to my attention thanks to Herr von Neurath's courtesy is the subject of careful investigations on the part of our Ministry of Foreign Affairs. As for the principle of abstaining from violence in mutual relations between the two countries, there is conformity of opinion on this point. As far as the external form of the document is concerned, I stated that no objections were raised, although it is rather novel.

Herr Neurath began to elaborate in more detail about the form of the document. He said that his lawyers were at first very reluctant, since they wanted to adorn everything with paragraphs. However, he declared that this form is more appropriate and better serves the purpose of the declaration.

Discussing the form of the document, I said that the Marshal also mentioned to Herr Moltke that such a document without paragraphs is more agreeable to him.

I further stated to Herr Neurath that before the conclusion of our investigations of the document we were anxious to receive some preliminary explanations (*Vorfragen*) as to certain points of the declaration. I pointed out that the first such preliminary question is the problem of the Polish-German arbitration agreement signed at Locarno, which is referred to in the document. I confirmed that this agreement contains a reference in some vital points to the Council of the League of Nations, that is, in Part II, Article 18, wherein it is stated that "if during a month upon conclusion of works of the permanent conciliatory commission both parties will not reach an understanding, the case, on request of one of the parties, will be brought before the Council of the League of Nations, which will rule in accordance with Article 15 of the Pact of the League."

I added that the Locarno agreements were in general negotiated with a view to Germany's entry into the League of Nations. I therefore asked whether there is not a difficulty arising from Germany's withdrawal from the League.

Herr von Neurath agreed that this point really seems to require some explanation. He is not so well acquainted with the juridical side of the problem and is therefore obliged to confer with Gaus.[14] He thinks, however, that the Locarno agreement was referred to because it is a negotiated arbitration agreement between Poland and Germany which could be applied in this case. If this agreement were to be refuted, in all probability a new arbitration and conciliation agreement would have to be negotiated between Poland and Germany. However, Neurath insisted that he was speaking of this matter without authority, owing to his lack of strict juridical information.

I stressed here that in my opinion a reference to the Kellogg Pact would be more in line with the intentions of both governments, and Herr von Neurath agreed. I also added casually, stressing that this was my personal opinion, that Locarno as a whole did not evoke special enthusiasm on our part.

I then passed on to paragraph four of the declaration, saying that we understand the affirmation that "both governments, in case it is impossible to settle controversial matters by direct negotiations, will seek a solution by other peaceful means, and especially by arbitration and conciliation" to mean that in such controversial matters both governments will seek adequate conciliatory proceedings or arbitration by way of a mutual understanding.

Herr Neurath said that he understands it in the same way.

Finally I asked Herr von Neurath what it meant that the agreement should be concluded for *at least* ten years, adding that we have no special objection to the length of time; however, bearing in mind that the text must possess a juridical value and be ratified, it is important to realize the meaning of the words "at least."

Herr von Neurath replied that this paragraph means that the agreement will be binding for at least ten years, and that only after this time may the possible notification of more precise dates of withdrawal take place.

I replied that I was satisfied with this explanation.

[14] Friedrich Gaus, director of the Legal Department of the A.A.

Referring to the whole complex of my questions, Herr Neurath said that it would be best if I would discuss the whole problem with Gaus, and expressed his desire that I should immediately get in touch with Gaus. However, I said that today I was rather busy and would contact Gaus next week, who in the meantime will be briefed by Herr Neurath on the matter. Herr Neurath expressed the opinion that in general it will be necessary for our lawyers to meet to discuss this text.

I put off the conversation with Gaus until next week, supposing that this would meet with your approval. Here I would like to add that, as I was informed by Herr von Bülow, who came to lunch at the Legation, the high government officials are leaving for a holiday period until January 9.

From my conversation with Neurath I drew the conclusion, first of all, that I was right in supposing that the text was elaborated on by the lawyers of the Auswärtiges Amt and not by the Chancellor's pen. I also wish to add that von Neurath told me that the Chancellor questioned him a few days ago about our point of view and that he replied that such matters always require more time for investigation.

In this respect I would like to call your attention to notices published yesterday and the day before in the *Völkischer Beobachter* from Warsaw, stating that the Polish government is taking a wait-and-see attitude in connection with the whole international situation. These notes, rather friendly to us in tone, make a comparison between the nervous tactics of Beneš and the calm reserve of the government in Warsaw.

Taking leave of Herr Neurath, I paid him a few compliments on the occasion of the Polish-German football match, stressing particularly the very friendly role toward us of the Sportsführer for the Reich, Herr von Tschammer und Osten. Herr Tschammer und Osten asked me yesterday, if possible, to lay stress in my conversation with the Foreign Minister of the Reich on the importance of such sport shows for mutual Polish-German relations.

On Monday, at 1 o'clock, I will have an audience with the minister of propaganda, Goebbels, and in the evening I will dine at Herr Neurath's. I advise you of this because I might have an opportunity to convey some of your wishes to Minister Goebbels or Neurath.[15]

Józef Lipski

[15] For the German version of this conversation, see *DGFP*, Series C, Vol. II, No. 131.

DOCUMENT 18   Lipski to Beck

Berlin, December 18, 1933
Strictly Confidential

I was received today by Minister Goebbels at the Ministry of Propaganda. I began by explaining to Goebbels the cause for the delay of my visit, which was due to my departure for Warsaw, where I stayed a little longer than expected. I conveyed your greetings to Herr Goebbels. Expressing his thanks, Goebbels said that he remembers with pleasure the conversation with you in Geneva.

After these opening remarks, Goebbels declared that he would like in the first place to have a basic talk with me about Polish-German relations. He added that he is a close collaborator of the Chancellor and that he knows him very thoroughly. He knows that if the Chancellor takes a certain line in politics, or if he promises something, he then holds to it closely regardless of difficulties. Goebbels knows that the Chancellor chose the line of understanding with Poland. Herr Goebbels called it a *modus vivendi*. In spite of certain resistance, the Chancellor is undoubtedly acting and will continue to act along this line. In Goebbels' opinion, the Chancellor would like to conclude a nonaggression pact with Poland. The understanding with Poland undoubtedly—Goebbels did not conceal it—will meet with certain obstacles; however, the Chancellor is determined to overcome them. Goebbels was quite frank in referring explicitly to the old Prussian caste of Junkers who, as he put it, led politics for four hundred years and are encumbered by certain formulas. The men of today who have come to power in Germany are new men, young, not compromised, originating from masses of Germans with nationalistic ideas, but who have nothing in common with the *alldeutsch* type striving for expansion at the expense of other nations. The *modus vivendi* with Poland will cause the Germans to suffer considerable sacrifices. But they are aware of more imminent dangers today and the necessity to subordinate secondary interests to them. Such a danger—in Goebbels' opinion—is Communism. The Western states have not grasped the threat of this danger. The condition in Germany was such that, as the Führer said, power could have been seized in the street. A bunch of irresponsible persons could have become masters of the Reich. This very danger of Communism compels Germany to seek an understanding with Poland, and from this angle Polish-German relations are of very basic importance.

Herr Goebbels embarked on a lengthy tirade, stressing that he was talking not as a diplomat but as a sincerely feeling German who belonged to the National Socialist Party. Goebbels wondered if any of the old-regime diplomats would dare to speak so openly with the Polish Envoy. Herr Goebbels was pleased to observe that on the Polish side he sees young people in responsible posts also. He mentioned how pleased he was with the conversation he had with you at Geneva. Would it be at all possible to talk in this manner with a representative of a state which would have to look back to its parliament? When the Chancellor says something, whether for the moment it is popular or not, public opinion accepts it. Everyone believes him, and everyone obeys him. Goebbels gave me to understand that it is they who are aware of the feelings of the masses, and that there is no estrangement between the leaders of the National Socialist camp and the masses.

Going on to matters concerning the press, in Goebbels' opinion it is essential that the press should not bait. He declared himself against an irresponsible press which starts conflicts, taking no responsibility for them.

In answer to this long flow of words, I said more or less this:

In Poland there has always prevailed a certain interest and understanding for the National Socialist idea, and that is why even in spite of very strong international agitation by propagandists, the press in Poland and opinion in general took an objective stand toward the German revolution. Goebbels confirmed this in full. I further stated that, in the period of fifteen years in the aftermath of the war, Polish-German relations had been poisoned by a campaign of hatred. Only since the Chancellor's coming to power and his first words spoken to my predecessor had a change occurred in these relations. My last conversation with the Chancellor was, especially in view of the international situation, a very important event. If under such circumstances we came to ask what should be done in the field of Polish-German relations in order to reinforce security jeopardized by Germany's withdrawal from the League of Nations, this was very proof of the Polish government's wish for, and a resulting tendency toward, good relations with Germany. The communiqué published on November 15 spoke out against resorting to power in mutual relations. The declaration of such a principle by statesmen of both states, fully responsible for their governments, was—I dared say—a clear confirmation of this tendency.

Herr Goebbels added that the communiqué means much more than a treaty signed, for example, with a state which has to refer to its parliament, in the face of which the government is absolutely powerless.

As to the question discussed much longer by Herr Goebbels than I have reported above, namely, Polish-German collaboration with regard to a not clearly defined danger of Communism, I replied more or less along these lines:

I stated that, looking at Poland, one should also bear in mind its history. I reminded him that Poland, as was also mentioned by the Chancellor during our conversation, was often the guardian of the West. I pointed to Vienna and the battle of Warsaw in 1920.[16] I said that, since I was in London at that time, I had had the opportunity to observe how deeply the Labor Party was undermined by subversive Communistic tendencies. We were eyewitnesses to it, since the Polish Legation was formally besieged for several weeks by communized elements. However, I added, the very territory of Poland is not adaptable to subversive experiments. This is a result, on the one hand, of the social structure, owing to the majority of agricultural elements, and, on the other hand, of the patriotic attitude of the population, which, under cover of subversive propaganda, hears the old aggressive tune of the former occupant.

Herr Goebbels agreed that this analysis was interesting but that Germany finds itself in a different situation, owing to a different social structure, and has no defense, like Poland, in a certain natural repulsion against outside infiltration. However, he thought that it makes no difference what elements of resistance are present in the struggle with subversive ideas. Of prime importance for international relations is the fact that a particular state refuses to be enslaved by these ideas. Goebbels also said that he would like me to look thoroughly into their principle of thinking, enter into the closest possible contact with persons in the

16 In the battle of Vienna (September, 1683) the Polish king, Jan Sobieski, defeated the Turkish Army. In the battle of Warsaw (August, 1920), Józef Piłsudski, chief of state and commander in chief of the Polish Army, defeated the Soviet Army and stopped their march to the West. Both battles are recognized as decisive battles in European history. See W. Jędrzejewicz, "Dziewietnaście decydujących bitew świata" [Nineteen Decisive Battles of the World], *Bellona* (London), 1963, Nos. 3–4, pp. 216–23.

Chancellor's camp, and in this way act for the establishment of good relations between the two states. "If that succeeds," Goebbels said, "I feel that both you and I will have great credit in the eyes of history."

Afterward, passing to the question of a press *détente* in propaganda— and this is interesting—Goebbels suggested that at first some resistance had been detected against a rapprochement with Poland, which he, by order of the Chancellor, was energetically suppressing. It was obvious that the resistance came from the old Prussian caste. . . .

Józef Lipski

Discussion by Lipski of specific points of the declaration took place on December 20 during a conference with the legal counselor of the Auswärtiges Amt, Gaus. Then came an interval due to the holiday season and a delay in Marshal Piłsudski's final decision.

DOCUMENT 19   Lipski to Beck

Berlin, December 20, 1933

Following my letter of December 16, I am now reporting on the result of the conversation I had today with Director Gaus to discuss the document in question.

Referring to my conversation with Minister Neurath of December 16, I stressed that, in its study of the plan of the Polish-German declaration, our Department came across a few items requiring additional preliminary clarification. I then posed the first question, namely, whether in view of Germany's withdrawal from the League of Nations further reference to the Polish-German Locarno arbitration agreement would still be valid.

Herr Gaus replied that this question was quite justified because, in connection with Germany's withdrawal from the League of Nations, a problem arises as to the consequences of this fact on the basic Locarno agreement, that is, to the Rhineland Pact automatically connected with the League's structure. On the other hand, Article 22, par. 1, of the Polish-German Arbitration Treaty, signed at Locarno, states as follows:

"The present treaty will be ratified. Ratification documents will be deposited with the League of Nations at Geneva, simultaneously with documents of ratification of the treaty concluded on this date between Germany, Belgium, France, Great Britain, and Italy.

"It will be enforced and binding under the same terms as the treaty mentioned above."

The Rhineland Pact problem connected with Germany's withdrawal from the League of Nations pertains to the field of general policy. Herr Gaus points to the recent debates on this subject in the parliaments of England and France. I am taking the liberty of mentioning here what was omitted in my previous report—that von Neurath confirmed to me on December 16 that the Locarno treaties are still binding. Germany is still a member of the League *de jure,* and therefore nothing formally is changed. Only after two years will Germany legally cease to be a member of the League. Herr Gaus, as a lawyer, is not in theory excluding the necessity of introducing adequate modifications into the Locarno agreements in this case. The Polish-German arbitration agreement might then also be subject to certain alterations. Herr Gaus understands our doubts with regard to Article 22, while he does not expect any difficulties with reference to the League of Nations as far as Articles 18 and 19 are concerned.

Herr Gaus further ascertained that, just because of these certain doubtful points, paragraph three of the declaration includes a provision "to exclude possible ambiguity," etc., and that the following paragraph states that both governments will seek solutions on controversial matters in arbitration and conciliation. The whole text, in his opinion, should be taken more from the political angle than as a purely formal juridical document.

I asked Herr Gaus whether my idea is correct about the obligation to seek a way of settlement by arbitration or conciliation in matters in which diplomatic proceedings fail.

In connection with this question Herr Gaus gave the following explanation:

The obligation to seek a solution of disputes by way of arbitration or conciliation could in practice be carried out (1) by application of the Polish-German Locarno arbitration agreement; (2) by application of a new Polish-German arbitration agreement, which, in case of withdrawal from the Locarno agreement, would have to be negotiated by the two governments; (3) by seeking in each separate case arbitration or conciliation procedures.

Herr Gaus envisages these three alternatives. He personally sees no objection to keeping the Locarno arbitration in binding force for both states, or perhaps replacing it with another agreement. However, he understands the doubts entertained by the Polish side.

He was anxious to explain that the Locarno agreement should not be considered a trap. Just two agreements were referred to—Locarno and Kellogg—since these are two political acts following the Versailles Treaty binding for both states.

I had the impression that Herr Gaus would be inclined to omit reference to the Locarno agreement completely, keeping only the reference to the Kellogg Pact.

He stresses that the text is simply a draft and gives me to understand that he is waiting for Polish counterpropositions on these points.

As to the term "at least for ten years," Gaus gave a reply analogous to Herr Neurath's.

Expressing thanks for the explanations, I stated that I would forward them for the information of the Ministry of Foreign Affairs in Warsaw.

Józef Lipski

Only on January 9, 1934, when Piłsudski arrived at the conclusion that France would not stand up to Hitler, was Lipski in a position to present to Neurath the Polish counterpropositions in connection with the declaration of nonaggression, expressing readiness for immediate signing.[17]

In the course of these difficult proceedings Lipski displayed his great talent as a negotiator and his profound knowledge of international juridical problems. Results of further conversations with Gaus are contained in two reports of Minister Lipski dated January 16.[18]

DOCUMENT 20 Lipski to Beck

Berlin, January 16, 1934
Strictly Confidential

On January 12 I had a call in the late evening hours from the office of the Minister of Foreign Affairs, informing me that Herr von Neurath

[17] For the notice by von Neurath and the Polish text of the proposition, see *DGFP*, Series C, Vol. II, No. 168.
[18] For the German version of the Lipski-Gaus conversation, see *ibid.*, No. 186.

requested that I call in the next few days on Director Gaus in connection with my previous conversations with Herr Neurath about the Polish-German declaration.

During your stop in Berlin on January 13, I was instructed to conduct conversations with Gaus in accordance with principles set out in Warsaw, and to take *ad referendum* doubtful questions that might arise in the course of the talks. You instructed me to keep in contact with you by wire at Geneva, and with Mr. Szembek, the undersecretary in Warsaw.

On January 16, I was received at 11 A.M. by Director Gaus. Referring to our conversation on these matters on December 20, 1933, Herr Gaus stated that Minister von Neurath, upon acknowledging the alterations introduced by us in the German text, directed him as a specialist to express his opinion on these alterations. Herr Gaus explained to Herr von Neurath the nature of the Polish alterations, although he wished to discuss them with me in order to be fully cognizant of their meaning.

Herr Gaus then stated that the German side—here he made reference to the Chancellor—attaches considerable importance to this document, and therefore it is not possible to deal with it superficially. Here I replied that we also take this declaration very seriously and that is why our Departments had to consider all details and why the work had to last a certain length of time.

Next Gaus mentioned that our conversations are just preparatory proceedings to the principal exchange of opinion between me and von Neurath with regard to the declaration.

Passing on to the text, Gaus stated that three principal points require clarification, while our other amendments are rather of an editorial character. From his statement it developed that he did not think that the omission of the words "just peace" from the second paragraph had any significance; neither did editing changes in paragraph five. With regard to certain definitions introduced by us in connection with the notification for nonextension of the declaration, he said they are rather in agreement with his ideas.

The three basic points referred to by Gaus are the following:

1) *Affirmation that the declaration cannot limit or change obligations for each of the contracting parties under the agreements concluded by them.*

This Polish amendment struck Neurath and particularly affected Hitler. Gaus explained to Neurath that the restriction deals with Poland's obligations under the Covenant of the League, agreements with France of 1921 and 1925, and agreements with Rumania.

Speaking of Hitler's reaction, Gaus stressed that the Chancellor wanted to bestow on the document a political character and free it from any juridical preciseness. Hitler—in Gaus's opinion—obviously cannot appreciate the meaning of our reserve from the technical point of view. Gaus suggested, stressing that he was speaking quite frankly and confidentially, that in the Chancellor's mind this restriction could evoke the impression of a desire to obtain from Germany the acceptance of these treaties, a certain affirmation of their inviolability, and a sort of fear that this formula might serve as a cover for some obligations of Poland unknown to Germany and directed against it.

With regard to this point, I made it clear that explanations given by Gaus and Neurath concerning Polish obligations covered by this formula are fully in accordance with the actual state of affairs. It is absolutely out of the question that the restriction ensuing from Polish obligations could serve as a cover for the intention to compel Germany to recognize the treaties. Besides, I confirmed that our treaties are registered at the League of Nations.

The conclusion that the declaration does not infringe on existing international obligations included in pacts concluded by Poland is indispensable to avoid a collision with the Covenant of the League.

Gaus tried to persuade me that this formula is unnecessary. The declaration merely says that neither state will resort to force in mutual relations in matters which may arise between them.

Stipulating that he was only quoting an example, Gaus touched on the possibility of a German-French military conflict, arising not out of Polish-German problems. In that case, in his opinion, the proposed Polish-German declaration would not create any obstacle for the obligations of Poland under the Polish-French alliance and the Covenant of the League (Article 16).

When I pointed out that the declaration is unthinkable with the omission of the affirmation about international obligations with regard to states like Germany, which are withdrawing from the League, and when I drew attention to a similar restriction included in our pact with Russia, Gaus quoted paragraph four of the preamble to the Polish-Russian pact, which reads as follows:

"Declaring that none of the obligations hitherto assumed by either of the Parties stands in the way of the peaceful development of their mutual relations or is incompatible with the present Pact."

He added that this phrasing is at any rate more digestible than our proposition. He, of course, made the reservation that his statement was just an opinion. In general, Gaus laid emphasis on the form which will cover this restriction, still keeping to his point of view that the restriction is superfluous and requesting that this point be reconsidered.

2) *The declaration cannot concern matters reserved under international law for exclusive competence of the states.*

As far as this reservation is concerned, Gaus agrees that it is inserted in various international texts, as, for example, in the Covenant of the League of Nations and in the General Act established by the League. He only asks why this restriction is necessary, since it is self-explanatory. He has often discussed this subject in the international field with Scialoja and other jurists, who were also against this formula, but still for the sake of tradition introduced it into texts. He would like to be informed whether our lawyers are taking this formula into consideration in practice. In case facultative arbitration were maintained in the declaration by consent of the parties from case to case, the formula would become even more superfluous.

For tactical reasons I accepted this point of view *ad referendum.*

3) *With regard to paragraph five, providing that controversial problems will be settled by peaceful means and in particular by conciliation and arbitration based upon an understanding between the contracting parties in each separate case.*

In view of our insertion of "in each separate case," Gaus asked whether we intend to recognize the Polish-German Arbitration Treaty signed in Locarno as nonexistent, since this treaty provides for obligatory arbitration more extensive than the suggested formula. Cancellation of this treaty is a question of principle, especially in connection with the whole set of these agreements. A broader concept of obligatory arbitration would be replaced by us with a more narrow agreement, which would mean a step backwards.

This is why Gaus insists on an absolutely basic reply on this point.

I answered that I would communicate with Warsaw on this matter.

Józef Lipski

DOCUMENT 21 Lipski to Szembek

Berlin, January 16, 1934
Strictly Confidential

My conversation today with Gaus, which lasted an hour and a half, concerned matters so entangled that it would be difficult to squeeze into a telegram the very substance of the problems. I therefore had to limit myself to telegraphing only points referred to by Gaus, while I took the liberty of sending a special courier to Warsaw who will deliver the enclosed report to you.

Minister Beck instructed me to forward to him copies of telegrams directed on this subject to Warsaw. Unfortunately, I cannot send him a copy of the report, and I am compelled to supply only an abbreviated telegram, which undoubtedly will not be sufficient basis for taking a decision.

Coming back to the conversation with Gaus, I must first of all say that neither my two conversations with Neurath nor my discussion with Gaus today give me the impression that the matter can be settled promptly. I also suppose that the German side, for deeper reasons, would tend to delay a decision for a certain time. In any case, if I would press for a more urgent finalization, this would prejudice my standing as a negotiator.

Of points referred to by Gaus, it seems to me that the most difficult to agree with is arbitration. In their original text the Germans went far beyond the Polish-German Locarno Arbitration Treaty, while we, on our part, have limited the Locarno agreement. For the German side it is difficult to step backward beyond 1925, and that is why Gaus in his statement points to the consequences of our withdrawal from the Locarno Treaty. This is of course a matter of argument. Nevertheless, Gaus is right when he declares that, if we state in the new agreement that arbitration and conciliation in Polish-German relations might only be applied upon agreement between the parties in each separate case, we are thus canceling the rules of the Polish-German Arbitration Treaty signed at Locarno, ruling for obligatory arbitration. The Locarno Treaty, despite its unsavory political aftertaste owing to its links with the Rhineland Pact, gives the advantage of excluding the possibility of arbitration in matters rooted in the past, and in general contains security clauses which give us good protection. This is best proved by the fact that since 1925 not a single case was brought to Locarno by Germany.

I may stress here that Gaus is not really insisting that reference be made to the Locarno agreement, since he is aware that this might be awkward for us politically. What he definitely does not want is a tightening of arbitration by the declaration.

For lack of time I was unable to disclose the whole of my argumentation in this report. Indeed, I did not fail to stress, in my reply to Gaus's evasive statement that our editing cancels the Locarno arbitration agreement, that this is by no means so.

Finally, I would like to add that I am thinking over the possibility of finding a way out of these particular points and shall not fail to send you by next courier my suggestions in this matter.

Józef Lipski

At that time Beck was in Geneva. In a telegram of January 17 to the Ministry of Foreign Affairs he expressed his view of the political situation.

DOCUMENT 22   Beck to the Ministry of Foreign Affairs

Code Telegram
Geneva, January 17, 1934
Received: January 17, 9 A.M.

From Lipski's verbal relation it develops that Hitlerite spheres are resolutely striving for a favorable conclusion to our negotiations. In appraising the German situation, the following points are striking: (1) anxiety about isolation, (2) considerable preoccupation with internal problems. Conflict between the Hitlerites and the German Nationals seems to be taking on a sharper aspect. The Chancellor's efforts lean toward an internal reform on a huge scale, a new administrative division of Germany, the completion of unification, and, in practice, the liquidation of the former states of Germany. March is mentioned as a date when the reform will be put into life.

According to the unanimous opinion from various sources in Geneva, the disarmament question will still be a subject for an exchange of opinion between Germany and France before it reaches the conference forum. A crisis in this problem is also foreseen for March. At the Council of the League I am conducting the agreed-to tactic of reserve, so far without objections. Please report on the contents of the telegram to the Marshal.

Beck

On January 19 Lipski was received by Marshal Piłsudski in Warsaw and acquired from him the final decisions.[19] The next day he had a conversation with Gaus,[20] and on January 25 he was received by Hitler.

DOCUMENT 23   Lipski to the Ministry of Foreign Affairs

Code No. 14   Berlin, January 20, 1934

After a long discussion, first of all I composed with Gaus the plan of a formula on international obligations in accordance with paragraph 4 of the Polish-Soviet pact, with the addition that these obligations are not infringed on by the declaration. Secondly, I composed a formula on matters concerning the exculsive competence of the states, in such a way that the declaration does not cover matters which under international law are considered as exclusively internal matters of one of the two states. Gaus will present both these formulas to Neurath and to the Chancellor with our explanations. With regard to the paragraph about arbitration and conciliation, I established—following your instructions —that we consider the agreements binding, including the Polish-German arbitration agreement, and that the words "in each separate case" were introduced by us because of a confusing clause of the said agreement in connection with Germany's withdrawal from the League of Nations. Gaus explained that this whole paragraph in the original German com-position lays no new obligations on the parties and speaks only about seeking a solution of disputes by peaceful means, citing arbitration and conciliation as examples. This paragraph sidesteps the question whether the agreement of 1925, binding for both states, may in the future require certain amendments. However, according to Gaus, the words "in each separate case" would be in contradiction with Article 16 of the 1925 agreement.

[19] See Namier, *Europe in Decay,* pp. 282–83 (footnote).
[20] For Gaus's version, see *DGFP,* Series C, Vol. II, No. 203.

I reserved further conversation over this point for Monday morning in the presence of Makowski.[21] Gaus told me that the German side is pressing for prompt finalization of the agreement.

DOCUMENT 24   Lipski to Beck

NO. 49/8/34   January 25, 1934
                                                Strictly Confidential

I was received today at 11 A.M. by Chancellor Hitler with the minister of foreign affairs of the Reich, von Neurath, also present. Chancellor Hitler first of all expressed his satisfaction that as a result of his conversations with my predecessor and with me an understanding had been reached which will take the form of a Polish-German declaration. This declaration should ensure an appropriate relaxation in Polish-German relations. The Chancellor availed himself of this occasion to pay a courteous compliment to Ambassador Wysocki and to my activity in Berlin.

For my part I stressed that I would like to extend to the Chancellor my thanks for the confidence shown in me and I confirmed that the Polish-German declaration will undoubtedly contribute to a relaxation of the atmosphere. I added that the Polish government duly appreciates the importance of the declaration, and I suggested that this was proved by the fact that last week I was summoned by Marshal Piłsudski, who requested a full report on the negotiations.

In a long declaration the Chancellor of the Reich pointed to the importance of an improvement in Polish-German relations. He underlined Poland's responsible role in the east. Talking about Russia, he said that in contrast with others he is not an optimist as far as Russia is concerned. Namely, he fears that in the future this giant, whose position in armaments is very threatening, could become a danger for Europe. He stressed that, in the field of tractors, for example, Russia is four times stronger than Germany. Discussing the Russian-Japanese conflict, he expressed the opinion that, in the face of such a dynamic trend in Japan, Russia will be compelled to abandon its position in the Far East. It could then direct the full impact of its pressure westward. A very serious danger might then occur for the civilization of the West, espe-

[21] Prof. Julian Makowski was chief of the Treaty Department at the Polish Ministry of Foreign Affairs.

cially since Russia is firmly entrenched in its Communistic doctrine. From this angle the Chancellor considers the role of Poland as very momentous. He said: Poland is the last barricade of civilization in the east. Besides, Poland has already played a similar role. (The Chancellor was making an allusion to the battle of Vienna.)

I stressed that Poland, in the course of its history, often played historic roles as a shield for Western culture, and I mentioned three famous battles: Legnica [Liegnitz, 1241], Vienna [1683], and Warsaw [1920].

Coming back to the Polish-German declaration, the Chancellor stated that it should not only give good results in Polish-German relations but should contribute to a *détente* in the whole of Europe.

Referring to a possibility of war, the Chancellor declared that any war would end in disaster for civilization. For instance, a war between Germany and France would bring about Bolshevism in Germany. Bolshevism in Germany would undoubtedly turn into Bolshevism in the whole of Europe. Because Germany is situated in the center and has so many inhabitants, the radiation would spread to other countries. No one would reap any advantages from the war. A possible shifting of frontiers, in the Chancellor's words, is quite secondary, a trifle as compared with the danger ensuing from the results of a war.

As far as Polish-German relations are concerned, the Chancellor's main concern is that the conviction that Germans and Poles are always *Erbfeinde* should be abandoned. This idea should be weeded out. Were not Polish-Danzig relations very entangled also, and at present were not these relations being arranged on the basis of mutual interests? For the Chancellor had declared to his men at the outset that the Polish nation must be considered *a reality. It is impossible to exterminate the Polish nation.* Both nations have to live side by side. If this principle is accepted, then in the future some solution might be found for both states to overcome difficulties. One thing is weighing on the Chancellor's heart, namely, that on both sides equally the rights of the Polish minorities in Germany and the German minorities in Poland must be respected, for in this field much can be done for a mutual *détente* and many frictions can be removed.

The Chancellor stressed that there were periods in history when we were fighting each other, but at other times we lived in friendship and collaboration.

Józef Lipski

The declaration of nonaggression between Poland and Germany was signed in Berlin on January 26, 1934, by Minister von Neurath and Envoy Lipski.[22] Ratification took place in Warsaw on February 24.

The German government informed its posts abroad on January 24 [23] that an understanding had been reached with regard to the declaration, and the Polish government did likewise on January 26.[24] Moltke was received by Beck on January 27, and Beck expressed his satisfaction over the signing of the declaration.[25] On January 30 Hitler stressed the positive aspect of the understanding concluded with Poland in his speech in the Reichstag.[26] Beck replied by his speech delivered at the Commission for Foreign Affairs of the Polish Senate on February 5.[27]

Finally, general remarks with regard to the signing of the declaration were formulated by Lipski in his report of February 5.

DOCUMENT 25   Lipski to Beck

NO. N/49/17/34   Berlin, February 5, 1934
                                                   Confidential

Public opinion in Germany and governmental spheres which were not kept abreast of the negotiations under way were in general taken aback by the signing of the Polish-German declaration on January 26. The secrecy of the negotiations was very strictly maintained, so that even representatives of the press with the closest links to the A.A. were kept in the dark in connection with the forthcoming understanding. The press, following instructions issued by top authorities, maintained a reasonable reserve, making no restrictions and drawing no conclusions which, in contradiction to the actual state of affairs, could evoke critical comments on the Polish side. This positive attitude of the press toward the Polish-German declaration could only be achieved owing to the fact that the whole press is at present under the control of the government. Nevertheless, German opinion—fed during fifteen years by anti-Polish propaganda—cannot change its attitude toward us from one day to the

[22] For the text of the declaration, see *DGFP*, Series C, Vol. II, No. 219, and *Polish White Book*, No. 10.
[23] For the telegram to Rome and Moscow, see *DGFP*, Series C, Vol. II, No. 211.
[24] For Beck to posts abroad, see *Polish White Book*, No. 11.
[25] For Moltke's telegram, see *DGFP*, Series C, Vol. II, No. 226.
[26] *Polish White Book*, No. 12.
[27] Beck, *Przemówienia, deklaracje, wywiady, 1931–1937*, p. 98; also *DGFP*, Series C, Vol. II, Nos. 230 and 244.

next, and therefore an atmosphere of deep-seated criticism, particularly among people linked with the former *Deutschnationale* camp and elements originating from the east, might be detected, checked by fear of the authority of the Chancellor, who took on himself the responsibility for the agreement with Poland. The Chancellor wanted to express this clearly to public opinion; that is why on the eve of the signing he received me and gave an order to the press to publish a communiqué about the audience with the Polish Envoy. In a lengthy speech before the Reichstag, the Chancellor also substantiated his policy toward Poland, in order to establish a direct impact on the masses of his adherents and prod them to change their hitherto negative stand toward Poland. It is very characteristic that all reference to Poland in speeches delivered by the Chancellor last year, and especially since May, 1933, always laid stress on our valor as a state, this point of view being in striking contradiction to pronouncements by his predecessors. It was obvious that the Chamber could not accept enthusiastically this passage of the Chancellor's speech. Being present in the Reichstag, I could observe the deep silence that at first prevailed when the Chancellor spoke about the understanding reached with Poland. Only gradually a slow reaction came from individual members of the Chamber and calls such as "sehr richtig" could be heard. When the Chancellor finished stating the necessity of balancing Polish-German economic relations, the applause came. It was evident that Hitler was exerting himself in order to impose his will on the audience when he referred to the rapprochement with Poland.

Rumors reach me from the Chancellor's entourage that he was personally very satisfied with the understanding with us. I was also told that the Chancellor is sympathetic toward the Polish nation, appreciating its deep patriotic feelings. The Chancellor's trump card when substantiating his policy toward Poland, and his chief argument, is that the danger threatening from the east might in the future become a reality. He envisages this danger in the Asiatic-Bolshevik penetration, as he calls it, and declares that Poland, true to its historic role, could shield Western, and also German, civilization against this pressure. In this connection the Chancellor always stresses that all matters dividing Poland and Germany, including the frontier problem, which is indeed painful for him as a German, are not to be compared with sacrifices which Germany would have to sustain in case of a war with Poland. He says that territorial gains would be incommensurable with losses, and the war would result in a disaster for European civilization. He wants to force public opinion to respect the Polish nation and accept the fact of the necessity for coexistence, even with prevailing difficulties, assuming that in the future, which he sees as a very long span of time, differences dividing the two nations may fade away.

When I observe this situation in the light of a certain evolution now under way in the Reich, I must agree that this ideology of the Chancellor is a great *positivum* for us, provided that it penetrates more profoundly into the masses of the German nation and reaches young elements, to whom the future belongs. Nevertheless, I must point out again that this whole atmosphere is emanating from the Chancellor himself, and that the people who surround him may only gradually become attracted to his ideas.

However, when discussing the Chancellor's ideology, I do not forget about possible advantages he might reap from the understanding with us, especially in the international field. Nevertheless, I am keeping this problem strictly within the frame of Polish-German relations. If we would accept as a positive factor the present trend in the Chancellor's policy toward us, then it seems to me that it would be highly desirable if in the near future the development of Polish-German relations would follow the line of the Chancellor's ideas. For as soon as elements hostile to us, which are still swarming within the bosom of the administration, slowly recover from the blow of the agreement of January 26, they will do their utmost to compromise—in the eyes of the Chancellor and his confidential ministers—any possibility of collaboration with Poland.

Fully realizing that the development of our relations with Germany does not depend exclusively on problems on the Warsaw-Berlin line, I am nevertheless taking the liberty of enumerating a few principal problems which influence the relations of the two states.

1) If in the near future the Polish-German tariff war is terminated, local opinion will note it as a positive result of the declaration of January 26.

2) Likewise, the attitude of our press with regard to German problems could be exploited to our advantage locally, especially since the present German regime is excessively sensitive to all kinds of international reaction.

In this field our advantages will be great, since the German press, in comparison with ours, has a world-wide scope.

3) A sensitive point for local opinion is the minority problem. The

Chancellor, in his last talk with me, asked that this matter be considered from the point of view of avoiding friction. At the same time he expressed his intention to ensure just treatment for Polish minorities in Germany.

4) In Germany anti-Polish activities are primarily concentrated within organizations created *ad hoc,* such as the Ostbund.

It is characteristic for the German nature that it needs an organization to keep it in a constant state of political tension. A German will lose his belligerent nationalistic attitude for lack of this element of tension.

If we strive to realize in practice the principles contained in the declaration of January 26, we will then be obliged to pay special attention to the eastern provinces of Germany, and to organizations which are still breeding hatred against Poland. Indeed, it would be desirable that our similar organizations, such as the Union for Defense of the Western Frontier [Związek Obrony Kresów Zachodnich], comply with the Reich government's action to curb the anti-Polish activities of the German organizations.

Finally, I would like to bring to your attention some of my observations with regard to the Baltic question, which, after the last revelations of the *Daily Herald,* evoked a big commotion in political circles here. It came to my knowledge that the opinion was fostered in the A.A. here that the plan of the Polish-Soviet declaration pertaining to the independence of the Baltic states was used by Poland to put pressure on Berlin to finalize the declaration of January 26. It is considered that this maneuver was quite successful in forcing the opposition in the A.A. to agree to a prompt finalization of the declaration.

I am citing this detail because in my opinion it is very characteristic. In general, fears are still prevalent here as to our common policy with Russia on the Baltic, and undoubtedly they saw in this a threat against Germany.

Józef Lipski

DOCUMENT 26   Lipski to Dębicki

February 8, 1934

Referring to my letter of the 7th inst., No. N/49/23/34, I would like to inform you that yesterday at the reception of President Hindenburg for heads of the diplomatic missions I had the opportunity to converse with Foreign Affairs Minister von Neurath.

Herr von Neurath was very well satisfied with what Mr. Beck said at the Commission for Foreign Affairs of the Senate with regard to Polish-German relations. I took this opportunity to advise Herr Neurath quite informally about Minister Beck's trip to Moscow planned for the near future. I mentioned as well that this trip will be in return for the visit of Chicherin to Warsaw in 1925 and the unofficial visit of Mr. Litvinov to Warsaw. The Soviet government has for a long time been looking forward to a return visit of the Polish Minister of Foreign Affairs.

Herr von Neurath, confirming that he had already been informed about this, characterized Mr. Beck's visit to Moscow as quite a natural thing. I further informed Herr von Neurath in confidence that the idea of a declaration on Baltic problems is no longer timely. Obviously satisfied, Herr von Neurath answered that he never saw any possible interest for Poland in tying itself up with Russia on Baltic problems. He added that this was his deep, purely objective, conviction.

Discussing Minister Beck's visit to Moscow, Herr von Neurath also added that he is not anxious to see Litvinov in Berlin, especially after his last speech, which made an unpleasant impression here.

Hitler also attended the Reichspräsident's dinner party. I approached the Chancellor and stressed that public opinion in Poland received with great satisfaction (*Genugtuung*) his words uttered at the last session of the Reichstag in connection with Polish-German relations.

In reply, the Chancellor expressed his warm appreciation for Minister Beck's speech at the Foreign Affairs Commission of the Senate. He manifested his keen pleasure in view of the rapprochement of the two nations, and stressed that we should now strive to establish collaboration in the economic field.

I also exchanged a few conventional words with President Hindenburg on the subject of Polish-German relations. The President also expressed his satisfaction with the agreement reached, adding that he hopes things will remain as they are.

Józef Lipski

Soviet Russia and the Baltic States
January—April, 1934

IN THE FIRST DAYS of January, 1934, news appeared in the European press with regard to the forthcoming Polish-Soviet agreement to guarantee the independence of the Baltic states.

DOCUMENT 27   Lipski to Beck

NO. N/128/1/34   Berlin, January 11, 1934
                                                              Strictly Confidential

News published by the London *Daily Herald* and the Finnish press on the alleged plan of a Soviet-Polish pact to guarantee the independence of the Baltic states reached Berlin the evening of January 4. The usually uniform, summit-disciplined press showed certain diverse tendencies, probably owing to the fact that this news came as quite a surprise to German official circles. Moreover, it was the holiday period when government officials were absent from Berlin. Neither Neurath nor Secretary of State von Bülow was at the Ministry of Foreign Affairs.

The newly formed official German News Agency, created by the merger of the Wolff Agency with the Telegraphen-Union, and headed by persons ideologically akin to the Hugenberg group, on the same day issued an official communiqué categorically denying rumors that Germany proposed a nonaggression pact with Poland in return for acquiescence to Germany's eastward expansion into non-Polish territories. However, the communiqué also stated that competent Soviet and Polish circles apparently harbored anti-German schemes with respect to the territory of the Baltic states. I took the liberty of calling your special attention to this paragraph by telegram.

Characteristically, the National Socialist press in the capital did not publish this communiqué, and tried to present the *Daily Herald*'s revelations as the usual anti-German assault by the Socialist press.

The remainder of the German press presented the proposed pact as a Soviet action and directed its attacks against Moscow.

Lithuania suffered the brunt of the criticism for its alleged friendly attitude toward the Soviet plans. Estonia and Latvia, on the other hand, demonstrated certain reservations with regard to the plans, while Finland took an utterly negative stand. Poland was generally spared by the press, and no critical comments were printed during the first few days. Only on January 10 did the *Völkischer Beobachter* publish correspondence from Warsaw blaming Poland for abandoning the trend it had followed up to that time, and returning—as the paper put it—to the old romantic period. The Warsaw correspondents of the *Berliner Börsenzeitung* and the *Vossische Zeitung* also pointed to Poland as a participant in the Baltic plans.

Considering that no government instruction could as yet be detected in the German press with regard to Poland's stand, it is possible that the German correspondents in Poland were somewhat disoriented as a result of the lack of unanimity in the Polish press.

Although at first they could base their conclusions on the clearly defined position taken by *Gazeta Polska,* later, as the result of a different interpretation provided by the *Agence Telegraphique d'Est* and *Ilustrowany Kurier Codzienny,* they became confused and reported to their German readers that conflicting reactions had appeared in Poland.

Following your telegraphic instructions received on January 5, and confirmed to me verbally in Warsaw on January 7, I made reference to the recent Baltic events during my conversation with Reich Foreign Affairs Minister von Neurath on January 9. I telegraphed my report of this conversation on January 9.

I began by stating that we again found ourselves in a period when many false rumors are being spread by the international press. I pointed to the *Daily Herald*'s version which stated that Germany allegedly offered Poland a nonaggression pact in return for a free hand in non-Polish territories in the east. I declared that *Gazeta Polska* denied this garbled news, and Neurath replied that he had already been informed about this.

Furthermore, I drew his attention to the fact that rumors are being deliberately spread about anti-German activities in the Baltic states, and that Poland is allegedly involved in these activities. I declared that the rumors were groundless. I stated that Poland's policy with respect to the independence of the Baltic states was always quite clear and open. Herr Neurath agreed with this point. For a great many years there was a divergence in this area between Polish and Russian policies. I mentioned the Communist putsch in Estonia and our efforts to draw the Baltic states into the pacts. I stated that, owing to a general improvement of political conditions in Eastern Europe, divergences between Polish and Russian policies had been reduced. Conversation on these subjects between Moscow and Warsaw could only be concerned with a rapprochement on these problems. However, these talks cannot be interpreted as Poland's participation in a Baltic pact directed—as the press mendaciously commented—against Germany. I added that, if the question of a Baltic pact were raised at all, the Polish government would undoubtedly approach Germany also, in accordance with its principle that all states concerned should participate in such a pact.

Herr Neurath replied that he was not taking all this so tragically. Rumors about the supposed intentions of German expansion in the Baltic zone should simply be ignored, since they were sheer nonsense. The latest plans concerning the maintenance of the Baltic states' independence are—in Neurath's opinion—symptoms of Mr. Litvinov's nervousness. Neurath had an opportunity to observe this when the Commissar for Foreign Affairs last passed through Berlin.

Litvinov's nervousness—according to Neurath—is due to the decline of Communism not only in Germany but in other countries as well; to the complicated situation in the Far East; to certain ideas of Rosenberg; and, finally, to the currently emerging rapprochement between Poland and Germany. Neurath says that Litvinov told him that this rapprochement is worrying him.

So far as Moscow's general attitude toward the Baltic states is concerned, Neurath commented that, as soon as Russia's imperialism gathers momentum in its natural drive toward the sea, it will undoubtedly push in the direction of these countries. Keeping them independent as long as possible is in accordance with German interests. However, from Neurath's words it was obvious that he considers the existence of the Baltic states dubious in the long run. He spoke with a certain irony about the Soviet guarantee for Finland, comparing it with assurances given by a wolf to a lamb.

Finally, Herr Neurath said that he doubts whether a guarantee for the

Baltic states, made together with Russia, would be a good policy for Poland, adding that this could expose us in the future to serious complications with Russia.

Herr Neurath thanked me for clarifying these matters. Bearing in mind the whole situation, I felt that it would be pointless to continue the conversation with Neurath on Polish-German problems without first giving him a reassuring explanation of the recent action on the Baltic, which must have greatly disturbed the local official—and especially Hitlerite—circles. Even if von Neurath were *au fond* somewhat skeptical about our declarations, the very fact that he was kept informed by us—as described above—should, in my opinion, make a rather good impression.

This was particularly advisable since in this way Chancellor Hitler, who is particularly interested in Russian affairs, will receive a certain *mise au point* from our side. For I must stress that, in all the conversations I have had in the course of the last months, either with Chancellor Hitler or with other members of the government, that is, with Goebbels, Darré, or Göring, they constantly brought up the problem of Bolshevism and Russia.[1]

Józef Lipski

The problem of a possible Polish-Soviet declaration guaranteeing the independence of the Baltic states became the subject of conversations between the German ambassador in Moscow, Rudolf Nadolny, and Commissar Litvinov, and was the subject of the Ambassador's correspondence with the Auswärtiges Amt.[2]

On March 28, 1934, Litvinov handed Nadolny a draft of a German-Soviet pact guaranteeing the independence of the Baltic states. This matter evoked lengthy conversations and correspondence, until Germany finally rejected the Soviet proposition on April 14.[3]

[1] For the German version of the Lipski-Neurath conversation, see *DGFP*, Series C, Vol. II, No. 169.

[2] *Ibid.*, Nos. 187, 240, and 251.

[3] *Ibid.*, Nos. 362, 364, 375, 376, 382, 390, 401, 415, 416, 417, 418, 421, and 423.

The Ukrainians in Germany and the Assassination of Minister Pieracki

June, 1934

THERE WAS a strong movement championing the cause of Ukrainian independence by Ukrainian nationalists active on Polish territory. This movement encompassed many factions, some of which cooperated with the Polish government and played an important role in the Warsaw Sejm. There were other factions striving clandestinely to achieve their goal by a revolutionary struggle against the Polish state. They were supported either by the Soviet Union (Ukrainian Communists) or by Germany and Czechoslovakia. Minority troubles in Poland coincided with the interests of these countries.

In 1929 a clandestine organization of Ukrainian nationalists was formed from the ranks of the former Ukrainian Military Organization (UON).

Its leaders, headed by Colonel Eugene Konowalec, resided predominantly in Germany and enjoyed the support of the German government. In Germany they also had their operational school to prepare future terrorists. In the territory of Eastern Galicia the UON undertook a series of attempts on Polish offices and outstanding politicians, as, for instance, the assassination of Tadeusz Hołówko, chief of the Eastern Department of the Ministry of Foreign Affairs (August, 1931). The same group assassinated Minister of the Interior Bronisław Pieracki on June 15, 1934, in Warsaw.

It is characteristic that in the Polish government both Hołówko and Pieracki represented a trend favoring far-reaching collaboration with the Ukrainians.

In Ambassador Lipski's papers there is the following note dealing with the assassination of Bronisław Pieracki:

On the initiative of Reich Foreign Affairs Minister von Neurath, Minister Beck stopped in Berlin on his way back to Warsaw from Geneva on June 7, 1934, and had a conversation with Herr von Neurath at his villa on Herman Göring Strasse.

I was present at this interview.

A few days before this meeting, Military Attaché Colonel Szymański informed me that he had been warned confidentially by the chief of the

Reich's Second Bureau that Ukrainian terrorists were preparing attempts on the lives of high-ranking persons in Poland. The German side stressed the fact that until the Polish-German understanding of January 26, 1934, the Reichswehr had been in close contact with terrorist Ukrainian elements and therefore wanted to warn Poland about the attempts in preparation. This was done to avoid their possibly being held responsible for anything that happened. The Military Attaché telegraphed this information to the Polish General Staff.

Considering this information to be of utmost importance, I instructed Colonel Szymański to report it personally to Minister Beck. Colonel Szymański did so, reporting at the Legation in my presence after Minister Beck returned from his conversation with von Neurath.

We were at that time living through a very turbulent period inside Germany. Within the ranks of the National Socialist Party serious frictions were occurring between the movement represented by Hitler and the adherents of Röhm. Röhm blamed Hitler for having deserted the ideals of National Socialism by following too moderate a line, negotiating with financial circles, and collaborating with the conservative Reichswehr. Röhm was striving to keep the S.A. the sole power ruling the National Socialist state. As head of these storm troops, he created a giant apparatus. During one of his speeches delivered at a meeting organized by Rosenberg at the Hotel Adlon, he quoted an S.A. membership figure of two million.

Beginning in March, 1934, our consul general in Munich, Mr. Lisiewicz, sent information to the Legation in Berlin from the Bavarian region about friction between Hitler and Röhm over the importance of the S.A. Röhm persistently refused to reduce the strength of the S.A., which Hitler obviously was considering doing under pressure from the Army. As a result of these tensions within the ranks of the Party, some people, such as General von Schleicher, started a series of intrigues in an attempt to dominate the situation. Violent changes in the Reich government would undoubtedly have an effect on Polish-German relations. For we have to bear in mind that the policy of a rapprochement with Poland, inaugurated with the agreement of January, 1934, was highly unpopular with German public opinion. Not only Prussian circles, but also the National Socialist Party, especially in the eastern provinces of the Reich, accepted the change of course toward Poland with utmost reluctance. Polish diplomacy in the Reich had to take various circumstances into account. Frictions within the ranks of the government itself had to be considered, as well as tense relations between the Auswärtiges Amt, recruited from former officials, and Party leaders. The Reichswehr was then not yet "gleichgeschalted." Some of the generals, for example Blomberg, were openly for Hitler. Others, for example Reichenau, were considered pronounced adherents of the regime and proclaimed their sentiments openly. Others still, in keeping with the old Prussian traditions, eyed the new regime warily. Finally, there were those who, like von Schleicher and von Bredow, plotted secretly and dreamt of seizing power. Under these circumstances, the atmosphere was tense with electricity.

The trip of Propaganda Minister Goebbels to Poland took place on June 12–15, 1934. I was following it with serious misgivings for fear that some anti-German manifestations might take place in connection with the trip. I assigned Mr. S. Dembiński, director of the Polish Telegraph Agency in Berlin, to the team of Herr Goebbels' staff. The Polish minister of the interior, Bronisław Pieracki, was to greet Goebbels at the airport in Warsaw upon instructions from the government, and was to bid him farewell at his departure for Cracow by air on June 16. The visit was not of an official character, since Goebbels came to Poland at the invitation of cultural circles to deliver a lecture on the ideology of National Socialism.

Two unpleasant incidents occurred during Goebbels' visit in Warsaw. During a reception at the German Legation, a rock was thrown from the street to the drawing room, breaking a windowpane. This was only a minor incident, but on the evening of the same day some of the press agencies reported from Warsaw that Marshal Piłsudski had fallen ill, and that the audience fixed for the next day would not take place. I was unable to investigate the source of this rumor fully, or to find out whether it was true that at the last moment there was some hesitation as to whether Goebbels should be received by the Marshal. This information was released by the Iskra agency, at that time directed by Colonel Scieżyński. The Marshal's failure to receive Goebbels would provoke a serious note of discord in Polish-German relations, spoiling the whole effect of the journey, particularly since Goebbels was known to be highly sensitive to any incidents of this sort.

I called the attention of the Minister of the Interior to this situation and in the early morning hours of the next day received a reply that the audience with the Marshal was definitely on. The anxiety on the German side that Goebbels be received by the Marshal may be demonstrated by the fact that, on the afternoon of June 14, at a reception of Reichspräsident Göring, von Ribbentrop—who was said to be already closely associated with the Chancellor—asked with obvious concern whether there was any truth in the rumors spread to the effect that the Marshal would not receive the Reich Propaganda Minister. I was able to reassure him on this point. Parenthetically, the conversation itself did nothing to improve Polish-German relations.

On June 15, Goebbels flew from Warsaw to Cracow, where he stayed for a few hours to visit the monuments of that city. In the afternoon I received information by telephone from Dembiński from Cracow that Goebbels had flown from Cracow via Wrocław (Breslau) to Berlin, where he was to land at Tempelhof at 4:30 P.M. At the same time I received information by telephone from American press sources that an attempt had been made in Warsaw on the life of Minister Pieracki. The Polish Ministry of Foreign Affairs confirmed this news by telephone. At 4 P.M. I arrived at Tempelhof airport to greet Goebbels. The chief of the Eastern Department of the A.A., Meyer, brought a telegram from Moltke about Pieracki's death. Goebbels was shocked by the news of the assassination, and from what was said by his entourage I surmised that they were worried lest the assassination in some way be connected with the Goebbels-Pieracki meeting in Warsaw. Foreign correspondents in Berlin, ill-disposed to the idea of the Polish-German rapprochement, gave wide circulation to this version. Our Legation had to counteract this propaganda. In the following days I began to receive from Warsaw news of reprisals applied by the government of Prime Minister Kozłowski against nationalists suspected of possible participation in the attempt, of the creation of a camp at Bereza, and of a great ferment in Polish public opinion. I could not believe that a Pole could have murdered Pieracki. An argument against the hypothesis that the deed had been done by the Ukrainian terrorists was that they had hitherto (as I was informed later) performed these acts of terror only in territories inhabited by Ukrainians. An investigation starting from similar assumptions at first went astray. Several days after the assassination I received an anonymous letter, written in Ukrainian from the vicinity of Szczecin [Stettin], pointing to the killer, who was allegedly a resident of a Ukrainian settlement near that city. I sent this letter to Warsaw immediately. However, I was later told that it did not aid in the investigation.

A few days later, when I had guests at the Legation, I received a telephone call at 11 P.M. from Warsaw from Minister Schaetzel, chief of the Eastern Department of the Ministry of Foreign Affairs. He told me that at 7 P.M. that day the alleged killer of Minister Pieracki had left Danzig aboard the ship *Preussen*. The ship was to land at Swinemünde at about 6 A.M. without stopping on the way. Schaetzel gave me a description of the person, asking me to do my best to arrange for his arrest. There was not a single moment to lose. Taking leave of my guests, I detained only Dembiński, the director of the Polish Telegraph Agency, and made a direct call to the headquarters of the Gestapo in Berlin, circumventing the A.A. At that late hour I would probably find no one present at that office; besides, I had no doubts but that the old Prussian clerks would take a negative attitude toward my intervention.

The officer on duty took my telephone call. Fortunately, no senior functionary was present. I gave the officer the details communicated to me from Warsaw, laying particular stress on the necessity of arresting the man upon his landing in Swinemünde. As the Gestapo functionary did not contradict me, and to all my demands replied in a dutiful tone, "Jawohl, Excellenz," I told him that in a few minutes Mr. Dembiński would come to assist him in this matter. We also called Counselor Lubomirski and started on a full night's work at the Legation. I issued personal telephone instructions to Polish Consul Sztark at Szczecin to proceed immediately by car to Swinemünde and call on Chief Police Commissary Opitz, who on orders from Berlin was to perform the arrest of the murderer upon his landing. Consul Sztark was further instructed at all cost to be present at the interrogation of the criminal. Dembiński acted very efficiently. He suggested that we send a radio message to the ship *Preussen* to confirm that the person in question, as described in our report, was indeed among the passengers and asking that he be watched and prevented from escaping. Upon further instructions from Warsaw, we obtained permission from the Gestapo for our agent Budny, who had trailed the murderer until the moment he boarded ship, to cross the frontier post near Wielkie Boże Pole that same night.

About 7 A.M. I received a telephone report from Consul Sztark about the arrest of this man. It took place in the following circumstances: The

captain of the *Preussen* replied to the radio message that there was a
person answering the description aboard ship and that he showed signs
of considerable nervousness. Even before the landing at Swinemünde,
several police functionaries arrived by motorboat and arrested the man,
taking him ashore discreetly. The interrogation took place in the presence of the Polish Consul. The man proved to be a Ukrainian. With
obvious satisfaction he learned that he was already on German soil. A
search of his travel documents revealed a brand new passport from the
consulate general of the Reich in Danzig. His name was Mikolaj
Łebed, and he had been the organizer of an earlier attempted sabotage
on a train at Gródek Jagielloński. The faces of the German functionaries
showed embarrassment at this obvious gaffe, since the Polish Consul
was present and wrote down a protocol.

In the morning hours I informed Warsaw about the arrest and received instructions to undertake steps for extradition immediately. Upon
consultation with my staff (Counselor Wyszyński) I decided not to take
the official routine channel through the A.A. but instead to approach the
top Party authorities directly. I ordered my secretariat to arrange a
meeting for me with the chief of the Gestapo, Himmler. The meeting
was fixed for 12 noon. A quarter of an hour before I was to leave the
Legation, Himmler telephoned that he had been suddenly summoned by
Hitler and on his way back from the Reich Chancellery would come to
the Legation.

About 1 P.M. Himmler arrived at the Legation with a large retinue.
Upon entering my office he was the first to mention the affair, declaring
in the Chancellor's name that it had been decided to hand over without
delay to the Polish authorities the Ukrainian arrested that morning. Herr
Himmler added that he had interrogated the person in question. The
man was the chief organizer of Pieracki's assassination, and he was to
be deported about 2 P.M. that day by plane to Warsaw. Himmler then
shifted the conversation to broader topics of Polish-German relations,
suggesting an understanding between the security organs of the two
countries.

Upon informing Warsaw of these developments, I gave instructions to
watch for the announced flight. At the hour fixed for the departure, I
received a telephone call from a representative of a Polish airline who
was present at the airport, informing me that the departure would not
take place. Upon confirmation of this news, the Legation was advised

that the departure would not take place that day. Our apprehensions that the German Intelligence Department, engaged in schemes with the Ukrainians, would object to turning the criminal over to Poland thus proved to be justified. It was also clear to me that the A.A., as well as the Reichswehr, was opposing the Chancellor's decision. I obtained a telephone connection with Himmler's office. I was first told that he was absent, and that he had left, but when I firmly insisted on the necessity of speaking to him immediately, Himmler took the call. I told him that I was calling him with reference to the information I had received that the plane had not left at the hour fixed for the departure. Himmler began to explain that a delay had occurred because the matter was more complicated than appeared at first. The man arrested was mixed up in other cases on German territory, which required further long investigations. However, he assured me that within a few days the man would be delivered to the Polish authorities. I replied firmly that I had already communicated the Chancellor's decision to Marshal Piłsudski, and that it was impossible for me to accept a change in the decision. I could not risk it, because this might have disastrous consequences for Polish-German relations. I let it be understood that under such circumstances I would consider my mission as ended. As far as German interests were concerned during legal proceedings, I assured Himmler that everything possible would be done to avoid unnecessary friction. I added that the German side would be free to obtain all information in the course of the proceedings through normal legal channels. In view of my very firm stand, Himmler weakened and declared that he would approach the Chancellor once more. It was obvious that if the matter were not settled immediately it would be impossible to obtain the extradition at a later date. Poland's political interest was at stake, since it was imperative to appease public opinion by showing that the coup had been organized by foreign terrorists and not by Poles. After a rather long wait, Göring telephoned at 4 P.M. He stated that as chief of the German Air Force he was not opposing the departure of the criminal to Poland, and that he had given orders to this effect. A moment later Himmler informed me that the matter had been settled and agreement secured for the immediate departure of a Polish plane to Poland with the arrested man aboard. Himmler added that at the earliest opportunity he would explain to me the causes for the delay.

Shortly before the purge of June 30, Funk, the secretary of state at the Propaganda Ministry, threw a large party at his villa near Berlin for the diplomatic corps and the Party. When we sat down at the table, I was astonished to see that a number of places were empty. Our hosts were obviously taken aback by the absence of their guests. It developed that the missing visitors were Röhm's adherents. Himmler arrived late, almost at the end of the dinner. In a casual conversation after dinner he began to explain why the departure of the plane to Poland had been delayed.

He put the blame for this on elements of the old regime who had allegedly collaborated with the Ukrainian terrorists against Poland. He solemnly declared that he had severed all ties with the terrorists. However, when after this conversation Warsaw forwarded a number of names of Ukrainian terrorists who were leading diversive anti-Polish action in the Reich, the Gestapo made no reply for a long time, or else just issued casual explanations. The extradition of Łebed took place only because the German government had been compromised by the collaboration of its consulate general in Danzig in Łebed's escape to Germany.[1]

[1] M. Łebed was tried in Poland and was sentenced to death, but the sentence was reduced to life imprisonment. When Poland was occupied by Germany, he was released from prison. At present he is in the United States.
    See Wojciechowski, *Stosunki Polsko-niemieckie, 1933–1938*, pp. 235–37, Roos, *Polen und Europa*, p. 154, and Szymanski, *Zły sąsiad*, p. 152.

The Eastern Pact

May—December, 1934

The declaration of nonaggression between Poland and Germany of January 26, 1934, resulted in a further *détente* in relations between the two countries, so that by February 7 a commercial agreement had already been signed by them. The German offer to coordinate with Poland the problem of the construction of the superhighway (autobahn) to East Prussia, as presented by von Moltke in his conversation with Beck on May 25, 1934, was probably connected with this agreement. Four years later the problem of a German superhighway across Polish Pomerania became one of the principal causes of the Polish-German conflict.

The matter of regional pacts of mutual aid was initiated by Louis Barthou, who became the minister of foreign affairs of France in the cabinet of Gaston Doumergue (this government was formed on February 9, 1934). He attempted to include Poland in this system during his visit to Warsaw (April 22–24). However, Poland did not support his plan of an Eastern Pact. The pact, in which Poland, the Soviet Union, Germany, Czechoslovakia, Lithuania, Latvia, Estonia, and Finland were to participate, was discussed by Barthou with Litvinov at Geneva (May 18–19). Von Moltke referred to this conversation in his discourse with Beck on May 25, 1934.[1]

The visit of the Reich propaganda minister, Dr. Josef Goebbels, to Warsaw on June 12–15 was a further sign of improved Polish-German relations. He came at the invitation of the Polish Intellectual Union and on June 13 delivered a lecture entitled "National Socialist Germany as an Element of European Peace." In the course of this lecture Goebbels declared, in part, that there was no problem in Europe which would necessitate a solution by war. The press in Danzig stated that this speech was also addressed to Paris, Moscow, Prague, and all countries which feared that National Socialism had imperialistic features and aggressive tendencies. Goebbels' speech had a favorable reception in Poland.

Lipski's report of June 22 gives an illustration of the general situation in European relations at the beginning of the summer of 1934.

[1] *DGFP*, Series C, Vol. II, No. 465.

DOCUMENT 28   Lipski to Beck

NO. N/49/78/34   Berlin, June 22, 1934

In connection with the telegram of June 21, in which I informed you about explanations given to me by the A.A. with regard to conversations of Hitler with Mussolini and of Neurath with Litvinov, I am now presenting the following information.

I have been able to observe recently a considerable increase in German diplomatic activities. In Polish-German relations, this was illustrated by Herr von Neurath's initiative in meeting you in Berlin and by Herr Goebbels' trip to Warsaw; in relations with other nations, by the Chancellor's meeting with Mussolini in Venice, by the travels of von Ribbentrop, the delegate for disarmament problems, to London and Paris, and, finally, by the conversation between Litvinov and von Neurath in Berlin as disclosed by the press. Beyond any doubt, this increased activity is due to the international situation of the Reich at present—namely, to its rather considerable isolation. At the same time the Reich strives to counteract French policy, which, since Barthou became minister of foreign affairs, tends to strengthen the French position by more pressure on London, an approach to Russia, reactivization of relations with Poland, and a tightening of links with the Little Entente.

Under these circumstances, I thought it desirable to obtain authoritative comments on moves in German politics which have taken place since your last conversation with Minister von Neurath.[2]

At the A.A. I was told that inquiries had come from various quarters about whether there was any connection between Hitler's trip to Venice and Goebbels' visit to Warsaw. As the dates coincided, they could not accept the fact as sheer coincidence. In spite of assurances by the A.A. that the day of Goebbels' arrival had been fixed long in advance, before it was known when Hitler would be able to leave for Italy, no one was willing to accept this explanation.

With regard to Hitler's meeting with Mussolini, the A.A. confirmed that the aim of this visit was, in the first place, to establish personal contact between the two dictators and to offer the opportunity for free discussion of the complex of international problems of interest to both

[2] *Ibid.*, No. 485. The meeting of Hitler with Mussolini in Venice took place on June 14.

countries. There was no question of any binding agreements. The German side is very well satisfied with the results of the meeting, since besides allowing for personal contact between the two statesmen, it also demonstrated a far-reaching community of opinion on international matters.

As for Austria, the A.A. communicated to me in strictest confidence that the Chancellor presented the matter to Mussolini in the following vein: any attempt to calm the situation in Austria would be impossible to achieve with the present Dollfuss government. The Chancellor observed that a neutral person should be placed at the head of the government. Under such neutral rule elections should be held, and only then would peace come to Austria.

The A.A. did not comment on Mussolini's point of view on this question, and it was impossible to press further for comment owing to the fact that the matter was rather ticklish. From other quarters, however, I learned that German government circles consider elections in Austria a possibility as a result of the Venetian talks. From the Italian press and correspondence in the *Temps* of Rome it could be concluded that Mussolini had won a victory over Hitler on the Austrian question. The German government supposedly is for the independence of Austria, and will coordinate its actions with the Italian government.

From the A.A. statements it is obvious—in my opinion—that Hitler is standing firm on the position he has repeatedly stated, which in short is that he is not acting against Austria's independence, but only requests that the population have the right to vote freely for the government of its choice. He is counting on a *Gleichschaltung* after the elections.

In the light of the A.A. statements it is also obvious that the present terrorist methods applied by Austrian Hitlerites are designed to prepare the way for the overthrow of the Dollfuss government.[3]

According to the A.A. information, during Hitler's conversations with Mussolini the question of Germany's relations with the League of Nations, as well as the matter of disarmament, was also touched upon, and

[3] For some time Austria had become a stage for many acts of terror, such as the destruction of roads and bridges and assassination attempts in public places. These acts were part of a systematic and organized action designed to wreck security and create difficulties for tourists, who contributed considerably to Austria's income. The action was conducted by Austrian National Socialist organizations under direction from Munich. In order to overcome the terror and sabotage, the government of Chancellor Dollfuss extended the competence of Austrian martial law, introducing the death penalty for these criminal offenses.

it was ascertained that the views of the two leaders are similar on these subjects.

With regard to the question of disarmament, Hitler referred to the stand taken by the German government in the known notes addressed to the Great Powers, which stressed that German demands should be considered an indispensable minimum.

Relations with the Western Powers—that is, with France and England—were also discussed, the problem of the Four-Power Pact, relations with Russia, the question of the Far East, but there was no mention of the Balkan pact or the triple agreement [Italy, Austria, Hungary].

Giving me further information on the plan of the Litvinov pact, which was also discussed in Venice, the Auswärtiges Amt described the situation as follows:

A few days before Litvinov's visit to Herr von Neurath, François-Poncet called at the A.A. and communicated the plan for the pact, based on the principles of consultation, nonaggression, and reciprocal aid with the participation of Russia, the Baltic states, Poland, Czechoslovakia, and perhaps also the Little Entente. The plan provided for a guarantee by France, without its actual participation in the pact. In return for the guarantees obtained by this pact, the Soviet Union, for its part, had to guarantee the Rhineland Pact.

On the very day of Neurath's departure for Venice, the Soviet Embassy called unexpectedly, suggesting that, on his way back from Geneva via Berlin, Litvinov be received by von Neurath. Neurath replied that he was leaving in a few hours, but, bowing to pressure, he received Litvinov.[4]

In the conversation with Litvinov the question of the pact was brought up. Litvinov did not present any plan in writing. The A.A., after its talks with Poncet and Litvinov, has some misgivings as to the authorship of the pact. The A.A. hints that the pact is rather a French product. Neurath told Litvinov that the plan for the pact is receiving careful attention. He stated that it possesses some positive elements, such as consultation and nonaggression. However, he stressed that the German government is negatively disposed with regard to the grouping of states involved in mutual assistance, since this means a return to the policy of alliances. Besides, owing to the restrictions in armaments, the German government would be unable to accept obligations under such a pact.

[4] On June 13, 1934.

The same explanations were repeated by the German chargé d'affaires in Moscow. Consequently, the press rumors that the German government had rejected the plan for the pact "purement et simplement" are not accurate. In his discussion with Litvinov, Neurath once more explained the stand of the German government toward the plan of the Baltic Pact as presented by Moscow some time earlier.

Herr von Neurath also implied to Litvinov that he desires good relations with Moscow.

Coming back to the Hitler-Mussolini conversations, I was told that the question of reciprocal assistance was also under discussion and that the Italian government shared the opinion of the German government on this matter absolutely.

The German government thought that the pact would grant the Franco-Russian alliance special influence. Also, by entering into the pact, Germany could be dragged into conflicts—as it was put—at the cost of money and blood.

It was further noted that Belgium would in principle be against the guarantee of the Rhineland Pact by Russia, as well as by Italy and England. According to the A.A. information, Finland is also negatively disposed to this project. The Finnish foreign minister, who was passing through Berlin, allegedly spoke of Soviet propaganda spreading news of a threat of German invasion of the Baltic states.

At the end of my interview I also asked about the recall of Nadolny from Moscow. This news was confirmed to me, but it was stressed that this was purely a personal matter and had nothing to do with a difference in political opinion, as was hinted by the foreign press. He will be succeeded by Count von Schulenburg, the envoy in Bucharest.

I must stress that the chief of the Eastern Department, who in the absence of the secretary of state was my informer, asked for my discretion and added that the German government would like to continue a permanent contact with the Polish government on the question of Litvinov's planned pact. Herr von Moltke will call on you next week to discuss this problem. Also von Bülow, the secretary of state, would like to see me upon his return to the office.

Finally, I am taking the liberty of making the following observation on the background of German-Russian relations:

According to information in the *Temps,* Mussolini pressed Hitler to modify his position toward Russia, to stop Rosenberg in his anti-Russian propaganda, which is highly irritating to Moscow, and to do this independently of the negative stand taken by Italy toward the mutual aid pact.

I presume that this was really so, and that Italy undoubtedly was using the argument that the anti-Soviet tendency of the German policy is contributing to the Soviet-French rapprochement, forcing Litvinov to look for guarantees.

I have reason to believe that the elements in Germany that are basically oriented toward the Soviets (primarily the circles close to the Reichswehr and the former Hugenberg camp) are using such arguments in order to ease German-Soviet tensions.

Józef Lipski

The problem of the Eastern Pact or the Eastern Locarno was the topic of a number of diplomatic conversations in Berlin and Warsaw, at the League of Nations, and in other capitals. On July 13 von Neurath informed Lipski about the French and British proposition.

DOCUMENT 29   Lipski to Beck

NO. N/49/100/34   Berlin, July 13, 1934
                                   Top Secret

This afternoon, quite unexpectedly, Neurath asked me to call on him without delay. Apologizing for summoning me to the A.A. so suddenly, von Neurath said that he was already anxious yesterday, after his talk with the British Ambassador [5] about the Eastern Pact, to inform me of its course, but his secretary forgot to telephone, and this was the reason for his asking me to call today.

Herr von Neurath submitted for my information two texts handed to him by Sir Eric Phipps, one containing the original French plan, and the other with British propositions accepted in London by Barthou. I am attaching copies herewith.[6]

He told me that, according to his information, Sir William Erskine presented a similar *démarche* to you.

[5] *DGFP*, Series C, III, 164–68.
[6] *Ibid.*, No. 85, enclosures 1 and 2.

Discussing the texts, von Neurath stressed their knottiness and the difficulty in deducing the consequences which might follow for the signatories of such agreements.

Regarding Part I, point *a,* he observed that the obligation of the participants of the pact to offer mutual assistance might result in the presence of the Red Army on the territory of Germany or Poland, which—as he jokingly remarked—would be no pleasure for either country. Neurath further called my attention to the fact that, according to the text, assistance would be extended immediately without consultation.

He especially stressed point 2, concerning the Franco-Russian agreement for mutual aid, as well as letter C of point 3, dealing with Russia's joining the League of Nations.

With regard to the counterpropositions on the British side, Neurath pointed to the very involved wording of point 3, dealing with equality of rights for Germany. In reply to the *démarche* of the British Ambassador, von Neurath replied that both texts would receive careful investigation. Without approaching the matter *ad meritum,* he limited himself to three questions posed to the Ambassador: namely, whether Great Britain intends to join the pact, which would endow the pact with special value; whether the Ambassador does not foresee that such a pact could turn against Great Britain, that is, in case of a conflict in India; and, finally, how the matter of *Gleichberechtigung* [equality] for the Reich in the field of armaments in connection with point 3 of the British plan should be understood.

With regard to this last question, von Neurath observed that point 3 of the British plan is constructed in such a way that only upon the conclusion of the pact could negotiations be started on the convention providing the acceptance of the principle of *Gleichberechtigung* for Germany. He added that it is beyond his comprehension how the German government could join such a pact prior to the settlement of the armaments problem.

The whole course of von Neurath's thinking was definitely negative to the project. Neurath wants to deal with the whole matter slowly and to withstand the pressure of the Great Powers. He made this obvious by planning to go on leave the following week. He stressed that even the threat that a Franco-Russian alliance would be concluded in case of a negative attitude by Germany toward the pact would not force the German government to abandon its position. A Franco-Russian alliance is no threat to us, he added, since we have no aggressive intentions. Besides, von Neurath thinks that if the French government had to defend the alliance with the Soviets before the Chamber of Deputies it would encounter serious opposition.

Neurath described the pact as a hegemony of strongly armed powers, making an allusion to France.

Since the afternoon press brought news of Sir John Simon's communication to the House of Commons on Mussolini's stand toward the pact,[7] I asked for Neurath's opinion regarding the Italian declaration. Von Neurath replied that he was also taken aback by the press announcements; only upon reading Mussolini's statement did he get the impression that this was a very skillful retreat by the chief of the Italian government from probable British pressure that he participate in the Eastern Pact.

Mussolini's declaration is not in the least contradictory with his basically negative point of view toward the pact, as he clarified it in his conversations with the Chancellor at Venice.

Neurath also told me that, in view of the information in the London press that Simon's speech was made in time to enable the Chancellor to take a stand during his speech tonight on the question of the pact, he had immediately contacted Hitler and asked him to keep silent on this point.

Closing the conversation, von Neurath promised to keep me further informed about developments in this matter.

From my side, I gave him to understand that we are rather critical toward these plans, and that we shall have to investigate them thoroughly.

Józef Lipski

Eighty-seven-year-old President Hindenburg died on August 2, 1934. Three hours later, a directive dated August 1 was issued stating that the offices of Chancellor and President had been combined and that Hitler had taken power as the head of state and commander in chief.

A plebiscite was held on August 19, and 90 percent of the people voted in favor of the above directive.

[7] In his speech in Commons on July 13, Sir John Simon read a telegram just received from Mussolini, who informed the Foreign Secretary that the attitude of Italy toward the Eastern Pact was identical with that of Great Britain.

In a private letter of August 17, Lipski wrote to Józef Potocki, vice-director of the Political Department of the Ministry of Foreign Affairs, as follows:

More than ever before Chancellor Hitler is the dominant figure in the Reich's political life. Since the passing of the decree of August 1, fusing the functions of President and Chancellor, Hitler grasps the maximum of power in his hands. This is a fact which is worrying more than one politically-minded German, since the whole system depends on one man, with the attendant dangers.

If one takes a better look behind the scenes, it is clear that the events of June 30 aggravate the internal situation even more, and their results may be felt as time goes on. Nevertheless, viewing the events of June 30 from the vantage of the most recent moves connected with the succession of Hindenburg, it must be admitted that Hitler came off well, liquidating Röhm and getting rid of Schleicher before the death of the Reichspräsident. I have even met with the opinion that Hitler, who has known for more than three months about the possibility of Hindenburg's sudden death, rushed things through.

In this connection, it seems quite significant that the last published testament of Hindenburg is dated May 11. Since June 30 Hitler has systematically taken advantage of all developments to further his ends. His rapprochement with the Reichswehr facilitated his take-over of presidential power and his control over the armed forces. All the moral credit enjoyed by the late President in Germany is utilized for the aims of the National Socialist Party. Hindenburg is made out to be the spiritual father of Hitlerism. Hindenburg's testament is announced a day before the plebiscite.

It is immaterial whether the rumors (rather unconvincing) making the rounds abroad, that the document was allegedly forged, have a basis in fact or not. It is a fact that German public opinion believes that Hindenburg's testament favored Hitler. Even in Austrian-German relations he evokes the ghost of Hindenburg. Papen calls on Hindenburg's authority and wishes in carrying out his mission.

Hindenburg is to be buried in Tannenberg with full honors. They have taken over his glory, and his body remains in the distant East Prussian soil. It is better not to have a new Mecca too close to the capital.

In connection with Bülow's note, about which I write separately, the law of August 1, gives rise to interesting reflections. The title *Führer und Reichskanzler,* and abroad *Der Deutsche Reichskanzler,* seems somehow to be less than the idea of the head of state in other countries. One automatically feels that something is still missing. It is possible that Hitler did not want to forejudge the matter, but left possibilities open for the future.

How does the matter of the monarchy look? In my opinion, it is not of present interest, especially until Hitler's program of uniting Germany, in the wide meaning of the word, that is, with Austria, is realized. The monarchy would be a stumbling-block that would probably make unification impossible. The monarchy could only be the crowning achievement of a *fait accompli*—a definite stabilization. Meanwhile, we are in the full process of evolution. Of course, the trump card of the monarchy could be thrown in as the last hope in case of the collapse of Hitlerism. But this possibility is not being considered at present.

In conclusion, I may say that I do not see the monarchy as a current problem, but I do feel that, as the internal situation in Germany develops, it is imperative to watch this aspect closely. A plebiscite is strictly a touch à la Hitler, a means of clearing the atmosphere. Also, it is an absolution for the events of June 30, the acceptance of the law of August 1 by the nation, a demonstration to foreign countries that, in spite of what is said, the Germans back Hitler and his regime. What are the horoscopes? Most of them, in my opinion, are assured in advance. An element in the election struggle is the lack of a strong S.A. as an agitating agent in the elections. There may be surprises there. I expect that those who come to the polls will vote "for." Nevertheless, there may be a sizable number of abstainers, although the authorities are trying to counteract this possibility by special implementing orders. One would have to have comparable figures from previous elections at one's disposal to evaluate the results. A few more words about Hitler himself. I saw him during the funeral ceremonies for Hindenburg and I spoke with him. Outwardly he has changed a lot; the smile has disappeared from his face. He looks gloomy. His closest collaborators say that the Führer is suffering inside because of the betrayal of June 30. There is a certain atmosphere of *unheimlich.* Past and future assassination attempts are constantly discussed.

If it is very successful, the plebiscite will serve to clear the atmosphere.

DOCUMENT 30   Lipski to Beck [8]

N. 128/20/34   Berlin, August 27, 1934
                                                Strictly Confidential

On Thursday, August 23, the secretariat of Minister von Neurath telephoned to the Legation asking whether I would be in Berlin next Monday. Next day I was advised that the Minister for Foreign Affairs of the Reich would like to have a conversation with me on August 27 at 11 A.M.

Expecting that the problem of the Eastern Pact would be raised in the conversation, I asked for your eventual directions, which I received yesterday.

Minister von Neurath broached the question of the Eastern Pact, remarking that he would like to have Polish-German collaboration in this matter. He thought this should be done discreetly to avoid false rumors, which are already being circulated abroad by hostile propaganda. Herr von Neurath alluded here to the allegations in *Echo de Paris* about supposed secret Polish-German clauses. The German government had the project of the pact carefully investigated by its jurists, with the result that its reservations were rendered even more justified. The German government intends to issue an answer to the authors of the project, who, in von Neurath's opinion, use camouflage. Such a reply, expressing German reservations, would be handed to the British government.

The German government would like to check with us on this matter and therefore the Chancellor of the Reich desires to see me today at 2 P.M.

He is now in Berlin for a few hours and returns in the afternoon to Berchtesgaden by plane. Neurath also leaves tonight.

Last week the idea of inviting me to Berchtesgaden was discussed. However, it was necessary to conceal it from the press. Herr von Neurath asked me to be discreet about what he told me with regard to the pact, until my conversation with the Chancellor. On my side, when talking about the pact, I followed your latest instruction, pointing to our

[8] Lapter, pp. 314–18.

unchanged attitude and stating that we had not made much progress in studying this problem, which appears obscure from many angles.

Herr von Neurath also informed me that the Chancellor will present to me the question of establishing embassies in Warsaw and Berlin.

He closed the conversation with a sigh alluding to Pless. I presented to him a number of arguments pointing to absolutely improper dealing by Pless with his income tax duties.

I came to von Neurath before 2 o'clock and went with him to the Chancellery. The Chancellor thanked me in the first place for my greetings on the results of the plebiscite. He then declared it to be his wish to raise the German Legation in Warsaw to the rank of an embassy.

Next the Chancellor remarked that he would like to discuss with us very frankly the subject of the Eastern Pact.

Parental claims upon this project seem to be rather ambiguous. The Chancellor's attitude to the pact is negative in principle. In the problem of equality the pact offers no solution, although here there is a certain difference of opinion between the British and Italians on one side, and the French on the other.

From what the Chancellor said, I gathered that something might be hammered out in connection with the pact.

The Chancellor further pointed out that, in accordance with the pact, the Soviets would come to the aid of the Reich in case of a French attack on Germany. The Chancellor said that this is not without a certain irony. He cannot imagine what country would welcome the Red Army on its territory. Germany is quite content with the Locarno British-Italian guarantees, as is Russia. Besides—the Chancellor observed—in case of a French assault the real defense will rest on the Germans alone. In his opinion, this is true of all states; that is, they can count only on their own forces.

The Chancellor further stated that the whole conception of the pact involves Soviet Russia's interest primarily.

He observes Russia from two angles, from its drive for expansion and its military power.

In the Chancellor's opinion the whole might of the Soviets is based on their Communist doctrine of international scope. Contrary to Hitlerism or Fascism, Bolshevism does not respect national frontiers. It is an illusion to think that Bolshevik expansion reaches a terminal point. He quoted the example of America, where they are again having trouble with Moscow. In every country the Soviets have their organizations that would start action on behalf of Moscow in case of a conflict. That is why he, Hitler, was ever against the policies of former German governments that strove to rely on relations with the Soviets.

Russia is a colossus of unlimited resources. To think that in a few oncoming years something might change in Russia is an error. A doctrine never changes.

Russia's military progress is enormous. The Chancellor quoted figures of planes, tanks, people under arms. He does not belong to those who close their eyes in the face of danger. He never ceases to point out this danger of Russia to his people. Presently a commotion is boiling up in the Far East. Nobody can foresee whether a conflict with Japan will take place. However, the Chancellor thinks that Russia's whole policy— to join the League, to sign the Eastern Pact, to remove prejudices against collaboration with capitalist states—points to the intention of the Soviets to safeguard themselves in the West in case of a conflict in the Far East. Hence to sign the pact would mean to support the Soviets. This obviously does not please the Chancellor in the least. German guarantees for Russia are against his point of view. In a raised voice he declared: No German soldier will fight for Russia, at least as long as I live. In his long deliberations the Chancellor said many things about Poland. He declared that he had decided to change his policies toward Poland when he saw the danger coming from the East. For Europe— and particularly for Germany—Poland is a shield against the East. He always says that to his people. In relation to this ominous problem, any Polish-German divergences under the treaty fade away. These, of course, are unpleasant matters for Germans, but they retreat to the back of the stage. Thus, for example, if Poland's access to the sea had been pushed eastward from East Prussia at Versailles, then the two states would long ago have become allies. Poland to the east—Germany to the west. Germans and Poles have to live side by side and they should know better than to Germanize or Polonize. France's rapprochement with Russia is not a surprise to the Chancellor. For many years he was of the opinion that, when Russia took on weight, France would seek an alliance with Russia at the expense of its friendship with Poland. That is why he opposed the Reichswehr's politics toward Russia.

Coming back to the Eastern Pact and reiterating his ideas, the Chancellor confirmed that Germany's joining the pact would reinforce the

Soviets, which he does not want in principle, and which he regards as detrimental not just for Germany but for Europe too.

In this situation Poland's position is crucial. If Poland, in spite of being a neighbor, would join the pact, this would deprive him of his main argument. He would then be obliged to revise his position, eventually to bargain to some extent with the Great Powers (he is not precise but it is clear that he has the *Gleichberchtigung* in mind). On the other hand, if he could be sure that Poland's attitude to the pact is also negative, then merely a tactical arrangement would suffice, which would be relatively simple.

Here von Neurath explained that the German government would reply to the British government prior to Geneva, itemizing its negative attitude. The Chancellor mentioned your possible meeting with von Neurath prior to the Geneva session.

In reply to the Chancellor's deliberations I stated that I would communicate them to my government. With regard to the pact I added that you had a discussion with Herr von Neurath some time ago and that a series of conversations had taken place between the two governments. I confirmed that nothing had changed in our attitude toward the pact, which was not especially enthusiastic, and that we saw a number of complications.

At the end of the conversation with the Chancellor I left with von Neurath for the Auswärtiges Amt to render its results precise.

1) In von Neurath's opinion the question of the embassy should now be positively settled. This decision of the two governments could be realized at a suitable moment, and the German government would conform to the desire of the Polish government.

2) Von Neurath asked me to communicate to my government the contents of the conversation with the Chancellor and obtain a reply of the Polish government as to its basic standing regarding the pact. In case the reply from Warsaw would confirm as negative a standing as that of the German government, he would in all probability still forward a reply to London at the end of this week. Von Neurath thinks it very advisable to specify reservations toward the pact to the Powers prior to the Geneva session, in order to prevent sudden undesirable decisions in Geneva. Neurath thinks that the best thing to do would be to have the pact dissolved. The Polish-German understanding should not—in his opinion—be outwardly revealed. He also understands that arguments used by each of the governments would be different.

As to meeting you prior to Geneva, von Neurath does not see any possibility of meeting in Berlin. He suggested your eventual transit through Stuttgart on your way to Geneva via Berlin, where the meeting could take place on his estate situated at 20 minutes' distance from the former town. Herr von Neurath is leaving today for Berchtesgaden with the Chancellor. He requests that the reply about the pact be forwarded to the Secretary of State. Owing to shortage of time before the departure of the courier, I have made only a brief résumé of the most important points of the conversation with the Chancellor.[9]

Józef Lipski

On August 30, in his conversation with Secretary of State von Bülow, Lipski announced the approval of the Polish government regarding the question of embassies (which went into effect on November 1) and presented the initial Polish opinion regarding the Eastern Pact.[10]

On September 6 Beck discussed the question of the pact with von Neurath.[11]

The assassination of Minister Barthou on October 9 temporarily held up conversations on the Eastern Pact, but his successor, Pierre Laval, renewed discussions and started diplomatic action in this matter.

DOCUMENT 31   Dębicki to Lipski

Warsaw, December 2, 1934

Following the instructions of Minister Beck, I am taking the liberty of quoting below his remarks, which, together with the text attached herewith, plus possible verbal comments of the bearer of this letter, Mr. Skiwski,[12] might help you, Mr. Ambassador, in your informative action, which is at present of great importance to Minister Beck.

I. (*a*) The reply of the French government to the Polish exposition of the Eastern Pact (both documents enclosed),[13] presented by Ambassa-

---

[9] For the German version, see *DGFP*, Series C, Vol. III, No. 177.

[10] *Ibid.*, Nos. 184 and 187.

[11] *Ibid.*, No. 194.

[12] Wiktor Skiwski was chief of the Press Department at the Ministry of Foreign Affairs.

[13] For the text of the exposition, see *DGFP*, Series C, Vol. III, No. 226; for France's reply, *ibid.*, No. 379.

dor Laroche on November 26, brings no new elements to the basis and system of the pact. It only contains concessions for the Polish thesis regarding Czechoslovakia and Lithuania. The Minister considers this reply a product of the bad traditions of the old Quai d'Orsay. He declared to the French government that he would have to make a study of it, and is keeping to his present position of reserve toward the planned pact.

(*b*) A further stage of this question is the Minister's conversation with Ambassador Laroche, a *compte rendu* of which I am enclosing herewith.[14]

(*c*) Finally, I am enclosing a memorandum of the conversation of Director Potocki with Herr von Schliep, held in consequence of the inquiry made by the German Chargé d'Affaires regarding the text of the French reply.[15]

II. Germany's stand on this question remains of essential importance for Minister Beck. Any shift in this stand would create a really new situation and force us to change our tactics. Therefore, it is most important and most urgent to obtain information about anything pertaining to German opinions on the whole problem of the pact. In order to collect such information, the Minister thinks it is indispensable that you, Mr. Ambassador, remain in Berlin. Although from conversations held so far with Herr von Moltke it develops that the German government still retains its negative attitude toward the pact, the impact of a possible change in this stand would result in such serious consequences that it is of the utmost importance to follow this problem as closely as possible, since it is the foremost problem facing us at present.

On the other hand, we are trying to find out whether the British campaign to legalize German armaments (resulting from recent speeches of Baldwin and Simon in the House of Commons) is at all connected with the question of the Eastern Pact, or whether it is being undertaken independently of it. If it turns out that the action of the British government and France's renewed efforts for the realization of the Eastern Pact have no interconnection and are being conducted independently, then this, in the Minister's opinion, could weaken the concept of the Eastern Pact. If, on the other hand, French policy succeeds in combining its efforts toward the realization of the plan with England's

---

[14] Enclosure missing. For the text of the conversation, see Laroche, p. 187.
[15] Notice missing.

initiative to legalize German armaments, the observation of the German position will become all the more important, since if both actions were combined, one of the chief German objections to the pact would fall and it could become for Germany the first genuine objective of political bargaining.

III. In the light of the above, strictly internal, considerations, Minister Beck requests that you declare to Herr von Neurath at the first opportunity that we made no promises as to the revision of our stand on the question of the pact, and that we are investigating the French reply, reserving judgment for the present. Up to now, the results of our studies on this reply are not very satisfactory. We are asking what the German stand is, declaring that we are ready to continue an exchange of opinions on this subject.

Dębicki

DOCUMENT 32   Lipski to Beck

Berlin, December 5, 1934
Strictly Confidential

On Monday, on the 3d inst., Skiwski brought me your verbal instructions regarding the Eastern Pact, as well as the letter of Director Dębicki, dated December 2, together with its enclosed texts and informative material.

I asked Reich Foreign Affairs Minister von Neurath for an audience on Tuesday and received a reply that, owing to important cabinet sessions, the Reich Minister was asking me to come on Wednesday at 12 noon.

At the cabinet session Minister von Neurath reported on foreign policy problems, particularly questions of the Saar. On Tuesday evening at Kiepura's concert I talked casually with Herr von Neurath, and we agreed that on the next day we would talk politics.

Arriving at Herr von Neurath's on Wednesday, I told him that I would like to discuss the question of the Eastern Pact, which had again become timely. I recalled that after your meeting with von Neurath at Stuttgart you had a conversation with Barthou at Geneva on the Eastern

Pact. At the request of the French Minister of Foreign Affairs you handed him an exposition in writing, not destined for publication because of the form of the document, since it was not a formal note but merely a summary of verbal explanations. Consequently, you informed Herr von Moltke about the contents of this document. I then handed this very document to Herr von Neurath, asking him to regard it as confidential.

I next stressed that after Barthou's death it seemed that the problem of the pact lost some of its timeliness; this was also the opinion of the A.A. I came across such statements in the course of several conversations. At present M. Laval is again taking up the problem of the pact. The French ambassador in Warsaw handed you a reply to his exposition of September 27. According to your instructions contained in Mr. Dębicki's letter, I mentioned that we did not make any promises to the French government so far as our attitude toward the pact was concerned, and that we are studying the French reply, reserving our opinion. I added that, although with regard to guarantees to Czechoslovakia and countries that have no diplomatic relations with us the French reply attempts to observe Polish restrictions, nevertheless, upon investigation of the text, no changes in the essence of the pact itself were discovered.

Here Herr von Neurath quickly rejoined that he had received the same impression, that nothing had changed in the very foundation of the pact.

At the end I remarked that it seems that our study of the French reply will take some more time; that we would like to know what the stand of the German government is and to remain in contact with them on this matter.

In reply Herr von Neurath said that he knows from Ambassador Köster that the French government intends to communicate to the German government the wording of the reply to Poland, and that it only awaits Warsaw's consent.

I explained that we gave a positive reply to Paris, which was obvious in itself.

Herr von Neurath firmly verified that the stand of the German government on the problem of the Eastern Pact was unaltered. He said he is quite sure that there is no possibility of any change, unless the essential foundations of the pact are altered, for the German government has no intention of being drawn into guarantees which might expose it to unpredictable conflicts.

This declaration was rather characteristic, since Neurath passed over in silence the question of equality of rights, but instead used the question of obligations for reciprocal assistance as an argument against the pact.

Herr von Neurath added that he would like further to keep in contact with me, and upon receiving the French reply to Poland he would like to take up this question again.

Herr von Neurath mentioned that he saw from the press that Mussolini is pushing his new idea. Knowing Mussolini, he is not surprised, for in such international situations the chief of the Italian government is trying to get into the forefront in the character of superarbiter. Herr von Neurath is only *au courant* of Mussolini's plan from the press. It would appear that a great many countries would be united in a pact of friendship. However, Herr von Neurath thinks that this apparently innocent concept conceals a hidden catch in the form of an obligation to limit armaments on the basis of the present status. This means that Germany would be granted its presently achieved armaments, thus limiting its ceiling, which is against its interests.

It was clear from the conversation with Herr Neurath that the German government's stand with regard to the Eastern Pact is still negative, and that it is rather satisfied that Warsaw received the last French reply with reserve, considering that the essence of the pact was unchanged.[16]

It was rather significant that von Neurath called the pact *Russenpakt.* May I remind you that Chancellor Hitler, in his conversation with me on August 27, 1934, stressed his reluctance to reinforce the Russian position in Europe as his main argument against the pact. At an audience of November 14 last, Hitler firmly assured me that his government, outside of economic relations, will not enter into any further understandings with Soviet Russia. Although I am aware that the circles of the Reichswehr and industry are drifting in the direction of a rapprochement with Russia, I nevertheless do not conceive the possibility that influence could be exerted on the Chancellor—given the present structure of power inside the Reich—to make him abandon his guiding policy line,

---

[16] The stand of the German government regarding the Eastern Pact was defined in the instructions to Ambassador von Moltke in Warsaw on December 15 (*DGFP*, Series C, Vol. III, No. 392), which he carried out in his conversation with Beck on December 20 (*ibid.,* No. 397).

all the more so since he regards the Eastern Pact as a trend toward French-Russian hegemony in Europe. Though the German-Russian rapprochement might have some attraction for certain German circles, a *détente* with Russia effected by the Eastern Pact cannot be advantageous to any German movement.

In his letter Mr. Dębicki asked whether British action to legalize German armaments has any connection with the Eastern Pact, in short, whether the Great Powers would agree to concessions on the armaments problem provided Germany joins the pact.

I shall keep you informed about all observations on this matter that I am able to make here. I did not want to take up this matter with Herr von Neurath, since I am very careful to avoid any topic with the Germans which would bring up the problem of equality of rights. I will only mention that von Neurath dealt with the matter of the pact independently of considerations of equality of rights. We could ask ourselves to what extent Germany is interested in the legalization of its armaments and what price it would be willing to pay for this move. Now, since the German government offered a certain ceiling in its notes to Great Britain and Italy, the situation has changed drastically. Germany has clearly contravened the provisions of Part V of the Versailles Treaty by arming, while the reaction of the Great Powers turned out to be just a platonic one. Public opinion has become used to German armaments, as could be observed even from the last debates in the House of Commons. If one of the leading British objections is that nothing precise can be learned about the state of German armaments, I presume that this objection is rather welcomed by the chief of the General Staff of the German Army. I think that, for the German government in the present period of Army expansion, it is more convenient to arm now, even against the letter of the treaty, than to agree to a restriction of armaments on a certain level, which would undoubtedly bring about controls.

If the tempo of German armaments has been accelerated during the last months, we have to assume that, besides other considerations, this is due precisely to a desire to create a *fait accompli* in face of the attempts of the Great Powers to limit the armed forces of Germany to a certain level.

Józef Lipski

Introduction of Conscription in Germany
January—May, 1935

DOCUMENT 33 Lipski to Beck

NO. 49/1/5/35   Berlin, January 24, 1935
Strictly Confidential

The annual dinner for the chiefs of diplomatic missions accredited in Berlin took place on January 22.

After dinner Chancellor Hitler conversed with several ambassadors, among others with me.

I began by declaring that I was very glad that in a few days Reichspräsident Göring will take part in a hunting party in Poland. The Chancellor was visibly pleased with this.

Next, the conversation turned to Polish-German relations in connection with the anniversary of the nonaggression declaration signed a year ago, on January 26. The Chancellor stressed in very cordial terms the importance of the rapprochement between the two nations. Deliberating on this topic, he said how false the thesis of Polish-German *Erbfeindschaft* had proved to be. Hitherto in our history there were periods when we collaborated, opposing the common danger from the east. We also had some dynastic ties. Here I mentioned the last visit of the lord mayor of Dresden, Zoerner, to Warsaw and Cracow and how warmly he was welcomed. The Chancellor—developing this theme—remarked that in some eight or nine years utterly different relations would prevail, when the two nations would get to know each other and would rid themselves of former prejudices. He added that of course there are some elements in Germany acting against Poland. These are the elements which, as he put it, would like to prevent his government from being successful in its foreign policy. Such elements undoubtedly exist in Poland also, the Chancellor remarked.

The Chancellor then went on at length about Russian problems and the danger from the east. He pointed to the information obtained from his military circles and the intelligence service that Russia had made enormous progress in the military field. A moment might come when both countries would have to defend themselves against invasion from the east. In his opinion, the policy practiced by the governments of his predecessors, and especially by the Reichswehr, based upon alliances with Russia against Poland, was sheer political nonsense. He himself at one time had clashed very bitterly with General von Schleicher, who wanted to get closer to Russia at Poland's expense. The Chancellor told him at that time that such a policy, even if it resulted in wrenching some territories from Poland, would lead to the resurgence of the worst danger for Germany, that is, the Soviet threat. He himself knows Bolshevism and has been combating it from the beginning, and here he brought up his struggle with Communism in Bavaria.

Talking about Marshal Piłsudski, the Chancellor said that he feels ashamed that only recently has he had the opportunity to learn more about the Marshal's life, and his esteem for the Marshal as a great statesman has increased even further. I took this occasion to thank the Chancellor for the kind gesture of sending Secretary of State Meissner to me to inquire about the Marshal's health, as a result of some press reports which had appeared a few weeks earlier.

Next, Hitler inquired about our stand toward the Eastern Pact. I replied, according to your instructions, that, as there were no changes in the basic structure of the plan for the pact, we are still reserving judgment. Finally, the Chancellor said a few very cordial words about Ambassador Wysocki.

We also talked about the Weisser Hirsch sanatorium near Dresden, and I thanked the Chancellor for his concern about my cure when he visited General Blomberg there.

At the close of the conversation, to which the Chancellor obviously wanted to lend a hearty tone, I said a few complimentary words about the results of the Saar plebiscite.[1] I remarked that this result is dispersing some false rumors peddled by the international press after the elections held in the Reich.

---

[1] A plebiscite was held in the Saar on January 13, 1935. The large majority of inhabitants (477,000 against 48,000) voted for the union of the Saar with the Reich. Hitler then declared that he had no territorial claims on France.

In connection with the above, I am also taking the liberty of stressing that at the same reception the French Ambassador expressed his conviction that he has lately felt a certain stiffening on the part of the Germans regarding the equality of rights. He also criticized the last speech of the Chancellor, stating that Hitler's previous public appearance was more moderate, since it was first discussed with von Neurath. M. François-Poncet was visibly disturbed by this state of affairs, and remarked that in the present situation reciprocal concessions and the search for a formula, etc., should be under discussion.

Also from other quarters I can detect a certain intensification of German demands regarding armaments since the settlement of the Saar problem. I refer to my report of the 8th inst., No. N/49/I/1/35, where I stressed that, in my opinion, military elements would not be willing at present to limit the ceiling of armaments and to allow controls. However, it is still difficult to judge what Germany's stand will be, and one can only make certain conjectures. Nevertheless, even now we can state that Germany will not be in a hurry to enter into negotiations and will rather keep to a position which would play into their hands from a tactical point of view.[2]

Józef Lipski

DOCUMENT 34 Lipski to Beck

NO. N/49/I/10/35 Berlin, February 5, 1935
Strictly Confidential

Referring to my telegrams of the 4th inst., I would like to report that on February 3 in the evening, when I met the French Ambassador at the races by chance, I learned that, together with the British Ambassador, he had presented the London resolutions to Hitler. The French Ambassador remarked that the text of the London resolutions was so cautious and subtle in wording that it should not have evoked any controversy from the German side. Nevertheless, the Chancellor strongly objected to two items, on which the Ambassador did not elaborate further. As far as

[2] The *Polish White Book* presents this report (No. 13) in an extensively abbreviated and considerably deformed version.

the plan of the air agreement was concerned, the Chancellor had a rather favorable opinion. The French Ambassador did not conceal his anxiety that the German government might jeopardize these negotiations, the results of which might prove so important, by its overly prejudiced stand. M. François-Poncet is of the opinion that this is the crucial moment for the shaping of international relations in Europe. Either Germany will accept international collaboration along the lines presented by the Great Powers, or a system of blocs and an armaments race will persist. Here the French Ambassador assumed that Poland would also have an interest in the success of the negotiations, since otherwise it would be compelled to abandon its present convenient position and declare itself on one side or the other. The Ambassador made a slight allusion to the fact that the Polish government, since it holds such an influential position in Berlin, could now render a useful service to the cause of peace.

I would also like to add that François-Poncet, who has read the protocol of Laval's conversation with you, told me that Laval is positively impressed by these talks.[3]

Talking about your last speech,[4] François-Poncet remarked that the German press is constantly intriguing to create friction between two allied nations. For example, it was stressed that the passage about France was especially brief as compared with the number of words you devoted to the relations with the Germans, etc. However, François-Poncet thinks that what is most important is that you confirmed the existence of a Franco-Polish alliance, which should be quite sufficient for his government.

On the following day the chief of the Eastern Department at the A.A. quite confidentially, informed me, on behalf of von Neurath, about the Chancellor's conversation with the ambassadors of France and Great Britain, which, as I mentioned before, was held on February 3. He handed me the text of the London resolutions in English, which had been presented to the Chancellor on this occasion. The text is nearly identical with the communiqué published the following day in the European press. I am enclosing a copy of the English text herewith.[5]

[3] For Beck's note of conversations with Laval on January 16 and 19, 1935, see *Diariusz*, I, 466–69.

[4] For Beck's speech of February 1 at the Commission for Foreign Affairs of the Diet, see Beck, *Przemówienia, deklaracje, wywiady, 1931–1937*, pp. 142–50.

[5] For the text, see *British Blue Book*, Cmd. 5143 of 1936, No. 5.

Minister Meyer declared that upon receiving this text the Chancellor in the first place firmly refuted the allusion that Germany has reputedly violated the armament clauses of the Treaty of Versailles. He declared that it was not Germany but the Great Powers who did not keep their respective obligations. As for Germany's joining the League of Nations, the Chancellor was supposed to have repeated his well-known position. Regarding the Eastern Pact, he took exception to the obligation of reciprocal aid.

Declaring that at present he was simply making a few comments based on superficial initial investigations that had taken place at the A.A. on the morning of February 4, Herr Meyer remarked that the text, which he considers quite interesting, will be given careful attention. As for the question of reciprocal aid in the Eastern Pact, Herr Meyer— evidently acting on instructions from the top—declared very explicitly that the German government would under no circumstances accept such stipulations. Herr Meyer stressed as a certain *novum* that it was noted in the text that Great Britain would take part in the consultations provided for by the Roman agreements in case the independence of Austria is threatened.

Regarding the accession to the air convention which was proposed to Germany, Herr Meyer gave me to understand that the stand of the German government might be positive. He added that such an agreement concluded between Great Britain, France, Italy, Belgium, and Germany could logically result from Locarno obligations which bind these states.

I am taking the liberty of remarking that the proposition of an air agreement is rather convenient for Germany, only because it grants the Germans an *a priori* military air force. Besides, it guarantees a possibility of removing from German-British relations the most drastic cause of friction.

Closing our conversation, Herr Meyer said that the German government would continue to keep me informed about these matters.

Not declaring myself at present as to the chances of success or failure of negotiations started between Germany and the Great Powers, I would just like to observe that the scope of the talks has become extensively broader, inasmuch as all problems (equality of rights, disarmament problems, Germany's entrance into the League of Nations, the Eastern Pact, the Central European Pact, Austria) are under discussion.

Here I shall recall the position presently held by Germany with regard to the particular problems encompassed by the negotiations.

The problem of the Eastern Pact. In principle a negative stand. The main argument used against the pact is the question of obligatory reciprocal assistance to the signatories of the pact.

The problem of the Central European Pact. Germany's position is declared in the memorandum to Italy and France, on which I reported in No. N/49/I/9/35 on the 5th inst.

When investigating this problem, it should be kept in mind that the German government would oppose anything that could in the future be an obstacle to its free action in relation to Austria.

Disarmament problems. Theoretically would demand absolute equality of rights with the Great Powers. As far as the limitations which would be accepted by the German government, it is doubtful whether it would still keep to its stand, as revealed in its last note in the spring of 1934. It is probable, as I mentioned in my previous reports, that Germany's demands were henceforth raised, and that military elements would oppose the establishment of limitations and controls.

Western air agreement. Stand of Germany positive in principle.

Germany's entrance into the League of Nations. Germany's stand is that the return of Germany depends on first obtaining equality of rights. Whether besides equality of rights the German government would also bring up the question of the League's reorganization is not yet quite clear, but my guess is that such a possibility might occur.

When evaluating the chances of negotiations so broadly conceived as a topic of conversations between the Great Powers and the government of the Reich, two points should be considered. First, that present-day National Socialist Germany is in a dynamic and not a static state. Therefore, a formula presented by the Western states that is too restrictive for Germany cannot be in line with the present development of Germany. Also, a too-extensive connection with democratic organizations in the West in the field of international collaboration, as for instance in the League of Nations, could not be very tempting to the regime. These *imponderabilia* will undoubtedly have an impact on the decision of the Reich government.

Józef Lipski

DOCUMENT 35   Lipski to Beck

NO. N/49/I/9/35   Berlin, February 5, 1935
                                                            Strictly Confidential

Referring to my telegram of the 4th inst., I am taking the liberty of
reporting as follows:

During my stay in Poland with Prime Minister Göring,[6] the chief of
the Eastern Department of the A.A. telephoned the Embassy, expressing
the wish to see me. As he explained to me on the 4th inst., he wanted to
hand me a memorandum addressed by the German government to
France and Italy in connection with their *démarche* in Berlin regarding
the Roman agreements.[7] Director Meyer declared to me that Ambassador Moltke was instructed to present this memorandum to you.

The memorandum, a copy of which is attached herewith,[8] contains a
statement in the introduction that the German government accepts as
self-explanatory the principles agreed to in the Central European Pact:
namely, nonintervention into the internal affairs of other states; interdic-
tion against the preparations on its territory of acts of terror directed
against another state. On this basis the German government expresses
its consent to undertake conversations to conclude an agreement which
would define the above principles.

The memorandum further poses five questions to the French and Italian governments, to which I would like to add the following explanations:

ad 1) The demand for a precise definition of the idea of nonintervention into another state's affairs is made in connection with the Austrian
situation. Already in my previous talks at the A.A. I heard musings on
whether financing of the Heimwehr should be regarded as mixing into
Austria's internal affairs. I presume that this point might serve the German government as a basis for bringing up the question of the Great

---

[6] Göring stayed in Poland at a hunting party from January 27 to January 31.
Besides hunting he had several conversations with Marshal Piłsudski, Beck,
Szembek, and others (see *Diariusz*, I, 218–21, 223–25, 230–31). For the German
version of this visit, see *DGFP*, Series C, Vol. III, No. 474.

[7] The Roman agreements were a series of agreements regarding Danubian
problems and African questions, signed in Rome on January 7, 1935, by Laval
and Mussolini.

[8] See *DGFP*, Series C, Vol. III, No. 460, enclosure on p. 866.

Powers' not opposing the right of a free vote for the Austrian population and not pressing for the suppression of the Hitlerite Party in Austria.

ad 2) Objections against the so-called *accords particuliers* were raised by the German government from the moment it had been informed about the contents of the Roman agreements. Undoubtedly, the Germans particularly fear any ties of Austria with other states, for example, with Italy, and therefore they introduce the restriction that such separate agreements have to be previously accepted by all signatories of the pact.

ad 3) The suggestion that Switzerland, and especially Great Britain, should be partners in the pact was probably caused by two reasons. It could be that the German government wanted to weaken the Central European Pact by expanding the number of signatories, thus neutralizing individual influences, or that it wanted to burden the negotiations with further demands.

ad 4) The Italian-French consultative agreement concerning Austria, as we know, evoked the strongest objections of the German government, which regarded it as a sort of protectorate over Austria. Hence the demand that, if the consultative pact were to be continued during the period of the Central European Pact, it should be extended to the full extent to cover reciprocal relations of all signatories of the Central European Pact.

ad 5) The fifth question derives logically from Germany's walkout at the League of Nations. However, bringing up this point makes it doubtful that Germany could enter the Central European Pact prior to its return to the League.

Recapitulating the above, one cannot help having the impression that by posing these questions the German government not only did not facilitate negotiations but actually complicated them, for these questions require solutions of problems pending between Germany and the Great Powers, such as equality of rights and the return of Germany to the League of Nations.

Józef Lipski

DOCUMENT 36 Lipski to Beck

NO. N/128/8/35   Berlin, February 14, 1935
                                                 Strictly Confidential

Referring to my telegram, dispatched tonight, I am taking the liberty of
reporting as follows:

This afternoon Foreign Affairs Minister von Neurath handed to the
ambassadors of France and Great Britain the reply of the Reich government to the London resolutions. At 6 P.M. I was received by von Neurath, who declared that in accordance with his promise to keep us
closely informed about the negotiations with the Western Powers on the
above matters he would like to hand me the text of the German reply.[9]

Leaving me some time to acquaint myself with the text, Herr von
Neurath added the following verbal comments:

The German government was rather pleased that the British and
French governments informed it of the results of the London consultations, even prior to issuing a joint communiqué. Therefore, the German
reply is maintained in a tone of courtesy and marked with the desire to
reach an understanding.

Herr von Neurath further confirmed that the German government
found in the text of the resolutions communicated to it, first of all,
reference to a number of problems previously discussed by the Powers
and the German government. Herr von Neurath enumerated here the
question of the Eastern Pact, the Roman agreements, and disarmament.
The German government did not deem it advisable to return to these
particular questions in its present reply. This reply is therefore general
in character, for as far as the Eastern Pact is concerned, the German
government has already explicitly stated its point of view and has nothing further to add. It regards this pact—and especially the clause of
reciprocal assistance (*assistance mutuelle*)—as not acceptable. The
French reply to the German government brought nothing new to this
problem. Therefore, the German government had nothing to add regarding the Eastern Pact; it would only have had to declare its negative
attitude.

With regard to the Roman agreements, Herr von Neurath referred to
questions already known to us, posed by the Reich government to the

[9] For the text, see *British Blue Book* for 1936, No. 6.

governments of Italy and France. Here too there was nothing more to say.

Regarding the disarmament problem, Herr von Neurath told me that it was certainly the French government and not the German government which broke off negotiations carried on last spring on this subject.

Therefore the Powers had to say the last word here, and not Germany.

Finally, von Neurath declared that the only *novum* is the proposition of the air pact. Therefore, this item was treated in detail in the German answer, and their stand on this matter was positive.

To my question as to the meaning of the statement in the German reply that the Reich government would like to negotiate in a more restricted group on the air pact, Herr von Neurath remarked that this passage, which, in his opinion, evoked a reaction on the part of the British ambassador, Sir Eric Phipps, was meant as a certain preparation for negotiations. Herr von Neurath, stressing that this is only his own opinion, remarked that the air pact, as an outgrowth of the Locarno agreements, would present no editing problem. It could be contained in two articles. In one it could be stated that the signatories of the agreement agree to mutual assistance without prior recourse to the League of Nations in case of attack by air. The second article could contain certain resolutions of a technical nature. Of course, Herr von Neurath has no illusions that considerable difficulties might arise in this matter.

Talking about the air pact, Herr von Neurath told me that he had a conversation with the Chancellor yesterday, during which the latter informed him of our discourse during the dinner for the Papal Nuncio.[10]

In this connection, Herr von Neurath asked me to inform you that he thinks it would be desirable at the present time to bring about a Polish-German conversation regarding the air pact, because he fears that if the question is raised about Polish-German mutual assistance in case one of these states is attacked by air, the problem would become timely and lead directly to the Eastern Pact. Russia undoubtedly would place a request for mutual assistance in air matters. Therefore von Neurath thinks it is better, in the present circumstances, to leave this question alone in Polish-German relations and await results of the conversations with the Western Powers. From the practical point of view, von Neurath repeated twice that in case of an air attack on us from the only side to be considered, that is, by Russia, we can count on the stand of Ger-

[10] In the Lipski documents the report of this conversation is missing.

many. Herr von Neurath remarked that in his conversation with the Chancellor he had told him the same thing.

I told Herr von Neurath that I could not give the Chancellor an authoritative reply the day before at the Nuncio's dinner to his concrete inquiry as to whether we would accept an air pact without Russia or not. I added that I had informed you about my conversation with the Chancellor.

Herr Neurath remarked that obviously I could not declare myself without consulting my government on such a matter—and that he was well aware of this. He repeated again his opinion that it would be better not to actualize the Polish-German air agreement. It was better to await further developments in the situation, and he added that the moment might come when it will become timely.

The above explanations of Herr von Neurath answer the question I put to myself after my conversation the day before with the Chancellor. I referred to it in my telegram of the 13th inst. I see from it that the idea of mutual air assistance in Polish-German relations came from the Chancellor and is not a result of suggestions from any third state. The Chancellor, who in the matter of security takes the Polish problem seriously, and probably taking into consideration the air negotiations with the Western Powers, did not want to leave a void on the Polish side.

Owing to a lack of time because of the courier's departure, I would only like to draw your attention to several issues in the German reply.

I seriously doubt whether passing over in silence the question of the Eastern Pact, the Roman agreements, and the disarmament problem, which Herr von Neurath tried to present as tactical moves, would meet with much enthusiasm on the part of the Western Powers, especially France, which tied all problems into one tight bundle.

The passage stating that the armaments race was caused by the policy of the Powers who were against disarmament as foreseen by the Versailles Treaty is a reply to an item in the London resolutions: namely, that the Powers cannot admit a one-sided violation of the treaty's disarmament clauses.

The suggestion to undertake direct German-British talks on the air pact is obviously a tactical move destined for public opinion in England.

In conclusion, it might be stated that the reply of the German government, as it is given, poses even more questions over the whole of the negotiations. It is most improbable that the air pact can be separated from the bulk of questions, and that Great Britain upon reaching an understanding with France in London would like to deal with this matter independently of the whole complex of other problems in the field of security covered by the forthcoming negotiations.

I stress that the text will be published on Saturday. Today the German press received only general information.

Józef Lipski

DOCUMENT 37   Lipski to Beck

N/128/12/35   Berlin, February 25, 1935
                                               Confidential

Referring to my telegram reporting on the conversation I had with Herr von Neurath on the 21st inst., I am taking the liberty of communicating as follows:

To begin with, I declared to Herr von Neurath that, in connection with my conversation with the Chancellor at the Nuncio's reception and the explanations von Neurath later furnished me with, I had written to you and had received your reply, which I would like to acquaint him with. I remarked that we very much appreciate the open and sincere manner of the Reich Chancellor's declaration regarding the possible extension of the air pact to Poland. I added that we shall adjust our relations with Germany in this matter accordingly.

Passing *ad meritum* of the problem, I pointed out that the air guarantee is quite a *novum* and that, as far as the wording of such an agreement is concerned, no precedent exists. We have had no possibility as yet to investigate fully the problem regarding the application in practice of this guarantee. I further added that we shall follow the negotiations closely, and in case attempts are made to extend the air pact to other groups of states also, we will discuss this matter with the German government.

With regard to my previous conversation with Herr von Neurath, I said that you had not as yet received any proposition from the Russian side to this effect. Nevertheless, you share the opinion that the Soviets will strive to bring up the Eastern Pact in other ways. I declared that our stand on this matter is unchanged.

In a discussion that followed the above explanations, Herr von Neurath remarked that he fully understands that Poland cannot at present declare itself regarding the air pact. The Chancellor's suggestion aimed in the first place at assuring Poland that in negotiations conducted in the West on this matter Poland would not be left out by the Reich.

I replied that it was just because of this idea of the Chancellor that I declared, on your behalf, at the start of this conversation, how highly we appreciate his approach to this matter.

Herr von Neurath's comment regarding the reception of the German note in London and Paris was that criticism stating that Germany allegedly grasped at the negotiations of the air pact while omitting other issues contained in the Anglo-French declaration was groundless. The Reich's stand regarding other issues, such as the Eastern Pact, Roman agreements, or equality of rights, has been explicitly stated in the course of the Reich's conversations with the Powers, which have been under way for some time. The only *novum* is the air pact. The Anglo-French declaration stated that negotiations on this subject should be begun promptly. It was therefore evident that in its reply to the declaration the Reich government gave priority to the air pact.

Regarding Simon's trip to Berlin or Neurath's to London, the Reich Foreign Minister observed that, unless such visits are properly prepared, the meeting of the ministers to discuss such difficult and intricate matters might be prejudicial if no positive result is attained.

Herr von Neurath promised to keep us *au courant* on this matter.

He then spontaneously touched on the question of Schuschnigg's trip to Paris and London. He told me that according to information he received it is not impossible that the problem of the future regime in Austria will be discussed to consider the idea of the return of the Hapsburgs. For the idea prevails of creating a *Reichsverweserschaft* as it existed in Hungary. Until the return of the Hapsburgs, supposedly Starhemberg would take this post. Now, von Neurath confided in me that in the Hapsburg question the German government is taking a stand of total *désintéressement* and has issued instructions to whom it may concern accordingly. The constitutional form the regime in Austria will wish to adopt is its own affair, so that the Reich has no intention of interfering.

In my further conversation with Herr von Neurath on this issue, I had the strong impression that this stand of the Reich is rather opportunistic, since Neurath is of the opinion that the Hapsburg question will render the situation still more confused. Of course, he does not believe that Austria can achieve normal relations. It was rather characteristic that in connection with this question Herr von Neurath made a slight allusion to the Italian-Abyssinian conflict.

Józef Lipski

On March 16, 1935, a bill was published in Germany introducing conscription and a build-up of the army.[11] In peacetime it was to be developed to twelve army corps and 36 divisions, totaling about 500,000 men. This was a final violation of Part V of the Treaty of Versailles.

Von Moltke, in his telegram of March 18 (*DGFP*, Series C, Vol. III, No. 536), reports how public opinion in Poland reacted to this news. (See also *Diariusz*, I, 242–43.)

DOCUMENT 38   Lipski to Beck

NO. N/133/a/10/35   Berlin, March 16, 1935
                                           Strictly Confidential

Today I was asked to call on Chancellor Hitler, who received me at 5:45 P.M. at the Chancellor's palace, with Herr von Neurath present.

Entering the palace, I met the British Ambassador, whom the Chancellor had received before my audience.

Chancellor Hitler opened the conversation by declaring that I was probably already informed about the conscription bill issued by the Reich, dealing with the build-up of the army. (Here I must note that before my departure for the Reich Chancellery I was informed by the representative of the Polish Telegraph Agency that Goebbels had just advised the press about the publication of the bill.) Chancellor Hitler stated to me that the issuing of the bill was due to the general situation that prevailed as a result of the Powers' armaments. He added that what is contained in the bill more or less corresponds to the actual state of the Reich's armaments. He further emphasized that this step of the Reich is

[11] For the English text, see Royal Institute of International Affairs, *Survey of International Affairs, 1935*, pp. 141–42.

devoid of any aggressive tendencies, since it is only of a defensive nature. Besides, the effective forces themselves defined in the bill by the Reich, as compared with those of its neighbors, manifest the peaceful tendencies of the Reich. Here the Chancellor cited 101 divisions in Russia, 41 divisions in France, and 30 divisions in Poland. He further stressed that the government of the Reich—provided conditions permit —will not try to avail itself of the figures drawn up in the bill. The bill, as the Chancellor conceives of it, would in no way mean a cancellation of talks with the Powers on limitation of armaments, which the government of the Reich is anticipating. The Chancellor also gave me to understand that he regrets handing this text to me so late, and without a Polish translation. It was obvious from his words that the decision of the Reich government must have been taken very hurriedly, probably in connection with yesterday's debate in the French parliament. Besides, the Chancellor told me that he interrupted his rest leave at Berchtesgaden and arrived in Berlin today.

Next the Chancellor took up the subject of future Anglo-German conversations. He stated that the Eastern Pact is for him the most difficult point in the program of talks, for the government of Great Britain exerts very strong pressure on the Reich government to bind itself to the Eastern Pact by a clause of mutual assistance. Now, under no circumstances will the Chancellor accept the clause of mutual assistance in relation to Russia. To confirm this stand of his, he told me that in the first place the Reich has no frontier with Russia. Furthermore, it is inconceivable for him that divisions of the National Socialist army could bring assistance to Communist Russia. Finally, he thinks that the whole construction of extending mutual assistance could of itself result in a situation in which Russia, supported by France, could start a conflict and shift the responsibility to Poland, for example. In such a case, it is inconceivable that, in accordance with the obligations of the Treaty, the German Army would have to act on the side of Soviet Russia. The Chancellor is ready to enter into pacts of mutual assistance with any other neighbor. He then cited Holland, Belgium, Poland, France, and even—adding that this would not be easy for him—Austria. In connection with Russia, such an obligation is out of the question.

Poland's position regarding the Eastern Pact is—in the Chancellor's opinion—of utmost importance. The Chancellor gave me to understand that he is very much concerned that we should maintain our position without change.

I explained to the Chancellor that Poland's stand toward the Eastern Pact—as is well known to the German government—is replete with reservations. I told him that we still have a pact of nonaggression with Russia.

Both the Chancellor and Neurath pounced on this point, stating that this pact should be enough.

In a discussion on this point, I said generally that we recognize all elements, such as nonaggression, consultations, and nonintervention, and that our pacts are based on these principles. Neurath, together with the Chancellor, eagerly agreed with me.

When the Chancellor once more stressed that the Eastern Pact will be the most difficult point to discuss with the British side, Neurath, addressing me, remarked that the best solution would be to oppose the British firmly on the idea of mutual assistance. The Chancellor then observed that the English would break their heads and find some solution.

I would also like to add that, in broad terms, the Chancellor described his conversation with the British as follows:

He said that in the field of armaments he foresees possibilities of discussion, and that the Reich government is in favor of the air triangle with England and France. Regarding the Danubian point, the Chancellor thought that on this also a settlement could be reached in spite of considerable difficulties with the problem of the definition of intervention.

When discussing the Eastern Pact, the Chancellor said that he does not understand why France, instead of agreeing to direct talks with Berlin in which Poland would possibly be included, was seeking channels via Moscow. Was it not easier, observed the Chancellor, to talk directly with Berlin after its declarations about Alsace and Lorraine? Here the Chancellor reiterated again that, regarding the Saar, he obviously had to claim the return of this territory to the Reich, since the population was totally German, while, with regard to Alsace and Lorraine, he went so far as to renounce any revindication. In his words, the population of Alsace and Lorraine draws toward Germany when it is under France; when under German authority, it is attracted toward France.

The whole misfortune of France, Hitler said, is that it has no Marshal Piłsudski. The parties are gambling politically with international problems. As an example of how a solution can be found to difficult problems, he pointed to Polish-German relations. He remarked that here it was psychologically impossible to waive so clearly a revindication of territories—as could be done regarding Alsace and Lorraine. We therefore had found a formula to renounce the use of power in our mutual relations.

I must add here that in justification of the conscription bill there is a passage regarding Polish-German relations on which, for lack of time, I do not dwell any longer.

Taking leave of the Chancellor, I asked about his health. I must add that in the course of the whole conversation he tried to speak in lower tones because of a sore throat. The Chancellor said that false rumors were spread by the press that he had caught a cold during the Saar demonstrations, for he had not been too well and the Saar affair aggravated his condition. The worst of it is that he has to deliver speeches, and this affects his vocal cords. "Breaking off my rest and leaving Berchtesgaden," said the Chancellor, "was not fortunate either, and I am not feeling very well."

When I took my leave, he asked me to present his respects to the Marshal.

The assistant of the military attaché—owing to the late hour and the departure of a special courier—is forwarding to the General Staff only the bill with the justification. He is also reporting to the chief of the General Staff that I had a conversation with the Chancellor on this subject. It is therefore possible that the chief of the General Staff will contact you for information about the contents of my report.

Józef Lipski

DOCUMENT 39   Lipski to Beck

NO. N/133/14/35   Berlin, March 23, 1935
                                   Strictly Confidential

Referring to my telegram of today, I am taking the liberty of communicating that, following your instructions contained in the telegram of March 22,[12] I had a conversation with Reich Foreign Minister Herr von Neurath at 12 noon today.

I told him that I had informed my government of the decision com-

[12] See *Diariusz*, I, 248–49 (conversations with Laroche of March 23 and 24); also Laroche, p. 207.

municated to me by the Chancellor on March 16 about the introduction of conscription. The Polish government instructed me to call the attention of the German government—in a quite friendly way—to the fact that the situation created by the introduction of conscription by the Reich government might result in complications in international relations. I added that these complications can at present not be evaluated. I also called Herr von Neurath's attention to the fact that, in case the League of Nations handles this problem, difficulties will naturally increase considerably. I gave Herr von Neurath to understand that the Polish government is concerned about the international situation caused by this problem. I then added a few words to the effect that the Polish press kept a quiet and reasonable tone in this difficult moment.

Herr von Neurath was evidently prepared for this statement of mine for, as I could observe, he had very precise answers to each particular item. First of all, he stressed that the League aspect is of the least concern to him. Of course, opening proceedings against the Reich government would not encourage him to join this institution (Germany will undoubtedly use this argument with Simon). He is quite aware that the situation might become rather embarrassing for some members of the Council. However, as far as the *meritum* of the matter is concerned, the League of Nations can only pass a declaration that the Treaty was violated. Such a declaration, however, would be merely a paper without further consequences.

Herr von Neurath further stated that in taking such a decision the German government naturally realized what difficulties it might encounter. However, the development of events compelled it to take such a step. He mentioned that the prevailing confusion was unbearable *à la longue*. Besides, even the British government claimed that it is known that Germany is arming, but it knows nothing definite about it. The German government was alarmed that Sir John Simon is setting out on his trip to Berlin totally misinformed, convinced that he will be able to bargain for too high stakes in particular fields of national defense. It was therefore better to play an open hand.

As to the results of Simon's trip, von Neurath was of the opinion that they might be meager. He added that he sees no possibility of discussing Germany's military forces, which are essential for the Reich's national defense, as drawn up by the bill. I could not be sure whether this declaration by von Neurath meant that any discussion regarding the ceiling on armaments was excluded in principle, or whether it was just a tactical statement designed to keep us from making a hint to the British side regarding any hopes for possible German concessions in this field.

Further, von Neurath mentioned that, as far as pacts are concerned, some solution might be found. However, he strongly confirmed that guarantees for mutual assistance are out of the question. Simon's trip— as von Neurath put it—will be rather of an informative nature. The British Foreign Secretary, in contrast to other Powers interested in this problem, such as France and Italy, is handicapped in his competence.

Passing to more general topics, Herr von Neurath stated that it should now be expected that France might dress up its understanding with Soviet Russia to take the form of a treaty. He thinks it would have come to this anyway.

He began to deliberate on the growing Russian imperialism. For the moment it might still be devoid of elements of immediate threat, but its aims are quite obvious. He remarked that it is quite clear that sooner or later this imperialism will reach for the Baltic states, for it is fluctuating either eastward or westward. Herr von Neurath even presumes that the aggressive tendencies of Russia, following in the footsteps of tsarist Russia, will also spread to the Balkans, so that the prewar situation will be restored with only a changed internal Russian constellation. Poland and Germany are the two states most threatened by this development of Russia, which is now showing the wish to intervene in European matters.

Closing our conversation, Herr von Neurath said that he will keep me *au courant* of his talks with Sir John Simon.

As I mentioned before in this report, I have the impression that Neurath—possibly because of your conversation with Moltke—was already prepared for our *démarche*. In spite of the fact that, in accordance with your instructions, I kept my statement in a friendly tone, the German Minister of Foreign Affairs must have understood the meaning of the expression of the Polish government's concern over the tide of international events as a discreet reminder that a violent decision by, and obstinate action on the part of, the Reich creates a rather awkward situation for us also.

As for Neurath's suppositions that in the field of pacts some settlement might be reached in the talks with the British, this explanation to some extent coincides with information forwarded by me in the letter of the 22d inst. addressed to Director Dębicki. On the other hand, I was rather astonished by the stiff approach of the Reich Foreign Minister regarding the possible discussion of the ceiling on German armaments, as based on the newly published bill. Since the bill did not precisely define the actual figures (and besides, information obtained by Captain Steblik showed that not all divisions were completed), it could be assumed that a margin for negotiations might be placed between the present actual state of build-up of the German Army and the full figure of armaments foreseen within the frame of the bill. Neurath's declaration seems to disperse this illusion. However, I must stress that the Reich Minister, who did not explicitly mention the ceiling, saying only in general terms that on the problem of equality of rights and of national defense as fixed in the bill there will be no bargaining, was so firm on the problem for tactical reasons only. [13]

Józef Lipski

DOCUMENT 40   Lipski to Beck

NO. N/128/30/35   Berlin, April 13, 1935
                                                    Strictly Confidential

In the afternoon of April 12 I was informed that Herr von Neurath had asked me to call at the A.A. on Saturday at 11:30 A.M. In the evening Ambassador von Moltke came to dinner to discuss certain economic matters in Polish-German relations. During the dinner I received your telephone call regarding Sir John Simon's declaration at Stresa concerning Herr von Neurath's explanations given to the British Chargé d'Affaires in Berlin about the Eastern Pact.[14] At the same time a repre-

[13] For the German version of this conversation, see *DGFP*, Series C, Vol. III, No. 553.

[14] The Stresa Conference of the ministers of Great Britain, France, and Italy lasted from April 11 to April 14. On April 12 Beck received news in Warsaw that Minister Simon allegedly declared that, in the conversation between Neurath and the British Chargé d'Affaires in Berlin, the German Foreign Minister had confirmed Germany's consent to join in a general pact of nonaggression. This pact foresaw the possibility of particular signatories of the pact contracting additional agreements of mutual assistance. Upon receiving this information, Beck instructed his cabinet director, Dębicki, to contact the Polish Embassy in Berlin immediately in order to obtain from Lipski the information whether the above news from Stresa was duly confirmed in Berlin. *Diariusz*, I, 267.

sentative of the Polish Telegraph Agency in Berlin confirmed the declaration of the British Foreign Secretary, with an annotation that both the
Deutsches Nachrichtenbüro and the A.A. declined any clarification in
this matter.

Herr von Moltke, whom I have informed to this effect, and who,
besides, saw that I had been called on the telephone by you, told me that
Herr von Neurath just wanted to inform me tomorrow about his conversation with the British representative. Moltke was of the opinion that
Simon's declaration was an indiscretion. When I told von Moltke that
you are leaving for Geneva this morning, he was even more upset by the
fact that the Polish government was not informed in time. He even tried
to arrange an interview with Neurath for me during the night, so that
you could be informed before leaving Warsaw. As he did not succeed in
reaching von Neurath, he advised Director Meyer to give me precise
information, which I duly cabled to you on the same night.[15]

This morning von Neurath asked me to call at the A.A. an hour later,
that is, at 12:30 P.M. and right from the start, apologizing that owing to
a misunderstanding he could not see me immediately after his conversation with the British Chargé d'Affaires, he declared that Chancellor
Hitler wanted to see me at once. Herr von Neurath explained briefly that
some inaccurate information appeared in the press regarding the reply
he gave to the British Chargé d'Affaires concerning the Eastern Pact. He
then read to me his own note from the conversation with Newton,
approved *post factum* by the Chancellor, and handed me one copy for
your strictly confidential attention. This copy is enclosed herewith.[16]

Then, accompanied by Herr von Neurath, I went to see the Chancellor, who told me more or less as follows:

He wanted to inform me personally about the actual situation in
connection with the conversation held yesterday between the Reich Foreign Minister and the British Chargé d'Affaires, because some of the
daily papers published misleading information, thus creating confusion.
For this reason the Chancellor this morning ordered that the British
representative be presented a *mise-au-point* in writing. It will appear in
the press, possibly tonight or tomorrow morning.[17]

The Chancellor then read to me the text of this document. The docu-

15 See *DGFP*, Series C, Vol. IV, No. 28.
16 See *ibid.*, No. 24.
17 *Ibid.*, No. 29.

ment states that during the conversation with Simon in Berlin Chancellor Hitler, as requested by the British side, communicated principles which might serve as a foundation for a nonaggression pact in Eastern Europe. These principles were limited to nonaggression, consultation, arbitration and conciliation, and nonassistance to the aggressor. Questioned by Simon as to whether the German government, having rejected mutual assistance in the Eastern Pact, would be prepared to agree that, within the frame of the nonaggression pact as proposed by the Reich, particular signatories could contract agreements of mutual assistance, the Chancellor gave a negative reply.

The document then passed to the last conversation of Neurath with Newton, stating clearly that the German government maintains its proposition for a nonaggression pact in Eastern Europe. This offer is made irrespective of whether particular signatories of the pact would contract additional agreements for mutual assistance. However, the German government made a reservation that it would not agree to any mention in the text of the pact about such agreements, and would not accept any notification that such agreements were contracted. Finally, the document confirms that agreements of mutual assistance are logically contradictory to the very idea of nonaggression pacts, anticipating in advance the bad will of the contracting parties. When reading this document, the Chancellor observed that after the last move on the British side he wonders whether it would not be best to withdraw the offer of the nonaggression pact made to Simon. Psychologically this would suit him best in the face of tactics applied by the Powers, who press for military agreements, disguising them in a formula of mutual assistance. However, if he did this, the whole world would denounce him as a warmonger. That is why he decided to give the above reply to the British side. The Chancellor stressed firmly that he is definitely unwilling to legalize such agreements, and that is why he excludes the possibility of formally binding them with the nonaggression pact in any way.

Here I mentioned that in my opinion, besides the formal side of legalizing such agreements, the danger exists of Soviet Russia's pressure on smaller states for contracting such agreements. I pointed precisely to the Baltic. Both the Chancellor and von Neurath very openly seconded my concern.

I thanked the Chancellor for his gesture, obviously designed to remove any resentment on our part for not being informed in time by the

German government regarding its last *démarche* to Great Britain. I also availed myself of the occasion to carry out your instructions conveyed to me yesterday by telegram. I said that you will pass through Berlin today on your way to Geneva, and that your intention is to observe the international situation, which in our opinion is far from clear, at firsthand. I further stated that the foundation and principles of Poland's foreign policy, known to the German government, will remain unaltered. Further, referring to one of your recent talks with Ambassador von Moltke, I said that you anticipate an extensive action on the part of the Soviets in Geneva to save at least some semblances of the Eastern Pact, and that probably they will exert strong pressure on smaller East European states to this end. I finally said that the Soviet-French bilateral pact is not a subject of special concern to us. Following your instructions, I added with some emphasis, so that both the Chancellor and von Neurath would realize our intentions, that the Polish government is not inclined to link Franco-Polish problems with Franco-Soviet problems, and that we shall follow this line in our relations with France.

After listening to these explanations of mine, the Chancellor passed next to considerations of a general nature. They would be rather difficult to render in detail in this report. As usual, the very basis of his deliberations was Soviet Russia. His attitude toward it is clearly negative.

He analyzed Russia from many angles, including economic expansion, and stated that it is a power which will be a serious threat to European civilization. That is why—in his opinion—and here he added that he was not talking now as a Chancellor but rather as a professor, a logical idea would be for all states to unite on nationalistic grounds in the name of solidarity and common effort to overcome this danger. Of course, he was talking only in a hypothetical sense.

I am taking the liberty of quoting some interesting points of his deliberations.

He said, for example, that if someone in Germany thinks that the Russian danger is meaningless, since Poland separates Germany from Russia, this problem should be viewed from a long-range historic perspective. In his opinion, Russia will be a danger for the whole West. If the West does not wake up—in his opinion—it may pay the price of its whole culture and civilization. Poland, of course, could—as he put it— keep its position in the east for some ten to fifteen years. However, for an effective opposition, the solidarity of all concerned is needed. From

this broad point of view all frictions between the states of Europe become unimportant.

Talking about war, he said that in his meditations he came to the
conclusion that Germany, if you consider the last centuries, lost millions
of people in wars, and the best ones too, reaching no goal and remaining
practically in the same spot. By contrast, England lost very few people.
Instead of spilling blood, England dominated the world. The best human
element, lost in Germany for nothing, remained in England and contributed to the realization of its great world policy.

Then the Chancellor talked about expansion being impossible in relation to Germany's neighbors, quoting figures of overpopulation. He
mentioned here that this has induced him to raise the colonial question
with the British. He needs an outlet for the population and also raw
materials. When Germany has access to raw materials from the colonies,
it will be able to increase its exports, which will allow it to import more,
and this will have only positive results for other countries trading with
the Reich. He said that he had to raise the colonial problem, since this is
a master problem. Of course, he is not for an immediate solution of this
problem.

Pointing out that Germany is not striving to enlarge its possessions,
he cited the fact that the Saar annexation cost the Reich a great deal.
Fifty thousand unemployed in the Saar took jobs away from half a
million people of the Reich. The deplorable economic condition of the
Saar is a heavy burden for the Reich today.

As far as Austria is concerned, the Chancellor said that his desire is
only to enable the population to express their will freely. However, if
this occurs, it would be impossible for the Reich to take over the burden
of a state of six million in such a deplorable economic condition. There
are some things, the Chancellor continued, which demand a strict accounting. He stressed here that he has quite enough problems and difficulties on the territory of the Reich.

Returning again to the question of Europe's relation to the Russian
problem, the Chancellor said that there is one method, which I have
already mentioned, namely, a certain solidarity in the stand of all states
of Europe toward this problem. There is also another method, he remarked, the one cherished by the British—which consists in shoving
away danger and in tactical gambling. England is playing with Russia
here in the sense of not allowing it to expand too far either eastward or

westward. The Chancellor said that such policies are clearly short-sighted. There are some people in England who understand the whole problem. They are not to be found, however, either in the government or in the Foreign Office.

Next the Chancellor raised the question of the Far East and the role of Japan as a dynamic factor, dangerous not only in the Far East but also, owing to its great vigor in economic competition, for the countries of Europe. He explained that in this respect Japan, though for different reasons, is as dangerous as Soviet Russia.

I must stress here that the above deliberations of the Chancellor were made to me, to some extent confidentially, with the provision that they not be revealed as some of his more deep-seated views.

Taking leave of the Chancellor, I thanked him for the audience and for giving me explanations regarding Germany's approach to the nonaggression pact in the east.

Herr von Neurath remained with the Chancellor alone for a moment, and later accompanied me to the A.A. for a short conversation. I talked with him for a moment about items contained in your instructions. I again stressed possible attempts by Russia with regard to smaller states situated in Eastern Europe. Talking about Hungary, whose position is somewhat delicate, Herr von Neurath said that he has persistently exerted pressure on Budapest to bring about an understanding with Yugoslavia. Before the assassination of the king the situation was easier. Neurath is of the opinion that Hungary will not find a common language with Czechoslovakia and Rumania. With Yugoslavia the object of contention is not so important. Besides, within the frame of the Little Entente, Yugoslavia represents a real value of strength.

At the end of our conversation Herr von Neurath asked me to present his respects to you, and to tell you that in case you return via Berlin he would be very glad to meet you. I will await your instructions in this matter.

Herr von Neurath and the Chancellor, in order to make a sort of demonstration for Geneva, are leaving today for vacations, but, as the Minister confided to me, he will probably be obliged to interrupt his leave several times.

Recapitulating the above conversations held today, I am taking the liberty of stressing that the declaration presented to the British Chargé d'Affaires yesterday did not formally change the stand of the German government regarding the question of the Eastern Pact. *Ad meritum,* however, by declaring its *désintéressement* in agreements of mutual assistance contracted outside the nonaggression pact in the east by its signatories, the German government has taken a step toward conceding compromise. It is essential to realize that the German government fully maintains its negative approach regarding the signing of a pact of mutual assistance between the Reich and the Soviets. Nevertheless, by the concession mentioned above, it undoubtedly opened the door for Russia to attempt to put pressure on the Baltic states in order to induce them to contract agreements of mutual assistance, and also rendered easier Franco-Russian action in relation to the Little Entente. That is why I raised this aspect of the problem in my conversation today.

Józef Lipski

The problem of Hitler's introduction of conscription and German violation of Part V of the Treaty of Versailles was placed before the Council of the League. Beck delivered a speech on April 16 at the Council, stressing the role played by Poland in the build-up of peace in Eastern Europe by the stabilization of Poland's relations with its neighboring Great Powers. On April 17 the Council of the League passed a resolution condemning the German action.[18] Poland voted for this resolution.

DOCUMENT 41 Lipski to Beck

NO. N/49/28/35   Berlin, April 25, 1935
                                              Strictly Confidential

As I already reported to the Vice-Director of the Western Department in my letter dated April 20, I was invited by Prime Minister Göring for Thursday, April 25, to his forest pavilion at Schorfheide. Minister Göring showed me a document, beautifully bound in silver, destined for the President of the Polish Republic as a member of *des Reichsbundes deutscher Jägerschaft.* He also displayed several other gifts for people participating in the hunting party at Białowieża. These objects will be

[18] For Beck's speech and the text of the resolution (both in French), see *Diariusz,* I, 496–501. For von Moltke's opinion on this matter, see *DGFP,* Series C, Vol. IV, No. 41, No. 49, and partly No. 75.

taken to Warsaw in the coming days by an aide-de-camp of Göring so that they may be handed out by Ambassador von Moltke.

During my stay of several hours at Schorfheide, Herr Göring expressed his desire to have a longer political talk with me. He declared that last Saturday he had a conversation with Hitler, who suggested that, independently of official Polish-German relations, he should take the relations between the two countries under his special protection. Herr Göring gave me to understand that this does not mean that he will do this officially. In his opinion, however, in such important matters a discussion might often be useful with persons on the German side who are not encumbered by the Reich's policies toward Poland as conducted by previous governments.

Herr Göring stressed that Foreign Affairs Minister von Neurath is a person thoroughly loyal to the Chancellor. On the other hand, he stated that he is not 100 percent sure whether other officials of that office strictly observe the line toward Poland as drawn up by the Chancellor. Here Göring added that, if it were up to him, he would have cleaned up the Auswärtiges Amt long ago. However, the Chancellor is perhaps too indulgent, and pays too much attention to the services rendered in the past by some of his collaborators who cannot adapt themselves to the new situation. Referring to the Chancellor's policy toward Poland, Herr Göring firmly stressed that it is not dictated by any premises of a tactical nature but is the result of a very deep grasp of this problem. On this point the Chancellor will not stand for any fluctuations or changes in direction.

Passing to the last Geneva session, Minister Göring said that the Chancellor fully understands the position taken by you. He asked Göring to bring this to my knowledge. In my conversation with Göring, I stressed the fact that your speech gave a clear and precise idea of our basic political line. Minister Göring agreed completely. He said that personally he admires the independent position taken by you in your speech, which was even more than they expected. As for voting for the Geneva declaration, I said that this was just a formal act, which was obvious both from your speech and your statements given to members of the Council. To this Göring replied that he understood the difference between the speech and the voting in a similar way. Finally, talking about Franco-Russian relations, I referred to the declaration[19] pre-

[19] *DGFP*, Series C, Vol. IV, No. 30.

sented to the Chancellor on your behalf and stated that we do not in the least intend to link our relations with France to Franco-Russian relations. Here I remarked that it was not in the interest of Poland, nor indeed of Germany either, to slam the door definitely in the face of Laval at Geneva, pushing him permanently into the arms of Russia. Göring understood our tactics on this point. He remarked that this might possibly contribute to a certain extent to some reaction in France against too far-reaching relations in its alliance with Russia.

I discussed more extensively the question of the Geneva session with Göring, since I assumed that the Chancellor may need some arguments for orienting himself to our position. Göring added that von Moltke was instructed to lodge a protest in Warsaw similar to the one lodged with other members of the Council, although this should be regarded as a purely formal act, without any further consequences. Göring spoke well of von Moltke, stressing that he is a loyal person, devoted to the Chancellor's policy toward Poland. In his further comments about certain elements who cannot adapt themselves to the new policy of the Chancellor, Göring pointed out that they took advantage of the voting in Geneva and some incidents in Pomerania to create an unfriendly atmosphere for Poland in Germany. However, the Chancellor reacted very firmly, issuing suitable instructions. From Göring's words I had the impression that it was precisely because of a certain reaction among these elements that the Chancellor had decided to entrust Göring with the special mission of taking an interest in Polish-German relations. Göring stated that on his part he had issued most strict orders to local authorities to avoid any drastic demonstrations against the Poles. Here I told him that you are acting in the same way with our local authorities. Göring even added that, in case we observe some shortcomings on the German side in this respect, he requests that we bring them to his attention, even if from our point of view it should be a matter of some undesirable German activity on the territory of Poland.

At the conclusion of our talk Göring once more very emphatically stated that the Chancellor wishes to maintain the best possible relations with Poland. Deliberating on the question of Polish-German relations, he repeated all the things he said during his stay in Poland. Therefore, there is no need to repeat them here. I would just like to stress that Göring declared again that the Chancellor is fully aware of the necessity of Poland's access to the sea, and that for him the problem of the Corridor does not exist in the field of close Polish-German relations. As usual strong anti-Russian note could be detected in Göring's deliberations, both toward the Soviets and toward any other possible regime in Russia.

Minister Göring laid stress on the fact that, in accordance with information received by his intelligence agents, he sees how efforts are made from many quarters to interfere with good Polish-German relations. He mentioned that Mussolini—obviously for fear that Germany allegedly has aggressive intentions toward Austria—is trying everywhere to act against the Reich. Göring vented sharp criticism of the policies of the Italian government. He mentioned here that he is aware of the overtures made by Rome to the Polish government. Although Göring tried to deal with this question rather casually, some anxiety could be noted in his words.

Passing to some practical action in Polish-German relations, Göring mentioned how pleased the Chancellor would be to welcome you at a convenient opportunity in Berlin. He added that after the visit of the British ministers in Berlin and your meeting with Suvich [20] in Venice, he thinks that such a visit would be very desirable, for two great nations who are neighbors should from time to time demonstrate their good relations by such contacts. Here I remarked that you had stopped in Germany on two occasions to converse with Foreign Affairs Minister von Neurath. However, on the advice of the A.A. these meetings were not publicized, and you mentioned to me that in case any further meetings were to take place it would be much better to give them some publicity. Herr Göring was of the same opinion, and discreetly observed that your visit in Berlin on some convenient occasion—for example, on your way to Geneva—would be very advisable.

The main aim of such a visit would be a direct contact with the Chancellor. Therefore, Göring thinks that it would not be so important to bestow on it a strictly official character, since this is always very burdensome for the guest, but it should rather be made an informal affair. Finally, in connection with contacts he made in Białowieża with General Fabrycy, General Sosnkowski, and other ministers, Göring said he would take great pleasure in being able to reciprocate for the hospitality extended to him at Białowieża by inviting some of these people for a stag hunt at Schorfheide in the fall. I promised that I would take this matter up in Warsaw.

At the close of our conversation I thanked him for his valuable expla-

---

[20] Fulvio Suvich, undersecretary of state at the Italian Ministry of Foreign Affairs.

nations and expressed my satisfaction that by authorization of the Chancellor I shall be able to address myself directly to him in case any difficulties arise in matters of interest to both our countries. I remarked that I would inform you about this conversation, adding that in the coming days I shall be in Warsaw, and upon my return I shall call on him again.

Recapitulating this conversation, I am taking the liberty of observing that the most important element is that the Chancellor, in spite of some rumors spread by elements rather unfriendly to us, understood Poland's position at the last session at Geneva. I consider the fact that Göring was entrusted with a mission to take care of Polish-German relations as positive for us. His position as prime minister of Prussia will enable him to assist us not only in the field of general politics but also in practical territorial matters.

From Göring's further comments it is worth noting that he expressed some anxiety about Italian efforts in Warsaw. Undoubtedly, fear can be detected that Italy may obtain from us some obligations regarding Austria, for this matter is of basic importance for the National Socialist Party.

A statement inside the Reich that the Chancellor's policy toward Poland is consistently pursued, and that in the field of international relations no essential difference of opinion exists on problems of basic importance for Germany, evidently makes the Chancellor even more willing to meet you.

Józef Lipski

DOCUMENT 42   Lipski to Beck

NO. N/128/38/35   Berlin, May 5, 1935
Confidential

Upon my return from Warsaw I had, on May 3, my first conversation with Herr von Neurath, foreign minister of the Reich, since the last Geneva session. Following your verbal instructions, I declared to him more or less as follows:

I remarked that I had returned from Warsaw, where I had the opportunity of discussing with you at length your trip to Geneva. I stressed, as

I had already mentioned to Herr von Neurath in our talk on March 23, that you were anticipating beforehand that the situation in Geneva would be particularly awkward. You decided to go to Geneva because you thought it to be unavoidable to state explicitly in your speech Poland's stand in connection with the international situation, inasmuch as the Soviets displayed an obvious tendency to save at least the appearances of the Eastern Pact, and pressure to this effect could be felt especially in relation to smaller states. After your conversation with Mr. Eden, the British delegation did not conceal any longer that it regards the concept of the Eastern Pact as dead and buried. Nevertheless, in view of the efforts made by the Soviets, you thought it necessary once more to define the negative position of Poland toward the Eastern Pact before the forum of states present at Geneva. Besides this, I stated that in your speech you presented existing Polish-German relations as a fully realistic, positive international element to be seriously taken into account by all states.

Regarding the Geneva resolution, I remarked that, both in your speech and in your conversations with some members of the Council, you expressed your *désintéressement* as to its text, considering it merely a formal act. Thus your speech was a competent expression of the stand taken by the Polish government.

I also made it clear that extending the discussions in Geneva would not serve Germany's interest; the best thing would be to close the problem. I also stressed—feeling that this argument is most agreeable for authoritative elements here—that breaking all ties with Laval would only serve to push the French Foreign Minister definitely into the Soviets' embrace.

In his reply Herr von Neurath remarked that he also understood the stand taken by you in Geneva in this way. He understood that Poland's position would be especially delicate and difficult. Public opinion in Germany was somewhat taken aback by the vote of Poland, but this did not last long. Herr von Neurath stressed that the resolution is unpleasant for the German government and that the Powers could word it differently, introducing, for example, an adequate preface. Herr von Neurath told me that immediately after the Geneva decision he went to the Chancellor to discuss with him future tactics. I could detect from his words that he was acting to prevent too violent a reaction to the Geneva resolution. Herr von Neurath remarked that the Chancellor would shortly deliver a speech on the Reich's foreign policy, referring to the note presented to the members of the Council, and would then bring up the whole matter. (As I found out, the Chancellor's declaration will probably be delivered on May 14.) [21]

Herr von Neurath also remarked that Moltke's protest in Warsaw was just a formality. The words of the Reich Minister of Foreign Affairs resulted—if in more diplomatic terms—in a confirmation of the comments I heard from Göring, which I reported on April 25, No. N/49/28/35; that is, that the Chancellor completely understood the stand taken by Poland in Geneva.

Next, Herr von Neurath rather casually talked about developments in the international situation. First of all, he stressed that from MacDonald's speech [22] it was clear that the British government still stands firm in its position of the resolution of February 3. Here he observed that since February 3 many things have changed. He added that MacDonald is again talking about the Eastern Pact which Germany should join. This point of the British Prime Minister's speech is not clear for the German government, since the German side has already said all it had to say on this matter. By the way, Neurath mentioned that the concession he made to Simon at Stresa, about which I reported on April 13, No. N/128/ 30/35, when he said that the German government maintains its offer for a nonaggression pact in the east regardless of whether agreements of mutual assistance will be contracted between particular signatories of the pact, had no effect whatever. At the given moment he might have rendered Simon's task at Stresa easier, but no consequences were drawn from it. Neurath's avowal that as a matter of fact he did then make a useless withdrawal from the position taken by the Chancellor toward the British Minister was sincere and quite disarming.

In acknowledging that since February 3 quite a lot has changed, Neurath pointed to the development of the situation regarding the

[21] Hitler's speech was delivered on May 21.

[22] On May 2 Prime Minister MacDonald delivered in the House of Commons a declaration expressing concern about German armaments, calling on Germany to join in international collaboration. Great Britain would not accept any new obligations on the continent, he declared. The British government was of the opinion that Hitler's proposal for a collective nonaggression pact in the east should not be rejected, but it felt that this offer should be balanced with the Franco-Soviet pact then being negotiated. Germany's stand regarding armaments rendered questionable the frankness of the Reich's declaration. The British government was trying not to create military alliances but to get the Powers to collaborate for peace. The understanding between Great Britain, France, and Italy meant just this.

Danubian plans. He has not as yet received from Simon the promised definition of "nonintervention." A few days ago he reminded the British Ambassador of this when the latter brought up the question of the Danubian agreement.

Regarding the conference presently taking place in Venice,[23] von Neurath said that its final result cannot be foreseen; even the date when the conference is to be held in Rome is as yet unknown. He laid some stress on certain misunderstandings between the partners of the proposed pact. According to information obtained from the Yugoslav minister, Yugoslavia would join the pact under the condition that the restoration of the Hapsburgs be excluded.

Regarding armaments, Herr von Neurath remarked that the Powers now have the last word, since Germany has nothing more to request in this field. He stressed that the forthcoming German-British sea conferences will be only of a preliminary character.

Upon these casual remarks of Herr von Neurath, I gave him some information about your meeting with Suvich in Venice.[24] I mentioned that this meeting was not planned in advance. When you decided to spend a short Easter vacation with Mrs. Beck in Italy, Signor Suvich proceeded to Venice. I explained that the conversation was of a general character. Besides, following your instructions, I stressed that in general Polish-Italian relations, with perhaps the exception of the period of the Four-Power Pact, have always been friendly. However, the two countries have no interests in common which would constitute a link between them. Adriatic problems, for example, and other matters of primary concern to Italy are of little interest to us.

I added that only in our relations with Hungary do we find a certain platform of common interest, since neither Warsaw nor Rome would like to see Hungary in complete isolation from the Little Entente.

Later in our conversation I hinted quite casually that, as far as I can see from the reports of our ambassador in Rome, it is rather characteristic that some sort of anxiety might be detected in Italy with regard to a possible expansion of Russia at the expense of the states of the Little Entente. Herr von Neurath took up this point, remarking that the Ital-

[23] On May 4 a conference began between the ministers of foreign affairs of Austria and Hungary and the Italian vice-minister, Suvich, in Venice, to discuss political problems in connection with the proposed Roman conference regarding the Central European (Danubian) Pact.

[24] On April 19.

ians are quite right; he is also of the opinion that modern Russia, acting within the pattern of the old tsarist Russia, will strive to spread its influence over the Balkans.

I then said to Herr von Neurath that you regret that on your way back, which was not via Germany, you could not avail yourself of Herr von Neurath's suggestion for a meeting. Nevertheless, on the occasion of passing through Germany, you would be very pleased to have an opportunity to talk with Herr von Neurath and present your regards to the Chancellor. I also added that this time it would not be advisable to keep the meeting secret; it should be revealed to the press.

Herr von Neurath eagerly agreed with this idea, adding that this very morning he had a talk with the Chancellor, who personally stresses the necessity of maintaining friendship with Poland. Therefore Herr von Neurath thinks that your meeting with the Chancellor would be most desirable. I did not mention any precise date for your visit, but only mentioned in passing that such an occasion might arise in the future. Von Neurath asked whether you will be in Geneva on May 20, and I replied that I did not know.

Closing my conversation with Herr von Neurath with a reference to some claims I have encountered in Warsaw regarding the alleged German agitation in our western provinces, which may possibly be inspired by the Reich, I laid stress on the necessity of avoiding any friction in relations between us. By the way, I mentioned that upon resolving the new Constitution [25] we are approaching elections and that on such occasions any irritating incidents should be avoided. I mentioned in passing that, acting accordingly, you had used your influence to put off demonstrations of the Silesian insurgents planned for May 3, and I learned with satisfaction from Prime Minister Göring that he on his part had issued strict orders on the German side.[26]

[25] The new Polish Constitution was signed by President Mościcki on April 23, 1935.

[26] On May 3, Poland's national holiday, a demonstration was to be held in Warsaw to commemorate the anniversary of three Silesian insurrections against Germany in 1919–21. About 5,000 uniformed insurgents were to attend. The Prime Minister, the Minister of the Interior, and the Vice-Minister of War were to be sponsors. In his conversation with Vice-Minister Szembek on April 24, Ambassador von Moltke called attention to the consequences of such demonstrations for Polish-German relations (*Diariusz*, I, 274). At the end of April, while in Warsaw, Lipski stressed that at this time such a demonstration was not advisable (*ibid.*, p 277). In spite of pressure on the part of Silesian deputies in the Diet, the Polish government canceled the insurgents' rally.

Agreeing with me, Herr von Neurath said that he had talked with Hess on this matter, and that orders were issued to this effect. Referring to the situation of Germans in Poland, Herr von Neurath observed that party quarrels among Germans in our country bring about certain frictions.

Next, I pointed out that I had handed to the Press Department of his Ministry material pertaining to some transgressions on the German side regarding the Polish-German press agreement, and I stressed the problem of demands about inscriptions on monuments.

Finally, I told Herr von Neurath that I shall be in Munich on May 12 to attend the opening of the Polish Exhibition, and on the 14th I will be in Hamburg. Regarding my stay in Munich, I mentioned that I shall of course pay a visit to Governor General Epp and that I also intend to call on Cardinal Faulhaber. I presumed that this courtesy visit of mine would not be misinterpreted. Herr von Neurath replied that he naturally has nothing against such a visit. However, he warned me against any contact with the Papal Nuncio in Munich, whose situation in relation to the German government is irregular.[27]

On the same evening I went with Prime Minister Göring to Spreewald for blackcock tooting. I took this opportunity to give Göring the explanations he asked for in our conversation of April 25.

First of all, I stated that you were very pleased to learn that the Chancellor had entrusted Prime Minister Göring with special care over Polish-German relations. On this occasion I repeated what I had already said to Neurath: that you would like to stop in Berlin at a convenient opportunity to see the Chancellor, and that such a visit—according to what we agreed to previously with Herr Göring—would be publicized by the press.

As to the invitations to the stag rutting in the fall, Göring would like to extend invitations to some personages who participated in the hunting party at Białowieża; I said that I had taken this matter up with you. You mentioned the names of General Fabrycy and Maurice Potocki. We will let him know about other possible names.

Finally, I once more discussed the Geneva problem with Göring. Göring again declared to me that the Chancellor fully understands our

[27] The Papal Nuncio officially recognized by the German government was Monsignor Cesare Orsenigo in Berlin. The Nuncio in Munich, who was there in accordance with the old concordat between Bavaria and the Vatican, was not recognized by the German government.

point of view; besides, he will talk it over with me at an available moment. According to Göring, the Chancellor is satisfied that you did not want to give France a definite push into the arms of Russia at Geneva.

I also gave Göring some information about your meeting with Suvich. It was typical that Göring told me that he negotiated on behalf of his government with the Italian government on the Four-Power Pact. He told Mussolini that Germany is not in the least interested in concluding this agreement. It is doing so just for the sake of German-Italian friendship. I could detect in Göring quite a lot of suspicion and dislike for Italy. When I mentioned to him some common Polish and Italian opinions regarding the Hungarian problem, Göring remarked that for Hungary the most appropriate thing to do would be to approach Yugoslavia. He himself is going to Yugoslavia in the near future, and he intends to act along these lines in Belgrade. In his opinion the differences between Hungary and Yugoslavia are insignificant as compared with the situation between Hungary and Czechoslovakia. That is why the German government is putting pressure on Budapest to relinquish its secondary demands on Belgrade. Göring mentioned that he is very well liked in Yugoslavia, and to prove it he said that he received many letters and telegrams on the occasion of his wedding, not only from official quarters, but also from a multitude of the local population.

I am taking the liberty of reminding you that I had already heard about the concept of Hungarian-Yugoslav rapprochement from the Reich Foreign Affairs Minister and duly reported it to you some weeks ago.

I next told Göring that you were very glad to hear that Göring will issue special orders to prevent German-Polish frictions. I mentioned the cancellation of the insurgents' rally, which was acknowledged with great satisfaction. He then said that, if we let him know about any anti-Polish action in Germany, twenty-four hours later he will issue orders and they will be carried out, whereas things are more difficult if claims concern the German minority in Poland. There, of course, the German government has no direct executive power. Besides, as Göring confided to me, very often elements prevail among this minority who are at odds with National Socialist tendencies. They think that Chancellor Hitler's government, through its understanding with Poland, abandoned the minority to the mercy of fate. I did not pursue further discussion with Göring on this subject. However, in my opinion, if adequate orders are issued for state and Party organs in the Reich to avoid any clash with Poland, this might also reflect on the behavior of Germans in Poland.

I was also interested in what Göring confided to me about Danzig. He said that it is only owing to the fact that the National Socialist majority is in power in Danzig that relations between Poland and the Free City are good. If the old parties had won the elections, the same quarrels and contentions would undoubtedly exist and the same methods would be applied as prior to Hitler's coming to power, since all the old parties continuously leaned toward dissension with Poland, opposing any kind of understanding. I fully agreed with this opinion of Göring.

Finally, I am taking this opportunity to mention that, during the declaration with regard to air-force problems made by Göring to the foreign press, Mrs. Męcińska, correspondent of the *Kurier Warszawski,* addressed several questions to him. These questions were so undiplomatic and nonpolitical that the Prussian Prime Minister lost his temper and reacted with a rather sharp reply. Göring commented at length about this, cursing the lack of tact on the part of the Polish lady correspondent. She later declared in the presence of the *Havas* representative and others that Göring is making very light of Poland's role in Eastern Europe.

I appeased the Prussian Prime Minister by stating that I personally and the whole staff of our Embassy have a well-established opinion regarding Mrs. Męcińska's political experience. Besides, I told him that I had already expressed my highest disapproval of the correspondent through the intermediary of the chief of the press of the Embassy.

Józef Lipski

The Death of Marshal Piłsudski
The Currency Conflict with Danzig
May—July, 1935

DOCUMENT 43   Lipski to Beck

NO. N/421/15/35   Berlin, May 15, 1935
                                                 Strictly Confidential

News of Marshal Piłsudski's death was received in Berlin on Sunday, May 12, at 10:30 P.M.[1] According to information I received on the next day from Secretary of State Meissner, the Chancellor of the Reich, who was informed during the night, was deeply shocked by this news. He immediately addressed a telegram of condolence to the President of the Polish Republic in words of high esteem for the late Marshal of Poland and sympathy of the German nation for the Polish nation. The Chancellor laid special emphasis on the fact that the Marshal's policy toward Germany brought about profound advantages for both nations and served the cause of peace. Orders were given to lower flags to half-mast on all government buildings in the Reich on May 13 and on the day of the funeral; General Göring was delegated to be a representative at the funeral in Poland; and it was announced that, contrary to all traditions hitherto observed, the Chancellor would personally attend services in Berlin: all these were Hitler's personal spontaneous decisions.

I will take the liberty of presenting a special report illustrating in detail the reaction in the Reich to the death of the Marshal. In the meantime I would only like to confirm that the reaction was very strong in governmental circles as well as in the wider spheres of the German community.

Yesterday, on the occasion of Göring's condolence visit at the Em-

[1] Marshal Piłsudski died on May 12, 1935, at 8:45 P.M.

bassy, I had a long conversation with him, and I am anxious to report to you on this without delay.

Minister Göring, who was delegated as a personal representative of the Chancellor, will attend the funeral of the Marshal escorted by a brigadier, an admiral, and two aides-de-camp. He expressed his desire for a meeting with you in Warsaw on Sunday, after the Friday funeral services in Warsaw and the Saturday ceremonies in Cracow. He also told me that he would like to obtain an audience with the President of the Republic and establish contact with General Śmigły-Rydz.

I could detect in Göring, who discussed these things with the Chancellor, a certain undertone of concern with regard to our future policy toward Germany. Of course, I did not fail to disperse all his doubts in this respect. General Göring, who spoke very openly, expressed his opinion that France will now do all in its power in order to draw Poland away from its policy toward Germany. In Göring's opinion, without Poland the Franco-Russian alliance will be of little use. Here Göring stressed with great satisfaction that, according to information the Chancellor received from Warsaw, in your conversations with Laval you stood your ground firmly as to your earlier point of view, excluding any possibility of Soviet troops crossing the territory of Poland. Herr Göring declares that the key to the peace situation is in the hands of Poland, and that, in case Poland goes over to the side of the Franco-Soviet alliance, an armed conflict will be unavoidable. Göring obviously spoke with me very frankly, stressing that he feels himself authorized to do so, owing to the fact of our long collaboration.

For my part, I told Göring that to my mind such an open exchange of opinion, free of diplomatic protocol, is most useful for our mutual relations. I confirmed that Marshal Piłsudski had defined so clearly the goals of Poland's policy in the fields of internal structure, organization of the armed forces, and foreign policy that Poland's idea of a nation is very strictly delineated for the future executors of the Marshal's policy.

Minister Göring also mentioned to me that on his shortly anticipated trip to Yugoslavia he would like to press for a Hungarian-Yugoslav rapprochement, and later on also for a Yugoslav-Bulgarian understanding. On this problem he would in all probability like to have an exchange of opinion with you to be quite clear as to whether this concept is in accordance with Poland's stand.

Talking about Czechoslovakia, Göring assumed that the Czechs are under the influence of Russia in the military field and that certain preparations of the air force in Czechoslovakia are directed not only against Germany but also against Poland.

As far as Rumania is concerned, Göring is very skeptical with regard to Minister Titulescu's moral caliber. Göring told me that, according to information in his possession, Rumania would agree to the possible crossing of Soviet troops across Rumania.

From all these considerations the result is that the Chancellor is very much concerned about Poland's stand, since he regards it as a central focus of further developments in the east.

Göring mentioned that if Laval is present at the funeral services in Poland he will not fail to contact him.[2]

Finally, Herr Göring returned to what he had already said during his last conversation with me, stressing very intensely the necessity of a meeting between you and Hitler in the near future.

In the end I would like to point out that, owing to the funeral of the Marshal, the Chancellor has postponed the date for convening the Reichstag from the 17th to the 21st of this month.

Józef Lipski

DOCUMENT 44   Lipski to Beck

NO. N/52/3   Berlin, May 23, 1935
                                            Strictly Confidential

When I took leave of Chancellor Hitler after the funeral services for the Marshal at Saint Hedwig's Cathedral, he expressed the wish to see me in the next few days. On Monday morning, May 20, I asked Secretary of State Meissner to let me know when I could be received by the Chancellor, and we agreed that this could only take place after the session of the Reichstag called for Tuesday evening. Early in the evening of Wednesday, May 22, I was advised that the Chancellor had invited me for 8:30 P.M.

---

[2] The conversation between Göring and Laval was held in Cracow on May 18. See *Diariusz*, I, 295–99 and 304.

Chancellor Hitler received me very informally; Neurath was not present, and the usual protocol was dispensed with.

He looked overtired after the oratorical exertion of the day before at the Parliament, where he talked himself hoarse. He told me that he has a gland in the throat which makes him hoarse when his voice is strained. He is considering the possibility of an operation to get rid of this gland.

I subsequently expressed to the Chancellor, in very cordial tones on behalf of the President of Poland and the government, our thanks for the token of sympathy extended to Poland by him, government circles, and the German community in the face of the mourning into which our country was plunged at Marshal Piłsudski's passing.

The Chancellor said that the death of the Marshal has moved him deeply. The figure of the Marshal always had a great attraction for him, and his desire was to meet the commander of the Polish nation.

He even considered the possibility of a meeting to take place in a train at the Polish-German frontier, although he understood what a sensation this would create in world opinion.

Hitler was also anxious to meet Mussolini, whom he considers one of the great national leaders, in spite of a deterioration in German-Italian relations.

The Chancellor also mentioned that he would like to meet Kemal Pasha.

Coming back to the subject of the Marshal, the Chancellor remarked that the death of the Marshal has become a cause for concern in connection with the continuance of the line of Polish foreign policy. However, Minister Göring gave him reassuring information upon his return from Warsaw.[3] I declared to the Chancellor that I am in a position to assure him very firmly that no change will occur in our policy toward Germany.

The Marshal defined very clearly the goals for internal administration, as well as the organization of the armed forces and foreign policy. For many years he had been training his collaborators for independent work following his instructions. The Marshal's teachings are obligatory rules for all of us.

[3] Göring stayed in Poland on the occasion of the funeral of Marshal Piłsudski from May 17 to May 24 (see Moltke's report of May 21, *DGFP*, Series C, Vol. IV, No. 98, and parts of his report of May 28, *ibid.*, No. 115, p. 223).

The Chancellor accepted this statement with satisfaction.

I further declared that the Marshal's policy was always based upon the genuine interest of the Polish state, rather than on abstract ideas, thus guaranteeing the absolute durability of his policy.

In his further deliberations, the Chancellor remarked that the Marshal was one of those exceptional statesmen who understood the reality of the international situation and steered the policy of his country in accordance with this concept.

Subsequently the Chancellor began to analyze his policy toward Poland. He declared that he was the first to get rid of the previous negative political attitude toward Poland, the so-called Rapallo policy, represented by the Reichswehr, headed by Groener and Schleicher. Even prior to his coming to power, he exerted pressure on Schleicher to break his relations with the Soviets, but in vain. The fact alone that Schleicher contributed to Soviet Russia's becoming a military power is sufficient justification for the end that he met. The Chancellor said that much worse things were also weighing against Schleicher, and it was embarrassing to talk about them now. It was a shame even to think about them. It could be concluded from these words that Schleicher's policies were not disinterested.

The Chancellor further stated that the opinion of the Reichswehr then was that a militarily strong Soviet Union could be a threat to Poland only, but not to Germany. This was a shortsighted policy. The only man who at that time understood the Chancellor's opinions was Blomberg. As commander of a corps in East Prussia, he was well versed in the problems of the East, in contrast with the men sitting in the offices of the Reichswehr in Berlin. Also General Reichenau, in the Chancellor's opinion, was well informed.

Talking about Russia, the Chancellor pointed to the danger threatening from that side. Then he stressed that the Marshal understood the Russian reality, just as the Chancellor—according to what he said at the Parliament yesterday—had a knowledge of Bolshevism. Statesmen in the West, I added, are commonly acquainted with Russia only through literature. This generality obviously pleased the Chancellor, since he repeated it several times during the conversation.

In his Eastern policy the Chancellor has taken the stand that a rapprochement with Poland gives much more to the Reich than dangerous relations with Russia. For Germany there exists the problem of finding territories for economic expansion—or room for its population—which Poland does not possess and cannot offer. He was reproached on the question of the Corridor, to which he retorted that compared with these enormous problems the Corridor is of no importance. What harm is there, if Polish-German relations are good, in crossing several tens of kilometers of Polish territory? In a few dozen years of good relations, they will forget about the Corridor in Germany, and in Poland also this problem will become less acute.

The Chancellor has an idea, about which it is too early to speak today, but which could be put into life in some fifteen years: namely, to establish a special railroad and a highway through Pomerania for transport purposes.

The Reich's policy toward Poland will not change, even if he is no longer here, for he has passed his ideas on to his collaborators. In case of his death, which may occur at any time—some idiot (*ein Narr*) can throw a bomb—he has two successors named.

The Chancellor says that his policy is shared by the whole nation. He confirmed that as a result of his speech yesterday [4] countless numbers of letters of congratulations are arriving from all sections of the country.

Who else opposes his policy? Certain aristocrats, some groups of the clergy, and a few old *Deutschnationale,* the last only because he removed them from power, since they have no arguments against his program. He considers Hugenberg to be a loyal man, while his opponents on the right wing are such people as Oldenburg-Januschau.

Next the Chancellor approached the armament problem. He says that some restriction of armaments should be introduced. He states that in some cases the technique of war has gone so far as to render its application impossible.

As an example he noted that close to the end of the war the Germans discovered the *Brandbomben,* but they could not take the decision of using them for fear that the same weapon might be used against them. The present inventions in the field of incendiary bombs make it possible to destroy whole cities, burn out whole forests, etc. Mutual struggle would thus end in complete ruin on both sides, and the future victor would find himself facing a desert, which would result in a catastrophe for him as well. Therefore, banning the use of certain military weapons is in the interest of all nations.

[4] For extracts from Chancellor Hitler's Reichstag speech, see *Polish White Book,* No. 18.

He also mentioned that the Russian factor will obstruct the restriction of armaments.

In the course of the conversation I also had the opportunity—following your instructions—to touch upon our general reservations as to the motives guiding many international circles when they promote plans for multilateral pacts. I stated that in all combinations of this kind we shall be very cautious, in order that real results obtained in our mutual relations are not jeopardized in any way.

The Chancellor also mentioned that he sees from Baldwin's words uttered in the British Parliament that his speech was received with some understanding by the British government.

I would like to stress that the whole conversation was of an informal character and that the statements were rather general, without exactness in separate items.

Owing to the Chancellor's intimate confidences concerning the internal affairs of the Reich, I am sending this report exclusively for your information.[5]

Józef Lipski

DOCUMENT 45   Lipski to Beck

NO. N/128/54/35   Berlin, June 7, 1935

In view of the cabinet crisis in France, which has been dragging on for some time already,[6] I was not in a hurry to contact the Auswärtiges Amt upon my return to Berlin, assuming that it would be convenient for you not to actualize your trip for the time being. I limited myself at present to a single informative talk with the chief of the Eastern Department, in the course of which I stated that in principle, according to what was discussed with Neurath and Göring, you would like to come to Berlin to meet the Chancellor and the Foreign Affairs Min-

[5] Inserted in the *Polish White Book,* the text of this report (No. 19) is incomplete and very distorted.

[6] On May 30 the Chamber of Deputies rejected the plan of granting financial power to the government, causing the resignation of the Flandin cabinet. On June 1 the Buisson cabinet was formed, but was overthrown June 4 in connection with a demand for economic warranties. On June 7 Laval became prime minister and minister of foreign affairs, with parliamentary support.

ister of the Reich. I added, however, that I was as yet unable to declare myself as to the date and form of this visit.[7]

On current affairs now under discussion by the Reich government with the Western Powers in connection with Hitler's last speech, I would like to give the following explanations, since they result from the above-mentioned conversation:

1. *The Problem of the Conformity of the Franco-Soviet Agreement with Resolutions of the Rhineland Pact*

On this matter the German government presented a memorandum to the French government on May 25, a copy of which was handed to you by Ambassador von Moltke.[8] As was announced in Paris, the German government is to have the reply of the French government in the next few days. The Auswärtiges Amt seems to attach a great deal of importance to this matter and is looking forward with great interest to arguments of the French government, since it feels that it will be very difficult to confirm that the two agreements are not in conflict with each other.

2. *The Problem of the Eastern Pact*

The French government, referring to the proposition of a nonaggression pact in the East presented by the Chancellor of the Reich to Simon during his stay in Berlin,[9] as well as the explanations on this problem offered by the German government to the British government during the Stresa Conference, handed to the German ambassador in Paris an *aide-mémoire* expressing the intention of undertaking negotiations with the German government on this matter.[10] Ambassador von Moltke was instructed to communicate to you the text of the French memorandum. In the meantime the Auswärtiges Amt is investigating the document, and I was advised that the matter of conformity of the Franco-Soviet pact with the Locarno agreement is being given priority.

3. *Naval Negotiations under Way in London*

As is known, these are preliminary talks, not destined to reach any final solution. Nothing special was communicated to me on this matter, be-

[7] For the German version of the conversation with Meyer, see *DGFP*, Series C, Vol. IV, No. 142.
[8] *Ibid.*, No. 107.
[9] *Ibid.*, No. 29.
[10] *Ibid.*, No. 127.

yond a general assumption that the conversations are following the normal line, and that after a short vacation period they will continue once more. However, it can be felt here that precautions will be taken to spare any irritation to Great Britain, for the local political spheres are concentrating on a solution to the impasse by means of an improvement in German-British relations.

4. *Problem of Italo-German Relations*

I was informed just in a general way that some sort of relaxation might be observed, appearing primarily in press relations. Nevertheless, it was stated that nothing happened which would go beyond normal diplomatic talks between the two countries, and that all rumors spread abroad about trading Austria for Abyssinia are of course a product of sheer imagination.

Józef Lipski

Poland's relations with Danzig did not enter into the sphere of activities of the Polish Ambassador in Berlin. Poland was careful to settle Danzig problems directly with the Senate of the Free City. It was only in emergency cases that Warsaw issued instructions for Lipski to negotiate on these matters from Berlin.

Such an emergency case was the tension in Poland's relations with Danzig in the summer of 1935.[11]

The conflict began on May 2 when, owing to financial difficulties in Danzig, the Senate of the Free City devaluated the Danzig gulden by 42.3 percent. This caused heavy losses for Poland, since customs income collected by Poland decreased automatically by an equal percentage. The Polish government made a proposition to balance the Danzig gulden with the Polish złoty. However, Arthur Greiser, the president of the Danzig Senate, opposed this proposal vehemently for fear that the złoty might completely replace the gulden.

This catastrophic situation in Danzig's finances constituted a grave political threat for Hitler, inasmuch as it could bring about the downfall of the National Socialist movement in the Free City. In their anxiety to avoid this calamity, political circles were ready to extend financial assistance to Danzig. On the other hand, however, these same political sponsors were well aware that in order to push Germany to the forefront as a large European power they had to continue expensive armaments, and they were reluctant at that

[11] See *Diariusz,* I, 320, 323–25, 522–25.

time to entangle themselves in the Danzig problems. At the same time economic circles (represented by Schacht, president of the Reichsbank) were unwilling to increase the normal monthly subsidy allotted for Danzig.

On June 11 Danzig introduced a currency control which constituted a direct blow to Polish industrialists who used the harbor of Danzig. Besides, this measure was illegal on the part of Danzig, since it was contradictory to the Polish-Danzig convention of November 9, 1920.

Under these circumstances the Polish-Danzig conflict deepened, with Hitler's obvious support and his promise of all possible aid in money and food in case Poland shut its frontier.

Two reports by Lipski dealing with the conflict follow.

DOCUMENT 46 Lipski to Beck

NO. G/3/8/35

Berlin, June 13, 1935
Strictly Confidential

In accordance with your recommendation received yesterday by telephone,[12] I called on Schacht this morning at 11 A.M. and made the following declaration:

I learned from the press that Herr Schacht is to proceed in the next few days to Danzig. I am calling on him in this connection to discuss the financial and economic situation in effect in the Free City at present, noting that my action is not an official *démarche* because—if for no other reason—Danzig is beyond the sphere of direct Polish-German relations.

I subsequently stressed that I would like to present to Herr Schacht our point of view on this problem, assuming this might be of assistance to him. I began by declaring that the relaxation in Polish-Danzig relations was the first stage heralding a Polish-German rapprochement. The Polish government accepted, as a principle, nonintervention in Danzig's internal affairs. Our stand in the face of internal political struggles waged on the territory of the Free City during the last years might serve as sufficient proof here. What Poland is pressing for is that its rights in Danzig, based on a number of agreements, be respected.

I was recently approached by top political spheres of the Reich, who expressed some anxiety about the situation now prevailing in the Free

[12] *Ibid.*, p. 316.

City, for fear of repercussions on Polish-German relations. I was requested to watch over this problem within the frame of my opportunities. Availing myself of this occasion, I had come today to have a talk with Schacht.

Coming back to the financial situation in Danzig, I stressed that it is causing justified anxiety. I confirmed that a successful economic development of the situation in Danzig is also of concern to Poland. Therefore, I stated that we would be ready to extend financial and economic aid. I added that this aid would take a form that would be politically unobtrusive for the government, under the condition of loyal economic collaboration with us. Finally, I pointed to the fact that it would be regrettable to have something go on in Danzig which is contradictory to Polish-Danzig agreements.

Here Herr Schacht inquired which acts of Danzig, in our opinion, are in contradiction with the agreements, to which I replied that I had in mind currency restrictions which, besides being contradictory to Article 195 of the Warsaw Convention, in practice are bound to expose to difficulties Polish interests in their transactions with the Free City and via the Free City. Herr Schacht reacted strongly to this point and tried to persuade me that the introduction of currency restrictions in the Free City, as a matter of fact differing from those issued in the Reich and aimed solely at stopping the exodus of gold from the Bank of Danzig, is not designed to hurt Polish interests. As for the contradiction with Article 195, he did not deny that it might be against the law, and he said that he would give this matter his attention.

Herr Schacht replied as follows: He is proceeding to Danzig in his capacity as president of the Reichsbank, at the invitation not of the Senate of the Free City but of the president of the Bank of Danzig. He will not have any contacts with the Senate, a political institution. The goal of his visit is to reinforce the position of Schäfer, whom he regards as quite a competent person. In his conversations he will obviously avoid any subjects embarrassing for Poland, since maintaining good relations with Poland is his heart's desire, as well as that of other members of the government. Although several years ago a rapprochement would have seemed unrealistic and impossible, such a fact had occurred in a form positive for both partners.

Schacht declared that the situation of the Bank of Danzig is quite good. The balance sheet shows that on 32 million gulden in assets (*Aussenstände*) there are bills worth 29 million gulden in circulation

(*Notenumlauf*). His opinion is that the crisis is purely psychological. Stronger nerves will restore a perfect currency situation in Danzig in two months. The gulden will become the most sought-after currency. That is why he wants to inject psychological resistance into the Bank of Danzig. He deems it to be necessary to introduce currency restrictions for a time. This might be a painful blow for some individuals, but it will have an immediate positive effect. In his opinion the whole matter is exaggerated and a result of artificial excitement. He is aware, of course, that the Senate of the Free City found itself in a difficult position with the elections over and the necessity of introducing the devaluation of the gulden immediately afterward.

With regard to Poland's financial and economic aid, Herr Schacht asked if we would be ready to give gold from the Bank of Poland to cover the gulden. I replied that some aid of this sort could be extended. In the field of economics, I answered Herr Schacht by stating that I understood that, in view of the complex of Polish-Danzig economic relations, some way might be found to reach out a helping hand to the Free City.

At the end of my conversation with Schacht, I stated that I only wanted, quite informally, to draw his attention to the Danzig aspect as observed from Warsaw. For his part, Herr Schacht stressed that in his opinion the financial situation should not be considered too tragically, that it will improve very soon, that he understands Poland's concern to have its interests in Danzig respected, and that certainly nothing will be done by the German government to jeopardize Polish-German relations.

In view of the position taken by Herr Schacht and his very strong dissociation from any political elements, both here and in the Free City, I did not deem it necessary to ask him to meet our representative in the Free City.

I would like to add that on my return to the Embassy I received a telephone call from the Auswärtiges Amt, informing me that they were advised of my conversation with Schacht and that they shared the point of view of the Reichsbank President. I replied that I had spoken with Schacht privately, since I had no authority to hold talks with the Reich government on the subject of Danzig.[13]

I quite understand that the German government was compelled to support Danzig financially in view of the difficult financial situation there. Undoubtedly, the mission of investigate the problem was en-

[13] See *DGFP*, Series C, Vol. IV, No. 149.

trusted to the most responsible factor in the Reich, namely, to Schacht. As far as I can see, the restoration work is proceeding on the following lines:

1) Compression of the inflated budget. Here, as was already confirmed by Greiser in his speech, the Reich is granting assistance in order to meet individual claims.

2) The Bank of Danzig, following Schacht's advice, will try to stop the exodus of the gulden by currency restrictions. Schacht thinks that, if the gulden remains as the only currency in the Free City, its exodus will stop as a result.

3) The assistance has become a matter of prestige, owing to the fact that the Reichsbank President is paying a visit to Danzig.

4) It is at present difficult to ascertain whether there are other invisible subsidies coming to Danzig from the Reich.

Regarding our assistance for the Free City, I am of the opinion—observing the situation from Berlin—that this matter is being used by the opposition elements in Danzig as a trump card to fight the National Socialist government, especially with regard to introducing gold currency in Danzig. Therefore, I imagine that it would be extremely awkward for the Senate to approach Poland with a proposition for aid.

Although my conversation with Schacht did not result—in my opinion—in any positive end with regard to our participation in extending aid to Danzig, nevertheless a concrete advantage was obtained, since it revealed the method of action of the Reich government regarding the financial crisis in the Free City.

Józef Lipski

DOCUMENT 47   Lipski to Beck

NO. G/3/11/35   Berlin, June 17, 1935
                                                     Strictly Confidential

Owing to the absence of Reichspräsident Göring from Berlin, only this morning could I discuss with him the situation in Danzig.[14]

With reference to what Göring declared to me on May 21 concerning Danzig problems, I opened the conversation by saying that I had wanted

14 See *ibid.*, No. 158.

to talk with him on this subject for several days. Unfortunately, this was not possible because of his absence from Berlin. I added that I had had a conversation with Schacht before he left for Danzig, but the President of the Reichsbank saw this matter from a purely financial angle. Göring replied that Schacht indeed does consider this question only as a currency problem.

I further declared to Göring that, realizing that a National Socialist Senate in Danzig is also most desirable from our point of view, since it brought about a rapprochement between the Free City and Poland, I would like to remind him that we have always kept aloof from internal Danzig problems. In spite of approaches repeatedly made by the opposition parties, we rejected any attempt to draw us into action against the Senate. I mentioned quite confidentially that the Polish minority in Danzig was advised not to join forces with the opposition at the time of the elections. Deliberating on this point, I pointed to our basic attitude regarding the situation of the National Socialist Senate.

Subsequently, I stressed that, owing to the introduction of the currency order without our knowledge, we were presented with a *fait accompli* that constituted a serious blow to our economic interests. I further illustrated with examples to Herr Göring how detrimental the currency regulations are both for our economic interests and for the genuine interests of the Free City. I mentioned that we had the possibility of taking this matter to the League but that you abstained from doing so, realizing that on the platform of the League such a case could be exploited by a number of elements to the detriment of Polish-German relations. I added that for the time being you had settled for a protest presented on the 13th inst., that the strongly worded protest was purposely softened for presentation to the press, and that, counting on the possibility of direct talks with the Senate, we had not as yet introduced any retaliatory measures. I said again that the only way out of this situation would be direct conversations between Poland and the Free City. Poland would then be able to offer certain financial and economic aid to the Free City, and I added in this connection that Mr. Roman is leaving tomorrow for Danzig with this aim in mind. I remarked that Mr. Roman is well known to the German side as a very able and reasonable negotiator, who conducted negotiations with the Free City for many years.[15]

[15] At this time Antoni Roman was Polish minister in Stockholm.

In the course of my deliberations Herr Göring several times gave me immediate explanations which, in brief, are as follows:

He stated that the Chancellor is taking a firm stand that the Danzig problem should under no circumstances create difficulties in Polish-German relations. Both Greiser and Forster are well aware of this. The Chancellor insists on supporting the National Socialist Senate in Danzig, not only for prestige reasons, but primarily because he knows that, if power in Danzig were seized by the opposition, this would be harmful for the Free City's policy toward Poland. The opposition parties would obviously immediately revert to the old policy against Poland.

Regarding currency regulations, Göring said that the Senate was ordered to advise the Polish government. As a proof of how the Chancellor is keeping watch over this matter from the point of view of Polish-German relations, Göring cited the fact that, when Greiser asked that a battleship be sent to Danzig to boost the Senate's prestige, the Chancellor replied that he would not do it, since a visit of the Germany navy to Gdynia should have priority. Also, Schacht's trip was solely aimed at keeping up spirits at the Bank of Danzig.

Regarding assistance for Danzig, Herr Göring said that, of course, both Germany and Poland are not very well off at present, and therefore assistance on a large scale is difficult. I mentioned here that, with good will, we might on our part find some means of easing Danzig's situation. Here I made the reservation that we are well aware that this aid should be devoid of any aspect which would compromise the National Socialist Senate in the eyes of the opposition.

Göring expressed great satisfaction over this clarification. He added that Greiser told him that it was apparently stated by our side that, in case the Free City does not accept Polish conditions, it would be economically ruined, and that it was also said—between the lines—that time has now come to cancel some of the rights of the Free City. When this was related to him, Göring allegedly declared in the presence of the Chancellor that he does not know what was said in Danzig; but he was in Warsaw and spoke with competent elements there, and he is well aware of the atmosphere in the Polish government, which is trying to maintain good relations with Germany. Here I remarked to Göring that possibly opposition circles are intriguing on both sides. We are not in the least interested in depriving the Free City of any rights whatsoever, and in economic talks certain ways can be found financially to support the currency.

Talking about Greiser, Göring said that Greiser does not please him, since his position is visibly turning his head a bit. But he praised Forster, stating that it was worth while to talk with him, since he is absolutely in favor of the maintenance of good relations with Poland. He therefore advised that Minister Roman should also talk with Forster.

Herr Göring during this whole conversation stressed authoritatively that nothing would be done by the German government to create difficulties in Polish-German relations, but that, on the contrary, pressure would be exerted on the Senate in this matter. In conclusion he said that he would immediately call Greiser and Forster by telephone in order to induce them to conduct their talks with Minister Roman in this spirit. He will also advise the Chancellor of our conversation.

Parenthetically I might add that Göring thought that you had a conversation with Greiser in Danzig. Herr Göring asked me to extend to you his thanks for approaching him on these matters and to assure you that the previous line is not subject to fluctuations. He remarked that it would be sheer nonsense if such a nutshell as Danzig were to complicate the all-important Polish-German relations.

Finally, Herr Göring said to me that he is very anxious for you to come to Berlin now. He has already announced this to the Chancellor. I replied that in principle you would be pleased to come, and that the Danzig problem, as well as Göring's absence from Berlin, has simply delayed your arrival a bit. Herr Göring also added that he counts on an understanding being reached in direct talks in Danzig. If any difficulties should arise, he is ready at any time with personal intervention, and thinks that in case of necessity you could take this matter up with the Chancellor.

I would like to add that the local press—in all probability inspired—passed over in silence the whole Danzig affair. The D.N.B. [Deutsches Nachrichtenbüro] is very thrifty with news to be circulated in Germany.

Józef Lipski

On July 18 the Polish government, having authority on customs problems, ordered that duty be levied in Danzig only on goods destined for the internal consumption of the Free City, while duty on goods bound for Poland via Danzig should be collected in Poland. This order could have resulted in economic catastrophe for Danzig, and certain German elements reacted by urging that Danzig be detached from Poland and united with the Reich. Von

Moltke, in a conversation with Beck, strove to iron out the situation, but the Danzig Senate aggravated the conflict still further by its order (on August 1) to admit customs-free those goods destined for internal consumption in the Free City.

Immediately following this order, Lipski, who at that time was in Warsaw, received instructions to return to Berlin for orientation on whether the government of the Reich supported the decision of the Danzig Senate.

On August 2 Lipski had a conversation with Secretary of State von Bülow. Bülow criticized sharply the action of the Senate and expressed the opinion that, in spite of this, Polish-Danzig negotiations would succeed in achieving the liquidation of the conflict (*DGFP,* Series C, Vol. IV, No. 244).

On the next day Lipski proceeded to Berchtesgaden, where Göring was taking part in a hunt. In his conversation with Lipski on August 4, Göring had words of sharp criticism for the order by the Danzig authorities, as being contrary to the Chancellor's guiding line. Their action had absolutely nothing to do with the Reich government. Göring was of the opinion that the conflict must be liquidated immediately. He was ready to summon Greiser to Berlin in order to use his influence on him to this effect. To Göring's question how this strife could be ended, Lipski explained that the Danzig authorities should withdraw their order and, in consequence, upon agreement that customs would be levied in a fixed currency, the Polish government would withdraw its order of July 18. Göring approved this solution and promised Lipski to arrange a meeting with Hitler.

This meeting took place on August 5 (*DGFP,* Series C, Vol. IV, No. 25). When the Ambassador outlined the course of the Danzig problem to the Chancellor, as he had previously to Göring who was also present, Hitler declared that his argumentation was quite clear and convincing. Hitler said that in his policies he gave priority to essential problems, subordinating second-rate problems to them. The Chancellor regarded good Polish-German relations to be of primary importance. With the situation developing in the east, the two states might face an omnific moment, and they should therefore coexist in friendship. Compared to these great interests, the Corridor quesion was of second-rate importance. Poland needed access to the sea; if deprived of it, the whole Polish nation would then turn against Germany. Returning to the Danzig question, the Chancellor stated that he was in favor of absolute respect of the *status quo* in the Free City by both Germany and Poland. This was the only way to avoid unnecessary conflicts. The problem of Danzig was a second-rate problem; it should not encumber Polish-German relations.

Bringing the conversation to an end, the Chancellor urged a prompt liquidation of the Danzig conflict, asking on what level this could be achieved. Göring quoted conditions of the agreement as discussed with Lipski. Without bringing up further details, the Chancellor thanked the Ambassador for coming to Berchtesgaden and asked him to communicate their conversation to Beck.

Once more, on August 6, Lipski had a conversation with Göring, first getting authorization from Beck by telephone to settle the conflict. Forster and Greiser accepted the Polish formula upon Göring's inquiry by telephone.[16] Beck's conversation with Greiser at Gdynia on August 8 (*DGFP,* Series C, Vol. IV Nos. 257 and 258) brought this conflict to a close, and aggressive orders on both sides were withdrawn. A number of relevant documents are cited in *DGFP,* Series C, Vol. IV, Nos. 65, 92, 97, 103, 112, 123, 126, 130, 133, 134, 143, 149, 150, 158, 214, 215, 224, 226, 227, 240, 244, 245, 247, 250, 251, 254, and 256.

[16] In his report to the Foreign Affairs Ministry dated August 15, Lipski presented the whole of this action from August 2 to August 6, as well as his conversations with von Bülow, Göring, and Hitler. This report is missing from Lipski's papers. Halina Trocka quotes from it and summarizes it in *Gdańsk a hitlerowski "Drang nach Osten"* (Danzig, 1964), pp. 58–60, while sentences from the conversation with Hitler are quoted literally as per Lipski's report, although with omissions.

German Refunds for Transit across Polish Pomerania
July, 1935—March, 1936

MINISTER BECK'S official visit to Berlin on July 3 and 4, 1935, was an important event in Polish-German relations. Beck, accompanied by Lipski, had his first long conversation with Hitler at that time. For details according to the German verson, see *DGFP*, Series C, Vol. IV, No. 190, pp. 398–407, and No. 192. For the Polish résumé of this conversation, see *Diariusz*, I, 330–32, 344–45, and 526. The official communiqué about this visit appears in *Polish White Book,* No. 20.

On June 20 negotiations were started in Berlin on the Polish-German trade agreement, which was signed in Warsaw on November 4, 1935.

DOCUMENT 48   Lipski to Beck

NO. N/52/4/35
Berlin, July 15, 1935
Strictly Confidential

Before my departure tomorrow for a three-week vacation, I called today on Secretary of State von Bülow, who is substituting for von Neurath during the latter's absence from Berlin.

Von Bülow expressed the German government's satisfaction with the results of your visit to Berlin, stressing that good Polish-German diplomatic collaboration in Warsaw and Berlin was developing so successfully as to render new achievements dispensable.

For my part I referred to the question of the current Polish-German trade negotiations. I pointed out that, following the suggestion for a broader understanding made by the German representative, Directors Sokołowski and Rose left for Warsaw to obtain authorization to negotiate on the basis suggested by the German side.

I remarked that this was not an easy problem, especially with regard to granting Germany the most-favored-nation clause.

· I confirmed that naturally we are most interested in satisfying agricultural demands. Here I emphasized that, in accordance with the suggestions of the delegation, our demands in this field cannot be reduced. I especially laid stress on the point that our total calculation is based on obtaining sufficiently high prices.

I said that both Herr Hemmen and Herr Ritter understand and support our stand; however, they are concerned about possible opposition from Herr Schacht's department. Therefore, I asked Herr Bülow to give his careful attention to this problem. Von Bülow, who agreed with my explanations, stated that he also understands our interest in striving to obtain the highest possible prices for agricultural products, and that this is a basis for a possible agreement.

I also asked Herr von Bülow, in case any difficulties arose, to receive Counselor Lubomirski in my absence, and if necessary to extend his assistance to him, which he willingly promised to do.

I subsequently took up the question of Sir Samuel Hoare's speech in the House of Commons.[1] The Secretary of State replied that Hoare's speech made an unfavorable impression on the German government; here he obviously had in mind the appeal made to the Chancellor to agree to the Eastern and Danube pacts. This is even more unpleasant if one bears in mind that the British government was well aware what was cooking backstage. It is obvious that the British, French, and Italian governments distributed parts between them. England is pressing for the air pact, France for the Eastern Pact, and Italy for the Danube Pact. At present Italy has ceased its pressure for the Danube Pact; the problem of the Eastern Pact, viewed from the angle of Franco-German relations, is more complicated. The British appeal calling on Germany to accept these pacts was very tactless under these circumstances. Such was the reaction of the German press. Herr von Bülow remarked further that he has spoken only with Herr von Neurath, who has not yet seen the Chancellor since Hoare's speech. Neurath and Bülow took a stand—which they expect will be shared by the Chancellor absolutely—that the appeal of the British Secretary of State should be dismissed without any reply.

Herr von Bülow stated that the German government will not stand for blackmail (he used a milder expression) by Great Britain in connection with the air pact. If he followed Britain's course, then after the Eastern

[1] July 11, 1935.

Pact the Danube Pact would be brought forward, and after the Danube Pact the return of Germany to the League of Nations, etc., etc. If the air pact is not concluded, it cannot be helped. Germany will continue to build up its air force; this build-up, von Bülow added, will be conducted only in accordance with real needs.

With regard to the Eastern Pact, Herr von Bülow remarked that he had recommended to the German ambassador in Paris, Köster, that he ask Laval informally whether France really intends to participate in the suggested Eastern Pact. Herr von Bülow stressed that Barthou's original proposition included France's participation, but in subsequent plans this participation was not explicitly mentioned. Bülow thinks that this will be a convenient tactical question, since it might open the possibility for a series of new arguments against the pact.

Next, observing that he would like to discuss a timely matter of importance, Herr Bülow referred to the question of the recent meeting of the representatives of the Baltic states at Riga.[2] He confirmed that the Auswärtiges Amt had received news that strong pressure was exerted from the Soviet side on the Baltic states to draw them, like Czechoslovakia, into the Franco-Soviet agreement. This was the subject debated at Riga, and the German Envoy reported from Riga, following his conversation with the Latvian Foreign Affairs Minister, that Latvia is beginning to lean toward the Russian-French plotting.

Herr von Bülow stressed that Ambassador von Moltke was instructed to inform you about this state of affairs.

Today, prior to my visit, the Latvian Envoy called on the Secretary of State and communicated to him the text of the resolutions passed at the conference of Baltic states in Riga.[3]

One of these points states that, in case the German government does not support its earlier declaration made at Stresa with regard to the Eastern Pact and the pact is not concluded, the Baltic states will then be compelled to join the Soviet-French agreement. The Secretary of State allegedly reacted very strongly to the point of view expressed by the Latvian Envoy. He said, in the first place, that in Stresa the German government only expressed its opinion, without taking on any binding obligations. Since the problem of the Eastern Pact is very complicated, it

[2] This was a conference of thirteen Latvian envoys from various countries that lasted from June 28 to July 3.

[3] See *DGFP*, Series C, Vol. IV, No. 208.

is not possible to present motions, as the Baltic states are prepared to do, basing themselves on explanations supplied by the German government to the Western Powers at one time. Von Bülow supposedly then pointed out that the Eastern Pact is nothing but a cover for a Soviet-French alliance.

He further declared to the Latvian Envoy that the German government is very positively disposed toward the Baltic states and their independence.

Although he could not agree to the conclusion of an agreement of mutual assistance with these countries, this did not indicate in the least his *désintéressement* in case other Powers threatened the independence of the Baltic states. Finally, von Bülow warned the Latvian Envoy against joining the Soviet-French system, which constitutes a threat for the independence of the Baltic states. He stressed that, faced with such an emergency, the German government could be compelled to revise its present attitude toward these states. Herr von Bülow told me that he strove to influence the Latvian side not to succumb to pressure exerted by the Soviets. He remarked that this pressure also has its basis in the field of economic relations. Herr von Bülow concluded by asking me to support, for my part, Ambassador Moltke's *démarche* to you aimed at obtaining the collaboration of the Polish government in taking action in Riga and Tallin to keep them in the present state of balance.

I remarked that, owing to my departure for a vacation tomorrow morning, I would write my report on the conversation with the Secretary of State today and dispatch it without delay for your attention.

I declared that in my opinion the wisest policy for the Baltic states would be to maintain their neutral position toward the Great Powers, and that such a stand is the best guarantee for their independence.

I stressed that our activities were always aimed at the preservation of independent Baltic states, without binding them with agreements which could prove detrimental to their independence. I also made allusion to the fact that Estonia's policy was the most forthright and well balanced.

The Secretary of State agreed with my opinion. He also added that the German envoys in Riga and Tallin had received appropriate instructions. As far as Kovno was concerned, in his opinion it was hopeless.

I also had a casual talk with Director Meyer. As far as I can judge, news coming from Riga has rendered the Auswärtiges Amt somewhat nervous. Probably this is due also to the absence of Neurath.

In order to inform you without delay, I took the liberty of sending a special courier.

Józef Lipski

DOCUMENT 49   Lipski to Szembek

NO. 1/3/45/35   Berlin, October 18, 1935
                                             Confidential

I am forwarding the enclosed report on a conversation held on October 11 between Minister Beck and Minister von Neurath after dinner at the Polish Embassy. This report gives only a general outline of the conversation, which was conducted in a very subtle manner.

I would like to add that on the same day at 7 P.M. Minister Beck called on Minister President Göring, by special invitation. The conversation also dealt with the Abyssinian question, and Herr Göring's arguments, if not so detailed, were more or less in agreement with von Neurath's opinions.

Herr Göring expressed his concern about progress made by the Soviets in Rumania, remarking that, in case a Soviet-Rumanian pact is concluded, he is convinced that the question of allowing Soviet troops to march through Rumania would be settled positively as well. Minister Beck, without involving himself in further discussion on this point, said only that the situation in Rumania is difficult indeed, and that the King seems to be more and more under the influence of Mr. Titulescu's policy.

Józef Lipski

Report on the Conversation of Foreign Affairs Minister Józef Beck with Reich Foreign Affairs Minister von Neurath, *held on October 11, 1935, in Berlin*

On October 11, on his way from Geneva to Warsaw, the Foreign Affairs Minister met with Reich Foreign Affairs Minister von Neurath at a dinner at the Embassy. The course of this conversation was as follows:

Both Minister Beck and Herr von Neurath agreed that the situation in connection with the Abyssinian conflict is very serious, more than a local struggle, and that in the long run it might constitute a danger for Europe.[4]

Minister Beck remarked that this time the impact of the situation could be felt at Geneva. He stressed that one thing has become obvious, namely, that the Second and the Third International had acted jointly, striving to regain their positions. Minister Beck had called the attention of the British delegation to this fact. Herr von Neurath was absolutely of the same opinion. Both ministers agreed in their supposition that the conflict could extend further owing to a miscalculation of the British situation by the Italians and vice versa.

They both realize that Italy's position is rendered more difficult because broad public opinion in all countries is taking the part of Abyssinia as a country attacked. Here Herr von Neurath quoted facts from Germany, remarking that he can hardly stop the press from attacking Italy.

Both ministers do not at present see any way out for Mussolini. They share the opinion that an Italian defeat would be very dangerous for relations in Europe and would only contribute to the reinforcement of the Third International.

Minister Beck stated that, although in principle Poland abstains from interfering with matters of no direct concern to our state, in this particular case, in the face of the seriousness of the situation, he did not shrink from participation in the Committee of Five, which is striving, within the limits of existing possibilities, to assist in settling the conflict.

Minister Beck emphasized the efforts made by Laval to find a way out of the situation. Herr von Neurath remarked that, if Laval were defeated, power would go to Herriot. Both ministers shared the opinion that too-strong British pressure on France, with the consequent downfall of Laval, would only bring about a closer Franco-Soviet association.

Herr von Neurath, remarking that he had had a conversation with the Chancellor that afternoon, declared that the German government considers the developing situation as a serious danger for Europe and is interested in the speediest possible settlement of the conflict. In this matter the German government is not following its own secondary inter-

[4] On October 2 Italy mobilized, and on the 3d Italian troops marched into Abyssinia. On the 5th the Council of the League of Nations was in session, and on the 7th the Council unanimously proclaimed Italy an aggressor. Poland voted for this motion.

ests but is taking a broader European point of view. Herr von Neurath stated that since the German nation lives in Europe it must take care of the development of this part of the world. Bearing these issues in mind, Herr von Neurath believes that at the right moment this point might be communicated to public opinion, thus favorably affecting the general situation. He thinks that if, for instance, the German government were approached with regard to sanctions, this could possibly be the occasion for this sort of action.

Minister Beck noted with appreciation the stand of the German government regarding the Anglo-Italian conflict. On this point he stressed that, as a result of his conversation with the Chancellor, he had expressed to the English his conviction that the government of the Reich desires its relations with Great Britain to take the best possible turn.

Herr von Neurath went on to confirm that, in the light of these issues, he could assure Minister Beck that nothing would occur with regard to Kłajpeda [Memel]. The fate of several thousand Memel Germans is a secondary issue compared with wide European interests. The German government, even now after the elections, will endeavor—if a reasonable reaction by the Lithuanian government prevails—to normalize its relations with Lithuania if possible.

Minister Beck, remarking casually that negotiating with the Lithuanian government is not an easy task, referred to his conversation with Lozorajtis. He stated that he told the Lithuanian statesman that for Poland to establish relations with Lithuania it is essential to know whether Lithuania has a self-governing policy. Minister Beck stressed to Herr von Neurath that a certain reaction can be detected in Lithuania against total surrender to Moscow's supremacy. Herr von Neurath agreed with this.

With regard to the Baltic states, both ministers were of the opinion that a certain amount of calmness and sobering down could be noted in these countries. Minister Beck thinks this is due partly to the fact that representatives of these states could observe in Geneva that the importance of Moscow in Western Europe is not so considerable as it seems locally. Mr. Beck stated that he appraises positively the visits of Scandinavian statesmen to the Baltic states.

Coming back to current Polish-German economic matters, Herr von Neurath stressed that he was advised that the delegation which is to negotiate with Poland is to leave for Riga. He asked if it would not be advisable that they go via Warsaw. Ambassador Lipski replied that in his opinion this is desirable, suggesting that the stopover take place next week.

Ambassador Lipski referred to the question of railway payments.[5] Minister Beck remarked that this matter is not exclusively a financial one but has a political aspect as well.

DOCUMENT 50   Lipski to the Ministry of Foreign Affairs

NO. N/51/58/35   Berlin, November 7, 1935
                                                        Confidential

On October 28, I was summoned by telephone by the Vice-Minister of Foreign Affairs to come to Warsaw on October 30 in connection with the question of German arrears in refunds for transit through Poland. On October 30 and 31, I was present at consultations on this matter conducted in the presence of Vice-Minister Szembek, Vice-Minister of the Treasury Koc, Director of Financial Turnover Baczyński, Director Potocki, and others. On November 1, I proceeded to Rabka with Vice-Minister Szembek and Director Baczyński in order to receive from Minister Beck final instructions for my conversations with the German government.[6]

Upon my return to Berlin, on November 3, I was received by Foreign Affairs Minister von Neurath on November 4 at 11:30 A.M. After a preliminary exchange of opinion regarding rumors about the alleged deviation from our present political line and my reassurances on this point, I passed to the subject of arrears in railway refunds. I declared that this matter had reached such dimensions that besides its financial aspect it now assumed a conspicuous political character. I pointed to the very negative reaction in the Polish government to Germany's tardiness in settling these refunds. I remarked that the economic department decided that granting further credits to German railways is impossible and that the only solution would be to issue orders to collect the arrears for transit on the frontier. In order to prevent this extreme solution, I tried

[5] These payments were connected with transit from Germany through Polish Pomerania to East Prussia. Contrary to the binding Paris Agreement of 1921, Germany withheld payment, which by the end of September, 1935, amounted to 29,500,000 zlotys. Germany tried to combine this question with other economic matters in the current trade negotiations; the Polish side requested that these debts be settled separately.

[6] For Lipski's conversations in Warsaw, see *Diariusz*, I, 391–95.

to find a way out in my conversations with the ministers. I stressed that the present government, whose main concern is to stabilize the budget, and which for this reason will have to increase the tax burden on the population, is even more reluctant to let such arrears jeopardize its recovery plans. I subsequently presented our suggestion requesting the immediate repayment of 42 million zlotys, indicating that after this refund is made we would be prepared to credit the German government for two years with an equivalent sum from the future flow of transit dues. The balance would be transferred to the German-Soviet-Polish triangle. I told Herr von Neurath that we would thus enable Herr Schacht to shift payments for raw materials, for example. I made it explicitly clear that the refund is indispensable and that nonpayment would have bad consequences for our relations.

Herr von Neurath replied that, as far as the field of foreign policy is concerned, this whole problem has been weighing heavily on him for months, and that he is doing his utmost to liquidate it. Of course, in this case he has to confer with the Chancellor and with Schact.

I added that up to now I had never embarrassed the Chancellor with either economic or financial matters, confining myself to purely political matters of a general nature. However, in view of the importance of this particular case, I would like him to advise the Chancellor that I am at his disposal for discussion on this problem.

In the course of the conversation, von Neurath also mentioned that the matter of our later crediting the sum of 42 million zlotys, upon repayment of the present arrears, is not too convenient a solution, for it still leaves a debt. In his opinion, the problem should be solved completely, in order to prevent its reoccurrence.

I laid stress on the urgency of the case, asking Herr von Neurath for a reply, possibly in the next few days, which he promised to give me.[7]

On the 5th inst., Counselor Gawroński was interpellated at the Auswärtiges Amt by the economic desk officer, Herr Bräutigam, about this matter in connection with my conversation with Herr von Neurath. Counselor Gawroński also took a determined stand.

Realizing from this conversation that the matter is receiving attention inside the department, I had a talk yesterday, on the 6th inst., with Minister President Göring, in the course of which, acting as I had previ-

[7] For the German version of this conversation, see *DGFP*, Series C, Vol. **IV**, No. 392. See also *ibid.*, No. 409.

ously with von Neurath, I insisted on the necessity for the refund of railway arrears.

Herr Göring noted all the details, remarking that he will have a talk with Schacht right away and will give me a reply, possibly on Monday.

On this occasion Göring told me that, when at the Council of Ministers the question of payment of membership fees to the League of Nations by the Reich government was presented, he strongly urged that this sum be given to Poland instead of to the League. The argument presented against this was that, if Germany does not cover its indebtedness to the League of Nations, it might still be regarded as subject to membership obligations, and this would be a political handicap for it.

As I wired yesterday, I am leaving for Munich for two days. I therefore assume that I shall not be in a position to give you further information on this problem before Monday.

Józef Lipski

DOCUMENT 51   Lipski to Beck

NO. N/320/151/35 Berlin, November 24, 1935
Strictly Confidential

My nearly two years of observations and experience in the field of so-called Polish-German moral disarmament found application in the declaration of January 26, 1934, and especially in the press agreement concluded on February 24, 1934.[8] These, in my opinion, can be of assistance in evaluating results achieved as well as obstacles continually manifested in this matter. A synthesis of this matter would also contribute to a proper orientation regarding our future action and tactics.

It should be taken into consideration that, in the post-Versailles pe-

[8] In February, 1934, press conversations were held in Berlin between Poland and Germany in connection with the nonaggression declaration of January 26, 1934. Participating on the Polish side were Wacław Przesmycki, chief of the Foreign Ministry Press Department and his deputy, Emil Rücker; on the German side, Director of the Press Department of the A.A. Aschmann and Counselor Jahnke of the Propaganda Ministry. The conversations concluded with a secret protocol established by the two sides on February 24 which defined a series of resolutions aimed at creating a friendly atmosphere and good-neighbor relations in the fields of the press, radio, theater, cinema, and periodicals. This protocol was supplemented at the next conference in Warsaw.

riod and until conversations were undertaken with Chancellor Hitler, German governments, regardless of their party line, systematically rejected all our suggestions that they abandon German press and propaganda action against Poland. The Polish government's endeavors, both during the period of Locarno and during the rule of Chancellor Brüning, took a very concrete form. We were permanently vigilant in this matter, approaching the Geneva institution with our claims and using the governments of France, England, and America as intermediaries. German propaganda against Poland, active inside the Reich, spread abroad to other countries.

It served two principal goals:

a) on the assumption that Poland is a foe of the Reich, to counteract our interests in all fields;

b) through a permanent revisionist action against Polish frontiers, to maintain, both in German and foreign minds, the concept that a peaceful coexistence between the two nations is impossible without territorial changes.

Starting with conversations with Chancellor Hitler, action described under (a) necessarily subsided and became pointless when, after the declaration of January 26, 1934, the German government accepted for propaganda use abroad the principle of displaying correct and friendly relations with Poland.

It was and will remain much more difficult to find brakes for the multicolored German propaganda generally labeled as revisionism. Here the Polish side, realizing that leaving this problem to the normal exchange of opinion through diplomatic channels (which would make permanent contacts necessary) would result in the need for a permanent objective procedure and definitely defined principles to oppose this action, suggested a press and propaganda understanding inaugurated by the signing of respective protocols on February 24, 1935.

The above press understanding, supplemented by protocols confirmed at the following conference in Warsaw, gives, according to the present *status quo*, a general outline of credit balance in our favor:

a) a generally correct stand and tone toward Poland by the popular daily German press;

b) cessation of the revisionist campaign against our frontiers by this press, especially against Pomerania. This is a positive result for us, particularly outside the Reich's frontiers. On the other hand, in spite of continuous efforts by the Embassy, we could not succeed in general in stopping harmful publicity in the local press, especially in the east. Of concern here are the publication of maps and other items sponsored by such organizations as the B.D.O. and V.D.A.,[9] demonstrations at the frontiers, etc. The results achieved in this sector are rather modest. Therefore, an even greater need exists to find ways and means to render this action as harmless as possible.

The resolutions of the present Polish-German protocol may sometimes be an insufficient basis for intervention. Of course, the Embassy is trying to extend the application of press protocols even to such fields as activities by the V.D.A. and B.D.O., although par. 2, section III, of the protocol gives little formal basis for this.

Closing these general remarks, I present below a synthesis of particular sections of German propaganda, asking that you give your careful attention to the following items:

I. Press

The popular political press is generally taking a correct attitude. Only one case of a serious deviation could be noted (the *Frankfurter Zeitung* on the occasion of the Danzig conflict). In the provincial press, especially the East Prussian press, the frontier press, and the Silesian press, anti-Polish notices and articles are still being printed.

Commenting very broadly on par. 9, section I, of the protocol, the Embassy protests the use of terms such as *Korridor* and even *abgetretene* (ceded) and/or *abgetrennte* (separated) *Gebiete*. The Embassy succeeded in obtaining some positive results here. *Der Gesellige* at Piła, a daily well known for its anti-Polish campaigns, recently began to use the term *Pomerellen* (No. 235 of October 8, 1935). Also, the Deutsches Nachrichtenbüro ceased to use the term *Korridor*.

An explicit definition of the Ministry's demands with regard to the use of the above-mentioned terms by German propaganda would greatly contribute to a further exploitation of the press protocol to our advantage. As for the terms *geraubte* or *entrissene Gebiete,* these are undoubtedly in contradiction with the contents of the press protocol. However, the same cannot irrefutably be deduced as far as such expressions as *Korridor, abgetrennte,* or *abgetretene Gebiete* are concerned.

[9] B.D.O.: Bund Deutscher Osten. V.D.A.: Volskbund für das Deutschtum in Ausland.

The number of press interventions initiated by us is therefore the result of a very broad interpretation of the protocol.

II. Books, Pamphlets, and Periodicals

In the course of the last year several books were published with anti-Polish tendencies, such as *Volk ohne Heimat,* by Christoph Kaergel; *Volk an der Grenze,* by Rudolf Fitzek; and *Annaberg,* by Kurt Eggers.

As the result of very scrupulously kept records at the Embassy, and based also on collaboration with the consulates, the number of interventions on this matter at the Press Department of the Ministry of Foreign Affairs reached the figure of 131. It would be useful if the press conference could determine more precisely the technique to be employed, as a guarantee of fuller consideration of our claims.

III. Schoolbooks

Obtaining changes in anti-Polish passages can only take place through a resolution passed by a mixed commission called on the basis of the press protocol. This is due to the fact that the Ministry of Education is the competent authority. Neither prompt nor sufficient results may be obtained simply by bringing to the knowledge of the German side questionable passages or books.

IV. Meetings, Demonstrations, Excursions to the Borderland

Centers dealing with problems in the east, particularly pertaining to Poland, are the V.D.A. and B.D.O., with affiliated organizations such as the Bund Heimattreuer Oberschlesier, Westpreussen, Thorner, Posener, etc. The whole complex of activities of these organizations is subject to control by the staff of the Führer's deputy, Reich Minister Hess. The Embassy is trying to deal with these activities within the frame of the press protocol, in the face of a determined stand by the German side and the very vague formulation of par. 2, section III, of the Warsaw protocol.

A check on V.D.A. and B.D.O. activities might be achieved by way of further special negotiations and utilization of the material accumulated by the Embassy.

V. Maps

Par. 1, section III, of the protocol regulates the question of maps with revisionist tendencies. The German side continues further to violate these resolutions, but recently, especially on official occasions (as, for example, the Reichsautobahnen propaganda map displayed abroad), the resolutions of the protocol have been observed in various instances.

VI. Films, Theater, Radio

In this sector anti-Polish propaganda cases are quite exceptional, and the *status quo* might be considered satisfactory.

VII. Monuments

The removal of monuments in existence for several years that were erected in connection with the loss of Polish territories by Germany should be the subject of special discussions at a Polish-German press conference, and if possible at the earliest opportunity. The press protocol, as I have already pointed out, still has many gaps, and efforts should be made to fill them in at future conferences. Hitherto, these conferences proved in practice to be of assistance in promoting some of our basic claims. Of course, the German side will not fail to display a whole arsenal of claims, directed mainly against our daily press. It is difficult to control our local press, while in Germany the local press is subject to absolute censorship by the government. When I compare the scope of anti-Polish action in Germany with anti-German tendencies in Poland I come to the conclusion that spontaneous rather than organized impulses may be noted in the press columns in Poland. On the other hand, where organizations exist subject to control by governmental censorship, principles of the agreement are observed. In Germany under the present regime there is no room for spontaneous reactions. The popular press observes the rules of the agreement, while the organizations whose goal it is to propagate revisionist ideas continue their task. They do this, however, with less impetus and without broad external propaganda effects. It should be added that, as far as the local press is concerned, it often commits sins against the agreement, particularly in the eastern region bordering Poland.

When the Ministry takes up the preparation of material for the press conference, I would appreciate it if the press desk officer of the Embassy would be summoned to Warsaw.

Józef Lipski

DOCUMENT 52   Lipski to Beck

NO. 51/62/35   Berlin, November 30, 1935
                                          Confidential

As I informed you in my telegram of November 25, I asked for an audience with Minister von Neurath to take place on November 28, immediately after his return from a short vacation, in order to receive a final reply with regard to railway refunds. I put the Auswärtiges Amt on notice that, since I was not in a position to wait any longer, I would place my inquiry very explicitly and precisely.

I still tried to influence the Chancellor indirectly. Specifically, I instigated a direct report to the Chancellor by General von Massow, a member of the S.S. with whom I am personally well acquainted. In his report the General referred to his conversation with me on the situation arising in connection with nonpayment by Germany of arrears in railway payments. As a result of this step, on November 28, I received a telephone call from the president of the Prussian Council of Ministers, Göring, whom I once more pressured strongly on this matter. I obtained a promise that he would take further steps in this respect.

I called on Herr von Neurath today at 11 A.M. Herr von Neurath declared to me that unfortunately he is not in a position to give me a positive answer. Efforts made by him to bring about the refund of these arrears have so far been unsuccessful, in the face of Schacht's declaration about a complete lack of foreign currency. Herr von Neurath seemed to me to be embarrassed, and he emphasized, from the point of view of his department, how awkward this matter is for him. The Chancellor, in his opinion, is well aware of this.

I answered Herr Neurath that the only thing I could do now was to report this negative stand to the Polish government. I remarked that on Wednesday of this week the Council of Ministers was to debate on the question of refunds. At your request this subject was postponed, awaiting the reply of the German government scheduled for the week-end. I pointed to serious complications caused to the Polish government by the nonpayment of such a considerable sum, and mentioned the heavy burdens laid on the population in order to balance the budget. I made allusion to the fact that the shortage of such an amount in foreign currency compels the Polish government to seek security elsewhere.

Finally, I said that I must warn Herr von Neurath that the Polish government will undoubtedly be obliged to undertake preventive measures.

Herr von Neurath replied that this is significant and that he understands the necessity. He added that, when the situation reaches a crucial point, the possibility of a concrete solution might arise. He also added that he personally is persisting in his efforts, but he hinted that his proposals up to now have been rejected by Schacht. At a convenient moment he plans to take the next step.[10]

From my conversation with Herr von Neurath today I concluded that, considering the opposition of Schacht, who is using the excuse of a shortage of foreign currency, the Reich Minister of Foreign Affairs has failed to enforce the solution for repayment of railway arrears in our favor. It is quite clear to me that in this situation it might even be convenient for von Neurath to have us undertake steps which would compel Schacht to change his point of view. That is why he so frankly stated to me that his endeavors had failed, and why he did not try to maintain the present situation, which he also considers untenable.

For my part, I did not make any further suggestions, in order to leave us a free hand in negotiations.

While I was dictating this report I received your instructions to be in Warsaw on December 2. I am therefore withholding further conclusions that I intended to suggest when I sent Counselor Lubomirski to Warsaw in connection with tactics to be applied.

I shall present these conclusions to you personally.

Józef Lipski

DOCUMENT 53   Lipski to Beck

NO. 1/90/35

Berlin, November 30, 1935
Confidential

In the course of today's conversation with Minister von Neurath regarding railway refunds, we also took up several matters of general policy.

In connection with the latest conversation of French Ambassador François-Poncet with Chancellor Hitler, Herr von Neurath said that this

[10] For the German version of this conversation, see *DGFP*, Series C, Vol. IV, No. 436. See also *Diariusz*, I, 412, 413, 416, 423–25.

meeting produced no practical results.[11] The French Ambassador raised several points. With regard to the Soviet-French pact, M. François-Poncet supports the thesis of its conformity with prevailing international obligations. He was anxious that the German government should withdraw its reservations and, as Herr von Neurath put it, give the pact its "blessing." However, the Chancellor, although he expressed confidence in Laval's peace policy, did not satisfy the above-mentioned wish of the Ambassador.

Subsequently the French Ambassador suggested that the German government should make a declaration that it has no aggressive intentions toward Soviet Russia. In reply, the Chancellor stressed that in the first place Germany has no common frontier with Russia. He jokingly observed that he would have to embark on a sort of "Argonauts' expedition." He further pointed to declarations he had already made many times. Von Neurath thinks that the French government is anxious to obtain such a declaration in connection with presentation to the French Chamber of the ratification of the Franco-Soviet agreement.

Finally, the French Ambassador asked whether the German government is still in favor of reduction of armaments and the conclusion of the air convention. Declaring his readiness in principle, the Chancellor considered the present moment to be rather untimely for such negotiations, owing to the general political situation and frantic rearmament by the countries concerned. On the other hand, he reiterated his statements made in the May speech [on May 21, 1935] with regard to restrictions of a number of means of waging war.

The communiqué which appeared after the conversation was published at the request of the French side. Its editing was not easy, since none of the concrete points raised by the French side met with a solution.

Von Neurath gave me to understand that he had the impression that the French initiative for the conversation was dictated by tactical reasons with regard to the British government. Von Neurath then deliberated on the internal political situation in France and on the chances of Laval's government remaining in power. He thinks that the fact of the approaching elections is playing into the hands of the Prime Minister, since no other statesman would venture to seek power under such circumstances.

[11] This conversation took place on November 21. After the conversation, on the same day, identical official communiqués appeared in the Paris and Berlin press, giving special importance to these talks.

In accordance with your telegram of November 27, I asked von Neurath about his opinion regarding England's relations with the Soviets in connection with the developments in the Far East. I said that you are taking an interest in this point. Herr von Neurath, also showing great interest in this question, told me that up to now the German government has not been informed of any actual political, or even financial, agreement between the British and Soviet governments. Von Neurath thinks it is too early for that. Nevertheless, the thesis of the German Foreign Affairs Minister is that the British government has a method of far-reaching calculations. Therefore, upon the liquidation of the Mediterranean problem, it will necessarily have to make a shift to Far Eastern problems. Besides, the situation developing there constitutes a serious threat for British interests. That is why the British government is already paying a good deal of attention to the countries which in a future showdown might become considerable trump cards in its hands. Russia, in his opinion, might be one of these countries. Herr von Neurath has already been struck by the fact that during Mr. Eden's trip to Moscow the British government suddenly began to proclaim a theory that Russia is not a danger from the point of view of Bolshevism. This, in Herr von Neurath's opinion, is a very characteristic symptom of the psychology of British policy. At the moment that a distant possibility appeared of a need for the Russian trump card, the hitherto proclaimed slogan of Bolshevik danger was brushed aside.

Von Neurath is watching this problem, as I have already pointed out, from a further and broader perspective; nevertheless, he thinks this matter should be closely followed. Herr von Neurath also feels that the strong position taken by the British government in the Mediterranean question—specifically, keeping full freedom of transit in its hands—is a symptom which can also be explained in connection with the future contest in the Far East. Von Neurath thinks that Great Britain will now liquidate Italy's action. He is pessimistic as to Mussolini's situation. If Great Britain succeeds in enforcing sanctions on oil, the power of Italy's national defense will be undermined. Besides, in von Neurath's opinion, the Italians, after their first easy successes on the territory of Abyssinia, are now encountering real opposition. Ending the conversation on this point, von Neurath said that in his opinion the only narrow escape for Mussolini in case he realizes his defeat, although a very risky one, is to address his nation with a declaration that the Great Powers stood in the way of the realization of the Italian program. In short, to shift all responsibility onto the Great Powers at the right time. Of course, von Neurath sees an ominous danger in such a step from the internal point of view of the Italians.

Józef Lipski

DOCUMENT 54   Lipski to Potocki

NO. N/51/66/35

Berlin, December 14, 1935
Confidential

Upon my return from Warsaw, in accordance with instructions received from Minister Beck,[12] I advised the Auswärtiges Amt on the 7th inst. through the intermediary of the Commercial Counselor that Herr Neurath's reply, which contained no counterproposition of any sort, will make a very bad impression in Warsaw. The Commercial Counselor also informed him that the question is now being discussed in Warsaw of putting into effect the disposition to collect dues for railway transit at the frontier. A copy of the memorandum on this conversation is enclosed.[13]

On the same day, during a dinner at the Embassy, I had a conversation about railway refunds with a member of the cabinet, Minister Frank, who, as is known, is the legal adviser of the Party and the government. I have close and friendly relations with Herr Frank. He told me confidentially that Schacht approached him with a request that he investigate the legal aspect of this problem. Frank was of the opinion that Poland's right to claim refunds is indisputable, despite the fact that this might cause a considerable burden for German finances. Herr Frank added that from his conversation with Schacht he had the impression that the latter considers Poland's currency position strong enough to meet a period of nonpayment.

In reply I pointed out how wrong Herr Schacht was in his calculations on this, stressing the burdens the Polish government has had to impose on the population in order to balance the budget and maintain the currency. Finally, discussing a possible way out of the situation, I sug-

[12] See *Diariusz*, I, 428, 432, 437–46.
[13] Enclosure missing.

gested that the German government pay a certain considerable sum and find a practical solution for the balance.

In principle, Herr Frank thought this suggestion was acceptable. For his part, simply as a suggestion, he cited the sum of 10 million reichsmarks for immediate refund. Obviously concerned over the refund for arrears, Herr Frank promised me personally to exert strong pressure and to discuss the problem with the Chancellor.

During the hunting party at Springe on the 9th inst., I had the opportunity to discuss this subject with Herr von Neurath. I told him that, according to information in my possession, Reich Minister Schacht is not quite aware of the difficulties the nonpayment of amounts due for railway transports is causing to our finances. Neurath was quick to answer that he gave Schacht adequate information. As a result, I agreed with Neurath that the German government should make a counteroffer, and I pressed for immediate payment of a certain sum.

On December 12 Counselor Lubomirski discussed this problem with the chief of the Polish Desk, Herr von Lieres. The latter was already in possession of Moltke's report on his conversation with you.[14] Lieres said that Moltke called his attention to the fact that the situation is serious, with the refund of amounts due still being dragged out. Herr von Lieres once more referred to measures taken on this matter by the A.A. These efforts have up to now been to no avail in the face of Schacht's declaration that he has no foreign currency (Schacht used the expression that he is *ganz nackt*). At present the Auswärtiges Amt is working on the plan of a counterproposition to be presented to us before the holidays. The Commercial Counselor was also informed accordingly.

As far as I could observe the attitude of all competent elements regarding this problem, a certain confusion and desire to make up for the bad impression can be noted. Reich Minister Frank took the longest stride in this direction when he declared to me outright that the situation as it stands today is *untragbar* from the point of view of the prestige of the Reich. Nevertheless, as I am being informed from all quarters, the foreign currency situation has deteriorated seriously, and endeavors to obtain a loan ended in a fiasco. Official *démentis* published to this effect are but a further confirmation that endeavors were undertaken.

In my opinion, it would be advisable to undertake concrete planning on our side as to how we could possibly use finances frozen in the Reich.

[14] See *DGFP*, Series C, Vol. IV, No. 455.

We could, for instance, buy up certain industries in Silesia, such as Wspólnota Interesów [Interessen Gemeinschaft], Pless, etc.; or make some purchases in Germany, for which amounts are earmarked in the budget of the Polish state; or, finally, investigate deals with the Russian triangle, a tobacco loan, etc.

Józef Lipski

DOCUMENT 55   Lipski to Beck

NO. N/128/86/35   Berlin, December 16, 1935
                                                Strictly Confidential

Today I was received by Reich Foreign Affairs Minister von Neurath at his request. Herr von Neurath opened the conversation by stating that he would like to inform me about the conversation which took place on the 9th inst. between the Chancellor and the British Ambassador.[15] Chancellor Hitler would like to see me on Wednesday, at 12:45 P.M., to renew our contact after a long interval. In the course of this audience he will probably give me more detailed information about the above-mentioned conversation. Herr von Neurath therefore limited himself to a brief outline of its essential points.

I stressed that I was grateful for today's reception in connection with your stop in Berlin this evening on your way from Geneva.

In a brief résumé of the Chancellor's conversation with the British Ambassador, Herr von Neurath said that Sir Eric Phipps asked whether the German government still intends to conclude an air pact with the Locarno states, as well as a disarmament agreement. The Chancellor said that he is positively disposed toward the concept of an air pact and the idea of disarmament. Nevertheless, with regard to armaments, the Chancellor's opinion is that time should not be wasted in general vague discussions. He formulated his claims for concrete restrictions of a certain category of weapons in his speech of May 21.

The British Ambassador further inquired whether the German government would be prepared to enter into an air convention with the Locarno states if some of them were linked by special agreements of the

[15] For Neurath's version of this conversation, see *ibid.*, No. 462.

same category. Questioned by the German side as to the meaning of such special agreements, the British Ambassador explained that in this case the creation of bases for the Royal Air Force on the territory of France and Belgium should be taken into consideration. The British Ambassador cited as the motivation for this necessity the distance separating England from the European operational base under the obligations of the Locarno agreements. To the question by the German side, which, I understand, was made ironically, that is, whether the British government would consider it necessary, owing to its Locarno obligations, to establish similar air bases on the territory of the Reich, the British Ambassador answered that such a necessity would not arise owing to the fact that, in case England's guarantee under the Locarno obligations would have to turn against France, the distance from the operational territory would be much shorter from the point of view of the Air Force.

With reference to the above question of Sir Eric Phipps as to whether the German government would agree to an air convention in case it were supplemented by separate agreements of the Locarno signatories, the Chancellor took an absolutely negative stand. He further added that, in case Great Britain engaged in building operational air bases on the territory of Belgium and France, the German government would be compelled consequently to move its operational air force bases westward. Herr von Neurath explained this to me as a cancellation of resolutions pertaining to the demilitarized zone. Besides, the Reich Chancellor declared to the British Ambassador that the concept of such bilateral agreements serving as an instrument for coordination of air forces with the Locarno states in the West should also be applied to the Franco-Russian alliance, in case it becomes a reality; for the German government in its evaluation of the question of armaments restrictions of air forces by means of a pact with Locarno signatories must give a lot of thought to the fact that Soviet air force bases were built on the territory of Czechoslovakia as a result of the Soviet-Czech agreement. The British Ambassador allegedly rejoined by referring to the German government's agreement expressed in Stresa. He received the answer that the Franco-Soviet agreement, which is undermining the Locarno principles, in the opinion of the German government, brought about a change in the situation. Deliberating at length on this subject, the Chancellor allegedly told Phipps that if, for instance, the Soviets attacked Poland, the German government could not remain passive. In that case France, under its agreement with the Soviets, would have to come out against Germany.

At first no communiqué was supposed to be issued on this conversation with Phipps. Herr von Neurath observed that in his opinion it would serve no purpose to issue a communiqué after each conference of an ambassador with the chief of the government, and that my conversation of Wednesday would not be communicated to the press. After the Chancellor's conversation with Phipps, the English press started to disseminate information, so that it became imperative to issue a communiqué. This communiqué appeared in a form similar to that published after the conversation of François-Poncet with the Chancellor.

To my inquiry as to whether Sir Eric Phipps had brought up the question of the Eastern Pact, Herr von Neurath replied that he had not. He added that, bearing in mind the Chancellor's point of view with regard to the Franco-Soviet agreement in connection with the air convention, the question of the Eastern Pact is probably buried for good; it already displayed very few signs of life.

I subsequently asked Herr von Neurath what had impelled the British Ambassador to approach the Chancellor at this particular moment. Herr von Neurath replied that he had also given some thought to this question and that, in his opinion, it was a sort of maneuver in connection with the previous conversation with Poncet.

I then directed the conversation toward the latest developments in the Abyssinian conflict. Neurath did not conceal his critical attitude with regard to the agreement between England and France.[16] He thought this lent a flavor of melodrama to the whole problem, administering a fatal blow to the prestige of the League. He is seeking an explanation for this unexpected change in Great Britain's position. He thinks that this might have been brought about by Laval's declaration that the French

[16] Prime Minister Laval reached an understanding with Great Britain's foreign secretary, Samuel Hoare, on December 8, 1935, regarding Abyssinia. Upon approval by the British government on December 13, this agreement was presented in the form of a note to the Italian government. The Anglo-French plan recommended that the Abyssinian government agree to cede to Italy a portion of its country, rectify the frontier, and create in South Abyssinia a zone for economic expansion and immigration for Italy. This plan met with violent reaction in England as being contradictory to the pact of the League of Nations and the concept of justice. It was the cause of Hoare's resignation on December 18. Prime Minister Baldwin declared on December 19 in the House of Commons that the government considered the Laval-Hoare pact nonexistent, and on December 22 the portfolio of foreign affairs passed to Anthony Eden.

government would not condone oil sanctions. This shifted the whole burden to the government of Great Britain, with all the ensuing consequences.

It might be considered a fact not without its amusing side that the recent developments in the Abyssinian situation have been exploited by local public opinion to express taunts on the subject of the blow that the Great Powers dealt to the high ideals of the League of Nations. Of course, the settlement of the conflict by means of an agreement between the Powers would deprive the German government of the very convenient situation it is presently enjoying in the midst of international turmoil.

Józef Lipski

DOCUMENT 56   Lipski to Beck

NO. N/52/11/35   Berlin, December 18, 1935
                                          Strictly Confidential

Following my report of December 16, N/128/86/35, I am taking the liberty of communicating to you that I was received today at 12:45 P.M. by Chancellor Hitler. The conversation lasted for over an hour.

The Chancellor started with a statement that, in view of developments in the political situation and in particular his conversations with the ambassadors of France and England which were so widely commented on in the press, he would like to have an informative talk with me. He observed that the press greatly exaggerated the real meaning of these conversations. Analyzing the purpose of the interventions of both ambassadors, the Chancellor thinks they were undertaken for reasons of diversion.

The Chancellor then gave a general outline of his conversations with the two ambassadors. His deductions are in accordance with what I related after my conversations with Neurath in my reports of November 30, No. N/1/90/35, and December 16, No. N/128/86/35. I am therefore limiting myself to communicating only the more important parts of these conversations, or those that Herr von Neurath did not mention to me.

Referring to his conversation with François-Poncet, the Chancellor remarked that the French Ambassador was anxious to push to the forefront the question of Laval's meeting with him. However, at the Chancellor's request, Neurath advised the Ambassador to drop this suggestion. In this connection the Ambassador confided to me that it is obvious that in the prevailing situation a meeting with Laval is out of the question. Under the present circumstances the Chancellor cannot meet with Mussolini, for example. The German government is taking a purely neutral stand toward the Abyssinian conflict. However, the Chancellor is rather anxious to maintain good relations with Great Britain, with whom he signed a sea pact. On the other hand, in spite of the unfriendly attitude of the Italian side, the Chancellor considers Mussolini and the Fascist regime positive elements. The Chancellor explained the anti-German attitude taken by the Italian government at the Stresa Conference as an effort to cajole the Great Powers in connection with the already planned action in Abyssinia. According to the Chancellor's words, the German government has no interest whatsoever in taking the part of one side or the other but wishes to remain totally aloof from the conflict. That is why it rejected the British suggestion that it participate in sanctions, as well as their demand to introduce certificates of origin. As far as coal supplies for Italy are concerned, the German government must consider the economic situation of the mines, where each ton of exported coal contributes to the reduction of unemployment. Germany has no intention of drawing any special profit from the present conflict. Export of arms to the belligerent countries was stopped in advance. The French, as the Chancellor put it, replied to this that Germany was not even in a position to supply arms, since it needs them for its own armaments. However, this is a misleading argument, for these small-scale orders could be executed. After all, the Chancellor continued, it is evident that any war industry, in order to maintain itself, has to export. That is why the German war industry is also exporting. If it is assumed that Germany, because of its withdrawal from the League of Nations, is drawing a profit from the present conflict, the Chancellor's reply is that he walked out of the League for quite different reasons than the Abyssinian question, which at that time was still unknown. He also ordered conscription without any knowledge of the oncoming conflict. To make a long story short, all his undertakings had nothing to do with the present development of the Abyssinian question. Certainly, the Chancellor draws some satisfaction from the fact that he is not obliged to sit in Geneva at this moment. As an illustration he noted that quite recently the English pressed him on the problem of sanctions, requesting the introduction of certificates of origin. Today, quite unexpectedly, they made a *volte-face*.

In the ensuing discussion on this subject I said, following your instructions, that we would describe our attitude toward the present situation as follows:

We are not tied to any special doctrine in relation to the League of Nations, that is, with regard to the limits of its competence in general or pertaining to certain regions. However, we deem it to be unquestioned that we are faced with *faits accomplis* enforced on us by certain rules passed in the course of events. I added that this, of course, has nothing to do with our relations with Italy, which are known to be friendly. On this occasion I also mentioned the efforts undertaken by you within the frame of the Committee of Five.

The Chancellor replied that he certainly understands our point of view, which lies beyond the sphere of our relations with Italy and pertains to certain methods of action of the Powers.

The Chancellor remarked in passing on the subject of the League that he sees from today's news that a plan is now being launched, possibly aimed also against Poland, to create a directorate of Four Powers in the League, including Germany. The Chancellor emphatically declared that he has not the slightest intention of entering such a combination.

Deliberating further on his conversation with François-Poncet, the Chancellor remarked that, in order to reinforce Laval, the Ambassador was eager to obtain the blessing of the German government for the Franco-Russian pact. The Chancellor called one of his previous conversations with the French Ambassador (already known to you) when the latter begged that Laval be saved at the cost of the Eastern Pact. The Chancellor then asked the Ambassador how long Laval might remain in power, to which he got the reply that it might be until the fall. The Chancellor then pointed out to the Ambassador that he deemed it impossible to bind his country to a harmful pact in order to prolong the life of a French prime minister by a few months. It was clear from the Chancellor's words that in the course of the last conversation François-Poncet used a similar argument, for Hitler reiterated that in spite of his esteem for Laval he could not jeopardize his vital interests. For this reason he denied the French Ambassador his consent for the Franco-Russian pact, motivating his refusal, first of all, on the fact that the definition of the aggressor remains in the hands of the countries involved. He illustrated this by the fact that in the Oual Oual case the aggressor is still not defined.[17]

With regard to the French Ambassador's wish that the Chancellor make a declaration that the German government has no aggressive intentions toward Russia, the Chancellor in the first place allegedly pointed out that he has no common frontier with Russia. On the other hand, he is not inclined to engage in erratic adventures.

From the conversation with the British Ambassador the following passages are worth commenting upon:

The Chancellor first of all told me that he was surprised that the British Ambassador did not utter a single word, as would quite naturally be expected, about Great Britain's *volte-face* on the Abyssinian problem.

With regard to the British Ambassador's question as to whether the German government is positively disposed to the idea of the air pact and the disarmament problem, the Chancellor's reply was affirmative. He cited a series of arguments in support of this, such as heavy expenses resulting from excessive armaments, etc. On the other hand, the Chancellor criticized the British Ambassador's idea of the application of bilateral agreements within the frame of the air pact. This point was analyzed by the Chancellor in more detail than in my conversation with Herr von Neurath. Specifically, Sir Eric Phipps allegedly suggested an air pact mentioning England, France, and Germany. Other states, it seems, were not mentioned by the Ambassador. But he ventured to suggest an idea that within the frame of this pact special air agreements could be included, such as, for example, French-English and French-Soviet. The Chancellor assumed that with such a concept the general pact would be just a purely formal act. On the other hand, only special pacts would be in force. In practice this could mean Germany's authorization for Soviet air bases in Czechoslovakia or Lithuania, for example. On this occasion the Chancellor said—and this is very significant—that for him Czechoslovakia is the great unknown, if only because of its internal political situation. For instance, he fears that Czechoslovakia may adopt the form of so-called National Communism.

[17] On December 5, 1934, there occured an encounter near Oual Oual on the Abyssinian-Italian Somaliland frontier. The Abyssinian government maintained that Somalis under the command of Italian officers were the aggressors. The Italians claimed that their troops were attacked by the Abyssinian Army which penetrated into Somaliland territory. The problem was never cleared up.

Hitler allegedly told Phipps that he cannot understand the French policy, which binds itself with Soviet Russia. But France is certainly safeguarded by England, and *besides it has a "Ruckversicherungsvertrag" with Poland.*

I consider this declaration of the Chancellor to be very significant.

In his further deliberations the Chancellor stated that he is firmly opposed to drawing Russia westward. As a National Socialist, he sees an ominous danger in Bolshevism. No matter how other states consider this problem, Germany would pay for the rapprochement with Soviet Russia with a social revolution. He is afraid that other countries would also pay for it heavily. He is for European solidarity, but such solidarity ends at the Polish-Soviet frontier. The air pact should have a more general scope, but only those countries should be admitted which are bound by the same principles of international policy. How is it possible to bind oneself to Soviet Russia, which preaches a world revolution?

Finally, the Chancellor also added that his answer to the British Ambassador's question whether nonactivation of the French-Soviet agreement would not change the situation was affirmative.

The above deliberations of the Chancellor could be viewed as general political considerations. I thought it also desirable in this connection to spell out to him certain points of ours.

I said in the first place that I would like to confirm my previous declaration made to the Chancellor that we are dealing with France irrespective of French-Soviet relations. I added that M. Laval was well informed by you about our stand in this matter. I confirmed that we shall not let ourselves become entangled in any deals. Following your instructions, I mentioned your conversation with Hoare during the last session in Geneva. In this conversation, in connection with a reference made by the British Minister to Franco-German relations, you remarked —in the form of a personal opinion—that France's Russian policy is a handicap for these relations. I mentioned in passing that some influences from Russia often cause a certain amount of nuisance for us.

Subsequently, passing to direct Polish-German relations, I remarked that it had not surprised us when, after the first change in the Polish government following the death of Marshal Piłsudski, a number of international elements spread various rumors with regard to a change in our foreign policy line. I stated that Poland's foreign policy, as outlined by Marshal Piłsudski, is primarily an independent Polish policy based exclusively on our interests. Therefore, all competent circles in Poland will follow this policy line. I added that it is quite understandable that opposition to good Polish-German relations exists in many international quarters. The campaigns opposing our rapprochement serve as a proof of this. But in order to avoid feeding this alien propaganda, we should immediately remove any possible friction from our relations. I said that in my estimation the last year had contributed to a successful development in our relations in the general political field, and that positive results had been achieved in cultural and social contacts.

The Chancellor approved this statement with satisfaction and remarked that, of course, a few years are needed to reach a broader détente.

Referring to the necessity of avoiding all possible difficulties, I stressed to the Chancellor that I had a question causing us considerable trouble and concern in the financial field.

Neurath, addressing the Chancellor on his own initiative, said that this concerned railway refunds.

The Chancellor replied that he had already heard about this matter and that, in his opinion, its settlement is indispensable. He will use his influence on Schacht.

I took advantage of this occasion to inform the Chancellor of our financial measures striving to balance the budget and stabilize the currency. I explained to him, well aware that such arguments impress him, the patriotic zeal displayed by the officials and the population in accepting the burdens imposed. However, I observed that under these circumstances the Ministry of Railways cannot be exposed to a permanent deficit from arrears for dues for transit.

The Chancellor asked if a portion could not be compensated by goods. Before I could reply, Neurath explained why this would not accommodate Poland, and the Chancellor understood. On the other hand, Neurath, stressing the necessity of presenting a counterproposition to the Polish government, remarked that a certain portion could be covered by the Soviet triangle, or some other deal, as, for example, Italian, etc. It was agreed that the Chancellor would speak with Schacht.

Subsequently we touched slightly on Rumanian and Baltic questions. Following your instructions I mentioned on the subject of Rumania that some reaction by public opinion could be observed against the excessive pro-Soviet tendencies of Mr. Titulescu. Neurath said that he had heard similar rumors and had received reassuring information a few days ago.

With regard to the Baltic states we also agreed that the problem has abated to a certain extent, and the Chancellor added that relations with Lithuania have also improved a little. He said that the problem of Kłajpeda [Memel], which is of secondary importance as a matter of fact, was to some extent embarrassing, evoking constant tension in German public opinion. But it was awkward for him to stop the press from commenting on persecutions of Germans at Kłajpeda.

At the close of the conversation, the Chancellor suddenly addressed this question to me: "Tell me, why did the British government retreat in the Abyssinian problem?" I replied that, according to information from London, the British Admiralty had certain misgivings as to the advisability of maintaining a concentration of the British fleet in the Mediterranean. Neurath interjected that he had similar information. I also thought that the situation in Egypt and the events in the Far East all compelled Great Britain to cut short the Abyssinian conflict. And finally I added that I had heard from Paris that Hoare allegedly surrendered to Laval.

Taking leave of the Chancellor, I extended New Year's wishes to him and thanked him for his support, which had facilitated me to carry out my mission during this year.

The Chancellor replied very warmly to the greetings, thanking me and my predecessor for such loyal cooperation with him.[18]

I dictated this report in a great hurry owing to the departure of the courier. In summary, I would like to call your attention to the following more important declarations of the Chancellor:

1) His assumption that the Polish-French agreement constitutes a safeguarding element for France. Together with our statement that Poland's relations with France are dealt with by us independently of French-Russian relations, it might be considered to a certain degree an acceptance by the German government of the French-Polish agreement as a *Rückversicherungsvertrag,* for France and for us, without encumbrances to our relations with Germany.

2) The emphatic declaration of the Chancellor that he will not go in for any deals such as the Four-Power Pact or a reorganization of the League of Nations.

3) Clarification at the very source that the problem of railway ar-

[18] For the German version of this conversation, see *DGFP*, Series C, Vol. IV, No. 470. A very condensed text is in the *Polish White Book*, No. 21.

rears is not viewed by the Chancellor from the political angle but simply as a financial difficulty, which does not take for granted what is going through Herr Schacht's head on this matter.

Józef Lipski

The problem of frozen German refunds for transit through Pomerania became considerably complicated at the beginning of 1936.

In Lipski's papers there is a handwritten notice on this matter:

In the first months of 1936 the problem of frozen railway arrears took a very sharp turn, threatening an open Polish-German conflict. On the Polish side the strongest pressure was exerted by the Bank Polski and the Ministry of Finance purely from a currency angle. Through my interventions (conversation with the Chancellor on December 18, 1935, and also with von Neurath),[19] my conversation with Schacht took place on February 15.[20] Schacht clearly gave me to understand that he was ready to liquidate the frozen amount, paying a certain portion in foreign currency and liquidating the balance by way of credits for goods or advancing the amounts due to the German side for the Polish government's take-over of German industrial companies in Upper Silesia (Wspólnota Interesów—Interessen Gemeinschaft).

As a result of this positive conversation with Schacht, I was to continue further conversation with him. However, I contracted a severe cold, and in consequence Warsaw was approached with a proposition to delegate someone else for these conversations. Mieczysław Sokołowski, vice-minister of the Ministry of Industry and Commerce, was appointed and arrived in Berlin. On the eve of the Rhineland occupation on March 6, 1936, Schacht took an absolutely intransigent stand as to payment of a portion of the refund in foreign currency, causing a breach in negotiations and the departure of Sokołowski. I asked for a meeting

[19] For the Beck-Neurath conversation of January 25, see *DGFP*, Series C, Vol. IV, No. 521; for the Lipski-Bülow conversation of January 30, *ibid.*, No. 528; for the Lipski-Neurath conversation of February 4, *ibid.*, No. 537.

[20] *DGFP*, Series C, Vol. IV, Nos. 551 and 567. It should be noted that on February 7 an order was issued by the Polish Minister of Communication limiting transit through Pomerania owing to arrears of refunds by German railways. Whereupon the German government announced a change in railway communications and the opening of permanent communications by sea between East Prussia and the Reich.

with Neurath for the next day. I received the answer that the Reich Minister asked me to meet instead with Secretary of State von Bülow, since he would be very busy that morning. Bülow received me on March 7, at 11 A.M.[21] At 12 noon the Chancellor was to deliver a speech at the Reichstag and it was presumed that the Rhineland problem would be the subject of the declaration.

On the evening of the 5th I gave a large dinner for Herr Goebbels and his wife. Mrs. Betka Potocka and Alfred [Potocki] were also present. The Germans gave no hint as to the text of the Chancellor's speech, in spite of the fact that all conversations revolved around this subject.

Coming back to my conversation with von Bülow, when I informed him that on the previous day a breach in the negotiations had occurred owing to Schacht's intransigent stand, this very stiff and unfriendly-to-us diplomat displayed an animation rare to him and expressed a desire to iron out the impasse. He promised to contact Schacht immediately and in general gave me the impression of being taken completely aback by this turn of events. His embarrassment was very obvious when I pointed out to him that this nonsettlement of the problem of arrears in railway refunds was forcing us to close the transit through Pomerania to East Prussia. Bülow's attitude became clear to me when, upon closing this point of the conversation, he handed me, at Neurath's request, the text of the declaration with regard to the remilitarization of the Rhineland to be presented by the Chancellor during his speech at the Reichstag at 12 noon. I maintained an absolutely noncommittal attitude; von Bülow emphasized that German detachments would only symbolically occupy the Rhineland.

I told Herr von Bülow when I took leave of him that, owing to pneumonia from which I had just recovered, I would not be present at the Reichstag. Immediately upon my return to the Embassy I telephoned Minister Beck to inform him in brief of the text of the declaration that Hitler would present to the Reichstag, even before the Chancellor's appearance. I wired to Warsaw at once the full text of the declaration handed to me by von Bülow.

Together with Counselor Lubomirski I decided to take advantage of the crisis caused by Hitler's breach of the Locarno Treaty to approach the German side with a proposition favorable for us in the settlement of railway arrears.

[21] *DGFP*, Series C, Vol. V, Nos. 22 and 62.

On the evening of the same day, March 7, Lubomirski met Koerner, Göring's secretary of state, at a dinner, and presented in a very dramatic way the consequences of Schacht's breach of negotiations for Polish-German relations against the background of the international crisis caused by the remilitarization of the Rhineland. He observed considerable nervous tension on the part of his German collocutors and a desire to settle the dispute with us. Consequently Göring took over the problem of the frozen railway arrears. . . .

During those critical days of March I had several long conversations with him. It was quite obvious that, under the threat of a conflict in the Rhineland case, he was anxious to make any sacrifice in order to settle the question of railway arrears to our satisfaction, and thus avoid a conflict on the Polish-German sector. He offered, without bargaining, a sum of several tens of millions of zlotys in foreign currency, with the balance of the debt to be liquidated in goods. The results of this understanding, jointly with an agreement for the future, were fixed under the supervision of Göring, who exerted decisive pressure on the German economic agencies. Technical negotiations finalized by an agreement lasted for some time.

The problem of German refunds for transit through Pomerania was settled on April 7, 1936, by a provisional agreement which was to remain in force to the end of 1936. It was agreed therein that beginning with March 25 current dues were to be paid by the Germans every month by way of a cash transfer amounting to a million and a half reichsmarks in gold. Two commissions were also formed to define the size of transit through Pomerania and the method of liquidation of the arrears. In the latter case the possibility of Germany's taking over refunds of the Polish tobacco loan in Italy was to be considered, as well as readjustment of accounts in connection with Poland's take-over of Wspólnota Interesów (Interessen Gemeinschaft) in Upper Silesia.

The settlement of the problem of refunds for transit through Pomerania took place on August 31 and December 22, 1936. Delegates of the ministries of Communication of Poland and Germany signed an agreement in Berlin for regulation of transit between East Prussia and the rest of the Reich, which was to become binding for 1937.[22]

[22] See *Diariusz*, II, 65, 386–87, 70, 72, 74–75, 79–80, 88–89, 91, 101–2, 105–6, 113–15, 138–41, 143–44, 150–54, 156–57. See also *DGFP*, Series C, Vol. V, Nos. 82, 107, 151, 261, 264, 276, 356, and 491.

Remilitarization of the Rhineland (March, 1936) and Blomberg's Directive (June, 1937)[1]

IN LIPSKI'S ARCHIVES there are no materials relating to the problem of the remilitarization of the Rhineland. At that time (February–March, 1936) Lipski was seriously ill with pneumonia; this might explain to some extent the lack of his reports. However, he had some contacts with certain persons in the Reich government and the diplomatic corps, as can be seen from his handwritten notes.

Lipski wrote an article about the Rhineland, which is quoted below. Although it relates to General Blomberg's operational directive of June 24, 1937, fully a year after the remilitarization of the Rhineland, it contains a number of interesting details illustrating the events of March, 1936.

It should be mentioned, as far as Blomberg's directive is concerned, that it pertains to the period of time from July 1, 1937, to approximately September 30, 1938. At that time the directive was still not planned as a German offensive action but was limited to defense in the east and west. This directive was changed by Hitler's order dated May 30, 1938: "to smash Czechoslovakia by military action in the near future." [2]

In Lipski's handwritten notes the following remarks may be found relating to the remilitarization of the Rhineland:

A few days prior to the marching of troops into the Rhineland, the Italian ambassador, Signor Bernardo Attolico, paid me a visit. It was an extremely difficult period for Italy because of sanctions imposed for the aggression against Abyssinia. Italy's vital interest was to see Germany engaged in a conflict with Great Britain and France on the Rhineland problem, thus relieving its own front.

Signor Attolico, using veiled language, touched on the Rhineland question, giving me to understand that the Reich now found itself in unexpectedly favorable circumstances to risk a step allowing it to get rid

---

[1] This article, entitled "Blomberg's Directive of June 24, 1937," was published in *Sprawy Międzynarodowe* (London), 1947, Nos. 2–3.

[2] *DGFP*, Series D, Vol. II, No. 221, enclosure.

of the treaty clauses pertaining to the demilitarization of the Rhineland.

I had the impression from Signor Attolico's words that he was probably in possession of some inside information on Germany's intentions, and that possibly Mussolini's advice might play a certain role in them.

With regard to Göring's opinion on the Rhineland question, Lipski notes the following remarks:

Göring was visibly terrified by the Chancellor's decision to remilitarize the Rhineland, and he did not conceal that it was taken against the Reichswehr's advice. I had several talks with him then. I found him in a state of utmost agitation, and this was just at the time of the start of the London Conference.[3] He openly gave me to understand that Hitler had taken this extremely risky step by his own decision, in contradiction to the position taken by the generals. Göring went so far in his declaration as to say literally that, if France entered upon a war with Germany, the Reich would defend itself to the last man, but that, if Poland joined France, the German situation would be catastrophic. In a broken voice Göring said that he saw many misfortunes befalling the German nation, bereaved mothers and wives.

In the course of these deliberations an aide-de-camp entered with news from London that Germany was to be invited to the London Conference. In his excitement Göring asked for my advice on what to do. I replied that of course I would accept the invitation.[4]

Göring's breakdown during the Rhineland period made me wonder about his psychological stamina. I thought this might be due to his physical condition, since he was using narcotics.

Here begins Lipski's article:

When on June 24, 1937, General Blomberg issued his "Directive for standardizing the preparation of the German armed forces for war," he already had several years of experience and of strenuous efforts to build up Germany's military potential behind him. Hitler cleared his path by his political moves. The declaration of the bill for general conscription, issued on March 16, 1935, contrary to the provisions of the Treaty of Versailles, met with only a formal protest on the part of the Great

---

[3] The London Conference of the Council of the League of Nations opened on March 14. It was decided to invite Germany to take part in the debates on the Franco-Belgian claim concerning the breach of the Locarno agreements.

[4] *Diariusz,* II, 411–14.

Powers that was agreed to at the Council of the League of Nations with Poland's participation. An understanding between the three Western Powers reached at Stresa,[5] aimed at forming a common front against Hitler's Reich, was a short-lived undertaking. Relations between France, Great Britain, and Italy were rapidly deteriorating because of the Abyssinian conflict. With the British government's rejection of the Hoare-Laval agreement of December, 1935 [6]—the last sheet anchor for keeping Italy on the side of Great Britain and France—the policy of sanctions prevailed, creating broad perspectives for German diplomacy. A rapprochement between Berlin and Rome followed that later took the form of a formal alliance.

Availing himself of this favorable international situation, Hitler decided to take another still more risky step, in spite of strong warnings by the Reichswehr. On March 7, 1936, German detachments marched into the demilitarized zone of the Rhineland. This came as no surprise to Paris, London, and Warsaw, since for a long time some new violent stroke by Hitler threatening the safety of France had been anticipated in connection with Germany's interventions against the Franco-Soviet agreement. From the top French military quarters Warsaw received assurances that the French government would counter by force any attempts to remilitarize the zone.

Shortly before March 7, 1936, upon his return from Paris, M. François-Poncet declared to me that, in case of a breach by Germany of the Rhineland Pact resolutions, France would resort to general mobilization. This would result in an armed conflict: "Ce sera la mobilisation générale, ce sera la guerre." The French Ambassador empowered me to make use of this declaration, which he defined as most authoritative. I immediately advised Warsaw accordingly.

In consequence of reports received as to Hitlerite intentions in the Rhineland, Marshal Śmigły-Rydz delegated a trusted officer of the General Staff to get in touch with our military attaché and investigate the condition of German preparations.

Therefore, it was not a surprise to Minister Beck when, upon receiving from Secretary of State Bülow on the morning of March 7 the text

[5] The understanding reached at Stresa by Italy, France, and Great Britain on April 14, 1935, established their common front against the breach of treaty obligations by Germany.

[6] See p. 240, footnote 16.

of the declaration that Hitler was to present an hour later to the Reich-stag, I immediately got in touch with Warsaw by telephone and commu-nicated to the Minister that German troops had begun to occupy the Rhineland.

The Polish government's reaction is known from various diplomatic publications. It was expressed in the immediate declaration of *casus foederis* to the French government.[7] France did not venture independent action, as Poincaré had in 1923.[8] The French government decided to approach Great Britain. The British government, under pressure of paci-fist tendencies in British society, pursued a policy of appeasement toward Hitlerite Germany. Under these circumstances, armed action was not taken against Hitler, nor was his offer exploited as a basis for setting up concrete claims.

The prestige of the Western Powers suffered a serious setback in Europe as a result of the Rhineland problem, expecially in such smaller countries as Belgium, Yugoslavia, and Poland.

Other events in the international field also contributed to reinforcing the German situation at that time. In July, 1936, civil war broke out in Spain. This drew Italy closer to Germany. Ciano's trip to the Reich in October of 1936 brought about the signing of a protocol by the Italian

[7] On March 7, 1936, Polish Foreign Affairs Minister Beck summoned the French ambassador in Warsaw, Léon Noël. "I declared to the Ambassador that in view of the information received on the action of the German troops, which in certain circumstances might threaten to become a French-German conflict, I asked him to inform his Government that should it come to any clash under conditions in accordance with the spirit of the alliance, Poland would not hesi-tate to carry out her obligations as an ally." (Beck, *Final Report*, p. 110.) Noël's version of the same conversation reads: "At the fixed hour I entered the elegant Raczynski Palace . . . . 'This time it is serious,' the Minister said to me. . . . Colonel Beck presently requested me, not without solemnity, to make the following communication to my government on his behalf and in the name of 'high authorities' of the Polish state: Poland is anxious under the circumstances to assure France that she will be true, in case of emergency, to the engage-ments binding her to your country." (Noël, p. 125.) See Noël's telegram to the French Ministry of Foreign Affairs on the same day, where Beck's dec-laration was presented in a very camouflaged form (*Documents diplomatiques français, 1932–1939,* 2 Série, Vol. I, No. 303; also Vol. II, No. 214). See also *Diariusz,* II, 110–11, and *DGFP,* Series C, Vol. V, No. 106.

[8] In December, 1922, when Raymond Poincaré was prime minister of France, the Reparations Commission agreed, against the opinion of Great Britain, that Germany was not carrying out delivery of coal and coke provided for in the reparations agreements. At that time Poincaré presented the question of sanctions against Germany, and, contrary to Great Britain's stand, French and British troops occupied the Ruhr basin.

Minister with Neurath and the approval by Germany of the Italian Empire.

News from Soviet Russia about Stalin's purge within top military ranks, including even Marshal Tukhachevsky, was evaluated by governing circles of the Third Reich, and particularly by the Reichswehr, as a serious weakening of possible Soviet war activities.

This explains why General von Blomberg, when he issued his orders, was inclined to draw an optimistic picture of Germany's international position.

"The general political position," wrote Blomberg, "justifies the supposition that Germany need not consider an attack from any side. The chief grounds for this are, in addition to the lack of desire for war in almost all nations, particularly the Western Powers, deficiencies in preparedness for war on the part of a number of states and of Russia in particular.

"Germany has no intention of unleashing a European war. Nevertheless, the politically fluid situation, which does not preclude surprising incidents, demands a continuous preparedness for war by the German armed forces (*a*) to oppose attacks at any time and (*b*) to enable the military *exploitation of politically favorable opportunities should they occur.*" [9]

Blomberg's directive provided for various hypotheses of war entanglements for which concentrated plans had to be drawn.

In general, military orders are drawn to meet various alternatives of action. The starting point, as a rule, is an evaluation of the political situation by authorities in control of the state's defenses. In the Third Reich, Hitler's word was law. From military orders we therefore can guess the general attitude of the dictator of Germany at that time. Blomberg's disposition was rather defensive in character. This was still before the storm. The marching of German troops and occupation were contemplated only in case of the Hapsburgs' restoration.

In regard to the hypothesis of a war on two fronts—with France in the west, and with Russia and perhaps Czechoslovakia in the east—the directive anticipated that Poland would at first remain neutral, or might assume a wait-and-see attitude. Poland's participation in the war on the side of Russia was considered improbable from the very beginning.

[9] *Trial of the Major War Criminals,* Vol. XXXIV, No. C-175. Emphasis added by Lipski.

The Lithuanian attitude was evaluated along the same lines. It was assumed that Lithuania would only take arms against Germany jointly with Poland, or if Soviet armies marched into its territories.

Regardless of this appraisal, the German command also made preparations in case Great Britain, Poland, and Lithuania entered the war at the outbreak of hostilities. Considering such a state of affairs as a calamity from the point of view of Germany's defenses, the leadership assumed that German political leaders would do their utmost to maintain the neutrality of Great Britain and Poland.

The Battleship *Leipzig* in Danzig and Danzig Problems [1]
Summer, 1936

IN SPITE OF the *détente* in relations between Poland and the Free City which could be noted in the second half of 1933 and following the Polish-German declaration of January 26, 1934, the entire period until the outbreak of the war was marked by continuous incidents in Danzig, often necessitating firm protests lodged by the Polish side in Berlin.

In the summer of 1936 a serious Danzig problem arose in the forum of the League of Nations, this time with the indirect participation of the Reich government. The very roots of the crisis were linked with the struggle of Nazi elements against the Geneva institution, represented in Danzig by Sean Lester, who protested against the *gleichschaltung* of the Free City in the form of liquidation of opposition parties. However, the immediate cause of the conflict was the visit of the battleship *Leipzig* to Danzig on June 25, 1936. In paying an official call, the commander of the *Leipzig* ignored the High Commissioner of the League of Nations. Lester referred the matter to Geneva, claiming a breach of binding agreements. The German side explained the behavior of the commander of the *Leipzig* by the fact that during an earlier visit to Danzig of the battleship *Admiral Scheer* in August, 1935, the commander of that ship had met representatives of the Danzig opposition, vehement adversaries of National Socialism and its Führer, at the reception given by the High Commissioner of the League of Nations, thus creating an embarrassing situation for the representative of the German Navy.

Arthur Greiser, president of the Danzig Senate, was summoned by the Council of the League of Nations on July 4, 1936, to explain the Danzig

---

[1] Published in *Bellona* (London), 1950, No. 1, under the title "Danzig Problems. From the Appearance of Senate President Greiser before the Council of the League of Nations in July, 1936, to Lord Halifax's Visit to Berchtesgaden in November, 1937."

problem. As far as the form and content of his appearance was concerned, it constituted an attack against the Geneva institution unprecedented in the international forum. Finishing his speech, Greiser walked out of the hall, provokingly sticking his tongue out at those present.

This escapade of Greiser caused general consternation. It was interpreted as the intention of the Free City to break relations with the League of Nations by way of *faits accomplis,* and with the Reich's blessing. However, the representatives of the Great Powers sitting on the Council did not manifest a desire for more serious engagements in defense of the statute of the Free City.

Under these critical circumstances, Minister Beck tried to determine to what extent Great Britain's support could be expected in Danzig matters. In a conversation with Minister Eden at the Carlton Hotel, with Tadeusz Gwiazdoski, vice-director of the Political Department of the Polish Foreign Affairs Ministry also present, Beck discussed the possibility of applying measures to prevent further possible action by the Senate and the German government aimed against the authority of the High Commissioner and the League of Nations. With this discussion under way, Beck addressed a question to Eden as to whether the British government would be willing to send a battleship to Danzig under the pretext of a normal visit of the fleet. This step, in Beck's opinion, would be the best measure to display to the German side the importance Great Britain attached to respect for the authority of the League of Nations in the Free City. However, Eden did not think it at all possible to approach his government with such a proposition.[2]

Finally, it was decided in League of Nations circles to entrust Poland with the settlement of this matter. The Council issued a resolution to confer a mandate on the Polish government for clarification of the *Leipzig* incident with the Reich government, as well as to obtain adequate assurances for the future.

On July 5 I received the following instructions by telegram from Minister Beck in Geneva:

[2] Memorandum by Gwiazdoski in Lipski's papers, File 9. The problem of the battleship *Leipzig* is related in more detail by Szembek, *Diariusz,* II, 231, 454–55, 457–72, 241–42, 476–80, and in *DGFP,* Series C, Vol. V, Nos. 419, 429, 430, 434, 435, 436, 437, 438, 443, 458, 467, 472, 473, 476, 524, 557, and 566.

DOCUMENT 57   Beck to Lipski

July 4, 1936

Today's appearance of Danzig Senate President Greiser definitely points to a German attack on the League of Nations. Simultaneously, a wish to respect our rights in Danzig was expressed in his speech. At today's open and secret meetings of the Council of the League of Nations I *still* gained the support of the League of Nations and of the Powers for the *present statute of the Free City.* The ambassadors of Great Britain and France will make a warning *démarche* in Berlin and we are faced with either a disagreement or an understanding with Germany. I shall dispatch additional details. Please obtain an immediate audience with the Chancellor, Göring, or Neurath and declare that in the Polish-German agreement we agreed to consider the problem of the Free City as a measure of our relations.

The visit of the battleship *Leipzig* and the appearance of the President of the Senate at the Council of the League of Nations indicate that Greiser has chosen the method of *faits accomplis* in violation of our agreement that Danzig should not become the object of strife between Poland and Germany. The Polish government is ready to consider the most complicated matters by way of direct discussions, but it would react immediately to any breach of the afore-mentioned agreement.

The statute of the Free City is undoubtedly clumsily formulated; however, it has served hitherto as a basis for Polish-Danzig and Polish-German relations. The breach of this statute must bring on conflict in case a change is not achieved by means of a mutual agreement.

The Polish government deems it possible to deliberate on this matter with Germany prior to the occurrence of events precluding in advance any such contact.

Beck

On the same day I had a long conversation with Göring, on which I reported to Minister Beck:

DOCUMENT 58   Lipski to Beck

NO. G/3/26/36   Berlin, July 5, 1936
Strictly Confidential

Following your telegraphic instructions dated July 5,[3] I had a conversation with Minister President Göring at 2 P.M. today, in the absence of the Chancellor from Berlin.

As a preamble to the execution of your instructions, I stated that on June 19 in my conversation with Secretary of State Koerner I had already raised the question of incidents in Danzig between the National Socialists and the parties of the opposition. On the next day, that is, on June 20, Herr von Neurath on his own initiative informed me about the attitude of the Chancellor with regard to the recent Danzig incidents and stressed that it was a matter of concern to the German government that the Danzig problem should in no way aggravate Polish-German relations. After these soothing explanations I left for a cure at the Lahmann Sanatorium where I read in the papers about Forster's article and the incident caused by the arrival of the battleship *Leipzig*. Yesterday—I continued—a bombshell exploded at Geneva and I received from Minister Beck instructions to present a certain declaration to Minister President Göring requesting him to inform the Chancellor accordingly.

Here Göring interrupted, remarking that the incident in Geneva was by no means directed against Poland's interests. It is a firm policy of the German government as well as of the Senate of the Free City not to infringe upon the rights of Poland and its citizens in Danzig. If during the recent incidents some Polish citizens were hurt, the offenders will be prosecuted. In spite of the fact that some Polish Communists demonstrated in Danzig, orders were issued that they should be left alone. Instructions were also issued to ignore the fact that the German opposition in Danzig used training premises belonging to Polish companies in Danzig. As far as Greiser's performance in Geneva is concerned, it was directed against Lester, who maintains contact with the opposition to the National Socialist Party in Danzig. Allegedly there is proof that Lester coordinates his action with Ziehm. Greiser's speech in the forum of the League was a sort of unloading of grievances accumulated for many years. The German government did not restrain him from this.

[3] The date should be July 4.

However, Göring assured me that, outside of this speech, nothing further will happen.

Here I interrupted Herr Göring to ask him to hear out your instructions. When I finished reading them, Göring promptly referred to the sentence that the Polish government assumes that no events whatsoever could take place to render Polish-German relations impossible to be continued. He stressed that he is in a position to declare most emphatically in the name of the Chancellor and on his own behalf that nothing will happen on the part of the German government and Danzig besides the Greiser speech. He is authorized to declare, in the name of the Chancellor, that, if requested by the Polish government, he can assure us quite categorically on behalf of the German government that

1) neither from the side of the Free City nor from the side of the German government will the Danzig statute, and particularly laws pertaining to Poland, be undermined in any respect;

2) there will never be any question of steps aimed at uniting Danzig with the Reich.

Here Göring once more confirmed that Greiser's whole performance resulted from Lester's behavior and from the fact that Greiser was summoned to Geneva in order to make an explanation, which was embarrassing from the German point of view.

In the course of the conversation I repeatedly underlined the fact that Poland, as a member of the Council, has certain obligations, and I mentioned the resolution of the Council dealing with the *Leipzig* incident. Herr Göring remarked that the Chancellor feels personally offended by the problem of the *Leipzig,* for Lester is blaming him, as commander of the armed forces, that the commodore of the fleet did not call on the High Commissioner, who only last year, in a most tactless manner, compelled a commodore of the German fleet to meet under his roof with a representative of the Danzig opposition who vehemently fights against National Socialism. Herr Göring confided to me that the Chancellor ordered him to declare to the British Ambassador that, if a diplomatic intervention takes place on the *Leipzig* problem, the Chancellor will withdraw his promise to join the League of Nations, for the Chancellor does not want to enter a League which deals in such a manner with orders he delivers to units of the German fleet.

Herr Göring repeatedly asked me to bring his argumentation to your attention and to assure you that not only will the statute be respected but also that other rumors spread all over the world about German aggressive tendencies are absolutely groundless. He also sought a formula for a solution which would avoid any complications of the situation in case I make a *démarche* in Berlin in consequence of the Council's resolution. So, for instance, he mused aloud on my possible questions to the German government (1) respecting the Danzig statute and (2) respecting the rights of Poland and its citizens, to which positive answers were given by the Chancellor.

Lipski

On the same day, July 5, 1936, Beck stopped in Berlin on his way back from Geneva and met with Göring in the evening at a dinner at the Embassy. In spite of Göring's endeavors to pour oil on troubled waters, the atmosphere was rather tense, since it was quite obvious that Greiser's behavior in Geneva was coordinated with the top authorities of the Reich. Göring's statements made to Beck did not differ from those he made to me during our afternoon meeting. It was evident that, in view of the great commotion in international opinion and Poland's firm stand, Berlin would content itself with that drastic anti-League demonstration and would abstain, at least for the time being, from further steps.

The next day the ambassador of France and the British chargé d'affaires intervened at Wilhelmstrasse, in accordance with what was agreed to in Geneva. They both received appeasing explanations. I informed the Ministry of Foreign Affairs accordingly in my report of July 6, 1936.[4]

DOCUMENT 59   Lipski to the Ministry of Foreign Affairs

NO. G/3/27/36   Berlin, July 6, 1936
                                          Strictly Confidential

The Counselor of the French Embassy telephoned Counselor Lubomirski today, stating that the French Ambassador, having received instructions to make a *démarche* on the Danzig problem to the German government, would like to coordinate his action with my intervention.

[4] *DGFP*, Series C, Vol. V, Nos. 436, 437, and 438.

On my direction, Counselor Lubomirski called on the Counselor of the French Embassy and communicated to him that yesterday I had had a conversation with Reichspräsident Göring concerning Greiser's last appearance in Geneva and had received appeasing explanations with regard to respect for the statute and abstention from any *faits accomplis*.

During this conversation at the French Embassy, Ambassador François-Poncet returned from the Auswärtiges Amt, where he had made his *démarche* to the counselor of the Ministry, Dieckhoff, who was in charge in the absence of von Neurath. The French Ambassador informed Counselor Lubomirski that Herr Dieckhoff also gave him reassuring explanations, remarking, however, that the problem of the revision of the Danzig statute was raised by Greiser's speech. Thus, Dieckhoff's statement is to some extent contradictory to Göring's declaration yesterday.

The British Embassy had also tried to contact me since morning. I received the chargé d'affaires, Minister Plenipotentiary Newton, who informed me that he had received instructions from his government to put pressure on the German government in order to obtain from it reassuring statements as to possible further occurrences to follow Greiser's action; and to mention the mandate granted to Poland to clarify the problem of the battleship *Leipzig,* expressing the hope that this might settle the dispute.

Mr. Newton tried to contact Dieckhoff yesterday, and this morning he called on him at the A.A. Herr Dieckhoff first of all made accusations against Lester for his activities in Danzig; he also complained about summoning Greiser to face the forum of the League. Herr Dieckhoff, contrary to what he allegedly said to the French Ambassador, assured Mr. Newton that the revision of the Danzig statute is at present not considered.

For my part I told Mr. Newton that yesterday I had had a conversation wtih Reichspräsident Göring, who also gave me some reassuring explanations. To Mr. Newton's question as to our stand with regard to the statute, I replied that it certainly is the very basis of the whole legal position at present. Mr. Newton also asked whether in our opinion the High Commissioner should safeguard the statute, as Lester did. I gave an affirmative reply, and said casually that the behavior of the High Commissioner in the field is naturally a matter of his personal methods.

In my discussions with the French and British embassies I followed the line of the position you took at Geneva; that is, I did not want to be pushed into a joint *démarche*. That is why I mentioned that I had already had a conversation with Göring yesterday. On the other hand, I maintained a friendly contact with the two ambassadors.

Analyzing yesterday's conversation with Göring, I conclude as follows:

Undoubtedly, Greiser's action in Geneva—coordinated, as we positively know, with the Chancellor and with Göring—was aimed at actualizing the problem of some revision of the statute. Fearing to jeopardize Polish-German relations in view of the reaction of Poland, Herr Göring yesterday deprecated the revision of the statute, at least for the near future. He probably assumed that such a moment would come, and possibly under circumstances more favorable for Germany, in the fall. Some contradictory explanations by Dieckhoff might be due to his misinformation in Neurath's absence, or perhaps he engaged on purpose in tactics which would lead to the question of revision.

Beyond any doubt, the French on their part, as I can see from their press, will bring this problem to the forefront.

Lipski

Obtaining formal assurances from the German government with regard to the *Leipzig* incident was a very embarrassing procedure. Following several burdensome conversations with Neurath, he informed me that Hitler finally agreed to the exchange of notes as proposed by the Polish government; the exchange took place in Berlin on July 24, 1936. The German note ended with a declaration that there was no intention to act against the statute and Poland's rights in the Free City. The Council of the League of Nations accepted the note as the execution of the mandate entrusted to the Polish government.

DOCUMENT 60   Lipski to the Ministry of Foreign Affairs

NO. G/3/46/36   Berlin, July 23, 1936
                                                 Confidential

In accordance with my telegram sent yesterday to the Ministry of Foreign Affairs, I was received at 12:30 P.M. by Director of the A.A. Dieckhoff, who is replacing von Neurath during his absence from Berlin.[5]

[5] *Ibid.*, No. 473.

Dieckhoff communicated to me that Chancellor Hitler expressed his agreement to the exchange of notes proposed by me regarding the incident with the battleship *Leipzig*. Herr Dieckhoff showed me a note signed by Herr von Neurath as a reply to our question. This note is identical with the text proposed by me to Neurath in my second conversation with him on July 9 (No. 6/3/30/36); only the last paragraph contains a slight, but not vital, alteration. This paragraph now reads:

"Hence no intention was suggested of acting against the Statute of the Free City or Poland's rights."

Herr Dieckhoff declared that he is authorized to exchange the notes with me immediately.

We agreed that the exchange of notes would take place tomorrow at 12:30 P.M.[6]

Herr Dieckhoff then communicated to me that Herr Neurath had confidentially expressed the desire that Minister Beck would use his influence in Geneva to induce a change in the post of the high commissioner of the League of Nations in Danzig. I availed myself of this occasion to remind Dieckhoff discreetly that this spring, at Greiser's request as related to me by Göring, Minister Beck had already arranged that Lester's mandate would not be prolonged beyond the fall. However, Greiser later expressed to the British his consent that the mandate be extended for another year. Herr Dieckhoff, deploring Greiser's unwise action, remarked that certainly with the extension of Lester's mandate only until fall the situation concerning the change of commissioners would have been much easier than at present.

Finally, Herr Dieckhoff remarked that he understands that the exchange of notes will not be reported in the Berlin press, since their publication will take place in Geneva.

Herr Dieckhoff plainly stressed in the conversation that the German side is anxious to have the matter settled as promptly as possible, and he gave vent to his concern that Polish-German relations might be endangered by the Danzig incidents. I mentioned in passing yesterday's talk of Greiser with Papée. However, since I had no information on this matter, I abstained from any comment.

I would like to add that, although the press here in general passed over in silence the anti-Danzig demonstrations on Polish territory, in competent circles they gave rise to a certain amount of agitation.

[6] For the text of the notes exchanged on July 24, 1936, see League of Nations, *Official Journal*, November, 1936, p. 1334.

Finally, I am taking the liberty of communicating to you a copy of a rather significant letter received by me from Staatsrat Boettcher of Danzig, who invites me, in Greiser's name, to Zoppot for the Wagnerian plays on July 26 to 28. Of course, I shall refuse.[7]

Józef Lipski

Further appeasing reassurances regarding Danzig were made by Hitler to the undersecretary of state at the Foreign Affairs Ministry, Count Szembek, on August 12, 1936, during his visit to the Olympic Games in Berlin.[8]

At Nuremberg in the trial against Weizsäcker a memorandum was presented on Danzig matters, signed by him on October 15, 1936, when he was still director of the Political Department.[9] It is written from the angle of negotiations to be started between the Senate of the Free City and the Polish government and illustrates the A.A.'s point of view on this problem at the time.

Weizsäcker poses the principle that the problem of Danzig cannot be dealt with separately from the Reich's foreign policy, for the relaxation of possible tension in Polish-German relations depends on how matters are treated in Danzig. Here he is drawing a practical conclusion that the Senate and the unruly Gauleiter Forster must act in close direct contact with the Auswärtiges Amt. The aim of the Danzig policy must be the return of the Free City to the Reich. Under present conditions this is impossible, unless a *coup d'état* is arranged. A *coup d'état* is at present not envisaged, since this would actualize the hitherto unsolved question of the Corridor. In his further deliberations, Weizsäcker considers the subordination of Danzig to the League of Nations as an inconvenient solution. Analyzing the possibility of transferring to Poland part of the League of Nations' right, or possibly even of nominating a Pole to the post of high commissioner, he reaches a negative conclusion. Under the prevailing good Polish-German relations, this would possibly cause a relaxation in the situation but, with a change for the worse, the

[7] Invitation not enclosed.

[8] *Journal*, pp. 196–98; *Diariusz*, II, 259–61; *DGFP*, Series C, Vol. V, Nos. 506 and 513.

[9] The text of the memorandum is in *DGFP*, Series C, Vol. V, No. 605. See also No. 609.

hand of Poland would weigh over Danzig, especially since the high commissioner is authorized, on his own responsibility, to call on the Polish armed forces to restore order to the Free City.

Weizsäcker confirms that under the legally binding statute the high commissioner is authorized to intervene in the Free City's internal affairs.

In his conclusion, he recommends that the Senate seek jointly with Poland a neutral successor to Lester; that it bring about a calming down in the internal situation of Danzig, so that at the next session of the Council of the League of Nations Poland would be able to declare that peace has been restored to the city; that it not grant any concessions in the negotiations with Poland which might in the future create difficulties for the return of Danzig to the Reich; and, finally, that permanent contact be maintained with the A.A. during the negotiations.

In 1937 a change occurred in the post of the high commissioner of the League of Nations in Danzig. Lester was succeeded by Professor Burckhardt, a Swiss (Swiss envoy in Paris, 1945–49). His candidacy— as is now obvious from German documents—was discreetly supported by Weizsäcker. They had been acquainted since 1920 and maintained close contacts until the outbreak of the war. At the Nuremberg trial Burckhardt presented an affidavit in defense of Weizsäcker.

At the Nuremberg trial Weizsäcker, when questioned about the memorandum on Danzig matters, replied verbatim as follows: [10]

"The later incorporation of Danzig as the final aim was justified not only because without a plebiscite Danzig had been taken away from Germany and was almost completely German, but also in a political sense this aim was justified because there was not one problem during the years beginning with 1920 with which the League of Nations had to make such constant and such useless efforts as the Danzig problem. A complete clarification of the Danzig question was essential for any practical European peace policy. I remind you that the Danzig problem at that time was somewhat similar to the Trieste problem, and I don't think that I am the only one who holds that opinion because the British foreign minister, Lord Halifax, one year after I wrote this memorandum, that is, in 1937, in autumn 1937, stated publicly that changes in the European order would have to come sooner or later and that one of

[10] At the session of the court on June 9, 1948 ("Trials of War Criminals," mimeographed transcript, p. 7835, Lipski's Papers, File 23).

these changes for him was Danzig, while another one was Austria, and so on and so forth."

This declaration of Weizsäcker is connected with Lord Halifax's mission to Hitler in November, 1937.

In the disclosed German documents we find a full report of the conversation that took place on November 19, 1937, at Berchtesgaden.[11]

The aim of Halifax's trip was to investigate possibilities for a large-scale British-German understanding, which was the goal of Neville Chamberlain's policy. Toward the end of 1937, with Hitler's power in a state of constant growth, the West showed an increased tendency toward a rapprochement with the Reich. This tendency was apparent not only in Great Britain but also in France. On this subject there is an interesting report by von Papen, dated November 10, 1937, on conversations he had with Minister of Finance Georges Bonnet, Prime Minister Chautemps, François Pietri, Champetier de Ribes, and a number of other politicians.[12]

In his conversation with Hitler, Lord Halifax in principle was of the opinion that the British-German rapprochement should not put a stress on Great Britain's relations with France and Germany's with Italy. He had the idea that, when an understanding between Berlin and London was reached, the four Western Powers would be called on to create common foundations for a lasting peace in Europe; in other words, a reversion to the Four-Power Pact.

Referring to the friendly attitude taken by the British government toward Germany on the problem of the premature evacuation of the Rhineland in 1930, on the cancellation of German war indemnities, and on the remilitarization of the Rhineland (in March, 1936), Lord Halifax remarked that the British side would not insist on maintaining the *status quo* in Europe as a condition *sine qua non*. Great Britain understood that it might be necessary to consider balancing the situation in the light of new conditions and correcting errors committed in the past. Great Britain was only concerned that such changes should be carried out peacefully without resorting to the threat of war. Referring to possible changes in the European system, Lord Halifax at one time pointed concretely to *Danzig, Austria,* and *Czechoslovakia.*[13]

In his reply Hitler engaged in a discussion on Czechoslovakia and

[11] *DGFP*, Series D, Vol. I, No. 31.
[12] *Ibid.,* No. 22.
[13] Emphasis added by the author.

Austria, while he passed over in silence Halifax's allusion to Danzig. Referring several times to Poland in the course of this lengthy exchange of opinion, the Chancellor expressed satisfaction with the good relations he had succeeded in establishing with this state in spite of difficulties inherited from the past.

It should be recalled that a few weeks before Halifax's visit, on the occasion of Polish-German declarations dealing with the treatment of national minorities (November 5, 1937), Hitler made a solemn declaration to the Polish Ambassador on the inviolability of the statute of the Free City and respect for Poland's rights in Danzig.[14] The government of Great Britain was duly informed about this.

Lord Halifax's stand was understood in Berlin as a sort of *désinté-ressement* on the part of Great Britain in the problem of Austria and the Sudeteland, and had a serious impact on Hitler's future decisions.

I do not know whether Warsaw at that time received any alarming news in connection with Halifax's mission. It is a fact, however, that the Ministry of Foreign Affairs, referring to the forthcoming visit of French Foreign Affairs Minister Delbos to Warsaw, urgently requested the Embassy in Berlin to supply more detailed information on Halifax's conversations with Hitler. At first Weizsäcker was reluctant to give such information, describing the meeting as personal and confidential, the results of which were transmitted only to Paris and Rome. When Lubomirski insisted, he referred the matter to Neurath, and with the latter's consent on the same day he gave a general outline of the conversation and characterized Halifax's opinion about Danzig as a vague remark to which Hitler did not react.

When Beck passed through Berlin on January 13, 1938, the Chancellor repeated to him word for word the declaration on the matter of respecting the legal situation in Danzig as made on November 5, 1937. In connection with rumors about the possibility of the withdrawal of the League of Nations from Danzig, Hitler confirmed during this conversation that his declaration was binding independently of the fate of the League of Nations.[15]

Here Lipski's article ends.

Coming back to the Danzig problems at the end of 1936, it should be stressed that Nazi elements in the Free City permanently maintained the

[14] *DGFP*, Series D, Vol. V, No. 19.
[15] *Ibid.*, No. 29.

explosive state of Polish-Danzig relations, in spite of the many promises made by Hitler and Göring.[16] For example, in October, 1936, the Danzig Senate issued a number of rulings of a commercial character detrimental to Poland's interests. On October 31 an armed Nazi band attacked a Polish home at Schönberg (near Danzig). The Commissioner-General of Poland in Danzig intervened in this case, and the Senate promised to investigate.

The Danzig Senate also created the Landesarbeitsamt, a labor exchange office, designed to render it impossible for Poles to obtain work. And again on November 7 the Commissioner-General had to intervene in this matter.

These incidents met with a strong reaction from the Polish community, especially at Gdynia, as well as from the Polish press.[17]

At this time Lipski twice discussed the problem of conflicts in Danzig with Göring (these reports are missing from Lipski's papers). According to what Szembek notes in his journal (Diariusz, II, 326), Göring "expressed a wish to remove all misunderstandings which had occurred in this matter. Next, in a most confidential manner, he told the Ambassador about Hitler's opinions on the problem of Pomerania and Germany's connections with East Prussia. Specifically, the Chancellor would wish—against compensations to be granted to Poland in another field—to obtain easier access for Germany to East Prussia. This might be achieved by the construction of a superhighway through Polish territory, as well as the creation, under Poland's supervision, of transit for German railways across Pomerania. Hitler thinks these plans cannot be realized at present, but he envisages them as projects for the future."

This inflammatory situation is described in the conversation of Beck with Ambassador von Moltke in Warsaw.[18]

At the beginning of September there was held in Nuremberg, as usual, a congress of the National Socialist Party. Lipski was there, together with the heads of other diplomatic missions.

DOCUMENT 61   Lipski to Szembek

NO. N/7/121/36   Berlin, September 16, 1936
                                  Strictly Confidential

I returned yesterday from the Congress at Nuremberg and I shall dispatch a detailed report by the next courier.

Following up the conversations you had with authoritative German elements during the Olympic Games in Berlin, I tried to present the

[16]*Ibid.*, Series C, Vol. V, Nos. 623, 628, 635, 636, and 639.
[17] See *Diariusz,* II, 314–16, 521–26, 325, 330, 534–35.
[18]See *Polish White Book,* No. 26, where the conversation is given in abbreviated form. The full text is in Lipski's papers, File 9.

results of General Śmigły-Rydz's trip to France in a suitable light.[19] I laid stress on the fact that Poland's foreign policy has remained absolutely unaltered, and that conversations were held on a purely bilateral military Polish-French ground. Easiest to digest for the German side is the argument that the revival of the Polish-French alliance contributes to the devaluation of the French-Soviet alliance, and also that it has an impact on the nationalistic shift in focus of the internal policy in France. This argument is most persuasive in the present psychological atmosphere of anti-Bolshevism in Germany. The press attaché of the Embassy, Mr. Wnorowski, followed this line in his interviews with the local press at Nuremberg. . . .

Although competent German circles allegedly understand and properly evaluate our recent moves in relation to France, popular reaction is rather unfavorable. A similar reaction may be observed among those personalities who after all were wrong in their assumption that contracting good Polish-German relations would once and for all definitely cut off the link uniting Warsaw with Paris.

A particular touchiness with regard to all symptoms in Poland's relation to Germany may be observed from press articles—acting as an instrument of public opinion—especially those against our press. In a number of communications from Warsaw in the local press yesterday and today, annoyance is obvious because of negative comments in our press with regard to the political meaning of the Nuremberg Congress. Here Smogorzewski's telegram in *Gazeta Polska* is an exception.

Under these circumstances I am taking the liberty of suggesting that influence be exerted on the Polish press (if possible on all its segments) to inspire it to comment most cautiously on German matters.

I would like to remark that the thesis of foreign correspondents attending the Nuremberg Congress as disclosed in the course of the first

[19] In connection with Polish-French military relations, two visits took place in August-September, 1936. General Gamelin, chief of France's General Staff, visited Poland on August 12–18, and General Śmigły-Rydz, general inspector of the Polish Army, visited France on August 30-September 6. He participated in the grand maneuvers of the French Army and had a number of conversations, finalized by the Rambouillet Agreement of September 6 with regard to Polish-French technical and financial collaboration. On the basis of this agreement Poland received a loan of 2 billion French francs, half of which was in gold and the other half in matériel. Of this second portion Poland received only 13 percent before the outbreak of the war. Problems of the military alliance of Poland with France are related in *Diariusz*, II, 433–39; for the stay of Śmigły-Rydz in Paris, see *ibid.*, pp. 488–97.

days of the conferences—that the Chancellor in his anti-Bolshevik declaration tried to impose on particular states the choice of either Communism or Fascism—does not correspond with the actual situation. I shall return to this question in my report. The Chancellor stated that Italy, a state which definitely threatened Bolshevism, is sympathetic to the National Socialist movement. The same is true of all other states which in their own way oppose the destructive action of Moscow. Nevertheless, he made the reservation that he is not imposing the system of National Socialism, labeled "made in Germany," on any foreign state.

I was invited to Rominten for September 28 and 29 by General Göring, with whom, unfortunately, I could not get in touch at Nuremberg. Neurath told me that he would also be at Rominten. I think that I should then talk more authoritatively with the ministers of the Reich. I would therefore like to be in Warsaw prior to this date and to have an audience with General Śmigły-Rydz, owing to some prejudices in this territory which are well known to you. I shall talk this over with Minister Beck tomorrow when he passes through Berlin on his way to Geneva.

Józef Lipski

From November 25 to November 28, 1936, Mr. Victor Antonescu, who became foreign minister of Rumania after Titulescu's resignation,[20] paid an official visit to Poland.

In the same month, two eminent Rumanian politicians, who were in opposition to the government, proceeded on a political trip to Western capitals.

In Berlin they called on Ambassador Lipski, about which Lipski writes in the reports that follow.

DOCUMENT 62   Lipski to Beck

NO. N/52/9/36   Berlin, November 20, 1936
                                           Strictly Confidential

From reports of our Legation in Bucharest dated October 28, No. 52/R/83, and October 30, No. 52/R/85, I learned of the planned trip of Messrs. George Bratianu and Atta Constantinescu to Berlin, Brussels, and Paris.

[20] *Diariusz*, II, 342–43, 553–54.

The politicians paid me a visit at the Polish Embassy on November 5. I had not seen either Bratianu or Constantinescu since our meeting in January of 1936, on which I reported at that time to the Ministry of Foreign Affairs in my letter dated January 27. Mr. Bratianu expressed satisfaction over the improvement in Polish-Rumanian relations since Titulescu's departure from government. He informed me about his recent conversations with the foreign minister of Rumania, Mr. Antonescu, and with Count Ciano in Rome. These have already been related in the above-mentioned reports of our Legation in Bucharest. He was visibly disturbed by Mussolini's last speech delivered in Milan,[21] a paragraph of which is devoted to the support of Hungarian revisionism. In connection with Count Ciano's visit to Berlin, Bratianu is wondering whether this speech is the result of opinions duly coordinated between the Italian and German governemnts.

In the course of a long debate I expressed the opinion that during Ciano's conversations with German statesmen they defined their points of view only with regard to Austria. This had been made clear in the press declaration of Italy's Foreign Minister at Munich, while no agreement—in the broader sense of the word—had been reached with regard to the Danubian basin. I am confirmed in this belief by the fact that governing spheres of Germany were rather critical of Mussolini's speech.

Mr. Bratianu told me that this time he would like to be received by the Chancellor of the Reich, especially since Mr. Goga, the head of another political party, had already obtained an audience with Hitler during the Olympic Games. He stressed that he would remain in constant contact with me and would inform me extensively about all his conversations in Germany, as well as about his impressions from Paris and Belgium.

After his talk with Göring, Mr. Bratianu is even more convinced that, as far as the Rumanian and Hungarian problems are concerned, no conformity exists between the Italian and German points of view. Rather, a rivalry prevails. Göring is definitely critical of Mussolini's speech. Göring also mentioned that while he was in Budapest for the funeral of Gömbös [22] he could see Ciano's obvious reserve toward any particularly friendly manifestations shown to him by the Hungarian side. Göring defined his attitude toward the Rumanian question by stating that

[21] The speech was delivered on November 1, 1936.
[22] General Julius Gömbös de Jákfa was prime minister of Hungary from 1932 to 1936.

the German government is ready to safeguard Rumania from Hungarian revisionism in the same way it protected Yugoslavia against it. But this on the condition that Rumania frees itself from commitments to Soviet Russia. Besides, Herr Göring drafted plans for possible German-Rumanian economic collaboration. He would be prepared to consider during the next six months all more concrete prospects for such collaboration with Rumania, within the frame of his four-year plan now under elaboration. Finally, Göring promised Bratianu that he would arrange a meeting for him with Hitler.

Messrs. Bratianu and Constantinescu left for Paris for a few days, and returned to Berlin on November 15. The next day Bratianu was received by Neurath, whose deliberations followed the same line as Göring's, but in a more prudent tone. Later, Bratianu was received by the Chancellor.

The Chancellor's deliberations can be recapitulated in the following three points:

1) The Reich would be prepared to influence Budapest to restrain its revisionist aspirations toward Rumania when it is assured that the Rumanian government would free itself from the influence of Soviet politics.

2) When Bratianu explained that they have an alliance with France and Poland, the Chancellor took the stand that these agreements create no obstacle for German-Rumanian collaboration.

3) The Chancellor laid special stress on tightening German-Rumanian economic relations.

In the Chancellor's reasoning there were also comments about Poland. He said, for instance, when he stated that the Reich cannot claim reunion of all regions inhabited by Germans beyond its frontiers, that for the sake of about 300,000 Germans living in Poland there is no reason to create difficulties in the relations between Poland and Germany.

The Chancellor also mentioned the Corridor, stating that, since a nation of 35 million needs access to the sea, this problem has been removed from the agenda.

These two passages dealing with Poland—mentioned to a Rumanian statesman—are, in my opinion, of great positive meaning, especially since they were uttered at a moment of persistent tension over Danzig problems.

About France the Chancellor allegedly repeated his previous arguments that he has no territorial quarrels with that country. Here he made a rather characteristic allusion—with regard to raw materials and colonial aspects—to a possible compromise with France in that field, not in the sense of territorial expansion in French colonies, but in the spirit of economic collaboration with France and its colonies. I am laying special stress on this point because this is the first time such an idea of the top German authorities has been brought to my knowledge.

On the next day Mr. Bratianu left Berlin, proceeding to Brussels for an audience with the King. He will then go to Paris to be received by Prime Minister Blum.

Mr. Bratianu also shared with me his impressions from an earlier stay in Paris for a couple of days. As a positive element of the situation in France he considered the fact that M. Daladier, minister of war, is to some extent purging the army of Communist elements. As far as the internal situation of France is concerned, Mr. Bratianu's opinion is rather pessimistic. French policy shows symptoms of considerable deterioration.

High-ranking factors in France made it clear to Mr. Bratianu that under the present circumstances Rumania cannot count on any kind of military assistance from France. As a symptom of France's reaction, March 7 was cited to Mr. Bratianu, followed by a declaration that the French soldier would only take up arms if the enemy crossed French frontiers.

Mr. Bratianu was rather impressed by the evaluation of the Czechoslovak situation made to him in Paris. The French are of the opinion that the position of Czechoslovakia is tragic, with the bulk of Hungarian revisionism concentrated in its direction. But competent spheres in France did not deem it possible to give assistance to Czechoslovakia in case of emergency.

The above conversations held in France and Germany further confirmed Mr. Bratianu in his basic thesis that Rumania must undertake a more independent policy based upon purely national interests. In his opinion, both Rumania and Poland should stay aloof from the struggle of the two blocs devoted to different ideologies. He first defined this policy line as neutral politics, evidently having Belgium in mind. However, he corrected this definition as inaccurate, referring to alliances his country is partner to. Mr. Bratianu thinks that it would be advisable to start a more active policy against Germany. Yugoslavia evidently represents some sort of bait for him as far as safeguarding Rumania against Hungary's revisionism is concerned.

When discussing all these problems, I tried to point to the fact that in the economic field no particularly positive results should be anticipated from collaboration with Germany, since the Reich finds itself on the path leading toward ever-tightening autarchy. Also, when Mr. Bratianu mentioned possible collaboration with Germany in the field of armaments, I tried to make it clear to him that regardless of the increase in economic turnover between the two countries, which in his opinion would be profitable for Rumanian export, certain caution should be observed, bearing in mind that Rumania, as well as Poland, should take into account its proximity to Soviet Russia.

Apart from these conversations with Messrs. Bratianu and Constantinescu, which must be kept in strict confidence, a few days ago I had a visit from the Rumanian envoy, Mr. Comnen, who just returned from Bucharest. From the long conversation I had with him I could deduce that Mussolini's last speech evoked strong dissatisfaction in Rumania. These ill-feeling will probably be exploited by Germany for its own ends.

Józef Lipski

DOCUMENT 63   Lipski to Beck

NO. N/52/10/36   Berlin, November 28, 1936
                                          Strictly Confidential

With reference to my report of November 20, No. N/52/9/36, I am taking the liberty of communicating that I received further information pertaining to Mr. Bratianu's conversations with the King of Belgium and M. Delbos, the foreign minister of France.

The Belgian King allegedly laid special stress on Belgium's tendency to conduct its own independent national policy. Therefore it will form its relations with particular states in accordance with its own national policy. The Belgian King referred here to Poland as a state that succeeded in basing its foreign policy on the interests of the country. The King of Belgium further stated that he is at present finalizing an agreement with Holland based on such principles. In his opinion, Rumania, through its alliance with Poland, should follow a similar policy.

The King was allegedly satisfied with Hitler's statement made to Mr. Bratianu with regard to the fact that the Reich would fully respect Belgium's sovereignty.

Mr. Bratianu was impressed very positively by his conversation with the Belgian King.

In his conversation with M. Delbos, Mr. Bratianu referred in the first place to his previous meeting with the French Foreign Minister several months ago, stating that Mr. Titulescu's resignation from the post of foreign minister resulted from Rumania's reaction—as foreseen by Mr. Bratianu—to the attempt to draw it into the orbit of Soviet Russia. Allegedly Mr. Bratianu quite bluntly declared to Delbos that pushing Rumania into an agreement with Russia had to be obviously understood in his country as a desire to shift to Russia obligations deriving from the French-Rumanian alliance. To this M. Delbos retorted that the chief aim of the French-Russian agreement was to draw Germany away from Soviet Russia, that is, to counteract a possible renewal of the Rapallo policy. At present the signing of the German-Japanese agreement, in the opinion of the French Foreign Minister, definitely canceled such a possibility. Therefore, the attitude of the French government toward an agreement with Russia might also be subject to certain alteration. M. Delbos, aware of the fact that 60 percent of the French nation desires an understanding with Germany, cannot oppose the establishment of closer contact between Rumania and the Reich. In his opinion, Rumania should follow the line of policy as pointed out by Poland. Here M. Delbos laid special pressure on his statement that, in spite of all appearances, the line of the French-Polish alliance had been constantly maintained, and that complete accord prevails between your opinions and those of the French government. A certain superficial misunderstanding has been removed by the trip of Marshal Śmigły-Rydz to France. This trip evoked symptoms of friendship for Poland in the French nation.

Mr. Constantinescu, who reported on the two above-mentioned conversations to me, stressed how deeply both he and Mr. Bratianu were impressed by the fact that the Belgian King, as well as M. Delbos, cited the foreign policy conducted by Poland as an example to be followed and laid stress on the alliance between Rumania and Poland. Mr. Bratianu stated that the closest possible collaboration with Poland is the basic foundation of his policy. Starting from this premise, he fought against Titulescu.

The above reports are evidently only fragmentary, since the conversations were only briefly reported to me by Mr. Constantinescu.

Expressing their satisfaction over the trip of Foreign Minister Antonescu to Warsaw, Messrs. Bratianu and Constantinescu declared their intention to visit Poland at the beginning of next year.

My observations with regard to the reception offered locally, as well as in Belgium and France, to Mr. Bratianu, in spite of the fact that he is going as a private individual, confirm my opinion that his position abroad has gained considerable weight since last year. Perhaps Titulescu's resignation contributed to this, since it forces the government to seek a factor to play a leading political role in Rumania.

Józef Lipski

Beck's Conversation with Neurath

January, 1937

WHEN HE WAS in Warsaw at the end of 1936 (on December 10), Lipski informed Vice-Minister Szembek about the internal situation in Germany, which he considered very difficult in the financial and economic fields.[1]

On January 11, 1937, at the annual reception of Chancellor Hitler for the diplomatic corps, Hitler, talking with Ambassador Lipski, expressed his hope for a positive solution to the Danzig problems and stressed the importance of the Polish-German agreement of January, 1934.[2]

Ten days later Minister Beck, on his way to Geneva to a session of the Council of the League of Nations, stopped for one day in Berlin and had a conversation of a general character with Minister von Neurath.

DOCUMENT 64 Memorandum on the
Conversation of Minister Beck with von Neurath,
the Reich Minister of Foreign Affairs,
held on January 20, 1937 (11:30 A.M.–1 P.M.)
in the presence of Ambassador Lipski

1. Danzig

Herr von Neurath began the conversation by stating that the first matter to be discussed would be the problem of Danzig. He added that, as he was informed, a Polish-Danzig agreement had been reached, thus bringing about a *détente* in the situation.[3]

[1] *Journal,* pp. 218–19.
[2] *Polish White Book,* No. 27.
[3] On January 6 negotiations were terminated in Danzig concerning Poland's rights in the Danzig harbor. The Senate of Danzig made a declaration confirming its readiness to respect all political and economic rights of Poland under the treaty and the agreement. The Polish government on its side stressed its readiness to respect and not to transgress on economic and legal relations binding under the statute of the Free City and obligatory agreements.

Minister Beck confirmed this, adding that additional talks on technical issues would follow. He did not wish to deal immediately with these matters under the new agreement, so that it would not look as though Poland was trying to exploit the situation because of its mandate in the League of Nations. Minister Beck underlined the fact that the Danzig problems evoked quite an uproar in public opinion recently, and he therefore deemed it advisable to deal with them from a proper angle in his speech delivered at the Senate Commission.[4] He stressed in this speech how necessary it was to respect mutual rights.

Minister Beck further told von Neurath that Poland was not demanding an extension of its rights, since it was only concerned with the maintenance of the balance.

Passing to the question of the high commissioner, Minister Beck stressed that he presented the principle that the new candidate should not have connections with the secretariat of the League of Nations. Herr von Neurath readily shared this opinion. In Mr. Beck's opinion the candidate should be a person belonging to a neutral country, independent and not subject to influence from the outside. Perhaps an army man with a good record of service.

As to the attributes of the commissioner, von Neurath mentioned casually that it would be desirable that he should keep aloof of internal matters.

Minister Beck replied loosely that some formulas for this have been provided.

The [Polish] government contacted the Senate formally with regard to the candidates, and some of these candidacies were discussed: two Norwegians, one Portuguese. Of course, the problem will be settled definitely in Geneva. Minister Beck added that, since he is in touch with Eden, he has reason to believe that the British Foreign Secretary shares his concept of the type of candidate.

Herr von Neurath stressed that these particular candidates are not known to him, and he thinks that Eden, in his capacity as *rapporteur*, would only welcome an agreement between Poland and Danzig which would relieve him of further difficulties. However, he agreed with Mr. Beck that some unexpected complications might, as always, be in store

---

[4] Beck's speech at the Commission for Foreign Affairs of the Polish Senate on December 18, 1936. See J. Beck, *Przemówienia, deklaracje, wywiady, 1931–1937*, pp. 272–73.

for us in Geneva. He therefore advised Greiser to be present in Geneva and to contact Minister Beck personally if necessary.[5] As for Forster, whom he considered a very unruly individual, von Neurath remarked that he had taken measures to keep him within the proper limits. Von Neurath requested that Forster should communicate with him, and he now does this when he comes to Berlin.

Forster intended to call on Minister Beck presently in Warsaw. Von Neurath had restrained him for the time being, since he thought this might not be convenient for Minister Beck. However, both Minister Beck and von Neurath were of the opinion that such a visit by Forster to Warsaw might be advisable at the right time. Herr von Neurath, confirming in principle that the Danzig problems should not weigh on Polish-German relations, referred to Hitler's statement on these lines made recently to Ambassador Lipski at the New Year's reception of January 11. Minister Beck also expressed the hope that Polish-Danzig relations would now take a normal course and he indicated that, acting in Danzig's favor, he had taken up the question of lowering the high commissioner's salary, which weighed so heavily on the modest budget of the Free City. Von Neurath stressed the importance of this measure, since the high figure of the salary aroused criticism.

2. *The Problem of the Raw Materials Committee in Geneva*

Minister Beck explained that he had received information that the secretariat of the League of Nations omitted Germany when it investigated chances for collaboration in this committee of some countries who were not members of the League and when it consulted these countries. Minister Beck, as a *rapporteur,* firmly took exception to such discriminatory methods. Minister Beck stated on this occasion that he would discuss with Herr von Neurath Germany's attitude toward the Committee of Raw Materials.

Herr von Neurath replied that for the time being the German government is not prepared to participate in the works of the Raw Materials Committee. The Chancellor, whom von Neurath asked some days ago about his opinion on this question, took the same point of view. Although von Neurath was not expecting much from the committee's activ-

---

[5] The chairman of the Council of the League of Nations nominated a Swiss, Professor Charles Burckhardt, as high commissioner of the League of Nations on February 17.

ities, he preferred not to slam the door for the future but just to wait and see how things develop.

Summing up his present activities on the problem in relation to Germany, Mr. Beck stated that there are two possible alternatives. Either he should declare at Geneva, referring to his conversation with von Neurath, that the German government will not join the committee, or he should admit a formal consultation, to which the German government will give its reply.

Following Herr von Neurath's idea not to slam the door on this matter, Minister Beck suggested the following solution: he will state in Geneva that in his talks with the German government he noted interest in the problem, but he is not certain whether under the present circumstances, if a consultation followed at a later stage, the Reich government would define its stand more precisely. Von Neurath expressed his appreciation for this suggestion and accepted it, remarking that at the consultation he would reply so as not to exclude further possibilities.

3. The Geneva Convention

Herr von Neurath, remarking that the term of the Geneva Convention on Upper Silesia expires in July, stated that it will be necessary for the two governments to give attention to this problem in order to find some solution.

Minister Beck replied that from the political point of view it is better that the situation prevailing thus far come to an end, and that the situation is becoming clear.

Von Neurath shared this opinion.

Minister Beck stated further that in case of technical problems requiring settlement prior to the expiration of the convention, such as in railway or mining matters, they should be discussed.

Ambassador Lipski stressed that he had just received such instructions from Warsaw dealing with railway questions, which he will submit to Herr von Neurath or, as they are of a purely technical character, to the Secretary of State.

Herr von Neurath, not going into details, limited himself to the remark that discussions on such technical and economic problems should be undertaken because they are so essential for the local population.

Minister Beck again laid stress on the fact that technical matters will have to be negotiated.

4. Spanish Matters

Herr von Neurath gave some explanations on this matter. He reported that the German government will give an answer to the British government in the coming days regarding volunteers. This answer, as well as the first one, will be positive. Herr von Neurath stated confidentially that the German government had already issued an order to stop shipments of volunteers. The Italian government allegedly is considering a similar prohibition. Von Neurath also mentioned similar British dispositions and the latest French law.

In von Neurath's opinion the next step will be the problem of controls, which is under discussion in the nonintervention committee. By these means, as he put it, they would reach "zur Einkapselung" of Spain. The Civil War would probably still go on, but without participation from the outside. Spain, which in von Neurath's opinion has no elements for becoming a Fascist state, would find some way to rule itself. There is just one thing that neither the German nor the Italian government would stand for, and that is a Communist state in Spain. This stand of the two governments is in the interest of the whole of Europe. Here Herr von Neurath, asking if Mr. Beck shared his opinion, stressed that it seems as if the Soviets have recently been backing out of the Spanish affair.

Referring to the recent tension in the case of Morocco, von Neurath declared that this whole anti-German campaign had no foundations whatever and that a talk between Hitler and François-Poncet had put an end to it. He agreed that naturally Germany receives, as compensation for war matériel, raw materials from mines in the zone occupied by General Franco (Rio Tinto and Morocco). He mentioned brass as an example. However, he remarked that with the end of war supplies, which of course is inevitable, the flow of raw materials from Spain to Germany will also cease.

5. Italy and England

Herr von Neurath corrected the current opinion that the newly reached understanding between Italy and Great Britain is not convenient for the German government. Without this understanding, he added, our whole friendship with Italy would be worthless. He personally persuaded Ciano to negotiate with England. Hitler, without contacting him, made a statement along the same lines to the Italian Foreign Affairs Minister.

Herr von Neurath was of the opinion that the Italian-British agreement did not remove basic controversies, which still exist. But it contributed to a clarification of the atmosphere of British-Italian relations, which at any moment, even for a trifle, could result in a conflict. Such a situation was a hindrance to any policy.

6. French-German Relations

Herr von Neurath noted a certain *détente* in the sector of French-German relations. He remarked that he could feel some inclination in Blum as well as in Delbos for a rapprochement with Germany. Presently it will be started by a resumption of French-German trade negotiations. But he cannot predict whether concrete results will be obtained in French-German relations. As usual, when dealing with France, Herr von Neurath thinks that, even if the French government desired an agreement with Germany, it might not be able to achieve it, since this could result in the downfall of the cabinet.

7. The Western Pact

Herr von Neurath observed that the events in Spain pushed the problem of the Western Pact into the background. It might, however, again become timely as the result of a certain relaxation in French-German relations.

Minister Beck made a longer statement defining our general concepts with regard to the Western Pact.

He pointed out that in principle we conceive of this pact as an understanding with Germany, and not against Germany. That is why he directed Ambassador Lipski to establish contact with the German government on this problem.

Bearing in mind that the old Locarno concept is no longer timely, Minister Beck stressed the available possibility of finding other forms of understanding. Realizing the difficulty created by the French-Soviet agreement, Minister Beck remarked that a certain reaction might be observed in French public opinion against excessive engagement with Soviet Russia. Here the Polish-French alliance is an instrument enabling French opinion to evolve in this respect. The defensive and bilateral character of this alliance is well known to the German government. Herr von Neurath agreed with this. In the Western Pact this Polish equivalent could relieve the situation. The fact that the Polish-French alliance was concluded before Locarno is an argument in support of this concept.

In his deliberations, Herr von Neurath also laid stress on the fact that the old Locarno concept is now out of date. The British, as he remarked, are holding on tight, as usual, to the old ideas, and therefore some time may pass until they change their minds. Herr von Neurath sees a considerable difference of opinion in the British and Italian points of view.

Von Neurath listened to Mr. Beck's statements with great interest. He remarked that the problem requires long-lasting negotiations, and added that he will maintain close contact with us.

8. Austria

Minister Beck stated that he would like to raise a point which Herr von Neurath might not be prepared to answer. Namely, he would like to have some idea as to the relation of the Reich toward the present Austrian government. Minister Beck stressed that this question is connected with a certain possibility of visits. He made the reservation that Poland has no special political interest in Austria. The two countries, however, have considerable economic ties, if only resulting from earlier trade between Małopolska [Galicia] and Vienna.

Herr von Neurath remarked that the best reply would be if he informed Minister Beck, for the time being quite confidentially, that in a month he intends to go to Vienna. Von Neurath confirmed an improvement in relations with Austria, defining it as the return to a normal situation. He stressed correct relations with the Austrian government.

In this connection, Minister Beck pointed to our unchanged stand with regard to the Danubian basin, which was defined at the time of the plan of the Danubian pact.

9. Rumania

Herr von Neurath pointed to a certain noticeable improvement in German-Rumanian relations, which occurred after Titulescu's departure. The only thing that causes him some anxiety is that Titulescu is allegedly recovering from his illness.

Minister Beck strongly lauded the very logical and quiet activty of Minister Antonescu.

10. Minister Beck brought up the problem of the D.N.B. [Deutsches Nachrichtenbüro] communiqué regarding the Kiel Canal.[6]

Herr von Neurath replied that this is not a new step concerning the canal; the problem was contained in the Reich's declaration on the Versailles Treaty resolutions with regard to water communications.

For in practice battleships passing through the canal were as a rule always reported to the German government. At present the only change consists in the fact that in answer to the notification the Reich government grants its consent.

Herr Neurath does not know for sure why the navy issued such a communiqué. It is possible that the communiqué was issued in answer to an inquiry by one of the Scandinavian countries.

11. Herr von Neurath touched casually on the matter of the unfriendly tone of the Polish press in relation to Germany, remarking that this also refers to newspapers close to the government.

Ambassador Lipski replied that Herr Neurath probably had in mind the *Kurier Poranny,* which cannot at present be regarded as a governmental press organ.

Minister Beck remarked that the solution of Danzig problems, so irritating to Polish opinion, will undoubtedly contribute to the calming of the tone of the Polish press.

Ambassador Lipski remarked that recently such a calming was already under way.

12. Minister Beck informed Herr von Neurath that the German Embassy in Warsaw obtained the agreement of the Polish government to the purchase of land for the building of new premises, by way of compensation for goods.

In February, 1937, Göring arrived in Poland for a hunting party. On February 16 he paid a visit to Marshal Śmigły-Rydz with Vice-Minister Szembek and Ambassador von Moltke also present. (For the contents of the conversation, see *Journal,* p. 221, and *Polish White Book,* No. 29. The final part of the conversation containing Marshal Śmigły's statement is missing from both summaries.) The Marshal stressed that he was determined to follow the policy line initiated by the late Marshal Piłsudski. He thought that

[6] The Kiel Canal was internationalized according to articles 381–86 of the Treaty of Versailles. The passage was open to all commercial and navy ships. On November 14, 1936, Germany unilaterally repudiated the international status of the canal.

Polish-German relations were slowly but steadily developing in a positive way. However, the Polish government was not in a position to exert its influence on public opinion to such a degree as the Reich government. The Marshal thought also that in this respect an improvement was shortly to be expected. The Marshal called attention to the fact that the youth in Germany was brought up in an anti-Polish spirit. He shared the opinion of Prime Minister Göring that, in case misunderstandings arose, they should be frankly clarified between the two parties.

As far as the attitude toward the Soviets was concerned, the Polish nation would not succumb to Communist influence. This was proved in a gallant way when Polish soldiers fought the Bolsheviks in 1919–20.

The Marshal, like Prime Minister Göring, did not think the Soviets would plan aggression. Nevertheless, he had the impression that in case of complications in Europe the Soviets would avail themselves of the situation to spread social disturbances in weak and more unsteady sectors. It was beyond conception that Poland would be on the side of the Bolsheviks in case of international conflict.

With regard to the alliance with France, the Marshal stressed that it was purely a defensive one, and he added that since Marshal Piłsudski's death this alliance had been neither extended nor altered. Prime Minister Göring declared that he was happy to have heard the above statement from the Marshal and that he would be able to repeat it to the Chancellor.

Later in the course of the conversation Göring supplied information about the war situation in Spain, where, in his opinion, the Soviets had already lost their game. Giving this information, he did not conceal the large number of German and Italian troops and armaments in the Spanish fighting.

In his notes Lipski complains of difficulties over the visits of Polish ministers to Germany. Fearing public opinion, they did not wish to engage themselves in German politics. Such was the case of the minister of justice, Witold Grabowski, whom Minister Frank invited to deliver a lecture in Berlin. He first agreed to come but later refused, and only decided to go to Berlin at the urging of the Ministry of Foreign Affairs and Marshal Śmigły-Rydz. In Berlin, besides holding other conversations, he was received by Chancellor Hitler.

Declaration about National Minorities
June—November, 1937

IN THE SUMMER and fall of 1937 negotiations were conducted by Poland and Germany on the situation of national minorities. The talks began on the initiative of the German government, which strove to find a legal way to increase the rights of the German minority in Poland. This minority, numbering about 740,000 (in 1931), was very well organized, was generally economically prosperous, had a system of German schools on a large scale, had its representatives in the Diet and Senate in Warsaw, and was constantly supported financially by the appropriate institutions in Germany. Besides, this minority was protected by a minorities agreement which Poland was obliged to sign in 1919 and which was in force until 1934. Nevertheless, Germans in Poland fought determinedly for more rights.

As compared with this situation, the Polish minority in Germany, although much larger in number (about 1,300,000 in 1938), was economically destitute, had a lower degree of consciousness in the national and political fields and a modest school system, and was faced with all kinds of obstacles raised by the German authorities regarding its cultural and economic development. It was also exempt from the protection that Germans in Poland enjoyed for so many years under the minorities agreement of 1919.

Therefore, when the German government presented a proposition for an agreement on the minorities problem, the Polish government accepted this proposition in order to obtain similar rights for the Polish minority in Germany.

In the course of conferences on the minorities agreement, Ambassador Lipski discussed with the Polish Ministry of Foreign Affairs the necessity of binding this minorities agreement to a certain degree with the agreement defining the inviolability of Polish rights in Danzig. A distinct difference of opinion between the stand taken by the authorities in Warsaw and that of the Ambassador in Berlin could be noted. This difference is related in Lipski's reports and the instructions of Beck, who, although he desired to obtain an additional German declaration with regard to Danzig, did not want to bind it to the minorities agreement. Hitler's declaration of November 5, 1937, to Ambassador Lipski brought a solution to this problem.

DOCUMENT 65 Lipski to Beck

NO. N/52/11/37   Berlin, June 19, 1937
                                                Confidential

Even before my return from Warsaw, Herr von Neurath, as you were
informed, asked me to call at the Auswärtiges Amt on Saturday the 19th
at 12 noon. In connection with news that submarine torpedo boats
belonging to the Red Spanish fleet had repeated their attack on the
battleship *Leipzig*,[1] Herr von Neurath informed me on Saturday morning that he had been summoned by the Chancellor for consultation.
Therefore the audience was postponed and the Foreign Affairs Minister
was pressed for time, which rendered difficult a detailed exchange of
opinion.

Herr von Neurath informed me that a few days ago the German
battleship *Leipzig*, on patrol duty in Spanish waters, had been torpedoed
by submarines of the Red Spanish fleet. On Friday, June 18, a similar
incident took place, rendering the situation serious. The German government cannot tolerate that its war units on patrol duty be exposed to
such risks. On this occasion the torpedoes missed their target. Nevertheless, at any time of such shooting the torpedo might hit the ship. As a
proof that the Madrid side did shoot at the German ship on purpose,
Herr von Neurath stated that although the Soviet navy remained silent
after the first shooting, the population on the side of the Reds was
informed about this fact. François-Poncet allegedly also confirmed this
to him. Under these circumstances the German government intervened
energetically at the London committee and is now awaiting measures to
safeguard the German side from such attempts.

Following such explanations, Herr von Neurath passed to the real
subject of our conversation.

I was invited to the Auswärtiges Amt to be informed that von Moltke
was directed by his government to present to you a proposition for a
declaration on minorities. Herr von Neurath observed that the minority
problems had become drastically complicated of late and he had great
difficulties in restraining the press and public opinion. This matter had

[1] The battleship *Leipzig* was attacked four times north of Oran on June 16–18,
1937, by Spanish submarines belonging to the government in Valencia.

reached the Chancellor himself. In von Neurath's opinion, such declarations would contribute to a relaxation of the atmosphere and would set an example for the local authorities to follow in selecting a proper line of conduct.

For my part, I mentioned that this matter is very ticklish for us, especially as compared with the situation of other minorities. I added that I already knew from von Moltke that he is awaiting proposals from Berlin to be presented to you. These proposals will be subjected to investigation by our side.

Next, we touched loosely with Herr von Neurath on the problem of negotiations now under way between Poland and Germany with regard to the expiring Geneva Convention.[2]

During the conversation Herr von Neurath mentioned his trip to the Balkans.[3] He stressed a positive development in the Yugoslav policy that is serving to improve relations with Yugoslavia's neighbors. He pointed to the considerable development of Belgrade in the last years, which impressed him even more since he had not visited this city since prewar times.

Then, following your recommendation, I invited Minister von Neurath, in the name of the Polish government, to visit Poland this summer. Herr von Neurath, requesting me to convey to you his thanks for the invitation, remarked that he had recently been traveling a good deal and that some interruption is advisable. He stressed that he was also compelled to give a negative answer at present to the suggestion of the French Ambassador that he visit Paris. He is going to London on the urging of the British government, without any definite program, and he knows that only a general exchange of opinion will take place. Moreover, he does not intend to take up any matters in detail, such as the Western Pact.[4] He asked that the date of his visit to Warsaw be postponed until autumn. Besides, in his opinion, there are no problems between us requiring settlement by way of such an official visit.

From the above pronouncements of Herr von Neurath I could draw

[2] On June 2, 1937, a new Polish-German railway agreement was signed following the expiration of the Upper Silesian convention of May 15, 1922.

[3] In the first half of June, Minister von Neurath paid official visits to Belgrade, Sofia, and Budapest.

[4] Von Neurath's visit to London, scheduled for June 23, was canceled on June 21 in connection with the *Leipzig* problem.

the conclusion that he thinks he has been traveling too much in the last period to various countries, and perhaps he feels overtired. At the same time he is somewhat concerned that the volume of his travels might reduce their prestige value. In the course of the conversation, in order to avoid the misleading impression that our invitation to Warsaw might in any way be connected with Herr von Neurath's visit to London, I mentioned his conversation with Minister Grabowski on this subject. Herr von Neurath agreed that on Minister Grabowski's suggestion he had expressed a desire to visit Warsaw, and that he still has such an intention.

Next I brought up the problem of the Western Pact, remarking that it might be noted that this problem is acquiring more concrete forms. I explained that hitherto we had not spelled out our point of view in writing but had simply conducted a loose exchange of opinions with particular countries. I stressed that, without prejudging our attitude of the future pact, I would like to state that the structure of agreements from 1925 on does not suit us, and I underlined among other aspects undesirable for us the excessive dependence on the League of Nations. I further explained that we see from the present exchange of correspondence between the Powers that an idea still prevails of concluding certain triangle agreements under the new pact between Great Britain, France, and Germany, and between Germany, France, and Italy. In this connection I observed that, under such a concept of triangles, a German-Polish-French triangle could be considered. Herr von Neurath quickly answered that in the first place, in his opinion, the whole idea of the pact is not yet ripe for realization. He referred to the difficulties existing between Great Britain and Italy, which encumber the possibility of reaching an understanding. As far as the concept of triangle agreements in the West is concerned, he does not see any real foundation for them, especially since the Italian government is against such a set-up. Herr von Neurath's attitude to the very idea of such triangles is negative, for in his opinion they would complicate the situation. He much prefers bilateral agreements, such as our agreement of 1934. The German government limited itself to conferences with the Western countries in order to avoid complications of the situation by other more extensive systems of pacts.

When I observed that our situation in the east is different, for besides our alliance with France we now have the 1934 agreement with the Reich, Herr von Neurath stressed that he considers the agreement with us to be of more importance than the concepts of some vague, more extensive pact. Bearing in mind this stand of the Foreign Affairs Minister, I confined myself to a statement that I only wanted to make a suggestion as to one of the possible variations.

With reference to the above report, I would like to explain that in my opinion Herr von Neurath's point of view does not preclude the possibility of further talks on this subject. I think that on the eve of his departure for London the Foreign Affairs Minister did not wish to commit himself to a more definite attitude toward us. On the other hand, this concept, which introduces quite a new element to the negotiations, might have taken him aback to a certain extent. Nevertheless, I may not exclude the possibility that the German government was told by the French government of our recent attempts in Paris. This seems even more probable, inasmuch as Herr von Neurath, in the course of the conversation, referred several times to his contacts with the French Ambassador; on the other hand, it is known to me that M. Delbos had a conversation with Ambassador Welczek with regard to the last French note. However, I must lay stress on the fact that Herr von Neurath's stand reflected a tendency well known to me—to separate the pact in the west from eastern problems.

This thesis recently appeared in the German press, and it could be observed in connection with the gradual growth of collaboration among the Four Powers in the London Committee of Nonintervention. In order to render the Minister of Foreign Affairs more conscious of the advantages to be gained by the German side from the concept of a triangle including Poland, eliminating the Soviets and Czechoslovakia from the pact, I chose an indirect way, by instructing Counselor Lubomirski to supply additional explanations on the problem to the office of the A.A. I intend to discuss these matters with Prime Minister Göring or other competent authorities of the Party at the next opportunity. I would begin these conversations from the angle that we on our part consider it desirable to maintain a friendly exchange of opinion and to collaborate with the German government on the problems of the Western Pact, and would like to know whether they reciprocate our point of view.

Józef Lipski

DOCUMENT 66   Lipski to Beck

NO. N/262/13/37   Berlin, August 6, 1937
                                               Strictly Confidential

Last Tuesday, on August 3, I had the opportunity to discuss at length
with Herr von Moltke the problem of the minorities and the Danzig
declaration. Von Moltke expected a separate declaration by the Auswärtiges Amt on the subject of our counterplan on the declaration about
minorities. However, the departments declared that they have to investigate the changes introduced by the Polish government into the German
plan. A conference with the respective departments will take place on
Monday, August 9. Until then, since he is not in a position to push the
problem forward, von Moltke will remain at home in Silesia and will
drop in for a day or two at Warsaw.

Availing myself of this occasion, I had a longer discussion with von
Moltke about the difficulties encountered by our minorities in Germany in
connection with the application of National Socialist rules. Only upon
reading the memorandum on Polish minorities in Germany did Herr von
Moltke realize the essence of the problem. However, he stated at the
same time that there is a complete lack of orientation on this problem
on the part of the central administration elements in Berlin. From this
point of view he thinks that an interministerial consultation might be
advisable, at which he will be able to expose this particular aspect of the
problem. Herr von Moltke still has no clear idea for a solution to this
problem. He considers that the question of exception to National Socialist rules would not be suitable for the declaration, and that the question
should rather be solved by way of an internal German bill.

Referring to the fate of the German minorities in Poland, Herr von
Moltke stressed that these minorities complain little about difficulties of
a cultural character but instead claim a systematic economic pressure.
Allegedly 80 percent of the minorities in Poland are unemployed. Herr
von Moltke added that the central authorities in Warsaw are not quite
aware of this, just as the central authorities in Berlin do not understand
that Polish minorities in Germany suffer from the subjection to National
Socialist laws.

Incidentally, I also referred in this conversation to the question of the high schools at Kwidzyń and Racibórz. Moltke replied that this question is quite clear, as far as its solution is concerned, in spite of difficulties with the application of a total system.

When I touched upon the Danzig declaration, Herr von Moltke answered that, unfortunately, this problem cannot be solved without von Neurath and the Chancellor. He added that personally he sees no objection to such a declaration, which in his opinion would have a favorable effect on bilateral relations. As Herr von Neurath is in the country and the Chancellor at Berchtesgaden, it is difficult to obtain a final decision. Neurath will probably have no opportunity to see the Chancellor prior to the opening of the Nuremberg Congress, which will take place on September 6.

When I mentioned the necessity of settling both matters and remarked that I am leaving for Monte Cattini on the 16th, Herr von Moltke observed that from your words he did not have the impression that the two acts should be connected and that, in his opinion also, this might not be advisable.

So, next week will bring a definition of the German point of view regarding alterations inserted by us into the German plan of the declaration and a possible coordination of the texts. On the 13th and 14th of this month Göring will be in Berlin for two days. I will avail myself of this opportunity to inform him about the state of negotiations and will take care to gain his support for the Danzig declaration.

I think that to present a declaration on minorities without obtaining at least an *accord de principe* with regard to the Danzig declaration would be dangerous. Therefore, if Moltke should return to Warsaw next week without a reply on Danzig, the solution to the minorities questions could be postponed until the Congress at Nuremberg. As I shall be in Nuremberg, I could take up the Danzig problem with von Neurath and the Chancellor.

Józef Lipski

DOCUMENT 67 Lipski to Beck

NO. N/262/16/37   Berlin, August 14, 1937

Following my letter of August 6, No. N/262/13/37, I am taking the liberty of reporting that Herr von Moltke, prior to his return to Warsaw on August 12, gave me a general idea of the results of local consulta-tions on the counterplan of our declaration on the minorities questions. In the German insertions to the text I was most concerned about the desire to cancel the paragraph of our preamble stating that the minori-ties questions are the exclusive concern of the internal affairs of each country. Von Moltke justified this demand by saying that the German side does not recognize this thesis, and therefore does not want to de-clare it officially. Referring to the agreement of 1934 and our principles in this matter, I stated explicitly to von Moltke that such a demand will not be accepted by Warsaw. He then informed me that this stand of ours is no surprise to him, and that he did not fail to point out to the Auswär-tiges Amt what difficulties might arise from such a German demand.

Von Moltke mentioned other alterations in a general way. On the item dealing with Church matters, I stressed the total neglect of Poles in Germany as far as the pastorate is concerned, quoting as an example that even our emigrants cannot obtain priests from Poland. I pointed to the last case when the departure to Saxony of a priest nominated by Primate Hlond was refused.

By the way, I would like to add that it would be useful to draw up a list of pastors in Poland who are citizens of Germany, in order that we may present this statistic to counter difficulties we have here concerning Polish priests.

As to my question on the application of National Socialist methods toward the minorities, von Moltke could as yet obtain nothing concrete; he only said that he had presented this problem *in extenso* to the repre-sentatives of the departments.

He did not mention Danzig at all.

It was obvious from the above that Moltke was working only with departmental clerks, without reaching competent authorities, who are on vacation. My meeting with Göring also did not materialize, since he did not return to Berlin as had been planned. All this makes me think that for the moment it is impossible to finalize the negotiations to our advantage, and that it is better to await the possibility of talking with competent authorities. Besides, I do not observe on the German side any special hurry in this matter, which was taken up on their initiative, and which could only be of interest for us if we obtain some positive results for our *minorities in Germany* and at the same time a clarification of the *Danzig question.*

Up to now the German text deals mostly with the demands of German minorities in Poland.

For the better orientation of the Ministry of Foreign Affairs I shall take the liberty of dispatching in the oncoming days a report prepared by the Association of Poles, dealing with the application of each of the particular National Socialist laws to the Polish minorities in Germany.

Józef Lipski

DOCUMENT 68   Lipski to Beck

NO. N/262/22/37   Berlin, September 22, 1937
Strictly Confidential

Following your verbal instructions received on September 7 during the trip from Warsaw to Berlin, I had a conversation on September 11 with Foreign Affairs Minister von Neurath at Nuremberg dealing with Polish-German negotiations on the question of minorities.[5] I reported on it by telegram from Munich on September 11. This conversation, completed by explanations given to me by Herr von Moltke at Nuremberg and on September 14 in Berlin, yielded the following results up to now:

1) With regard to the declaration, it was decided that it will be published after your return to Warsaw, and that a date will be fixed to prevent other political moments, such as Mussolini's arrival in Germany, from absorbing public attention.[6] The two governments will therefore still have to agree on the date.

---

[5] For von Neurath's version of this conversation, together with the Polish plan of the declaration on the Danzig problem, see *DGFP*, Series D, Vol. V, Nos. 1 and 2.

[6] Minister Beck proceeded to Geneva on September 7 for the eighteenth session of the Assembly of the League of Nations, paying a visit on the way to

2) Herr von Moltke returned to matters *ad* point 1 of the declaration, suggesting the restoration of the wording in accordance with the Polish counterplan presented by you at the time. In my discussion on this subject with von Moltke on September 14, I introduced a formula most adequate for the interests of our minorities in Germany, which reads as follows:

"Mutual respect for the German and the Polish nationality in itself precludes any attempt to assimilate the minority by force, to question membership in the minority, or to hinder profession of membership in the minority. In particular, no pressure of any kind will be exerted on youthful members of the minority in order to alienate them from their adherence to such minority."

Herr von Neurath accepted the text of this formula, and the Auswärtiges Amt informed the Embassy accordingly on September 17.

I enclose the text of the declaration in German with the altered Article 1, together with a Polish translation of the first part of this article.[7]

3) In order that the German government would have in writing our restrictions regarding the consequences of some National Socialist laws for Polish minorities, on September 15 I forwarded the promised memorandum on this matter to Herr von Neurath. Copy enclosed.[8]

4) Regarding the Danzig formula, Herr von Moltke explained that von Neurath's statement to the effect that he allegedly understood from the Ambassador's report that we are interested in a one-sided declaration must be a misunderstanding, since as a result of his talk with you Moltke stated clearly in his report that the declaration is to be two-sided. Interpellated by von Moltke, Herr von Neurath did admit that the Ambassador's report raised no doubts in this respect, and that it was the Foreign Affairs Minister's own mistake. Herr von Moltke told me that the Chancellor will decide on this matter, and that it is a *novum* that we are now pushing forward the concept of a confidential exchange of notes on this problem instead of an official declaration. In spite of the fact that Herr von Moltke seemed to realize the purpose of a clarification of the Danzig problem between the two governments to be the appeasement of

---

Minister Delbos in Paris (September 8 and 9). The return to Warsaw took place on September 30. Mussolini's stay in Germany on an official visit lasted from September 25 to September 29.

[7] See *DGFP*, Series D, Vol. V, No. 18.

[8] Enclosure missing in Lipski's papers.

the competent authorities in Poland, nevertheless he was not quite sure whether the Chancellor would accept such a suggestion.

Under these circumstances I am trying to influence the Chancellor via Göring, with whom, however, it is difficult to establish contact, owing to the maneuvers and Mussolini's arrival, as well as his absorption with the Four-Year Plan.[9]

Józef Lipski

DOCUMENT 69   Lipski to the Ministry of Foreign Affairs

Telephonogram
NO. 107   Berlin, October 7, 1937
                                             Received October 7, 7:50 P.M.
                                             *Confidential: for the Minister
                                             only*

Replacing the absent von Neurath and on his instructions, the Secretary of State declared to me that he cannot accept our suggestion for an exchange of notes on the Danzig problem. He referred to the principle which was accepted by the German government for nonconfirmation of particular resolutions of the Versailles Treaty. He tried to persuade me that the Chancellor's declaration of nonviolability of the Danzig statute should be sufficient for the Polish government.

In my reply, however, I explicitly stated why we consider the declaration to be necessary. I abstained from any discussion of the declaration on minorities.

I shall try to find out tomorrow through Göring whether the opposition stems from the A.A. or whether the Chancellor has really taken such a decision.[10]

Lipski

[9] Lipski talked with Göring on September 29, asking for his support in reaching a common declaration of the two countries on the Danzig question. Neurath presented this matter to Hitler, who accepted Neurath's stand not to link the declaration on minorities with the declaration dealing with Danzig (*DGFP*, Series D, Vol. V, Nos. 6, 7, 8, 9, and 10). See also the conversations between Lipski and Szembek of October 4 (*Journal*, p. 243).

[10] For Secretary of State Mackensen's version of this conversation, see *DGFP*, Series D, Vol. V, No. 11.

In Lipski's papers there is the following handwritten note:

After my conversation with Secretary of State Mackensen on October 7, I wanted to see Göring immediately. In his absence I had a conversation [on October 8] with Secretary of State Koerner [in Göring's office]. In very precise terms I criticized the negative German attitude with regard to the Danzig formula proposed by me. I went so far as to state that, if the Chancellor supported the negative stand of the Auswärtiges Amt on this problem, I would consider my mission as terminated. Koerner tried to iron out the problem and promised to discuss it seriously with Göring.[11]

DOCUMENT 70 Lipski to the Ministry of Foreign Affairs

Telephonogram   Berlin, October 18, 1937
NO. 117   Received: October 18, 7:30 P.M.
                             Secret

Although during today's conversation von Neurath asked me to inform you that he will not be able to carry through the bilateral declaration on the Danzig problem proposed by us, he nevertheless showed willingness to find a solution in a different way acceptable to us.

He is also considering the following solution: that after receiving our minorities the Chancellor would, at a special audience, give me a verbal declaration on the Danzig question. In this connection, a communiqué appeared which followed the line of appeasing public opinion on Danzig matters.

I told von Neurath that I would communicate our point of view to him on Friday. I shall be in Warsaw on Thursday and relate to you another essential point for the conversation with von Neurath.[12]

Lipski

In a personal note on his conversation with von Neurath on October 18 and later with Beck, Lipski writes:

[11] For Koerner's version of this conversation related by Mackensen, see *ibid.,* No. 12.
[12] For von Neurath's version of this conversation, see *ibid.,* No. 13.

I referred to Forster's statement that Danzig is a *Zwergstaat* which sooner or later must disappear. I stressed the harmfulness of such statements by the Danzig Gauleiter. Herr von Neurath, as usual, said a few soothing words, alluding to the necessity of our having a special talk about this sometime.

I reported this to Beck. Beck instructed me to tell von Neurath casually, referring to his statement, that Beck also feels that the necessity may arise to discuss an understanding on the Free City of Danzig question.

DOCUMENT 71   Lipski to the Ministry of Foreign Affairs

Telephonogram
NO. 119
                            Berlin, October 23, 1937
                            Received: October 23, 5:55 P.M.
                            Secret

I communicated to Neurath your reply expressing agreement to the solution on the Danzig matter proposed in coded telegram No. 117. Following your wishes, I outlined verbally items of the communiqué from the anticipated conversation with the Chancellor. Neurath promised to work on the text and clear it with me.

Neurath will present the proposed solution to the Chancellor, who returns tomorrow, and will communicate the result to me.

Neurath said that, owing to the Chancellor's short stay in Berlin, the Chancellor's reception for the minorities and the audience with me, as well as the issuance of the declaration, will have to take place in the next few days.[13]

In this connection please advise the Civil Chancellery [of the President of Poland], since the receptions for the minorities by the Polish President and the Chancellor are to take place on the same day. Only after my next conversation with Neurath will it be possible to establish whether the reception by the Chancellor will take place prior to or after the declaration.

Lipski

[13] For von Neurath's version of this conversation, see *ibid.*, No. 16.

On November 3, 1937, Vice-Minister Szembek proceeded to Berlin to take part in the opening of the Hunting Exposition, where Poland also had a pavilion. Szembek handed Lipski Beck's instructions cited below for the conversation with Hitler, which was to take place on November 5.

After a luncheon at the Embassy on November 4, Szembek had occasion to have a talk with Göring, which Szembek related in his *Journal*, pp. 244–49. See also *Polish White Book*, No. 30.

DOCUMENT 72   Beck to Lipski

November 3, 1937

In your conversation with the Chancellor on the Danzig matters, I request you to declare that you are authorized by the Polish government to convey thanks for the declaration which was presented by Ambassador Moltke in the Chancellor's name to Minister Beck on September 6, namely, that neither the Chancellor nor the Reich has the intention of violating Polish rights in Danzig. The Polish government values this declaration highly, for the unanimous opinion of government authorities, as well as of the population at large in Poland, will always consider the Danzig problem a test case for Polish-German relations. And this in spite of the fact that the Danzig problem does not seem to have such objective importance. Please state further that we wish to explain that, if the Polish government raised this question on the occasion of the publication of the declaration on minorities, this was only due to the fact that it is not possible to create an atmosphere of confidence in Poland for relations between Poland and Germany without peace on the Danzig sector.

Please remind the Chancellor that, as far as the free development of the German population in Danzig is concerned, the Polish government abstained from participation in any international plotting, or any anti-German action by international elements.

Nevertheless, cardinal principles exist in respect to the life of the Free City to which the Polish government will never be indifferent. These principal Polish rights and interests, defined in the Polish-Danzig convention in Paris in 1920, seem to be threatened of late. Namely, we noted that the National Socialist Party in Danzig began to attack not only what was considered as the Geneva doctrine in Danzig but also the principles of the said Polish-Danzig convention.

The Polish Ambassador in Berlin has been working and continues to work for the great idea of a Polish-German understanding, but he must warn that the course of events in Danzig might spoil the positive effect of the present new effort (the minorities declaration) designed to consolidate Polish-German relations.

In case the Chancellor inquires what the crux of the matter really is, please answer that the rights and interests of Poland which you are referring to depend in the first place on the matter of the harbor and railways; next, on the situation of the Polish minorities; and, finally, on the customs system and the currency connected therewith. Also, forms of conduct of the Senate, considered from the angle of the afore-mentioned Paris Convention entrusting the foreign policy of Danzig to the Polish government, are of vital importance.

Regardless of the results of the conversation, I ask you to negotiate with Neurath the forms of the communiqué about the conversation with the Chancellor in such a way as to omit the paragraph with regard to conformity of opinion on the Danzig question.

Beck

On November 5, 1937, a declaration was published in Warsaw and Berlin by the Polish and German governments regarding treatment of national minorities. Simultaneously, President Mościcki received Ambassador von Moltke and a delegation of the German minorities in Poland, and Chancellor Hitler received Ambassador Lipski and a delegation of the Polish minorities in Germany. In the conversation with Lipski, Hitler made a declaration with regard to Danzig. Pertinent official communiqués were also issued.

Lipski's report which follows cites the wording of the declaration about Danzig. The text of the declaration on national minorities and other details may be found in the *Polish White Book*, Nos. 32, 33, 35. The text of Lipski's report of November 5 (*Polish White Book*, No. 34) is very much abbreviated. *DGFP* cites documents on this matter (Nos. 18 and 19).

DOCUMENT 73 Lipski to Beck

NO. N/262/31/37   Berlin, November 5, 1937
                                                      Strictly Confidential

I was received by the Chancellor at 12:15 P.M. today, with the Reich
foreign affairs minister, von Neurath, also present.

The Chancellor began the conversation by expressing satisfaction
with the finalization of the declaration on the problem of minorities. For
my part, I started my deliberations by remarking that the date of November 5 marks a certain anniversary. On that day four years ago I
received from Marshal Piłsudski basic instructions for my conversation
with the Chancellor of the Reich, which took place on November 15 and
which resulted in the agreement of January 26, 1934. I further stated
that, in spite of difficulties of an internal and external political nature,
the Polish government accepted the Chancellor's suggestion on minorities declarations designed to bring about a relaxation of Polish-German
relations in this sector. President Mościcki, together with Marshal
Śmigły-Rydz and Minister Beck, took a broad view of this matter. If in
the course of discussions on this subject we also referred to a relaxation
in the Danzig sector, it was because we strove for a general *détente*.
When, following your instructions of November 3, I then pointed out to
the Chancellor that his declaration presented by Ambassador von
Moltke to Minister Beck on September 6 relating to Danzig was duly
appreciated by the Polish government, the Chancellor for his part defined his stand, and he did so in a most precise manner. Specifically, he
stated point by point that

1) in the legal-political situation of Danzig no changes will occur
("an der rechtspolitischen Lage Danzigs wird nichts geändert werden");
2) the rights of the Polish population in Danzig have to be respected;
3) Poland's rights in Danzig will not be violated.

The Chancellor firmly declared that the agreement concluded by him
with Poland will be respected, and this applies also to Danzig. The
promise he makes will be kept. There is no question of any surprise
action. The Chancellor only desired the German population in Danzig to
adopt a system of rule most suitable for the Germans. Besides, such a
state of affairs is the best safeguard against possible complications, since

it is a protection against sallies by particular political parties. The Chancellor asked me to communicate the above declaration to the Polish government. He laid special stress on the fact that it is his desire that it should be known to Marshal Śmigly-Rydz. This undoubtedly relates to the fact that in my conversations I referred several times to the person of the Marshal and laid stress on the mistrust prevailing in these matters in our army command.

In reply, I acknowledged the above declaration, expressing my thanks for it to the Chancellor. In the course of further discussion on this point, I stated that we always abstained from intervention into the internal development of the German population in Danzig. We rejected all offers by the Danzig opposition. In the international forum we were careful to avoid entanglements in intrigues. I also mentioned that our rights and interests connected *with the existence of the Free City* are defined in the Polish-Danzig convention of 1920 as well as in later agreements.

Next, and just in a general sense, I added on my own that Danzig should certainly be a link—a center where Polish-German interests can work together. I pointed here to the important historic role Danzig played in olden times in trade with the Polish Kingdom and even far beyond its frontiers.

Here the Chancellor twice emphasized that Danzig is connected by its interests with Poland ("Danzig ist mit Polen verbunden").

Further, according to your instructions, I tried to shift the conversation to the domain of general politics. We first took up the subject of direct conversations, which had proved successful now and in the past, on Polish-German relations. And lately, as the Chancellor remarked, they had also yielded positive results with Belgium. Here the Chancellor called attention to the difficulties of applying such methods to regimes with overcomplex parliamentary systems, and he mentioned France. He illustrated by means of a number of his endeavors aimed at improving relations with France, as, for example, in the problems of disarmament. Unfortunately, they were of no avail, for at the moment of a possible understanding a part of the French press started a strong campaign.

About Czechoslovakia the Chancellor said that he cannot understand the government in Prague, which, in the situation in which it finds itself—surrounded by Germany and Poland, as well as by Hungary—has done nothing to settle the minorities question. A reasonable government in Prague would undoubtedly take the necessary measures to find a way out of the impasse by means of an agreement on these matters.

Regarding colonies, the Chancellor said that he is presenting the colonial thesis, and will realize it, but naturally not by means of war. Jokingly he remarked that he would not declare war even for the Cameroons. The colonial problem, in his opinion, has now passed from the European to the global level. If Germany is accused of the fact that the colonies would supply it with only 10 to 15 percent of its food and raw material needs, the Chancellor's reply to this is that this corresponds to the monthly consumption of the Reich, which is a very high figure. Today, in economic questions, the Reich government has to consider even the smallest states, and with some of these, as, for example, Belgium, relations are developing successfully. From the angle of economic interests, the Chancellor cannot remain indifferent to the internal development of these states, because in smaller states the Communist system immediately disrupts all commercial turnover; Red Spain might serve as an example. On the other hand, economic life in Spain under General Franco is developing to some extent.

Talking further about Spain, the Chancellor stated that he has no political interests there and that he does not intend to introduce National Socialism into Spain. In general, he will stay away from the problems of the Mediterranean, since they are very dangerous. If he were offered a portion of Morocco, he would willingly turn it down for the same reasons. If he had such possessions, he would have to build a tremendous naval war base, with all the risks this involves.

When discussing certain international diversions against the agreements, I pointed to the action of the Soviets, who still resort to this method. The Chancellor agreed with this, citing the incident of the Spanish submarines.

I would like to stress that the whole conversation was conducted on very friendly terms, and the Chancellor seemed to be very well satisfied with the understanding achieved with Poland.

Józef Lipski

DOCUMENT 74   Lipski to Beck

NO. N/52/22   Berlin, November 19, 1937
                                             Strictly Confidential

Upon my return to Berlin I found an invitation from Göring for a hunting party at Springe on November 18, which I attended before leaving for my vacation. On this occasion I had the opportunity to discuss political subjects with him at length.

As I had hunted in the Poznań region on November 15 with Marshal Śmigły, to whom I once more related in detail my conversation with the Chancellor on the Danzig problem, I told Göring that the Marshal accepted with satisfaction the Chancellor's declaration, which will undoubtedly also contribute to smoothing out the Danzig situation. I went over again the items agreed to with the Chancellor. Göring, who now seemed to be very well disposed toward us, said that he had talked with Forster, who is very anxious to be received by you. In order to follow strictly the guiding lines fixed in his conversation with the Chancellor, Forster said that the prohibition against establishing parties in the Free City does not apply to the Polish population. However, in his conversation with you he would like to find a solution which would render impossible the infiltration of German Socialist elements into the Polish parties in Danzig.

Göring thinks that in principle we should have nothing against this, since burdening themselves with German Socialists does not seem to be in the interest of the Danzig Poles.

I seized this opportunity to mention to Göring the present economic negotiations between Poland and Danzig. I did this on purpose in order to be able to exert pressure, via Göring, on the Party elements in Danzig, in case the need, as referred to me by Wachowiak,[14] should arise.

Today reprints appeared in the German press, nearly *in extenso,* from *Political Information* on the subject of the last conversation with the Chancellor about Danzig.

I think that our *mise au point* will have a very positive effect both locally and abroad.

Among other subjects, Göring brought up the Russian problem, stat-

14 Stanisław Wachowiak, former deputy to the Diet, was the Polish political leader in Poznań and Silesia.

ing that the leaders of the National Socialist Party headed by the Chancellor profess the principle that Germany's attitude should be negative not only to Soviet Russia but also to a possibly nationalist Russia, which will always be a threat to the Reich as an unpredictable Asiatic colossus. He set this opinion against certain contradictory judgments prevailing in Reichswehr circles.

Next he said that Russia's military aspirations seem to be concentrated at present on the Rumanian sector and in the region of the Baltic states, including Finland. He posed the question whether Poland would remain neutral in case of some action on the part of the Soviets in these regions. I remarked that we have an alliance with Rumania. In relation to the Baltic states, our policy is that they should maintain their independence from Russia.

Göring was not yet prepared to discuss Halifax's mission,[15] stating that a decisive talk will take place at Berchtesgaden with the Chancellor. He only stated that Germany cannot afford to loosen its ties with Italy and Japan. Göring felt that support of Japan, in his opinion, would be a move in Poland's interest also, since it would check Russia in the Far East.

Göring quite openly counts on an invitation for a hunting party in Poland. I discussed this matter with General Fabrycy.

Józef Lipski

The following note (not dated) was found in Lipski's papers:

The Problem of Marshal Tukhachevsky's Assassination [16]

Göring communicated to me strictly in confidence that Soviet Marshal Tukhachevsky, during his visit to London for the funeral of King George V, approached the Reichswehr through secret channels, offering

---

[15] Lord Halifax, at that time Lord President of the Council, came to Berlin on the occasion of the Hunting Exposition. Although his visit was of a private character, he was delegated by Prime Minister Chamberlain to establish contact with government authorities, and especially with Hitler. The conversation with the Chancellor took place on November 19 (*DGFP*, Series D, Vol. I, No. 31). Some information about this conversation was given by Weizsäcker to the Polish chargé d'affaires, Lubomirski, on December 2 (*ibid.*, Nos. 53 and 54).

[16] Mikhail Tukhachevsky, marshal of the Russian Army, was executed in June, 1937, together with seven prominent Soviet generals.

closer collaboration. This matter reached Chancellor Hitler, who emphatically rejected the offer.

Göring gave me to understand that the Reichswehr elements would have been more agreeable to an understanding with the Soviets, but Hitler prevented it.

I communicated this news to the Foreign Affairs Minister [Beck] who, so far as I know, did not make any further use of it. This indiscretion of Göring in front of the Polish Ambassador was, in my opinion, an attempt to persuade the Polish side that, as far as Hitler and the Party were concerned, it could be taken for granted that their attitude toward the USSR was negative. At the same time it served as a sort of warning that failure to join Hitler in an agreement against Russia might have grave consequences for Poland.

Hitler Discloses His Designs [1]
November, 1937

AFTER LONG and onerous Polish-German negotiations, the two governments promulgated simultaneously on November 5, 1937, the declaration regulating principles for the treatment of national minorities. In connection with the issuing of this declaration, I was received on the same day at 12:15 P.M. by Hitler in the Reich Chancellery, in the presence of von Neurath.

In the course of the conversation Hitler made a declaration ordering respect for the statute of the Free City of Danzig, the rights of Poland, and the interests of the Polish population in Danzig. During a later exchange I pointed to the role Danzig should perform as the natural harbor of the Polish hinterland, and recalled the importance of this city in old Polish times. Then Hitler twice firmly stressed that Danzig was bound to Poland ("Danzig ist mit Polen verbunden").

For several months the Polish government strove to bring about a clarification of the German stand on the Danzig problem. This became imperative in the face of the National Socialist campaign directed at that time against Polish interests in the Free City, with the knowledge and blessings of Gauleiter Forster. My concern was to induce an exchange of notes with the German government on this problem in order to give a more formal character to the pledge, which would be a bilateral commitment in writing. However, I met with obstacles on the part of the Auswärtiges Amt. At one time an acute clash resulted from Undersecretary Mackensen's refusal to accept my proposed text, previously confirmed by Göring. Mackensen hid behind von Neurath's decision. Under these circumstances it was necessary to clarify the Chancellor's stand.

Hitler's declaration was a sort of compromise solution, not very satisfactory.

[1] Printed in Sprawny *Międzynarodowe* (London), 1947, Nos. 2–3.

From the Reich Chancellery I proceeded to the French Embassy for a reception M. François-Poncet was giving for Göring and the international delegations visiting the Hunting Exposition in Berlin. At the entrance to the reception salons of the Embsssy I met the newly appointed British ambassador, Sir Nevile Henderson, whom Chamberlain entrusted with the mission to seek an understanding with Hitler. When I informed him of the result of my conversation with Hitler, Henderson, turning to his French colleague, remarked jokingly that Piłsudski had bought Hitler's shares at their lowest, while Great Britain and France wanted to buy them at the highest rate. This expression was very characteristic of the atmosphere prevailing at that time.

On the afternoon of the same day, a consultation was held at the Reich Chancellery that was enveloped in the deepest mystery. Hitler, Göring, Neurath, Blomberg, Fritsch, and Raeder took part in it. A report of this meeting written down by Colonel Hossbach fell into the hands of the Allies and was widely utilized at Nuremberg. It constitutes one of the most important documents of the prosecution, for it reveals the date when Hitler made the decision to choose the road of conquest.[2]

Opening the conference, Hitler remarked that he wanted to explain his principal idea for the necessity of German expansion. He requested that in case of his death this speech be considered his political testament. (Hitler often mentioned death when he spoke of his future plans. I heard such declarations of his several times.)

As usual, Hitler tried to explain his point of view in long and intricate deliberations. Analyzing the possibilities of finding a solution for the needs of the German nation and wondering if this could be achieved by autarchy or by an increase in Germany's share of foreign trade, or perhaps by increased international collaboration in the industrial field, Hitler concluded that, as far as raw materials were concerned, a system of autarchy might be applied to a limited extent only, for autarchy brings no solution when a nation has to be fed. Hitler's conclusions were also negative as far as the possibility of increasing Germany's share in the world's economy and the effectiveness of such a measure were concerned.

On the basis of these economic premises, Hitler concluded that the German nation, with a crowded population of 85 million, needed space to live (*Lebensraum*).

Illustrating with events from the history of the Roman and British

[2] *DGFP*, Series D, Vol. I, No. 19 (so-called Hossbach paper).

empires to show that those powers achieved accession of territories only by risky conquests, Hitler declared that Germany today faced the problem at a time when the *greatest conquests* could be achieved at the lowest risk.

This confession of Hitler renders his future actions more understandable.

In his further deliberations on the international situation, Hitler described Great Britain and France as potential enemies of the Reich. Besides these two states, Hitler also pointed to Russia and the smaller European states surrounding it as elements of power with which Germany must reckon. In this speech the dates for the war were fixed.

According to Hitler's calculations, the war was to take place in the years 1943–45. After this period Germany would begin to lose its ascendancy over its adversaries. The war could occur earlier in two cases: if social tension in France reached such a culminating point that the French Army would be unable to fight against the Germans, at which point the moment would come to occupy Czechoslovakia; or if a conflict erupted in the Mediterranean between Italy on the one hand and England and France on the other.

Hitler considered the necessity of occupying Czechoslovakia and Austria of primary importance. He explained this by a strategic need to remove the threat from the south in case of war with the West. However, it is quite probable that even then Hitler foresaw the possibility of subjugating Czechoslovakia without war, for he voiced the supposition that Great Britain and even perhaps France had ceased to count on Czechoslovakia. Besides, he was right when he argued that Great Britain's stand would be decisive for the behavior of France.

"If the Czechs were overthrown and a common German-Hungarian frontier achieved, a neutral attitude on the part of Poland could be the more certainly counted on in the event of a Franco-German conflict. Our agreements with Poland only retained their force as long as Germany's strength remained unshaken. In the event of German setbacks a Polish action against East Prussia, and possibly against Pomerania and Silesia as well, had to be reckoned with."

Elsewhere in the speech, when the probable reaction of France and Russia was considered in case of German warfare against Czechoslovakia and Austria in 1943–45, it was mentioned that Poland's position in such a conflict would depend on the dimensions and speed of German action.

Hitler presumed that Poland would not be inclined to stand up against a victorious Germany, with Soviet Russia at its back.

Hitler's deliberations on the Italian policy showed a striking lack of orientation. It turned out that he wanted to use his Italian ally as an instrument of his political strategy. He wished to bring about a conflict between Italy and France and England over the Spanish problems. He believed this war to be close at hand and even defined its anticipated dates. Neurath had some misgivings on this occasion. Blomberg and Fritsch were of the opinion that Great Britain and France should not be regarded as potential foes of Germany. They warned against taking lightly the military strength of France, and pointed to difficulties in conquering Czechoslovakia fortifications.

Hitler was not swayed by these arguments. Just a few months later, on February 4, 1938, Neurath, Blomberg, and Fritsch were relieved of their posts.

Attempts to Draw Poland into the Anti-Comintern Pact[1]
November, 1937

THE ANTI-COMINTERN PACT between Germany and Japan was signed in Berlin on November 25, 1936. [2] British political circles were amazed by the fact that on the German side the signature apposed to the act was that of Herr Ribbentrop, at that time the Reich's ambassador in London. Ribbentrop regarded the Anti-Comintern Pact as his achievement and his exclusive domain. He obstinately elaborated the concept of creating a league of states linked with the Third Reich against Communism and tried to gain Great Britain's consent to his plans. A special office in Berlin under Ribbentrop's leadership worked on anti-Comintern problems. Its activities were not controlled by the Auswärtiges Amt, thus creating a twofold policy that became a source of misunderstandings and frictions at the Wilhelmstrasse.

To the official pact between Germany and Japan a secret protocol [3] was attached which stated at the outset that Soviet Russia, supported by its armed forces, was trying to realize the goals laid out by international agencies. Article I provided that, in case of unprovoked aggression on the part of the Soviet Union against one of the participants of the pact, no action would be taken by the other side to reinforce the position of the USSR and that a consultation would follow immediately, aimed at safeguarding the common interests of the signatories. Article II contained an obligation not to conclude political agreements with the Soviet Union contradictory to the spirit of the pact.

A year later, on November 6, 1937, the Italian government joined the German-Japanese Anti-Comintern Pact,[4] under the clause providing

[1] Printed in *Bellona* (London), 1950, No. 1.
[2] For the text, see *Documents on International Affairs, 1936*, pp. 297–99.
[3] For the text, see *DGFP*, Series D, Vol. I, No. 463, footnote 2a.
[4] For the text, see *ibid.*, No. 17.

for the participation of other states. The problem of Poland's participation in the pact was discussed again and again by the original signatories, as can be proved by certain documents contained in *Documents on German Foreign Policy,* Series D, Volume I.

One of these documents [5] relates to a German-Japanese consultation in Berlin, organized on August 13, 1937, by the Ribbentrop office. This office delegated the following persons to the meeting: Dr. von Raumer, as director; Professor Langsdorf, as an expert on Rumania; and Dr. Kleist, as an expert on Polish problems. Representing Japan were these delegates: Count Mushakoji, ambassador in Berlin; General Oshima, military attaché in Berlin; General Sawada, military attaché in Warsaw; and Lieutenant Colonel Yoshinaka, representing the Japanese Foreign Affairs Ministry.

Opening the session, Dr. von Raumer mentioned the possibility of enlisting other states for collaboration against the Communist International, stressing the importance of drawing Rumania and Poland into the work. The Japanese Ambassador remarked that he had had a short conversation on this subject with the Polish Ambassador, and that he was convinced that a close collaboration with these two states would be very difficult to achieve. As far as Poland was concerned, its internal situation was not clear. Colonel Koc and his nationalistic camp encountered strong opposition from traditional right-wing circles, the adherents of which were opposed to the government and were now energetically fighting against Colonel Koc and his political group. Colonel Koc was supported, first of all, by the group of colonels and some of the left-wing circles. On the other hand, National Democrats, who were zealous adversaries of Communism and the Jews, and at the same time dogged foes of Germany, were now on the side of the national opposition.

Dr. Raumer agreed that these were difficult problems. However, in his opinion, it was necessary from the very beginning to choose the right path, and to act with energy. General Sawada suggested that a friendly atmosphere toward Germany be created in Poland and that pressure be exerted on Poland. He proposed a friendly gesture in the field of German minorities, an area so important for Poland, simultaneously suggesting that strong pressure be exerted by means of manifestations of power on the Polish frontier through a concentration of armed forces

[5] *Ibid.,* No. 479.

(maneuvers, fortifications), or even going so far as to occupy Kłajpeda [Memel] or possibly Lithuania.

Agreeing in theory with these tactics, Dr. von Raumer expressed doubt as to their consequences in practice. In conclusion, he suggested that one or more persons be found among the Poles to lead the anti-Communist drive, persons who at the same time would be in close contact with the government. He mentioned the name of Colonel Koc. Further, von Raumer suggested that the Japanese should exert their influence on the National Democrat circles in Poland, bearing in mind that the Germans had no connections whatever in those spheres. Those present agreed with this suggestion.

The attitude of the Polish government toward the anti-Comintern problem was determined in the circular telegram sent by Minister Beck on November 9, 1937, to representatives abroad. The instructions read as follows:

"No proposals to join the Italian-German-Japanese protocol [Anti-Comintern Pact] were hitherto addressed to Poland. Besides, Poland could not participate in such a protocol owing to its specific situation as a neighbor of the USSR and its basic stand against blocs. If asked, please inform accordingly."

The conversation held by the Polish ambassador to the Quirinal, Wysocki, with German Ambassador von Hassell on November 10, 1937,[6] follows these lines. Referring to his discussion with Beck before leaving Warsaw, Wysocki remarked that Poland wanted peace with Russia and that its participation in the Anti-Comintern Pact would be regarded by Moscow as a hostile demonstration. Wysocki's remarks on the reaction of the Italians to the agreement of November 6 are worthy of careful attention. He was taken aback by the optimistic judgments of Ciano, who was simply drunk with enthusiasm over the creation of such a powerful coalition. The Italian Minister thought that Great Britain would be so impressed by the fact of the coalition that it would seek to approach the Axis. Wysocki was even more surprised by the arrogant tone of the article in the semiofficial *Correspondenza Diplomatica* that attacked Chamberlain. This article, as Wysocki rightly supposed, was written by Mussolini himself. In the same report Hassell quoted a correct remark made by the counselor of the Soviet Embassy,

[6] *Ibid.,* No. 18.

confirmed by future events, that the pact was certainly an aggressive alliance against Russia; nevertheless, its first blow was destined for Great Britain.

In a later telegram of November 17,[7] Hassell reported on the conversation with Ciano on the subject of Poland's and Brazil's participation in the pact. Ciano thought that the United States would exert pressure on Brazil not to join the agreement. Poland would not take a positive decision because of its eastern neighbor. From Ciano's further deliberations it developed that for the time being he was not inclined to extend the partnership of the pact. He was anxious to maintain the full prestige of the coalition of the Three Great Powers. In any case, he did not intend to draw in smaller states such as Austria or Hungary. On January 12, 1938,[8] the German envoy, Erdmannsdorf, reported from Budapest that Ciano did not propose to Austria or Hungary to join the pact, since he was satisfied with their pledge of solidarity. Only large states should sign the pact. Ciano suggested that steps should be taken to get Poland and Spain to join. Drawing in Brazil, thus creating a breach in the ideological bloc of the democratic states on the American continent, would be very profitable. However, it was doubtful whether the President of Brazil could stand up to the opposition of the United States.

Upon taking over the Ministry of Foreign Affairs on February 4, 1938, Herr von Ribbentrop made some attempts to induce the Polish government to join the pact. Beginning in March, 1938, these endeavors lasted more than a year and came to an end when, following the March crisis in 1939, Poland and Great Britain provided each other with mutual guarantees. In order to get a full picture, it is worth while to establish a chronological chart of Ribbentrop's actions:

March 31, 1938: on the occasion of a general exchange of opinion on Polish-German relations, Ribbentrop suggested to the Polish Ambassador that Poland join the Anti-Comintern Pact.[9]

September 27, 1938: at the moment of the worst tension over the Sudetenland problem, Ribbentrop reiterated to the Polish Ambassador the question of Poland's attitude to the Anti-Comintern Pact.[10]

October 24, 1938: Ribbentrop proposed to the Polish Ambassador a

[7] *Ibid.,* No. 27.
[8] *Ibid.,* No. 97.
[9] See below, Document 83, p. 357, and *DGFP,* Series D, Vol. V, No. 34.
[10] See below, Document 109, p. 427.

broad Polish-German collaboration within the framework of the Anti-Comintern Pact in connection with a general settlement of Polish-German problems, the so-called *Gesamtlösung* offer.[11]

January 26, 1939: in his conversation with Ribbentrop in Warsaw, Minister Beck explained the reasons why the Polish government would not be in a position to join the Anti-Comintern Pact.[12]

Attempts to bind Poland more tightly to the Reich were not limited to Poland's joining a multilateral pact. Even before such a concept arose, beginning with 1935, the German side made a number of proposals, such as military cooperation, alliance against Russia, an air pact, etc.

To all these proposals Poland's attitude was negative.

[11] See below, Document 124, p. 453, and *DGFP*, Series D, Vol. V, No. 81, pp. 104–7.
[12] See *Polish White Book*, No. 56, and *DGFP*, Series D, Vol. V, No. 126.

Weighty Decisions of the Third Reich [1]
November, 1937—February, 1938

THE PERIOD from November, 1937, to February, 1938, was far-reaching in its consequences for the foreign policy of the Third Reich. On November 5, 1937, at a secret consultation in Berlin, Hitler, in the presence of Göring, Blomberg, Fritsch, Raeder, and Neurath, declared his decision to enter on the path of conquest. The war was to take place in the years 1943–45. It could be waged earlier in case the internal situation of France showed symptoms of debility, or if an armed conflict ensued between Italy and France and Great Britain. In the latter event, Austria and Czechoslovakia would become the first victims of Hitler.

The visit of Lord Halifax to Berchtesgaden opened perspectives to Hitler for an earlier solution of the Austrian and Sudetenland problems. He was faced with the problem whether to negotiate first with Great Britain, or whether to take immediate action for the realization of his plans. An understanding with Great Britain would indeed secure colonial advantages. Nevertheless, in Halifax's opinion, the colonial problem might only be settled positively within the frame of a global agreement, together with the security problem (disarmament), Germany's relation to the League of Nations, and an explicit definition of German claims in Central Europe, since this last matter was of special concern to France. At the consultation on November 5, speaking about the necessity of *Lebensraum* for the German nation, Hitler said, without mincing words, that Germany faced the problem of the greatest conquests with the smallest risk.

Still, other factors weighed on Hitler's decision. In spite of the power in his grasp as an absolute ruler of a populous and powerful nation situated in the heart of Europe, Hitler was afraid of the future (a symptom so very characteristic of political gamblers). He preferred im-

[1] Printed in *Bellona* (London), 1950, No. 1.

mediate solutions, which entailed great risks, to a long-term policy. His personal ambitions and a nervous, bouncing temperament also pushed him toward prompt solutions. His whole system was based on permanent dynamism.

His chief adviser, Ribbentrop, who enjoyed Hitler's ever-growing confidence, was opposed beforehand to the plan for Halifax's visit. He told me this already in September, 1937, at the Congress in Nuremberg. This was the period of the last months of his ill-fated mission in London, which made of him a dogged foe of Great Britain.

In a personal, strictly confidential memorandum of January 2, 1938, to the Chancellor,[2] Ribbentrop presented his point of view as to the future of German-British relations, recommending at the same time tactics of action. This important document provides a key to deciphering German political moves that followed.

I quote an extract of the conclusions reached by Ribbentrop:

1) Great Britain is lagging with its armaments and is therefore trying to gain more time.

2) Great Britain believes that in its competition with Germany time is playing into its hands. It plans to exploit its greater economic possibilities in the field of armaments, as well as to extend its treaties; for example, with the United States.

3) Halifax's visit should be considered as camouflage, just a pretext to investigate the situation. British Germanophiles on the whole play only such roles as are assigned to them.

4) Great Britain and its Prime Minister do not recognize in Halifax's visit the possibility of setting the basis for an understanding with Germany. Their trust in National Socialist Germany equals Germany's confidence in Great Britain. That is why they fear that they may some day be compelled to accept solutions detrimental to them. In order to counter this eventuality, England is making military and political preparations for a war with Germany.

The final conclusions of Ribbentrop are as follows:

1) Externally, further understanding with Great Britain to safeguard the interests of Germany's allies.

2) Keeping it strictly secret, to create with iron perseverence a coalition against Great Britain by tightening Germany's friendship with Italy and Japan, as well as by drawing in all other nations whose interests

[2] *DGFP,* Series D, Vol. I, No. 93.

correspond directly or indirectly to German interests. Establishing close and confidential collaboration of the Three Great Powers in order to reach this goal.

3) The question arises whether France, and as a result also Great Britain, will take up arms in case Germany engages in conflicts in Central Europe. This will depend on the specific conditions, on the speed with which the adversary will be conquered, and, finally, on the military situation. On this matter Ribbentrop wishes to present his personal point of view to Hitler.

In his final remarks there is an interesting paragraph relating to the role Ribbentrop attributed to Edward VIII in maintaining good German-British relations. After his abdication, which in the German Ambassador's opinion had a political foundation, Ribbentrop lost all hope for a possible agreement.

"Henceforth," writes Ribbentrop, "regardless of what tactical interludes of conciliation may be attempted with regard to us, every day that our political calculations are not actuated by the fundamental idea that England is our most dangerous enemy *will be a gain for our enemies.*" [Emphasis added by Ribbentrop.]

A month after dispatching this opinion, Ribbentrop replaced von Neurath, who was known for his pro-British sympathies.

The line drawn in the memorandum was of vital interest for the future formation of Polish-German relations. Ribbentrop's guiding idea was to create a coalition against Great Britain, in which, besides Germany, Italy, and Japan, smaller states whose interests corresponded with those of Germany were also to collaborate. Drawing Poland into the orbit of the pact was of obvious importance for Germany. Poland was to play the role of a bulwark in the East in case of Germany's conflict with the West, and of an ally in a war with Soviet Russia. This might explain Ribbentrop's endeavors in relation to Poland dating from March, 1938.

The Anti-Comintern Pact, created in principle against the Soviets, was gradually transformed into a tool of the German policy to check Great Britain. A great war alliance would grow out of it later on, while its two original signatories, Germany and Japan, would conclude non-aggression pacts with the Soviet Union.

Beck in Berlin
January, 1938

AMONG THE PAPERS of Józef Lipski there is a document (in Polish) written by him under the general title "Polish-Czech Relations, Observed from Berlin, in the Period from November, 1937, to the Conference in Munich." This work numbers twenty-two typewritten pages and was probably intended to be inserted in the memoirs of the author. It has never been published. It is included here in slightly altered form; the full texts of related documents, often given by the author in considerably abbreviated form, have been added.

In the second half of 1937, according to our information, we were in a position to assume that the moment was near when the Third Reich would actualize the Austrian and Czech problems on a nationalistic level.

On September 29, 1937, I was received by Göring at Karinhall in connection with our request for an exchange of notes on the Danzig problem on the occasion of the minorities declarations. Göring, who on the preceding day had received Mussolini at Karinhall, told me emphatically that the Duce stopped before a map showing Austria included in the Reich. Mussolini, without a single critical remark, simply said that the Reich was promptly realizing its program and, looking at Czechoslovakia, he added that this state was cutting deep into the German organism. Göring commented on this fact as a proof that Mussolini was taking the matter of the *Anschluss* for granted.

Minister Beck was of the opinion that Hitler, intending to settle the problem of Austria and the Sudetenland on the nationalistic level, wanted to exclude from this showdown the Polish-German minorities question, and that was why the Reich government intended to conclude an agreement with Poland on these matters. I, for my part, pressed for the necessity of binding the German side to an agreement on Danzig in connection with the minorities declaration. In case of the Reich's refusal,

I thought we should not finalize the minorities compromise. After extensive discussions with the Germans, the Danzig problem reached a semi-solution by means of Hitler's declaration of November 5, 1937. During the conversation with the Chancellor, when general problems were discussed, Hitler mentioned casually that he could not understand the rulers of Prague who, in their country's situation, surrounded as it was by Germany, Poland, and Hungary, did nothing to take care of the minorities question. A reasonable Czech government would, in Hitler's words, do all that was possible to take up these problems with its neighbors.

Although I did not know it at the time, on that same day, November 5, 1937, Hitler held a consultation with Göring, Neurath, Blomberg, Fritsch, and Raeder. The consultation lasted for four hours. Hitler concluded his deliberations by declaring that he had decided to gain living space (*Lebensraum*) for the German nation by conquests. From his detailed analysis of the plans it was clear that Austria and Czechoslovakia were at the top of the list in Hitler's aggressive strategy.

In the second half of November, Lord Halifax arrived in Germany on a mission from the British government. Halifax's conciliatory attitude toward German revisionist designs weighed considerably on Hitler's later decisions with regard to Austria and Czechoslovakia. During this period I was still unaware of the result of German-British conversations. Göring, whom I questioned on November 19 about the subject of these talks, was not able to give me an answer, since the decisive conversation of Halifax with Hitler was to take place that very day at Berchtesgaden.[1] He only said that Germany could not afford to loosen its ties with Italy and Japan.

On his way to Geneva for the session of the Council of the League of Nations, Beck stopped in Berlin on January 13–14, 1938, for an exchange of opinion with Hitler and the Reich's ministers. These conversations, besides covering Polish-German matters, dealt with all international problems. Beck, whom I accompanied to all the conversations, was able to see clearly the German plans for the near future. The conversations covered a very wide range of problems: German-French, German-British, and German-Soviet relations, the situation in Spain, the

[1] See *DGFP*, Series D, Vol. I, No. 31. On Beck's recommendation, Prince Lubomirski, chargé d'affaires in Berlin, questioned Weizsäcker on December 2 in Lipski's absence about the main subjects and viewpoints treated in the Halifax visit (*ibid.*, Nos. 53 and 54).

question of the Far East, and Germany's relations with the League of Nations. The most important of the Polish problems under discussion was the case of Danzig. . . .

From the outpourings of Hitler and the German ministers it was apparent unequivocally that the Reich was approaching the realization of its plans relating to Austria and Czechoslovakia.

Neurath's opinions were most characteristic; he always was more reserved and more cautious than his colleagues. . . .

Göring, declaring that to the German way of thinking the Austrian problem was an internal matter (he said so, without mincing words, to Flandin),[2] stressed that Austria's annexation by the Reich must follow sooner or later. . . .

In general, however, the Chancellor's stand was less adamant than Neurath's and Göring's. He said, for example, that he would like to arrive at an understanding with Czechoslovakia if, he added, he were not compelled to act in a different way. . . .

Minister Beck listened to these deliberations, maintaining a certain reserve in his pronouncements. Only with regard to Austria did he remark to Neurath that Poland had economic and transit but not political problems with that country. He also expressed himself in a similar way to Göring. He pointed to the difficulties in minorities problems encountered by Poland in Czechoslovakia. Referring to the forthcoming visit of Horthy to Poland, Beck stated that he was acting in order to improve Hungarian-Rumanian relations by trying to stiffen Rumania in relation to the Soviets.

During Beck's visit in Berlin news came of the fall of Chautemps' cabinet and the postponement of the meeting of the Council of the League of Nations until the formation of a new government. Beck decided to stay in Berlin another day and to proceed later to Cannes, in order to spend some time awaiting the meeting. On the day when Beck was to depart for Geneva (January 15) the Yugoslav prime minister, Stoyadinovich, arrived in Berlin. The Auswärtiges Amt approached me with a suggestion that Beck take part in a dinner that night in honor of the Yugoslav guest. The purpose of this invitation was obvious. On the eve of the action against Austria, the German side was anxious to display the semblance of an East European bloc under Berlin's leadership.

[2] Pierre Flandin, who had been French prime minister (1934–35) and minister of foreign affairs (1936), paid an unofficial visit to Berlin in the second half of December, 1937.

I therefore advised Beck not to accept the invitation for dinner, and instead proposed his immediate departure for Cannes. In spite of technical difficulties made by the German railways administrations, evidently by order of the A.A., Beck succeeded in leaving Berlin in time.

The German government obtained from Stoyadinovich, who was closely tied to Germany, an agreement for the *Anschluss,* a promise that Yugoslavia would oppose the possible return of the Hapsburgs to Austria, and a promise that it would mobilize in case of a legitimist revolution in that country.

DOCUMENT 75   Report
on the Conversation of Foreign Affairs Minister Beck
with Reich Foreign Affairs Minister von Neurath,
in the presence of Polish Ambassador Lipski,
on January 13, 1938, at 11:30 A.M.

NO. N/52/3/38   *Strictly Confidential*

1) Minister von Neurath opened the conversation by stating that he had observed Minister Beck's extensive activity of late. Minister Beck mentioned his exposition delivered at the Commission for Foreign Affairs of the Diet and yesterday's debate.[3] Such explanations serve the cause well. Herr von Neurath said that in the times of the old regime, when he had dealings with the parliament, the deputies were more reasonable when debating on problems in smaller groups, but in the forum of the parliament, when they addressed the electorate, demagogy flared up. Minister Beck remarked that it is our habit to have speeches delivered on foreign policy and national defense by members of the cabinet exclusively at the commission, since this renders matter-of-fact debate possible.

Minister Beck stated that in his exposition he wanted to describe precisely Poland's stand with regard to the problems of the League of Nations, even before the Geneva session.

A conversation ensued on the subject of the League. Neurath asked the Minister whether, in his opinion, some new plans for the League's

[3] Beck delivered his exposition on January 10, 1938, and participated in the discussion on January 12, 1938. See Beck, *Przemówienia, deklaracje, wywiady, 1931–1939,* pp. 331–40.

reorganization would be revealed at Geneva. The Minister thought this would not take place; Neurath shared this opinion.

Nevertheless, Minister Beck added that, bearing in mind that principal debates might always result from speeches of one of the delegates, he preferred in anticipation to define Poland's position.

Herr von Neurath pointed to a number of approaches made by the Western states to the German government (he also mentioned Halifax) actualizing the question of the League's reorganization. However, no concrete plans were presented; instead, endeavors were made to secure a plan of reorganization from the German government. To clear up the situation, after Italy's withdrawal from Geneva, the German government presented a declaration whereby it finally canceled its participation in the League. This was intended as a total blow to abolish the present structure of the League. ("The League of Nations must become completely kaput.") [4] Of course, Neurath was not excluding the possibility that some new form of international collaboration might be created in the future, replacing the present Geneva.

2) In connection with the discussion on the League of Nations, Neurath remarked that he had in mind a point and, not wishing to forget it, he wanted to bring it up immediately, namely, the problem of the Danzig flag. [5]

He wanted to assure us that this question is not at all timely and is of no importance to the German government. If in the future Danzig should desire, for example, to place a swastika on its flag, this would be the subject of a previous understanding between Danzig and Poland.

This gave rise to a conversation on Danzig in connection with the situation at the League. Minister Beck pointed to a certain improvement in Polish-German relations of late, adding that our relations are being discussed directly with the Senate. He mentioned recently concluded economic agreements. He remarked that Polish-Danzig matters were dealt with (in the last period) outside of the League's arbitrament. It might be necesssary, owing to the situation at the League, to investigate

[4] The Great Fascist Council decided on December 11, 1937, that Italy should withdraw from the League of Nations. The German Information Bureau proclaimed on December 12 a declaration by the German government supporting Italy's stand and stating that Germany's return to the League of Nations would never again be considered.

[5] Forster, the gauleiter of Danzig, wanted to add the swastika to the Danzig flag or to introduce a flag with a swastika.

(*überprufen*) this question, as mentioned at the time to Ambassador Lipski by Neurath. Herr von Neurath remarked that the present High Commissioner of the League in Danzig shows much more discretion and calmness in office, and does not sound the alarm for every petty detail. He heard from London that there is some intention there of withdrawing the Commissioner. He does not know whether this is still timely. He thinks that Danzig matters could be discussed either now or at a later date. He would appreciate it if Minister Beck would find out at Geneva what the consensus is there on this question.

Minister Beck remarked that it is essential that the League's withdrawal from Danzig should not coincide with a simultaneous aggravation of our relations. Von Neurath shared this opinion. For his part he exposed the thesis that, in case a revision of the League's situation in Danzig is undertaken, changes in the High Commissioner's rights should not be made. Minister Beck said that in this instance he is of the definite opinion that either the League will remain in Danzig under the present conditions or will withdraw from there entirely.

Neurath ascertained in conclusion that talks on this subject might be opened between Poland and Germany now or at a later date. From his words it was rather obvious that the German government is not in a hurry. Neither did Minister Beck insist particularly on expediting this solution.

3) Herr von Neurath touched upon the change in the cabinet in Rumania, asking the Minister's opinion. For his part, he thought that the government of Prime Minister Goga showed too much speed in its basic decisions.[6] Neurath had issued instructions to the German press to curtail their enthusiasm for the new government, which would only place a trump card in the hands of their opponents.

Minister Beck stated that two basic changes might be observed in the conditions in Rumania:

a) a definite withdrawal from the pro-Soviet policy propagated by Titulescu,

b) a structural change in the rule of the Rumanian state, which was based upon the old tradition of liberal prewar governments.

The Minister cannot predict what the fate of Goga's rule will be. With such radical changes in the system, he is afraid it might be safer to rely

[6] The Rumanian government of Tatarescu resigned on December 27, 1937. The next day a new cabinet was formed by Professor Octavian Goga.

on the organization emanating from below than to impose concepts from the top. It is therefore possible that, in case Goga fails, the King, who today is a competent factor in Rumania's politics, will choose a government with more middle-of-the-road tendencies. In his speech the Minister stressed Poland's attitude toward Rumania: nonintervention in internal affairs, but continued observance of the Polish-Rumanian alliance. On this level Polish-Rumanian relations cannot be exposed to any harm.

Herr von Neurath stressed that the German government, within the limits of its possibilities, also countered Mr. Titulescu's policy. If Mr. Titulescu claimed that he was for an understanding with Germany, von Neurath could confirm that such offers had been made; however, the German government had no confidence in the person of Mr. Titulescu and therefore all proposals made a few years ago through Envoy Comnen were rejected. Neurath remarked that German-Rumanian economic relations are prospering well.

4) With regard to Hungary, Minister Beck pointed to Horthy's trip to Poland,[7] stressing the friendship uniting the two countries. Referring to the paragraph of his speech wherein he mentioned the coordination of Laval's plan with Mussolini, Minister Beck remarked that he simply wanted to stress the positive aspect of this plan, which provides for certain collaboration of the Danubian states, placing them all on the same level, since this is exactly Poland's point of view. Herr von Neurath said that the German government's attitude toward this plan is a critical one, partly because it provided for Austria's independence. Besides, Minister Beck added, Poland does not conduct any *Grosspolitik* in the Danubian countries.

He stated that the Polish government is trying to assist in a certain rapprochement between Rumania and Hungary. He is of the opinion that Rumania would thus achieve more freedom in its policy with Soviet Russia; this might have a salutary effect on Rumania's internal situation.

Minister Neurath stressed that the German government also supports a Rumanian-Hungarian rapprochement.

5) With regard to Austria, Neurath complained that relations are not developing well, although on his part he has taken measures to improve them. However, he encounters a special personal resistance in Schusch-

[7] The visit of Regent Horthy to Poland took place February 5–9, 1938.

nigg, so that he is rather pessimistic as to the possibility of easing the situation. As a matter of fact, relations are so tense that Neurath does not exclude the possibility of an outburst inside Austria.

Minister Beck remarked that Poland has only economic relations with Austria; we have no special political interests there.

6) With regard to Czechoslovakia, Neurath called attention to the fact that relations with that country are not good. Attempts for improvement have yielded no results. A difference exists between the principles proclaimed by Mr. Beneš and repeated by the Czech Envoy with regard to the minorities in the Sudetenland and the real state of affairs.

Minister Beck stressed that, in spite of a liberal constitution, the Czechs are introducing the most drastic police-state forms with regard to the minorities.

Minister Neurath emphasized that, if the Czechs kept to the original Masaryk concept, they could exist at least for some time longer. But, as matters stand today, "This stump will have to be severed sooner or later."

7) Questioned about relations with the Western countries, Minister Beck said: "Im Westen nichts neues" ["All quiet on the Western Front"]. Neurath confirmed this. He remarked that there were loud repercussions on his fifteen-minute talk with Delbos at the station in Berlin.[8] Minister Beck confirmed this, remarking that Delbos had expressed to him satisfaction at this gesture of Neurath, a gesture that undoubtedly contributed to the easing of the atmosphere.

Minister von Neurath had a favorable opinion of Delbos. Minister Beck was of the same opinion, adding that in Warsaw Delbos showed the full understanding of a realistic statesman for Poland's need to carry on an independent foreign policy.[9]

Minister Beck remarked that he had the impression that Delbos desires to deal with all problems together, while Germany wants to settle each problem separately. Neurath replied that he had discussed this subject in a railway car with Delbos, and that he had the impression that the French Minister is not completely negatively disposed toward the German thesis.

On the other hand, Minister von Neurath expressed his very negative

[8] En route to Warsaw, Delbos had a short conversation with Neurath (at the latter's request) at the station in Berlin, *DGFP*, Series D, Vol. I, No. 55.
[9] Minister Delbos' official visit to Warsaw took place on December 3–7, 1937. Afterward Delbos proceeded to Bucharest, Belgrade, and, via Budapest, to Prague.

impression of his talk with Flandin. He said that Flandin belongs to the category of French ministers who have not learned anything. That is why Neurath did not arrange for an audience for him with the Chancellor.

8) About the Western Pact, Herr von Neurath said that this matter is not at all timely and that such a pact seems to be pointless, since it can be done without.

9) With regard to colonies, Neurath stated that it will probably be some time before England presents some proposals. He added that sooner or later this problem will appear in concrete form.

10) Spain: with regard to Franco's defeat at Teruel, von Neurath described this as an event which will postpone the settlement of the situation in Spain.

Minister Beck remarked that, according to information in his possession, the Red Spanish Army has improved considerably.

Neurath confirmed this, and added that because of this Berlin had advised General Franco to open the promised offensive as soon as possible. However, General Franco, as Mussolini declared to Neurath, is not taking into consideration two factors: time and money. Neurath added that in general it is not easy to deal with Spain.

Both von Neurath and Minister Beck agreed that today a defeat such as the one at Teruel might not create such misgivings as existed a year ago concerning the possible victory of the Reds and the spread of Bolshevism.

Minister Beck underlined that, in spite of Russia's internal isolation, the Comintern is still functioning very strongly abroad.

11) With regard to the Far East, Herr von Neurath described the situation as follows: for Japan it is not easy. Neurath does not consider the danger of Japanese entanglements with Soviet Russia, bearing in mind that, following Stalin's purge of the army, Russia's combat value is not sufficient for a conflict with Japan.[10]

Here Mr. Beck observed that the eastern Soviet Army was less affected by the executions.

Minister von Neurath maintained his opinion that he does not fear Russia's action against Japan; in his opinion, the difficulty lies in the dragging out of the conflict, which is also due to serious misunderstandings in Japan with regard to relations with China, in particular in the

[10] On June 11, 1937, Marshal Tukhachevsky and seven Soviet generals were sentenced to death in Moscow.

higher echelons of the army, the navy, foreign policy, etc. This renders the conclusion of peace with China very complicated. It should also be considered that Chiang Kai-shek remains an element of permanent anti-Japanese counteraction in the vast territory of China. He symbolizes China's national rebirth. Japan has taken up arms in order to put an end to this national revolution symbolized by Chiang Kai-shek.

In conclusion, von Neurath said that the Chancellor would like to see Minister Beck, if he could spare some time for this meeting.

Minister Beck replied that naturally he would consider it a great honor to be received by the Chancellor.[11]

DOCUMENT 76   Report on the Conversation of
Foreign Affairs Minister Beck at Lunch with General Göring,
in the presence of the Polish Ambassador in Berlin, Lipski,
on January 13, 1938

NO. N/52/3/38

The conversation with Göring was partially carried on during the luncheon, with Mrs. Göring present. This part was purely general in character. First of all, it concerned the development of the internal situation in Rumania. Minister President Göring has certain misgivings as to whether Goga is strong enough to realize his program. He thinks that in case he fails the Iron Guard will appear on the stage.

Minister Beck expressed an opinion similar to that he had described to Herr von Neurath.

They both agreed that the great danger which threatened as a result of Titulescu's policy of rapprochement with the Soviets had now been removed.

Further, the forthcoming visit of Göring to Poland was discussed. Beck invited him formally in the name of the Polish President. The date was fixed at about February 11, which was quite acceptable to Göring.

After lunch, when Mrs. Göring left, a political discussion began. Questioned by Göring as to whether any special political moves are expected to take place in Geneva, Minister Beck replied negatively. He

[11] For the memorandum prepared for Neurath for his conversation with Beck, see *DGFP*, Series D, Vol. V, No. 25; for Neurath's version of this conversation, *ibid.*, No. 28.

referred to his speech at the Commission for Foreign Affairs of the Diet when he defined Poland's stand toward the League of Nations.

With reference to Danzig, Beck observed casually that a certain easing in the situation might be noted. Göring confirmed this, adding that we might count on him in these matters if necessary.

Minister President Göring pointed out that it would be desirable if Forster could be received by Minister Beck so as to disperse the last shade of misunderstanding. Minister Beck answered that this is being taken into consideration. Minister Chodacki is already in contact with Forster. Following the Minister's return to Warsaw, he will probably be in a position to receive Forster.

The last minorities agreement was described by Göring as a great *positivum,* and he gave voice to his satisfaction over such a successful development in Polish-German relations.

It is now essential that the lower ranks, such as mayors and voivodes, should conform to the governmental policy. He is always ready to help as far as the German side is concerned. Minister Beck mentioned that pertinent orders had been issued on the Polish side. Such problems as the release of members of German minorities sentenced at the Chojnice trial had also been settled.

Defining particular problems of the Reich's policy, Göring stressed that there are certain problems which in the nature of things should reach solution sooner or later. First among these problems is the reunion of Austria with the Reich. He illustrated by using this example: if in the place of Czechoslovakia a thoroughly Polish state existed, only ruled by factors other than those in Warsaw, would it not be quite natural that the whole Polish nation would long for reunion with the sister nation? That is why Austria, in the minds of the German people, is regarded as their internal affair. Herr Göring had presented this point in quite categorical form to Flandin, who asked for what price Germany would abandon the idea of annexing Austria. Halifax had shown much more understanding for this problem. Göring told him quite explicitly that the Reich government is striving for a peaceful union of Austria with the Reich. Nevertheless, he hinted that, if this way achieves no result, an outburst might occur. Germany, as Göring put it, will settle this matter without regard to others. It has no misgivings about France. In case of an Italian protest, any realistic politician in Europe will understand that, if Mussolini comes to Germany and delivers speeches binding for his policy, he will not act without contacting Berlin on the most important problem that could divide the two countries, namely, on the problem of Austria. Of course, it is rather awkward to publicize this. Here Göring cited the example of the map which he showed to Mussolini at Karinhall, in which Austria was united with Germany. To this Mussolini only observed that he could see on this map that Czechoslovakia was cutting too deeply into Germany.

Göring added that Schmidt [12] has been informed by him about this, so that the Austrian government is quite aware of the real state of affairs.

With regard to Czechoslovakia, Herr Göring observed that he cannot understand the Czech policy. This country, extended in a long line, lives in tension with Germany, Poland, and Hungary. The German minority in Czechoslovakia is not like the minorities in other countries, since it is well knit and numbers about four million people. He does not understand what the Czechs are counting on. French assistance is nothing but an illusion, the more so since new German armaments on the western frontier of Germany would render France's assault difficult even today. And in a year such an assault would be out of the question. Here Göring had critical words for the Maginot line, because soldiers in such fortifications are unwilling to leave them and fight. That is why the German government applied a system of dispersed defense points, which seems far better.

Herr Göring does not conceal that he considers the existence of the Czech state in its present form as impossible.

He inquired about Polish minorities inhabiting the Cieszyn [Teschen] region. When he talked about Hungarian-Czech relations, Minister Beck remarked that Hungary had failed in one point of its policy, namely, with regard to national minorities. Göring confirmed this, adding that Germans who went over to Yugoslav rule from Hungarian rule were of the same opinion.

As to the future of Polish-German relations, Göring declared that cutting Poland off from the sea would result in the thrust of a population of 40 million against Germany. Therefore, it would constitute political nonsense. In case of other compensations for Poland in the east, Germany would like in the future to have some convenient communication by railway through Pomerania. It does not aspire to anything else.

---

[12] Guido Schmidt, secretary of state in the Austrian Ministry of Foreign Affairs (July, 1936-February, 1938), later foreign affairs minister (February-March, 1938).

With regard to Austria, a subject to which Göring returned again, Minister Beck remarked that, as he had already told Neurath today, Poland has only economic interests there. Göring, who understood this allusion, replied that in the economic field an understanding will always be possible.

DOCUMENT 77 Report on the Conversation of
Foreign Affairs Minister Beck with Chancellor of the German Reich
Hitler *in the presence of Reich Foreign Affairs Minister*
von Neurath and Ambassador of the Polish Republic in Berlin Lipski,
on January 14, 1938, from 12 P.M. to 1:30 P.M.

Strictly Confidential

In very lengthy deliberations the Chancellor described his views on particular international problems and brought up the affairs of the Reich. In the field of international politics these deliberations concerned the relation of Germany to France and the internal French situation, German-British relations, with special stress on colonial affairs, the attitude toward Bolshevism and German-Russian relations, the attitude toward Austria and Czechoslovakia, the situation in the Far East, and the attitude of the German government toward the League of Nations.

In the course of these long deliberations, the Chancellor repeatedly referred to Polish-German relations and made a declaration with regard to Danzig.

1. Polish-German Problems

These problems are left out of this report for the whole of the conversation, to be dealt with as a separate point.

Minister Beck thanked the Chancellor for expressing a desire to see him during his stay in Berlin.

He found that Polish-German relations are developing successfully, and pointed to the agreement concluded on November 5, 1937.

The Chancellor said he was glad to see Minister Beck in Berlin and for his part repeatedly stressed during the conversation that the successful development of Polish-German relations constitutes one of the rare positive factors in the present inflamed international situation. On this occasion he confirmed his firm decision to keep to the same line of action. He expressed his sincere satisfaction with Minister Beck's last exposition at the Commission for Foreign Affairs of the Diet, and laid stress on the importance for the international situation of such a warning voice about the League of Nations.

In his general thesis the Chancellor confirmed his basic line that frontier corrections would by no means be commensurate with the sacrifices, and therefore would not make sense.

With regard to Danzig the Chancellor stated literally that on November 5, 1937, he had made a declaration to the Polish Ambassador. He would like to repeat this declaration to the Minister. He put it this way: that Poland's rights in Danzig will not be infringed upon, and that, moreover, the legal status of the Free City will remain unaltered. Polish-German relations, the Chancellor added, are of essential and decisive importance in this matter for him also. He only wished that the local German population could adopt a form of government which would suit it best, and which as a result would contribute to the maintenance of peace. The Chancellor gave firm assurances that the declaration made by him is binding. Further in the course of the conversation he mentioned that it is binding irrespective of the fate of the League.

With regard to the flag, the Chancellor assured us that this matter will be canceled. He added that he will talk it over with Forster and Greiser. He mentioned that he does not wish to complicate matters internally for the Minister by this question.

Minister Beck's statements can be recapitulated as follows:

Taking note of the Chancellor's declaration on Danzig, with a mention that he had discussed this matter with Neurath in order that our relations not be exposed to difficulties by a third party, such as the League, which today is the stage for surprises. It was mentioned that the Minister and Neurath went through a general review of problems of concern to the two states.

Affirmation that Polish-Rumanian relations are developing successfully. Mention of Horthy's visit to Poland and attempts to improve relations between Hungary and Rumania, thus reinforcing Rumania's resistance in its policy toward the Soviets. Underlining that in these problems the opinion of the Polish and German governments is uniform.

Stressing difficulties encountered by Poland with regard to its minorities in Czechoslovakia.

Underlining that besides this we are not conducting particularly large-scale politics in the Danubian basin.

2. France

The Chancellor remarked that he had just been informed that Chautemps' cabinet has fallen. Critical evaluation of the internal situation in France. Remark that if Blum would now seize power Communist tendencies would be strengthened. Fear of possible Communism in France, which would undoubtedly spread to Belgium and Holland. Opinion that the only nationalistic and stable element in France is the army; nevertheless, the army alone, without political leadership, cannot play a decisive role in the life of the country. If no political spheres will take the responsibility for engaging the army in politics, the army alone will not do so.

The optimistic opinions of people who say that there are right-wing movements in France are based on a false appraisal. These people only see the political pendulum swinging to the right and again to the left. They do not realize that the clock itself moves to the left.

From the egoistic point of view, Germany would welcome the weakening of France; however, wisdom and a well-conceived self-interest advise against it. With the present political and economic ties between the European countries, a breakdown in a neighbor's economy might signalize a Bolshevik revolution next door, and should therefore be cause for concern. Distant Spain is proof of this. Germany could not remain indifferent if Communism were to appear on its western frontier.

3. Czechoslovakia

Communism in the west is even more of a threat since there is a country bordering on Germany in the east which is yielding more and more to Moscow's influence. This country is Czechoslovakia. The Chancellor cited information received from there with reference to Soviet influence on the press, cinema, theater, etc. Czechoslovakia is one of the countries in the opinion of some in which a little flame (*Feuerchen*) might be fanned or extinguished at will. All those who argued this way were mistaken; when they want to extinguish the fire it is already too late and the fire overtakes them.

The Chancellor was very critical of Czech politics. He declared that Czechoslovakia is not a uniform nation, like, for example, Poland. The very name shows that Czechoslovakia is *ein Nationalitätstaat*. Its policy should be adapted thereto. But it is not, and this evokes conflicts with regard to the treatment of minorities. The Chancellor would like to find a peaceful solution here also, unless he is compelled to act otherwise.

4. Austria

Besides this difficult problem, as the Chancellor put it, there is another one which is causing him concern—Austria. If legitimistic attempts take place in Austria, the Chancellor declared with absolute firmness that he would not hesitate to march immediately into Austria. This would be done as quickly as lightning. By no means would he let the Hapsburgs in. This problem goes beyond Austria and concerns the territory of the Reich. In the Hapsburgs' entourage there is talk about an emperor of Germany. Religious considerations are also utilized here.

This passage of the Chancellor's statements is exceedingly decisive.

5. The Soviet Union

The Chancellor deliberated at length on his attitude toward Communism, stating very firmly that his negative stand is inviolable. In this connection he mentioned some opinions as to a possible national evolution in Russia. Similar opinions also prevailed at the Reichswehr. It was assumed that Soviet military elements would continue to impose their line. The opposite happened; Russia today is in the full swing of Communism and the generals are dead.

6. Great Britain

The Chancellor criticized Great Britain for misinterpreting the German situation. England refuses to understand the Reich's real need for colonies. This need results from the very structure of German economy, which cannot be fed without colonies. England grants the rights for colonies to everyone, even to the smallest states, except the Reich. The Chancellor illustrated Germany's need for raw materials by examples. In addition, he pointed to the fact that young vital elements of the Reich need territories for their expansion. In Germany everything is forbidden to them. They trample on each other's toes. Everywhere there are signs on what is prohibited. These young elements seek expansion in expeditions, for example, to Tibet. Sooner or later England will see how indispensable the colonies are for Germany. The old German colonies are not exploited by Great Britain. England's concept is that Germany should receive colonies from the smaller states. However, the German government has no claims on these states, which did not take the colonies from Germany.

France shows more understanding for Germany's colonial claims, but it is hiding behind Great Britain.

7. *The Far East*

The Chancellor is of the opinion that Japan will definitely win and that China will have to accept onerous peace conditions. He does not think that Russia, in its present situation, will constitute a serious threat to Japan. America and England, in spite of their loud promises, will certainly do nothing. China will be left to its fate. The Abyssinian situation will be repeated. There was a moment when Chiang Kai-shek had a chance to make peace. Then all the League spheres throughout the globe were shouting that China should fight to the very end, promising the assistance of other nations. In practice nothing came out of all this. The Negus also had a chance to make peace with the Italian government, saving a part of his state, possibly in the form of a protectorate. He trusted the League and lost.

8. *The League of Nations*

The Chancellor expressed sharp criticism of the system of the League, which consists in imposing far-reaching obligations on states. The Chancellor was very sarcastic, illustrating his opinion with examples. He declared that, with the prevailing League system, all those who trust it 100 percent, especially the smaller states, will always be made fools of, since the Great Powers always back out in time. That is why the German government will never again return to the League, and here the Chancellor was quite determined. There are moments when the League becomes more or less popular; this depends on the Great Powers' interests. At present Great Britain is again playing the card of the League in connection with the situation in the Far East. The League is the forum in which Great Britain furthers its interests.

9. *Germany's Internal Affairs*

The Chancellor pointed to economic difficulties in connection with the necessity of feeding 68 million people. Looking at things from this angle, he considered any convulsion in Europe to be of great danger. This dictates the necessity for a peaceful policy. He elaborated in detail on the subject of creating new raw materials.

He stressed the durability of his cabinet. Some of his collaborators have been at his side for fifteen years already. The ministers of his cabinet, with a few exceptions, are not being replaced.

About Schacht he said that, pressed by the Chancellor, Schacht had taken over the Ministry of Economy after Schmidt's illness. However, he had always shrunk from this department, since his profession is banking. Every six months since then he had handed in his resignation, since he was unwilling to take the responsibility for economic matters.

General Remarks of the Chancellor

The Chancellor referred to the fact that his offers of disarmament, fixing the ceiling at 200,000 and later at 300,000 men, had not been accepted at the time. If a compromise had then been accepted, this fact would have had a favorable impact on Germany's economic life. Money would have been spent for productive aims instead of for armaments. As an illustration, he cited that the necessity to make armaments at such a pace delayed by four years the creation of a cheap motor car (the Volkswagen). Only now was its production being realized. This would be a gigantic enterprise, employing 65,000 people. The price of the car would not exceed 900 marks, which would be advantageous for the idea of savings. The Germans must be thrifty to meet the requirements of the national economy. With the goal of buying a cheap car in mind, an individual would be willing to save.

In connection with the cabinet change in France, the Chancellor stated that with a perpetual change of statesmen any kind of policy becomes impossible. Today there is one French minister with whom contact is established; tomorrow a new individual, a complete stranger, appears, with whom things have to be taken up from the very beginning. Hitler alluded to the fact that on the Polish side there was a permanent team of competent people.[13]

[13] See *Polish White Book,* No. 36, where this conversation is published in a very concise form. For the German version of the conversation, see *DGFP,* Series D, Vol. V, Nos. 29 and 30.

Changes in the Reich's Top Rulers
Conversations with Göring in Warsaw
The Anschluss
February—March, 1938

ON FEBRUARY 4, 1938, fundamental changes took place in the organization and staff of the top rulers of Germany. Dismissed from their posts were Reichswehr Minister Field Marshal von Blomberg, Commander of the Army General Fritsch, and Foreign Affairs Minister von Neurath, as well as seven Army generals and six Air Force generals. In addition, thirty-six generals were transferred to different positions.

Chancellor Hitler did away with the office of the Reichswehr minister and established the post of commander in chief, himself assuming supreme command over the armed forces. General Wilhelm Keitel was nominated chief of the General Staff, and General Walter von Brauchitsch became commander of the Army. At the same time Hitler promoted General Göring, commander in chief of the Air Force, to the rank of field marshal.

Joachim von Ribbentrop became foreign affairs minister, and von Neurath was relegated to the rather unimportant leadership of the newly created Secret Council for Foreign Affairs in the Chancellor's office.

These changes, worked out in the strictest secrecy, came as a total surprise to Germany itself, to other countries, and to the diplomatic corps in Berlin. In Lipski's papers the following personal note was found:

Note with Regard to the Events of February 4, 1938

Following many insistent requests from Warsaw to introduce the Polish Ballet (created on the occasion of the *Exposition des arts décoratifs* in Paris) into the Reich, I approached Minister Goebbels to accept jointly with me the patronage of this enterprise. Goebbels accepted, agreeing to performances of the ballet not only in Berlin but also in a number of other German cities.

The gala performance at the Goebbels Opera in Berlin was fixed for a few days prior to the events of February 4, 1938. The Chancellor promised to attend. On the same day, an hour before the performance, I got a telephone call from the Secretary of State and the Reich Chancellery that Hitler, in spite of his best intentions, would be unable to attend. He hoped to have an opportunity to see the ballet in some other German city, for example, in Munich. At the opera I sat in a box with von Neurath, Goebbels, Rauscher, and Funk. I felt that there was something in the wind and that grave political complications were under way which prevented the Chancellor from attending. After the ballet there was a big reception at the Embassy, attended by von Neurath, Goebbels, and many high-ranking German dignitaries, as well as the whole corps de ballet. One half of the income from the first performance went to the Wintershilfe, and the other half for Polish needs. Goebbels presented me with a check.

Meanwhile, the Austrian problem was swelling into a crisis. On February 12 a meeting took place at Berchtesgaden between Austrian Chancellor Schuschnigg and Hitler, and on February 15 identical official communiqués were published in Berlin and Vienna, declaring that the two countries were determined to observe the principles of the agreement dated July 11, 1936,[1] and to consider them as a fundamental basis for mutual peace relations.[2] The terms presented in the form of an ultimatum by Hitler were accepted by Schuschnigg. In Vienna the cabinet was reshuffled, and Hitler's appointee, Seyss-Inquart, became minister of the interior and security. Amnesty was also proclaimed for political offenders (mainly for National Socialists).

On February 20 Hitler delivered an important speech at the Reichstag, presenting a detailed analysis of the Reich's foreign policy. He declared that Germany would never return to the League of Nations. With regard to Austria and Czechoslovakia, he remarked that 10 million Germans were living in those countries. A legal and governmental separation from the Reich could not result in a divorce so far as the rights of the population were concerned. With good will, as had been demonstrated, a solution might be found to problems of national minorities. However, a state which strove to prevent such an understanding in Europe by force might one day provoke an act of force.

With regard to Poland, Hitler laid stress on ever-increasing friendly relations. The Polish state respected national relations in Danzig, and the Free City and Germany respected the rights of Poland.[3]

In Lipski's papers there are two personal notes on these questions and a report to Beck dated February 19 (still prior to Hitler's speech).

[1] For the text of the agreement, see *DGFP*, Series D, Vol. I, Nos. 152 and 153.
[2] For the text of the communiqué, see *Survey of International Affairs, 1938*, II, 53–54.
[3] For the paragraph referring to Poland, see *Polish White Book*, No. 37.

Austria

On the afternoon of February 11 Austrian Envoy Tauschitz called by telephone, asking to be received immediately.

Showing some nervousness owing to the situation prevailing in Austria's relations with the Reich, he asked me if I was of the opinion that the changes which had taken place on February 4 in the top posts of the Reich's leadership were connected with Germany's intentions toward Austria.

In the course of a long conversation dealing with the political situation, I expressed my views as to the real plans of Germany with regard to his country.

When Tauschitz left, I received a report that Austrian Chancellor Schuschnigg was arriving the next day at Berchstesgaden. I think that when Tauschitz came to discuss this matter with me he had already been informed about the intended visit. However, a few days later he tried to persuade me that when he called on me he had known nothing about Schuschnigg's visit, and he begged me to believe that he had no intention of keeping this visit secret from me.

February 15, 1938

Herr von Ribbentrop, nominated the Reich's foreign affairs minister on February 4, took office on February 10. He confined himself to leaving visiting cards with the ambassadors, instead of paying the usual personal call.

He established official contact with the chiefs of the diplomatic missions by inviting them to a reception at Kaiserhoff on February 15.

I had only a brief exchange of opinion with him. He was not enthusiastic when I mentioned Göring's visit to Poland, whence I was just returning. In general, even social contact with him was rather difficult, to say nothing of a political discussion, for he had the habit of monologizing without heed to the *meritum* of the arguments of his opponent.

DOCUMENT 78   Lipski to Beck

NO. 1/13/38   Berlin, February 19, 1938

As of February 13, 1938, events in German-Austrian relations took such a rapid turn that I was obliged to communicate with you by telegram, almost on an hour-to-hour basis, on the more outstanding facts. I would like to report now on the fundamental stages of developments in this matter on the eve of the Chancellor's speech, which undoubtedly will concentrate on the outstanding political moment in the Reich's modern history: Hitler's conversation with Schuschnigg. This event is closely connected with the decisions taken on February 4.

From the conversation you had with the leading authorities of the Reich during your stay in Berlin on January 13–14, it was evident that the German government had decided to settle the Austrian problem in one way or another. May I just recall the statement of the usually reserved von Neurath, then in charge of the A.A., that, bearing in mind Schuschnigg's resistance, he saw no possible way of solving the situation by German-Austrian negotiations, and that therefore he was not excluding the possibility of an outburst inside Austria.

From these conversations, and especially from Göring's declarations, it was clear that, analyzing the reaction of the Western Powers interested in this problem, the German government came to the conclusion that Great Britain was leaving the Reich free to act (Halifax's conversations in Berlin).[4] France cannot afford any action, while the Italian government, as a result of Mussolini's conversations during his trip to Germany, also agrees with the idea of Austria's annexation to Germany. Finally, the Chancellor himself definitely stressed at that time that in case of an attempt to realize the legitimist idea he would not hesitate to march into Austria.

I am aware that the Austrian problem was discussed later on by German statesmen with Prime Minister Stoyadinovich when he visited Berlin. This occurred just after you left Berlin on January 15. A pledge was allegedly obtained from Stoyadinovich that the Yugoslav government would oppose the possible return of the Hapsburgs to Austria, and that Yugoslavia would mobilize in case of a legitimist revolution.

The consul general in Munich, [Konstanty] Jeleński, in his report dated February 1, No. 3/N/156, informed you about his conversation with Austrian Consul General Jordan. Herr Jordan was of the opinion that the legitimist movement in Austria would not be the only pretext for an open German intervention; he had most serious misgivings as to the possibility of an internal outburst through the National Socialist

[4] The Hitler-Halifax conversation of November 19, 1937 (*DGFP*, Series D, Vol. I, No. 31).

organizations in Austria. The Austrian Consul then pointed to a plan he was informed about—the creation of a provisional National Socialist government in Salzburg supported by the Austrian Legion, in order to seize power in Austria. He also mentioned the increase of financial subsidies granted by the Reich to Austrian National Socialists.

Here the question arises whether the changes ordered by the Chancellor in the army and the foreign service on February 4 were directly connected with the Austrian problem. It is impossible to prove beyond any doubt. I think that the complications caused by Blomberg's marriage were the very last straw that broke the camel's back, forcing the Chancellor to make a final decision in the domain of the commander in chief of the Reich's armed forces. However, it cannot be overlooked that the men who left on February 4, especially the military, represented the old Prussian, Protestant ideological trend, basically hostile to the reunion with Austria. It must also be added that the chiefs of the army, such as General Fritsch, who had to base their opinions on purely realistic considerations of the army's preparedness for war, often used their influence to mitigate decisions taken from the political angle. This was the case with remilitarization of the Rhineland, intervention in Spain, etc. So it is not impossible that in the Austrian problem also these elements would be in opposition to the use of the army as a trump card in the diplomatic gamble, at a moment when this army was not yet ready for action.

On the other hand, it was quite obvious that after February 4 Hitler was badly in need of a huge political showdown on the Austrian problem to erase the unpleasant memories of public opinion at large caused by changes in the leading posts of the army. Nevertheless, the following question arises, which I heard, for instance, from the Italian Ambassador: how was it possible that precisely at a time of weakness caused by changes in the top brass of the army the moment was chosen by the German side to hand an ultimatum to Schuschnigg, threatening him with consequences going so far as the use of force (*Machtpolitik*)? I think that in this case, as in the case of the remilitarization of the Rhineland when the risk was far greater, Chancellor Hitler took this risk, and won.

Whether, in case Schuschnigg refused the ultimatum, German armed forces would actually have been used for operations in Austria is still an open question. Besides this extreme, other means were at Hitler's disposal in case Schuschnigg rejected his conditions: the agreement of July,

1936, could be revoked; diversion could be started inside Austria by National Socialists supported by Party formations from the Reich. I was told here that Papen used the argument with Schuschnigg that the peace policy based on the July agreement would end at the moment he left Austria. Anyhow, the impact of the pressure exerted by Hitler's government, whether there was any bluff behind it or not, had its effect.

At any rate, this fact is worth noting, as far as concerns methods that the German government is now introducing to realize its plans in the field of foreign policy.

The atmosphere on the same evening at the reception the Chancellor gave for the diplomatic corps might serve to illustrate the state of tension which existed on February 15 until the German proposition was accepted. Even at 8:30 P.M., prior to the publication of the communiqué, General Field Marshal Göring took me aside and said how glad he was about his intended trip to Poland; however, he wanted to say as frankly as usual that this trip might have to be postponed if a row with Austria occurred ("Wenn wir mit Oesterreich krach bekommen").

The Chancellor, as I have already telegraphed, expressed to me his lively satisfaction with the agreement achieved, and headed very significantly that Czechoslovakia would now follow in the footsteps of Austria. However, in Göring I noted a certain dissatisfaction and concern on that day. From what I heard later, I had the impression—although unconfirmed—that, taught by experience, he preferred to go deeper into action immediately instead of pushing step by step, where some possible surprise might be in store that would cause long-term friction. Very characteristic was Secretary of State Mackensen's opinion that Schuschnigg's political suicide must have cost him quite a lot. Von Neurath, with a note of melancholy, observed to one of my colleagues that von Ribbentrop was now reaping the fruits of his work, for the initiative and the elaborated plan for Schuschnigg's meeting with Hitler were his. At the Auswärtiges Amt it was said that conversations on Schuschnigg's arrival at Berchtesgaden had already lasted for some weeks, and that the events of February 4 had brought about a certain interruption. . . .

Józef Lipski

Between February 23 and 26, 1938, Field Marshal Göring was in Poland at a hunting party. During this visit he had a conversation with Marshal Smigły-

Rydz (see *Journal,* pp. 275–77, and abridged text in the *Polish White Book,* No. 38), as well as two conversations with Minister Beck.

DOCUMENT 79 First Conference of Minister Beck
with Göring in Warsaw, February 23, 1938

NO. N/52/6/38   Berlin, February 28, 1938
                                                   Strictly Confidential

On February 23, 1938, Göring had two conversations with Minister Beck. Résumé of the principal points of the first conversation held before noon at the Foreign Affairs Ministry, with Ambassadors Moltke and Lipski present.

1. Austria

On the Chancellor's recommendation, Göring informed Minister Beck, in strict confidence, about the circumstances of the Hitler-Schuschnigg conversation.

1) The German government had received of late information based on documents that the Austrian government was taking a new direction in its foreign policy, namely, that it was establishing close contact with the Czechoslovak government. There was the risk that through taking this path Austria would enter the orbit of Czech-Soviet politics. This situation called for prompt action.

2) Under these circumstances, the Chancellor was compelled first to take basic measures of an internal character in order to gain more freedom of action. This was achieved by centralizing in his own hand all the elements needed for the operation (events of February 4).

3) Without mincing words, the Chancellor communicated to Schuschnigg the information in his possession; he made him face the alternative—either to sever talks with the Czechs and make an agreement with the Reich, or to break with the Reich, with all the ensuing consequences. Schuschnigg chose the agreement.

4) Schuschnigg was told explicitly that the understanding achieved at Berchtesgaden was just the beginning of a rapprochement between the Reich and Austria.

5) The agreement consisted of granting power to the National Socialists (under Seyss-Inquart), admitting them to the *Vaterländische Front,*

and filling government posts with them; furthermore, granting an amnesty, a considerable economic rapprochement, for which the delegates to the economic negotiations with the Reich had already been nominated.

Göring mentioned ore when referring to the economic agreement. Czechoslovakia was to be eliminated from the Austrian market (coal) and was to be replaced by trade with the Reich. As a further step, a customs union was envisaged.

Austria's policy in foreign affairs was to conform to the Reich's guiding lines. For instance, persons who had acted or were acting to the detriment of the German ideology were to be dismissed from Austrian diplomacy. Göring said that there were people who had been forced by Vienna to act against German interests, as, for example, Tauschitz in Berlin. Those, of course, would not be purged. Closer military contacts, indispensable under such an agreement, were to be established between the two armies.

6) Göring declared that things had taken a more rapid turn in Austria than was foreseen by the German government. In other words, the idea of National Socialism was spreading ever more broadly.

7) In spite of a certain pressure from the Austrian side, Chancellor Hitler did not use the word "independence" in his speech at the Reichstag on February 20.

8) Göring pointed to a probable attempt on the part of Schuschnigg to shield himself in his speech from excessive attacks by the opposition. He thinks that Schuschnigg will say that Austria's independence was not encroached upon, since relations remained within the frame of the agreement of July, 1936. A certain anxiety could be detected in Göring in connection with Schuschnigg's forthcoming speech.

9) The French government had intervened through Ambassador Poncet with Ribbentrop on the Austrian problem. The Foreign Affairs Minister of the Reich replied that he was not in a position to answer his question, since this was *eine Familiengelegenheit* between Germany and Austria.

II. Rumania, Hungary, Czechoslovakia

1) Göring pointed to the fact that the internal situation of *Rumania* is disturbing. He hinted that although Goga's cabinet was welcomed by the German government, nevertheless Berlin was aware that Goga went much too fast and had no support from the masses. The present gov-

ernment, with a patriarch at the helm, evokes some misgivings. The German government's main concern is that Rumania might fall under Soviet influence. In his opinion, Goga's downfall was certainly due to international intervention and Soviet threats.

Minister Beck, who was in possession of information from Envoy Arciszewski, [5] did not consider Rumania's internal situation so alarming. He thought that King Carol had trump cards in his hand with which to dominate the situation. At one time the King had decided to dismiss Titulescu, that is, the element most obedient to Soviet dictation. Minister Beck shared Göring's opinion that Goga had no mass support; besides, he wanted to carry out basic reforms through administrative channels. This, plus financial difficulties, had caused his downfall. As far as Soviet threats were concerned, the Rumanian government knew that it could count on assistance under the alliance with Poland.

2) Minister Beck stressed that, in order to stiffen Rumania against the Soviets, it was important that Rumania should feel at peace on the Hungarian frontier. Therefore, Minister Beck was endeavoring to procure a rapprochement between *Hungary* and Rumania.

Göring pointed to the difficulty in obtaining such an understanding, given Hungary's intransigent attitude. He allegedly heard from some Hungarians the thesis that, in view of the open Bessarabian problem, Hungary could, in case of a future Soviet-Rumanian conflict, grab Transylvania. When Göring answered the Hungarians that besides Transylvania and Bessarabia there still remained the former Rumania, he was told that the remaining part of Rumania could fall under Poland's protectorate. Göring declared that with such an atmosphere prevailing it was rather difficult to plan a rapprochement between Hungary and Rumania.

3) *Czechoslovakia* was touched on casually, and Göring remarked that it remains under the influence of Soviet Russia's policy. Minister Beck remarked that he does not see what other policy Czechoslovakia could adopt. It always adopts radical solutions. At one time it builds on the concept's of Beneš; if there is a reaction against this, it pushes Hodža and his thesis to the forefront.

In Lipski's papers there is a note with reference to his conversation with Beck after the first Beck-Göring conference:

[5] Mirosław Arciszewski, Polish minister to Rumania (1932–38); later he was assistant undersecretary of state in the Ministry of Foreign Affairs.

After this conference I had a conversation with Beck, at which time I returned to my idea of approaching the German side with some conditions with a view to stabilizing Polish-German relations. I assumed that upon the realization of German intentions toward Austria and Czechoslovakia the Reich's power would increase tremendously. We should therefore place our demands in advance. I suggested extending the declaration of nonaggression for twenty years, with an adequately worded introduction which would secure the *status quo* in our mutual relations. I suggested that this agreement could be signed on the occasion of Ribbentrop's visit to Warsaw. Beck agreed to this in principle, stressing additionally the necessity of securing an agreement on Danzig.

In addition, in view of the danger that in the Czechoslovak problem Germany might act over our head, I proposed definitely to declare to Göring our interest in that country, with which we have a long frontier-line. Such a reservation was to be made without going into details.

DOCUMENT 80   Second Conference of Minister Beck with Göring, in Warsaw, on the Evening of February 23, 1938, with Just the Two of Them Present, *after dinner at the Foreign Affairs Ministry*

Minister Beck said that, as far as *Austria* is concerned, as he had already stated at one time in Berlin, we have no political interests there, only transit and economic interests.

Göring replied that he had considered this point of view as it was communicated to him by the Minister in Berlin, and that Poland's interests would be adequately taken into account.

Beck stressed that, in contrast to Austria, we were seriously interested in the *Czech* problem from a twofold standpoint:

1) in a certain region of Czechoslovakia,

2) in the possible method of settling Czech problems ("die Art und Weise der eventuallen Lösung").

ad. 1) Göring replied that Poland's interests "in Mährish Ostrau" will not be infringed upon ("werden nicht berührt").

ad. 2) Göring acknowledged this statement, remarking that from the German side there would be no surprises for Poland. In case of any anticipated action in this respect, Warsaw would be informed in time.

Göring declared that the Chancellor had full confidence in Poland's

foreign policy as directed by Minister Beck. The Chan
people in Poland to know that, as long as Poland's policy co.
the Marshal's [Piłsudski] guiding idea, the Reich would observe
as agreed to with Poland.

Minister Beck replied that Poland would continue its line based on
reciprocity, and he added that the leading authorities in Poland had no
misgivings as to the development of Polish-German relations. But
abroad our mutual relations were regarded as a temporary arrangement.
Therefore the Minister suggested extending the act of 1934 on the occasion of Ribbentrop's possible visit to Warsaw.

Minister Beck remarked that this was just a vague idea.

Göring reacted in a very positive way to this idea, adding that the
Chancellor had directed him to investigate how Polish-German relations
could be reinforced in order to dispel the tensions existing on the Polish
side.

Minister Beck remarked that he saw two possible ways:

1) by an adequate solution of the Danzig problem, adding that anything accomplished to appease the situation in the Free City would
contribute to better mutual relations,

2) by the possible extension of the agreement of 1934, as mentioned
above.

Göring declared that the agreement should be extended for 20–25
years, so as to make it clear that Polish-German relations were based
upon a solid foundation. He suggested that, during the signing in Warsaw, the mutual tendencies of the two countries toward peace should be
expressed in an adequately worded preamble, which would serve to
influence public opinion at large.

Considering this matter to be strictly confidential, Göring will first
discuss it with the Chancellor.

Events in Austria signalized that the dramatic crisis in the *Anschluss*
problem was near at hand. On March 9 Chancellor Schuschnigg announced
in his speech at Innsbruck that the plebiscite fateful for Austria's future
would take place on Sunday, March 13.
Lipski noted on March 9:

On March 9, I had a farewell dinner at the Embassy for Mr. Comnen,
the newly appointed foreign affairs minister of Rumania. Among others,
the Austrian Envoy was present. Half an hour before dinner I received

news by telegram from Gawroński [6] of the planned plebiscite in Austria. Gawroński got his information from President Miklas. As seen from Berlin, it was clear that the announcement of the plebiscite would push Hitler to occupy Austria. I kept this secret from my guests, and only after dinner did I disclose the news to them. Reaction to the news about the plebiscite had already started by 9 P.M. Participants of my party were receiving telephone messages from Berlin from their embassies there and their legations in various capitals. The evening came to an end in an atmosphere of general excitement.

On March 10 Hitler decided on a military occupation of Austria, issuing special orders to General Keitel. On March 11 Chancellor Schuschnigg tendered his resignation to President Miklas. On March 12 German troops marched into Austria.

DOCUMENT 81   Lipski to the Ministry of Foreign Affairs

NO. 39   Berlin, March 12, 1938
                                         Received: March 12, 1938, 12 P.M.
                                         Secret Code

Göring told me that he counts on Poland's stand on the Austrian problem being the same as that taken by Minister Beck in Göring's conversation with Beck in Warsaw. He added that the Chancellor will be obliged to Poland for such a stand. I stated that our stand is unaltered and that we have only economic and transit interests in Austria. Göring replied that the German government will be all the more willing to consider these Polish interests.

Received: Warsaw, Rome

Lipski

The following is Lipski's personal note completing the telegram.

The conversation with Göring took place at a big reception given by him on the evening of March 11, 1938, at the Club for Airmen on the premises formerly occupied by the Prussian Herren Stube.

[6] Jan Gawroński, Polish minister to Austria, 1933–38.

Before this reception I attended a dinner at Czech Envoy Mastny's, where an atmosphere of utter tension and depression prevailed. I went to Göring's reception together with Prince Olgierd Czartoryski. Göring told me that Mussolini had given his consent for the *Anschluss* in reply to Hitler's letter handed to him by Prince Philip of Hesse. He remarked that German troops were entering Austria to safeguard peace; that only in the industrial centers of Wilden and Wiener Neustadt might some local riots be expected. Otherwise, the whole of Austria was for Hitler.

He mentioned his conversation with Henderson, which had taken place just a moment before.[7]

During this reception bands were playing continuously and many couples danced in the large hall, while diplomats clustered at round tables were engaged in animated discussions. I sat at the table of ambassadors, presided over by Göring. Next to me sat Prince Bismarck, who rather tactlessly asked me repeatedly why I was so gloomy. He tried some ersatz merrymaking.

We left the reception with Czartoryski in a mood of utter disgust, convinced that the Reich was racing toward an inevitable catastrophe of war. In the Embassy we were on night-duty service. On my return to the Embassy I sent a telegram informing Warsaw of the entrance of German troops into Austria and reporting on my conversation with Göring. In a second telegram I described my answer to Göring's question about our stand. This declaration of Göring with regard to consideration of our economic interests in Austria I utilized later on in my trade negotiations with the Reich, gaining 800,000 tons of coal in export to Austria.

A decision on this matter was communicated to me, with Vice-Minister Sokołowski present, by the undersecretary of state at the Ministry of Economics of the Reich, Herr Brinkmann. (During the stay of Minister of Commerce Roman in Berlin this problem was not settled, and only after his departure did we ram through, together with Herr von Moltke, this principal Polish demand.) [8]

[7] Henderson, pp. 124–26.
[8] See also *DGFP*, Series D, Vol. V, No. 35.

Resumption of Polish-Lithuanian Relations
Spring, 1938

POLAND AND LITHUANIA had no diplomatic relations for twenty years, a striking anomaly for two neighboring states over such a long period of time. A frontier incident which occurred on the night of March 10, 1938, when a Polish soldier was killed, compelled the government of Poland to intervene. On March 17 an ultimatum was dispatched to Lithuania through the Polish Legation in Tallin, with an expiration date of March 19, requesting that diplomatic relations be resumed prior to March 31; the Lithuanian government accepted the ultimatum, and relations between Poland and Lithuania were established on the date fixed.[1]

In the papers of Ambassador Lipski there is a personal note on this matter.

Note with Regard to the Ultimatum to Lithuania

Our action toward Lithuania was not coordinated with the Reich. The guiding idea of Poland's policy had been a constant tendency to normalize Polish-Lithuanian relations on the principle of the *status quo*. Beck tried to counteract the gradual growth of the Reich's power, and Poland's security became the axiom of his foreign policy.

I discussed this problem with him after his Berlin visit in the middle of January, 1938. The incident during which a Polish soldier, Stanisław Serafin, was shot by the Lithuanian frontier guards gave rise to Warsaw's large-scale action to exert pressure on Kaunas to resume diplomatic relations with Warsaw.

This action, which coincided with the *Anschluss,* quite erroneously gave the impression to international opinion that Warsaw and Berlin were acting jointly. This conviction contributed to a large extent to Kaunas' acceptance of the Polish ultimatum. Upon receipt of the Polish note fixing the date for an answer at March 19, the Lithuanian govern-

[1] See *DGFP,* Series D, Vol. I, Nos. 321–39; also *ibid.,* No. 33, and *Journal,* pp. 293–97.

ment addressed itself to the Great Powers, among others to Moscow, asking for advice. These Powers advised Kaunas to accept the Polish conditions, under the impression that Warsaw's step was covered by Berlin.

As a matter of fact, the situation in the sector of Polish-German relations was then as follows: on March 15 the tension in Polish-Lithuanian relations became so violent that a crisis could be expected at any time. A commotion within diplomatic quarters became very obvious; I could observe it at an evening reception at the Persian Embassy. Saulys, the Lithuanian envoy, approached me and, visibly excited, told me that Warsaw was seeking a conflict with Lithuania. I purposely kept my reserve.[2] In a longer conversation with me, Taffe, the Estonian envoy, stressed that this was the best occasion for the resumption of Polish-Lithuanian relations. A number of diplomats turned to me for information. The Soviet Chargé d'Affaires showed great excitement. He conversed with the Lithuanian Envoy.

Chancellor Hitler left for Austria. Göring was replacing him as head of state. Minister Beck was in Italy; his return was expected on March 16 at noon. On the morning of the 16th I received a telephone call from Göring at Karinhall inviting me to come over and inform him about the situation. I was without any instructions from Warsaw, and I could only act in accordance with the line of general political concepts and my personal intuition.

Göring told me that Ribbentrop had telephoned him from Munich, asking for information on the development of our relations with Lithuania, in order to transmit it to the Chancellor.

The German government was anxious to obtain more detailed information in view of the possible entanglements on Germany's frontier as a result of the Polish-Lithuanian conflict. Taking refuge in the lack of detailed instructions, I explained to Göring in general outlines the Polish-Lithuanian situation, stressing that it was impossible to maintain the present state on the frontier. I mentioned that the last frontier incident was proof that the void in Polish-Lithuanian relations threatened serious consequences at any moment. I was therefore of the opinion that the Polish government would be compelled to draw conclusions from this and to request that Lithuania resume relations. Göring showed understanding for our point of view. He stressed Germany's interest in Kłaj-

[2] See *DGFP*, Series D, Vol. I, No. 322.

peda [Memel], otherwise expressing his *désintéressement* with regard to Lithuania. Nevertheless, he came out with a question about Russia's stand and inquired whether the Polish government did not fear possible complications on that side. In accordance with general directives, I replied that we did not foresee any danger, adding that we were taking the Russian risk upon ourselves.

In addition, I promised Göring to keep him *au courant* of the development of events. Göring put through a telephone call to Munich and communicated our conversation to von Ribbentrop.

Our further exchange of opinion related to the assurances given by the Reich government to the Czech Envoy (see report dated March 16, 1938, No. 37/38) [3] and relations with Russia. Herr Göring came out with an open offer for Polish-German military collaboration against Russia. He stressed on this occasion that he could not conceive how Poland would be able, in the long run, to take the whole burden of Russia's threat on its shoulders. His present offer was even more detailed than those made previously.

Göring's stand on the Lithuanian question, confirmed by his telephone call to the Chancellor, enabled me to give a factual explanation to the Polish government upon Beck's return to Warsaw with regard to the position taken by the German government on our possible action against Lithuania.

This, in my opinion, had even greater importance when one bears in mind that this information could have an impact on the decision of the Polish government.

In reply to my telegram, the Ministry of Foreign Affairs forwarded to me a definition of the Polish stand with regard to the ultimatum to Lithuania, to be transmitted to Göring. A reservation was made therein that German interests in Kłajpeda would be respected by the Polish side, in case an armed Polish-Lithuanian conflict followed the rejection of the Polish request. I communicated this news to Göring in the late evening hours of March 17, when I retired unexpectedly for a short time from a dinner at the Embassy, leaving behind a large group of guests. I simply passed the news on to Meissner that I would leave for a moment to meet with Göring.

The next day, on March 18, Herr von Ribbentrop, who was back in

[3] See below, Document 82, p. 356.

Above left: Major Józef Lipski, London, November, 1951

Above: Józef Lipski, Berlin, October 3, 1933

Right: Foreign Minister Józef Beck and Ambassador Józef Lipski

Top: Ambassador Lipski showing the Wawel sculptured heads to German Chancellor Hitler at the Polish Arts Exhibition in Berlin, March 29, 1935. Between Lipski and Hitler, Professor Mieczysław Treter, organizer of the exhibition

Bottom: Conversation between Lipski and Hitler at the annual dinner for the chiefs of diplomatic missions, Berlin, January 22, 1935

Top: Memorial mass for Marshal Piłsudski on May 18, 1935. Ambassador Lipski greeting Hitler on the steps of St. Hedwig's Church in Berlin

Bottom: Alfred Rosenberg's monthly reception for foreign diplomats and foreign press at the Adlon Hotel, Berlin, March 7, 1938. Left to right: Lipski; Dr. Otto Dietrich, Reich press chief and secretary of state of the German Propaganda Ministry; Rosenberg; Hamdi Arpag, Turkish ambassador

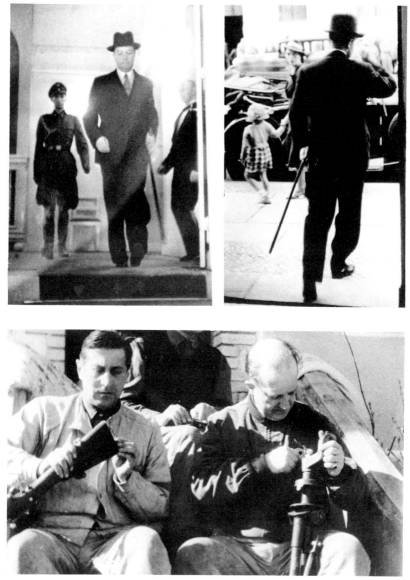

Top left and right: Ambassador Lipski leaving the Auswärtiges Amt after his last interview with Ribbentrop on August 31, 1939

Bottom: Former Ambassador Lipski and Henryk de Malhomme (left), former First Secretary of the Embassy in Berlin, as cadets at Coëtquidan, Brittany's boot camp, October, 1939

Top: Private Lipski and "frères d'armes" at Guère, Brittany, May, 1940, before leaving for the Maginot Line

Bottom: General Józef Haller greeting Private Lipski at Coëtquidan, Brittany

This page: General Kazimierz Sosnkowski with Lieutenant Lipski in the Middle East, 1943

Opposite above left: General Władysław Anders and Major Lipski in Italy, 1944

Opposite above right: Major Lipski with commanding officer Colonel St. Zakrzewski after taking Ancona, 1944

Opposite: Major Lipski in a happy reunion with Colonel Antoni Szymański, former military attaché in Berlin, after the latter's release from prison in Russia

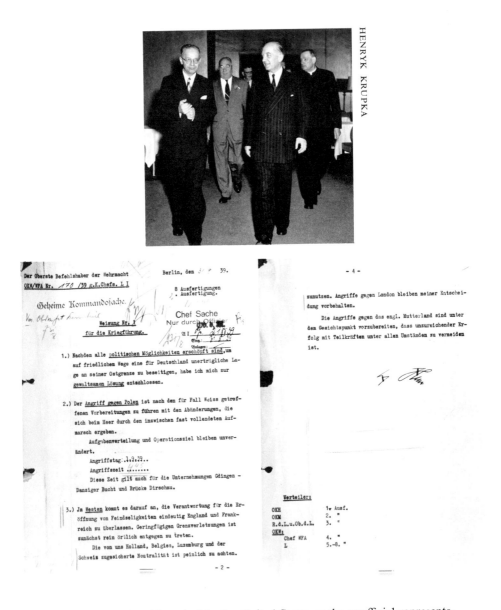

Top: Lipski after his arrival in the United States as the unofficial representative of the free Poles. At a reception in New York with Msgr. Felix Burant

Bottom left and right: The first and fourth pages (including Hitler's signature) of the German order for the attack on Poland at 4:45 A.M. on September 1, 1939. The time of attack was added in pencil at the last moment.

Berlin, got into the Polish-Lithuanian problem by inviting me for a conversation.

He declared [4] that Lithuanian Envoy Saulys had called on him and had tried to explore the German government's attitude with regard to Poland's demand dispatched to Kaunas. Herr von Ribbentrop told me that he had advised the Envoy to accept Poland's request.[5] He thought that Kaunas would do so. I expressed thanks to Herr von Ribbentrop for his position on this problem.

The French ambassador, M. Poncet, sent to me a well-known French journalist, Sauerwein, to explore the situation. It was rather difficult for me to play an open hand with him, since French journalists are known for their lack of discretion. I could not possibly reveal that our step toward Lithuania was dictated by our desire to shield ourselves in that region against Germany. I must admit that M. Sauerwein grasped our aims, sparing me the necessity of spelling out the situation, and he promised to refer the matter to competent French authorities.

Upon our dispatch of notes to Lithuania, Minister Saulys called me by telephone expressing his desire to see me without delay. In spite of the fact that I had a high opinion of Mr. Saulys as a patron of a rapprochement between our two nations, I could not comply with his demand. Meeting with him at a moment when Warsaw had sent a note requesting an answer by a fixed date, I could thwart the action of my government.

On the morning of March 19, I received news from Warsaw that the Kaunas government had accepted our request. I immediately approached the Lithuanian Envoy personally, asking to be received. We shook hands. He realized that I was sorry to have had to refuse his demand to see me a few days earlier. Very tactfully, he did not even mention it. The conversation now took a very friendly turn. This day of March 19 was a day of great satisfaction for me. . . .

The annexation of Austria by the Reich pushed the problem of Czechoslovakia to the forefront in international affairs. Lipski gives an account of this situation in his report dated March 16, 1938.

[4] *DGFP*, Series D, Vol. I, No. 334.
[5] *Ibid.*, Nos. 328 and 332.

DOCUMENT 82   Lipski to Beck

NO. N/37/38   Berlin, March 16, 1938
                                                              Confidential

Assurances received by Czech Envoy Mastny from Field Marshal Göring [6] and Minister von Neurath [7] that the German government has no
aggressive intentions toward Czechoslovakia were passed over in total
silence by the German press. This fact is characteristic, for it denotes
that it was not the intention of the German government to appease its
public opinion with regard to the Czechs.

The first spontaneous intervention by the Czech Envoy took place on
March 11 at a reception given by Minister President Göring, when news
came that German troops had marched into Austria. Later, Envoy
Mastny had a long conversation with von Neurath. He finally intervened
with Field Marshal Göring in connection with airplanes flying over the
territory of Czechoslovakia. [8]

Mr. Mastny, as he confirmed to me personally, was satisfied with the
assurances given, which were echoed in the speech of British Prime
Minister Chamberlain. [9] Field Marshal Göring, with whom I had a conversation today on Polish-Lithuanian relations, also confirmed his talk
with the Czech Envoy. He told me that not only did the Reich have no
aggressive intentions, but it is to be hoped that relations with Czechoslovakia may now improve. He asked Mr. Mastny if it was true that Czechoslovakia had taken some mobilization measures that might bring about
reaction on the part of Germany. Mr. Mastny, upon communicating
with Prague by telephone, advised him immediately that this news was
absolutely incorrect. [10]

As to the flight of German planes, Herr Göring remarked that there
was a lot of misinformation in the news in possession of the Czech side,
and that this matter had been cleared up in the conversation with Envoy
Mastny with an air expert present.

Deliberating on the Czechoslovak problem, Herr Göring told me that

[6] *DGFP*, Series D, Vol. II, No. 74.
[7] *Ibid.*, Nos. 78 and 80.
[8] *Ibid.*, Nos. 75–77.
[9] For the speech of Chamberlain on March 14, see *ibid.*, No. 84.
[10] *Ibid.*, No. 72.

the Reich government expects the Czech government to ease relations in the field of minorities and nonextension of Czech-Soviet relations. He added, however, that he does not think that in the long run Czechoslovakia can exist in its present form.

From the above deliberations of Göring it could be concluded that for the moment no violent action against Czechoslovakia by the Reich should be expected, provided that the basic line toward this state—known to you—is maintained in the future.[11]

It is very characteristic that the *Deutsch-Diplomatisch-Politische Korrespondez,* No. 49 of March 15, writing about recent events in Austria, mentions, for the first time so explicitly, that Hungary also still has unsettled national questions beyond its frontiers.

Józef Lipski

DOCUMENT 83   Lipski to Beck

NO. N/52/9/38   Berlin, March 31, 1938
                                            Strictly Confidential

With the Polish-Lithuanian conflict under way, I had just one conversation, on March 18, with the newly appointed foreign affairs minister, Herr von Ribbentrop, since he was traveling a good deal and I had no occasion to discuss with him in more detail problems pertaining to Polish-German relations. Last week Herr von Ribbentrop was also absent from Berlin, so that I could not be received by him until today.

To begin with, I would like to remark that the new minister continually stresses his positive and even friendly attitude toward Poland, which I have no reason to doubt. However, his personal style of holding office reveals that he is not quite *au courant* of particular problems and questions. The present secretary of state, von Mackensen, will leave the Auswärtiges Amt soon for the Embassy in Rome. Since his relations with Ribbentrop are not too friendly, the information service supplied to the Minister on the part of the A.A. leaves much to be desired.

May I add that von Mackensen's post will probably be filled by the present political director, Baron von Weizsäcker.

[11] See also the Lipski-Szembek conversation (*Journal,* p. 297).

Referring to my stay in Warsaw, I conveyed today your best greetings to Herr von Ribbentrop. When we touched casually on the successful liquidation of the Polish-Lithuanian conflict, I told him that you were obliged to Herr von Ribbentrop for the position he adopted on this matter at the time. I mentioned that the German Ambassador in Warsaw has already been advised accordingly.

Passing to Polish-German relations, I pointed to their successful development based on the declaration of January, 1934. I stressed that certain methods of action were established, based upon direct exchange of opinion in matters of interest to the two states. Thus, no surprises are in store, thanks to this system of mutual information. I added that, as the Chancellor confirmed in his speech at the Reichstag on February 20, this agreement had prevailed against many odds, facilitating a solution in the minorities question by a joint declaration of the two governments on November 5, 1937.

From these deliberations I went on to recall the conversation which took place in Warsaw on February 23 between you and Marshal Göring. At that time Göring said that the Chancellor had instructed him to investigate what could be done to reinforce Polish-German relations and to remove the tension which undermines Polish public opinion; to which you replied that anything that could be done to ease the situation in Danzig would have a positive effect on our opinion. I also mentioned that you promoted the idea of a possible extension of the agreement of January 26, 1934, hinting on my part that this could be done on the occasion of the planned visit.

To my great surprise, I noted that Herr von Ribbentrop had not yet been informed about this conversation. He explained that in the meantime the events in Austria had completely absorbed the whole government. Herr von Ribbentrop said that naturally he was not prepared to make a factual statement prior to consulting Göring. In the first place, he wondered whether such a well-functioning agreement contracted by the leaders of the two nations would not be weakened in the eyes of public opinion by an ill-timed extension.

I pointed to the fact that precisely by an extension would the provisional character of the agreement be removed; which, although it does not exist for competent authorities of the two states, is often exploited by international circles for opinion at large.

Herr von Ribbentrop, whose doubts might be due to a lack of orientation on the problem, promised to reflect on this question. Under these circumstances I did not insist further. Also in connection with Danzig, I simply referred to the Chancellor's declaration made to me on November 5, 1937, and repeated to you on January 14, 1938, as well as to the public statement contained in the Chancellor's speech of February 20.

As to the way the declaration of the two governments with regard to national minorities is working, Herr von Ribbentrop mentioned that he is not yet in a position to be acquainted with this matter. I gave him a general outline of this problem. I availed myself of this occasion to touch upon the census fixed for May 17, and now postponed because of Austria's annexation to the Reich. I did this presuming that, since the registration is being postponed and since as a result of the incorporation of Austria the bill calling for the census might be altered, the current moment is well chosen to present our reservations. I note here that I had already mentioned our objections to the head of the Political Department, Baron von Weizsäcker. Now, just in a general form, I presented the census problem to Herr von Ribbentrop, adding that I would forward to him an informative memo in the next few days.

Herr von Ribbentrop showed interest in Polish-German press relations. We discussed the departure of the German press delegation to Warsaw for a press conference on April 4–5. Herr von Ribbentrop remarked in general terms on the necessity of also influencing the opposition press in Poland. I stated that, as far as certain national organs of the opposition were concerned, they had recently changed their tone for a more positive view of the Polish-German policy.

For my part, I expressed the need of checking the German press in its propaganda campaign which exaggerates even the most insignificant minority incidents in Poland. I remarked that on our part we are hushing up such incidents concerning our minorities in Germany.

Herr von Ribbentrop also mentioned the unfortunate case of the correspondent of *Kurier Warszawski,* Mrs. Męcińska, with regard to the alleged German point of view on the Polish-Lithuanian conflict. He pointed to the Chancellor's dissatisfaction with this press incident, the more so since the German stand on this problem was correct and friendly toward Poland. I replied that Polish official quarters were most critical of this press release by a person who is also quite unqualified politically and is impressed by gossip. I stated that necessary steps have been taken by us to impress on *Kurier Warszawski* the necessity of recalling this correspondent from Berlin. In case this does not succeed, we would not protest if permission to remain in the Reich would be denied to her.

Finally, referring to the point of your conversation with Göring regarding the reinforcement of Polish-German relations, Herr von Ribbentrop made the reservation that he was not speaking officially but just as a friend, and asked me not to report the conversation to Warsaw. He took up a question which is weighing heavily on his heart: that of a wider anti-Comintern collaboration. He stressed that these matters are being worked on by a special bureau of his. Collaboration with Italy and Japan is yielding very interesting and positive results. At present a special commission has been formed to this end. Herr von Ribbentrop asked what Poland's reaction would be to this kind of collaboration.

With the reservation that I was also speaking quite informally, I stressed first of all that we are fighting Communism by all possible means inside Poland. We also react if it is infiltrated from abroad, and here I cited our last note to Czechoslovakia.[12] (By the way, my impression was that Herr von Ribbentrop only learned of this note from me, in spite of the fact that Ambassador von Moltke was duly briefed by the Polish government.) I further mentioned that we have a secret understanding with German security elements to this effect which is functioning satisfactorily, so that in practice we, like the Germans, are fighting Comintern activities on all sectors. Nevertheless, as far as outside manifestations are concerned, we must bear in mind our very special situation as an immediate neighbor of Soviet Russia, the more so since we are also under the obligations of our alliance with Rumania.

Herr von Ribbentrop said that naturally he brought up this issue quite informally, asking me again not to make any official use of it.

Since in the course of our conversation Herr von Ribbentrop was repeatedly called away from the office, I cut short the discussion and brought up no further problems of international politics.[13]

Józef Lipski

[12] In this note the Polish government made a firm declaration about Communist and diversive action directed against Poland from the territory of Czechoslovakia. In its reply of May 5, the Czech government declared that necessary steps would be taken to render this kind of action impossible in the future. The Polish government took due notice of the Czech declaration, provided that concrete results of action by the Czech authorities would follow.

[13] For the German version of this conversation, see *DGFP*, Series D, Vol. V, No. 34.

DOCUMENT 84   Lipski to Beck

NO. 7/70   April 9, 1938
                                                              Secret

With reference to my report of February 12, No. N/7/17/38,[14] I am
taking the liberty of informing you that, in connection with the nomination of Herr von Ribbentrop on February 4 to the post of foreign affairs
minister of the Reich, further changes followed in German diplomacy,
published by the press on April 2, covering the head office of the Auswärtiges Amt and a number of posts abroad.

Former Secretary of State von Mackensen became ambassador in
Rome, and his place was taken by Baron von Weizsäcker, formerly head
of the Political Department of the A.A. When Herr von Neurath left the
post of foreign affairs minister on February 4, Herr von Mackensen
made no secret that he would not remain in his post. For the son-in-law
of the former Foreign Affairs Minister, whose relations with Herr von
Ribbentrop (as I mentioned in my report) were not too cordial, the
situation at the A.A. became embarrassing, the more so since in his
capacity as secretary of state von Mackensen would have to maintain
contact both with Foreign Affairs Minister von Ribbentrop and Neurath
as president of the Privy Council (*Geheimsrat*).

During his short stay in office as secretary of state, which lasted just a
year, Herr von Mackensen did not cut a particularly remarkable figure. I
was under the impression that he lacked technique, elasticity, and a
quick grasp of matters indispensable in such a post. Herr von Mackensen and his wife genuinely welcomed the fact of their transfer to Rome,
since they had become acquainted with that country some years earlier.

The newly appointed secretary of state, Baron von Weizsäcker, is a
talented diplomat, highly intelligent and very flamboyant. He has always
been well disposed toward nationalistic ideas, and he is a man of confidence of the Party. I would like to remark that an outstanding professional in the post of secretary of state was particularly needed by Herr
von Ribbentrop, who is not a career diplomat and is not very fond of the
technicalities of his office.

Herr von Ribbentrop transferred to the A.A. the former counselor of

[14] Not included in this series of documents. It contained details with regard to
changes at the Auswärtiges Amt made on February 4, that is, the resignation of
Minister von Neurath, the appointment of Ribbentrop to this post, and his
biography.

the German Embassy in London, Herr Woermann, to become his new collaborator as head of the Political Department.

If we take into consideration that Herr Bohle is secretary of state at the A.A. for the problems of Germans abroad, that recently Herr Keppler was nominated to a similar post at the A.A. as secretary of state for Austrian affairs, we note that at present this ministry numbers four secretaries of state. This situation naturally evoked some misgivings on the part of the former ministerial directors, who were thus pushed into the background. It is more characteristic that the highest ranking director, Head of the Legal Department Gaus, was offered an autographed portrait of the Chancellor as a sort of compensation.

Vacant Embassy posts were now offered to Mackensen in Rome, von Dirksen in London, von Papen in Ankara, and General Ott in Tokyo.

As I mentioned before, the candidacy of Herr von Moltke was considered for London. Finally, the Chancellor decided to keep him in Warsaw, since he was well oriented in Polish-German relations and had a good reputation in Poland. I heard from people friendly with von Moltke that he was not very anxious to go to London. A large family and a landed estate in Silesia, which he often visits from Warsaw and looks after personally, probably influenced his decision.

Some circles close to the A.A. are of the opinion that Herr von Dirksen's nomination to London is not a very good choice, as he is allegedly much too bureaucratic for London.

In the last appointments, Herr von Ribbentrop did not neglect the chief of his special bureau, von Raumer, who was nominated minister plenipotentiary and will probably soon go into the diplomatic service.

Besides, I was informed that a number of young men from the Party would soon be introduced into the A.A. in order to "pump in some fresh blood."

Józef Lipski

DOCUMENT 85 Lipski to Beck

NO. N/L/82/38

May 19, 1938
Strictly Confidential

Rumors and unconfirmed reports are currently circulating here about the results of conversations during Chancellor Hitler's stay in Italy.[15] As the dictators of Italy and Germany were mostly conversing without witnesses, it is even more difficult to obtain reliable details. That is why I refrained for the time being from transmitting information not issued from official quarters. I was awaiting an occasion, upon my recovery from the flu, to discuss these topics with members of the German government. In the last days I took this subject up with the secretary of state at the Auswäriges Amt, von Weizsäcker, and the Chancellor's secretary of state, Lammers.

Herr von Weizsäcker limited himself to a few explanations of a general character, without going into details. In the first place, he stated that the visit did not, in principle, add any new aspects to German-Italian relations, or to the so-called Axis. No document was signed in Rome. Herr von Weizsäcker did not conceal the fact that there was some negative reaction to the *Anschluss* on the part of public opinion in Italy. Nevertheless Mussolini—a great statesman—considered this move to be a historic necessity. Chancellor Hitler's emphatic and so-well-justified declaration on the inviolability of the German-Italian frontier contributed to the appeasement of opinion in Italy. Besides, added von Weizsäcker, with the *Anschluss* already an accomplished fact, a tension permanently present in German-Italian relations was removed. At present a common frontier has become an element of rapprochement and further collaboration.

As for news spread by the press about the alleged dealing out of spheres of influence between the Reich and Italy in certain regions, as, for example, the Danubian basin, the Secretary of State called such rumors products of sheer imagination. In order to understand fully the very essence of German-Italian relations—von Weizsäcker said—careful attention should be paid to the speeches delivered by Mussolini and Hitler at the Venetian Palace. These texts reveal everything.

[15] Hitler's trip to Italy from May 2 to May 10 was to pay a return visit to Mussolini, who had come to Germany in September, 1937.

To my allusion about French-Italian relations, the Secretary of State only remarked that in this sector also an understanding would probably be reached, the more so since matters are not very complicated. Recent endeavors to extend the life-span of Red Spain were, in Herr von Weizsäcker's opinion, weighing on the relations of Italy with France. If once and for all a decision was taken to ease the situation in Spain, the conflict should not be prolonged by supporting the hopeless cause of the Red Army.

With reference to the reception of Ambassador Wysocki by Hitler, the Secretary of State explained that previous notice given to Ambassador Wysocki that the audience was not possible was caused by fear of establishing a precedent, especially since very high-ranking persons were also trying to obtain an audience with Hitler. I learned from a report from Rome that, upon refusal on the part of the German Embassy, a personal friend of Ambassador Wysocki, Secretary of State Meissner, obtained the audience for him. I therefore think that Herr von Weizsäcker tried to explain the behavior of the German Embassy in Rome. Von Weizsäcker also explained that Hitler made an exception for Ambassador Wysocki out of regard for his very positive role in the Polish-German rapprochement at the time National Socialism came to power.

If Weizsäcker in his deliberations did not throw too much light on the real meaning of the conversations in Rome, Secretary of State Lammers went a step further and was more explicit in his explanations. He stated that the journey to Rome was not just a demonstration but had resulted in concrete political advantages. In his opinion, the moment for the meeting—following the Italian-British agreement [16]—was well chosen, for otherwise Germany would be held responsible for possible difficulties in reaching this agreement.

Herr Lammers rather significantly stressed that the fruits of the Rome visit would only ripen in its aftermath. And he added that Germany is aware that Italy must have a free hand in the Mediterranean, just as Germany is striving to have freedom of action in some other regions.

With regard to the Chancellor's declaration as to the inviolability of the German-Italian frontier, Herr Lammers explained that the Chancellor launched upon a most emphatic and basic statement on the subject of German-Italian relations. He also added that the inhabitants of Tyrol

[16] The Italo-British agreement was concluded in Rome on April 16, 1938, clearing up a number of problems dividing these two states of late.

feel badly hurt by such a settlement. However, the greater good turned the scale in this case.

As Lammers is close to the Chancellor, I laid special emphasis on the fact that Ambassador Wysocki, as well as Polish governmental circles, greatly appreciated the fact that the Chancellor granted an audience to Wysocki. Herr Lammers replied that the Chancellor was pleased to grant it, owing to Ambassador Wysocki's merit in the cause of Polish-German relations.

As yet, I have had no opportunity to converse with Ribbentrop and Göring on the subject of the visit in Rome. However, it might be stated that, in spite of the *Anschluss* and certain negative repercussions caused by it to public opinion in Italy, the Axis is in full swing. Matters of overwhelming weight of interest were probably decisive for the maintenance of full collaboration between the two states. In my opinion this collaboration should be taken into consideration very seriously in concrete international situations. The last speech of Mussolini in Genoa is very characteristic in this respect.[17]

From what I could gather from a remark made casually to Counselor Lubomirski by Herr Woermann, the second secretary of state, it seems that the German government was warned and informed in advance about the tenor of Mussolini's speech in Genoa. The speech gives the impression of a certain challenge to France via Italy at a moment when the Sudetenland case is on the carpet. It is worth while to quote here from Hitler's speech at a banquet in the Venetian Palace, where he stated:

"Thus a bloc of 120 million people was formed in Europe ready to guard their eternal rights for life and to counter all forces which would oppose the natural development of these states."

Józef Lipski

DOCUMENT 86 Lipski to Beck

NO. N/L9L/38   Berlin, May 28, 1938
                                               Strictly Confidential

With reference to my report of May 19, No. N/L/82/38, I am taking the liberty of informing you that lately I have had occasion to discuss

[17] Mussolini's speech of May 14 on Italian foreign policy.

the results of Hitler's trip to Italy with Italian Ambassador Attolico, who returned to Berlin after a long illness.

Signor Attolico spent the last period of his illness in Italy and was present in Rome during the demonstrations in honor of Germany's Führer. Chancellor Hitler paid him a courtesy visit at his Roman villa.

Signor Attolico told me, and I also heard this previously from Weizsäcker, that after the *Anschluss* the reaction in Italy was openly hostile to the Germans. During the first days of Hitler's stay in the Italian capital, this could allegedly be clearly observed. Even Mussolini and his entourage were visibly taken aback by this atmosphere. Only after Hitler's speech delivered at the Venetian Palace, and especially the passage stressing the inviolability of the Italian-German frontier, was the tension in feelings relieved, so that in Naples the reception was much warmer, reaching a diapason in Florence.

The Italian Ambassador thinks that, although the *Anschluss* was painful to take at the start, in the long run it removed a source of friction from German-Italian relations. In his opinion the words spoken by Hitler carry historic meaning. The Ambassador also explained that, since Mussolini's speech as a matter of course was less expressive, this shortcoming had to be balanced. Mussolini did so in the speech delivered in Genoa.

The Ambassador also strongly confirmed that nothing had been signed during the conversations between the two dictators. Questioned about Italian-French negotiations, Signor Attolico remarked that an error was possibly committed by not requesting an immediate nomination of an ambassador. On its side, the French government overloaded the negotiations with a lot of problems which, in the opinion of the Italian government, do not concern France in the least, as, for example, the Suez question, the Red Sea, etc. Besides, the French side started to mangle such delicate matters as Tunisia, thus making a mess of the negotiations.

Józef Lipski

The Problem of the Sudetenland
Summary, 1938

A NUMBER of incidents occurred in the Sudetenland in connection with county elections in Czechoslovakia fixed for May 22–29 and June 12, 1938.

The tension reached its climax on May 19–21 when two Sudetenland Germans were killed by the Czech police near the town of Eger on the Czech-German frontier. The situation became so serious that the Czech government mobilized two classes of reservists on May 21. They were partially released on June 18.

The press in the West published news about the concentration of German troops on the Czechoslovakian frontier.

Lipski writes about these events in his memoirs.

Alarming news about the alleged German mobilization against Czechoslovakia came as a surprise to me. I had no regional reports dealing with the alleged German concentration on the Czechoslovakian border. Disturbed by the alarms sounded by the Western press, I approached the British Embassy and received the information that Henderson had ordered his staff to get ready to leave.[1]

At that time Minister Beck passed through Berlin on his way to Stockholm.[2] Upon discussing the matter, we decided that he should proceed with his trip. Owing to a longer stay at the station, Beck dictated in the car a reply to the French government's exposition addressed to us with regard to Czechoslovakia. (The text of Beck's telegram is not in my possession.)

On May 21 Ambassador Lipski noted his conversation with Göring:

At Göring's invitation I had a conversation with him.

Göring declared that the attitude taken by Great Britain and France on May 19–21 creates obstacles for a speedy realization of German demands with regard to the question of minorities in Czechoslovakia.

[1] This matter is related in Henderson, pp. 137–38.
[2] Beck left Warsaw on May 22 and arrived in Stockholm on May 24.

He suggested, rather casually and confidentially, the possible extension of economic pressure on Czechoslovakia on the part of Germany, Poland, and Hungary as a common action. The goal of this pressure was to be the realization of the demands of these states in relation to Czechoslovakia.

Keeping my reserve on this problem, I limited myself to the answer that the next time I was in Warsaw I would present this matter to the Foreign Affairs Minister.

Warsaw adopted a "wait and see" attitude in this matter. Beck, as usual, replied by a series of questions, which I was not able to present to Göring until our next meeting, held on June 17, 1938.

Lipski writes further in his memoirs:

As confidentially revealed by General Bodenschatz,[3] in answer to the stand taken by the Western Powers during the May crisis, Hitler gave orders for the building of fortifications on the western frontier of the Reich. And he wanted them built at full speed, fixing the deadline for a deal with Czechoslovakia at the fall of 1938. During my stay in Warsaw at Whitsuntide, I reported on this problem, asking the Minister to issue, in case of an emergency, evacuation instructions for the diplomatic posts in Germany. (The same instructions detailed at that time were applied later at the outbreak of the Polish-German war on September 1, 1939.) Besides this, I also warned the minister of the treasury, Eugene Kwiatkowski, about a possible conflict in the fall. Minister Kwiatkowski, disturbed by this news, which threatened his economic plans, told me half-jokingly that if I repeated the news to Marshal Śmigły the army would put an even greater strain on his budget. The top-brass of the army was, of course, informed about Bodenschatz's revelations.

DOCUMENT 87   Lipski to Beck

NO. N/52/18/38   Berlin, June 19, 1938
                                                  Strictly Confidential

Upon my return to Berlin after Whitsuntide, on June 7, I immediately called on Field Marshal Göring. I was informed that he was leaving Berlin the same day for about a week and would only be able to receive me upon his return.

[3] Karl Bodenschatz, a general of the Luftwaffe.

In the meantime I was able to draw a more precise picture of the situation which prevailed here following the events of May 19–21. I could do so on the basis of information received from a series of casual conversations with Minister von Ribbentrop and Secretary of State von Weizsäcker,[4] as well as with the ambassadors of France and Great Britain.

The position taken by Great Britain and France during these May days obviously contributed to the application of more circumspect methods in the Czech problem, in order to spare the Reich the risk of an international conflict.

During the debates which, as I heard, took place with the participation of representatives of the army, the Chancellor's opinion prevailed against more radical tendencies represented by some Party dignitaries. It is very characteristic that Ambassador Henderson, who plays first fiddle in this matter, told me that the only person showing moderation and reserve is the Chancellor himself. His entourage is, in the opinion of the Ambassador, fanatical and lacking in sufficient experience. The Chancellor personally, at a farewell audience for the Egyptian Envoy, firmly laid stress on his peaceful attitude, remarking that he would not wage war for the Sudetenland question.

Transition to more circumspect and to some extent more dragged-out tactics in the Sudetenland problem met with a certain disillusion in Party circles, not excluding, as I felt, even Göring himself. But especially disappointed was Himmler, who is very bellicose in his attitude toward Czechoslovakia. A glorification campaign by the West European press with regard to Anglo-French action on May 19–21, which compelled the Germans to retreat, was a severe blow for the Party elements to take.

This situation became a fertile ground for internal criticism which erupted against states supposedly hampering Germany's freedom of action. From a number of quarters information reached me that in circles close to the army rumors were being circulated that the unexpected attitude of Poland had rendered void Germany's undertaking in the Sudetenland problem, which was to have been settled in the above-mentioned days of May.

I am reporting these rumors, simply for the sake of information, without precluding whether they originated from actual ignorance of the

---

[4] See *DGFP*, Series D, Vol. II, No. 255.

real state of affairs or were spread intentionally by German or foreign factors hostile to us. As a matter of fact, I did not observe any such reaction on the part of the competent authorities.

Possibly there was just a temporary impulse of dissatisfaction caused by a failure in prestige combined with a desire to shift the blame to other states.

This passing wave of reaction in the face of the Sudetenland problem will, in my opinion, have no impact on the question itself in the long run, for German goals remain unchanged for the future. Besides, public opinion is being maintained in a state of tension by the press campaign, so as to actualize the problem inside Germany and abroad. A possible understanding by way of negotiations between representatives of Sudetenland Germans and Prague is excluded in advance. Secretary of State von Weizsäcker expressed his opinion to this effect to me.

On June 17, I was received by Göring at Karinhall. The conversation lasted for over an hour and consisted this time of a rather general exchange of opinion. From Göring's mood I had the impression that the Sudetenland matter, though still timely, had been to some degree slowed down, as if there were a lack of final decision as to what to do next.

I opened the conversation with a remark that immediately upon my return from Warsaw I had wanted to see Göring, but unfortunately, owing to his departure, our conversation had been delayed. Göring mentioned that he was in the west of Germany for a couple of days to inspect fortifications on the French frontier. I consider this detail to be of utmost importance under the present circumstances, and I shall return to it at the end of my letter. Next, I told Göring that, after our conversation of May 21, I had proceeded to Warsaw to report on it personally to you, since I was not prepared to deal with this problem in writing. Finally, following your instructions, I gave an answer to Herr Göring to his suggestion for possible economic pressure to be exerted on Czechoslovakia jointly by Germany, Poland, and Hungary.

1) Göring did not give a direct answer to your question as to what, in that case, would be the requests put to the Czech side. Only from his deliberations which followed could one get some idea of the German stand. Namely, he explained that, with regard to the realization of demands dealing solely with minorities, a total economic isolation of Czechoslovakia would be too costly an operation. Such action would only pay if the total disintegration of Czechoslovakia were considered.

Moreover, Göring did not conceal the fact that this is bound to occur some time, and he called Czechoslovakia an inconceivable creation.

Without further defining the German concept, in spite of my repeated attempts to question him, Göring referred to his conversation with you of February 24 and tried to learn something about our plans.

With matters at a standstill I also did not play an open hand, confining myself to referring to what you said on February 23. Still returning to the conversation with you, and recalling that the German government takes into consideration our interests in a certain region, Göring hinted in a very camouflaged way that the German side also understands our interests stemming from the geographical situation, and that in this case Hungary should also consider this aspect. Since we had previously discussed the subject of the excessively long stretch of Czechoslovakia on Poland's southern frontier, I think that Göring undoubtedly had in mind Carpathian Ruthenia.

2) With regard to possible gradual economic pressure, Herr Göring remarked that such an eventuality would be considered by the German side. On the basis of calculations he concluded that for Poland the greatest difficulty would consist in the problem of transit lines southward. Here I added that transit to our Baltic ports should also be taken into consideration. Herr Göring further stated, also in very general terms, that, with such an eventuality in mind, transit from Poland to Italy, for example, should be moved through the Reich's territory, and in such a way as not to burden Poland excessively. This operation would be most costly to Germany, with direct turnover disrupted, the more so since the Reich is importing many raw materials, such as wood, etc., from Czechoslovakia. No conclusion was reached, and the deliberations were rather general in character. Herr Göring ended his deliberations on this issue by a statement that this matter should be dealt with in a circumspect manner.

In our conversation we touched on a number of other questions. Göring mentioned, for example, that the Czech Envoy in Warsaw allegedly received instructions to declare confidentially to the Polish government that our minorities would receive more far-reaching rights than the Sudetenland. To this I replied that I had no information to this effect, and that some time ago Prague had assured us that our minorities would enjoy the same rights as those granted to other minorities. Herr Göring remarked that naturally Poland could not accept anything else. Göring further deliberated on the consequences that would follow if France attacked the Reich because of the Sudetenland question. On this occasion he tried to illustrate Germany's military power from the most favorable angle. In this connection he said that he had given orders to reinforce fortifications on the French frontier and extend them on the northern sector up to Holland in a wide belt. As far as the German air force is concerned, in the present state of development it is, in his opinion, nearly equal to Anglo-French aviation taken jointly. He did agree that great efforts are being made in England and France, but results are not expected sooner than in two years. He analyzed the productivity of an economic system at the disposal of a totalitarian state as compared with the difficulties in armaments encountered by democratic states. He cited England's problems with its air defense.

The conversation then shifted to Soviet Russia. Göring gave voice to rather serious concern that Rumania could panic under pressure from the Soviets and agree to grant transit to Soviet aviation, or even to let troops march across its territory.

I remarked that our collaboration with Rumania is designed to stiffen that state against Russia. I pointed to the recent visit to Warsaw of the Rumanian Chief of the General Staff.[5] I emphasized the necessity of safeguarding Rumania from the Hungarian side, and here as always Göring agreed.

I availed myself of this occasion once more to lay stress categorically on our stand against any attempt to use our territory for transit of Soviet troops. I confided to him that we had recently repulsed an attempted overflight of Soviet planes, which news he received with visible satisfaction. He also talked about international forces interested in the outbreak of a world war, which I on my part particularly stressed. Naturally the question of the Jews and Bolshevism was not left out of our discussion, and here Göring suggested that, in case the Jews and the Third International pushed Europe into war, then the Soviets, as *tertium gaudens,* would remain on the margin.

At the end of the conversation Göring especially underlined the common interest uniting Poland and Germany, which might in the future result in serious concrete advantages to be derived from their relation. He remarked that, in case of a Polish-Soviet conflict, Germany, in its own well-understood interest, could not refrain from giving assistance to

[5] The chief of the General Staff, General Jonescu, arrived in Warsaw on May 30, 1938.

Poland. He added that perhaps today Russia is comparatively weak, but who knows if in the future it would not become strong enough.

He insisted that Poland should understand that the Reich has no revisionistic designs whatever on Poland, for example, in Pomerania. Such ideas might dwell in the minds of small middle-class people, but never in the minds of responsible politicians. National Socialist Germany, as he put it, is not anxious to annex foreign nationals to the Reich. And that is why German aspirations in Europe come to an end with the settlement of the Austrian and Sudetenland problems. Afterward colonial problems might arise, said Göring.

My conversation with Göring was a further confirmation of my observations in the Sudetenland problem, on which I had the honor of reporting at the beginning of my letter.

Józef Lipski

We further read in Lipski's personal notes:

The German side was at that time seriously concerned about Rumania's reaction to Soviet requests of transit for their troops. Rumania's policy was similar to ours in this matter. This subject came up in every conversation with Göring. Germany began to threaten Rumania with its possible collaboration with Hungary in case Rumania yielded to Soviet pressure. Misgivings as to the alleged military agreement between Germany and Hungary grew deeper in Rumania with Keitel's visit to Budapest in June, 1938. I wrote about this in detail in my letter of June 21.

DOCUMENT 88 Lipski to Beck

NO. N/52/23

Berlin, June 21, 1938
Strictly Confidential

In my report on my conversation with General Field Marshal Göring at Karinhall on June 17, I pointed to the serious misgivings of the President of Ministers that Rumania might be terrorized by Soviet pressure and agree to the overflight of Soviet aviation, and even to the marching of troops through its territory. I did not mention in my letter of June 19 that Herr Göring remarked in a discussion on this point that it would be worth while to influence Rumania to stiffen its stand against Soviet transit claims. The argument might be used that, in case Rumania grants a free hand to the Soviets, Hungary might stand up against it. This declaration of Göring, which I did not at first consider too seriously, is now taking on considerable weight in the light of the information I received yesterday from the Rumanian Envoy. Mr. Djuvara informed me that, according to news from Budapest, German-Hungarian military collaboration has been developing rapidly of late. There is circumstantial evidence that the Hungarian General Staff arrived at an agreement with German military authorities to coordinate their possible action against Czechoslovakia from the Hungarian side. This understanding was presumably so close that the Hungarians agreed to the marching of German troops through their territory. German action through Hungary would bestow a number of advantages on Germany: quicker and more effective action against Czechoslovakia, better protection in the Sudetenland from war operations, and, finally, better chances for an assault from the Hungarian side, where Czech border fortifications are not so strong as on the border facing Germany. The Rumanian Envoy also pointed to the recent visit of General Keitel to Budapest where, in his opinion, these matters were discussed. As you know, I have for years been on close friendly terms with the Rumanian Envoy, who is firmly in favor of the Polish-Rumanian alliance and categorically opposes the idea of the transit of Soviet troops through Rumania. He criticizes Minister Comnen's weak stand on this matter. I repeated to him what Göring told me: that he feared that Rumania may cede to Soviet pressure for transit of troops and overflight of planes. I added that I had no confirmation of Göring's information as to the allegedly far-advanced state of German-Hungarian military collaboration against Czechoslovakia. However, I called his attention to the fact that the evasive attitude of Bucharest with regard to the military transit of the Soviets might push Germany into military collaboration with Hungary against the Soviets. The Rumanian Envoy confided in me that he wants to report on this matter to the King, for in spite of the fact that the Soviet problem has been raised in his conversations with the Chancellor, Göring, and von Ribbentrop, Bucharest has not as yet given a definite reply that he could communicate to the German side.

Owing to my feelings of close friendship with Mr. Djuvara, I am very anxious to keep my report secret. I wish to add to the above information that I have as yet been unable to obtain more precise information about the German-Hungarian military collaboration. Questioned by me on this, the Hungarian Envoy here replied that General Keitel was paying a return visit for Hungarian Landwehr Minister Roeder's visit to Germany. My personal opinion is that, since Germany is concerned about the evasive stand of Rumania toward the Soviets (it might have heard about the overflight of planes), it is seeking support from Hungary.

Józef Lipski

In the period of June–July, 1938, the problem of Polish minorities in Germany and German minorities in Poland resulted in a series of conversations in Berlin and Warsaw. In Lipski's papers there are no documents on these events. They are dealt with extensively in the German version (*DGFP*, Series D, Vol. V, pp. 52–74).

We quote further from Lipski's personal notes:

On August 5 Beck passed through Berlin,[6] and I then had the opportunity to communicate to him my observations with regard to Czech-German relations. Too-strong anti-Czech accents in the Polish press were a handicap in my trump-card negotiations with Germany. My intention was to reach an understanding to stabilize Polish-German relations in the future.

Beck told me then that without pressure on the press on the part of the Foreign Affairs Ministry in support of our claims from Czechoslovakia, the press would engage in an opposite campaign, rendering our strategy impossible. I completed the information given to Beck verbally by means of a detailed letter dated August 11.

DOCUMENT 89   Lipski to Beck

NO. N/1/137/38   Berlin, August 11, 1938
                                                          Strictly Confidential

Since you passed through Berlin on August 5, when I had the opportunity of reporting to you verbally on the development of the situation in the Sudetenland as observed from the local angle, I obtained information that throws additional light on the matter.

Rather interesting is the opinion of the British Ambassador, who

[6] Beck paid an official visit to Oslo between August 1 and August 4 and was on his way back to Warsaw via Berlin on the 5th.

shows great independence of judgment. He recently told one of my colleagues that in his opinion Prime Minister Chamberlain took a great personal risk in sending Lord Runciman to Prague. The Ambassador laid special stress on the fact that Runciman's mission is taken most seriously by the British side, for a basic settlement is at stake and not just a short-term superficial solution. If Lord Runciman, in spite of his endeavors, fails to achieve an agreement, it will then become obvious that the Czech side is to blame, and that the Germans are right to state that in view of the unyielding attitude of the Czechs the only solution is to act by force. The British Ambassador let it be understood that in such case the British government would abstain from any further responsibility. It is also known to me that Sir Nevile tried to influence the Rumanian and Yugoslav envoys to have their governments exert pressure on Prague. He did this, as he confirmed, on his own responsibility, without being instructed by his government accordingly. Following further information, Belgrade and Bucharest duly intervened in Prague, advising the Czech government to make concessions.

I had further opportunity to converse with American Ambassador Wilson upon his return from Warsaw and Prague.[7] Owing to his acquaintance with Beneš when he was envoy to Switzerland, the President of the Czech Republic invited him to visit Prague for a conversation. Ambassador Wilson told me that Beneš, who in the past displayed self-confidence and composure, now impressed him as a man under pressure seeking for an emergency exit. Beneš denied the allegation that he is the main source of resistance against Sudetenland demands, and stressed his peaceful policy. Beneš was ready to approve a local self-government within the frame of the national electoral group, but he declared that the Sudetenland claim for territorial self-government could not be granted. In answer to my question Ambassador Wilson also explained that Beneš did not agree to the granting of *Staatsvolk* status to the Sudetenland Germans. The American Ambassador was rather surprised by the fact that, while competent elements in Prague are aware of how serious the situation is, public opinion at large seems to be insufficiently informed.

Finally Mr. Wilson, remarking that he was speaking from a personal point of view, said that he is under the impression that Chamberlain's choice of Lord Runciman, who belongs to the Liberal Party, was made

[7] See *Foreign Relations of the United States: Diplomatic Papers, 1938,* I, 540–44.

from the angle of England's internal politics, and possibly in accordance with French policy.

Yesterday at the reception given by the Italian Ambassador for Marshal Balbo, I had an opportunity for a casual conversation with General Field Marshal Göring. Göring said that he would like to talk to me in the next few days to discuss—naturally, as usual, privately and confidentially—the possibilities of a further Polish-German rapprochement in certain fields. He mentioned, as an example, the problem of discontinuing mutual spying action, in addition to some exchange of information regarding Russia and Czechoslovakia.

With regard to the Russian problem, he made a casual remark that this would become timely after the settlement of the Czech question. He referred to his idea that, should a Polish-Soviet conflict occur, Germany could not remain neutral and not come to the aid of Poland. He denied rumors that Germany would march into the Ukraine, stressing that the Reich's interests are concentrated in the first place on putting a stop to Bolshevik action. On the other hand, Poland, in his opinion, might have some direct interests in Russia, for example, in the Ukraine.

During the discussion on this point I informed Göring about Szembek's conversation with Comnen and the latter's emphatic statement against the transit of Soviet troops through the territory of Rumania.[8] Göring received this explanation with satisfaction.

Questioned about developments in the Sudetenland problem, Göring replied that it is now nearing its settlement ("die Sache geht jetzt zu Ende"). He is of the opinion that the Czech state will cease to exist as a creation made up of various nationalities: Germans, Slovaks, Hungarians, Ruthenians, and, finally, of some number of . . . Czechs. Göring mentioned casually that the moment is near when a decision should be taken and agreement reached on how to settle this matter. In Göring's opinion the Western Powers are beginning to realize how impossible the situation has become. In his opinion, England's mediation is just a *pro forma* affair. Prague's chief speculation is based upon its relation with the Soviets.

It was very characteristic that in the course of these deliberations Göring remarked that *Italy would naturally intervene* in case the Reich were attacked by France because of the Sudetenland conflict.

In view of the situation in connection with Lord Runciman's media-

[8] See *Journal*, pp. 325–26.

tion and the forthcoming visit of Regent Horthy to Germany, and bearing in mind the above statements of Göring that the Sudetenland problem is close to its crucial point, I thought it advisable to go one step beyond my usual limits in my conversation with Göring. With this in mind, I stressed that already at the Paris conference Czech policy strove for a common frontier with the Soviets, excessively stretching their territory on our southern border. This cut us off from our common frontier with Hungary, to the detriment of Polish-Hungarian interests based upon centuries of tradition of the two countries. Göring replied that he understands the necessity of a Polish-Hungarian frontier.

My further exchange of opinion with Göring was restricted to our immediate relations, such as the situation of our seasonal workers, whose efficiency is highly valued by the Field Marshal, and whose number he would still like to increase next year. We also touched on the successfully achieved Polish-German economic agreement, as well as the social insurance agreement.

At the same reception I had an opportunity to speak briefly with the Hungarian Envoy in Berlin. Following your directives, I referred to Regent Horthy's visit to the Reich, stating that I would consider it a great honor to be able to pay him my respects during his stay in Berlin. Envoy Sztojay seemed pleased and said that in all probability Horthy would receive me on August 24.

I further laid stress on the importance of the present moment for our common relations, adding that Warsaw and Budapest were in close contact. Asking him to keep this in strict confidence, I privately remarked that I had some misgivings as to whether in dealings on the question of the Sudetenland Hungarian and Polish interests in Czechoslovakia would not be overlooked. The Envoy seemed to share this opinion. I further added that I was observing Runciman's mission with a touch of skepticism in view of Prague's resistance to acceptance of the principal demands on the Sudetenland. However, I remarked that I did not yet see clearly a definite German line. I therefore thought that it would suit our interests to safeguard them in advance. Envoy Sztojay shared this opinion. He firmly stressed how important it is for Hungary to be sure of Poland's support. However, I could feel a certain hesitation when, for example, he expressed his concern about Yugoslavia's attitude, or Rumania's power of resistance with regard to possible Soviet claims for transit.

The following outline emerges from the conversations reported on above, which I shall take the liberty of turning into a factual report only after a longer talk with Göring:

The German government does not believe in the success of Runciman's mission, and the more radical elements, among whom I am also placing General Field Marshal Göring, are of the opinion that the problem can be settled only by force. If Beneš really rejects the claim for *Staatsvolk* and territorial autonomy, then the agreement seems to be more than doubtful. However, England could present Czechoslovakia with the choice of either accepting German conditions or facing England's retreat, which would leave Czechoslovakia in a tête-à-tête with the Reich. So, the moment of crisis might be close at hand. Chancellor Hitler, as I was informed from several reliable sources, declares to the outside that he would not wage war over the Sudetenland problem. This stand of the Chancellor corresponds with opinion at large, excluding more fanatical elements of the Party and youth, which is anxiously watching over the possibility of international war entanglements. Such information is reaching me from all over the territory. Nevertheless, among the older elements, memories of the great war lost in spite of the colossal preparations of 1914 carry a certain weight. At the same time, however, feverish preparations are being made to protect the Reich in case of a possible conflict with the West. This may be observed from fortifications built without regard to the material and human effort expended.

I would also like to call your attention to the recently very intensive contacts between Italian and German military spheres. May I just cite the recent visit of General Pariani, chief of the Italian General Staff, and the present visit of General Balbo. Besides the above-mentioned utterances of Göring with regard to the possible checking of France and Italy in case of a German-Czech conflict on the Sudetenland, I would like to lay stress on a rather characteristic passage in Marshal Balbo's speech delivered in reply to Göring's speech on the 10th inst.:

"Germany and Italy will remain unconquered if under the leadership of Mussolini and Hitler they will jointly realize their policy." ("Deutschland und Italien werden unbesiegbar bleiben, wenn sie, geführt von Benito Mussolini und Adolf Hitler, ihre Politik gemeinsam verfolgen.")

Józef Lipski

During the official visit of Regent Horthy in Berlin (between August 22 and August 28), Ambassador Lipski called on him on August 24 in the former Chancellor's palace. Lipski noted this conversation in his personal papers: [9]

This conversation, during which the Regent spoke very warmly about Poland, expressing the hope that the two countries might in the future share a common frontier, threw some light on his dislike of the National Socialist system and a certain concern over the risky policies of the Third Reich. He asked me confidentially to advise Warsaw that he would shortly send a trustworthy person to Poland to discuss the changing situation.[10] He emphasized that time was running short. He had a negative opinion about Rumania as our partner with regard to Russia. He was very much embarrassed by the commotion created by the publication of a communiqué from the conference in Bled.[11] The Regent labeled this matter an intrigue perpetrated against him in connection with his trip to Germany. He shifted responsibility for what happened to the Hungarian Foreign Affairs Minister.[12]

DOCUMENT 90   Note of Director Łubieński for Ambassador Lipski

August 25, 1938 [13]

The Soviets

Mr. Ambassador has confirmation that the Polish government will always oppose Soviet intervention in European problems.

[9] See also *Sprawy Międzynarodowe* (Warsaw), 1958, Nos. 7–8, pp. 70–71.

[10] Count István Csáky. director of the cabinet of the Hungarian Foreign Affairs Minister, stayed in Warsaw on October 5–6 and held conversations with Beck.

[11] On August 23 a communiqué was issued by the conference of states of the Little Entente and Hungary at Bled. This communiqué stated that the provisional agreement reached "includes the recognition by the three States of the Little Entente of Hungary's equality of rights as regards armament, as well as the mutual renunciation of any recourse to force between Hungary and the States of the Little Entente" (text in *Documents on International Affairs, 1938,* I, 284). See also Horthy, pp. 162–63.

[12] "During the state visit Regent Horthy told the Führer informally that Hungary was prepared to advocate in Warsaw that Poland return the Corridor to Germany. The Führer requested the Regent to refrain from taking such a step." *DGFP*, Series D, Vol. V, No. 52. See also Horthy, p. 156.

[13] The date of the note is not correct. Michał Łubieński, director of Minister Beck's cabinet, must have delivered this note before August 24, for on that day the conversation between Lipski and Göring (Document 91) took place, during which the Polish Ambassador used the instructions contained in the note.

Czechoslovakia

We do not believe that this country is capable of existing; we do not see any signs of change in its policy. The West is becoming tired of the Czech problem. The greatest obstacle for Germany in this question is that, in the West, German policy is described as a big adventure (Poland, of course, does not believe this). The dragging out of the Czech problem is creating an ever-increasing combustive situation.

Hungary

The most stabilized element in that region, our eternal friends, etc. Are they capable of an effort? How far might they be relied on?

Poland

Stress explicitly that various great efforts were made of late to draw Poland into some anti-German deals, but they were flatly rejected.

At present they are trying to use Danzig matters as a lever to undermine Polish-German relations. Danzig, it must be admitted, is now disorganized. We do not know with whom to talk there. Praise Greiser slightly, without blaming Forster.

Czechoslovakia

Slovakia must at any rate get autonomy either from the Czechs or from the Hungarians. Carpathian Ruthenia is a junk pile of political intrigues not worthy of occupying oneself with.

Poland-Germany

If there are some concrete proposals it should be declared that, since these are new aspects, they should be taken *ad referendum*. One thing, Mr. Ambassador, you have to say on behalf of your government: that nothing ever said in Berlin will be used by us against Germany. The initiative belongs to them, but we are not evading them.

According to the conversation, please investigate whether Minister Beck could not stop in Berlin for a personal conversation on his way to Geneva on September 7.

Japan

Mr. Ambassador, you have to quote the words of Marshal Piłsudski, that for Russia a war with Japan would always be only a colonial war, and that a real national war might be only a European war.

Poland

Ever-growing consolidation of public opinion at large toward foreign policy (Arciszewski-Niedziałkowski).[14]

DOCUMENT 91　Conversation of Ambassador Lipski
with General Field Marshal Göring
on August 24, 1938

Strictly Confidential

Göring returned to the question of sending to Warsaw the hunting car presented by him to the President of the Polish Republic. His aide-de-camp, Captain Menthe, who will proceed to Warsaw with the chauffeur, will present the car to the President on his behalf. Göring thought this way might be more suitable than a letter from him to the President. He remarked that the technicalities will be settled by his aide-de-camp's office in agreement with the Embassy.

Göring stated that he had again issued orders regarding the overflight of German planes in the restricted zone near Hel. The last case reported to him by the Embassy (conversation of Lubomirski with Director Grutzbach on August 22, 1938) is subject to investigation. The airman was punished for violating the zone. On the other hand, it might be possible that he did not see the rockets fired as warning signals.

Göring remarked that he had not yet had an occasion to talk with Regent Horthy and his staff, who will only arrive in Berlin this afternoon. He wanted to stress that the German government exerted pressure on Budapest to conduct negotiations so as to avoid collective obligations with the states of the Little Entente but to enter into agreement separately with Belgrade and Bucharest, omitting Prague. Göring remarked that Stoyadinovich followed the line of these suggestions at the Bled conference (if I understood correctly). Thus, in Göring's opinion, Hungary would be free to act, as he put it, in the last stage, its action anticipated to follow only a few days after that of the Germans. Göring described Hungary's stand as somewhat soft (*flau*).

[14] Tomasz Arciszewski (1877–1955) and Mieczysław Niedziałkowski (born 1893; executed by the Germans in 1940) were leaders of the faction of the Polish Socialist Party before the war which opposed the Polish government.

He then began to deliberate on the Czech question. As he had in previous conversations, he pointed to tendencies prevailing in Czech military circles to bring on an international military conflict as the only solution to the situation. In case of a victorious war these elements believe that they would completely defeat the minorities which make up the Great Czech state.

Analyzing the position of the Western Powers from the angle of a possible international armed conflict, Göring remarked that England might be ready with military strength in aviation not sooner than at the end of 1939, especially in antiaircraft defense. He said that the British land force is minimal. Their navy is really powerful, but the new units are still under construction, since England, up to the moment of the Abyssinian war, neglected its armaments. Besides, England has a number of troubles; for example, in the Mediterranean, in Spain, and in the Far East. From Göring's words it resulted that international propaganda is spreading rumors overrating England's preparedness to take up arms.

Applying the same analysis to France, Göring pointed to the enormous fortifications built on the western frontier of Germany, where about 400,000 people are at work. In opposition to the Maginot Line, which is very deep, and therefore renders maneuvers by concentrated units very difficult, the Germans are creating a more elastic system by building a whole series of defense lines. Regarding French aviation, Göring observed that very considerable shortcomings have existed, and only recently have steps been taken to raise it to an adequate level.

On this occasion Göring stressed that in case of French mobilization Mussolini would also mobilize, and France is aware of this.

Agreements with the Soviets and the Czechs are becoming a burden to France.

General Vuillemin[15] told him that the French-Czech agreement operates exclusively via the League, should unprovoked aggression be confirmed. Göring answered General Vuillemin that, if this was the case, there would never be a war between the Reich and France, since the Germans will not be the aggressors. Very significantly Göring told me here that obviously either the Germans would be attacked or they would be provoked, as, for example, in case of riots in the Sudetenland.

Continuing his hypothetical deliberations about the war, Göring ob-

[15] General Joseph Vuillemin, chief of the French Air General Staff (after February 22, 1938), paid a state visit to Berlin on August 16.

served that some lessons of the world war were not wasted. So, for instance, the Germans would not open an offensive but would sit in their fortifications and repulse attacks, causing heavy losses to their enemies.

Returning to the Czech problem, Göring cited the British opinion that in a matter of time everything could be settled. He does not share that opinion. He cannot conceive how the Czechs could agree to any concessions, since their state is composed of so many nationalities. For instance, if in order to make things even with Poland they would grant it all concessions, then similar concessions would have to be made to all other minorities. Therefore, the situation is at an impasse.

Following your instructions, I replied to these declarations that we also do not believe the present Czech creation can exist any longer. Nor do we see any change in the Czech policy. I added that of late efforts have been made to draw us into anti-German deals but that the Polish government rejected these offers categorically. I ascertained that international propaganda presents German policy as pushing ever new claims and provoking conflicts. Poland, I added, does not believe this. Here Göring reacted very strongly, saying that indeed propaganda imputes to Germany intentions of new territorial demands.

He passed on to Polish-German relations, declaring that the German government would be ready to do anything in order to deny such groundless opinions. He mentioned that it was ready to extend the agreement of January 26, 1934, for twenty-five years. He described the foundation of German-Polish relations as based upon the Reich's decision to recognize Poland's territorial state, since this is to a certain degree more digestible for Germany, inasmuch as the territories ceded to Poland did belong to it prior to the partitions.

I returned to the Hungarian problem. I stressed Polish-Hungarian friendship, describing Hungary as an element of stabilization in the Danubian basin. Referring to the expression Göring used earlier—that the Hungarians are a bit *flau*—I came out with the question whether, in his opinion, they are mature enough for independent action. I remarked that the untimely death of Gömbös [16] was a heavy loss of Hungary. Göring confirmed my opinion, as well as my judgment that still not enough understanding might be observed in Hungarian statesmen on nationality problems (*völkisch*).

In discussion on this item, important opinions of Göring are worth

[16] Julius Gömbös, the Hungarian prime minister, died on October 6, 1935.

noting. First of all, he remarked that Germany has no precise understanding on this matter with Hungary, nor does it have any with Poland.
On the other hand, Germany is aware of Hungary's interests in Czechoslovakia, and the same relates to Poland. The Germans envisaged that,
in case Germany undertook any action, Hungary would join. Germany
is taking on itself the task of restraining Belgrade from acting against
Hungary. It expects that Warsaw would act along the same lines toward
Bucharest in order to prevent any action. It would be most embarrassing
if Hungary did not make a move, since Czech forces could then retreat
to Slovakia. Evidently, Germany would not demand military assistance
from Budapest or Warsaw, if only for the reason that this would look
derisory in view of Germany's predominance over Czechoslovakia. But
Germany understands that under such circumstances Poland would occupy the region of interest to it. In practice it might occur that Polish
and German units would meet somewhere.

In connection with these deliberations of Göring, I stressed that Poland is closely united with Slovakia, owing to links of race and language.
The ties are even closer since we have no claims to Slovakia. I observed
that the evolution of the Slovak nation had progressed rapidly, especially in the last years, and I said that it is imperative that Slovakia be
granted autonomy from either one side or the other—from the Czechs
or the Hungarians.

Göring eagerly confirmed that this is a necessity. He added that Germany is fortunately in such a position that these matters are of no
concern to it. On the other hand, there is the question of relations between Warsaw and Budapest, and Poland's good influence on Hungary.
In his opinion Hungary should grant the autonomy which was refused
by Czechoslovakia.

With regard to Sub-Carpathian Russia I observed, following instructions, that it is a place where international intrigues abound, adding that
this land was taken away from Hungary solely for the purpose of giving
Czechoslovakia access to Russia.

We further touched upon Polish-German relations. I followed my
instructions on the Danzig problem. I stated that we observed a certain
lack of organization in the territory of the Free City, and that this
renders normal business difficult. I said that, although conversations
with Forster were satisfactory, he has no executive power. I praised
Greiser as a well-balanced person. However, I stated that the Commis-

sioner is encountering obstacles, that some incidents are again poisoning the atmosphere, and that this situation is being exploited by elements hostile to a Polish-German rapprochement. Göring carefully noted my remarks.

Since during our conversation he implied that secret service action might be discontinued, I stressed, following your instructions, that we should both refrain from influencing minorities in such a way that they would take up political action.

Göring understood my idea, particularly since I casually mentioned the matter of the *Deutsche Vereinigung* at Bydgoszcz. He noted this point.

On this occasion he voiced some ideas as to whether it would not serve the cause best if German minorities in Poland were to return to Germany, and vice versa. He observed that in view of the shortage of workers in Germany he has given orders to make it easier for a number of members of the German minority in Silesia to return to the Reich. This evoked a loud protest from local German authorities, who objected to the weakening of the German element in Poland. To this Göring replied that, since the frontier is recognized, it is in the Polish-German interest to have as few minorities on either side as possible.

At the end of the conversation I asked Göring whether he would be in Berlin in the first half of September, in case you pass through Berlin and would like to meet with him. Göring said he would be in Berlin on September 6 and 7 and would be very glad if such a meeting could take place. On this occasion he would like to show you Karinhall.

Supplement to the Report on the Conversation of Ambassador Lipski with General Field Marshal Göring
on August 24, 1938

Strictly Confidential

The following points were omitted from the report:

1) To the passage dealing with Slovakia it should be added that, in case basic territorial changes take place in Czechoslovakia, Poland would naturally be entitled to request an agreement which would definitely settle the situation in the Danubian basin.

2) With regard to Polish-German relations, Göring remarked casually that there are people in Germany who declare that Poland intends to annex East Prussia. He personally does not believe that Poland would

be willing to absorb a larger number of Germans. In his opinion, Poland's legitimate aspirations would rather tend toward the fertile Ukraine. On this occasion Göring denied Germany's claims on the Ukraine.

3) Göring stressed that a certain rapprochement of Polish and German military spheres would be highly desirable.

4) Göring declared that upon settlement of the Czech question the Reich would issue a top-level statement to acknowledge the achievement of definite stabilization. Poland would also profit from this act.

5) Upon leaving at the end of the conversation, Göring expressed the hope that we might still have some peaceful times before us.

In his personal papers Lipski writes:

I had the impression from this conversation that this was the psychological moment to impress on Germany the necessity of accepting our demands. I thought that this could be done in connection with Beck's planned visit to Berlin. This inspired me to write on the 26th [of August] a letter to Director Łubieński.

DOCUMENT 92   Lipski to Łubieński

Berlin, August 26, 1938
Strictly Confidential

Dear Director:

With reference to our last conversation about the possibility of Minister Beck's stopping in Berlin on his way to Geneva, I would like to advise you that I must be in Nuremberg on September 7, for on that day Chancellor Hitler is giving a reception for the diplomatic corps. So the only date available for the Minister to meet with Göring and Ribbentrop would be September 6.

Perhaps under these circumstances it would be advisable to postpone this meeting to a post-Geneva period.

Reflecting on Polish-German relations in the light of my last conversations with Göring, I would like first of all to state that the German government is aware that unless Poland remains neutral the solution of the Sudetenland problem might take an undesirable turn. The Germans must also realize that, even with the most favorable settlement of the

Czechoslovak problem, our possible gains are infinitely less than Germany's. I therefore think this to be the moment to achieve some positive solutions in Polish-German relations. These are:

1) extension of the declaration of January 26, 1934;

2) some kind of declaration similar to the one issued by the German government regarding Alsace and the frontier with Italy and at present with Hungary.

I quote a passage from Hitler's speech delivered at a banquet in honor of Horthy:

"This steadfast *connection,* based upon an imperturbable bilateral confidence, will in the first place be of extreme value for both nations— when, following historical events, we shall as neighbors have found *our final historical frontiers.* I am convinced that it will not only serve the interests of our countries but that also, *in close cooperation with Italy, which is friendly toward us, it will become a pledge of a worthy and just common peace.*"

I noticed that Göring reacted to my statement that international propaganda is accusing Germany of having ever-increasing territorial aspirations. Göring kept repeating the words: What can be done to remove Poland's distrust? He mentioned, on his part, the extension of the 1934 agreement. Although I am not valuing highly declarations and texts in international relations, since only real power and interests remain the decisive factors, nevertheless there is a certain vacuum in territorial problems in our relations with Germany, especially since France, Italy, and Hungary received precisely termed declarations. It is rather worth noting that Göring mentioned for the first time Poland's aspirations with regard to East Prussia. This might be an occasion to take advantage of in order to endow such a declaration with bilateral features. However, considering our relations with the Western states, it would be awkward to stage such Polish-German demonstrations at present. Still, some sort of *pactum de contrahendo* could be obtained in both matters if presented at the proper moment.

Nothing definite was obtained on Horthy's case. Some *querschusses* were made to him here, probably by the Czechs and the French; for example, rumors were circulated yesterday that Prime Minister Imredy must return to Budapest immediately.

Yesterday, at the evening performance of the opera, Horthy again mentioned to me the possibility of sending a special trustworthy delegate to Minister Beck. However, he gave me a piece of advice, which I deem to be most characteristic and communicate very confidentially, not to use code when relating my conversation with him. Maybe you could make confidential use of this with our code service.

Józef Lipski

P.S. According to what I could observe, the Hungarians did not sign anything here and did not take on any binding obligations. I was informed most confidentially that Prime Minister Imredy allegedly confessed to a third party that in case of an armed German-Czech conflict in the Sudetenland they would not move unless they could join Poland's action.

J.L.

We continue from Lipski's personal papers:

In the first days of September I was in Warsaw, where I discussed all of these problems with Minister Beck. With regard to the Czech problem, Beck laid much more stress on the settlement of the Danubian problem than on the Teschen Silesia question, which he considered to be just a starting point. Although the problem of a common Polish-Hungarian frontier through Carpathian Ruthenia was more or less clearly defined, I could not find any clear concept about Slovakia. It was just stated generally that Slovakia should be granted autonomy either by the Czechs or by the Hungarians.

I also did not feel that Beck definitely wished to present our demands to Germany in order to stabilize our relations. Obviously, he did not want to bind himself to Germany by new agreements with regard to Czechoslovakia. In principle he was not against stopping in Berlin on his way to Geneva. However, bearing in mind that at that time his relations with the League were vacillating, since he feared the pressure of the Western Powers in Geneva he deferred a decision to come to Germany, preferring to stop in Berlin on his return trip.

I had inadequate information about our relations with Paris and London. At the Foreign Affairs Ministry the opinion prevailed that France, and consequently Great Britain also, would not move in aid of Czechoslovakia. With regard to preventing Soviet troops from marching through Polish territory, our stand was categorical. Our action in Bucharest followed this line.

DOCUMENT 93 Lipski to Beck

NO. N/52/30/38   Berlin, September 5, 1938
                                       Strictly Confidential

This morning, upon my return from Warsaw, I had a personal telephone
call from Field Marshal Göring. He wanted to know how the matter
stands concerning your possible stopover in Berlin on your way to
Geneva, which I had mentioned in my last conversation with him.

I answered that, owing to a shortage of time, the meeting would have
to be postponed. I added that the chief of the Minister's cabinet, Director Łubieński, will be at Nuremberg.

Göring very emphatically informed me that he would have explanations for the Minister of the utmost importance ("Aufklärungen aller-
wichtiger Art"), which could not be dealt with via diplomatic channels,
and that the Chancellor, whom he advised of the planned visit, attached
considerable importance to it. Göring further questioned whether a
meeting could take place after Geneva. I said that I would immediately
contact you on this matter. Göring continued by saying that in the
aftermath of Geneva this meeting would be still more interesting for
him, since you would be informed about the position and attitude of the
Western Powers.

He fears, however, that considerable pressure will be exerted on Poland in Geneva by these states. According to his information, such
pressure is now being exerted by the Western Powers on Italy, Yugoslavia, and Poland. Italy, as he stated before, took a negative stand to
such propositions ("Haben eine kalte Schulter gezeigt"). Now the full
impact is on Belgrade and Warsaw. I told Göring that I was just back
from Warsaw and that I could assure him that our policy line remains
unaltered. Göring also remarked that the German side would be ready to
go far in Polish-German relations to our advantage.

I established with Göring that I would immediately contact you with
regard to the possible meeting. In case it could take place even now, on
which Göring did not insist so much in the course of the conversation,
the dates convenient would be Wednesday the 7th or Thursday the
8th.

For the meeting on your return trip, if the date could be September 20
or the next few days following, Göring suggests Rominten in East Prus-

sia, where he would stay during this period. In case you travel through Germany at a later date, Berlin. He thinks the meeting in East Prussia might be convenient for you, since it would cause no extra detour. He asked me, in that case, to accompany you as a guest at a hunting party. Göring stressed that this approach of his should be regarded as a direct unofficial contact with us owing to our close relations.

Since I have to leave for Nuremberg tomorrow evening, September 6, and since I have to give a reply to Göring before I leave, I am taking the liberty of sending Major Kowalczyk by plane to Warsaw; he can return to Berlin by night train.

For my part I would like to add to Göring's statements the following explanations:

The Chancellor and Göring, fearing that Poland's stand toward the German-Czech conflict might change in Geneva under pressure from the Western Powers, wanted to establish direct contact with you prior to the Geneva session. Undoubtedly in such conversations the German side would be likely to offer a gesture toward Polish-German relations.

The question is whether the German attitude toward us would be more expansive now or after Geneva? I think that, according to your opinion in our conversation yesterday, more favorable conditions might be available in the future, while at present, especially prior to Geneva, excessive obligations could be expected. Therefore I tried to persuade Göring to arrange the meeting for after Geneva. If, however, you would still prefer to see him now, there is a standing invitation for Wednesday or Thursday.

Józef Lipski

DOCUMENT 94   Łubieński to Lipski

Warsaw, September 6, 1938

In reply to the letter brought yesterday by Major Kowalczyk, I hasten, as instructed by the Minister, to communicate to you the following:

1) A meeting on the way to Geneva is out of the question, since the Minister does not know when he might be able to leave Warsaw (regardless of sleeping-car reservations).

2) On the other hand, the Minister seriously considers the possibility of the meeting after Geneva, probably just after September 20, and therefore perhaps at Rominten. The Minister would present the final proposal as to the date from Geneva, after seeing how long a period of time will be necessary to conduct the conversations there. The Minister does not intend to stay in Geneva any longer than required for establishing the necessary contacts.[17]

3) You may, however, when informing Göring with reference to the Minister, state that, as far as Geneva is concerned, Poland's policy is known for its resistance to pressure or yielding to concessions. On the other hand, information about the atmosphere prevailing in the world is naturally desirable in order to form a judgment on the situation.

M. Łubieński

[17] Finally Beck did not go to Geneva and the meeting with Göring did not take place.

The Party Congress at Nuremberg
September 7–12, 1938

ON THE EVENING of September 6 Ambassador Lipski proceeded with other members of the diplomatic corps to Nuremberg to attend the annual congress of the National Socialist Party. This provided him with an opportunity for a number of political conversations.

DOCUMENT 95   Ambassador Lipski's Conversations at Nuremberg, *September 7–12, 1938*

Strictly Confidential

I. With Field Marshal Göring on September 9, 1938

1) The planned meeting with Minister Beck. It was agreed that on his way back from Geneva Minister Beck would be able to meet with Göring; if the date were September 20 or immediately thereafter, the meeting would take place at Rominten; if at a later date, in Berlin. In case Minister Beck did not go to Geneva, the Ambassador on his part suggested a meeting at Rominten, where Beck could arrive by car from Augustowo. Göring was very pleased with this suggestion.

2) Göring was concerned about press attacks on Minister Beck. It had come to his knowledge that some press organs allegedly started a campaign against the Minister's policy. From further deliberations it became clear that these rumors were instigated by Forster. The Ambassador gave mitigating explanations.

3) The Ambassador pointed to certain steps taken toward us by the Western Powers, in particular England, in connection with the international situation. Göring, in his last conversation with the Ambassador, recalled such overtures made toward Italy, Yugoslavia, and Poland. The Ambassador laid stress upon the fact that Poland's policy did not cede

to pressure and followed a set line. He added that we valued more highly a sincere cooperation with the Reich than passing advantages. It was obvious that some international elements were against good Polish-German relations. Arguments used in an attempt to sway public opinion in Poland were (*a*) the problem of Danzig; (*b*) the thesis that the Reich interposes ever new claims. *Ad a*), Göring remarked that he had summoned Forster and had admonished him that Danzig matters should not complicate Polish-German relations. *Ad b*), Göring is aware how difficult it is to persuade Polish opinion that the Reich has sincerely given up revisionist aspirations concerning Poland. In his opinion, the fact that during the last five years the Reich's policy has been scrupulously observed in respect to the Polish state should confirm the sincere intentions of Germany. He referred to pronouncements by leading elements of the Reich during this period in relation to Poland, all of which aimed at influencing German public opinion in a way positive for Polish-German relations.

4) *Czechoslovakia.* Göring declared that the Karlsbad points [1] request, among other things, dissolution by Czechoslovakia of the pact with Russia. Göring does not believe in the possibility of an agreement with Czechoslovakia. If the Czech government were to make an agreement, it would do so with the intention of breaking it. Even if Beneš were to accept its conditions, military elements would come out against it. From Göring's words it was clear that he is convinced that the necessity will arise to act by force. Göring shared the Ambassador's opinion that international armed conflict should be avoided. Göring thinks the problem should be placed on the League's agenda in order to define the aggressor. The Germans, though not members of the League, will be able to prove that they were not aggressors. Before a decision is taken by the League, action in the field might already be finished. In Göring's opinion, France is simply looking for an honorable way out. England also is not willing to go to war and is exerting really strong pressure on Prague.

5) The Ambassador drew attention to the fact that there are international elements striving to provoke a conflict among the European powers. The Second and Third International and the masonic lodges are

[1] See *DGFP*, Series D, Vol. II, No. 135.

among them. There ensued a longer discussion about masonic lodges, the Ambassador stressing the fact that French and British lodges remain in close contact. He also pointed to the fact that Beneš has considerable support from the lodges. Göring rather significantly questioned the connections of Jan Masaryk, the Czech envoy in London.

6) *Rumania.* The Ambassador raised the question of the Havas Agency communiqué about the alleged Rumanian-Soviet agreement for Russian transit through Rumania. He pointed to the *démenti* issued by Bucharest.[2] Göring questioned in detail the internal Rumanian situation, the King's role, his internal political plans, and, finally, the position of the new Rumanian envoy in Berlin, Djuvara.

7) *Russia.* Göring stressed that in the future the real Russian attack against Germany could not be directed through Rumania or the Baltic states but only via Poland. Göring remarked that in case of a Polish-Russian conflict the Reich would come to Poland's assistance. A discussion followed about the situation in Russia and the strength of Russian armed forces.

8) *Hungary.* Göring revealed a number of confidential bits of information from his conversations with Horthy (the first point, not mentioned here, was told to the Ambassador for his information under a word-of-honor plea for secrecy). Göring declared quite openly to the Hungarian side that under no circumstances would Germany act as intermediary in matters of interest to Hungary and Poland. The Hungarian government should settle these matters directly with Warsaw. Göring acted in this way in order to deprive Budapest of any illusions in this respect. Göring also pointed out to Horthy the necessity of granting broad autonomy to Slovakia. He did this in consequence of his last conversation with the Ambassador. Horthy was not too eloquent on this point. Göring was under the impression that, in spite of Hungarian statements that in case Czechoslovakia were attacked by another state no Hungarian government could maintain itself in power unless it decided to act, Hungary would probably go into action very late.

   [2] On September 7 the official Rumanian agency Rador issued information denying the news that Rumania had agreed to the flight of Soviet planes over its territory. On September 18 the same agency issued a categorical denial of repeated rumors with regard to Rumania's consent for transit of Soviet troops through its territory.

9) Horthy allegedly told the Chancellor that it would take England ten years to forgive Hungary if it attacked Czechoslovakia today. Hitler, upset by such a naïve concept, replied that if this action took place in five years, when England would be armed to the teeth, it would be even less ready to forgive. Göring confirmed that territorial matters between Hungary and Poland are of no concern to Germany. The Germans are not prepared to pull chestnuts out of the fire for the Hungarians.

10) *Italy.* The Rome-Berlin axis is based upon the principle that neither of the states can allow the other to be defeated. Ideological solidarity is at stake here.

II. With Minister of Foreign Affairs Ribbentrop at a Reception Given by Hess on September 7, 1938

Ribbentrop declared to the Ambassador:

1. Germany's position has never been so strong as it is now.

2. Ribbentrop has not yet examined the last proposals presented in writing by Beneš. He is studying them now.[3]

3. Chancellor Hitler would never again let another May 21, 1938, happen. May 21 was a provocation against the Reich. In case such a provocation were repeated, the Chancellor would react immediately.

III. With Minister Ribbentrop on September 10, 1938

1) The Ambassador stated that on his way back from Geneva Minister Beck is expecting a personal meeting with Minister Ribbentrop. The Ambassador is not yet in a position to state if or when the Minister will go to Geneva. The Ambassador stressed that our [Polish] participations in the Council is also not yet resolved.

With regard to currently circulated rumors, the Ambassador remarked that our policy is not yielding to external pressure. Poland's policy is unanimous throughout the government, being a heritage of Marshal Piłsudski. The Ambassador pointed to certain proposals extended to Poland by the Western Powers, adding that sincere cooperation with the Reich means more to us than passing advantages. International propaganda is striving to undermine Polish-German relations, making use of the Sudetenland problem. It operates with two arguments: (*a*) the Danzig problem (a short historical outline of Polish-German conversations on Danzig and the Chancellor's declaration of

[3] *DGFP*, Series D, Vol. II, No. 440, pp. 714–19.

November 5, 1937); (*b*) instilling public opinion with the idea that the Reich is resorting to ever new claims.

The Ambassador mentioned that with the settlement of the Czechoslovak problem we would have to expect a much stronger campaign.

2) *Relation to Poland.* Herr von Ribbentrop emphasized the necessity of good Polish-German relations; this was his own conviction regarding the common interests linking the two states. His personal view was confirmed by the line adopted by the Chancellor. As long, therefore, as the Chancellor desired to maintain him in his present post, he would work positively for the development of Polish-German relations.

Granted this assumption, minor issues disturbing Polish-German relations must be settled in a friendly spirit.[4]

3) *Czechoslovakia.* Ribbentrop: We strive for a solution by agreement. Beneš, as yet, has not granted any adequate concession. Misgivings as to Beneš' frankness. Remark that the Chancellor would never allow the provocation of May 21 to recur again. In such circumstances the Chancellor would definitely act by force, ignoring international repercussions, since then Germany's honor would be at stake.

Ribbentrop called attention to the anomaly of the signing of the Franco-Czech agreement at a moment when Germany was weak. The agreement was to serve the Czechs as an instrument to exert pressure on the Germans. In Ribbentrop's opinion, Great Britain would not budge on the Sudetenland case. France would encounter unyielding resistance with regard to armed intervention. Germany is now stronger than ever. The Ambassador declared it to be most important that the problem be solved locally to avoid international conflict. Ribbentrop replied that evidently no government would lightheartedly jump into an international brawl. Ribbentrop questioned our position on the Czechoslovak problem. The Ambassador replied that we are interested in a certain region. He stressed the necessity of autonomy for Slovakia. He pointed to the pro-Russian policy permanently pursued by Czechoslovakia, displayed in the geographical composition of the Czechoslovak state at the Peace Conference. In the course of further deliberations on this issue, when the Hungarian question was raised the conversation had to be interrupted.

4) *Rumania.* The Ambassador raised the question of the Havas

[4] *Polish White Book,* No. 40.

communiqué about the alleged Rumanian-Soviet understanding with regard to the transit of troops. He pointed out that this rumor is false. He stressed that approximately on May 21 there were attempts on the part of the Soviets for an overflight of the Polish territory toward Czechoslovakia. We rendered them void. Ribbentrop showed interest in this information.

5) *Italy*. Ribbentrop laid stress on his statement that all he could say is that direct relations between Hitler and Mussolini are based upon far-reaching confidence.

IV. With Minister Ribbentrop on September 12, 1938

During a military parade, Ribbentrop mentioned casually that he wanted to continue discussions with the Ambassador but had been prevented from doing so these last days. The Ambassador remarked that he was proceeding to Warsaw to contact Minister Beck and learn about his views on the situation, particularly with regard to the stand taken by the Western Powers and Russia. The Ambassador also pointed to the official British declaration published the previous day.[5]

Ribbentrop seemed not to attach special attention to this. The Ambassador observed that the passage on the exchange of opinion between the British and American governments made him think. They decided to continue their conversations immediately upon the Ambassador's return from Warsaw.

V. Conversation with von Moltke on September 7, 1938
after Lunch in the Diplomat's Train

Moltke was visibly disturbed by the prospect of an international conflict. He suggested that rumors are current that from my discussions with Göring on August 24 last it was evident that I was optimistic concerning Great Britain's position. I corrected this statement, declaring that I did not express myself as to the possible stand of Great Britain. Talking frankly, Moltke asked what Poland's position would be in case of a conflict. In his opinion Poland would remain neutral. It would occupy the region of interest to it in Czechoslovakia only in case the conflict is localized for certain. Ambassador Lipski did not reply explicitly, hinting that the opinion of Ambassador Moltke rather follows the right trend. He stressed the necessity for a local settlement.

[5] *DGFP*, Series D, Vol. II, No. 458.

VI. *Conversation with Secretary of State Weizsäcker on September 11, 1938*

The Secretary of State, visibly disturbed by the possibility of an international conflict, told the Ambassador, underlining his friendly and sincere approach, that if we are expecting the possibility of an outbreak of an international conflict, we should openly and without reserve confirm this to the authorities of the German government; for, bearing in mind their attitude, words uttered in a diplomatic form are not necessarily considered. The Ambassador referred to his conversations with Göring and Ribbentrop during which he insisted that an international conflict should be avoided. Weizsäcker said that he could not observe any reaction, and that stronger words should be used.

REMARK: I know that similar words were also spoken to the Italian and Belgian ambassadors here.

VII. *Conversation with von Moltke on September 12, 1938 during a Lunch at the Grand Hotel*

Ambassador Lipski advised Moltke that he would tell von Ribbentrop that he is going to Warsaw to get in touch with the government in connection with the international situation and the Nuremberg conversations.

VIII. *Conversation with von Moltke on September 13, 1938, in Berlin*

Ambassador Lipski informed Moltke about his conversation with Minister von Ribbentrop on the preceding day. Ambassador Moltke said he is staying in Berlin, since the Minister of Foreign Affairs wants to continue his conversations with him. He asked for permanent contact with Ambassador Lipski through the counselor of the German Embassy in Warsaw, Scheliha. Ambassador Lipski expressed satisfaction with the passage of the Chancellor's speech dealing with Poland.[6] He added, and this was his own conviction, that he would consider it as most desirable, bearing in mind the international situation and the atmosphere prevailing in Poland, that a certain act should take place following the Chancel-

---

[6] In his speech at the Congress at Nuremberg on September 12 Hitler, speaking about Poland, said: "In Poland a great patriot and a great statesman was ready to make an accord with Germany; we immediately proceeded to action and completed an agreement which was of greater importance to the peace of Europe than all the chattering in the temple of the League of Nations at Geneva."

lor's speech, namely, a declaration about our mutual frontiers, something like that which was granted to Italy. Moltke showed understanding for such a concept.

IX. Conversation with the British Ambassador on September 11, 1938

Ambassador Henderson remarked that, unfortunately, competent German elements do not understand the British position and do not take it seriously. They continually insist that Great Britain could not be interested in entering a conflict over the Sudetenland. Henderson remarked further that his government had already long ago considered the necessity of revising the treaty. He is only concerned that this revision be executed by peaceful means. The Ambassador told him that with such a revision Germany would obtain the Sudetenland; Poland, Teschen; Hungary, its part. (Henderson cited 700,000 Hungarians in Czechoslovakia.) The Czechs with Slovakia would, in his opinion, form a uniform and united state. Henderson sharply criticized the Czech government and Beneš, adding that chances for a conflict increase with the delay.

X. Conversation with the Hungarian Envoy on September 11, 1938

He very confidentially disclosed that Horthy would shortly proceed to Rominten as a private guest of Göring. Ambassador Lipski called the attention of the Hungarian Envoy to the necessity of quick action on the part of the Hungarians in view of the rapid course of events. In addition, he stressed the necessity of considering the fact that the Czechoslovak problem would develop on the basis of plebiscites. In such an event, broad action should be considered. The Hungarian Envoy admitted that he is fully aware of this, and that a broad scope of autonomic rights should be promised beforehand.

Conversations with Chamberlain
at Berchtesgaden and Godesberg
September 15–26, 1938

WE QUOTE from Lipski's personal papers:

From Nuremberg I proceeded to Warsaw with a short stop in Berlin.

In Warsaw I finally obtained precise instructions with regard to our requests in relation to Germany. They were to be embodied in three documents:

1) a Polish-German declaration similar to the Italian-German one;

2) an extension of the nonaggression declaration of January 26, 1934;

3) a precise definition in writing of the Chancellor's declaration on Danzig of November 5, 1937, safeguarding our economic interests by assuring free development of Polish trade in the Free City.

When I was taking the night train for Berlin on September 14, a clerk of our Ministry of Foreign Affairs who brought the diplomatic mail informed me that, according to broadcast information, Chamberlain was coming to Berchtesgaden the next day. The West had capitulated. It was too late to present our demands to Germany.

I raised these demands as early as September 16 in my conference with Göring. He did not refute them, but even added a few items, such as a possible exchange of population, the avoidance of friction in the minorities field, and the question of the superhighway to East Prussia. However, in a very characteristic way he added that the settlement of these matters should be postponed to a later period, after the settlement of the Czech crisis. Chamberlain's arrival changed the whole situation to the advantage of Germany. Göring was in high spirits, acknowledging Chamberlain's visit as a great success for Hitler. He started to give advice for the benefit of Poland and Hungary, how these two states should act in order not to jeopardize their interests in relation to Czechoslovakia when the Sudetenland question was settled.

Following Minister Beck's instructions, during the same conversation I presented our definite requests with regard to the plebiscite in Teschen as well as the common Polish-Hungarian request on a plebiscite in Slovakia.

Late in the evening of September 15, on Beck's instructions, Lipski telephoned State Secretary Weizsäcker at Berchtesgaden, informing him that, in case the Czech problem was settled by plebiscite, the Polish government would categorically request an adequate solution of the Teschen region and would under no circumstances retire its claim. This stand was fully agreed to by the Hungarians.[1]

DOCUMENT 96   Lipski to Beck

NO. N/52/31/38   Berlin, September 16, 1938
                                                       Strictly Confidential

I. Referring to my telegram of today's date, I report information received through the Auswärtiges Amt on the Hitler-Chamberlain conference,[2] this being more precise than the information wired after my conversation with Göring.

The conversation was sincere in tone and lasted for several hours. The Chancellor presented a demand for the immediate settlement of the Sudetenland question in one way or another, insisting openly on the annexation of the Sudetenland to the Reich. He made it clear that the situation calls for an immediate decision, and that in case of delay he would not hesitate to use force.

Chamberlain accepted this request of the Chancellor to seek a solution, reserving the decision to his cabinet. He took a plane today for London, where at 12 noon a session of the Council of the cabinet was to convene, followed by a consultation with the French government. A further meeting of Hitler with Chamberlain is planned probably for next Monday in the vicinity of Cologne. During this meeting the execution of the decision is to be discussed. The next stage of conferences is to deal with British-German subjects. Göring considers Chamberlain's coming

[1] For the German version, see *DGFP,* Series D, Vol. II, No. 508.
[2] The Hitler-Chamberlain conference at Berchtesgaden took place on September 15 (*ibid.,* No. 487, pp. 786–98.)

to Berchtesgaden as a great personal success for Hitler. As far as the plebiscite is concerned, Göring and his staff have misgivings as to whether it is at all possible. I could feel that the Field Marshal is still speculating on the possible occupation of the Sudetenland by German armed forces. He remarked casually that it would be well if we could be prepared for any eventuality.

II. Göring was alarmed by the possibility of a settlement of the Czechoslovak problem at present exclusively with regard to the Sudetenland, which would leave sources of further conflicts in this region. He therefore advises that Poland should categorically insist on a plebiscite in the region inhabited by Polish population, using all possible means of pressure, agitation, etc., as well as approaching the Western Powers in this respect. He is giving similar advice to the Hungarians. In his opinion Slovakia should place a request for a plebiscite supported by Poland and Hungary. He has some misgivings here as to whether Hungary is acting promptly enough with regard to autonomic concessions. He understands the necessity of a common Polish-Hungarian frontier, which —as he put it—would join in Slovakia. It was obvious that Göring was anxious to separate Slovakia from the rest of Czechoslovakia, in order thus to create a Czech state economically dependent on the Reich.

Following your instructions, I categorically communicated our stand with regard to the plebiscite in Teschen as well as our common demand with the Hungarians for a plebiscite in other parts of Slovakia.

III. Reflecting upon Chamberlain's decision to proceed to Berchtesgaden, Göring remarked that a change in the front had occurred in Paris, with London following suit.

As, in accordance with your instructions, I was to present our demands, I informed Göring in strict confidence that even at the last moment the British side had made some approaches to us that were not accepted.

I then passed to our problems.

1) Referring to Hitler's speech at Nuremberg, I presented the concept of a declaration on Polish-German relations similar to that exchanged by Hitler and Mussolini.[3] I am refraining from citing here the

[3] In his speech on May 7, 1938, at the Palazzo Venezia in Rome during a state visit to Italy, Hitler gave assurances on the stabilization of the present German-Italian frontier (Brenner Pass), the inviolability of which was an integral part of German-Italian friendship. (The text is in *Documents on International Affairs, 1938*, II, 32–34; see also *DGFP*, Series D, Vol. I, Nos. 759, 761, and 767.)

arguments used to this effect. I mention that Göring was quite positively disposed toward this idea.

2) I brought up the necessity of removing permanent frictions in the Danzig region through a definition in writing of the Chancellor's declaration dated November 5, 1937, and repeated to you on January 14, 1938. I stressed that, in my opinion, the definition should underline the necessity of a guarantee for Polish economic interests in the Free City through a free development of Poland's trade. I laid stress on the thesis that Danzig is a product not of the Treaty of Versailles but of history.

Göring also accepted this point positively, adding on his part that he does not expect any difficulties in a formulation which would reserve to Poland the freedom of trade. In his opinion the agreement should be based on two premises: Poland, as it was stated, would not intervene in the development of the German population in the Free City; and, on the other hand, Danzig would consider the interests and economic rights of Poland, which are of essential need to its own development. Göring remarked that, if it were not for Poland, the Reich would not be in a position to assure Danzig of its present commercial turnover, for at best East Prussia, with a port of its own at Królewiec [Königsberg], could serve as a hinterland for Danzig. In conclusion he added that immediately upon the settlement of the Czechoslovak problem we should get together, possibly with economic experts, to investigate Poland's economic problems in Danzig. He thinks a suitable solution could be reached without difficulty. Here I brought up customs matters as an example.

To recapitulate, I stated that the Polish government considers Polish-German relations as a long-range problem, that in order to conduct such a policy it is indispensable to create an atmosphere of confidence, that in my opinion this could be achieved by way of three things:

1) a declaration similar to the Italian-German one,

2) the removal of frictions from Danzig problems in the field of Poland's economic interests,

3) an extension of the declaration of January 26, 1934.

Göring on his part mentioned the necessity of avoiding dissent in minority cases, and I replied that, with these three conditions settled, things would improve on our side. Here Göring returned again to the possible exchange of minorities, that is, the removal of some of the landowners from Poland to Germany. The General Field Marshal also brought up the question of the superhighway to East Prussia.

IV. As to your possible meeting with Göring, in view of the fact that events are moving so rapidly, he suggested that in case of emergency such a meeting could take place somewhere near the border.

Józef Lipski

DOCUMENT 97   Lipski to Beck

September 17, 1938
Code

1) Yesterday Göring invited the Hungarian Envoy and exerted his influence on him for action regarding Hungary's claims.

2) In my conversation with the Italian Ambassador I raised the subject of our thesis, stressing the necessity of settling all minorities questions in Czechoslovakia in order to achieve a definite stabilization of relations in that region. The Ambassador showed full understanding, stressing that this conforms with Mussolini's stand.

Lipski

We quote from Lipski's personal papers:

On September 19 I was informed that Hitler desired to receive me the next afternoon at his residence in Berchtesgaden, and that for this purpose a plane would be placed at my disposal at Tempelhof airport. I was also informed, from other sources, that Hungary's prime minister, Imredy, and the Hungarian chief of the General Staff were invited to Berchtesgaden for the same day. I was therefore not quite sure whether a common German-Hungarian-Polish consultation would take place. Minister Beck, informed accordingly, succeeded in sending his instructions on September 20.

DOCUMENT 98   Beck to Lipski

Warsaw, September 19, 1938
Strictly Confidential

Please adopt the following directives in the conversation with the Chancellor:

1) The Polish government declares that by its stand it has paralyzed the possibility of Soviet intervention on a wider scope in the Czechoslovak problem. Pressure exerted by us on Bucharest achieved the desired result. Our current maneuvers in Volhynia were understood by Moscow as a warning.

2) Poland considers Soviet intervention in European affairs as intolerable.

3) We consider the Czechoslovak Republic to be an artificial creation convenient for certain doctrines and combinations, but one that does not take into account the concrete needs and sound claims of the states of Central Europe.

4) In the course of the last summer the Polish government four times rejected propositions to join international interventions in Czechoslovakia.

5) Poland's direct claims in the problem under discussion are restricted to the Teschen-Silesian region, that is, not far beyond the Teschen and Frystat districts plus access to the Bohumin railway station [Oderberg].

6) Bearing in mind our immediate proximity, we are interested in a general settlement of the Czechoslovak crisis. We consider favorably the idea of a common frontier with Hungary, since we are cognizant of the fact that the geographical scope of the Czechoslovak Republic was meant to serve as a bridgehead for Russia. In this problem we lack the definite decision of Hungary, whose role here is vital. From our point of view, Hungarian aspirations have more chances in Carpathian Ruthenia. Slovakia could only be considered within the frame of broad autonomy. We are not convinced that these problems are properly prepared by the Hungarians, and Poland could not possibly settle the matter for them.

7) According to recent information, the Western Powers might try to maintain the present concept of Czechoslovakia with partial concessions to Germany. On September 19 we protested such a solution.

We place our local claims categorically. We communicate confidentially that frontier control is reinforced. On September 21 we shall have considerable military forces in the southern part of Silesia. We formally declare that this grouping of troops is not directed against Germany.[4]

8) From the Polish side, the further course of events depends, in the first place, on the decision of the government, but also on the feelings of public opinion at large. In this field, especially for the future, a stabilization of Polish-German relations is essential. Attention is called here to the following problems:

a) The Danzig problem has a key role for the atmosphere. With this in mind and owing to the League of Nations' bankruptcy, a simple agreement stabilizing the situation in the Free City seems indispensable.

b) An explicit formula with regard to the frontiers, similar to the German-Italian one, might contribute to a paralysis of international intrigues trying to come between Poland and Germany.

c) Extension of the 1934 pact might be an additional factor for stabilization of the situation.

REMARKS

I. The item relating to Hungary to be settled by you, depending on the conversation, in a dialogue or *à trois* with the Hungarian Prime Minister.

II. Please bear in mind that the exceptional importance of the situation calls for a bold approach to problems, far stronger than in normal negotiations.

III. If necessary, especially on the Chancellor's initiative, I am ready for personal contact with the Chancellor or Göring, in spite of possible technical or political difficulties.

IV. If in doubt, take matters *ad referendum*.

Beck

From Lipski's personal notes:

At Berchtesgaden audiences were arranged separately for the Hungarian ministers and for me. I agreed with Ribbentrop on a communiqué

---

[4] On September 20 a Polish Telegraph Agency communiqué announced that frontier control of Poland had been reinforced on the Czech frontier by special detachments of frontier guards. On September 22 news appeared about keeping in service certain units of the Polish Army's older lists and reservists called for maneuvers.

which only confirmed the fact that I had been received by Hitler. On the other hand, the communiqué relating to the conversation with the Hungarians brought up the *meritum* of the problem.

DOCUMENT 99   Lipski to Beck

September 20, 1938
Strictly Confidential

The Chancellor received me today in Obersalzberg in the presence of the Reich minister of foreign affairs, Ribbentrop, at 4 P.M. The conversation lasted for more than two hours.

The Chancellor had previously received the Hungarian Prime Minister and the Chief of the General Staff of Hungary.[5]

Audiences for the Polish and Hungarian sides were arranged separately. In like manner, the press communiqué relating to the reception for Prime Minister Imredy deals with the *meritum* of the problem, while the communiqué relating to my audience simply acknowledges the fact of the reception. I coordinated this with Minister of Foreign Affairs von Ribbentrop.

Chancellor Hitler opened the conversation with me with a statement that events had taken a different turn than he first expected. He then gave a historical outline of the Sudetenland problem, starting from his speech at the Reichstag this February. He laid special emphasis on the events of May 21 which compelled him to take a decision on May 28 to accelerate rearmaments and fortifications in the west. He then remarked that he was taken aback to a certain extent by Chamberlain's proposition to come to Berchtesgaden. It was of course impossible for him not to receive the British Prime Minister. He thought Chamberlain was coming to make a solemn declaration that Great Britain was ready to march. He would, of course, then reply that Germany was aware of such a possibility. The Chancellor declared to Chamberlain that the Sudetenland problem must be settled peacefully *or by war,* resulting in the return of the Sudetenland to Germany. As a result of this conversation Chamberlain, persuaded of the necessity of separating the Sudetenland,

[5] For a recapitulation of the conversation with the Hungarian ministers, see *DGFP,* Series D, Vol. II, No. 554.

returned to London. Up to now the Chancellor has had no further news about London's decisions. Neither has he definite information as yet about the date of the meeting which allegedly is to take place tomorrow. However, incoming news seems to indicate that the Chancellor's claims will be honored. Nevertheless, a version is circulating that the settlement of the Sudetenland problem will be executed not by self-determination but by a new delineation of frontiers. Allegedly where there is an 80 percent German majority, the territory would go to Germany without a plebiscite. The Chancellor declared that he prefers the plebiscite and is standing firm on this. He would of course insist on a plebiscite in order to secure votes for people who left the territory after 1918. The status of 1918 must be restored. Otherwise, it would mean acceptance of Czechization, which has been under way since 1918.

Occupying the Sudetenland by force would, in the Chancellor's opinion, be a fuller and more definite solution. However, the Chancellor declares that, in case his claims are recognized, then it would not be possible for him not to accept them before his people, even if the rest of the Czechoslovak problem remained unsolved. That is why the Chancellor wonders what could be done with the balance of the problem concerning Hungary and Poland. He therefore invited the Hungarian Prime Minister and me to confer on this problem.

In reply I declared that I would like to present in detail Poland's point of view. I did this following the guiding directive contained in points 1 to 7 inclusive of your instructions dated September 19. In view of the shortness of time, I just want to underline that when discussing the Teschen problem I twice stressed that the territory in question does not reach far beyond the districts of Teschen-Frystat *and access to the railway station of Bohumin* [Oderberg].

With regard to Hungarian demands, I particularly emphasized the question of Carpathian Ruthenia, calling attention to the strategic moment with regard to Russia, the spreading of Communist propaganda over this territory, etc. I had the impression that the Chancellor was particularly interested in this problem. This was even more apparent when I mentioned to him that the Polish-Rumanian frontier is comparatively narrow, and that through a common Polish-Hungarian frontier via Carpathian Ruthenia we would obtain a broader barrier against Russia.

I wish to add that I pointed out in respect to Carpathian Ruthenia that this territory, not claimed by Slovakia, was entrusted to Czechoslovakia only as a mandate. The very low level of population is strongly mixed; as a matter of fact, Hungary has its greatest interests there.

Defining our stand with regard to the region of Poland's direct interest (Teschen), I stated:

a) that we had approached London, Paris, Rome, and Berlin categorically requesting a plebiscite when this idea was brought up for the Sudetenland,

b) that we had approached the same Powers yesterday with regard to news spread about the alleged plan of territorial delimitations (I presented our declaration in writing to Ribbentrop),[6]

c) that Poland's position is especially strong in view of the assurance received from Prague, which was confirmed at that time by London and Paris, that our minorities in Czechoslovakia would enjoy the same status as the most privileged other minorities.

I concluded, when questioned by the Chancellor, that we would not retreat at this point from recourse to force if our interests were not recognized.

Analyzing further tactics to apply in settlement of the Czechoslovak problem as a whole, the Chancellor stated:

1) If his conditions are not accepted by Chamberlain, the situation is clear, and according to his warning he would use armed force to annex the Sudetenland to the Reich.

2) In case the Sudetenland condition is accepted and guarantees are claimed from him for the rest of the Czechoslovak territory, he would take the position that he might grant such a guarantee only in case a similar guarantee is given by Poland, Hungary, and Italy. (He considers the introduction of Italy important to counterbalance French and British guarantees.) He understands that neither Poland nor Hungary would issue such guarantees prior to the settlement of the problem of their minorities. Here I gave assurances on behalf of the Polish government.

3) For my confidential information, remarking that I could use it at my discretion, the Chancellor declared today that, in case a conflict would arise between Poland and Czechoslovakia over our interests in Teschen, Germany would be on our side. (I think that a similar declaration was made by the Chancellor to the Hungarian Prime Minister,

[6] For the text, see *ibid.*, No. 553.

though I was not told so.) The Chancellor suggests, in such an eventuality, that we undertake action only after the Germans occupy the Sudeten Mountains, since then the whole operation would be shorter.

Further in the conversation the Chancellor very strongly stressed that Poland is an outstanding factor safeguarding Europe against Russia.

From other long deliberations of the Chancellor the following results were clear:

a) that he does not intend to go beyond the Sudetenland territory; naturally with armed force he would go deeper, especially since, in my opinion, he would then be under pressure from the military elements who for strategic reasons push toward the subjugation of the whole of ethnographic Czechoslovakia to Germany;

b) that besides a certain line of German interests we have a totally free hand;

c) that he sees great difficulties in reaching a Rumanian-Hungarian agreement (I think the Chancellor is under Horthy's influence, as I reported to you verbally);

d) that the cost of the Sudetenland operation, including fortifications and armaments, adds up to the sum of 18 billion RM;

e) that upon settlement of the Sudetenland question he would present the problem of colonies;

f) that he has in mind an idea for settling the Jewish problem by way of emigration to the colonies in accordance with an understanding with Poland, Hungary, and possibly also Rumania (at which point I told him that if he finds such a solution we will erect him a beautiful monument in Warsaw).[7]

[7] Lest Lipski's words be misinterpreted, we give the following facts:

In 1937 there were about 3,350,000 Jews in Poland; most of them were concentrated in cities (Białystok, 43 percent Jewish; Stanisławów, 41.4 percent; Warsaw, 30.1 percent) and small towns. The Jews living in rural areas made their living as agricultural brokers. However, as agricultural cooperatives developed in Poland, these middlemen were no longer needed and the Jews were deprived of this means of livelihood; they were left destitute and with no means of support. This had nothing to do with anti-Semitism; it was solely a natural economic development. The Jews in Poland, with their traditional clannishness, posed a serious problem in the overpopulated Polish state. The Polish government felt that a partial solution to this problem would be for them to emigrate, principally to Palestine.

The matter was considered so serious that Polish delegates to the League of Nations, in October, 1936, insisted that some immediate solution would have to be found, one possibility being the creation of a Jewish state in Palestine as a natural

Following your instructions, I also brought up Polish-German relations in the above conversation. I must mention that the moment was not especially well chosen, since the Chancellor was very much absorbed by his approaching talk with Chamberlain. I referred to the Danzig question, suggesting the possibility of a simple Polish-German agreement to stabilize the situation in the Free City. I cited a series of historical and economic arguments. In reply the Chancellor mentioned that we have the agreement of 1934. He also considers it desirable to take another step forward, instead of simply taking the position that force should be excluded in our relations, and to make a definite recognition of frontiers. He referred here to the concept of the superhighway connected with railways, which you are already familiar with. The width of such a belt would, in his words, reach about thirty meters. This would be a certain *novum*—a time when technical means would serve politics. He said he would not bring this up now, since it could be realized later on. Under these circumstances I did not discuss the matter any further.

At the close of the conversation I referred to your possible meeting with the Chancellor in the near future in case of necessity. The Chancellor accepted the suggestion with satisfaction, remarking that this might be desirable, especially after his conference with Chamberlain.

For his part, Ribbentrop asked me to find out if you would be ready to make a declaration regarding Polish demands to Czechoslovakia similar to that made by the Hungarian Prime Minister, in order that it might be used in the conversation with Chamberlain. Besides, Ribbentrop stated that the German press will give wide publicity to our action regarding minorities in Czechoslovakia.

The above report has been dictated by me before the departure of the courier after my return by plane from Berchtesgaden, so please forgive any possible shortcomings.

Józef Lipski

---

home for Jewish émigrés. The Polish government further stressed that additional territories for émigrés would have to be found to house the large number of Jews. Polish ambassadors discussed this matter with Paris, London, and Washington.

It should be noted that during this same time the Polish government was giving financial aid to the Zionist organization of Vladimir Zabotynski; also, with the approval of Minister Beck and Marshal Śmigły-Rydz, the Jewish Military Organization (Irgun Tsevai Leumi) was training several hundreds of its instructors at secret military courses in Poland. (See Pobóg-Malinowski, II, 614–29.)

DOCUMENT 100   Lipski to Beck

Telegram   September 22, 1938

The Hungarian Envoy asked me again yesterday about Rumania's stand in the possible Hungarian-Czech conflict.

The Rumanian Envoy, who is realistic about the situation, upon arriving at an understanding with the Yugoslav Envoy, telegraphed the King that a basic change in Czechoslovakia is to be expected. He pointed to the necessity of a prompt reorientation of Rumanian policy toward an understanding with Warsaw and Belgrade in order definitely to balance relations with Budapest, compensating Hungary on the Czechoslovakian side.

Lipski

Received: Warsaw, Rome, Budapest, Bucharest

On September 22 and 23 a conference of Chancellor Hitler with Chamberlain took place at Godesberg.[8]

Lipski notes in his personal papers:

Mr. S. Dembiński, the director of the Polish Telegraph Agency, represented the press on the Polish side.

On the second day of consultations Ribbentrop reported to me by telephone Hitler's rejection of a nonaggression pact and guarantee for Czechoslovakia. The Undersecretary [Woermann] handed the German memorandum which Chamberlain undertook to execute in Prague.[9] The Auswärtiges Amt expressed satisfaction over Warsaw's firm reply to the Soviet note. The Polish Ministry of Foreign Affairs asked for wide publicity by the German press regarding our reply.[10] Beck's instructions arrived with maps dealing with three variants of our claims in the Teschen region.

[8] See *DGFP*, Series D, Vol. II, Nos. 562, 572, 573, 574, and 583.
[9] For the text, see *ibid.*, No. 584, pp. 908–10.
[10] On September 23 Vladimir Potemkin, vice-commissar for foreign affairs in Moscow, handed to Polish Chargé d'Affaires Tadeusz Jankowski a note declaring that if the Polish government did not deny the news of a concentration of Polish troops on the Czech frontier, and if Polish troops crossed the frontier, the Soviet government would be compelled to denounce the Polish-Soviet pact of nonaggression. Upon telephone contact with Warsaw, Mr. Jankowski presented a note to Potemkin to the effect that the Polish government had the incontestable right, without rendering account, to undertake all measures which ap-

DOCUMENT 101   Beck to Lipski

Warsaw, September 23, 1938

In view of the shortly expected possibility of the beginning of concrete conversations regarding our territorial claims on Teschen Silesia with the German government, I am enclosing herewith three variants of a map illustrating our above demands.[11]

Variant A represents the maximum of our territorial claims, covering the whole territory of Silesia proper beyond the river Olza, and *also Moravska Ostrava and Vitkovice.*

Variant B covers the same region, the southern part of Frydek district excluded.

Variant C is an alternative for Variant B (*Moravska Ostrava and Vitkovice excluded*); it represents the minimum of our claims.

More detailed instructions on this matter will be forwarded to you by telegram.

Beck

DOCUMENT 102   Lipski to Beck

Refer to code of telegram of   Berlin, September 23, 1938
   September 22   *Telegram by code*

I was informed in strict confidence that the minister of foreign affairs of Rumania, Comnen, at present in Geneva, undertook measures against the Hungarian action. He resents the excessive growth of Hungary and threatens that in the event of Hungarian aggression a *casus foederis* might take place. I think that he is under the influence of Geneva circles. To counteract this, I am approaching local authorities and competent

---

peared to it necessary for the security of Polish territory. The Polish government was aware of the possibility of the denunciation of the nonaggression pact. Orally Mr. Jankowski also added, in accordance with instructions, that the Polish government was all the more astonished over the Soviet step since the Polish government had taken no special measures on the Polish-Czechoslovak frontier. (*DGFP*, Series D, Vol. II, No. 582, No. 593, and, for text of notes, No. 621.)

[11] There are no maps in Lipski's papers.

foreigners with the thesis that the moment has come for a definite under-standing between Rumania and Hungary that would give an outlet to the Hungarians in Czechoslovakia. I am stressing that this is in conformity with the opinion of the governments of Poland, Germany, and Italy.

Lipski

Received: Warsaw, Budapest, Bucharest, Rome

DOCUMENT 103   Lipski to Beck

Berlin, September 23, 1938
Telegram by code

The Italian Ambassador communicated to Ribbentrop the text of Ciano's conversation with the British Ambassador.[12] Ciano stated that satisfying Polish and Hungarian demands is imperative for the regula-tion of the Czechoslovak question. Asked about Italy's guarantee for Czechoslovakia, Ciano replied that he cannot presently take a stand, and that in any case such a guarantee would not be granted unless Polish and Hungarian claims were satisfied.

Lipski

Received: Warsaw, Rome

DOCUMENT 104   Lipski to Beck

NO. N/1/171/38   Berlin, September 24, 1938

Since the conference of the Chancellor with Chamberlain yesterday lasted until 1:30 A.M., it was impossible for me, in spite of several telephone calls, to obtain detailed information regarding its results.

This morning I received a communication from Godesberg that Rib-bentrop and Secretary of State Weizsäcker will see Chamberlain off at the airport and that the Secretary of State will probably return to Ber-

[12] See *DGFP*, Series D, Vol. II, No. 571.

lin in the evening. Von Ribbentrop will remain with the Chancellor's staff for several more days.

This morning I received the German memorandum sent to me by Undersecretary of State Woermann which, in accordance with the communiqué issued yesterday, is to be presented by Chamberlain to the Czech government. I am enclosing this memorandum herewith, remarking that the Auswärtiges Amt asked for strictly confidential handling of same.[13]

I also went this very morning to Undersecretary of State Woermann in order to obtain more details.

To my question as to why the British side did not in principle agree with the above memorandum, Woermann replied that it is his understanding that a difference of opinion occurred over the German claim to occupy by armed force a part of the Sudetenland (red line). It allegedly would be difficult for Chamberlain to accept this condition and impose it on public opinion. However, the Secretary of State remarked that as a matter of fact the British and German points of view did not differ greatly.

To my question whether a deadline is stated in the memorandum, Woermann replied that, since in point (1) of the memorandum it is stated that a part of the Sudetenland territory is to be occupied on October 1, the deadline is thus determined.

The memorandum refers to a map in several places. However, I was not able to secure one from the Secretary of State, who made the excuse that he did not have it yet, since it had been decided on in Godesberg.

I also raised the question of the general mobilization ordered by the Czechs,[14] stressing that yesterday was a day marked by international activities aimed at creating a specific atmosphere. Among these maneuvers I included also the Soviets' note to us. The Secretary of State expressed great appreciation for our firm reply, stressing that the German press published special commentaries on the Soviets' action and our reply. With regard to Czech mobilization, Woermann was not very much concerned about it, since the army had already been mobilized. The press also, although it attacked this order, is not particularly up in arms.

Questioned about other matters under discussion, especially during

13 Missing from Lipski's papers. For the text, see *ibid.*, No. 584.

14 Czech mobilization was proclaimed on September 23. The next day France called to arms some categories of reservists.

the last conversation of Hitler with Chamberlain, Herr Woermann was unable to give me any explanation. Neither did he have any details as to whether the problem of the Soviet-Czech agreement had been discussed. I asked him for prompt information with regard to principal motifs of the Hitler-Chamberlain conferences to be communicated to you either by me or by von Moltke.

Józef Lipski

DOCUMENT 105   Lipski to Beck

Receptus code No. 134 (GMP)   Berlin, September 26, 1938
                                       Coded

I executed your instructions with regard to Ribbentrop. At Godesberg a discussion *ad meritum* dealt exclusively with the Sudetenland question. The problem of a general solution was only touched upon casually. Our problems and those of the Hungarians were referred to indirectly in connection with the proposal of a nonaggression pact. The Chancellor brought it up by remarking that such an agreement would become an instrument in the hands of the Czechs against the aspirations of the Polish and Hungarian minorities. The Chancellor also rejected the proposal for a guarantee without Poland, Hungary, and Italy.

Ribbentrop, referring to our conversation at Berchtesgaden, confirmed this stand of the Chancellor most firmly. I consider this to be of importance in view of the rumors that the Czechs are returning to the concept of a nonaggression pact.

Lipski

DOCUMENT 106   Lipski to Beck

Berlin, September 26, 1938
Secret Code

Ribbentrop told me in strictest confidence that Chamberlain secretly assured the Chancellor at Godesberg that he is taking it upon himself to communicate the memorandum, but he cannot endorse it officially.

Today Wilson is coming to see the Chancellor on behalf of the Foreign Office. I was indirectly informed that Chamberlain's situation has become awkward. Ribbentrop assured me that, although the Chancellor is at present very much absorbed by the Sudetenland problem, he is standing firm on the Polish and Hungarian demands.

Ribbentrop suggested that, upon acceptance of the memorandum and the occupation of the Sudetenland planned for October 1, a closer definition of Polish and Hungarian demands should take place.

Lipski

DOCUMENT 107   Lipski to Beck

NO. N/1/172/38   Berlin, September 26, 1938

I am taking the liberty of supplementing the two telegrams sent today after this morning's conversations with Secretary of State Weizsäcker and Minister of Foreign Affairs Ribbentrop with the following information:

I had difficulty in securing sufficient information about the real meaning of the conference at Godesberg, inasmuch as both Minister von Ribbentrop and Secretary of State Weizsäcker returned to Berlin only today.

Besides, the international press has been full of false rumors to misguide foreign observers.

Under these circumstances, the only reliable document resulting from this conference was the German memorandum communicated to the representatives of Poland, Hungary, and Italy here. I forwarded it with my letter of September 24, No. N/1/171/38.

May I also remind you that on the second day of the conference at Godesberg von Ribbentrop communicated to me at about 1 o'clock that the Chancellor had rejected the plan of a nonaggression pact and guarantee for Czechoslovakia, about which I immediately reported by wire.

A version confidentially circulated by the British side among representatives of the Polish press at Godesberg (Director Dembiński of the Polish Telegraph Agency) informed me that the crisis at Godesberg stemmed from the Chancellor's demand to settle simultaneously the whole complex of Czechoslovak problems, that is, Polish and Hungarian demands. Allegedly the tension was eased when the Chancellor, in his final nocturnal conversation with Chamberlain, withdrew this demand.

The Hungarian Envoy, who called on me this morning, also made the statement that the Chancellor yielded to British pressure in his last talk with Chamberlain, when the latter declared that he must leave Godesberg the next day. The Hungarian Envoy thinks that the Chancellor's decision was also influenced by pressure on the part of German military circles, who feared an international conflict. Top officials of the Auswärtiges Amt, who, as I have observed, always warn about the possible action of England and France, might have also used some pressure. The Hungarian Envoy also expressed anxiety over information in his possession that the Czech government, although it accepted the German memorandum for the time being, would return to the question of a nonaggression pact not for the whole territory of Czechoslovakia but for the newly delimited German-Czech sector, and that the Chancellor under British pressure might agree to this. I declared to the Hungarian Envoy that I consider this to be out of the question in view of the stand precisely defined to me by the Chancellor during our conversation at Berchtesgaden.

After this meeting with the Hungarian Envoy I had a conversation at the A.A., first with Weizsäcker[15] and afterward with von Ribbentrop.

From explanations given it develops that in factual conversations at Godesberg the Chancellor restricted himself to discussions on the Sudetenland problem only. In his opinion, discussing the whole complex of problems on his initiative would only complicate the matter. On the other hand, our problem and that of the Hungarians were indirectly brought up when the Chancellor rejected the plan of a nonaggression pact and a guarantee. Ribbentrop told me that the Chancellor refused the nonaggression pact, arguing that it would become an instrument in the hands of the Czechs against the aspirations of the Polish and Hungarian minorities. The guarantee was rejected by the Chancellor on the principle that he would have to make it dependent on whether it would also be granted by Poland, Hungary, and Italy. Ribbentrop added that the question of the guarantee was rather weakly proposed by the British

[15] For the German version of this conversation, see *DGFP*, Series D, Vol. II, No. 608.

government, since it was rather inconvenient from the traditional angle of British policy.

Weizsäcker made an interesting remark about the guarantee, stating that it would not surprise him if Beneš, giving up the idea of guarantees by other countries, would claim them only from France and England, and insist on this as a condition for acceptance of the German memorandum.

To my question concerning the real cause of the crisis at Godesberg, Ribbentrop replied that after the conversation at Berchtesgaden Chamberlain strove to find a more digestible form of the problem of the transfer of the Sudetenland territories to serve to the West. This would confirm the information I communicated to you after my conversation with Woermann, namely, that Germany's claim to occupation of the territories by armed force before October 1 evoked Chamberlain's serious reservations.

Nevertheless Ribbentrop, in strictest confidence, asked me to inform you that Chamberlain personally pledged to the Chancellor that he would take measures to push the memorandum through. Officially, of course, this could not be disclosed, and hence it was mentioned in the communiqué that the British Prime Minister would present the memorandum to the Czech government.

In Ribbentrop's reception drawing room, I met the ambassadors of Great Britain and Italy. The British Ambassador just had time to remark that he considers the situation to be critical. The Italian Ambassador, following news from Rome, expressed anxiety that Chamberlain's position is becoming awkward. I could imagine that Mussolini feared the British Prime Minister's position might be compromised. The Italian Ambassador told me that on Mussolini's recommendation he would call on Ribbentrop and ask him to influence Hitler not to aggravate the situation further by his speech today. He would propose that Hitler declare that he is ready to grant a guarantee upon reaching an understanding with Czechoslovakia's neighbors (Poland and Hungary) and Italy.

To my question whether the Chancellor in his speech today would take up the question of settling the whole Czechoslovak problem, Ribbentrop replied that as yet he had not received the text of the speech. He is still to confer with the Chancellor today.

More definitely from Weizsäcker's statements, and less explicitly from

Ribbentrop's declarations, it was clear that Hitler, for the time being, as long as the Sudetenland problem remains unsolved, has to concentrate on this question. Nevertheless, von Ribbentrop assured me that Hitler stands firm on the Polish and Hungarian demands.

Furthermore, Ribbentrop, in rather general terms, said he sees two possibilities. First, it is possible that the Czech government will accept the memorandum, in which case the territory will be peacefully occupied. In such an event, he suggested that it might be advisable to meet with us in order to discuss further proceedings in the Polish and Hungarian matter. I replied evasively, as we had mentioned in Berchtesgaden, that the possibility would exist for your meeting with the Chancellor. The second alternative von Ribbentrop considers is the possible necessity for Germany to march into Czechoslovakia. And here he asked whether in such an eventuality we would march as well. I replied that naturally I could not express myself on this matter, since the decision is up to the government. Quite personally I mentioned that, if our demands were not met, force might possibly be used in either case—whether in marching or settling the problem by peaceful occupation of the territory by Germany.

Von Ribbentrop remarked at the end of the conversation that it would be well, for operational reasons, to be in contact if necessary, to which I did not reply.

Von Ribbentrop remarked that he is at my disposal at any time, that he considers the closest contact as desirable, and that, in case something particularly important results from the conversation with Wilson, he will inform me immediately.

Józef Lipski

On the same day (September 26) Hitler delivered a speech at the Sport Palace—with a long section about Poland. (See *Polish White Book,* No. 42.)

Munich and the Teschen Silesia Problem
September 27—October 21, 1938

IN THE AFTERMATH of the Sudetenland issue, the Teschen Silesia problem was raised, particularly with regard to Bohumin (Oderberg).

On September 27 the British ambassador in Warsaw, Sir Howard William Kennard, communicated to Minister Arciszewski, acting vice-minister of foreign affairs, that he had seen a copy of the map attached to the German memorandum. On that map, Bohumin was located in the red zone to be occupied by the Germans immediately, and Moravska Ostrava and Frydek (Friedeck) in the green zone, to be subject to a plebiscite.[1]

Polish action to secure Bohumin was begun.

The same day Beck sent instructions to Lipski, written in the form of a private letter using the friendly term of second singular form. In his private papers, Lipski stresses that points 8, 9, and 10 of these instructions were not carried out by him.

Beck informed Ambassador von Moltke on the same day about Poland's stand with regard to Teschen Silesia (*DGFP,* Series D, Vol. II, No. 652).

DOCUMENT 108   Beck to Lipski

Warsaw, September 27, 1938

Dear Ambassador:

In the rapid flow of events I am sending instructions in telegraphic style for your conversation and your own orientation.

1) Beneš, in his letter to the President, explicitly agrees that it is necessary to rectify our frontiers in order to improve relations between Poland and Czechoslovakia for the future. No closer definition of political conditions.

2) I received simultaneously a notice from the British and French

[1] See *DGFP,* Series D, Vol. II, map 1.

governments confirming our territorial *revindications légitimes* in Teschen Silesia.

3) Today a reply was dispatched by plane containing acknowledgment by the President that territorial problems were essentially the factor spoiling the good-neighborly relations between the two countries. Further action is referred by the President for agreement between the governments.

4) At the same time I recommended to Papée that he present a note demanding immediate agreement in the following matters:

a) acceptance of the principle of rectification on the basis of the desires of the population in connection with the Polish-Czech agreement of 1918–19;

b) a guarantee that this important decision of the governments is timely through formal occupation by Polish forces of the districts of Teschen and Frystat, since they have an incontestable Polish majority.

The request for immediate agreement is motivated by the grave situation, but it does not bear the character of an ultimatum with a time limit.

5) Today the French Military Attaché presented to us the map of German claims attached to the Chancellor's memorandum. In accordance with this map, the Bohumin region is marked in red, as being contained within the frame of the *Sofortprogram* occupation, while a considerable part of the territory east of the river Ostravica (see map "C") is included in the plebiscite region.

6) Under these conditions the problem should be solved promptly, in order to avoid political dissent or, even worse, a military clash between us and the Germans.

7) Within the limit presently considered by you as possible, please inform any one among the competent political leaders of the Reich about our point of view.

To define the general scope of our interests use map "C"; others are not valid. If necessary, show the map of our immediate claims forwarded today to Prague, which you will find enclosed. Do this in order to avoid friction and, in emergency, to find a prompt realistic compromise. In this occasion refer to your conversation with the Chancellor at Berchtesgaden.

8) Not insisting on indiscretion, express the expectation that we

would be informed about the start of any possible military action. We guarantee not to use this information to the detriment of the Reich's interests.

9) For your confidential information I add that we have at our disposal forces under arms capable of action. Relative to the development of the situation we could take prompt action following the outbreak of a German-Czech conflict.

10) Politically you can confirm that (a) our stand against the admittance of Soviet intervention is categorical and (b) we would not issue any more extensive guarantees to Czechoslovakia without Germany and Hungary.

Beck

DOCUMENT 109   Lipski to Beck

NO. N/1/182/38   Berlin, September 27, 1938
                                       Strictly Confidential

I. Today I was summoned for a conversation at the Auswärtiges Amt by Weizsäcker at 7 P.M.; afterward, at the invitation of Ribbentrop, I conferred with him.

Weizsäcker informed me of the result of today's conversation of Sir Horace Wilson with the Chancellor, and he read the stenograph to me.[2] The Chancellor took the stand in this conversation that the German memorandum has to be accepted by the Czech government, and that he would not retreat from this stand. During the conversation Sir Horace Wilson—here I quote the stenograph—defined possible English action against Germany: "If Czechoslovakia refuses the German memorandum, no one knows where the ensuing conflict will end. If Germany attacks Czechoslovakia, France will fulfill her treaty obligations to Czechoslovakia. If this occurs and French forces were thereby to become actively engaged in hostilities with Germany—whether or not this would occur, he did not know—then Britain would feel herself obliged to support France." Herr von Weizsäcker explained that Wilson de-

[2] *Ibid.*, No. 634.

fined these words, remarking that he was quoting Chamberlain's ideas correctly.

I remarked to Weizsäcker that this formula is typical of British policy. Weizsäcker mentioned that in the course of the conversation Wilson pointed to the possibility of a British-German understanding on a number of questions. Of course, he also laid firm emphasis on the necessity of avoiding a calamity. He allegedly promised, at the end of the discussion, that he would act along these lines.

Herr von Ribbentrop, with whom I conversed later, is of the opinion that the British government will still exert firm pressure on Prague for acceptance of the memorandum. Questioned by me as to whether tomorrow's date at 2 P.M. is still in effect, the Secretary of State replied that he asked me for strict secrecy in order that this term not be precisely revealed. In consequence the time limit is elastic.

II. Furthermore, following your telegram, 1 informed the Minister of Foreign Affairs, as well as the Secretary of State, where we stand in our conversations with Prague. I stressed that we would not let ourselves be led into a trap and would request concrete settlements.[3]

III. Herr von Weizsäcker, who had a map of the General Staff before him, stressed that he would suggest that our military attaché establish a demarcation line with a competent expert of the General Staff, so as to prevent a collision between the two armies in case of a possible clash.[4]

I answered von Weizsäcker that in the first place it was important to establish with him the territory of our political interests in Czechoslovakia. As Herr Weizsäcker had no such map at the moment, I agreed that I would discuss this problem with him tomorrow in the morning hours. The problem of possible delimitation between military factors was postponed for the present.

IV. When my conversation with the Secretary of State passed to more general topics, we raised the question of France's and England's position. Von Weizsäcker told me that, unfortunately, the A.A. is not adequately informed about the position of France, for French Ambassador François-Poncet has not appeared at the Auswärtiges Amt for a fortnight, collecting his information from other sources, and Ambassador Welczek is absent from Paris. The Secretary of State, however, stated

[3] *Ibid.*, No. 639.
[4] *Ibid.*, Nos. 644 and 666.

that a considerable stiffening of French public opinion might be observed.

V. In a general exchange of opinion with von Ribbentrop he stressed that, as I already mentioned, the British side would still exert firm pressure on Prague. He thinks that the British side would do its utmost to avoid armed conflict and to settle the problem peacefully. He expects a local conflict. However, as he declared, he does not exclude the possibility of a general conflict, for which he is prepared. Referring to my previous conversations with him, I stressed how important the localization of the conflict is.

As far as Russia is concerned, von Ribbentrop's views are on the optimistic side.

To Herr Ribbentrop's question whether, in case the memorandum is executed by peaceful means, we would have recourse to military action, I replied that I was not in a position to forejudge the stand of my government.

Von Ribbentrop further raised the hypothesis that the Czechs would not accept the momorandum; then, as he put it, the Czechs would be destroyed. He lightly touched on the question whether in that case we would march. At this point I could deduce from Ribbentrop's words that in his opinion the Polish government, feeling that the eastern frontier was a great weight on its shoulders, would enter into action upon orienting itself whether the operation was a local flare-up or a world war. In case Germany occupies the whole of Czechoslovakia, von Ribbentrop considers it useful to establish in more detail the political and military interests. He asked me to draw your special attention to this point and obtain instructions on this.

VI. In conclusion, I am taking the liberty of stating that:

1. Further conversations on the German memorandum are useless, owing to the final decision of the Chancellor as declared to Wilson.

2. I would appreciate instructions agreed upon with the General Staff in view of the concrete proposition by the Secretary of State to create a demarcation line on our interests in the Teschen region.

3. Also, instructions as to Ribbentrop's motion, in case of military action and transgression by Germany of the line of its immediate interests in Czechoslovakia.

Józef Lipski

The following is Lipski's handwritten note relating to the report of September 27, 1938, on his conversation with Ribbentrop.

When I returned from the Auswärtiges Amt Ribbentrop called me on the telephone, inviting me at 10 P.M. to Kaiserhof for a conversation. Ribbentrop apologized for troubling me again on the same day, but he was in need of some explanations.

I dined together with Counselor of the Embassy Lubomirski and Colonel Szymański, the military attaché, in one of the restaurants near the Adlon (I do not remember its name), and I proceeded to Kaiserhof. I anticipated some very essential question in relation to the threatening conflict in the Sudetenland.

But Ribbentrop, returning to the conversation I had with him when he took office in March, 1938,[5] in a rather discreet manner asked me what our position would be to a suggestion to join the Anti-Comintern Pact.

A discussion ensued on this topic, while Ribbentrop made some evasive statement that he would like to have an idea about our stand with regard to conversations he was engaged in with the Japanese side. He underlined that collaboration with Japan was giving good results.

For my part I stressed our point of view, known already to Ribbentrop from our previous conversation. I pointed out that, having a common frontier with the Soviets, we did not want to bind ourselves by a pact against Russia. On the other hand, I laid stress on our negative attitude to Soviet attempts at marching through or overflight of our territory.

The conversation did not achieve concrete results, aside from a statement that on Ribbentrop's request I would inform Beck about his suggestion. Ribbentrop did not lay stress on urgency.

Bearing in mind that, as was disclosed later on, this was the vital moment of decision—war or peace over the Sudetenland—Ribbentrop, as I suppose, wanted discreetly to find out about our stand in case of a conflict; in the last days, both Moltke at Nuremberg and Ribbentrop at Berchtesgaden and again in a conversation on September 27 at the Auswärtiges Amt had asked if and under what circumstances Poland would act.

[5] See Document 83, p. 360.

On September 28 Ambassador Lipski received by special planes two instructions, both dated the same day, with regard to the delimitation of zones in Teschen Silesia.

DOCUMENT 110   Beck to Lipski

Warsaw, September 28, 1938
Strictly Confidential

With regard to your conversations as to the delimitation of our and German interests in Teschen Silesia, we have worked out here the problem of Bohumin [Oderberg] with Marshal Śmigły-Rydz.

The Military Attaché received technical instructions and a clear map by the same courier. The railway problem, as I had already stressed to you before the meeting at Berchtesgaden, is of prime importance.

We have established with Marshal Śmigły that the first conversations based upon the military instructions will be conducted by you, while only afterward should the Military Attaché approach the General Staff (in accordance with this morning's instructions sent by earlier plane), with the exception of cases when immediate German operation would necessitate establishing immediate contact with the German command.

So the enclosed instructions for the Military Attaché are for the moment also instructions for the Ambassador. For lack of time, I do not repeat details separately.

I quote the latest information: in accordance with Krofta's statement, Prague will accept all our demands, but it is playing for delay in the usual Czech manner.

On the Soviet frontier, two days ago we had a series of demonstrations by larger Soviet detachments in the region of Minsk and in other smaller sectors, in addition to larger groups of planes close to our frontier. Yesterday and today all was peaceful. The character of the demonstrations was obviously political, sometimes taking rather grotesque forms. For the time being they are of no special importance from the military angle. Only a desire to call our attention to these demonstrations, which we are ignoring, is apparent.

However, please mention these demonstrations casually in Berlin.

Beck

DOCUMENT 111 Beck to Lipski

Pro memoria dictated by Minister Beck as instructions to Ambassador Lipski on September 28, 1938

In reply to your report of today and as a supplement to my instructions of yesterday, I communicate as follows:

1) Clarification of delimitation of German and Polish interests in Teschen Silesia is essentially a very important and urgent matter, since a clash of any sort might cause disastrous consequences.

2) The method chosen by you, namely, first political conversation and only as a result thereof an understanding between the General Staffs, is the only correct one. Marshal Śmigły-Rydz shares this conclusion and will issue instructions to the Military Attaché.

Under these circumstances it is necessary to compare in Berlin the original German map attached to the memorandum (we are naturally interested only in the northeastern sector) with our map "C" and the map attached to the note to Prague. Political conclusions can be drawn only from such a confrontation. Please telegraph or forward by rented plane the position taken by the Germans at such a confrontation.

3) With regard to the plebiscite in the zone between the western frontier of the Teschen and Frystat districts (map sent to the Czechs), it could be negotiated that this might be settled in the future in case the conflict is averted. Most urgent and drastically in need of explanation is the Bohumin region.

Most confidentially I communicate to you that if a rough-and-tumble German plan calls for the immediate occupation of this territory, possibly a slight compromise could be offered, bearing in mind, however, our interests in the railway tract to Bohumin.

I remind you that at present the railway line reaching this station on the Czech territory belongs to the Germans. I am citing this point for orientation, in case of action *in extremis;* for the present please clarify the problem.

DOCUMENT 112   Lipski to Beck

NO. N/1/183/38   Berlin, September 28, 1938
                                                      Strictly Confidential

This morning at 12:30 I was received by the Secretary of State whom, in accordance with our agreement of yesterday evening, I confronted with the map attached by the German government to the memorandum and with our map "C."

It appeared that the German red line reaches fairly deeply into the Bohumin region, while the line proposed by the Germans for the plebiscite oversteps into the region between our "frontier proposed" line more or less from Frydek to Silesian Ostrava, and in some places either oversteps or cuts back from the Teschen and Frystat districts.

In addition, Herr von Weizsäcker showed me a demarcation line established by the General Staff on which, as he put it, the German Army would stop in case of military action without overstepping it eastward. This line ran more or less alongside the above-traced line of the German plebiscite in the Frydek district, reaching to the north and joining the German red line to the east of Bohumin.

I declared to Weizsäcker that the German government in its demarcation overstepped the Polish region at two points: Bohumin and Frydek. I laid most pressure on the Bohumin problem, referring to the Chancellor's tacit consent at Berchtesgaden.[6]

The Secretary of State mentioned that he had to find out why this took place, and that he would confer with me again today.

For my part I remarked that in view of the situation the problem must be definitely settled today.

May I add that I showed to the Secretary of State a map attached to our note sent to Prague with our red line traced, stating that westward of the red line in the district of Frydek a plebiscite should be held, in accordance with our proposition to Prague.

At 6:30 P.M., together with Counselor Lubomirski, I had another consultation with Secretary of State Weizsäcker; Counselor Altenburg was also present. It was established as follows:

1) The German government withdraws its red line from the territory of Bohumin, transferring it to the line "frontier proposed" on map "C." In the sector west of Olza to Koblów, the German red line runs further

---

[6] See Document 99, p. 409.

westward, leaving Moravska Ostrava for a plebiscite. Von Weizsäcker remarked that the withdrawal of the red line from the Bohumin region could be executed in connection with the anticipated alterations at the conference in Munich tomorrow.[7]

2) With regard to the overstepping of the German plebiscite line into the Frydek district, the Secretary of State presented the concept of a possible plebiscite for Germany, Czechoslovakia, or Poland. He implied that the German government had no territorial claims here, rather being concerned with the exchange of population to compensate for other territories. Besides, bearing in mind the change in the situation, in his opinion the question of the plebiscite territories will have to be reconsidered, so that any definition at present would be pointless.

In consequence we agreed as follows:

The German government will not settle the plebiscite in the district of Frydek prior to a consultation with us.

3) In view of the altered situation, the Secretary of State remarked that for the moment he does not deem it necessary to discuss the question of the German military demarcation line in the event of armed occupation. Here I observed that, in my opinion, the military demarcation line should follow the line of the Oder and Ostravica rivers. I laid some stress on the fact that in any case the Secretary of State should consider our "frontier proposed" line as the frontier of our region, adding that I was making this statement in the event of our military action.

The Secretary of State acknowledged my statement.

Józef Lipski

Map enclosed.[8]

DOCUMENT 113   Lipski to Beck

NO. N/1/184/38   Berlin, September 28, 1938
                                            Strictly Confidential

Yesterday's situation resulted in increasing international tension. Herr von Ribbentrop summoned me for still another nocturnal conversation,

[7] The communiqué convoking the conference in Munich was issued on September 28.
[8] See *DGFP*, Series D, Vol. II, No. 666. The map is missing from Lipski's documents.

bringing up other topics (the Anti-Comintern Pact), on which I am reporting separately.[9] I simply mention that the matter under discussion is of no urgency, but is rather interesting as an indication of the attitude of the German government toward Russia.

The majority of diplomats here, not excluding the Italian Ambassador, who was in direct contact with Ciano and Mussolini, are of the opinion that we are quickening our pace in the march toward a European war. Comments were circulated that international circles are using the atmosphere observed in France and England for a showdown with competent Powers.

Today, right from this morning, a very strong diplomatic action could be observed here. The Chancellor first received the British Ambassador, who presented some plan considered as not acceptable.[10] Next, the French Ambassador called on the Chancellor, presenting a plan on behalf of the French government in more concrete form.[11] Finally, the Chancellor also received the Italian Ambassador acting in the name of Mussolini. Constant attempts were also made by President Roosevelt to reach Berlin directly.[12]

As a result of these endeavors, and after a direct telephone conversation between Mussolini and Hitler that allegedly cut the Gordian knot, a meeting is to take place tomorrow in Munich between Hitler, Mussolini, Chamberlain, and Daladier.

Under these circumstances, the general mobilization planned by the German government in case the memorandum is not accepted by the Czech government by Wednesday at two o'clock is to be postponed for twenty-four hours. The Secretary of State, however, told me that military orders are still being issued.

Next von Weizsäcker informed me that a certain willingness to compromise was noted on the part of France and Great Britain with regard to the peaceful occupation by German forces of a certain red line, and to the extension of international control over the remaining part of the territories destined for a plebiscite, as well as over some other territories. He added that delimitation of frontiers under the plebiscite is planned with the assistance of an international committee.

[9] This report is missing from Lipski's documents. Résumé in handwritten note (*supra*, p. 427).
[10] *DGFP*, Series D, Vol. II, No. 655.
[11] *Ibid.*, Nos. 648 and 656.
[12] *Ibid.*, No. 653.

The Secretary of State evaluated the situation as follows: a peaceful settlement is anticipated. Naturally, a possible failure to agree should still be considered.

I saw the Hungarian Envoy today, who had called on Göring to discuss Hungarian revindications. Göring will also attend the conference at Munich. The Hungarian Envoy hopes that Mussolini will very firmly support the Hungarian cause.

Józef Lipski

On September 29 a conference was held in Munich.[13] Lipski notes in his private papers:

Director Dembiński departed for Munich as a representative of the Polish Telegraph Agency. The Ministry of Foreign Affairs instructed me, while the conference was under way, to inform the Italian delegation about the alleged sabotage by Prague of the agreement with us on Teschen. This was accomplished by Dembiński.

DOCUMENT 114   Lipski to Beck

NO. N/1/186/38   Berlin, September 30, 1938
                                               Strictly Confidential

Referring to my telegram of today I confirm that von Ribbentrop telephoned me from Munich expressing his conviction that the Polish government would probably be satisfied with the way Polish interests were secured at yesterday's conference. He also acknowledged that the German government, in accordance with my agreement with the Chancellor at Berchtesgaden, made the granting of a guarantee to the future Czechoslovak state dependent upon the settlement of Polish and Hungarian problems. The Italian Ambassador confirmed to me today that Mussolini made a similar declaration.

I made it clear to Ribbentrop, while extending my congratulations to

[13] For the program, memoranda, and resolutions, see *ibid.*, Nos. 669, 670, 674, and 675.

him and the Chancellor, that the burden of the problem now weighs on us. Here Ribbentrop remarked that the formula regarding Polish and Hungarian interests accepted yesterday by the conference should be convenient for us since it deals with the whole Czechoslovak question.

I tried discreetly to sound von Ribbentrop out with regard to France's and England's guarantee for Czechoslovakia. Ribbentrop said that he does not know exactly what guarantee these two states gave to Czechoslovakia. This matter was dealt with between France, England, and Prague. Herr von Ribbentrop thinks that the declaration of England and France about the guarantee for Czechoslovakia, contained in an additional protocol, was executed by these states out of consideration for their public opinion and that of Czechoslovakia.

I was further informed by the Minister of Foreign Affairs that Prague had been notified of the agreement tonight, and that there can be no possible doubt as to its acceptance. Today at 5 P.M., as foreseen by the agreement, a committee will meet to discuss the evacuation.

I later saw the Italian Ambassador. He ascertained that Mussolini was practically leading the conference, presenting a concrete plan to settle the strife in a way acceptable to all parties.

The Polish-Hungarian question had naturally also been presented by Mussolini; he did so at the final nocturnal debate. Mussolini set a term of one month for these matters to be settled directly between Prague, Budapest, and Warsaw, while Chamberlain insisted on three months; a compromise proposition of two months suggested by Mussolini was not accepted.

However, the Italian Ambassador stressed the importance of the fact that the principle of direct negotiations between Warsaw and Prague had been maintained.

In answer to my question, the Italian Ambassador explained that Polish and Hungarian questions had not been dealt with *ad meritum* at all.

In accordance with your instructions transmitted to me by Director Łubieński, I immediately took steps to obtain first of all a map provided for *ad* point 4 of the agreement. I approached the German side and the Italian Ambassador on this. The Italian Ambassador gave me his map, and I had a copy of it made. The Secretary of State of the Auswärtiges Amt also sent a map on which the sectors for evacuation are marked. As the two maps agree, I am forwarding the German map. For the sake of order, I enclose the text of the agreement.

Józef Lipski

(add. to Document 114)
enclosures:
Map
Text[14]

DOCUMENT 115   Lipski to Beck

NO. 1/194/38   Berlin, October 1, 1938
                                                Strictly Confidential

Yesterday, September 30, in the evening hours, Undersecretary of State Woermann telephoned to ask whether it was true that the Polish government had sent an ultimatum to Prague. In reply I stated that up to then I knew only that the Polish government would make a serious decision that evening.[15]

This morning I was asked by Woermann to call him at the Auswärtiges Amt at 11:30 A.M. It was impossible for me to get in touch either with General Field Marshal Göring or with Herr von Ribbentrop prior to this meeting, since they were taking part in greeting the Chancellor upon his arrival in Berlin at 10:30 A.M.

Before I left for the Auswärtiges Amt, the British ambassador, Sir Nevile Henderson, called by phone, very upset by our ultimatum to Prague. He said that he had instructions to get in touch with the German government on this matter. He pointed to the "disastrous consequences military action against Czechoslovakia would entail for Poland during

---

[14] Both enclosures are missing from Lipski's documents.

[15] The decision to send an ultimatum was reached in Warsaw on September 30 in the afternoon, and the Polish Minister in Prague handed to Minister of Foreign Affairs Krofta the ultimatum note on the same day at 11:40 P.M. for a term of twelve hours, that is, until October 1 at noon. For the text see *Documents on British Foreign Policy, 1919–1939*, Third Series, Vol. III, Document No. 101. See *Journal*, pp. 342–43. See also Wojciechowski, *Stosunki polsko-niemieckie, 1933–1938*, pp. 484–85.

such a delicate international period." Poland would lose all sympathy in England and the United States. I tried to explain the situation to the Ambassador, advising him, as a sole remedy, that his government should influence Prague to accept our ultimatum.

Immediately afterward there was another telephone call; this one came from the Italian Ambassador who, although he did not threaten us with the wrath of the Italian people, was hurt and accused us of undermining Mussolini's work: the result of Munich, which had saved the peace. I explained that our ultimatum followed the lines of this conference, which left the problem of Teschen for direct settlement between Warsaw and Prague.

I then started for the Auswärtiges Amt. Undersecretary Woermann asked me to confirm the military demarcation line established by me with Secretary of State von Weizsäcker in the event of a Polish-Czechoslovak war. I confirmed that our demarcation line runs alongside the rivers Oder and Ostravica, and that the Polish General Staff, in accordance with my previous report, would keep to this line.

Herr Woermann did not wish to commit himself with regard to the political situation, remarking that Herr von Ribbentrop would receive me in a moment, after he got in touch with the Chancellor. He read to me Moltke's telegram on yesterday's conversation with you, when you asked if, in the event of an armed Czech-Polish conflict, we might count on the friendly attitude of the Reich government, as well as on a similar position by Germany in case of an armed conflict of Poland with the Soviets.[16]

Immediately afterward I was received by Herr von Ribbentrop, who informed me that the French, British, and Italian governments are exerting pressure on the German government to advise the Polish government to extend the term of the ultimatum. He was expecting a telephone call from Ciano at any moment. I set forth the situation to von Ribbentrop, concluding by stating that the ultimatum expired at 12 noon, that is, in a couple of minutes. Von Ribbentrop remarked that the Chancellor had told him that, if Poland waited for three months, not a single Pole would be left in Teschen Silesia. Although I could detect some embarrassment on his part, probably because of the Munich agreement with the Powers and the Hitler-Chamberlain declaration, von Ribbentrop tried to extricate himself from the Anglo-French-Italian pressure. Called on the tele-

[16] For von Moltke's telegram, see *DGFP*, Series D, Vol. V, No. 54.

phone by Ciano, von Ribbentrop went to another room, returning to inform me that the Italian government, through its ambassador in Warsaw, this morning advised an extension of the ultimatum.

He then described the attitude of the Reich government as follows:

1) In the event of an armed Polish-Czech conflict, the German government would maintain a friendly attitude toward Poland.

2) In case of a Polish-Soviet conflict, the German government would take a far more than friendly attitude toward Poland, and he clearly hinted that the German government would come to Poland's assistance.

3) Von Ribbentrop would reply along these lines to the British, French, and Italian governments: that he hopes no armed conflict will occur between Poland and Czechoslovakia if Prague accepts Poland's claims. He would add that, bearing in mind the situation prevailing in Teschen Silesia, he cannot give advice to the Polish government.[17]

I was next invited to Field Marshal Göring's. Making the reservation that he was expressing his own opinion, he declared that the Reich government would give no advice to the Polish government in such a situation, being aware that Warsaw would not accept such advice, and that it would be right not to do so. He further stressed that in connection with military operations it might be important for our military authorities to know that the German pressure on Czechoslovakia could be much more effective upon the occupation of Sector IV, that is, on October 7. Finally—and he laid special stress on this—in case of a Soviet-Polish conflict, the Polish government could count on aid from the German government. It is absolutely out of the question that the Reich would not help Poland in its struggle with the Soviets.

Next, the conversation with Göring passed to general subjects, on which I am commenting separately in other reports.[18]

From Göring's attitude it was obvious that he is completely in agreement with the Polish government's point of view. In a conversation by telephone with me when the ultimatum was accepted, he characterized our step as "a very bold action performed in excellent style."

Ribbentrop also told me in the afternoon that the Chancellor today at lunchtime expressed to his entourage great appreciation for Poland's policy.

[17] For Ribbentrop's memorandum of his conversation with Lipski and Ciano, see *ibid.*, No. 55.

[18] These reports are missing form Lipski's documents, outside of a handwritten note dated October 1.

I must stress that our step was evaluated here as an expression of great strength and independent action, which represents the best guarantee of our good relations with the government of the Reich.

Józef Lipski

The following is Lipski's handwritten note of his conversation with Göring:

Göring joined in the conversations I had with Woermann and Ribbentrop on October 1 at the invitation of the Auswärtiges Amt on the ultimatum sent by the Polish government to Prague. In addition to his invitation by telephone, which already occurred after 12 noon (the term for the expiration of the ultimatum), I had a conversation with him at his residence in Berlin. I found him overjoyed by the result of the Munich conference, which he called a great success for Germany.

With his usual directness, he said that "now probably Poland also will draw consequences from the changed situation and change its alliance with France for an alliance with Germany." He was very well satisfied with his conversation with Daladier. Allegedly it would result in the French Prime Minister's striving to carry through elections to enable him to tighten French relations with Germany.

I maintained my reserve with regard to these revelations of Göring. With regard to our ultimatum to Prague on Teschen Silesia, Göring asked why we were asking for so little, and why we did not want to annex Moravska Ostrava to Poland, where obviously there was also some Polish population. I replied that our demand was restricted to Teschen Silesia, to which Göring insisted that, availing ourselves of the occasion, we should extend our claims.

On my return to the Embassy I received a telephone call from Göring. He asked, somewhat embarrassedly, that I not repeat his deliberations to Warsaw with regard to Moravska Ostrava. It was quite clear to me that he had probably been admonished by the Chancellor or by Ribbentrop that he should not display to the Polish side Germany's *désintéressement* with regard to Moravska Ostrava.[19]

[19] In this matter attention should be called to a memorandum by Secretary of State Weizsäcker dated October 4: "Field Marshal Göring told me today, with regard to the territory south of the southwestern corner of Silesia, that it must by all means become German. Should a dispute develop about it with the Poles, a deal could be made over Danzig. Otherwise it would be best to pass it to the Czechs." *DGFP*, Series D, Vol. V, No. 58.

DOCUMENT 116   Lipski to Beck

NO. N/1/198/38   Berlin, October 4, 1938
                                                Strictly Confidential

On October 3 Secretary of State Weizsäcker, in the course of a casual
conversation at the Auswärtiges Amt, told me that for the sake of order
he would like to compare our maps again.[20] For this purpose Counselor
Lubomirski met with Undersecretary of State Woermann in the evening
at the Auswärtiges Amt and confirmed that the German map copied
from ours on September 28 (see my report of 9/28, No. 1/183/38) is
in conformity with what was agreed between me and Weizsäcker on the
above date. Counselor Lubomirski was under the impression that
Woermann has had some difficulties with his authorities over the problem of the Bohumin region. Woermann mentioned casually the planned
Oder-Danube canal, which would possibly run across Polish territory.
However, he did not raise any other objections with regard to the established line.

This morning Secretary of State Weizsäcker called me by telephone,
remarking that probably Minister von Ribbentrop would like to see me
in connection with the intersection of lines in one spot on the delimitation of the territory.[21]

Herr Ribbentrop did not telephone during the day, but Undersecretary of State Woermann asked me to call on him at 6 P.M. He told me
that Herr Ribbentrop had a cold and could not receive me, and had
instructed him to declare as follows:

"The inclusion of Oderberg in the Polish zone is a new matter of fact.
Since, however, we will have to discuss the drawing of the frontiers, the
problem of Oderberg can then become the subject of debates."

I call attention to the fact that, in the first version of the declaration,
instead of the words "a new matter of fact" (*neue Tatsache*), Woermann said "a surprise" (*eine Überraschung*).

In a very outspoken manner I stated that I must categorically protest
that there could not possibly be any mention of any "surprise." On this
occasion I referred to your basic conversation on the problem of the
Polish region with Field Marshal Göring, to my conversation with the
Chancellor at Berchtesgaden, when I clearly discussed Oderberg, as well

[20] For the memorandum by Weizsäcker of his conversation, see *ibid.*, No. 57.
[21] *Ibid.*, No. 60.

as to a virtual and unequivocal agreement reached on this matter on September 28, on the basis of maps, with Secretary of State Weizsäcker.

Woermann, visibly embarrassed, replied that he had received his instructions, that the formula showed by itself the spirit of the forthcoming talks on these matters, and that besides this declaration no details were known to him.

For the sake of order I took literal notes of Woermann's declaration and told him sharply that I did not conceive how I could report such a declaration to my Minister. Woermann started to explain, very evasively, that in the conversation of September 28 Secretary of State Weizsäcker only discussed the line in the event of war. This, of course, is absolutely untrue. I corrected this statement, saying that, on the contrary, we were delimitating for a peaceful territorial occupation on the eve of the Munich conference. This put an end to the conversation.

Upon my return to the Embassy and a consultation with Counselor Lubomirski, we checked details, and I communicated to Woermann as follows:

I had studied the declaration as presented to me. I was not in a position either to accept it or to bring it to the knowledge of my government. I stated that I was unable to do so because the declaration is based upon untrue premises that the Oderberg matter was allegedly a *novum* for the government.

I asked Woermann to communicate this to Herr von Ribbentrop.

Woermann tried to explain that I could communicate any declaration to my government. Nevertheless, I replied firmly that I could not do it. The Secretary of State still observed that I might possibly communicate it to the Minister of Foreign Affairs. I replied that formally I was unable to do so.[22]

May I add to the above that, in my opinion, the Auswärtiges Amt possibly made inadvertent concessions on September 28 and is now under pressure from competent authorities. They are trying to make a narrow escape, creating a basis for future negotiations. I could not determine whether the German side is interested in a canal or access to Oderberg [Bohumin] by railway.

[22] For Woermann's version of the same matter, see *ibid.*, No. 61. See also Hitler's agreement to leave Bohumin on the Polish side (*ibid.*, No. 62), and the rejection by the Germans of a petition of this city (*ibid.*, No. 63).

In case von Moltke approaches you on this matter, I am taking the liberty of asking you to reject this declaration.

I think that under these circumstances it would be advisable to occupy the Bohumin region without delay.

Józef Lipski

DOCUMENT 117 Lipski to Beck [23]

NO. N/1/204/38

Berlin, October 6, 1938
(Personal)
Strictly Confidential

This morning Ambassador von Moltke paid me a visit, remarking that he had received a telegram about my conversation with Undersecretary of State Woermann regarding Oderberg. Without further delay, and without discussing this matter with the Minister, he had immediately left for Berlin in order to get in touch with his authorities and, naturally, to remove the problem from the agenda. I explained the whole matter to von Moltke and why I had protested so vehemently to Undersecretary of State Woermann. Moltke fully shared my point of view.

He returned in the afternoon, stating quite confidentially that he finally realized how the matter stands. On the German side three points are essential:

1) the canal the German government is planning to build between the Oder and the Danube would have to run across the territory ceded to Poland by the Czech government;

2) the Berlin-Wrocław-Vienna railway line goes through Oderberg, crossing Polish and then Czech territory, necessitating the passing of six frontier stations;

3) the city of Oderberg itself has a majority of German population, and some objections have been raised in this connection.

Von Moltke agreed that all these matters should have been discussed peacefully in advance, and that undoubtedly the German side is to blame here. Nevertheless, the German side would like at present to iron

[23] For the Polish text, see *Sprawny Międzynarodowe* (Warsaw), 1958, No. 9, pp. 111–13.

out the situation and avoid hurting Poland. Moltke suggested that the Germans would like to adopt the following plan, bearing in mind, of course, that the Polish red line cannot be infringed upon:

1) With regard to the canal, the Germans would like to obtain assurances that the Polish government will agree in the future to its passage through Polish territory.

2) With regard to the railway, the German side would like to have its line on the Polish sector come up to the Czech frontier.

3) With regard to Oderberg, the German government would require some special minority guarantee.

Regardless of the result of his consultations, Moltke mentioned that he sees a solution in prompt negotiations on the problem with the Polish government upon his return to Warsaw. This might take place either tomorrow morning or the next day.

I promised von Moltke, upon his special request, that our conversation would be kept secret, as being strictly private.

Realizing it to be of importance that you should be warned about a possible *démarche* on this matter, I would like, for my part, to lay stress on the following:

With regard to the canal, which in any case would have to pass through the territory of other states, in my opinion such an assurance could be given—upon orienting ourselves which way the canal would run (von Moltke did not know this).

Regarding the railway problem, I think some agreement might be reached, especially since, as I was informed by Director Łubieński, a part of this railway has hitherto been in German hands.

Concerning the guarantee for minorities, I would be very careful not to go further than the provisions of the declaration of November 5, 1937.

I think that von Moltke will probably approach you with a concrete proposal for a compromise with regard to particular points, suggesting that negotiations be finalized in Warsaw as promptly as possible. Moltke understands the necessity of keeping the matter absolutely secret. If the news leaked out, it would appear to public opinion at large that there is frontier strife between Poland and Germany.[24]

[24] Upon his return to Warsaw, von Moltke had a conversation on this matter with Szembek on October 7 (*Journal*, p. 346, and *DGFP*, Series D, Vol. V, No. 66).

DOCUMENT 118   Lipski to Beck [25]

NO. N/1/207/38   Berlin, October 8, 1938
                                                Strictly Confidential

In addition to my report of the 6th inst., No. N/1/204/38, I am taking the liberty of informing you as follows:

On the 7th inst. I was invited by Secretary of State Weizsäcker to the Auswärtiges Amt for a conversation. Weizsäcker referred to my conversation with Undersecretary of State Woermann on October 4. He mentioned that this conversation had been referred to the top authorities of the Reich, who had justified my point of view ("Ihr Standpunkt ist von den höchsten Stellen gewürdigt worden"). General Field Marshal Göring wanted to declare this to me personally but he was unfortunately prevented from doing so. Von Ribbentrop is also bedridden with a cold. That is why the Secretary of State communicated this to me.

Next, von Weizsäcker stated that he would like to inform me about the instructions von Moltke received for his conversations in Warsaw. Von Weizsäcker added that he would just give me an outline, since details would be presented by von Moltke.

Specifically, the German government would like to present several matters to us in a friendly way for settlement in connection with the takeover of Teschen Silesia by Poland.

1) Of concern were communication problems in connection with the line crossing Bohumin on the Annaberg-Oderberg-Vitkovice line; here he added that this concerned certain property of the German railways.

2) In connection with the planned Oder-Danube canal, consent should be given to the building of this canal through our territory in the future.

3) The German side was concerned that the German minorities in the territories occupied by Poland should not be treated worse than hitherto. The Secretary of State mentioned that quite a number of claims had been made with regard to Voivode Grażyński's action. He also stated that the German side would like to have a consulate at Teschen.

The whole conversation was marked with the highest degree of courtesy on the part of Secretary of State Weizsäcker.

[25] For the Polish text, see *Sprawy Międzynarodowe* (Warsaw), 1958, No. 9, pp. 113–14.

Further continuing our conversation, I asked the Secretary of State to authorize Counselor Altenburg to hand over the map of Sector V to Counselor Lubomirski. He promised to do so.

We touched casually on the Hungarian question, and Weizsäcker showed particular interest in the newly formed Slovakian government. He also expressed a desire to be kept informed about the recent conversations of Count Csáky with you in Warsaw.

I finally brought up the subject of Carpathian Ruthenia with the map in hand. At this point I referred to our discussion in detail with Chancellor Hitler at Berchtesgaden.[26]

Józef Lipski

DOCUMENT 119   Lipski to Beck

Telegram by Code No. 154

Berlin, October 12, 1938
Received: October 13, 9 A.M.
Secret

During a conversation to which he invited me, the Secretary of State declared that in view of certain rumors in the Polish press [27] he wanted to warn me that the German government is not uninterested in Moravska Ostrava and Vitkovice. He communicated to me confidentially that the German government nevertheless would not call for a plebiscite in this region. However, it will place a reservation with the Commission [28] tomorrow; in case another party (read Poland) should be interested in Vitkovice and Moravska Ostrava, the German government would then request a plebiscite.

I declared conclusively that we do not claim Moravska Ostrava and Vitkovice, and that we would not go beyond the black line as communicated to the German government. I therefore confirmed that there is no difference of opinion between us.

Owing to my declaration, the Secretary of State considered the German government's reservation as purposeless and will not place it before the Commission tomorrow.

[26] For the German version of this conversation, see *DGFP*, Series D, Vol. V, No. 65.
[27] Von Moltke writes about this in his telegram of October 10. *Ibid.*, No. 68.
[28] The International Commission for Executing the Terms of the Munich Agreement.

We acknowledged that consequently the region of Moravska Ostrava and Vitkovice would remain as a Czech territory between Poland and Germany.

Following instructions, I informed the Secretary of State about the direction of our negotiations with Prague with regard to the establishment of the Polish-Czech frontier in the region of Frydek.[29]

Received: Warsaw and Prague

On October 18 Beck went to Rumania for a conversation with King Carol, which took place at Galati on October 19. Before his departure, instructions were sent to a number of Polish ambassadors, Lipski among them; he was asked to try for a *neutralité bienveillante* with Germany with regard to transferring Carpathian Ruthenia to Hungary. Lipski was also to discuss all problems with Göring (Szembek, *Journal*, pp. 356–59).

On the 18th Lipski conferred with Weizsäcker on the problem of Carpathian Ruthenia. The report on this conversation is missing from Lipski's documents; for Weizsäcker's version, see *DGFP*, Series D, Vol. V, No. 75, pp. 96–98.[30]

Upon his return to Warsaw Beck sent instructions to Lipski on October 20 containing information about his conversation with the King.[31]

Lipski had a conversation with Göring on October 21, and on October 22 he repeated the same things to the director of the Political Department, Woermann (*DGFP*, Series D, Vol. V, No. 80; the report on the conversation with Woermann is missing from Lipski's documents).[32]

DOCUMENT 120   Beck to Lipski

Warsaw, October 20, 1938
Strictly Confidential

I communicate information and guiding lines for the conversation with Göring:

1) I had a conversation with King Carol yesterday which lasted for several hours, partly in the presence of Comnen, and partly alone. Prince Hohenzollern-Sigmaringen was also there.

[29] During those days Lipski was in Warsaw (see his conversation with Szembek on October 10 and that of Szembek with Beck on October 11, *Journal*, pp. 349–52). For the German version of Lipski's conversation with Weizsäcker, see *DGFP*, Series D, Vol. V, No. 69; also, on the same matter, Nos. 70, 71, and 74.

[30] See also von Moltke's report of October 19 (*DGFP*, Series D, Vol. V, Nos. 76 and 79).

[31] See Beck, *Final Report*, pp. 165–67.

[32] Regarding Carpathian Ruthenia, see also von Moltke's report of October 25, *DGFP*, Series D, Vol. V, No. 83, and Weizsäcker's information sent to Ribbentrop on October 22, *ibid.*, Series D, Vol. IV, No. 83.

I was under the impression that the King wanted to take advantage of the present situation to achieve a basic relaxation in his relations with Hungary. However, he has to cope with the feelings of many political circles in Rumania, and the main difficulty lies in Comnen's tendentious reporting to the King. Together with Prague, Comnen is pursuing his dream of a Czechoslovakia serving as a political corridor binding Rumania with the West. Comnen even goes so far as to weave fantastic plans for drilling tunnels for a new railway, once Hungary occupies the ethnographic territories which cut across the only railway artery hitherto. The King is not taking this seriously. One of the principal arguments suggested to the King against the Hungarian Carpatho-Ruthenian concept is the pressure allegedly exerted by the Reich against this concept. The "entourage of Marshal Göring" is even being quoted as a source of German policy on Ruthenia.

The King listened with satisfaction to my arguments contradicting Comnen's concepts. He is taking an interest in our *bons offices* between Rumania and Hungary, while he is very reticent about any allusions regarding frontier corrections to the advantage of Rumania in the eastern point of Ruthenia. He has scruples about his former allies—the Czechs. He, as well as Comnen, was deeply troubled by my remark that it is difficult to conceive how the Czechs can in the future be responsible for the control of Carpathian Ruthenia, and in consequence how they can guarantee that it would not become a settlement center for all kinds of destructive agitators among immigrant elements.

Please evaluate, on the basis of your own orientation, how far Göring should be informed about these details, besides the point of the alleged German policy which must be brought up.

2) Please utilize your talk with Field Marshal Göring to develop the following marginal argumentation:

Carpathian Ruthenia was invented during the Peace Conference to supply Russia with a bridge into Europe. Later, hopes were nourished, and are still timely, of creating on this territory a kind of springboard, some political cadre designed to exert influence on the real Ukraine at present situated within the frame of Soviet Russia. According to our opinion and our experience of 1918–20, as well as our present observation, this concept is proving to be sheer fiction. Neither Carpathian Ruthenians, nor the undoubtedly much more accomplished Galician Ruthenians, have any chance of controlling national movements in the real Ukraine. They are, and will always remain, a foreign element whom the local population will reject. The language, religion, and political concepts of these various Ruthenians of ours have very little in common with the real Ukraine; besides, in liberation movements, emigration, even of political groups—and particularly an artificially cultivated breed actually of alien origin—never represents a decisive factor. All this, taken together, is absolute fiction, and the Germans had an opportunity themselves to learn the value of all these pseudo-Ukrainians used for action on the sides of the Dnieper.

3) I report for your information that Prince Hohenzollern suggested to me at Galati the proposition that in case of an increase of difficulties in the Carpathian region we should foster the idea of calling a conference of representatives of Hungary, Czechoslovakia, Rumania, and Poland. The idea was that within the frame of such a consultation Rumania would join our thesis on the indispensable basic territorial revision of the former Czechoslovakia, thus bringing about a general relaxation in the whole region.

4) Please ask Göring, and if necessary also Ribbentrop, about the character of German mediation undertaken today between Prague and Budapest, communicating to Göring our readiness for contact and our agreement of opinion on the problems which you have already presented at the Auswärtiges Amt.

5) Our conversations with the Czechs as to the final delimitation are proceeding, while we have limited our claims to rather insignificant extensions of the occupied territory in Silesia, so that not only is there no question of crossing the Ostravica, but on its eastern bank we are prepared to give up Polish Ostrava and its mining region.

Beck

DOCUMENT 121   Lipski to Beck

Berlin, October 21, 1938
Strictly Confidential

In my conversation today at Karinhall with Field Marshal Göring, I utilized all the information and instructions received from you in the last days.

For lack of time before the plane leaves, I am not presenting extensive deliberations but am limiting myself to a short, broad outline of the conversation.

1) When I mentioned that Poland is trying to influence Budapest in order to attenuate Hungarian claims with regard to Slovakia, Göring said that German mediation was wrecked by the Hungarian claim to Koszyce [Kosice]. Göring thinks that this claim was quite unjustified from the ethnographical angle, as well as because of the importance of this point for Slovakia.

2) After I explained our point of view regarding Carpathian Ruthenia, which Göring noted carefully and today showed great personal understanding for, he asked me how this demand could be taken care of in practice. Seeking for a solution, we reached the common opinion that in a country 80 percent illiterate it is hardly possible to speak of self-determination. Göring agreed with my opinion that France and England are expressing their *désintéressement* in this matter.

In conclusion I stated that if we and Germany are in accord in this respect and the Italians, as I am informed, are also for it, then there is no objection to the settlement of the problem. Göring added here that naturally under these circumstances Hungary could occupy Ruthenia.

3) I discussed the results of your trip to Bucharest, criticizing Comnen's activity. Göring, for his part, holds an opinion similar to ours.

When I said that in the King's presence Comnen used the argument that Germany is opposing a common Polish-Hungarian frontier through the annexation of Ruthenia to Hungary, Göring exploded, declaring that he cannot conceive on what basis Comnen dares to make such a statement. Also, when I pointed out that Comnen still thinks in categories of the Little Entente, Göring declared that it was high time for the Little Entente to be formally buried, since in fact it does not exist any more.

During the conversation I tried to lay stress on the difference of opinion between the King and Comnen.

4) Asked about German mediation with regard to Hungarian demands, Göring replied that as far as Ruthenia was concerned the German government had taken on no obligations whatsoever. I stressed how important it was that the German side should do nothing in this matter.

Summing up the above conversation I state that I found Göring more understanding than on previous occasions on the subject of the settlement of the problem of Carpathian Ruthenia along the lines of our thesis. However, and I particularly stress this, he said that he does not know what conclusions might have been reached by the Chancellor in the last days, since he would not see him until next week. Therefore, Göring's revelations should not be taken as authoritative declarations of the German government.

It was rather interesting that Göring remarked that the Chancellor is facing very difficult problems with regard to Czechoslovakia as such, since Prague made very far-reaching attempts to come to an agreement with Germany, even to the extent of evoking certain suspicions in Berlin. Göring added that there are Czechs who approach him with propositions that Czechoslovakia be annexed into the German *organismus* autonomically. This might influence the Chancellor to make a prompt settlement of Hungarian revindication in order to deal with the Czechs on economic problems only afterward.

I shall try to see Ribbentrop as soon as possible; if necessary, I shall even go to Munich.

Yesterday I received very confidential information that Comnen gave orders to verify your declaration that Germany is not in the least interested in the matter of Ruthenia, to see whether it corresponds with reality, and that on this occasion all arguments against our common frontier with Hungary should be used.

I would ask you, for the sake of my friend, not to disclose this fact. I am doing all I can to undermine Comnen's activities.

Józef Lipski

Göring's notebook, in which he made very short notes on conversations conducted, was found after the war. In it he noted the above conversation he had with Lipski on October 21, 1938. The following note was published, somewhat abbreviated, by the *Daily Herald* (London) in the issue of July 11, 1945, after the paper had previously shown it to Ambassador Lipski, who at that time resided in London. Upon taking note of its contents, on July 6 Lipski sent his comments on the note to the editor; these appeared, with some deletions, in the *Daily Herald* on July 12.

The full text of the translation of Göring's note and the full text of Lipski's declaration are given below.

DOCUMENT 122   Göring's Note

LIPSKI   October 21

Information on Poland's intentions. Keep contact, avoid misunderstandings.

Problem Hungary-Slovakia: pressure on Hungary for giving way, but only toward Slovakia.

Problem Carpatho-Ukraine. Poland is interested, but not territorially. At Versailles, 1919, separation of Poland from Hungary was demanded. Ethnical mixture, in the south Hungarians down to the line Uzhorod-Munkacz.

Poland fears that a center of future troubles might develop there. The country tends toward Hungary. Should be a bridge toward the question of a Great Ukraine. But for the Great Ukraine this little territory does not mean anything. Different religions! Ruthenians are not Ukrainians. The Communist center for the Balkans against Poland was, and is, established there.

For Poland such a center for a hardening of Ukrainians is very alarming. Would lead to a stiffening of Ukrainian question in Poland.

Therefore Polish desire that this territory come to Hungary, so that it may be controlled.

Propaganda in the West that common frontier could be a danger for Germany. That would be absurd.

Information on Bucharest. The visit there took place on the King's initiative. The King's ideas. Understands interest to achieve better understanding with Hungary. Comnen exercises bad influence on policy. Completely taken in by Geneva. He alleges that Germany is opposed to solution of a common frontier. Beck denies it. Comnen is still a supporter of the idea of granting assistance to the Little Entente. If there was an agreement with us and Italy one might achieve a clear solution.

I protest against the treatment inflicted on the Germans on the Polish territories. Sending documents to Lipski. Stern warning sent to Warsaw to treat the Germans well.

DOCUMENT 123   Notes on Lipski's Conversation
with Göring on October 21, 1938

On identifying this particular conversation in my diary, I would like to submit the following remarks concerning the document at present in possession of the *Daily Herald*.

The conversation in question took place at Karinhall on the morning of October 21, 1938. I forwarded a detailed account to the Polish Foreign Office and luckily I am in possession of a copy of that report.

The prints which I have been given appear to be photographs of loose notes taken down in Göring's hand. The notes are a rough and incomplete summary of the points raised in our conversation; the arguments used by both Göring and myself are presented in some confusion and give no indication of the theme used by either party.

As regards the political background of the conversation, the following facts should be noted.

The Nazi leaders, intoxicated as they were at that time by their easy triumph at Munich, increased their activities in Eastern Europe. In connection with the Hungarian claims to Slovakia and Carpathian Ruthenia, Nazi activities concentrated mainly on the Ukrainian question; Vienna, which was then the headquarters of the Ukrainian terrorists (under the auspices of Himmler), became the center of this agitation in which every form of subversive intrigue and seditious propaganda was fully utilized. The Germans had two objects in bringing the Ukrainian problem to the fore. Firstly, they hoped by preaching the idea of separation of the Ukraine from Russia to injure the USSR; secondly, they thought that by making Carpathian Ruthenia a fictitious focus of Ukrainian nationalism and an unwelcome center of German propaganda on Poland's very doorstep they would be striking an indirect blow at Poland. Czechoslovakia, substantially weakened as a result of Munich, was consequently incapable of coping with German intrigues in so distant a region.

The aim of the Polish government was to stabilize conditions in Central Europe as far as possible. It strove to reduce Hungarian claims to Slovakia. As regards Carpathian Ruthenia, however, Poland favored its return to Hungary, to which country it had belonged before the Treaty of Trianon. Moreover, Polish diplomacy was striving to effect a rapprochement between Bucharest and Budapest.

A common frontier between Poland and Hungary would have formed a considerable obstacle to German ambitions in the east. Accordingly, they were resented in the Wilhelmstrasse.

Ribbentrop had retired in the period following Munich to Bavaria. There he made himself inaccessible to the diplomatic corps in Berlin. Information reached us, however, that he was busy contacting, among others, his Ukrainian agents and that the idea of a joint German-Italian ruling on the territories being disputed by Budapest and Prague was being formed. In the circumstances, I had to approach Göring in order to stress the Polish point of view.

The Soviet ambassador, Mr. Merekalov, was obviously interested in this question. It transpired, from conversations which I had with him at the time, that he was fully aware of the German aims. These events had considerable influence on the Soviet-Polish Declaration, signed in Moscow on November 26, 1938, reaffirming the will of both parties strictly to adhere to the agreements actually reached in the preceding years (for example, the nonaggression pact of 1932).[33]

J. Lipski
former Polish Ambassador in Germany

London, July 6, 1945

[33] See *Polish White Book,* Nos. 160 and 161.

Ribbentrop Puts Forth Claims to Poland
October 24—December 15, 1938

DOCUMENT 124   Note Concerning Ambassador Lipski's Conversation
with Reich Minister of Foreign Affairs von Ribbentrop
at Berchtesgaden on October 24, 1938

Polish Embassy in Berlin
Strictly Confidential

IN A CONVERSATION on October 24 over luncheon at the Grand Hotel in
Berchtesgaden, at which Herr Hewel was present, Herr von Ribbentrop
put forward to the Polish Ambassador a proposal for a basic settlement
of issues (*Gesamtlösung*) between Poland and Germany which, as he
expressed himself, would remove the causes of future strife. This included the reunion of Danzig with the Reich, while Poland would be
assured of retaining railway and economic facilities there. Poland would
agree to the building of an extraterritorial superhighway and railway line
across Pomerania. In exchange, von Ribbentrop mentioned the possibility of an extension of the Polish-German agreement by twenty-five
years and a guarantee of Polish-German frontiers. As a possible sphere
for future cooperation between the two countries, the German Foreign
Minister specified joint action in colonial matters, the emigration of
Jews from Poland, and a joint policy toward Russia on the basis of the
Anti-Comintern Pact. Herr von Ribbentrop asked the Ambassador to
communicate his suggestions to Minister Beck. He would like to discuss
these matters with him with the Ambassador's participation.

In his reply, Ambassador Lipski referred to the Chancellor's declaration on the Danzig question made to him on November 5, 1937,[1] and
repeated to Minister Beck in Berlin on January 14, 1938.[2]

[1] See Document 73, p. 303.
[2] See Document 77, p. 334.

The Ambassador also pointed to the importance of Danzig as a port for Poland, and repeated the Polish government's principle of noninterference in the internal life of the German population in the Free City, where complete self-government is established.

Finally, the Ambassador stated that he would like to warn von Ribbentrop that he could see no possibility of an agreement involving the reunion of the Free City with the Reich. He concluded by promising to communicate the substance of this conversation to Minister Beck.

After the conversation von Ribbentrop invited the Ambassador again to call on him and, mentioning the issue of the union of Carpathian Ruthenia with Hungary, put to him the question whether he was raising it with the German government as a Polish demand. He added that, if the Polish government agreed to the German concept regarding Danzig and the superhighway, the question of Carpathian Ruthenia could be solved in accordance with Poland's wishes on the matter. Ambassador Lipski answered that his only task was to inform the German government of Poland's attitude in regard to Hungary's demand in Carpathian Ruthenia, since Poland had already informed the Italian government.

The Conversation with Minister of Foreign Affairs von Ribbentrop
at the Grand Hotel, Berchtesgaden, on October 24, 1938

October 25, 1938
Strictly Confidential

Herr von Ribbentrop invited me for luncheon. The liaison officer between the Auswärtiges Amt and the Reich Chancellery, Herr Hewel, was also present.

I. In the first part of the conversation general issues were discussed, while von Ribbentrop deliberated at length on the international situation preceding the Munich Conference. He declared that he had been convinced all the time that a world war was out of the question. His arguments were based upon a calculation of power; he had been assured that, in case France mobilized, Italy would also mobilize, and if France attacked, Italy would attack France. From his calculations it ensued that in this conflict France would be isolated.

For my part, in the course of these deliberations I pointed to the action of international agencies which had been started on the very day of the Godesberg Conference with a protest lodged by Moscow against Poland.[3] I laid stress on our firm and determined stand on this matter.

II. Hungary's Revindications

Herr von Ribbentrop exposed at length his personal objections to the Hungarian way of behavior. He recalled that during Horthy's visit the Chancellor quite frankly told the Regent that he had decided to act on the problem of the Sudetenland, and he advised the Hungarians to be ready for any eventuality. During this visit, to the utter surprise of the German government, Kanya showed Ribbentrop a communiqué from Bled,[4] which evidently made the worst possible impression in Berlin. The Hungarian side, during this visit, constantly warned against war entanglements, owing to the Anglo-French stand. It came to Ribbentrop's knowledge that upon their return to Budapest the rumor was spread there that he was conducting a madman's policy. Ribbentrop's resentment centered mainly on Kanya.

He further mentioned that on the eve of the Godesberg Conference the Chancellor invited Imredy to Berchtesgaden and gave him detailed information on the situation.[5] On Imredy's request, the Chancellor firmly supported Hungarian claims at the conference in Munich. Hungarians knew all about this, but not a single word of thanks followed, since they considered that German efforts were self-explanatory.

Next, von Ribbentrop discussed the problem of the German government's mediation. In the conversations with Darányi[6] at Berchtesgaden the Hungarian ethnographic line was discussed. It was established that Bratislava would remain outside the line and that Nitra would be subject to a plebiscite; Koszyce [Kosice] would remain within the Hungarian line, while Uzhorod and Munkacz [Munkacevo] would fall beyond the line (as far as I could understand, they were to be subject to a plebiscite).

Ribbentrop used his influence on Chvalkovský[7] to accept such a

---

[3] See p. 413, note 10.

[4] See p. 380, note 11.

[5] *DGFP*, Series D, Vol. II, No. 554.

[6] Kálmán Darányi, former prime minister (1936–38) and minister of agriculture in Hungary. See his conversation with Hitler and Ribbentrop of October 14 (*ibid.*, Series D, Vol. IV, Nos. 62, 63, and 65).

[7] František Chvalkovský, foreign minister of Czechoslovakia from October, 1938, to March 1939. See the Ribbentrop-Chvalkovský and the Hitler-Chvalkovský conversations, *ibid.*, Nos. 55 and 61.

Hungarian line and discussed it also with the Slovaks and representatives of Carpathian Ruthenia.[8]

The Slovaks were hurt by the Koszyce question; the representative of Carpathian Ruthenia was rather pleased that Uzhorod and Munkacz had been left outside the line of claims.

Ribbentrop emphasized here that he did not take any sides and was acting merely as a mediator.

When the results of these conversations were communicated to Budapest by Erdmannsdorf,[9] the Hungarian government bluntly rejected the proposal, in spite of Darányi's earlier approval. Under these circumstances the German government withdrew from mediation and washed its hands of the matter. The Italian side, informed about this, is allegedly also discouraged to some extent by the Hungarian methods.

Ribbentrop is of the opinion that, as matters stand, talks will continue for the time being between Budapest and Prague.

Asked about arbitration, he replied that at present he does not think arbitration could take place; besides, he raises the following objections:

1) Whether, with two other signatories of the Munich Agreement, arbitration with the participation of Germany and Italy would be possible.

2) In case of arbitration, its execution should be guaranteed. Here a military engagement would possibly be needed.

For my part, in accordance with my instructions, I only stated that, in case Germany and Italy agree on arbitration, Poland would join it also.

In my discussion with Ribbentrop I laid special detailed emphasis on our stand regarding the Polish-Hungarian frontier and Carpathian Ruthenia. I am not repeating my arguments here. I think that Ribbentrop was impressed by the Ukrainian argument contained in your instructions.[10] In conclusion he said that he would still reconsider this matter in the light of my deliberations. He asked whether we had territorial claims to Ruthenia; I replied that we did not, that we limited ourselves to support of Hungarian claims to that country.

Ribbentrop pointed here to difficulties created by Rumania's attitude, stressing the Reich's desire to maintain good relations with that country.

[8] *Ibid.*, Nos. 72 and 73.

[9] Otto von Erdmannsdorf, German minister in Hungary. See his report of October 20, 1938, *ibid.*, No. 75.

[10] Point 2 of Beck's instructions of October 20 (see Document 120, pp. 446–47).

He was also informed that Rumania does not insist on a territorial revision in Carpathian Ruthenia to its advantage.

I told him of certain details of your conversations at Galati, showing the contrast between the King's attitude and Comnen's policy.

III. German-French Rapprochement

Ribbentrop mentioned that a desire for a rapprochement might be felt on this sector. He referred to the fact that the Chancellor spoke along these lines to Ambassador François-Poncet and that a certain document, similar to the Hitler-Chamberlain declaration, might be expected.[11] He also mentioned the twenty-five-year nonaggression pact. However, he added that all this is not for immediate action, and that an exchange of opinion with England and Italy must take first place. Here he made the reservation that this agreement should not be considered a sort of Four-Power Pact, since it would only be a bilateral German-French understanding.

IV. General Policy

With regard to general policy, Ribbentrop dwelt on Germany's general endeavors to enter a phase of peaceful development. He pointed to the Chancellor's declaration that he has no further territorial claims.[12]

With regard to *colonial* problems, he remarked that this matter is becoming a reality, and that Germany will consistently strive to achieve its demands.

He laid special stress on the Japanese victory in China as a point detrimental to the British position.

V. Military Matters

He mentioned in brief a new system of German fortifications in the west constructed in accordance with Todt's system, which, in his opinion, is superior to the construction of the Maginot Line. Allegedly trials on the Sudetenland line built on the French model showed that a heavy caliber German shell breaks through such fortifications.

[11] For the text, see *DGFP*, Series D, Vol. II, No. 676.
[12] In his speech at Saarbrücken on October 9, Hitler said: "As a strong state we are prepared at any time for a policy of understanding with our neighbors. We have no demands on them. All we want is peace."

VI. Polish Matters

Ribbentrop stressed that in conversations with him the Chancellor kept returning to his idea of finding a solution to the Jewish problem through an organization for the purpose of emigration. We had an exhaustive talk on this subject. Ribbentrop interrogated me at length on the Jewish situation in Poland.

Speaking about our action with regard to Teschen, Ribbentrop remarked that the Chancellor repeated again and again to the circle of his collaborators his appreciation for our determined move, stating: "The Poles are tough guys. Piłsudski would be proud of them."

Józef Lipski

The problem of Ribbentrop's suggestion (*Gesamtlösung*) was referred to the Minister in my personal letter.

J.L.[13]

On October 31 instructions were prepared in Warsaw for Ambassador Lipski; however, he could not execute them until November 19. These instructions are published in the *Polish White Book*, No. 45 (pp. 48–50), but in paragraph 2 the following sentence is missing:

"On the other hand, our determined attitude in the period of final tensions, when Poland did not join in the international anti-German action on a large scale, was the best proof of the Polish government's loyal intentions." [14]

On November 2 arbitration took place in Vienna (the Vienna Award) between Hungary and Czechoslovakia in connection with the transferral to Hungary of Czechoslovak territory and the delimitation of new frontiers. Minister Ribbentrop and Minister Ciano served in the capacity of arbitrators.

[13] A copy of this letter is missing from Lipski's documents. After his conversation with Ribbentrop at Berchtesgaden, Lipski immediately proceeded to Warsaw to report on it to Beck. On October 29 he discussed this matter "d'une façon assez pessimiste" with Szembek (*Journal*, p. 366).

For the German version of this portion of the conversation, *see DGFP*, Series D, Vol. V, No. 81, pp. 104–7. In the *Polish White Book*, No. 44, this conversation is published in the form of Lipski's letter to Beck, and not as a note.

[14] H. Batowski is wrong in stating that "the translated text published in the *Polish White Book*, No. 45, is a full and exact translation of the Polish original." (Batowski, *Kryzys dyplomatyczny w Europie*, p. 147, note 36.)

DOCUMENT 125   Lipski to Beck

NO. N/1/223/38   November 9, 1938
                                                 Strictly Confidential

From my conversation with the Italian Ambassador I learned many
details concerning the Vienna Award. With the reservation that his report was confidential, he disclosed to me that, although in Rome Ciano
and Ribbentrop agreed to concede Uzhorod and Munkacz to Hungary,
the German side changed its mind on the eve of the arbitration, raising
objections against the Hungarian demands regarding these cities. The
German government used the argument that, since the countries of the
Berlin-Rome Axis were acting for the first time before international
public opinion in the role of arbitrators, any hint of bias should be
avoided. However, in Vienna Ciano categorically stood by the Rome
agreement to concede Uzhorod and Munkacz to Hungary. According to
Signor Attolico, nothing more could be obtained, particularly since the
Hungarians were in very bad form for negotiations. For instance, from
Carpathian Ruthenia not a single petition of the population for union
with Hungary had been forwarded to the arbitrators.

Answering my question, the Ambassador explained that, besides the
establishment of an ethnographic line, nothing had been settled in
Vienna, not even the possible guarantee for Czechoslovakia.

In Signor Attolico's opinion, upon its being separated from Uzhorod
and Munkacz, Ruthenia would face an acute problem in the future.
However, he thinks that in view of the tension accumulating at present
on this problem, especially on the part of the German government, a
public discussion of this matter, in the form of press polemics, such as is
taking place in Poland, would be harmful rather than useful for the
future realization of the common Polish-Hungarian frontier. For the
German government it is a matter of prestige, with Berlin engaged as
arbiter in Vienna.

As far as the guarantee for Czechoslovakia is concerned, Signor Attolico thinks that, if Berlin reached final agreement with Czechoslovakia
in particular fields and Prague would require a guarantee, the Reich
government would probably grant it. That is why the Ambassador would
prefer to press that the guarantee problem be postponed, rather than
settle for prompt action. In accordance with this information, under the

present changed circumstances the British government shows considerably less interest in the guarantee and is rather unwilling to grant it. This might be a sort of argument for Berlin.

When our conversation turned to Rumania, the Ambassador agreed with me that the Rumanian government, owing to Comnen's erroneous appraisal of the situation, has taken a negative stand toward the common Polish-Hungarian frontier. The Rumanians will not avail themselves of this occasion to improve their relations with Budapest with the help of Poland and Italy.

In the opinion of the Ambassador, it would be advisable to wait until after the visit of the Rumanian King to London. That visit is absorbing the monarch and his entourage to such an extent that any steps on the part of Rome and Warsaw in Bucharest should be undertaken only after this visit.

In connection with the above conversation and the [Polish] Ministry's telegram of the 7th inst. reporting on the alleged communication by the Reich government to the Hungarian government that it regards the Vienna Award as a final settlement of the Hungarian-Czechoslovakian frontier problem, and that it is interested that Czechoslovakia should remain within the frontiers established in Vienna, I would like to state that such a declaration is in conformity with official statements by the German authorities. May I recall here a fragment of Foreign Minister Ribbentrop's speech delivered on the 8th inst. at the banquet for the foreign press, which reads as follows:

"The arbitration decision which was pronounced by Italian Foreign Minister Count Ciano and myself, after the most thorough consideration and the most careful weighing of all interests involved, has now finally determined the frontier between Hungary and Czechoslovakia on the basis of ethnography."

This, in my opinion, does not actually preclude the possibility that the rest of Carpathian Ruthenia left outside Hungary could not be dealt with in the future. However, the approach to this problem from the propaganda angle should, in my opinion, be somewhat altered and cannot be based on the claim for a common Polish-Hungarian frontier, for this argument contradicts the arbitration based upon ethnographical ground. As far as this place [Berlin] is concerned, the problem could be more successfully promoted if it originated from the real internal development of the situation in Carpathian Ruthenia. As a matter of fact, I would not be surprised if, in spite of the present situation, the problem of Ruthenia, especially with the growing Ukrainian activity within the territory, would in the future return to haunt Bucharest and force the course of its tactics accordingly. Some outpourings made to me by Mr. George Bratianu would confirm such a point of view.

Finally, I would like to call your attention to the passage of von Ribbentrop's speech of the 8th inst. regarding the Reich's relations with Czechoslovakia, which reads as follows:

"If, following the final delineation of its frontier, the Czechoslovak government is ready to recognize fully the new reality and adopt a completely new orientation in its policy toward Germany, a reconciliation with this state, as well as a final settlement between the two nations, is possible."

From this declaration it might be deduced that the Reich's possible guarantee to Czechoslovakia would depend on a previous basic agreement of these states between themselves and the dissolution by Prague of the network of its present alliances.

Józef Lipski

On October 15 a decree of the Minister of the Interior, dated October 6 and issued jointly with the Minister of Foreign Affairs, was published in Poland in connection with the establishment abroad of a one-day control of Polish foreign passports.[15] This order went into effect on October 29 (the date for the control was later postponed until November 15).

Controlled passports received a pertinent annotation by Polish consulates. In cases in which circumstances might call for a revocation of citizenship, the consul could refuse the annotation, thus depriving the owner of a Polish passport of the possibility of crossing the Polish frontier.

In connection with the territory of Germany this problem could involve many thousands of Jews, formally Polish citizens, who, often having no connection with Poland whatsoever, could not obtain from the consuls the annotation indispensable for crossing the Polish frontier. Therefore, the Auswärtiges Amt strongly protested against this order, fearing that thousands of Jews who did not register in the period discussed would lose their right to return to Poland and would remain in Germany permanently. At the same time the A.A. informed the Polish government that the German authorities would start immediately to expel Jews from Germany.[16]

[15] *Dziennik Ustaw Rzeczpospolitej Polskiej,* 1938, No. 80, item 543.
[16] *DGFP,* Series D, Vol. V, No. 84. For Polish explanations, see *ibid.,* Nos. 88, 89, and 91; also *Journal,* pp. 363–65 and 374–75.

According to German calculations, by October 29, 17,000 Jews, citizens of Poland, were expelled from Germany and forced to cross the Polish frontier. Polish authorities threatened retaliations and the expulsion of the same number of Germans.

Under these circumstances Polish-German negotiations were started on November 2 in Berlin [17] with the participation of Lipski, who was later replaced by Counselor Lubomirski. This was a period of an extremely violent anti-Semitic drive in Germany, culminating in pogroms of Jews on November 8 and 9. These pogroms, inspired by governmental circles, were connected with the assassination in Paris of a German diplomat, Ernst vom Rath, by a young Polish Jew, Hershel Grynszpan, whose parents were expelled from Germany at that time.

Polish-German talks on this matter were concluded with a provisional agreement on January 24, 1939.[18] Jews expelled in October could return for the time being to Germany in order to liquidate their financial affairs.

DOCUMENT 126   Lipski to Beck

Berlin, November 12, 1938
(Personal)
Strictly Confidential

1. With reference to my handwritten letter of November 5, I am taking the liberty of communicating to you that until now my planned meeting with the foreign minister of the Reich, von Ribbentrop, has not taken place. I would like to recall that on the eve of the Vienna Award, on November 1, I announced at the secretariat of the Minister of Foreign Affairs my return from Warsaw, stating that I was at the disposal of Herr von Ribbentrop. I repeated the same thing to Secretary of State von Weizsäcker on November 3, as well as to Ambassador von Moltke. At the banquet for the foreign press on November 7, von Ribbentrop was present, but he left for Munich immediately after dinner to attend a celebration to be held there on November 8 and 9. I had no opportunity for an exchange of opinion, and the Minister only told me in passing that he would be back in Berlin from November 10 on. This was confirmed by his secretary, on his own initiative, with the explanation that owing to the many travels of the Minister lately it was impossible to fix a

17 *DGFP*, Series D, Vol. V, Nos. 92, 95, and 107.
18 *Ibid.*, No. 127.

meeting, but that the conversation could be arranged for November 11 or 12.

In the meantime, as I was informed, Herr von Ribbentrop, who returned just for a short while to the capital, left Berlin again, I believe, on November 10.

Of course, I do not deem it necessary that I press for this conversation, especially since Ribbentrop's initiative made to me at Berchtesgaden came from the German side. It also seems to me impossible to discuss the subjects raised at Berchtesgaden with any other official, unless I described in detail to von Ribbentrop the stand of the Polish government on this whole problem. Here I make the only exception for Herr von Moltke, who was the first to bring up the topic of Danzig in a conversation with me. As the ambassador accredited to us, he should have authoritative information on what limits beyond which we cannot go in this matter.

Considering the tactics applied by Herr von Ribbentrop, I must first of all mention that he is an unreachable minister for all diplomatic representatives accredited here. I was told yesterday by the American Ambassador that he has to leave for the United States to report to Roosevelt, and he has been vainly hunting for Ribbentrop for six weeks.

As far as our problem is concerned, I think that, following your interview, the position Chodacki [19] took toward Greiser, and certain explanations of Moltke, Ribbentrop must realize that our answer with regard to Danzig will not be a positive one. Possibly, in view of the unclear situation with regard to the Western states, he is not too anxious to start conversations with us, or possibly he would like to open them at a more convenient moment for the Reich government. The way in which both the Chancellor in his speeches and the local press here treated French-German relations for some time shows a desire to bring about a relaxation on that sector first of all.

Negotiations with Poland are possibly planned for a time following the finalization of an agreement with France.

It is rather characteristic that since the Munich Conference Polish-German relations have not improved but are considerably cooler.

All recent declarations of the Chancellor are openly unfriendly toward England; in spite of the fact that he is attacking the opposition, the

[19] Marian Chodacki, commissioner-general of the Polish government in Danzig from February, 1936, to September 1, 1939.

method he is using is nevertheless making it far from easy for Chamberlain to carry out his policy of rapprochement with the Reich.

I think that the recent anti-Jewish excesses on the whole territory of Germany, which reached hitherto unprecedented dimensions and could not be attributed to a mob impulse, since they were organized by Party organs, will further deepen the controversies existing between the Germany of the present era and the Anglo-Saxon world.

I am at a loss to judge whether these events will render difficult M. Daladier's policy of rapprochement with the Reich. Nevertheless, observing from this locality at a moment of a certain rapprochement between Paris and Berlin, any apparent improvement in the attitude of France toward Poland would be a very positive element for us in Berlin.

Information is reaching me from French industrial circles that their attitude toward Poland has considerably improved. These spheres call attention to the fact that at present, when Russian prestige has waned in Paris, it would be possible, through the use of material means, to influence the French press to write in a pro-Polish spirit, thus winning over wider circles of public opinion for us.

2. Our negotiations on Jewish matters, upon a definition of our common stand and to some extent a balancing of opinions, were arrested for lack of decision by competent German authorities. It is necessary to stress that the atmosphere created about the Jewish problem is weighing heavily on the German negotiators, including high-ranking officials who are simply anxious to save their own skins. I therefore think that a certain dose of patience is needed, all the more so since our decree and orders have remained in force.

I gave an order to the consulates that Jewish passports are very rarely to be stamped; beginning with November 15, when the *sursis* granted in Warsaw expires with regard to the revocation of citizenship, energetic action should be taken in the execution of this law.

Finally, I am taking the liberty of also calling your attention to the Ukrainian problem, and to its aspect now developing in the local territory.

Upon the occupation of Vienna, the local Ukrainian headquarters were transferred to the Reich. They consisted in the majority of groups of the Konowalec type, whose active character pushed them to the front line. A number of local organizations are dealing with Ukrainian matters, for instance, Ribbentrop's office, Rosenberg's office, certain offices of the Propaganda Ministry, and, last but not least, the German Intelligence Service. All these elements, as far as can be observed, at present lack a precise directive from the top as to the line to follow in such a complicated affair. But they are bursting with dynamism, and the groups most harmful to us, such as the Jaryj and Melnyk type, are taking advantage of this atmosphere. I conversed today with Professor Smal-Stocki, who is to report his observations to Director Kobylański.[20] For my part, I would only like to ask for your opinion whether, when the occasion presents itself, I should not take this matter up in more detail with high-ranking German officials, for instance with von Ribbentrop or Göring, in order to establish our point of view, for with some young, inexperienced leaders here the conviction is growing that the Ukrainian problem might be solved even without Poland, and the idea of penetration via Carpathian Ruthenia and Rumania is being inseminated. These, of course, are utopian ideas but, nevertheless, being presented by Ukrainian elements hostile to us, they might result in serious friction with Germany on the Ukrainian problem.

Józef Lipski

DOCUMENT 127   Lipski to Beck

Berlin, November 19, 1938
Strictly Confidential

In accordance with the conclusions contained in my letter to you dated November 12, I did not take any further steps to hasten my conversation with the Reich minister of foreign affairs, Herr von Ribbentrop.

On November 18 I was informed that Herr Ribbentrop would receive me at the Auswärtiges Amt on the 19th inst. at 12:30 P.M.

The conversation took the following course:

Herr von Ribbentrop opened the conversation by remarking that since our last meeting at Berchtesgaden on October 24 he has had no opportunity to see me because he was constantly traveling, and lately he

[20] Roman Smal-Stocki, professor of Warsaw University, secretary of the Ukrainian Institute in Poland. See his conversation with Szembek upon his return from Germany (*Journal*, pp. 376–78).

Tadeusz Kobylański, chief of the Eastern Division of the Polish Ministry of Foreign Affairs.

was absorbed in the problem of the assassination of the secretary of the Embassy in Paris, vom Rath.

I only mentioned that upon my return from Warsaw I called at the secretariat of the Minister, announcing that I was ready to meet him.

Next, in accordance with your instructions contained in your letter of October 31, I informed von Ribbentrop that I had acquainted you with his suggestion (*Anregung*) made at Berchtesgaden regarding a Polish-German agreement which would finally stabilize mutual relations between the two countries, and that you had requested me to communicate our attitude in answer.

To give greater weight to my arguments I availed myself of my written instructions, and exactly and emphatically communicated their contents to the Reich Minister of Foreign Affairs. Herr von Ribbentrop listened attentively to my exposition without discussing particular points.

I noticed that he was impressed by my statement that any tendency to incorporate the Free City into the Reich must inevitably lead to a conflict, not of a local character only, but one also jeopardizing Polish-German relations in their entirety. I concluded my exposition by quoting Marshal Piłsudski's opinion that the Danzig question would constitute a criterion for evaluating Germany's relations to Poland, adding a number of other explanations of a general nature.

In his reply Herr von Ribbentrop stated that the Reich desired to maintain the best possible relations with Poland, just as it did with Italy, and assured me that all his emphasis was in this direction. In a very friendly tone he stated that it was his desire to hold conversations with Poland, not in a diplomatic manner, but entirely as between friends, frankly and openly. He remarked that he had just conversed with the newly appointed French Ambassador, using diplomatic language.

Referring to the idea contained in your instructions, he stated that during the Czechoslovak crisis Polish-German relations stood the test to the advantage of both parties. Poland's determined attitude helped the Germans to achieve their demands while German action enabled Poland to recover Teschen Silesia. Here Herr von Ribbentrop was discursive, reverting to the history of the last crisis, and repeating a statement already known to me that in the political constellation of that time France was actually isolated and that he was all the time convinced that neither France nor England would move to the defense of Czechoslovakia. A certain *novum* was his explanation that a meeting of foreign ministers of the Reich and Italy had been planned, for the day the conference of Munich was later held, to be attended by Generals von Keitel and Pariani also, in order to establish common military action in case of an armed conflict of Germany with the Western Powers. Von Ribbentrop quoted this detail to me in order to stress that the Reich could absolutely count on Italy's military aid. The fact that the Italian and German General Staffs were to meet only on the day of Germany's mobilization would, in my opinion, point to the lack of a basic coordination for the event of war. Herr von Ribbentrop emphasized in his further deliberations Germany's military superiority at that time, remarking that at present the situation has become even more favorable for the Reich.

Reverting to Polish-German relations, von Ribbentrop emphasized that he would like to know that Germany conceived of relations with Poland on a very broad political plane, and that he had no intention of simply raising one question after another with Poland. He added that negotiations with Poland were of quite a different character from those with Mr. Beneš for Czechoslovakia. In the course of his argumentation he declared that for years you had been pursuing a definite and consistent course in Polish foreign affairs. I replied that, if the Reich conceived of its policy toward Poland on broad lines, then I had no fear as to our relations. Von Ribbentrop said that in any case he had more than once confirmed this in his conversations with me.

Von Ribbentrop then explained how the suggestion he had communicated to me at Berchtesgaden had arisen: taking as basis the Chancellor's conviction as to the necessity for maintaining the best of relations with Poland, which was a fundamental principle in Reich policy, he had been trying to find a solution which would completely stabilize the situation. He had talked only indefinitely (he used the word "vaguement") with the Chancellor on the subject, and on the basis that Danzig was a German city he had himself put forward his suggestions. (It was worthy of note that von Ribbentrop discreetly gave it to be understood that he was responsible for the initiative in this matter, leaving the Chancellor out of it.)

He returned again and again to his explanation that his sole desire was to achieve stabilized relations and that he had sought for a solution for this reason. He alluded to the interview you gave to the Hearst representative,[21] which he understood as the adoption of a negative

[21] Beck's interview given to Mr. Hillmar of the Hearst Press on October 29, 1938 (see *Polish White Book,* No. 46, p. 51).

attitude on the matter, and he revealed some disappointment that this had been done in a public statement. I said nothing to this. He also mentioned that he would gladly have a talk with you.

We discussed the Danzig question itself in general terms only. When he reverted to my statement that any tendency to incorporate Danzig into the Reich would lead to a conflict in Polish-German relations, I reaffirmed it most decisively. I added that the Danzig question was most irritating for our public opinion, the more so since we have made such great concessions to Danzig in respect of freedom of development for the German population and choice of their own form of government. I did not fail to mention the irritation caused by the activities of chauvinistic party elements, and specified Mr. Forster. With reference to our conception of the matter, I quoted Chancellor Hitler's words in his Reichstag speech on February 21, 1938. When speaking of Danzig, he said: "The Polish state respects national relations in that city, and that city and Germany respect the rights of Poland."

With regard to our suggestion of a Polish-German agreement guaranteeing the existence of the Free City, von Ribbentrop indicated that he could not express an opinion, and that he must study further and reflect still more on this whole problem in the light of my statement. Incidentally, he mentioned that apparently new irritation had arisen in Danzig in connection with postboxes, and asked me to raise the matter in Warsaw.

In the course of the conversation von Ribbentrop asked me what our attitude was with respect to the superhighway. I replied that my discussion in Warsaw had been primarily concerned with the Danzig question, so I could not give him any definite answer on this point. I simply expressed my personal belief that it might be possible to find a solution.

In its further course the conversation dealt with the Jewish problem; the Minister sharply criticized the attitude of the American government and President Roosevelt, pointing to the summoning of Ambassador von Dieckhoff to Washington.[22] He expressed his deep conviction that there would be anti-Semitic outbursts in America in the future, and that those now ruling the country would pay heavily for this. In his opinion the real power in the United States is lodged neither with the government nor the city but with the farmers. I availed myself of the discussion on this

[22] The American Ambassador in Berlin had been summoned to Washington and left Berlin on November 17.

subject to recall to the Minister that the Polish delegation in Warsaw for negotiations with the Reich on the Jewish problem is awaiting a reply from the German side in order to conclude the negotiations. The Minister promised to have this matter investigated.

Herr von Ribbentrop is leaving for Berchtesgaden in connection with the credentials to be presented to the Chancellor on Monday and Tuesday by a number of ambassadors and envoys, among others, the Belgian and French ambassadors.

Presentation of credentials at Berchtesgaden is explained by the fact that owing to the reconstruction of the Reich Chancellery in Berlin there are no adequate premises in the capital for these receptions.[23]

Józef Lipski

Immediately after his conversation with Ribbentrop, Lipski proceeded to Warsaw to report on it to Beck and Szembek.[24] The Danzig question came to the forefront. At that time Beck invited to Warsaw the high commissioner of the League of Nations in Danzig, Professor Burckhardt, in order to converse with him.[25] On November 22 Beck had a conversation with Ambassador von Moltke.[26] Lipski returned to Berlin with Beck's instructions to continue talks on the Danzig problem.

At that time, Poland conducted a series of exploratory conversations with Soviet Russia, with whom relations had deteriorated during the Munich period. A joint communiqué was published on November 26, stressing the durability of the contracted agreements between the two countries, including the nonaggression pact of 1932, and announcing an expansion of trade relations.[27]

In his report of December 3, Lipski informed Beck about his conversation with Ribbentrop.

[23] The *Polish White Book* published this report of Lipski with certain omissions (No. 46). For the German version, see *DGFP*, Series D, Vol. V, No. 101, pp. 127–29.

[24] For the Szembek-Lipski conversation on November 22, see *Journal*, pp. 379–80.

[25] For the conspectus, see *DGFP*, Series D, Vol. V, No. 102. See also Burckhardt, pp. 256–57.

[26] For Beck's note, see *Polish White Book*, No. 47; for Moltke's report, *DGFP*, Series D, Vol. V, No. 104, wherefrom, however, Danzig problems were omitted.

[27] *Polish White Book*, No. 160; see also the reports of Schulenburg, German ambassador to Moscow, to the A.A. of December 3, *DGFP*, Series D, Vol. V, No. 108, and von Moltke's reports of November 27, *ibid.*, No. 105.

DOCUMENT 128   Lipski to Beck

NO. N/1/243/38   Berlin, December 3, 1938
                                                   Secret

Following your instructions of November 25, No. P. I/MOR/386, with
regard to Danzig, on November 30 I asked to be received by the Foreign
Minister of the Reich. I had a conversation with him on Friday, December 2.

Unwilling to keep the discussion exclusively on the subject of Danzig
(I sent my report dated December 2, No. G/3/112/38,[28] on this subject), on this occasion I raised several other topics in the international
field. Since, in spite of the generally correct attitude taken by the German press, I could note a certain disorientation in local official circles
regarding the recently published Polish-Soviet communiqué, I availed
myself of this occasion to explain it to the Minister of Foreign Affairs of
the Reich, in accordance with your instructions telegraphed to me on
November 28. I deemed the occasion to be even more expedient, bearing in mind that von Ribbentrop, as the chief author of Anti-Comintern
agreements with Japan and Italy, might be a bit touchy about the communiqué, inasmuch as twice already since this spring he came out with
the suggestion that Poland should make up its mind to join this
agreement.

Upon stating that the Polish-Soviet communiqué has been repeatedly
misinterpreted and presented under a false aspect by the international
press, I added that I would like to make a few comments on it.

I recalled that tension entered Polish-Soviet relations in connection
with the Czechoslovak crisis, taking the form of military demonstrations, overflight of Polish territory by Soviet planes, our counteraction to
this, frontier incidents, etc. I added that this situation was obviously
aggravating and could not persist. The Polish-Soviet communiqué is
nothing but a reversion to the previous state of affairs, based upon the
nonaggression agreement. Also, normal trade transactions are under
way again in the economic field, as they were prior to the tension in
Polish-Soviet relations. Finally, some incidents are being liquidated.

Herr von Ribbentrop gave me to understand that he sees our position
in this matter. He simply expressed some regret that I had not informed

[28] This report is missing from Lipski's papers.

him in due time about it, since the communiqué came as a surprise and he could not give adequate information to the Chancellor. He made a slight allusion to the fact that, if only with regard to its three million Jews as colporters of Communism, Poland should not be very much interested in getting too close to Moscow. Here I pointed out that lately Poland's internal situation shows a strong consolidation of national forces and increasing executive power. I took some time to throw more light on this point.

Herr von Ribbentrop here laid some extra pressure, as he had also during this conversation with regard to another point, on the fact that the Reich is very much interested that Poland should be as strong a barrier as possible against Bolshevism.

From this subject he passed to the internal situation of France, remarking that in spite of Daladier's considerable victory the French situation cannot be regarded as stabilized. On the contrary, he still foresees strong attacks from the left wing inspired by the Comintern. He added that it has come to his knowledge that the Comintern has opened a new central office. I agreed that Communist activity continues to act vigorously outside of Russia.

Next, I inquired about the results of conversations with the Rumanian King.[29] Herr von Ribbentrop gave me the following explanation:

The Chancellor allegedly raised the question of Rumania's relations with the Soviets. King Carol pointed to his anti-Soviet attitude; however, he made the reservation that Rumania, as a country smaller than the Reich and a neighbor of Russia, must act with more prudence in this respect than Germany. Here the King referred to the Polish-Rumanian alliance.

The necessity of closer economic ties between Germany and Rumania was also discussed. I know that the King had special conversations with General Field Marshal Göring on these problems in Leipzig. Therefore, von Ribbentrop did not give me more extensive details on this matter. To my question about the news which had appeared in the press about the supposed plans to construct a pipeline for Rumanian oil, von Ribbentrop replied that he considers it a fantastic and unreal idea. However, he might still ask Göring about it. I think that, with regard to German-Rumanian economic relations, I might get some more details on

[29] During a private visit of King Carol in Germany he had, in Ribbentrop's presence, a conversation with Hitler on November 24 (*DGFP*, Series D, Vol. V, No. 254), and on November 30 a conversation with Göring (*ibid.*, No. 257).

December 6, at the hunting party at Springe which Göring will attend.

Finally Herr von Ribbentrop told me that the assassination of Codreanu and his associates [30] made a most unfavorable impression in German circles. It is beyond conception how national leaders could be murdered in such a way. Von Ribbentrop let it be understood that German spheres are wondering whether this step was taken with King Carol's blessing.

On the occasion of the conversation about the visit of the Rumanian King, Herr von Ribbentrop brought up the question of Hungarian claims. He sharply criticized Mr. Kanya's tactics, while he laid special stress on the recent attempts to interpret falsely the German declaration to Rome. He remarked that two weeks after the Vienna Award, to which the parties agreed and which, even in Mussolini's opinion, gave 95 percent to the Hungarian side, Hungary suddenly, without consulting Germany, tried to campaign for the remaining 5 percent. Von Ribbentrop naturally criticized the Hungarians for their slowness in the past, and for being misinformed by Darányi at Berchtesgaden with regard to Munkacz and Uzhorod. [31]

He told me that, naturally, a negative attitude could be detected in the Rumanian King toward Hungarian demands, but the German side did not inform the King about the note sent by the German and Italian governments to Budapest, about which the Polish government had also been advised. [32]

From von Ribbentrop's words I could not detect any change in attitude regarding problems of Carpathian Ruthenia, which was to be expected after what General Field Marshal Göring told General Fabrycy. It was only characteristic that he underlined the fact that immediately after the arbitration Hungary wanted to take action on Carpathian Ruthenia. [33]

Józef Lipski

[30] Corneliu Codreanu, founder of the Legion of the Archangel Michael, and in 1931 of the Iron Guard, was assassinated on November 30, 1938, together with thirteen members of the Iron Guard.

[31] For the occupation by Hungary of territories of Carpathian Ruthenia on November 20, see *DGFP*, Series D, Vol. IV, Nos. 128, 129, 131, 132, 133, and 134. With reference to Darányi, see Document 124, pp. 455-56.

[32] *Ibid.*, No. 132.

[33] For Ribbentrop's version of this conversation, see *ibid.*, Series D, Vol. V, No. 106.

DOCUMENT 129 Lipski to Beck

NO. 1/246/38

Berlin, December 7, 1938
Strictly Confidential

Referring to my report of December 3, No. 1/244/38, I would like to communicate that tension developed in German-Rumanian relations in connection with the assassination of Codreanu and his associates. According to information from confidential sources, during King Carol's visit to Berchtesgaden the Chancellor allegedly remarked that in Germany, if a patriotic national leader like Codreanu were deprived of freedom for his activities, he would certainly be taken to a fortress and not to a prison. To this remark King Carol is said to have replied that the prison regimen of Codreanu was not too onerous. A few days later news came that Codreanu had been shot, and thereafter the Chancellor allegedly ordered Germans who were recipients of Rumanian decorations on the occasion of King Carol's visit to Germany not to wear these decorations.[34] Besides, the Chancellor adopted an utterly negative attitude toward Rumania since, in his opinion, Codreanu's assassination would have terrible repercussions on Rumania's internal situation and cohesion. This information explains why during our conversation on Friday, December 2, von Ribbentrop repeatedly asked himself whether the King was really informed about the fact that Codreanu had been shot. As other adherents of the Iron Guard movement were later also executed, no doubt remains that they must have been removed with the King's knowledge.

This might also explain why the German press, at first restrained and only repeating rumors which had appeared on this subject in other countries, including Poland, has taken a much sharper tone in the last few days. *Der Angriff* of December 6 brings a paraphrased assault on the King under the title: "The Story about the King and His Jewish Mistress." Against the background of the internal German situation it tries to explain that Codreanu's assassination was perpetrated on the instigation of international Jewry.

The Rumanian Envoy here was to intervene in connection with the *Angriff* article and the press campaign.[35]

[34] See *ibid.,* No. 261, footnote.
[35] See also the report of the German Legation at Bucharest of December 4 (*ibid.,* No. 260).

I think that the above events will weigh heavily on the personal relations of the King with Hitler and the leading elements of the Reich for some time. Nevertheless, it should not be forgotten that at present, after the solution of the Czechoslovak problem, competent German spheres are very much interested in Rumania as a result of the desire to control the Danube basin economically. Rumania, with its natural resources (grain, oil) and since it controls the Danube outlet into the Black Sea, has particular attraction for Germany. On the other hand, it borders on the Soviet Union, and specifically on the geographical line of Russia at which German expansion is aiming. That is why, in spite of a temporary tension, Germany will not cease in its endeavors to penetrate into Rumania. Collaboration would only be jeopardized by a deeper crisis in the internal Rumanian situation, which would possibly take place as a result of a struggle with the Iron Guard.

Józef Lipski

On December 8 Beck sent another set of instructions to Lipski in connection with his continued conversations with Ribbentrop. The text of these instructions is missing from Lipski's papers, as well as from the archives of the Ministry of Foreign Affairs in Warsaw; [36] however, in Szembek's *Journal,* under the date of December 7, there is a fairly accurate text for, as Szembek writes, Beck dictated it to him.[37]

"He [Beck] outlined his opinion on Ribbentrop and on the interior situation of Germany. He stated that the principles of the pact of 1934 had withstood the impact of recent events. However, today misunderstandings were occurring between us and the Germans; it would be necessary to clarify and dismiss them by direct contact between Beck and Ribbentrop. (Addressing me directly, Beck stressed that this seemed to him of even more importance because Ribbentrop had made some advancements to us, to which, as a matter of fact, we did not respond.) Lipski should invite Ribbentrop to come to Warsaw. This visit must not be just a courtesy visit. The question of Danzig would have to be approached, as well as the question of a declaration with regard to frontiers and the prolongation of the 1934 pact. Lipski would have to make a previous survey of all these problems with Ribbentrop. As far as Danzig was concerned, our *desiderata minima* would be that Hitler repeat his declaration according to which the question of the Free City could not constitute a cause for a conflict in Polish-German relations. Lipski could show some approbation for the highway, but unofficially, while chatting with

[36] Batowski, *Kryzys dyplomatyczny w Europie,* p. 152.
[37] *Journal,* p. 385.

Ribbentrop, stressing at the same time that this affair would be of no avail to the Danzig question. Lipski should not enter upon other subjects with the German minister that would otherwise become the object of conversation for the two ministers. The starting point of Lipski's conversation with Ribbentrop should be that none of our political activities were directed against the vital interests of Germany."

Lipski refused to execute these instructions, and Beck was annoyed by this.[38]

A few days later Lipski explained this matter to Szembek: [39]

"He [Lipski] explained to me why he thought it impossible to execute—in the way they were meant—the latest instructions of Beck. The questions that were being pushed to the front had recently been discussed many times between Lipski and the German government. Lipski was persuaded that Ribbentrop would come to Warsaw, but he judged that the ground should be prepared in advance. Hitler would like, so it seemed, to see Beck."

This attitude of Lipski prompted his being summoned to Warsaw in order to achieve an agreement on a *démarche* toward Ribbentrop. Lipski spent a few days in Warsaw and returned to Berlin on December 14 with new instructions for his conversation with Ribbentrop.

In November a new conflict arose between Danzig and Poland in connection with Poland's issuing of commemorative postage stamps on November 11 on the occasion of the twentieth anniversary of Poland's rebirth. In this series there was a 15-grosz stamp representing King Jagiełło and Queen Jadwiga, at whose feet two crossed swords were laid as symbols of Poland's victory over the Teutonic Knights at Tannenberg (Grunwald) in 1410. Also, a series of four stamps was issued bearing the inscriptions "Polish Post— Port of Danzig" and "Danzig in the XVI Century," illustrating the transaction of the sale of grain by Polish merchants to Danzig merchants.

The issuing of these stamps provoked a sharp protest by the Danzig Senate, presented to Marian Chodacki, the commissioner-general of the Polish Republic in Danzig. The Senate declared that the motifs on these stamps offended the feelings of the German population of Danzig.

The Commissioner-General made the reservation in his reply that he did not deem it necessary to discuss this matter, since it involved internal orders of the Polish authorities, who decided for themselves what motifs might be placed on Polish postage stamps.

In the Polish reply it was stressed that according to the reasoning contained in the Senate's protest it should be recognized as inadmissible to represent in art and literature any historical events, for each event from the history of a nation might be a recollection unpleasant for its neighbors or certain groups.

At the same time, the Polish answer expressed the conviction that the Danzig Senate probably would not be anxious to support such an opinion,

[38] *Ibid.,* p. 387.
[39] *Ibid.,* p. 389.

thus absolving the Commissioner-General from solving the riddle why the recollection of a battle fought by Poland over five hundred years ago with an organization of a religious-political character, against whom Danzig was fighting alongside Poland, should be especially offensive for the inhabitants of the Free City of Danzig.

The Commissioner-General further underlined that the introduction of special postage stamps with the inscription "Polish Post—Port of Danzig" indicated that the Polish Republic possessed its own postal service at the port of Danzig, which remained under joint administration—and this corresponded with the rights Poland was entitled to. as well as with reality.

It was also stressed that the principal theme for the stamps of Polish post in Danzig was drawn from a painting by Van der Block of 1608 which adorned the Chamber of the Danzig City Hall.

The Commissioner-General further stressed that this picture, representing the golden era of Danzig's economy when the Free City collaborated with the Republic of Poland, evidently did not hurt Danzig's feelings, since in the Chamber where it was hanging official receptions by the Senate were held. The Commissioner-General also stated that it was not in his power to change the fact that in the sixteenth century Danzig belonged to Poland.

Besides the protest of the Danzig Senate, Ribbentrop in his conversation with Lipski on November 19 declared his objections (see the text of Ribbentrop's version, *DGFP*, Series D, Vol. V, No. 101, p. 129). Taking this into consideration, and in order not to complicate relations with Danzig during the period of preparation for Ribbentrop's visit to Warsaw, the Polish government decided to withdraw the stamp with Jagiełło and Jadwiga with the two swords; instead, on March 2, 1939, another stamp was issued, which aroused great interest among philatelists, at the same price and with the same personages, but without the swords.[40]

DOCUMENT 130   Łubieński to Lipski

Telephonogram   Warsaw, December 10, 1938
To: Ambassador Lipski in Berlin   *Secret*
From: Director of the Minister's Cabinet, Michał Łubieński

Please hold up for the time being execution of instructions dated December 8. Instead please call on Minister Ribbentrop and declare to him:

    1) Inquire whether the message given by you to von Weizsäcker [41]

---

[40] *Ilustrowany Kurier Codzienny* (Cracow), December 11, 1938.

[41] The message referred to regarding the French-German declaration signed in Paris on December 6 during Ribbentrop's visit, had been presented by Lipski on December 5 to Woermann, not to Weizsäcker (*DGFP*, Series D, Vol. V, No. 109).

has been duly transmitted to Ribbentrop. Express surprise that the friendly position of the Polish press with regard to Herr Ribbentrop's trip and the Paris declaration has been ignored in German communiqués (as well as by the press).

2) You have been summoned to Warsaw, and in this connection you are asking if Minister von Ribbentrop would possibly like to communicate something to the Minister. Minister Beck of late referred repeatedly in his instructions to the lack of *einer direkten Aussprache* with Ribbentrop. The Ambassador would revert to this matter after his return from Warsaw.

3) If by chance von Ribbentrop questions you about the problem of the postage stamps, please state that the stamp with the picture of Jagiełło and Jadwiga with two swords of the Teutonic knights at their feet will be withdrawn from sale.

DOCUMENT 131   Lipski to Beck

NO. N/52/46/38   Berlin, December 15, 1938
                                         Strictly Confidential

I had a conversation with the minister of foreign affairs of the Reich, von Ribbentrop, today, and proceeded to execute the instructions you gave me verbally yesterday in Warsaw.

I opened the conversation by stating that you had summoned me to Warsaw to discuss the whole complex of problems pertaining to Polish-German relations. I referred to your extensive conversation with Ambassador von Moltke yesterday evening, which was already known to Ribbentrop.[42] I pointed to the fact that while Polish-German relations had stood firm during the Czechoslovak crisis as a weighty element of peace, nevertheless a number of misunderstandings had occurred since which resulted in bad feeling. This situation is driving us to the conclusion that an exchange of opinion between you and Minister von Ribbentrop would be desirable and useful.

Herr von Ribbentrop replied that he had already mentioned such a necessity at Berchtesgaden.

I responded that I was instructed by you to suggest a visit of von Ribbentrop to Warsaw.

[42] See *ibid.*, No. 113.

Herr von Ribbentrop declared that he would willingly consent to an exchange of visits and would come to Warsaw with pleasure. However, he would still like to discuss this matter with the Chancellor in more detail before the holidays, since he is expected in Berlin. (He added that he would also report then on all conversations hitherto held with us.) In principle he thanks you for your invitation.

Here it was possible for me to imply that in 1935 you paid an official visit, and that at that time a return visit had been planned, but it had never taken place. I also mentioned that you were in Germany several times unofficially.

Herr von Ribbentrop further stressed that, in his opinion, it would be desirable to have such visits preceded by suitable diplomatic preparations, and he thinks that you would share this opinion. He inquired in a general sense what subjects would be raised during this visit.

I cited as general topics the Danubian complex, that of the East and of the Baltic countries, referring to the precedent of similar visits in the past. I stressed that problems would be discussed in which the interests of the two states coincide, or could coincide.

On his own volition, von Ribbentrop mentioned problems of immediate Polish-German relations, asking about the superhighway.

I remarked that this problem had been referred to you and that it is being discussed in Warsaw, but that, naturally, this matter can only be dealt with within the frame of *der Gesamtlösung*.

With regard to Danzig, I referred to Chodacki's memorandum handed to Herr von Ribbentrop, pointing to the fact that local authorities there deliver speeches of the kind that perforce poison the atmosphere.

Defining further the course of the conversations, we established the following:

Herr von Ribbentrop expresses thanks for your invitation and will take up this matter with the Chancellor. Up to January 10, that is, until the Chancellor's reception for the diplomatic corps, he will be on leave; as a matter of fact, he already began his vacation but had to interrupt it. After January 10 he would like to bring up through diplomatic channels the subjects to be discussed with you in a concrete form. He indicated a desire for an exchange of opinion with me during this period as well.

Besides the above question of the visit, which ran through the whole conversation, we also discussed the following subjects:

1) I pointed out to Minister Ribbentrop that Ukrainian propaganda,

which makes use of Germany's name, is obviously detrimental to our relations. To illustrate this, I handed him a pamphlet by Jaryj written in German about the Ukraine, showing on the cover a Great Ukraine reaching up to Warsaw and Cracow. Besides, I remarked that in Warsaw we continually receive information from the territory of Slovakia about anti-Polish activity conducted there, which claims to be inspired by Germany.

Herr von Ribbentrop mentioned that he will have the problem investigated. When he deliberated on the Ukraine as an anti-Russian element, I replied that we have nothing against this, as long as such propaganda deals with territories situated outside the frontiers of the Republic.

Talking more generally about Russia, I recalled that Poland really is the state constituting a barricade against Communist, as well as imperialistic-panslavic, Russia.

2) For his part, von Ribbentrop laid special stress on the way the German minority is treated in Teschen. He remarked that this matter, which he has been personally investigating on the basis of reports and claims, has become detrimental for our relations. He urgently requested me to refer this problem to you, asking that the activities of the local authorities be investigated.

As far as I know, von Moltke approached our Ministry of Foreign Affairs on the same problem.[43] I think it would be advisable to investigate this matter more closely.

3) I expressed thanks that we were informed about the results of the Paris talks, while I pointed out our stand, which I had explained to Secretary of State Woermann on the eve of von Ribbentrop's departure for Paris.[44]

4) Stressing that we have navigational interests at Kłajpeda [Memel], in view of the fact that negotiations with Lithuania were under way, I inquired about this matter.

Von Ribbentrop answered rather noncommittally, remarking that France and England, as signatories of the convention,[45] had approached the Secretary of State on this matter. He was of the opinion that the signatories of the convention had had the opportunity, in the

[43] *Ibid.,* No. 113, last paragraph.
[44] *Ibid.,* No. 109.
[45] Reference is made to the convention concluded by the Great Powers with Lithuania on May 8, 1924, with regard to Kłajpeda territory under Lithuanian sovereignty.

course of many years, to care for the Kłajpeda population. However, they did nothing. From Ribbentrop's words it was clear that he is passing over this question. He further stressed that Kłajpeda is a German city. To my remark that I raised this question in connection with our trade interests, von Ribbentrop remarked that, in keeping with our good-neighbor policy, our economic interests would always be resolved satisfactorily.

At one phase of the conversation, when Ribbentrop was speaking of his positive attitude toward Polish problems, he gave way to some sort of regret that his intentions in the conversation at Berchtesgaden might possibly have been minsunderstood to some extent—hence our strong reaction to it.

Here I made a reply of a general character, saying that he could be assured that our leading authorities understand his intentions, while I pointed out that local authorities, for instance in Danzig, are jeopardizing an accord by their activities.

At the end of the conversation von Ribbentrop remarked that, if we are led by the principles drawn up by Marshal Piłsudski and Hitler in 1933, then we will undoubtedly reach agreement. However, he added that here it would be essential for the Polish side to understand certain principles of German policy.

As a result of this conversation, I have the following comments to make:

I assume that the Chancellor will accept the idea of Minister Ribbentrop's trip to Warsaw, perhaps will even suggest a meeting with you. I also think that the idea of diplomatic preparations would suit you too. Under these conditions, we have to be prepared for concrete conversations beginning January 10. Before this date it would be necessary to gain possession of material concerning Danzig, which I took the liberty of suggesting to you while I was in Warsaw. We should also state precisely our stand with regard to the superhighway (from press information and the planning of German superhighways disclosed recently, it would appear that a superhighway is intended for the narrowest northern sector, to unite Królewiec [Königsberg], Danzig, and Szczecin).

Besides, material should be collected concerning German-Ukrainian joint action detrimental to Polish interests, and possibly data on the anti-Polish activity of German diplomatic agents or others in Czechoslovakia and Lithuania.

In connection with my telegram of today regarding the statement made to Counselor Lubomirski by Reich Minister Frank, I am taking the liberty of suggesting that Frank should be informed even more fully than before with regard to the problems of Danzig and the Danubian complex, with a mention of the Ukrainian agitation. This matter seems to me particularly important since Minister Frank will undoubtedly report his conversations directly to the Chancellor. The orientation he achieves from his Warsaw conversations will constitute a serious factor for Hitler's decision, especially on the Danzig question, as well as on the Ukrainian problem in the light of our interests.[46]

Józef Lipski

[46] Frank was in Poland in the middle of December, 1938.

Beck's Visit to Berchtesgaden and Ribbentrop's to Warsaw. Hitler's Speech at the Reichstag
January, 1939

IN HIS REPORT of December 15, 1938, Lipski advanced the supposition that Hitler would suggest a meeting with Beck. In his conversation with Moltke on December 20, Beck brought up the possibility of a preliminary Polish-German discussion of problems prior to Ribbentrop's official visit to Warsaw.[1] As it was Beck's intention to spend the Christmas holidays at Monte Carlo, it would be possible for him to stop in Berlin on his way back. Hitler availed himself of this suggestion, and Beck's conversations with Hitler and Ribbentrop took place on January 5, 1939, at Berchtesgaden, and with Ribbentrop on January 6 in Munich.

These conversations added no new elements to the prevailing situation. The German side insisted again that Danzig must be reunited with the Reich, and that Poland should agree to an extraterritorial superhighway and railway line across Pomerania. However, Hitler exerted no special pressure in this matter, promising Poland access to the sea and assuring it that there would be no question of a *fait accompli* in Danzig. Ribbentrop was more aggressive regarding this problem, and received a stronger *repartie* from Beck, who said that for the first time he was pessimistic about Polish-German relations.[2]

Beck informed Polish representatives abroad about the substance of these talks by a telegram dated January 10.[3] The mitigating wording of the telegram contrasted with Beck's concern about the further development of Polish-German relations evident from his conversation with Ribbentrop. Immediately upon his return to Warsaw he considered it to be "my duty to warn the President of the Republic and Marshal Śmigły-Rydz of these alarming symptoms which could result in a war." [4]

[1] *DGFP*, Series D, Vol. V, No. 115.

[2] *Polish White Book*, Nos. 48 and 49; *DGFP*, Series D, Vol. V, Nos. 119 and 120; Beck, *Final Report*, pp. 171–72; *Journal*, pp. 404–8.

[3] For the German circular telegram to representatives about the conferences, see *DGFP*, Series D, Vol. V, No. 121.

[4] Beck, *Final Report*, p. 172. In Beck's book the date of this conversation is erroneously cited as January 4. Beck returned to Warsaw on January 7, after conversations with Hitler and Ribbentrop, and the conversation with the President could only have taken place on January 8 or 9.

DOCUMENT 132   Lipski to Beck

NO. N/1/11/39   Berlin, January 23, 1939

I received strictly confidential information from the Hungarian Envoy regarding the stay of Count Csáky, foreign minister of Hungary,[5] in Berlin from January 16 through the 18th.

Csáky came at the invitation of the Germans. Some time ago, in his conversation with Envoy Sztójay, Ribbentrop suggested that German-Hungarian relations should be improved by a visit of Csáky to Berlin.

The Hungarian Envoy explained that of late a critical attitude toward Germany had increased considerably in Hungary, as manifested in many press articles. Count Bethlen's intervention in one of these articles hurt German feelings, and even top spheres took offense at it. These symptoms of opinion in Hungary compelled the Reich government to try to smooth out relations.

Count Csáky commented with satisfaction on his conversations in Germany. In the course of these conversations the German side went to great lengths to explain that, if Hungary's demands were not met, Hungary was to blame, not Germany. Stress was laid on the fact that Hungary did not go into action under the most favorable circumstances. It was mentioned that in its solutions the German government had to observe ethnographic principles, as agreed to at the Munich Conference.

Further, it was stressed that the military action which Hungary wanted to undertake at a certain moment against Carpathian Ruthenia was far too risky in view of the potentiality of a Czechoslovak war, the more so since at that time Germany had already released its recruited forces.

From further German deliberations it was clear that the Reich government does not regard the Czechoslovak situation as definitely settled. Allegedly Count Csáky had the impression that under the right conditions the Carpatho-Ruthenian problem could be reconsidered in the future. From the German side, it was mentioned that the Reich did not oppose the Polish-Hungarian frontier, and in general German spokesmen underlined the need for good relations between Poland and Hungary. They also insisted that the Reich desires to maintain as good relations as possible with Poland.

[5] For Minister Csáky's conversation with Hitler on January 16, see *DGFP*, Series D, Vol. V, No. 272; for his conversation with Ribbentrop, *ibid.*, No. 273.

The Chancellor allegedly denied rumors circulated by the foreign press about his alleged plans for the Great Ukraine. A seeming result from what was said by the German side was that in the future the Ukrainian problem at any rate could not be solved without Poland's participation.

The Hungarian envoy, Sztójay, whom I kept informed about the results of your conversations at Berchtesgaden, remarked that the German explanations to Count Csáky were in conformity with what has been said to us at Berchtesgaden.

As far as the guarantee for Czechoslovakia is concerned, Ribbentrop allegedly said to Csáky that Germany would not grant it unless a similar guarantee is granted by other states. To my question whether these "other states" meant the Powers participating in the Munich Agreement, or neighbors, Envoy Sztójay replied that Count Csáky understood this point to mean that the neighbors of Czechoslovakia were concerned.

By the way, I would like to add that the Hungarian Envoy, in view of his departure two days ago for Budapest, instructed his chargé d'affaires to communicate to me today that Secretary of State Weizsäcker, in his conversation with him with regard to guarantees, defined Germany's position thus: that the guarantee for Czechoslovakia would not be granted until Czechoslovakia is consolidated. There is therefore a certain deviation between Ribbentrop's statement and that of Weizsäcker.

According to explanations of Envoy Sztójay, Hungary's admission to the Anti-Comintern Pact would probably take the form of a declaration made by Count Csáky to the representatives of Italy, Germany, and Japan, with the formal signing of the agreement at a later date. This delay is due to difficulties in obtaining approval of the Japanese government with regard to the text, which has to be dispatched to Tokyo.

To my question as to the attitude of Hungary toward the League of Nations, I was told that the Hungarian government has decided to leave the Geneva institution. The date foreseen for the withdrawal is spring—April or May. The Envoy was at a loss to explain why this date had been chosen. From words of Mr. Ottlik, a Hungarian journalist accompanying Count Csáky, I could judge that the withdrawal from Geneva would take place at a suitable time.

Finally, Envoy Sztójay informed me that he thinks that German-Czech relations have considerably cooled off and that Chvalkovský would get a bad reception here, which subsequently proved to be true.

In brief, the Hungarians are of the opinion that the German Reich will for the time being conduct a policy of appeasement toward the Eastern states, while its attention will concentrate on events in Spain and the Mediterranean basin.

I must add that, prior to the above conversation with the Hungarian Envoy, Count Csáky informed me through Mr. Ottlik that he was pleased with his conversations here, particularly since the Germans had stressed that they are anxious that relations between Poland and Hungary should develop satisfactorily.

Józef Lipski

On January 25–27 Ribbentrop came to Warsaw on an official visit. Weizsäcker prepared a note for the visit dated January 23, informing Ribbentrop about the problems to be discussed in Warsaw.[6] In his conversations with Beck, Ribbentrop once more returned to the problem of Danzig and the superhighway, but Beck again categorically rejected the proposals. It was only agreed that, in case the League of Nations withdrew from Danzig, a joint Polish-German declaration would be issued for the maintenance of the *status quo* in the Free City until agreement was reached on this matter between Poland and Germany.[7]

A circular telegram sent by Beck to representatives abroad on January 31 again did not reveal the essence of a deeper conflict between Polish and German interests.

DOCUMENT 133   Lipski to Beck

NO. N/49/22/39

February 2, 1939
Secret

Prior to relating in a separate report the speech of Chancellor Hitler delivered at the session of the Reichstag on January 30 last, I would like to draw your attention to passages dealing directly or indirectly with Polish-German relations.

[6] *Ibid.*, No. 125.
[7] For the Polish version of this conversation, see *Polish White Book*, Nos. 50–56; also Beck, *Final Report*, pp. 173–74, and *Journal*, pp. 411–17. For the German version: *DGFP*, Series D, Vol. V, No. 126. See also Florian Miedziński, "Rozmowy Becka z Ribbentropem i Gafencu w sprawozdaniach warszawskiego meża zaufania senatu gdanskiego," *Przegląd Zachodni* (Poznań), 1965, No. 4, pp. 295–311 (document texts in German).

A direct passage about Poland reads as follows:

"We have just celebrated the fifth anniversary of the conclusion of our nonaggression pact with Poland. There can scarcely be any difference of opinion today among the true friends of peace as to the value of this agreement. One only needs to ask oneself what might have happened to Europe if this agreement, which brought such relief, had not been entered into five years ago. In signing it, the great Polish marshal and patriot rendered his people just as great a service as the leaders of the National Socialist state rendered the German people. During the troubled months of the past year the friendship between Germany and Poland has been one of the reassuring factors in the political life of Europe." [8]

Further passages of the Chancellor's speech deal with Hungary, Yugoslavia, and economic relations with Bulgaria, Greece, Rumania, and Turkey are touched upon in a single sentence.

This statement follows: "Germany is happy to possess today friendly frontiers in the west, south, and north," and then general reference is made to the attitude toward the western and northern states. Finally, he warns Czechoslovakia against returning to Beneš' ideas.

The above passage about frontiers is characteristic for its omission of eastern frontiers. Despite the fact that relations with Poland are especially dealt with, and that reference to the frontiers is interwoven among other questions, nevertheless some consistent tendency might be detected here. I wish to recall that in his speech of September 12, 1938, on the occasion of the closing of the Reichstag in Nuremberg, Hitler used this sentence:

"Germany has today on *all* sides completely friendly frontiers."

However, this was later changed by D.N.B. to "on *many* sides" [emphasis added in both cases by Lipski].

In contradiction to the statement that Germany forced concessions from other states (Austria, Czechoslovakia) by military pressure, the Chancellor declares that, in regions where the English and other Western Powers have nothing to expect, Germany restored to millions of its compatriots the right to self-determination, and he adds next:

". . . and I need not assure you, my representatives of the German Reichstag, that in the future also we will not put up with it when Western Powers simply try to intrude in certain matters concerning us only,

8 *Polish White Book,* No. 57.

in order, through their intervention, to harm natural and rational solutions."

In my opinion, this statement is not void of meaning with regard to relations between Western and Eastern Europe.

Yesterday, at a reception of the Finance Minister, I congratulated von Ribbentrop on words of appreciation the Chancellor addressed to him in his speech. The Foreign Minister of the Reich did not conceal his satisfaction with regard to these words of the Chancellor, and said they were a surprise to him.

At the same time he stressed how pleasant his stay in Poland was. He added that efforts should be made to have Polish-German relations develop satisfactorily, and he made reference to his conversation with you in Warsaw, saying that he is counting on my help to find a solution in these matters. He recalled that the Chancellor treats these matters "von der hohen Werte" ["of high value"].

As this took place on a purely social level, there was no opportunity to expand the discussion.

I would like to add that von Ribbentrop and all the German officials who accompanied the Minister to Warsaw expressed their satisfaction over the reception they met with in Poland.

Minister Ribbentrop is leaving for a ten-day vacation; he is coming back for a few days, and then is leaving again for a week.

Józef Lipski

DOCUMENT 134   Lipski to Beck

NO. N/7/7/39

February 7, 1939
Secret

With reference to my report of the 2d inst., No. N/49/22/39, where I raised points dealing with Polish-German relations contained in the speech delivered by the Chancellor at the Reichstag on January 30 last, I am now taking the liberty of analyzing this speech more extensively.

Upon the reunion of Austria and Sudetenland with the Reich, and thus the achievement of the most essential demand of National Socialism—the union of all Germanic countries—the question arose as to what Hitler would attempt to do next.

Bearing in mind the fact that in connection with the Carpatho-Ruthenian problem the Ukrainian question began more intensely than before to absorb the minds of the so-called annexes of the local Ministry of Foreign Affairs (Ribbentrop's office, Rosenberg's office, certain sections of the Ministry of Propaganda, the Institute for Eastern Europe), it was commonly supposed that the Chancellor would start a wide-ranging eastern program. Others suggested that the year 1939 would be devoted to colonial problems.

Chancellor Hitler spent the last two months of 1938 at Berchtesgaden in order to arrive at a decision as to the basic line of his policy. Your conversation with the Chancellor at Berchtesgaden on January 6 [9] provided some orientation to the Polish government in this respect.

Hitler's Reichstag speech of January 30, 1939, defined the guiding lines for the Reich's foreign policy, as well as its internal affairs, for the near future.

In contrast to his speech delivered last year (on February 20, 1938), when the problem of Austria and the Sudetenland was quite unequivocally presented,[10] the Chancellor drafted only the principal goals of the Reich in the domain of foreign policy, without spelling out how and when he intends to realize his demands. This probably derives from the very problem of colonialism.

The Chancellor's speech is so extensive that a detailed analysis would take too much space in this report. I therefore limit myself to the most essential matters, omitting material already familiar from other speeches of the Chancellor.

First of all, attention is arrested by the calm, matter-of-fact tone of the speech and his restraint from aggressive accents against other states. This exterior garb of the speech has caused the foreign press to label it a peace speech. I think that this kind of reasoning needs some correction. Although this speech is calmer than usual, it nevertheless contains statements which leave no illusions as to the fact that Germany will realize its demands in a very decisive manner.

I. It is characteristic that Chancellor Hitler, as far as the sequence and direction of his aspirations is concerned, has followed consistently his basic program, namely, *the revision of the Versailles Treaty*.

[9] The date is in error; it should be January 5.
[10] See p. 340.

Pushing the sequence of claims to the forefront, he passed over in silence eastern problems, reserving them for a later date.

This is undoubtedly the first speech of the Chancellor in which he has taken such a deeply motivated stand on the problem of claims for the return of colonies. He based these claims neither on premises of justice nor on prestige, but on the economic needs of the German nation. The Chancellor supported his claims to the Western Powers for the return of the colonies by the argument that the Reich is bound either to export at any cost—which would consequently be detrimental to the interests of these states—or to recover its colonies. He declared that, because the victorious states of the Great War are reluctant to settle the colonial problem, only the first alternative is left to Germany. The Chancellor predicts that, in case the Powers undertake to hamper German export, the Reich will undertake "a desperate economic drive."

In connection with his colonial demands the Chancellor stresses the common interest uniting the Reich and Italy, saying:

"Germany understands that other nations want their share in the riches of the world, to which they are entitled by their numbers, courage, and value; a decision has been taken, in recognition of these rights, to act jointly (with Italy) for the sake of common interests."

In conclusion regarding the colonial point, it is worth mentioning that a tendency runs through Hitler's speech to support Italy in its Mediterranean action, undoubtedly expecting that this is the way to render colonial questions timely. On the other hand, as I mentioned before, the Chancellor is threatening England and France—in case the colonies are not recovered—with disorganization of their trade markets by means of increased export.

II. It is characteristic that the Chancellor did not mention Russian subjects at all; the words "Ukraine" and "Russia" were not uttered in the speech (outside of the usual invectives against Bolshevism). The Chancellor's statement that in *the north, west, and south the Reich possesses peaceful frontiers, with an omission of the eastern frontier,* should undoubtedly be understood as a sort of reservation about the Czechoslovak question (Hitler hopes that Czechoslovakia will not fall into Beneš' errors in politics) and the Danzig and Kłajpeda [Memel] questions.

The special traditional passage about *Poland,* about which I reported on February 2, No. N/49/22/39, confirms the desire to continue a policy based upon the 1934 agreement.

To other states of the *Danubian basin* the Chancellor refers in the sense of increased economic ties with them, while he has particularly warm words for Hungary, which joined the Anti-Comintern Pact, and also Yugoslavia.

With regard to the *Baltic and Northern states,* the Chancellor welcomes their intention to remain neutral, and thus escape obligations under Article 16 or the Pact of the League of Nations.

III. As far as Germany's relations with the *Western Powers* are concerned, attention is first of all arrested by the fact that the Chancellor did not mention a single word about the *French-German declaration* signed in Paris by Ribbentrop and Bonnet.

While German opinion at large was utterly different toward France than toward England a few months ago, when negotiations and the signing of the declaration were under way, at present the Chancellor in his speech repeatedly poses his demands to both states simultaneously, or tries to identify them in his criticism as democracies. So, for instance, he says:

"Germany has no territorial claims against England and France, outside of the return of German colonies."

He adds, however, that "this problem is not in the category of problems which would demand war solutions."

Throughout the whole speech runs a polemic with statesmen and pressmen of the so-called democratic states who are critical of the system and activities of the Reich. Nevertheless, even here a moderation more marked than usual may be observed. Even against America his polemic is more or less restricted to repulsing complaints directed against Germany, while a statement is made that Germany desires peace and friendship with America also. The supposition that the speech would contain an assault against Roosevelt was not realized.

IV. In the field of relations with foreign states, the most definite passage clearly relates to *Italy*. The Chancellor motivates the rapprochement of the two nations on the ideological premises of the Fascist and National Socialist systems, the common history of national rebirth in Italy and Germany, as well as a common action in the period of the Abyssinian war and the events of 1938.

A categorical declaration that the Reich would come to Italy's assistance in case it was drawn into war is contained in the following sentence:

"It might just serve the cause of peace that there is no doubt but that a war against Italy today, for whatever cause it might be unleashed, would call Germany to the side of its friend."

(It is characteristic that in the translation of this passage for the use of the French press, the German official press agency added to the word "war" the adjective "ideological," a word not to be found in the official German text.)

The passage about the Reich's determination to assist Italy constitutes a sort of answer to the declaration made by Mussolini some time ago with regard to the Czech conflict, which was later confirmed in the speech of Count Ciano.

V. German-*Japanese* relations are treated on the level of their anti-Bolshevist principles. However, the actual Anti-Comintern Pact is referred to rather loosely in the form of a hypothesis for the future:

"The Anti-Comintern Pact might one day perhaps become a crystallization point for a group of powers whose main goal would be no other than to ward off the threat to the peace and culture of the world from a satanic phenomenon."

Closing the analysis of the part of the speech pertaining to international relations, I wish to underline the Chancellor's words that he believes in a lasting peace. I think that these words should be understood thus: that the Chancellor supposedly believes it possible to achieve his demands by way of political and economic pressure, without having recourse to military action.

VI. In the field of internal politics, the following more important issues are worth noting:

1) The declaration that the reunion of Austria and the Sudetenland with the Reich constitutes the crowning of a thousand years' struggle to unite all German tribes into one state.

2) *Outlining National Socialist tasks* for the future, unlimited in time, and striving for the creation of "a true people's community." To bring about the situation that all the elements of the German community predestined to become leaders would have the possibility to come to the top, creating a new leading sphere. Here the Chancellor is getting rid of all class prejudice. I quote a characteristic passage:

"For in the mass-millions of a nation there are talents enough to

occupy successfully all made-to-measure posts. This offers the best safeguard for the state and for the community against revolutionary designs
of individuals and destructive tendencies of the times. For danger ever
threatens only from those overlooked, never just from the negative critical groups or the malcontent. . . . The true revolutionists on a world
pattern are in all times those who were misunderstood or who were not
admitted to be leaders by nature by a presumptuous, sclerotic, secluded
community layer."

Besides these statements of a general nature, the speech brings no
new points in the field of internal reforms.

3) Justifying his anti-Jewish action, the Chancellor refers to the
suffering sustained by the German nation during the period of the Treaty
of Versailles until the liberation by National Socialism—the Jews being
the main culprits causing this ordeal. He argues with the democracies
which take pity on the Jews but are unwilling to help them by granting
territory for Jewish emigration. He states that National Socialism will
consistently follow its policy on this issue. Special attention should be
given to the passage suggesting that European states otherwise having
difficulties in agreeing might reach a common platform on the Jewish
problem:

"It is quite possible that over this problem, sooner or later, a union
will take place in Europe spontaneously among those nations that could
not easily find a way to each other."

In connection with confidences I heard at one time from the Chancellor, it is not impossible that he is considering Poland here also, as well
as other East European countries.

4) An extensive passage is devoted to the two religions: Catholic and
Protestant.

In reply to attacks of the democracies that there is persecution of
churches in Germany, the Chancellor states that:

a) no one has hitherto been persecuted in Germany because of his
religious attitude;

b) large funds are contributed every year from the state budget, as
well as by the provinces and communities, to both churches; the land
and forest estates of the churches in Germany amount to 10 billion
marks, with an income of 300 million per year;

c) not a single church has been closed and no pressure has been
exerted on church rites;

d) in case the churches continue their complaints, the National Socialist state is ready, following the example of France, America, and other states, to *bring about a division between the church and the state.* Then follow attacks against clergymen for their political attitude or moral offenses.

With regard to the Protestant church, the Chancellor states that he strove to create one great state church in Germany out of the separated, dispersed churches. This attempt met with opposition on the part of the bishops and had to be abandoned.

The above deliberations of the Chancellor relating to the Catholic church do not deal with the basic difficulties which exist between the totalitarian National Socialist system and the church, for example, in the field of education of the youth, etc. The enumeration of governmental subsidies for the churches as well as the state of their property might contain a certain threat that, after the confiscation by the state of Jewish property, their turn will come.

5) The principal part of the speech relates to economic problems.

It should be stressed that such a pessimistic evaluation of the Reich's economic situation was heard for the first time from Hitler. In this respect the speech is very skillfully constructed, since economic problems are closely tied with the demands for a just division of the world's riches. So here also there is a scapegoat: the powers now in possession of German colonies.

With regard to the Reich's financial system, the Chancellor repeats statements previously contained in other speeches that wages, as well as prices and currency, should be maintained at a certain fixed level. In his system currency is based not on gold but on the increasing capacity of production. With regard to a different system applied by other states, the Chancellor is of this opinion:

"In other countries they take the wrong way. Production is prevented, national property is raised by an increase in wages, the purchasing value of money is thereby lowered, and depreciation of currency finally results."

The Chancellor agrees that the German system is in itself unpopular, remarking:

"I agree that the German way is in itself an unpopular one, since it means nothing else but that any rise of wages can forcibly derive only from an increase in production."

As guidance for the future the Chancellor recommends rationalization of industries and reinforcement of technical organization. The capital market should therefore be more open to technical development of enterprises and free from governmental burdens (loans).

This statement is similar to the exposition contained in the well-known letter of Hitler addressed to the new president of the Reichsbank, Funk, after Schacht's resignation (see report No. N/7/2/39, dated January 23, 1939).[11]

Next, the Chancellor predicts the reorganization of the Reichsbank in accordance with principles also expressed in the above letter.

The Chancellor's speech, which also stresses the necessity of reinforcing armaments, brings no precise answer to the question by what means, in the long run, the Reich intends to finance the *Arbeitsbeschaffung* and armaments. However, one thing is clear, that the Reichsbank will have to take over an even more considerable burden than hitherto in this respect.

The Chancellor's economic deliberations sound similar to Schacht's ideas on one essential issue. Schacht, as I often wrote, considered the autarchy system a *malum necessarium* but not a final goal. His intention was to bring about, in the final stage, normal relations in economic exchange between the Reich and the rest of the world, and to increase this turnover. The Chancellor is getting close to this truth when he poses as a guiding principle the necessity of exporting at any cost, which means nothing but an increase of the Reich's share in international trade.

If the Chancellor presents the return of the colonies as an alternative, it is worth recalling that Schacht was one of the most zealous adherents of the colonial thesis, being fully aware that this was the way for the Reich to get access to raw materials and food supplies that would guarantee its economic independence.

Józef Lipski

[11] This report is missing from Lipski's papers.

Further Aggravation of Polish-German Relations
February—March, 1939

ON JANUARY 29, 1939, an incident took place at a cafeteria in Danzig which caused further complications in Polish-Danzig relations. On that day a group of Polish students of the Danzig Polytechnic were at the Café Langfuhr, talking in Polish. German students present in the café started to shout: "It is forbidden to speak Polish here." One of the German students hit a Pole, and a general fight broke out.

Two weeks later the owner of the Café Langfuhr forwarded a letter to the Fellowship Society of Polish students, advising them that he did not wish Polish students to frequent his premises. The Poles ignored this letter and appeared at the café on February 12. German students placed a sign at the entrance with the inscription: "To dogs and Polish students entrance is forbidden! The poor dogs!" A new scuffle started among the students.[1]

This incident was the source of many riots between Polish and German students on the premises of the Polytechnic, where lectures were temporarily suspended in order to calm the youths.

News about these incidents in Danzig upset students in Polish universities, and anti-German demonstrations were staged in Poznań, Cracow, Lwów, and other cities.

In Warsaw, on February 25 a group of students demonstrated before the building of the German Embassy, a windowpane was broken by a rock, and anti-German slogans were shouted. On Beck's orders, the chief of protocol of the Polish Ministry of Foreign Affairs expressed words of regret to Ambassador Moltke.[2]

This incident was even more embarrassing and troublesome for the Germans, since it happened during the official visit to Warsaw of Minister Ciano. (Ciano was in Warsaw from February 25 to March 1.) Consequently, Ribbentrop reacted strongly in his conversation with Lipski on February 28.[3]

[1] *German White Book*, No. 195; see also *Ilustrowany Kurier Codzienny* (Cracow), February 20, 1939, where a picture is shown of a card with an inscription offensive to Poles.

[2] *German White Book*, No. 146; also *DGFP*, Series D, Vol. V, No. 137.

[3] *DGFP*, Series D, Vol. V, No. 131. The Polish version of this conversation is missing from Lipski's papers.

Lipski took up the question of the incidents in Danzig in his conversation with Hitler and Göring on March 2.

DOCUMENT 135   Lipski to Beck

NO. G/3/27/39   March 2, 1939
Strictly Confidential

Yesterday at the Chancellor's reception for the diplomatic corps I had occasion for a casual exchange of opinion with Chancellor Hitler and also with Göring with regard to the recent student incidents in Poland caused by the situation in Danzig.

Immediately after the reception I sent you a short telegraphic account describing only the background of the two conversations, which I am now supplementing more extensively.

In my conversation with the Chancellor I followed the instructions contained in your telegram of the 1st inst.[4] I first mentioned the regrettable student demonstrations before the Embassy in Warsaw, stressing that they were being exploited by the elements of the opposition. The Chancellor did not make too much of these incidents.

I further pointed out that these incidents were provoked by the anti-Polish sign posted in Danzig and the ensuing beating of Polish students. I stated that public opinion in Poland is especially touchy about Danzig matters, and that this sensitivity has been on the upswing lately because German policy toward Danzig is not clear to Polish public opinion. I added that, naturally, this situation is being exploited by elements of the opposition.

The Chancellor replied that Danzig problems are ticklish. That is why he thinks that they should be determined by a solution which would totally remove all complications. In the course of his deliberations he stressed that as long as he, as a partner of Marshal Piłsudski in the Polish-German agreement, is in charge of the Reich's policies, there will be no conflict. In Poland, at the head of Polish foreign policy, stands Minister Beck, "a very clever and noble man." Nevertheless, in the future someone might take the Chancellor's place in Germany, just as some changes may occur in the political leadership in Poland. Therefore, it would be desirable to reach an agreement on this matter before

[4] Missing from Lipski's papers.

then. Such an agreement, though bilaterally painful, would remove forever all misunderstandings—as was done at the Brenner Pass. The Chancellor remarked that Germany's approval of the Corridor is not an easy decision. He added that there are more Germans in Pomerania than Poles in Danzig. He also mentioned that some time ago he was strongly attacked by the *Deutschnationale* for his policy toward Poland. Such an attack on him by Oldenburg-Januschau took place at Neudeck, while the late Field Marshal Hindenburg extended his support to him. If he had not removed the *Deutschnationale* from rule, he could not have reached an agreement with Poland. Naturally, Socialists and Communists did not take any interest in these matters.

The Chancellor also mentioned that it is quite natural that many elements desire to spoil Polish-German relations. He stressed that he understands that you also came upon elements who attack you for your policy toward Germany.

The Chancellor closed the conversation in a positive tone concerning our relations.

Next, I had a conversation with Göring. He remarked that the student demonstrations in Warsaw as such would not have meant much to him if they had not coincided with Minister Ciano's visit to Warsaw. As he learned from the Italian side, Ciano was greatly embarrassed to hear shouts for the Italians and against the other partner of the Axis.

He discreetly inquired whether it was true that some military elements took part in the demonstrations, which I denied. Göring replied that he also thought it to be impossible, since the demonstrations were conducted against the government and you.

For my part, I laid pressure on the necessity of promptly liquidating student incidents in Danzig by acceptance of a Polish proposal to settle the matter by way of a commission.

Göring said that he sent a special clerk to Danzig to investigate who the author of the offensive inscription against Poland was. If we are in possession of any information, he would be obliged if we would share it with him. I understood that he might suspect the possibility of a provocation against Polish-German relations.

For my part, I underlined the sensitivity and hurt feelings of Polish public opinion with regard to the situation in Danzig.

Göring showed understanding. He said that he personally is always trying to iron things out and check such incidents. Stressing that he spoke as a friend, he said that, in his opinion, these matters should be discussed on some occasion. He added that, as long as the Chancellor and he control the government, these matters can always be balanced (*ausbalancieren*). Following the trend of his ideas, he declared that it cannot be denied that Danzig is a German city, while it is a known fact that Poland needs the port of Danzig. If Poland, he went on, had not built Gdynia, this would be even more obvious. Nevertheless, even so Poland's interest is sufficiently evident.

Göring understands the great difficulties this problem is causing inside Poland. He added that it was a misfortune that Marshal Piłsudski died too early, for only a person like him could make a decision on such a problem. Göring closed this point by stating that he is hoping for the best, since we always did find a solution, even in difficult situations.

Göring also added that he is often approached by people from East Prussia and Silesia with many claims and complaints. However, he pays no attention to them. In order to illustrate how the Chancellor cares for our interests, he stressed that, when decision was taken regarding Bohumin, many local Germans tried to influence the Chancellor to re-unite that territory with Germany. However, the Chancellor took the position that Poland's interests had to be taken into consideration there.

Göring remarked that rumors spread by the Western press about alleged German plans for a Great Ukraine are sheer fiction. About Carpathian Ruthenia he said that this problem could still be resolved.

The above conversations of yesterday, which, as I already mentioned, were conducted rather casually in a loose exchange of opinion, made it clear that the Chancellor did not feel personally hurt by the Warsaw anti-German demonstrations, as I had first feared, since he might have suspected that they constituted a reply to his suggestions with regard to Danzig. On the other hand, these demonstrations must have shown both to the Chancellor and to Göring how very irritating the Danzig problems are for public opinion in Poland. From this angle, the demonstrations might even be of some use; under the condition, however, that they will not be repeated and will not result in consequences undesirable for this opinion.

It is rather characteristic that both the Chancellor and Göring laid pressure on the fact that as long as they are directing the Reich's policy there will be no conflict over the Danzig problem. It could be gathered from this that no drastic solution is planned, and that the Chancellor remains willing to come to an understanding with Poland on this issue.

My aim was to prove to the Chancellor and to Göring how very strongly our public opinion is reacting on these matters, so that no illusion would remain in this respect among top elements here.

Finally, I was under the impression that the Party elements in Danzig and those on our border undoubtedly exerted pressure on the political leadership to obtain concessions for the northeastern region of the Reich, which must feel to a certain extent overlooked and neglected after the reunion of Austria and the Sudetenland. This might also be felt as a reaction in the territory.

I would also like to add that Göring, who just underwent a rigorous reducing regimen (he lost over 45 lbs.), looks very tired and is leaving in a few days for four weeks in San Remo.

Józef Lipski

On March 15 the annexation of Czechoslovakia to the Reich took place, about which Moltke informed Beck officially on the same evening.[5] Poland recognized the newly proclaimed independence of Slovakia on that day and sent a chargé d'affaires to Bratislava. However, when Slovak Minister President Tiso made an agreement with Hitler on March 16, and Hitler extended a protectorate over Slovakia, the Polish Ministry of Foreign Affairs reacted with concern and sent instructions by telephone to Lipski on March 17.[6]

On March 15 the Czechs accepted the Hungarian ultimatum to give up Carpathian Ruthenia, and on that day Hungarian troops entered this territory. On March 16 they reached the Polish frontier.

DOCUMENT 136   Łubieński to Lipski

Telephonogram   March 17, 11:07 A.M.
                                                     Secret

Instructions for Ambassador Lipski for the conversation with Field Marshal Göring.

1) Yesterday evening Minister Arciszewski invited Ambassador von

[5] *DGFP*, Series D, Vol. VI, No. 4.
[6] See *ibid.*, Nos. 12 and 18. For the text of the German-Slovak treaty, see *ibid.*, No. 40.

Moltke and asked for a genuine interpretation of the Tiso-Hitler declaration.

2) The very fact of placing us in the face of ever new decisions without previous notification does not contribute to the creation of a good atmosphere in Polish-German relations.

3) Besides, please stress that you are talking without being instructed.

DOCUMENT 137   Lipski to Beck

NO. 54   Berlin, March 17, 1939
                                Received: March 17, 17:10 [5:10 P.M.]
                                Coded

From my conversation with Göring, to whom I mentioned that I was speaking without being instructed, the following are the results:

I. German-Slovak negotiations in Vienna on the form of the *Schutzstaat* are being finalized.

II. The principles are, approximately, as follows: maintainance of Slovakian sovereignty, defense from external threats, common foreign policy, financial aid, probable customs and currency union.

III. I made clear our relation to Slovakia, which took us by surprise with this decision; bad impression in Poland.

Göring stated that the decision about the *Schutzstaat* is final; he said he will call the Chancellor's attention to Polish interests connected with this problem, so that, for instance, there would be no German garrisons in central and eastern Slovakia.

IV. I could feel in Göring a desire to maintain good relations with us; he referred on this occasion to his last conversations with the Chancellor. Nevertheless, he explained the failure to communicate with us (besides the unexpected, even for Germany, turn of events) by a certain dissatisfaction on the part of Hitler caused by the fact that the Warsaw demonstrations put him in an awkward position with Mussolini.

Details in my report today.[7]

In Lipski's papers there is a handwritten sheet of paper with very short remarks, from which the trend of the Ambassador's thoughts—in those crucial days after the annexation of Czechoslovakia by Hitler and the extension of the Reich's protectorate over Slovakia—may be pieced together.

[7] Report missing from Lipski's papers.

On March 19 Lipski proceeded to Warsaw to discuss matters of personal concern with leading factors in Poland. Prior to his departure he had two conversations with Robert Coulondre, French ambassador in Berlin. These conversations, as Lipski noted, dealt with the question of the Polish-French-British alliance. Coulondre's opinions, very pessimistic as to the possibility of checking Hitler's expansion, are contained in his long report to Paris dated March 19.[8] Coulondre presumed that Hitler's next blow would be directed eastward, toward Rumania and Poland, giving these states the alternative, as he had to Austria and Czechoslovakia, of a massacre of the population and destruction of cities or acceptance of German terms. Besides, Coulondre did not exclude the possibility that Hitler might first attack France and England, before they reached the level of the Reich in their armaments. Coulondre's comments were in favor of an increase, jointly with England, of the military potential of the two countries, especially in the air force, avoiding any publicizing of this armaments build-up.

Coulondre dispatched his report on the same day that he had the conversation with Lipski. It may be assumed that the Ambassador of allied France had informed the Ambassador of allied Poland about the pessimistic tenor of his report.

Lipski arrived in Warsaw with the intention of resigning from the post of ambassador in Berlin. He saw clearly that all his work of many years to establish peaceful relations between Poland and Germany had been ruined. He thought that his resignation might, as he writes in his note, help "to bring the country back to its senses."

The Ambassador's intention to resign sprang up some time earlier (such is the opinion of persons close to him). After his conversation with Ribbentrop at Berchtesgaden on October 24, 1938 (Document No. 124), Lipski understood that the policy he had been conducting was coming to an end; that neither written nor verbal promises and obligations of Hitler and Ribbentrop could be trusted; and that possibly it would serve the cause to change Polish ambassadors in Berlin.

Now, after Hitler's occupation of Prague, Lipski decided to present this matter formally to Beck.

On the morning of March 20, upon his arrival in Warsaw, Lipski was informed about disturbances in the capital and about "demonstrations against Beck, when words against me were also uttered." On the same day he had a conversation with Beck and Marshal Śmigły-Rydz, during which he presented his resignation and reported on his conversations with Coulondre. Both the Minister and the Marshal were upset by this information.[9]

Lipski's resignation was not accepted, and during the day he received a

[8] *Livre jaune,* No. 80, pp. 87–92.
[9] Three days after the conversation with Lipski, on March 23, Marshal Śmigły-Rydz issued special instructions to the western inspectors of the army (who in case of war would take command of the armies), defining the war tasks of their armies. *Polish Armed Forces in the Second World War,* Vol. I, Part 1: "September Campaign, 1939" (London, 1951), p. 271.

telephone message from Berlin that Ribbentrop was awaiting him for a conversation.

In Warsaw, Lipski encountered intentions of a Polish-British rapprochement. For some time already Beck had intended to go to London.[10] With regard to conversations with the British, Lipski made the reservation "for my part to keep the Polish-British rapprochement absolutely confidential until all security military measures between the three [Poland, England, and France] were achieved."

On the evening of March 20 Lipski departed for Berlin, where he had a conversation with Ribbentrop the next day. In this conversation Ribbentrop once more repeated the German propositions that Danzig be returned by Poland and an extraterritorial superhighway and railway line be constructed across Pomerania, and in exchange he guaranteed that Poland would keep Pomerania and its access to the sea.[11] He complained about Polish student excesses and talked about Polish-German minority negotiations, about which no joint communiqué had been agreed to.[12]

Lipski, for his part, stressed Poland's concern over Germany's solution of the Slovakia question, which definitely had an anti-Polish aspect.

Ribbentrop suggested that Beck should come to Berlin to discuss basic matters with him and Hitler, and advised Lipski to proceed in the next days to Warsaw to refer this offer to Beck.

On the following day, March 22, Lithuania was compelled to sign an agreement ceding Kłajpeda (Memel Territory) to the Reich.[13]

On that day Lipski arrived in Warsaw in a highly pessimistic mood.[14]

He wrote in his note: "My appraisal is that the situation is far more dangerous than Warsaw realizes." Waiting for Beck, he had a conversation in the hall with Beck's secretary, Starzeński, and "several other officials of the Polish Ministry of Foreign Affairs, who were of a different opinion."

Germany's position with regard to Danzig and the superhighway had been very bluntly defined by Ribbentrop in his plan of instructions for von Moltke dated March 23.[15] However, Hitler did not consent that it be sent to Warsaw.

[10] *DGFP*, Series D, Vol. V, Nos. 130 and 140.

[11] For the contents, see *Polish White Book*, No. 61, and *DGFP*, Series D, Vol. VI, No. 61.

[12] These negotiations were held in Berlin from February 27 to March 3. See *DGFP*, Series D, Vol. V, Nos. 128, 132, and 134.

[13] For the text of the agreement, see *ibid.*, No. 405.

[14] See the Lipski-Szembek conversation of March 22, *Journal*, p. 433.

[15] *DGFP*, Series D, Vol. V, Nos. 73 and 88.

DOCUMENT 138   Memorandum on the Conference of Senior Officials
with the Polish Minister of Foreign Affairs
on March 24, 1939

Secret

Minister: The tension of the situation requires an investigation of the
whole complex of problems. The situation is serious and it cannot be
ignored. And it is serious because one of the elements hitherto timely
for the definition of the state's situation, that is, Germany, has lost
its calculability, with which it was endowed even amidst difficult
problems.

Therefore a number of new elements have appeared in our politics
and a number of new problems in the state.

As far as the basic line of action is concerned, a straight and clear line
has been established with the top factors in the state. We defined with
precision the limits of our direct interests, and beyond this line we
conduct a normal policy and undertake action dealing with it as with
normal current work. Below this line comes our Polish *non possumus*.
This is clear: we will fight. Once the matter is put this way, chaos is
overcome by a considerable share of calm, and thinking becomes
orderly.

Where is the line? It is our territory, but not only that. The line also
involves the nonacceptance by our state, regarding the drastic spot that
Danzig has always been, of any unilateral suggestion to be imposed on
us. And, regardless of what Danzig is worth as an object (in my opinion
it may perhaps be worth quite a lot, but this is of no concern at the
moment), under the present circumstances it has become a symbol. This
means that, if we join that category of eastern states that allow rules to
be dictated to them, then I do not know where the matter will end. That
is why it is wiser to go forward to meet the enemy than to wait for him
at home.

This enemy is a troublesome element, since it seems that he is losing
the measure of thinking and acting. He might recover that measure once
he encounters determined opposition, which hitherto he has not met
with. The mighty have been humble to him, and the weak have capitulated in advance, even at the cost of honor. The Germans are marching
all across Europe with nine divisions; with such strength Poland would

not be overcome. Hitler and his associates know this, so that the question of a political contest with us will not be like the others.

I started with the extreme problem, in order to establish immediately an outlet for our thinking on this matter. On this basis we shall start international action. We have arrived at this difficult moment in our politics with all the trump cards in our hand. This does not speak badly for us.

I would like you, Gentlemen, to use your influence on your junior colleagues in order to bestow on our Ministry the bearing commensurate with these serious premises.[16]

Lipski attended this conference at which Beck defined the political line for Poland to follow. The next day Lipski received instructions within the frame of this policy and proceeded immediately to Berlin, requesting a meeting with Ribbentrop.

These instructions are contained in the *Polish White Book* (No. 62) with a number of basic omissions, and with the complete elimination of the last paragraph dealing with Russia. In Lipski's papers there is the full text, which reads as follows:

DOCUMENT 139   Beck's Instructions to Lipski

Warsaw, March 25, 1939
Strictly Confidential

With reference to the questions addressed to you on the 21st inst. by Herr von Ribbentrop relating to the complex of Polish-German relations, please communicate the following reply:

1) As in the past, so now, the Polish government attaches full importance to the maintenance of good-neighborly relations to the utmost extent with the German Reich.

The Polish government has given definite proof of this by the fact that in 1933 it was first to adopt a friendly attitude toward the Third Reich by opening conversations with a view to eliminating difficulties—conversations which led to the Polish-German declaration of January 26, 1934.

[16] Szembek quotes this memorandum in his *Journal* (pp. 434–35) but not *in extenso*.

It will be appropriate, at this moment, to remind the German Reich of the friendly attitude adopted by the Polish government toward the first National Socialist Senate of the Free City of Danzig.

During the five years following, in all its political activity in the international sphere, the Polish government always refused to take any part in action directed against the interests of the German Reich.

Finally, it is a known fact that in 1938 the firm attitude of the Polish government, marked with understanding for national German revindications, contributed in a great measure to the avoidance of the catastrophe of war.

2) In regard to questions on which agreement has hitherto always been achieved, but concerning which the German Reich has recently put forward new proposals, namely, on the question of transit between the Reich and East Prussia and on the question of regulating the future of the Free City of Danzig, the Polish government considers that:

a) It has no interest in hindering the German government's free communication with the Eastern Province of the Reich. For this reason also, despite many changes which have occurred in recent years by comparison with the previous state of affairs (for instance, the payment of transfers), the Polish government not only has not placed any difficulties in the way of privileged rail transit but has arranged the financial side of this transit in accordance with German interests. This being its attitude, the Polish government is quite willing to study together with the German government the possibility of further simplification and more facilities in rail and road transit between Germany and East Prussia, so that German citizens shall not encounter unnecessary difficulties while using these communications. To this end technical experts could set to work to draw up plans which would by degrees render possible an improvement also in the technical aspect of these communications. All facilities granted on Polish territory could only exist, however, within the limits of Polish sovereignty, and therefore extraterritorial status for ways of communication could not be considered. With this exception, the Polish government's intentions are in the direction of the most liberal treatment of the German *desiderata*.

The solution of the problem, however, depends upon the attitude the German government adopts in regard to my suggestions in the following point.

b) So far as the status of the Free City of Danzig is concerned, the Polish government recalls that it has for a long time now made references to the necessity for a settlement of this issue by way of an understanding between Warsaw and Berlin, this because it would correspond to the essence of the problem, and all the more because the League of Nations is losing the possibility of fulfilling the obligations it has undertaken in the matter.

From previous conversations it is clear that there is no difference of opinion as to the basic approach to the problem, that is, that the Polish government in no way hinders the free national life of the Free City of Danzig, while the German government has declared its respect for Polish rights and interests in the spheres of economy, communications, merchant marine, and the Polish population on the territory of the Free City. As the entire problem is contained in these two points, the Polish government considers it would be possible to find a solution based on a joint Polish-German guarantee to the Free City of Danzig. Such a guarantee would need to meet the aspirations of the German population on the one hand, and to safeguard Polish interests on the other, which interests for that matter are synonymous with the interests of the population of the Free City, considering that the City's well-being has, for centuries, been based upon Polish maritime trade.

The problem of the superhighway is primarily of a technical nature. In the opinion of the Polish government it should be studied by technical experts. On the question of the Free City of Danzig it would be advisable first to have a discussion of political principles between the government of the German Reich and the Polish government so as to ensure that in this organism, in the Chancellor's words employed in February last year, the national conditions of the Free City on the one hand, and the rights and interests of Poland on the other, would be respected.[17] To ensure a stabilization of conditions in our part of Europe, the Polish government considers it desirable to carry on conversations on all these questions as quickly as possible, so as to find a basis for a lasting consolidation of good-neighborly relations between Poland and Germany.

I request you to add orally, and with some emphasis, that Marshal Piłsudski explicitly stressed to me that the method of handling the Polish-

[17] See *Polish White Book*, No. 37.

Danzig problem would be a touchstone of Polish-German relations. I ask you to add that you would be grateful if this opinion were brought to the Chancellor's notice.

You can present your statement, *in extenso* or recapitulated in the form of a memorandum, to the Reich Foreign Minister. On this occasion please add that, if there is a question of my possible meeting with the Reich Chancellor, I always regard this contact as a factor of immeasurable importance, not only to relations between our countries, but to general European policy. Yet I would add that in the present difficult situation I think it indispensable that such conversations should be prepared for by a previous elucidation of the above-mentioned questions, at least in outline form. For, in the atmosphere existing today, personal contacts which yielded no positive results might prove to be a retrogressive step in relations between our states. That my government would desire to avoid.

Please add at the same time that we must now devote great attention to our mutual relations. For owing to Germany's latest steps in regard to both Slovakia and Lithuania, of which the Polish government was not informed even at the last moment, although they concerned territories situated right on the frontiers of the Polish Republic, the general atmosphere demands clarification, and the methods of progress utilized by both governments must be chosen with particular caution.

In case the conversation turns to the subject of relations with Soviet Russia, please, recalling my conversation with von Ribbentrop in Warsaw and my explanation given to the Chancellor at Berchtesgaden, confirm that we always considered Russia's access to European politics a dangerous thing. Also please stress that we consider blocking the penetration of Communism into Poland one of the supreme tasks of our state.

Beck

Lipski executed the instructions of March 25 on the next day when he was received by Ribbentrop. The Polish Ambassador handed the Minister of Foreign Affairs a memorandum containing the main points of the instructions. Once more Ribbentrop stressed that a basis for conversations with Poland might be his conditions presented in the conversation of March 21.

He considered Polish military measures carried out at that time as a strange answer to his proposal for a final settlement of Polish-German relations.[18] The conversation gave no positive results. Ribbentrop stubbornly insisted on Danzig's incorporation into the Reich and on an extraterritorial superhighway in exchange for a twenty-five-year nonaggression agreement and a guarantee of the frontier with Germany. The Polish side was for a settlement of the Danzig question between Germany and Poland, without basically changing the status of the Free City, and was ready to further facilitate transit through Pomerania, maintaining Poland's sovereignty on that territory.[19]

On March 27 anti-German demonstrations took place at Bydgoszcz. Ribbentrop availed himself of this occasion to summon Lipski and deliver a strong protest. Stressing that, to the "generous proposal which Germany had made to Poland," Poland had replied evasively, the Reich Foreign Minister considered that relations between the two states "were therefore deteriorating sharply." [20]

[18] On March 25 Admiral Canaris, head of the Intelligence Department, telephoned the Auswärtiges Amt about Polish mobilization orders as follows: "1) Some 4,000 Polish troops are concentrated at Gdynia. 2) The troops of a garrison previously stationed in the southern part of the Corridor have been transferred to the immediate vicinity of the Danzig frontier. 3) Poland has mobilized three age-groups. All these measures concern only the northern part of Poland; in the other districts of the country there is nothing to report militarily. General Keitel does not believe in any aggressive intentions on the part of the Poles." *DGFP*, Series D, Vol. V, No. 90.

[19] See *Polish White Book*, Nos. 63 and 64, and *DGFP*, Series D, Vol. II, No. 101, with enclosed text of Polish memorandum.

[20] The report on this conversation is missing from Lipski's papers. For the German version, see *DGFP*, Series D, Vol. II, Nos. 108, 118, and 126. See also *Journal*, pp. 437–38, for Szembek's conversation with Moltke on March 24.

Hitler's Hesitation as to the Direction of Attack [1]
January—March, 1939

IN MY ARTICLES I called attention to a series of facts denoting certain hesitations by Hitler—from Munich until the spring of 1939—as to the sequence of future political and strategic moves of the Third Reich. My suppositions were confirmed by the declarations of Hitler himself, as well as by the general assumptions of his policy in relation to England, France, and, at that period also, Poland. The book of German Ambassador von Hassell contains a number of details in confirmation of my thesis. As far as the relations with Poland are concerned, German policy shows in its moves two seemingly contradictory tendencies. One of them is a drive for territorial revision with regard to Danzig and Pomerania; the other, a desire to gain Poland's partnership in a coalition formed under the leadership of Germany. Ribbentrop's proposals of October 24, 1938, the so-called *Gesamtlösung,* take both of these tendencies under consideration. Requests for Danzig's reunion with the Reich and for an extraterritorial superhighway and railway line across Pomerania represent no less than a reduced program of territorial claims, while an offer to Poland that it join in the Anti-Comintern Pact and in collaboration on colonial and emigration matters is in keeping with the broad aspirations of Hitlerite policy.

Upon the rejection by Poland, on November 19, 1938, of the claim to Danzig, the German side apparently made some gesture of withdrawal. A few days later Moltke (on November 22) told Beck that Ribbentrop was considering Polish-German relations on the level of high policy, and that Poland's reply of November 19 made him better realize that is was impossible for Poland to give up the Free City.

The German Ambassador gave assurances that he was always warn-

[1] Printed in *Bellona* (London), 1950, No. 1, under the general title "New Contributions Concerning the Outbreak of the Polish-German War in 1939."

ing his government not to have illusions concerning this problem. Such illusions persisted within Party circles, especially in Forster, the gauleiter of Danzig, who was always inciting Hitler's entourage.

The German government outwardly pretended that no changes had occurred in its relations with Poland. During Ribbentrop's visit to Paris on December 6, 1938, in connection with the signing of the French-German nonaggression pact, Georges Bonnet declared that France had two agreements: one with Poland and another with Soviet Russia, the free action of which was formally provided for in the document prepared for signing.[2] To which Ribbentrop replied: "I know them both. I know about your pact with Russia, supervised by the League of Nations, and your alliance with Poland. These points do not constrain us. As a matter of fact, we ourselves have the best relations with the Poles, with whom we are also bound by an agreement."

In spite of the signing of this pact between France and Germany, the atmosphere in French-British circles was very tense with concern. This is confirmed by M. Georges Bonnet's description of the conference held by him and Daladier with Chamberlain and Halifax at the Quai d'Orsay on November 20 with regard to the mutual defense of the two countries.

"The dialogue between the French and British ministers is a good illustration of our mutual concern. We were far from believing that the Munich Agreement canceled the danger of war in the east. And what is more, we even asked each other who would first receive the German blow in the west—England or France? Mr. Chamberlain did not share the opinion of M. Daladier, who thought that France—owing to its geographical position—would be attacked first in case of a conflict. Mr. Chamberlain thought, owing to the present attitude taken by Germany, it was more probable that strife would erupt between England and Germany, and then England would suffer the first blow. Experts should investigate the problem of possible aggression against England by Germany and the means of assistance on the part of France."[3]

On January 5, 1939, Beck was to meet with Hitler at Berchtesgaden. Secretary of State Weizsäcker prepared material for the conversation. He handed it to Ribbentrop on January 2, 1939,[4] with the following conclusions:

[2] Bonnet, *Fin d'une Europe*, p. 38.
[3] *Ibid.*, p. 55.
[4] *DGFP*, Series D, Vol. V, No. 119 (footnote).

a) Poland should do more for our minorities.

b) Poland should at present remain satisfied with small economic advantages, in case Kłajpeda [Memel] shortly becomes German.

c) It will probably become evident from the conversations whether it is still too early to determine Poland's attitude toward other points of our eastern policy. Beck should understand how very weak his position is and that we await the moment when he becomes more conciliatory.

From this opinion it is clear that the Auswärtiges Amt did not urge a prompt Polish-German solution in accordance with Ribbentrop's proposals of October 24, 1938. Weizsäcker confessed at the Nuremberg trial that, since Poland lost sympathy in the West upon its occupation of Teschen Silesia, he counted on a further deterioration of its relations with France and England, and in consequence on more concessions on its part.

A report from the Berchtesgaden conference was distributed to German posts by a circular telegram dated January 10, 1939. It was signed by Weizsäcker, who undoubtedly must have confirmed the text with Ribbentrop, who was present at the Hitler-Beck conversation. The text of the telegram is as follows: [5]

"The visit of Foreign Minister Beck, which was motivated by a Polish desire to discuss the new situation, took place in a friendly atmosphere. It was noted on both sides that the agreement of January, 1934, had provided its worth and continued to form the basis of German-Polish relations.

"More particularly the question of Danzig was discussed, but did not reach a practical stage. The Führer reassured Beck with respect to the alleged danger of *faits accomplis* being engineered in Danzig, and confirmed Poland's need for access to the sea. The question of Memel was touched upon briefly. The Führer also dissipated Polish misgivings regarding Germany's Ukraine policy. No agreements of any kind were reached. Beck repeated the familiar Polish explanation of the origin of the Polish-Soviet declaration, which became necessary on account of numerous border incidents.

"The Reich Foreign Minister accepted in principle Beck's invitation to Warsaw extended at the end of last year. The date is still open."

From these instructions it is evident that, in spite of the fact that no agreement had been reached on the Danzig problem along the line of

[5] *Ibid.*, No. 121.

German claims, the German government continued to avoid open conflict with Poland.

Upon his return to Warsaw Beck, as he told me himself, warned the President of the Republic and Marshal Śmigły-Rydz that the situation on the Danzig problem was becoming serious.[6] Polish diplomacy intensified its activity in Paris and London.

As yet we have no access to the full German documentation with regard to Ribbentrop's visit to Warsaw (January 25–27, 1939). We only know that on January 13 Ribbentrop issued an order to Forster to desist from new steps in Danzig until his return from Warsaw.[7]

Among the measures planned for the near future were:

a) introduction of the official Hitlerite salute in Danzig,

b) introduction of the German flag,

c) formation of an S.S. *Totenkopf* detachment.

In the same instructions for the Gauleiter of Danzig, it was also mentioned that upon his return from Warsaw Ribbentrop would have a consultation with him, and at that time a decision would be made as to whether these measures would have to be introduced, or whether they would become unessential in view of a general understanding with Poland.

A series of articles appeared in Germany written by P. Kleist, a member of the Polish Desk at Ribbentrop's office.[8] Kleist accompanied the Reich Foreign Minister to Warsaw in January, 1939. The main aim of this visit was, in his opinion, to obtain from the Polish government basic consent for collaboration with Germany against the Soviet Union. Ribbentrop's conversations with the President of the Republic and Marshal Śmigły-Rydz yielded no results. As Kleist put it, "The Poles always skillfully avoided this subject."

Late on the afternoon of January 26 Ribbentrop held a conversation with Beck at the Brühl Palace on principles of the whole complex of Polish-German problems. In accordance with Beck's desire, I agreed with Ambassador von Moltke that we would leave the foreign ministers to converse alone, in order to facilitate a freer exchange of opinion. The conversation lasted for more than two hours. High-ranking officials gathered in the German Embassy had to wait a long time before they could take their places at the dinner table.

7 *DGFP*, Series D, Vol. V, No. 122.
8 *Die Zeit*, October, 1949, I: "Die Reise nach Warschau."

In this basic conversation Beck once more stressed Poland's negative stand with respect to Danzig's reunion with the Reich. Passing to the other problem no less urgent for Hitler, he cut himself off unequivocally from Poland's participation in the Anti-Comintern Pact.

Ribbentrop's mission therefore, proved to be a failure. Kleist called it "the collapse of an attempt on the part of Germany to overcome the problem of Danzig and the Corridor by way of an anti-Soviet solution in conjunction with Poland." Kleist presumably had in mind compensations for Poland at the expense of Soviet Russia in exchange for Danzig and the Corridor.

With growing distrust in the West as to the results of the Munich policy, Polish credit was on the rise. London received at that time disturbing news from Germany. Bonnet writes that according to information received on January 29 at the Quai d'Orsay by the British ambassador in Paris, Hitler, influenced by Ribbentrop and Himmler, was turning over in his mind the idea of striking against the Western Powers as an inaugural operation, with a later assault in the east. This information originated from high-ranking Germans whose sincerity was beyond any doubt. Other similar news was received from foreigners, hitherto Germanophiles, who were in contact with leading German personalities.

"As yet, there was no reason to suppose that Hitler had declared himself for some definite plan. Information in our possession pointed to the fact that he could:

"1) Encourage Italy to support its claims by force and, taking advantage of his obligations toward Italy, enter into war.

"2) Attack Holland. By becoming master of Holland and its coastline, Germany would try to dictate its conditions to Great Britain, at the same time paralyzing France. In the meantime, it could draw Poland, and possibly also other states, to its side by luring them with promises of colonial compensation.

"3) Put colonial claims in the form of an ultimatum.

"4) Attack England by air and, upon this surprise assault, undertake land and sea operations against the Western Powers.

"We received information from high-ranking Germans according to whom such a surprise attack was being prepared." [9]

At that time President Roosevelt communicated to the Dutch envoy information according to which the President had been advised "from

[9] Bonnet, *Fin d'une Europe,* pp. 126–27.

three reliable sources that Germany was allegedly determined to turn against the West, in all probability at a moment when Italy officially placed its territorial claims." [10]

In connection with Ciano's trip to Warsaw (February 23), the French government feared that the Polish government might collaborate on colonial problems. Activities of the Maritime and Colonial League (Liga Morska i Kolonialna) were disturbing for Paris, as was clear from Noël's report. On the request of the French government, Beck made a declaration that he would not support Ciano's colonial plans and, as Noël put it, he kept his word. [11]

Such was the picture of the situation prior to Hitler's occupation of Prague.

Public opinion in Poland was seriously disturbed by incidents involving students in Danzig. Hostile demonstrations against the German Embassy in Warsaw during Ciano's visit gave vent to these feelings. The irritating problem of Carpathian Ruthenia, as well as anti-Polish action of German agents in Slovakia, further inflamed the atmosphere.

Camouflaging the growing conflict with Poland during this period in the field of international relations became a characteristic feature of German tactics. Berlin still hoped to achieve its aim by direct conversations with Warsaw under more convenient political circumstances (after the occupation of Prague).

Germany did not want to drop the Polish card, which was of basic value to the Reich in Hitler's vast plans in the west and east.

Polish diplomacy, on its part, did everything in its power to avoid a conflict with Germany, and therefore remained outwardly discreet. After November, 1938, it tried to balance relations with Soviet Russia that had deteriorated owing to events in Czechoslovakia. Primarily, Polish diplomacy sought stronger support in the West. The restraint displayed by the Polish government in informing the Western Powers about the growing Polish-German tension might also be explained by fear that Poland's international position would be weakened in the eyes of the West.

[10] *Ibid.*
[11] *Ibid.*, p. 129.

Further Hesitation of Hitler [1]
March, 1939

THE PERIOD of the occupation of Austria and the Sudetenland, which was so thoroughly investigated during the Nuremberg trial, did not provide much new material concerning direct Polish-German relations. Documents brought before the International Military Tribunal dealt, in the first place, with German activities which confirmed the aggressive attempts of the leaders of the Third Reich in relation to Austria and Czechoslovakia.

Sir Hartley Shawcross,[2] British prosecutor, in discussing German preparations for aggression against Poland, cited two documents [TC-76 and GB-31] stressing the connection between Germany's action against Czechoslovakia and Poland. One of these documents contains instructions of the Auswärtiges Amt regarding tactics to be used in the problem of Czechoslovakia in order to avoid conflict with the Western Powers and not evoke an undesirable reaction on the part of Poland. This document, destined for Ribbentrop, is dated August 26, 1938.

In opening remarks it is stated "that the most pressing problem of German policy, the Czech problem, might easily but does not have to lead to a conflict with the Entente. Neither France nor England is looking for trouble regarding Czechoslovakia. Both would perhaps leave Czechoslovakia to itself if it should, without direct foreign interference and through internal signs of disintegration due to its own faults, suffer the fate it deserves." Warning against the use of force to settle the Czech problem, the Auswärtiges Amt advised promoting the catchword popular in London circles: "autonomy for the Sudetenland." This kind of

[1] Printed in *Sprawy Międzynarodowe* (London), 1947, Nos. 2–3.
[2] There is a mistake in name here. This part of the indictment was read not by Shawcross but by Colonel Griffith-Jones on the thirteenth day of the Nuremberg trial, December 5, 1945 (*The Trial of German Major War Criminals*, Part II, p. 133).

method seemed desirable to the Foreign Affairs Ministry also in connection with relations with Poland, for encroachment of frontiers by Germany in the southeast would forcibly cause a reaction among Poles owing to frontier questions existing in the north and northeast. It is further stated in the document:

"The fact is that, after the liquidation of the Czech question, it will generally be assumed that Poland will be the next in turn. But the later this assumption penetrates international politics as a firm factor, the better. In this sense, however, it is important for the time being to carry on the German policy under the well-known and proved slogans of 'the right to autonomy' and 'racial unity.' Anything else might be interpreted as pure imperialism on our part and create the resistance to our plan by the Entente at an earlier date and more energetically than our forces could stand up to."

Shawcross also quoted General Jodl regarding the strategic importance of occupying Czechoslovakia for the future war with Poland. Jodl assumed that "the bloodless solution of the Czech conflict in the autumn of 1938 and the spring of 1939 and the annexation of Slovakia rounded off the territory of Greater Germany in such a way that it then became possible to consider the Polish problem on the basis of more or less favorable strategic premises." [3]

It could therefore be assumed that Hitler had been determined in advance to inflict armed aggression on Poland, upon capturing Czechoslovakia, and that events took exactly the course provided for them in his original plans and expectations. Was it so in fact?

In order to reply to this question, it would be necessary to investigate, from the material now made available, not only the development of Polish-German relations from Munich until the spring of 1939, but also the attitude of the Reich government toward France and Great Britain, as well as to establish the circumstances under which Nazi policy in relation to Russia underwent a change in May, 1939, or perhaps already in the middle of April.

The closer we come to the date of the outbreak of the war, the fuller and more abundant in detail becomes the Nuremberg documentation. In the last days of August, 1939, the course of events is fixed nearly from hour to hour.

---

[3] Speech of Colonel Taylor (not Shawcross) on the twenty-seventh day of the trial (January 4, 1946) quoting from Jodl's paper of 1943 (Doc. L-172, USA-34).

Let us first listen to Hitler himself, the person most responsible for the course of events. In his speech delivered to commanders of German armed forces, on August 22, 1939, when he disclosed his final decision to attack Poland within the next few days, Hitler used these words to motivate his decision:

"It was clear to me that a conflict with Poland had to come sooner or later. I had already made this decision in spring, but I thought that I would first turn against the West in a few years, and only afterward against the East. But the sequence could not be fixed. One cannot close one's eyes before a threatening situation. I wanted to establish an acceptable relationship with Poland in order to fight first against the West. But this plan, which was agreeable to me, could not be executed since essential points had changed. It became clear to me that Poland would attack us in case of a conflict with the West." [4]

At a conference with commanders of the armed forces on November 23, 1939, that is, already after war operations against Poland, Hitler confirmed his previous statements. Here are his words:

"One year later, Austria came; this step also was considered doubtful. It brought about a considerable reinforcement of the Reich. The next step was Bohemia, Moravia, and Poland. This step also was not possible to accomplish in one campaign. . . . It was not possible to reach the goal in one effort. It was clear to me from the first moment that I could not be satisfied with the Sudeten-German territory. That was only a partial solution. The decision to march into Bohemia was made. Then followed the erection of the Protectorate and with that the basis for the action against Poland was laid, but I was not quite clear at that time whether I should start first against the East and then the West or vice versa. Moltke often made the same calculations in his time. Under pressure the decision came to fight with Poland first." [5]

Hitler's attitude toward France left no doubt from the moment he started to build up the National Socialist Party. In *Mein Kampf* he called France the eternal enemy of Germany. He consistently strove to weaken France's position in Europe from the time he came to power. However, outwardly his action toward that country was camouflaged by a pretended desire for an agreement on the basis of Germany's renunciation of its territorial claims. In the first years of his rule, Hitler achieved

[4] *Trial of the Major War Criminals,* Vol. XXVI, No. PS-798.
[5] *Ibid.,* No. PS-789.

his greatest success at the expense of direct French interests, owing to France's internal weakness which compelled it to abandon its independent policy. Among his victories were the reunion of the Saar with Germany and the remilitarization of the Rhineland. In November, 1937, Hitler was absolutely aware of France's dependence on Great Britain. This became even clearer to him after Munich. He then started to act toward loosening relations between Paris and London. The German-French declaration of December 6, 1938, signed by Ribbentrop and Bonnet, was, for the German side, aimed at neutralizing British influence.

In contrast with his early anti-French arguments, Hitler declared himself in *Mein Kampf* for an agreement with Great Britain. He condemned Wilhelm II for bringing about a war between the German and Anglo-Saxon races. His emissaries traveled to England prior to 1933. They did not succeed, judging by the failure of Rosenberg's mission. Ideological programs and ideas of anti-Bolshevik crusades did not find a fertile soil in the British community. Hitler, however, was obstinate. The choice of Ribbentrop for the office of delegate extraordinary for disarmament matters had been decided on because of his allegedly widespread relations in the Anglo-Saxon world, about which that weird ambassador of the new regime was so eager to boast. In spite of some initial successes, primarily the conclusion of a sea pact between Great Britain and the Reich in 1935, the later mission of Ribbentrop as ambassador to London ended in utter failure. The anti-Comintern plans with which he approached the English, with the idea of thus gaining a free hand for the Reich in the East, failed completely. From an advocate of a rapprochement with Great Britain, he then became its most dogged adversary. Plenty of proof might be found to this effect in the Nuremberg documents.

In a personal, strictly confidential memorandum sent from London on January 2, 1938, to the Chancellor of the Reich,[6] describing the complex of German-British relations, Ribbentrop reached the following conclusions:

1) England is late with its armaments and therefore wants to gain time.

2) England believes that in the competition with Germany time is playing into its hands. It is counting on exploiting its larger economic

[6] *DGFP*, Series D, Vol. I, No. 93.

potential in the field of armaments, as well as on extending its treaties, for example, with the United States.

3) Halifax's visit should be regarded solely as a desire to investigate the situation and as a camouflage. English Germanophiles also are only playing the roles they have been assigned to perform.

4) England and its Prime Minister do not see in the visit of Halifax any possibility of creating the basis for an understanding with Germany. They have only as much confidence in National Socialist Germany as the Germans have in England. That is why they fear that some day they might be forced to accept solutions not agreeable to them. In order to cope with this, England is preparing militarily and politically—in case of emergency—for a war with Germany.

And here are Ribbentrop's final conclusions:

1) Outwardly, further agreement with England to safeguard the interests of Germany's friends.

2) In utter secrecy, creation, with unflinching persistence, of a coalition against England, namely, by tightening the friendship with Italy and Japan, as well as by winning over all nations whose interests are linked directly or indirectly with German interests. To establish close and confidential collaboration between the diplomacies of these three Great Powers in order to achieve the goal sought.

Not even a whole month elapsed from the time this memorandum was written before Joachim von Ribbentrop became foreign minister of the Reich. It is therefore easy to guess how Hitler reacted to the advice of his London emissary.

The Chamberlain-Hitler agreement at Munich brought no change in the situation. It conformed with Ribbentrop's recommendations in keeping up the appearances of an agreement with Great Britain. Hitler's speech delivered at Saarbrücken came as an unpleasant surprise to English Munich-adherents. At the same time information reached the British government from German opposition circles about military and particularly air plans of Germany directed against England.

Against the background of this general situation my conversation with von Ribbentrop took place at Berchtesgaden on October 24, 1938.[7]

Ribbentrop presented a concept of a large-scale Polish-German

[7] See Document 124, p. 453.

agreement, calling it "eine sekulaere Loesung" ["a solution for centuries"]. In exchange for Danzig's reunion with the Reich and the extraterritorial superhighway and railway line across the Pomeranian Corridor, the German government would disclaim further aspirations to the Polish western provinces and would extend the nonaggression declaration by a further twenty-five years. But this was not the end of the German proposal. Ribbentrop suggested that Poland should join the Anti-Comintern Pact and that there should be Polish-German collaboration on colonial problems. This would be equivalent to Poland's joining a coalition formed under Hitler's leadership.

Theoretically speaking, Hitler could have abstained from burdening his proposals that Poland enter within the orbit of German politics with the highly irritating problems of Danzig and the superhighway. He might have expected that, if Poland were joined with Germany, it would have later surrendered to the will of Germany's dictator on territorial questions. Or did Hitler still, after so many rejected attempts, have some hope of persuading Poland to renounce its relations with the West and its independent position between Germany and Russia? Were the return of Danzig and the superhighway just to be a tribute, which Hitler was in the habit of claiming in advance in exchange for the so-called friendship offered by the Third Reich to its future satellites? Hitler must have had, of course, to consider local pressure from the Reich's eastern provinces. After the Saar and the Rhineland, after Austria and the Sudetenland, the German eastern provinces must have felt neglected. Gauleiters who kept promising for years that a great day would come in Danzig just could not wait to see it come. The Prussian Junker caste, whose influence reached as far as the Reich Chancellery, did not tire in its agitation for the reunion of the Corridor with Germany. In Hitler's concept, the demand for the return of Danzig and the possession by Germany of an extraterritorial superhighway represented a minimum program of German claims, since it was possible to execute this program under convenient international circumstances without an armed conflict with Poland. Hitler and his immediate entourage believed this to be possible, in spite of unequivocal warnings on the part of Polish diplomacy. General Keitel's order issued on November 24, 1938,[8] that is, just five days after my conversation with Ribbentrop, when on behalf of Minister Beck I gave a reply to the proposal of October 24, stating that any

[8] *Trial of the Major War Criminals,* Vol. XXXIV, No. C-137.

attempt to incorporate the Free City into the Reich would evoke a Polish-German conflict, confirmed this belief. Keitel's order anticipated the occupation of Danzig by surprise attack. However, it contained a clear reservation that this operation should not mean a war with Poland. The occupation of the Free City was to take place at a politically convenient moment, under the appearance of a revolt in the city. Another interesting detail contained in the order was a message that German forces in East Prussia, destined for the occupation of Danzig, should not be simultaneously engaged in the move on Kłajpeda [Memel], in order that, if necessary, these two operations could take place at the same time. It is worth recalling that, when in March, 1939, Hitler occupied Kłajpeda, the Polish command—counting on the possible synchronization of the two operations—took steps for a military cover of the Free City of Danzig.

The Nuremberg files contain quite a lot of material dealing with German activities in relation to Slovakia and Carpathian Ruthenia for the period of the March crisis after Munich. There is not so much material to enlighten us with regard to German moves against Poland.

The published memoirs of former German Ambassador von Hassell, who was executed on Hitler's orders after the July, 1944, attempt, correct this shortcoming to a certain extent. Among other things, Hassell reports on a conversation held with Weizsäcker on December 16, 1938. The Secretary of State, who talked very openly with his colleague and friend, defined the policy of Ribbentrop and Hitler as one definitely leading to war. He also pointed to some hesitation among the top authorities of the Reich whether to turn immediately against England, safeguarding Poland's neutrality to this end, or to move eastward to liquidate the Polish and Ukrainian problems and occupy Kłajpeda. Hassell gives no explanation as to what Weizsäcker had in mind when he spoke of the liquidation of Polish and Ukrainian questions.

Under the date of January 26, 1939, von Hassell noted in his memoirs, following further information from Weizsäcker, that there was a peaceful atmosphere also with regard to the East, where at most they would like to start something with Poland (on that day Ribbentrop was in Warsaw). At the same time, in Weizsäcker's opinion, Hitler's program anticipated a total occupation of Czechoslovakia.

Ribbentrop's conversations with Beck in Warsaw produced no results. The Reich Minister met with firm resistance regarding the incorporation of Danzig into Germany. He also once more had the occasion to learn from his conversation with Minister Beck about Poland's negative attitude toward joining anti-Comintern agreements. Upon his return to Berlin Ribbentrop, as appears from Hassell's report, influenced Hitler to liquidate the Czechs in the first instance, leaving Danzig and the Corridor question to be settled later. Hassell, who notes this detail as a result of information received from von Nostitz, a German diplomat who at that time was assigned to the Auswärtiges Amt, adds his own commentary that if the Corridor question were placed ahead of the Czech problem there was a chance to arrive at a solution agreeable to German demands. Hassell justifies this assumption by the fact that only after Prague was occupied did the resultant deep shock strike international public opinion, causing a change in the Powers' attitude toward Hitlerite Germany. According to further information from von Nostitz, Ribbentrop, owing to his tactical mistake and his erroneous appraisal of the reaction in England, for a few weeks fell into disfavor with Hitler.

Ribbentrop undoubtedly thought that, owing to the occupation of Prague and the extension of the German protectorate over Slovakia, a militarily threatened Poland would be readier for concessions. That is why on March 21, immediately upon the termination of the Czech operation, he renewed his claims against Poland.

Hitler's attitude toward Poland during these critical days of March is disclosed by a note on the conversation held by the commander in chief of the Land Army, General Brauchitsch, with the Reich Chancellor [9] on March 25, 1939. This very important document, to which not enough attention was paid during the Nuremberg trial, is of particular value in taking stock of the situation at that time.

I quote verbatim paragraphs dealing with Poland:

"*Danzig problem.* L. [Lipski] is returning from Warsaw on Sunday, March 26; his mission there was to inquire whether Poland was ready to make an arrangement about Danzig. The Führer left Berlin on the evening of March 25 and does not wish to be here when L. returns. For the present R. [Ribbentrop] is to conduct the negotiations. The Führer *does not* wish to solve the Danzig question by force, however. He does not wish to drive Poland into the arms of Britain by this means.

"A possible military occupation of Danzig could be contemplated *only* if L. gave an indication that the Polish government could not justify

[9] *DGFP*, Series D, Vol. VI, No. 99 (emphasis appears in the official text).

voluntary cession of Danzig to its own people and that a *fait accompli* would make a solution easier for it."

When making such a supposition, Hitler possibly thought about some instances from the negotiations with Czechoslovakia. However, they could not possibly be applied in Poland's case.

"*The problem of Poland.* For the present the Führer does not intend to solve the Polish question. However, it should now be worked upon. A solution in the near future would have to be based on especially favorable political preconditions. In such a case Poland would have to be so beaten down that, during the next few decades, it need not be taken into account as a political factor. In a solution of this kind the Führer envisages an advanced frontier, extending from the eastern border of East Prussia to the eastern tip of Silesia. The questions of evacuation and resettlement still remain open. The Führer does *not* wish to enter the Ukraine. Possibly a Ukrainian state might be established. But these questions too still remain open."

Further directives in the note dealt with problems of Slovakia and the Protectorate.

It transpires from this document that Hitler feared that Poland might bind itself with England. He still made the solution of the Polish problem dependent on favorable international circumstances. Nevertheless, his future plans concerning Poland, together with the question of the future frontier, were clearly drafted in his mind.

On March 31, 1939, Chamberlain made a declaration in the House of Commons granting a guarantee to Poland in case its independence were threatened.

Three days later, on April 3, 1939, Keitel signed the first order dealing with preparations for war with Poland (code: "Operation White").[10] We see on the order in Hitler's handwriting a postscript that military preparations were to be finished by September 1, 1939.

The London conversations of Minister Beck were followed with utmost attention by the German government. News about the text of the Polish-English communiqué of April 6, stating that England and Poland united themselves with a bilateral guarantee, evoked a reaction of utmost dissatisfaction in Berlin. The German government evaluated this step as Poland's entry into the orbit of British politics. A conversation I had on that day with Weizsäcker left no illusions in this respect.

[10] *Ibid.,* Nos. 149 and 185.

Gisevius, author of the well-known book *Bis zum bitterem Ende,* and one of the leading witnesses at the Nuremberg trial, writes of Hitler's reaction when he learned about England's guarantee for Poland.

Gisevius' chief, the famous Admiral Canaris, head of the German Intelligence Service, returned one day from the Reich Chancellery, shocked by the state in which he found Hitler. Bad news had come from London. The British had decided to grant a guarantee to Poland. Canaris confirmed this news to Hitler, adding on his part that any further step to the east would bring about an armed conflict.

At this Hitler flared up with rage. Infuriated, he ran across the room, hammering with his fists against a marble table and spewing forth a tirade of the worst curses. His eyes glaring malevolently, he hissed a venomous threat: "I shall prepare a diabolic beverage for them."

Gisevius was of the opinion that this was the first hint of a pact with Stalin.

Breach by Hitler of the
Nonaggression Declaration of 1934
March—July, 1939

THE OCCUPATION of Prague by Germany and the liquidation of the Czecho-slovak state met with the determined reaction of British political circles. On March 21, Sir Howard Kennard, ambassador of Great Britain in Warsaw, presented to the assistant vice-minister, Mirosław Arciszewski, a memoran-dum regarding the declaration by four states—Great Britain, France, the USSR, and Poland—announcing immediate consultations as to steps to be taken in order jointly to counteract any action threatening the political independence of any of the European states.[1]

In answer, Beck proposed to Halifax a bilateral Polish-British declaration in the same spirit instead of a multilateral declaration.[2] On March 30 Am-bassador Kennard advised Beck that Chamberlain intended to make a decla-ration in the House of Commons to the following effect:

"In the event of any action which clearly threatened Polish independence, and which the Polish government accordingly considered it vital to resist with their national forces, His Majesty's government would feel themselves bound at once to lend the Polish government all support in their power."

Beck acknowledged this statement, and Chamberlain delivered his speech in the House of Commons.[3]

In order to discuss these matters, Beck proceeded to London on April 2. However, counting on a possible German reaction, especially in Danzig, he held a conference on April 1, prior to his departure, with senior officials of the Polish Ministry of Foreign Affairs and with General Wacław Stachiewicz, chief of the General Staff.

[1] *Polish White Book*, No. 65.
[2] *Ibid.*, No. 66.
[3] *Ibid.*, Nos. 68 and 69.

DOCUMENT 140   Director of the Minister's Cabinet

April 1, 1939

Conference in Minister Beck's office on the Danzig problem.
Present: Messrs. General Stachiewicz, Vice-Minister Szembek, Minister
Arciszewski, M. Łubieński, T. Kobylański.

Minister Beck does not think that we face an immediate decisive conflict
over Danzig. However, we must be prepared for that eventuality and be
in possession of emergency means which represent a compromise between military action and diplomacy.

The Minister envisages the following possibilities of a conflict:

I. Direct German military intervention in the form of trespassing of
troops or landing of detachments. In that case our immediate counteraction follows in accordance with principles established by the General
Staff. Entry of the fleet alone, without landing of detachments, would be
dealt with as a diplomatic incident. In case of illegal entry of the German fleet into the Danzig harbor, our navy will not salute it in this
port.

II. An internal Danzig putsch, that is, a case where initiative remains
in the hands of the Senate or the Danzig Party.

Version A. Political declaration for reunion with the Reich. In the
first stage only a diplomatic incident is created. On our side a protest is
lodged in Danzig and in Berlin. Note to the German government should
be formulated as follows: the Polish government supposes it to be only a
sally of the local authorities; the German government should recognize
that this cannot be tolerated by the Polish government. If the German
government does not take this declaration under consideration, we shall
consider this a violation of Polish rights and interests. Recognition by
the Reich results in a Polish-German incident and our reaction as *ad* p. I
(hypothetically).

Version B. Attack on Polish state organs in Danzig takes place, active
reaction follows as *ad* p. I, but in proportion to the extent of the attack.

In case of an incident, railway orders are issued (Chief of the General
Staff):

I. If the incident is confined to the Danzig territory only, transit
communication at the sector of all transit lines across the Danzig territory is closed;

II. if Germany participates in the incident, all privileged transit is closed;

III. active reaction follows and mobilization orders are issued; a complete halt in communications.

General principles:

1) We are interested in maintaining the incident, as long as possible, within a local frame. Transfer of the quarrel to the level of Poland-Germany should not occur on our initiative but on the Reich's.

2) In case of a German ultimatum, answer that we cannot take it into consideration. In general do not get involved in any discussion as to yes or no. Act only on the basis of the Danzig or German *Uebergriff*.

3) In any case, the Minister is interrupting his trip and is returning to Warsaw.

In the evening hours of April 2, Beck, passing through Berlin, conversed with Lipski in the Nord Express. In a short note the Ambassador wrote that he called Beck's attention to the fact that, according to Attolico, the Italian ambassador in Berlin, a reguarantee on the Polish side would be considered by the German government as the end of its conversations with Poland. Lipski, therefore, suggested that the reguarantee should be linked with the Polish-French alliance, which was connected with the French-British alliance.

Lipski advised that nothing be done which might be interpreted as contradictory to the declaration of January 26, 1934. Beck replied that Director Józef Potocki was carrying with him documents relating to Lipski's negotiations regarding the 1934 declaration, and that they would do their best to avoid controversy in London. Verbal instructions for Lipski read as follows:

1) Any Polish-British agreement will be bilateral, defensive, and in the character of a reguarantee,

2) Poland will not join the anti-German bloc.

Lipski also stressed the "fairly great tension in Berlin" and remarked that he preferred to converse with Weizsäcker rather than with Ribbentrop, who rendered the situation more acute.

On April 3 Lipski sent the following telegram to Beck:

DOCUMENT 141 Lipski to Beck in London

April 4, 1939

The local inspired press information contains very clearly a tendency to represent British action as trying to encircle Germany. Reference is made to the Chancellor's speech [4] predicting counteraction in anticipation of the attempt at encirclement. Insinuations addressed to Poland are beginning to appear openly.

I therefore think it would be desirable for Polish-German relations still to lay special stress outwardly in London on our attitude toward Germany, based upon the 1934 agreement.

Dirksen is absent from London. I suggest that perhaps the German Chargé d'Affaires and the Italian Ambassador could be received and our position explained to them, the more so since I feel a certain anxiety here from the Italian side that the rapprochement with England might complicate relations with Germany.

Lipski

A joint Polish-British communiqué about the necessity of contracting a bilateral pact of mutual aid in order jointly to counteract any action in case the independence of the two states was threatened was published in London on April 6, 1939. Poland took on the obligation to aid Great Britain in case of aggression.[5]

On the same day, even prior to the publication of the communiqué, Secretary of State Weizsäcker summoned Lipski to declare to him that German proposals in relation to Poland were no longer valid, since Poland's reaction to them had taken the form of military orders. On the basis of press information in respect to Beck's conversations in London, Weizsäcker was at a loss to understand how they could be in conformity with the spirit of the 1934 declaration.

Lipski, for his part, strongly criticized German policy in the last weeks, which acted by surprise against Poland, and stressed the necessity of reinforcing Poland's security.

Contents of the Lipski-Weizsäcker conversation were published in the *Polish White Book*, No. 70, but with a couple of omissions. After the first paragraph, the following sentence of Lipski was omitted: "I further stressed that we are not aiming for any association with Russia." At the end two sentences were omitted: "We did not go deeper into the matter, especially since this was only a first general exchange of opinion after a longer interruption of more than three weeks in my personal contacts with the Auswärtiges Amt. Herr Weizsäcker finally stressed that the German government is maintaining absolute calm, and he said that he regrets that our relations have taken such a course."

[4] Hitler's speech of April 1 at Wilhelmshaven on the occasion of the launching of the battle cruiser *Tirpitz*.
[5] *Polish White Book*, No. 71.

Weizsäcker's account of this conversation is different; he insists that a sharply toned statement was made to the Polish Ambassador.[6] During the Nuremberg trial, Weizsäcker finally conceded that the text of the *White Book* was rather more reliable.[7]

This was one of Lipski's last conversations with Weizsäcker. With Ribbentrop Lipski had one more conversation, on August 31, 1939, at 6:30 P.M.— ten hours before Germany attacked Poland.

After May, 1939, the number of Lipski's reports to the Ministry diminishes. He is more and more isolated from the A.A. and he visits Warsaw more frequently. The counselor of the Embassy, Prince Stefan Lubomirski, in the character of a chargé d'affaires, filled in for him in Berlin.

On April 8 Beck, in bad health, was returning from London via Berlin to Warsaw. In the morning at the station in Berlin he was greeted by Dornberg, chief of the A.A. protocol. Lipski writes in his personal notes that Beck was not yet ready and had to dress in a great rush. "He did not look well, and I was chagrined to see him exchange a few sentences with Dornberg in a hoarse voice." Lipski, together with the military attaché, Colonel Szymański, accompanied Beck by train to Frankfurt-an-der-Oder. In his conversation with Beck, Lipski called attention to the fact that demonstrations on the Polish side in honor of Beck's return should not take the form of an anti-German agitation. Beck issued orders that calm should be observed. Lipski further communicated to the Minister that the atmosphere in Berlin was becoming more tense from day to day and that the results of the London conversations further contributed to the deterioration of Polish-German relations. The whole German press overflowed with invective regarding the policy of encirclement applied by Great Britain and Poland to Germany. Lipski related to Beck his conversation with Weizsäcker of April 6, stressing his unwillingness to confer with Ribbentrop. To Beck's question about Göring's role, Lipski answered that he thought Göring's prestige had gone down. There were rumors that Göring was against the occupation of Prague. It was a fact, however, that Ribbentrop's influence on the Chancellor had become stronger. Hitler believed Ribbentrop in his evaluation of British policy, that is, that England would not go to war. Here Beck remarked that this concept was absolutely false and dangerous.

In conclusion, Lipski stressed that war was coming, but not immediately.

Colonel Szymański gave a pessimistic analysis of the situation.[8] He described it as dangerous, using the German term "Aufmarschbereitschaft— Richtung nach Osten" ("Preparation for marching up—direction toward the east"). The German *Ordre de Bataille* provided for the use of 60–70 divisions in 48 hours, and German drill-mobilization made it possible to place this force on Polish frontiers. However, Beck thought this opinion to be too

[6] *DGFP*, Series D, Vol. VI, No. 169. See also the characteristic instructions for Moltke of April 5, *ibid.*, No. 159.
[7] "Trials of War Criminals," mimeographed transcript, pp. 7839–40.
[8] Szymański, pp. 128–31.

pessimistic; he explained to Lipski the character of the agreement with England and thought that an understanding on Danzig might still be reached on the conditions stated by Poland.

Lipski and Szymański took leave of Beck in Frankfurt and returned to Berlin by plane.

Between April 18 and April 20 Gafencu, the foreign minister of Rumania, paid a visit to Berlin and had a conversation first with Ribbentrop and then with Hitler. Lipski noted in his papers that he had occasion to talk with Gafencu after his meeting with Hitler. The Chancellor used very strong words against Poland.[9]

On April 28 Hitler delivered a major address at the Reichstag in which he deliberated on the complex of international relations. With regard to Poland he disclosed for the first time German proposals for a settlement of the Danzig question, the extraterritorial superhighway and the railway line through Pomerania, as well as the twenty-five-year pact of nonaggression. Poland had rejected this generous offer, had mobilized its army, and by the agreement with England had infringed on the declaration of nonaggression of 1934, which, under the circumstances, should be considered void.[10]

On the same day (April 28), immediately before Hitler's speech at noon in the Reichstag, the German chargé d'affaires in Warsaw, Krümmer, handed Vice-Minister Szembek a memorandum dated April 27 containing a reiteration of all the charges against Poland from the Chancellor's speech.[11]

DOCUMENT 142   Lipski to Beck

NO. N/52/30/39   Berlin, April 29, 1939
                                                              Secret

I am evaluating as follows Chancellor Hitler's speech delivered at the Reichstag on April 28, which had been anxiously awaited by German and international opinion:

1) Chancellor Hitler followed the trend of diplomatic, rather than military, action.

2) The chief aim of this action is to weaken or else loosen the united front which was formed (between the Powers of the East and the West) after the occupation of Bohemia, the extension of the *Schutz* over Slovakia, and the take-over of Kłajpeda [Memel].

[9] *DGFP*, Series D, Vol. VI, No. 234.

[10] For the text of Hitler's speech relating to Poland, see *Polish White Book*, No. 75.

[11] For the text, see *ibid.*, No. 76, and *DGFP*, Series D, Vol. VI, Nos. 276 and 274. See also *Journal*, pp. 449–50.

3) While the polemic with England and the breach of the naval agreement constitute two of the principal features of the speech, it nevertheless resulted in direct pressure being brought to bear on Poland.

The fact that the Chancellor decided on tactics designed to loosen the front created to counteract German aggression indicates that the method adopted by the Powers of granting mutual support to each other in case of aggression proved to be effective. Its future success, in my opinion, depends on the partners' consistent willingness to keep their previously adopted positions.

Here I would like to mention that in my conversation today with the French Ambassador [12] we came to identical conclusions, and he assured me very definitely, on the basis of his constant contact with Prime Minister Daladier, that the French government would keep firmly to its adopted line. At the same time he urged that efforts be made to see that London, owing to Chamberlain's inclination for negotiations, does not stray from the adopted path. The Ambassador stated that the principle that Poland alone has the right to define the limits of its concessions to Germany should be respected.

Analyzing yesterday's speech of the Chancellor in a general review, I would like to call attention to the following details:

I. The reply to Roosevelt, which was to be the pivot of the speech, is dealt with on the level of skillful propaganda polemics, while essential political aspects relate to other fields.[13]

II. Most striking is the paragraph concerning German-*English* relations. It is conciliatory, reiterating Hitler's old concept of maintaining the best of relations with the British Empire. It might be possible to read between the lines an idea with regard to a partition of the world between England and the Reich. This had already been told to me by Minister Gafencu after he met with Hitler. At the same time, Hitler attacks England for the policy of encirclement and on this basis revokes the naval agreement.

Beyond any doubt, action undertaken by Great Britain against German aggression and the decision of Parliament to introduce conscription [14] are the reasons for the change of tone toward Great Britain. This

---

[12] *Livre jaune,* No. 115.

[13] See Roosevelt's telegram to Hitler of April 15 (*DGFP*, Series D, Vol. VI, No. 200).

[14] On April 26, Chamberlain informed the House of Commons that Great Britain intended to present a bill for compulsory military service.

tone, compared with invective cast by the German press and local statesmen against England, is most striking.

III. Although Hitler is sticking to his previous attitude toward *France,* namely, that upon settlement of the Saar problem territorial questions have been resolved, nevertheless there is a slight warning to France that renunciation of Alsace-Lorraine cannot be taken for granted, but that it stems from the desire to surrender national demands to higher international interests.

IV. Arguments justifying the occupation of Bohemia are clearly lacking in logic. The argument that the Czech element insinuated itself within the German tribe to create an enclave is groundless from the historical point of view. All this portion of the speech, barren of real arguments, is the weakest part.

V. The paragraph about a possible *guarantee for Rumania's frontiers* (about which I reported in my telegram) [15] is not contained in the speech. Instead, Hitler used an unguarded expression uttered by the Rumanian King to him at Berchtesgaden that Rumania should be entitled to a direct corridor through Carpathian Ruthenia and Slovakia toward the Reich. He used it to deny his aggressive intentions toward that country.

VI. Lengthy deliberations about *Lithuania* might not be explained solely by the question of uniting Kłajpeda with the Reich. Here tendencies should be considered for economic occupation of this country, as well as of the *Baltic states.*

VII. Through the speech runs a clear note that *Western Powers* should keep away from *Central and Eastern Europe.* The Chancellor explains that he could envisage their financial collaboration. Nevertheless, he adds that financial aid, as in the Czech instance, would result in military action of the Eastern states against the Reich.

VIII. A characteristic statement in confirmation of my earlier observations that the Chancellor felt that *without the Munich Agreement* a more favorable *solution of the Czechoslovak* problem could have been achieved by the Reich.

The statement that the Chamberlain-Hitler consultative agreement dealt exclusively with German-British relations, and that the Munich Agreement has nothing to do with Czech and Moravian problems, as well as that the appeal for arbitration made by the Hungarians and

[15] Missing from Lipski's papers.

Czechs on the matter of frontiers for Slovakia excluded the other two partners of Munich, might only be evaluated in the light of documents. Prime Minister Chamberlain himself will be the most competent interpreter of whether the Chancellor is right or wrong in his deliberations.

IX. In his speech the Chancellor returns repeatedly to the idea of *Lebensraum*. Explaining the annexation of Austria and Bohemia to the Reich, he states that within the frame of the present Great Reich there is not a single territory which had not long ago belonged to the Reich, had not been connected with it, or had not been under its sovereignty.

X. While there is a traditional paragraph about friendship *with Italy,* and praise for *General Franco* as the conqueror of Bolshevism, *Japan* is mentioned only by a single word, which undoubtedly results from the negative attitude Japan took with regard to efforts to change the Anti-Comintern Pact into a military alliance directed against England and France. Here I might mention in passing that, contrary to its previously employed practice, the German press for the first time printed information about Chinese successes in their offensive against Japan.

XI. The Chancellor made a characteristic statement that war would end in the destruction of European culture by *Bolshevism.*

XII. The portion devoted to Poland this time is particularly extensive; it maintains a rather realistic tone and is devoid of a clearly aggressive note. It is, however, bent to conform to the German thesis.

In other parts of the speech Poland is only mentioned in connection with the Teschen Silesia problem and Carpathian Ruthenia, as striving for a common frontier with Hungary.

In the main paragraph about Poland the following points are worth noting:

1) Reference by the Chancellor to the provision of the 1934 declaration which reads as follows:

"Each of the two governments, therefore, lays it down that the international obligations undertaken by it toward a third party do not hinder the peaceful development of their mutual relations, do not conflict with the present Declaration, and are not affected by this Declaration,"
and reference to the fact that in practice the provision had only been granted to Poland.

This statement is inaccurate, inasmuch as in 1934, as well as now, the German government was bound by the Treaty of Rapallo and the Berlin agreement with the Soviets. The fact that the negotiators in the 1934 declaration mentioned the hitherto accepted international obligations in relation to third parties is self-explanatory, since they could only make declarations in respect to contracted agreements. Besides, and this we have to bear in mind, these agreements were not disclosed to the parties, and it was only considered that these agreements were not in contradiction with the declaration.

The Chancellor speaks on this occasion about the Polish-French alliance but does not mention the Polish-Rumanian alliance, which, as a matter of fact, refers to Soviet Russia. However, he also fails to mention obligations under Article 16 of the Covenant of the League of Nations. I pass over here the legal argumentation to ascertain the conformity of the 1934 declaration with the Polish-British pact.

2) With regard to *Danzig,* I draw attention to the fact that the following is mentioned:

"The Danzig problem must at the latest, with the gradual extinction of this disastrous institution [the League of Nations], be discussed at any rate."

This might explain why the Chancellor opened a discussion on the subject of Danzig. At the same time this is also a loophole to postpone the settlement of the problem.

3) The statement that the Corridor and the superhighway through the Corridor have no military importance; their meaning is only of a psychological and economic nature.

4) At point 1 of the German offer, mention that Danzig returns "as a free state" to the Reich, which was not spelled out in conversations by the German side, while in the German note is only mentioned "return of Danzig to the Reich."

5) At point 2 of the offer, underlining that Germany had to obtain a *superhighway* and *railway line* for its use across the Corridor, of the same *extraterritorial* character as the Corridor is for Poland. The editing is not clear; it may be designed for a German audience, to show that the problem of the Corridor would thus also be settled.

6) At point 1 of the German concessions, it is said that all *economic rights in Danzig* would be granted to Poland. This would mean that this concerns also the customs union.

Note here that mention is also made of "the safeguarding of Poland's economic interests in Danzig" and of the "far-reaching settlements of the remaining problems for Poland in the field of economy and communication with the reunion of Danzig with the Reich."

7) The Chancellor states that he offered us a *twenty-five-year pact of nonaggression.*

In my report on my conversation with Ribbentrop of March 21, I only find an offer as to the guarantee of our frontiers. The question of the extension of the nonaggression pact had been brought up in previous conferences by the German side. I fail to remember whether von Ribbentrop, talking about the guarantee on March 21, also referred to the possibility of extending the pact. If so, he did it only very casually.

8) Also in connection with *Slovakia,* von Ribbentrop in the conversation of March 21 only mentioned that it would be possible to discuss it.

The Chancellor, however, speaks about guaranteeing the independence of the Slovakian state by Germany, Poland, and Hungary, which in practice would mean withdrawal of Germany's unilateral position in that country.

The note states Germany's readiness to consider also Poland's interests when securing Slovakia's independence.

9) Both paragraphs regarding our answer as to Danzig and the superhighway are inaccurate and minimize our counteroffer. Here we have to keep to my note handed to Ribbentrop on March 26.

10) The final statement of the Chancellor in the paragraph regarding Poland, of basic importance, is worded quite inexplicably, for an explanation is required to clarify the meaning of "readiness for a new agreement with Poland under the condition that such a *solution would be based on a quite clear obligation equally binding for both parties.*"

Józef Lipski

In Warsaw Lipski for a second time handed Beck his resignation from the post of ambassador to Berlin,[16] this time in writing. In his opinion, after Hitler's renunciation of the nonaggression declaration of 1934, which had been the major achievement of Lipski's efforts, his further stay in Berlin was purposeless. Beck agreed with Lipski's argumentation; he conferred about the resignation with President Mościcki, but finally for the time being did not accept it. In any case, he considered the possibility of recalling Lipski from

[16] *Journal,* p. 451; see also the conversations between Szembek and Lipski (*ibid.,* p. 456), and between Szembek and Beck (*ibid.,* pp. 465 and 478).

Berlin and delegating him to the Embassy in the Vatican (a post which was filled by Kazimierz Papée, previously envoy in Prague), and replacing him in Berlin with Vice-Minister Szembek.

Beck's speech at the Diet on May 5 [17] came as an answer to the German speech and memorandum. Beck stressed in it that the 1934 declaration had been an event of great importance, bringing positive values into the lives of Poland, Germany, and Europe. Therefore, the breach of it by Hitler was not a meaningless act. Danzig was of enormous importance for Poland as an outlet to the Baltic, and Poland would not let itself be cut off from the Baltic. Poland was ready to make further transit concessions through the Pomeranian Corridor. However, Beck did not see any reason "to restrict our sovereignty on our own territory." Poland was ready to conduct further negotiations with the Reich in order to maintain peace, as the Chancellor mentioned, but under the condition that the Reich maintain its "peaceful intentions" and "peaceful methods of procedure." Beck closed his speech with the statement that "peace, like almost everything in this world, has its price, high but definable. We in Poland do not recognize the conception of peace at any price! There is only one thing in the life of men, nations, and states which is beyond price, and that is honor."

On that day the Polish chargé d'affaires in Berlin, Lubomirski, presented to Secretary Weizsäcker a memorandum dated May 5 containing the Polish answer to the German memorandum of April 28.[18] In principle it followed the same line as Beck's speech.

DOCUMENT 143   Lipski to Beck

NO. N/52/175/39   May 24, 1939
                                                           Secret

In respect to the political-military alliance [19] contracted on May 22, 1939, between the Reich and Italy, and with reference to my report of May 22, No. N/52/159/39,[20] I am taking the liberty of communicating as follows:

The government here bestowed on the act of the signing of the alliance an exceptionally festive and demonstrative character for internal and foreign propaganda purposes. The Chancellor of the Reich person-

[17] *Polish White Book*, No. 77.
[18] For the text, see *DGFP*, Series D, Vol. VI, No. 334, or *Polish White Book*, No. 78; see also *DGFP*, Series D, Vol. VI, No. 335.
[19] Pact of Friendship and Alliance between Germany and Italy (Pact of Steel); for the text, see *DGFP*, Series D, Vol. VI, No. 426.
[20] Missing from Lipski's papers.

ally attended the signing ceremony. An exchange of telegrams followed between the King of Italy and the Chancellor. Both foreign ministers were recipients of highest-ranking decorations (von Ribbentrop received the Annunciata). The Reich government prepared a most pompous reception for Ciano. The two foreign ministers broadcast speeches which were afterward repeated to representatives of the press (texts were enclosed with my report No. N/52/159/39 of May 22).

So much about the exterior frame of this historic act, as it is called by the German press.

Analyzing the document itself, first of all it strikes one by its considerable deviation from the type of the hitherto-contracted alliances between the states. It does not, in my opinion, deserve the title of either an offensive or a defensive alliance. It represents a *sui generis* international instrument based upon a common ideology of Germany and Italy. I should say that it is an understanding aimed at coordinating the dynamics of Fascism and Hitlerism, and at creating a common flow of their activities in order militarily to bind Hitlerite Germany with Fascist Italy.

Within a number of circles, both on the German and on the Italian side, the achievement of such an extensive alliance between the two countries evokes anxieties and forebodings. On the German side, the slogan "the strong man is most powerful alone" is popular, and where memories of alliances with the Austro-Hungarian Monarchy, Italy, and Rumania evoke bitter echoes from the period of the world war, elements of former diplomacy and the army in particular have misgivings about such strong links binding the policies of the Reich with Italian policy. Critical voices may be heard in those spheres even today. Nevertheless, close ties with Italy, at a moment when the Reich is faced with the British action of so-called encirclement, are regarded by decisive factors and the Party as a far-reaching success. And they are trying to make the best of it abroad.

With regard to the Italian side, I shall restrict myself to communicating the information I received from Envoy Gawroński. He has contacts with Italian military figures who came to Berlin on the occasion of signing the alliance. In accordance with this information, even General Pariani [21] himself is seriously prejudiced against the signing of a military pact. His anxieties are shared by other army men as well. With the Italians, this attitude might be considered the mentality of the weaker

[21] General Alberto Pariani, Italian chief of the General Staff of the Army.

fearing the stronger, as well as consideration for the unfavorable position of Italy in case of a world war, into which they would be plunged, for example, in the east, by German policy.

The Italian side lays special pressure—when commenting on the agreement—on the fact that the Italian government, through consultations, has the possibility of influencing the German government and of checking its actions.

Ambassador Attolico, with whom I conferred today, interprets Article I of the alliance [22] thus: that consultation, as it is stated *expressis verbis* in this article, concerns not only *common interests* but also *problems dealing with the complex of the European situation,* and as such it must bring about agreement in order to make the alliance valid. To my question as to the concept of "warlike complications" contained in Article III,[23] Signor Attolico explained that this sentence was used because it was more explicit than the previously employed concept of aggression, which is always a subjective one.

With regard to Article VI,[24] the Italian Ambassador only remarked that it is expressed in a general form and concerns friendly countries and those which in the future would like to approach the Axis.

I think that annexes to the agreement might exist which were not given publicity.[25] I received indirectly from the Italians information that there are three annexes, namely, to Article VI, for military collaboration, and allegedly—and this sounds incredible—even a division of interests after the possible war. Many Italians who arrived here commented on the alliance in a very inconsistent way. They even went so far as to state that in the first place the alliance is an act directed against the West, and especially against France, which would be the first to receive

[22] Art. I. The High Contracting Parties will remain in continuous contact with each other in order to reach an understanding on all questions affecting their common interests or the general European situation.

[23] Art. III. If, contrary to the wishes and hopes of the High Contracting Parties it should happen that one of them became involved in warlike complications with another Power or Powers, the other High Contracting Party would immediately come to its assistance as an ally and support it with all its military forces on land, at sea, and in the air.

[24] Art. VI. The two High Contracting Parties are aware of the significance that attaches to their common relations with Powers friendly to them. They are resolved to maintain these relations in the future also and together to shape them in accordance with the common interests which form the bonds between them and these Powers.

[25] There was one secret additional protocol consisting of two paragraphs. *DGFP*, Series D, Vol. VI, pp. 563–64.

the blow. The Italian Ambassador, however, tried to comment on the situation to the effect that there is now a possibility of a vast international understanding which would even comprise disarmament. He did not fail to observe that the main obstacle at present is the Danzig problem.

Also the German press, as I mentioned before, declares that the Western Powers must now make a decision whether they are willing to try for a just peace, acting jointly with the Axis.

Józef Lipski

DOCUMENT 144   Lipski to Beck

NO. N/52/214/39   Berlin, June 5, 1939
Strictly Confidential

Within the last few days I had a long conversation with French Ambassador Coulondre. I report on the more important points:

1) M. Coulondre first of all stated that not only he, but also the British Ambassador, gave the German government to understand unequivocally that in case of German aggression against Danzig their two governments would immediately take a position on the side of Poland. This statement has reached the knowledge of top elements of the Reich.

2) The French Ambassador thinks that the completion of agreements with Russia by England and France would have a decisive impact on the Reich, in restraining it from any aggressive moves. He is informed that General Keitel's and General Brauchitsch's opinion is that, with Russia's entry into the antiaggression front, the chances for the Reich to win the war would be nil. However, without Russia, both of these generals think that the Reich has a chance to win the war.

M. Coulondre, who knows conditions in Russia, is well aware that Russia's entry into the pacts would be less important from the military angle than from the psychological point of view.

I would like to stress that I share M. Coulondre's opinion that Russia's entry into an agreement with England and France would have a decisive meaning in restraining the Reich from aggressive steps.

Józef Lipski

The following handwritten note is among Lipski's papers under the date of
June 27, 1939:

I gave a farewell dinner party for Ambassador Labougle, who had
been transferred to Santiago, and his wife. It was attended by ambassadors and a few envoys. From the German side, only a few unofficial
guests attended.

During my whole stay in Berlin I had the most cordial relations with
M. and Mme Labougle. He was quite an expert on Germany, having
served as secretary of the Argentinian Legation during the last war.

The premises of the Argentinian Legation belonged to Frau von
Stamm, who had considerable estates in Argentina. A few years prior to
the outbreak of the war, Frau von Stamm donated her palace to Argentina. The interior of the building was in the most outrageous bad taste—
a vestige of the worst era.

Among the last Germans I met before the war broke out were the von
Stamms (she was Baroness Wolff), the von Tries, and Frau von Recht-
hofen, who spoke in panic about the threat of war.

The bulk of society, with relations deteriorating, steered clear of our
Embassy.

From the Party, Lutze [26] and his wife behaved properly up to the end.
Among the socialites, the worst behaved was Frau von Dirksen's clan.
Her son kept himself far removed. Besides, his behavior toward his
Polish business partner was simply scandalous.

DOCUMENT 145   Lipski to Beck

NO. N/52/266   Berlin, June 28, 1939
                                          Strictly Confidential

I am taking the liberty of communicating the following observations and
information from the local territory:

1) The ambassador of Argentina, Labougle, who, after many years
spent in Berlin, will be transferred to Santiago de Chile, had an audience
with Hitler at Berchtesgaden a few days ago.

Labougle informed me yesterday that in the course of the conversation the Chancellor also brought up Polish problems.

[26] Victor Lutze, chief of the S.A.

As usual, Hitler's deliberations were lengthy and not very clear. The Ambassador had the impression that the Chancellor expects, as it were, some initiative on our part toward Germany in connection with problems which have caused tension between the two states (Danzig, the superhighway). Besides, the Chancellor presented Poland as the aggressive side, referring to Poland's claim to East Prussia, etc. He even had knowledge of such details as the speech delivered by a certain Polish general who, according to the German press, promoted the reunion of Opole-Silesia and East Prussia with Poland.[27] According to the Ambassador's relation, in his conversation with him Hitler did not consider Poland and England as the No. 1 foes but directed the brunt of his attack against President Roosevelt. As could be noted, the Chancellor was obviously hurt by the fact that Roosevelt ignored his speech of April 28. He also blamed the United States for opposing economic negotiations between the Reich and the states of South America.

The Chancellor's reaction to the Ambassador's suggestion that it is indispensable to restore confidence in international relations was positive.

When Mr. Labougle and I analyzed the Chancellor's deliberations more closely, he remarked that he is not in a position to conceive clearly how the Chancellor envisages the further development of events and what his goal seems to be. The tone of his words was rather appeasing.

The fact that Hitler was especially aggressive toward the United States might easily be explained if we bear in mind that he was talking with a representative of South America.

In connection with the fact that Hitler presented Poland as a state with aggressive intentions toward the German Reich, I would like to refer to my previous reports. I called attention in these reports to the fact that the German side is very eager to catch even the slightest hints from the speeches of unions and Polish organizations and political parties which advocate reunion of East Prussia and Opole-Silesia with Poland, for this provides the Germans with an excellent weapon for interior action which strives to unite the German community in the face of the encirclement policy conducted under the leadership of England. That is why the argument of our aggressive tendencies is being exploited by German propaganda abroad also, especially for Anglo-Saxon states. Even today, the latest resolutions of the National Party, claiming East Prussia and the Oder frontier, are printed by the *Völkischer Beobachter*

[27] *DGFP,* Series D, VI, 819.

with the annotation that British opinion has not been informed about these Polish tendencies.

2) I am receiving information from various sources about differences of opinion to be detected among eminent leading local personalities with regard to the international situation.

However, in my opinion no special attention should be paid to these possible discords, for as long as Hitler is in command he decides all basic problems of the state.

Nevertheless, it is worth while noting some symptoms of personal animosity or of rapprochement among certain persons on the basis of kindred ideas. In Goebbels' offices some kind of rivalry exists in the field of foreign propaganda.

I know that Ribbentrop is not satisfied with Goebbels' last speeches. He even expressed his feelings in the presence of several members of the diplomatic corps.

I heard, however, from a reliable source that Goebbels got his instructions directly from the Chancellor, evidently behind the Foreign Minister's back, whose feelings thus were hurt.

Göring, as he allegedly disclosed to one of the diplomats, has ceased to act in international politics. He stands now on the margin of these affairs, unless they directly concern his competence (the four-year plan, the air force).

Nevertheless, symptoms exist that this certain eclipse of his is only temporary. I heard that of late such personalities as Lutze, chief of the S.A., Himmler, and military personages such as General von Brauchitsch are gravitating toward him.

3) Recently a number of rumors reached me that the German side is preparing certain moves concerning Polish-German relations for August.

Such information was communicated by the Consulate General at Leipzig in its report of June 23, No. N/3/a/55/39.

The French Ambassador also has some information pointing to certain preparations for August. M. Coulondre suggests in this connection that German tactics with regard to Danzig might strive to create on the territory of the Free City a military force, camouflaged for the time being, out of elements immigrating from the Reich. Then would come the proclamation of reunion with the Reich in such a way as to shift over to Poland—in the eyes of public opinion—the responsibility for possible reaction to such a step taken by Danzig.

On this occasion he suggested that it might perhaps be advisable for the governments of Poland, France, and England to get together in advance, and to warn the German government that a violation of the statute of the Free City is subject to the Polish-French-British guarantee.

I am taking the liberty, while reporting on the above suggestions of M. Coulondre, of calling your attention to the fact that on our part a restriction of this sort has already been lodged with the government of the Reich. It was contained in your declaration to Ambassador von Moltke on March 29, 1939.[28] I do not know whether the governments of France and England are aware of this. I think it could possibly serve as a basis for action of these governments in Berlin.

Józef Lipski

DOCUMENT 146   Lipski to Beck

NO. N/297/II/151/39   Berlin, July 27, 1939
                                   Strictly Confidential
                                     Urgent

Re: Tactics of German authorities
     relation to Polish minorities

Referring to previous reports on the same subject, and particularly to report No. N/303/23 of July 11,[29] I would like to give you a general picture of the situation in which the Polish minorities find themselves in Germany, in connection with tactics recently applied by the German authorities.

I. Press Action Rendered Impossible

In spite of the difficult and ever-worsening situation of the Polish minorities due to numerous acts of oppression and terror at present, this minority has ever-fewer possibilities of presenting its case in the press. This has been achieved by German police authorities in the following way:

1) Secret state police, in spite of the fact that preventive censorship does not exist in Germany, requested the editors of three daily Polish

[28] *Ibid.*, No. 118.
[29] Missing from Lipski's papers.

papers in Germany, namely, the editors of *Nowiny, Naród,* and *Gazeta Olsztyńska* (two remaining papers, *Dziennik Berliński* and *Głos Pogranicza,* are printed jointly with those mentioned above, as reprints), to present to police headquarters for approval the first-edition copy of each issue of these dailies. Upon presentation of the copy for approval, the editors are obliged to continue the printing of the issue (allegedly in order to avoid delays in publication), but they can distribute the papers only after the police grant their approval. Thus, in case the distribution of the paper is prohibited, the editors' offices are not only exposed to losses on the already printed issues but, owing to the lateness of the date, they cannot repeat the issues.

Prohibition of distribution has already been ordered several times in the case of each of the above-mentioned daily papers. Usually they confiscate the whole issue, without stating a reason or citing the questioned articles. Thus the editors are even unable to repeat the issue with the omission of certain articles, while for propaganda reasons the effect of white censorship patches would serve the cause well.

The editor of *Naród* was even refused the right to print in following editions a notice about the confiscation; other editors cannot disclose the reasons for the confiscation of the paper.

Although the Gestapo does not disclose the reasons for the confiscation, nevertheless from the hitherto fairly numerous cases it can be observed that:

a) For *Naród* those issues are confiscated with any mention of terror against Polish nationalism, of unfavorable acts of authorities, or of protests lodged by the Union of Poles. The Gestapo explicitly requested the editor of *Naród* not to insert notices about the oppression of Poles.

b) For the *Gazeta Olsztyńska* issues are confiscated which contain news subject to Gestapo restrictions.

c) Confiscations of *Nowiny,* according to the editor, are made in the following way: the Gestapo confiscates issues containing news which evokes the Gestapo's disapproval. Besides, the Gestapo withholds permission for distribution until it is informed that a corresponding issue of *Kattowitzer Zeitung* was not confiscated. If it was confiscated, *Nowiny* is confiscated regardless of its contents.

As a result, in a part of the Polish press, among others, in *Dziennik Berliński,* the reader does not find either notices about oppression of the Polish population or white patches, and cannot orient himself as to the real condition of the Polish minority. As the press in Poland and the Western press drew their information on the fate of Poles in Germany from the Polish press in Germany, mainly from *Dziennik Berliński,* news about oppression of the Polish population in Germany disappeared from the press in Poland and from the press in the West. In contrast to this, news about oppression of the German population in Poland is multiplying in the Western press. This is not devoid of a certain political meaning.

A further fact should also be noted: in recent days the editors of *Nowiny* and *Głos Pogranicza* were notified by the paper producers' union that the union is not interested in supplying paper for the dailies of the Polish press and is discontinuing the supply. As there is an allocation of paper to the daily newspapers in the Reich, and there are no other sources from which to acquire paper, and as the editors of the journals in question evaluate that their stock of paper will last for two weeks, we have to envisage the possibility of the suspension of publication of these papers.

II. *Freezing of Organization Life*

In the last week the Gestapo in Westphalia has been conducting intensified action against Polish organizational life, on which report No. N/197/II/147, dated July 18, completed by telegram,[30] was sent by the Embassy.

According to news recently received, the fourteen persons arrested in the first days have all been released after interrogation, while there is no further information about a number of other people arrested in the following days of interrogation.

Without going into the details here of the many house searches, police interrogations, and prohibitions to hold meetings, even in private apartments, I am concentrating only on the essential things.

1) All persons interrogated and examined were prohibited to communicate to anyone the fact and the contents of the political interrogation.

2) All these people were forbidden to leave their permanent addresses and communicate with their organizations.

Thus, the Westphalian District of Unions of Poles is even deprived of legal means of informing its headquarters about what happened, and

---

[30] Missing from Lipski's papers.

conversely the headquarters of the Union of Poles cannot legally obtain any information concerning the District, which renders any kind of intervention impossible.

It is also worth mentioning that, after the Gestapo released the offices of the Westphalian District of the Union of Poles, clerks were allowed to remain on the premises of the office but were prohibited from communicating with other organization centers.

In case the method adopted by the Gestapo in Westphalia is extended to other regions, a total paralysis and freezing of organizational activities of the Union of Poles will take place. The perfidy of the method consists in the fact that the organization remains in existence, and no action is apparently taken either against the organization or its members, but the organization is dead.

III. Threat to the Existence of Schools

School authorities conducted detailed investigations of three schools in Warmia and six in the borderland, exposing in all cases a number of shortcomings of a constructional and hygienic nature. As a result of the survey, all investigated schools plus eleven schools in the borderland, or twenty schools in all, are threatened with being closed. At the same time, instructions were issued to publicize this in the press. As far as we can judge, German authorities thus want to enforce the reopening of three German schools allegedly closed recently in Poland (at Gniezno, Międzychód, and Wolsztyn). During the survey, the German commission explicitly declared that the threat of closing Polish schools corresponds to the closing of German schools.

Let us stress here that for the closing of three German schools the reaction was to threaten the closing of twenty Polish schools, that is, 40 percent of the number of Polish schools in Germany.

From the above remarks it is evident that the situation exists where the total liquidation of Polish organizational life in Germany might take place without any propaganda effect to our advantage, while in contrast to this each attempt to reduce the German state of possessions in Poland meets with unfavorable comments in the Western press.

Under these circumstances, I am taking the liberty of formulating certain general motions with regard to informing public opinion on the one hand, and on the other hand in respect to the very *meritum* of the minority problems.

I. Informing Public Opinion

In view of certain information about the German attack on the minority sector, expected relatively soon, it seems to me that there arises the necessity of building an information apparatus that would enable us not just to fill the lack which lately occurred in informing Western opinion about the actual situation of Polish minorities but also to refute the possible offensive of German propaganda. The following points can be delineated here:

1) The Ministry is always informed about any hostile acts against Polish nationals through detailed statements of all events forwarded periodically to Section E. II.[31]

2) Bearing in mind the confidential character of this material, as well as consequences which might threaten the interested organizations and persons belonging to the minority at the hands of the German authorities in case this material is published, not all of it may be printed in the press. However, some of this material could be published in the local press in Poland as well as in the Western press, under the condition that press releases are given in the following form: "We learn from refugees recently arrived from German territory that . . ." Obviously, only in this manner could facts generally known and obvious to anyone in the given locality appear in print, such, for instance, as the breaking of windowpanes, assaults, attacks on schools, liquidation of associations or meetings, extradition, arrests, expropriations, demonstrations, etc., while more confidential information could not be used.

3) It would seem advisable to exploit with precision in the local press in Poland and the West all information still appearing in the Polish press in Germany, especially in *Nowiny* and *Gazeta Olsztyńska*.

4) For lack of more profuse and printable material of a concrete nature, even now the preparation of a series of basic articles from various fields of life of Polish minorities in Germany should begin, with the aim of using them at the proper moment. I am taking the liberty of suggesting that synthetically prepared material recently supplied by particular consulates to Section E. II of the Ministry might be of considerable assistance.

5) I recently approached Editor K. Smogorzewski with regard to several such general articles, in order to dispatch them to our embassies

[31] Section of Poles Abroad of the Consular Department of the Ministry of Foreign Affairs.

in London and Paris. They would be published (without the signature of the author) in the Western press.

6) It would also serve a purpose, in my opinion, to hold off insertion in the Polish press of any notices about action taken by the Administration, or any other acts unfavorable for German minorities in Poland if they do not directly concern cases of acts against the state, for such comments are being reprinted by the German and foreign press. Obviously, it would also be advisable to reduce press comments about the ill-treatment of German minorities in Poland in the press of that minority.

II. Tactics on the Minority Sector

Abstaining from forming concrete conclusions in this field because of the variety of aspects of the matter as such, as well as a lack of precise information as to the whole complex and details of action conducted in relation to German minorities in Poland by the Ministry of the Interior (the only information is what I find daily in the German press), I would just like to state clearly the necessity of a basic definition of our tactics in the field of minorities as early as possible, for the basic question arises whether, in the face of new acts of oppression by the German side in relation to the Polish population and the impossibility of establishing whether they occur on German initiative or as a reaction to the treatment of German minorities in Poland, we have further to tolerate German organizational life, or to resort to fighting more energetically against this minority, using the same methods which are at the disposal of the German side. However, in the event of applying repressions we should bear in mind the standards resulting from the strict numerical ratio between the two minorities. So, for instance, for each Polish school closed in Germany, to liquidate eight German schools in Poland (the numerical ratio of the number of schools, 50:400) and define in detail methods of action. It is difficult, of course, to say now whether the choice of such a method would result in the final liquidation of organizational life of both minorities, or rather whether it would restrain the German side from further oppressing the Polish minority.

Józef Lipski

The Polish-German Crisis [1]
March—April, 1939

ON MARCH 29, 1939, President of the Senate Greiser and Dr. Boettcher [2] called on Weizsäcker to obtain information of Polish-German conversations with regard to Danzig. They were informed of the course of discussions held on March 21 and 26, 1939, between the Reich Foreign Minister and the Ambassador of Poland in Berlin. [3]

Greiser came out with a question as to what the further action of Danzig toward Poland should be, to which the Secretary of State cautiously replied that, while the situation should not be made easy for the Polish government, on the other hand Poland should not be provoked. Weizsäcker was of the opinion that it might be possible to push Poland onto the track of a policy which would weaken it internally (*Zermürbungspolitik*). This might render the Polish government more conciliatory when settling a number of German demands, one of which was Danzig. Danzig should continue to apply the same tactics as during the previous weeks and months.

To Greiser's question as to how he should behave toward the high commissioner of the League of Nations, Burckhardt, Weizsäcker thought that Burckhardt's return to Danzig was for the time being undesirable, since it might be feared that the Polish Commissioner-General would abuse Burckhardt's authority for the interests of Poland and of the Committee of Three. Weizsäcker also dissuaded Greiser from appearing before the Committee of Three in London if an invitation were extended to him.

---

[1] Printed in *Bellona* (London), 1950, No. 1, under the general title "New Premises on the Outbreak of the Polish-German War in 1939."

[2] Victor Boettcher, Staatsrat, Director of the Department of Foreign Affairs of the Danzig Senate. For the memorandum of von Weizsäcker, see *DGFP*, Series D, Vol. VI, No. 124.

[3] *Ibid.*, Nos. 61 and 101, and *Polish White Book*, Nos. 61 and 63.

On the same day (March 29, 1939), the Hungarian Envoy in Berlin, referring to his last audience with Hitler, questioned Weizsäcker about the result of Polish-German conversations with regard to Danzig.[4] He hinted that Hungary's foreign minister, Csáky, would be ready to use his influence in Warsaw to bring about a compromise with Germany. Weizsäcker rejected this idea as futile. During the discussion Weizsäcker commented on his point of view, explaining that since his Austrian days Hitler had remained prejudiced against all that was Hungarian, and especially against the Hungarian upper classes; therefore it was out of the question that Count Csáky could serve as mediator.[5]

A few days later, on April 5, after England's guarantee for Poland and while Beck was still in London, Weizsäcker sent instructions for Moltke in Warsaw.[6] I quote them in extenso, since they are a key to the further tactics of Germany:

"Lipski will probably be received here again before Easter. At this interview he will be told the following with reference to his last conversation with the Foreign Minister.

"Our offer to Poland will not be repeated. The Polish government had apparently not fully understood the significance of this offer. We could not help that. The future would show whether Poland had been well advised. The counterproposal put forward by Lipski had, as was known, already been rejected by the Foreign Minister as a basis for negotiations.

"End of the statement to Lipski.

"Please do not enter into any further material discussions on the German offer and the Polish counteroffer. We must prevent Poland from throwing the ball back to us and then maneuvering us into the position of appearing to have let a Polish offer go unheeded. Other principal missions have likewise been instructed not to enter into serious discussions on the Polish question but rather to evade the subject calmly and not to give any indication of further German intentions."

These instructions were written two days after Hitler signed German military dispositions against Poland on April 3, 1939.[7] In the light of

---

[4] DGFP, Series D, Vol. VI, No. 123.
[5] Depositions made by Weizsäcker on June 8, 1948.
[6] DGFP, Series D, Vol. VI, No. 159.
[7] The directive of April 3, 1939, was signed by Keitel. Enclosure II contained "Operation White" directed against Poland (ibid., No. 149). Hitler signed a final directive dealing with operations against Poland and the occupation of Danzig on April 11 (ibid., No. 185).

these instructions, it becomes clear to us why Moltke evaded seeing Beck upon his return from London and left Warsaw for a long time.

On the next day, April 6, 1939, on Weizsäcker's invitation, I had a conversation with him.[8] This conversation was overshadowed by the British-Polish guarantee. During the Nuremberg trial it was established that at that very moment the German propaganda thesis of the "blank check" allegedly issued by Great Britain to Poland was born.

According to Weizsäcker's depositions, Ribbentrop kept hoping to the end that Great Britain would not execute its guarantee toward Poland. Hitler shared his Minister's expectation. In this connection, it is worth while to recall telegraphic instructions Lord Halifax sent to Ambassador Henderson in Berlin on May 13, 1939, which were inserted into the documents of the trial. The contents of this telegram, a copy of which was forwarded for the attention of the British ambassador in Rome, fell into the hands of the Italians, who happened to know the English code. At that time Mussolini was anxious to hold Hitler back from war action. He therefore instructed Count Ciano to communicate the text of the telegram to the German ambassador in Rome, Herr von Mackensen. The instructions, in very firm terms, acknowledged to the full extent the obligations of the government of Great Britain toward Poland in case of war, confirming that the guarantee also covered Danzig.[9]

The Polish-German declaration of January 26, 1934, put an end for a number of years to German open propaganda in France and England against the western frontiers of Poland. This created a rather awkward situation for the Auswärtiges Amt when in the spring of 1939 the revisionist campaign had to be launched again. It was necessary to brush up long-forgotten French and English utterances which had been gathering dust in the files. In the instructions of May 10, 1939, to German embassies in Paris and London, Weizsäcker recommended compiling declarations of eminent French and British personalities who at one time had made statements against resolutions of the Versailles Treaty with regard to Danzig and the Corridor.[10] Such statements, commented the instructions, might be found in the archives of the Locarno period as well as in the aftermath of Locarno.

[8] *Polish White Book*, No. 70 (also *DGFP*, Series D, Vol. VI, No. 169).
[9] *DGFP*, Series D, Vol. VI, No. 377.
[10] "Trials of War Criminals," mimeographed transcript, No. N.G. 2019 (Lipski's papers, File 22).

In his instructions dated July 4, 1939, addressed to a number of embassies and legations, Weizsäcker informed about the situation in Poland to be used in conversations.[11] The purpose of these instructions was to show that two contradictory tendencies—chauvinist and moderate—were in conflict in Poland. The chauvinist group was composed of various private societies, party organizations, clerks of local administration, and primarily of the military element. This group instigated anti-German demonstrations, dreaming of annexing East Prussia and waging a battle for Berlin. Minister Beck was numbered among the moderate group—"for we had reason to believe that Minister Beck, though without a definite program, was yet seeking a settlement with Germany."

A memorandum of July 4, 1939, about the stay of the Ministry counselor, Altenburg, in Danzig, is a good illustration of German propaganda methods with regard to the Free City.[12]

A number of other documents originating from the Auswärtiges Amt deal with the technicalities of preparation of the diplomatic side in case of war. Most of them are signed by Weizsäcker or Woermann.

Among the latter's files, under the date of August 26, 1939, there is his report on a conversation with the Polish Ambassador, who lodged a protest with regard to serious frontier incidents (two Polish notes), as well as concerning the break in telephone communication of the Polish Embassy in Berlin with Poland, and of the Polish Embassy with Polish consulates on the territory of the Reich.[13]

The intensity of German incidents on August 25, 1939, was connected with Hitler's originally fixed date of August 26, 1939, at dawn for the attack on Poland.

[11] *Ibid.*, No. N.G. 2323; see also *DGFP*, Series D, Vol. VI, No. 592, note 7.
[12] "Trials of War Criminals," mimeographed transcript, No. N.G. 2025.
[13] *DGFP*, Series D, Vol. VII, No. 331.

Final Endeavors
August, 1939

AMBASSADOR LIPSKI gave a detailed relation (see pages 574–610) of events of the last month prior to the outbreak of the war. We are limiting ourselves here to the exposition of documents pertaining to this period that have been preserved in Lipski's papers. They do not cover this period fully. During that tragic month, the tempo of work at the Polish Embassy in Berlin and at the Ministry of Foreign Affairs in Warsaw was so feverish that quite a number of documents might easily have been mislaid both in Berlin and in Warsaw. Nevertheless, the documents presented below, together with Lipski's description referred to above, give a full and correct illustration of the tension in Polish-German relations on the eve of war, as seen from the post of the Polish Ambassador in Berlin.

The following is Lipski's handwritten note, dated August 9, 1939.

On August 8, I was in Warsaw for conversations with Minister Beck. I was received on the same day by Marshal Śmigły-Rydz, who inquired about the situation in Germany.

My statements took the following trend:

1) German armaments and preparations for war are in full swing.

2) It is difficult to have an exact orientation at present as to the precise German plan. From the German point of view, upon defeating Poland, Germany would come upon the USSR in the east while it was at war with the Allies in the west. Under these circumstances the war with Poland would not bring them a solution—element of a local contest.

3) We should be prepared for any eventuality.

I then left with Beck for Nałęczów, where I spent a day and a night. One of the American correspondents called on Beck while I was there. On the evening of August 9 we were informed about Weizsäcker's declaration handed, in my absence, to Lubomirski.[1]

---

[1] The declaration dealt with the problem of Polish customs inspectors in Danzig. Weizsäcker termed the Polish demands an "ultimatum," remarking that, with the Polish side threatening reprisals, Polish-German relations would suffer. For the text of the declaration, see *DGFP*, Series D, Vol. VII, No. 5.

Beck got the report and said: "Now it begins." He decided to return to Warsaw in the early morning hours.

At the Ministry of Foreign Affairs I met Arciszewski, with whom I made an appointment for lunch. Beck went to Śmigły-Rydz.

At lunch Arciszewski confided to me his anxiety that Beck might answer too sharply. I was quite in accord with this opinion and we agreed that we would try to use our influence in rendering the form of the declaration less adamant, so it would outwardly show the furthest-reaching good will on our part with regard to Danzig, where we met with sabotage and the undermining of our rights. We exposed our point of view to Beck. However, he obstinately kept to his own concept and decided that Arciszewski would present the declaration in accordance with the text edited by him.

DOCUMENT 147   Lubomirski to the Ministry of Foreign Affairs

Berlin, August 10, 1939
Secret

On August 8 the British ambassador, Henderson, invited me for a talk. He opened the conversation by expressing his concern over the development of the situation in Danzig. From his approach to this question I got the impression that conversations he had had of late with Secretary of State Weizsäcker, as well as with other Germans, were not without an impact on his judgment. It seemed to me that he accepted German information with a certain dose of faith; I was confirmed in this impression by a certain detail: namely, when I communicated to him a detailed genesis of our last note addressed to the Danzig Senate, Henderson took from his desk the manuscript of a report he had apparently prepared according to these conversations, and he made some alterations in it.

Henderson next developed his point of view as follows:

From information in his possession, he knows that Chancellor Hitler has not yet taken any decision on how to settle the problem of Danzig. He might use force to achieve a solution, or proceed by peaceful means. Radical German elements, among whom Forster and Zarsky [2] should be

[2] Wilhelm Zarsky, editor of *Der Danziger Vorposten*.

numbered, who right now are in Berchtesgaden for consultation with the Chancellor, are pushing the Chancellor to act on impulse. They represent the matter in such a way as to make it appear that Poland has aggressive tendencies toward Danzig. Under such circumstances, it would be wise to abstain from any action which would provide grist for the radicals' mill, and possibly accelerate Hitler's decision, for Henderson thinks that everything possible should be done to make the crisis last until late into the autumn, or even until spring, when the situation will be quite different. In following this idea, Henderson reached the conclusion that it might be desirable to establish a certain diplomatic contact, purely informative, between the Polish Ambassador in Berlin and Secretary of State von Weizsäcker. At present Weizsäcker is replacing Ribbentrop. Experience shows that contact with Ribbentrop is not very essential, for Ribbentrop relates to the Chancellor his conversations with diplomatic representatives from memory only, and not too precisely. On the other hand, Weizsäcker is an experienced official, and each conversation with him, in the form of an exact note, is being forwarded to the Chancellor. Here Henderson made the reservation that it is not his intention to advise concrete talks with Weizsäcker about Danzig. He only thinks that through normal diplomatic contact the question could be clarified and thus the tendentious versions presented to Hitler by his entourage could be counteracted. As an example of tendentious informing of the Chancellor by his collaborators, Henderson cited an incident which took place after the occupation of Prague. Upon his arrival in Prague, the Chancellor expressed his wish to pay a hospital visit to injured members of the German minority about whom the German press had reported at length. The Chancellor's entourage faced quite a problem, since such victims did not exist at all. Finally, Hitler received a delegation of "wounded Germans" whose heads were bandaged *ad hoc*.

To my remark that the German side shows evident ill-will by provoking difficulties in Danzig, obviously striving to increase tension by creating incidents and by conducting a falsification campaign in the press, which accuses the Polish side of aggressive tendencies while it strives for conquests, Henderson remarked that German behavior toward England is far from correct also, but in his opinion the duty of a diplomatic representative is to maintain contact with official factors of the government of the state to which he is accredited. That is why, if the situation does not deteriorate basically, he intends to accept, even this year, an invitation to take part in the Congress of the Party at Nuremberg. He explained the German activity which strives to intensify tension by saying that the Chancellor possibly figures that with strong tension it will be easier for him to settle problems.

St. Lubomirski.

DOCUMENT 148   Invitation to Ambassador Lipski to Attend a Hunting Party

Chief-Hunting-Master Scherping   Berlin, August 11, 1939

H. Excellency
Mr. Ambassador Lipski

Berlin, W. 35
Kurfürstenstrasse 135

Your Excellency,

On behalf of General Field Marshal Göring, hunting master of the Reich, I take the liberty of inviting Your Excellency for hunting in the state forests.

As I perceive from my list, Your Excellency has already killed red deer, elk, and chamois in the German preserves, but no muffle-ram; I would like to suggest to Your Excellency hunting this year for muffle-ram.

The best time to hunt a muffle-ram is October or November, since the ram is in full hair then. Of course, it can also be killed at an earlier date merely as a trophy.

If Your Excellency would wish for a good stag to deerstalk at rutting season, I would take the liberty to ask for a reply, and then I would immediately send information with regard to preserve and time to Your Excellency.

With the assurance of my deepest respect and with *Weidmannsheil* [a hunter's greeting], I am, Your Excellency, very sincerely

Scherping

DOCUMENT 149   Lipski to Beck

NO. W/52/440   Berlin, August 15, 1939

Yesterday I had a visit from the British Ambassador, who came to share with me his opinions on the political situation.

He remarked first of all that the declaration of the German government of August 9 with regard to Danzig [3] and the reply of the Polish government dated August 10 [4] had resulted in a considerable deterioration in the situation. The Chancellor felt particularly hurt by the last paragraph of the Polish declaration. When Ciano raised the Danzig problem in Salzburg,[5] the German side presented to him the exchange of the declarations in question, stressing that the honor of Germany, as well as that of the Axis, was at stake. Thus the Italian side had to abandon its moderator's mission in the case of Danzig.

Besides, the argument of Germany's honor made its appearance in the columns of the German press after the conference of Salzburg.

Repeating this version—probably heard from the German side—Ambassador Henderson told me that he is awaiting further explanations on the results of Italian-German conversations from his colleague in Rome.

I may add that I did not fail to clarify to Henderson the very essence of the German declaration and to explain more precisely our reply.

In his further deliberations the British Ambassador gave way to his concern that, if the hitherto absolutely negative line of policy toward Germany is maintained, we will be entangled in a war in a short time. In his opinion, Hitler would not knuckle down even if faced by a coalition reinforced by Russia. Since March the parties have not been on speaking terms, while the situation is becoming ever more complicated and the conflict is deepening.

London, the Ambassador told me, took the stand that we should abstain from any conversations with the Reich. Besides, the internal situation in England is such that Chamberlain could do nothing for peace at present, and neither could Mussolini. The Ambassador thinks

---

[3] *DGFP,* Series D, Vol. VII, No. 5.

[4] *Polish White Book,* No. 86.

[5] Ciano conversed with Ribbentrop in Salzburg on August 11, and with Hitler in Obersalzberg on August 12 and 13 (*DGFP,* Series D, Vol. VII, Nos. 43 and 47; see also Editor's Note, p. 35).

that, as matters stand now, only France or Poland could take a step toward Germany to save peace.

Sir Nevile thinks that there is just time until the Congress in Nuremberg; then, if Hitler takes a position in his speech, it will be too late.

To quote a characteristic feature of Henderson's deliberations, here is what he said: if after seven months of war it will be necessary to strive for peace, it is better to find a peaceful solution now.

Henderson has the idea, for example, that Poland should declare to the German side that it considers it essential to calm the minds on the German and Polish side first, which would make it possible to demobilize troops in Poland and Germany, and only afterward (without spelling out the time limits) to open conversations to find a solution for Danzig.

In Henderson's opinion, such a declaration would strengthen considerably Poland's position. In accordance with his words, German government circles reduce the Polish-German strife to Danzig only, stressing that Hitler has already given up the Corridor question. Besides, the French Ambassador confirmed to me that Welczek recently made a similar statement to Bonnet.

I cited to the two ambassadors totally contradictory reports from the German press, with recent aspirations even for Silesia. Finally Henderson repeated what he previously said to Counselor Lubomirski: that Secretary of State Weizsäcker told him that he has no contact whatsoever with me.

I replied to the Ambassador that in this case it is the German side that is making demands. I am always at the disposal of the German government, if it has anything to communicate to me, while on my part the line of the Polish government is strictly defined.

Recapitulating, I may observe that I noticed that the British Ambassador was visibly upset by the prospect of an armed conflict. I am sure that he will act in London to find some solution to the situation.

For my part I told him that what is causing most concern in international relations is the complete lack of confidence in Hitler's government, as a result of the bitter experiences of the past. I added that, in my opinion, persuasion is hardly a weapon to be used with Germany.

Besides, of course, I expressed my best intentions to do everything possible to avoid the catastrophe of war.

Although Henderson did not say so, from what he said to Lubomirski it was clear that he is anxious first of all to secure more time.

Coulondre, who was quite calm and composed, told me yesterday more or less the same things.

Józef Lipski

DOCUMENT 150   Lipski to Beck

NO. N/52/449/39   Berlin, August 17, 1939

Today, in the afternoon hours, I had the visit first of the British Ambassador and then of the French Ambassador.

The two ambassadors informed me about conversations they had on August 15 with Secretary of State von Weizsäcker.[6]

Sir Nevile Henderson read to me a long report on his conversation forwarded to Lord Halifax,[7] of which I shall try to give a general outline.

Herr von Weizsäcker, who, as the Ambassador thinks, is working to prevent war, stated that while in his last conversation with the British Ambassador on August 4 he evaluated the situation rather calmly, considering it to be better than it had been at the same time last year as far as peace was concerned, it has since become very serious. Weizsäcker blames this

1) on the Polish ultimatum to Danzig regarding customs inspectors;

2) on the declaration of the Polish government dated August 10 in reply to the German declaration of August 9 (allegedly, especially the last passage of our reply caused a sharp reaction from the Chancellor); and, finally,

3) on the alleged growing violence perpetrated against the German population in Poland. According to the Secretary of State's words, the situation, beyond any measure, is reaching crisis proportions.

The British Ambassador replied to these statements by (1) pointing to the illegal militarization of Danzig, (2) stressing that the Polish government, in the last passage of its declaration dated August 10, only stated that it would consider as an act of aggression any possible intervention of the German government to the detriment of *rights and interests of Poland under the treaty,* and (3) stating that the Polish

[6] *Ibid.,* Nos. 64 and 66.
[7] *British Blue Book,* No. 48.

Ambassador, for his part, had informed him of persecutions of Polish minorities in Germany.

Herr von Weizsäcker further stated that Poland is conducting a suicidal policy, that Russian assistance for Poland in case of war would be of minor value, and that in case of a conflict Germany would enter into an agreement with Russia to the detriment of Poland. Von Weizsäcker observed that he cannot conceive how England can guarantee the irresponsible action of Poland, and expressed the opinion that such a guarantee would not be valid in case Poland caused the conflict.

Sir Nevile observed that Poland is conducting a prudent policy and that each of its steps of a basic character is agreed upon with the British government.

Weizsäcker interrupted, saying that the ultimatum for the Free City of Danzig regarding customs inspectors, as well as the reply to the German declaration of August 9, had not been agreed upon with the British side.

Sir Nevile firmly stated that England would come to Poland's assistance in case of German aggression. With regard to the British guarantee for Poland on the matter of Danzig, he referred to Lord Halifax's declaration.

Further statements of the Ambassador on the British guarantee for Poland, repeated in the course of this long conversation, were quite explicit and followed the line of our policy.

At a certain point of the report the Ambassador mentioned that he felt that Weizsäcker was making very light of the specific gravity of British military action.

Talking about the prevailing impasse, Weizsäcker remarked that under the present circumstances any step by the German side in order to reduce tension with Poland has become impossible. The Secretary of State also stated that Minister Beck's speech of May rendered difficult the resumption of conversations. Namely, it stated that such conversations could only proceed upon the principles defined in this speech, thus creating a prestige obstacle for Germany.

In conclusion I note that von Weizsäcker was trying to present us as an irresponsible partner; he added that there are only a few men in Poland who have a reasonable concept of the situation, but their position is of no importance.

Henderson got the impression from this conversation that a total impasse now prevails in Polish-German relations, and if the situation continues it will threaten to end in an armed conflict. He fears that, if events are allowed to take their course, then either at Tannenberg or at Nuremberg [8] the Chancellor might go so far that conflict will be inevitable. Henderson's thesis is that the Chancellor is misinformed by his entourage; they do not inform him about Polish arguments, but rather stir him up. That is why Henderson returned to his previous idea of my meeting with Göring and telling him things he might bring to the knowledge of the Chancellor. I recall that in his previous conversation with me (report No. N/52/440/39 dated August 15) Henderson proposed a formula in which the two partners should return to the *status quo* on Danzig of March, and do their best to appease public opinion in both countries. Only then could conversations be started. I did not conceal from Henderson that with the present German approach such propositions could hardly achieve a positive result. I cited news from the German press, which for the past two days has categorically urged the reunion of Danzig and even of the Corridor with the Reich. Henderson thinks that this is rather an answer to our claims to East Prussia. Looking for a way to avoid war, he thinks that the invitation to the stag hunt in the autumn sent to him by Göring through Scherping, as well as to me, could serve as an occasion to meet the General Field Marshal.

Next I had a visit from French Ambassador Coulondre. Referring to his conversation with Weizsäcker, he called special attention to the fact that the Secretary of State posed the same question to Henderson and to him: namely, would France come to the assistance of Poland in case Poland provoked military action by Germany? [9]

M. Coulondre told me that, reading Weizsäcker's camouflaged thoughts, he declared in an absolutely emphatic way, leaving no room for the slightest doubt, that France would always stand at Poland's side. He stressed that in March French public opinion felt threatened at the very heart of freedom. As a result, the alliance with Poland had been reinforced. M. Coulondre placed this alliance on the level of the *indissoluble common security of France and Poland.*

M. Coulondre was under the impression that this categorical declaration of his had not been understood by Weizsäcker but—since the Secretary of State was striving to hamper whatever unpredictable step might be contemplated by the top German factors—he accepted the declara-

---

[8] Celebrations at Tannenberg were to take place on August 27, but were called off earlier. The annual congress of the National Socialist Party was to be held at Nuremberg on September 2–11, but did not take place because of the war.

[9] *Livre jaune,* No. 194.

tion rather as an argument to be presented to those authorities. Today M. Coulondre already had certain confirmation that his declaration had been circulated further. M. Coulondre is of the opinion, which I share wholeheartedly, that only a determined stand taken by England, France, and Poland can save the peace. Only this can stop Hitler's risky policy. He fears just such reticence as in 1914 paved the way for the outbreak of the war. Even today, in certain German circles the supposition prevails that England would soften in the last moment. The French Ambassador does not believe this; nevertheless, he thinks that such rumors should be denied by the British side.

In connection with this, I remark that I told Henderson that such opinions were repeated to me. They resulted from misinterpretation of certain British probing of the German position. I was referring here to news supplied by an informant of Consul General Chiczewski with regard to this subject (Chiczewski's report No. 3/N/a/62/39 of August 12, 1939).[10]

Henderson was positive here, stating that he never met with a shadow of a doubt on the part of competent German factors as to England's determination to fulfill its obligations toward its allies.

Returning to Coulondre's conversation with the Secretary of State, I stress that Weizsäcker shared the Ambassador's opinion that the war would only turn to the advantage of Trotsky, as Coulondre put it.[11]

I am taking the liberty of recalling to you that last year during the Czech crisis Weizsäcker was one of the German diplomats who did everything possible to avoid war. I therefore do not doubt that he is now following the same line. According to Coulondre's information, Ambassador Welczek in Paris and Count Schulenburg in Moscow also strongly recommend prudence to the German government.

Finally, Coulondre evaluates the result of the conference at Salzburg thus: that Ciano did not yet take on any obligation, leaving the final word to Mussolini and a possibility to act further for peace. Ambassador Attolico left Salzburg for Rome and has not yet returned to Berlin.

Józef Lipski

---

[10] Missing from Lipski's papers.

[11] Weizsäcker finished his memorandum of the conference with Coulondre in these words: "In conclusion the ambassador assured me of his willingness to cooperate in any way in preserving peace. A European war would end with the defeat of all, even present-day Russia, and the victor would not be Stalin, but Trotsky" (*DGFP*, Series D, Vol. VII, No. 64, p. 71).

DOCUMENT 151   Lipski to Beck

NO. N/52/450/39   August 18, 1939
                                                  Strictly Confidential

I would like to take up in a more concrete way a number of problems in connection with my last reports:

1) I would like to know whether you consider it desirable in principle that I should try to meet Göring.

I am enclosing a copy of an invitation I received for stag hunting in the autumn,[12] which might make it easier for me to renew, even at present, my contact with Göring. In case you consider such a conversation to be desirable, I would like to have, under the present circumstances, definite instructions as to the subjects I should take up.

For my part, I think that reference could be made in a general way to intentions wrongly attributed to Poland and to mendacious propaganda. Poland's consistent policy should be underlined, with a slight hint to Russia, stressing that we are going to fight if aggression takes place. And inquire in whose interest this European war would be waged.

Such a conversation with Göring, if it could take place at all, would rather be aimed at presenting to Hitler, through Göring, our determined, but not aggressive, standpoint.

2) At present, the worst tension in Polish-German relations appears on the sector of minorities. This tide is clearly reaching a crescendo. Bearing in mind that this sector, from the international angle, is particularly inconvenient for us, in addition because of other minority problems in Poland besides the German, I am trying to do my best to supply documentary proof about the persecutions of our minorities in Germany. Special files, containing more than 600 incidents, were recently handed to the British and French embassies. Nevertheless, even in a man so devoted to us as Coulondre, I can detect anxiety. He fears that our minorities measures may cause a Polish-German conflict, judging that sector to be particularly exposed.

Observing these matters from Berlin, as well as from the Polish territory, I came to the conclusion that coordination is indispensable between our Ministry of Foreign Affairs and the activities of our local administration.

3) I am taking the liberty of suggesting that it might be desirable,

[12] See Document 148, p. 556.

even prior to Tannenberg and Nuremberg, to issue some official declaration explaining that the loyal German minority has nothing to fear and can live peacefully in Poland, developing its own culture, while anti-Polish incidents and organizations created for diversion will be persecuted with absolute determination. I think that such a declaration could be issued by the Prime Minister or the Minister of the Interior to a representative of the German minorities in Poland—one most digestible for us.

4) Yesterday invitations for Nuremberg arrived. The time limit for reply is fixed at August 26.

You would therefore oblige me by sending me a decision in connection with my reports No. N/52/442/39 of August 15 and No. N/52 443/39 of August 16.[13]

Józef Lipski

DOCUMENT 152   Beck to Lipski

August 19, 1939
Coded

I think it advisable to accept Göring's invitation. Please telegraph exact date of stag hunt. Possibly come first to Warsaw to discuss instructions for conversations.[14]

Beck

DOCUMENT 153   Lipski to Beck

NO. N/52/464/39   Berlin, August 21, 1939
Strictly Confidential

Our Consulate General in Prague has for some time been receiving information that Germany is considering possible changes in the formal legal structure in the territory of the Protectorate to the benefit of the Czechs. The report of our Consul General in Prague, No. 52/C/15 of

13 Missing from Lipski's papers.
14 For the Lipski-Göring conversation, see pp. 590–92.

August 16, a copy of which is enclosed herewith, brings some recent news.[15] In my opinion, this matter should have most careful attention.

The above information, if accepted as reliable, would show that tendencies of the German side to take a milder course toward the Czechs, including changes in the structure of the Protectorate, might, in my opinion, aim to (1) win over the Czechs with the war approaching (I recall that similar steps of a tactical nature were often taken toward the Polish population in the region of Poznań when Prussia, and later on the Reich, had to face an international crisis) or (2) serve as a springboard for action toward the Western world which the Chancellor would take during the Congress of "Peace" at Nuremberg.

The first alternative is a purely tactical local maneuver that would have no broader political meaning.

However, the second hypothesis, camouflaging some deeper German attempts, could become a threat to our interests.

If, as a matter of fact, the Chancellor decided at present to make even a fake exit from the Protectorate, after a military, political, and economic subjugation of the Czechs, he could present it as an intention to return to the Munich policy, thus restoring the ethnographical principle obliterated by the occupation of Prague. The Chancellor could do this by offering this cheap concession to the West in order to add more weight to the Danzig demand on the ethnic level.

Józef Lipski

The following is Lipski's handwritten note of August 20, 1939.

On the afternoon of August 20 [16] I took a plane for Warsaw to discuss with Beck my oncoming meeting with Göring. I prepared a letter for Göring in Berlin, signed it, and left it in the hands of the Embassy staff to await orders from Warsaw. In the letter I referred to the invitation sent in Göring's name for a hunting party in the autumn, and I mentioned that I would like to extend personally my thanks for it. I left the date *in blanco*. In my conversation with Beck I received no margin for negotiations, only general instructions to ask Göring whether it was worth while for our two states to enter into a conflict, and to repeat to him our basic political principles.

[15] This report has been omitted.
[16] Error in date; it should be August 21.

In the evening, after dinner, General Stachiewicz joined us.[17] In the course of the conversation he asked whether we should expect a German attack against Poland on all fronts simultaneously. I confirmed this absolutely unequivocally. Beck praised the antiaircraft defense of the capital, which allegedly numbered a hundred heavy artillery guns. In general, as usual, he appeared well satisfied with our military power.

In the morning I awoke (I stayed at the Brühl Hotel) to the news of Ribbentrop's trip to Moscow. This was a terrible moment for me. The two adversaries shook hands against us.

In the morning I met Beck, who was disturbed. I gave orders by telephone to Berlin to send the letter to Göring immediately, dating it August 20,[18] and I left by plane for Berlin at noon.

My greatest concern was that in the face of the German-Soviet pact the West might weaken and start to withdraw the support it had hitherto shown to us.

German opinion at large accepted the pact with joy, as proof that there would be no war.

However, in the Party itself, particularly among Party doctrinaires, symptoms of sharp criticism could be noted.

The enthusiasm of the masses soon evaporated in the face of the growing danger of war in spite of the German-Soviet pact.

On August 23 a nonaggression pact was signed between Germany and the Soviet Union.[19] On August 26 the Soviet ambassador in Warsaw, Nicolas Sharonov, called on Minister Beck, about which Beck informed the Polish Embassy in Moscow (and other posts) by telegram as follows:

DOCUMENT 154 Beck to Grzybowski

Warsaw, August 26, 1939
(Telegram No. 240)

Yesterday's visit of Sharonov under the pretext of a second-rate frontier incident was supposedly aimed to show that in spite of the Soviet-German pact relations between Moscow and Warsaw remain unchanged.

Beck

[17] General Wacław Stachiewicz, chief of the General Staff.
[18] The date should be August 21.
[19] For the text, see *DGFP*, Series D, Vol. VII, Nos. 228 and 229.

DOCUMENT 155   Beck to Raczyński

Polish Embassy, London   August 28, 1939
                                                              Secret Code

The British Ambassador consulted me about the answer to Hitler.[20]

I agreed to inform the German government that Poland is ready for negotiations, and asked for a definition of what the British government means by the concept of "international guarantee." Please treat the whole matter of consultation as strictly confidential.

Beck

DOCUMENT 156   Szembek to Representatives Abroad

Warsaw, August 29, 1939
(Telegram No. 263)

Within the past few days the representative of Germany at Bucharest declared to Rumanian political factors, showing the relative instructions from Berlin, that German-Soviet conversations on a nonaggression pact had been going on for the past two and one-half months, and that all details of the pact were established in advance.

Please, Mr. Ambassador, exploit the above fact in the light of Voroshilov's declaration that only the negative attitude of Poland toward staff conversations of the Soviet's with England and France caused the agreement with Germany.

Szembek

DOCUMENT 157   Declaration of Minister Szembek[21]
to the Allied Ambassadors

Warsaw, August 29, 1939

Please declare to Allied ambassadors:

1) The concentration of German forces on the Polish frontier is growing continuously.

[20] See *British Blue Book,* Nos. 72 and 74.
[21] See *Journal,* p. 497.

2) German forces entering Slovakia constitute a further threat to the Polish state.

3) Frontier incidents and aggressive action of the Reich on the territory of the Free City leave no doubt as to the aggressive intentions of the Reich.

4) The Polish government received from most reliable sources, including the government of Great Britain, explicit warnings about the planned attack on Poland by surprise in the next few days.

5) Under these circumstances the President of the Republic, on a motion of the government, proclaimed general mobilization.

6) General mobilization is but a completion of the previously issued military directives, which called to arms three fourths of the Polish Army.

7) Introduction of a state of war is not intended. Dispositions usually supplementing mobilization will be limited to a minimum.

8) The Polish policy remains unchanged.

DOCUMENT 158   Beck to Representatives Abroad

Warsaw, August 30, 1939
(Telegram No. 269)

The mobilization order which we postponed yesterday so as not to hamper action in Berlin was executed today. Please stress that, in spite of its official name, this mobilization is, as a matter of fact, a disposition on a smaller scope than the preparedness for war of units previously called to arms. In accordance with mobilization techniques, publication by posters will be utilized.

Beck

The last days of August were a continuum of tension and feverish work for the Polish Embassy in Berlin. This is evident, among other things, from a note, quoted below, of the first secretary of the Embassy, Mr. Henryk Malhomme, from his conversation with Ambassador Henderson.

With regard to a sentence of the Ambassador included in this note expressing his wish that his words be repeated to Malhomme's compatriots, it should be remembered that in August, 1939, Ambassador Henderson was hopelessly ill with cancer, a fact of which he was aware. After the outbreak of the war he retired from all other work and devoted himself completely to his book *Failure of a Mission: Berlin, 1937–1939*. The manuscript was ready in December, 1939, and the first edition appeared in London (Hodder & Stoughton) in April, 1940. Another book of his, a collection of short personal reminiscences, *Water under the Bridges*, was written in seclusion in the last months of his life.

Ambassador Henderson died on December 30, 1942.

Excerpts from Notes of Mr. Henryk Malhomme, First Secretary of the Polish Embassy in Berlin

I spent most of the night of August 30 to August 31 working in the offices of the Embassy.

That night Ambassador Lipski had a long conversation with the British ambassador, Sir Nevile Henderson, and he returned to the Embassy only at 4 A.M.

After a short exchange of opinions with the Ambassador, we retired to have some rest. For the past few days I, as well as the majority of the officials, had moved to the Embassy to facilitate our work. We had bedrooms assigned there.

That night I did not sleep for long, for already at 7 A.M. I was summoned by the Ambassador.

I received instructions to proceed immediately to the British Ambassador, who had expressed the desire, in the course of his telephone conversation with Ambassador Lipski, that one of the Embassy staff should call on him without delay.

The choice fell on me.

I presented myself at the British Embassy at 8 A.M. I found the same strain of work there. It was obvious that the members of the Embassy had just left the offices.

Immediately upon my arrival I was led to the Ambassador's study.

I found Sir Nevile absolutely changed; he looked at least ten years older. He looked worn out, and the strain of several nights spent behind his desk was evident.

He greeted me with the words: "Malhomme, I do not like war" ("Malhomme, je n'aime pas la guerre"), and repeated them several times. It was clear that he was wondering how to start the conversation.

I replied that I did not like war either, but that unfortunately the decision was in the hands of a single man who was, so it seemed striding toward it consistently.

After a longer moment of silence, Sir Nevile told me that he was glad that Ambassador Lipski had delegated me, since he had known me for a long time, ever since the Belgrade days. What he was going to say was rather in the nature of a personal confidence, and therefore it would be easier for him to talk with someone he knew well.

He then explained to me that he had done his utmost to stop the war, and that until the last moment he would work to maintain peace; however, at present he had lost almost all hope that the conflict could be settled by peaceful means, if only for the reasons just mentioned by me.

Of late he had been under the impression that the Poles did not understand him and regarded him as a sympathizer of Germany unfriendly toward Poland. As a matter of fact, this was not so. He had many true friends in Poland; he knew Poland well because of his passion for hunting, and he had grown fond of the country and its people.

In case of war Poland would undoubtedly be destroyed and would lose its independence. For a long time Great Britain and France would not be able to come to its assistance. Probably after long years the war would be won by Great Britain, and Poland would recover its independence, but losses sustained by it would be irreparable.

These, and no other, were the motives of his endeavors to settle the Polish-German conflict by peaceful means.

He now considered that his mission had come to an end, and he would like me, when the war was over, to repeat his motives to my compatriots.

I thanked him for his confidence and we parted with a long handshake.

When I left the Embassy I met the former ambassador of the Reich in Rome, von Hassell, on the Unter den Linden.

I was absolutely taken aback when he approached me and, in spite of the tension in Polish-German relations, greeted me with exceptional warmth, even manifesting cordiality. He told me that he was going to the Auswärtiges Amt to, as he put it, save the peace. Of course, he was acting primarily in Germany's interest, but if he succeeded, he would also render a great service to all mankind. He thought that Poland would have to make some concessions which, however, would be much better for it than the results of a war. Taking leave of him, I stressed that we were also doing everything possible to settle the conflict, the sources of which were not in our country but in his.

DOCUMENT 159   Lipski to the Ministry of Foreign Affairs

NO. GMS/5165   Berlin, August 31, 1939
                       Received: August 31, 1939, 10:55 A.M.
                       Cipher-Code, incoming No. 243

According to Henderson's information, the German terms prepared for a fully empowered Polish plenipotentiary:

I. A demobilized Danzig returns to Germany.

II. Gdynia remains with Poland.

III. Within a year a plebiscite in the Corridor, the southern boundary of which to run from Marienburg [22] through Grudziądz, Bydgoszcz, Schonlanke [Trzcianka]. Plebiscite on the basis of population of 1919. Decision by absolute majority.

IV. Commission for the plebiscite: England, Italy, France, and Russia.

Lipski

DOCUMENT 160   Lipski to the Ministry of Foreign Affairs

NO. 242   Berlin, August 31, 1939
                       Received: August 31, 1939, 11:45 A.M.
                       Secret

Coulondre has told me that Henderson's informative giving the impression that the Germans were prepared to wait only until 12 comes from Ribbentrop's circles. Coulondre thinks that we, for our part, might tell the German government after 12, in keeping with our reply to Roosevelt and the British government, that the Ambassador in Berlin is always at the disposal of the German government. This would be a gesture for peace.

Of course the German government might use such a step for propaganda purposes, saying that we are giving in.

Lipski

[22] This is a mistake; it should be Marienwerder.

DOCUMENT 161   Beck to Lipski

Telephonogram to the Polish   Warsaw, August 31, 1939
Ambassador in Berlin

With reference to your reports, please request an interview with the
Minister of Foreign Affairs or the Secretary of State, and inform him as
follows:

Last night the Polish government was informed by the British government of an exchange of views with the Reich government as to the
possibility of direct understanding [23] between the Polish and the German governments.

The Polish government is favorably considering the British government's suggestion and will make them a formal reply on the subject in
the next few hours at the latest.

End of declaration for the Ministry of Foreign Affairs. Next passage
for the Ambassador's information.

Please do not engage in any concrete discussions, and if the Germans
put forward any concrete demands, say you are not authorized to accept
or discuss them and will have to ask your government for further
instructions.

DOCUMENT 162   Lipski to the Ministry of Foreign Affairs

NO. 239   Berlin, August 31, 1939 [24]
                                        Received: August 31, 2 P.M.

For the Minister

Lubomirski arriving tomorrow noon by plane. Please receive him
immediately.

Lipski

[23] The Ambassador was also informed that the word "understanding" was
meant in the sense "communicating with each other" and should therefore be
translated as *Verständigung* and not as *Vereinbarung*. The Ministry also instructed the Ambassador that, as he had already requested an interview in the
Auswärtiges Amt (in accordance with previous instructions), he was not to
insist on being received at once.
[24] The date should be August 30.

DOCUMENT 163 Lipski to the Ministry of Foreign Affairs

NO. GMS 5185   Berlin, August 31, 1939
NO. 244   Received: August 31, 1939, 2:45 P.M.
                      Cipher telephonogram, incoming
                      Secret

The British Ambassador sent to me, accompanied by the Counselor of the Embassy, a Swede, Dahlerus, who is a friend of Göring and who is acting as a mediator between England and Germany. Dahlerus confirmed that Göring, in opposition to the extremists who wanted to annex to Germany the whole Prussian territory, limited his claims to Danzig and the Corridor, as per coded telegram No. 243. I shall telephone conditions by press cipher as strictly confidential.[25] . . . with the British Counselor separately. Of course, I did not discuss with D.

I regard *démarche* D. as a further symptom of pressure on us, which took especially drastic form today. I react calmly, very firmly.

Lipski

These are the last telegrams sent by Ambassador Lipski to Warsaw.

In the *Polish White Book*, No. 147, pp. 141–52, there is a final report of Lipski covering his whole activity in Berlin from September, 1933, to August, 1939.

[25] A few words are illegible here.

The Last Month before the Outbreak of the War [1]
August, 1939

Hitler Resolves upon War against Poland

IN THE EARLY HOURS of April 8, 1939, Minister Beck was traveling through Berlin on his return journey from London. With the military attaché, Colonel Szymański, I met him at the Zoo Station and traveled with him as far as Frankfurt-an-der-Oder. First of all we reviewed the political situation. Then Colonel Szymański gave an account of the military position, stressing its gravity in connection with the information received that the dispositions of the Reichswehr were concentrating upon an operation directed to the east. Colonel Szymański's military considerations reckoned with the possibility of an early German initiative, which actually took place later. Nevertheless, the outlines of his account turned out to be accurate. It appears from Reichswehr documents now in Allied hands that—from April 3 on—preparations for "Operation White" (code name for the war against Poland) were advancing at great speed.

On April 11 Hitler issued further orders, containing detailed instructions for "Operation White" (Appendix II) aiming at the occupation of Danzig (Appendix III) and the organization and exercise of power in East Prussia in case of a warlike conflict (Appendix IV).[2]

On May 10 Hitler signed the order on the "uniform preparation for war by the armed forces," which in its Part VI contained instructions for economic warfare.[3]

Already in these first orders the basic political outlines of the war against Poland appeared. The principal object was to localize the war with Poland. The German supreme authorities considered this possible,

[1] Printed in *Sprawy Międzynarodowe* (London), 1947, No. 4, under the title *Stosunki polsko-niemieckie w świetle aktów norymberskich.*
[2] *DGFP*, Series D, Vol. VI, No. 185.
[3] *Trial of the Major War Criminals*, XXXIV, 402–8.

in view of the inner weakness of France, which might prevent England from entering the war.

The directives of April 11 assumed the entry of German troops into Slovak territory in order to attack the southern flank of Poland as well as rapidly to occupy Pomerania and to cut off Poland from its ports in the Baltic. Economic directives prescribed the occupation of industrial plants in Poland without damaging them, especially in Upper Silesia and Teschen Silesia. The whole operation should be mounted in such a manner that the attack could be launched before general mobilization had been proclaimed.

The discussion in detail of these directives of the Reichswehr against Poland is outside the scope of this article. Moreover, the subject is more a matter for military examination. It is a most unusual case that after a war we should be able to know exactly what were the enemy's plans, on the basis of statements of members of the High Command and authentic General Staff documents. The documentation in our possession makes it possible to reconstruct the German strategic plan against Poland and the subsequent stages through which it passed. Hitler considered himself to be not only a statesman but also a strategist. We know from the Nuremberg documents that he surprised his entourage, including many outstanding specialists in military art, by the great scope of his strategic conceptions, by his profound knowledge of the subject, including the most trifling details, and above all by his remarkable memory. In discussions he outstripped his generals and discarded their schemes, replacing them by his own conceptions, which proved to be right, especially in the first period of the war.

The indisputable superiority of Hitler over his associates increased his inborn vanity and megalomania, which chiefly accounted for his defeat, particularly since he lacked the main elements of science and true insight into international politics.

Hitler's speeches addressed to his most trusted associates should be considered the true expression of German policy, since he was a paramount factor in the Third Reich, in domestic affairs as well as in foreign policy. As regards the aggression against Poland, the Nuremberg Tribunal considered the exposition addressed by Hitler on May 23 to a meeting of his commanders in chief as inculpating him most.[4]

The minutes of this meeting were taken by Lieutenant Colonel

[4] *DGFP*, Series D, Vol. VI, No. 433.

Schmundt, Hitler's aide-de-camp. The conference was attended by Göring, Räder, Brauchitsch, Keitel, Milch, Halder, Bodenschatz, Schnievindt, and others of lower rank. Hitler opened his address with a general survey of Germany's position. He reached the same conclusions as on November 5, 1937 (in spite of the fact that Austria and Czechoslovakia had since been annexed), that Germany needed vital space (*Lebensraum*) to solve its economic problems; this could not be achieved without "incursions into alien territories." In the way of ascension to power Germany met the resistance of Great Britain, which considered all new claims as disturbing the balance of power. England was consequently the driving force against Germany. No longer believing in the possibility of peaceful settlement with Great Britain, Hitler reached the conclusion that it was necessary to be prepared for a conflict, which would be a life-and-death struggle. As the first stage of this war, Hitler planned an attack against Poland. One can follow the course of his reasoning from short minutes made by Schmundt:

"The Pole is not a fresh enemy. Poland will always be on the side of our adversaries. In spite of treaties of friendship, Poland has always been bent on exploiting every opportunity against us. It is not Danzig that is at stake. For us it is a matter of expanding our living space in the east and making food supplies secure and also solving the problem of the Baltic states." And further on: "The problem 'Poland' cannot be dissociated from the showdown with the West. . . . Poland sees danger in the German victory over the West and will try to deprive us of victory." Then follows his definition of Polish-Russian relations in the light of German interests: "Poland's internal solidarity against Bolshevism is doubtful. Therefore Poland is also a doubtful barrier against Russia." Here is manifest Hitler's discontent with the refusal by Poland of many of his anti-Russian proposals. In the concluding part of his address Hitler stated that the attack against Poland must be launched at the first occasion. But at the same time the conflict with Poland should not drag Germany into war with Great Britain and France; the main and nearest objective of German policy would be to isolate Poland.

Most striking is the change of tone toward Soviet Russia. There are no more aggressive accents and threats. The judgment becomes more objective: "Economic relations with Russia are only possible if and when political relations have improved. In press comments a cautious trend is becoming apparent. It is not ruled out that Russia might disinterest herself in the destruction of Poland. If Russia continues to agitate against us, relations with Japan may become closer."

Further military orders of Hitler and his generals in June, July, and August, 1939, only carried out the general directives established at this conference in May.

Danzig as the Trump Card in the German Game

August, 1939, began with an outbreak of new Nazi provocations in Danzig. Some Polish customs inspectors on the frontier between the Free City and East Prussia were informed on August 4 by the local Danzig authorities that after 7 A.M. on August 6 they would be prevented from carrying out their duties. In view of such drastic violation of fundamental Polish rights, the Polish government, which displayed great patience and forbearance in face of the remilitarization of the Free City carried out by the Hitlerite organization, was compelled to react abruptly. The note delivered that very day by the Polish Commissioner-General to the President of the Senate, presuming that the orders issued by minor officials must be due either to a misunderstanding or to a wrong interpretation of the respective instructions, left an open door for retreat to the authorities of the Free City. Nevertheless, the note asked that the orders be canceled within a prescribed time, namely, by August 6 at 6 P.M.; informed the Senate that the Polish customs officials would be instructed to serve in uniform and armed; and in the last instance announced that any further interference with the discharge of the customs control would call forth reprisals.[5] The President of the Senate on the following day immediately gave reassuring oral explanations, and only three days later—namely, on August 7—evidently after getting into touch with Berlin, sent a reply to the Polish note in which it was denied that any alleged orders directed against Polish customs inspectors had been issued and took exception to the attitude adopted in the matter by the Polish government.[6] For a short while it was believed in political circles that the customs conflict was, if only for the time being, wound up owing to the peremptory, but at the same time moderate, line adopted by Poland, supported by the Western Powers, who were supplied by Warsaw with full information on the course of events. In this particularly tense situation the Polish press showed as a rule more

[5] *Polish White Book*, Nos. 82 and 83; *DGFP*, Series D, Vol. VI, Nos. 773 and 774.
[6] *Polish White Book*, No. 84; *DGFP*, Series D, Vol. VI, No. 780.

discretion and forbearance than the press in the West, where much too optimistic conclusions were drawn from an alleged withdrawal by the Danzig Senate.

As a matter of fact, as early as August 9, during my short stay in Poland, where I had to report to the Foreign Minister and Marshal Śmigły-Rydz on the development of the situation in Berlin, news reached Warsaw in the late hours of a statement made that day by Secretary of State Weizsäcker to Polish Chargé d'Affaires Lubomirski in connection with the last incident in Danzig.[7] In its statement the German government took a strong view of the contents of the Polish note to the Senate on August 4, declaring that another Polish ultimatum or threat of reprisals would lead to aggravation of Polish-German relations.

The German step raised a question of principle, since the government of the Reich was interfering in relations between Poland and Danzig in a moment of increasing tension, when an action against the Danzig statute and Polish rights and interests in Danzig was initiated by an order from Berlin and closely followed directives from there. Minister Beck, in a conversation with me, took the view that the German move meant the opening of a final stage in the contest with Poland. After consultation with Marshal Śmigły-Rydz he instructed the assistant of the Undersecretary of State, Arciszewski, to inform the German Chargé d'Affaires in Warsaw of the text of the Polish government's reply contesting the German right to interfere in relations between Poland and Danzig and warning that the Polish government would consider any future intervention by the German government to the detriment of Polish rights in the Free City as an act of aggression.[8] The last reservation was a simple repetition of a formal statement made by Minister Beck to Ambassador Moltke on March 28, 1939,[9] in reply to Ribbentrop's declaration that "Polish aggression against the Free City of Danzig would be regarded by the Reich government as aggression against Germany itself." Ribben-

---

[7] *Polish White Book*, No. 85 and *DGFP*, Series D, Vol. VII, No. 5. In his report of August 9, Polish Chargé d'Affaires Lubomirski, citing Weizsäcker's statement in German, adds: "Secretary of State von Weizsäcker again underlined the verbal character of this declaration. Outside of this, he refrained from any personal remarks or comments, mentioning that he had only the above to declare."

[8] For Mr. Archiszewski's statement to Herr Von Wuhlisch, see *Polish White Book*, No. 86, and *DGFP*, Series D, Vol. VI, No. 10.

[9] *Polish White Book*, No. 64.

trop then used this expression in a conversation with me when sharply criticizing military measures taken by Poland during the occupation of Memel by Hitler, when there was a danger of a simultaneous German invasion of Danzig.[10]

After my return to Berlin, Counselor Lubomirski informed me of a conversation in the British Embassy on August 8, at Sir Nevile Henderson's request. . . .[11]

A few days later, on August 14, I had a long talk with the French ambassador, Coulondre, to whom I was bound by an old friendship and who was my precious support in those exhausting days. Coulondre, while not sparing any effort to preserve peace, was of the opinion that in no case should the mistakes made in the solution of the Czechoslovak problem be repeated, for the sake of France's security.

Coulondre's position was not an easy one, with a personality so wavering as M. Georges Bonnet, then French foreign minister. Being well acquainted with the German mentality, the French Ambassador was aware of the impossibility of preventing Hitler from starting a war. In his view the only efficient manner of repressing the Nazi impulses was to maintain a compact allied front, if possible extended to Russia. Being afraid that Hitler might have had some illusions about the French attitude in the event of German aggression against Poland, Coulondre never ceased to stress to the Germans that France would take up arms in the case of aggression, and would give immediate assistance to its ally. As may be presumed from the very weak protection left by the Germans on the western front during the September campaign, Hitler did not believe in the offensive spirit of the French Army and its High Command. According to Keitel's evidence, in September, 1939, there were on the western front, including reserves in the Rhineland and behind the West Wall, roughly twenty German divisions, only five of which were first class.

As I had been constantly in touch with the British and French ambassadors I had the opportunity of following the maneuvers of the Germans to throw upon Poland the responsibility for the ever-increasing tension in the political situation. Secretary of State Weizsäcker, who during the occupation of Prague had scrupulously avoided any contacts with foreign diplomats, now appeared as a conciliating factor, trying to find

10 *Ibid.*, No. 63.
11 See Document 147, pp. 554–56.

some outlet from a difficult situation and to preserve peace. In this way he made use of some credit which he had with foreign diplomats, in order to disparage Poland in their eyes as a reckless factor in international politics. In this way the German Foreign Office played the role detailed to it by Hitler, within his general political-strategic scheme. At the head of this Office, by the way, was Ribbentrop, who was entirely devoted to Hitler and was a most fanatical protagonist of the use of force in international politics. One of the most essential tasks of the Polish Embassy in Berlin was to counteract this German propaganda by the rectification of false news spread by German broadcasting stations and the press. As the main object of German attacks was concentrated on minority problems, the Embassy passed to the representatives of the Western Powers all details of the persecution of the Polish population in Germany. In mid-August the French and British embassies received a list of 600 instances of gross offenses against the Polish minority, the whole structure of which, as well as its cultural and economic institutions, was being destroyed extremely ruthlessly.

The disappointing visit of Ciano to Salzburg served to launch new accusations against Poland. On August 14 Sir Nevile Henderson told me that the Germans were spreading rumors, according to which Hitler, deeply hurt by the last passage of the Polish government's statement on Danzig, had declared to Ciano that German honor was involved from now on, and consequently also Axis honor.[12] This made it impossible for the Italian Foreign Minister to use his influence to stop the warlike impulses of the Dictator of the Reich. Henderson was not yet in possession of the report of his colleague in Rome on the Ciano-Hitler meeting. Nevertheless, as the German press after the Salzburg conference availed itself of the arguments of German honor, the Ambassador drew very pessimistic conclusions. Being fully aware of the military unpreparedness of Great Britain and its Allies, and not trusting Russia, Henderson made every effort to gain time at least. He regretted that Polish and German diplomacy had not discussed fundamental problems since the spring, confining themselves to delivering mutual protests and complaints.

Were there any bases for such talks in view of the described general German attitude? The Polish government voiced the Polish opinion, rejecting all claims to the incorporation of Danzig into the Reich and to extraterritorial corridors across the Corridor, stating in its reply of

---

[12] See Document 149, p. 557.

March 26, 1939, the extent of possible concessions.[13] The German government did not then accept the compromise proposed by Poland, and more and more peremptorily insisted on acceptance of the demands affecting the independence of Poland. In this state of affairs Poland received the English guarantee. From that time on the German government declined any conversations with the Polish government. Moltke, invited by Beck after his return to Poland, did not call at the Polish Foreign Office, and left Warsaw for a long time.

On April 28, 1939, Hitler denounced the nonaggression pact with Poland, to which Beck answered in a speech delivered in the Polish Diet on May 5.

Henderson did not sufficiently explore the true reasons for the Polish-German conflict, which was bound up with the general European situation, and was closely connected with the main aims of Hitler's policy and his wide plans for conquest. The British Ambassador was under the illusion that a catastrophe might be avoided by talks and arguments. Having for many years closely watched the development of the situation in the Third Reich, and being well acquainted with Hitler's mentality, I had no such hopes in this respect. Hitler used to make decisions and carry them out, basing himself on his own directives and taking into account only the real strength of the adversary. As I believed at that time, Hitler might have been inclined to believe then that by conflict with Poland he might incur too great a risk, and that its outcome would not profit him, if he were to face an unfriendly Russia in the east after the occupation of Poland. For this reason there were still some hopes of preserving peace, in spite of German military preparations and increasing tension, so long as the German-Soviet pact was not signed.

Differences between the Axis Partners at the Time of the Outbreak of the War

What was the course of events in the first half of August, 1939, in the light of the Nuremberg documents? The memoirs of Ciano and the German records of the Salzburg conversations supply a fair amount of documentation divulging the true designs of Hitler and his tactics at that period.

In spite of assurances given more than once by Ribbentrop to the Italian Ambassador in Berlin that the Reich government would not go to

[13] *Polish White Book*, No. 63.

extremes in its claims against Poland, Mussolini did not trust his ally. Disturbed by the development of German-Polish relations in the first half of August, he sent Foreign Minister Ciano to Germany for an exchange of views with Hitler and Ribbentrop. Having arrived in Salzburg on August 11, 1939, Ciano went to Fuschl, Ribbentrop's residence, where he held his first conversation with him. He related it as follows: "While we were waiting to be seated at the dinner table, Ribbentrop informed me of the decision that the storm must break, as he would have talked with me of a minor, ordinary administrative measure. 'Well, Ribbentrop,' I asked, 'what do you want? The Corridor or Danzig?' 'Not that any more,' he said, gazing at me with his cold expressionless eyes, 'we want war!' "

At the Nuremberg trial, on April 1, 1946, Ribbentrop denied having said this: "I told Count Ciano that Hitler was resolved to settle the Polish problem by any means; Hitler ordered me to tell Ciano this. It is simply preposterous to affirm that I said 'we want war,' for one does not say such things even to one's best and most faithful ally—certainly not to Count Ciano." Had he confessed to having made such an announcement Ribbentrop would have condemned himself for a crime against peace.

We have an account of the subsequent conversation held on August 12, 1939, at Obersalzburg between Ciano and Hitler, at which Ribbentrop also took part. It was made by Minister Plenipotentiary Schmidt, chief German interpreter, who attended all important conferences. It appears from this bulky document that the discussion was concerned with an essential question—the time of the outbreak of the war.

When Hitler put forward the reasons for the immediate outbreak of hostilities, Ciano offered stubborn resistance, trying to win two or three years' delay. In connection with this point they argued about the possibility of localizing the conflict. Hitler replied that "he personally was absolutely convinced that the Western democracies would, in the last resort, recoil from unleashing a general war."

Trying to convince his Italian ally that in view of the present strategic position the risks of war with the Western Powers were considerably less, owing to the present military superiority of the Axis, than they would be in a few years, Hitler stated that the destruction of the Polish war potential could only be beneficial to the Axis. Since the Poles had clearly shown that in a conflict they would side with the enemies of

Germany and Italy, a quick liquidation of Poland at the present moment could only be of advantage for the unavoidable conflict with the Western democracies. Should a hostile Poland remain on the German eastern frontier it would tie up not only eleven East Prussian divisions but even more German units in Pomerania and Silesia. By an earlier liquidation of Poland this necessity would be eliminated. Generally speaking, the best thing would be for the pseudo-neutrals to be eliminated one after the other, concluded Hitler, indicating Yugoslavia and other Balkan states, unreliable from the Axis point of view. A further reason brought forward by Hitler with the purpose of reassuring Ciano as regards France was his statement that after a quick defeat of Poland the Germans would have 100 divisions available on the western front, which would compel France to withdraw its armies from all fronts, including units stationed on the Italian Frontier.

Hitler gave his opinion of the Polish war potential and the internal situation as follows: "The quality of the Polish Army was extremely uneven. Alongside a few crack divisions there was a host of units of inferior quality. Poland's antitank and antiaircraft defenses were very weak. At present France and England could send it no supplies. But, if Poland were given economic assistance by the West over a fairly long period, it could secure these arms, and Germany's superiority would thereby be diminished. Over and against the fanatics in Warsaw and Cracow there was a rural population in other districts which was quite indifferent. Furthermore, the comparison of the population of the Polish state should be taken into account: of the 34 million inhabitants there were 1½ million Germans, some 4 million Jews, and approximately 9 million Ukrainians, so that considerably less than the total population were actual Poles, and, as he had already said, even the fighting qualities of the Poles could not be considered uniform. In these circumstances, Poland would be defeated by Germany in a very short time."

Hitler adapted his argument on Danzig to his Italian interlocutor, comparing Danzig, "the Nuremberg of the North," to Italian Trieste. He stressed that the east, the northeast, and the Baltic states were within the German sphere of interest, comparing the importance of this area for Germany with the Mediterranean, which undoubtedly constituted the Italian sphere of interest.

The reasons put forward by Ciano for postponing the conflict were of no avail: he referred to the Duce's idea for an international conference, but Hitler maintained a negative attitude. Eventually he proposed the issue of a declaration which would lead to a gradual withdrawal of support by the Western Powers from Poland, which in turn would eventually force Poland to accept the German claims. Hitler's answer was that he had no time to lose in settling the Polish problem. After autumn had set in, military operations in Eastern Europe would be more difficult. From September to May, Poland was a great marsh and entirely unsuited to any kind of military operations. In fact, Poland could occupy Danzig in October, and was probably ready to do so, when Germany would be unable to do anything about it, since the use of artillery against Danzig and the destruction of the town were out of the question.

After Hitler's statement Ciano asked bluntly how soon the Danzig question must be settled. Hitler replied, "By the end of August," repeating his well-known accounts of offers most advantageous to Poland, which were alleged to have been refused as the result of British intervention. He gave warning that he was prepared to use the occasion of the next Polish provocation—an ultimatum, some brutal ill-treatment of Germans, an attempt to starve out Danzig, or something of the kind —for the invasion of Poland within forty-eight hours and the final settlement of the problem in such a way. In his opinion it would greatly improve the Axis position, as would the liquidation of Yugoslavia by Italy.

Hitler concluded that such action against Poland must be expected at any moment.

In the last passage of Schmidt's minutes it is said that the conversation was interrupted for a short time because Hitler received telegrams from Moscow and Tokyo.

When the conversation was resumed Ciano was told that the Soviet government agreed to the dispatch of a German envoy to Moscow for political negotiations.

German Camouflage Goes On

From mid-August the tension between Germany and Poland increased from day to day. The war of nerves was at its peak. The Hitlerite propaganda machinery, which had stood the test during the occupation of Austria and Czechoslovakia, was working with great skill and precision. Its weakness consisted in such methods of propaganda as spreading false rumors and simply inventing some facts, which were used not for the first time and were consequently well known to foreign observers.

The action of camouflage recommended by Hitler at the meeting with his commanders in chief on May 23 [14] was systematically carried out. Nevertheless, the intensive military preparations and troop movements did not escape the attention of Polish and Allied observers. The concentration of German divisions against Poland was ascertained with great precision. The military attaché at the Polish Embassy in Berlin, Colonel Szymański, maintained a day by day contact with his French and British colleagues, as did the three Allied ambassadors among themselves.

The Tannenberg celebration fixed for August 27, at which Hitler was to make a speech, and which was to have been attended by the military attachés invited on this occasion, was part of the German camouflage measures, serving among other things to cover mobilization action in East Prussia. On August 17, 1939, the heads of diplomatic missions received, as in previous years, invitations to the annual Party Congress at Nuremberg, for the first half of September. It was asked that answers to these invitations be given before August 26, 1939, the date previously appointed by Hitler for the invasion of Poland. But what was most unexpected was an invitation sent to me in mid-August by Oberjäger-meister Scherping, on behalf of Göring, to a hunt in the Prussian game preserves.[15] From May on I had had no close contact with Göring. This move on his part was a puzzle to me, but I soon heard that the British Ambassador had received a similar invitation.

On August 17 I was informed in detail by Ambassadors Henderson and Coulondre of their conversations with Weizsäcker, held on August 15. . . .[16] At the end of this long and sometimes tumultuous exchange of views with the British Ambassador, Weizsäcker let it be understood unequivocally that Germany reckoned on an understanding with Russia to the detriment of Poland. After Moscow's approval of the start of political conversations, transmitted to Hitler on August 12,[17] Weizsäcker was in a position to play this trump card with the representative of Great Britain.

[14] *DGFP*, Series D, Vol. VI, No. 433.
[15] See Document 148, p. 556.
[16] See Document 150, pp. 559–62. See also *DGFP*, Series D, Vol. VII, Nos. 64 and 66.
[17] See *DGFP*, Series D, Vol. VII, No. 43, pp. 48–49, and No. 50.

Last Visit to Warsaw

The events subsequent to August 21, 1939, were fully disclosed in the Nuremberg trial. It would take many volumes to comment on all evidence brought to light by this trial. The Tribunal aimed firmly to establish the guilt of crimes against peace caused by launching a war of aggression accompanied by violation of international agreements. The defendants strove to portray in the most favorable light their part in the events which occurred in the last days of August. To this effect they supplied the Tribunal with vast evidence and called many witnesses for the defense, among them the famous Dahlerus. The arguments put forward by the defense, aiming sometimes even at charging Polish diplomatic representatives in connection with German proposals summed up in sixteen points, were much like the tactics of the German Foreign Office on the eve of the war. Nevertheless, in this case the official German documents which were in Allied possession spoke for themselves, refuting the statements of the defendants and putting witnesses in a most awkward position.

The events which occurred on August 25, 1939, and also the sixteen points of the German demands which raised wide discussion and numerous comments in the press are of particular importance for the history of German-Polish relations.

In the afternoon of August 21 I flew to Warsaw for one day. I had some urgent business which had to be transacted orally.

To my suggestion to accept the invitation sent to me on behalf of Göring and to write to him proposing a meeting, Beck answered in the affirmative,[18] asking me to come to Warsaw for a few hours to receive detailed instructions.

German military preparations were going to such lengths and tension was increasing to such a degree that one had to reckon with the outbreak of war at any moment. Orders to the Embassy and to the consular posts in Germany in the event of war had already been issued for some time, and were gradually put into force. Final decisions had still to be given on some particular points, among them the question of evacuating part of the staff and their dependents, as well as taking over the protection of Polish interests in Germany, in the case of war, by a neutral state.

[18] See Document 152, p. 564.

Other matters to be discussed referred to problems closely connected with our relations with the Western Powers, in view of German attempts to discredit Poland in their eyes. I always advised the most prudent treatment of minority problems and the coordination of all moves by the home authorities with the directives of the Foreign Office. For years hostile propaganda had been exploiting the minority problems, and that had left some traces. Even in circles friendly to us opinions were expressed that Poland might be represented in an unfavorable light in connection with minority incidents. The problem became still more delicate through the fact that the Hitlerite Reich, in the last months before the outbreak of the war, quite openly used the German minority in Poland for diversionist and propaganda purposes.

I was received by Minister Beck at Brühl Palace in the evening hours. I received general directions for my conversation with Göring. The purpose of this conversation was to be the rectification of false accusations against Poland, stressing the consistent Polish policy toward Germany within the general framework of the nonaggression pact of 1934, emphasizing our fortitude regarding defense against aggression, and in the last instance putting the question: Whose ends would a European war serve? The main idea of the meeting with Göring should be an attempt to exercise some influence on Hitler through him, following Henderson's advice to some extent, who always asserted that Hitler was misinformed by his entourage and men like Ribbentrop. Before the conversation with the Foreign Minister was brought to an end, General Stachiewicz, chief of the General Staff, called. Minister Beck asked me to call on him again the following day in the morning before I flew back to Berlin. For a while we three exchanged among ourselves our views on the political and military situation. Beck, reviewing different assumptions, took into account the possibility of German aggression confined to Danzig and the cutting off of Pomerania. In view of the extent of German preparations I did not agree with this opinion. The Danzig problem, which had been an object of constant worry and preoccupation to the Foreign Minister since spring, had become the outpost of an undisguised struggle led by Hitlerite Germany against Poland. By putting this problem forward and with it absorbing Polish and international public opinion, Germany was trying to obscure the true picture of the situation. This circumstance also had its consequences in influencing some Polish military moves. I replied to a question put by General Stachiewicz, stating peremptorily that we must reckon with a German attack along the whole front, including the Slovak sector.

In the early hours of the following day Warsaw was informed by a communiqué published in Berlin during the night that Ribbentrop was soon to fly to Moscow for negotiations over a nonaggression pact. This news profoundly upset Polish public opinion, aware of the political situation. I gave the order by telephone to the Embassy in Berlin to send my letter to Göring, dated August 21 and signed by me before my departure. I found Beck in the Foreign Office, profoundly worried, although he maintained an apparent calm. Our interview was short. I was in haste to get to the airport.

In view of the big diplomatic success scored by Hitler, considerably strengthening the German strategic position, I was very much disturbed as to what might be the repercussions in the West from the new German agreement. Beck expressed the opinion that Great Britain would keep its pledges to Poland.

Being aware that there were no more chances to preserve peace, I left Warsaw with great anxiety.

Hitler's Speech to the Commanders in Chief

In the files of the "Oberkommando der Wehrmacht" at Flensburg the Allied authorities found copies of the two speeches addressed at Berchtesgaden on August 22, 1939, to the German commanders in chief.[19] The purpose of the meeting was, according to Hitler's own words, to inform the commanders of his decision to begin war operations in the next few days, and in connection with this "to strengthen their confidence."

That day Hitler was in high spirits, feeling that he had reached the peak of his successes.

From the picture of the situation given by him it clearly appeared that the situation was so favorable for Germany that it would be more advisable to start the war at once instead of waiting two or three years more. His own personality was a very important factor which influenced his decision. "No one will ever again," said Hitler, "have the confidence of the whole German people as I have. There will probably never again be a man with more authority than I possess. My existence is therefore a

[19] *DGFP*, Series D, Vol. VII, No. 192.

factor of great value. But I can be eliminated at any time by a criminal or a lunatic."

On the enemy's side, in Hitler's opinion, there were no outstanding personalities. He also stressed as particularly favorable factors for Germany the fact that the Duce and Franco were in power. Economic reasons were summed up by Hitler in the following words: "It is easy for us to make decisions. We have nothing to lose, we have everything to gain. Because of our restrictions, our economic situation is such that we can only hold out for a few more years. Göring can confirm this. We have no other choice, we must act." His further arguments pointed out the rivalry between France and England in the Mediterranean, the increasing tension in the Near East, the uneasy position of the British Empire, the weakness of France, the internal decomposition of Yugoslavia, the position of Rumania threatened by Hungary and Bulgaria, and the lack of an outstanding personality in Turkey after the death of Kemal Pasha. Hitler confessed that the creation of a Greater Germany was a big political achievement, but open to question on the military side since it was gained by a bluff on the part of the political leaders. It must now be tested in war. He stressed that his Polish policy was contrary to popular feeling in Germany. From the difficulties met by Poland in obtaining a loan from England for rearmament, Hitler drew the conclusion that England did not really want to support Poland. It did not want to risk eight million pounds in Poland, although it had put half a billion into China.

The enemy hoped—said Hitler—that Russia would become our enemy after the conquest of Poland. The enemy did not reckon with my great capacity to take decisions. The publication of the nonggression pact with Russia was a bombshell. The consequences cannot be overlooked. The effect on Poland will be tremendous. "Now Poland is in the position in which I wanted her."

In his second speech there were the following most significant announcements:

"The destruction of Poland has priority. The aim is to eliminate active forces, not to reach a definite line. Even if war breaks out in the West, the destruction of Poland remains the priority. A quick decision is in view because of the season. I shall give a propagandist reason for starting the war—no matter whether it is plausible or not. The victor will not be asked afterward whether he told the truth or not. When starting and waging a war, it is not right that matters, but victory. . . . New German frontier delimination according to sound principles, and possibly a protectorate as a buffer state."

Expressing his conviction that Germany would be equal to the task, Hitler concluded that the start would probably be ordered for Saturday morning (August 26, 1939).

The Last Meeting with Göring

On August 23, 1939, the British government took an initiative to save peace. On that day Sir Nevile Henderson conveyed to Hitler a personal letter from Chamberlain in which the British government—in spite of the announcement of the German-Soviet agreement—while confirming its pledges to Poland, expressed its readiness to discuss with the Reich government all questions arising between Germany and England, if only a proper atmosphere of confidence could be created, and finally called for direct negotiations between Germany and Poland on minority questions.[20] The first news of a negative outcome of the conversations between Henderson and Hitler was told to me on the night of the same day by the Belgian ambassador, Davignon, at the house of the Rumanian envoy, Crutzescu, where I also met Prince Ghica, former Rumanian foreign minister, who was passing through Berlin. All present were profoundly depressed.

The following day I had a telephone call from Göring's office. Referring to my personal letter, the aide-de-camp asked me whether I would like to meet the Field Marshal. To my reply that I was ready to call on him at any time, the aide-de-camp gave me a significant answer, asking me to call the same day at 5 P.M., "since later on it might be too late." The meeting took place at Göring's Berlin residence and lasted one hour. Göring made the reservation that the conversation was a private one. He started by saying that the policy of maintaining good relations with Poland, for which we had both cooperated for so many years, had foundered and he was examining the reasons for that turn of events. Then followed a long exchange of views, each of us mutually advancing his arguments. Göring complained among other things of our distrust of Germany and of Hitler's pledges, which he always observed on the Polish side. In his opinion the distrust greatly contributed to rendering

[20] *Ibid.*, No. 200; see also *British Blue Book*, Nos. 56, 57, 58, and 59.

impossible cooperation between the two states. He tried to convince me that Hitler was sincere when he declared that he dismissed the Corridor problem. That sounded rather cynical in the light of the frantic German campaign for the revision of Poland's western frontier. As regards Danzig, Göring admitted that the decision had been taken to annex this city to Germany. When I referred to the formal pledges made on many occasions before me by the Chancellor to respect the statute of the Free City and Polish rights in Danzig, Göring replied that Poland should have no illusions on this point, in view of the action led by the National Socialists in the Free City. Even in Danzig questions "we have had our tussles, but things between us would never have got so far ("wir hätten uns gerauft, aber es wäre nicht so weit zwischen uns gekommen") without British intervention. We would never have been placed in such a position as we are at present." "What does Mr. Beck expect?" Göring kept repeating. Even in the case of England's intervention that country was quite unable to give Poland efficient assistance.

Alluding to the German-Soviet agreement, I pointed out that Poland had followed a consistent policy toward both Germany and Russia in agreement with the nonaggression pacts with these countries, refusing to side with one of them against the other. Göring did not deny this. I put to him then the question whether the German-Soviet agreement would not in its consequences turn against the Reich, provoking war in Europe, which must profit only the Soviets. Göring looked down and did not answer. After a while he admitted that German foreign policy had made a *volte-face* of 100 degrees, but that was Great Britain's fault. One must keep in mind that Germany had to choose between Great Britain and Russia. The pact with Russia would have far-reaching consequences. "From now on we have to agree on all our moves toward Poland with Soviet Russia." The last words of Göring remained deeply impressed in my mind.

Referring to my continuous efforts for fourteen years to normalize Polish-German relations and establish a possible cooperation between the two countries, I said that I remained at this crucial moment in Berlin (Moltke left Warsaw in July) in order that I might be at the Chancellor's disposal if he wanted to ease the tension with Poland. Göring assured me that he would inform the Chancellor accordingly.

It appeared from the conversation with Göring and from his behavior that he considered the war with Poland to be a foregone conclusion. He expressed regrets that he should, on the Führer's order, fight in the opposite camp to me, and he took leave of me with a theatrical gesture.

Events of August 25, 1939

In the last days before the outbreak of the war there were rumors in Berlin of the alleged hesitations of Hitler as regards starting the war. Much evidence points to the fact that the attack against Poland was originally ordered for August 26 and then postponed.

From August 23 reports were coming in of incidents provoked by German groups along the Polish frontier. These incidents assumed vast proportions on August 25, and on the following day the tension was still increasing.[21] At this time an incident occurred which threw light on the German plans. On the night of August 25 to 26 a German detachment, starting from Slovak territory and stealing through woods, attacked the railway station at Mosty and the railway tunnel in the Jablonka Pass. In the morning it was destroyed by a Polish detachment of the 21st Mountain Division.[22] The German lieutenant who commanded the detachment confessed that he had carried out this task in connection with the outbreak of the war. The Germans withdrew immediately from this incident. The commander of the 7th German Infantry Division expressed his regrets to General Kustroń for an incident caused by "an irresponsible man." This fact could not be fully used by Polish propaganda, since there was so much news of incidents multiplying from hour to hour.

When on August 26 I lodged a protest against the violation of the Polish frontier with Undersecretary of State Woermann,[23] the Embassy obtained news circuitously that on August 25 in the late afternoon the Polish Consulate at Marienwerder [Kwidzyń] was occupied by the police and Consul [Edward] Czyżewski interned with all his staff. This step by the German authorities must have been connected with the general measures which had been taken in the event of war on the territory of East Prussia, which was under special watch.[24] In reply to an intervention by the Polish Embassy, the German Foreign Office was unable to

[21] See *Polish White Book*, No. 116.
[22] Gisevius, in his book *Bis zum bitteren Ende*, states wrongly that this German detachment maintained the Jablonka Pass for a whole week until the war broke out.
[23] *DGFP*, Series D, Vol. VI, Nos. 330, 331, and 335.
[24] *Ibid.*, No. 336.

state any valid reason which might have explained this step of the local authorities in East Prussia. Owing to our intervention, Consul Czyżewski, with all his staff, left a few days later for Lithuania via Königsberg. They thus had the chance to escape the fate of their colleagues from other consular posts in East Prussia, some of whom died in German prisons during the war, such as the consul in Allenstein [Olsztyn], Bohdan Jałowiecki; the attaché to the consulate in Königsberg, Witold Winiarski; and the clerk of the same consulate, Emil Schuller.[25]

Our assumption that the date of August 26, 1939, was originally chosen for the outbreak of the war was confirmed in the Nuremberg trial, and the course of events of that day was set up with full precision on the ground of the evidence given by the defendants and documents produced before the Tribunal. Hitler's main idea was to localize the conflict with Poland. He believed that he could achieve this by his agreement with Russia; he anticipated a government crisis in England and in France under the shock of the news of the German-Russian agreement; and he was sure that he would compel Poland to surrender. The position taken by the British government and conveyed to him by Henderson on August 23, as well as the declarations of the British ministers in the House of Commons and the House of Lords (August 24), had shaken his confidence that the Western Powers would not come to Poland's assistance.[26] This may explain the approach by Hitler to Great Britain with a comprehensive offer, as well as his conciliatory gesture toward France. Between the conversations held on August 25, first with Henderson at 1:30 P.M., then with Coulondre at 5:30 P.M., Hitler issued an order at 2 P.M. to start the attack against Poland at dawn the following day.[27]

At the same time conversations were held between Rome and Berlin, as disclosed in Ciano's memoirs. In the night from August 24 to August 25, Ribbentrop advised Ciano by telephone that the situation had become critical on account of Polish "provocation." The following day,

[25] Consul Bohdan Jałowiecki was imprisoned in Königsberg and in concentration camps Hohenbruch and Działdowo, where he died in February, 1941. Witold Winiarski, imprisoned in Königsberg, died in concentration camp Działdowo in August, 1941. Emil Schuller committed suicide in prison in Königsberg in May, 1941. In Lipski's papers (File 31), there is a list of 51 Polish foreign service employees arrested by the Germans, 27 of whom were executed or died in concentration camps.

[26] *British Blue Book*, Nos. 56 and 64.

[27] *DGFP*, Series D, Vol. VI, No. 265 and Editor's Note on p. 302, as well as *Livre jaune*, No. 242.

before noon, Ciano called twice on Mussolini, who was perplexed whether he should stay outside the conflict or declare his allegiance to Hitler. At 2 P.M. Hitler sent a communication to Mussolini, through Mackensen, that he would start an armed intervention, asking for an "Italian understanding." The Italians availed themselves of this last passage. Mussolini's answer was conveyed to Hitler through Attolico at 3 P.M. The Italian ally refused to take part in the war, alleging that Italy was not ready for the time being, and that it could not intervene unless supplied "with the military supplies and the raw materials." [28] Shortly afterward even worse news reached Berlin, namely, that on the same afternoon a treaty of alliance between Poland and England had been signed.[29]

Under interrogation Ribbentrop said the following about the steps he had taken when this news was communicated to him: "When I heard this news from Press quarters, subsequently confirmed by the Reich Chancellery, I went at once to the Führer and, hearing that military steps had been taken against Poland, I asked him to withdraw and stop the advance. Hitler hesitated for a moment and then agreed with me. He gave orders to his military adjutant—I think that Marshal Keitel called at the same time—to convene the generals and stop the military measures which had already been started. Hitler told me on that occasions that he had received two items of bad news that day and assumed that news of the attitude adopted by Italy must have reached London immediately, which accounted for the final signing of the treaty of alliance." [30]

Keitel also made a statement on this subject: "I was surprised by an urgent call from Hitler to the Reich Chancellery. He told me to 'stop everything at once, and to call Brauchitsch. I need time for negotiations.' I telephoned to the Commander in Chief of the Army and transmitted to him the order, and he was called to Hitler." [31]

Göring supplemented Ribbentrop's and Keitel's statements by saying: "On the day when England gave its formal guarantee to Poland, that was on August 25, 1939, the Führer called me on the telephone and told me that he had stopped the planned invasion of Poland. I asked him

[28] *DGFP,* Series D, Vol. VI, Nos. 266 and 271.

[29] For the text of the Anglo-Polish Agreement of Mutual Assistance, see *Polish White Book,* No. 91. For the secret protocol, see Jędrzejewicz, *Poland in the British Parliament, 1939–1945,* I, 191, and III, 513–17.

[30] *Trial of the Major War Criminals,* 94th day of the trial, March 29, 1946.

[31] *Ibid.,* 99th day, April 4, 1946.

whether this was just temporary or for good. He said, 'No, I will have to see whether we can eliminate British intervention.' " [32]

The Affairs of the Sixteen Points

After August 25 the Nazi leaders redoubled their efforts to neutralize Great Britain, and in this way France also, in the conflict with Poland. The principal roles were clearly shared out. Hitler took the direction of the whole action. Ribbentrop, as foreign minister, carried out his orders in conversations held with the British government through Henderson. Finally, Göring—with the knowledge and consent but allegedly behind the back of Ribbentrop—in great secrecy initiated unofficial steps with London, using Dahlerus as his trusted confidant.

The history of the exertions of Dahlerus, a Swedish industrialist, who in this tragic period meddled in negotiations for peace with utterly irrelevant proposals, being completely in the dark as regards German designs, as he confessed at Nuremberg, was widely discussed during the trial. Even before the trial started and he was himself cited as a witness by Göring, Dahlerus had published a book in Swedish in which he related his adventures in detail.[33] We learn about Dahlerus' past life from these memoirs, written in the form of a report and imbued with an exaggerated feeling of the historic importance of his mission and displaying his gullibility. He was thoroughly acquainted with Germany and England, having stayed as an industrialist in both countries for a long time. He came into contact with Göring in 1934 over personal matters: Göring helped him in the settlement of the financial affairs of Dahlerus' future wife, a German by birth, and in return Dahlerus took care of Göring's stepson, who was staying in Sweden. After 1935 they both met a few times each year, which gave Dahlerus the opportunity of making the acquaintance of the rulers of the Third Reich. From close observation Dahlerus reached the conclusion that, while Hitler and his protégé Ribbentrop were aiming at war for territorial conquests, Göring inclined toward peaceful settlement, as tested during the Sudetenland crisis in 1938.

Dahlerus was extremely worried that the breach between Germany and England was widening because of the lack of understanding among the Nazi rulers, including Göring, of British policy and of the firm

[32] *Ibid.,* 87th day, March 21, 1946.
[33] Dahlerus, *The Last Attempt.* See also *The Times Literary Supplement* (London), May 25, 1946, for the article "An Interloper in Diplomacy."

decision of the British nation to resist all further German aggression. When the tension between Germany and Great Britain was increasing in the summer of 1939, it occurred to him that it would be useful if Göring could get into direct touch with prominent representatives of the British nation for a free exchange of views, outside the well-worn ruts of diplomacy. For this purpose, on June 24, 1939, he left Sweden for London, where over dinner at the Constitutional Club he met leading men from the industrial, financial, and commercial worlds, and held a discussion with them on the subject of British-German relations. At the request of the Britons who attended the conference a summary of the discussion was made, consisting of a few paragraphs.

The conclusions of the British participants were that the British nation had reached the limit of its patience and would not put up with any further conquests. The British nation, nevertheless, wished to live in peace with the German nation and did not see any valid reason for an armed conflict, the more so as the Germans could gain much more by agreements than by war. The British party stressed the pledges to Poland, also as regards Danzig. It was clearly pointed out that the occupation of Danzig would mean war with Poland and that Great Britain would automatically be involved in war with Germany.

Pursuant to this meeting, Dahlerus arrived in Berlin on July 5 and on the following day was received by Göring, to whom he produced the conclusions of the London conversation, suggesting a meeting between German and British statesmen. As Göring persisted in saying that the English guarantee to Poland was a bluff, Dahlerus proposed to summon to Berlin three persons who had attended the conference at the Constitutional Club and who were staying at that time in Copenhagen. They were to confirm the opinion expressed by Dahlerus to Göring. With Göring's approval three Englishmen, among them Spencer, reached the Reich capital on July 7; they confirmed what had been discussed in London, met a German general, detailed to show them the Air Ministry, and after a tour of the city left Berlin the following day. On July 8 Dahlerus was told that Hitler had accepted the idea of an interview of the British group with Göring, provided that strict secrecy was preserved. In this way they met on August 7, 1939, at Sonke Nissen Koog, a place in northern Schleswig. Before that, on July 20, Dahlerus was received by Lord Halifax, who was interested in the idea of the meeting, but emphasized that the British government would not take part in the conference. For this reason there were no members either of the government or of Parliament among the Britons who attended the conference. Dahlerus did not disclose in his memoirs the names of those who were present, whose number was seven, except for Spencer.

On the German side the meeting was attended by Göring, with General Bodenschatz and other high officials. According to Dahlerus' recital of the meeting, which lasted some hours (Göring stayed at Sonke Nissen Koog from 10 A.M. to 6 P.M.), it was confined to the presentation by both parties of their points of view in a friendly atmosphere and with mutual recriminations. Göring, who was more and more cheerful and outspoken, alluded once to the fact that Germany had abstained from criticizing the Soviet Union for some months past, and to the Rapallo pact as still being valid. When the British representatives pointed out the recurring German method of putting on the agenda the minority problem, as an introduction to the incorporation of certain areas into Germany, Göring assured them "upon his word as a statesman and an officer" that Germany's demand for Danzig and the Pomeranian Corridor did not aim at the encirclement of Poland, and that Germany would not raise any further territorial claims after the settlement of the Danzig problem. The meeting was closed with the adoption of a recommendation of both governments to convene an official conference, attended by delegates with full powers. Dahlerus writes that the meeting became more and more cordial and was closed by mutual toasts, and that its outcome gave hope for a peaceful settlement of outstanding difficult problems.

The next day the British representatives raised a proposal before Dahlerus to extend the conference of the two powers to France and Italy also, which meant that Poland as well as the Soviets would have been excluded. Dahlerus went after Göring to the island of Sylt to obtain his agreement. Göring, who seemed to be satisfied with the outcome of the meeting, expressed the opinion "that the conference of the four powers would be agreed to by the German government, provided it was well prepared."

Returning to Sweden full of good hope, Dahlerus told his English friends three days later that Germany agreed to a secret meeting of the four powers, and that Sweden would be the most agreeable meeting place for them. Dahlerus felt elated as his dreams took shape. New chances for saving the peace were secured, but he omits to state that it could be done only at the price of a new Polish Munich. He urged the Swedish minister of state to suggest that Sweden accept its responsibilities and not refuse its hospitality should it be requested to grant it by the British and German governments.

"And now," further writes Dahlerus, "an episode occurred, inexplicable to me, pregnant with consequences." The negotiations came to a complete stop. A dilettante diplomatist was unable to understand that.

On August 23 Göring summoned Dahlerus from Stockholm by telephone to come at once to Berlin. The zealous Dahlerus was at Karinhall the next day. Göring delivered a long speech in which he told Dahlerus that the German political and military position had greatly improved owing to the treaty with Russia. Assuring him that Germany sincerely desired an understanding with Great Britain, Göring asked Dahlerus to go immediately to London and declare to the British government on his, Göring's, behalf that he was ready to risk all his authority in order to achieve this end. Distrusting the German Foreign Office—which must have meant that he placed no reliance on Ribbentrop—he was trying his own channels to make contact with London.

On August 25 at 1:30 P.M. Dahlerus landed at Croydon, at the moment when Hitler was seeing Henderson, and less than an hour before he ordered the attack against Poland. As Dahlerus confessed afterward, he knew nothing about that.

Stating the reasons for which he had taken upon himself this mission to London, Göring explained at Nuremberg as follows: "During all these negotiations it was not a question, as far as I was concerned, of isolating Poland and keeping England out of the matter, but rather it was a question, since the problem of the Corridor and Danzig had come up, of solving it peacefully as far as possible along the lines of the Munich solution." [34] Göring was fully aware that the acceptance of German territorial claims would deliver Poland lock, stock, and barrel to Germany, canceling all its alliances with the Western Powers. Moreover, from August 23, 1939, Germany was bound to Soviet Russia by a secret protocol which stipulated the delimitation of the spheres of interest between these powers along the Narew, Vistula, and San in the case of any territorial and political changes in the areas belonging to the

[34] *Trial of the Major War Criminals,* Testimony of Göring on the 85th day of the trial, March 19, 1946.

Polish state.[35] Infringement of the territorial status of Poland would automatically bring into force the German-Soviet agreement, which meant the partition of Poland between Germany and Russia. Göring believed that it would be possible to settle the Polish problem by cunning and artful devices without risking war with the coalition.

The French ambassador in Berlin rightly assessed the German aims, drawing the attention of his government, in a telegram of August 26, to the necessity not to commit two essential mistakes when negotiating with Germany: the first would be if the international guarantee for Poland were stipulated without the necessary precision. M. Coulondre warned against the second mistake in the following words: "The second stumbling block would be to lend oneself to intrigues aimed at dissociating the Allies. No pressure of the sort to demoralize Poland could be exerted. Danzig is merely the point of least resistance at which the Reich tries to break into Poland. M. Lipski said to me last night: 'What the Germans want is to place their hands on Poland and one day to have the Polish Army at their disposal.' Negotiations, and this is a preliminary condition, can only start if all threat of force is discarded." [36]

An official stage of the German-British negotiations was reopened by a conversation between Hitler and Henderson on August 25. Then followed Henderson's flight to London on the 26th, his return to Berlin on the 28th, and a conversation with Hitler the same day at 10:30 P.M. In these negotiations the British government took a favorable stand toward the question of reaching an agreement with the Reich if the differences between Germany and Poland were settled peacefully.

At the same time Dahlerus was carrying on his job. On August 25 he called on Halifax who, in view of the news from Berlin that official negotiations had been reopened, thanked him for his further services for the time being. Nevertheless, when Göring warned him on the telephone at night that the war might break out at any moment under the shock of the signing of the Anglo-Polish Treaty of Mutual Assistance, Dahlerus saw Halifax again the morning of the next day, obtained from him a personal letter to Göring, and flew to Berlin. The same night he met Göring and then was received by Hitler. After a long monologue and a hysterical violent outburst, Hitler asked Dahlerus to return immediately

---

[35] For the text of the Treaty of Nonaggression between Germany and the USSR and the Secret Additional Protocol, see *DGFP*, Series D, Vol. VI, Nos. 228 and 229.

[36] *Livre jaune*, No. 248.

to England, conveying through him orally his proposals to the British government, summed up in six points which differed considerably from the note handed over through Henderson. In return for friendship offered to England, Hitler wished to secure its assistance in obtaining Danzig and the Corridor—Poland to retain Gdynia and to be given a free port in Danzig. He demanded adequate guarantees for the German minority in Poland, but at the same time agreed to guarantee Poland's future frontiers.[37]

On August 27 Dahlerus was received at Downing Street by Chamberlain and Halifax in the presence of Cadogan and Horace Wilson. The British negotiators were in a rather awkward position, being confronted by two reports on the German demands, one officially conveyed by Henderson, and the other unofficially transmitted by Dahlerus. Their position could not fail to increase the English distrust of Hitler and his government. When the meeting was over, Cadogan explained to Dahlerus the British stand toward Hitler's proposals and said that the British government recommended direct German-Polish negotiations and asked for the participation of Germany, Russia, France, Italy, and Great Britain in the international guarantees for Poland.

Returning to Berlin on August 27 at 11 P.M., Dahlerus informed Göring of the results of his endeavors in London. After seeing Hitler, Göring decided that the situation was taking a favorable turn.

At this crucial moment for Poland the bonds of alliance to the Western Powers put on its shoulders a heavy and responsible duty to follow a line of conduct imbued with the maximum good will in spite of hostile German maneuvers.

To the appeal addressed to Poland and Germany by the Belgian King on behalf of the Oslo group, as well as by President Roosevelt, the President of Poland replied in the affirmative, agreeing to direct negotiations between the two powers concerned, respectively to the application of conciliation procedures and the participation of an impartial and disinterested factor.[38]

---

[37] Hitler's six points in his talk with Dahlerus were to cover the following: (1) An agreement or alliance of Germany with England. (2) England must help Germany in the annexation of Danzig and the Corridor. (3) Germany would guarantee the western frontier of Poland. (4) There must be an agreement on the matter of German colonies. (5) The treatment of German minorities would be guaranteed. (6) The Germans would agree to fight for the British Empire anywhere it might be attacked. (Testimony of Dahlerus in Nuremberg on the 85th day of the trial, March 19, 1946.)

[38] *Polish White Book*, Nos. 87, 88, 89, and 90.

On August 28, after a consultation between the British Ambassador in Warsaw and Mr. Beck on the answer to be given to the German note of August 25, the British government was authorized to convey to Berlin the news that Poland was ready for conversations.[39]

In connection with this decision of the Polish government, a meeting took place on August 29 in the afternoon, at Mr. Beck's house, attended by a small number of higher officials of the Polish Foreign Office. The object was to choose the Polish delegate and the place where the talks should be held. During the meeting Mr. Beck spoke on the telephone with President Mościcki and Marshal Śmigły-Rydz in order to reach a common agreement on these two matters. The opinion prevailed that it would not be advisable for Mr. Beck himself to go to Berlin, or to another place, in view of the precedents set by Schuschnigg and Hacha. As regards the place for the conference, it was recommended to hold it either in a town near the frontier or in a railway coach close to the Polish-German frontier, in order to avoid the use by the Germans of their ill-famed means of pressure. During the discussion of the names for the Polish emissary several names were put forward, among others that of Mr. Anthony Roman, minister of trade and industry, former Polish envoy in Stockholm, who on some occasions had led the negotiations with Danzig. Eventually Beck gave his preference to the Polish Ambassador in Berlin, an official diplomatic representative to Germany, as the most suitable man for reopening and carrying out the negotiations.[40]

At almost the same time, a few days before this meeting at the Polish Foreign Office, I obtained from a good German source a confidential piece of news—transmitted to me by Dr. Wnorowski, press attaché at the Embassy for many years—which appeared to me to be vitally important and which I immediately conveyed to Warsaw. The Auswärtiges Amt was allegedly preparing a draft of German claims to Poland, but the whole document must be drafted in such a way as to create the appearance of a conciliatory spirit on the German side and yet be quite unacceptable to Poland on its merits. The purpose of the document was to provoke a rupture between Poland and the Western countries.

On the evening of August 28 Henderson transmitted to the Chancellor the answer of the British government, which, among other things, recommended a peaceful settlement of the Polish-German dispute by

[39] *British Blue Book*, Nos. 72 and 74.
[40] According to the notes made by Mr. Paweł Starzeński, secretary to Mr. Beck.

way of direct discussions with safeguards for Poland's essential interests, and stressed the necessity of granting international guarantees to Poland by the five Great Powers. The note also said that His Majesty's government "has already received a definite assurance from the Polish government that it is ready to negotiate on that basis." In the exchange of views which followed between Hitler and Henderson the Chancellor raised his price, asking not only for the return of Danzig and the whole Corridor but also for the rectification of the frontier in Upper Silesia to the advantage of the Germans.

When Henderson was received at the Reich Chancellery the next day at 7:15 P.M., Hitler handed him the German reply.[41] While fully maintaining German demands for the return of Danzig and the Corridor and the safeguarding of the German minorities in Poland, the note declared that Germany was prepared to enter into discussion with Poland if the Polish emissary arrived by Wednesday, August 30, 1939. This condition sounded like an ultimatum and was considered as such by the Allied governments. It provoked a sharp reply from the British Ambassador, and an extremely vivid discussion with Hitler followed. Moreover, the German note contained reservations, the meaning of which is today quite obvious in the light of the claims of the secret Soviet-German protocol, namely, that "in the event of a territorial rearrangement in Poland, the German government could no longer give a guarantee without the USSR." There was also a paragraph which said that the German government would immediately draw up proposals for a solution acceptable to itself and would, if possible, place these at the disposal of the British government before the arrival of the Polish negotiator.

After his return from the Reich Chancellery, Henderson told me of the text of the German note, and we had a long conversation on the situation arising from it.

In order to ascertain the opinions prevailing that evening in the Reich Chancellery it is worth while to refer to the evidence given by General Bodenschatz, Göring's trusted man and his liaison officer with the Reich Chancellery. During the interrogation Bodenschatz stated unequivocally that Hitler wanted war with Poland. He said then that he was present at the Reich Chancellery that evening when Hitler handed Henderson his conditions with the demands for the return of Danzig and the Corridor,

[41] *DGFP*, Series D, Vol. VI, No. 421, and *British Blue Book*, Nos. 78, 79, and 80. See also Henderson, pp. 262–68.

and stressed that after all the discussions between the Chancellor and the British Ambassador he was under the impression that Hitler did not at all wish Poland to accept his conditions. At the hearing Bodenschatz was more cautious in his statement, in which he said the following:

"I was not present at the conference. If I said that, I did not express myself correctly. I was not at the conference that the Führer had with Henderson, but I was standing in the antechamber with the other adjutants, and in the hall one could hear the various groups, some saying one thing, some another. From their talks I gathered the conditions which Henderson received for the Poles in the evening—that the deadline for answering these questions, which was noon of the next day, was so short that one could conclude that there was some intention behind it." [42]

Bodenschatz's account, while not quite accurate in details, speaks for itself, since during conclusive discussions at the Chancellery all those present in the antechamber were usually the highest and most initiated members of the party.

When cross-examining Ribbentrop, Sir David Maxwell Fyfe put a straightforward question:

"Q. Now did you really expect after the treatment of von Schuschnigg, of Tiso, of Hacha, that the Poles would be willing to send a fly into the spider's parlor?

"A. We certainly counted on it and hoped for it. I think that a hint from the British government would have sufficed to bring that Ambassador to Berlin.

"Q. And what you hoped was to put the Poles in this dilemma, that either the terms would stand as a—to use Hitler's phrase—propagandist cause for the war, or else you would be able, by putting pressure on the Polish plenipotentiary, to do exactly what you had done before with Schuschnigg and Tiso and Hacha, and get a surrender from the Poles." [43]

The evening of August 29 was really a crucial moment. Göring was fully aware of that and, being extremely worried by the critical turn caused by the outcome of the conversation between Henderson and Hitler, summoned Dahlerus that very night and set him moving. He requested him to go at once to London and confidentially say there that

[42] *Trial of the Major War Criminals,* testimony of Bodenschatz on the 77th day of the trial, March 8, 1946.
[43] *Ibid.,* 96th day of the trial, April 1, 1946.

Hitler was preparing a magnanimous offer to Poland (*grosszügiges Angebot*), that he had decided to deliver to Poland on August 30 a note offering such lenient terms that Poland would be able to accept them and England would recommend acceptance. The previous day Hitler had been busy with this draft, and for this reason the last disagreement with Henderson was most regrettable. Besides the annexation of Danzig by the Reich, Hitler's proposals would ask for a plebiscite in the Corridor on the lines of the one held in the Saar. Special lines of communication would be granted to the state which was the loser in the plebiscite.

Dahlerus, as a good tradesman, wanted to know the kind of goods he had to deal with. Göring replied that the matter was still under consideration, but tore out a page from the atlas and drew a line for the plebiscite area, reaching as far as Lodz.[44]

The indefatigable Dahlerus was in the plane by 5 A.M. and landed at Heston at 9 o'clock. He carried out Göring's commission before Chamberlain and Halifax in the presence of Cadogan, and did not fail to repeat the story concocted by Göring for British ears about the shooting by Polish soldiers of eight German refugees trying to cross the Warta. This story had "utterly shocked" Hitler.

On this occasion Dahlerus got the impression that the patience of the British government was at the breaking point and that it was becoming more and more suspicious of Göring's maneuvers and initiatives. Trying to discard these suspicions, he telephoned from Cadogan's office to Göring and obtained the information that the German document was ready and contained more favorable terms for Poland than those told to Dahlerus at night.

When all again met, Chamberlain declared that he had to summon another cabinet meeting in order to review the situation, after which new instructions would be forwarded to Henderson. Then Dahlerus had a separate talk with Cadogan, who produced an idea that the discussions between Poland and Germany should be held not in Berlin but rather in a neutral country. Dahlerus telephoned again to Göring, who became angry, saying that it was "nonsense," for the conversations must be held in Berlin where the Chancellor was. At 11 P.M. Dahlerus landed at Tempelhof airport.

[44] *Ibid.*, 85th day of the trial, March 19, 1946. During the trial Göring explained that the line he had drawn had delimited the area with a German population.

On August 30 the atmosphere in Berlin was tense, and this atmosphere was felt also in the diplomatic corps. Many heads of diplomatic missions called on me that day. In the evening Coulondre called also, as usual self-possessed and calm. He communicated to me the news obtained from most confidential quarters that the attack on Poland originally planned for August 26 had subsequently been postponed, that Hitler was hesitating as regards war operations, and that he had had a nervous breakdown in recent days. This information showed also that in certain high German military quarters the opposition to risking war with France and Great Britain was increasing. This opposition was coming to a head. It was therefore most important to gain time. I then discussed with Coulondre how to proceed in connection with the German demand for a Polish emissary to be sent to Berlin. Together we reached the conclusion that the best solution would be my announcement to the German government that I, in my capacity as ambassador, was ready at any time to enter into contact with them. It would be a further proof of our good will, and would at the same time give a possibility of reopening negotiations. Any trust in Hitler and his entourage was already out of the question, and extreme caution was recommended in order to avoid the well-known Nazi methods of blackmail and pressure.[45]

Warsaw was informed in detail of the official conversations between London and Berlin through the British ambassador, Kennard, who took the advice of the Polish government and agreed on the procedure with them. I obtained my information from Henderson, contacts with whom were rather casual and did not give the whole picture of the exchange of views between Warsaw and London. My contact with the Foreign Office in Warsaw was made more and more difficult by the German authorities. Telephone conversations were often interrupted. The dispatch of telegrams met with obstacles. The wireless station of the Embassy was the only means left for communication with the head office. In view of these circumstances I asked Counselor Lubomirski to go to Warsaw in the early hours, and it was arranged that he would go by road to Poznań, then by plane to Warsaw, and would return as soon as possible.[46] It had great weight with me that Lubomirski might give Beck the latest news, sound his opinions, and obtain his authorization for the

[45] See *Livre jaune,* No. 296.
[46] See Lubomirski, "Ostatnia misja z Berlina," *Wiadomości* (London), 1943, No. 182.

establishment of contact with the Reich government. When I was going to rest in the late hours, Henderson telephoned me, at 2 A.M., asking me to come over. I found him highly excited after a violent discussion with Ribbentrop. The account of this discussion is well known from official British publications and from Henderson's book.[47] It is known that, after presenting the reply of his government to the British note of August 29, Ribbentrop read out in German at top speed the German proposals for the Polish emissary, consisting of sixteen articles. When asked by Henderson for the text, Ribbentrop refused, stating that these proposals no longer existed because the Polish representative had not arrived in Berlin within the prescribed time. Explaining his behavior toward the British Ambassador, Ribbentrop stated as follows:

"I should like to state here once more under oath that the Führer had expressly forbidden me to let these proposals out of my hands. He told me that I might communicate only the substance of them, if I thought it advisable, to the British Ambassador." [48]

Dahlerus informed Göring of the incident with Ribbentrop the same night. Then Göring authorized him to convey by telephone the text of the sixteen points to the counselor of the British Embassy, Forbes [Sir George Ogilvie-Forbes]. At Nuremberg Göring stated the following: "To do this was, as I have already said, actually an enormous risk, since the Führer had forbidden that this information should be made public at present."

The purpose of this document was manifest. It was not to constitute a basis for normal negotiations with Poland but was to serve as a trump card in the perfidious game of Hitler. The draft was undoubtedly the result of thorough researches by the best experts of the Auswärtiges Amt. By no means could it have been dictated by Hitler. A well-informed student of Polish-German relations could immediately discover the hidden poison dart concealed in the highly polished, glib words of the document, which, should it be put into execution, would strangle Poland with iron claws. If we examine, for instance, the principles on which the plebiscite in Pomerania, presented as Hitler's magnanimous offer, was to be arranged, we find they were drafted in such a way that the outcome was considered as a foregone conclusion.

[47] British Blue Book, No. 92; Henderson, pp. 269–71; and DGFP, Series D, Vol. VI, Nos. 461 and 458 (Hitler's sixteen proposals).
[48] Trial of the Major War Criminals, testimony of Ribbentrop on the 94th day of the trial, March 29, 1946.

Today it is obvious that Hitler did not take into account any plebiscite at all. But his prudent advisers took their precautions to provide for all contingencies. The Polish forces, police, and administrators should leave the plebiscite area in Pomerania, leaving all power in the hands of a commission composed of representatives of France, Great Britain, Italy, and Russia. The poll would take place only a year later. In such a way, during this whole time Poland, whose vital problem of access to the sea was at stake, would have to live in a state of anxious uncertainty, while Nazi propaganda could be freely carried out under the protective wings of its two allies, Soviet Russia and Italy. The right to vote should belong to the Poles as well as Germans born in the plebiscite area before January 1, 1918, or who lived there before that date. Germans who left Pomerania after 1918 were entitled to come back and take part in the poll. Consequently, all Polish inhabitants settled in Pomerania after the Versailles Treaty, as well as all the Polish generation born on this territory after January 1, 1918, would have to stay as passive witnesses of a tragic plebiscite.

On the memorable night of August 30, Henderson was unable to memorize the text of all these sixteen articles, and even more to understand the far-reaching consequences of this portentous document. In our conversation he was able only to reproduce to me some provisions concerning the plebiscite. Nevertheless the offer, as such, impressed him as being "on the whole not too unreasonable." For this reason he urged me to approach Ribbentrop, still on the same night, with the request to convey to me the terms with reference to his conversation with the British Ambassador.

I considered that to approach Ribbentrop in such circumstances would have meant asking him to deliver me an ultimatum, which in view of the well-known attitude of Hitler and Ribbentrop would be understood as our surrender and appropriate use made of the step. Since Ribbentrop was really so eager to reach an understanding with Poland by negotiations, it was completely inexplicable that he should refuse to hand to Henderson the text of the sixteen articles. I put forward an argument to the British Ambassador that I could not act in such an important matter without the knowledge of my government, and promised him to get in touch with Warsaw immediately. I did this as soon as I returned to the Embassy, sending the appropriate telegrams.[49] I suc-

[49] See Document 159, p. 571.

ceeded in informing Lubomirski before his departure for Warsaw of my conversation with Henderson.

In the early hours Henderson telephoned me that he had received information according to which the German government would be disposed to wait only until 12 o'clock. He asked for an answer from Warsaw and wished to see me once more. Being unable to leave the Embassy premises, since I was waiting for instructions, I sent to Henderson the first secretary of the Embassy, Malhomme, whom Henderson knew from Belgrade. . . .[50]

From the early hours the Embassy was seized by feverish activity. My colleagues of the diplomatic corps called without previous warning. Coulondre called also and told me that Henderson's information about 12 o'clock came from Ribbentrop's entourage. The Italian Ambassador, a consummate diplomat and a friend of mine, terrified by the prospect of war and its consequences for Italy as the Axis partner, exercised the heaviest pressure on me that morning. He was seconded by the Hungarian envoy. Other heads of missions, with the Papal Nuncio, kept inquiring about the development of the situation. In this flood of calls the British Ambassador, having previously warned me on the telephone, sent to me the counselor of the Embassy, Sir George Ogilvie-Forbes, accompanied by an individual unknown to me, who introduced himself as a friend of Göring and *homme de confiance* of the British government. He was Dahlerus. I saw him then for the first time, and I had no knowledge whatever of the role of go-between he had played with Berlin and London. In the conversation that followed Dahlerus stated that Göring was opposing the extremists of the Party who wanted to annex to Germany the whole part of Poland taken by Prussia after the partition of Poland, and made a proposal limited to Danzig and the Corridor.

To my astonishment Dahlerus began to read aloud from a handwritten page those famous sixteen articles which had raised such a storm. Pretending that there was no time to lose, Dahlerus urged me to go immediately to Göring, accept his terms and sign them, and then the whole problem would be settled and we would be able to shoot stags together. In order to stop this ghastly business I told him that I could not understand what the matter was about, and asked Dahlerus to dictate the contents of the note to my secretary, Miss Gimzicka.

When I was left alone with Forbes I told him of my dissatisfaction

50 See p. 569.

with his bringing to me an unknown individual who put forward proposals infringing the territorial integrity of the Polish state. I warned him against the discussion of Poland's territorial problems, as it would bring about moral breakdown and military collapse in Poland. I insisted that the only course to be followed was the maintaining of a united front by England, France, and Poland, and I added that Poland would defend itself in any case.

Dahlerus handed me the typewritten text, and our conversation came to an end.

My meeting with Dahlerus, described in his book, had been an item vividly discussed at the Nuremberg trial. The defense made use of a passage from Dahlerus' account, according to which I was alleged to have said to Forbes, when we were left alone, that I was not interested in German proposals, since I was convinced that riots would break out in the event of war and the victorious Polish Army would march into Berlin.

Sir David Maxwell Fyfe, when cross-examining Dahlerus, put to him the following questions, undoubtedly basing himself on Forbes's account of the conversation with me:

"And did not Sir George Ogilvie-Forbes tell you that Lipski made his opinion quite clear, that the German offer was a breach of Polish sovereignty, and in his view Poland and France and England must stand firm and show a united front, and that Poland, if left alone, would fight and die alone?" Dahlerus' answer was "Yes." [51]

The same day Beck summed up the Polish attitude to Lubomirski, who had just arrived in Warsaw to carry out his mission. The Foreign Minister informed him that pursuant to the conversation with the British Ambassador he had sent instructions to Berlin, ordering the Polish Ambassador to establish immediate contact with the German Foreign Minister and the Secretary of State respectively.[52] Beck added also that the Polish government consented to enter into discussions with the Reich under the condition that both parties would be on an equal footing and that Poland would not be faced with *faits accomplis* before the discussions ended. The instructions from Warsaw reached me at 12:40 P.M. I immediately asked for an interview with Ribbentrop, but it did not take place until 6:30 P.M.

[51] *Trial of the Major War Criminals,* cross-examination of Dahlerus by Maxwell Fyfe, 85th day of the trial, March 19, 1946.
[52] *Polish White Book,* No. 110, and Document 161, p. 572.

In his book Hassell writes that he was entertained at lunch by Ambassador Moltke that day and was told by the latter that Ribbentrop was reluctant to receive the Polish Ambassador. At 3 P.M. Weizsäcker telephoned me, asking in which capacity I wished to be received by the Foreign Minister. I answered that I was asking for an interview in my capacity as Ambassador in order to remit a communication from my government.[53]

When I was driving to the Auswärtiges Amt in the Wilhelmstrasse for the last time, a big crowd filled the road. A cordon of S.S. was keeping order. In the hall downstairs and along the staircase members of the S.S. in uniform were posted. Before I reached the first floor I was photographed several times. Nobody was waiting in the familiar oblong reception room with portraits from Bismarck's time; this room was between the study of the Foreign Minister and that of the Secretary of State on duty. Involuntarily I glanced at the desk, Empire style, on which six years before I had signed the declaration of nonaggression with Neurath.

Shortly afterward the door opened and for the last time I had occasion to speak with Ribbentrop. I handed him the communication of the Polish government, which ran as follows:

"Last night the Polish government was informed by the British government of an exchange of views with the Reich government as to the possibility of direct negotiations between the Polish and German governments. The Polish government is favorably considering the British government's suggestion and will make a formal reply on the subject within the next few hours."

The interview was short. Ribbentrop's manner was icy.[54]

At 9 P.M. the sixteen proposals were broadcast by Berlin Radio Station, with the addition that they had been rejected by Poland. It is known that these proposals had never been communicated to the Polish government. They were simply a "propagandist reason" for starting the war, in accordance with Hitler's announcement at the meeting of his commanders in chief on August 22.

[53] *Polish White Book*, No. 111, and *DGFP*, Series D, Vol. VI, No. 475.
[54] *Polish White Book*, No. 112, and *DGFP*, Series D, Vol. VI, No. 476.

Last German Moves in Danzig before the War [1]
August, 1939

AT THE END of May, 1939, the high commissioner of the League of Nations, Burckhardt, was in Berlin, where he met first with Ribbentrop and then with Weizsäcker (the note from this last interview is dated June 1).[2]

Burckhardt intended, although rather reluctantly, to spend the summer months in Danzig, hoping that his very presence there might have some effect contributing to calm excited minds. He kept hoping that no new steps would be taken in the Free City during this period which would force him to take decisions which could afterward be interpreted as anti-German. From Burckhardt's statements that followed it was evident that he tried to use his influence in Berlin in order to alleviate tension with Poland. He mentioned that he had a conversation in Warsaw with Beck, who hoped that it might be possible to reopen Polish-German conversations on a broader level and in a more peaceful atmosphere. Burckhardt further confirmed that from his interview with Lord Halifax, as well as with other British officials, he got the impression that England would keep its obligations in relation to Poland in case of a conflict. However, he added that, according to information obtained from the British Ambassador in Warsaw, a special commission formed at the suggestion of the British side was touring the western provinces—on behalf of the Polish Ministry of the Interior—to supervise the correct treatment of German minorities problems.

When referring to these matters, it seems that the High Commissioner acted with Beck's knowledge. As a matter of fact, Beck made such peaceful advances through the good offices of several other persons.[3]

---

[1] Printed in *Bellona* (London), 1950, No. 1, under the general title "New Premises on the Outbreak of the Polish-German War in 1939."

[2] *DGFP*, Series D, Vol. VI, No. 464; see also Burckhardt, pp. 317–19.

[3] See Gafencu, *The Last Days of Europe*, and Peter Kleist, "Hammer, Sickel und Hakenkreutz," *Die Zeit* (Hamburg), October 13, 1949.

In defiance of binding agreements, as of spring, 1939, Germany began to form military detachments on the territory of Danzig, at first clandestinely, and later on more and more openly. By July the militarization of the Free City already had become quite obvious. At that time General Keitel approached the Auswärtiges Amt for its opinion on the performance of artillery drill exercises in Danzig, in the course of which twelve light guns and four heavy caliber guns, hitherto hidden in the city, would be brought out into the open. In his letter dated July 14, Weizsäcker suggests the postponement of such a demonstration until Poland committed some new tactical error.[4]

The German fleet command was also ready for demonstrations in Danzig. Vice-Admiral Schnievindt urged the Auswärtiges Amt on July 14 for a reply concerning the visit of war-cruisers planned for the end of the month.[5] The problem was of such scope that it could not be decided without Hitler's agreement. Weizsäcker refers to it in his opinion dated July 19.[6] Evasively and with caution, Weizsäcker adds this significant sentence: "For we must always bear in mind that a solution of the Danzig question might occur by force of arms, and that we must put the blame for this on the Poles, while the dispatch of this naval unit to Danzig would be interpreted internationally as a prelude to the generally awaited German-Polish conflict."

In the first days of August a Polish-Danzig conflict broke out with regard to customs inspectors. This matter was to drag on until the end of August, when the frontier between Danzig and East Prussia was formally opened.

In the middle of August Undersecretary of State Keppler delegated to Danzig his trusted collaborator, a National Socialist by conviction, a certain Veesenmayer. (He was to play an important role later in the Balkans and in Hungary.) Vessenmayer confessed at the trial that he had never before been in Danzig, and even at the last moment asked that he not be entrusted with this mission. However, as a National Socialist he had to obey, "so it was always his luck that he was always sent where a fire was to break out."

In Danzig the consul general, Grolman, quarreled with Forster, and the Auswärtiges Amt was left without information. It was necessary to

4 *DGFP*, Series D, Vol. VI, No. 670.
5 *Ibid.*, No. 687, footnote.
6 *Ibid.*, No. 687.

find a liaison between that office and the very ambitious and well-protected Gauleiter, who was accustomed to making policy on his own. So the choice fell on Veesenmayer.

In spite of ever-deepening tension in relations in the Free City and open violation by the Danzig authorities of Polish right for control of customs, the Polish government, in order to show its good will, expressed agreement to undertake conversations for the reduction of the number of customs inspectors. These conversations were started by Commissioner-General Chodacki with President of the Senate Greiser on August 18. Next Maksymowicz, chief director of the Customs Board in Warsaw, came to Danzig, in his capacity of professional negotiator.

A note signed by Weizsäcker, dated August 19, shows the conclusion of Veesenmayer's report as to what methods, recommended by the Gauleiter [7] should be used in negotiations with Poland. Forster declared that pressure should be exerted on Poland to the utmost limits. From the conversation with Chodacki it resulted that Poland was ready to withdraw twelve inspectors within the period of eight to fourteen days. Conversations between experts were to start on August 21. Forster was of the opinion that the immediate withdrawal of fifty customs officials should be requested. In case the Poles gave in again, further requests were to be made to render the negotiations impossible. Veesenmayer asked for instructions. Weizsäcker gave the following answer: "I agree with your views on the conduct of negotiations on the customs officials controversy. Negotiations must, however, be conducted in such a way, and pressure on Poland in other respects must be so applied, that the responsibility for the breakdown of the negotiations and for all consequences falls on Poland." [8]

On August 22 Veesenmayer sent Weizsäcker a detailed plan of action set in five points: [9]

"1) A final breakdown after long negotiations on the question of customs officials. Blame on the side of the Poles.

"2) Then comes the complete removal of all Polish customs officials and the abolition of the customs frontier with East Prussia.

"3) There follows reaction one way or the other on the part of the Poles.

[7] *DGFP*, Series D, Vol. VII, No. 119.
[8] *Ibid.*, No. 139.
[9] *Ibid.*, No. 176.

"4) Thereupon the arrest of numerous Poles in Danzig territory and the clearing of numerous Polish arms dumps; the discovery of these arms dumps is assured.

"5) If this does not produce sufficient action by the Poles in reply, then finally the Westerplatte is to be attacked."

Veesenmayer was not yet informed as to the decision on this matter during Forster's conference at Berchtesgaden.

According to a later report of Veesenmayer dated August 24, points 1, 2, 3, and 5 of the above plan were approved by Hitler.[10]

The Polish desk officer at the A.A. [Bergman] received a report by telephone on August 23 from Grolman, the consul general in Danzig. It reads as follows: [11]

"1) At noon today the Danzig Senate will pass a resolution to offer Gauleiter Forster the post of head of state of the Free City of Danzig. Greiser then will have the post of head of the Danzig government.

"2) In Danzig-Polish negotiations the Danzig representative will demand the immediate withdrawal of fifty Polish customs inspectors. We expect the Poles to refuse this demand. A statement is then to be made about 6 P.M. saying that the negotiations have broken down through the fault of the Poles.

"3) The *Schleswig-Holstein* will come to Danzig instead of the cruiser *Königsberg,* perhaps even tomorrow. The reason for this is that this ship is armed with 28 cm. guns with which it could reach the Hel peninsula from its berth [near the Westerplatte].

"4) Last week berths were already prepared in Danzig harbor for several more warships.

"5) A British steamship berthed in the port of Danzig, which was scheduled to stay three days longer in Danzig to take on cargo, has today received orders from Britain to sail immediately."

No comment is needed on these documents.

10 *Ibid.,* No. 244.
11 For the full text, see *ibid.,* No. 197.

Slovakia on the Eve of the Polish-German War [1]
August, 1939

IN SPITE of bonds of genuine friendship between the Polish and Slovakian population, as well as of racial kinship of languages and the common Catholic faith of the two nations, fate would have it that, during the crisis of March and at the outbreak of the war, Slovakia became a trump card and an instrument in Hitler's hands in his action against Poland.

Some errors of Polish policy, such as minor frontier alterations (which were, besides, of no special importance for the interests of the Polish state), carried out late in the autumn of 1938, provoked public opinion in Slovakia, paving the way for German operations. This, however, had no decisive impact on Slovakia's attitude toward Poland, which at that time was the object of various conflicting influences. The disproportion of strength between the Third Reich and Poland, which could not effectively oppose German plotting on the territory of Slovakia in the aftermath of Munich, determined the outcome.

When on March 13, 1939, Hitler coerced Tiso to separate Slovakia forthwith from the Czech state, the Third Reich established a protectorate over that country. [2]

An agreement defining the mutual relations of the two states [3] was signed on March 23, 1939, by the German and Slovakian governments. Under this agreement Germany was entitled to station garrisons in Western Slovakia up to the line of the Little Carpathians, the White Carpathians, and the Jawornik Mountains. The agreement also provided for the organization of Slovakian armed forces, modeled on the German Army, and obliged Slovakia to conduct its foreign policy in close understanding with the German government.

[1] Printed in *Bellona* (London), 1950, No. 1, under the general title "New Premises on the Outbreak of the Polish-German War in 1939."

[2] *DGFP*, Series D, Vol. VI, No. 10.

[3] *Ibid.*, No. 40.

In relation to Poland this agreement in practice was nothing but the creation out of Slovakia of a base for the concentration of German armed forces, which would facilitate an attack from the south. Resolutions of the agreement were applied in practice on the eve of the war.

At the moment when Hitler decided to start war operations against Poland (Ribbentrop was in Moscow at that time), Woermann sent telegraphed instructions to the German envoy at Bratislava on August 23, 1939,[4] ordering him to communicate forthwith their contents to the Slovakian government. These instructions were a blatant confirmation that the marching of Polish troops into Slovakia was to be expected at any moment. In order to protect Slovakia from a surprise attack, the Reich government requested the Slovakian government immediately to express its agreement to the following:

a) In order to protect the northern part of the country, the command of the Slovakian Army should immediately be taken over by the commander in chief of the German Army.

b) The chief commander of the German air force should have access to the Spiz [Zipser]-Neudorf Airport, and, if necessary, should be able to issue general orders to stop all planes from leaving Slovakia.

In exchange for this the German government was ready to

a) defend the Slovakian frontier against Hungary,

b) return to Slovakia, in case of war with Poland, territories ceded to Poland in 1938,

c) give a guarantee that in case of a Polish-German war Slovakian forces would not be used outside of their country.

On August 26, 1939, the Slovakian envoy in Berlin, Černak, called on Woermann. He expressed satisfaction over the promise of the return to Slovakia of the territory ceded to Poland in 1938 in case of a Polish-German war. The Envoy also asked whether the German government would be ready to return to Slovakia the territory allotted to Poland in 1920. Woermann replied that in this matter he would have to consult before making a decision. In his opinion Slovakia's request would meet with approval.[5]

On August 29, 1939, Černak reiterated his request to Woermann regarding the territory lost in 1920.[6] Woermann confirmed the friendly

---

[4] *DGFP*, Series D, Vol. VII, No. 214.
[5] "Trials of War Criminals," mimeographed transcript, No. N.G. 2774.
[6] *DGFP*, Series D, Vol. VII, No. 468.

attitude of the Germans to this problem, but he could not make a binding decision on his own. Černak then asked whether declarations regarding the territory of 1938 would remain binding also in case the German-Polish conflict were settled peacefully. To this Woermann gave a negative reply. The Slovakian Envoy asked on behalf of his government for an extension of the German promise in case of a peaceful settlement.

Finally, Woermann expressed thanks for the friendly attitude toward Germany taken in the last days by the Slovakian government, and particularly for the proclamation of Prime Minister Tiso.

In his conversation with the Slovakian Envoy on August 31, 1939, Weizsäcker accepted with satisfaction the request for the return to Slovakia of the 1938 territory in case of a peaceful settlement of the conflict with Poland, as well as of the 1920 territory in case of war. Weizsäcker remarked that he was not in a position to grant a formal agreement in the two matters for lack of time, owing to the tense international situation.[7]

[7] *Ibid.*, No. 488.

Remarks on the Trial against German Diplomacy
at Nuremberg
1948–1949

LIPSKI gave two lectures in London about the second Nuremberg trial of 1948–49, one, on June 26, 1949, at the Polish Institute of Research on International Affairs, and the second on June 13, 1951, at the Polish School of Political Sciences. The texts of these lectures are included in Lipski's papers.

As some of the same problems were referred to by the lecturer (although in different form) in both lectures, and as some parts of them were printed in *Bellona*,[1] in this section the main texts of the two lectures are connected into a single entity.

Lipski's affidavit on Weizsäcker's case, referred to by him in his lectures, is given *in extenso* in the following section.

Introduction

In the aftermath of the war years, and upon the termination of the Nuremberg trial, memoirs of German politicians, army men, and diplomats began to appear. Among the diplomats who recently published their memoirs are: Herbert von Dirksen, former ambassador in Moscow, Tokyo, and London (until the outbreak of the war); Erich Kordt, for long years secretary to Ribbentrop, a brother of Theo Kordt, known for his depositions at Nuremberg and counselor of the Embassy in London; Paul Schmidt, interpreter of the Auswärtiges Amt in Weimar times and under Hitler; and primarily Ernst von Weizsäcker, former secretary of state at the Wilhelmstrasse from the spring of 1938 to 1943, and later ambassador at the Vatican. In this category of memoirs should also be included the reminiscences of Peter Kleist, who before the war was a clerk in Ribbentrop's office with special assignment to eastern problems.

The reading of these books clearly shows the goal they are striving to

---

[1] See "The Polish-German Crisis," p. 549; "Last German Moves in Danzig before the War," p. 611; "Slovakia on the Eve of the Polish-German War, p. 615.

achieve. The authors' concern is not only to whitewash themselves of the accusation that when collaborating with Hitler's regime they were blind executors of the Third Reich's aggressive policy. They have something more in mind. These memoirs are to serve as propaganda tools for the German population, as well as for public opinion at large. In each of these books a declaration is repeated that it was not Germany, at least not Germany alone, which was guilty of the calamities that befell Europe in the last thirty years.

Weizsäcker, who, owing to his position, has the most to say, clearly shifts responsibility to the Western Powers and their smaller East European allies. He accuses them of not giving sufficient assistance to the democratic Weimar Republic, of being too long in opposition to Germany's equality of rights. This was the cause for the growth of German nationalism, which later on burst out into Hitlerism.

Another propaganda trick is to underline the importance of the actually rather doubtful movement of German resistance, which allegedly already strove to overthrow the Nazi regime in the prewar years. On this subject men from the Canaris Intelligence Service and agents of the Gisevius type are writing extensively. The post-mortem memoirs of Ambassador Ulrich von Hassell also contain many details on this subject.

Weizsäcker complains that the resistance movement was not properly understood in the West and that attempts to overthrow Hitler during the Sudetenland crisis were thwarted by Chamberlain's visit to Berchtesgaden. The former Secretary of State further claims that during the war the principle of unconditional surrender, resolved at the Roosevelt-Churchill conference in January, 1943, clipped the wings of the German resistance.

Besides these general theses there are also to be found in these memoirs arguments brought against Poland. Among others, there is the statement that the British guarantee granted to Poland in the spring of 1939 was to some extent "a blank check." This British *démarche* supposedly stiffened Poland's stand, rendering its understanding with Berlin impossible. The German memoir writers accuse Poland, since it was in possession of a British cover, of indulging in anti-German demonstrations connected with violence against German minorities, thus provoking Hitler.

German diplomats also refer to the idea of German revisionism in the east. Von Dirksen's claims to this effect are the furthest reaching. He claims not only the Corridor for Germany but also Upper Silesia and a part of the Poznań region. It is worth recalling that, at the time of the Weimar Republic, von Dirksen was for a number of years chief of the Eastern Department of the A.A., to which Polish problems belonged.

Erich Kordt says that in October, 1939, in a memorandum worked out by him which was to serve as a basis for peace negotiations with the West and which was confirmed by a group of German generals belonging to the anti-Hitler opposition, he set, as one of the conditions, the reunion of East Prussia with the Reich and the return of the Polish part of Upper Silesia. This solution, in Kordt's opinion, was to secure for the Reich an overwhelming influence over a rump Poland, as well as over Czechoslovakia, whose frontiers with the Reich remained within the frame of the Munich agreements.

The Auswärtiges Amt and Poland

Prior to discussing the trial itself against top officials of the Auswärtiges Amt, I would like to make a few comments with regard to the role played by this office in relation to Poland in the interwar period.

German diplomacy, with which we had to deal before 1939, had been trained in the Bismarck tradition. The "Iron Chancellor," founder of a united Germany under the Prussian dynasty of the Hohenzollerns, was a model statesman in the eyes of the average clerk of the foreign service. He was someone who, owing to farsighted and skillful diplomacy, supported by concrete power, was able to contribute important gains to his fatherland through victorious warfare. And by a prudent policy of alliance and reinsurance he succeeded in maintaining his conquests. Bismarck's ideas on Polish problems were well known. He regarded the rise of the Polish state as a threat to Prussia. He used the definition that Poland would become an advance guard of France to the east of Germany. In the Berlin Prussian camarilla this opinion was deeply rooted.

If after World War I critical voices were raised in Germany regarding the foreign policy of prewar Germany, these reservations were directed at the period of the reign of William II, after Bismarck's removal from office. Widespread rumors circulated about the mysterious role of Baron Holstein, an éminence grise of that epoch. Almost continuously secluded in his study at the Wilhelmstrasse, he struck terror not just in his own office but also among top governing spheres of the state. His influence on the course of events was of utmost importance, although it was detrimental to German's policy. Criticism concerned the loss of Russian reinsurance (*Rückversicherungsvertrag*), the impulsive action of William II which caused unnecessary friction and inflammation, expecially in relation to England. The blame was also laid on the weak and inefficient political leadership which succumbed to great pressure from military circles and was driven into a war unfortunate for the future of Germany.

The downfall of the monarchy and the introduction of the republican system did not result in basic changes in the clerical staff of the German Foreign Affairs Office. Only a few nonprofessional diplomats, chiefly from the so-called *November-Socialisten,* were admitted to this resort. These were men who joined Social Democracy at the outbreak of the November, 1918, revolution, some of them just for a short time. To these exceptions belonged Ulrich Rauscher, later envoy of Germany in Warsaw. He played a positive role in Polish-German relations during the great economic liquidation negotiations conducted between the two states in the years 1927–30.

The Auswärtiges Amt, and particularly its Eastern Department (*Ost Abteilung*), was a forge of anti-Polish policy, conducted by German governments in the aftermath of the Treaty of Versailles. Within its walls the definition was born of Poland as a season-state (*Saisonstaat*). German diplomacy, in connection with the Reichswehr, created a basis for the agreement with Soviet Russia at Rapallo, which was, under different conditions, a sort of return of Germany to the policy of Bismarck. The Auswärtiges Amt kept to a stand of revision of frontiers with Poland. In the midst of the most complicated Polish-German relations, whole tactics were directed from the revisionistic angle. If at special periods when, for the sake of higher interests, the German government was compelled to agree to some concessions on a larger scale in relation to Poland, as, for example, at the liquidation agreement of October, 1929, connected with the introduction of the Young Plan, the most stubborn resistance was usually encountered on the part of the bureaucrats at the Wilhelmstrasse.

The signing of the Polish-German nonaggression declaration of January 26, 1934, when Hitler was already in power, was pepper in the eye of that office. In negotiations on this agreement, officials of the Eastern Department of the A.A. did not participate; conversations went on at the highest level with Hitler, Minister of Foreign Affairs von Neurath, and the confidential legal counselor, Gaus.

Under Hitler, the prestige of the Auswärtiges Amt declined. A number of facts contributed to this decline.

Decisions of principle in international affairs were taken by Hitler alone, who personally received ambassadors and representatives of foreign governments on matters of special import. In the long run, as his power grew and the regime became more self-confident, the myth of professional diplomacy slowly sank in the horizon, giving way to dilettantish high-spirited improvisation.

High-ranking Party dignitaries began to enter the domain of the Ministry of Foreign Affairs.

Alfred Rosenberg, the Party ideologist, created an office of his own, "Aussem-politisches Amt," which made direct contacts abroad. Göring's ambitions also reached into the international field. He performed many missions on behalf of the Chancellor. He went to Italy, to Yugoslavia, to Hungary. As of the spring of 1935, he was plenipotentiary for Polish-German relations.

Propaganda Minister Goebbels had his extensive press apparatus and exerted considerable impact on the formation of relations between the Reich and particular states. Finally, Ribbentrop, after he became the delegate for disarmament, opened an office in Berlin which was in a way a miniature of the Auswärtiges Amt. This office had its delegates in various capitals, and they informed their chief behind the backs of official German representatives. The office's special field was anti-Comintern problems. When Ribbentrop became ambassador in London, this cell continued its activities.

There were two ministers of foreign affairs in the time of Hitler, Neurath and Ribbentrop. The first was a professional diplomat of the old school, with great experience gained in long years of service abroad and at headquarters. He had no great personal ambitions. Called to the government of von Papen in 1932, he remained under Hitler until February, 1938. Hitler had confidence in him. Neurath tried generally to impose a soothing influence on the dynamic trend of Nazi policy. However, he was not a fighter, in the best meaning of that word. He shielded his office, as best he could, from internal disintegration, but was helpless in the face of Party initiatives that intruded into the field of international politics. Weizsäcker, who for several months in 1933 performed the functions of chief of personnel of the Auswärtiges Amt, writes that at that very period the first "house cleaning" was undertaken at the office.

Prince Waldeck acted on behalf of the Party, whose ranks he had joined. Such "house cleanings" afterward occurred from time to time when National Socialists such as Wilhelm Keppler or Ernst Bohle took over high-ranking posts of undersecretaries of state for special commitments.

A chief personality and official manager of the office was the secretary of state. In Weimar times, when foreign ministers were usually recruited from representatives of political parties, the position of a professional secretary of state was a very responsible one, and his voice had weight on international decisions. In the first years of Hitler's regime this post was held by von Bülow, a nephew of the former Chancellor, who in his time had achieved fame for introducing in the Prussian Chambers the anti-Polish resolution for expropriation (1908). Upon Bülow's death, a short interregnum prevailed caused by difficulties in having a candidate approved by the Party. Finally, von Neurath succeeded in introducing his son-in-law, Hans von Mackensen, son of the famous field marshal of World War I, whose name carried weight in Party spheres.

Changes made by Hitler in February, 1938, in the top military brass after the famous affair of Blomberg's marriage extended also to the Auswärtiges Amt. To the removed Neurath, to dry his tears, was offered the direction of the so-called Council of State, which in practice had no voice or power. Then came the era of Ribbentrop, who, in the light today of German documents, depositions, and memoirs of his close collaborators as well as reports of foreign diplomats, played an outrightly sinister role as confidential adviser to Hitler. He bears the major responsibility for the outbreak of the war. A few months after his nomination, Ribbentrop nominated Weizsäcker secretary of state. Weizsäcker became the leading personality in the trial against German diplomacy at Nuremberg.

The Trial

For the prosecution of major German war criminals, Great Britain, the United States, Soviet Russia, and France contracted an agreement on August 8, 1945, creating adequate legal bases for future trials. Three categories of crimes were established by this agreement: crimes against peace; war crimes; and crimes against mankind.

The greatest *novum* in international law is the determination of the idea of a crime against peace. The definition reads as follows:

". . . planning, preparation, initiation or waging of a war of aggression, or a war in violation of international treaties, agreements or assurances, or participation in a common plan or conspiracy for the accomplishment of any of the foregoing."

After the termination of the main trial at Nuremberg, on November 15, 1947, a bill of indictment was placed with the Secretariat General of American War Tribunals at Nuremberg against a number of diplomats and high-ranking German personalities, twenty-one persons in all, for crimes against peace, crimes against mankind, and war crimes.

On December 19, 1947, the case was transferred to the Fourth Military American Tribunal at Nuremberg, and proceedings were opened on January 7, 1948. The sentence was published on April 11, 1949. The dimension of the trial may be judged by the fact that the files of court proceedings cover 28,085 pages of print; 9,067 documents were attached to the files, making a total of 39,000 pages. Justification of the sentence is written in 800 pages, not counting the *votum separatum* deposited by Judge W. Powers.

Among the personalities who found themselves on the defendants' bench, the group of German diplomats were at the forefront. As a matter of fact, this was a trial against the Auswärtiges Amt of the Third Reich. Persons in this trial who arouse the most interest on our part are Secretary of State Ernst von Weizsäcker and Undersecretary of State Ernst Woermann. Other diplomats on the defendants' bench were Steengracht von Moyland, Weizsäcker's successor in the post of secretary of state after 1943; Karl Ritter, for long years chief of the Economic Department at the A.A., former ambassador in Rio de Janeiro, who during the war served as liaison for the office with the German commander in chief; and, finally, Otto von Erdmannsdorf, envoy to Budapest, later assistant chief of the Political Department at the A.A. Besides these professional diplomats, names of persons appeared in the trial to whom special missions were entrusted by the Wilhelmstrasse, owing to their Party membership. Among these are Wilhelm Keppler, Ernst Bohle, and Edmund Veesenmayer, known for his diplomatic activities in Danzig on the eve of the outbreak of the war and for his later military action in the Balkans. The remaining defendants who were included in the trial of the diplomats were selected rather at random. That is why this trial was called the "omnibus" trial. Besides former Finance Minister of the Reich Schwerin von Krosigk and Food Minister

Walter Darré, there were to be found two secretaries of state at the Reich Chancellery, Otto Meissner and Hans Lammers, as well as Director of the Reichsbank Puhl, Director of the Dresdener Bank Rosche, Göring's deputy in the four-year plan, Koerner, Chief of the S.S. Intelligence Department Walter Schellenburg, Chief of the Reich's Press Otto Dietrich, and others. Only Erdmannsdorf and Meissner were released. The latter was a faithful servant of all regimes, performing functions in the civil chancellery under Ebert, Hindenburg, and Hitler. All those remaining were sentenced by the Tribunal to prison from four to twenty-five years.

Character of the Sentence

The sentence contains some important points of a broad political meaning. As the trial was pending before an American Tribunal, Soviet problems were brought out in fuller relief than during the main Nuremberg trial. The political situation of Germany had also changed to its advantage, and the defense took full advantage of this, presenting much bolder theses.

1) The defense used the principle of *Tu quoque* ("and you too"), claiming that the co-culprit of a crime cannot pass judgment on the same case. The presentation of this thesis, confirmed by Soviet Russia's partnership in the aggression against Poland, aimed to undermine the legal foundations upon which the Nuremberg sentences were based. The Tribunal took a negative stand on the point of view of the defense in this matter, declaring as follows: [2]

". . . the defendants have offered testimony and supported it by official documents which tend to establish that the Union of Soviet Socialist Republics entered into a treaty with Germany in August 1939, which contains secret clauses whereby not only did Russia consent to Hitler's invasion of Poland, but at least tacitly agreed to send its own armed forces against that nation, and by it could demand and obtain its share of the loot, and was given a free hand to swallow the little Baltic States with whom it had then existing nonaggression treaties. The defense asserts that Russia, being itself an aggressor and an accomplice to Hitler's aggression, was a party and an accomplice to at least one of

[2] *Trials of War Criminals before the Nuremberg Military Tribunals under Control Council Law No. 10*, XIV, 322.

the aggressions charged in this indictment, namely, that against Poland, and therefore was legally inhibited from signing the London Charter and enacting Central Council Law No. 10, and consequently both the Charter and the Law are invalid, and no prosecution can be maintained under them.

"The justifications, if any, which the Soviet Union may claim to have had for its actions in this respect were not represented to this Tribunal. But if we assume *arguendo,* that Russia's action was wholly untenable and its guilt as deep as that of the Third Reich, nevertheless, this cannot in law avail the defendants or lessen the guilt of those of the Third Reich who were themselves responsible."

2) The court dealt with the arguments of the defense that in view of the fact that Germany had an unjust peace treaty imposed on it and had to take recourse to force to free itself of the resolutions of the treaty its acts in consequence could not be regarded as aggression. The court took the stand that a moment always comes when the prevailing *status quo,* regardless of the conditions under which it came into existence, should be regarded as lasting, at least as regards the change of such status by violence and aggression.

The court's argument was a reference to Hitler's declaration with respect to territorial clauses regarding Austria, Czechoslovakia, and Poland, as well as to nonaggression pacts concluded by Germany with those states. These pacts and declarations created, in the opinion of the court, that very state of relaxation and permanence of the prevailing situation. The court stated as its motives that those declarations were made without compulsion and that the pacts were contracted freely.

3) A politically important statement on motives of the sentence refers to Hitler's agreement with Stalin:

"He [Hitler] did not dare to make the attack in the face of the British and French guarantees to Poland until he had secured his eastern boundaries from possible attack by Russia. This he did by means of the German-Soviet Treaty of August 23, 1939. There he not only protected himself; but apparently by giving the Soviets a free hand in the Baltic States and in Bessarabia and by agreeing to share the loot in Poland, he gained a partner. As long as the Polish State existed, it is sheer nonsense to talk about Hitler's fear that the Soviets might attack. Whatever may have been the attitude of Poland toward Germany, there can be no question that had the Russians attacked the Reich, Poland and the Baltic States for their own preservation would have been thrown to the side of Germany, and the suspicion which Poland felt toward Russia would have made a Polish-Russian alliance wholly unlikely. If a Russian offensive took place in the north, it could only go through Poland, and if it took place in the south, Hungary and Rumania were bound to stand alongside the German forces." [3]

4) During the trial Weizsäcker sharply criticized Poland's prewar foreign policy. His main arguments dealt with the British guarantee issued to Poland, as he put it, a "blank check" in treating the German minorities in Poland and in Poland's relation to the Free City of Danzig. In addition, his criticism was aimed at Poland's stand durng the Munich period and its action toward Lithuania in March, 1938.

Under these circumstances the American prosecutor approached me officially, requesting me to present my deposition with regard to the points attacked by Weizsäcker.

The points referred to by the prosecutor in his letter were dealt with in the extensive statement deposed by me under oath at the American Embassy in London on September 23, 1948. This deposition contains four principal chapters:

a) an outline of Polish-German relations from Hitler's coming to power to March, 1939;

b) the problem of the British guarantee for Poland and a refutation of the German thesis about a "blank check";

c) rectification of German statements with regard to alleged persecution of German minorities in Poland;

d) a true picture of the Polish-Danzig strife with regard to customs inspectors.

Forwarding the Final Prosecution Brief to me on November 18, 1948, the prosecutor remarked: "Your testimony has been invaluable in bringing the affairs of German foreign policy into the true historical and legal perspective." In his motions the prosecutor availed himself of the material contained in my deposition, quoting literally part of the passage dealing with the British guarantee for Poland (refutation of the German thesis about a "blank check") and the passage rectifying the false statement about the persecution of Germans in Poland.

[3] *Ibid.*, p. 355.

More Important Documents Concerning Polish-German Relations
Disclosed at the Trial

During the trial against Weizsäcker, as well as at the main Nuremberg trial, the prosecution presented a number of documents from archives of the German Auswärtiges Amt. Some of them, although not so sensational as Hitler's directive or the dispositions of the German headquarters, have their meaning for the history of diplomacy. They throw some light on the activities of the Auswärtiges Amt, and particularly on that of the Secretary of State and his immediate collaborators; they reveal the form through which German diplomacy tried to camouflage the most drastic dispositions of the Hitlerite leaders of the Third Reich's foreign policy. Weizsäcker, who at the trial condemned Hitler's policies and vented his bile on Ribbentrop, who was the object of hatred of German professional diplomats, deprecated authorship of certain notes which he had personally handed to foreign representatives. For instance, Weizsäcker confessed on June 16, 1948, that the declaration on Danzig presented by him on August 9, 1939,[4] to Polish Chargé d'Affaires *ad interim* Lubomirski, as recommended by the Reich government, did not originate from him but was written by Hitler's order and forwarded to him for delivery without alterations. As a matter of fact, Weizsäcker agreed that this declaration was unfortunate, while he did not abstain from criticizing the final paragraph of the Polish government's reply, referring to remarks contained in Noël's book on this subject.[5]

In the files was found a circular telegram to German representatives abroad (a copy to the Embassy in Warsaw) signed by Weizsäcker, referring to the exchange of notes of August 9 and 10, 1939, between Berlin and Warsaw. The telegram, dated August 14,[6] reads:

"You are requested not to initiate any conversation in your capital on the German and Polish statements. If you are questioned about it, the Foreign Minister asks you to say that the Polish communication is a further proof of the megalomania and the warmongering policy of the Polish rulers. If Poland chooses to run amok now it will have to bear the responsibility and the consequences. We cannot understand how any Powers could still be prepared to further such an insane policy or even to encourage it, thereby making themselves jointly responsible."

[4] *DGFP*, Series D, Vol. VII, No. 5.
[5] Noël, pp. 397–98.
[6] *DGFP*, Series D, Vol. VII, No. 57.

Weizsäcker insisted that Ribbentrop and not he had written these instructions. He stated that on purpose he often did not alter the very individual style of Ribbentrop, thus signaling to the recipients at the posts from whom the instructions originated. To illustrate his depositions, Weizsäcker quoted the fact that at the time Ribbentrop recommended that he communicate to the officials of the Auswärtiges Amt that they should use most categorical language, adding that if any of them indulged in defeatist remarks they would be shot in their own offices. At the conference of directors of the ministry Weizsäcker repeated this declaration literally, to which someone present asked jokingly: "In whose office? Weizsäcker's or Ribbentrop's?"

When during the trial reports were shown to Weizsäcker from his conversations with foreign representatives, from which it was obvious that he was wholeheartedly defending Hitler's official policy, he tried to explain that diplomatic language, for people of Ribbentrop's type, was beyond comprehension. That is why he was obliged to elaborate these reports to fit the level of the readers.

My conversation with Weizsäcker of April 6, 1939, dealing with the British guarantee for Poland was included in the *German White Book* published during the war.[7] In the German version of this conversation the tone allegedly used by the Secretary of State when addressing me was presented in a version considerably at variance with the truth. At that time he probably wanted to display to Ribbentrop his smart dealings with the Polish Ambassador, unaware that the time would come for him to face a tribunal. When asked at the proceedings about this conversation, Weizsäcker had no choice but to make reference to the *Polish White Book*,[8] where our exchange of opinion is stated in conformity with the truth.

With great skill, displaying himself to be an agile diplomat, Weizsäcker was able to answer the questions, presenting more and more arguments when efforts were made to drive him to the wall in connection with documents bearing his signature. He was far from questioning the guilt of Hitler and Ribbentrop for starting the war with Poland; on the contrary, he accused them both of aggressive intentions. He based his defense on proving that he personally, though harnessed in the Reich's diplomatic machine, was against aggression and, in secret from the Nazi

[7] *German White Book,* No. 212, p. 242, or *DGFP,* Series D, Vol. VI, No. 169.
[8] *Polish White Book,* No. 70.

top echelon, was acting to save the peace. Until July, 1939, he still did
not see any immediate threat of war. When he found out that Hitler was
decided on aggression, he began to act, particularly toward London and
Rome. His explanation of his methods of action is often lost in diplomatic finesse. Allegedly what he strove to achieve was that French and
British diplomacy should restrain Warsaw, hinting to the Poles that they
would obtain no assistance from the West if they persisted in provoking
(*sic*) Hitler. On the other hand, he wanted British and French diplomacy to make Hitler understand categorically that in case of aggression
against Poland both Powers would fulfill their obligations toward that
state. Weizsäcker tries to present his conversations in the last months
before the war with the ambassador of France and particularly the
ambassador of Great Britain from that angle. Weizsäcker also referred
to his attempts to stop Hitler's aggression by means of the mediation of
Mussolini. His contacts with Attolico, the Italian ambassador in Berlin,
constitute a large chapter in his trial. His further argument was that he
wanted to gain time in order, as he put it, to get through the critical
month of August.

Weizsäcker did not conceal at the trial that his opinion with regard to
the contents and form of the British guarantee for Poland was critical.
He stated that in any case the guarantee should not have been issued in
such form and publicly. His statements with regard to the German-Soviet pact were, in my opinion, of most interest. He confessed that he
regarded the agreement of Hitler with Stalin as "catastrophic for peace,"
since Hitler was persuaded that with this pact in his grasp he could
attack Poland without any risk. Weizsäcker referred to steps undertaken
by him in order to warn London about the threat of an agreement with
Russia (confidential mission of Erich Kordt to England in June, 1939,
and later conversations with Henderson). This, however, did not stop
him from participating in diplomatic action for a rapprochement with
Moscow and counteraction against an understanding of the Western
Powers with Soviet Russia.

Analysis of Documents

1. Polish-Danzig Problems. We find in the files three documents relating to Polish-Danzig problems dating prior to January, 1939.

The first document is a memorandum of October 15, 1936, signed by
Weizsäcker,[9] at that time political director. It deals with conversations

to be undertaken between the Senate of the Free City and the Polish government. The first five points of the instructions deal with general considerations; point 6 contains motions.

Here is a recapitulation: It is agreed that the Danzig problem cannot be separated from the Reich's general foreign policy, owing to the fact that relaxation or tension in Polish-German relations depends on how the problem of Danzig is developing. Consequently, the Senate must collaborate closely with the Auswärtiges Amt. Weizsäcker explains this point by the necessity of holding Forster tightly in check, for his exuberant activity might be dangerous in relations with Poland, which at that time were developing rather satisfactorily.

The second point states that Danzig policy should be aimed at the return of the Free City to the Reich. This is not possible under present circumstances, unless by a *coup d'état*. A *coup d'état* is not to be considered at present, since this would actualize the hitherto unsolved question of the Corridor. Weizsäcker's commentary on this point (deposed at the trial on June 9, 1948) reads as follows:

"The later incorporation of Danzig as the final aim was not only justified because without a plebiscite Danzig had been taken away from Germany and was almost completely German, but also in a political sense this aim was justified because there was not one problem during the year beginning with 1920 with which the League of Nations had to make so constant and so useless an effort as the Danzig problem. A complete clarification of the Danzig question was essential for any practical European peace policy. I remind you that the Danzig problem at that time was somewhat similar to the Trieste problem, and I do not think that I am the only one who holds that opinion because the British foreign minister, Lord Halifax, one year after I wrote that memorandum, that is in 1937, stated publicly that changes in the European order would have to come sooner or later and that one of these changes for him was Danzig, while another one was Austria, and so on and so forth."

The memorandum further points out that subordination of Danzig to the League of Nations would be inconvenient; it refers to the necessity of replacing Lester and considers the possibility of transferring part of the League's powers to Poland and nominating a Pole as high commis-

[9] "Trials of War Criminals," mimeographed transcript, No. N.G.-1998 (Lipski's papers, File 22).

sioner of the League. However, he arrives at the conclusion that this would be undesirable. Under the prevailing good Polish-German relations this would relax the situation, while if those relations deteriorated the Polish hand could weigh on Danzig, especially since the high commissioner was authorized to call on Polish forces to restore order in the Free City.

In point 5 the question of the high commisioner's right to intervene in the Free City's internal affairs in accordance with the statute is discussed. A motion follows that an attempt should be made to soften the actual situation.

Then motions follow, expressed in seeking a successor to Lester, jointly with Poland, and restoring order in the internal situation of Danzig so as to give Poland the opportunity to declare at the next session of the League of Nations that an appeasement has been accomplished. In conversations with Poland no concessions should be allowed which in the future might render difficult the return of Danzig to the Reich. And finally, contact with the Auswärtiges Amt should be maintained during negotiations with Poland.

The next two documents, one of February 8, 1937,[10] and the other undated,[11] relate to candidates for the post of high commissioner in Danzig. Weizsäcker gives priority to Burckhardt; second comes Rothmund; and third, Reimers. Weizsäcker instructs Greiser what tactics should be applied to deal with the Polish side. Burckhardt should not be pushed before his candidacy is presented. In the second document, Greiser reports that Poland's commissioner suggested Reimers, to which he protested. Then the Polish side suggested Burckhardt; Greiser declared that this candidacy seems to be possible, but he reserved his answer. Now Greiser would give his formal consent for Burckhardt.

It should be recalled that Weizsäcker and Burckhardt were acquainted since 1920 and maintained close contact. Burckhardt's name appears in the document of July 15, 1938, signed by Schliep, in charge of the Polish Desk at the A.A.[12] It refers to an invitation to be sent to Burckhardt for the Nuremberg Congress.

Owing to attacks by the Swiss left-wing press, Burckhardt would prefer (according to a report of the German consul general in Danzig) to avoid this invitation. The A.A. shared this opinion.

[10] *Ibid.*, NG-5403.
[11] *Ibid.*, NG-5402.
[12] *Ibid.*, NG-5404.

2. Beck's Visit to Berchtesgaden and Ribbentrop's to Warsaw. On January 5, 1939, Beck was to meet with Hitler at Berchtesgaden. Weizsäcker prepared material for the conversation. Presenting it to Ribbentrop on January 2,[13] he made the following motions:

a) Poland should do more for the German minority.

b) Poland should now be satisfied with small economic profits in case Kłajpeda [Memel] shortly became German.

c) It would probably ensue from the conversation that it was still too early to establish Poland's stand toward other points of Germany's eastern policy. Beck should understand how weak his position was and that Germany was waiting for a moment when he would be more flexible.

From this note it could be gathered that the A.A. did not at that time exert pressure for a quick solution of Polish-German problems as suggested by Ribbentrop on October 24, 1938.

The basic line of German policy at that time is confirmed by a circular telegram sent by Weizsäcker on January 10, 1939,[14] to representatives abroad, evidently on the instructions of Ribbentrop, who took part in the conference together with Hitler:

"For information and guidance in your conversations:

"The visit of Foreign Minister Beck, which was motivated by a Polish desire to discuss the new situation, took place in a friendly atmosphere. It was noted on both sides that the agreement of January, 1934, had proved its worth and continued to form the basis of German-Polish relations.

"More particularly, the question of Danzig was discussed, but a practical stage was not reached. The Führer reassured Beck with respect to the alleged danger of *faits accomplis* being engineered in Danzig, and confirmed Poland's need for access to the sea. The question of Memel was touched upon briefly. The Führer also dissipated Polish misgivings regarding Germany's Ukraine policy. No agreements of any kind were reached. Beck repeated the familiar Polish explanation of the origin of the Polish-Soviet declaration, which had become necessary on account of numerous border incidents.

"The Reich Foreign Minister accepted in principle Beck's invitation to Warsaw extended at the end of last year. The date is still open."

After Beck's visit to Hitler, Ribbentrop and Gauleiter Forster deter-

[13] *DGFP*, Series D, Vol. V, No. 119, note 3.
[14] *Ibid.*, No. 121.

mined their tactics on the territory of Danzig. In a note dated January 13, 1939, and signed by Hewel,[15] it is stated that no new steps should be taken on the territory of Danzig prior to Ribbentrop's return from Warsaw. The measures contemplated were, in part:

  a) official adoption of the German salute,

  b) adoption of the German flag,

  c) formation of a Death's Head (*Totenkopf*) unit of the S.S. in Danzig.

Upon Ribbentrop's return from Warsaw, it would be decided whether these measures should be applied or whether they would become dispensable in view of a "global" settlement of the question with Poland.

On the eve of Ribbentrop's departure for Warsaw, on January 24, 1939, I had a conversation with Weizsäcker. It was preceded, on my recommendation, by an exposition, by our press attaché, Wnorowski, to Herr Kleist of Ribbentrop's office. This was an intervention by the Polish side in a number of matters which, rather characteristically, coincided in the last days. The exposition concerned a map published by the *Völkischer Beobachter* on January 24, 1939, showing Danzig reunited with the Reich, and news from Kaunas, in the same issue of the paper, in which a request for the return of Wilno to Lithuania was printed. It also dealt with the withdrawal, by the order of the Auswärtiges Amt, of a communiqué about reaching a temporary Polish-German agreement regarding the expulsion of Polish Jews from Germany, as well as postponement of the signing of this agreement.

Documents from January, 1939, although they give a very superficial illustration of the attitude of German governmental factors, nevertheless represent valuable premises for the history of their period. We know today from other sources that at that time Hitler was hesitating about the future direction of attack—west or east.

Documents show that the Auswärtiges Amt, estimating that the Polish card in the West was losing its value, judged that it might be possible to force Poland into concessions on the question of Danzig. The A.A waited, however, for a more suitable moment. This is confirmed by Weizsäcker, who at the trial on June 9, 1948, deposed as follows:

"The Polish position during these years was by no means strengthened. I have already mentioned that in international politics Poland had been considered, after Munich, a so-called hyena; it had been weakened

15 *Ibid.*, No. 122.

to such a point that, according to my own conviction, if one could only apply a certain amount of patience, the necessary compromise between Warsaw and Berlin would have been achieved without any special intervention."

Here the question arises whether such an opinion did not change the sequence: first Czechoslovakia and afterward Danzig. However, it is significant that Weizsäcker took an active part in preparations for the occupation of Prague, and that he was convicted for that very reason.

Another characteristic feature is a certain convergence in German and Polish tactics to keep secret the growing strife between the two states. Germany continued to count on reaching its goal by way of direct conversations with Warsaw. It also tried to keep the Polish card, in view of its broad schemes in Europe. Polish diplomacy strove to avoid conflict with Germany. However, it started to seek reinsurance in the West, trying simultaneously to balance its relations with Soviet Russia. It would not serve Poland's interests to show its cards too early, since this might weaken Poland's position abroad, rendering its rapprochement with the West more complicated.

Affidavit of Ambassador Lipski in the Case of
von Weizsäcker during the Nuremberg Trials
1948–1949

ON AUGUST 2, 1948, William H. W. Caming, chief prosecutor in the trial of twenty-one Germans in Nuremberg, wrote to Lipski, who was at that time residing in London, inviting him to the trial at Nuremberg in order to testify in the case of the accused former secretary of state, Baron von Weizsäcker. In the event that Lipski could not appear in person, he was asked to present a written affidavit.

In his letter, enclosing the pertinent documents from Weizsäcker's hearings,[1] Mr. Caming wrote:

"The defendant Weizsacker has not denied that he faithfully executed the orders of the late von Ribbentrop. His defense pursues two lines of reasoning. Firstly, although participating in the German diplomatic mobilization for aggression against Poland, he secretly committed himself to every possible effort to maintain the peace through contacts with British Ambassador Henderson and Italian Ambassador Attolico. (Upon cross-examination, this defense was substantially destroyed.) Secondly, he contended that the greater proportion of the guilt for the provocation of the German-Polish conflict fell upon Poland. He emphasized that the Polish government willfully permitted the persecution of German ethnic minorities in Poland proper, which activities reached a crescendo in violence in August, 1939. Further, he contended that the British guarantees in March and April, 1939, presented the Polish government with a "blank check," permitting it to maintain an unbridled policy of intimidation and lawlessness against Germany and Danzig. Thirdly, he contended that the Polish authorities provoked the Danzig customs dispute in August, 1939, and their actions further contributed to the deterioration of conditions in Danzig. He described the Polish governmental leaders as jackals and hyenas who slyly attempted to secure territories and rights for themselves at the expense of their neighbors."

Lipski chose the form of presenting an affidavit in writing and sent it to the Chief Prosecutor at Nuremberg on September 23, 1948.

On April 11, 1949, sentence was passed on Weizsäcker, confining him to prison for seven years for his part in the occupation of Czechoslovakia in

[1] Lipski's papers, File 24.

March, 1939, and the transportation of Jews for annihilation from Slovakia and France. By the decision of the high commissioner, John J. McCloy, of January 31, 1951, the sentence was commuted to time served.

Lipski's affidavit reads as follows:

60 Pelham Court
London, SW 3

In the statement which I am submitting below I was able to refer to my diplomatic dispatches from Berlin, many of which were published in the *White Book* issued by the Ministry of Foreign Affairs of the Republic of Poland (concerning Polish-German and Polish-Soviet relations, 1933 to 1939). Moreover, a number of these reports was put before the International Military Tribunal of Nuremberg at the trial of the Major War Criminals, sentenced for their participation in the planning, preparation, initiation, and waging of a war of aggression against Poland.

I had been in charge of German problems at the Ministry of Foreign Affairs in Warsaw between 1925 and the autumn of 1933, first as chief of the German Section and subsequently as head of the Western Department there. Between 1925 and 1930 I took part in numerous negotiations with the German government, and myself concluded a series of agreements, the most important of which was the Liquidation Treaty of October 31, 1929, connected with recommendations of the Young Plan. The Polish-German Trade Agreement, on which I had been working for many years, signed in Warsaw on March 17, 1930, was to have complemented this Liquidation Treaty; it was never ratified by the Reichstag on account of opposition from Prussian agrarian circles against the importation of agricultural produce from Poland.

I was, moreover, in touch with German diplomacy in international conferences at Locarno (October, 1925), The Hague (July, 1929, and January, 1930), and Lausanne (July, 1932). In September, 1933, I was appointed Polish minister to Berlin, and ambassador in October, 1934. I held the latter post until the outbreak of war in 1939.

At the time of Hitler's accession to power, in January, 1933, Polish-German relations had reached a critical stage owing to the Nazis' anti-Polish agitation. In order to ease the tension which had then developed, a meeting was arranged through Polish initiative on May 2, 1933, between my predecessor in Berlin, Mr. Wysocki, and Hitler, as a result of which "the Chancellor laid stress on the firm intention of the German government to maintain its attitude and its actions strictly within the limits of the existing treaties" (communiqué issued on May 3 by the Wolff Agency on the interview between Chancellor Hitler and Mr. Wysocki).

A further step toward the improvement of relations was the Polish-German declaration of nonaggression, which was negotiated and signed by myself on January 26, 1934.

In the said declaration, concluded for a period of ten years, both sides agreed to abstain from the use of force for the purpose of reaching a decision in possible disputes. This pact became the basis for mutual relations between the two countries in the years which followed.

The value which the Germans at that time attached to their relations with Poland can be seen from numerous subsequent statements: for example, Hitler's speeches to the Reichstag on May 21, 1935, March 7, 1936, January 30, 1937, and February 20, 1938, of which the following words might be quoted:

"It fills us, in the fifth year following the first great foreign political agreement of the Reich, with sincere gratification to be able to establish that in our relationship to the state with which we had perhaps the greatest differences, not only has there been a *détente,* but in the course of these years a constant improvement in relations has taken place."

Moreover, also in Hitler's Sport Palace speech of September 26, 1938, and even in the Reichstag speech of January 30, 1939 ("We have just celebrated the fifth anniversary of the conclusion of our nonaggression pact with Poland. There can scarcely be any difference of opinion today among the true friends of peace with regard to the value of this agreement . . .").

The beginning of a crisis in German-Polish relations that revealed its full gravity at the end of March, 1939, might be traced back to the late autumn of 1938 when, after having occupied Austria and the Sudetenland, the Nazi government came to its decision for further territorial aggrandizement at Poland's expense. However, even earlier, the Bohumin (Oderberg) incident had already given grounds for dispute between Berlin and Warsaw.

Bohumin had belonged to the former Cieszyn Principality, mainly inhabited by a Polish population, and had constitued, ever since 1920 when this territory was occupied during the Polish-Bolshevik war by the Czechs, a bone of contention between Poland and Czechoslovakia. When, in the summer of 1938, the problem of Czechoslovakia's national minorities was raised in the light of the Czech-German dispute over the Sudetenland, the Polish government received an assurance from France, as well as from the Czechoslovak government, that the Polish ethnic minorities in the Cieszyn province would be granted the same privileges as any other minority.

Thus, on the eve of the Munich Conference, when it had become evident that the Sudetenland would be ceded to Germany, the Polish government instructed me to endeavor to fix with the German government a demarcation line on the map which would leave the Cieszyn District outside the German claims.

This step became essential owing to information received on September 27, 1938, by the Ministry of Foreign Affairs in Warsaw from the British Ambassador that at the Godesberg Conference the strategically vital Bohumin junction (one of the most important railroad junctions in Central Europe) had been included in the German claims and that the so-called Red Line which delimited these claims entered well into the Cieszyn area.

I then clearly agreed with Herr von Weizsäcker (at a conference on September 28, 1938, in the presence of Counselor Altenburg and Counselor of the Polish Embassy Lubomirski) that Bohumin was to be left outside the German demarcation line. Nevertheless, on October 4 the Auswärtiges Amt endeavored to revoke the agreement which we had reached on September 28. This met with a protest from the Polish side. Moreoever, at that period there coincided some alarming activities of organized Nazi bands in the Bohumin district.

Therefore, the Defendant's (Herr von Weizsäcker's) statements regarding the Cieszyn matter seem misconstrued, to say the least, coming from so highly graded a representative of the Auswärtiges Amt of that time.

At a talk I had at Ribbentrop's invitation at Berchtesgaden on October 24, 1938, the Reich Foreign Minister raised for the first time the demand to incorporate Danzig into Germany. This was contrary to the attitude hitherto shown by the German government, as proved by numerous statements made in the highest quarters.

The understanding between Germany and Poland as far as Danzig was concerned was based, ever since 1934, on the principle of noninterference on the part of Poland into the life of the German population of the Free City, with due reciprocal consideration on the part of the Danzig anuthorities to Polish rights and interests, the statute of the Free City, and the Polish population.

Official statements which confirmed this state of affairs were made to me personally, among others by Hitler on November 5, 1937, reiterated by him before Minister Beck in Berlin on January 14, 1938, finally in a public utterance in his speech to the Reichstag on February 20, 1938, in the following words:

"The Polish state respects the national conditions in this state and both the city of Danzig and Germany respect Polish rights. And so the way to a friendly understanding has been successfully paved, an understanding which, starting from Danzig, has today succeeded, in spite of attempts by certain mischief-makers, in finally taking the poison out of the relations between Germany and Poland and transforming them into a sincere, friendly cooperation."

The demands for the return of Danzig to Germany and the creation of an extraterritorial highway and railroad through Polish Pomerania were accompanied, among others, by proposals for Poland's accession to the Anti-Comintern Pact. Ribbentrop had already earlier, that is, in March and September of that year (1938), made similar suggestions in his talks with me; these had, however, always been turned down by the Polish government.

In reality, the so-called *Gesamtlösung* which Ribbentrop had proposed merely boiled down to the wish to open the question of the Corridor and the surrender of Danzig to Germany. This was tantamount to severing Poland's access to the sea. The joining of the Anti-Comintern Pact by Poland would automatically have forced it to give up its treaty of alliance with France, put it at loggerheads with Russia, and ultimately drawn Poland into the orbit of the Nazi policy of conquest.

Ribbentrop's action, thus understood by the Polish Minister of Foreign Affairs, resulted in a reassertion by the mutual Polish-Soviet declaration of November 26, 1938, that "the relations between the Polish Republic and the Union of Soviet Socialist Republics are and will continue to be based to the fullest extent on all the existing agreements, including the Polish-Soviet Pact of nonaggression dated July 25, 1932."

The demands put forward by Ribbentrop on October 24 came up again in the talks between Hitler and Beck at Berchtesgaden on January 5, as well as during Ribbentrop's trip to Warsaw on January 25-27,

1939. This period was characterized by a growing tension in Polish-German relations, the smoldering flame being strongly fanned by anti-Polish agitation in Danzig and the highly disturbing movements of German agents working on the Ukrainian and Slovakian questions, of which movements the Polish government was well aware.

That the Polish government's fears regarding Danzig were well conceived has now been proved by the publication at the Nuremberg trial of General Keitel's instructions of November 24, 1938, which referred to the occupation of Danzig at a politically opportune moment by means of an internal putsch.

The German methods at that time might well be illustrated by document N.G. 2771 of January 13, 1939, signed by the liaison officer between the Auswärtiges Amt and the Reich Chancellery, Hewel. This document recommends a delay in the issue of certain new instructions for Danzig, among others the official introduction of the German salute, introduction of the German flag, the formation of the Death's Head units of the S.S., etc., until the time when the results of Ribbentrop's trip to Warsaw were known.

The crisis in Polish-German relations reached a crucial stage in the later part of March when, in equal surprise to both the Polish Government and Polish public opinion, Hitler occupied Prague, German military formations entered Slovakia, a protectorate over that country was established, and Lithuania was forced to give up Memel.

Poland felt itself threatened both from the north and from the south. A feeling of anxiety invaded the whole Eastern European atmosphere.

With regard to Lithuania, I would like to make it clear, in connection with the Defendant's (Herr von Weizsäcker's) allegations as to Polish policy, that a considerable rapprochement between Lithuanians and Poles had been achieved since Poland's drastic step of the preceding March (1938) to bring about the establishment of normal diplomatic relations with that country.

Poland's attitude at that moment (March, 1938) was dictated exclusively by considerations of security and was devoid of any other aims.

It was in these circumstances that, on March 21, 1939, Ribbentrop reiterated his demands to me, laying strong emphasis on the urgency of the matter. When I reported the course of this talk in my dispatch to Warsaw, I expressed my view on the situation in the following words:

"Herr von Ribbentrop's suggestion of a conversation (Beck-Hitler) and his emphasis on its urgency are a proof that Germany has resolved to carry out its eastern program quickly, and so desires to have Poland's attitude quickly defined."

In spite of the most unfavorable circumstances for negotiations, the Polish government did not shrink from further discussions. At my next meeting with Ribbentrop, on March 26, I handed my government's counterproposals for a solution of the Danzig problem in the bounds of a bilateral Polish-German agreement and suggesting the creation of a Polish-German commission in order to provide the best possible facilities for communications between the Reich and East Prussia. Ribbentrop, however, presented his case in such a manner that the German demands were to be accepted as a whole, refusing to commit himself in any way whatsoever as to the merits of the Polish counteroffer, regarding which, in consequence, complete silence was deliberately imposed by the German government.

Such a form of negotiation was a departure from both the letter and the spirit of the Polish-German declaration of January 26, 1934.

Ribbentrop, on March 26, and Weizsäcker, on April 6, 1939, gave me ample expression of their indignation regarding the Polish military measures which were taken as a result of the March incidents. With regard to these measures, I should like to point out that the Polish orders had strictly local meaning and were of a purely defensive character, being moreover entirely justified in view of the large-scale German military moves in the vicinity of Poland's borders; alarm was also felt over the demonstrations held near the Polish Baltic coastline in connection with Hitler's triumphant visit to Memel. There was a feeling of deep concern in the Polish government with regard to the danger of a surprise occupation of Danzig. It can now be seen from Keitel's order dated November 24, 1938, that these fears were not without substance.

With reference to Herr von Weizsäcker's statement concerning Poland's attitude in the last months before the outbreak of the war:

I

On the question of the British guarantee to Poland and the effect which that guarantee had on Polish-German relations, I would like to say the following:

The British guarantee, given as it was in the face of a threat from

Hitler to the security of Eastern Europe, was aimed at deferring him from further conquests; by then it was generally realized that his next move would most likely affect Poland, now strategically weakened by the occupation of Prague and the placing of the Slovakian wedge in the reach of the German military system. Conceived as a weapon of peace, it was by no means contrary to the Polish-German declaration of non-aggression dated January 26, 1934. Furthermore, this declaration was based on the Paris Pact of August 17, 1928, which stipulated a general renunciation of war as an instrument of national policy; both Germany and Poland were cosignatories of this pact.

On his way through Berlin to London in the beginning of April, 1939, the Polish Minister of Foreign Affairs told me that in its further relation-ship to Germany the Polish government was determined to adhere to the principles of the 1934 declaration. I confirmed that to Secretary of State von Weizsäcker on April 6. Mr. Beck saw no reason why, after the Polish-British guarantee, Polish-German relations should not return to their previous satisfactory state, provided, of course, that the German government had a sincere intention of respecting mutual interests in accordance with the 1934 declaration. It was for this reason that, im-mediately after his return from London to Warsaw, Mr. Beck invited German Ambassador von Moltke in order to give him an adequate version of the results of his London visit and thus to resume a firmer exchange of views between Warsaw and Berlin. However, the German Ambassador declined to face Mr. Beck, and left Warsaw ostentatiously. He only returned to his post after Hitler had broken off unilaterally the declaration of nonaggression with Poland and the naval pact with Great Britain. Herr von Moltke never again approached Mr. Beck but kept aside, in complete reserve.

The Polish-British guarantee evoked sharp resentment in German government circles, as became evident to me at my next conversation, on April 6, with Secretary of State von Weizsäcker. He then adopted a highly critical attitude with regard to the Polish-British agreement and put to doubt the explanations which I offered.

As I had supposed at the time, the British guarantee came as a shock to Hitler and upset his calculations. Hitler's intentions with regard to Poland have now been made clear by document No. R. 100 concerning his conversation with General Brauchitsch of March 25, 1939; I quote the relevant clause:

"Problem Poland. For the time being, the Führer does not intend to solve the Polish question. However, it should now be worked on. A solution in the near future would have to be based on specially favorable political conditions. In that case Poland shall be knocked down so completely that it need not be taken into account as a political factor for the next decades. The Führer has in mind such a solution, a border line advanced from the eastern border of East Prussia to the eastern tip of Upper Silesia."

After the Polish-British guarantee, the Germans altered their tactics. Purposely avoiding all further talks with the Polish government, their endeavors were centered on putting Poland into bad odor. Their aim became to achieve Poland's isolation. Thus the German propaganda machine was put to work and one of its products was the slogan of the "blank check" given by the British government to Poland.

I should like to make it clear that the whole idea of a "blank check" was pure invention. In reality it was quite the other way round. The British-Polish guarantee imposed on Poland the duty to coordinate its actions with both the British and the French governments in matters which might have evoked friction with the Germans. The Polish government took care to observe this provision as strictly as possible and was extremely cautious in all its actions, as can well be seen from the diplomatic dispatches of the British and French ambassadors then accredited to Warsaw.

From information which I kept on receiving in the last months preceding the outbreak of war from my colleagues in the Berlin diplomatic corps, especially from the French and British ambassadors, I knew that Secretary of State von Weizsäcker had been swamping them with arguments purporting Polish responsibility for the growing tension. I was forced to endeavor to rectify the deluge of false news about the situation in Poland which was being given to foreigners and distributed to the radio and press; this brought about critical comment from the Auswärtiges Amt with regard to the Polish Embassy's activities.

II

With regard to the defendant von Weizsäcker's statements as to the situation of the German minorities in Poland, I would like to state that, first of all, the question of the German minorities in Poland as well as of the Polish minorities in Germany was governed by the following provisions:

a) by the treaty between the principal Allied Powers and Poland, signed at Versailles on June 28, 1919;

b) by the Polish-German convention regarding Upper Silesia, of June 15, 1922;

c) by the appropriate clauses of the Polish Constitution and by the German Constitution of Weimar.

With the accession to power of National Socialism in Germany and after the German exit from the League of Nations, the problem of minorities underwent a deep change.

On the one hand, the Nazi totalitarian system, having taken up the theories of racism, brought out a new legislation in the exclusive favor of Germanic interests (*Deutschtum*) which automatically curtailed the development and life of the Polish minorities. On the other hand, the Third Reich endeavored to subordinate, for the furtherance of its own aims, all the German minorities in other countries (that is, in Poland) and use them as a tool for its policy of expansion.

To substantiate the above statement, it is enough to recollect the succession of events in the Sudetenland in the autumn of 1938, on the details of which full light was thrown at the Nuremberg trial.

As to Herr von Weizsäcker's statement regarding the alleged abuse suffered by the German minority in Poland in the period preceding the German aggression, I wish to state that the Polish government was well aware, thanks to the Czech precedent, of the Nazi methods of using the minorities as an implement of political action and diversion. It was for that reason, when the Germans embarked upon a war of nerves against Poland, using Danzig and the minorities problem as a background, that the Polish government gave express warning to the administrative authorities to take the greatest care in dealing with infringements on the part of German minorities and to take action only with regard to instances of sabotage or open provocation. The Polish Prime Minister was in constant touch with the voivodes (provincial governors) and had regular conferences with them in the presence of representatives of the Ministry of Foreign Affairs. A senior official of the Ministry of Foreign Affairs was on tour in the summer of 1939 through the western provinces of Poland, in order personally to verify the strict execution of the government's orders.

In order to substantiate what has been said above, I would like to quote some reports of the French and British ambassadors in Warsaw for the period directly preceding the outbreak of the war, as published in the *Livre jaune français, Documents Diplomatiques, 1938–1939* (Imprimerie Nationale, Paris, 1939), and in the *Documents Concerning German-Polish Relations* (H.M. Stationery Office, London, 1939):

No. 102. A report from April 17, 1939, in which the French Ambassador defines the German war of nerves against Poland in the following manner:

"The German tactics toward the Poles seem very clear: The Reich propaganda machine is doing its best to disturb them, play on their nerves, tire them by the multiplicity and persistence of false news, criticisms, and more or less veiled threats, endeavoring either to evoke a change of opinion among the Polish people or to weaken the moral resistance of this potential adversary."

The Ambassador points out the instructions given to correspondents of the German press in Poland to overpublicize even the smallest incidents, and mentions the rumor spread by German agents in Silesia that the German Army was to enter on April 24; the report ends with an assertion that the Polish authorities and population "are showing remarkable calm."

No. 107. The French Ambassador stated on April 29, 1939:

"Contrary to German allegations, the Polish population has displayed great calm up till now and the functioning of the authorities is bent on utmost moderation. This fact has been ascertained by all foreign observers. . . . Furthermore, the most serious incidents noted recently in the Reich press were due to German provocations."

Some examples of these provocations follow.

No. 142. June 22, 1939. The French Ambassador reiterates that for three months Poland has been kept in a state of tension. He states:

"At the beginning of that period, it was possible to doubt whether, under these circumstances, Polish public opinion could long endure in its calm, without losing some degree of its determination. The trial has turned out entirely in the Poles' favor."

No. 52. August 24, 1939. A detailed report of the British Ambassador rectifying false statements regarding alleged abuses committed against the German minorities:

"While I am of course not in a position to check all the allegations made by the German press of minority persecutions here, I am satisfied from enquiries I have made that the campaign is a gross distortion and exaggeration of facts. Accusations of beating with chains, throwing on barbed wire, being forced to shout insults against Herr Hitler in chorus, etc., are merely silly, but many individual cases specified have been disproved."

There follow several examples of ungrounded statements of German propaganda.

No. 55. August 27, 1939. Wire from the British Ambassador:

"So far as I can judge, German allegations of mass ill-treatment of German minority by Polish authorities are gross exaggerations if not complete falsifications.

"2. There is no sign of any loss of control of situation by Polish civil authorities. Warsaw—and, so far as I can ascertain, the rest of Poland —is completely calm.

"3. Such allegations are reminiscent of Nazi propaganda methods regarding Czechoslovakia last year.

"4. In any case, it is purely and simply deliberate German provocation in accordance with fixed policy that has since March exacerbated feeling between the two nationalities. I suppose this has been done with the object of (*a*) creating war spirit in Germany, (*b*) impressing public opinion abroad, (*c*) provoking either defeatism or apparent aggression in Poland.

"5. It has signally failed to achieve either of the two latter objectives.

No. 276. August 28, 1939. The French Ambassador writes:

"The ill-treatment, murders, etc., of which the Poles are being accused by Chancellor Hitler are pure slander. The denials given by the Polish authorities cannot be doubted. It is impossible for Germans to have been killed in the vicinity of Danzig or Bielsko without some information about it. It should be stressed besides that the Germans have failed to provide a single precise fact, a single name, or a single date."

No. 281. August 28, 1939. The French Ambassador, while refuting invented statements of the German press, gives the following explanation:

". . . the instances of pillage by bands of insurgents in Silesia are a product of invention in every detail. Captain Blacha, their alleged leader, has been dead for two years."

In the mutual declarations made on November 5, 1937, by the Polish and German governments regarding the principles governing the treatment of the minorities, it was stated that "the above principles can in no way affect the duty of the minorities to give complete loyalty to the state to which they belong."

This rule was strictly adhered to by Polish minority organizations in Germany, whose activities were limited to cultural, benevolent, and economic matters. It was hardly so with the German minority in Poland, gathered together in Nazi organizations and governed by Party discipline and directives from the Reich. In the war of nerves against Poland, it became an implement of disruption by the spreading of false rumors and provocative action. On the outbreak of the war, the German minority entered on preplanned subversive operations, thus becoming an advance guard of Hitler's Army. This was revealed at the time of the campaign in Poland and was confirmed by documents seized by Polish military authorities. (See Appendix I.)[2]

To complete the picture of the minorities problem, I refer to a memorandum of the Polish Embassy in Berlin dated August 26, 1939, which described the situation of the Polish minority in Germany on the eve of the outbreak of the war. (See Appendix II.)[3]

I might add that in the middle of August, 1939, the Polish Embassy in Berlin handed to the French and British embassies a list of over 600 cases of persecutions of the Polish minority in Germany within recent months. These included arrests, deportations, religious persecutions, measures against schools and the press, compulsory removal from the frontier zones, and the destruction of property.

Such incidents became more and more widespread and grew in violence as the date of the German aggression approached.

III

With reference to defendant von Weizsäcker's statement regarding the conflict over the customs inspectors in Danzig, August, 1939:

The Free City of Danzig, under the care of the League of Nations represented by the high commissioner, was, in accordance with its statute and constitution, a demilitarized area.

In the spring of 1939, contrary to the existing legal status, military

[2] Instructions to be brought to the notice of troops engaged against Poland, Polish Ministry of Information. *The German Fifth Column in Poland*, pp. 149–52.
[3] *Polish White Book*, No. 93.

units began to be formed on the territory of the Free City—clandestinely at first, more boldly and openly as time progressed. Old, disused barracks were being prepared to accommodate troops. Young men, organized under S.S. and S.A. colors, received military training in Danzig by instructions (army officers) posted from the Reich, or were sent for that purpose to Germany. Growing numbers of "tourists" were arriving in Danzig from adjacent East Prussia. From May, 1939, the militarization was getting more and more noticeable. By now, closed formations of troops were beginning to parade openly in the streets, unarmed at first, later carrying small arms. In July, 1939, the military unit formed on Danzig free territory under the name of the *Freikorps* under the command of General Eberhard, who came from Germany for this purpose, had grown to the strength of one division.

In spite of such blatant provocation, to the accompaniment of inflammatory speeches by Party members and dignitaries visiting the Free City from the Reich, the Polish government did not allow itself to lose temper.

The Free City of Danzig formed part of the Polish customs area in accordance with the provisions of the Treaty of Versailles and of the Paris Convention of July, 1920. Subsequent executive agreements, in particular the Polish-Danzig agreement of October 24, 1921, made detailed arrangements as to the application of Polish customs regulations and control through Polish inspectors.

Until the spring of 1939, cooperation between Polish and Danzig customs executives on the whole progressed on reasonable and appropriate terms. Friction inevitably arose when, together with the militarization of the Free City, the smuggling of arms and ammunition from East Prussia began. At that time, a violent press campaign against the control exercized by Polish customs inspectors was unleashed, both in Danzig and inside the Reich. A series of incidents was provoked with the aid of Nazi bands, the most noteworthy of which was the coup against the customs office in Kalthof on May 20, 1939.

The Danzig Senate simultaneously endeavored, in its letter of June 3, 1939, to the Polish Commissioner-General, to curtail the inspectors' scope of competence to that of mere document control. In its subsequent letter of July 29, 1939, the Senate went even further by stating that it did not consider itself any longer under obligation to adhere to the agreements regarding the Polish inspectors. This was rejected by the

Polish Commissioner-General in his letter of August 3, which simultaneously expressed his readiness to discuss the matter as a whole.

In accordance with the Senate's letter of July 29, the chief of Danzig customs, in a letter dated August 4, 1939, informed the chief Polish customs inspector that the Danzig customs offices would no longer recognize the Polish inspectors posted on duty in the frontier zone sectors. On the same day, the superintendents of four Danzig customs posts on the East Prussian frontier verbally informed the Polish inspectors on duty that as of 7 A.M. on August 6 they would no longer be admitted to work.

The timing of this step and the general sequence of events, with the Senate's letter of July 29, 1939, and the Danzig customs directorate's letter of August 4, 1939, made it clear that an attempt to breach the customs barrier between the Free City and the Reich was being made.

This time, the Polish government felt compelled to oppose the threatened violation of one of its most vital rights in the Free City; hence the note from the Commissioner-General to the Danzig Senate dated August 4, 1939.

The President of the Senate on the following day gave oral reassuring explanations, and only three days later, namely, on August 7—evidently after getting in touch with Berlin—sent a written reply to the Polish note. This note, while denying the order issued on August 4, endeavored to charge the Polish authorities for the tension which had arisen.

Nevertheless, for a short time it was believed in political circles that the customs conflict was, if only for the time being, wound up owing to the peremptory but at the same time moderate line adopted by Poland. The Polish press showed discretion and forbearance in order not to complicate matters.

However, on August 9, 1939, the German government intervened in the direct relations between the Free City and Poland, when Secretary of State von Weizsäcker made the known statement to the Polish Chargé d'Affaires in Berlin on August 9. Herr von Weizsäcker refused to enter into any discussion on the subject with the Polish Chargé d'Affaires.

In these circumstances, the Polish government had no other way than to state that it could see no legal basis that could be held as justifying any interventions in the relations between Poland and the Free City and made a strong reservation against possible attempts on the part of the German government to infringe on the agreed Polish rights in Danzig.

In its endeavors, nevertheless, to find a way to a compromise, the Polish government started conversations with the Free City authorities as of August 16 (Chodacki-Greiser). For that reason, the director of the Central Customs Office, Mr. Maksymowicz, was especially delegated from Warsaw to Danzig. In spite of the fact that the unceasing contraband war matériel from Germany to Danzig hardly warranted a cut in the force of customs inspectors there, Mr. Maksymowicz received instructions to make substantial concessions in that respect, as a good-will gesture. The discussions gave no results since Polish concessions only evoked further demands on Danzig's part.

I was told at that time that the Auswärtiges Amt was endeavoring to charge Poland with the responsibility for the events in Danzig. This was also confirmed to me by Sir Nevile Henderson on August 27 when he told me of his conversation with Herr von Weizsäcker two days before.

That Danzig served merely as a trump card in the German game against Poland can be seen from Hitler's sentence at a conference on May 23, 1939:

"Danzig is not the subject of the dispute at all. It is a question of extending our living space."

September 23, 1948

J. Lipski

Select Bibliography

I. *Official Documents*

Czechoslovak Sources and Documents, No. 2. *Struggle for Freedom.* New York, 1943.

Degras, Jane, ed. *Soviet Documents on Foreign Policy, 1917–1941.* 3 vols. London, 1951–53.

Documents on International Affairs, 1939–1946. Ed. by A. J. Toynbee. Vol. I: March–September, 1939. London, 1951.

France. Ministère des Affaires Étrangères. *Documents diplomatiques, 1938–1939: Pièces relatives aux événements et aux négociations qui ont précédé l'ouverture des hostilités entre Allemagne d'une part, la Pologne, la Grande-Bretagne et la France d'autre part. (Livre jaune français.)* Paris, 1939.

—— *Documents diplomatiques français, 1932–1939.* 2me série (1936–1939), Tome I, II. Paris, 1964.

Germany. Auswärtiges Amt. *Documents and Materials Relating to the Eve of the Second World War.* Vol I: November, 1937–1938. Vol. II: Dirksen papers, 1938–1939. Moscow, 1948.

—— *Documents Concerning the Last Phase of the German-Polish Crisis.* Berlin–New York, 1939.

—— *Documents on German Foreign Policy, 1918–1945.* Series C: 1933–1937, Vols. I–V. Series D: 1937–1945, Vols. I–II, IV–VII. Washington, 1949–62.

—— *Documents on the Events Preceding the Outbreak of the War.* New York, 1940.

—— *Documents on the Origin of the War.* Berlin, 1939.

—— *Dokumente zur Vorgeschichte des Krieges. (Weissbuch, No. 2.)* Berlin, 1939.

—— *The German White Paper: Full Text of the Polish Documents Issued by the Berlin Foreign Office.* New York, 1940.

—— *Nazi-Soviet Relations, 1939–1941: Documents.* Dept. of State Publication 3023. Washington, 1948.

—— *Negotiations for the Solution of the Sudeten German Question. (White Book, 1938, No. 1.)* 1938.

—— *Polish Acts of Atrocity Against the German Minority in Poland.* Berlin–New York, 1940.

—— *Polish Documents Relative to the Origin of the War.* 1st series, No. 3. Berlin, 1940.

—— *Weissbuch der deutschen Regierung: Urkunden zur letzten Phase der deutsch-polnischen Krise.* Basel, 1940.

—— *Zweites Weissbuch der deutschen Regierung: Dokumente über die Entwickelung der deutsch-polnischen Beziehungen und die Ereignisse von 1933 bis zur Gegenwart.* Basel, 1940.

Great Britain. Foreign Office. *Correspondence Showing the Course of Certain Diplomatic Discussions Directed Towards Securing an European Settlement, June 1934 to March 1936.* Parliament, Papers by Command, Cmd. 5143. London, 1936.

—— *Documents Concerning German-Polish Relations and the Outbreak of Hostilities Between Great Britain and Germany on Sept. 3, 1939. (British Blue Book.)* London, 1939.

—— *Documents on British Foreign Policy, 1919–1939.* 2d series, Vol. I. 3d series, Vols. I, VII. London, 1949–54.

Nazi Conspiracy and Aggression. 8 vols. and suppls. A–B. Washington, 1946–48.

Poland. Ministerstwo Spraw Zagranicznych. *Official Documents Concerning Polish-German and Polish-Soviet Relations, 1933–1939. (Polish White Book.)* London, 1940.

—— *Polskie Siły Zbrojne. Komisja Historyczna. Polskie Siły Zbrojne w drugiej Wojnie Światowej.* Vol. I: *Kampania wrześniowa 1939;* part 1: Polityczne i wojskowe położenie Polski przed wojną. London, 1951.

—— *"Przeglad Informacyjny Polska a Zagranica."* Warsaw, Ministry of Foreign Affairs. Secret. Mimeographed. Years 1933–39.

Sbornik dokumentow o wnieszniej politikie SSSR. Vols. I-III. Moscow, 1944.

Survey of International Affairs. Ed. by A. J. Toynbee. 1935, Vol. I. 1938, Vols. II–III. 1939, Vol. I. London, 1936–52.

The Trial of German Major War Criminals: Proceedings of the International Military Tribunal Setting at Nuremberg, Germany, 20th Nov. 1945 to 1st Oct. 1946. London, 1946–50.

Trial of the Major War Criminals: Nuremberg, 14 Nov. 1945–1 Oct. 1946. 42 vols. Nuremberg, 1947–49.

"Trials of War Criminals." Mimeographed transcript of trials of war criminals before the Nuremberg Military Tribunals.

Trials of War Criminals before the Nuernberg Military Tribunals under Control Council Law No. 10, Nuernberg, Oct. 1947–April 1949. Vols. XII–XXIV, *Case 11: U.S. vs. Von Weizsäcker ("Ministries case").* Washington, 1951–52.

United States. Department of State. *Foreign Relations of the United States: Diplomatic Papers.* 1938, Vol. I. 1939, Vol. I. Washington, 1955–56.

—— *Peace and War: U.S. Foreign Policy, 1931–1941.* Washington, 1943.

II. *Other Sources*

Batowski, Henryk. "August 31st, 1939 in Berlin," *Polish Western Affairs* (Poznań), Vol. IV, No. 1 (1963).

—— *Kryzys dyplomatyczny w Europie, jesień 1938–wiosna 1939*. Warsaw, 1962.

—— "O dyplomacji niemieckiej, 1919–1945," in Paul Schmidt, *Statysta na dyplomatycznej scenie* (Polish translation), pp. 563–626. Cracow, 1965.

—— *Ostatni tydzień pokoju*. Poznań, 1964.

—— "Rumuńska podróż Becka w październiku 1938 r.," *Kwartalnik Historyczny* (Warsaw), No. 2 (1958), pp. 423–37.

Beck, Józef. *Dernier rapport: Politique polonaise, 1926–1939*. Neuchâtel, 1951.

—— *Final Report*. New York, 1957.

—— *Przemówienia, deklaracje, wywiady, 1931–1937*. Warsaw, 1938.

—— *Przemówienia, deklaracje, wywiady, 1931–1939*. 2d ed. Warsaw, 1939.

Benedykt, Stefan. "Zajazd O.R.P. 'Wicher' na Gdańsk," *Wiadomości* (London), No. 108 (1948).

Bonnet, G. E. *Défense de la paix*. Vol. I: *De Washington au quai d'Orsay*. Vol. II: *Fin d'une Europe: De Munich à la guerre*. Geneva, 1946–48.

Breyer, Richard. *Das Deutsche Reich und Polen, 1932–1937: Aussenpolitik und Volksgruppenfragen*. Würzburg, 1955.

Bullock, A. L. C. *Hitler, a Study in Tyranny*. New York, 1952.

Burckhardt, C. J. *Ma mission à Danzig*. Paris, 1961.

Cerruti, Elisabeth. *Memoirs*. London, 1952.

Chudek, Józef. "Polska wobec wrześniowego kryzysu czechosłowackiego 1938 r.," *Sprawy Międzynarodowe* (Warsaw), No. 4 (1958), pp. 72–79.

—— "Rozmowy Beck-Göring z 23 lutego 1938," *Sprawy Międzynarodowe* (Warsaw), No. 5 (1960), pp. 53–57.

—— "Sprawa Bogumina w dokumentach polskich," *Sprawy Międzynarodowe* (Warsaw), No. 9 (1958), pp. 108–14.

Ciano, Galeazzo. *Ciano's Diplomatic Papers*. London, 1948.

Cienciala, Anna. "The Significance of the Declaration of Nonaggression of January 26, 1934, in Polish-German and International Relations: A Reappraisal," *East European Quarterly*, No. 1 (1967).

Coulondre, Robert. *De Staline à Hitler: Souvenirs de deux ambassades, 1936–1939*. Paris, 1950.

Craig, G. A., and Felix Gilbert. *The Diplomats: 1919–1939*, Princeton, N.J., 1953.

Cyprian, Tadeusz, and Jerzy Sawicki. *Agresja na Polskę w świetle dokumentów*. 2 vols. Warsaw, 1946.

—— *Sprawy polskie w procesie norymberskim*. Poznań, 1956.

Czarnecki, Bogdan. *Fall Weiss: Z genezy hitlerowskiej agresji przeciw Polsce*. Warsaw, 1960.

—— "Gdy Niemcy chciały z Polską pokoju: Z genezy polsko-niemieckiego układu z 26 stycznia 1934 r.," *Sprawy Międzynarodowe* (Warsaw), No. 12 (1958), pp. 69–82.

—— "Od 'Monachium' do kryzysu kwietniowego 1939 r.: Z historii niemieckich przygotowań do agresji," *Sprawy Międzynarodowe* (Warsaw), No. 10–11 (1958), pp. 55–69.

Dahlerus, J. B. E. *The Last Attempt.* London, 1947.

Dębicki, Roman. *Foreign Policy of Poland, 1919–1939, from the Rebirth of the Polish Republic to World War II.* New York, 1962.

Dirksen, Herbert von. *Moskau, Tokio, London: Erinnerungen und Betrachtungen zu 20 Jahren deutschen Aussenpolitik, 1919–1939.* Stuttgart, 1949.

Dodd, Martha. *My Years in Germany.* London, 1939.

Dodd, W. E. *Ambassador Dodd's Diary, 1933–1938.* London, 1941.

Dopierała, Bogdan. *Gdańska polityka Józefa Becka.* Poznań, 1967.

Flandin, P. E. *Politique française, 1919–1940.* Paris, 1947.

François-Poncet, André. *Souvenir d'une ambassade à Berlin, septembre 1931–octobre 1938.* Paris, 1946.

Gafencu, Grigore. *The Last Days of Europe.* London, 1947.

Gamelin, M. G. *Servir.* Vol. II: *Le prologue du drame (1930–août 1939).* Paris, 1946.

Gąsiorowski, Z. J. "The German-Polish Non-aggression Pact of 1934," *Journal of Central European Affairs,* XV, No. 1 (1955), 3–29.

—— "Stresemann and Poland before Locarno," *Journal of Central European Affairs,* XVIII, No. 1 (1958), 25–47.

Gawroński, Jan. *Moja misja w Wiedniu 1932–1938.* Warsaw, 1965.

Gelbert, Ludwik. "Anulowanie przez III Rzeszę polsko-niemieckiej deklaracji z 26 stycznia 1934 r.," *Sprawy Międzynarodowe* (Warsaw), No. 6 (87) (1959), pp. 78–94.

The German Fifth Column in Poland. London, 1940.

Gisevius, H. B. *Bis zum bitteren Ende.* Zurich, 1954.

Hassell, Ulrich. *Vom anderen Deutschland: Aus den nachgelassenen Tagebüchern, 1938–1944.* Vienna, 1948.

Henderson, Nevile. *Failure of a Mission: Berlin, 1937–39.* London, 1940.

Hilger, Gustav, and A. G. Meyer. *The Incompatible Allies: A Memoir History of German-Soviet Relations, 1918–1941.* New York, 1953.

Hitler, Adolf. *Mein Kampf.* London, 1939.

—— *The Speeches of Adolf Hitler, April 1922–August 1939.* Ed. by N. H. Baynes. 2 vols. London–New York, 1942.

—— *Table Talk, 1941–1944.* London, 1953.

Horthy, Nicolas. *Memoirs.* New York, 1957.

Jędrzejewicz, Wacław. "Dziewiętnaście decydujących bitew świata," *Bellona* (London), No. 3–4 (1963), pp. 216–23.

—— "The Polish Plan for a 'Preventive War' Against Germany in 1933," *The Polish Review* (New York), XI, No. 1 (1966), 62–91.

Jędrzejewicz, Wacław, ed. *Poland in the British Parliament, 1939–1945.* Vol. I: March, 1939–August, 1941. New York, 1946.

Jurkiewicz, Jarosław. *Pakt wschodni: Z historii stosunków międzynarodowych w latach 1934–1935.* Warsaw, 1963.

—— "Polska wobec planów paktu wschodniego w latach 1934–1935," *Sprawy Międzynarodowe* (Warsaw), No. 3 (84) (1959), pp. 18–51.

—— "Węgry a Polska w okresie kryzysu czechosłowackiego 1938 r. (nieopublikowane dokumenty)," *Sprawy Międzynarodowe* (Warsaw), No. 7–8 (1958), pp. 69–73.

—— "Wizyta Prezydenta Rauschinga w Warszawie w grudniu 1933," *Najnowsze dzieje Polski, materiały i studia z okresu 1914–1939* (Warsaw), III (1960), 163–82.

Keyserling, R. W. *Unfinished History.* London, 1948.

Kleist, Peter. *Zwischen Hitler und Stalin, 1939–1945: Aufzeichnungen.* Bonn, 1950.

Komarnicki, Tytus. *Piłsudski a polityka wielkich mocarstw zachodnich.* London, 1952.

—— *Rebirth of the Polish Republic: A Study in the Diplomatic History of Europe, 1914–1920.* London, 1957.

Korbel, Josef. *Poland Between East and West: Soviet and German Diplomacy Toward Poland, 1919–1933.* Princeton, N.J., 1963.

Kordt, Erich. *Nicht aus den Akten: Die Wilhelmstrasse im Frieden und Krieg; Erlebnisse, Begegnungen und Eindrücke, 1928–1945.* Stuttgart, 1950.

—— *Wahn und Wirklichkeit: Die Aussenpolitik des Dritten Reiches; Versuch einer Darstellung.* 2d ed. Stuttgart, 1948.

Kozeński, Jerzy. *Czechosłowacja w polskiej polityce zagranicznej w latach 1932–1938.* Poznań, 1964.

Kozłowski, Eugeniusz. "Stosunki polsko-niemieckie przed II Wojną Światową: Dokumenty z Archiwum Generalnego Inspektora Sił Zbrojnych," *Najnowsze dzieje Polski, materiały i studia z okresu 1914–1939* (Warsaw), III (1960), 195–261.

Krasuski, Jerzy. *Stosunki polsko-niemieckie, 1919–1925.* Poznań, 1962.

—— *Stosunki polsko-niemieckie, 1926–1932.* Poznań, 1964.

Kremer, Jan. "Remilitaryzacja Niemiec w roku 1935," *Sprawy Międzynarodowe* (Warsaw), No. 2 (119) (1962), pp. 56–64.

Kuźminski, Tadeusz. *Polska, Francja, Niemcy, 1933–1935: Z dziejów sojuszu polsko-francuskiego.* Warsaw, 1963.

Laeuen, Harald. *Polnisches Zwischenspiel: Eine Episode der Ostpolitik.* Berlin, 1940.

Lapter, Karol. *Pakt Piłsudski-Hitler: Polsko-niemiecka deklaracja o niestosowaniu przemocy z 26 stycznia 1934 roku.* Warsaw, 1962.

Laroche, J. A. *La Pologne de Piłsudski: Souvenirs d'une ambassade, 1926–1935.* Paris, 1953.

Lipski, Józef. "Nowe przyczynki dotyczące wybuchu wojny polsko-niemieckiej w 1939 r.," *Bellona* (London), No. 1 (1950), pp. 16–40.

—— "Przyczynki do polsko-niemieckiej deklaracji o nieagresji," *Bellona* (London), No. 1–2 (1951), pp. 18–37; No. 3, pp. 3–21.

658   SELECT BIBLIOGRAPHY

—— "Rzut oka na zagadnienie granic polsko-niemieckich," *Bellona* (London), No. 2 (1947), pp. 3–11.

—— "Stosunki polsko-niemieckie przed wybuchem wojny w świetle aktów norymberskich," *Sprawy Międzynarodowe* (London), No. 2–3 (1947), pp. 11–26; No. 4, pp. 24–51.

—— "Uwagi o polityce i strategii," *Bellona* (London), No. 4 (1946), pp. 3–13.

Lipski, Józef, E. Raczyński, and S. Stroński. *Trzy podróże gen. Sikorskiego do Ameryki.* London, Gen. Sikorski Historical Institute, 1949.

Łossowski, Piotr. "Stosunki polsko-niemieckie w latach 1933–1939 a klęska wrześniowa," *Wojskowy Przegląd Historyczny,* No. 1 (1963), pp. 132–62; No. 1 (1964), pp. 189–226.

Louis Ferdinand, Prince of Prussia. *The Rebel Prince: Memoirs.* Chicago, 1953.

Łubieński, Michał. "Ostatnie negocjacje w sprawie Gdańska," *Dziennik Polski i Dziennik Żołnierza* (London), Dec. 3, 1953.

Lubomirski, Stefan. "Fałszowanie prawdy historycznej przez przemilczenie faktów," *Dziennik Polski i Dziennik Żołnierza* (London), Nov. 26, 1957.

—— "Ostatnia misja z Berlina," *Wiadomości* (London), No. 182 (1943).

Lukacs, J. A. *The Great Powers and Eastern Europe.* New York, 1953.

Łukasiewicz, Juliusz. "Pamiętniki." Unpublished manuscript in the Józef Piłsudski Institute of America, New York, N.Y.

—— "Sprawa czechosłowacka w 1938 r. na tle stosunków polsko-francuskich," *Sprawy Międzynarodowe* (London), No. 6–7 (1948), pp. 27–56.

Macartney, C. A. *October Fifteenth: A History of Modern Hungary, 1929–1945.* 2 vols. Edinburgh, 1957.

Mackiewicz, Stanisław. *Colonel Beck and His Policy.* London, 1944.

—— *O jedenastej, powiada autor, sztuka jest skończona: Polityka Józefa Becka.* London, 1942.

Meissner, Otto. *Staatssekretär unter Ebert, Hindenburg, Hitler: Der Schicksalsweg des deutschen Volkes von 1918–1945, wie ich ihn erlebte.* Hamburg, 1950.

Miedziński, Bogusław. "Droga do Moskwy," *Kultura* (Paris), No. 188 (1963), pp. 74–86.

—— "Pakty Wilanowskie," *Kultura* (Paris), No. 189–90 (1963), pp. 113–32.

Morgenstern, T. "Wejście O.R.P. 'Wicher' do Gdańska w 1932 r.," *Bellona* (London), No. 1 (1953), pp. 44–48.

Namier, L. B. *Diplomatic Prelude, 1938–1939.* London, 1948.

—— *Europe in Decay: A Study in Disintegration, 1936–1940.* London, 1950.

—— *In the Nazi Era.* London, 1952.

Noël, Léon. *L'aggression allemande contre la Pologne.* Paris, 1946.

Pajewski, Janusz. *Problem polsko-niemiecki w Traktacie Wersalskim: Praca zbiorowa.* Poznań, 1963.

Paul-Boncour, Joseph. *Entre deux guerres: Souvenirs sur la IIIᵉ République.* 3 vols. Paris, 1945–46.

Petresco-Comnène, N. M. *Preludi del grande dramma.* Rome, 1947.

Pobóg-Malinowski, Władysław. *Najnowsza historia polityczna Polski, 1864–1945.* 3 vols. London, 1956–61.

Raczyński, Eduard. *In Allied London.* London, 1962.

Rauschning, Hermann. *Gespräche mit Hitler.* Zurich, 1940.

Roos, Hans. *Geschichte der polnischen Nation, 1916–1960: Von der Staatsgrundung im ersten Weltkrieg bis zur Gegenwart.* Stuttgart, 1961.

—— *A History of Modern Poland from the Foundation of the State in the First World War to the Present Day.* London, 1966.

—— *Polen und Europa: Studien zur polnischen Aussenpolitik, 1931–1939.* Tübingen, 1957.

Rose, Adam. *La politique polonaise entre les deux guerres.* Neuchâtel, 1944.

Schmidt, Paul. *Statist auf diplomatischer Bühne, 1923–45: Erlebnisse des Chefdolmetschers im Auswärtigen Amt mit den Staatsmännern Europas.* Bonn, 1949.

Schuman, F. L. *Europe on the Eve: The Crises of Diplomacy, 1933–1939.* New York, 1939.

Seton-Watson, R. W. *From Munich to Danzig.* London, 1939.

Shirer, W. L. *The Rise and Fall of the Third Reich: A History of Nazi Germany.* New York, 1960.

Smogorzewski, K. M. *Czy dziejowy zwrot w stosunkach polsko-niemieckich?* Poznań, 1934.

—— *Poland's Access to the Sea.* London, 1934.

Sokulski, H. "Wojna celna Rzeszy przeciwko Polsce w latach 1925–1934," *Sprawy Międzynarodowe* (Warsaw), No. 9 (1955), pp. 39–40.

Sontag, R. J. "The Last Month of Peace, 1939," *Foreign Affairs,* April, 1957, pp. 507–24.

Stanisławska, Stefania. *Polska a Monachium.* Warsaw, 1967.

—— "Umowa Göring-Beck z 23 lutego 1936 r.," *Najnowsze dzieje Polski, materiały i studia z okresu 1914–1939* (Warsaw), III (1960), 183–93.

—— *Wielka i mała polityka Józefa Becka, marzec–maj 1938.* Warsaw, 1962.

Starzeński, Paweł. "Marzec 1939," *Wiadomości* (London), No. 323 (1952).

—— "Powrót do Warszawy," *Wiadomości* (London), No. 329 (1952).

—— "Umowa z Anglią," *Wiadomości* (London), No. 326 (1952).

Stroński, Stanisław. "Polska i Niemcy, 1937–1938: Czechosłowacja i z Karpat nad Bałtyk," *Wiadomości* (London), No. 405 (1954).

Szembek, Jan. *Diariusz i teki Jana Szembeka, 1935–1945.* Vol. I, 1935. Vol. II, 1936. Ed. by Tytus Komarnicki. London, 1964–65.

—— *Journal, 1933–1939.* Paris, 1952.

Szymański, Antoni. "Fragmenty niemieckich przygotowań wojennych w ostatnim przedwojennym półroczu 1939 r.," *Bellona* (London), No. 3 (1954), pp. 4–11.

—— *Zły sąsiad: Niemcy 1932–1939 w oświetleniu polskiego attaché wojskowego w Berlinie.* London, 1959.

Taylor, Telford. *Sword and Swastika: Generals and Nazis in the Third Reich.* New York, 1952.

Trocka, Halina. *Gdańsk a hitlerowski "Drang nach Osten."* Danzig, 1965.

Turlejska, Maria. *Rok przed klęską, 1 wrzesień 1938–1 wrzesień 1939.* 2d ed. Warsaw, 1962.

Wandycz, P. S. *France and Her Eastern Allies, 1919–1925: French-Czechoslovak-Polish Relations from the Paris Peace Conference to Locarno.* Minneapolis, 1962.

Weizsäcker, E. H. *Erinnerungen.* Munich, 1950.

Wheeler-Bennett, J. W. *Munich: Prologue to Tragedy.* New York, 1948.

—— *The Nemesis of Power: The German Army in Politics, 1918–1945.* New York, 1954.

Wiskemann, Elizabeth. *The Rome-Berlin Axis: A History of the Relations Between Hitler and Mussolini.* London, 1949.

Wojciechowski, Marian. "Polska i Niemcy na przełomie lat 1932–1933," *Roczniki historyczne* (Poznań), XXIX (1963), 152–75.

—— *Stosunki polsko-niemieckie, 1933–1938.* Poznań, 1965.

Wolski, Aleksander. "Pakt polsko-niemiecki z 1934 r.," *Sprawy Międzynarodowe* (Warsaw), No. 6 (26) (1953), pp. 64–77.

Wysocki, Alfred. "Początek dramatu," *Tygodnik Powszechny* (Cracow), No. 7 (525), Feb. 15, 1959.

Zaleski, August. *Przemowy i deklaracje.* Warsaw, 1929.

Zay, Jean. *Souvenirs et Solitude.* Paris, 1946.

Index

PERSONNEL
Human Resource
Management

PERSONNEL
Human Resource Management

Fourth Edition

Robert L. Mathis
University of Nebraska at Omaha

John H. Jackson
University of Wyoming

West Publishing Company
St. Paul   New York   Los Angeles   San Francisco

A study guide has been developed to assist you in mastering concepts presented in this text. The study guide reinforces concepts by presenting them in condensed, concise form. Additional illustrations, examples, and exercises are also included. The study guide is available from your local bookstore under the title, *Study Guide to Accompany Personnel: Human Resource Management*, fourth edition, prepared by Sally A. Coltrin and Roger Dean.

Copy editing: Theresa Castle
Art design: Art by AXYA
Composition: The Clarinda Company
Cover design: Steve Holler

Library of Congress Cataloging in Publication Data

Mathis, Robert L., 1944–
    Personnel : human resource management.

    First-3rd eds. published under title: Personnel : contemporary perspectives and applications.
    Bibliography: p.
    Includes index.
    1. Personnel management.   I. Jackson, John Harold.
II. Title.
HF5549.M3349   1985   658.3   84-27116
ISBN 0-314-85276-X
1st Reprint—1985

To

Jo Ann Mathis
who manages me

R. D. and M. M. Jackson
who have been
successful managers of
people for many years

Contents
in Brief

Contents

Chapter 2 ■ Personnel in the Organization 23

Chapter 3 ■ Human Behavior and Personnel 55

Chapter 5 ■ Implementing Equal Employment 109

SECTION III
STAFFING THE ORGANIZATION AND ITS WORK 145

Chapter 6 ■ Designing Jobs and Work 147

Chapter 8 ■ Human Resource Planning and Recruiting   207

Chapter 9 ■ Selecting Human Resources   235

SECTION IV
TRAINING AND DEVELOPING HUMAN RESOURCES   273

Chapter 10 ■ Orientation and Training   275

Chapter 15 ■ Employee Benefits 429

Chapter 18 ■ Human Resource Research and Information Systems   525

Preface

The fourth edition of this book continues the tradition established by the first three. Every effort has been made to cover all relevent new ideas and developments in personnel since the last edition. New terms, new methods, and new research have all been carefully integrated into the successful format. Certainly not everyone who reads this book will become a personnel manager. In fact, most students who take a personnel course never become personnel specialists. However, everyone who works in any organization will contact personnel management—both good and bad. Anyone who does become a manager must be able to manage personnel activities. We feel every manager's personnel actions can have major consequences for the organization.

A unique feature of the book is specifying the "area of contact" between operating managers and the personnel unit. This concept is a way to view the division of responsibilities between operating managers and the personnel unit. Although this division will vary depending on the size of the organization, its technology and history, and other factors, clearly there is a group of personnel activities for which someone in the organization *has to take responsibility*. The "interface" concept used throughout the book addresses how this responsibility is divided.

This book examines the major activities in personnel or "Human Resource" management completely but concisely. We are gratified by the reception of the previous editions and feel the changes and additions suggested by users of the third edition have made the book even better.

Change is a constant companion for anyone writing or working in the field of personnel/human resource management, as it is if one has a well-recognized and accepted basic text in the field. It is the field of personnel and the demands of it that require a revision every three years.

The fourth edition reflects the authors' continuing efforts to have the most current and comprehensive personnel text on the market. Every line and word of existing content has been reviewed and revised as deemed necessary for the book to keep its "cutting edge". Consequently, the revision has several important new interest problem/program/practice in an actual organization in order to illustrate the nature of the content to follow. Within each chapter, vignettes entitled Personnel in Practice capture specific practices by firms such as Apple Computer, Miles Laboratories, Manpower, and others. At the end of each chapter a futuristic issue in personnel in the content area is highlighted. Issues covered include working-at-home (telecommuting), genetic testing, merit pay for teachers, and many others.

The fourth edition opens with revised content which highlights some of the changes occurring in how human resources are being creatively managed and personnel is being practiced. Chapter 2 provides enhanced coverage of the role of personnel in the organization and public personnel management.

Major revisions have been made in the chapters on equal employment opportunity in order to update the content in light of changes and intervening court decisions. Several new landmark cases are discussed.

Section III on staffing begins with a new chapter that highlights the many issues and concerns in Chapter 7 revolving around work design, work schedules, quality of work life, and productivity. Job analysis is now the primary topic covered in Chapter 7. More details on the preparation of job descriptions and methods of job analysis are included. In Chapter 8, the Human Resource planning sections have been significantly upgraded and changed.

In the training and development section, enhanced and expanded coverage of career planning and pathing has been included. Also, the performance appraisal chapter has been moved to this section to emphasize the developmental aspects of appraisal.

Major attention has been devoted to restructuring and expanding the section entitled Compensating Jobs and People. More information on the construction of pay structures and grades is included. By splitting incentives and benefits coverage into 2 separate chapters, it was possible to add significantly expanded coverage of executive compensation. The new chapter 15 is tightly focused on benefits. More coverage has been added on health care cost management and on new benefit options.

The last three sections include significant additions and updating. For instance, updated content reflects changes in OSHA regulations and court decisions. Specific detailed content on employment-at-will and improved coverage of human resource information systems have been added. Emerging trends in union membership and the many changes in bargaining relationships in terms of give-backs and the use of bankruptcy are discussed. Finally, an enhanced and expanded final chapter identifies some emerging trends and speculates upon the changes that will be coming to personnel management by the year 2000.

In addition, over one-third of the cases within the text are changed and a broad-based case that touches many areas of personnel has been included after the last chapter. Another new feature is an appendix on getting a job to help students prepare resumes and prepare for interviews.

A greatly improved instructor's manual is also available which has over 1700 test questions in it, as well as detailed chapter outlines. This manual is the most comprehensive and complete ever available in the personnel market. Also, an excellent study guide, which has been revised and expanded, is available to enhance the learning potential of this text. Transparency masters are offered as a separate package.

ACKNOWLEDGMENTS

Producing any book requires assistance from other people. Some of the cases included in the book reflect the reality of modern personnel management because they summarize the experiences of practicing managers and former students too numerous to detail.

The authors are especially grateful to those individuals who provided reviews and numerous helpful comments. In particular, the following persons deserve special mention:

John A. Belt, Wichita State University
Katherine Bruce, Anne Arundel Community College
Gary Cameron, Washburn University
Roger A. Dean, Washington and Lee University
Daniel R. Hoyt, Arkansas State University
Gerald H. Kramer, University of Wisconsin-Platteville
Donna E. Ledgerwood, North Texas State University
Betty Jo Licata, Ohio University
Dave Roberts, San Joaquin Delta College
Yitzchak M. Shkop, University of Illinois at Chicago
Cary D. Thorp, University of Nebraska-Lincoln
William Traynor, California State University, Long Beach

In addition, Gary Cameron and Daniel R. Hoyt contributed heavily to the content of the instructor's manual accompanying the text. Also, Roger Dean, working from the excellent base provided in other editions by Sally Coltrin, has revised the study guide that accompanies this edition. Students George Stilphen and Steven Howell provided valuable research assistance.

Excellent secretarial support was provided by Anita Carson, Deb Van Horn, and Shirley Hanson. Special recognition goes to Jackie Mulherin for her word processing skills and to JoAnn Mathis for her assistance with many miscellaneous but necessary details. Finallly, the comments of numerous ASPA friends and former students helped the authors make the text a more effective learning resource.

The authors wish to note that many of the examples cited in cases and the body of the text occurred in real situations, but specific references to existing organizations are coincidental. We feel confident that this edition has fulfilled what we perceive to be a real need in the study of personnel and the management of human resources.

Robert L. Mathis
Omaha, Nebraska

John H. Jackson
Laramie, Wyoming

To the Reader

This book is designed to aid you, the reader, as you learn more about personnel management. As you use this book, you may find value from the following tips:

1. Familiarize yourself with the learning objectives at the beginning of each chapter. The learning objectives indicate what you should know after reading and studying a chapter.

2. Outline each chapter for study purposes by noting the boxed definitions and the main, second level, and in-paragraph headings.

3. Read the case at the beginning of the chapter which illustrates the type of problems the information in the chapter would help you resolve.

4. As you read the chapter, notice the idea check questions and see if you can answer them. Each idea check relates directly to one of the learning objectives. If you cannot correctly and completely answer an idea check, go back and re-read the section immediately preceding the idea check.

5. After reading the chapter, answer the review questions. Also, if your instructor has requested you to use the student supplement, read the summary in that supplement and answer the sample questions in it.

6. Read the short ending case and answer the questions on it by applying ideas from the chapter.

7. For additional study assistance, you might wish to purchase the study guide written to accompany this text, which is authored by Professors Sally Coltrin and Roger Dean.

If you let this book and the learning features in it aid you, your study of personnel management will be easier and more enjoyable. With the knowledge you acquire, you will be able to become more effective in your chosen career field.

PERSPECTIVES ON PERSONNEL MANAGEMENT

New approaches and perspectives on personnel management have emerged recently. They have changed to meet the demand for effective ways to manage people in organizations. New approaches use analysis of human behavior to help organizations improve existing working environments and plan those of the future.

These approaches did not just happen. They are the product of 25 years of development. In the last ten years dramatic developments in the field have altered its traditional image. This text provides perspectives on important traditional, current, and emerging practices to help the reader develop a practical, realistic, and modern view of personnel management.

This first section (1) examines differing views of personnel management, (2) defines and places personnel management in an organization context and (3) examines leadership, group behavior and communication. Chapter 1 presents the nature of Human Resources or Personnel Management. Different views of "who is a personnel manager?" How do you handle employee differences?, and how you learn about Personnel Management form the basis for defining personnel. The "interface" concept is used to reconcile these differences. An interface is a point of contact between a specialized personnel unit in an organization and other managers. The concept is used to illustrate that certain "people activities" must be attended to by *someone* in any organization.

Chapter 2 places personnel management in an organizational context and views an organization as an open system. Typical personnel activities are considered and the role of personnel in public organizations and international personnel Management are covered.

Chapter 3 examines the human resource by considering four basic intraorganizational processes: motivation, leadership, group behavior, and communication. Knowledge of each of these behavioral processes is fundamental to managing human resources in organizations. The purpose is not to duplicate the coverage given these topics in other courses such as Organizational Behavior, but to give a concise summary of their major impacts on the design of personnel systems.

Human Resource Management and Personnel Activities

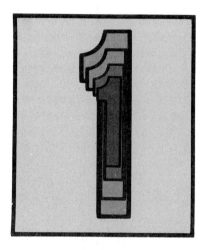

When you have read this chapter, you should be able to:

1. Discuss how personnel management has changed.
2. Explain the three sets of views used to define personnel management.
3. List and define each of the seven personnel activities.
4. Identify factors that affect the emphasis a specific personnel activity receives in a firm.

PERSONNEL AT WORK
MANAGING HUMAN
RESOURCES FOR PRODUCTIVITY

TRW, Inc. has gained a reputation as a company that manages change well. As far back as the 1930's when the chief executive officer picked one of every five employees for a face-to-face discussion, TRW has been sensitive to its employees. In the changing times of the 1980's, TRW has continued to manage its human resources creatively.

At 10 of its plants all the employees, including production workers, are on salary; these plants also have no unionized employees. Only one-third of TRW's entire workforce is unionized, whereas competitors have a much higher percentage of unionized workers. When TRW has negotiated with unions, it has been able to cut the number of job classifications, gain more flexibility in making work assignments, and work out agreements so employees can do maintenance on their own machines.

However, TRW's creative management of human resources has not been limited to production workers. Changes also were made to improve the productivity of software writers. The writers were put in individual windowless offices with state-of-the-art computer equipment, unlike the large "bullpen" area in which the writers had worked previously. TRW found that productivity jumped 39 percent in the experiments the first year. The Vice President of Systems Information said the results were so good the company was "reluctant to believe them."

The reasons given by the writers and programmers for the improvement were surprising. Predictably, they loved their new electronic gadgets, but simple changes such as privacy and comfortable chairs helped too. Dennis Hacker relates, "I'd close the door and grind away at my work; the next thing I knew I was getting hungry. I'd realize it was 6 P.M. and I'd worked right through the day."

As the U.S. work force changes, efforts to increase productivity will have to focus more on white collar employees. By the year 2000, they will make up 77 percent of the work force. The improvement of white collar productivity depends on analyzing how people use their time. For the software writers, TRW wanted to eliminate time wasted on filing, attending meetings, or staring out the window. To do this, the writers themselves were asked what it would take to generate more programs. The result was the radically redesigned work environment and a computer that performs many of the activities on which people had wasted time before.

The long-range effect of TRW's efforts to improve employee productivity over its whole range of products—from car parts to satellite systems—will be seen in the future. Such efforts reveal the importance of creative management of human resources.[1]

1

"The Human Resources function has undergone a transition from being an organizational stepchild to being a premiere force in an organization's ability to grow."

—D. R. Briscoe

The successful management of human resources is one of the keys to the performance of an organization. As TRW and many other employers have discovered, better management of human resources can be a major source of productivity improvement. Public relations documents often describe people as "the most important resource" a firm has. An example is IBM, which has been extremely successful in the computer industry due, in large part, to its ability to attract and retain skilled employees and managers. It is significant that IBM also has the reputation of having sound, forward-looking personnel management policies and practices.

Some managers feel that personnel management is primarily a "business" profession or activity. However, managers in both the private and public sectors depend on their human resources to be successful. Large corporations, banks, universities, advertising agencies, small retail stores, hospitals, manufacturing firms, and governmental agencies all must tap the talents of their people if these organizations are to accomplish their objectives. A production supervisor, hospital administrator, grocery store manager, mayor—any managers in any organization—will succeed only if that manager can deal with people.

But the days when a "concern for people" was all that was necessary for success in personnel matters are long past. Responding to people's needs, expectations, and legal rights in work organizations has become much more demanding and complex. Laws and regulations at the international, federal, state, and local levels impose limitations on what managers can and cannot do in managing employees. Nondiscriminatory recruiting, selection, and promotion criteria must be identified and used. Sound, coordinated, and legal wage and salary systems must be designed and implemented so that employees feel fairly compensated for their efforts. Personnel policies that help rather than hinder the accomplishment of work must be designed. These areas and many others require a good understanding of the basics of "personnel" or "human resource" management. These terms are used interchangeably throughout the book.

Personnel management has changed greatly in a relatively short period of time. In a 1970 survey, one respondent noted that personnel management had begun to move away from the image of "social, recreation, and fund drive leader."[2] A 1983 survey made the extent of change quite clear. More than 98 percent of the chief executive officers surveyed said they now consider personnel to be a top management function.[3]

Another study asked personnel executives if their departments had changed in structure or authority in the preceding two or three years. About 60 percent said changes had occurred, with several respondents noting that the personnel director now reports directly to the president of the organization, rather than to a vice president.[4] A later study for personnel departments in transition placed the figure at 74 percent.[5]

Some other trends in personnel management that will continue through the 1980's include:

- Assisting line management in long-range personnel planning.
- Improving quality of worklife.
- More involvement in "social responsibility issues," such as anticipating and responding to governement regulations and consumer pressures.
- Developing and implementing computer systems in personnel activities.
- Designing and changing the structure of organizations.
- Assisting operating managers with their communications.

These and other emerging trends will continue to raise the importance of personnel-related activities. One survey of top executives found that 65 percent of the non-personnel executives predicted that personnel executives will become more heavily involved in developing corporate strategy and policy in the years ahead.[6]

It is clear that personnel management has changed and continues to change. But, many personnel practitioners do not have any formal training in modern personnel management.[7] The same can be said for many operating managers with whom personnel managers must work. As Figure 1–1 shows, the number of personnel jobs has increased dramatically since 1950. (These figures include professionals as well as non-professionals, such as clerical employees). Yet the rate at which personnnel professionals are being trained is much slower. This gap in training appears even larger when one realizes that all managers need personnel training to properly manage such activities as performance appraisal, discipline, and Equal Employment Opportunity compliance.

This book provides you with a basic understanding of the tools and

FIGURE 1–1
Growth in personnel jobs in the United States.

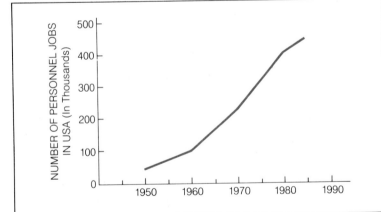

(SOURCE: H. G. Heneman, Jr. "Quo Vadis PAIR," *Personnel/Human Resource Division Newsletter, Academy of Management,* March 1980, p. 3.)

SECTION I PERSPECTIVES ON PERSONNEL MANAGEMENT

concepts of personnel management. Whether or not you ever make personnel your career, information on the management of human resources will be important to you in the years ahead.

But who is a personnel manager? What exactly is personnel management? Which managers should do what jobs in managing people? Answers to these questions will help define personnel management.

TOWARD A DEFINITION: VIEWS OF PERSONNEL MANAGEMENT

Not everyone agrees on what personnel management includes. One reason is that in different organizations personnel activities vary or there are differing distributions of responsibilities for activities. For example, in one medium-sized bank all new non-management employees are hired by the personnel department. In another equally successful company, new employees are screened by the personnel department but actually selected by the supervisors for whom they will work. Which is "right"? The answer seems to be that if it is working well for the company, it is right for that firm.

Historical, philosophical, and other differences result in a slightly different emphasis being given to personnel activities in each organization. The way an organization views personnel management can be determined by its response to three key issues:

1. Who is a personnel manager?
2. How do you handle individual employee differences?
3. How do you learn personnel management?

Who Is a Personnel Manager?

On this issue, one perspective is that personnel management is limited to only one part of the organization, the *personnel department*. This department handles "people" problems. Another perspective contends that *all managers* are personnel managers, and that it is only through the effective management of human resources by all managers that work gets done.

Those who believe that the personnel department is best qualified to handle all personnel problems feel that there are advantages to having all personnel activities performed at one place. The personnel department "handles people," in the same manner that the finance department handles the management of capital and cash, and many personnel departments can be very good at it.

Figure 1–2 shows a typical organization chart. Personnel is shown in the chart as a distinct unit, just as marketing, finance, and purchasing are separate specialized units. A major problem with this "functional" structure is that personnel management may become narrowly defined as *only* those areas with which a "personnel department" directly deals. For example, the personnel department might make wage surveys, but it might not work with middle-level managers on allocation

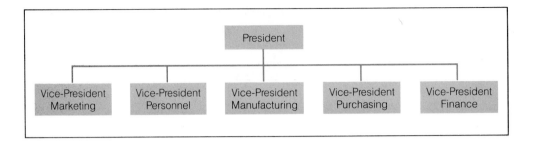

```
                              ┌─────────────┐
                              │  President  │
                              └─────────────┘
         ┌──────────┬──────────┼──────────┬──────────┐
┌────────────┐┌───────────┐┌──────────────┐┌─────────────┐┌───────────┐
│Vice-President││Vice-President││Vice-President││Vice-President││Vice-President│
│  Marketing  ││  Personnel  ││ Manufacturing ││  Purchasing ││   Finance  │
└────────────┘└───────────┘└──────────────┘└─────────────┘└───────────┘
```

FIGURE 1–2

Personnel as a Functional Unit in Amalgamated Products.

of production bonuses, because that is "the production department's job." This split can result in activities that need to be done by a person with training in personnel going undone.

Those who share the perspective that personnel management is spread throughout the organization feel that all managers have some personnel responsibilities. Sales managers, head nurses, manufacturing supervisors, corporate treasurers, college deans, and retail store managers are all personnel managers because their jobs are closely tied to their employees' effectiveness. However, it is unrealistic to expect an accounting department supervisor, for instance, to be extremely knowledgeable about such personnel activities as equal employment laws and insurance benefit plans.

How Do You Handle Individual Employee Differences?

The second issue that helps define the role of personnel management relates to how individual differences are considered in an organization. One perspective assumes that management should use formal, *standardized techniques* for handling all people. These techniques will be effective because if everyone is treated in the same manner, the result will be "fair" treatment. Certainly, standard techniques, if they are .well-designed, *can* be the basis for making some personnel decisions. But overuse of standard procedures emphasizes organizational uniformity, conformity, and predictability. It also assumes that people will be just as rational and predictable as the organization expects them to be. However, they obviously are not always that way.

Another view holds that *individual human differences* must be incorporated in the design and operation of personnel management activities. One can argue that employees' individual qualifications and personalities have such a great impact on personnel decisions that formal personnel procedures always require exceptions. Carried to its logical extreme, this view would mean that the job of a personnel manager should be to maximize employee individuality and satisfaction.

However, organizations need a reasonable degree of standardization and uniformity. Clearly, what is appropriate for one organization and its employees may not be best suited to another. Adjusting to individual needs must be done, but this adjustment must be balanced with the overall needs of the organization.

How Do You Learn Personnel Management?

A final question to help define personnel concerns how one learns personnel management. One view is that personnel management is an *applied field* that should be learned by focusing on techniques for handling people. Another view argues that *understanding basic human nature* through theories of psychology, sociology, or anthropology is the appropriate training for personnel management.

Certainly, learning that personnel is only a series of techniques can lead to a loss of the "big picture" about why the techniques are followed. A manager must have an ability to predict the effects of new personnel policies and practices. This understanding is often based on a good underlying "theory" about human nature. Yet, personnel *is* an applied field and the research and theories from the behavioral sciences only help when they are applied to the problems of people at work in real organizations.

In reality, successful personnel management contains elements of all the above viewpoints. The specific blend that occurs in a given organization depends on its strengths, weaknesses, history, and other variables. It is important to realize that contact with human resources activities in an organization cannot be limited solely to a personnel department. All managers are involved. Yet the personnel unit provides support in those areas in which other managers do not have expertise. Therefore, cooperation between the personnel unit and the other managers is very important for successful human resources management.

Can you discuss three sets of issues about personnel management?

INTERFACES
are areas of contact be-
tween the personnel
unit and other manag-
ers in an organization
that occur in critical personnel activities.

SHARING PERSONNEL
RESPONSIBILITIES: THE "INTERFACE"

Cooperation between people who specialize in personnel management and other managers is critical to organizational success. This cooperation requires contact, or **interface,** between the two groups. These points of contact occur within seven major activities, which will be outlined later, that focus on the employees in an organization. These activities are ones that must be addressed by someone when an organization has employees. For example: Who will do what jobs? How much will they be paid? Who is doing a good job? The idea is that personnel management involves shared responsibility for these activities.

The contact between the personnel unit and the operating managers is best based on who is most qualified to perform various parts of a personnel activity. For example, who is responsible for improving a poor safety record at a manufacturing plant? The personnel department has responsibility for safety because it compiles information on work-related injuries. But the production supervisors and managers share that responsibility because it is their control of the actual work situations that will change employee behavior. However, in all organizations, *someone* must manage the "people-related" activities; they cannot be left to chance. Clearly, personnel management is a concern of *both* the managers *and* the personnel unit in an organization.

The size of an organization is often a key consideration in determining who will do what. In a very small organization, such as a small retail store, no specialized personnel unit may exist. Instead, the owner-manager will hire the clerks, handle the payroll, train new employees, and perform any other needed personnel activities. However, a large retail chain will usually have a specialized personnel unit.

Value of the Interface Concept

The interface approach in this book helps to identify people-oriented activities that must be performed in all organizations. The responsibility for proper management of personnel activities, such as interviewing, training, or performance appraisal, is placed on both managers and personnel specialists. As an example, Figure 1–4 illustrates how some of the responsibilities in the process of selection interviewing might be divided between the personnel unit and other managers.

Whether interviewing or appraising employee performance, a man-

FIGURE 1–3
Interface Between Person-
nel Unit and Other Man-
agers.

PERSONNEL UNIT	MANAGER
■ Develops legal, effective interviewing techniques ■ Trains managers in selection interviewing ■ Provides interviews and testing ■ Sends qualified employees to managers who want to do final interview ■ Does final interviewing and hiring for certain managers and job classifications	■ Decides whether to do own final interviewing ■ Receives training from personnel in interviewing ■ Does actual final interviewing and hiring where appropriate ■ Provides feedback to personnel on hiring decisions and reasons for not hiring

FIGURE 1—4
The Selection Interviewing Interface Between the Personnel Unit and Other Managers.

ager must consider both the situation and the people involved to determine the most appropriate approach to handling problems. For example, consider the appraisal of a nurse's performance. The head nurse and/or personnel director must choose the most appropriate appraisal method, given the situation and the nurse involved. This approach differs greatly from prescribing an appraisal technique for "any situation," or from examining appraisal problems in the absence of having to solve them. It also requires cooperation between the head nurse and personnel specialists, but the end result is a much more adaptable and effective personnel system.

PERSONNEL MANAGEMENT is a set of activities focusing on the effective use of human resources in an organization.

Use of the "Interfaces" in This Book

The division of responsibilities, or interfaces, will be developed throughout the book. In each chapter a figure will show a particular division of personnel responsibilities, or interfaces, and who typically performs what portion of them. However, these illustrations are not attempts to indicate "the one way" all organizations should perform the activities. They illustrate how these activities can be divided. We now have enough information to define personnel management and discuss the seven major personnel activities that require attention in any organization.

Personnel Management Defined

The reconciliation of the various viewpoints discussed earlier in this chapter emphasizes that **personnel management** is a set of activities that must be managed. All organizations with people in them must deal with specific personnel activities of work analysis, staffing, training and development, appraisal, compensation, maintenance, and union relations. Notice that the definition emphasizes the personnel *activities*, not who performs them.

PERSONNEL ACTIVITIES

The major activities that must be managed by the personnel unit and/or other managers are presented in the center portion of Figure 1–5. These activities are:

- Work analysis
- Staffing the organization
- Training and development
- Appraisal of employees
- Compensation
- Maintenance of work environment
- Union relations

Environmental forces that affect an organization are shown in Figure 1–5 as an external boundary surrounding the organization. These forces include legal, societal, and interorganizational factors. The development of an organization as a system, open to environmental factors, and the relationship of the personnel unit to the total organization are concepts discussed in Chapter 2. One critical environmental force, equal employment legislation, is described in Chapters 4 and 5.

Intraorganizational forces of leadership, motivation, and group behavior are organizational processes of special interest to personnel focusing on human behavior. These forces are behavioral processes rather than specific personnel activities, and are discussed in Chapter 3.

Work Analysis

Work analysis focuses on a job as a unit of work. The specialization of narrow jobs versus the humanization of broader jobs is one consideration in *job design*. Chapter 6 discusses productivity and how it relates to the design work into jobs. Once the design of work is established, jobs can be analyzed, and *job descriptions* and *job specifications* can be written. The nature of these activities and their implications for human behavior are discussed further in Chapter 7.

A good working relationship between an employee and a job does not just happen. It requires analysis of the job to be done and proper design of the work the employee does. Job design that considers people's behavioral desires is becoming increasingly important.

Comprehensive analysis of jobs also has implications for equitable pay systems. Why does a word processing specialist earn more pay than a keypunch operator? The answer has to be that one job requires more knowledge, skills, and abilities than the other. But without good job analysis it is difficult to justify the difference.

Staffing the Organization

Staffing emphasizes the recruitment and selection of the human resources for an organization. *Human resource planning* and *recruiting* precede the actual *selection* of people for positions in organizations. Choosing the right person for the job involves the use of such data sources as application blanks, interviews, tests, background investigations, and physical examinations. The staffing interface is examined in Chapters 8 and 9.

Human resource planning, affirmative action, equal employment opportunity, and *structured interviewing* are terms that were seldom used 30

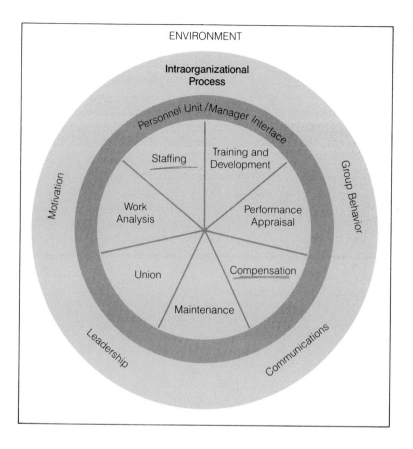

FIGURE 1–5
Model of Processing Activities.

years ago. Yet, these modern procedures reflect that no single area has changed as much in personnel as staffing. Much of the change is for the better because it has forced a more professional approach to matching people and jobs, and has cut major costs to both the organization and the individual associated with a mismatch. But the change has brought with it problems unheard of 20 years ago, as the "Personnel in Practice" that follows illustrates.

Training and Development

Training and development includes the *orientation* of new employees, the *training* of employees to perform their jobs, and the *retraining* of employees as their job requirements change. Encouraging the *development* and *growth* of more effective employees is another facet. Training and development are examined in Chapters 10 and 11.

Assessment of training needs, training evalation, career planning, and *management development* have been growing in importance. However, training costs—like anything else—are increasing, and management has a right to know whether or not it is receiving at least a dollar's worth of benefit for every dollar spent in training. Further, as jobs requiring special training become more common in organizations of all kinds, specialized types of training and development will continue to grow.

Appraisal of Employees

Performance appraisal focuses on how well, employees are doing their jobs. Appraisals are useful in making *wage and salary decisions,* in specifying areas in which additional *training and development* of employees is needed, and in making *placement* decisions. Knowledge of the approaches to appraisal and the types of appraisal methods is essential in implementing an appraisal system. The behavioral and legal consequences of appraisal are also a primary concern, and are discussed in Chapter 12.

Performance appraisal is poorly done by managers in many organizations. Yet, as the cost of keeping unsatisfactory employees continues to grow, performance appraisal will become even more critical. The cost associated with unrecognized excellence and potential is at least as great. Further, proper appraisals are often needed as evidence in equal employment and termination situations that end up in court. Well-designed, properly implemented appraisal systems, perhaps more than any of the other activities, require the cooperative efforts of the personnel unit and operating managers in an organization. The importance of performance appraisal can be summed up in one very simple question: If employees do not know how they are doing, how can they improve?

Compensation

Compensation deals with rewarding people through *pay, incentives,* and *benefits* for performing within the organization work. The behavioral side of compensation and the meaning of equity and reward to the employee are underlying considerations. Building on job analysis, the *job evaluation* activity determines the relative worth of each job. Also, special types of compensation fall within this interface. Compensation activities are discussed in Chapter 13, 14, and 15.

Pay is of great importance to employees. Although they obviously need pay to purchase life's necessities, the motivating (or demotivating) effect of pay is also a major factor. Meanwhile, compensation administration is becoming increasingly complex, legislation has greatly changed benefit plans, and changes in white-collar jobs will make the tie between productivity and compensation even more complex. New approaches and new ideas about compensation and benefits are vital if strides in productivity are to be made.

Maintenance

The emphasis in maintenance activities is somewhat different from that in other personnel activities. Maintenance functions emphasize consistency, stability, continuity, and an acceptable work environment. The physical and mental health and safety of employees are key parts of this interface.

The Occupational Safety and Health Act of 1970 (OSHA) has forced management attention to the *health and safety* areas. The effects of various substances in the work environment on employees are just being discovered. Creation of a safe and healthy work environment is an evolving process for most organizations. Largely because of OSHA, but also because of increasing management awareness of its social responsibilities to the public and its employees, personnel health and safety will continue to grow in importance.

Maintenance also includes *personnel coordination* and *personnel records and research.* In addition to developing and implementing policies, managers must communicate with employees and keep abreast of the personnel activities in their organizations. Maintenance activities are presented and discussed in Chapters 16, 17, and 18.

Union Relations

Union-related activities are very important because they affect both an employer's bottom line and personnel activities. An understanding of unions requires an overview of the development of the organized labor movement in the United States, the current state of unions, and the international dimension of unions.

The prime contact a union and an employer occurs at two levels. One is at the formal organizational level and occurs when the union becomes the agent representing the employees of an organization. Once an organization is unionized, a contract must be negotiated through union-organization discussions and collective bargaining—a process in which behavioral considerations play a vital role. At another level, a continuing union-organization relationship focuses on settling disputes and grievances that arise during the duration of a labor agreement. Because effective union relations may play a significant role in the management of human resources, a discussion of unions is vital. Union-management relations are discussed in Chapters 19 and 20.

For some organizations labor unions will increase in importance in the years ahead. In other organizations and industries, a rethinking and reformulation of existing union-management relationships may be necessary for the industries to grow and remain viable. The steel industry is an example of an industry in which this reexamination appears to be occurring. At the same time, in white-collar and pink-collar areas unions are becoming more of a force to be dealt with.

Can you briefly identify the seven major
sets of personnel activities?

EXTENT AND SCOPE OF PERSONNEL ACTIVITIES

FIGURE 1–6
Personnel's responsibility for activities.

A survey conducted by the American Society of Personnel Administration (ASPA) and the Bureau of National Affairs (BNA) found that the personnel unit's responsibility for different activities varies considerably.[10] Figure 1–6 shows that personnel is usually responsible for records, reports, and personnel information (90 percent). The department is seldom responsible for travel or janitorial services (8 percent). The activities listed in Figure 1–6 provide a good picture of how personnel people spend their time.

Activity	Percent of Companies (631)			
	Extent of Personnel Department's Responsibility			No Such Activity at Company/Facility
	All	Some	None	
Personnel records/reports/information systems	89	10	1	*
EEO compliance/affirmative action	86	12	1	1
Insurance benefits administration	85	10	5	*
Unemployment compensation administration	83	11	5	1
Wage/salary administration	79	18	3	*
Workers' compensation administration	77	14	9	*
Personnel research	75	6	1	18
Job evaluation	69	25	4	3
Pre-employment testing	66	9	3	22
Induction/orientation	62	34	3	1

FIGURE 1–6
(Continued)

Activity	Percent of Companies (631)			
	Extent of Personnel Department's Responsibility			No Such Activity at Company/Facility
	All	Some	None	
Health/medical services	62	12	11	15
Promotion/transfer/separation processing	61	36	2	1
Retirement preparation programs	61	10	5	24
Vacation/leave processing	60	30	9	*
Recreation/social/recognition programs	58	29	8	5
Tuition aid/scholarships	58	19	12	11
Pension/profit-sharing plan administration	57	26	10	7
Employee assistance plan/counseling program	57	18	4	22
Recruiting/interviewing/hiring	56	42	2	*
Complaint/disciplinary procedures	54	43	2	1
Attitude surveys	48	9	5	38
Employee communications/publications	47	28	20	5
Human resource planning	46	40	4	10
Executive compensation administration	46	26	20	8
College recruiting	45	16	4	35
Safety programs/OSHA compliance	44	37	17	3
Union/labor relations	44	15	3	39
Outplacement services	42	7	1	50
Supervisory training	40	44	12	4
Relocation services administration	40	19	7	34
Performance evaluation, nonmanagement	39	44	14	4
Management development	36	44	11	9
Suggestion systems	32	17	10	41
Food services	32	6	28	34
Thrift/savings plan administration	31	13	8	47
Community relations/fund drives	30	35	28	7
Management appraisal/MBO	27	38	13	21
Career planning/development	26	41	5	28
Security measures/property protection	26	16	52	6
Organization development	24	43	13	20
Stock plan administration	21	11	9	59
Skill training, nonmanagement	20	42	31	7
Productivity/motivation programs	17	49	13	21
Payroll processing	15	24	58	3
Public relations	14	30	48	8
Administrative services (mail, phone, messengers, etc.)	14	17	66	3
Library	10	5	37	48
Travel/transportation services administration	8	19	48	26
Maintenance/janitorial services	7	8	79	6

* Less than 0.45 percent.

SOURCE; ASPA-BNA Survey, #47, "Personnel Activities, Budgets, and Staffs," June 21, 1984, p. 2. Reprinted from *Bulletin to Management,* copyright 1984 by the Bureau of National Affairs, Inc., Washington, D.C.

CHAPTER 1 HUMAN RESOURCE MANAGEMENT AND PERSONNEL ACTIVITIES

Industry Differences

Another study found that some industries place a greater emphasis on some personnel activities than do others.[11] For example, labor relations and safety receive more emphasis in the steel industry, while in the petroleum industry more time is spent on wage and salary matters. These differences are not surprising when one realizes that the basic steel industry is heavily unionized and that the work is done in potentially dangerous circumstances. However, the petroleum industry has a high percentage of professionals (such as engineers and geologists) who require more complex pay systems.

Size Difference

The size of the firm also influences the amount of time spent on various personnel activities. Larger firms spend a higher percentage of time on wage and salary concerns and benefits than do smaller firms. They also spend more time on labor relations. However, smaller firms spend more time on general personnel administration.

One interpretation of these differences has to do with the mix of duties handled by personnel and operating managers. In the smaller companies, operating managers handle more of the tasks handled by personnel departments at larger companies. However, costs are another matter. While total personnel administration costs go up as a firm grows, the cost per employee drops because the cost is spread over more people. Figure 1–7 illustrates this cost relationship.

Unionization Differences

The amount of time and money spent in different personnel activities varies with the degree of unionization in a company as well. Organizations with from zero to 50 percent of the work force covered by collective bargaining agreements have more people in the personnel area than those with more union representation.[12] This difference is explained by the fact that these firms must either deal with two work forces (unionized and nonunionized), or spend a lot of time to keep parts of the company nonunion. As the amount of workforce unionization increases in a company, personnel activity decreases because many traditional personnel activities are specified in the union contract. Therefore, the number of personnel professionals making decisions can be reduced.

FIGURE 1–7
Costs of the Personnel
Function by Company
Size.

Company Size	Average Dollar Per Year Spent on Personnel Administration	Average Cost Per Employee
Up to 250 employees	$110,000	$690
250–499 employees	$181,800	$488
500–999 employees	$340,938	$495
1000–2499 employees	$566,000	$438
2500 or more employees	$1,785,695	$383

SOURCE: Adapted from *Personnel Policies Forum*, No. 560, BNA, 1983, p. 23.

PERSONNEL TODAY AND TOMMOROW

QUALITY OF WORKLIFE—WHISTLING WHILE YOU WORK?

Personnel-management has many concerns. One that affects human resources specialists and most other people as well is the "quality of work life." It is safe to say that most people want what they would consider a "good quality" life. Because most of us spend some 40 to 50 years of that life on the job, the quality of life at work is an important issue.

Many employees would not have found "quality" in the work life people faced just 60 to 70 years ago. Employees did not question the boss; they simply did what they were told to do. There were far fewer paid holidays, and workdays were often 10 hours, with 6- or even 7-day workweeks. Paid vacations were viewed as a major benefit, as was health insurance. Yet these benefits now are taken for granted. For these and other reasons quality of work life now has different meanings to most employees than it did to their grandparents.

There are as many definitions of quality of work life as there are people, but common factors include:

1. Participation in decisions that affect employees.
2. A chance to continue to develop employee skills and knowledge.
3. Making the job more meaningful.
4. Career advancement.
5. Open communication and reduced management/non-management status differences.
6. Providing feedback and financial incentives for cost savings where possible.
7. A voice in workplace innovation.

It is clear from looking at the list above that people want a say in their jobs, they want to feel more a part of the company and of the work, and they want to be able to profit by doing a good job. That realization, however, is a long way from solving all the quality of work life issues. Workers in the past might not have recognized the need for quality of work life concerns when their main concern was getting some time off to rest. Likewise you may not recognize the quality of work life concerns future generations of workers will have. But one fact is certain: quality of work life will continue to be of major interest to those who work for a living.

SUMMARY

■ Successful personnel (human resource) management is essential to organizational success. The personnel department itself has evolved dramatically in recent years.

■ Three issues help define personnel.

1) Who is a personnel manager? The answer is: both the personnel specialist and other managers in the organization. 2) How do you handle individual differences? A certain amount of control and structure are necessary, but the differences of individuals must be recognized as well for a personnel system to work. 3) How do you learn personnel management? The answer is that managers need theories and concepts to understand the application of techniques.

■ An interface is a point of contact on personnel activities between the personnel manager and the line manager.

■ Personnel management is a set of activities focusing on the effective use of human resources in an organization. The personnel activities referred to are: *work analysis, staffing, training* and *development, appraisal, compensation, maintenance,* and *union relations.*

■ Studies show that certain activities get more or less emphasis in a company depending on industry, company size, and the degree of unionization.

REVIEW QUESTIONS AND EXERCISES

1. The field of personnel management has changed—but how has it changed?

2. Each set of differing viewpoints on personnel management is concerned with a slightly different issue. What are the three issues and the viewpoints in each?

3. Define personnel management and explain how the differing viewpoints can be reconciled into a definition.

4. What are the seven sets of personnel activities and what is the nature of each set?

5. What determines the emphasis given major personnel activities in a firm?

Exercise

a. Interview a manager to learn how he or she views personnel management. Then, based upon the discussion, categorize the views according to those presented in this chapter and explain your classification.

Ten years ago Albert Phillips opened his own retail store and sold un-painted furniture. His store was located in Lakeside, a small city in the southeastern part of the United States. Although his business was somewhat slow at first, it grew steadily.

Many more sales, stock, and clerical personnel were hired. However, it soon became evident that Mr. Phillips was not able to effectively service all potential customers. Warehouse space also was badly needed.

Because Phillips Furniture Store was situated in a central location, Mr. Phillips was hesitant about relocating. As an alternative to relocat-ing, Mr. Phillips opened a satellite store in an outlying district to attract a new source of customers, as well as to provide better service to his current customers. Mr. Phillips eventually expanded his business into several neighboring towns until he had a total of six stores. When Mar-tin Furniture, a small manufacturing firm that supplied some of the furniture for Phillips, became financially unstable, Mr. Phillips was able to gain control of the manufacturing plant.

At the end of last week you were called into Mr. Phillips' office, and he said to you, "I have been pleased with your progress with us as a management trainee since you joined the company ten months ago." He explained that he felt that the company had gotten large enough to need a personnel manager. Previously, all managers handled most of their own personnel activities, usually on a "casual" basis. Mr. Phillips said that, with the acquisition of the manufacturing firm, "It's time for us to get our personnel activities organized, and you're the person to do it."

When asked why, he said, "I reviewed your personnel file and no-ticed you had a course in personnel management listed on your college transcript." Faced with both the challenge and the promotion, you ac-cept. Now you are trying to decide, "What am I, now that I'm a per-sonnel manager?"

Questions

1. How would the interface concept help you in defining your role at Phillips Furniture?

2. On what activities would you tell Mr. Phillips you intend to focus? Why?

3. What would be your first actions, and why?

NOTES

1. Adapted from *Forbes,* July 18, 1983, p. *37* and *Wall Street Journal,* September 22, 1983, p. 35.

2. "BNA Policy Guide", *Personnel Management,* No. 560 (Washington, D.C.: Bureau of National Affairs, 1983), p. 18.

3. *Ibid.*

4. *Aspects of the Personnel Function,* PPF Survey #127, (Washington, D.C.: Bureau of National Affairs), October, 1979.

5. R. Foltz et. al., "Senior Management Views the Human Resource Function," *Personnel Administrator,* September, 1982, pp. 37–51.

6. *Wall Street Journal,* February 12, 1980, p. 1.

7. H. G. Heneman, Mr., "Quo Vadis PAIR," *Personnel/Human Resource Division Newsletter, Academy of Management,* March 1980, p. 3.

8. Adapted from *Wall Street Journal,* July 28, 1982, p. 1.

9. Adapted from M. H. Sekas, "Dual-Career Couples—A Corporate Challenge," *Personnel Administrator,* April 1984, pp. 37–45.

10. "BNA Policy Guide", *Personnel Management,* No. 560, p. 15.

11. O. A. Ornati et. al., *The Personnel Department: Its Staffing and Budget,* (New York: AMA Research and Information Service, 1982).

12. *Ibid.,* p. 42.

Personnel in
the Organization

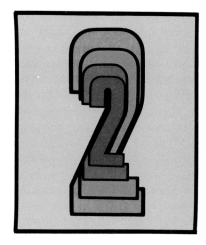

When you have read this chapter you should be able to:

1. Tell what an organization is and why it is an open system.
2. List the three organizational subsystems.
3. Define organization structure, line, and staff.
4. Discuss a matrix organization.
5. Discuss three factors affecting the decentralization of the personnel department.
6. Compare a personnel generalist and a specialist.
7. Identify three differences between public and private sector personnel management.
8. Discuss changes caused by the Civil Service Reform Act.
9. Define expatriate and discuss international staffing, training, and development activities.
10. Identify three expatriate compensation practices.

PERSONNEL AT WORK:

BUILDING THE HUMAN RESOURCES DEPARTMENT AT OTASCO

OTASCO began operations 65 years ago when three brothers opened a tire store in Okmulgee, Oklahoma and called it Oklahoma Tire and Supply Company. The company has grown significantly since then, and today the renamed OTASCO has over 600 stores in 14 states in the South and Southeast. These stores are served by four warehouses distributed throughout the marketing area. The corporate headquarters is in Tulsa. OTASCO is a specialty retailer with marketing emphasis primarily on automotive supplies and service, appliances, lawn and garden equipment, toys, sporting and camping goods, hardware, and housewares. While the company always has been concerned about its employees, as late as 1981 it had not developed a formal personnel or human resources unit.

In 1980, under the direction of its general counsel, Jerry Goodman, OTASCO began to look at areas in which future company growth might occur. This examination was carried out through strategic planning sessions and incorporated the results of an organizational study conducted by the management consulting firm of Arthur Young and Company. In 1981, upon his appointment to the presidency of OTASCO, Jerry Goodman began the search to fill three new positions identified in the consultant study as crucial to the future success of the organization. Among them was the position of corporate director of human resources.

Until this time, OTASCO's personnel activities had been limited to administering the hourly pay and employee benefits programs, providing employee counseling, and assisting supervisors in recruiting new employees. The person responsible for personnel split his time between personnel responsibilities and the direction of the company's sales contests and general management meetings. The new position represented a greatly expanded human resources role.

In August 1981, Richard Messer was hired as the new Director of Human Resources. His initial responsibilities during the first 12 months were organizational design, recruiting, and incentive compensation.

The consultant study also had indicated the need for a number of organizational structure changes. As a result, several administrative functions were pulled from existing organizations and grouped under a new General Services Department: the mail room; building maintenance and cleaning; the receptionist and phone system; the word processing section; lease cars; space planning, office supplies, and equipment purchasing; and printing. At the same time, the Human Resources Department was expanded. The security function was moved from the Distribution Department to Human Resources and was transformed into a loss prevention unit responsible for worker's compensation, general liability insurance, employee health and safety, and corporate security programs. *The reporting relationship of the Editor of Employee Communications also was transferred to Human Resources. Messer was given the responsibility for both areas as Director of Human Resources and General Services.*

In addition to completing the basic restructuring of the Human Resources and General Services departments, a Personnel Assistant also was added during the first year to conduct recruiting for hourly jobs and to coordinate employee relations activities in the headquarters. (In later years a Manager of General Services was hired to report to Messer, who then was named Vice-President of Human Resources.) Also, executive searches for the chief financial officer and chief marketing officer were conducted and the executive compensation program was restructured during the first year.

During the second year the Human Resources staff was expanded to include a compensation analyst—a position needed as the company revised its compensation structure to include a new job evaluation procedure, job grades and ranges, new bonus plans, and a formalized merit pay program. The new analyst also assisted in the implementation of a quality circles program in the company.

The recruiting activity also became more formalized, and with the addition of job posting and requisition procedures and approval of all staffing needs, an employment representative and a Human Resources Planning and Staffing Manager were added to the staff. Two new staff members also were added to the publications group in order to produce a new employee publication.

By the end of 1983 OTASCO had evolved from a one-person Personnel department to a multifaceted Human Resources department. Training and development of existing employees became a primary task for 1984. A new personnel payroll system was implemented in that year as well and more emphasis was placed on the management of benefit expenses. In addition, other human resource professionals were added in various store operations regions and warehouses. In summary, the department has continued to grow as it helps OTASCO build for the future.[1]

An ORGANIZATION is a goal-oriented system of coordinated relationships between people, tasks, resources, and managerial activities.

"People acting together as a group can accomplish things which no individual acting alone could ever hope to bring about."

Franklin D. Roosevelt

The evolution of a specialized personnel unit at OTASCO illustrates how the management of personnel activities has grown and changed in many organizations. However, the role of a personnel unit may differ from organization to organization. An understanding of organizations is necessary because they share certain characteristics that affect the practice of personnel management. This chapter demonstrates how personnel fits into the organization and how its character differs in various organizational settings.

THE ORGANIZATION

An **organization** is a goal-oriented system of coordinated relationships between people, tasks, resources, and managerial activities. For example, a hospital is an organization attempting to provide health care through the combined efforts of administrators, doctors, nurses, and technicians. Administrators primarily act to direct and coordinate the efforts of the hospital employees. An organizational structure is established by staffing a hospital with an administrator, director of nursing, director of housekeeping, and chief surgeon to guide the hospital's efforts to provide quality health care. The number of beds, the types of laboratory and radiological equipment, and the financial resources available also affect the overall operation of the hospital.

Can you define an organization?

Classical Organization Theory

Many approaches have been used in the past to try to understand organizations and how they operate. At one time, organizations were thought of in terms of a "universal organizational design," complete with a set of principles. This concept has been given the title of "classical organization theory."

Classical theory has been criticized for being too restrictive and inadequate because, in its rigid definitions, it failed to account for the varying environments in which an organization operates. In the mid-1980s there is a need for greater flexibility of all elements of an organization to meet challenges both inside and outside the organization. Some of the classical "principles" may apply and some may not, depending on the circumstances. As an example, in some manufacturing firms a quality-control inspector reports to the plant manager. In others, quality control may not be a separate job because employees check the quality of their own work.

Systems Approach to Organization

The systems approach to studying and analyzing organizations is a useful way to emphasize the whole organization and the interrelationships of its parts. The major implication of the systems approach is that an organization must be examined as a whole, including its parts or "subsystems," and as a part of the environment around it. For example, a public university is a system with subsystems (such as the colleges of business, arts, or engineering) and may be part of a state system including other public universities in the state.

A system, whether a biological one such as the human body, or a social one such as a business organization, has four major components: *inputs, processor, outputs,* and *feedback.* Figure 2–1 shows the relationship of these components to each other and to the organization, in this case a bank.

Open Systems. The basic difference between an open system and a closed system is that the open system affects and is affected by its environment. The closed system tries to operate as a self-contained unit with little regard for its environment. Note in Figure 2–1 some examples of external forces that affect the internal operations of a bank.

Using the systems approach, the organization is viewed as an open system, or a "living" entity that takes resources from its environment, processes them, and returns outputs to the environment. In other words, it is a "transformation system" which changes inputs into outputs.

It is important to realize that as an open system, the organization is continually dependent upon inputs from the environment. Too much

FIGURE 2–1
Simple Bank System and its Components.

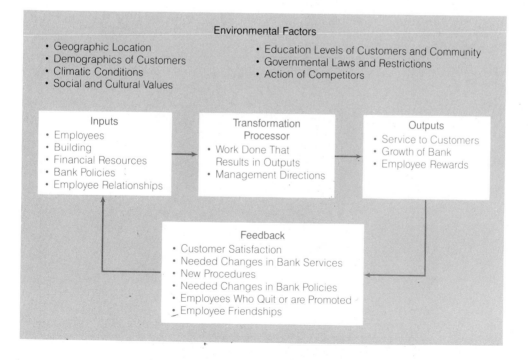

CHAPTER 2 PERSONNEL IN THE ORGANIZATION

27

managerial concern with the internal aspects of an organization, such as coordination, control, or job design, ignores the relationship of the system to its environment. This nearsightedness may be fatal to the existence of the organization. For example, a small bank that does not take into consideration deregulation in its industry or the actions of a financial conglomerate such as American Express may lose customers.

The most important argument for an open systems approach to studying organizations is the increasingly complicated and unstable environment in which most organizations exist. For example, laws on equal employment opportunities (EEO) and occupational safety and health (OSHA) have significantly affected the selection and promotion of employees and working conditions in many organizations. With the rapid growth of technology, the expansion of operations into foreign countries, and continued social and political change, organizations and their personnel activities are constantly pressured to adjust to changing environments.

Can you explain why an organization must be viewed as an open system?

ORGANIZATIONAL SUBSYSTEMS

One way to view an organization is to see it as a system composed of interrelated parts or subsystems in which everything interacts with everything else. Figure 2–2 shows three interacting characteristics of an organization. The interrelated nature of the three components, indicated by the arrows, reflects the fact that change in one of the variables can result in a change in any or all of the others. The characteristics of the people who are employed in an organization, for example, depend on the nature of the work and the design of the organization. In turn, the characteristics of the people *affect* each of the other components as well.

FIGURE 2–2
Organizational subsystems.

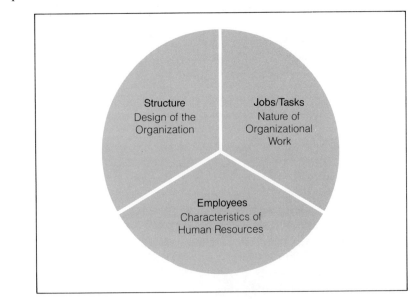

Consider what happened in the payroll department of Coastal Petroleum Company when a computer was introduced to process payroll. First, people had to be trained. New specialists were hired, which resulted in new social groupings—new carpools, lunch groups, and so on. In addition, new facilities were needed to accommodate the added equipment. The department was reorganized, and a new layer of management was needed. The design that worked well with 25 bookkeepers simply did not work well with the new computer staff.

This example emphasizes that an organization is a dynamically-linked whole, not just a collection of parts. A manager can change any of the variables but must realize that all components are interrelated.

As the complexity and number of tasks and people grow, there is an increased need for organizations to do what individuals alone cannot do; thus organizations grow and require the redesign of their structures. The subsystem that focuses on the design of the organization is examined in this chapter. The other two subsystems are discussed in later chapters.

Can you identify the three organizational subsystems?

Design of the Organization

Organization design results in an **organization structure**, which is a formally-designed framework of authority and task relationships.[2] The growth of a structure generally begins when a very small organization adds more people. Suppose an individual has an idea: a store that will carry merchandise selling for 5 and 10 cents. The stores are enthusiastically received and the entrepreneur must eventually move to a larger building, hire more employees, and open new stores. Soon the founder becomes overburdened because it is impossible for one person to direct all of the stores effectively. At this point, an entrepreneur like Frank W. Woolworth must get organized!

Organizations "coordinate" the efforts of their human resources by giving some direction to people's behaviors. Whenever two or more people get together—for any purpose—someone must be "in charge." Thus, the foundation of an organizational structure based upon formal authority is laid.

Can you define organization structure?

Authority

Authority as the right to use resources to accomplish goals can be derived in two ways: formally or informally. Formal authority exists originally in the governing body of an organization. For example, if the organization is a corporation, the stockholders hold formal authority for making decisions. However, the formal authority is delegated to the board of directors and to the president, who delegates some of this authority to various vice-presidents, who in turn delegate authority to operating managers, and so on down through the organization.

ORGANIZATION
STRUCTURE
is the formally-designed framework of authority and task relationships.
AUTHORITY
is the right to use resources to accomplish goals.

Formal Authority. A manager attains formal authority by accepting a position as a manager. For instance, when Sharon McDonald agrees to become Office Services Manager, she acquires the formal right to direct the office workers. It is even possible under certain circumstances for her to fire a worker who will not accept her formal authority. This action may seem rather harsh, but it may be necessary in some situations. However, the concept of formal authority has been modified in many modern organizations. Even in the military, where absolute authority and right to command have traditionally been a basis for issuing orders, there is a growing recognition that formal authority and commands are not the only way to guide people.

Informal Authority. Informal authority is a concept often used along with formal authority in describing leadership. Instead of having a formal designated position, an "authority figure" emerges from the group or is given authority by subordinates. This view of authority emphasizes that authority comes from the "consent of the governed." Individuals who accept direction and guidance from another have indicated that they believe the person has a legitimate right to direct their actions.

Line and Staff

A distinction can be made between two types of formal authority. The traditional distinction between line and staff refers not only to differences in formal authority, but to differences in function or type of work performed for an organization.

Line. A line function is generally considered to be the operating branch of the organization or that portion directly concerned with producing the product or service. In a manufacturing firm, the portion of the organization directly involved in production of goods is the line function. Other departments, such as the purchasing and management information systems departments, provide a staff function to support those production activities. Line functions, according to classical organization theory, are those directly involved in the major "business" of the organization.

Line authority can be described as the right of a manager to demand accountability from subordinates for their performance. It includes the right to command subordinates.

Staff. Staff functions commonly refer to people or positions that provide an advisory or support function. For example, the line aspect of a university is the faculty; and the athletic and business operations are staff functions. In Figure 2–3 the president, the vice-president of operations, and the division plant managers make up the line organization, while the others are staff units.

The traditional view of staff authority is that it is advisory in nature. Consequently, staff gives advice or assists line managers, but the staff people do not command and direct line managers to follow their advice. Instead, line managers decide whether or not they will accept the advice offered by staff people.

Typically, line officials consult staff people for their expertise when a decision is to be made. The real authority or influence of a staff department emerges from that department's ability to make worthwhile and significant contributions to solving the problems facing line em-

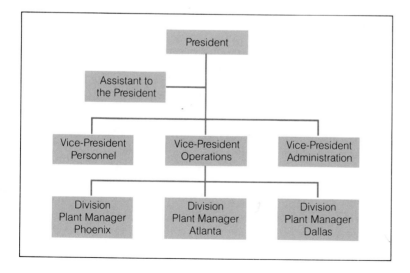

FIGURE 2–3
Line and Staff in a Manufacturing Firm

ployees. A staff department that can provide useful advice or service to the line departments may soon do more than just advise. For example, a staff legal department may actually begin to make decisions on legal matters for a company president. In recent years, as organizations have changed, line/staff distinctions have become less meaningful.

Can you differentiate between line and staff?

Matrix Organization Structure

A nontraditional form of organization, the matrix organization, offers a different environment for personnel management. As Figure 2–4 shows, in a **matrix organization** two organization structures exist at the same time—a conventional functional organization and a "project team" organization.

The project teams are created and dissolved as the situation demands. People may join a project team to tackle a certain project, retain their positions in the conventional organization, and return full-time to them when the project is completed. A project manager in charge of the team draws expertise from wherever he or she finds it in the organization.

The ultimate result of the matrix format is that a functional personnel specialist, for instance, may report to two bosses: the director of the personnel function and the project manager. The personnel specialist is responsible for coordination of all personnel activities related to the project. With two bosses, the potential for conflict is heightened, especially if the personnel director and the project manager disagree on how a personnel activity is to be managed. Because such conflict is possible, it is especially important to manage the organizational interface between the functional manager and the project manager so that needed personnel activities can be performed on the project in a manner that considers the personnel requirements of the entire organization.

Since its beginnings in the defense and aerospace industries, the matrix organization form has spread to many other areas. Industrial firms using a matrix format in some or all areas of operation include Dow Corning, TRW Systems, General Electric, Equitable Life Insurance,

FIGURE 2–4
Matrix organization.

FUNCTIONS	PROJECT/PRODUCT/SERVICE				
	A	B	C	D	E
Accounting					
Engineering					
Marketing					
Personnel					
Purchasing					

Shell Oil, and Citicorp.[4] Nonindustrial users include certified public accountant (CPA) firms, hospitals, real estate development companies, law firms, and various governmental agencies.[5]

Can you discuss a matrix organization structure?

PERSONNEL'S ROLE IN ORGANIZATIONS

One reason for creating a separate personnel department is to have better coordination of personnel activities. This coordination can be seen in an analogy. In some universities, student advising is handled by individual faculty members. Each professor may have 70 to 80 students to advise on courses to take, degree requirements, and the like. However, because most professors do not work with the details of the degree requirements regularly, far too frequently a number of students discover (usually in their senior year) that they are missing a course because they have been incorrectly advised. As a result, many schools have centralized advising in the deans' offices by providing a staff of trained advisors. These advisors are specialists who have detailed knowledge of the specific degree requirements, future course offerings, and the paperwork deadlines that must be met by students.

Likewise, organizations often establish a department that is composed of individuals with specialized knowledge of personnel activities. It is unlikely that a sales manager or maintenance supervisor will have detailed knowledge of government regulations on wages and hours or equal employment opportunity. Also, if every manager or supervisor keeps his or her own personnel files, the result will be inconsistent and overlapping efforts.

As an organization grows in size, the need for a separate personnel department grows. One survey found that there is an average of 1.1 personnel employees for every 100 workers in an organization. It also found differences in the number of personnel employees by industry. The average bank or other finance industry firm had more personnel employees per 100 workers than nonbusiness or health care organizations, for example. Also, firms with less than 250 employees had a higher average (1.7 per 100 workers) than larger organizations.[6] As might be expected, the number of personnel employees needed to serve 200 employees is not significantly different than the number needed to serve 300 or 800 employees. The same activities simply must be provided for more people.

Views of Personnel Responsibilities

In one study, groups of personnel directors, top executives, and line managers from different organizations were asked to rank activities that personnel departments did perform and should perform in their organizations.[7] As Figure 2–5 shows, there was some disagreement between the groups all of which were in unionized organizations. Respondents in nonunionized organizations (not represented in Figure 2–5) had greater agreement among their responses.

	RANKINGS		
PERSONNEL ACTIVITIES	Personnel Directors	Executives	Line Managers
Affirmative Action/EEO	1	1	1
Recruiting	2	3	5
Employment Selection	3	2	7
Grievances	4	5	15
Wage & Salary Administration	5	6	6
Discharges	6	8	10
Vacations/Leaves	6	10	13
Insurance Benefits	8	4	4
Discipline	9	9	16
Layoffs	10	13	17
Transfers	11	16	12
Retirement	12	12	3
Promotions	13	15	14
Collective Bargaining Negotiations	14	7	7
Pay Structure Design	15	11	2
Selection Testing	16	14	9
Incentive/Merit Program	17	17	11

SOURCE: G. W. Bohlander, H. C. White, and M. N. Wolfe, "The Three Faces of Personnel . . . ," *Personnel*, July-August 1983, p. 16.

From this study, it is clear that the "proper" role of personnel has not been determined. Further, it is inappropriate to say that all management people want the personnel unit to perform a certain activity; views of the "appropriate" division of duties have changed over time and vary among different organizations. The division of personnel activities depends upon which specific activities have been assumed by personnel specialists. A study such as the one reported here can be done easily in any organization to determine what personnel specialists and other managers think the ideal division of duties should be.

Historical Perspectives on Personnel

Personnel as the managing of people in organizations is as old as the human animal. Minimum wages have existed since at least 1800 B.C. Division of labor, span of control, hierarchy, and incentive plans have been in existence nearly as long.

But personnel management as a specialized area in organizations really began its growth at the beginning of the 20th century. Before that time most hiring, firing, training, and pay adjustment decisions were made by supervisors. Early personnel departments were primarily clerical in nature. Such work as keeping payroll and retirement records, arranging stockholder visits, managing school relations, and organizing company picnics were often the major tasks of the personnel departments.

With the greater importance of collective bargaining following the rise to prominence of unions in the 1940s and 1950s and the social legislation of the 1960s and 1970s, the role of the personnel department has changed in many organizations. Many kinds of legislation now directly affect any organization employing people. As a result, personnel departments are becoming much more professional.

THE ORGANIZATION OF THE PERSONNEL DEPARTMENT

Even though the personnel department has normally been considered an advisory or service department, the distinction is becoming more clouded. In some organizations certain duties, often considered operating or line duties by nature, have been assigned to the personnel department. For example, hiring management trainees to work in the manufacturing division of a larger corporation could be considered a line activity because the success of hiring directly affects future operations. However, very often hiring is done by the personnel department. Such delegation of direct decision-making authority to the personnel department is neither unusual nor a problem as long as both sides agree on who is to do what, as was emphasized in the first chapter. How personnel activities are coordinated and structured within personnel departments varies considerably from organization to organization.

Centralized vs. Decentralized Personnel Departments

Centralization and decentralization are the end points on a continuum, as organizations are seldom totally centralized or decentralized. Instead, the degree to which authority to make personnel decisions is concentrated or dispersed determines the amount of decentralization that exists. **Centralization** is the extent to which decision-making authority/responsibility is concentrated within the organization, whereas **decentralization** exists when that decision-making authority/responsibility is distributed downward.

Size. One factor that affects the degree of decentralization is organizational size. In a small organization of less than 200 employees, the personnel staff is likely to be small (2–3 people), so all specialized personnel activities will be concentrated and centralized. However, in a large corporation like U.S. Gypsum, which has several divisions and operating subsidiaries that are geographically dispersed, it is unrealistic to concentrate all personnel department activities in the corporate headquarters in Chicago.

Management Philosophy. Another factor affecting the degree of decentralization is the prevailing management philosophy. In some firms top management may want to make most personnel-oriented decisions. This philosophy results in relatively few personnel policies being formulated at lower levels in operating divisions. Instead, emphasis is placed on uniformity and consistency of policy throughout the corporation. However, in other firms that have geographically dispersed operations or numerous divisions and products or services, personnel policy-formulation often is widely diffused, resulting in greater decentralization.

Specialization. The need for highly specialized knowledge is a third factor that affects the degree of decentralization of personnel acitivites. Some personnel activities must be concentrated because of the intensive knowledge or degree of uniformity required. Consider a large corporation such as Firestone Corporation. All employees are part of a corporate pension plan, which must comply with federal legislation. Because highly specialized knowledge is needed to comply with such complex regulations, pension reporting, planning, and administration are centralized in the corporate personnel staff. Other areas that often are centralized are equal employment compliance and reporting, compensation administration, and human resource planning.

As a result of all of these factors, personnel departments can be highly centralized or decentralized. However, regardless of the structure, there usually will be a need for individuals who are generalists and those who are specialists.

Can you discuss three factors affecting the decentralization of a personnel department?

Personnel Generalists and Specialists

A wide variety of jobs can be performed in personnel departments. The common job titles listed in Figure 2–6 illustrate the number of

FIGURE 2–6
Personnel Generalists and Specialists.

GENERALISTS	SPECIALISTS
Vice-President of Personnel	Employee Manager
Human Resources Director	Training Director
Director of Industrial Relations	Compensation Specialist
Personnel Assistant	Benefits Clerk
Personnel Clerk	Job Analyst
Personnel Technician	Personnel Interviewer
Employee Relations Administrator	Labor Relations Specialist
Personnel Manager	EEO/Affirmative Action Coordinator
Corporate Personnel Director	Human Resource Information Systems Specialist
	Safety Coordinator
	Career Planning Specialist
	Testing Technician
	Corporate Recruiting Manager
	Pension/ERISA Compliance Manager

areas in which career personnel professionals can work. There are job opportunities in specific personnel areas and for personnel generalists who are knowledgeable in several areas.

Personnel Generalists. As a firm grows large enough to need someone to focus primarily on personnel activities, the role of the personnel generalist emerges. Someone who has responsibility for performing a variety of personnel activities is a **personnel generalist**. In one study, smaller organizations (those with less than 10,000 employees) were found to have 47 percent of their personnel staff classified as generalists, compared to 37 percent in larger organizations. The authors of the study projected that growth in the demand for generalists will be greatest in smaller organizations.[8]

Personnel generalists often are characterized as having broad knowledge of personnel activities and some knowledge and/or expertise in several areas of personnel. Their responsibilities span the personnel field. As Figure 2–7 shows, Richard Messer, Vice-President of Human Resources at OTASCO, is a personnel generalist who has a staff of specialists with widely varying responsibilities in the personnel area.

Generalists may be specialists who entered the personnel field and have "grown up" with a company. Or they may be individuals who transferred into the personnel field from some other area, (such as sales, accounting, or operations). Regardless of how they become generalists, the growing complexity of personnel activities forces generalists to maintain an adequate knowledge of numerous personnel activities. Such expansion in all personnel areas points to a greater need for personnel specialists.

FIGURE 2–7
OTASCO Human Resources Department.

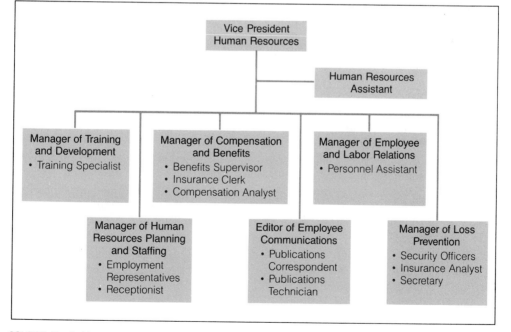

SOURCE: Used with permission of OTASCO.

Personnel Specialists. Individuals who have in-depth knowledge and expertise in a limited area of personnel are **personnel specialists**. Intensive knowledge of an activity such as benefits, testing, training, or affirmative action compliance typify the work of personnel specialists.
Because of the in-depth knowledge required of specialists, advanced
education in a specialty area may be useful.

Growth in organization size and complexity is one factor contributing to the need for specialists. For example, a midwestern computer
software development firm started in 1975 with five employees. By
1980, the firm had 80 employees and had hired a recent college graduate to manage recruiting, employee benefits, and personnel record
keeping. By 1984 the firm had 260 employees, and a personnel director
with a staff of four, including a full-time technical recruiter, a benefits
specialist, and an employment interviewer. Except for the personnel
director, who was a generalist by virtue of her growth with the firm,
the others in the personnel department were specialists.

Another factor contributing to the growth in personnel specialists is
the proliferation of laws and regulations affecting personnel activities.
OSHA, EEO, ERISA, worker compensation, unemployment insurance,
and wage/hour laws are some of the areas in which specialized, in-
depth knowledge and experience can be helpful, especially if the organization is large and geographically dispersed.

Personnel activities outside the U.S. are another area in which specialized knowledge and experience is required for multinational firms.
Some of the special aspects of international personnel management are
highlighted in the next section. Both personnel specialists and generalists in the public sector also face unique challenges, which are discussed in the next section.

*Can you explain the difference between a
personnel generalist and a personnel specialist?*

PERSONNEL IN PUBLIC ORGANIZATIONS

Management of human resources is not restricted to organizations operating in the private sector.[9] It is necessary, too, in the public sector,
where employment has grown enormously in the past 50 years. Today
nearly one of every five working Americans is employed directly by
some level of government—local, state, or federal.[10]

While many similarities exist in the personnel practices of private
and public sector organizations, there are several notable differences,
stemming from the distinctly different environments in which they operate. Before examining a few of these differences, it is important to
stress that personnel management in public sector agencies follows
many of the same practices that have emerged in the private sector in
the 20th century. The U.S. Civil Service System was established in the
1880s to reduce political patronage and favoritism in the selection of
governmental employees. As a result, many state and local governmental bodies established "merit systems" and formal personnel poli-

cies and procedures. However, personnel management in the public sector has a slightly different character.

Public/Private Sector Differences

Significant differences between the public and private sectors include: the basic goals and orientation, demands for accountability and openness, restrictions on political activity, and the type of top executives each sector requires. However, one must remember that despite these differences, the effective management of human resources must occur in the public as well as the private sector.

Political vs. Profit Rationale. One obvious difference is that a public organization is a political entity, whereas a private sector corporation has a profit-making orientation. Accountability for the political consequences of actions in the public sphere greatly affects the environment in a governmental entity.

The politicizing of the public sector occurs partly because many of the services it offers are monopolies. In most cities, only one police department, fire department, or street cleaning department exists. Residents cannot stop doing business with the city and buy the services elsewhere. In one community the city government attempted to change the method of garbage collection from twice per week to once per week. At the same time, the use of newer trucks and computer scheduling of routes resulted in the need for significantly fewer sanitation workers. The furor over the proposed changes resulted in 12 public hearings, numerous witnesses appearing before the city council, a threatened "sick-out" by all unionized city employees, and the submission of citizen petitions. Ultimately, the plan was implemented, but with a phased-in approach which significantly reduced the savings originally projected. In contrast, a private corporation generally can change how it offers its services or its prices with little or no public exposure.

Public Accountability and Scrutiny. Public sector managers also face greater scrutiny and media attention because of their public accountability. In the private sector, personnel suspension or termination decisions often are made without public coverage. However, many local and municipal bodies have established personnel boards whose actions are covered by newspaper, television, and radio reporters.

An additional complicating factor is that often it is difficult to determine how well a public organization has performed its service. For example, the level of expenditures per child may reveal little about how well a public agency working with handicapped children has done its work. Expenditures of $2 million per year to repair streets say nothing about the quality or the necessity of the work done. Whereas private firms often use earnings per share, profit after taxes, or return on assets to measure their viability, most public sector organizations have no comparable outcome or performance measures that are widely understood or used.

Heightened visibility also requires public employees to be more careful than their private sector counterparts about their conduct. Possible public exposure of actions forces public employees to demonstrate ethical standards that are beyond question. As a result, public employees must be especially careful about any appearance of impropriety. In a town in Kentucky a newspaper reporter followed city street workers for a week and timed the length of their coffee breaks. The following Sunday a front-page "expośe" appeared, requiring responses by the city manager, public works director, and the city council. In another city, the local newspaper listed all of the phone calls made by an officer with a public utility on the utility's credit card. When it was determined that some calls were personal in nature, the officer ultimately had to repay the utility for those calls and resign his position. Similar incidents in private corporations are usually handled without public exposure and with far less expenditure of time and money.

"Whistle-blowing." Another set of differences between the public and private sectors concerns restrictions and rights that impact public employees but not private sector employees. For instance, many governmental employees are required to sign loyalty oaths. At the same time regulations have been passed to ensure that public employees have adequate freedom of speech, especially when they speak out on administrative actions.

One of the touchiest areas involves protection for individuals who are labeled "whistle-blowers" by publically revealing official wrongdoing. When do employees have the right to speak out with protection from retribution? When do they violate the confidentiality of their jobs? Often the answers are difficult to determine. A widely publicized case involved an employee in the U.S. Defense Department who revealed that significant cost overruns on an airplane contract were being concealed from the U.S. Congress. Attempts were made by his superiors to transfer him, demote him, or fire him. The "whistle-blower" ultimately left the Defense Department, but not before a series of public hearings and investigations were held. "Whistle-blowing" is an important right, but one which can be abused.

Petty complaints and minor "scandals" can be reported by disgruntled employees and then may be blown out of proportion by news media. Often these "revelations" are of little significance and may be traced to personality conflicts with a supervisor or some other minor cause. For this reason, the rights of those accused of wrongdoing by "whistle-blowers" also must be protected.

Political Involvement of Governmental Employees. There are laws at all levels of government that limit the rights of public employees to participate in political campaigns and hold political offices. The best known law is the federal Hatch Act.[11] The act and subsequent amendments prohibit federal employees from lobbying, campaigning for candidates for public office, partisan political fundraising while on duty, holding elective office, or holding office in a political party. Some states also have similar laws.

The impact of these laws is to restrict how public employees participate in the political process. Also, limitations on the right to strike and participate in collective bargaining are placed on many public employee unions at all governmental levels. A fuller discussion of public unionism is presented in Chapter 19, which examines the union movement in general.

Popularity vs. Expertise. Another factor affecting the public sector is the process used to select top public policy managers. A person with little or no public administration experience can be elected mayor, city council member, school board member, or governor. Personal popularity often counts more in an election than public sector experience. A dentist, lawyer, housewife, or farmer who runs for public office may be a sincere, intelligent person, but it is unlikely that any of them have had much public sector personnel or managerial experience. The number of "amateurs" who assume public sector positions also is affected by the extent to which the public personnel system can be characterized as a patronage or merit system.

Patronage vs. Merit Systems

The process of appointing someone to a public sector job as a reward for past political support and friendship is at the heart of a patronage system. A merit system is one in which accomplishments control the selection, compensation, and continuity of individuals who are employed.

Patronage. The greater the number of jobs available for patronage appointments, the greater is the opportunity for inexperienced or unqualified individuals to be named. These individuals may include relatives, longtime supporters, or even people with dubious pasts.

The extent of patronage varies greatly. For example, the State of Wisconsin has less than 50 patronage positions, whereas the governor of the Commonwealth of Pennsylvania has approximately 50,000 patronage positions at his disposal.[12] Consequently, a change in governors has a much greater impact on public employees in a patronage-oriented state. Abuses of patronage have led to the adoption of a merit system by many public entities.

Merit System. In a merit system an attempt is made to establish uniform and impersonal policies and procedures to govern the selection, compensation, and continuity of public employees. A merit system operates through adequate publicity, open opportunity to apply for positions, realistic job-related standards, and ranking of candidates on ability.[13]

Selection in a merit system can occur through three approaches: 1) *open competition,* 2) *noncompetitive examinations,* and 3) *exempted positions.* For positions subject to open competition, standardized tests for various positions are given, and candidates for employment or promotion are ranked on the bases of those tests. Selection of one of the top candidates on the list is required. When noncompetitive examinations are used, the appointing manager may select the employee, subject to certain qualifications. Exempted positions are those that are filled without any testing. Included in this category are lower-level laborer jobs, jobs requiring confidential or personal assistant work, part-time jobs, and those not filled using the other methods.[14]

The standardization of procedures under a merit system represents both the major advantage and disadvantage of such a system. The advantage is the impersonality and fairness inherent in a system in which everyone is treated in a uniform and standard manner (at least theoretically). However, the standards and procedures also can result in a burdensome, paperwork-dominated system that is relatively rigid and slow. Additional arguments advanced by advocates and critics of the merit system are beyond the scope of this text.

Can you identify three differences between public and private sector personnel management?

Civil Service Reform Act of 1978

To make the U.S. federal government operate more efficiently, the Civil Service Reform Act was passed in 1978. The act eliminated the Civil Service Commission and replaced it with the Office of Personnel Management (OPM) and the Merit Systems Protection Board (MSPB).

Forces for Change. Two forces led to the passage of this act: 1) union pressures, and 2) the need for better management practices. Unions composed of federal government employees have grown over the last 20 years, despite restrictions that limit union activity to noneconomic issues. Also, because of inflexibility that developed under the old U.S. Civil Service System, it was difficult to provide greater rewards for exceptional performers and burdensome to remove poor performers.

Pay and Performance Revisions. Several major revisions included in the Civil Service Reform Act brought the federal personnel system closer to practices prominent in the private sector. For example, government executives now can earn *pay bonuses* for outstanding work. Under the old system, standard pay raises were granted almost automatically to all employees. Also, ineffective performers in the upper levels can be demoted more easily now because an improved system of appraising employee performance, coupled with a less cumbersome appeals process, allows greater flexibility in removing poor performers.[15]

Decentralization. Another important facet of the Civil Service Reform Act of 1978 is the provision that allows greater decentralization of personnel management activities. Within general management controls, individual federal agencies can tailor personnel management activities to their own operating circumstances. This decentralization adds greater flexibility and responsiveness, as two Navy research and development (R & D) laboratories found.

Managers in public organizations must be able to translate their expertise into creative solutions. Likewise, managers operating in inter-

NAVY R & D LABS DECENTRALIZE PERSONNEL

As a result of the Civil Service Reform Act of 1978, federal agencies may obtain authorization to conduct experiments in the delivery of personnel activities. In California, two Navy research and development laboratories were restructured to allow greater managerial control over local personnel activities.

Typically, in R & D situations, a project manager directs a project and various technical specialists are assigned to it. However, in these laboratories numerous restrictions on the assignment and evaluation of the specialists inhibited the flexibility of the project manager.

After undertaking an experiment with revised personnel practices, several changes were made. The pay classification structure was revised to include fewer levels, and managers were given more flexibility to set pay within the new ranges. Specialized performance appraisal standards were identified for spe-

cific positions and managers met with employees to set individual performance objectives. Pay increases were then linked to each individual's accomplishment of objectives. Greater flexibility in reducing the work force was given to managers, with performance ratings being the first consideration used to make retention or dismissal decisions.

The results of the experiment generally were positive. Managers spent more time with performance appraisals and pay decisions and they found the more simplified classification system to be beneficial. However, managers felt that there still were unnecessary rules and regulations limiting their flexibility. Nevertheless, the experiment illustrates that the reforms being implemented since the passage of the Civil Service Reform Act of 1978 are changing the face of public personnel management.[16]

national organizations need to recognize the importance of effective personnel administration in the success of their organizations. As more and more firms engage in cross-national trade, managing personnel activities in an intercultural environment will be of increasing importance. International personnel management is highlighted in the next section.

Can you discuss changes in federal personnel management as a result of the Civil Service Reform Act of 1978?

INTERNATIONAL PERSONNEL MANAGEMENT

With the growth of international trade, the management of human resources has become more internationalized. A growing number of U.S. firms have established plants and operations overseas and firms from

An EXPATRIATE
is a person working in a
country who is not a
national citizen of that
country.

other countries have purchased U.S. companies. The degree of internationalization that has occurred is illustrated by the following data:[17]

■ Overseas U.S. investments total more than $200 billion.
■ Many U.S. firms have a sizable percentage of sales and profits overseas. (See Figure 2–8)
■ Foreign firms own over 50 percent of such U.S. firms as American Motors, Shell Oil, and NorthAmerican Phillips.
■ Foreign firms own 100 percent of Lever Brothers, Volkswagen of America, and Grand Union, as well as many others.

Individuals who are not citizens of the countries in which they work are **expatriates**. Multinational corporations (MNCs) face many problems in sending employees abroad. One major concern is the cost of making a mistake. It has been estimated that it costs $16,000 to $20,000 to place a person overseas, and another $10,000 to bring that person home if he or she quits prematurely.[18] When all relevant direct and indirect costs are included, the costs likely are two to three times those figures. Another study determined that an executive making $45,000 per year with a spouse and two children who is transferred from an average U.S. city would pay approximately $11,300 per year more in housing expenses when transferred to Geneva, Switzerland, or $3,300 more if transferred to Paris, France. Also, costs of goods and services in London were estimated to be over 20 percent more than in the average U.S. city.[19]

The character of personnel activities varies significantly according to the location of the company. Some countries, such as Zambia and Japan, expect top management positions to be filled by executives from their own country. Other countries have requirements on the percentage of jobs that may be filled by foreigners. U.S. citizens who are transferred to Saudi Arabia, for example, must adjust to cultural and religious codes concerning the role of women and the prohibition of liquor, among other factors.

FIGURE 2–8
Foreign Activities of U.S.
Firms.

Firm	Foreign as % of Total Revenue	Foreign as % of Total Opening Profit
Bank America	44.7	47.4
Safeway Stores	24.4	45.9
Dow Chemical	52.3	74.0
Coca Cola	40.4	57.6
NCR	46.0	42.3
H. J. Heinz	36.3	37.9
Colgate Palmolive	54.6	47.8
Gillette	53.3	53.0
Quaker Oats	37.5	27.3
Morrison-Knudson	38.3	11.3

SOURCE: *Forbes*, July 2, 1984, pp. 129–133.

These and other problems lead some people to turn down overseas jobs. As the number of working spouses increases, overseas transfers to locations where spouses may find limited employment opportunities often mean income losses. Consequently, international personnel management practices focus heavily on staffing, training and development, and compensation.

Staffing

Many companies have the misguided notion that a good employee in a domestic operation will make a good expatriate. This idea has cost companies many thousands of dollars in mistakes. One study of expatriate failure found poor selection to be the cause in 80 percent of the cases.[20] Poor staffing for international assignments occur for two reasons. The first is poor identification of the qualifications that differentiate between effective and ineffective expatriate managers. A second problem is poor identification of family and career issues that negatively impact expatriate employees.[21]

Selection for International Assignment. The selection process for international assignment should provide a realistic picture of the life, work, and culture to which the expatriate may be sent. The procedure for avoiding failure is a multistep process. First, a comprehensive description of the job to be done should be prepared. Responsibilities that would be unusual in the home nation should be noted. Those noted might include negotiating with public officials, interpreting local work codes; or responding to ethics, morals, and personal issues such as religious prohibitions and personal freedoms. Throughout the selection process, especially in the selection interviews, it is crucial to assess the adaptability and cultural empathy of the potential expatriate.[22] The ability to accept and adapt to different customs, managment practices, laws, religious values, and infrastructure conditions is important. For example, in Nigeria the local telephone system is so inefficient that overseas calls can be made more easily than crosstown calls, especially in Lagos, the capital city. A U.S. citizen who is accustomed to the convenience and reliability of the U.S. phone system must not become impatient and angry when confronted with such delays.

The preferences and attitudes of a spouse and other family members also are major staffing considerations. The availability of good schooling opportunities, the roles of men and women in the foreign country, and the availability of employment opportunities for the spouse must be considered by the potential expatriate. According to one study, expatriate selection failures can be attributed to the following factors, in order of importance.[23]

- Spouse inability to adapt.
- Employee's inability to adapt.
- Other family-related problems.
- Employee's personal and emotional maturity level.
- Lack of technical expertise.
- Weak motivation to work overseas.

The importance of spouse and family concerns has led to efforts to identify how suitable the family members of the potential international employee are for overseas assignment. The expatriate employee may have an easier adjustment than the spouse because of involvement in work activities. For example, a major engineering design firm sent a male project manager to Saudi Arabia. However, because of cultural restrictions on women (such as prohibitions against women driving cars and restrictions on dress and appearance), the manager's wife became very unhappy. Ultimately, the project manager resigned and returned to the U.S. to work for another firm.

A related problem is the promotion and transfer of foreign citizens to positions in the United States. Special training to ease the adjustment of foreign managers and their families may be required. The acceptance of a foreign boss by a U.S. worker is another concern. All of these problems point to the importance of training and development for international adjustment.

Internationalizing Training and Development Activities

Some special training and development programs and activities must be established for international assignments.[24] As illustrated in Figure 2–9, these activities have three distinct concerns:

■ Orientation and training of expatriate employees and their families before taking the international assignment.
■ Continuing employee development in which the employee's broadened skills can be fitted into career planning and corporate development programs.
■ Readjustment training and development to prepare employees for a return to the home country culture and to prepare the expatriate's new subordinates and supervisor for the returnee.

FIGURE 2–9
International Training and Development.

The value in having effective international training and development activities is evident when one considers the cost of a premature return of an expatriate manager can be $80,000 or more.[25] The impact of foreign assignments on their careers is a significant concern of expatriates. To address this concern, career planning for expatriates is important.[26]

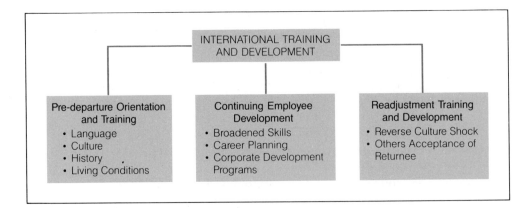

PERSONNEL IN PRACTICE

INTERNATIONAL PREPARATION

What is the weather like in Brussels? How fast can an individual learn a little of a foreign language? Can a person bow with the proper degree of respect?

Answers to these questions and many others are part of the training for individuals selected to work outside the U.S. for multinational corporations. A major oil company offers a three-day intensive orientation seminar to employees going to Kuwait. At Hewlett-Packard a film entitled "Going International" is used to prepare employees for living and working overseas. The film sets the stage for follow-up discussions. Westinghouse International pays for an outside course on culture of the Middle East for employees going there. These programs and many others include an introduction to a country and its language, religion, history,

and geography. Even executives who go for short business trips for some firms receive some orientation to the customs and culture of a country.

The president of a Miami-based export-import firm feels that U.S. business people have to think the way those in the other country think to do business in that country. A personnel manager for Hewlett-Packard, who has worked in Singapore says, "My advice is: Don't go abroad with preconceived notions. Whatever they are, they'll be wrong. Go with a sense of humor, be open, be receptive, and roll with the punches." And a businessman who spent two years in Brussels indicated that he wished his company had warned him that it rained nearly every day there.[27]

Repatriation. A major difficulty can arise when it is time to bring expatriates home. While they have been away, many changes may have occurred. At Economic Laboratory (a cleaning products firm) overseas work can mean "out of sight, out of mind." G. D. Searle and Company has admitted it has had trouble finding jobs for returning overseas workers. Studies have shown that returning employees face anxiety in three areas: 1) personal finances, 2) reacclimatization to U.S. life-style, and 3) readjustment to the company.[28]

Can you define an expatriate and discuss some aspects of international staffing and training and development activities?

Compensation

Compensation for expatriates can be a significant problem. Determining compensation for employees working in another country requires that a number of concerns be considered.[29] Some of the considerations are:

■ Adjustment of an employee's basic salary to consider the area pay averages and living costs.

■ The amount to be paid, if any, as a foreign service premium, especially in dangerous or remote locations.

■ Supplemental payment for travel and vacation costs back to the home country for the expatriate and family.

■ Additional payment for children's educational costs and for personal transportation while in the foreign country.

Economic Recovery Tax Act of 1981. Individuals who work in another country are subject to the tax laws of the countries in which they are located. Thus, expatriates could be subject to double taxation (from both the U.S. and the foreign country), unless some relief was provided through the U.S. tax code and by employers. The Economic Recovery Tax Act of 1981 removed some penalties that were previously in existence. Effective in 1982, the act allows a U.S. citizen to exclude the first $75,000 earned abroad from U.S. income taxes, and the exclusion increases each year by $5,000, to $95,000 in 1986. Also, U.S. expatriates can reduce their U.S. tax bill by deducting foreign income taxes up to the maximum U.S. rate. To qualify for the exclusion, a U.S. expatriate must reside or be present in the foreign country for 330 days of the 12 months of the tax year.[30]

Tax Equalization Plan. Another plan used to protect an expatriate from negative tax consequences involves the use of a tax equalization plan. Under this plan the company adjusts an employee's base income downward by the amount of estimated U.S. tax to be paid for the year. Thus the employee only pays the foreign country tax. The intent of the tax equalization plan is to insure that expatriates will not pay any more or less in taxes than they would pay if they had stayed in the U.S.[31]

In the future, more personnel specialists and operating managers may live and work in countries outside the United States. The growth of the American-based multinational corporation typifies the importance of viewing an organization as a system affected by environmental factors such as culture, language, climate, politics, and social changes.

Can you identify three compensation practices that are used with expatriates?

PERSONNEL TODAY AND TOMORROW

TRAINING IN GIFT-GIVING

As more and more U.S. firms do business in other countries, a special area of knowledge and training for employees is required—*gift-giving*. Because of U.S. restrictions through the Foreign Corrupt Practices Act, a fine line exists between gift-giving, which is legal, and bribery, which is illegal. In addition, the "proper" ways to give and refuse gifts may be as important as the items offered or the quality of the goods offered.

In Japan, for example, red denotes good health and is an acceptable color for wrapping a present. However, a white ribbon symbolizes a funeral, bold colors are disliked, and Western-style bows are viewed as unattractive. In China the best way to show appreciation and to develop further business is to sponsor a banquet. After the dinner, giving a small personal gift such as a small plaque, piece of artwork, or other collector's item must be done very discreetly.

In Arab countries it is acceptable to give books and gifts to children. However, giving a present to an Arab's wife or wives is not condoned. And if someone admires an object owned by an Arab too openly, that person may end up being given the object of admiration.

U.S. managers and executives need to know about customs like these if they are to be successful in international business. Training in such customs and practices should be part of the personnel training programs for individuals who will live or travel out of the U.S. for business purposes.[32]

SUMMARY

■ An organization is a goal-oriented system of coordinated relationships between people, tasks, resources, and managerial activities.

■ Currently the most useful way to view each organization is as an open system affected by the environment and subject to change.

■ The three major subsystems of organizations are: 1) nature of organizational work, 2) design of the organization, and 3) characteristics of human resources. As parts of an open system, the components are interrelated.

■ Design of an organization requires the development of an organization structure, which is a formally designed framework of authority and task relationships.

■ Authority can be either formal or informal. The formal authority of line and staff formation varies in different organizations.

■ A matrix organization is one in which both a functional and project organization exist at the same time.

■ The need for a separate personnel department grows as an organization grows.

■ Personnel departments can be highly centralized or decentralized, depending upon the size and management philosophy of the organization, as well as the need for specialized knowledge in personnel/human resources management.

■ Personnel departments are composed of personnel generalists and personnel specialists. A generalist has broad knowledge of a number of personnel activities, whereas a specialist has intensive knowledge of a limited set of activities.

■ Personnel management in the public sector is somewhat different because of political activity, public accountability and scrutiny, restrictions on employee rights, the popularity of top officials, and the existence of a patronage and merit system.

■ The Civil Service Reform Act of 1978 significantly changed the way personnel activities are managed in U.S. government.

■ Unique concerns affect the management of personnel activities of expatriates, who are persons working in a country other than their country of citizenship.

■ Staffing, training and development, and compensation activities are those most affected by international personnel management concerns.

REVIEW QUESTIONS AND EXERCISES

1. What is an organization? Why must organizations be viewed as open systems?

2. What are the three organization subsystems?

3. How do the concepts of line and staff relate to authority and organization structure?

4. What is a matrix organization and why is it a "different" type of organization?

5. What factors affect the degree of centralization or decentralization of personnel activities within an organization?

6. Which would you rather be—a personnel generalist or a personnel specialist? Why?

7. Discuss the following statement. "Even though the same personnel activities must be performed in any organization, personnel management in the public sector differs from personnel management in the private sector."

8. Why does the passage of the Civil Service Reform Act of 1978 represent a significant shift in the way personnel activities are managed in the U.S. government?

9. Assume you have just been offered a job in Nigeria with a U.S.-based corporation. What staffing and training and development issues would you want addressed?

10. Personnel management in international settings is increasingly important to U.S. firms. What are some compensation issues?

Exercises

a. Interview a public sector personnel manager and a private sector personnel manager and ask them to discuss their views of the differences between the two sectors in the way personnel activities are managed.

b. Talk with two different employees in the same personnel department—a specialist and a generalist. Find out what each likes and dislikes about his or her job and the differences in knowledge and experience each requires.

c. Identify a specific foreign country and assume you were offered a transfer and promotion to that country as a sales manager with a U.S. construction firm. Research and list differences in customs and culture between where you are now living and that country. Then decide if you would accept or reject the offer, regardless of the salary involved.

CASE

CREDIT SERVICE COMPANY

Harold Stanley started Credit Services Company about three years ago. The company is a data processing service bureau that specializes in charge account billings, charge card production, and credit record processing. The firm started small but has now grown to 75 employees. Stanley has done all the recruiting and selection since the firm began. Most of the personnel activities had been carried out on a very informal and haphazard basis by Stanley or the supervisors. Because of time pressures and the many other demands on him, Stanley hired Victoria O'Donnell, a recent college graduate, as the firm's first personnel manager.

O'Donnell was determined to set up a true personnel department. Since the firm has grown rapidly, O'Donnell could see that the firm would probably have to add 75 to 100 more employees over the next two years to keep up with the projected sales increase. Within a short period of time O'Donnell had redesigned the application blank and had established a personnel file for each employee. She discovered that the firm had many women employees but no female supervisors. Also, there was a noticeable lack of employees from racial minorities. Therefore, O'Donnell developed a detailed plan to head off potential equal employment problems. She also developed a revised selection procedure in which she did most of the selection interviewing.

Stanley voiced support for O'Donnell's selection efforts. However, he was very adamant that he wanted to be able to have the final say over any new employee hired. Also, Stanley voiced strong feelings about the government telling him who he could hire or not hire. As he said, "I'll hire whoever I damn well please." O'Donnell was quite concerned by this reaction, since it looked as if she was not going to be given the flexibility she needed to do what she felt should be done.

Questions:

1. Discuss why it is important to look at Credit Service Company as an open system.

2. Identify the authority and structural problems that may exist.

3. If you were O'Donnell, how would you proceed in trying to implement your plans?

NOTES

1. Used with permission from Richard J. Messer and OTASCO.

2. R. D. Middlemist, M. A. Hitt, and R. L. Mathis, *Management: Concepts and Effective Practices*, (St. Paul, MN: West Publishing Co., 1983), p. 583.

3. Reprinted by permission of *Forbes*, February 6, 1978, p. 95

4. "How to Stop the Buck Short of the Top," *Business Week,* January 16, 1978, pp. 82–83.

5. Stanley M. Davis and Paul R. Lawrence, *Matrix* (Reading, MA: Addison-Wesley, 1977).

6. "Personnel Activities Budgets and Staffs" ASPA-BNA Survey No. 46, (Washington D.C.: The Bureau of National Affairs, 1983), pp. 6–7.

7. G. W. Bolander, H. C. White, and M. N. Wolfe, "The Three Faces of Personnel . . . ," *Personnel,* July-August 1983, pp. 12–22.

8. Don Prock and Bob Henson, "The Educational Needs of and the Future Labor Market Demand for Human Resources Managers," *Personnel Journal* 56 (December 1977), pp. 602–607.

9. The authors acknowledge the assistance of Professor Edward Twardy for providing ideas on public personnel administration.

10. For statistical data on workforce distribution, see *Budget of the United States Government, Fiscal Year 1984, Special Analyses* (Washington, D.C.: U.S. Government Printing Office, 1983).

11. Hatch Political Activities Act, 53 Stat. 1147 (1939) and Hatch Political Activities Act, 54 Stat. 767 (1940).

12. Martin Tolchin and Susan Tolchin, *To the Victor Belong the Spoils* (New York: Random House, 1971), p. 96.

13. O. Glen Stahl, *Public Personnel Administration,* 8th ed., (New York: Harper & Row, 1983), pp. 35–45.

14. Adapted from Stahl, *Ibid.*

15. Donald Klinger, "Federal Labor Relations After the Civil Service Reform Act," *Public Personnel Management Journal* 12 (1982), pp. 172–183.

16. Adapted from the Gilbert B. Siegel, "The Personnel Function: Measuring Decentralization and Its Impact," *Public Personnel Management Journal,* 13 (Spring, 1983), pp. 101–115.

17. *Forbes,* July 2, 1984, pp. 115–126.

18. "International Employment is a World Apart," *PMA News,* February 1981, p. 3.

19. Wallace McDonough, "Europe vs. U.S. Living Costs Vary Greatly," *Personnel Administrator,* December 1982, pp. 53–54.

20. W. Holmes and F. Piker, "Expatriate Failure—Prevention Rather than a Cure," *Personnel Management,* December 1980, pp. 30–32.

21. John Rehfuss, "Management Development and the Selection of Overseas Executives," *Personnel Administrator,* July 1982, p. 39.

22. J. Newman, "Determinants of an Expatriate's Effectiveness: A Theoretical and Empirical Vacuum," *Academy of Management Review,* 3 (July 1978), pp. 655–661.

23. Rosalie Tung, "U.S. Multinationals: A Study of Their Selection and Training Procedures for Overseas Assignments," *Academy of Management Proceedings, 1979,* pp. 298–301.

24. Afzalur Rahim, "A Model for Developing Key Expatriate Executives," *Personnel Journal* 62 (April 1983), pp. 312–313.

25. A. D. Lanier, "Selecting and Preparing Personnel for Overseas Transfers *Personnel Journal* 58 (March 1979), pp. 160–163.

26. Cecil G. Howard, "How Best to Integrate Expatriate Managers in the Domestic Organization," *Personnel Administrator,* July 1982, pp. 27–33.

27. Adapted from Susan Nelson, "Learning to Work Overseas," *Nation's Business,* March 1984, pp. 59–60.

28. L. Clague and N. B. Krupp, "International Personnel: The Repatriation Problem," *The Personnel Administrator,* April 1978, pp. 29–33.

29. Details and additional data are available in Burton W. Teague, *Compensating Foreign Service Personnel,* Report no. 818 (New York: The Conference Board, Inc., 1982).

30. Linda M. Stillabower and Lawrence C. Phillips, "Employment Overseas and the Tax Home Issue: Exclusion versus Deductions," *Taxes—The Tax Magazine,* March 1983, pp. 202–207.

31. Bruce A. Searle, "How ERTA Will Benefit Expatriate Americans," *Management Review,* March 1982, pp. 20–21.

32. Adapted from Bruce A. Jacobs, "Beware of Rites When Bearing Gifts," *Industry Week,* October 18, 1982, pp. 75–76.

Human Behavior and Personnel

When you have read this chapter, you should be able to:

1. Define motivation.
2. Discuss problems encountered in identifying what factors motivate employees.
3. Describe four views about why people behave as they do.
4. Explain and compare the three major leadership approaches.
5. Define what a work group is and discuss at least five characteristics of groups.
6. Give examples of three barriers to successful communication.

PERSONNEL AT WORK
EMPLOYEE INVOLVEMENT AT FORD

At Ford's plant in Edison, New Jersey, workers assemble Escort and Lynx automobiles. Each worker does a job in about a minute before starting the cycle again. The repetition of putting headlights, door locks, or dashboards in again and again dulls the senses. It is exactly the setting for the kind of old-fashioned management that has been practiced on American assembly lines for years. But a different approach based on better understanding of human behavior has produced results the old methods could not match.

Foreman Donald R. Hennron formerly berated employees for omitting a bolt or failing to tighten a screw. He was a "hard-nosed disciplinarian" by his own admission. Yet, there has not been a disciplinary hearing at the Edison plant for a year now. Instead of yelling at an employee who made a mistake, Hennron and other supervisors try to find out what went wrong. In turn, workers are getting over their hostile feelings toward management. Before, when workers spotted defects they simply kept quiet—they were not motivated to see things change. Now they call the foreman or stop the line to fix it. They also volunteer ideas for improvement. "Ford has discovered that to build a good car they've got to have harmony", says the president of the local United Auto Workers union.

Foremen no longer "control people." They coach them, do planning, and make sure directions have been communicated clearly. Ford's worker participation program, called Employee Involvement (EI), puts more pressure on the foremen, but results in fewer defective cars reaching the street. Foremen must accept the idea that workers may know more about jobs than they do. The workers also can stop the assembly line if a defect keeps them from doing their jobs properly. The thought of a worker shutting down an entire line would not have been approved of by old Henry Ford. Yet, listening to groups of workers and using a participatory leadership style has improved quality, reduced absenteeism, and lessened hostility. All are evidence that workers' motives have changed in a favorable direction under the innovative EI program.

The greatest number of problems with worker participation programs have been the result of resistance by supervisors. The attitudes of many Ford line supervisors have been negative because they see increased worker involvement as undercutting their supervisory power. In order to reduce this resistance, supervisory discussion groups have been used to address the fears and concerns of supervisors. Also, special training of supervisors in how to work with and foster employee involvement has been useful. In summary, motivation of workers and supervisors and somewhat different leadership styles have been necessary for programs such as Fords EI program to succeed.

"In the electronic era, managers should seek to unify rather than to divide and conquer."
HARVARD BUSINESS REVIEW

This book is not about behavior. But to understand how personnel activities and practices affect and are affected by employees, certain basics of behavior must be understood. As Ford Motor Company found out, sometimes motivation can be improved through the use of employee involvement. Other personnel decisions are greatly influenced by basic human behavior. For example, how can a firm design compensation systems or predict the effect of incentives if there is little understanding of motivation? How can managers shape management development activities to improve leadership ability if they do not understand leadership? How can supervisors deal with work slowdowns by group members if they have no understanding of group dynamics? How can a human resource specialist deal with rumors, formal company communication programs, and interviewing without a knowledge of the basics of communication?

The purpose of this chapter is not to provide detailed examination of human behavior but to highlight key considerations for understanding human behavior at work. Interpreting and using these insights are essential to effective human resource management. The areas of human behavior emphasized here are the concepts of motivation, leadership, group behavior, and communication.

MOTIVATION

Motivation is concerned with the "whys" of human behavior. It attempts to account for the "drives" and "wants" of an individual rather than just focusing on the individual's actions. From observing behavior, one often can infer motives.

Motivation is an emotion or desire operating on a person causing that person to act. People usually act for one reason: to obtain a goal. Thus, motivation is a goal-directed drive and, as such, it seldom occurs in a void. The words *need, want, desire,* and *drive* are all similar to *motive.*

Importance of Motivation

Most managers agree that the success of any organization is determined by the efforts of the people in it. Also, managers often say that problems relating to employee behavior are the most perplexing. Questions that arise include: "How do you get people to do what you want them to do?" and "How can one be sure that people will do their work without a supervisor constantly watching them?" Because the human resources in an organization are an important part of how well it performs, these questions are of major concern to managers.

Can you define motivation?

Approaches to Understanding Motivation

It is often difficult to determine why employees behave as they do simply by observing their behavior. People's actions cannot always be directly related to their conscious or subconscious thoughts. Nor are these actions always related to obvious daily occurrences. For example, if an employee has an argument with her supervisor and fails to report to work the next day, it may appear that her behavior is a result of the confrontation. However, her behavior may actually be motivated by a combination of factors including overwork, family illness, or some other problems.

Multiple Causes. Different people may have different reasons for behaving in the very same manner. For example, one manager may join a service club because it is a good place to make business contacts; another may join because of the social environment; still another joins because of the interesting programs and speakers at the club. Thus, three different "whys" can underlie the same behavior, further complicating the process of inferring motivation from behavior. For example, the motivations people have to pursue a certain career can spring from quite different sources.[2] Personality, background, experiences, group effects, or many other factors can impact a person's career choice.

Multiple Behaviors. In addition, the same motive may result in different behavior. For example, if Jan Welch wants a promotion, she may concentrate on performing her job exceptionally well. But Bill Broust, who also wants a promotion, may take a different approach: He may try to "apple polish" the boss to get the promotion. Another manager, who also wants the promotion very badly, may be afraid to do anything at all for fear he will fail. The motivation for these three behaviors is the same, but it cannot be determined simply by viewing the behavior of the three managers.

Motivation As a Subject. Approaches to understanding motivation differ because many individual theorists have developed their own views and theories of motivation. They approach motivation from different starting points, with different ideas in mind, and from different backgrounds. Among the various viewpoints are Herzberg's theory of work motivation, Maslow's approach to motivation, and Porter and Lawler's model of motivation. The wide variety of views is evidence that no one approach is considered to be the only correct one. Each has made its contribution to the understanding of human behavior. The perspective taken here is to provide a practical view of the important approaches to motivation.

Many managers' views of motivation are based upon assumptions about what goals people are expected to achieve as employees. For example, if a sales manager says he wants to "motivate" his employees, he is really saying he wants his employees to select the goals that *he* wants them to seek—goals he considers best for salespeople in his division. His employees are undoubtedly motivated, but perhaps not toward doing what he would have them do. Figure 3–1 illustrates such a managers's model of motivation. This view, although widely held by managers, is too restrictive, as will be shown.

Can you discuss problems in identifying what motivates employees?

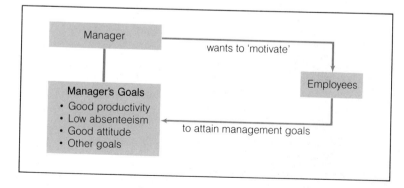

FIGURE 3–1
Managerial model of motivation.

The study of motivation over the last century has been focused partly on answering the question "What is the basic goal of man?" Managers have operated with their own preconceived ideas of basic human goals. Over time, four major assumptions about human nature and the mainsprings of motivation have emerged.[4] These assumptions have been translated into managerial philosophies and views of employee motivation. One of the most long-lived approaches is based on the assumption that people are rational-economic beings.

Rational-Economic View

The rational-economic view basically suggests that humans reasonably, logically, and rationally make decisions that will result in the most economic gain for themselves. Therefore, employees are motivated by the opportunity to make as much money as possible and will act rationally to maximize their earnings. The assumption is that money, because of what it can buy, is the most important motivator of all people.

This explanation of human motivation is weak because a great deal of behavior does not reasonably follow from the rational-economic assumption made about human nature. For example, if employees are primarily interested in maximizing their economic return, why do some of them turn away from the potential profits of piece-rate production and others refuse to take overtime? Obviously, the rational-economic assumptions have some limitations.

"In my book, fulfilling oneself and making money hand over fist are synonymous."

From Wall Street Journal, Permission: Cartoon Features Syndicate.

Social View

The social view of human nature suggests that all people can be motivated to perform if a manager appeals to their social needs. A predominant emphasis of this viewpoint management literature is: "Happiness and harmony in the group leads to productivity," or "A happy worker is a productive worker."

Human Relations. The social view of human nature has led to the human relations approach, in which humans are viewed as a bundle of attitudes, sentiments, and emotions. Managers are told that to be effective they should use "image management" to convince workers of their importance to the company. Employee participation in the decision-making process (as long as they cannot harm the operation) is supposed to lead to feelings of harmony, loyalty, and satisfaction.

Unfortunately, proponents of this view often went to extremes to explain motivation from just one variable, as earlier proponents of money as a motivator had done. In fact, not everyone is motivated primarily by harmony and cooperation, and many were suspicous of the sincerity of the human relations approach.

Self-Actualizing View

During the late 1950s and early 1960s the ideas of another group of management thinkers, many of whom were trained in the behavioral sciences, became very popular. They assumed that people are beings striving to reach self-actualization. This concept means that a person wants to reach his or her full potential, and is illustrated by the ideas of Abraham Maslow, Douglas McGregor, and Frederick Herzberg.

Abraham Maslow. A clinical psychologist, Abraham Maslow, developed a theory of human motivation that continues to receive a great deal of exposure in management literature.[5] Maslow classified human needs into five categories. He suggested that there is a fairly definite order to human needs, and until the more basic needs are adequately fulfilled, a person will not strive to meet higher needs, Maslow's well-know hierarcy is comprised of: (1) physiological needs, (2) safety and security needs, (3) belonging and love needs, (4) self-esteem needs, and (5) self-actualization needs.

An assumption often made by those using Maslow's hierarchy is that workers in modern advanced societies have basically satisfied their physiological, safety, and belonging needs. Therefore, they will be motivated by the need for self-esteem, the esteem of others, and self-actualization. Consequently, conditions to satisfy these needs should be present at work; the job itself should be internally meaningful and motivating.

Douglas McGregor. The concepts behind the self-actualization view perhaps were best expressed by Douglas McGregor, who presented two opposite sets of assumptions he believed were basic to most managers. Summarized in Figure 3–2, one set was labeled Theory X and the other

FIGURE 3–2

A summary of Theory X and Theory Y (McGregor).

THEORY X	THEORY Y
■ People dislike work and will try to avoid it.	■ People do not inherently dislike work.
■ People have to be coerced and threatened with punishment if the organization's goals are to be met.	■ People do not like rigid control and threats.
■ Most workers like direction and will avoid responsibility.	■ Under proper conditions, people do not avoid responsibility.
■ People want security above all in their work.	■ People want security but also have other needs such as self-actualization and esteem.

SOURCE: Douglas McGregor, *The Human Side of Enterprise* (New York: McGraw-Hill, 1960), pp. 33–45.

Theory Y.[6] McGregor felt that managers typically held one of these sets of assumptions about human nature and acted in keeping with those assumptions. However, McGregor argued that people are really more like Theory Y than Theory X. A key point in McGregor's Theory Y is that work is itself a motivator of most people.

Frederick Herzberg. In the late 1950s Frederick Herzberg and his research associates conducted interviews with 200 engineers and accountants who worked in different companies. The result of this research was a theory that, like Maslow's, has been widely discussed in the management literature.[7] Maslow identifies basic human needs, while Herzberg's work relates factors in the job to a person's motivation.

Herzberg's Motivation/Hygiene theory assumes that one group of factors, *motivators*, accounts for high levels of motivation to work. Another group of factors can cause discontent with work. These factors are labeled *hygiene*, or maintenance, factors. Figure 3–3 compares Herzberg's motivatiors and hygiene factors with Maslow's need hierarchy.

FIGURE 3–3

Maslow's and Herzberg's ideas compared.

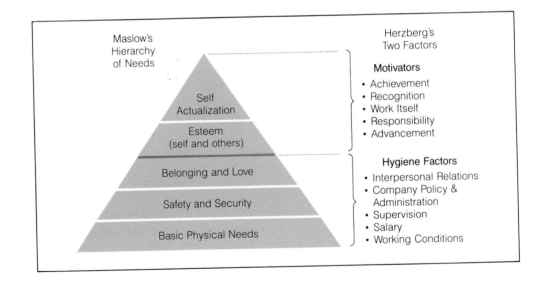

The implication of this research for management and personnel practices is that the hygiene factors provide a base that must be carefully considered if dissatisfaction is to be avoided. But even if all these maintenance needs are addressed, people may not necessarily be motivated to work harder. Only motivators cause more effort to be exerted and more productivity to be attained.

Herzberg's work has been the subject of much controversy, revolving around his research method and later attempts to replicate his findings. The controversy still continues.

The self-actualizing school of thought, with its sometimes moralistic requests to improve the job and let the individual achieve self-actualization, has given way to the recognition that everyone is somewhat different and that job situations vary. To understand motivation and human behavior, one must understand the interactions between individual characteristics and the characteristics of the situation. The fourth approach to motivation and human behavior recognizes that people are "complex."

Complex View

The complex view basically suggests that each person is different and a variety of items may prove to be motivating, depending upon the needs of the individual, the situation the individual is in, and what rewards the individual expects for the work done. Theorists who hold to this view, such as Victor Vroom and Lyman Porter and E. E. Lawler, do not attempt to fit people into a single category. Instead they accept human differences.

Victor Vroom. Vroom noted that people act to obtain goals.[8] But whether they will act at all depends on whether they believe their behavior will help them achieve their goal. In charting a path to a goal, people choose among various actions based upon their prediction of the outcome of each action. For example, does hard work lead to more money in the pay envelope? Some people think that it does, and others think that it does not, depending upon past experiences with hard work and earning more money.

Another critical element is how much the person wants the money (or any other outcome). If Lisa Harmon does not really want a promotion, offering her a promotion that requires relocation to another city will not be highly attractive to her. To put it another way, a person's motivation depends on: (1) his or her expectation that a particular behavior will result in a desired outcome or goal, and (2) the value the person assigns to that outcome. Numerous other researchers have added to Vroom's model.

Lyman Porter and E. E. Lawler. Porter and Lawler contend that the above relationship should be expanded to include perceived equity or fairness as a variable that influences job behavior. Perception is the way an individual views the job. Figure 3–4 contains a simplified Porter and Lawler model. This view is further affected by what people *expect* to

FIGURE 3–4
Porter and Lawler motiva-
tion model.

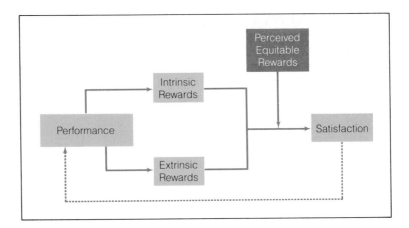

SOURCE: Adapted from Edward E. Lawler, III. and Lyman W. Porter, "The Effect of Performance on Job Satisfaction," *Industrial Relations* 7, October 1966.

EQUITY
is defined as the per-
ceived fairness of what
the person does (inputs)
compared with what the
person receives (out-
comes).

receive from jobs. If their *expectations* are not met, they may feel they have been unfairly treated, and they may become dissatisfied.[9]

Suppose that a male department store clerk is motivated to expend effort on his job by selling men's wear. From his job he expects to receive two types of rewards: intrinsic (internal) and extrinsic (exter-nal). For this salesclerk, intrinsic rewards could include a feeling of accomplishment, a feeling of recognition, or other motivators. Extrinsic rewards might be such items as pay, benefits, good working condi-tions, and other hygiene factors. The salesclerk compares his perfor-mance to what he expected and to both types of rewards he receives. This comparison is made from his perception of his performance and his rewards. He then reaches some level of satisfaction or dissatisfac-tion. Once this level is reached, it is difficult to determine what he will do. If he is dissatisfied, he might put forth less effort next time, or he might work harder to get the rewards he wants, or he might just accept his dissatisfaction. If he is highly satisfied, it does not always mean he will work harder. He may emphasize quality, or he may say, "I got what I wanted."

The essence of the Porter and Lawler view of motivation is the im-portant role of perception. It also shows that performance leads to sat-isfaction rather than satisfaction leading to performance, if a feedback loop is present.[10]

Equity As a Motivator. People want to be treated fairly, not just in the rewards they receive, but also in such areas as vacations, work assign-ments, and even penalties assessed. Fairness in management literature is referred to as **equity,** which relates to inputs and outcomes. Inputs are what a person brings to the organization. They include educational level, age, experience, productivity, and other skills or efforts. The items received by a person, or the outcomes, are the rewards obtained in exchange for inputs. Outcomes include pay, benefits, recognition, achievement, prestige, and any other rewards received. Note that an outcome can be either tangible (such as economic benefits) or intangi-ble (internal rewards such as recognition or achievement).

The individual's view of fair value is critical to the relationship between performance and job satisfaction because one's sense of equity is an exchange and comparison process. Assume you are a laboratory technician in a hospital. You exchange talents and efforts for the tangible and intangible rewards the hospital gives. Then you compare your inputs (what you did) to your outcomes (what you received) to determine the equity of your compensation. As Figure 3–5 shows, the comparison process also includes the individual's comparison of inputs/outcomes to the inputs/outcomes of other individuals. Thus, you also will compare your talents, skills, and efforts to those of other laboratory technicians or other hospital employees. Your perception—correct or incorrect—significantly affects your valuation of your inputs and outcomes. A sense of inequity occurs when the comparison process results in an imbalance between inputs and outcomes.

If Inputs Exceed Outcomes. One view of equity theory research suggests that if an employee is under-rewarded (more inputs than outcomes), the employee will tend to reduce his or her inputs.[11] If, like the lab technician mentioned above, you feel that your rewards have been fewer than your inputs, you will attempt to resolve the inequity. Your reactions can include some or all of the following: increased dissatisfaction, attempts to get compensation raised, quitting the job for a more equitable one, changing your perceptual comparison, or reducing your productivity. All these actions are attempts to reduce the inequity.

If Outcomes Exceed Inputs. One way a person may attempt to resolve this type of inequity is by putting forth more effort. If you feel that you receive more rewards than you deserve, you might work harder to justify the "overpayment." Or you might process the same number of laboratory samples, but do so more accurately and produce higher-quality results. Other actions could include a recomparison, whereby you might decide that you evaluated your efforts inaccurately and that you really were not overpaid.

Regardless of the action taken, you will make some attempt to relieve the inequity tension. Research evidence on the type of action you are most likely to take is mixed.[12] Because they can affect motivation, feelings of inequity have important implications for the design and ad-

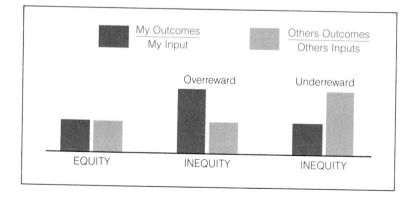

FIGURE 3–5
Equity evaluations.

ministration of compensation programs, staffing, training, and performance appraisal.

Importance of Complex View. The complex approach to motivation is important in that it moves away from the simplistic assumptions of the other three views. Work motivation really *is* very complex. It depends on both the individual and the environment in which the individual works. The important conclusion to be drawn from this view is that a manager must attempt to match individual needs and expectations to the types of rewards available in the job setting.

In sum, the current state of knowledge about motivation emphasizes that motivation really does depend upon the individual and the individual's job situation. Managers who must direct or lead these "complex" people must have a basic understanding of leadership and its relationship to motivation.

Can you describe four views about why
people behave as they do?

LEADERSHIP

Management and leadership are not exactly the same concepts but they overlap a great deal. Management implies formal authority, while leadership may not have any connection with formal authority. Managers have been given positions with formal authority to perform their jobs, including directing the actions of others. The responsibility for seeing that work gets done accompanies this authority. Leadership, however, does not require formal authority from "above" in the organization. It does not even have to occur in a formal organizational environment. A street gang, for example, will have a leader, though perhaps not a formally-appointed one. This leader is not a "manager" in the common sense of the word.

The distinction between leadership and management is not always clear. Employees obey or follow managers partially because they must. If employees consistently refused to cooperate, they would not be employed very long. On the other hand, people may obey or follow leaders including for entirely different reasons, physical attractiveness or superior knowledge.

The manager does not always have to be a leader to be effective, but some key ideas about leadership can be useful to the manager. For example, Jessica Harbeck, a new accounting supervisor, may rely on giving "orders" rather than using persuasion with Fred Abbott, a 60-year-old employee. If Jessica does not understand the difference between being a manager (having a formal position) and being a leader (having followers), she may find that after a while giving an order may not work with Fred, and a different kind of relationship is needed.

The successful manager's concern with leadership focuses on obtaining the very best performance from employees. Some employees do only the minimum number of tasks required of them. But most managers prefer effective and creative employees who can help management.

Leadership Approaches

Many different approaches have been taken to understanding leadership. It has been studied with varying degrees of rigor for centuries.

Trait Approaches. Early studies on leadership were done by psychologists who examined the personality traits of leaders. Leaders were thought to be dominant extroverts who possessed traits of self-confidence, empathy, and intelligence.

Even earlier approaches focused on the "Great Leader" theory. This method assumed that a better understanding of leadership could be gained by studying the personalities and behaviors of famous leaders. Such study certainly can be interesting, but what worked for Susan B. Anthony, George Washington, and Benito Juarez years ago may not

necessarily be applicable in today's world or in a different set of circumstances. Although many famous leaders shared certain traits, it
must be remembered that many other individuals with the same traits
failed to become leaders.

Style Approaches. During the last few decades, several attempts have
been made to classify leadership into its basic dimensions. The Ohio
State Leadership Studies have significantly affected our knowledge of
leadership. Through the use of sophisticated statistical techniques, two
basic dimensions of leader behavior were isolated: *initiating structure*
and *consideration.*

Initiating structure may involve scheduling, maintaining, and communicating standards of performance; emphasizing that deadlines be
met; and assigning group members to particular tasks–in other words,
a concern with productivity, costs, and getting the work done It has
also been called the *production-oriented* style.

Behavior that shows **consideration** includes explaining why decisions were made, consulting group members before making decisions,
listening to group members' problems, doing personal favors for group
members, and performing other such actions. Leaders characterized by
consideration have been called *people-oriented* leaders.

Managers who score high on initiating structure may be very effective and successful on performance measures such as productivity,
profit, and efficiency. They are commonly rated very well by their superiors. Managers who score high on consideration tend to have high
morale in their work groups, lower employee turnover, and lower
grievance rates than those who are low on consideration.

In general, those who believe in this style approach to leadership feel
that effective leaders are those who score high on both initiating structure *and* consideration (see Figure 3–6); they are concerned with their
people and concerned with getting the job done. However, viewing
leadership only as a combination of initiating structure and considera-

FIGURE 3–6
Leadership style
approach.

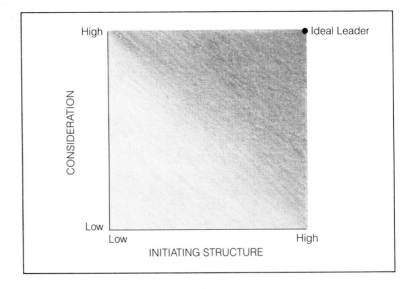

tion presents a problem because there is little evidence to show how successful a leader with a people-oriented or production-oriented approach, or both, will be in different situations.

Situational Approaches. Differences in the leadership situation, such as the size and style of the organization, the nature of tasks, or how well the leader relates to the followers, all may make a difference in the effectiveness of a given leadership style. For example, people tolerate more authoritarian leadership in larger groups than they do in small groups. Viewing leadership "contingently" in this way has brought a higher level of sophistication to the study of leadership.[14] It suggests that leadership style is really determined by the conditions under which the leader is operating. Production-oriented leadership may be more effective under some conditions and people-oriented leadership under others. These issues are still being researched, but some general guide lines are available.

Fred Fiedler. Since the 1950s Fiedler and his associates have been researching leadership by studying nurses, steel company crews, consumer sales cooperatives, church groups, athletic teams, factory workers, aviation cadets, and others. The main conclusion of all this research is that the *effectiveness* of the leader depends upon both the *leadership style* and the *favorableness of the situation.* Fiedler concludes that in either very favorable situations or very unfavorable situations, production-oriented leadership works best. In other situations, where poor leader-member relations, weak position power, or unstructured tasks combine to make the situation moderately unfavorable, the people-oriented leader is more effective.[15]

Path-Goal Approach. Another researcher, Robert House, has tried to identify those situations in which a leader's consideration or initiating-structure behavior affects employee performance or satisfaction.[16] His approach is based upon the path-goal motivation ideas of Vroom and of Porter and Lawler mentioned earlier. House argues that a leader can affect (1) intrinsic rewards of work, (2) intrinsic rewards associated with achievement, (3) extrinsic rewards associated with achievement, (4) the clarity of the "path" an employee will follow to achievement, and (5) the probability that achievement will be rewarded.

This theory predicts that a considerate leader is important if the work itself is boring and uninteresting: "If you have a bad job, you don't need a bad boss, too." When the job itself is stimulating, consideration is less important.

The leader's ability to use initiating structure is important when the job is unstructured or ambiguous or when a crisis occurs. If the job is already well structured, a high degree of structure from the leader is unnecessary and irritating.

This approach to the situational nature of leadership represents another attempt to identify what leadership style is most appropriate in a given situation. As more research is done on the path-goal approach and similar theories, managers will have a better grasp on ways to improve leadership effectiveness.[17]

Vroom and Yetton. Vroom and Yetton have developed a model to help a leader choose an approach to decision-making situations. The alternatives in the model differ according to how much the leader solicits input from subordinates and how much subordinates are involved in the decision-making process. Their model consists of a set of questions about the situation to which a leader must answer yes or no. On the basis of these answers, certain decision styles are rejected as inappropriate. After the entire sequence of questions has been answered, one or more styles remain that meet all requirements for quality and acceptability. The major considerations of this model are the quality of the decision and the probability that it will be accepted by subordinates.[18]

Hersey and Blanchard. The continuing evolution of the situational approach is illustrated by the model developed by Hersey and Blanchard.[19] Their *life cycle leadership theory* ties the maturity of subordinates to leadership styles. Based on the two leadership dimensions of task behavior and relationship behavior (similar to initiating structure and consideration), Hersey and Blanchard assert that as people change from immature to mature, the appropriate leadership styles change. For leading someone who is relatively immature, a high task, low relationship style is most effective. However, for leading highly mature people, a low task, low relationship style is most appropriate. In between these two maturity extremes, the most appropriate styles are high task, high relationship and high relationship, low task in nature.

This theory illustrates that as additional situational factors affecting leadership emerge, new concepts are blended with earlier theories. Hersey and Blanchard have blended employee maturity with ideas derived from some of the style approaches.

Can you explain and compare the three
major leadership approaches?

Leadership Effectiveness

Certain kinds of leadership skills can be learned and are an important part of many management training programs. Successful leadership also depends upon an individual's personality. Because changing leadership styles.is often very difficult, placing individuals in a situation more compatible with their leadership styles may be more effective. It is much easier to move a manager to a job that fits her or his leadership inclinations than it is to try to change the individual's way of leading.

An important part of effective leadership is a basic understanding of how individuals behave as members of groups. Group forces generally can and do affect management operations. The impact of work groups on productivity and operations demands that group behavior be discussed when considering behavioral characteristics of employees.

GROUP BEHAVIOR

Groups of employees can make a manager's job easy or impossible. Managers must understand the behavior and characteristics of groups, especially work groups, to effectively direct progress toward organizational goals. A bowling team, friendship group, or coffee break clique are groups. But a **work group** is a collection of individuals brought together to perform organizational work.

Work groups frequently have varied and overlapping social arrangements. For example, a work group of 20 people in a government office may have several subgroups, which develop because of social considerations, carpools, or physical location. Regardless of the type of work situation, a work group shares certain basic characteristics in common with groups in many other settings.

Group Characteristics

Informal groups frequently develop common "codes of behavior" to help attain group goals. During the growth, development, and maturity of a group, a collective bond develops which guides members' attitudes and actions as a group. This group understanding is called a **norm**.

Norms. Norms may develop in any group and function as a group's "code of behavior" for many reasons. Norms define a variety of group concerns, such as: which other groups to associate with, how other groups are to be viewed, and what behaviors or expressions are appropriate within the group. For example, detectives in a police department may have a group norm that implies that officers on parking patrol are to be viewed as inferior. As numerous studies have revealed, norms can even dictate acceptable productivity rates, and group quotas may be different from the formal quotas posted by management.[20] An example of conflict between the expected corporate code of behavior and group and individual norms is the pressure to give to United Way drives. This conflict is described at the end of this chapter in the "Personnel Today and Tomorrow vignette.

Cohesiveness. Groups differ in the degree of "cohesiveness," or closeness among members. A highly cohesive group is one in which the members place a high value on group membership and are very attached to the group. Members of highly cohesive groups tend to accept group goals more than members of less cohesive groups. Group sanctions tend to be much more effective in a cohesive group. For example, if an X-ray technologist is a member of a close-knit X-ray department, negative comments about his attire from other group members will carry more weight than if he were unconcerned about his membership in the department.

Status. As a group develops, each member's position and power in it tends to become organized into a status system. This **status** is the relative social ranking an individual has in a group.

Even in work groups, status usually results in a "pecking order" comprised of an informal leader and perhaps second- and third-level members. Status symbols may include dress, office size, desk size, number of pictures in the office, or a private office with a door and a window. These symbols serve a purpose because they allow people

A WORK GROUP
is a collection of individuals brought together to perform organizational work.
NORMS
are expected standards of behavior, usually unwritten and often unspoken, that are generally understood by all members of a group.
STATUS
is the relative social ranking an individual has in a group or organization.

who are knowledgeable about the status system to identify a person's "place" in the system.

Group Composition. The success of a group is partially determined by the individual characteristics of group members. Age, sex, ethnic background, marital status, experience, and educational levels are important considerations. If the individual characteristics of a group's members are very similar, individual member satisfaction usually will be higher than in a group with diverse members. In homogenous groups, members tend to be more friendly and have higher group spirit. However, groups whose members have quite different characteristics (heterogenous groups) tend to be more productive.

Groups composed of diverse individuals are likely to be superior in arriving at inventive solutions and new ideas because many different approaches to problems are presented by different people. For instance, when the product line supervisor for a ski-wear firm needed some new ideas for next year's product line, she called in people with very different backgrounds to brainstorm the problem: people from engineering, sales, design, and public relations. They did not always agree on an idea, but they provided a wide variety of ideas on the product line.

Size. The size of a group tends to affect individual performance in the group. Size certainly can affect the speed with which decisions can be made in a group. For example, at one university the management department has only 6 faculty members; at another, the management department has 25. Decisions about course assignments and curriculum will probably be easier in the smaller department. Also, as the number of members in a group increases, role definitions can be clearer because face-to-face communication is reduced. Generally, it is safe to say that management becomes more difficult and communication becomes more important as group size increases. Decision-making also takes more time as size increases if everyone continues to be involved in making the decisions.

*Can you define a work group and discuss
the characteristics of groups?*

COMMUNICATION

Communication is a behavioral process that affects motivation, leadership, and group effectiveness. Interpersonal communication occurs both formally and informally in organizations, and it maybe written, spoken, or nonverbal. Communication affects the management of people as much as or more than any other process over which management has influence. Communication is the method by which new policies are passed along, changes are implemented, and instructions are given.

The basic communications process is presented in Figure 3–7. Before a message can be conveyed, formally or informally, it is encoded or

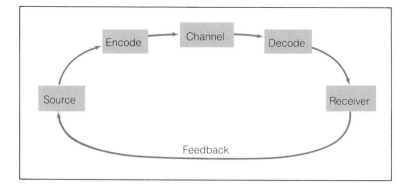

converted to symbolic form (made into words, for example); then it is passed by way of a channel (or medium) to the receiver who decodes (or retranslates) it. The desired result is the transfer of reasonably accurate meaning from one person to another. However, the process is subject to many failures.

Communication Barriers

Communication barriers are often mentioned by managers as being critical and persistent. Better communication comes about when people are aware of semantic, technical, and perceptual barriers.

Semantic Barriers. The semantic barrier is a barrier of words. Communication can be difficult because words or symbols can have different meanings. For example, the word *fire* can mean either a flame or to discharge an employee.

The way people use words can build semantic barriers. For example, the use of technical language, or "jargon," simplifies in-group communication (such as in a group of CPAs). But if the CPAs use the technical words when communicating with others who do not understand the language, real barriers to understanding are erected.

Technical Barriers. Technical problems can prevent a message from conveying the intended meaning. If you were in a room talking with friends and a rock band was playing loudly, you might not accurately hear what was said. Likewise, any message can be interrupted by noise before it reaches the receiver. Both noise and physical barriers can be technical problems in oral communication. You cannot always assume that messages sent will be received as intended.

Lack of effective listening habits is a technical barrier that does lie with the receiver. People talk past each other for several reasons. Often they do not listen but simply wait for their turn to speak. Or they seek only the information that is consistent with what they want to hear—a result of perceptual barriers.

Perceptual Barriers. Perceptual problems occur because people have different mental frameworks. If Maria attempts to tell Paul about a dog,

Paul conjures a visual image of a dog. Maria may be talking about a chihuahua, while Paul may be thinking about a German shepherd.

Emotion can set up perceptual barriers. The stronger the feelings, the less likely people are to communicate clearly. If a supervisor is appraising an employee's performance, at the end of which she will (or will not) recommend a salary increase, the employee will probably become defensive at any suggestion of inadequate performance. The employee is less likely to hear suggestions for improvement because of greater interest in the salary adjustment recommendation.

Informal Personnel Communication

An important part of organizational communication is carried out through informal information channels. These channels interweaving throughout an organization are referred to as the "grapevine." Just as jungle drums in old Tarzan movies indicated trouble, the grapevine often reflects employee and organizational problems. A well-known expert on the organizational grapevine, Keith Davis, says that effective supervisors and managers should monitor the grapevine as a supplement to formal information channels.[21] The absence of a grapevine in a company might be evidence that employees are too scared to talk or that they care so little about the company that they do not want to talk about it.

Managers should be aware of current grapevine messages and listen for major distortions. Activity in the grapevine depends on how important a topic is and the presence (or absence) of official communication on it. Studies also show that a minority of employees account for a majority of the information brought into and discussed throughout the organization.[22]

To be effective, both formal and informal communication should be matched to the receiver. The message should be transmitted over appropriate media using the right symbols at a level meaningful to both the sender and the receiver. Personnel communication also must match the medium and the message to the purpose. Take the case of a personnel director who wants to tell managers about a change that will affect their relations with union stewards. If the personnel unit does not care whether managers receive the message, they can post it on the bulletin board in the cafeteria. However, if the personnel unit wants to be sure the managers receive the message, a memo will be sent to the managers.

Can you give examples of three barriers to successful communication?

PERSONNEL TODAY AND TOMORROW

NONCONFORMITY AND CORPORATE PRESSURE: I WON'T GIVE AT THE OFFICE

Terri Ware got a message from the boss: "Give to the United Way, or else." She refused, so she was fired from her part-time job as a bank teller. The president of the company said, "I've had 100 percent participation from my employees for years and I'll be damned if one person is going to come along and change that." He offered her the job back only after the firing received publicity. This incident, which occurred at First Federal Savings and Loan in Cumberland, Maryland, may or may not be unusual.

Employees may not be dismissed over fundraising conflicts, but they are subjected to more subtle forms of pressure. Of course, companies can apply pressure because they do have power over jobs and salaries. At Chase Manhattan Bank many employees fill out their contribution cards in front of a supervisor who reads the donation amounts in the employee's presence. At AT&T workers are informed of "suggested" contribution levels and their bosses are rewarded if the levels are reached. The 100 percent participation goal receives significant emphasis at AT&T, where 96 percent employee participation is the average and many units end the drive at or over 100 percent of the targeted amounts.

At Chase Manhattan "team captains" call meetings to give employees payroll deduction cards. One participant watched as his supervisor read every card as it was turned in. The supervisor called several people to the front to "correct" their cards when they indicated they were not giving.

Some workers rebel. A Union Carbide worker says, "Last year I gave money because they called me into a meeting and gave me the pitch and then handed me the card. This year I just skipped the meeting, and I won't give either."

Although the United Way is resented by many workers, it actually evolved as a way to protect them. Its nearly exclusive right to collect money at the workplace was meant to protect workers from an onslaught of outstretched hands. Instead, one hand—the United Way—collects and distributes money. The United Way says it discourages coercion, but acknowledges it has no control over how the money is raised. It hired a pollster who studied donor attitudes and found that 15 percent of workers felt coerced into giving.

Experts say image promotion is behind the emphasis on giving at most companies. "Companies want to look good in comparison with their competitors in the industry. It just looks better to say that all the employees gave."[23]

SUMMARY

■ Major behavioral concerns in personnel—motivation, leadership, groups, and communication—have been the focus of this chapter.

■ Motivation deals with the "whys" of human behavior.

■ Four major views of human nature are: rational-economic, social, self-actualizing, and complex.

■ Maslow's hierarchy of needs, McGregor's Theory X and Theory Y, and Herzberg's motivation/hygiene theory all assume that self-actualization is a major motive at work.

■ The complex view of motivation includes the expectancy and equity theories and recognizes the current situations people in organizations face.

■ The "trait" and "style" approaches to leadership were early attempts to understand the phenomenon.

■ Current leadership ideas emphasize the situational nature of leadership, in which the successful manager/leader must be able to diagnose the appropriate style to be used in a situation.

■ A leader can affect followers' rewards and the path to those rewards; in so doing, he or she can affect motivation.

■ Cohesive groups can enforce norms best.

■ Each group has a status structure and the composition of the group is affected by the size and cohesiveness of the group.

■ Communication barriers may be semantic, technical, or perceptual in nature.

REVIEW QUESTIONS AND EXERCISES

1. What is motivation?
2. Why is it so difficult to identify the causes of behavior?
3. Which views about basic human nature do you see as most compatible with your own values?
4. "An effective leader must be a good diagnostician." Discuss.
5. What group characteristics would likely be involved in a situation where the work group was engaged in a work slowdown?
6. How can communication barriers lead to management failure?

Exercises

a. List what you believe to be your last boss's philosophy of motivation. What motivation theory (theories) did he or she appear to practice. What differences were there in the ways other employees reacted to this style? What additional intrinsic and extrinsic rewards could your boss have used that might have improved employee performance?

b. Describe activities in which "miscommunication" occurred. Then list the three types of communication barriers and give specific examples of how each type contributed to the miscommunication.

CASE

THE NEW PROJECT DIRECTOR

Cliff Wallen was hired by Eastern Data Corporation (EDC) three years ago. He joined EDC because of the advancement possibilities and because he wanted to live in New England. Two years ago he was promoted to Project Coordinator, and had 4 subordinates assigned to him. During a recent reorganization, he was promoted to Project Director and given authority over a group of 16 people.

Wallen was delighted to be offered the promotion because it meant that he had finally "made it in management" without the help of his father, president of an industrial supply firm, who had offered him a management position with the family business before he joined EDC. For three years Wallen had heard his father's derogatory comments about how he would have been better off joining the family firm. Also, the promotion carried with it a 15 percent salary increase, which would be quite useful because Wallen and his wife had been wanting to buy a house.

Although Wallen was pleased with the rate at which he was climbing the corporate ladder, he knew that some others were not. Several people in Wallen's group felt John Lorton should have gotten the promotion to director because he had been with the company for 15 years and they felt Lorton knew more about the technical aspects of the job. Also, Lorton turned down a managerial position a few years ago, a decision that many felt had hurt his chances of getting a promotion in the future. Others in Wallen's group felt that someone should have been brought in from outside the department. This action would have prevented people in the group from feeling that one group member was chosen over another. They also did not feel that anyone in the group, including Wallen, was qualified to be director.

The director whom Wallen replaced was well liked, well respected, and did a good job before he resigned to take a job at another firm. As Wallen sips a cup of coffee on Sunday night, the evening before his first day as Project Director, he knows he faces a big challenge to fill the shoes of the former director and to win the cooperation of his new subordinates.

Questions:

1. Apply some motivation concepts and analyze Cliff's reasons for taking the new job.

2. What type of leadership style would you recommend to Cliff? Why?

3. Describe how group forces may affect Cliff's work and what he might do to "manage" them.

NOTES

1. Adapted from, "The Old Foreman Is on the Way Out, and the New One Will Be More Important," *Business Week*, April 25, 1983, p.74.

2. M. London, "Toward a Theory of Career Motivation," *Academy of Management Review*, 8 (October 1983), pp. 620–630.

3. Adapted from H. S. Byrne, "Republic Air's Wolf Tackles Labor Costs, Undirected Growth to Cure Ailing Carrier," *Wall Street Journal*, May 24, 1984, p. 39.

4. The authors acknowledge the influence and contribution of Edgar Schein, *Organizational Psychology*, 2nd ed. (Englewood Cliffs, NJ: Prentice-Hall, 1970), in framing and structuring the various assumptions and approaches to motivation.

5. A. H. Maslow, *Motivation and Personality* (New York: Harper & Row, 1954).

6. Douglas McGregor, *The Human Side of Enterprise.* (New York: McGraw-Hill, 1960), pp. 33–45.

7. F Herzberg, B. Mausner, and B. Snyderman, *The Motivation to Work* (New York: John Wiley & Sons, 1959).

8. Victor H. Vroom, *Work and Motivation* (New York: John Wiley & Sons, 1964).

9. Edward E. Lawler, III, and Lyman W. Porter, "The Effect of Performance on Job Satisfaction," *Industrial Relations* (October 1966).

10. T. Mitchell, "Motivation: New Directions for Theory, Research, and Practice," *Academy of Management Review*, 7 (1982), pp. 80–88.

11. For a concise explanation of equity theory, see Michael R. Carrell and John E. Dittrich, "Equity Theory: The Recent Literature, Methodological Considerations and New Directions," *Academy of Management Review*, 3 (1978), pp. 202–210.

12. R. Vecchio, "Predicting Worker Performance in Inequitable Settings," *Academy of Management Review* 7 (1982), pp. 103–110.

13. Adapted from Janet Guyan, "Apple Lured President from Pepsi with Patient Persuasion and Cash," *Wall Street Journal*, April 15, 1983, p. 29.

14. See J. C. Wofford, "An Integrated Theory of Leadership," *Journal of Management* 8 (1982), pp. 27–47.

15. Fred E. Fiedler, "Engineer the Job to Fit the Manager," *Harvard Business Review*, September-October 1965, p. 119.

16. Robert House, "Path-Goal Theory of Leader Effectiveness," *Administrative Science Quarterly* 16 (1971), pp. 321–338.

17. For example see, J. Fulk and E. R. Wendler, "Dimensionality of Leader-Subordinate Interactions: A Path-Goal Investigation," *Organizational Behavior and Human Performance* 30 (1982), pp. 241–264.

18. A good source is D. Hellriegel, J. Slocum, and R. Woodman, *Organizational Behavior*, 3rd ed. (St. Paul, MN: West, 1983), pp. 413–418.

19 P. S. Hersey and K. H. Blanchard, *Management of Organizational Behavior*, (Englewood Cliffs, NJ: Prentice-Hall, 1977).

20. D. Feldman, "The Development and Enforcement of Group Norms," *Academy of Management Review* 9 (1984), pp. 47–53.

21. Keith Davis, *Human Behavior at Work* (New York: McGraw-Hill, 1977), pp. 278–286.

22. R. Keller and W. Holland, "Communicators and Innovators in Research and Development Organizations," *Academy of Management Journal* 26 (1983), p. 742.

23. Adapted from D. J. Blum, "Donor's Backlash," *Wall Street Journal*, January 12, 1982, p. 1.

SECTION CASE I

IONA'S IRE

Iona Eden worked in the housekeeping department of the Parker House Hotel as an area maintenance specialist. The Parker House Hotel is a large convention facility with several restaurants and meeting rooms in the downtown area of a large midwestern city. The hotel employes approximately 250 people in full- and part-time positions. The housekeeping department is composed of approximately 100 employees with a manager, several assistant managers, and eight supervisors.

Eden, a women in her late fifties, had been employed by the hotel for three years and was responsible for cleaning a specified area in the hotel as assigned by her supervisor, Reggie Hays. Eden was also a maintenance specialist trainer for new employees.

Because of rotating schedules different supervisors might rotate such that one supervisor was not always with the same shift, although when a supervisor was gone, another on-duty supervisor would take responsibility for two or more areas. Each employee was assigned to a supervisor, but when that supervisor was gone the employees of that area would report to the substitute supervisor.

Eden resigned from the hotel citing unfair treatment by Ralph Murphy, the substitute supervisor for her area. One month later Eden filed a charge of discrimination based on age against the hotel with the state Equal Opportunity Commission. In her suit against the hotel Eden claimed that she felt compelled to resign because of unfair treatment by Murphy over the three years she had worked at the hotel. She also stated that she had asked for her job back if the problems between herself and Murphy could be resolved but she had not been allowed to tell her side of the story before the decision was made not to rehire her. Furthermore, she claimed that Murphy had singled her out on several occasions for extra work rather than assigning extra work to other employees.

Investigation of the charge against the hotel indicated that Eden had threatened to resign on several occasions over misunderstandings and errors in her personnel file. In each of these misunderstandings, the problem was re-

solved and Eden was satisfied. These incidents were minor in nature and not documented except for the changes made in her file—a change in her starting date and a change in her vacation hours. The starting date error went back to the time the hotel took over the housekeeping duties from a private contractor and hired their personnel.

Eden had worked for Murphy for several months right after the hotel assumed responsibility for its own housekeeping and had several encounters with him during this time and over the three years she worked at the hotel. Usually the encounters involved the cleaning of guest rooms, which were an addition to the regularly assigned rooms in Eden's area of responsibility as provided for in her job description. The housekeeping department's policy was that all empty rooms were to be cleaned by 3:30 P.M. and the rooms took priority over other areas for cleaning. Eden had resisted being assigned additional rooms on several occasions when Murphy was the substitute supervisor in charge. None of these incidents had ever resulted in written action by a supervisor, however.

The event that caused Eden to resign began on a Friday when Reggie Hays, her regular supervisor, was gone. Murphy observed Eden wearing her street clothes, a half hour before her scheduled quitting time, which was against hotel policy. He confronted her but took no action at that time. Instead, he discussed the incident with Hays for his opinion as her supervisor.

On the following Monday, Hays met with Eden and discussed the incident as reported by Murphy. Eden's reason for the early change was that her son was picking her up after work to take her out to dinner for her birthday and she wanted to be ready when he arrived. She also indicated that she had finished her assigned work. She gave no reason for not asking Murphy for an exception to the policy.

Hays re-emphasized the hotel's policy on street clothes but did not take further action since this was the first time Eden had violated the policy.

Eden left Hays's office and immediately went

to the assistant manager's office and resigned, citing unfair treatment by Ralph Murphy. She then proceeded to the manager's office and to the vice-president's office, each time giving her resignation and citing unfair treatment. All these actions were inconsistent with the hotel's established procedures for grievances and resignation.

Reggie Hays and the assistant manager of the department then met with Eden, discussed her desire to resign, and provided her with a resignation form, which she completed.

Eden took an authorized day off and then called in sick on five consecutive days, using all her accumulated sick leave. This left her with four days of her two-week notice. On the last day of her notice, she went to Reggie Hays and asked to be reinstated on the condition that the unfair treatment by Ralph Murphy be stopped.

Hays met with the assistant manager and then the manager of the department to discuss her request. Their decision was to accept her original resignation for the following reasons:

1. The temper outbursts displayed by Eden when she felt that the hotel's policies were wrong or that her records were not as they should be.

2. Eden had violated the hotel's procedure concerning grievances by resigning to three levels of management.

3. Eden had a problem accepting authority.

4. A replacement for her position had been hired during the two-week notice period and was to start the next working day.

QUESTIONS

1. In what ways is the "interface" concept of personnel management illustrated in this case?

2. How have organizational authority and structure problems contributed to the difficulties at Parker House Hotel?

3. Discuss how communication barriers and problems are present in the case.

4. If you were a consultant to the management of the hotel, what would you recommend to resolve this situation? What recommendations would you make to prevent future problems of a similar nature?

EQUAL EMPLOYMENT OPPORTUNITY

Before considering the individual activities in Human Resource management, there is one area of which the reader must be aware. Equal Employment Opportunity (EEO) permeates all facets of an organization's operations. It affects all other activities and should therefore be covered early in a textbook.

Chapter 4 examines the legal constraints presented by EEO in-the staffing process of an organization. Title VII of the Civil Rights Act of 1964 and landmark court cases have provided the general guidelines in this area. The different strategies for complying with EEO regulations are covered. Different concepts of validity also are explained.

Chapter 5 looks at issues associated with implementing EEO in an individual organization. Sex discrimination, handi-capped, and seniority issues are a few concerns viewed. Also, the charge processing of the Equal Employment Opportunity Commission and the components of Affirmative Action programs are examined. Affirmative Action and EEO recordkeeping requirements are important issues, of the discussion, as are reverse discrimination and age discrimination.

Equal Employment

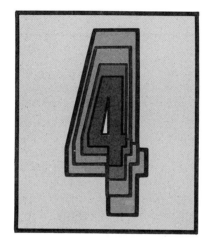

When you have read this chapter, you should be able to:

1. Briefly explain five legislative acts that deal with equal employment issues.
2. Describe the two most prominent equal employment enforcement agencies.
3. Identify and discuss four landmark equal employment opportunity (EEO) cases.
4. Discuss the two strategies to comply with the 1978 Uniform Guidelines.
5. Explain three means of validating employment methods.

PERSONNEL AT WORK
PAYING FOR DISCRIMINATION

Discrimination can be expensive, as a number of nationally-known firms have discovered. Whether the discrimination was based on age, sex, race, or other factors, a variety of U.S. employers have paid for discrimination. Some examples are:[1]

■ *A school district was ordered to pay a woman gym teacher $6,000 for illegal sex discrimination because of inferior working conditions. Unlike the boys' gym, the girls' gym lacked adequate light and ventilation, had no private office for the gym teacher, and lacked private shower and toilet facilities.*

■ *CF&I Steel Corporation agreed to pay $500,000 to 331 Hispanic employees for discriminating against them in promoting workers to supervisors. Also, CF&I agreed to pay $200,000 to 263 women in the production and maintenance departments for sex discrimination in promotions.*

■ *To settle employment discrimination charges over a 10-year period, General Motors agreed to pay $42.5 million. Included in the settlement were funds for special educational, training, and development programs for minorities and women. The agreement settled over 700 separate cases and covered all GM plants in the U.S.*

■ *United Airlines was ordered to pay $18 million in damages for violating age discrimination statutes. Thirty flight engineers who had been forced to retire at age 60, along with 82 pilots who were prohibited from transferring to flight engineer positions after age 60 received individual settlements up to $440,000, even though United was following a Federal Aviation Administration regulation prohibiting commercial pilots to fly after age 60. The jury awarded the defendants back pay and double damages. On appeal to the U.S. Supreme Court, the jury decision was overturned and a new lower court hearing was ordered.*

■ *John Folz, a hotel manager from Marriott Hotel Corporation who contracted multiple sclerosis was awarded back pay, front pay, and reinstatement of health care benefits. Although Marriott attempted to justify Folz's dissmissal as based on poor job performance, a federal district court rejected this argument.*

Not figured in the direct dollar costs of the above cases is the impact of discriminatory treatment on the productivity, turnover, and attitudes of employees and former employees. The experiences of these firms clearly demonstrates that discrimination does not pay in the long run.

"Our equality lies in the right, for each of us, to grow to our full capacity, whatever it is."

PEARL BUCK

As the opening examples of the costs of discrimination indicate, the days are past when employers can manage their work forces in any manner they wish. Laws have been passed prohibiting discrimination against individuals on the following common bases:

■ Race/ethnic origin/color (Black, Hispanic, Oriental, Pacific Islanders, American Indians, Eskimos, etc.)
■ Sex (women)
■ Age (individuals 40–70)
■ Physical and mental limitations (handicapped)
■ Military experience (Vietnam-era veterans)
■ Religion (special beliefs and practices)

The term "discrimination" has been used in many ways. The dictionary definition is a neutral one that identifies discrimination as recognizing the difference between, or differentiating between, items or people. For example, employers must discriminate between candidates for a job on the basis of job requirements and the candidate's qualifications. To simplify discussion of discrimination regulation, individuals who are covered under equal employment laws are referred to as "members of a protected class" or **"protected-group members."** To implement laws barring discrimination, several regulatory agencies have developed guidelines and regulations. Because of the importance of EEO the requirements mandated by federal, state, and local governments, this chapter and the next one focus on the nature and impact of this influence on personnel management practices.

EQUAL EMPLOYMENT LAWS AND REGULATIONS

Over the past three decades various laws have been passed that require employers to provide equal opportunity for people to be employed and to progress in their employment. Figure 4–1 contains a listing of the major EEO laws and regulations affecting employers. However, this discussion provides a basic outline of the subject and specific coverage of some of the most important areas.

1964 Civil Rights Act, Title VII

Discrimination against many minority groups is now clearly prohibited by law. The keystone of the structure of antidiscrimination legislation is the Civil Rights Act of 1964. Section 703A, Title VII, of the 1964 act states that:

It shall be unlawful employment practice for an employer (1) to fail or refuse to hire or to discharge any individual or otherwise to discriminate against any

PERSONNEL IN PRACTICE
"WOMEN NEED NOT APPLY?"

For many years and in many U.S. firms women were not considered for overseas jobs. Because of cultural values and historical traditions in some foreign countries, women who worked as professionals were a rarity, if such employment was allowed at all. Countries in the Middle East and Orient, in particular, still are problem areas for assignment of women. Unaccompanied women have difficulty obtaining visas to enter some countries. Also, the male-dominated culture of Japan has posed significant problems for women who attempt to represent U.S. firms to top-level Japanese executives.

Some observers believe that a shift toward acceptance of women for overseas assignments has begun. The decision by a large bank to send the first woman manager overseas ultimately was made at the top of the organization. Those women who do obtain overseas assignments are expected to be more qualified professionally and personally than men in similar positions, according to many observers. However, a growing number of women are interested in international assignments, as evidenced by the increasing numbers of women students at the American Graduate School of International Mangement in Arizona.

With the backing of some major U.S. firms, women appear to function effectively in foreign countries once the initial reluctance to send them is overcome. A woman executive with the Bank of America in Tokyo said, "If you are capable and you're in a position where you can demonstrate results quickly, being a woman is not an issue. Companies such as Sunoco, General Electric, Xerox, Levi Strauss, Citibank, and American Express have women executives overseas in Latin America, Nigeria, Russia, Great Britain, Mexico, Japan, China, and Brazil.

A related problem has been encountered by women in the U.S. who work for foreign-based firms. Some Japanese firms with U.S. operations have demonstrated reluctance to promote women into executive positions. Those positions have appeared to be "reserved" for Japanese nationals. Consequently, some discrimination charges have been brought against these firms.

In general, although signs of progress are appearing, for many companies offering overseas jobs, the unwritten practice still is: "Women need not apply." However, continued progress and enforcement of equal employment regulations can be expected to reduce the extent of this practice in the future.[3]

individual with respect to his compensation, terms, conditions, or privileges of employment because of such individual's race, color, religion, sex, or national origin; or (2) to limit, segregate or classify his employees in any way which would deprive or tend to deprive any individual of employment opportunities or otherwise inadvertently affect his status as an employee because of such individual's race, color, religion, sex, or national origin.

SECTION II EQUAL EMPLOYMENT OPPORTUNITY

ACT	YEAR	PROVISIONS
Title VII, Civil Rights Act	1964	Prohibits discrimination in employment on basis of race, religion, color, sex, or national origin.
Executive Orders 11246 and 11375	1965 1967	Requires federal contractors and subcontractors to eliminate employment discrimination and prior discrimination through affirmative actions.
Age Discrimination in Employment Act (as amended)	1967 1978	Prohibits discrimination against persons ages 40–70, and restricts mandatory retirement requirements, except where age is a "Bona Fide Occupational qualification."
Executive Order 11478	1969	Prohibits discrimination in the Postal Service and in the various government agencies on the basis of race, color, religion, sex, national origin, handicap, or age.
Pregnancy Discrimination Act	1978	Prohibits discrimination against women affected by pregnancy, childbirth, or related medical conditions. Requires that they be treated as all other employees for employment-related purposes, including benefits.
Equal Pay Act	1963	Requires equal pay for men and women performing substantially the same work.
Vocational Rehabilitation Act, Rehabilitation Act of 1974	1973 1974	Prohibits employers with federal contracts over $2,500 from discriminating against handicapped individuals.
Vietnam-Era Veterans Readjustment Act	1974	Prohibits discrimination against Vietnam-era veterans by federal contractors and the U.S. government and requires affirmative action.

The Civil Rights Act was passed by Congress in 1964, and took effect in 1965. It set up the mechanism for bringing about equality in hiring and job opportunity. As is often the case, the law contains ambiguous provisions which give great leeway to the agencies who enforce the law.

FIGURE 4–1
Major laws related to equal employment opportunity.

Who is Covered? Title VII, as amended by the Equal Employment Opportunity Act of 1972, covers:

■ All private employers of 15 or more persons who are employed 20 or more weeks per year
■ All educational institutions, public and private
■ State and local governments
■ Public and private employment agencies
■ Labor unions with 15 or more members
■ Joint (labor-management) committees for apprenticeships and training[4]

Any organization meeting one of these criteria is subject to rules and regulations of governmental agencies set up to administer the act.

Executive Orders 11246, 11375, and 11478

Beginning with President Franklin D. Roosevelt and continuing through the passage of the Civil Rights Act of 1964, numerous executive orders have been issued that require employers holding federal government contracts to be nondiscriminatory on the bases of race, color, religion, national origin, or sex. An executive order is issued by the President of the U.S. to provide direction to governmental departments.

During the 1960s, by executive order, the Office of Federal Contract Compliance Programs (OFCCP) in the Labor Department was established and given responsibility for enforcing nondiscrimination in government contracts. Under Executive Order 11246 issued in 1965 and amended by Executive Order 11375 in 1967, and updated by Executive Order 11478 in 1979, the Secretary of Labor was given the power to:

■ Publish the names of noncomplying contractors or unions
■ Recommend suits by the Justice Department to compel compliance
■ Recommend action by Equal Employment Opportunity Commission (EEOC) or the Justice Department to file suit in federal district court
■ Cancel the contract of a noncomplying contractor or blacklist a noncomplying employer from future government contracts

As enforced, these orders have required employers to take affirmative action to overcome the effects of past discriminatory practices. A detailed discussion of affirmative action is in Chapter 5.

Age Discrimination in Employment Acts

The Age Discrimination in Employment Act of 1967, amended in 1978, makes it illegal for an employer to discriminate in compensation, terms, conditions, or privileges of employment because of an employee's age.

It is unlawful (1) to fail or refuse to hire or to discharge or otherwise discriminate against any individual, applicant, or employee 40 to 70 years old as to compensation, terms, conditions, or privileges of employment because of age, or because he has opposed an unlawful employment practice or taken part in asserting his rights against an employer who has unlawfully so discriminated, (2) to limit, segregate, or classify employees so as to deprive any employee 40 to 70 years old of employment opportunities or adversely affect his status as an employee because of his age, (3) to use printed or published notices or advertisements indicating any preference, limitation, specification, or discrimination based upon age, (4) to reduce the salary rate of any employee in order to comply with the act.[5]

The 1978 amendment to the 1967 Age Discrimination Act stated that employees in private business having at least 20 persons on the payroll can no longer be forced to retire prior to age 70. Federal workers cannot be forced to retire at any age. Pension law, however, requires full vesting of pension rights no later than age 65 if the employee has at least 10 years' service. Employees may continue to retire at age 65 with full benefits if they desire. However, businesses can retire a high-level executive with a retirement income of $27,000 or more at age 65, as long as he or she is in a "high-level policy-making position," and has been in that job for two years.[6]

The act does not apply if age is a *Bona fide* occupational qualification. For example, it was ruled legal for a bus company to refuse to hire an entry-level driver age 45 or more, because of training, experience, and licensing requirements. Nor do the prohibitions against age discrimination apply when an individual is disciplined or discharged for good cause, such as poor job performance. Older workers who are poor performers can be terminated just like anyone else.

A person's ability to do a job does not necessarily decrease with increased age. Unless jobs require heavy, physical labor, workers from 65 to 75 generally perform as well as younger workers. Older workers tend to be more accurate, can compensate for age difficulties with experience, have increased responsibility, and tend to change jobs and be absent less frequently than younger workers. However, they generally have less ability to work at high speed, less capacity to memorize, and a slower rate of learning.[7]

Equal Pay Act of 1963

As a part of amendments to the Fair Labor Standards Act (FLSA) in 1963, 1968, and 1972, the Equal Pay Act attempts to prohibit wage discrimination on the basis of sex. As the Wage and Hour Division of the U.S. Labor Department states:

The equal pay provisions of the FLSA prohibit wage differentials based on sex, between men and women employed in the same establishment on jobs that require equal skill, effort, and responsibility and which are performed under similar working conditions.[8]

To qualify, jobs must be "substantially" the same, but not necessarily identical. For example, one midwestern department store chain was assessed $750,000 in back pay for paying women who managed women's ready-to-wear departments less than male managers of men's wear departments.

Pay differentials on the basis of merit or seniority are not prohibited if they are not based on sex discrimination. However, the lower pay that women have traditionally received for the same jobs that men perform can no longer be justified on the basis of future promotability.

"The motion has been made and seconded that we obey the law."

From Wall Street Journal, Permission: Cartoon Features Syndicate.

Paying a man more because the employer believes the man has a greater possibility of staying with the organization is not allowed. In the past, some employers felt women should be paid less because the employer believes the man has a greater possibility of staying with the organization is not allowed. Also, some employers felt women should be paid less because they might quit to marry, become pregnant, or have to move because their spouses were transferred. However, such concerns often are not true and, in any event, they cannot be used to justify pay differences.

Comparable Worth Issue. Although discussed later in more detail, it seems appropriate to mention the issue of comparable worth here. The concept underlying comparable worth is that jobs having comparable knowledge, skills, and abilities should be paid at comparable levels. One view is that it is discriminatory to have a situation in which jobs of comparable worth have unequal levels of compensation. Another view is that supply and demand, rather than discriminatory actions by an employer who "follows the market," is what creates such disparities. Nevertheless, employers must be mindful of future cases and rulings on the comparable worth issue when developing pay systems.

Pregnancy Discrimination Act

In 1978, a federal law, the Pregnancy Discrimination Act (PDA), was passed as an amendment to the Civil Rights Act of 1964. This act requires that women employees "affected by pregnancy, childbirth, or related medical conditions will be treated the same for all employment related purposes."[9] The major impact of the act was to change maternity leave policies and employee benefit systems. Under the PDA, pregnancy must be treated just like any other medical condition. The same provisions regarding disability insurance and leaves of absence must apply to pregnant employees as to all other workers. A more detailed discussion of the impact of the PDA is contained in the next chapter.

Vocational Rehabilitation Act

Disabled and handicapped people have special discrimination problems because they often are not considered for jobs they could perform. To deal with their concerns, in 1973 Congress passed the Vocational Rehabilitation Act, and in 1974 it passed 12 amendments officially titled the Rehabilitation Act of 1974. These acts constitute the basis for federal intervention concerning employment of the handicapped.

Generally, the effect of the law and subsequent executive orders is as follows:

1. Federal contractors and subcontractors with contracts valued at more than $2,500 must take affirmative action to hire qualified handicapped people.

2. Contractors have an obligation to inform all employees and unions about their affirmative action plans and to survey their internal labor forces to locate qualified handicapped employees.

3. The Architectural Barriers Act of 1968 attempts to ensure that buildings financed with public money are accessible to the handicapped.

It should be noted that private businesses that do not have federal contracts *are not covered* by the act. However, they may be subject to state laws that prohibit discrimination on the basis of physical or mental disability.

Vietnam-Era Veterans Readjustment Act

Concern about the readjustment and absorption of Vietnam-era veterans into the workforce led to the passage of the Vietnam-Era Veterans Readjustment Act. The act requires that affirmative action in hiring and advancing Vietnam-era veterans be undertaken by federal contractors and subcontractors having contracts of $10,000 or more.

State and Local Employment Laws

In addition to the federal laws and orders, many of the states and municipalities have passed their own laws prohibiting discrimination on a variety of bases. Often these laws are modeled after federal laws; however, they can require different actions or prohibit discrimination in areas beyond those addressed by federal law. For example, in several cities in California laws have been passed to prohibit discrimination against individuals who do not smoke or who have differing sexual preferences.

Can you explain five acts that deal with equal employment issues?

ENFORCEMENT AGENCIES

Several governmental agencies have the power to investigate illegal and discriminatory practices. The two most prominent of these agencies are the Equal Employment Opportunity Commission and the Office of Federal Contract Compliance Programs.

Equal Employment Opportunity Commission (EEOC)

The EEOC was created by the Civil Rights Act of 1964 to be the agency responsible for enforcing the employment-related provisions. The agency initiates investigations, responds to complaints, and develops guidelines to enforce Title VII regulations.

The EEOC has been given expanded powers several times since 1964 and is the major agency involved with employment discrimination. Where the courts have upheld the EEOC's finding of discrimination, they have ruled that remedies include back pay and remedial "affirmative action." Over the years the EEOC has been given the responsibility to investigate equal pay violations, age discrimination, and handicapped discrimination, in addition to areas identified by Title VII of the Civil Rights Act.

Commission Membership. As an independent regulatory agency, the EEOC is composed of five members appointed by the President and confirmed by the Senate. No more than three members of the commission can be from the same political party and members serve for seven years. In addition, the EEOC has a staff of lawyers and investigators who do investigative and followup work for the commission.

Office of Federal Contract Compliance Programs (OFCCP)

Whereas the EEOC is an independent agency, much like the Interstate Commerce Commission or the Federal Aviation Administration, the OFCCP is part of the Department of Labor. The OFCCP was established by executive order to ensure that federal contractors and subcontractors have nondiscriminatory practices. A major thrust of OFCCP efforts focuses on requirements that federal contractors and subcontrators take affirmative action to overcome the effects of prior discriminatory practices. Affirmative action plans are discussed in detail in the next chapter.

Can you describe the two most prominent
equal employment enforcement agencies?

LANDMARK COURT CASES

The laws discussed above that establish the legal basis for Equal Employment Opportunity generally have been written in a broad manner. Consequently, it is only through application of the laws to specific organizational situations that the laws truly affect employers. The broad nature of the laws has led the enforcement agencies, especially the EEOC, to develop guidelines and to enforce the acts as they deem appropriate. However, agency rulings and the language of those rulings have caused confusion and differing interpretations by employers. Interpretation of the ambiguous provisions in the laws also changes as the membership of the agencies change. Consequently, the court system must resolve the disputes and issue interpretations of the laws. Even the courts, especially lower level courts, have issued conflicting rulings and interpretations. The ultimate interpretation has often rested on decisions by the U.S. Supreme Court, although Supreme Court rulings, too, have been interpreted differently.

The important point to be remembered is that equal employment opportunity is a dynamic, evolving concept that often appears to be confusing because of conflicting decisions and rulings by courts and agencies. The cases discussed next are regarded as major precedent-setting decisions.

Griggs v. Duke Power

In March of 1971, the Supreme Court's decision in the case of *Griggs* v. *Duke Power Company*[10] put some teeth in the Civil Rights Act. As a result, companies must be able to prove that their selection procedures do not tend to discriminate. The Griggs case dealt with a promotion and transfer policy which required individuals to have both a high school diploma and to obtain a satisfactory score on two professionally developed aptitude tests. One of the tests was the Wonderlic Intelligence Test, which blacks failed at a higher rate than whites. In addition, fewer blacks had high school diplomas than whites.

The U.S. Supreme Court ruled that Title VII of the Civil Rights Act prohibits not only overt discrimination, but also practices which are fair in form but discriminatory in operation. This decision established two major points: 1) it is not enough to show a lack of discriminatory intent if the selection tool results in a *disproportionate effect* that discriminates against one group more than another or continues a past pattern of discrimination, and 2) the employer has the burden of proving that an employment requirement is directly job-related. Consequently, the use of the intelligence test and the high school diploma requirements were ruled to be not job-related.

Albemarle Paper v. Moody

The 1975 Supreme Court case of *Albermarle Paper* v. *Moody*[11] reaffirmed the idea that any "test" used for selecting or promoting employees must be a valid predictor or performance measure for a particular job. The term "test" includes such items as performance appraisals used for promotion decisions. The Court also found that if it can be shown that any selection test has an adverse impact (evidenced by hiring or promotion, for instance, that does not result in a pattern similar to minority representation in the population), the burden of proof for showing the test is valid falls upon the employer. Employment tests also must be sound predictors of a person's future job success.

Washington v. Davis

A 1976 Supreme Court decision in a case involving the hiring of police officers in Washington, D.C., represents a slightly different emphasis. In this case the issue was a reading comprehension and aptitude test given to all applicants for police officer positions. The test contained actual material that the applicants would have to learn during a training program. Also, the city could show a good relationship between success in the training program and success as a police officer. The problem with the test was that a much higher percentage of women and blacks than white men failed this aptitude test.

The court ruled that the city of Washington, D.C., did not discriminate unfairly because the test was definitely job-related. The implication of this case is that if a test is clearly related to the job and tasks performed, it is *not* illegal simply because a greater percentage of minorities or women do not pass it. The crucial outcome is that a test must be specifically job-related, and cannot be judged solely on its adverse impact.[12]

Kaiser Aluminum v. Weber

In this 1979 case Brian Weber, a white steelworker, charged Kaiser Aluminum and his union, the United Steelworkers, with "reverse discrimination." Weber sued because he was denied admission to a training program even though he had more seniority than some black workers admitted to the program. Because blacks were underrepresented in crafts jobs at Kaiser, a voluntary quota system and special crafts training programs were agreed to by the company and the union. Under the agreement 50 percent of the slots in a crafts training program were reserved for the blacks.

The U.S. Supreme Court ruled that because the company and union voluntarily agreed to the affirmative action plan that gave preference to blacks, the plan did not violate Title VII provisions. The key portion of the decision says "The inference that Congress did not wish to ban all voluntary, race-conscious affirmative action is further supported by its use of the word 'require' rather than 'permit' in Title VII." The relevant sentence from Title VII says that "nothing in Title VII shall be interpreted to 'require' any employer to grant preferential treatment to any group, because of that group's race. . ." Also, because the preference policy did not require discharging white workers and replacing them with black workers, the plan was a temporary measure used to eliminate racial inequality.[13]

Some experts have indicated that the Supreme Court really "ducked the issue" by using one word as the basis for the decision. The *Weber* case did provide some guidance, but it did not settle the legal status of "reverse discrimination" once and for all,[14] as the discussion on reverse discrimination in Chapter 5 indicates.

Texas Department of Community Affairs v. Burdine

This 1981 U.S. Supreme Court case focused on sex discrimination. Joyce Burdine was denied a promotion that was given to a male and was then terminated during a staff reduction. Consequently, Burdine charged sex discrimination was the basis for the actions against her.

The court decision dealt with the burden of proof required by individuals charging discrimination and by employers who must defend their actions. First, an individual must prove a *prima facie* case that he or she is a member of a protected group, applied for a job that was available, and was rejected. If that is proved, the burden of proof shifts to the employer, who must "articulate a legitimate nondiscriminatory reason" for taking the action in question.[15] Prior to this decision, employers had a greater requirement to prove they did not discriminate rather than forcing the individual to prove that the employer did discriminate. This decision also clarified the shifting character of EEO decisions by the Supreme Court.

Ford Motor Company v. EEOC

The Supreme Court in 1982 held that an employer may cut off its liability for back pay awarded as a result of a discrimination case by making an unconditional offer of reinstatement to the individual charging discrimination. If the individual refuses a job substantially equivalent to the one he or she was denied, the individual forfeits the right to back pay. An unconditional offer of employment does not require the employer to provide the employee with either retroactive seniority or back pay. The employee may continue the lawsuit in an effort to be awarded those damages.[16]

Arizona Governing Committee v. Norris

The Supreme Court in 1983 held that an employer's deferred compensation plan violated Title VII because female employees received lower monthly benefit payments than men upon retirement, despite the fact that women contributed equally to the plan. Although the difference in benefit payments was due to sex-segregated actuarial tables which reflected that women, as a class, live longer than men, the court rejected the employer's defense that sex may be used to predict longevity.[17]

   The impact of the decision was that many pension plans had to be revised. Regardless of longevity differences, men and women who contribute equally to pension plans must receive equal monthly payments. Over 450,000 pension plans containing over 25 million workers were affected by this decision.[18]

Memphis Firefighters, Local 1784 v. Stotts (1984)

This 1984 landmark case clarified and reinforced the concept that a bonafide seniority system cannot be overturned to protect individuals hired through an affirmative action plan. Understanding the facts in the case helps to clarify the impact of the decision.

   In 1981, city budget problems in Memphis forced a decision to be made to layoff a number of city workers. Carl Stotts, a black firefighter, filed suit asking the U.S. District Court to protect blacks and other minorities from layoff in order to maintain gains in employment made by protected group members. Otherwise, the seniority provisions of "last hired, first laid-off" would result in many protected group members being released. Although the District Court ruled for Stotts, a U.S. Supreme Court decision reversed this ruling.[19]

   The Supreme Court decision said, "It is inappropriate to deny an innocent employee the benefits of his seniority. . .", especially when those seniority rights are contrasted with the rights of other individuals under an affirmative action plan. Although this case did not directly address "voluntary affirmative action or hiring goals," it did provide an indication that further Supreme Court decisions on the viability of affirmative action are likely.

   *Can you identify and discuss at least four
   landmark EEO cases?*

ADVERSE IMPACT occurs when there is a substantially different rate in hiring, promotion, or other employment decisions which works to the disadvantage of members of protected groups.[21]

To implement the provisions of the Civil Rights Act of 1964, and the interpretations of it based upon court decisions, the Equal Employment Opportunity Commission and other federal agencies developed compliance guidelines and regulations. However, each governmental entity had a slightly different set of rules and expectations. Finally, in 1978 the major government agencies involved agreed upon a set of uniform guidelines.

Uniform Guidelines on Employee Selection Procedures

The 1978 guidelines apply to the EEOC, the Department of Labor's OFCCP, the Department of Justice, and the Office of Personnel Mangement.[20] They provide a framework used to determine if employers are adhering to federal laws on discrimination.

These guidelines affect virtually all phases of personnel management because they apply to tests and other selection procedures used in making employment decisions, including but not limited to the following:

- Hiring (qualifications required, application blanks, interviews, tests)
- Promotions (qualifications, selection process)
- Recruiting (advertising, availability of announcements)
- Demotion (why made, punishments given)
- Performance appraisals (methods used, how used for promotions and pay increases)
- Training (access to training programs, development efforts)
- Labor union membership requirements (apprenticeship programs, work assignments)
- Licensing and certification requirements (job requirements tied to job qualifications)

The guidelines apply to most employment-related decisions, not just the initial hiring process. Within the guidelines two major means of compliance are identified: 1) "No Adverse Impact" Strategy, and 2) Job-Related Validation Strategy.

"No Adverse Impact" Strategy. Generally, when courts have found that there is discrimination, they have found that the most important issue is the *effect* of employment policies and procedures, regardless of their *intent*. A practice, however harmless in intent, that results in an adverse impact on members of a protected group is considered discriminatory. The *Griggs* v. *Duke Power* decision is an example of such a ruling. **Adverse impact** occurs when there is a substantial under representation of protected group members in employment decisions.

The Uniform Guidelines identify the "no adverse impact" strategy in the following statement:

These guidelines do not require a user to conduct validity studies of selection procedures where no adverse impact results.[22]

When the percentage of protected workers in any job classification is not proportional to their representation in the surrounding population or work force, strong evidence of discriminatory practices and adverse impact exists. A company that has only 3 percent minority employees when the minority workforce in the area is 15 percent will have to show that its hiring is truly nondiscriminatory.

Some have skeptically suggested that this approach comes down to "getting your numbers in line." A partial rejection of the idea that discrimination can be avoided simply by meeting quotas was voiced in a 1982 U.S. Supreme Court decision in *Connecticut* v. *Teal*.[23] The Court said that because Title VII focused on the individual instead of a protected group as a whole, arriving at the proper *"bottom-line"* results does not eliminate the discrimination suffered by individuals. Though the Court's ruling somewhat restricts the application of the "no adverse impact" strategy, personnel professionals still should be aware of the principle since court decisions can shift over time. A caution for employers attempting to use the "quota" approach is that to meet this compliance requirement there must be no adverse impact at *all levels* and in *all job groups*. Consequently, "getting the numbers in line" is not really as easy or risk-free as it may appear to be.

Under the guidelines, adverse impact is determined using the "⅘ rule." The ⅘ **rule** points to discrimination if the selection rate for any protected group is less than 80 percent (⅘ of the selection rate for majority groups).

An example (Figure 4–2) shows how one phase of a firm's employment practices are evaluated for adverse impact. In Midville the labor force is 20 percent black and 60 percent white. In Orbus Company, which has 600 employees, 108 of the employees (18%) are black. Consequently, there is no adverse impact because ¹⁸⁄₂₀ equals 90%. Another

The ⅘ RULE states that discrimination generally occurs if the selection rate for a protected group is less than 80 percent of the selection rate of the majority group.

FIGURE 4–2
Adverse impact example.

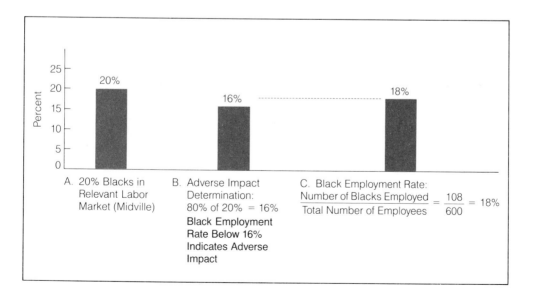

A. 20% Blacks in Relevant Labor Market (Midville)

B. Adverse Impact Determination: 80% of 20% = 16% Black Employment Rate Below 16% Indicates Adverse Impact

C. Black Employment Rate:
$$\frac{\text{Number of Blacks Employed}}{\text{Total Number of Employees}} = \frac{108}{600} = 18\%$$

example of the ⅘ rule is shown in Figure 4–3. Assume that Standard Company interviewed both men and women for manufacturing assembly jobs. Of the men who applied, 40 percent were hired; of the women who applied, 25 percent were hired. As shown, the selection rate for women is less than 80 percent (⅘) of the selection rate for men because ²⁵⁄₄₀ equals 62.5%. Consequently, Standard Company does have an "adverse impact" in its employment process.

The major advantage of the ⅘ rule is that it is a yardstick that employers can use to determine if they have adverse impact. For areas in which adverse impact exists, employers may then turn to the other compliance strategy of validating that employment decisions are based on job-related information. However, as described later, U.S. Steel managed to violate both strategies.

Job-Related Validation Strategy. The idea that employment practices must be valid involves such practices and "tests" as job descriptions, educational requirements, experience requirements, work skills, application forms, interviews, paper and pencil tests, and performance appraisals. Hence, the concept of validity affects many of the common tools used to make employment and promotion decisions.

Validity simply means that a "test" actually predicts what it says it predicts. For a general intelligence test to be valid, it must actually measure intelligence, not just a person's vocabulary. Therefore, an employment test that is valid must measure the person's ability to perform the job for which he or she is being hired.

A test is said to be valid for selection purposes if there is a significant statistical relationship between performance on the test and performance on the job. The better a test can predict satisfactory and unsatisfactory performance on the job, the greater its validity. Applicants'

FIGURE 4–3
Determining adverse impact.

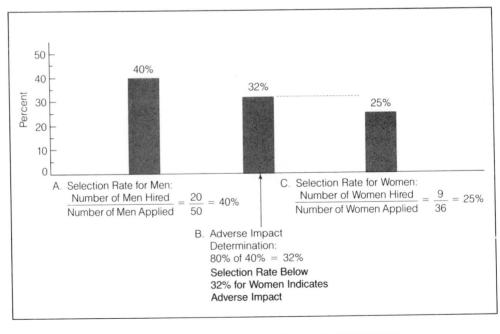

RELIABILITY
refers to the consistency
with which a test mea-
sures an item.

PERSONNEL IN PRACTICE

NONCOMPLIANCE AT U.S. STEEL

U.S. Steel Corporation had the unique experience of being found in violation of both of the equal employment compliance strategies because of its employment practices at its Fairless Hill, Pennsylvania plant. To understand the decision, it is first necessary to describe the employment situation.

Between 1972 and 1981, U.S. Steel had approximately 50,000 applicants for the 7,000–10,000 positions at the plant, most of which were for entry-level laborer jobs. Most of the applicants met the job specifications in terms of physical condition, literacy, and age. As jobs became available, applicants were called for interviews, and U.S. Steel kept a running tally to see what percentage of minorities were hired. If more minorities were needed, more blacks were called for interviews. A group of black applicants who were not hired filed suit claiming race discrimination because the black hire rate (18 percent) should have been in proportion to the black applicant rate (26 percent), even though the work force in the area was 9½–11½ percent black.

The ruling in a federal district court in Pennsylvania was for the applicants. The court decision said that the actual applicant flow rate of 26 percent should have been used as the target percentage because it represented the actual available work force, not a hypothetical one in the area. Consequently, the "no adverse impact" strategy used by the company was rejected.

U.S. Steel also claimed that it used valid hiring procedures to identify the most qualified candidates and the lower rate of blacks selected was due to the inferior qualifications of the blacks. Determination of who was the most qualified was made by supervisors who conducted the interviews. However, the court ruled that the interviewers had not been trained in interviewing and the hiring criteria of education, experience, no prior criminal record, attitude, personality, alertness, and initiative were too vague and subjective. Consequently, the hiring procedures were ruled to be too subjective, open to bias, and non-systematic.[24]

The result was that U.S. Steel had violated not just one, but both of the compliance strategies identified in the 1978 Uniform Guidelines. This case illustrates how the guidelines and the strategies stated in them require careful application in practice.

scores on valid tests can be used to predict their probable job performance by computing *correlation coefficients*. Correlation coefficients are a measure of the extent to which any two measures move together. Acceptable validity coefficients may be as low as .30 for "practical significance", due to intervening variables.

Along with determining validity, it is important to check the reliability of tests. **Reliability** is a consistency measure. For a test to be reliable, an individual's score should be about the same every time the individual takes it (allowing for the effects of practice). Unless a test measures a trait consistently (or reliably), it is of little value in predicting job performance. Acceptable reliability coefficients are quite high—a correlation of .80 or better.

Another dimension of reliability is the "internal consistency" of a measure or test. For example, assume both a supervisor and the supervisor's boss complete a performance appraisal for an engineer. If the two ratings of the engineer's performance are quite different, the performance appraisal is not very reliable. The relationship of validity and reliability are shown in Figure 4–4.

Can you discuss the two strategies to comply with the 1978 Uniform Guidelines?

VALIDITY AND EQUAL EMPLOYMENT

If a charge of discrimination is brought against a company and adverse impact is established, the company must be able to demonstrate that its employment procedures are valid. By valid, it is meant that the employment "tests" are related to the job and the requirements of the job.

General aptitude and psychological tests, such as those dealing with mental abilities, are very difficult to validate because a test must measure the person for the job and not the person in abstract, as emphasized in *Griggs* v. *Duke Power*. The Uniform Guidelines recognize three types of validity:

1. Criterion-related (predictive and concurrent)
2. Construct validity
3. Content validity

These types of validity, as they relate to employment practices, are discussed next.

Criterion-Related Validity

Employment "tests" of any kind attempt to predict how well an individual will perform on the job. The "test" is labeled the *predictor* and the desired job knowledge, skills, abilities, and behaviors are called the *criterion variables*. Careful analysis of the jobs for which the test is being used as a predictor is necessary. This job analysis determines as exactly

FIGURE 4–4

Relationship of validity and reliability.

		Valid?	
		NO	YES
Reliable?	YES	Common but illegal and poor management practices	Most desirable, legally required
	NO	Common but illegal and poor management practices	Impossible condition

SOURCE: Contributed by Dr. Roger A. Dean, Washington and Lee University.

as possible what knowledge, skills, abilities, and behaviors are needed for each task in the job. Tests are then devised and used as predictors to measure different dimensions of the criterion-related variables. Examples of "tests" are: requiring a college degree, scoring 50 words per minute on a typing test, or having five years of banking experience. These predictors are then validated against the criteria used to measure job performance, such as performance appraisals, sales records, or absenteeism rates. Some court cases, such as *Albermarle Paper* v. *Moody*, have pointed out the difficulty in using subjective performance appraisals by supervisors as the criteria against which the tests are validated. However, if the predictors do satisfactorily predict job performance behavior, they are legally acceptable and quite useful in selection.

Within criterion-related validity there are two different approaches: 1) predictive validity, and 2) concurrent validity. Predictive validity is a "before-the-fact" approach, while concurrent validity represents an "at-the-same-time" approach to validity.

Predictive Validity. This method of validating employment practices is calculated by giving a test and then comparing the test results to the job performance of those tested. Figure 4–5 outlines the predictive validity process.

The following example illustrates how a predictive validity study might be designed. A retail chain, Eastern Discount, wants to establish the predictive validity of requiring one year of cashiering experience, a "test" it plans to use to hire cashiers. Obviously, the retail outlet wants a test that will do the very best job of separating those who will do well from those who will not. Eastern Discount first hires 30 people, regardless of their cashiering experience. Sometime later (perhaps six months) the performance of employees who joined the company with and without cashiering experience is compared with the 30 employees' job success. Success on the job is measured by such yardsticks as absenteeism, accidents, errors, or results of performance appraisals. If those employees who had one year of experience demonstrate better

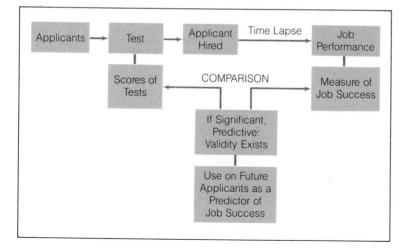

FIGURE 4–5
Predictive validity.

performance, as statistically compared to those without such experience, then the experience requirement is considered a valid predictor of performance and may be used to hire future employees.

In the past, predictive validity has been preferred by EEOC because it is presumed to give the strongest tie to job performance. However, predictive validity requires: 1) a fairly large number of people, and 2) a time gap between the "test" and the performance. As a result, it is not useful in many situations. Because of this and other problems, another type of validity often is used—concurrent validity.

Concurrent Validity. Concurrent means "at the same time." As shown in Figure 4–6, when an employer uses concurrent validity, current employees instead of newly-hired employees are used to validate the test. The test is given to current employees and the scores are correlated with their performance ratings as determined by such measures as accident rates, absenteeism records, or supervisory performance appraisals. A high correlation suggests that the test is able to differentiate between the better and the poorer employees.

A major potential drawback of concurrent validity is that those employees who performed poorly in their jobs are no longer with the firm and therefore cannot be tested, and the extremely good employees may have been promoted or may have left the organization for a better job. Thus, the firm does not really have a representative range of people to test. Another problem is that any learning that has taken place on the job influences the test score. Therefore, applicants taking the test without the benefit of on-the-job experience might score low on the test, but might be able to do the job well.

Construct Validity

A second type of validity, construct validity, is based on an idea or characteristic inferred from research. Most tests are designed to measure something; that "something" is typically an intangible or abstract construct, such as the intelligence quotient (IQ), which attempts to

FIGURE 4–6
Concurrent validity.

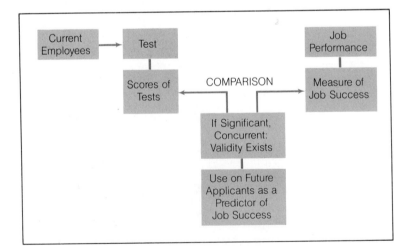

measure a person's basic intelligence. Other common constructs for which tests have been devised are creativity, leadership potential, and interpersonal sensitivity. Because a hypothetical construct is used as a predictor in establishing this type of validity, personality tests and other such constructs are more likely to face questions concerning their legality and usefulness than other measures of validity.

Content Validity

This type of validity uses a logical and nonstatistical approach. A test is said to be content-valid if a person performs an *actual sample* of the work done on the job. Thus, an arithmetic test for a cashier contains some of the calculations that a cashier would have to make on the job. Content validity is especially useful if the work force is not large enough to accommodate better statistical designs. Content validity is a solid alternative because its basic requirement is a good analysis of what tasks one performs in a job. By knowing exactly what is done, a test can be derived using an actual work sample.

In a metropolitan U.S. city a personnel specialist analyzed and rated the tasks of current firefighters to establish a test for firefighter applicants. Then, at a training center, a test was devised that reflected a realistic sample of a firefighter's job. Instead of having applicants lift weights to test strength, all applicants were required to drag a 75-pound hose up three flights of stairs in a four-minute period. This test represented the average conditions firefighters actually face in a real fire.

Another example is the structured interview used by a financial institution. The questions in the employment interview are tailored to the actual job being sought by an applicant. Questions for a teller focus specifically on customer service and experience with computer terminals. However, questions for an accounts payable clerk deal with accounting experience and numerical problem identification.

Growth of Content Validity. Many practitioners and specialists see content validity as a way to validate staffing requirements using a commonsense approach. Employment requirements are viewed in terms of job requirements rather than through more statistically-oriented methods. In the *Washington v. Davis* case discussed earlier, the Supreme Court also appeared to give support to the content validity approach because the training course test given by the police department represented actual training materials used by police officers.

Embodying modern views of personnel management, the legislation and court decisions mentioned earlier are forcing employers to make changes that should have been made earlier. Using an invalid instrument to select, place, or promote an employee has never been a good management practice, and now it is illegal. Management also should be concerned with using valid instruments from the standpoint of the efficiency of operations. Use of invalid tests may result in screening out individuals who might have been satisfactory performers or the hiring of less-satisfactory workers. Many organizations are increasing

LOOKS AREN'T EVERYTHING

Is attractiveness a job-related requirement for a TV news anchor? Is ugliness a protected characteristic under equal employment regulations? These questions illustrate an emerging area of discrimination that is based on appearance.

The most publicized case of appearance discrimination has been the case of Christine Craft, a TV news anchor. In 1981, KMBC in Kansas City replaced Craft as an anchor because she was "too old, unattractive, and not deferential enough to men," according to the station manager. During the trial in the court case filed by Craft against KMBC, testimony was given about Craft's two years at the station. After being hired, Craft was required to meet with a clothing and cosmetics consultant. However, her male co-anchor received few similar demands. Also, Craft contended that she was hired for her journalistic skills and the station had made fraudulent promises when she was hired. The jury in that trial awarded Craft $500,000, but the judgment was thrown out by the judge as excessive and a new trial ordered. In the second trial, Craft again won and was awarded $325,000.

Other individuals have brought cases of employment discrimination based upon appearance because of being too fat or unattractive. A woman weighing over 300 pounds was rejected for employment as a clerical worker for an electric utility. In another case an airline fired a woman flight attendant for being too unattractive and overweight. Employers lost in both cases because of their inability to prove any direct job-related value in their requirements.

These situations and others like them illustrate that the subject of equal employment opportunity is a constantly changing area. For occupations and industries in which public presence and image is deemed important by managers, the desire for physically attractive individuals as employees may conflict with the job-related requirements of equal employment regulations. Experts who commented on the Craft case indicated that an increasing number of similar cases is likely in other industries besides the television industry. Stay tuned to see the future of appearance discrimination.[25]

the use of instruments that have been demonstrated to be valid. In one sense, the current requirements have done management a favor because they force employers to do what they probably should have been doing previously—using job-related employment procedures.

Can you explain three types of validity?

SUMMARY

■ Equal employment opportunity laws prohibit discrimination against protected-group individuals.

■ The 1964 Civil Rights Act, Title VII, is the most significant equal employment law, but there are several others that address specific discrimination problems:
  ■ Executive Order 11246, 11375, and 11478
  ■ Age Discrimination in Employment Acts
  ■ Pregnancy Discrimination Act
  ■ Equal Pay Act
  ■ Vocational Rehabilitation Acts
  ■ Vietnam-Era Veterans Readjustment Act
■ The Equal Employment Opportunity Commission (EEOC) and the Office of Federal Contract Compliance Programs (OFCCP) are the major federal equal employment enforcement agencies.
■ There have been a number of landmark cases concerning discrimination in personnel practices. These court cases have helped define what enforcement agencies consider to be discrimination.
■ The 1978 Uniform Guidelines are used by the enforcement agencies to examine hiring, promotions, recruiting, and other employment practices.
■ Under the 1978 guidelines two alternative compliance strategies are identified: 1) "no adverse impact" strategy; 2) job-related validation strategy.
■ Adverse impact is determined through use of the 4/5 rule.
■ Job-related validation requires that "tests" measure what they are supposed to measure (validity) in a consistent manner (reliability).
■ There are three types of validity—criterion-related, construct, and content.
■ The two approaches of criterion-related validity are predictive validity and concurrent validity. Whereas predictive validity is a "before-the-fact" measure, concurrent validity uses tests and criteria measures available at the same time.
■ Construct validity shows a relationship between a measure of an abstract characteristic, such as intelligence, and job performance.
■ Content validity is growing in use because it shows the job-relatedness of a measure based upon the fact that it is a sample of the actual work to be performed.

REVIEW QUESTIONS AND EXERCISES

1. Various laws have been passed to provide equal employment protection for a number of groups of people. Identify five protected groups and the appropriate laws and briefly describe each law.
2. What agencies enforce equal employment opportunity regulations?
3. Identify the impact of each of the following court cases:
  a. *Griggs* v. *Duke Power*
  b. *Albermarle Paper* v. *Moody*
  c. *Washington* v. *Davis*
  d. *Memphis Firefighters Local 1784* v. *Stotts*
4. Why is validation considered to be a more business-oriented strategy than a "no adverse impact" strategy of complying with the 1978 Uniform Guidelines?

CHAPTER 4 EQUAL EMPLOYMENT

5. Explain what validity is and why content validity is growing in use compared to the construct and criterion-related types.

Exercise

a. Think about a job you have now or have had in the past. Then identify the "work samples" from that job that could be used as a part of a content validity test. Be specific and identify how you would "score" performance on the test and how it relates to ongoing job performance.

CASE:
KEEP ON TRUCKIN'?

Tim Roe owns a small trucking firm that specializes in local and metropolitan area deliveries in a large city in the United States. All employment activities are handled by Roe who has always hired employees on the basis of three qualifications:

1. They must have a high school diploma
2. They must pass a short paper-and-pencil test which is given to all applicants
3. They must have a valid driver's license if applying for the position of driver

The short test was devised by Roe from sample questions found on a General Education Degree (GED) Equivalency Test. The test consists of 33 vocabulary and mathematical questions, each worth 3 points. Anyone scoring below 70 is automatically rejected.

Last month two drivers quit, so Roe advertised in the local paper for two new drivers. Ten people applied for the openings, but Roe rejected four applicants because they were not high school graduates. Three others were rejected because of test scores below 70. The two white males who were hired scored the highest on the test, had high school degrees, and also had valid driver's licenses.

This week Roe was notified that two equal employment complaints had been filed against him and his firm. One complainant, a woman, alleges that the test does not measure a person's ability to drive and is not a valid predictor of job success. The other complainant, a minority man, alleges that the high school diploma requirement is not related to ability to do the job and unfairly discriminates against minorities. Roe is trying to decide how to respond to these complaints.

Questions

1. Identify and discuss problems with the validity of Roe's test?
2. What changes would you recommend he make?

NOTES

1. *Resource,* December 1982, p. 12, and *Resource,* November 1984, p. 12.
2. Civil Rights Act, 1964, Title VII, Section 703A.
3. Adapted from "A Rush of Recruits for Overseas Duty," *Business Week,* April 20, 1981, pp. 120–127 and other general news sources.
4. U.S. Equal Employment Opportunity Commission, *Affirmative Action and Equal Employment,* (Washington, D.C.: U.S. Government Printing Office, 1974), pp. 12–13.
5. Age Discrimination in Employment Act of 1967, as amended in 1978.
6. *Ibid.*
7. R. J. Paul, "Mandatory Retirement—Some Research Findings," paper presented at 1978 Midwest Business Administration Association, Chicago.
8. Wage and Hour Division, U. S. Department of Labor, *Handy Reference Guide to the Fair Labor Standards Act* Washington, D.C.: U.S. Government Printing Office, 1978), p. 4.
9. Public Laws 95–555, 92 Stat. 2076, October 31, 1978.
10. *Griggs v. Duke Power Co.,* 401 U.S. 424 (1971).
11. *Albemarle Paper Co. v. Moody,* 74–389 (1975).
12. *Washington, Mayor of Washington D.C. v. Davis,* 74–1492 (1976).
13. *Kaiser Aluminum and Chemical Corp. v. Brian F. Weber,* 78–435 (1979).
14. David E. Robertson and Ronald D. Johnson, "Reverse Discrimination: Did Weber Decide the Issue?" *Labor Law Journal,* 31 (November 1980), pp. 693–699.
15. *Texas Department of Community Affairs v. Burdine,* 25 FEP Cases 113 (1981).
16. *Ford Motor v. EEOC,* 29 FEP Cases 121 (1982).
17. *Arizona Governing Committee v. Norris,* 103 S.Ct. 3492, 32 FEP Cases 233 (1983).
18. *Resource,* July 1983, p. 1.
19. *Memphis Firefighters, Local 1784 v. Stotts,* (1984).
20. "Adoption by Four Agencies of Uniform Guidelines on Employee Selection Procedures (1978)," *Federal Register,* August 15, 1978, Part IV, pp. 38295–38309.
21. *Ibid.,* Sec. 16B, P38307, as adapted.
22. *Ibid.,* Sec. 1B, P38296.
23. *Connecticut v. Teal.*
24. *Green v. U.S. Steel,* ED PA, July 18, 1983, No. 76-3673 as reported in *Resource,* September 1983, p. 7.
25. *Omaha World Herald,* January 14, 1984; and *Time,* August 14, 1981, p. 17.

Implementing Equal Employment

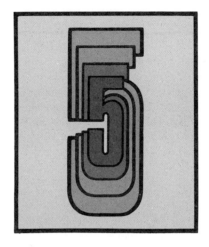

When you have read this chapter, you should be able to:

1. Identify typical EEO record-keeping requirements.
2. List the three stages of the EEO investigation process.
3. Define affirmative action.
4. Explain BFOQ and its relationship to "business necessity."
5. Discuss three sex-based discrimination issues.
6. Identify three age-related discrimination issues.
7. Apply the "reasonable accommodation" idea to discrimination on the grounds of religion and handicapped status.
8. Identify two indirect bases of discrimination which have been the subject of lawsuits.
9. Define reverse discrimination as a legal concept.

PERSONNEL AT WORK
TAKING AFFIRMATIVE ACTION

Employers who have taken equal employment opportunities seriously have found that a genuine commitment to EEO can help both work relationships and productivity. The experiences of two major corporations illustrate this commitment.

Merck and Company, a large pharmaceutical manufacturer with 61 plants and over 15,000 employees, has taken affirmative action seriously, especially the requirement to implement programs and to train employees in the impact of discrimination and why affirmative action is important. Affirmative action training is done through a program entitled Phase III, which is a structured, one-day group discussion. The typical group contains 10–15 employees and is led by one of the 1,000 specially-trained Merck managers. Using videotaped situations that depict typical discrimination problems such as sexual harrassment, reverse discrimination, and subtle forms of discrimination, participants discuss their feelings and attitudes about affirmative action and race and sex bias. Nearly every employee has participated in a session, and post-session feedback from attendees has been overwhelmingly positive.

Merck's efforts illustrate the firm's commitment to equal employment and affirmative action. In addition to reinforcing the company's compliance with externally-imposed requirements, Merck reveals its desire to enhance work relationships between and among employees with widely differing backgrounds.

Similar efforts have been carried out in the Celanese Fibers Group. Over 1,400 persons have participated in workshops entitled "Improving the Quality of Work Life." The workshops have used a confrontational approach and include male/female and black/white confrontation situations.

During the workshops, mixed sex and race groups are asked to discuss problems such as sexual harassment, patronizing behavior by whites, and other common work situations. By having employees express their feelings and their attitudes about such situations, the participants are forced to evaluate the accuracy or inaccuracy of their own biases and prejudices. The ultimate goal of the Celanese workshops appears to have been reached: to get workers to discover that their interests are similar to those of others. From that discovery, better working relationships can develop.[1]

*"There are, in every age, new errors to be
rectified and new prejudices to be opposed."*
SAMUEL JOHNSON

The efforts made by Merck and the Celanese Fibers Group illustrate what can be done to implement equal employment and affirmative action. The resources devoted by these employers demonstrate their commitment to EEO. However, many employers have neither the resources nor the understanding of equal employment requirements to take such steps. It is important for those employers to understand how to comply with the regulations and requirements of the enforcement agencies. Also, it is helpful for those employers to know what actions on the part of other employers have led to findings of discrimination. Information on those areas is presented in this chapter.

EEO COMPLIANCE

Employers must comply with all of the regulations and guidelines covered in the previous chapter. To do so, it is important for managers to be aware of what specific administrative steps are required and how charges of discrimination are investigated.

EEO Records

Through several enforcement agencies, the federal government has required employers to survey workforces and maintain records on the distribution of minority individuals in the work force. All employers with at least 20 or more employees are required to keep records that can be requested by the Equal Employment Opportunity Commission (EEOC) and the Office of Federal Contract Compliance Programs (OFCCP).

One small manufacturing firm in the southwestern U.S. with 40 employees did not keep any EE0-related records. Because it was located in a small town, the owner of the company, Mr. Ryan (not his real name) felt that keeping such records was a waste of time and a government imposition. Subsequently, a woman who applied for a manufacturing job was not hired. She then filed a discrimination complaint with the state equal employment agency. When the investigator checked on the complaint, he asked Ryan how many women worked in the company the previous three years, what jobs they held, and the number of women who had applied for plant jobs in those three years. Without any records, Ryan had no defense. The result was a substantial penalty imposed on Ryan and his firm in the form of back pay and penalties. In addition, he had to give the complainant a job with retroactive seniority. Without adequate records on past practices Ryan and his firm were subjected to even greater pressure and penalties than

FIGURE 5–1
Annual Reporting Form
EEO-1.

Standard Form 100
(Rev. 12-76)
Approved GAO B-180541 (R0077)
Expires 12-31-78

EQUAL EMPLOYMENT OPPORTUNITY
EMPLOYER INFORMATION REPORT EEO-1

Joint Reporting Committee

- Equal Employment Opportunity Commission
- Office of Federal Contract Compliance Programs

Section A — TYPE OF REPORT
Refer to instructions for number and types of reports to be filed.

1. Indicate by marking in the appropriate box the type of reporting unit for which this copy of the form is submitted (MARK ONLY ONE BOX).

(1) ☐ Single-establishment Employer Report

Multi-establishment Employer:
(2) ☐ Consolidated Report
(3) ☐ Headquarters Unit Report
(4) ☐ Individual Establishment Report (submit one for each establishment with 25 or more employees)
(5) ☐ Special Report

2. Total number of reports being filed by this Company (Answer on Consolidated Report only)_____

Section B — COMPANY IDENTIFICATION *(To be answered by all employers)*

OFFICE USE ONLY

1. Parent Company
   a. Name of parent company (owns or controls establishment in item 2) omit if same as label

Name of receiving office		Address (Number and street)		a.
City or town	County	State	ZIP code	b.
			b. Employer Identification No.	

2. Establishment for which this report is filed. (Omit if same as label)
   a. Name of establishment

Address (Number and street)	City or town	County	State	ZIP code	c.
b. Employer Identification No.	(If same as label, skip.)				d.

3. Parent company affiliation (Multi-establishment Employers: Answer on Consolidated Report only)
   a. Name of parent—affiliated company   b. Employer Identification No.

Address (Number and street)	City or town	County	State	ZIP code

---

Section C — EMPLOYERS WHO ARE REQUIRED TO FILE *(To be answered by all employers)*

☐ Yes ☐ No 1. Does the entire company have at least 100 employees in the payroll period for which you are reporting?

☐ Yes ☐ No 2. Is your company affiliated through common ownership and/or centralized management with other entities in an enterprise with a total employment of 100 or more?

☐ Yes ☐ No 3. Does the company or any of its establishments (a) have 50 or more employees AND (b) is not exempt as provided by 41 CFR 60-1.5, AND either (1) is a prime government contractor or first-tier subcontractor, and has a contract, subcontract, or purchase order amounting to $50,000 or more, or (2) serves as a depository of Government funds in any amount or is a financial institution which is an issuing and paying agent for U.S. Savings Bonds and Savings Notes?

NOTE: If the answer is yes to ANY of these questions, complete the entire form; otherwise skip to Section G.

SECTION II EQUAL EMPLOYMENT OPPORTUNITY

FIGURE 5–1
(continued)

Section D—EMPLOYMENT DATA

Employment at this establishment--Report all permanent, temporary, or part-time employees including apprentices and on-the-job trainees unless specifically excluded as set forth in the instructions. Enter the appropriate figures on all lines and in all columns. Blank spaces will be considered as zeros.

JOB CATEGORIES	OVERALL TOTALS (SUM OF COL B THRU K)	NUMBER OF EMPLOYEES									
		MALE					FEMALE				
	A	WHITE (NOT OF HISPANIC ORIGIN) B	BLACK (NOT OF HISPANIC ORIGIN) C	HISPANIC D	ASIAN OR PACIFIC ISLANDER E	AMERICAN INDIAN OR ALASKAN NATIVE F	WHITE (NOT OF HISPANIC ORIGIN) G	BLACK (NOT OF HISPANIC ORIGIN) H	HISPANIC I	ASIAN OR PACIFIC ISLANDER J	AMERICAN INDIAN OR ALASKAN NATIVE K
Officials and Managers											
Professionals											
Technicians											
Sales Workers											
Office and Clerical											
Craft Workers (Skilled)											
Operatives (Semi-Skilled)											
Laborers (Unskilled)											
Service Workers											
TOTAL											
Total employment reported in previous EEO-1 report											

(The trainees below should also be included in the figures for the appropriate occupational categories above)

| Formal On-the-job trainees | White collar | | | | | | | | | | |
| | Production | | | | | | | | | | |

1. NOTE: On consolidated report, skip questions 2-5 and Section E.
2. How was information as to race or ethnic group in Section D obtained?
   1 ☐ Visual Survey 3 ☐ Other — Specify ....
   2 ☐ Employment Record ....
3. Dates of payroll period used –

4. Pay period of last report submitted for this establishment

5. Does this establishment employ apprentices?
   This year? 1 ☐ Yes 2 ☐ No
   Last year? 1 ☐ Yes 2 ☐ No

Section E — ESTABLISHMENT INFORMATION

1. Is the location of the establishment the same as that reported last year?
   1 ☐ Yes 2 ☐ No 3 ☐ Did not report last year 4 ☐ Reported on combined basis

2. Is the major business activity at this establishment the same as that reported last year?
   1 ☐ Yes 2 ☐ No 3 ☐ No report last year 4 ☐ Reported on combined basis

OFFICE USE ONLY

3. What is the major activity of this establishment? (Be specific, i.e., manufacturing steel castings, retail grocer, wholesale plumbing supplies, title insurance, etc. Include the specific type of product or type of service provided, as well as the principal business or industrial activity.

e.

Section F — REMARKS

Use this item to give any identification data appearing on last report which differs from that given above, explain major changes in composition or reporting units, and other pertinent information.

Section G — CERTIFICATION (See Instructions G)

Check one
1. ☐ All reports are accurate and were prepared in accordance with the instructions (check on consolidated only)
2. ☐ This report is accurate and was prepared in accordance with the instructions.

Name of Certifying Official	Title	Signature		Date
Name of person to contact regarding this report (Type or print)	Address (Number and street)			
Title	City and State	ZIP code	Telephone Area Code	Number	Extension

All reports and information obtained from individual reports will be kept confidential as required by Section 709 (e) of Title VII

CHAPTER 5 IMPLEMENTING EQUAL EMPLOYMENT

they might otherwise have been. According to one EEO lawyer, "Many EEO lawsuits are won or lost on statistics, regardless of merits of the case."[2] It is for such reasons that all employers should maintain adequate employment records.

Notice Posting. Under the Civil Rights Act employers are required to post an "officially approved notice" in a prominent place where employees can see it. This notice states that the employer is an equal opportunity employer and does not discriminate. Usually this notice is posted on a bulletin board next to the time clock or in another prominent place.

Annual Reporting Form. The most basic report that must be filed with the EEOC is the annual report form EEO-1 (Figure 5-1). All employers with 100 or more employees (except state and local governments) or subsidiaries of another company that would total 100 employees must file this report. Also, federal contractors who have contracts of $50,000 or more and financial institutions in which government funds are held or savings bonds are issued must file the annual report. The annual report must be filed by March 31 for the preceding year. The form requires employment data by job category, classified according to various protected groups.

Application Flow Data. Under EEO laws and regulations employers may be required to show that they do not discriminate in the recruiting and selection of protected groups. For instance, the number of women who applied and the number hired may be compared to the selection rate for men to determine if adverse impact exists. The fact that protected group identification is not present on company records is not considered a valid excuse for failure to provide the data required.

Because racial data are not permitted on application blanks or other preemployment records, the EEOC allows a "visual" survey or a separate "applicant information form" that is not used in the selection process. An example of such a form is shown in Figure 5-2. Notice that this form is filled out voluntarily by the applicant and the data must be maintained separately from all selection-related materials.

EEO Record Retention. All employment records must be maintained as required by the EEOC, and "employer information reports" must be filed with the federal government. Further, any personnel or employment record made or kept by the employer must be maintained for review by the EEOC. Such records include application forms and records concerning hiring, promotion, demotion, transfer, layoff, termination, rates of pay or other terms of compensation, and selection for training and apprenticeship. Even application forms or test papers completed by unsuccessful applicants may be requested. The length of time documents must be kept varies, but generally three years is recommended as a minimum time period.

FIGURE 5–2
Applicant Flow Data Form.

THE C COMPANY

THE FOLLOWING STATISTICAL INFORMATION IS REQUIRED FOR COMPLIANCE WITH FEDERAL LAWS ASSURING EQUAL EMPLOYMENT OPPORTUNITY WITHOUT REGARD TO RACE, COLOR, SEX, NATIONAL ORIGIN, RELIGION, AGE OR HANDICAP AS WELL AS THE VIETNAM ERA READJUSTMENT ACT. THE INFORMATION REQUESTED IS VOLUNTARY AND WILL REMAIN SEPARATE FROM YOUR APPLICATION FOR EMPLOYMENT.

A   MONTH   DAY   YEAR   APPLICATION DATE
1   6

B   [ ][ ]—[ ][ ]—[ ][ ][ ][A]   APPLICANT SOCIAL SECURITY NUMBER
7   16

C   FIRST INITIAL   D   MIDDLE INITIAL
17   18

E   LAST NAME
19   32

F   STREET   ADDRESS
33   58

G   CITY   STATE (first 2 letters)   ZIP
59   71   72 73   74   78

H   1/ EEO CODES   EEO CODES 1/

A—White Male   F—Hispanic Female (Spanish Origin)
B—White Female   G—American Indian/Alaskan Native Male
C—Black Male   H—American Indian/Alaskan Native Female
D—Black Female   I—Asian or Pacific Islander Male
E—Hispanic Male   J—Asian or Pacific Islander Female
(Spanish Origin)

I   MONTH   DAY   YEAR   BIRTH DATE
80 81   82 83   84 85

J   ARE YOU HANDICAPPED—Impairment which substantially limits one or more of a person's life activities   NO —LEAVE BLANK   YES—ENTER 'Y' Ask for Form 2
86

K   ARE YOU A DISABLED VETERAN—   30% V.A. Compensation or discharged because of disability incurred in line of duty   NO —LEAVE BLANK   YES—ENTER 'Y' Ask for Form 2
87

L   ARE YOU A VIETNAM ERA VETERAN—   180 days Active Duty between Aug. 15, 1964 & May 7, 1975   NO —LEAVE BLANK   YES—ENTER 'Y' Ask for Form 2
88

JOB YOU HAVE APPLIED FOR (see reverse side) _____

LOCATION APPLICATION IS MADE FOR _____
(City or Town)   State

TO BE COMPLETED BY OFFICE ACCEPTING APPLICATION

[ ] DIVISION

DEPT. APPLICATION IS MADE FOR _____

EEO STAFF USE ONLY
90   99

M   REFERRAL SOURCE
89   A—Walk in/Write in
B—Ad Response
C—State Employment Agency
D—College Placement Office
E—Minority Referral Agency
F—CETA Referral
G—Private Employment Agency

Applicant's Signature

CHAPTER 5 IMPLEMENTING EQUAL EMPLOYMENT

Keeping good records, whether required by the government or not, is simply a good personnel practice. Complete records, including individual records, are necessary in order for an employer to respond when a charge of discrimination is made and a compliance investigation begins.

Can you identify typical EEO record-keeping requirements?

EEO Compliance Investigations

When a discrimination charge is received by the EEOC or a similar state or local agency it is usually processed in stages. The stages shown in Figure 5–3 represent the increasingly more involved actions that result when a complainant and an employer continue to disagree.

In the first stage, the charges are filed by an individual, a group of individuals, or their representative. Then the specifics of the charges are reviewed to determine if the agency has jurisdiction. If jurisdiction exists, the EEOC's major thrust turns to gathering information on the specifics of the charge. The complainant is asked for details about why he or she feels discrimination occurred and what settlement is desired. The charge is then served on the employer who is asked to respond.

The second stage involves conciliation efforts by the agency and the employer. If the employer agrees that discrimination occurred and agrees with the proposed settlement, the charge-processing ends at that point. However, if the employer disagrees with the charges and/or the proposed settlement, continued discussions and further investigation of facts may be required. If no agreement and settlement is reached, the charge is formalized into a lawsuit against the employer.

FIGURE 5–3
EEO Investigation Process.

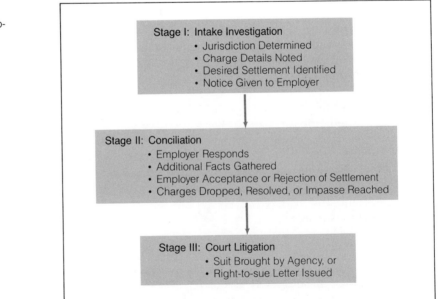

Stage I: Intake Investigation
- Jurisdiction Determined
- Charge Details Noted
- Desired Settlement Identified
- Notice Given to Employer

Stage II: Conciliation
- Employer Responds
- Additional Facts Gathered
- Employer Acceptance or Rejection of Settlement
- Charges Dropped, Resolved, or Impasse Reached

Stage III: Court Litigation
- Suit Brought by Agency, or
- Right-to-sue Letter Issued

The court litigation stage involves a legal trial in the appropriate state or federal court. At that point both sides retain lawyers and rely upon the court to render a decision. If either party disagrees with the court ruling, appeals can be filed with a higher court. The U.S. Supreme Court becomes the ultimate adjudication body.

Individual Right-To-Sue. It is important to note that if the enforcement agency decides that it will not bring suit on behalf of the complainant, the individual has the right to bring suit. He or she can request a right-to-sue letter from the agency and bring suit within 90 days after receiving the letter. The suit usually is brought in the U.S. District Court having jurisdiction in the area.

One of the ways in which employers and regulatory agencies try to reduce the potential for discrimination is through *affirmative action.* This effort requires continuing commitment by an employer to improve its equal employment opportunity posture, rather than merely a one-time effort to comply with certain standards or to resolve an individual charge.

Can you list the three stages of the EEO investigation process?

AFFIRMATIVE ACTION

Affirmative action means that an employer sets goals and positive steps that will be taken to guarantee equal employment opportunities for protected group personnel. Affirmative action focuses on the hiring, training, and promoting of protected groups where there are deficiencies. An Affirmative Action Plan (AAP) is a formal document that is available for review by employees and enforcement officers.

Who Must Have An AAP?

Affirmative Action Plan requirements are enforced by the OFCCP. Employers who meet OFCCP regulations must have a formally-prepared AAP.

The two major conditions that are considered are: 1) the number of employees, and 2) the size of the contract. As a result of concerns about the paperwork demands on employers, adjustments in the requirements have been made in the last few years. Also, the contract size varies depending upon the protected group under consideration. Different levels apply to the handicapped than apply to race- and sex-related employment. The differences are due to the different laws upon which the regulations rest.

Development of an Affirmative Action Plan

There are a number of suggested steps for developing an effective AAP, as noted in Figure 5–4. The most important step is the first one:

1. Issue written EEO policy and Affirmative Action Commitment.

2. Appoint a top official with responsibility and authority to direct and implement the program.

3. Publicize the policy internally and externally.

4. Survey present minority and female employees by department and job classification.

5. Develop goals and timetables to improve utilization of each protected group where underutilization has been identified.

6. Develop and implement specific programs to achieve goals.

7. Establish internal audit and reporting systems to monitor programs.

8. Develop supportive in-house and community programs.

developing a policy that indicates a commitment to affirmative action. In a survey of contract compliance officers, the two most important parts of compliance efforts were found to be: 1) evidence that top management is seriously committed to EEO policies, and 2) evidence that violations of those policies are enforced.[3]

Contents of The AAP

The contents of an AAP and the policies flowing from it must be available for review and dissemination to managers and supervisors. Many plans are very long and require extensive staff time to prepare. One small firm with 150 employees has a plan that is 48 pages long, while the plan for Mutual and United of Omaha Insurance Companies is over 1,000 pages long. The table of contents of a plan for a small employer is shown in Figure 5–5.

FIGURE 5–5
Sample Affirmative Action
Plan.

I Policy Statement

II Dissemination of Policy
  1. Internal
  2. External

III Responsibilities

IV Required Utilization

V Goals and Timetables

VI Identification of Problem Areas

VII Dissemination of AAP

VIII Audit and Reporting

IX Sex Discrimination

X Support of Action Programs

XI Consideration of Minorities

XII Religious and National Origin Guidelines

XIII Handicapped Policy

XIV Veterans of Vietnam Policy

Examination of Figures 5–4 and 5–5 together reveals that the table of contents of a plan reflects the basic steps taken to develop the plan. For example, the policy statement that is written begins the actual plan.

Can you define affirmative action?

EQUAL EMPLOYMENT AND MANAGEMENT PRACTICES

A wide variety of managerial practices have been affected by equal employment and affirmative action regulations. Some management practices have been upheld and some have been found to be illegal. It is sometimes difficult to draw general conclusions from court decisions because each court approaches each situation with a legal analysis of that particular situation, rather than trying to establish ideological patterns. At times, different courts have reached different conclusions when viewing similar situations. As a result, inconsistencies exist.

Business Necessity and BFOQ

Title VII of the 1964 Civil Rights Act specifically states that employers may discriminate on the basis of race, sex, religion, national origin, or color if the characteristic can be justified as a *"bona fide* occupational qualification reasonably necessary to the normal operation of the particular business or enterprise."[4] The concept of business necessity builds upon the establishment of a **Bona Fide Occupational Qualification (BFOQ),** that is, a legitimate reason why an employer can exclude persons on otherwise-illegal bases of consideration.

What constitutes a BFOQ has been subject to different interpretations in various courts across the country. For example, employment reasonably can be restricted to one sex on the basis of "authenticity," such as when women actresses portray women characters. Also, BFOQs exist on the basis of "community standards of morality" or "propriety," as when male rather than female restroom attendants are required in men's restrooms. However, it should be noted that the definition of a BFOQ has been increasingly narrowed as a result of court rulings over the years, as Southwest Airlines discovered.

Education as BFOQ

Educational requirements often are based upon "business necessity." Most employers have identified minimum education requirements for some jobs. An employer who requires a minimum level of education, such as a high school diploma, must be able to defend the requirement as essential to the performance of each job. For instance, equating a degree or diploma with the possession of math or reading abilities is considered questionable. Having a global requirement of a degree cannot always be justified on the basis of the need for a certain level of ability.[6] In cases involving educational requirements, "the job for which the requirement is specified, the degree in question, the legal authority, the adjudication strategy, and the defense each influences the outcomes of the cases."[7] What this means is that employers can use educational requirements as selection criteria, but should use them only in situations in which the educational requirements represent a "business necessity" for job performance.

Can you define BFOQ and how it relates to "business necessity" concept?

SEX DISCRIMINATION

Title VII of the Civil Rights Act prohibits discrimination in employment on the basis of sex. However, as with racial discrimination, it has taken a series of court decisions and EEOC rulings to determine exactly how broad that prohibition really is.

Discrimination in Job Assignments

The composition of the work force in the United States has changed as a growing number of women have entered it. Most estimates indicate that by 1990 women will compose half of all workers in the U.S. One result of this change is the movement of women into jobs traditionally held by men. More women are obtaining jobs such as welders, railroad engineers, utility repair specialists, farm equipment sales representatives, sheet metal workers, truck drivers, and carpenters. With this movement, many bases of discrimination in the assignment of women to jobs have been questioned.

One case involved a county sheriff's department. The Sheriff's Department had a practice of assigning all new deputy sheriffs to the county jail. However, because of concern for the privacy rights of the mostly-male inmates, the majority of jobs at the jail were reserved for males only. As a result of a suit by some women, the court decided that the Sheriff's Department had not proven that the sex-based reasons for discrimination in the assignment of jobs were justified. Also, the court held that the Sheriff's Department had not proved that it would have been difficult or impossible to rearrange the work schedules for females so they would not have to perform strip searches or other duties that would have impinged on the male inmates' privacy rights.[8]

In another case, Title VII action was brought against the U.S. Center of Military History (USCMH). There were three applicants for the position of Deputy Divison Chief, two of whom were women. After the one male applicant was selected, the two women brought separate suits against the USCMH. The USCMH contended that the man had better qualifications, a Ph.D. degree in history, more diverse experience, and more extensive historical writing experience. However, the Ph.D. had not been listed as a requirement for the job and the court ruled that having a Ph.D. would not be of any significant value. Further, evidence indicated that the women had wider ranges of experience than did the man and that the man's only writing experience was in an area that was eliminated shortly after he as hired. The women received back pay and damages as a result.[9]

Restrictive State Laws. In the past many states had laws to "protect" women by requiring that they be restricted to a certain number of working hours a week or by specifying the maximum weight a woman was allowed to lift (25 pounds in several states). The EEOC has disputed these laws in court, and in most cases, the restrictions have been ruled invalid because they conflict with federal law and are not reasonable grounds for denying jobs to women.

Height/Weight Restrictions. Many of the cases involving discriminatory use of height/weight restrictions were actually sex or race discrimination cases. Employers had used them to keep out women or members of traditionally-short minority groups. For example, the state of Alabama violated Title VII in setting height and weight restrictions for correctional counselors. The restrictions (5 feet 2 inches, and 120 pounds) would exclude 41.14 percent of the female population of the country but less than 1 percent of the men. The Supreme Court found that the state's attempt to justify the requirements as essential for job-related strength failed for want of evidence. The Court suggested that if strength was the quality sought, the state would have adopted a strength requirement.[10]

Sexual Harassment

In 1980 the EEOC issued guidelines designed to curtail sexual harass-ment. A variety of definitions of sexual harassment exist, but generally **sexual harassment** refers to actions that are sexually-directed, un-wanted, and that subject the worker to adverse employment condi-tions.[11]

The EEOC guidelines indicate that unwelcome sexual advances, re-quests for sexual favors, or verbal or physical acts of a sexual nature that affect decisions about employment conditions, promotions, and pay raises constitute sexual harassment.[12] In the first year after the EEOC issued its guidelines, over 300 sexual harassment complaints were filed by women workers. The cases involved women who refused sexual advances and subsequently were fired, transferred to less desir-able jobs, or faced such continuing harassment that they resigned. An official of the EEOC testified that of 118 charges that were substanti-ated, 106 were caused by supervisors or other managers.

Numerous cases have been filed and heard since the guidelines were issued. In the *Bundy* v. *Johnson* case in 1981, a female vocational reha-bilitation specialist (Bundy) suffered from sexual propositions and sex-ual intimidation, and was passed over for a promotion. She filed a complaint within the department, but no investigation occurred. The court decision favored Bundy and found that a violation of Title VII occurred "where an employer created or condoned a substantially dis-criminatory work environment, regardless of whether the complaining employee lost any tangible job benefits."[13]

It also appears that the granting of favored treatment to an employee who has an affair with a supervisor discriminates against other em-ployees who did not receive favored treatment. In one case, a Veterans Administration supervisor promoted an employee with whom the su-pervisor was having an affair. Another employee filed a discrimination charge for being denied the promotion. The court ruled in favor of the second employee.[14]

Sexual harassment by supervisors and managers who expect sexual favors as a condition for a raise or promotion is totally inappropriate behavior in a work environment. This view has been supported in a wide variety of cases, including one in which a woman U.S. Army officer was punished for sexually harassing an enlisted man. A few sexual harassment cases also have been filed involving a manger and an employee of the same sex. However, the vast majority of situations have involved harassment of a women by a man.

Preventing Sexual Harassment. To protect themselves from sexual harassment charges, employers must take affirmative action to avoid sexual harassment. Some actions suggested by the EEOC guidelines include:

1. Developing a policy on sexual harassment and distributing a copy of the policy to all employees.
2. Identifying ways in which individuals who feel they have been harassed can report the incidents without fear of retaliation, and creating procedures to ensure that complaints are satisfactorily investigated and acted upon.
3. Communicating to all employees, especially to supervisors and managers, concerns and regulations regarding sexual harassment, and the importance of creating and maintaining a work environment free of sexual harassment.
4. Disciplining offenders by using organizational sanctions up to and including firing the offenders.
5. Training all employees, especially supervisors and managers, about what constitutes sexual harassment and alerting employees to the issues and behaviors involved.

All of these actions aim at prevention. Court cases make it clear that employers have a duty to do more than publish a policy.[15] Employers generally have been held responsible for sexual harassment unless the employer takes appropriate action once an employee complains of harassment. Employers also are responsible for sexual harassment of an employee by a fellow employee if the employer knew (or should have known) of the conduct. This policy holds unless the employer can show that immediate and appropriate corrective action was taken.[16]

Pregnancy Discrimination

As a result of the 1978 passage of the Pregnancy Discrimination Act (PDA) many employers had to change their employee benefits policies. The act requires that pregnant employees be treated just like any other employee for the purpose of benefits. The major effect of the act has been that an employer no longer may have a policy for maternity leaves different from the policy used for other personal leaves or medical disabilities. Also, an employee who takes such a leave is assured a job provided that she returns in the agreed-upon time frame, though the job to which she returns does not have to be the same job at the same rate of pay. It is also a violation of the act to refuse to hire a woman who is pregnant. A 1983 survey of firms found that 45 percent of the firms were violating the PDA; most of the violaters were firms with less than 100 employees.[17]

A U.S. Supreme Court decision in a case involving a shipbuilding worker extended the PDA provisions to the wives of male employees by requiring that an employer's medical insurance plan provide the same pregnancy coverage and benefits given to married female employees.[18] Some firms have extended coverage to female employees who adopt children. Finally, in some situations male employees have been granted paternity leaves in either birth or adoption situations.[19]

Compensation Issues and Sex Discrimination

A number of concerns have been raised about employer compensation practices that discriminate on the basis of sex. At issue in several compensation practices is the extent to which men and women are treated differently, with the women most frequently receiving less compensation or benefits. Equal pay, comparable worth, and unisex pensions are three prominent issues.

Equal Pay. The Equal Pay Act, an amendment to the Fair Labor Standards Act enacted in 1963, forbids employers to pay lower wage rates to employees of one sex than to the other sex for equal work performed under similar working conditions. The act applies only to employees subject to the minimum wage provisions of the Fair Labor Standards Act. Exceptions are made when differences in pay are based on some factor other than sex, such as seniority or performance. Tasks performed only intermittently or infrequently do not make jobs different enough to justify significantly different wages.

Application of the Equal Pay Act can be seen in a case involving male and female janitors and cleaners. In this case, there were two groups of school custodians—male janitors and female cleaners. The employers contended that the duties of the janitors and cleaners were substantially different because the janitors had to operate buffers and shampooers but the cleaners did not. Consequently janitors were paid more than cleaners. However, a U.S. District Court ruled that the work required of both janitors and cleaners was, overall, "substantially similar in skill, effort, and responsibility." The difference in job tasks was of little consequence because such work was unskilled and required no special training or knowledge. The court ruled that each group had to expend the same amount of effort and had to work in the same conditions. Because the employer had failed to prove that the pay differences were not sex-based, appropriate adjustments and back pay were ordered.[20]

Comparable Worth. The **comparable worth** idea extends the concept of equal pay to require that employers provide "equal pay for jobs that require comparable knowledge, skills, and duties." Instead, of comparing the actual duties performed in jobs, the comparable worth concept advocates comparing jobs in four areas:

- Knowledge and skill level
- Effort
- Responsibility
- Working conditions[21]

A major reason for the development of the comparable worth idea is the continuous gap between the earnings of women and men. According to Census Bureau statistics the income of full-time working women is about 60 percent of men's earnings. In addition, the market rates for many jobs held primarily by women are lower than rates for jobs dominated by men.

Employers traditionally have tied pay for their jobs to what other employers pay for similar jobs. Advocates of comparable worth assert that using market rates perpetuates the gap in earnings between men and women working full-time, even though they are employed in distinctly different jobs. However, having courts or some government agency evaluate and price jobs, as some advocates have suggested, may not be a realistic alternative either.

Men and women appear to view the comparable worth idea very differently. In one study, approximately 84 percent of the women felt that the earnings gap was a result of conscious or unconscious bias in hiring and in setting wage rates, whereas less than 50 percent of the men felt the gap was caused by similar reasons.[22]

Using comparable worth, also called "pay equity," employees performing jobs that are comparable, even though they may have significantly different duties, are supposed to be paid equally.[23] But the grounds for determining comparability of jobs is a subject of much dispute. For instance, some nurses in Denver filed suit because their salaries were less than the salaries of tree trimmers and painters. In this case, the court decided that comparing jobs of entirely different skills was beyond the scope of existing laws.[24] In another case, *County of Washington v. Gunther*,[25] a group of prison matrons who were paid less than prison guards filed suit. The U.S. Supreme Court decided, by a very narrow 5 to 4 margin, that Gunther could file a sex discrimination suit under the Civil Rights law, even if the jobs involved were not equal jobs. The Court emphasized that it was not defining what must be done to prove sex discrimination in compensation and that it was not ruling on the "comparable worth" issue. The ultimate result of this case was to set up further court cases in order to clarify specifically the legal status of comparable worth and equal pay issues.[26]

The greatest victory for advocates of comparable worth occurred in the state of Washington. A union representing state employees filed suit claiming that approximately 15,000 women employees were paid significantly less for performing work of comparable value to that performed by men. A federal district judge ordered the state to pay approximately $200 million in raises and $650 million in back pay and pension fund increases to women employees. Estimates at the time were that the state would be forced to increase taxes and/or cut the workforce by 20 percent[27]. As expected, the ruling has been appealed to a higher court. Nevertheless, the impact of the comparable worth idea is apparent. If the comparable worth idea ultimately is affirmed at all levels of the courts, the cost to employers may be as much as $150 billion a year, according to estimates by the American Society of Personnel Administration.[28]

Unisex Pension Coverage. A final area of concern about sex-based differences in compensation has been labeled "unisex" pension coverage. The *Arizona Governing Committee* v. *Norris* decision held that pension plan payments based on sex were a violation of law if men and women contribute equally.[29] This ruling required employers to construct pension plans that relay on "unisex" mortality tables instead of the separate tables for men and women that traditionally were used. "Merged gender" tables do not reflect the fact that women generally live longer as a group.

Can you discuss three sex-based discrimination issues?

AGE-RELATED DISCRIMINATION

For many years race and sex discrimination cases overshadowed age discrimination cases. However, starting with the 1978 amendments to the Age Discrimination Act of 1967 (ADEA), a dramatic increase in age discrimination suits occurred. From 1979 to 1981 age-based suits doubled, and the number has continued to rise.[30]

Over 40 Age Discrimination

Age discrimination can occur in many ways. A common instance is seen when an employer wishes to reduce a work force. By eliminating older workers, an employer also may be reducing the most costly portion of the work force. Age discrimination also occurs when an employee over 40 is replaced by a new, younger employee. A third type of age discrimination occurs when an individual over the age of 40 is denied employment or a promotion because the employer feels that the applicant is "too old" or "not young enough." An analysis of almost 100 age discrimination cases revealed that over 70 percent of the age discrimination cases dealt with terminations.[31] The case involving Liggett & Meyers illustrates how discrimination on the basis of age is viewed by a court.

Insuring that age discrimination does not affect employment decisions requires a number of practices. These practices are not useful exclusively for age discrimination situations, but they should be used in all circumstances.[32] It is important that documentaion of performance be completed by supervisors and managers. Care must be taken that references to age ("good old Fred" or "need younger blood") in conversations with older employees are not used. In addition, terminations must be handled carefully and must be job-related and performance-based. In one case, the U.S. Supreme Court found that an employer is free to discharge older employees who are unfit because the ADEA does not require that unfit employees be retained, but it did indicate that older workers must be free from discrimination merely on account of their age.[33]

PERSONNEL IN PRACTICE
SMOKE AND FIRE AT LIGGETT & MEYERS

Due to decreasing sales volume, Liggett & Meyers, a major tobacco-producing firm, hired new top management in 1971. The new management conducted a detailed analysis of the company's work force and determined that a reorganization of managerial personnel was needed. The company implemented a termination policy providing for separation pay upon termination except where termination was for unsatisfactory performance. During the reorganization, many employees were terminated for unsatisfactory performance and were denied separation payments.

The court found that many of the "unsatisfactory discharges" were not supported by documentation. In the sales force the firings began with regional managers. All of the regional managers who were terminated were replaced by younger individuals. Of 15 department managers who were employed before the reorganization, 11 were either demoted or replaced. Many of these employees also were replaced by younger individuals. From January 1971 through July 1974, the company hired 81 individuals and two managers in the sales force and only one was over 40 years of age. The company also reorganized its California operations and again discharged older management personnel and replaced them with younger employees.

The company also had instituted personnel changes in the tobacco leaf department, in which a total of 34 individuals were terminated, 23 through forced early retirement. There were no written standards or criteria used for picking the employees to be discharged. The decisions were reached by discussing with supervisors who to terminate. The oldest supervisor was terminated; the oldest eight head buyers were terminated; 13 buyers were terminated, including the seven oldest and six above the age of 48; and the oldest buyer trainee was terminated. The court also found that age was a factor in some of the personnel changes made in the operation center and in the legal department.

Overall, the court found that the early retirements or forced resignations were not voluntary but tantamount to a direct discharge. It summarized the company's policy as follows: "The company, losing sales, brought in a new broom who was sweeping clean, starting with the older employees precisely because they were older." The court rejected the company's argument that many of these employees were discharged for poor performance, noting that they had been employed by the company for a substantial time and that the personnel files had little evidence of prior unsatisfactory performance.

As a result of the decision against the company, Liggett & Meyers was ordered to pay back wages and damages to the affected individuals. The case illustrates how age discrimination can occur, and what the results can be.[34]

Child Labor

The other side of age discrimination is reflected in restrictions against younger workers, especially those under the age of 18. Child labor laws, found in Section XII of the Fair Labor Standards Act, set the minimum age for most employment at 16 years. For "hazardous" occupations, 18 years is the minimum. A list of 17 hazardous occupations is contained in Figure 5–6.

The law is quite strict for 14- and 15-year-olds, who may essentially hold only clerical, office, and retail food service jobs, pump gas, or do errand and delivery work. They can work only between 7 A.M. and 7 P.M. during the school year and are restricted to an eight-hour day and a 40-hour week. These provisions do not apply to newspaper delivery, theatre performances, and children working for their parents in farming and similar occupations.

Many organizations require age certificates for employees because the Fair Labor Standards Act places the responsibility on the employer to determine an individual's age. Asking for an age certificate helps an employer avoid unknowingly hiring someone who is too young to perform hazardous jobs. These certificates may be issued by a representative of a state labor department, education department, or by a local

FIGURE 5–6
Child Labor and Hazardous Occupations.

1. Manufacturing or storing explosives
2. Driving a motor vehicle and being an outside helper
3. Coal mining
4. Logging and sawmilling
5. Using power-driven wood-working machines*
6. Exposure to radioactive substances and to ionizing radiations
7. Operating power-driven hoisting apparatus
8. Operating power-driven metal-forming, -punching, and -shearing machines*
9. Mining, other than coal mining
10. Slaughtering, or meat-packing, -processing, or -rendering*
11. Using power-driven bakery machines
12. Operating power-driven paper-products machines*
13. Manufacturing brick, tile, and related products
14. Using power-driven circular saws, band saws, and guillotine shears*
15. Wrecking, demolition, and shipbreaking operations
16. Roofing operations*
17. Excavation operations*

*In certain cases, the law provides exemptions for apprentices and student learners in these occupations.

SOURCE: Employment Standards Administration, Wage and Hour Division, U.S. Department of Labor, *Child Labor Requirements in Nonagricultural Occupations.* WH Publication #1330, (Washington D.C.: U.S. Government Printing Office, July 1978).

school official. In various states these certificates may be referred to as *age certificates, employment certificates, work permits,* or *working papers.*

> *Can you identify three age-related discrimination issues?*

OTHER BASES OF DISCRIMINATION

Discrimination can occur on many bases, some not as visible as race, sex, or age. The sections that follow illustrate how some more indirect "indicators" of protected group status have been used by employers and viewed by courts.

Religion and Discrimination

Title VII of the Civil Rights Act also identifies discrimination on the basis of religion as illegal. However, religious schools and institutions can use religion as a BFOQ for employment practices on a limited scale. A major guide in this area was established in a U.S. Supreme Court case involving Trans World Airlines (TWA).

TWA v. Hardison.[35] Hardison worked for TWA in Kansas City and was a member of the Worldwide Church of God, which forbids working on Saturday. However, under the terms of a union contract, low-seniority workers such as Hardison could be called to work special assignments on Saturdays. TWA offered to change the work assignment, but the union objected. Then TWA tried other alternatives, but none were acceptable to Hardison and the union. Ultimately, Hardison refused to work on Saturday, was discharged, and filed suit. The ruling by the Supreme Court was that an employer is required to make *reasonable accommodations* of an employee's religious beliefs. Because TWA had done so, the ruling denied Hardison discrimination charges.

"Reasonable Accommodation." Offering alternative work schedules, making use of compensatory time off, or otherwise adjusting to employees' religious beliefs are recommended. However, once "reasonable" accommodation efforts (a somewhat vague standard) have been made, the employer is considered to have abided by the law.[36]

Discrimination Against the Handicapped

Another area in which the "reasonable accommodation" concept is important is in the employment of handicapped individuals. As mentioned in Chapter 4, the two major pieces of federal legislation on discrimination against handicapped persons are the Vocational Rehabilitation Act of 1973 and the Rehabilitation Act of 1974. Under Section 503 and 504, affirmative action and nondiscrimination in employment of handicapped persons are required.

A handicapped person is someone who has a "physical or mental impairment that substantially limits one or more major life activities, or has a record of, or is regarded as having such an impairment."[37] Those persons who qualify for protection under the act are those who have obvious disabilities such as the absence of a limb or sight. Also, those who are mentally retarded or suffer from emotional illness, drug addiction, and alcoholism are considered handicapped. But, the user of drugs or alcohol who physically or for safety reasons would be unable to perform job duties is excluded.[38] Employers are required to provide "reasonable accommodation" for handicapped individuals to insure that illegal discrimination does not occur.

"Reasonable Accommodation" for Handicapped. There are two areas in which reasonable accommodation for handicapped must occur. The first is to insure access to work areas for individuals who are handicapped. Steps, extremely narrow corridors, and/or absence of elevators, may prevent an otherwise qualified handicapped person from applying for employment because of an inability to get to the employment office. Accessibility to restrooms and equipment of them for the use by handicapped persons also are required so that architectural barriers do not result in discrimination against a handicapped person.

Many new buildings have been constructed to provide handicapped access, but many older buildings do not do so. Reasonable accommodation includes actions that do not place an "undue hardship" on an employer.[39] In determining undue hardship, factors such as costs, employer size, and the type of facilities all can be considered. However, there are few specific rules upon which an employer can rely because every situation is considered on its own merits by courts.

A second focal point for discrimination is in the assignment of work tasks to specific job categories and exclusion of handicapped persons from those job categories. An employer can demonstrate reasonable accommodation by modifying jobs, work schedules, equipment, or work area layouts so that a handicapped person can be employed. Some examples include teaching sign language to a supervisor so that a deaf person can be employed, limiting the use of pre-employment physicals which may be used only for specific jobs, or having another worker perform minor duties.[40] For example, one firm made reasonable accommodation for an employee in a wheelchair by moving some furniture to widen an aisle and having another employee file the correspondence typed by the handicapped employee.

A legal action involving three blind case workers in the Pennsylvania Welfare Department illustrates how reasonable accommodation was applied in one situation. As the caseworkers' jobs became computerized, the blind workers needed readers to assist them in their jobs and they asked the state to pay for the readers. A District Court ruled that the caseworkers qualified for their jobs and ordered the state to provide readers to assist them because their handicap could be accommodated without undue hardship.[41]

In a number of surveys, handicapped employees have been found to be good, if not better, workers than nonhandicapped workers. Attitude, training, appropriate placement, and a supportive work setting all are important considerations that affect the success of a handicapped employee.[42] Discrimination against handicapped employees is not a defensible practice and appropriate accommodation can help an employer enhance the work force.

Can you apply the "reasonable accommodation" idea to discrimination on the bases of religion and handicap?

Other Types of Discrimination

Numerous other factors have been found to have adverse impact on one or more protected groups. For an idea of the extent to which discrimination has been found to occur, consider three specific areas.

Conviction and Arrest Records. Generally, courts have held that conviction records may be used if the offense could be considered job-related in nature. For example, a bank could use an applicant's conviction for forgery as a valid basis for rejection. However, some courts have held that only job-related convictions that have occurred within the most recent 5–7 years are allowed.[43] Consequently, employers inquiring about convictions often add a phrase such as, "Indication of a conviction will not be an absolute bar to employment."

A telephone company had the policy that it would not hire individuals who had criminal convictions. In response to a suit by members of a racial minority, a U.S. appeals court ruled that the company's policy was a legitimate business necessity because its insurance policy excluded coverage for theft losses when the company had knowledge of a record of dishonest conduct.[44]

Use of arrest records, as opposed to conviction records, has generally been viewed with suspicion by courts in employment discrimination cases. Statistics indicate that in some geographic areas, a greater number of minorities are arrested than nonminorities. Consequently, using arrests, not convictions, may have an adverse impact on some groups protected by Title VII.

National Origins and Citizenship. A continuing issue confronting politicians, labor leaders, employer groups, and many U.S. workers is the rights of individuals from other countries, especially non-citizens. At the same time, it is recognized that the rights of individuals born outside the U.S. who are citizens must be respected. In late 1980, the EEOC proposed guidelines to deal with discrimination based upon national origin.

One of the most problematic issues is that of the rights of persons who are in the U.S. illegally. These illegal aliens are often called *undocumented workers* because they do not have the appropriate documents from the Imigration and Naturalization Service. Except for national security reasons, court rulings generally have given non-citizens protection against discrimination because Title VII of the Civil Rights Act specifically mentions "national origin" along with race, sex, and other criteria as illegal discrimination bases.[45] Only through passage of an immigration bill by Congress can protection for undocumented workers (illegal aliens) be removed. In both 1983 and 1984 changes in U.S. immigration laws which would have placed penalties on employers for hiring undocumented workers were considered by Congress. But agreement between both bodies and the President was not reached.

Closely related to the rights of undocumented workers is the issue of requiring English in the workplace and/or prohibiting the speaking of a foreign language at work. The few court decisions in this area have rejected attempts by employers to ban speaking foreign languages at all times in work areas. However, some court decisions have supported the idea that some business operations require communication in a single language.[46]

Seniority and Discrimination. Conflicts between EEO regulations and company practices that give preference to employees on the basis of seniority represent another problem area. Employers, especially those with union contracts, frequently make layoff, promotion, or internal transfer decisions by giving employees with longer service first consideration. However, the use of seniority often means that there is an adverse impact on protected group members, who may have been the most recent workers hired. The result of this system is that protected group members who have gotten jobs through an affirmative action program are at a disadvantage because of their low levels of seniority. They may find themselves "last hired, first fired" or "last hired, last promoted."

Numerous conflicting and contradictory court decisions have been made in cases that deal with seniority and discrimination. In a case involving firefighters and police officers in Boston, the Supreme Court overturned a lower court ruling that required affirmative action goals to be given preference over seniority-based layoff provisions in a Massachusetts state law. When the city of Boston faced budget cuts, it instituted layoffs, and the result was that protected group members were adversely affected.[47]

Even clearer support for a bona fide seniority system was given by the Supreme Court in 1984 in the Memphis firefighters case. The decision in that case said, "Mere membership in the disadvantaged class is insufficient to warrant a seniority award."[48]

These two decisions appear consistent with an earlier Supreme Court decision that seniority systems are not invalid just because they perpetuate the effects of past discrimination. The decision involved alleged discrimination by a trucking company against blacks and Spanish-surnamed persons who sought employment as line drivers. Those who were hired were given lower-paying and less-desirable jobs as servicemen or city drivers and, when they sought to transfer to line jobs, they could not carry over their seniority. The Court concluded that the seniority system was entirely *bona fide*, applying equally to all races and ethnic groups. To the extent it locked employees into non-line-driver jobs, it did so for all.[49]

All of these cases illustrate a continuing concern between providing equal opportunity for groups that have suffered past discrimination and protecting the rights of white or male employees. Underlying all of these seniority-oriented decisions is the issue of reverse discrimination.

Can you identify at least three indirect bases of discrimination which have been subject to lawsuits?

REVERSE DISCRIMI-
NATION
may exist when a per-
son is denied an oppor-
tunity because of prefer-
ences given to protected
group individuals who
may be less qualified.

REVERSE DISCRIMINATION

At the heart of the concept of affirmative action is an emphasis on the rights of individuals who are members of protected groups. However, when someone or some group is given special attention, individuals not in that group may complain that they are being discriminated against in reverse. The concept of **reverse discrimination** implies that a person is denied an opportunity because of preferences given to protected group individuals who may be less qualified.

Key Cases

The most significant cases in which reverse discrimination has been claimed provide some support for affirmative action programs and reject the idea of reverse discrimination. Unfortunately, they have not provided clear guidelines for employers.

In the *Univeristy of California Regents* v. *Bakke* case Bakke, a white man, applied to the University of California at Davis Medical School and was denied admission.[50] The university had set aside 16 places in each beginning class for ethnic minority persons. Bakke was denied admission even though he had scored higher on the admissions criteria than minorities who were admitted. Thus, Bakke felt he suffered "discrimination in reverse" and sued for admission.

The Supreme Court reached a somewhat nebulous decision by ruling 5 to 4 that Bakke should be admitted but that admission plans that consider race as a factor are not illegal. The nine justices wrote six different opinions, with the swing decision being written by Justice Louis Powell, who said, "Equal protection cannot mean one thing when applied to one individual and something else when applied to a person of another color." However, Powell also ruled that preserving racial diversity was a legitimate goal of the university but having a specific number of reserved slots was illegal. Powell stated that "race or ethnic background may be deemed a 'plus' in a particular applicant's file, yet it does not insulate the individual from comparison with all other candidates for the available seats."

The ultimate effect of the Bakke decision was to set up further court tests in order to clarify the legal status of reverse discrimination concerns. The *Kaiser Aluminum* v. *Weber* case, discussed in the previous chapter, was another court test.[51] Again, the Supreme Court decided by a very narrow margin to reject Weber's charge of reverse discrimination.

Several years later a 1984 Supreme Court decision supported a racial quota system that required one black promotion for every white promotion given in the Detroit Police Department. The policy was adopted by the city of Detroit because other less severe measures had not significantly increased the number of black officers on the police force.[52]

The 1984 Supreme Court decision in the Memphis firefighters case protected the seniority rights of white males, even when the seniority system adversely impacted blacks and other protected groups in a lay-off situation.[53]. However, despite all these legal actions, many white males, some politicians, some union leaders and members, and numerous professional and trade associations have openly opposed affirmative action, while awaiting a definitive supportive decision from the Supreme Court. The nature of this opposition is highlighted in the "Personnel Today and Tommorrow" section at the end of the chapter.

Can you define reverse discrimination as a legal concept?

MANAGERIAL GUIDE TO EQUAL EMPLOYMENT INQUIRIES

Discrimination may occur in many widely spread areas, as the preceeding discussion has indicated. To narrow the focus, Figure 5–7 contains some general guidelines for pre-employment inquiries. All those inquiries labeled as "may be discriminatory" have been so designated because of findings of adverse impact in a variety of court cases. This inclusion does not mean that in all situations the practices would be illegal, but they should be used only if they specifically reflect a "business necessity." Although many different questions are asked in interviews and on application blanks, not all of them may be permitted under existing equal employment regulations. This list, developed by an equal employment enforcement agency, illustrates the care managers must take to avoid the appearance, as well as the actual act, of discrimination. Regarding name, it may be necessary for a potential employer to know if applicants had ever worked under other names if individuals, primarily women, had gotten married and were now applying under a new name. In order to check reference information with former employers, educational institutions, or the employers' own files in the case of former employees, this information could be needed. On the seventh item, citizenship, employers should monitor legislative changes which may be enacted by Congress to control illegal immigration, because some past proposals would have required employers to be penalized if they hired undocumented workers. Related to this area, questions about an applicant's language skills should be limited to those situations in which workers will have job-related reasons for using the language. For example, a governmental agency that is hiring a social worker to assist in neighborhoods in which Spanish is the predominant language could legitimately inquire if an applicant speaks

FIGURE 5–7
Guidlines to Lawful and
Unlawful Pre-employment
Inquiries.

Subject of Inquiry	It is not discriminatory to inquire about:	It may be discriminatory to inquire about:
1. Name	a. Whether applicant had ever worked under a different name	a. The original name of an applicant whose name had been legally changed. b. The ethnic association of applicant's name
2. Birthplace & Residence	a. Applicant's place of residence, length of applicant's resident in State and/or city where employer is located.	a. Birthplace of applicant. b. Birthplace of applicant's parents c. Birth certificate, naturalization or baptismal certificate
3. Race or Color	a. General distinguishing characteristics such as scars, etc.	a. Applicant's race or color of applicant's skin
4. National Origin & Ancestry		a. Applicant's lineage, ancestry, national origin, descendants, parentage or nationality b. Nationality of applicant's parents or spouse
5. Sex & Family Composition		a. Sex of applicant b. Dependents of applicant c. Marital status
6. Creed or Religion		a. Applicant's religious affiliation b. Church, parish or religious holidays observed
7. Citizenship	a. Whether the applicant is in the country on a visa, which permits him to work or is a citizen	a. Whether applicant is a citizen of a country other than the United States.
8. Language	a. Language applicant speaks and/or writes fluently	a. Applicant's mother tongue, language commonly used by applicant at home
9. References	a. Names of persons willing or proved professional and/or character references for applicant	a. Name of applicant's pastor or religious leader
10. Relatives	a. Names of relatives already employed by the Company	a. Name and/or address of any relative of applicant
11. Organizations	a. Applicant's membership in any union, professional service or trade organization	a. All clubs, social fraternities, societies, lodges, or organizations to which the applicant belongs where the name or character of the organization indicates the race, creed, color, or religion, national origin, sex or ancestry of its members
12. Arrest Record & Convictions		a. Number and kinds of arrests and convictions unless related to job performance.
13. Photographs		a. Photographs with application or before hiring b. Resume with photo of applicant.
14. Height & Weight		a. Any inquiry into height and weight of applicant, except where it is a bona fide occupational requirement
15. Physical limitations	a. Whether applicant has the ability to perform job related functions	a. Whether an applicant is handicapped, or the nature or severity of a handicap
16. Education	a. Training an applicant has received if related to the job applied for	a. Educational attainment of an applicant unless there is validation that having certain educational backgrounds (i.e., high school diploma or college degree) is necessary to perform the functions of the job or position applied for
17. Financial Status		a. An applicant's debts or assets b. Garnishments

SOURCE: Used with permission of City of Omaha, Nebraska, Human Relations Department.

Spanish fluently and/or give a Spanish language test to the applicant. However, a retailer in Houston who inquired about languages spoken or written by all applicants might be accused of using the inquiries to discriminate against Hispanic individuals.

Queries about relatives who may work for the company are acceptable, but care should be taken with so-called nepotism policies which prohibit any relatives from working for a firm. Anti-nepotism policies have affected women more than men in many circumstances. For example, in one insurance firm a man and woman in the same department started dating and ultimately got married. Upon their marriage the couple was told that one of them would have to quit or the company would designate one to be terminated. Because the man's job was a higher level one, the woman was forced to quit and find other employment. Other firms only require that relatives cannot work directly for or with each other or be placed in a position where potential collusion or conflicts could occur.

One item which may need clarification is education, item number sixteen. It is not illegal to inquire about education an applicant has attained provided that "automatic cut-offs", which may be used by an employer, are determined to be specifically job-related. As was made clear in *Griggs v. Duke Power* and other cases, requiring a high-school diploma for employment in any job in a company would be questionable. But inquiring about the highest grade completed would be acceptable, provided that the information would be used in a manner appropriate to the specific job applied for by an applicant.

It should be emphasized that employers still can obtain needed information about applicants as long as the information cannot be used for discriminatory purposes. Each case regarding discrimination is considered on its own merit, and while precedents such as those discussed earlier certainly do apply, they are not guarantees that an employer will or will not be charged and found guilty of discrimination. Employers must be aware of precedents and of the intent and interpretation of the law by the EEOC and other enforcement agencies. As additional court decisions are made, employers should keep informed of changes that occur.

After-Hire Inquiries

Once an employer tells an applicant he or she is hired (the "point of hire"), inquiries that were prohibited earlier may be made. After hiring, medical examination forms, group insurance, and other enrollment cards containing inquiries related directly or indirectly to sex, age, or other bases may be requested. Photographs or evidence of race or religion or national origin also may be requested after hire for legal and necessary purposes, but not before. Such data should be maintained in a separate personnel records system in order to avoid their use when making appraisal, discipline, termination, or promotion decisions.

PERSONNEL TODAY AND TOMORROW

SOME ARE MORE EQUAL THAN OTHERS?

At the end of his book *Animal Farm*, George Orwell identified a single commandment: "All animals are equal but some animals are more equal than others." That commandment represents how some feel about affirmative action programs. Examples of this viewpoint include:

■ Linda Chavez, appointed by President Reagan to the Civil Rights Commission, was quoted as saying, "I think we should be against discrimination against anyone of any color, and we should be against special preference for anyone of any color."[54]

■ A survey done by the Anti-Defamation League of B'nai B'rith, a major Jewish organization, showed that only 1.5 percent of those interviewed felt that giving special privileges to minorities was the best way to correct past discrimination. Only 20 percent said employers should be required "to hire a certain percentage of minority groups for all positions, even if this means more qualified persons are not hired."[55]

■ Officials from the Labor Department appointed during the Reagan Administration testified before Congress: "Goals to measure progress are proper and defensible. Preferential treatment or quotas are not proper or defensible. Although we continue to require that contractors set goals, we will not insist on or support anything that operates as a quota."[56] Significantly, the department houses the Office of Federal Contract Compliance Program (OFCCP), which enforces many affirmative action requirements.

As would be expected, spokespersons for organizations representing protected groups have rejected the above ideas about affirmative action. One writer said, "The need for exceptional measures to remove the stubborn residues of racial caste clearly outweigh the arguments against strong affirmative action."[57] Obviously, affirmative action will continue to be debated as future shifts in political, social, and economic conditions continue to reflect diverse views about affirmative action.

SUMMARY

■ Implemention of EEO requires a number of actions. One is to comply with the appropriate record-keeping requirements, such as completing the annual report (EEO–1) and keeping applicant flow data.

■ Many employers must develop Affirmative Action Plans that identify problem areas in the employment of protected-group members and goals and steps to overcome those problems.

■ Employers must be able to defend their management practices as being based on a Bona Fide Occupational Qualification (BFOQ) as a business necessity.

■ Sex discrimination has resulted in unequal job assignments, sexual harassment, pregnancy discrimination, and unequal compensation.

■ Age discrimination is an increasing problem area which must be addressed by employers.

■ Reasonable accommodation is a strategy that can be used to deal with discrimination on the bases of religion and handicapped status.

■ Discrimination has been found to occur when using such indirect measures as conviction/arrest records, national origin and citizenship, and seniority, although business necessity has been used successfully as a defense.

■ Reverse discrimination is the concept that a person is denied an opportunity because of preferences given to protected-group individuals who may be less qualified.

■ Managers should become knowledgeable about employment inquiries that are acceptable and those which may be illegal.

REVIEW QUESTIONS AND EXERCISES

1. Discuss: "How can I report race to the EEOC when I cannot ask about it on my application blank?"

2. How is an EEO complaint investigated and resolved?

3. What is affirmative action? Why is it important?

4. Evaluate the following statement by the president of a small company: "I can hire or promote whomever I please, as long as I get someone who can do the job."

5. Sex-discrimination concerns have turned to areas such as comparable worth, unisex pensions, and sexual harassment. Define and discuss each one.

6. Why are age discrimination issues growing in importance?

7. Give two examples of reasonable accommodation that would apply to discrimination based on religion or handicapped status.

8. Respond to the following comment made by the president of small company: "It's getting so you can't ask anybody anything personal, even their name, before you hire them."

9. Do you favor or oppose affirmative action plans that result in reverse discrimination against whites, males, or other nonprotected groups? Why or why not?

Exercises

a. Talk with two individuals who are members of different protected groups about any incidents of employment discrimination they have experienced. Describe the situations and write them up as cases like the one at the end of this chapter. Then present them to others in your class to discuss.

b. Contact two employers and obtain a copy of any application forms they use. Then use the guide to inquiries (Figure 5–7) and identify any questions that may be illegal. Then return the forms to the employers and discuss your critique of their forms.

CASE

DISCRIMINATION?

Ruth Wittman, a black woman, was employed as an operator of a check reader-sorter machine in a bank. After two years on the job, Wittman was discharged for being habitually absent and tardy. She filed an official charge of discrimination with the district office of the Equal Employment Opportunity Commission (EEOC). She listed the following allegations.

1. Although the bank had terminated her employment because of excessive absenteeism, a white employee in her department, who had as many absences as she had, was not terminated or reprimanded by the department manager.

2. A white worker in the department was allowed to leave the building during working hours, whereas she was not.

3. A white employee was assigned lighter blocks of processing work.

4. She was restricted by the assistant department manager from having conversations with her coworkers. When she discussed this problem with the department manager, he did not seem to understand the problem and failed to correct it.

The bank made the following responses to the allegations.

1. No employee in the entire bank had a combined absence-tardiness record as poor as that of Wittman. Written documentation was furnished that Wittman had been counseled on 54 separate occasions in a two-year period concerning excessive absenteeism and tardiness.

2. Bank policy prohibits employees fom leaving the building during working hours except under unusual circumstances and then only with management permission. The department manager stated that he administers this policy in a completely fair manner without regard to race or color.

3. All blocks of work in the department are assigned on a random basis without regard to race or color. Employees in training programs normally have lighter work loads until the training period has been completed.

4. A grievance procedure is outlined in the employee handbook. If an employee is not satisfied after talking with the department manager, he or she is encouraged to talk with the personnel officer or another officer of the bank.

Questions

1. Based upon Wittman's allegations, discuss how the idea of adverse impact applies.

2. What specific documents and evidence would the bank need to provide to justify its decision?

3. If you were the EEOC District Director, what decision would you make? Why?

NOTES

1. *Resource*, September 1982, p. 2, and Charles M. Kelly, "How to Reduce Bias on the Job—and Increase Productivity," *Management Review*, February 1983, pp. 14–18.
2. Jeffrey C. Pingpank, "Preventing and Defending EEO Charges," *Personnel Administrator*, February 1983, p. 36.
3. Kenneth E. Marino, "Conducting an Internal Compliance Review of Affirmative Action," *Personnel*, March-April 1980, pp. 24–34.
4. Title VII, Section 703e, Civil Rights Act of 1964.
5. Adapted from *Wall Street Journal*, June 15, 1981, p. 16.
6. *U.S. v. Georgia Power Company*, 5 FEP Case 588 (1973).
7. Ronni Merritt-Haston and Kenneth N. Wexley, "Educational Requirements: Legality and Validity," *Personnel Psychology* 36 (1983), pp. 743–753.
8. *Hardin et al. v. Stynchcomb et al.*, #80–9000 (November 22, 1982).
9. *McKenney v. Marsh; Zeidlilc v. Marsh*, #81–2051 and 81–2592 (March 2, 1983).
10. *Dothard v. Rawlinson*, 45 LW4888.
11. Gary N. Powell, "Sexual Harrassment: Confronting the Issue of Definition," *Business Horizons*, July-August 1983, pp. 24–28.
12. U.S. Code 24 CFR 1604.11.
13. *Bundy v. Johnson*, 641 F.2d 934 (D.C. Cir. 1981).
14. *Toscano v. Ninno*, DDE, 8/31/83, #82–315 – WKS.
15. Elizabeth C. Wesman, "Shortage of Research Abets Sexual Harrassment Confusion," *Personnel Administrator*, November 1983, pp. 60–65.
16. U.S. Code 24 CFR 1604, 11(d).
17. John P. Kohl and Paul S. Greenlaw, "The Pregnancy Discrimination Act," *Personnel Journal* 62 (September 1983), pp. 752–756.
18. *Newport News Ship Building and Dry Dock Co. v. EEOC.*, U.S. 77 LEd2d 89, 103. S. Ct. (June 20, 1983).
19. Nancy Norman and James Tedeschi, "Paternity Leave: The Unpopular Benefit Option," *Personnel Administrator*, February 1984, pp. 39–43.
20. *EEOC v. State of Rhode Island et al.*, 95 LC 34524 (D.C.-R.I., 1982).
21. Judy B. Fulghum, "The Newest Balancing Act: A Comparable Worth Study," *Personnel Journal* 63 (January 1984), pp. 32–38.
22. Benson Rosen, Sara Rynes, and Thomas A. Mahoney, "Compensation, Jobs, and Gender," *Harvard Business Review*, July-August, 1983, pp. 170–190.
23. Clarence Thomas, "Pay Equity and Comparable Worth," *Labor Law Journal*, 34 (January 1983) pp. 3–12.
24. *Lemons v. Denver*, (DC Colo. 1978), 17 FEP Cases 906.
25. *County of Washington v. Gunther*, 457 US 161 (US SCt 1961).
26. For a review of cases and issues, see Elizabeth A. Cooper and Gerald V. Barrett, "Equal Pay and Gender: Implications of Court Cases for Personnel Practices," *Academy of Management Review* 9 (January 1984), pp. 84–94.
27. *Wall Street Journal*, December 6, 1983, p. 10.
28. Charles R. Day, Jr., "Comparable Worth: A Smoldering Issue is Ready to Burn Once More," *Modern Office Procedures*, July 1983, pp. 72–80.
29. *Arizona Governing Commission v. Norris*, 103 S.Ct. 3492, 32 FEP Cases 233 (1983).

30. Tony Mauro, "Age Bias Charges: Increasing Problem" *Nation's Business,* April 1983, pp. 44–46.

31. Robert A. Snyder and Billie Brandon, "Riding the Third Wave: Staying on Top of ADEA Complaints," *Personnel Administrator,* February 1983, pp. 41–47.

32. *Ibid.*

33. *EEOC v. Wyoming,* 31 FEP Cases 75 (March 2, 1983).

34. *EEOC v. Liggett & Meyers, Inc.,* 29 FEP Case lb 11 (E.D. N.C. 1982).

35. *Trans World Airlines v. Hardison,* 432 U.S. 63(1977).

36. For a more detailed discussion, see Charles J. Hollon and Thomas L. Bright "Avoiding Religious Discrimination in the Workplace," *Personnel Journal* 61 (August 1982), pp. 590–594.

37. 29 U.S. Code Section 706(7) (B) (Supp. IV 1980).

38. Jon M. Nold, "Hidden Handicaps: Protection for Alcoholics, Drug Addicts, and the Mentally Ill Against Employment Discrimination . . . ," *Wisconsin Law Review,* 1983, pp. 725–750.

39. Gerber DeJong and Raymond Lifchey, "Physical Disability and Public Policy," *Scientific American,* June 1983, pp. 40–49.

40. More case histories and examples can be found in Gopal C. Pati and John I. Adkins, Jr., *Managing and Employing the Handicapped* (Lake Forest, Ill: Brace-Park Press, 1981).

41. *U.S. News & World Report,* August 8, 1983, p. 67.

42. Sara M. Freedman and Robert T. Keller, "The Handicapped in the Workforce," *Academy of Management Review* 6 (July 1981), pp. 449–458.

43. Eric Matusewitch, "Employment Rights of Ex-Offenders," *Personnel Journal* 61 (December 1983), pp. 951–954.

44. *U.S. News & World Report,* November 21, 1983, p. 78.

45. Paul S. Greenlaw and John P. Kohl, "National Origin Discrimination and the New EEOC Guidelines," *Personnel Journal* 60 (August 1981), pp. 634–636.

46. John G. Kruchko and Lawrence E. Dube, Jr., "English in the Workplace: A Rule or an Option?" *Personnel Administrator,* October 1982, pp. 43–46.

47. *Boston Firefighters Union v. Boston Chapter NAACP.*

48. *Memphis Firefighters, Local 1784 v. Stotts,* 1984.

49. *International Brotherhood of Teamsters v. U.S.,* 45 L.W. 4506, 1977.

50. *University of California Regents v. Bakke,* 438 U.S. 265 (1978).

51. *Kaiser Aluminum and Chemical Corp. v. Brian F. Weber,* 78–435 (1979).

52. *U.S. News & World Report,* January 23, 1984, p. 75.

53. *Memphis Firefighers, Local 1784 v. Stotts.*

54. Quoted in Universal Press Syndicated column by James J. Kilpatrick, November, 1983.

55. *Resource,* December, 1983, p. 3.

56. Stephen C. Swanson, "Affirmative Action Goals: Acknowledging the Empolyer's Interest," *Personnel Journal* 62 (March 1983), p. 218.

57. Thomas Nagel, "Caste Struggle," *The New Republic,* January 23, 1984, p. 13.

SECTION CASE II

THE INTERVIEW

Lenore Johnson responded to the following advertisement in a local newspaper:

> Repair Supervisor
> 12 repairmen,
> major brands
> LARGE RADIO & TV CO.
> address
> phone number
> An Equal Opportunity Employer

Johnson is a young, aggressive, black woman. She has been employed by an electronics manufacturing company as an assembly person for three years and as a line leader for the last year. She has an amateur radio operator's license and is studying for a commercial radio telephone license. Her work record at the ABC Electronics plant has been good. Her department manager's comments on her last performance appraisal indicated that she had good promotion potential.

The owner of LARGE RADIO & TV is an elderly gentleman who started the business many years ago. He has 16 employees; 4 are salespeople and 12 are repairmen. He feels very proud of his accomplishments and is very much "his own man."

Johnson filled out the application blank (Figure 1) and was given an interview. The interview was held at the repair shop with several interruptions from customers' phone calls and questions from salespeople and repairmen. The owner described the job by making references to the previous supervisor in glowing terms ("He was a great guy. He was always in here early to open up and make coffee, and he usually was the last one to leave"). The previous supervisor was retiring because of health problems, and the owner did not want to run the shop by himself again. He was planning to go into semi retirement and wanted someone who would keep the place going so he only had to "check in on things" once a day.

The owner asked Johnson to take a four-page "electronics knowledge" test that had been developed by a local trade association. The owner left her to complete the test while he attended to another interruption. When she had completed the test, she waited for the owner to return. When he did so, he briefly scanned the test. He asked her who her boss was at ABC

LARGE RADIO AND TV CO.
APPLICATION FOR EMPLOYMENT

1. Name: _____

2. Background in Radio/TV:

3. Your working habits:

4. What is your driving record?

5. Why do you want this job?

6. Do you realize if we get any collection calls or garnishment of wages on you, that you will be immediately dismissed? Yes _____ No _____

7. Do you use tobacco?

8. Are you in debt?

9. What are your hobbies?

I hereby affirm that my answers are true and correct.

Signed _____

FIGURE 1
LARGE RADIO AND TV CO. Application for employment.

Electronics because "I know most of the guys over there." She told him who her boss was and stated that he had written performance reviews that reflected her good work as a supervisor. When asked why she wanted to leave ABC Electronics, she stated that she wanted to advance herself and hoped to have a business like LARGE RADIO & TV someday.

The owner then asked her if she felt she would have any difficulty supervising 12 men. She replied that while most of the people she had been supervising were women, she had also supervised several men at the plant and felt that she would have no more problems than anyone else.

She asked what the normal working hours were for the shop. He replied that the shop was open from 7:30 A.M. to 4 P.M. every day except Sunday. "However," he said, "most of the men are still here at 5 or 5:30 P.M." He added that occasionally they would have a sale and the shop would be open until 9 P.M.

Noticing the wedding band on her finger, he asked, "Will your husband mind if you have to work late once in a while?" She replied that she didn't think that had anything to do with the job, and that she expected to have to work some extra hours.

He asked if she was good with figures "since the previous supervisor had done almost all the paperwork," and added, "You women are usually good with numbers." She said that she felt her arithmetic skills were adequate and that she had been responsible for the assembly-line paperwork at ABC Electronics. "My line produced 13 different models of television sets last year, and I was responsible for meeting production goals and making sure that the levels of inventory for my line were sufficient," she replied.

"Do you know anything about trucks?" he asked. "Glen used to take care of the little problems with the service vans. Of course, we always sent the trucks to a repair shop if it was something serious." She replied that she had little automotive experience.

The owner concluded the interview by thanking her and indicated he would make his decision "soon."

After two weeks without word from the owner, she called to find out if she was still being considered. She was told that he had hired someone else.

When she inquired why she had not received the job, the owner said that he felt that the young man he had hired had stronger technical skills and that he would become a good supervisor. She pressed for details and found out that the young man was a recent graduate from an area technical school, but had no supervisory experience. The owner had interviewed the young man over lunch at a cafe and had accepted his technical school diploma as a substitute for the test she had taken.

QUESTIONS

1. What grounds, if any, does Johnson have for an EEO complaint?
2. How should she proceed?
3. Characterize the professionalism of this selection process.

STAFFING THE ORGANIZATION AND ITS WORK

The first phase of staffing any organization is understanding the components of jobs. When a person is hired, both management and the individual must have a clear understanding of the job the new employee will perform. A job is an organizational unit of work, and Chapter 6 examines job design and its effects on people.

Job design is viewed as it has evolved historically up to and including the use of the job characteristics model. This chapter also looks at innovative scheduling and time usage, including part-time employment, job sharing, and compressed work weeks.

Further, advantages and disadvantages of flex-time are examined.

Chapter 7 considers Job Analysis—the process of getting information about the jobs people do in the organization. Various job analysis techniques are described and the impact on the behaviors of the people in those jobs is considered as well. Chapter 8 examines Human Resource planning and the development of an appropriate group of persons to be considered for possible employment. Human Resource planning, a longer-range form of determining the need for human

resources, is one focus in recruiting. A short-range focus is also discussed.

Once a pool of applicants has been accumulated, the actual selection of persons for employment takes place. The selection can be made using a variety of data sources as a basis for selection decisions. Application blanks, interviews, tests, physical examinations, references, and assessment centers may all be used. Finally, the method of offering employment to a person is examined. Chapter 9 presents the information on selection.

Designing Jobs and Work

When you have read this chapter, you should be able to:

1. Define job design and describe its nature.
2. Explain the difference between job enrichment and job enlargement.
3. Identify the five components of the job characteristics model.
4. List advantages and disadvantages of flex-time.
5. Differentiate among part-time employment, job sharing, and compressed workweeks.
6. Give an example of a quality of work life program.
7. Define Organization Development and discuss two general approaches to it.
8. Identify several reasons why people resist change and discuss how change can be managed.

PERSONNEL AT WORK

BEING A BANK TELLER

Mary Williams, a reporter for the Wall Street Journal, *struck a deal with First Pennsylvania Bank whereby she would train for two weeks then work as a teller for a week (at no pay) to experience firsthand the teller's job.*

Williams noticed that tellers and bankers view the job of teller differently. Many bankers believe that tellers are too expensive and cannot do the job as well as machines. On the other hand, many tellers argue that the job is an unpleasant one. It took two weeks of training to get ready to be a teller. In addition to learning how to handle checks, cash, deposit slips, and the like, today's tellers often are trained in what banks call S & S (sales and service). Banking has become more competitive since deregulation and the banks have tried to train their people to sell their products. To fulfill their selling roles, tellers learn such tips as not to fold their arms when people speak to them and not to cringe when a customer smells bad. They are taught to offer traveler's checks if someone mentions a vacation or to offer an IRA if a customer complains about taxes.

About 93 percent of the tellers are female. They earn a median wage of $198 per week, 2 to 9 percent less than other bank office workers. As a group, banks have not always had a reputation for having the best personnel practices. For example, in 1982, Daiwa Bank Ltd. of Los Angeles won the "Scrooge of the Year" award for making female employees serve tea on their knees to management. And in 1978, Cleveland's National City Bank won the award for paying some tellers so little that they qualified for food stamps.

Now some bankers feel they must improve the teller's job because they see change as a way to survive deregulation. One Boston bank has "hidden" tellers, and customers must make appointments to see them. Other banks are giving tellers new titles, such as "customer service representatives." However, as Williams' First Pennsylvania experience shows, there are some problems that seemed to be inherent in the job.

The typical day started at 8:15 A.M. when she took her money bin, logged onto the computer, and began counting overnight deposits. The work went faster if she stood up (which she did). Flat feet and varicose veins are often the teller's merit badges. By midmorning her hands were black from handling money. At 3 P.M., when the bank closed, the cash in the drawer had to be reconciled with the accounts on the computer. That took an hour. Then it was time to "nurse my feet and turn my mind back on."

Rude customers and foot and leg problems are some of the more obvious problems with the job. Boredom and an attitude among customers that the teller can only handle the most simple transactions are others. By 10:30 A.M. on the third day Williams had decided the job was not for her, but she finished out the week—probably very glad that this experience was only for a story, not for a career.[1]

"The British created a civil-service job in 1803 calling for a man to stand on the Cliffs of Dover with a spyglass. He was supposed to ring a bell if he saw Napoleon coming. The job was abolished in 1945."

ROBERT SOBEL

The way people look at work and jobs has evolved gradually over the years. The design of many jobs has changed too, while others, such as the Dover bell ringer, continue even though the need has long since disappeared. Other jobs, like the bank teller's job, are changing now. Job design considers the *content* of jobs and the effect of jobs on employees. Today more attention is being paid to job design for three major reasons:

1. Job design can impact *performance* in certain jobs, especially those jobs in which employee motivation can make a substantial difference.[2] Lower costs through reduced turnover and absenteeism also seem to be related to good job design.
2. Job design can affect *job satisfaction*. Because people are more satisfied with certain job configurations than with others, it is important to be able to identify what makes a "good" job.
3. Job design can affect both *physical and mental health*. Problems, such as hearing loss, back problems, and leg problems, can be directly traced to job design, as can stress and related blood pressure and heart disease.

Designing and redesigning jobs requires cooperation by personnel professionals and operating managers. Figure 6–1 shows how a large organization that has a separate personnel unit divides the duties. In a small organization the operating managers have to perform all activities.

The managers are mainly responsible for developing work procedures, identifying performance standards, and designing and supervising the performance of work in jobs. The personnel unit attempts to determine the effects of job design and to suggest changes when research reveals job design is having negative effects.

PERSONNEL UNIT	MANAGERS
■ Monitors need for job redesign company-wide	■ Actually design jobs with help from personnel unit and employees
■ Researches and provides information on effects of various designs on performance, satisfaction, and health	■ Supervise performance on jobs as designed, and make needed adjustments
■ May identify experts in various kinds of redesign to help when needed	■ Monitor productivity, turnover, and other factors as indicators of need for redesign
	■ Identify new jobs for initial design

FIGURE 6–1
Job Design Responsibilities.

A POSITION
is a collection of tasks performed by one person.

A JOB
is a grouping of similar positions.

RESPONSIBILITIES
are obligations to perform certain tasks and duties.

Every job is composed of *tasks*, *duties*, and *responsibilities*. Although the terms "position" and "job" are often used interchangeably, there is a slight difference in emphasis. A **position** is a collection of tasks, duties, and responsibilities performed by one person. A **job** may include more than one position. Thus, if there are two persons operating postage meters in a mailroom, there are two positions (one for each person) but just one job (postage meter operator).

A government manual notes that a task is composed of motions and "is a distinct identifiable work activity," whereas "a duty is composed of a number of tasks and is a larger work segment performed by an individual."[3] Because both tasks and duties describe activities, it is not always easy or necessary to distinguish between the two. If one of the employment supervisor's duties is to "interview applicants," one task that is a part of that duty would be "asking questions."

Responsibilities also go with jobs. They are the reason managerial jobs are usually more highly paid. **Responsibilities** are obligations to perform certain tasks and duties.

Person/Job Fit

Not everyone would be happy as a physician, as an engineer, or as a dishwasher. But certain people like and do well at each of those jobs. The person/job fit is a simple but important concept that involves matching characteristics of people with characteristics of jobs. Figure 6–2 depicts the person/job fit. Obviously, if a person does not fit a job, either the person can be changed or replaced, or the job can be changed. In the past, it was much more common to make the round

FIGURE 6–2
Person-Job Fit.

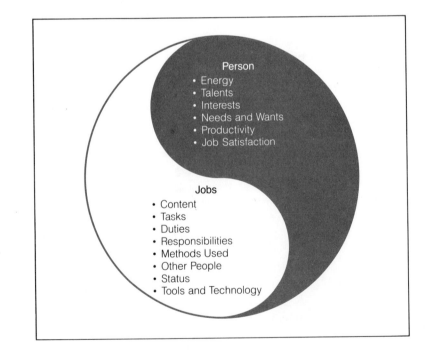

Person
• Energy
• Talents
• Interests
• Needs and Wants
• Productivity
• Job Satisfaction

Jobs
• Content
• Tasks
• Duties
• Responsibilities
• Methods Used
• Other People
• Status
• Tools and Technology

person fit the square job. Titles such as farmhand or factory hand suggested that *hands* were hired, not the whole person. However, successfully "reshaping" people is not easy to do. By redesigning jobs, the person/job fit can be more easily improved. Jobs may be designed properly when they are first established or redesigned later. In either case, the term used for the process is usually **job design.**

Job design has been a part of the revival of American productivity that is taking place following the grim productivity picture of the 1970s. Three recessions since 1973 and a shrinking share of world markets provided the motivation for the turnaround. Job design was not solely responsible, but it has played an important role. For example, increased efforts to involve employees in their jobs (to gain from their brains as well as their backs) have paid dividends.

Tandem Computers, Inc. of Cupertino, California, has developed the idea of employee involvement in a comprehensive manner. Ordinary line workers have all production and performance data available when they want it. They take short courses in statistical analysis and measurement, and then assume responsibility for tracking data relative to their jobs. Such information may include quality test results, incoming parts failure, work-in-process cycle times, and unit cost measurement, all available from computer terminals on the job.[4] This policy represents quite a change from the structure of most production jobs, and results in deeper employee involvement.

JOB DESIGN
refers to a conscious effort to organize tasks, duties, and responsibilities into a unit of work to achieve a certain objective.

NATURE OF JOB DESIGN

Identifying the components of a given job is an integral part of job design. Designing or redesigning jobs encompasses many considerations, and a number of different techniques are available to the manager. Job design has been equated with job enrichment, a technique developed by Frederick Herzberg, but job design is much broader than job enrichment alone.

Job design must consider:

- *Content* of the job
- *Methods, tools,* or *technology* used
- Their combined *effects* on the people during the job
- *Relationships* with other people at work that are likely to develop through interpersonal contact

Job design has not always been as comprehensive as the above list suggests, however. A brief review of the history of job design shows how it has evolved.

Can you define job design and describe its nature?

History of Job Design

With the industrial age people found employment outside agriculture, and many jobs evolved into simply machine-tending jobs. People were controlled by rules, and management's job was to enforce those rules. The idea that jobs could be satisfying to people's needs was not widely held. The prevailing work ethic led most people to associate hard work with "goodness," regardless of the nature of the work.

Scientific Management. The concept of scientific management approached job design from the standpoint of trying to achieve maximum efficiency—the greatest amount of work in the least amount of time. It was built on three major ideas:

■ *Division of labor*—jobs were broken into their smallest component parts because each part could then be done with greatest efficiency. A person was then put in charge of each of these small jobs. These smaller jobs required only unskilled workers because they could be learned quickly.

■ *Standardization*—The "one best way" to do a particular job was discovered through study and then everyone performed it that way. The advantages were seen in efficiency, ease of training, and reduction of wage and training costs.

■ *Specialization*—Specialization results from division of labor. As people specialize in small narrow jobs, they become very good at them. Specialization has continued to increase as organizations have become larger and more complex.

Specialization, however, can result in some problems as well. Among the problems are an inability to communicate with specialists in other areas and a shortage of people trained to see the entire picture of the organization's business. Further, petty jealousies, territoriality, and stereotyping often result. Boredom and a low sense of achievement also can result from specialization and overly-narrow jobs. Specialization does have major economic advantages and can be satisfying when it allows a person to develop an expertise.

Where the concepts of scientific management are used to design jobs, common characteristics seem to develop:[5]

■ Work speed is determined by the machine
■ Employees do the same small task over and over
■ Skill requirements are low
■ Each job is only a tiny fraction of the finished product
■ People cannot develop relationships because of noise and physical separation
■ Staff specialists control any meaningful job changes

Unfortunately, because many workers do not like jobs designed in this manner, they often perform at minimum levels.

Job Enlargement/Job Enrichment

Attempts to alleviate some of the problems encountered in excessive job simplification fall under the general headings of job enlargement and job enrichment. **Job enlargement** involves broadening the scope of a job by expanding the number of different tasks to be performed. **Job enrichment** means that the depth of a job is increased by additional responsibilities for planning, organizing, controlling, and evaluation.

An assembly line worker is very restricted in choosing what is done and when it is done, and therefore has very little *depth* in the job. The vice-president of purchasing has a wide job *scope* because that position has a great variety of managerial duties. Enlarging job scope means adding more similar operations to a job.

Job Rotation. The technique known as **job rotation** can be a way to break the monotony of an otherwise routine job with little scope by shifting a person from job to job. For example, one week on the auto assembly line, John Williams attaches doors to the rest of the body assembly. The next week he attaches bumpers. The third week he puts in seat assemblies and then rotates back to doors again the following week. Job rotation need not be done on a weekly basis. John could have spent one-third of a day on each job or one entire day, instead of a week, on each job. It has been argued, however, that rotation does nothing to get at employee boredom. Rotating a person from one boring job to another may help somewhat in the short term, but the jobs are still perceived to be boring. Job rotation, however, does develop an employee who can do many different jobs.

Increasing Job Depth. Increasing job depth involves increasing the influence and self-control employees have over their jobs. One might increase job depth by adding variety, requiring more skill and responsibility, providing more autonomy, and adding opportunities for personal growth. Giving an employee more planning and control responsibilities over the tasks to be done also increases job depth. However, simply adding more similar tasks does not increase job depth.

Examples of actions that increase job depth include:

■ Giving a person a whole job rather than just a piece of a job to do
■ Giving more freedom and authority to do a job the way the employee sees fit
■ Increasing accountability for work by reducing external control
■ Expanding assignments so employees can learn to do new tasks and develop new areas of expertise
■ Giving feedback reports directly to employees rather than to management only

Supporters of increased job depth contend that the additional challenge and responsibility lead to higher productivity, lower absenteeism, and higher motivation. They say that work designed in this way will be more meaningful and satisfying, and therefore employees will be more productive. However, some recent research has shown that while job enrichment results in substantial improvements in employee attitudes, it may not necessarily lead to greater productivity.[6]

Not all employees want their jobs enlarged in scope or depth. What they want depends on their motivations, expectations, and the desired

JOB ENRICHMENT is increasing the depth of a job by adding employee responsibility for planning, organizing, controlling, and evaluating the job.

JOB ROTATION is the process of shifting a person from job to job.

rewards. For example, when a towel rack manufacturer attempted to enlarge some jobs by giving workers the latitude to assemble, package, and label five-piece towel racks, the experiment was unsuccessful. The work force was primarily older, long-service employees who felt secure with the routine to which they had become accustomed. They were successful in resisting the change in job design, even though some of the younger workers would have agreed to the change.

Can you explain the difference between job enrichment and job enlargement?

JOB CHARACTERISTICS AND JOB DESIGN

Individual responses to jobs vary. A job may be fascinating to you but not to someone else. It is useful for a manager to know what effect a job has on different people.

Depending on how jobs are designed, they may provide more or less opportunity for employees to satisfy job-related needs. For example, a sales job may provide a good opportunity to satisfy social needs, whereas a training assignment may satisfy a person's need to be an expert in a certain area. A job that gives you little latitude to do anything *your* way may not satisfy your creative or innovative needs. One well-respected theory suggests that a job will be satisfying to the individual doing it when three critical "psychological states" are created.[8] Those states are:

■ The person must find the work *meaningful*. This means the work counts for something important in *that person's* own system of values. For example, Fred Smith feels that working with children is important and he finds his job as an elementary school teacher meaningful to him. On the other hand, his brother cannot understand why Fred chose to be a teacher.

■ The person must feel *responsibility for the results* of the work. There must be a feeling that "I am personally liable for this getting done." If the employee feels that work outcomes depend on the boss, the rules, luck, other people, or other uncontrollable factors, personal responsibility is not established.

■ The person doing the job must have *knowledge of results* before his or her work will be satisfying. If there is no feedback on whether the work has been done well or poorly, there is no basis for feeling good or bad about the results. For example, in one radio assembly plant workers were very insulated from the results of their work. If a radio did not work correctly, the inspectors would find it and correct it. The worker who made the mistake never knew about it. Supervisors received weekly reports on errors but the workers never saw them. As a result, error rates were very high at this plant.

The job characteristics model developed by Hackman and Oldham relates the occurence of these psychological states to five characteristics that may be present in jobs. Figure 6–3 shows that *skill variety, task identity,* and *task significance* stimulate meaningfulness of work. *Auton-*

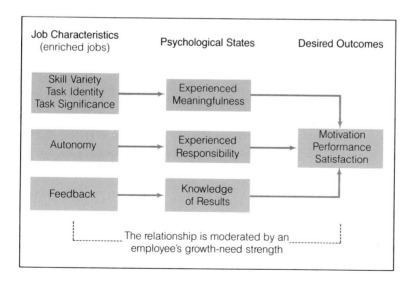

FIGURE 6–3
Job Characteristics Model.

omy stimulates responsibility, and *feedback* provides knowledge of results. The following is a description of each:

- *Skill Variety*—The extent to which the work requires several different activities for successful completion. The more skills involved, the more meaningful the work.
- *Task Identity*—The extent to which the job includes a "whole" identifiable unit of work, carried out from start to finish, with a visible outcome. It is more meaningful to make a pair of shoes from start to finish than simply to nail on the heels, even though the skills may be about equal in difficulty.
- *Task Significance*—The amount of impact the job has on other people. A job is more meaningful if it is important to other people for some reason. For instance, a soldier may experience more meaningfulness when defending his or her country from a real threat than when merely training to stay ready in case such a threat arises.
- *Autonomy*—The extent of individual freedom and discretion in the work and its scheduling. More autonomy leads to a greater feeling of personal responsibility for the work.
- *Feedback*—The amount of clear information received about how well or poorly one has performed. Feedback leads to a greater understanding of the effectiveness of one's performance and contributes to the overall knowledge an employee has about the work.

Jobs designed to take advantage of these important job characteristics are more likely to be positively received by employees. Such characteristics help distinguish between "good" and "bad" jobs. Recent studies have shown very little difference between men and women in their preferences for the above job characteristics. Both ranked meaningfulness of work as the most important factor.[9]

Can you identify each of the five components of the job characteristics model.

Other Design Elements

Several other options are available in designing jobs. These options, which may be used in conjunction with the design features above, include: the design of jobs to encourage professionalism, the physical setting of work, and group vs. individual job designs.

Professionalism. Some jobs can be designed so that "professionals" are used to do the work. This "professionalization" presents some interesting advantages and disadvantages. Lawyers, accountants, and physicians, as well as master plumbers, electricians, and medical technicians, are equipped with the necessary knowledge to do certain kinds of work as a result of their training. Consequently, they often require less direct supervision in getting that work done. In essence, they design the jobs themselves.

The automation of many office and clerical jobs can be used to "professionalize" a job. If several clerical workers spend part of their time

WORK LAYOUT CHINESE STYLE: FUNG SHUI

Work design includes not only tasks, duties, and responsibilities, but also the physical layout of the work. This concept seems simple enough, but in China it has at least one twist that Western personnel professionals often have not experienced. *Fung shui* is an ancient custom originating in nature worship, taoism, and principles of yin and yang. It literally means "wind and water" and is built on the simple idea that if man-made objects are placed in harmony with nature, they bring good fortune; it not, they can create havoc.

Historically, the concept of *Fung shui* was based on simple logic. Villages were placed facing south to absorb the sunlight, people did not build their kitchens near the outhouse, or eat in the stable area. *Fung shui* men, who understood such considerations, became highly valued.

But *Fung shui* has now become a mystical religion. "Invisible forces" (called Ch'i) run throughout the world and can be manipulated by the knowledgeable *fung shui* practitioner, according to current legend. Some foreign business people initially hire *fung shui* men to put Asian customers at ease or to please their Asian employees. Others simply say they see no reason to doubt the process. For example, a Canadian businessman keeps a mirror pointing out his window (as recommended by his local *fung shui* expert) to deflect bad luck emanating from across the street. Mirrors are often used this way, and office "mirror wars," in which bad *fung shui* is aimed at others, can create serious morale problems.

A banker keeps a tank of five black fish near his desk to absorb the bad luck. When they die their owner is supposed to be pleased, because that is proof that they have done their job. The dead fish are then replaced with new fish. Sometimes there is more to job design than meets the eye!![11]

typing, combining the typing tasks into one job may allow the creation of a word processing specialist position. The individual who fills the word processing slot is able to learn about computers and automated office equipment and the individual can develop a greater degree of professionalism.

However, using professionals may present some problems as well. They tend to relate to their profession rather than to the employer. Also, they may have different expectations about treatment and pay. Still, when the stiuation is right, designing a job so that professionals can be used can offer some real advantages.

Physical Setting of Work. Designing jobs properly requires consideration of the physical setting of a job. The way the work space surrounding a job is utilized can influence the worker's performance of the job itself.

Several job-setting factors have been identified, including: size of work area, kinds of materials used, sensory conditions, distance between work areas, and interference from noise and traffic flow.

Temperature, noise, and light levels affect job performance. For example, performance drops as temperature goes above or below the 68–70°F. range.[10] Older people usually need more light to do the same work than younger people do. Noise decreases performance on complex mental tasks, tasks requiring speed, or high levels of perceptual capacity.

"Personal space" is another factor to be considered. Some people need more space than others, and space needs vary from culture to culture. But violation of space requirements makes people feel either isolated or crowded. Both reactions may cause stress and related health problems.

Group versus Individual Jobs. Typically, a job is thought of as something done by one person. However, where it is appropriate, jobs may be designed for groups. The use of groups or "work teams" has been found to increase satisfaction with the job and decrease turnover.

The Volvo plant at Kalmar, Sweden, has successfully made use of work teams in building automobiles. A work team has responsibility for assembling a complete car component such as the engine or the body. In this way, the team can become expert on a whole subassembly of a car, and members can influence work procedures and work rates.[12]

General Motors has tried a team job concept at its Livonia, Michigan, engine plant with good results. In one team, for example, 23 group members rotate among 12 or 13 jobs on the line, 6 engine repair jobs, and 4 or 5 housekeeping jobs. The teams meet weekly on company time and decide when to award raises and rotate jobs. They even suggest redesign of the work. Livonia uses fewer employees per engine assembly and has higher quality ratings than comparable plants. The scrap rate, which reflects the amount of unused materials, has fallen by 50 percent and worker suggestions have saved $1.2 million.[13]

Job Design Summarized

For innovations such as those discussed above to be successful, they must be a part of the original design of jobs or part of a thorough redesign. Further, such considerations as pay (individual incentives v. group incentives) and time requirements (length of shift, eight-hour day, flex-time, four-day workweek) are best built into the job design.

Job design involves the consideration of such factors as specialization and simplification, job rotation, professionalism, enlargement of scope, job depth, the personal desires and motivations of employees, and job characteristics. Because of the impact of these considerations, job design is crucial and requires analysis and understanding of employees and organizations.

ALTERNATIVE WORK SCHEDULES

FLEX-TIME
refers to variations in
starting and quitting
times but assumes that
a constant number of
hours (usually eight) is
worked each day.

Working arrangements are a part of job design. One type of working arrangement that has been in transition lately is the traditional eight-hour, five-day workweek schedule. Organizations have been experimenting with many different possibilities for changing work schedules: the four-day, 40-hour week; the four-day, 32-hour week; the three-day workweek; and flexible scheduling. Changes of this nature require some major adjustments for organizations, but in some cases they have been very useful. One type of schedule redesign is flex-time.

Flex-Time

Under **flex-time,** employees work a set number of hours but vary starting and stopping times. Flex-time requires each person to work the same number of hours. However, the traditional starting and ending times of the eight-hour work shift can vary up to one or more hours at the beginning and end of the normal workday. The total span of possible work hours is labeled *bandwidth time.*

As shown in Figure 6–4, these hours include a *core time* when all employees must be present. Bandwidth and core times can be adjusted to fit the particular needs of an individual employer or operation.

Flex-time allows management to relax some of the traditional "time-clock" control of personnel. The system, which has won wide acceptance in the United States, has been applied in heavy industry, department stores, banks, insurance companies, and many other businesses. Although the flex-time system has been adopted mainly by white-collar and clerical workers within these organizations, it also has been successfully applied to manual production work.

One organization that has made effective use of flex-time is the Social Security Administration (SSA). Some interesting results that are now apparent are:

1. At least 70 percent of the employees liked flex-time better than the traditional work schedule.
2. Ninety percent of the employees liked helping to decide their work hours.

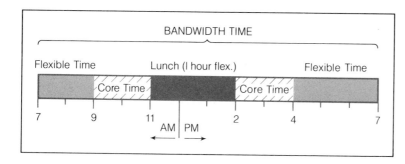

FIGURE 6–4
Flex-Time Illustrated.

3. 80 percent of the employees were able to set up better child-care arrangements.

4. Annual leave usage and tardiness were generally decreased.

5. As measured in a variety of ways, productivity of employees rose.[14]

U.S. companies using flex-time include: Exxon, Pacific Gas and Electric, Hewlett-Packard, Smith Kline Corporation, John Hancock Life Insurance, Continental Telephone, Sun Oil, Occidental LIfe, and Samsonite. Several federal agencies also are using flex-time. Figure 6–5 shows the percentage of flex-time use by industry and occupation.

Flex-Time Variations. Other forms of flex-time include flex-tour, gliding time, maxiflex, and variable working hours. Sometimes these terms are used interchangeably, but differences do exist. *Flex-tour* is a flexible system that requires employees to choose starting and stopping times from an established list of various times. Once these times are selected, the employee must adopt this schedule until given the opportunity to choose new times. Under *gliding time*, daily variation in starting and stopping times is allowed, but employees must work a set number of hours per day as determined by the company. *Maxiflex systems* do not

FIGURE 6–5

Use of Flex-Time.

OCCUPATION AND INDUSTRY	NUMBER (THOUSANDS)	PERCENT
All occupations	7,638	11.9
Professional and technical workers	1,914	15.8
Managers and administrators	1,622	20.2
Sales workers	878	26.5
Clerical workers	1,296	9.8
Craft workers	753	7.4
Non-transport equipment operators	387	4.4
Transport equipment operators	388	14.3
Laborers	214	7.3
Service workers	569	8.7
Occupations excluding professional and technical workers, managers and administrators, and sales workers	3,608	8.1
All industries	7,922	11.9
Mining	83	10.6
Construction	439	10.1
Manufacturing	1,516	7.9
Transportation and public utilities	620	11.7
Wholesale and retail trade	1,633	14.7
Finance, insurance and real estate	725	17.1
Professional services	1,555	11.4
Other services	696	16.9
Federal public administration, except Postal service	404	24.9
Postal service	47	7.6
State public administration	125	14.4
Local public administration	148	8.9

SOURCE: U.S., Bureau of Labor Statistics, news release, February 24, 1981.

require core times for all days, and they allow employees to carry hours forward. *Variable working hour systems* remove the core time from flex-time. Workers contract with their supervisors to work for a specific amount of time on a daily, weekly, or monthly basis.

Time Recording. Various time-recording methods can be used in a flex-time system, including manual systems, time clocks, time meters, and computer logs. Most organizations use either manual systems or time clocks. In a manual system, employees keep daily records of hours worked, using an honor system and sign-up sheets. The advantages of the manual system are that it costs very little and demonstrates trust in employees. The disadvantages include high administrative costs, the absence of a visual indication of the employee's presence, and the possible friction between individuals concerning actual hours worked.

In a time-clock system, employees insert time cards into the clock upon arrival and departure. The clock punches the time on the cards. The advantages of a time-clock system include low cost and evidence of actual hours worked. The disadvantages include the psychological stigma and inherent resentment of "clocking in," and increased administrative costs of calculating actual hours worked.

Advantages of Flex-Time. Flex-time systems can have both positive and negative effects on employees. One of the most important benefits attributed to flex-time is the increase in the employee's control over his or her time. For instance, appointments are easier to schedule. When a worker is under a fixed time schedule, he or she often must take time off from work for medical or dental appointments. Under a flex-time program, such appointments can be scheduled during the flexible bands, and the employee does not have to take off valuable time from work.

Flex-time also allows the employee to devote more time to his or her family. Parents can arrange to be home when their children come home from school, and can take a more active part in their children's day. It also allows them to transport their children to and from activities. If both parents are on flex-time, the family can spend more time together as a unit or can vary their schedules in order to share housekeeping and family responsibilities.

Another important benefit concerns commuting and transportation. Flex-time allows employees to schedule their work hours around traffic rush hours. If employees can avoid rush hours, they will probably be able to cut down on commute time and cost. Tensions and anxieties associated with driving to work during rush hours also can be eliminated.

Flextime tends to abolish certain employee "privileges." Often, salaried employees can come and go as they please, while hourly workers are tied to a fixed schedule. This difference can lead to resentment on the part of hourly workers and abuse by the salaried workers. Under a flex-time program, these "privileges" are eliminated because everyone can come and go as they please, within the limits established by the organization.

Disadvantages of Flex-Time. Although the disadvantages of flex-time for employees appear to be few, some have been reported. One of the most important is that overtime hours can be reduced. Certain workers may need overtime pay in order to maintain their standard of living, and flex-time has the potential of reducing the take-home pay of these employees.

A second disadvantage concerns workers who take frequent, short breaks from work. Under a fixed time system, these breaks are usually paid. However, under a flex-time system, these breaks may be counted as unpaid. A few employees may not receive additional responsibilities or decision-making power if they are the only employee available in a work area at certain times due to the schedules used by other workers. Others may experience a disruption in their social lives when the members of their work group go on different schedules. Also, some employees may experience increased family demands because they can be away from work at times normally part of an 8 to 5 schedule. Other employees may experience disappointment with the system if it does not live up to their expectations. Finally, some supervisors may be inexperienced in the use of flex-time and may administer it poorly, while other supervisors may be overly diligent in checking on employees' comings and goings. The longer organizational workday also leads to increased costs for utilities, receptionists, and other necessities. Figure 6–6 summarizes other advantages and disadvantages of flex-time.

Can you list several advantages and disadvantages of flex-time?

Compressed Workweeks

In a compressed workweek a full week's worth of work is accomplished in less than five days. Common schedules that are used include:

- Four days with ten-hour days
- Three days with twelve-hour days
- Four-and-one-half days with four nine-hour days and one four-hour day (usually Friday)
- The ⁵⁄₄–9 plan whereby the employee alternates five-day and four-day workweeks, working nine hours per day
- The work weekend of two twelve-hour days, paid at premium rates.

Notice that condensing of working hours does not significantly change the total length of time worked. It simply changes the number of hours per day per employee on any given day, and usually results in a longer working day and a decrease in the number of days worked per week.

Part-Time Employment

Another alternative work schedule is the employing of people on a part-time basis rather than for 40 hours a week. Although the use of

	DIRECTION OF EFFECT	FREQUENCY AND SIZE OF EFFECT
Labor Performance and Costs		
Productivity	more	⅓–½ of all users; 5–15% gain in output per worker
Absence and lateness	less	½–¾ of all users; 7–50% less absence; lateness virtually eliminated
Turnover	less	½ of all users
Overtime pay	less	⅓–⅗ of all users
Capital and Production Operations		
Utilities and overhead	more	20–25% of all users
Equipment and facilities utilization	better	No systematic data; case studies suggest gains are frequent but small
Scheduling, coverage, communication	often less sometimes more	35–40% of all users report these outcomes to be worse under flex-time, but about 25% report them to be better
Management and Personnel Administration		
Supervision	less	About 20% of all supervisors feel adversely affected in terms of control and scheduling
Timekeeping	often more costly	13% of all firms use flex-time accumulators, costing minimum $50 per employee; for others, no change in timekeeping methods; cheating is infrequent
Recruiting	easier	Easier for 65% of all users
Training	Less cross-training	Cross-training occasionally done, but with little or no out-of-pocket costs

SOURCE: Adapted from Stanley D. Nollen, *Managing Time in a Changing Society* (Scarsdale, NY: Van Nostrand Reinhold/Work in America Institute, 1982), p. 15.

FIGURE 6–6
Economic Effects of Flex-Time on User Firms.

part-time employment is not new, several variations of it are. These variations include: permanent part-time employment, job sharing, work sharing, and temporary part-time work. All are becoming more common and are helping to address the changing needs of the work force. If more part-time jobs were available to individuals with small children and/or families, more single parents, elderly people, or handicapped people would opt for this choice. In one survey, 79 percent of employees aged 55 to 64 said they would prefer part-time work to retiring completely. Retired workers especially were interested in working part-time in order to bolster pensions eroded by inflation.[15]

According to the U.S. Bureau of Labor Statistics, about 22 percent of all employed people in the U.S. are part-time workers (workers putting in less than 35 hours a week on average, including temporary workers). This figure is up one-third from a generation ago. One-third of employed women work part-time and one-eighth of all men are part-timers. Young and old people are especially likely to work part-time. Part-time employment is concentrated mainly in trade and service industries and among service, sales, and clerical workers. There is relatively little part-time employment in manufacturing firms (4.3 percent) and among managers (6.2 percent).[16]

The major reason that organizations use part-time employees is to solve scheduling problems. However, part-timers may cost the firm more than a full-time worker on a per-hour basis because some labor costs, such as the number of machines or terminals, are fixed regardless of the number of hours worked. In addition, unions often oppose part-time employment because it increases job competition and may damage the interests of their full-time members. Part-timers may be willing to work for less pay or few benefits.

Permanent Part-Time Employment. Permanent part-time employment has several potential advantages: savings on overtime payments, reducing straight wage costs, reducing unit labor costs, increasing productivity, reducing fatigue, and cutting absenteeism. Also, many employers do not provide the full range of benefits, such as medical insurance and pension plans, to part-time employees, so part-time employment can bring significant cost savings to an organization. Potential disadvantages include: increased administration costs, increased training costs, and more communication problems.

Job Sharing

Job sharing is a situation in which two part-timers share one full-time job. It can be accomplished either by a horizontal division, in which both employees are responsible for all the job requirements, or a vertical division, in which each employee is responsible for a distinct portion of the job. Jobs that require continuous full-time coverage and extensive on-the-job training are best handled through job sharing, thus ensuring staffing of the job on a full-time basis. For example, a medical clinic may have two radiological technologists filling one full-time job. Job sharing is especially well suited in such demanding and stressful work as health care, social service, and teaching.[17]

The potential advantages of job sharing include: reduced turnover, increased efficiency, greater continuity, and higher productivity. Turnover rates are high in jobs that are tedious or highly stressful, but the sharing of such jobs may result in a reduction in turnover. Also, many times a full-time job does not suit a worker's personal needs. Job sharing offers one way of recruiting and maintaining a highly capable employee who may otherwise have left. This attraction has been particularly true with women who want to have more time to spend with their children, but want to work part-time as well. For example, two women may share a job and child raising duties by splitting an accounting position.

Efficiency may increase in shared jobs because peaks of work can be covered more effectively. Also, by having two bodies as well as two minds, the sharers can literally be in two places at once if a heavy workload arises. Job sharing permits greater continuity in the job because one sharer can carry on with at least half the work if the other becomes ill, leaves the job, or takes a holiday or a medical leave. Theoretically, higher productivity should also result from sharers working shorter hours at higher energy levels.

When considering the use of job sharing, some potential disadvantages should be considered. First, the awkward divisions of responsibility created through the sharing of one job often lead to an increase in delays. For example, completion of a report by one sharer may be delayed until that same individual returns to work. These delays can result from poor managerial planning, improper administration, or faulty selection of personnel. Second, more time may be needed to allow for communication from supervisors and managers to job sharers, and for some overlap between the two sharers. Efficient time management is essential in order to overcome this problem. Finally, additional costs (such as insurance payments) may be incurred and could negate potential benefits.

Work Sharing

Historically, when U.S. employers have suffered serious downturns in business, they have had to lay off employees. (See Figure 6–7, which illustrates the relationship between recessions, unemployment, and part-time employment). In general, layoffs have a destructive impact on employees, families, businesses, and communities. Instead of laying off employees, the organization can consider work sharing as an agreeable alternative.

Work sharing reduces work time on a percentage basis for all employees or a segment of employees within a firm. This alternative permits the employee to maintain his or her job, although it results in a reduction in hours worked and in wages earned. In times of recession, this practice fills the need for job security by maintaining a full complement of employees and spreading out the available benefits among the entire work force. For example, Motorola, Inc. used work sharing in its Phoenix, Arizona, plant during the 1982–83 recession. To cut production, the organization realized that employees either would have to be laid off or everyone would have to work fewer hours. Choosing the latter option, Motorola cut 3½ hours from each machine operator's 36-

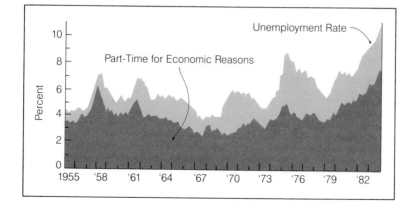

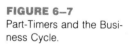

FIGURE 6–7
Part-Timers and the Business Cycle.

QUALITY CIRCLES
are small groups of em-
ployees that meet on a
regular basis to discuss
ways to improve pro-
ductivity and to cut
costs.

hour workweek. Pay for the average worker was cut from $253 to $213 per week, but unemployment benefits paid to those workers restored $12.[18]

Work sharing is not widely used, but interest is spreading. It is most popular in Arizona, California, and Oregon where workers can collect unemployment compensation for the time they do not work.

Productivity is maintained because skilled employees are retained and loss of morale resulting from layoffs is avoided. Also, retraining costs are avoided because employees are not "bumped" in bad times and added in good times. Employees favor work sharing because they keep their jobs and benefits. Work sharing also preserves the goals and objectives of affirmative action because it enables minority and women workers to keep their jobs though they may not have seniority. Unions achieve greater bargaining flexibility and are able to retain their membership. Finally, net unemployment costs are not increased in most states and society as a whole is less disrupted. However, when work sharing is chosen as an alternative to layoffs, employees with longer service do experience reduced incomes, a situation which would not happen if less experienced employees were laid off instead.

Conclusions on Alternative Work Schedules

Probably the single greatest obstacle to new work schedules is the old autocratic belief, deeply imbedded in the customs and practices of management, that rigid work schedules are essential to efficiency. Before adopting any new schedule, management should carefully analyze the characteristics and objectives of the organization to determine if the new schedule is a viable alternative. If a new schedule is adopted, the managerial practices may need to be changed. Employees and supervisors will need more self-management and less control from the top. The new schedules place an emphasis on trust and responsibility, communication, adaptability to workers needs, and equity.

Can you differentiate among part-time employment, job sharing, work sharing, and compressed workweeks?

QUALITY OF WORK LIFE

A number of new job design concepts are being tried as part of productivity management programs. Many of these include attempts to improve the quality of work life.

Quality Circles

Quality circles (QCs) are small groups of employees that meet on a regular basis to discuss ways in which they can improve productivity and cut costs. Generally a QC is composed of about ten employees who meet for an hour or so on a regular basis. The group members receive data from the group leader, often a manager or supervisor, and discuss specific work-related issues. Proposed solutions to existing problems, as well as new methods and ideas, are discussed and the recommendations made are forwarded to management for review and decision-making. Then the recommendations and management decisions are fed back to the group. Participation in QCs generally is voluntary, but it is common for a high percentage of employees to participate.

Where QCs have been used, workers often have been given productivity bonuses as a reward for their cost-cutting and productivity ideas. Northrop Corporation, a manufacturer of aircraft and defense-related items, has set up QCs in production and office areas. Many other firms, including Nucor Steel, Nashua Corporation, International Harvester, General Electric, and Honeywell, also have made use of similar programs.

The jury is still out on many of these efforts. Honeywell noted that getting management to respond to suggestions was difficult. In another situation, the United Auto Workers union (UAW) felt General Motors was using the technique to eliminate jobs and made the company put the program on hold.[19] Generally, however, quality circles are credited with an initial boost in productivity.

Quality of work life (QWL) is composed of more than just quality circles. The concept also includes *worker involvement, better communication, more self control by employees, better job design,* and *shared decision-making.* QWL is often linked with productivity improvement, but it need not be. The two are separate concepts.

Japanese Management and Theory Z

The philosophy behind QWL seems to be what is often referred to as the Theory Z approach to managing, which includes:

- Long-term employment
- Consensual decision-making
- Individual responsibility
- Slow evaluation and promotion
- Informal control
- Holistic concern for employees[20]

This philosophy is a blending of Japanese and traditional American management styles. Perhaps the best examples of what QWL advocates espouse are Japanese-run American subsidiaries. Japanese managers have achieved success with American workers, sometimes where American managers have failed.

Sanyo. The Sanyo plant in Forest City, Arkansas, is one example. When Sanyo took over the television plant (which produced TVs for Sears) quality was so bad that bankruptcy was close and only 500 workers were left. "Michi" Sohma, the Vice President for Administration, opened his door to the union leaders and talked to them as friends. He told them, "I cannot do everything you ask but I will openly tell you whatever we decide and why."[21] Then Japanese technicians were brought over to work side-by-side with American workers. They were there to act as role models, not teachers.

At first, the Americans felt the Japanese were overly concerned with "minor details" like putting the labels on perfectly straight. But this attention to detail showed their greater dedication to quality, compared to what the Americans had experienced previously. The reject rate dropped from 10 percent to below 2 percent, and morale improved and the Americans developed an affection for the Japanese technicians. There are still problems and frustrations, but the plant is now on a sound footing.

Nissan. The Nissan plant at Smyrna, Tennessee, sits on 800 acres and has a capacity of 240,000 cars and trucks per year. Texas-born and Ford-trained Marvin Runyan, President of Nissan USA, admits that the Japanese bosses did not believe American workers could produce Japanese-level quality at first.[22] Runyan tries to put some of the Japanese-style commitment to work by cultivating the American team spirit and sense of equality. Bosses wear the same uniforms as workers do, park in the same lot, and eat in the same cafeteria.

Nissan insisted that prospective employees commit themselves by taking extensive training in welding, hydraulics, pneumatics, electronics, and so on, on their *own* time *with no extra pay*. The workers maintain their own equipment, and are organized into work teams of 18 to 26 people. They rotate jobs and are cross-trained in many other jobs. As employees learn new skills, their pay increases. They are also responsible for getting their own parts to the line as needed.

The Smyrna plant seems to be a big success. The United Auto Workers union has tried to organize the plant but workers have insisted they do not need a union. The Nissan and Sanyo experiences seem to suggest that productivity and quality the problems are not so much the fault of the American worker, but of the traditional American ways of managing employees and designing jobs. An emphasis on both quality of production and QWL issues improves both production and satisfaction with the work.

Can you give an example of a quality of work life program?

ORGANIZATION DEVELOPMENT AND WORK RESTRUCTURING

Whether the focus is job redesign or quality of work life enhancement, such methods face some major challenges. Some efforts have failed, but roadblocks can be overcome if they are recognized. Figure 6–8 shows the reasons for success and the roadblocks identified in a review of successes and failures of recent work redesign efforts.

FIGURE 6–8
Success Factors and
Roadblocks in Work
Restructuring.

SUCCESS FACTORS	ROADBLOCKS
Preconditions	Sociopolitical
Apparent need for change because of:	Undefined need for program
Competition	Program mandated by higher levels
Labor-management relations	Diffuse objectives
Technological advancement	Unilateral decision to proceed
Low performance against standards	
	Lack of management commitment
Strong managerial commitment	Conservatism
Investment mentality	Desire for cosmetic change
Willingness to examine managerial styles and policies	Change in leadership
Theory Y values	Program serves political rather than organizational needs
	Theory X values
Adequate resources for change	
Finance	Inadequate resources for change
Time	Finances
	Time
Planning for change	
Clear objectives	Poor planning
Advanced management training	Broad-brush design
Collaborative approach	Piecemeal implementation
Use of expert resources	Inadequate training/understanding of program implications
Tailor-made design	Unrealistic expectations
	Exclusive orientation toward increased profit
Quality of Process	
	Labor-management difficulties
Agreed-upon theory of change	Lack of early union involvement
Shared values	History of poor relations and mistrust
Shared information	
Participation in decision-making	Lack of shared vision
Training for all levels	No clear theory of change
	No plans for diffusion
Collaboration with labor	Absence of review and adjustment mechanisms
Institutionalized labor-management study group	
Use of information at all levels	Technological
Clear program focus	Insufficient technological change to permit new work arrangements
Evaluation criteria provide program direction	
Specific attention to unique local problems	New technology exceedingly complex relative to skills of workers
Technological change	
Technological replacement	Environmental
Changes in work arrangements that increase feedback and worker control over problems	Shift in demand for products
Continuity of Change	Pressure for uniformity from larger organization
	Isolation of early success
Evaluation criteria specified in advance	Policy constraints
Turnover managed carefully	Lack of hierarchical support
Plans for diffusion made early in program	Unanticipated external change
Expectations managed throughout	Financial
	Program viewed as last-ditch effort
	Overabundance of resources obscuring need for change
	Pressure to maintain current level of performance
	Stiff competition
	Cost/benefit ratio unfavorable
	Inflexibility of reward systems

SOURCE: Reprinted, by permission of the publisher, from "Overcoming the Roadblock in Work-Restructuring Efforts," by William A. Pasmore, *Organization Dynamics*, Spring 1982, pp. 58–9. © 1982 AMACOM Periodicals Division, American Management Associations New York. All rights reserved.

CHAPTER 6 DESIGNING JOBS AND WORK

ORGANIZATION
DEVELOPMENT
is a value-based process
of self-assessment and
planned change, involv-
ing specific strategies
and technology, aimed
at improving the overall
effectiveness of an orga-
nizational system.

Organization Development

A collection of ideas and techniques called **Organization Development**
(OD) has emerged which can help organizations deal with changes.
OD attempts to help organizations better understand current and po-
tential problems and provides alternative methods of solving them.

Value-Based. The commonly accepted view of OD as value-based refers
to efforts which have an explicitly humanistic bias. The values underlying most attempted OD changes are:

1. Providing opportunities for people to function as human beings
rather than as resources in the productive process
2. Providing opportunities for each employee to develop his or her full
potential
3. Seeking to increase the effectiveness of the organization in terms of
all its goals
4. Attempting to create an environment in which it is possible to find
exciting and challenging work
5. Providing opportunities for employees to influence the organization, the environment, and the way they relate to work
6. Treating each employee as a person with complex needs, all of
which are important at work and in life

Approaches to Organization Development

Improvements in the effectiveness of the organization can be made by
changing people or technology, as shown in Figure 6–9. For example,
in the Bennett Supply Company, the productivity of the work force has
been low, costs have been rising, and the absenteeism and turnover
rates are rising. Jack Bennett, the company's president, is trying to decide how to reverse these trends and help the organization work better. He might appropriately begin with *action research*, attempting to
gather information on problems and make appropriate changes. He
can either do this research himself or hire a consultant to help him.
After changes are carefully planned, the effects can be monitored.

From this research Bennett might try to make changes in the interpersonal *processes* of his firm. Actions to build more team spirit and to

FIGURE 6–9
Organization Development
Model.

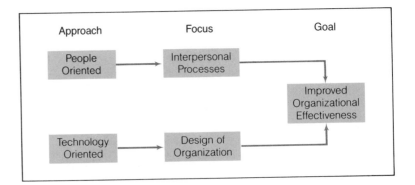

develop a climate might be taken so that employees can express their feelings more openly and honestly. Or, Bennett might want to change *technology* by bringing a new means of performing jobs in the company. He might also change *structure* variables by adding another level of management to the hierarchy. All these "targets" for intervention, or change, are legitimate. The ones appropriate for Bennett Supply depend on the firm's particular situation and management's assessment of it.

People Approaches. OD techniques can include several types of intervention, or planned change. The *survey feedback method* is a process in which data are systematically collected (usually by analysis of questionnaires from members of the organization), summarized, and the results fed back to employees.

Team building (group development) means developing a good working relationship among group members. Techniques such as T-group or laboratory training are useful in team building.

Intergroup development attempts to solve problems of contact between groups in an organization. For example, intergroup development might focus on minimizing or resolving conflicts between departments. These approaches (survey feedback, team building, and intergroup development) can have a positive effect on the attitudes of those involved.

Technological Approaches. Technological approaches to OD focus on changing in the nature of work or the design of the organization, or both. The OD change efforts are deeply rooted in engineering, sociology, psychology, and economics.

One technological approach would be exploring the possibilities of job redesign. Organizational design changes include removing levels of the management hierarchy and giving lower units in the organization more opportunity for self-direction. Creating new authority and responsibility patterns are other design change possibilities.

*Can you define Organization Development
and discuss two general approaches to
OD?*

Resistance to Change in Work Organizations

Successful changes, especially those concerned with personnel administration in an organization, do not simply happen—they are carefully planned. Planning for change requires an understanding of why people resist change.

Employees resist change in many ways. Wildcat strikes, quarrelling between employees and supervisors, requests for transfers, absenteeism, frequent job changes, and reduction in output are all ways employees can resist change. Most people have a need to maintain stability in their environments. When their stability is threatened by change, a number of concerns can cause resistance.

Economic Loss. Employees who are concerned about possible changes in income are prone to resist change. For example, the employees of a clock manufacturer feared they would lose their jobs if the company switched to manufacturing electronic clocks instead of mechanical clocks.

Status Loss. Another fear is that a change will detract in some way from an employee's status. For example, if a change means a new job but a smaller office, a manager might resist because he or she views the smaller office as a loss of status or importance.

Uncertainty. Resistance may be caused by a fear of uncertainty. Employees may be unwilling to learn something new because they are uncertain they will be able to do the required operations. A cashier at a supermarket resisted the change to electronic cash registers because he feared he would not be able to operate the new machine rapidly and accurately.

Inconvenience. Another cause of resistance to change is inconvenience. All people develop habits which provide a sense of security in their day-to-day existence. When they are thrown into new situations, the old habits and old ways of operating may no longer apply and new patterns of behavior may have to be developed.

Interpersonal Disruptions. A final cause for resistance to change is that change may be perceived as a threat to interpersonal relationships. When a change means becoming part of a new work group or being separated from close friends in the existing work group, a person is likely to balk. For this reason a person may hesitate at being transferred to a new job, even though it would mean a promotion and a raise. The disruption of old friendships and the effort involved in establishing new ones may cause resistance.

Positive Aspects of Resistance to Change. Resistance to change is not necessarily bad. Obviously, too much resistance to change can be disruptive for the organization and can even lead to extreme acts such as sabotage or efforts to disrupt production. However, managers can make a mistake by assuming that because people resist change, change must always be forced upon them, which is not necessarily the case.

Too much resistance to change is an indication that something is wrong in the way the change is being introduced, just as fever indicates infection in the human body. On the other hand, a complete lack of resistance to change may indicate that employees are so afraid to oppose change that they are unwilling to express their concerns in an unfavorable organizational climate.

Strategies for Reducing Resistance to Change. If, despite good planning and consideration of the human and social factors involved, resistance to change still appears, what can a manager do to handle it? Several strategies are available.

One possibility is to make change tentative, that is, to introduce it on a *trial basis* at first. This approach is especially appropriate if the employees have had an opportunity to participate in the decision-making process. If the employees have not participated in the decision, resistance may be greater. Careful *two-way communication* also can help reduce resistance. Many times resistance is based on a lack of understanding, and if managers will really listen to employees' suggestions, problems can be reduced.

Another possibility is to provide an *economic guarantee* to employees. If an employee refuses to move to a new job, a guaranteed reimbursement for all relevant costs can be offered. It is quite common in union contracts for management to guarantee that no union member will suffer economic loss as a result of technological change. Although guarantees are extremely useful in removing such opposition, they can also be expensive. However, when the cause of resistance to change is economic in nature, a manager should consider some type of economic incentive as a way to gain employee cooperation.

Assessment of OD

As a field of study, OD has made both academics and personnel practitioners aware of the need for planned change. It has contributed to the knowledge of personnel professionals by emphasizing that an understanding of the nature of organizational subsystems is basic to analyzing the operation of the entire organization. However, much more research is needed for OD to become the systematic body of knowledge OD advocates would like it to be. Therefore, OD should be seen as a useful strategy for changing organizations, provided that change is systematic and that many organizational units and members are involved.[23] Continued research on OD may reveal new and more precise means of effectively changing organizations.

*Can you identify several reasons why peo-
ple resist change and how it can be managed?*

Personnel's Role

The role of personnel specialists in job design, work scheduling, QWL, and OD varies from one organization to another. However, it is not uncommon in these areas for personnel specialists to act as the source of ideas and evaluation for upper management. While actual implementation of these decisions may be someone else's responsibility, personnel professionals need a working knowledge of these concepts in order to influence job design efforts.

PERSONNEL TODAY AND TOMORROW

ROBOTICS—BETTER JOBS OR FEWER WORKERS?

One fact that has been driven home to American management in the last several years is that people cost money and cause problems in jobs that machines can do just as well. As a result, the shift toward replacing people with machines, especially in those jobs that are routine, has accelerated.

Unions, understandably, have been concerned about automation taking jobs. This concern is not new, but the current emphasis on raising productivity through automation promises to spread the "robot revolution" much more widely. White collar jobs, for example, may soon be affected. Lexicons, machines that type directly from speech, are coming into use. Ultimately, they may eliminate 50 percent of all clerical and stenographic jobs.

Today's robots bear no resemblance to those of science fiction. They are often merely mechanical arms linked to a computer, not very different from automated machines. Regardless of whether these new machines are considered to be true robots or merely automatic machinery, experts have estimated that sometime after 1990 it will be possible for such machines to replace manufacturing employees in the automotive, electrical equipment, machinery, and fabricated-metals industries. The pace of these changes will depend on the relative costs of labor and robots. Supply, demand, and business cycles will affect the speed of change too.

Many countries in Western Europe have been quite concerned about the effects of automation on the institution of work. Some European authors have even prophesied the end of societies based upon the work ethic. In Japan (currently the leader in robots), concerns also seem to be mounting. Japan's unions have not opposed automation to date because the lifetime employment system has helped workers find other jobs if they are displaced. But unions have now begun their own studies of what the impact of robotics will be. For example, massive introduction of robots has led to workers being transferred from one city to another. Because of severe housing shortages, such transfers have caused serious dissatisfaction among workers.

Yet, new jobs *are* being created by the new technology. Many managers have been slow to realize that workers *can* learn new skills associated with the new equipment. One college professor points out that in the 1880s it was thought that only mechanics could drive cars—but the average person soon learned to operate an automobile.

The picture that is likely to emerge is one of evolution rather than revolution. Industry must be able to afford robots before buying them, a fact that will lengthen the time before robots make much impact on a workforce of 100 million.

There has been much speculation about how people in the robotized future would cope with the loss of meaningful jobs and how society could distribute wealth without strong ties to work and income. Perhaps the best teacher in this case is the past. Previous waves of automation have caused unemployment in the short term, but they have forced corresponding changes in the work force. Increased education, shorter workweeks and workdays, longer training, earlier retirement, child labor laws, and welfare and unemployment payments have all had roles in easing adjustments to new technologies. Americans have been successful in translating productivity gains from automation into higher standards of living instead of less work, and this pattern has held for centuries. Certainly work has changed, and it will continue to change, but work is here to stay.[24]

SUMMARY

■ Job design affects the performance, satisfaction, and health of the job holder.

■ A job is a grouping of similar positions.

■ Matching people and jobs is important, but sometimes in case of a mismatch, jobs are more easily changed than are people.

■ Job design began formally with scientific management, which was based on division of labor, standardization, and specialization.

■ Job enlargement, job enrichment, and job rotation have all been used to redesign jobs.

■ The job characteristics model suggests that three critical "psychological states" (a sense of meaningfulness, responsibility for results, and knowledge of results) can be influenced by five different characteristics of jobs (skill variety, task identity, task significance, autonomy, and feedback from the organization).

■ Professionalism, social ecology, and group job designs have all been considered in job redesign.

■ Work schedule arrangements are a part of job design. Recently some alternative schedules have gained popularity.

■ Flex-time allows people to vary daily starting and quitting times.

■ Permanent part-time employees help solve scheduling problems and may tap a good job market segment.

■ Job sharing occurs when two part-timers share one full-time job.

■ Work sharing, as a reduction in every employee's hours, is used to avert layoffs.

■ Compressed workweeks accomplish a full week's work in less than five days.

■ Quality of work life movements have usually included worker involvement, communication, employee self control, job redesign, and shared decision-making.

■ Organization Development is a process of assessing and changing the organization. It may be necessary with major job redesign efforts.

■ People resist change because they fear economic loss, status loss, uncertainty, inconvenience, and the loss of friends.

CHAPTER 6 DESIGNING JOBS AND WORK

REVIEW QUESTIONS AND EXERCISES

1. What is the nature of job design and why is it important?
2. What differences exist between job enlargement and job enrichment based on job scope and job depth?
3. List the five components of the job characteristics model and give an example of each from a job you have held.
4. Assume you are a plant manager and wish to establish a flex-time schedule for certain departments in the plant. How would you justify your plan to upper management?
5. Which of the alternative work schedules would be most appealing and least appealing to you? Why?
6. What are the essential elements of a Quality of Work Life (QWL) program?
7. How do the two approaches to organization development illustrate the nature and definition of OD?
8. Describe a work-related change you have observed or experienced? In what ways did you and your co-workers resist the change? Why?

Exercises

a. Using the characteristics model, analyze your professor's job. Compare that analysis to similar analyses for a grocery store checker and a first-level supervisor in an assembly plant.
b. Find a company using flex-time in your community and interview both a manager and an employee about how it works for them and what they specifically like and dislike about it.

CASE
COLLEGE BOOKSTORE

The College Bookstore is located on the campus of a large southern university. The university classes operate on a quarter system, which requires the bookstore to order textbooks quarterly for the beginning of each new term. The number of new textbooks to be received, priced, and shelved at the start of a new term is extensive.

There are basically five different operations involved in getting books from the receiving dock to the retail shelves. They are:

1. Transporting the boxes from the receiving dock to the pricing area, using a two-person cart.
2. Unboxing and sorting the books in each shipment.
3. Checking a shipment against the purchase order to ensure that the correct titles and quantities were shipped by each publisher.
4. Placing a price tag on each book.
5. Shelving books in appropriate locations, using one-person book carts.

Because of the volume of books involved at the beginning of each term, student helpers are usually hired for about two weeks before each term to process the incoming books. These temporary employees usually work six to eight hours a day on the textbook receiving process.

Questions

1. How does job design apply to this case?
2. **a.** How many jobs would you have under a job simplification approach?
   b. Why might job rotation be considered?
   c. Why might a job enlargement strategy be considered?
3. How might the job characteristics model be applied to this case?

NOTES

1. Adapted from Mary Williams, "The Teller's Lot Is Not a Happy One, Experience Attests," *Wall Street Journal*, December 29, 1983, p. 1.

2. R. W. Griffin, *Task Design: An Integrative Approach* (Glenville, IL: Scott, Foresman, 1982) pp. 62–70.

3. U.S. Civil Service Commission, *Job Analysis*, BIPP 152–35, (Washington, D.C.: U.S. Government Printing Office, 1973), p. 1.

4. "The Revival of Productivity," *Business Week*, February 13, 1984, p. 100.

5. C. R. Walker and R. H. Guest, *Man on the Assembly Line* (Cambridge, MA: Harvard University Press, 1952).

6. C. Orphen, "The Effects of Job Enrichment on Employee Satisfaction, Motivation, Involvement, and Performance: A Field Experiment," *Human Relations* 32 (1979), pp. 189–217.

7. Adapted from "In a Pro-Labor Area of Canada, Alcan Plant Resists Repeated Attempts at Unionization," *Wall Street Journal*, November 18, 1983, p. 25.

8. J. R. Hackman and G. R. Oldham, *Work Redesign*, (Reading, MA: Addison-Wesley, 1980), pp. 72–73.

9. W. B. Lacy, J. L. Bokemeier, and J. M. Shepard, "Job Attribute Preferences and Work Commitment of Men and Women in the United States," *Personnel Psychology* 36 (Summer 1983) p. 315.

10. I. D. Griffiths and D. A. McIntyre, "The Effect of Mental Effort on Subjective Assessment of Warmth," *Ergonomics*, 1975, p. 18.

11. Adapted from E. S. Browning, "Some Chinese Simply Won't Make a Move Without Fung Shui," *Wall Street Journal*, December 19, 1983, p. 1.

12. P. G. Gyllenhammer, *People at Work* (Reading, MA: Addison-Wesley, 1979).

13. "A Plant Where Teamwork is More Than Just Talk," *Business Week*, May 16, 1983, p. 108.

14. H. Gorlin Company, *Experience With Flexible Working Schedules* (New York: Conference Board, 1982).

15. J. M. Rosow, "Punch Out the Time Clocks," *Harvard Business Review*, March-April, 1983, p. 16.

16. *Ibid.*, p. 13.

17. M. Syrtt, "How to Make Job Sharing Work," *Personnel Management*, October 1982, p. 45.

18. H. Klein, "Interest Grows in Worksharing Which Lets Concerns Cut Work-weeks to Avoid Layoffs," *Wall Street Journal*, April 7, 1983, p. 27.

19. "Quality Circles Draw Mixed Reviews from Some Workers and Bosses," *Wall Street Journal*, December 13, 1983, p. 1.

20. W. G. Ouchi and A. M. Jaeger, "Type Z Organizations: Stability in the Midst of Mobility," *Academy of Management Review* 3 (1978), pp. 305–314.

21. "How the Japanese Run U.S. Subsidiaries," *Dun's Business Month*, October 1983, p. 34.

22. J. Cook, "We Started From Ground Zero," *Forbes*, March 12, 1984, p.

23. M. A. Hitt and R. L. Mathis, "Survey Results Shed Light Upon Important Development Tools," *Personnel Administrator*, February 1983, pp. 87–97.

24. S. A. Levitan and C. M. Johnson, "The Future of Work: Does It Belong to Us or To the Robots?" *Monthly Labor Review*, September 1982, pp. 10–14; "What's Coming Next in Robotics?" *Dun's Business Month*, November 1983, pp. 70–72; and "Japan: The Robot Invasion Begins to Worry Labor," *Business Week*, March 29, 1982, p. 46.

The Job Analysis Process

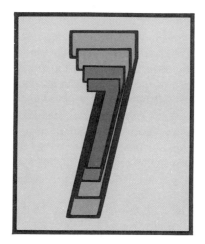

When you have read this chapter, you should be able to:

1. Define job analysis and indicate three uses of job analysis information.
2. List and discuss four ways to gather job analysis information.
3. Distinguish between functional job analysis (FJA) and the position analysis questionnaire (PAQ) as job analysis methods.
4. Discuss how behavioral considerations affect job analysis.
5. Outline the requirements for a legal job analysis system.
6. Explain the relationship between a job description and a job specification.

PERSONNEL AT WORK

PAMIDA USES JOB ANALYSIS TO GET ORGANIZED

Pamida is an employee-owned retail chain that serves the upper Midwest with 165 stores in twelve states. Its outlets, which are predominantly in rural communities, provide a wide variety of merchandise, from automotive and sporting goods to clothing. Pamida employs 4,500 people.

In its first 20 years, Pamida had no formal wage and salary system, nor did it have a program to develop and maintain job descriptions. Development of a complete wage and salary system meant creating job descriptions for all jobs in the company.

The process began with the employees in Store Operations, because that area had the greatest number of people. Job analysis questionnaires were sent to selected employees throughout the company. In some stores, all employees completed questionnaires; in other stores, only one category of employees was sampled; and in another group of stores, supervisors completed questionnaires on the employees supervised. Over 300 questionnaires were returned to the newly-hired Compensation Manager. After analysis, distinct jobs were defined and job descriptions were written, after which they were reviewed for accuracy by Store Operations management.

The analysis and resulting job descriptions resolved several thorny organizational issues for Store Operations. Title usage throughout the company became standardized. Whereas one job had been variously referred to as Bookkeeper, Office Manager, Secretary, *and others, the job title now became* Office Clerk. *Different levels of* Store Managers *and* Assistant Managers, *were established according to the store size responsibilities. The job of* Area Leader *consolidated the activities previously performed by individual department heads and gave store managers greater flexibility in assigning work to employees. Also, an organization chart was developed for each store, based upon store size and sales volume.*

Job descriptions were also written for hourly and salaried positions at the home office. Questionnaires were used to obtain information and, where necessary, personal interviews were used to clarify details. Draft descriptions were reviewed by the supervisor, the employee, and the respective vice-presidents.

Today, to keep job descriptions current, supervisors review employees' job descriptions at each performance appraisal and notify the Human Resource Department when any significant change occurs in jobs so that the job descriptions can be revised. All changes are coordinated through the Compensation Manager. The result of this job analysis process for Pamida has been a much more rational and organized system for jobs and pay.[1]

"Lots of folks confuse bad management with destiny"
ELBERT HUBBARD

To develop selection and training programs, classify jobs for pay purposes, and improve performance appraisals, management must have precise information on jobs. This chapter is concerned with how to get that information. Most methods require that a knowledgeable person describe what goes on in the job, or make a series of judgments about specific activities required to do the job.

This information is usually provided by the employee doing the job, the supervisor, and/or a trained job analyst. Each source is useful, but each has drawbacks. The supervisor would seem to be the best source of information on what *should be* done, but the employee knows most about what actually *is* done. However, both may lack the skills needed to use a job analysis questionnaire and write up the results. As the description of Pamida's process makes clear, job analysis requires a high degree of coordination and cooperation between the personnel unit and operating managers.

Responsibility for Job Analysis

The responsibility for job analysis depends upon who can best perform various aspects of the process. Figure 7–1 is a typical division of job analysis responsibilities in organizations that have a personnel unit. In small organizations, managers have to perform all the work interface activities in Figure 7–1. The personnel unit supervises the process to maintain its integrity, and writes the job descriptions and specifications for uniformity. The managers assist and may request analysis or reanalysis when it becomes necessary.

PERSONNEL UNIT	MANAGER
■ Prepares and coordinates job analysis procedures	■ Completes or assists in completing job analysis
■ Prepares job descriptions and job specifications	■ Reviews and maintains continuing accuracy of job descriptions and job specifications
■ Periodically reviews and assists managers in maintaining current job descriptions and job specifications	■ May request job analysis or reanalysis
■ Checks on manager's inputs to make sure they are properly done	■ Develops performance standards with assistance from specialists
■ May seek outside experts in difficult or unusual analysis	

FIGURE 7–1
Job Analysis Responsibilities.

Job analysis is the most basic personnel activity because it identifies what people do in their jobs and what they need in order to do the job satisfactorily. For example, if a supervisor tells an employee, "You are a grocery clerk," that clerk may not know what behavior is expected, because there are many different tasks and duties a grocery clerk could do. But when an individual is hired for a job with specific written duties and responsibilities, the manager can then expect certain work to be done.

Job analysis usually involves collecting information on characteristics of a job that differentiate it from other jobs. Information that can be helpful in making that distinction includes:

- Work activities
- Behaviors required
- Working conditions
- Interaction with others
- Performance expected
- Machines and equipment used
- Personnel requirements
- Supervision given and received

Conventional job analysis looks at the job from the standpoint of the demands the job makes on an employee. When completed it provides a description of acceptable performance and helps to identify the kind of person that should fill the job. It has been characterized as "worker requirements–oriented." But it has been argued that jobs should be described in terms of the satisfactions that employees receive from them as well—a "worker reward" approach.[2] Such an approach might depend on the job characteristics model described in the previous chapter. However valuable, the "worker reward" approach is not yet widely used.

Can you define what job analysis is?

END PRODUCTS OF JOB ANALYSIS

Job analysis is a process that identifies the components of a job, which then can be communicated to employees so they know exactly what to do. Figure 7–2 shows that job analysis serves as the basis from which job descriptions, job specifications, and job evaluations are prepared.

Job Description

Basically, the job description indicates what is done, why it is done, where it is done, and briefly, how it is done. As such, the **job description** is a summary of the tasks, duties, and responsibilities in a job. *Performance standards* should flow directly from a job description, telling what the job accomplishes and what performance is considered satisfactory in each area of the job description. The reason is clear. If employees know what is expected and what constitutes good or poor performance, they have a much better chance of performing acceptably.

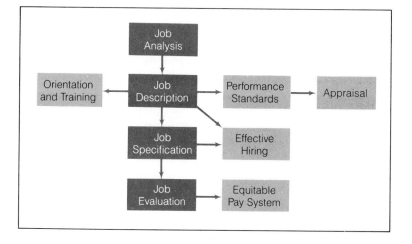

FIGURE 7–2
Job Analysis: Most Basic
Personnel Activity.

Unfortunately, performance standards are often omitted from job descriptions.

JOB SPECIFICATIONS
list the skills, knowledge, and abilities an
individual needs to do
the job satisfactorily.

Job Specification

The job description describes the job; the job specification defines the qualifications of the person needed for the job. The major use of the job specification is as a guide in recruiting and selecting people to fill jobs. A **job specification** lists the skills, knowledge, and abilities an individual needs to perform the job satisfactorily. An example of a job specification for a clerk-typist might be: "Types 50 words per minute with no more than 2 errors; successful completion of 1 year of high school English, or passing of an English proficiency test."

Job Evaluation

A job evaluation uses job analysis information to determine the worth of a job in relation to other jobs so that an equitable and meaningful wage and salary system can be established. Because job evaluation is such an integral component in the compensation of human resources, it is discussed in detail in Chapter 13, which deals with compensation issues.

Uses of Job Analysis Information

Good personnel management requires both the employee and the manager to have a clear understanding of the duties and responsibilities to be performed on a job. Job analysis helps develop this understanding by focusing on a unit of work and its relationship to other units of work. Because it identifies the tasks which make up a job, job analysis is necessary for EEO compliance and often is essential for defense when EEO complaints are filed.

Recruitment. Job analysis is used in planning how and where to obtain employees for anticipated job openings. An understanding of the skills needed and the types of jobs that may be open in the future enables managers to achieve better continuity and more effectively plan the staffing of their organization. For example, in Witlow Corporation, a small manufacturer of electric equipment, a recent job analysis showed that the *Accountant II* job, which traditionally required a college-trained person, really could be handled by someone with high school training in bookkeeping. As a result, the company can select from a greater number of available candidates and may save a considerable amount of money in salary costs.

Employee Selection. Selecting a qualified person to fill a job requires thorough knowledge of the work to be done and the qualifications needed for someone to adequately perform the work. Without a clear and precise understanding of what a job entails, a manager cannot effectively select someone to do the job. If a retail store manager has not clearly identified what a clerk is to do, it is difficult to know if the person hired must be able to lift boxes, run a cash register, or keep the books.

Compensation. While it is assumed that people are to be paid for their work, individuals should be paid more for doing more difficult jobs. Job analysis information can be used in a job evaluation to give more weight, and therefore more pay, to jobs with more tasks, duties, and responsibilities.

Training and Orientation. By providing a definition of what comprises a job through job analysis, the supervisor can easily explain to a new employee the boundaries of the employee's unit of work. It is difficult for an employee to perform well if there is confusion about what the job is and what is supposed to be done.

Career Planning and Development. As with training, job analysis information can be helpful in career planning by showing an employee what *will be* expected of a person in jobs he or she may choose to move to in the future. It also can point out areas that an employee might need to develop to further a career.

Performance Appraisal. By comparing what an individual employee is supposed to be doing (based on job analysis) to what an individual has actually done, the value of the individual's performance and competency can be determined. The ultimate objective for any organization is to pay people for performance. To do this fairly, it is necessary to compare what individuals should do, as identified by performance standards, with what they actually have done.

Can you name three uses of job analysis information?

Job analysis does not have to be a complicated process. However, the systematic investigation of jobs should be done in a practical, logical manner. The process of collecting and using information about a job is aimed at determining what work is done, how it is done, why it is done, and what skills and abilities are needed by someone to do it.

Information about jobs can be gathered in several ways. Four common methods are: (1) observation, (2) interviewing, (3) questionnaires, and (4) jury of experts. Some combination of these approaches may be used depending upon the situation and the organization.

Observation

Observation may be continuous or based on work sampling. The manager or job analyst observes the individual performing the job and takes notes to describe the tasks and duties performed.

Use of the observation method is limited because many jobs do not have complete and easily-observed job cycles. For example, complete analysis of the job of a pharmaceutical sales representative would demand that the observer follow the sales representative around for several days. Furthermore, many managers may not be skilled enough to know what to observe and how to analyze what they see. Thus, observation may be more useful in repetitive jobs and in conjunction with other methods. Managers or job analysts using other methods may watch the performance of parts of a job to gain a general familiarity with the job and the conditions under which it is performed. This observation will help them better apply some of the other job analysis methods.

Work Sampling. Work sampling differs from observation in that it does not require observing each detailed action throughout an entire work cycle. Instead, a manager can determine the content and pace of a typical workday through statistical sampling of certain actions rather than through observation and timing of all actions. Work sampling is particularly useful for clerical jobs.[3]

However, work sampling is not always well received. For example, in the Idaho Department of Health and Welfare, work sampling was instituted to increase efficiency. Seven randomly-selected times a day, a whistle was blown. The 30 workers were required to fill out forms describing what they were doing at the moment the whistle went off. Data was then collected and analyzed to determine better ways to design the jobs.

However, the workers' reactions were that the process was insulting, degrading, and disruptive. One secretary fumed, "It is insulting to my intelligence the way they go about these things." Another noted, "Yesterday morning there wasn't a single whistle. They all blew in the afternoon and everyone was sitting on pins and needles afraid to take a break or go to the bathroom." Another said the study did not bother her but the focus on secretaries did. "I think everyone should be a part of it, not just the clerical staff," she said. Because of such reactions,

I. PERSONAL INFORMATION	
1. Name (Last, First, Middle)	8. Department
2. Social Security Number	9. Board, Commission, Bureau, Institution (Where applicable)
3. Official Title of Position	10. Division, Section, Unit
4. Work Title of Position Part-time __ Permanent __ Full-time __ Temporary __ Seasonal __	11. Work Address (Mailing Address)
5. Years in Present Position	12. Regular Schedule of Hours and Shift Rotation (If Any)
6. Name and Class of Immediate Supervisor	DATE ANALYST
7. Name and Class of Next-Higher-Level Supervisor	CLASSIFICATION TITLE

FIGURE 7–3
Job Analysis Interview
Form.

the study was ultimately dropped. It should be noted that work sampling methods can include random observations without the whistle-blowing.

Interviewing

The interview method of gathering information requires that the manager or personnel specialist visit each job site and talk with the employees performing each job. Usually a structured interview form is used to record the information. Such a form is shown in Figure 7–3. Frequently, the employee and the employee's supervisor must be interviewed to obtain a complete understanding of the job. During the job analysis interview, the manager or personnel specialist must make judgments about the information to be included and its degree of importance.

II. DIFFICULTY OF WORK

Percent of Time	TASK STATEMENTS 13. Performs what action? To whom or what? To produce what? Using what tools, equipment, work aids, processes?

14. What *KNOWLEDGE*, procedures, practices, policies, and other guidelines do you use in the performance of the duties you listed? (Include any subject areas, technical knowledge, or specialized knowledge. Qualify the knowledges as *much, some, general, extensive.*)

15. What *ABILITIES/SKILLS* are required for the position? (Explain the abilities and/or skills required to perform the job, such as the ability to write reports, to train new employees, to type, to operate a bulldozer, etc.)

16. What minimum level of education/training and experience is needed for successful performance of the duties and responsibilities of the position? (Include licenses and/or certificates, special courses, etc.)

17. How much time did it take you to reach a satisfactory level of efficiency in the position and what kind of training did you receive to reach this level?

III. RESPONSIBILITY

18a. List name and class titles of employees under your *immediate supervision.* (If more than ten, list only class titles and number in each class.)

18b. Extent of Supervision:
— Assign work   — Train workers   — Discipline
— Oversee and review work   — Performance rating   — Plan methods, procedures,
— Approve work   — Recommend hiring, firing, pro-   work flow
     motion   — Others (explain)

19. What guidelines are used in completing your tasks? (Include reference works, manuals, precedents, oral and written instructions, textbooks, standard methods, procedures, etc.)

20. *Who* reviews or checks your work? *How* is it reviewed? *When* is it reviewed?

21. What happens when an error is found? How would it be found? How soon would it be found? Give specific examples.

22. Does this position require unusual physical demands such as standing, stooping, pulling, climbing, lifting or any special physical requirements such as eye–hand coordination, keen hearing, etc.?

23. In what working conditions is this position performed? Are there any hazards? Is work done in extreme weather conditions?

24. Does this position entail responsibility for the safety of other employees or the public?

25. Describe any contact (in person, by telephone, or by letter) with people other than your supervisors or subordinates you make as a regular part of your work. Describe how often, with whom, and why you have these contacts.

26. Does this position involve travel? Describe.

FIGURE 7–3
(Continued)

The interview method can be quite time-consuming. If Jones Computing Service has 30 different jobs and the job analysis interviewer spends 30–45 minutes on each interview, the time involved for interviewing and obtaining the analysis information will be extensive. The time problem will be compounded if the interviewer talks with two or three employees doing the same job. Furthermore, professional and managerial jobs are more complicated to analyze and usually require a longer interview.

For these reasons, combining the interview with one of the other methods is suggested. For example, if Lorraine Bowen has observed an employee perform a job, she can check her observation data by also interviewing the employee. Likewise, the interview is frequently used as a follow-up to the questionnaire method.

Questionnaire

The questionnaire is a widely used method of analyzing jobs and work. A survey instrument is developed and given to employees and managers to complete. Sometimes it is beneficial for the employee and supervisor to complete the questionnaire independently. Discrepancies can be highlighted and explored during interviews. At least one employee per job should complete the questionnaire, which is then returned to the supervisor or manager for review before being used for the preparation of job descriptions.

The major advantage of the questionnaire method is that information on a large number of jobs can be collected inexpensively in a relatively short period of time. However, follow-up observation and discussion are often necessary to clarify questions arising from inadequately-completed questionnaires and other interpretation problems. The questionnaire method assumes that employees can accurately analyze and communicate information about their jobs. That may not be a valid assumption in all cases. For these reasons, the questionnaire method is usually combined with interviews and observations to clarify and verify the questionnaire information.

Jury of Experts

The jury of experts approach is similar to the interview method except that it uses a group of people. Members of the group are usually experienced job incumbents and/or supervisors. The method is expensive because of the number of people involved, and it usually requires the presence of a representative from the personnel department as a mediator. However, it does bring together a large body of experience concerning a particular job in one place at one time.[4] It is probably most appropriate for certain difficult-to-define jobs.

SPECIFIC JOB ANALYSIS METHODS

There are many ways to analyze the information about the job once it has been gathered. One study of various methods found that each had strengths and weaknesses and that a combination of methods was generally preferred over one method alone.[5] The increased costs of combining methods paid off in clearer results for the job analysts. Although many methods are available and new ones continue to be developed,[6] this discussion will be confined to the two most widely used methods: functional job analysis (FJA) and the position analysis questionnaire (PAQ).

A STUDENT LEARNS JOB ANALYSIS FIRSTHAND

An undergraduate student recently had the opportunity to serve as an intern in the personnel department of a large city government. She worked in the job analysis division. At our request, she agreed to describe in her own words what was involved in the job analysis process in that organization.

Activities

I have mainly been conducting job studies. At first, I observed other analysts conduct the studies. Now I am in the position to complete my own studies with minimum assistance.

The procedure used to conduct the job studies is as follows:

1. The employee completes a 20-day worksheet log, which chronologically orders all of the work duties.

2. The employee completes a position analysis questionnaire.

3. After the log and questionnaire are received at the personnel department, I take them, analyze them, and write interview questions.

4. Next, I conduct the interview with the employee.

5. A rough draft of the report is then dictated. The objective of the job study is to see if the duties and responsibilities of the position have changed any since the employee took over the position. The report gives a very detailed description of the position, which is necessary for analysis. It is important to give extensive coverage to those duty characteristics that are related to the various class specifications, (such as technical knowledge, independence, or responsibility for error).

6. Next, I read the report to the employee and make any requested changes that are relevant, until the employee concurs with the contents of the report.

7. The report is then reviewed with the immediate supervisor. Once the supervisor agrees with the report, I have a final draft typed.

8. Next, I analyze the report to see if the position is properly classified. My decision after my analysis must be supported by as many reasons as possible. The report is then reviewed by my boss.

Functional Job Analysis (FJA)

Functional Job Analysis (FJA) is a method of analyzing jobs by constructing standardized statements and job descriptions that can be used in a variety of organizations.[7] A functional definition of what is done in a job can be generated by examining the fundamental components of *data, people,* and *things.*

Within each of these classifications a hierarchy of functions exists; the levels of this hierarchy can be identified by numbers. Figure 7–4 shows the levels and numbers associated with the dimensions of a job. The lower the number under data, people, and things, the more involved the job is in dealing with those functions. These numbers, as

FIGURE 7-4

Work Functions from *Dictionary of Occupational Titles.*

DATA (4th Digit)	PEOPLE (5th Digit)	THINGS (6th Digit)
0 Synthesizing	0 Mentoring	0 Setting Up
1 Coordinating	1 Negotiating	1 Precision Working
2 Analyzing	2 Instructing	2 Operating-Controlling
3 Compiling	3 Supervising	3 Driving-Operating
4 Computing	4 Diverting	4 Manipulating
5 Copying	5 Persuading	5 Tending
6 Comparing	6 Speaking-Signalling	6 Feeding-Offbearing
	7 Serving	7 Handling
	8 Taking Instructions-Helping	

SOURCE: U.S. Department of Labor, *Dictionary of Occupational Titles*, 4th ed. (Washington, D.C.: Government Printing Office, 1977) p. xviii.

well as those providing other information, can be used to identify and compare important elements of jobs by using the *Dictionary of Occupational Titles* (DOT), a standardized data source provided by the federal government.

Using the identification code for *Director of Athletics,* (090.117–022), a brief description can be given of how the DOT is used. The first three digits (090) indicate the occupational code, title, and industry designations. The next three digits (117) represent the degree to which a director of athletics *typically* has responsibility and judgment over *data, things,* and *people*. The final three digits are used to indicate the alphabetical order of titles within the occupational group having the same degree of responsibility and judgment.

The value of the DOT is in the wide range of jobs described (as shown in Figure 7–5). A manager or personnel specialist confronted with preparing a large number of job descriptions can use the DOT as a starting point. Then the job description from the DOT can be modified to fit the particular organizational situation. The importance of the DOT is demonstrated by the fact that job descriptions based on the DOT are considered satisfactory by federal employment enforcement agencies.

Functional job analysis is advocated as being easy to learn and use because statistical percentages can be assigned to each of the three dimensions (things, data, people) following the preparation of a task statement. A detailed explanation of the procedures involved in FJA is not appropriate here, but it is relevant to note that use of the DOT and FJA can be helpful to managers who are not personnel specialists. FJA can be used in developing occupational "career ladders" by identifying jobs requiring progressively more skill or responsibilities. This identification can clarify promotion and career ladders. Also, because FJA is standardized, statistical data can be developed for personnel decision-making areas such as test validation. However, because FJA is primarily narrative in nature, quantitative job evaluation is difficult. The Position Analysis Questionnaire can help quantify job classifications.

FIGURE 7–5

Sample Job Titles and Descriptions from *Dictionary of Occupational Titles*.

090.117-022 DIRECTOR, ATHLETIC (EDUCATION)

Plans, administers, and directs intercollegiate athletic activities in college or university. Interprets and participates in formulating extramural athletic policies. Employs and discharges coaching staff and other department employees on own initiative or at direction of board in charge of athletics. Directs preparation and dissemination of publicity to promote athletic events. Plans and coordinates activities of coaching staff. Prepares budget and authorizes department expenditures. Plans and schedules sports events, and oversees ticket sales activities. Certifies reports of income produced from ticket sales. May direct programs for students of physical education.

151.047-010 DANCER (AMUSE. & REC.)

Dances alone, with partner, or in group to entertain audience: Performs classical, modern, or acrobatic dances, coordinating body movements to musical accompaniment. Rehearses dance movements developed by CHOREOGRAPHER (amuse. & rec.). May choreograph own dance. May sing and provide other forms of entertainment. May specialize in particular style of dancing and be designated according to specialty as ACROBATIC DANCER (amuse. & rec.); BALLET DANCER (amuse. & rec.); BALLROOM DANCER (amuse. & rec.); BELLY DANCER (amuse. & rec.); CHORUS DANCER (amuse. & rec.); INTERPRETATIVE DANCER (amuse. & rec.); STRIP-TEASE DANCER (amuse. & rec.); TAP DANCER (amuse. & rec.).

160.162-010 ACCOUNTANT, TAX (PROFESS. & KIN.)

Prepares Federal, state, or local tax returns of individual, business establishment, or other organization: Examines accounts and records and computes tax returns according to prescribed rates, laws, and regulations. Advises management regarding effects of business, internal programs and activities, and other transactions upon taxes and represents principal before various governmental taxing bodies. May devise and install tax record systems. May specialize in particular phase of tax accounting, such as income, property, real estate, or Social Security taxes.

166.117-018 MANAGER, PERSONNEL. (PROFESS. & KIN.)

Plans and carries out policies relating to all phases of personnel activity. Recruits, interviews, and selects employees to fill vacant positions. Plans and conducts new employee orientation to foster positive attitude toward company goals. Keeps record of insurance coverage, pension plan, and personnel transactions, such as hires, promotions, transfers, and terminations. Investigates accidents and prepares reports for insurance carrier. Conducts wage survey within labor market to determine competitive wage rate. Prepares budget of personnel operations. Meets with shop stewards and supervisors to resolve grievances. Writes separation notices for employees separating with cause and conducts exit interviews to determine reasons behind separations. Prepares reports and recommends procedures to reduce absenteeism and turnover. Contracts with outside suppliers to provide employee services, such as canteen, transportation, or relocation service. May keep records of hired employee characteristics for governmental reporting purposes. May negotiate collective bargaining agreement with BUSINESS REPRESENTATIVE LABOR UNION (profess. & kin.)

709.684-026 BIRD-CAGE ASSEMBLER (WIREWORK)

Fabricates wire birdcages, using handtools and drill press: Cuts wire to specified length, using wirecutter. Positions metal plate in *jig*, and drills holes around circumference of plate, using drill press. Fits ends of wires into holes in plate, and fastens upper ends of wire together to form cage.

SOURCE: U.S. Department of Labor, *Dictionary of Occupational Titles*, 4th ed. (Washington, DC: Government Printing Office, 1977), pp. 66, 86, 91, 98, 665.

Position Analysis Questionnaire

A second method is the Position Analysis Questionnaire (PAQ), a standardized instrument for job analysis. Each job is analyzed in terms of the job "elements" in the PAQ. A manager using the PAQ checks the behavioral elements that apply on a six-point rating scale. The way in which the PAQ structures job elements makes it possible to analyze almost any type of position or job. It is easily quantified and can be used to conduct validity studies on tests. The PAQ also can be translated into a job evaluation system to ensure internal pay fairness, giving consideration to the varying demands of different jobs.

The PAQ is divided into six divisions, with each division containing numerous job elements. The divisions include:

- Information Input—Where and how does the worker get information to do the job?
- Mental Process—What levels of reasoning are necessary on the job?
- Work Output—What physical activities are performed?
- Relationships with Others—What relationships are required to perform the job?
- Job Context—What working conditions and social contexts are involved?
- Other—What else is relevant to the job?[8]

The PAQ has been found to be relatively stable even when attempts are made to manipulate information and the interest level of employees varies.[9] It has also been used successfully to classify positions into job families based on an analysis of job description narratives, which are readily available in most companies.[10]

Can you distinguish between the PAQ and FJA?

BEHAVIORAL AND LEGAL ASPECTS OF JOB ANALYSIS

When systematically analyzing jobs, managers must be aware of two general concerns. One is the reaction of employees to such an intensive look at their jobs. The other concern is the impact of governmental constraints, especially from equal employment opportunity guidelines, on job analysis and its outcomes. First, the impact of human behavior on the job analysis process must be considered.

Behavioral Aspects of Job Analysis

A detailed examination of jobs, while necessary, can be a demanding and threatening experience for both managers and employees, depending on the situation. For example, in one shoe manufacturing firm, Phil Goetz had worked very hard in the packing department for many years. Everyone knew Goetz worked hard, but because he was a hard worker no one ever really questioned what he did. When a new manager came to the packaging department, he felt a job analysis was in order. Goetz violently resisted any attempt to analyze his job and refused to cooperate with the analyst. He was sure he would be put back to work packing shoes eight hours a day instead of working on the many different projects with which he was involved.

Employee Fears. One fear that some employees have is that clearly analyzing, specifying, and defining their jobs will put a "straitjacket" on them. Just like the shoe packer, they feel creativity and flexibility may be limited by formalizing the duties, responsibilities, and qualifications needed for a job. However, it does not necessarily follow that analyzing a job will limit job scope or depth.

Another concern that some employees have is a fear about the *purpose* of a detailed investigation of their jobs. The attitude that "as long as someone doesn't know precisely what I am supposed to be doing, then I am safe," may generate attempts to hide the uniqueness of a job. The employee's concern is that someone must feel they did something wrong if such a searching look is taken at their jobs. Consequently, explanation of the job analysis process and of why it is being done should be part of any job analysis.

Resistance to Change. As jobs change, there is a continued need to update and revise job descriptions and job specifications to make them more meaningful. As would be expected, people become used to working within the defined boundaries of responsibilities. When an attempt is made to change those "job fences," fear, resistance, and insecurity are generated. Suggesting it is time to revise job descriptions provokes anxiety because the employees' safe and secure job worlds are threatened. Their jobs may be changed and they may have to take on new and difficult responsibilities.

Because resistance in this situation is a natural reaction, managers should expect it and be prepared to deal with it. Perhaps the most effective way to handle this problem is to involve the individual in the revision process. Allowing Diane Morris, a purchasing analyst, to help reexamine her job and play a vital role in the development of the new job description and job specifications can help overcome a certain amount of the fear and anxiety she may feel. However, this uneasiness may not actually disappear until she becomes accustomed to working under the new setup. Because jobs change, supervisors and managers should expect to continually strive to overcome resistance as changes in jobs and work occur.

In addition, as work changes and becomes more complex, especially at managerial and administrative levels, it is more difficult to analyze and determine exactly what constitutes a job. For example, trying to write a job description for the president of a corporation is very difficult, because of the extensive and often varied nature of the job. Likewise, clearly identifying the tasks, duties, and responsibilities of a head nurse or a university dean is difficult because of the wide scope, flexibility, and complexity of their activities.

In some organizations managers review the job description during each performance appraisal interview. This review enables the job holder and the supervisor to discuss whether the job description still adequately describes the actual job.

Overemphasis on Current Employees. A good analysis and the resulting job description and specification do not describe only what the individual currently holding the job does and that individual's qualifications. The person may have unique capabilities and the ability to expand the scope of the job to assume more responsibilities. The company would have difficulty finding someone exactly like that individual if he or she left. Therefore, the job description and job specifications should not be merely a description of what the person currently filling the job does.

Managerial "Straightjacket." Through the information developed in a job analysis, the job description is supposed to capture the scope of a job. However, some employees may use job descriptions in order to limit managerial flexibility, thus putting a "straightjacket" on a manager. Consequently, some nonunion employers refuse to show job descriptions to their employees. This refusal makes it difficult for an employee to say, "I don't have to do that because it is not in my job description." In some organizations with a unionized work force, very restrictive job descriptions exist.

A good example of using job descriptions to restrict work occurred in the early 1980s when air traffic controllers "followed the book" and caused havoc with airplane departures and landings at major airports. The attitude, "It is not in my job description," can become very burdensome for a management involved in changing an organization, its technology, and jobs in response to changing economic or social conditions.

Can you identify how behavioral considerations affect job analysis?

Legal Aspects of Job Analysis

In addition to behavioral concerns, managers must also be aware of the legal impact of job analysis. The equal employment discussion in Chapter 4 continually made reference to the need for "job-relatedness" in staffing activities. A job analysis provides the basis for job-relatedness through the development of job descriptions and job specifications. In a sense, it is the foundation for many personnel activities.

Federal equal employment opportunity enforcement guidelines clearly indicate that a sound and comprehensive job analysis is required for selection criteria to be validated. Without a systematic investigation of a job, an employer may be using requirements that may not be specifically job-related.[12] For example, if a trucking firm requires a high school diploma for a dispatcher's job, the firm must be able to indicate how such an educational requirement matches up to the tasks, duties, and responsibilities of a dispatcher. The only way the firm might be able to justify the requirement would be to identify the knowledge, skills, and abilities needed by the dispatcher and to show that they could only be obtained through formal education.

A careful review of the criteria used by the courts in their assessment of job analysis shows certain standards are expected. These standards, in addition to being legally necessary, also provide a view of a professional job analysis process. The standards are shown in Figure 7–6.

In summary, it is extremely difficult for an employer to have a legal staffing system without performing a sound job analysis. Consequently, job analysis truly is the most basic personnel activity, primarily because it focuses on the jobs employees perform.

Can you outline the requirements for a legal job analysis?

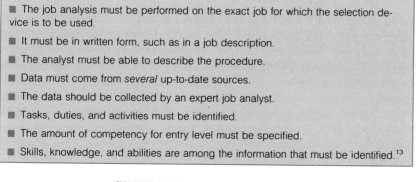

■ The job analysis must be performed on the exact job for which the selection device is to be used.

■ It must be in written form, such as in a job description.

■ The analyst must be able to describe the procedure.

■ Data must come from *several* up-to-date sources.

■ The data should be collected by an expert job analyst.

■ Tasks, duties, and activities must be identified.

■ The amount of competency for entry level must be specified.

■ Skills, knowledge, and abilities are among the information that must be identified.[13]

FIGURE 7–6
Legal Standards for Job Analysis When Validating Selection Instruments.

The output from job analysis is usually a job description and job specifications for the job that has been studied. Both are compiled and prepared to summarize concisely the job analysis information for each job. Job descriptions and job specifications should be accurate, readable, understandable, and usable.

Job Description Components

The typical job description, such as the one in Figure 7–7, contains three major parts. These parts are described below.

Identification. The first part is the identification section. In this part the employee's job title, department, and reporting relationship are presented. Additional information such as the date of analysis, a job number, the number of employees holding the job, and the current pay scale of the job occupants can also be included.

General Summary. The second part, the general summary, is a concise summation of the general responsibilities and components that make the job different from others. One personnel specialist has characterized the general summary statement as follows: "In 25 words or less, describe the essence of the job." In Figure 7–7 the listing of major accountabilities serves as the general summary.

Specific Duties. The third part of the typical job description, the specific duties section, contains clear and precise statements on the major tasks, duties, and responsibilities performed. The most time-consuming aspect of writing job descriptions is this listing of specific duties.

Writing Job Descriptions

In writing job descriptions it is important to use precise action verbs that accurately describe the employee's tasks, duties, and responsibilities. For example, avoiding the use of vague words such as *does* or *handles* is important. Also, specific duties should be grouped and arranged in some logical pattern. If a job requires an accounting supervisor to prepare several reports, among other functions, statements relating to the preparation of reports should be grouped together.

A guide to writing a job description for a social welfare job is shown in Figure 7–8. The manager preparing the job description should use precise and clear language but should not fall into the trap of writing a motion analysis. The statement, "Walks to filing cabinet, opens drawer, pulls folder out, and inserts material in correct folders," is an extreme example of a motion statement. The specific duty statement, "Files correspondence and memoranda to maintain accurate customer policy records," is sufficiently descriptive without being overly detailed.

FIGURE 7–7
Sample Job Description:
Benefits Manager.

Date: March, 1984 | Job Title: Benefits Manager

Div. Administration | Dept: Personnel | Sect:

Reports to: Personnel Director

Supervises: N/A

Education: College degree in personnel or business administration preferred but not essential.

Experience: Considerable experience with employee group insurance programs preferred.

Major Accountabilities

1. Insures (ERISA) compliance and reporting for all pension and welfare benefits, keeping a current knowledge of (IRS) and (DOL) regulations.

2. Coordinates employee benefits and services.

3. Counsels employees regarding benefit problems.

4. Manages the office in the absence of the personnel director.

Duties and Responsibilities

1. Maintains ERISA reporting calendars for (TSA), retirement plan, (LTD) and life insurance, health insurance.

2. Prepares and files appropriate reports to IRS, DOL, and employees, including gathering and verifying information from all insurance companies and/or other sources.

3. Maintains ERISA records for retirement plan. Correlates and insures accuracy of records with trustee, actuary, and legal counsel.

4. Calculates retirement benefits and processes forms, including vested terminations; early, normal, and late retirement, including "joint" and "survivor" and "lump sum" cash-out benefits.

5. Counsels employees regarding benefits at the time of transfer in status, termination, and retirement. Monitors pay period benefits reports, insuring accuracy.

6. Processes garnishments on employees.

7. Approves requests for educational assistance and makes payments and receives reimbursements to the hospital.

8. Administers absence control program, monitoring excused and unexcused absences, records and insures that proper disciplinary action is being executed according to established policy and procedures. Maintains records and distributes reports on absenteeism to department heads and personnel director.

9. Manages salary security program, including processing of claims insuring proper reporting to insurance companies and employee understanding of life insurances and LTD benefits and procedures.

10. Manages health insurance program, including counseling employees regarding benefits and claim procedures; pays billings and insures proper payroll input for deductions.

11. Administers TSA program (including conducting annual reopenings with broker and counseling employees regarding benefits), and maintains records insuring correct salaries, deductions, and billing procedures.

12. Receives and processes unemployment compensation claims and verifies and pays quarterly billings.

13. Ensures accurate and timely payment of terminal benefits.

14. Conducts and analyzes benefits surveys in order to maintain pay competitiveness with area hospitals.

15. Recommends changes in benefit policy and practices.

16. Performs other duties as assigned.   Used with permission.

FIGURE 7–8
Writing a Job Description
of a Social Welfare Job.

PERFORMS WHAT ACTION? (VERB)	TO WHOM OR WHAT? (OBJECT OF VERB)	TO PRODUCE WHAT? (EXPECTED OUTPUT)	USING WHAT TOOLS, EQUIPMENT, WORK AIDS, PROCESSES?
Asks ques-tions/listens Records answers	To/of applicant On eligibility form	In order to deter-mine eligibility	Eligibility form Eligibility criteria in manual Interviewing tech-niques

This task statement now reads: "Asks client questions, listens and records an-swers on standard eligibility form, using knowledge of interviewing techniques and eligibility criteria in order to gather information from which client's eligibility for food stamps can be determined."

SOURCE: U.S. Civil Service Commission, *Job Analysis: Developing and Documenting Data. A Guide for State and Local Governments*. BIPP 152–85 (Washington, D.C.: Government Printing Office, 1973), p. 6.

It is not the intent of this section to provide a detailed guide to writing a job description, but only to highlight some of the key ideas a manager should remember in writing or revising job descriptions.[14] Some job descriptions contain other sections about materials or machines used, working conditions, or special tools used. This information is often included in the specific duty statements or in a comments sections. Also, the final statement in many job descriptions is often the *miscellaneous clause*, often a phrase such as, "Performs other duties as needed upon request by immediate supervisor." This statement is included to cover the abnormal and unusual situations that comprise a very small part of an employee's job. Having such a statement is an attempt to prevent an employee from saying, "It's not covered in my job description."

One of the challenging aspects of writing job descriptions involves describing executive and upper management–level jobs. Because of the wide range of duties and responsibilities, those jobs often are described in more general terms than jobs at lower levels in the organization.

Job Specification

The job specification, a logical outgrowth of a job description, attempts to describe the key qualifications someone needs to perform the job satisfactorily. Specific factors identified often can be grouped into three categories: skills, knowledge, and abilities (SKAs). Factors within these categories include education, experience, work skill requirements, personal requirements, mental and physical requirements, and working conditions and hazards. A job specification for a remote visual display terminal operator might include a required education level, a certain number of months of experience, typing ability of 60 wpm, a high degree of visual concentration, and ability to work under time pressure.

A job specification can be written by talking with the current holder of the job about the qualifications needed to perform the job satisfac-

"I know I'm overqualified, but I promise to
use only half my ability."

torily. But caution should be exercised so that the characteristics of the
current job occupant are not used as the sole basis for the job specification statements. Opinions of supervisors are often used in determining qualifications. Checking the job requirements of other organizations with similar jobs is another means of obtaining information for
job specifications.

Critical Skills, Knowledge, and Abilities (SKAs). In writing any job specification, it is important to list only those SKAs essential for satisfactory
job performance. Only job-related items which are nondiscriminatory
should be included. For example, a high school diploma should not be
required for a job unless the manager can demonstrate that an individual with less education cannot perform the job as well. Because of that
concern, some specification statements read: "High school diploma, or
equivalent acceptable experience." In some technical jobs the exact
knowledge can be indicated: "Must have thorough knowledge of PL-1
and COBOL computer languages." Figure 7–9 is one example of this
approach.

A process for developing relevant SKAs has evolved very recently in
the public sector. Using a content validity approach that focuses only
on critical job-related criteria, this process uses a group of experts in a
job, including employees holding the job, to identify clear, recogniz-
able, and ratable SKAs. These SKAs then become the basis for selecting
employees.[15]

*Can you describe how a job description and
a job specification are closely linked?*

CLASS TITLE: Systems Project Leader

CHARACTERISTICS OF THE CLASS:
Under direction, is responsible for work of considerable difficulty in supervising a project team in the plan, design, and implementation of a major data processing project.

Incumbents are responsible for supervising a team of programmer/analysts in the design, installation, and implementation of a system and functions with complete independence within the framework of the assignment. This level is distinguished from
the EDP Programmer/Analyst III by having responsibility for planning, designing, and
implementing a total project and may assign responsibility at the job level to EDP
Programmer/Analyst III. This level is distinguished from the EDP Systems Project
Manager who has the responsibility for managing several project teams.

EXAMPLES OF DUTIES:
Supervises and participates as a member of a project team in systems design and
implementation; plans and designs automated processes determining applications
and computer requirements, conducting feasibility studies, scheduling projects and
implementation of activities; coordinates the development and implementation of
projects working with users and DP personnel to maintain schedules, to identify/re-
solve problems, and to maintain effective communication with users and DP management; assists users in planning and the development of new systems and maintenance, modification and enhancement of existing systems to identify/resolve
problems, assure that schedules are being met, provide better service, and maintain
effective communication links; prepares written instructions/descriptions for use in
developing user procedures and programming specifications; supervises the activities of programming staff in the development of coded instructions for digital computer processing and may perform programming functions as required; plans and
develops test data files, testing sequence and reviews test results for adherence to
programming and operations standards.

KNOWLEDGE, ABILITIES, AND SKILLS:
Considerable knowledge of electronic data processing equipment capabilities; considerable knowledge of application systems design techniques and procedures; considerable knowledge of project organization, management, and control; good knowledge of the principles and techniques of programming and digital computers; good
knowledge of the principles of supervision; some knowledge of statistics. Ability to
analyze data and situations, reason logically, draw valid conclusions, and develop
effective solutions to systems problems; ability to design procedures for processing
data with digital computers; ability to prepare comprehensive reports; ability to analyze and evaluate the progress of the system being developed; ability to speak and
write effectively.

MINIMUM QUALIFICATIONS:
Two years experience equivalent to an EDP Programmer/Analyst III.

Using Job Descriptions and Job Specifications

Once job descriptions and specifications are prepared, the manager
should provide feedback to the current job holders, especially those
who assisted in the job analysis. One feedback technique is to give
employees a copy of their own job descriptions and specifications for
review. Giving the current employees the opportunity to make corrections, ask for clarification, and discuss their job duties with the appropriate manager or supervisor enhances manager-employee communications. Questions about how work is done, why it is done that way,
and how it can be changed are topics that arise.[17] When employees are
represented by a union it is essential that union representatives be included in reviewing the job descriptions and specifications. Otherwise,
the possibility of future conflict is heightened.

Performance Standards. An important use of job descriptions and specifications is to generate performance standards for each of the job responsibility statements. Because performance standards list what is satisfactory performance in each area of the job, the employee can be given a clear idea of what is expected. The development of clear and realistic performance standards can prevent the communication problems that often arise when an employee's performance is appraised.

Staffing. A good job specification is useful in the selection process because it provides a specific set of qualifications for an individual to be hired for a specific job.[18] Clarifying what type of person is to be recruited and selected definitely helps a manager, supervisor, or a personnel specialist. Likewise, a well-written job description can be used to give applicants an initial picture of what they will be doing if they are hired.

PERSONNEL TODAY AND TOMORROW
TRACKING NEW JOB CATEGORIES

Change is a constant, and change in jobs is no exception. Jobs and oc-cupations change today at a rapid rate as companies adjust to a chang-ing business environment. But this change is not just a modern phenom-enon. In fact, jobs and careers have changed from the beginning of time. Long ago, food gathering was done by women, while men did the hunt-ing. Then came a period where most people engaged in subsistance farming. Jobs changed from hunting and gathering to plowing, planting, and harvesting.

In the Middle Ages, the newly emerging jobs were those done by crafts workers and artisans. During the Reniassance, business, trade, and manufacturing were the "hot" job classifications. Next the Industrial Revolution pulled many people off the farms and put them into factories.

Today we are in what is called the *post-industrial* period. Predictions are that by the year 2000, 80 percent of the work force will be engaged in the "information" industry. Professional workers, such as lawyers, ac-countants, teachers, professors, engineers, reporters, and librarians, have always been information workers.

New jobs and careers have emerged, died, and been replaced. Ele-vator operators, bowling pin setters, linotype operators, milkmen, and hundreds of other job categories have passed, or are passing away.

Not all traditional jobs will die off, of course. The U.S. Bureau of Labor Statistics estimates that there will be 600,000 jobs for janitors between now and 1990 compared to just 200,000 for computer systems analysts; 800,000 jobs for fast food workers, and only 88,000 jobs for computer operators. But new jobs and careers are emerging so fast that such in-formation as the education or training needed, working conditions, and typical earnings, cannot be developed fast enough to keep up with the changes.

Consider, for example, the Industrial Hygienist. This new specialty con-sists of people who evaluate and control health hazards where people work. Industrial hygienists can head off worker compensation claims and spot potential hazards that most people do not notice. For example, one group of computer room employees were experiencing headaches and nausea on a regular basis. An industrial hygienist discovered that some-one had blocked a vent and that the gas water heater burner was not taking in enough air, thereby creating carbon monoxide and making peo-ple sick.

In another case, tennis ball testers commonly suffered a tendon disor-der in their wrists. The solution was to change the work routine so that they squeezed a ball only when their wrists were not bent. Even "clean" industries can cause problems, such as the hazard of lead poisoning among those who do soldering work in electronics plants. As other new jobs develop, analyzing them and deciding how people should be trained to do them will present new challenges.[19]

SUMMARY

- Management needs information on what people do in their jobs for training, wage and salary decisions, and performance appraisal. Job analysis provides that information.
- Job analysis is a systematic investigation of the tasks, duties, and responsibilities required in a job, and the skills, knowledge, and abilities necessary to do the job.
- The end products of job analysis are job descriptions, job specifications, and job evaluation.
- Job analysis information is also used in recruitment, selection, and career planning, thus making it a basic personnel activity.
- There are four common methods of gathering job analysis information: observation, interviews, questionnaires, and a jury of experts. In practice, a combination of methods is often used.
- Functional Job Analysis (FJA) uses standardized task statements and job descriptions to examine data, people, and things.
- The Dictionary of Occupational Titles (DOT) can be used with FJA to analyze jobs.
- The Position Analysis Questionnaire (PAQ), a structured questionnaire, also is widely used to analyze jobs.
- Job analysis, while seemingly very straightforward, has several behavioral implications that managers should consider: employees' fear of the process, resistance to change, a tendency to overemphasize the current job holder's qualifications, and the danger of job descriptions putting a "straightjacket" on managerial flexibility.
- Legally, job analysis must conform to ideas of the courts about what is good job analysis. This conformity is especially true if the information is used in validating tests or in other EEO-related decisions.
- Writing job descriptions and job specifications, especially for executive jobs, can be tricky. But once prepared, the two tools provide good feedback to jobholders.

REVIEW QUESTIONS AND EXERCISES

1. Clearly define and discuss the relationship among job analysis, job descriptions, and job specifications.
2. "Job analysis is the most basic personnel activity." Discuss.
3. In two sentences each, describe the four common methods of analyzing jobs.
4. How do human behavior and governmental considerations affect the job analysis process?
5. Construct a form for a sample job description. Why is a job description necessary before developing a job specification?
6. Explain the reasoning behind each of the legal requirements for job analysis as you see them.

Exercises

a. Write a job description and a job specification for your current (or last) job.

b. Have the class interview your instructor to get job analysis information for his or her job and write up a job description and job specification for that job.

CASE

WHAT DOES AN ADMINISTRATIVE SUPERVISOR DO?

Several months ago Humphrey Millhouse, Regional Director of the Federal Bureau of Environmental Management, started hearing rumbles of discontent from several of his branch managers. The regional headquarters of the Bureau, located in a large metropolitan city, is the hub for ten branch offices scattered throughout the region. Upon checking out the rumors, Millhouse found that most of the complaints concerned the discrepancy between the broad range of duties for which Administrative Supervisors were responsible and the compensation they received.

Upon further investigation, it appeared that there were conflicting perceptions of what duties were required for a person in charge of an administrative group. Many of the Administrative Supervisors felt they were not receiving credit for all their responsibilities, while personnel specialists who prepared the position classifications felt that the Administrative Supervisors were claiming they were responsible for the same duties others were also performing.

Many of the managers to whom Administrative Supervisors reported expressed concern about recruiting and retaining competent help. The managers complained that headquarters did not recognize the knowledge required, the degree of difficulty, or the responsibility that goes with the position of Administrative Supervisor. They claimed that this lack of recognition had caused the job to be underpaid, leading highly qualified personnel to "dead-end" at unjustly low salary grades.

As a result of these complaints, Millhouse established a task force at headquarters, composed of representatives from six different divisions, to identify the problems that needed to be resolved and to develop ideas on how to solve them. At the first meeting of the task force, it was decided that an inventory of administrative functions was needed to define what should be done by the technical and support-level employees who reported to the Administrative Supervisors. Also, the task force attempted to identify what responsibilities should be performed at the branch offices and what should be performed at headquarters. At subsequent meetings, it was determined that input was needed from the branch offices. Managers in each branch were asked to make up lists of all the responsibilites and duties performed by their Administrative Supervisors. The task force has just received all of the lists from the branch managers and is now trying to decide what to do from this point.

Questions

1. Describe why job analysis may be useful in clarifying the duties of an Administrative Supervisor.
2. What is your reaction to the manner in which the task force chose to obtain information on the Administrative Supervisor jobs?
3. What steps would you recommend that the task force follow from this point? Why?

NOTES

1. Used with permission, Pamida, 1984.
2. B. Schneider, *Staffing Organizations* (Pacific Palisades, CA: Goodyear Publishing, 1976), p. 32.
3. W. H. Weiss, "How to Work-Sample Your People," *Administrative Management,* June 14, 1982, pp. 37–38, 49–50.
4. J. Markowitz, "Four Methods of Job Analysis," *Training and Development Journal,* September 1981, p. 116.
5. E. L. Levine et al., "Evaluation of Job Analysis Methods by Experienced Job Analysts," *Academy of Management Journal* 26 (1983), pp. 339–348.
6. M. H. Banks et al., "The Job Components Inventory and the Analysis of Jobs Requiring Limited Skill," *Personnel Psychology* 36, (1983), pp. 57–66.
7. A concise, detailed explanation of FJA is contained in Dale Yoder and Herbert G. Heneman, Jr., eds, *ASPA Handbook of Personnel and Industrial Relations Vol. 1, Staffing Policies and Strategies* (Washington, DC: Bureau of National Affairs, 1979).
8. E. J. McCormick and J. Tiffin, *Industrial Psychology,* 6th ed. (Englewood Cliffs, NJ: Prentice Hall, 1974), p. 53.
9. R. D. Arvey et al., "Narrative Job Descriptions as Potential Sources of Job Analysis Ratings," *Personnel Psychology* 35, (1982), pp. 618–629.
10. A. P. Jones et al., "Potential Sources of Bias in Job Analytic Procedures," *Academy of Management Journal* 35, (1982), pp. 813–828.
11. Adapted from B. A. Jacobs, "Title Wave Engulfs Corporate America," *Industry Week,* April 19, 1982, pp. 111–112.
12. For example, see T. M. Stutzman, "Within Classification Job Differences" *Personnel Psychology* 36 (1983), pp. 503–516.
13. Adapted from D. E. Thompson and T. A. Thompson, "Court Standards for Job Analysis in Test Validation," *Personnel Psychology* 35 (1982), pp. 865–874.
14. For a detailed guide on preparing and writing job descriptions see *Job Analysis,* U.S. Civil Service Commission, or R. I. Henderson, *Compensation Management* (Reston, VA: Reston Publishing, 1983), Chapter 7.
15. For detailed information, see Robert Otteman and J. Brad Chapman, "A Viable Strategy for Validation: Content Validity," *The Personnel Administrator,* November 1977, pp. 17–22.
16. Adapted from M. J. Gannon, "Managerial Ignorance," *Business Horizons,* May–June 1983, p. 27.

17. V. K. Manaktala, "Job Descriptions: Making Subordinates Accountable," *Supervisory Management*, January 1983, pp. 27–29.

18. E. A. Fleishman, "Evaluating Physical Abilities Required by Jobs," *Personnel Administrator*, June 1979, pp. 82–90.

19. Adapted from S. N. Feingold, "Tracking New Career Categories," *Personnel Administrator*, December 1983, pp. 86–94; and S. L. Jacobs, "Industrial Hygienists Increase Firm's Output and Efficiency," *Wall Street Journal*, March 5, 1984, p. 29.

Human Resource Planning and Recruiting

When you have read this chapter, you should be able to:

1. Define human resource planning and identify the stages of the human resource planning process.
2. Discuss the importance of assessing external and internal factors and auditing current jobs and employee skills.
3. Identify common items in a human resource plan.
4. Define recruiting, and diagram a typical recruiting process.
5. Identify three internal recruiting sources.
6. List four external recruiting sources.
7. Describe three advantages and disadvantages of internal and external recruiting.

PERSONNEL AT WORK

TRUTH OR GOBBLEDYGOOK IN RECRUITMENT ADVERTISING

On returning from a two-year employment contract overseas, L. O. Baier found himself reading the recruiting ads for personnel/human resource jobs. What he found was a surprising amount of jargon and very few ads that said just what a company was seeking.

On the subject of salaries, consider these excerpts:

Send confidential resume including salary history and salary requirements to . . . . We offer an *attractive* salary.
Send a detailed resume and letter. . . . We offer an *excellent* compensation package.
Send your resume including salary history to. . . . Our system offers a *competitive* package of compensation benefits.
You are required to send your resume including salary history/requirements to. . . . We offer an *excellent* benefits package including stock options and bonuses.

Frustrating? Wait until you try to determine company size. There's a Fortune 50, 100, 200, 300, 500, and 1000; along with companies that describe themselves as major, prestigious, outstanding, well-known, *and even as* a flagship operation.

To clear things up, "specific" qualifications are named for these positions: What's needed is "a heavy hitter" with a "firm grasp" moving on the "fast track" capable of sustaining a "high energy level" from a still higher "visibility position" impacting the "bottom line."

If you find it hard to believe such jargon would really be used, look at this Wall Street Journal *ad for a human resource generalist:*

Director opportunity with prestigious Fortune 100 organization committed to providing rapid advancement opportunities to fast track achievers who can continue to enhance a state-of-the-art human resource function. This high profile individual, who possesses excellent managerial and intervention skills, technical achievements and dynamic personal characteristics will interface with executives recognized for their growth oriented business results. Initiative, potential and progression through meaningful exposure is more important than years of experience. Respond in strict confidence to . . . .

As Baier commented, "Hard to believe, isn't it, that grown adults would have the courage to print such a collection of nonsense? I have read through the newspapers for New York, Boston, Philadelphia, Baltimore, and Washington, D.C. Included were some 300 or more pages of classified ads. Only one—that's right, only one ad in over thousands—said clearly what it wanted, what it would pay for this experience, and how to respond . . . It was two columns wide and two inches deep and contained three compound complex sentences. Unfortunately, it didn't say where the company was located. But then three out of four isn't bad."[1]

"Thorough planning is an open road to great accomplishments."

A. L. ROMANOFF

An important part of personnel management is providing the organization with a staff of employees to do its work. Sometimes efforts to do so are poorly conceived, as L. O. Baier discovered. Nevertheless, it can be done well. Staffing encompasses three distinct activities: *human resource planning, recruiting,* and *selection.*

Human resource planning is tied to the overall strategic planning efforts of the organization. It is the attempt to forecast the future supply and demand for human resources needed by the organization. *Recruiting* focuses on generating an adequate number of qualified applicants for managers to review. *Selection* is the stage at which individuals actually are screened and either rejected or offered employment. The first two of these activities are discussed in this chapter, while selection is examined in the next chapter.

HUMAN RESOURCE PLANNING

Planning for human resources must consider the allocation of people to jobs over long periods—not just for the next month or even the next year. **Human resource planning** (hereafter called *HR planning*) is the process of analyzing and estimating the need for and availability of employees. Factors to consider include the current level of skills in an organization and the expected vacancies due to retirement, promotion, transfer, sick leave, discharge, or other reasons. Human resource planners also try to foresee any expansions or reductions in operations and technological changes that may affect the organization. On the basis of such analyses, plans can be made for shifting employees within the organization, laying off or otherwise cutting back the number of employees, or retraining present employes, as well as for recruiting and hiring new people. Because of its focus on organizational needs, HR planning must be part of the overall strategic planning process in an organization.

Strategic Planning for Human Resources

Strategic planning is a term often used to identify organizational efforts to prepare for the future. The future is forecasted through assessment of a wide range of factors that may impact the organization. Although it is common to identify strategic planning with areas such as finance and marketing, it is people, as human resources, who will ultimately determine the future financial resources of the organization. Also, it is people who must manage and staff the sales effort used to market the goods or services of the organization. Consequently, human resource planning must be tied to overall organizational planning efforts.

The overall objectives of an organization should reflect human resource considerations. One writer has observed, "In planning corporate strategy, it is essential that an organization be fully aware of its present work force capacity as well as its future work force needs."[2] So, HR planning should be seen as a twofold activity: (1) it provides input for overall organizational planning efforts and (2) it identifies the actions needed to ensure that enough qualified people are available to meet those objectives.

THE PROCESS OF HR PLANNING

One of the most challenging responsibilities managers face is identifying and planning for the people who will be needed as the organization grows and changes. HR planning is especially important in emerging, highly technological fields such as computer design and telecommunications. The general process of HR planning is illustrated in Figure 8–1.[3]

The first stage of HR planning is to identify and assess relevant future *external and internal factors*. From this overall plan, organizational objectives are set and more specific plans are developed. For example, if a retail chain plans to double its number of stores from 100 to 200 in a 5-year period, the firm must identify the number and types of new employees needed to staff the new stores. A *human resource needs forecast* then can be made by comparing the number of people and the skills that will be needed by the anticipated labor force at the time of

FIGURE 8–1
HR Planning Process.

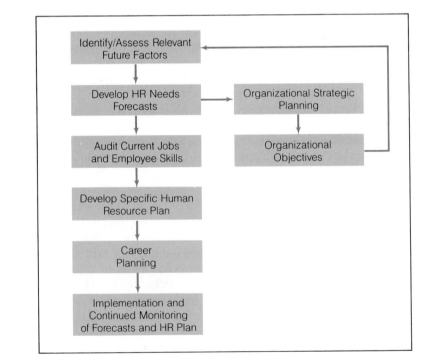

the expansion. Using this data as a base, the firm then must *audit current jobs and employee skills*. This audit compares the jobs that currently exist in the organization to those that are forecasted. It also includes an inventory of existing employee skills. This inventory identifies the skills and capabilities of current employees so that the firm can build on its existing reservoir of workers, as well as drawing on human resources outside the organization.

The actual *human resource plan* is formalized by drawing together all the data generated from the above processes. This plan represents an "action" model to guide managers and the organization over the planned time period—usually three to five years. To individualize the plan, *a career and succession planning system* is designed so that individuals will have the necessary skills when those skills are needed in the future. Throughout the entire process, *continual monitoring* of internal and external factors is important to identify whether the forecasted conditions are actually occurring. If not, then the human resource plan should be modified to reflect changing conditions. The remainder of this chapter will examine each phase of this process.

Assessment of External and Internal Factors

To staff an organization, managers must anticipate and respond to a variety of changes over which they have little, if any, control. The organization must draw from essentially the same labor market—private, public, and military—that supplies all employers. Significant changes in wages, working conditions, and demand in other sectors of the labor market can radically change the availability of job applicants. For example, when a large new employer comes into a community, all organizations drawing employees from that market are affected. Many factors can affect the supply of labor available to an employer and to the general economy. Some of the more significant ones are identified in Figure 8–2.

Can you define human resource planning and identify the stages of the HR planning process?

FIGURE 8–2
External Factors Affecting HR Planning.

Governmental Influences. One of the major external forces that must be considered when doing HR planning is governmental influences. Historically, certain minority groups and women have been discriminated against in staffing. As a result, staffing must be done by individuals knowledgeable about the numerous legal requirements involved in equal employment opportunity regulations.

Other government policies also can affect HR planning. For example, government trade policies and restrictions on importing Japanese cars affect the plans of automakers like General Motors, Ford, Chrysler, and American Motors because, under a "closed-import" policy, more U.S.–built cars may be sold. Also, foreign firms may establish more U.S.–based manufacturing operations. An "open-import" policy, on the other hand, creates an entirely different economic environment.

Economic Conditions. The general business cycles of recessions and boom times can also affect HR planning. Such factors as interest rates, inflation, and economic growth can affect both organizational plans and objectives and the availability of human resources. There is a considerable difference between finding qualified applicants in a 5 percent–unemployment market and in a 9 percent–unemployment market. In the 5 percent–unemployment market, significantly fewer qualified applicants are likely to be available for any kind of position. Those who are available may be less employable because they are less-educated, less-skilled, or unwilling to work. As the unemployment rate rises, the number of available qualified candidates rises too.

Population and Work Force Shifts. In the next two decades the United States will have a gradually aging labor force, a fact that reflects both the aging of the post–World War II "baby boom" generation and increased longevity nationwide.[4] Yet the work force has been expanding dramatically with the increased number of women who have joined the ranks of the employed. Beginning in the mid-1980s, as the "baby boom" passes, a reduction in the labor force growth rate is likely. After that, a relatively smaller number of people will be looking for entry-level jobs.

Another important consideration is that the number of technical jobs demanding high skill levels is expected to grow at a much more rapid rate than other jobs. According to projections made by the U.S. Bureau of Labor Statistics in 1983, several significant population and work force changes are expected from the mid–1980s to 1995:[5]

■ The total labor force will grow more slowly during the next decade than during the past decade.
■ Women will account for a greater proportion of labor force growth in the decade ahead (nearly two-thirds) than they did over the past decade.
■ Blacks and other minority groups will account for a greater proportion of overall labor force growth, about one-quarter during the next decade.
■ The younger members of the labor force, aged 16 to 24, will decline in absolute numbers.

■ The number of prime-age members of the labor force, those aged 25 to 54, will grow at a rate one percent faster than the total labor force.

Geographical and Competitive Conditions. The *demand* for workers from *other employers* in a geographical region also affects the labor supply. If, for example, a large military facility is closing or moving to another geographical location, a large supply of very good civilian labor, previously employed by the military, may be available for a while. On the other hand, the opening of a new plant may decrease the supply of potential employees in a labor market for some time.

Another factor affecting the supply of human resources is the *net migration* in a particular geographic region. For a time after World War II, the population of northern U.S. cities grew rapidly and provided a ready source of labor. The recent shift of population growth to the "Sunbelt" is an important new HR planning concern.

Competitors are another important external force in staffing. Failure to consider the competitive labor market and to offer pay scales and benefits competitive with organizations in the same general industry and geographical location may be a mistake. Underpaying or "undercompeting" may result in a much lower quality work force. The impact of *international competition* also must be considered, as well as numerous other external factors.

Internal Factors. HR planners also must evaluate the impact of a number of internal factors. Overall organization strategy for the opening or closing of facilities, shifting of products or services offered, and other changes must be considered. For example, if a firm plans to open a number of new facilities in the next five years, this expansion may lead to a more decentralized data processing system. Such possibilities should be considered when human resource plans are developed.

Nature of Forecasting

Forecasting is an attempt to predict future changes in human resource needs. Although some rather advanced techniques have been developed, forecasting is far from an exact science. Forecasts generally take historical data and project them into the future. This method is adequate, but the manager must keep in mind that the historical data are based on trends that may be changing.

Forecasting Periods. Human resource forecasting should be done over three planning periods: *short range, intermediate,* and *long-range.*[6] The most commonly used planning period is short-range, usually over a period of six months to one year. This level of planning is almost routine in many organizations because very few assumptions about the future are necessary for such short-term plans. These short-term forecasts indicate the best estimates of the immediate personnel needs of an organization. Intermediate and long-range forecasting are much more difficult processes. Intermediate plans usually project one to five years into the future and long-range plans extend beyond five years.

Forecasting Human Resource Demand. HR planning attempts to match the forecasted *demand* for people with the anticipated *supply* of available workers. To identify the demand, two basic approaches can be used: (1) calculating the demand for people on an organization-wide basis, using the *average demand* for the entire organization over a period of time; and (2) considering *individual units* in the organization, rather than the entire organization. For example, a forecast that Apex Corporation needs 75 new employees next year might mean less than a forecast that Apex Corporation needs 25 new people in sales, 25 in production, 10 in accounting, 5 in personnel, and 10 in the warehouse. This unit breakdown obviously allows for more consideration of the specific skills needed than the aggregate method does.

Forecasting Methods. Models for forecasting human resource needs range from a manager's best guess to a very rigorous and complex computer simulation. Simple models may be quite accurate in certain instances, but complex models may be necessary in other circumstances. For example, complex models are required in work-load scheduling, military staffing, or airline staff scheduling.[7]

Figure 8–3 is a chart that identifies four different types of models and their uses. It is beyond the scope of this text to provide a detailed discussion of the numerous methods available. Anyone interested should consult the source listed beneath the figure.

Audit of Current Jobs and Employee Skills

A comprehensive job analysis of all current jobs provides the base upon which to build an *employee skills inventory.* Knowing what jobs are currently being performed logically leads to an audit of current employees and their skills.

TYPE OF MODEL	TECHNIQUES	APPLICATIONS
Simple forecasting models	Judgmental forecasts Rules of thumb Staffing standards Ratio-trend analysis Time series	Rudimentary forecasts of available supply and demand under stable conditions
	Delphi technique	Long-range forecasting
Organizational change models	Succession analysis Markov/stochastic processes Renewal models	Replacement analysis and blockages Probability-based flow forecasts
	Regression analysis	Correlations to project changes
Optimization models	Linear programming Nonlinear programming Dynamic programming	Future needs defined by constraints
	Goal programming	Future needs identified to achieve defined objectives
	Assignment models	Matching individuals with anticipated vacancies
Integrated simulation models	Corporate models: combined techniques	Total entity simulation linked with corporate planning

SOURCE: James W. Walker, *Human Resource Planning* (New York: McGraw-Hill, 1980), p. 132.

Employee Skills Inventory. A basic source of data useful in developing an employee skills inventory is an employee's personnel file. One piece of data likely to be included in a skills inventory is an individual's performance appraisals that identify each person according to the quality of his or her work. This information is then combined by work group to pinpoint the level of performance in a work unit. For example, combining the performance ratings of the eleven people in one company's management group shows that the company has a high percentage of very qualified managers; nine of the eleven are rated *good* or *excellent* overall.

Charts giving an overview of the employee situation may be plotted for each department in an organization. When overall data are charted the accumulated information may show which departments need external candidates to fill future positions. Likewise, the inventory may indicate where there is a reservoir of trained people that the employer can tap as it meets future conditions.

The internal inventory must also consider some factors over which the organization has little control. For example, some employees will die, leave the firm, retire, or otherwise contribute to a reduction in the current employee force. Internal planning must utilize forecasts about these factors.

Information noted in the individual employee skills inventory may include the following:

- Previous jobs held
- Tenure in current job
- Educational and training qualifications
- Specific knowledge and skills
- Prior work performance
- Past and current compensation
- Mobility factors

The skills inventory can be as simple as a five-item form or as sophisticated as a computerized employee information system. One caution should be kept in mind: All information that affects a person's promotability or selection for promotion must meet the same standards of job-relatedness and non-discrimination as those used when initially hiring employees.

Human Resource Information System. Most managers feel they have a good idea of the talent available in their organization. But that information is not always current or complete, nor is it in a form that can be used to forecast future needs. However, many employers have developed computerized information systems to help manage employee skills inventories in large organizations. Such systems usually include data on:

- Individual demographics
- Career progression
- Appraisals
- Skills

- Interests
- Training/education
- Target positions
- Performance ratings
- Geographic preferences
- Promotability ratings

These data can be used to generate output that provides a useful inventory of talent when vacancies occur.

Can you discuss the importance of assessing external and internal factors and auditing current jobs and employee skills?

Development of a Human Resource Plan

With all the data collected and forecasts and assessments done, an organization has the necessary information for the formalization of a human resource plan that considers both supply and demand factors. Typical human resource plans project three to five years ahead. Attempting to forecast events more than five years in the future might be beneficial, but so many imponderables exist that many mangers prefer the three- to five-year time period. It is long enough to provide time for adjusting the current work force situation, but it is short enough to allow a reasonable consideration of future external and organizational factors.

A human resource plan can be extremely sophisticated or rather rudimentary. Regardless of the complexity desired, a human resource plan ultimately should answer the following questions:

1. What are the specific skills employees now have?
2. How many current employees will stay with the organization?
3. What types of people (in terms of EEO) are they?
4. What jobs now exist?
5. What changes in current jobs will occur?
6. What is the current employee potential for upward movement?
7. What new skills must current employees have in the future?
8. How many and which types of people (in terms of EEO) will be needed in the future?
9. What jobs will exist in the future?
10. How must company policies and practices change to be compatible with future employee requirements?
11. Where will the organization obtain the needed future employees?[8]

An organization must keep accurate records of its labor requirements in order to take steps to fill them. Recruiting methods should be planned to stimulate an increase of applicants when needed. The organization also needs to know where possible sources of labor are, and the approximate number and quality of potential workers from each source.

Matching of Supply and Demand. The ultimate purpose of a human resource plan is to enable managers in the organization to match the supply of labor that has been identified as available with the demands that have been forecasted. If the necessary skill level does not exist in the present work force, employees may need to be trained in the new skill or outside recruiting may need to be targeted. For example, one organization, unable to hire computer programmers, decided to train its own employees in a pilot project. The managers for whom the programmers worked found that the retrained employees consistently met or bettered job requirements.

Such programs can be costly and time-consuming. However, internal retraining may be considered if the necessary skills are not available in the organization's available work force. If a computerized human resource information system exists, reports analyzing the available data can provide information on both internal supply and demand. For example, it is possible to determine the following:

- Open positions
- Difficult-to-staff positions
- "Blocked" career paths
- Useful training positions
- Attrition data
- Affirmative action information

Career and Succession Planning

The human resource plan provides a "road map" for the future that managers and employees can use. This map should identify where employees are likely to be obtained, when the employees will be needed, and what training and development employees must have. Through career and succession planning, employee career paths can be tailored to individual needs that are consistent with organizational requirements. A discussion of career planning can be found in Chapter 11.

Implementation and Continued Monitoring

All of the effort involved in HR planning will be futile unless action is taken to implement the plans made. To ensure that the plans continue to be appropriate, they should be reviewed over time. Changes in the internal and external environments should be monitored so that their effects on the human resource plan can be considered.[9]

Benefits of Planning. Some of the potential benefits of an effective HR Planning system are:

1. Upper management has a better view of the human resources dimensions of business decisions.
2. Personnel costs may be less because management can anticipate imbalances before they become unmanageable and expensive.
3. More time is provided to locate talent because needs are anticipated and identified before the actual staffing is required.

RECURITING
is the process of genera-
ting a pool of qualified
applicants for organiza-
tional jobs.

4. Better opportunities exist to include women and minority groups in future growth plans.

5. Development of managers can be better planned.

In summary, the degree of HR planning done reflects the extent to which an organization attempts to plan and control its need for human resources. This planning will determine whether the firm shapes its participation in the labor market or is shaped by labor market situations.

Can you identify items common in a human resource plan?

NATURE OF RECRUITING

The objective of the recruiting process is to provide a sufficiently large group of qualified candidates so that satisfactory employees can be selected. **Recruiting** is the process of generating a pool of qualified applicants for organizational jobs. If the number of available candidates only equals the number of people to be hired, there is no selection—the choice has already been made. The organization must either leave some openings unfilled or take all the candidates.

Recruiting Process

The steps in a typical recruiting process are identified in Figure 8–4. Recruiting efforts translate human resource plans into action and also fill openings when unexpected vacancies occur. Even during periods of reduced hiring, implementation of long-range plans means keeping in contact with outside recruiting sources to maintain visibility and maintaining employee recruiting channels within the organization. These activities are essential when the recruiting activity must be stepped up on short notice.

Usually, a manager notifies someone in the personnel unit that an opening needs to be filled. A common way in which recruiting efforts are triggered is by the submission of a *requisition* to the personnel unit, much as someone would submit a supply requisition to the purchasing department. The personnel representative and the manager must *review the job description and specifications* so that both have clear and up-to-date information on the job duties and the specific desired qualifications. For example, whether a job is for a computer programmer or for a systems analyst would significantly affect the screening of applicants and the content of a recruiting advertisement. By becoming familiar with the job, it is easier to identify the minimum qualifications needed for someone to satisfactorily perform the job.

Following this review, the actual recruiting effort begins by a check of *internal sources* of recruits available through transfers, promotions, and job postings. Then *external resources* are contacted as required, and all applicants are screened through the selection process. *Follow-up* is necessary to evaluate the effectiveness of the recruiting efforts and to

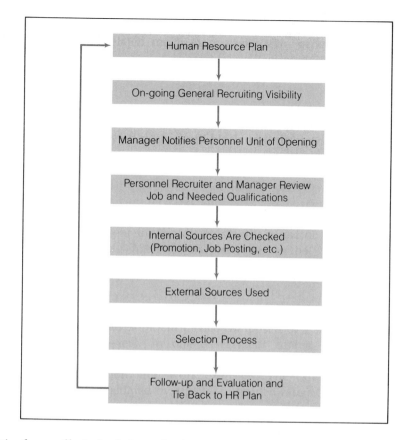

FIGURE 8–4
Recruiting Process.

Human Resource Plan

On-going General Recruiting Visibility

Manager Notifies Personnel Unit of Opening

Personnel Recruiter and Manager Review Job and Needed Qualifications

Internal Sources Are Checked (Promotion, Job Posting, etc.)

External Sources Used

Selection Process

Follow-up and Evaluation and Tie Back to HR Plan

tie those efforts back into the human resource plan and ongoing recruiting activities.

Evaluation of Recruiting Activities

Important activities for proper evaluation of recuriting include:

1. Determining and categorizing recruitment and selection efforts by job in light of long-range and short-range needs
2. Monitoring conditions in the employment market
3. Reviewing/developing effective recruiting material
4. Recording the number and quality of applicants from each recruiting source
5. Following up on applicants to obtain their views on the effectiveness of recruiting efforts
6. Conducting cost-benefit audits of recruiting efforts.

Audit of Recruiting Costs and Benefits. One reason for evaluating recruiting activities is to audit and manage recruiting costs. An audit can reduce costs by identifying the impact of various recruiting practices on the "bottom line" of an organization and by showing how the organization can use its recruiting dollars better.

One firm conducted a companywide audit of recruiting costs and practices. The total recruiting costs in the firm were over $700,000, in a year in which total net income was $5 million. The audit information was used to achieve better coordination of recruiting plans between divisions. Also, the firm changed its major recruiting source from outside agencies to targeted media advertising. The result was that the following year the recruiting costs for the firm had dropped to $200,000 even though more employees were hired![10] Although the extent of the savings may be unusual, many employers waste or do not make effective use of a portion of their recruiting expenditures, so follow-up and evaluation of recruiting activities is an important responsibility.

Recruiting Responsibilities

In most large organizations, the HR planning and recruiting functions are coordinated through the personnel department. This department maintains and analyzes human resource plans with other departments as part of a perpetual recruiting effort.

Often other managers help in the recruiting effort by determining the skills and qualifications needed by individuals who will fill vacancies in their areas. Figure 8–5 shows a typical distribution of responsibilities between the personnel department and managers for human resource planning and recuiting. In small organizations, and even in some divisions of large organizations, several different managers may work on recruiting.

Systems of Recruiting

There are several systems used in recruiting employees. The systems vary according to the intensity and continuity of efforts.

The most preferable system is a *continuing program* that anticipates the need for qualified individuals tied to human resource plans. While extensive recruiting efforts are usually associated with an immediate need for employees, recruiting efforts are usually associated with an immediate need for employees, recruiting efforts are usually associated with an immediate need for employees, recruiting efforts are usually associated with an immediate need for employees, recruiting efforts should not be limited to such periods. Input from employees can be a

FIGURE 8–5
Human Resource Planning and Recruiting Responsibilities.

PERSONNEL UNIT	MANAGERS
■ Proposes objective for HR planning	■ Determine qualifications and anticipate needs
■ Designs HR planning data systems	■ Identify and monitor career plans of employees
■ Collects data from managers to prepare human resource plans	
■ Forecasts recruiting needs	■ Determine management succession
■ Assists in career planning and training to accomplish planned goals	■ Assist in recruiting effort
■ Plans and conducts recruiting efforts	■ Provide management review of recruiting efforts
■ Audits and evaluates recruiting activities	

useful part of a continuing program. One firm gives a $25 savings bond to each employee recommending someone who is eventually hired.

In addition, an organization must engage in *specialized recruiting*. Such recruiting efforts are directed at the particular type of individual the organization wants to hire for an immediate or unanticipated opening. For example, recruiting college-educated electronics engineering employees is a more specialized process than recruiting accounting clerks.

The *recruiting campaign* is a concentrated drive for a short period of time. It is used mainly when large numbers of new people are required quickly.

Can you define recruiting and diagram a typical recruiting process?

RECRUITING SOURCES

To build on HR planning, employers must translate plans into action. They must also fill openings when unexpected vacancies occur.

Applicants come from a wide variety of sources. It is tempting to evaluate these sources on the basis of effectiveness, but such an effort is difficult because the sources can vary greatly and because different organizations have vastly different needs.

Internal Sources

Among internal recruiting sources are: present employees, friends of employees, former employers, and former applicants. Promotions, demotions, and transfers also can provide additional people for an organizational unit, if not for the entire organization.

Using internal personnel sources has some advantages over external sources. First, it allows management to observe an employee over a period of time and to evaluate that person's potential and specific job behavior. These factors cannot be easily observed off the job. Second, an organization that promotes its own employees to fill job openings may provide added motivation to its employees to do a good job. Employees may have little motivation to do more than just what the job requires if management's policy is to hire externally. This concern is why internal sources of qualified applicants are generally considered first.

Job Posting and Bidding. One procedure for moving employees into other jobs within the organization is a *job posting and bidding* system. Employees can be notified of all job vacancies by posting notices, circulating publications, or in some other way inviting employees to apply for jobs. In a unionized organization, job posting and bidding can be quite formal; the procedure often is spelled out in the labor agreement. Seniority lists may be used by firms that make promitions based strictly on seniority.

A job posting system gives each employee an opportunity to move to a better job within the organization. Without some sort of job post-

JOB POSTING AT MILES LABORATORIES

Miles Laboratories, Inc., is a leading pharmceutical drug and medical products manufacturer and supplies. As a result of questions and interests expressed by managers and employees at its nine plants, the *Miles Job Opportunity Program* was created.

The program applies to a majority of the salaried employees throughout its U.S. operations. However, sales, technical support, and customer service employees who work in field locations outside of company plants are not covered because of relocation and logistical considerations. Also, postings at one location are not sent to the other plants. Employees can only post for jobs at their own location, although movement between locations may occur if employees are considered for promotion to other locations.

The operation of the program begins with dissemination of a job posting announcement based upon a supervisory requisition. With the exception of the two lowest entry-level job grades, no external recruitment is done until internal sources, such as job posting, are used. An employee interested in a posted job files an application which is screened by a personnel representative and the supervisor of the posted job. Only after screening is completed and a qualified applicant is chosen to be interviewed is the employee's current supervisor notified. Interviews are then conducted. Unsuccessful applicants are notified by the personnel representative, who may discuss career interests and training needs with the rejected employee. If an employee is successful, a job offer is made to the employee after the current supervisor is notified of the intended offer.

To ensure that the program operated smoothly, a training program was developed and presented to over 500 supervisors. During training, the program was described, guidelines on interviewing were reviewed, and supervisors' questions were answered. Concerns about counseling rejected employees and the ability to replace employees who post successfully were common ones voiced by supervisors. These concerns are ones usually experienced in most job-posting programs, of which the one at Miles Laboratories is typical.[11]

ing and bidding, it is difficult to find out what jobs are open elsewhere in the organization. The most common method of notifying current employees of openings is by posting notices on bulletin boards in locations such as employee lounges, cafeterias, and near elevators.[12]

Job posting and bidding systems can be ineffective if handled improperly. Jobs should be posted *before* any external recruiting is done. A reasonable period of time must be allowed for present employees to check notices of available jobs before external applicants are considered. When employees' bids are turned down, they should be informed of the reasons.

Many potential problems must be worked out: What happens if

there are no qualified candidates on the payroll to fill new openings? Is it necessary for employees to inform their supervisors that they are bidding for another job? How much notice should an employee be required to give before transferring to a new department? When should job notices not be posted? These questions must be adequately anticipated. In any event, a mechanism such as job posting and bidding helps an employer tap the talents of current employees, as the discussion of the program at Miles Laboratories illustrates. (See "Personnel in Practice.")

Recruiting Through Current Employees. A reliable source of people to fill vacancies can be reached through current employees who may know of good prospects among their families and friends. The employees can acquaint potential applicants with the advantages of a job with the company, furnish letters of introduction, and encourage them to apply.

This source is usually one of the most effective methods of recruiting because many qualified people can be reached at a very low cost to the company. In an organization with a large number of employees, this approach can provide quite a large pool of potential employees. Most employees know from their own experiences about the requirements of the job and what sort of person the company is looking for. Often employees have friends or acquaintances who meet these requirements.

However, a word of caution is appropriate here. When the organization has an underrepresentation of a particular minority group, word-of-mouth referral has been considered a violation of Title VII of the Civil Rights Act.

Former Employees. Former employees are also a good internal source of applicants. Some retired employees may be willing to come back to work on a part-time basis or may recommend someone who would be interested in working for the company. Sometimes people who have left the company to raise a family or complete a college education are willing to come back to work. Individuals who left for other jobs might be willing to return for a higher rate of pay. Also, as noted in Chapter 6, job sharing and flex-time programs may be useful with retirees or others who previously worked for the organization. The main advantage in hiring former employees is that their performance is known.

A senior vice-president at New York's Chemical Bank says, "The days of discriminating against people who previously left are gone." Previously, notions of corporate loyalty had kept many firms from rehiring those who left. American General Insurance Company of Houston, however, regards returning employees as among its most loyal workers. And Kentucky Fried Chicken hired a former junior officer as its president even though in the interim he had worked for Church's Fried Chicken.[13]

Previous Applicants. Another source of applicants can be found in the organizational files. Although not truly an internal source, those who have previously applied for jobs can be recontacted by mail, a quick and inexpensive way to fill an unexpected opening. Although "walk-ins" are likely to be more suitable for filling unskilled and semiskilled jobs, some professional openings can be filled by applicants for previous jobs. One firm that needed two cost accountants immediately contacted qualified previous applicants and was able to hire two individuals who were disenchanted with their current jobs. Some of the more unusual "walk-in" approaches are highlighted in the "Personnel in Practice" entitled *"Here I Am, Recruit Me."*

Can you identify three internal recruiting sources?

External Sources

If internal sources do not produce an acceptable candidate, several external sources are available. These sources include schools, colleges and universities, employment agencies, temporary help firms, labor unions, media sources, and trade and competitive sources.

School Recruiting. Schools may be a good source of new employees for many organizations. A successful recruiting program with these institutions is the result of careful analysis, thorough training and planning, and continuing contact with the individual schools.

Major considerations for such a recruiting program are:

1. School counselors and other faculty members concerned with job opportunities and business careers for their students should be contacted regularly.
2. Good relations should be maintained with faculty and officials at all times, even when there is little or no need for new employees.
3. Recruiting programs can serve these schools in ways other than the placement of students. For instance, the organization might supply educational films, provide speakers, or arrange for demonstrations and exhibits.
4. It should be recognized that many organizations compete for their share of the capable graduates. Continuing contact and good relations provide a better opportunity to secure the best graduates.
5. The extent and scope of this recruiting program will depend on needs. However, a long-range view of recruiting is more desirable than a campaign approach.
6. Some larger schools have a centralized guidance placement office. Contact can be established and maintained with the supervisors of these offices; they are in a good position to help plan and conduct recruiting activities.

School counselors are generally interested in the employer's policies and working conditions and will cooperate with an organization that treats its employees fairly. Promotional brochures that acquaint students with starting jobs and career opportunities can be distributed to counselors, librarians, or others. Participating in career days and giving tours of the company to school groups are other ways of maintaining good contact with school sources. Cooperative programs in which students work part-time and receive some school credits also may be useful in generating qualified applicants for full-time positions.

College and University Recruiting. At the college or university level, the recruitment of graduating students is a large-scale operation for many companies. Most colleges and universities maintain placement offices where employers and applicants can meet. However, college recruiting presents some interesting and unique problems.

The major determinants that affect the selection of colleges at which an employer interviews are:[15]

■ Current position requirements
■ Past experience with placement offices and previous graduates
■ Organizational budget constraints
■ Cost of available talent
■ Market competition

College recruiting can be very expensive. Therefore an organization should determine if the positions it is trying to fill really require a college degree. A great many positions do not; yet many employers insist upon filling them with college graduates. The result may be disgruntled employees who must be paid more and who are likely to leave if the jobs are not sufficiently challenging.

There is a great deal of competition for the top students in a college and much less competition for those further down the ladder. One study pinpointed attributes that recruiters seem to value most highly in college graduates; poise, oral communication skills, personality, appearance, and written communication skills all came in ahead of grade point average.[16] (To aid you, the reader, in the college recruiting process, Appendix A, which follows the last chapter, is a special section entitled *Getting a Job*. This section looks at resume preparation, interviewing, and other phases of the staffing process from the perspective of a college student.)

Employment Agencies. Every state in the U.S. has a *state* employment agency. These agencies operate branch offices in many cities throughout the state and do not charge fees to applicants or employers.

Private employment agencies also are found in most cities. For a fee collected from either the employee or the employer, these agencies will do some of the preliminary screening for an organization and put the organization in touch with applicants. These agencies differ considerably in terms of the level of service, costs, policies, and types of applicants they provide. Employers can reduce the range of possible problems with these sources by giving an employment service a good definition of the position to be filled, including such details as job title, skills needed, experience and education required, and pay ranges available.

Some employment agencies focus their efforts on executive, managerial, and professional positions. These *search firms* may work on either a retainer basis or for a fee based upon the pay level of the hired employee. Those fees may range as high as 33 percent of the employee's first-year salary. Most employers pay the fee, but there are some circumstances in which the employee will pay the fee. For placing a high-level executive job, a search firm may receive $300,000 or more counting travel expenses, the fee, and other compensation. The size of the fees and the aggressiveness with which some search firms pursue candidates for openings has led to the firms being called *headhunters*.

Temporary Help. Perhaps the most accessible and immediate source of certain types of help is the temporary help agency. These agencies supply secretarial, clerical, or semiskilled labor on a day-rate basis. As Figure 8–6 indicates, temporary employees are used for a variety of reasons. The use of temporary help may make sense for an organization if its work is subject to seasonal or other fluctuations. Hiring temporary help may be more efficient than hiring permanent employees to meet peak employment needs, in which case the employer either has to find something to keep employees busy during less active periods or must resort to layoffs.

Labor Unions. Labor unions are a source of certain types of labor. In some industries, such as construction, unions have traditionally supplied workers to employers. A labor pool is generally available through a union, and workers can be dispatched to particular jobs to meet the needs of the employers. The hiring hall is usually the contact point.

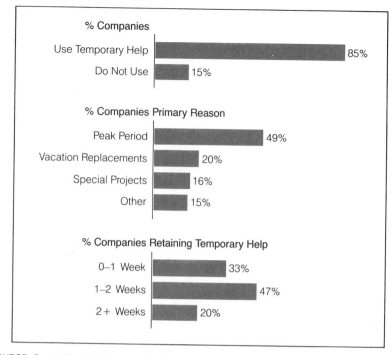

FIGURE 8–6
Use of Temporary Help.

SOURCE: *Central New York Business Review*, reported in Sam Dickey, "The Generalist," *Management World*. December 1980, p. 24.

In some instances unions can control or influence recruiting and staffing needs. An organization with a strong union may have less flexibility than a non-union company in deciding who will be hired and where he or she will be placed. Unions also can work to an employer's advantage through cooperative staffing programs, as they do in the building, trade, and printing industries. Such cooperativeness has not been the case in manufacturing. There, union shops have given management a free hand in hiring, while unions have insisted on strong seniority provisions for promotions.

Media Sources. Media sources—newspapers, magazines, television, radio, and billboards—are widely used and familiar to many people looking for a job. Almost all newspapers carry "help wanted" sections and these are frequently a source of applicants for many organizations. For example, the *Wall Street Journal* is a major source used to recruit managerial and professional employees.

Newspapers are useful because there is a short lead time—usually two or three days—for placing an ad. For positions that must be filled quickly, newspapers may be a good source. However, newspaper advertising can lead to a great deal of "wasted circulation" because most newspapers do not aim to reach any specialized employee markets. Often applicants are only marginally suitable, primarily because employers do not describe the jobs and the necessary qualifications very well. Many employers have found that it is not cost-efficient to schedule newspaper ads on days other than Sunday.

When using recruitment advertisements employers should ask five key questions:

- What do we want to accomplish?
- Who are the people we want to reach?
- What should the advertising message convey?
- How should the message be presented? In which media should it run?[17]

Two studies shed some light on the use of ads. In one, the Bureau of National Affairs found that eight out of ten companies use newspaper advertising to recruit professional, managerial, technical, and plant personnel.[18] However, another study that rated the effectiveness of recruitment sources found that newspapers and college placement were poorer sources of employees (based on performance, absenteeism, and work attitudes) than either journal and convention contacts or self-initiated (personal) contacts.[19]

Other media sources include general magazines, television and radio, and billboards. These sources are usually not suitable for frequent use, but may be used for one-time campaigns aimed at quickly finding specially skilled workers. General Electric once used a billboard at a major plant to advertise its openings for welders. Radio ads have also been tried by some employers.[20]

Trade and Competitive Sources. Other sources for recruiting are *professional and trade associations, trade publications,* and *competitors.* Many professional societies and trade associations publish a newsletter or magazine containing job ads. Such publications may be a good source for specialized professionals needed within an industry. Ads in other specialized publications or listings at professional meetings also can be good sources of publicity about professional openings.

An employer also may meet possible applicants who are currently employed by a competitor at professional associations and industry meetings. Some employers directly contact individuals working for a competitor. Employees recruited from these sources spend less time in training because they already know the industry.

Can you list four external sources for applicants?

INTERNAL VS. EXTERNAL SOURCES: A COMPARISON

There are pros and cons associated with both promotion from within (internal recruitment) and hiring outside the organization (external recruitment) to fill openings. Figure 8–7 summarizes some of the most commonly cited advantages and disadvantages of each source.

Promoting from within generally is thought to be a positive force in rewarding good work. However, if followed exclusively, it has the major disadvantage of perpetuating old ways of operating. Recruiting externally for professionals such as accountants or computer programmers may be cheaper than training them. It also infuses the organization with new ideas that are needed from time to time. But

FIGURE 8–7
Internal vs. External
Sources.

	Advantages	Disadvantages
Internal	• Morale of Promotee • Better Assessment of Abilities • Lower Cost for Some Jobs • Motivator for Good Performance • Causes a Succession of Promotions • Have to Hire Only at Entry Level	• Inbreeding • Possible Morale Problems of Those Not Promoted • "Political" Infighting for Promotions • Need Strong Management Development Program
External	• "New Blood", New Perspectives • Cheaper than Training a Professional • No Group of Political Supporters in Organization Already • May Bring Industry Insights	• May not Select Someone Who Will "Fit" • May Cause Morale Problems for Those Internal Candidates • Longer "Adjustment" or Orientation Time

recruiting from outside the organization for any but entry-level positions presents the problem of adjustment time for the new persons. A serious drawback to external recruiting is the negative impact that often results from selecting an outsider instead of promoting a current employee.

One survey of 262 employers found that the following services were used for filling managerial and professional jobs:[21]

- College recruiting   35%
- Newspaper advertising   19%
- Employment agencies   12%
- Referrals   11%
- Unsolicited resumes   10%
- In-house training programs   6%
- Executive recruiters   4%

Most organizations combine the use of internal and external methods. In organizations that operate in rapidly changing environments and competitive conditions, a heavier emphasis on external sources may be necessary. However, for those organizations existing in environments that change slowly, a heavier emphasis on promotion from within may be more suitable.

Can you describe three advantages and disadvantages of internal and external recruiting?

CHAPTER 8   HUMAN RESOURCE PLANNING AND RECRUITING

PERSONNEL TODAY AND TOMORROW
"INTO THE RECRUITING POOL"

NCR is a large computer and technology-based manufacturer that uses college recruiting to fill about 1,500 jobs per year. In an average year, over 10,000 employment inquiries are mailed directly to its world headquarters in Dayton, Ohio. Additionally, company representatives interview over 11,000 people at approximately 250 colleges and universities. In one recent year, recruiters made 937 visits and averaged over 11 interviews per visit. In order to track this recruiting volume, computerization became imperative.

NCR's automated recruiting data system, developed in 1981, stores data on both institutions and students visited. For each college or university NCR maintains data on the college placement office, lodging and transportation information, all NCR recruiting schedules at the institutions, and any gifts or donations made by NCR to the institution. For each student interviewed, a "mini-resumé" is entered in the computer data base.

Based upon this data, NCR has composed several different letters for different applicant circumstances. By entering the name of an individual and designating the appropriate letter through a code number, a "personalized" response can be sent. Likewise, contacts with college placement offices can be standardized.

From this data base NCR can compute a cost-of-hire report by student, by university, and offer status, which identifies the average cost per interview and average cost per hire. The computer program also can generate interview schedules, recruiter reports, and applicant listings by area. The value of the system is evident when one considers that NCR can interview an electrical engineering graduate in Massachusetts today and by tomorrow have the graduate's qualifications available at virtually every NCR facility. Similar data bases are now being established by other firms to marry technology to recruiting.[22]

SUMMARY

- Staffing is accomplished through three major processes—human resource planning, recruiting, and selection.
- Human resource planning (HR planning) focuses on analyzing and identifying the future needs and availability of human resources for the organization.
- HR planning is tied to the broader process of overall strategic planning.
- The process of HR planning requires analysis and assessment of external and internal forces, development of forecasts, auditing of current

jobs and employees, development of a human resource plan, career and succession planning and monitoring.

■ Many external and internal factors must be identified and their impact assessed as part of HR planning.

■ Forecasts of human resource needs can be done for three time periods using a variety of methods.

■ The purpose of the actual human resource plan is to match human resource supply and demand factors by indicating specific answers to a number of questions.

■ An audit of current jobs and employee skills identifies the existing human resources available to the organization as it plans for the future.

■ Human resource plans should be implemented and their progress monitored so that plans can be altered as future conditions change.

■ Recruiting is the process of generating a pool of qualified applicants for organizational jobs through a series of activities.

■ The costs and benefits of recruiting efforts should be audited to assess how well HR planning and recruiting responsibilities are being performed by the personnel unit and operating managers.

■ Two general groups of recruiting sources exist: (1) internal sources and (2) external sources. An organization must decide whether it will look primarily within the organization or to external sources for new employees—or use some combination of each.

■ Current employees, former employees, and previous applicants are the most common internal sources available.

■ External recruiting sources include schools, colleges and universities, employment agencies, temporary help firms, labor unions, media, and professional or trade sources.

■ The decision to use internal or external sources should consider the advantages and disadvantages associated with each.

REVIEW QUESTIONS AND EXERCISES

1. What is human resource planning and why is it important?

2. Assume you have to develop a human resource plan for a local hospital. What specific external and internal factors would be important for you to consider? Why?

3. Discuss why HR planning must precede career planning for individual employees if it is to be effective.

4. Suppose you had to find a new sales representative. How would you proceed?

5. Your secretary has just resigned. You have decided to recruit within your organization. How would you proceed?

6. You need a computer programmer. What external sources would you use? Why?

7. You are vice-president of administration in an insurance company and need to hire a controller. Discuss what factors you would consider in deciding to recruit outside rather than promoting someone from inside your firm.

Exercises

a. Find two box employment ads in the *Wall Street Journal* or the local newspaper and clip them out. Then compare their contents to the experience recounted by L. O. Baier at the beginning of the chapter. What good points and weak points can you see in each ad? What changes would you make in the ads? Why?

b. Visit your local college placement office and interview the director or another staff member. Ask him or her to describe the common mistakes made by employer representatives and students during on-campus recruiting efforts.

CASE

THE "FRIENDLY" RESTAURANT

Banta's Restaurant is a very successful privately-owned operation. Banta's has earned many industry awards in the past several years, including the National Tourist Three-Star Award and Platinum Plate Award. Employees are aware of Banta's fine reputation; however, lately tension has been increasing. The primary reason is that while Banta's has recently doubled the size of its facility and significantly renovated the interior of the restaurant, it has not hired enough new employees. Consequently, most employees have been working over 50 hours per week with double shifts. Although the present employees are well-trained, well-paid, and secure in their jobs, the stress is beginning to affect employee morale. It seems that many of the employees feel that Banta's management has no plans to reduce the work load pressures.

Hiring at Banta's is done almost entirely through internal recruiting methods. Friends of current workers are responsible for over 50 percent of current employees in the present work force. The management of Banta's likes current employees to recommend people they have worked with in the past. Likewise, past employees of Banta's have been welcomed back under many circumstances. However, Banta's internal recruiting system is not presently providing an adequate pool of applicants.

Current employees feel that the recruitment interview, as presently used, is informal (it is done during work hours by the restaurant manager's assistant) and seems to focus on the applicant's personality more than the specific qualifications needed to perform the job. They are also concerned about the head manager's reluctance to hire additional help fast enough or to utilize any external recruiting methods to help eliminate the problems caused by having too few employees.

Questions

1. How would human resource planning have helped Banta's reduce some of the problems described above?

2. What are the advantages and disadvantages associated with the current exclusive use of internal sources for applicants?

NOTES

1. Adapted from L. O. Baier, "Job Searching and the Advertising Dilemma," *Personnel Administrator*, April 1984, pp. 22–23. The American Society for Personnel Administration, 606 North Washington Street, Alexandria, VA 22314, $30 per year.

2. John F. DeSanto, "Work Force Planning and Corporate Strategy," *Personnel Administrator*, October 1983, p. 33.

3. Some of the information in the following sections has been adapted from Robert L. Mathis, "Managing and Planning Human Resources," *Ideas in Management* (Cleveland, OH: Association for Systems Management, 1979), pp. 98–105.

4. Malcolm H. Morrison, "The Aging of the U.S. Population: Human Resource Implications," *Monthly Labor Review*, May 1983, pp. 13–19.

5. H. N. Fullerton and John Tschetter, "The 1995 Labor Force: A Second Look," *Monthly Labor Review*, November 1983, pp. 3–10.

6. James W. Walker, *Human Resource Planning*, (New York: McGraw-Hill, 1980), p. 104.

7. *Ibid*, pp. 129–142

8. Mathis, "Managing and Planning," p. 104.

9. G. G. Alpander, *Human Resource Management Planning* (New York: AMACOM, 1982).

10. Rick Stoops, "Managing Recruitment Costs," *Personnel Journal* 62 (August 1983), pp. 612–615.

11. Adapted from Robert B. Cummins, "Miles Laboratories, Inc. Creates a job Posting Program," *Personnel Administrator*, June 1983, pp. 41–45.

12. L. S. Kleiman and K. J. Clark, "An Effective Job Posting System," *Personnel Journal*, February 1984, pp. 20–25.

13. "Rehiring Employees. . . ." *Wall Street Journal*, December 4, 1979, p. 1.

14. Adapted from *Wall Street Journal*, October 26, 1982.

15. D. L. Chicci and C. L. Knapp, "College Recruitment from Start to Finish," *Personnel Journal* 59 (August 1980), pp. 653–657.

16. A. Biltstein, "What Employers are Seeking in Business Graduates," *Collegiate Forum*, Winter 1980–81, p. 7.

17. Bernard S. Hodes, "Planning for Recruitment Advertising," *Personnel Journal* 62 (May 1983), pp. 380–384.

18. "Remember the Classifieds," *Personnel Journal* 59 (November 1979), p. 736.

19. J. A. Breaugh, "Relationships between Recruiting Sources and Employee Performance, Absenteeism and Work Attitudes," *Academy of Management Journal* 24 (March 1981), pp. 142–147.

20. Rick Stoops, "Radio Advertising As an Effective Recruitment Device," *Personnel Journal* 61 (January 1981), p. 21.

21. *Personnel Administrator*, March 1984, p. 15.

22. Adapted from James E. Lubbock, "A Look at Centralized College Recruiting," *Personnel Administrator*, April 1983, pp. 81–84.

Selecting Human Resources

When you have read this chapter, you should be able to:

1. Define selection, and explain several reasons for having a specialized employment unit.
2. Diagram a typical selection process in sequential order.
3. Discuss the reception and application form phases of the selection process.
4. Identify two general test types and some usage concerns.
5. Discuss three types of interviews and six key considerations or problems in the selection interview.
6. Construct a guide for conducting a selection interview.
7. Explain how and why privacy concerns affect background investigations of applicants.
8. Identify why medical examinations can be useful in selection.

PERSONNEL AT WORK
REALITY-BASED EMPLOYMENT

Manpower, Inc., a Milwaukee-based supplier of temporary office help, identified a need for a better system of selecting clerical employees. These employees are supplied as temporary replacements or hired out as additional help to businesses throughout the world. Clerical workers supplied by Manpower include typists, word processing operators, data entry clerks, stenographers, transcriptionists, accounting clerks, and others. The reality-based selection system developed by Manpower has been labeled the "Manpower Predictable Performance System."

At the heart of this reality-based employment system is job analysis. Manpower conducted detailed job analysis studies of a cross-section of clerical jobs in order to identify the following items: (1) tasks performed in given jobs; (2) the frequency with which the tasks are done; (3) the importance of the tasks to each job; (4) the knowledge, skills, and abilities required; and (5) the environment in which the jobs are performed. The result of all of this effort is a detailed task checklist, with appropriate special supplemental lists, for many office clerical jobs. Clients of Manpower provide information for the completion of these checklists, which enables Manpower to achieve a better match of its employees to the work that employers need done.

In addition, Manpower developed a "30-Questions Interview" to aid in screening individuals. This interview has questions grouped into four categories: work interests, work experience, business skills, *and* interpersonal skills. *Additional special supplemental interview questions are used for the more technical areas of data entry and word processing.*

The next phase of the Manpower Predictable Performance System involves testing. In the "Typing Plus" test, applicants are given a handwritten letter with 43 errors in it; they must correct the errors and type it in 20 minutes. According to Manpower sources, the test more nearly reflects the actual content of letters typed by many clerical workers than the traditional typing test used by many employers. Manpower customers have reported greater satisfaction with Manpower employees who have passed the "Typing Plus" test.

Manpower asks supervisors of the temporaries at the customer sight to complete a brief performance appraisal. Ratings of ability, skill level, adaptability, as well as quantity and quality of work help assess the accuracy of the interview & testing process, and provide input for future matching to assignments. Employees with consistant "Excellent" ratings receive special recognition. Hands-on training for a variety of word processors and personal computers results in temporary employees upgrading their skills to a level sufficient to function effectively in today's automated office environment.

The development and implementation of its Predictable Performance System cost Manpower over $5 million. However, reactions from its managers, employees, and customers confirm that it was money well spent.[1]

"The power of choice must involve the possibility of error—that is the essence of choosing."

HERBERT SAMUEL

The systematic efforts taken by Manpower, Inc. to select employees emphasize the importance of employee selection. More than anything else, personnel selection should be seen as a *matching process*. How well an employee is matched to a job affects the amount and quality of the employee's work. This matching also directly affects training and operating costs. Workers who are unable to produce the expected amount and quality of work can cost an organization a great deal of money, time, and trouble.

Proper "matching" also is important to the individual applying for a job. The wrong choice of a vocation or improper job placement can result in wasted time for the employee, who could be getting useful experience in a more suitable field. In addition, poor placement can result in an unhappy individual or even in dismissal if the employee cannot do the job.

Effective staffing requires constant monitoring of the match between person and job. It is not just a one-time effort ending with the initial placement.

NATURE OF SELECTION

Selection is the process of picking individuals who have relevant qualifications to fill jobs in an organization. The selection process begins when a manager or supervisor sends a request to the employment office, or the staff member in charge of personnel, that an employee is needed to fill a certain vacancy. A job description, based on job analysis, identifies the vacancy. A job specification, which may also accompany the request, describes what kind of person is wanted to fill the vacancy. Employment or personnel specialists then use the job description and specifications to begin the recruiting process. The pool of applicants generated by recruiting activities must be narrowed down and one person selected to fill the job.

Selection Responsibilites

The selection portion of the staffing process is shown in Figure 9–1. In different organizations these activities are done to a greater or lesser degree by personel specialists or managers.

Until the impact of equal employment opportunity regulations became widespread, the basic selection process was performed in a rather unplanned manner in many organizations. In some companies, each department screened and hired its own employees. Many managers insisted upon selecting their own people because they were sure no one else could choose employees for them as well as they could. This practice still prevails in many organizations, especially smaller ones.

FIGURE 9–1
Selection Responsibilities.

PERSONNEL UNIT	MANAGERS
■ Provides initial employment reception ■ Conducts initial screening interview ■ Administers appropriate employment tests ■ Obtains background and reference information ■ Refers top candidates to managers for final selection ■ Arranges for the employment physical examination, if used ■ Evaluates success of selection process	■ Requisitions employees with specific qualifications to fill jobs ■ Participates in selection process as appropriate ■ Interviews final candidates ■ Makes final selection decision, subject to advice of personnel specialists ■ Provides follow-up information on the suitability of selected individuals

Other organizations maintain the traditional practice that the personnel unit does the initial screening of the candidates, while the appropriate managers or supervisors make the final selection. As a rule, the higher the level of the position, the greater the likelihood that the ultimate hiring decisions will be made by operating managers rather than personnel specialists.

Multiple government regulations concerning employment practices have removed the possibility of managers doing their own selecting in many organizations. However, careful relations between the department manager doing the selecting and other parts of the organization are still needed. Many organizations have established a specialized part of the personnel unit to handle employment.

The Employment Office

Selection activities may be centralized into a specialized organizational unit that is part of a personnel department. This specialization often depends on the size of the organization. In smaller organizations, especially those with less than 100 employees, a full-time personnel specialist or unit may be impractical.

The employment division of the personnel unit is generally concerned with the following operations: (1) receiving applicants, (2) interviewing applicants, (3) administering tests to applicants, (4) conducting background investigations, (5) arranging for physical examinations, (6) placing and assigning new employees, (7) coordinating follow-up of these employees, (8) termination interviewing, and (9) maintaining adequate records and reports.

Advantages. Some of the more important reasons for coordinating the employment function within such a unit are:

1. It is easier for the applicant because there is only one place to apply for a job.
2. It helps coordinate contact with outside applicant sources because

issues pertaining to employment can be cleared through one central location.

3. It frees operating managers to concentrate on their operating responsibilities. This release is especially helpful during peak periods.

4. It can provide for better selection because it is done by a specialist trained in staffing.

5. The applicant is more assured of consideration for a greater variety of jobs.

6. Selection costs may be cut because duplication of effort is avoided.

7. With increased government regulations affecting the selection process, it is important that people who know about these rules handle a major part of the selection process.

Can you define selection and explain why it is advantageous to have a specialized employment unit?

Selection Activities and Public Relations

In addition to matching qualified people to jobs, the selection process has an important public relations dimension. Discriminatory hiring practices, impolite interviewers, unnecessarily long waits, inappropriate testing procedures, and lack of any follow-up letters can produce very unfavorable impressions of an employer.

Poorly-executed selection processes can considerably damage the image other departments have worked hard to build. In one situation, a student who applied for a part-time clerical job was treated rudely and waited 45 minutes for an interview, after being told that she would be interviewed immediately. She finally left without being interviewed and made a point of telling her friends not to apply for a job at that firm.

SELECTION PROCESS

Certain steps are taken to process applicants for jobs in most organizations. Variations on this basic progression depend upon organizational differences, including factors such as size of the organization, nature of the jobs to be filled, the number of people to be selected, and the pressure of outside forces such as EEO considerations.

The process shown in Figure 9–2 is a typical selection process and Pete Dickens is a typical applicant. He comes to the organization and is directed to the employment office where he is received by a receptionist. Some firms conduct a very brief interview to determine if an applicant is or is not qualified before the person is given an application form. In Dickens' case, the receptionist gave him an application form to complete. The completed application form serves as the basis for an initial screening interview. After the interview, Dickens may be told that he does not fit any positions the company has available.

But if he is deemed to have the minimum necessary qualifications,

FIRE THE PERSONNEL OFFICE
By Andy Rooney

Looking for work is one of the worst things to have to do. There's nothing good about it. You don't really know how to get started, you feel like a jerk and it's demeaning every step of the way. You'd rather no one knew you were doing it.

There aren't many of us who haven't looked for work at some time in our lives. There are 10 million Americans doing it right now, today, and I feel terrible for them.

Considering that just about everyone has looked for work, it's amazing how lousy the people with jobs are to the people without them. You'd think they'd never looked for jobs themselves. You'd think they were born with jobs.

Once a person gets to be in the position of hiring or firing someone, he or she seems to forget what it's like to be unemployed. Why is that?

The person who interviews you always acts as if he or she was president of the company. You know darn well it's just a flunky's job but you don't dare let on you know that because your application could end up in the wastebasket. When he turns away from you and walks to a desk or a file cabinet you feel like giving him a swift kick in his smug tail.

I remember the first time I looked for work. There were hundreds of classified ads in the paper under the Help Wanted heading and I figured it was going to be easy.

Well, it didn't take me long to find out that the number of Help Wanted pages in the classified section of the newspaper has very little to do with getting a job.

First, you count out all the ads looking for nuclear physicists, registered nurses, animal trainers and, if you don't know anything about computers, you count out the ads looking for computer programmers.

As soon as you get some experience looking in the classified section, you get discouraged. You begin to read the classifieds the way you read the phone book when you're looking for one number. You know all those hundreds of listings don't mean anything. You get to spot the ones looking for door-to-door salesmen to work on commission only. There's usually one or two categories that mean anything to you. If anything is listed there, you're probably too late.

Unemployment is as much of a mystery as cancer and almost as bad. I've never understood why there should be any real unemployment. Do we mean there isn't any work to be done anywhere in the country? Do we mean people have everything they want to eat? Everything they need by way of housing?

What we need is a president who can figure out a way to match up those 10 million unemployed with the 10 million Help Wanted ads. And when that's done, I hope everyone fires those people in the personnel office.[2]

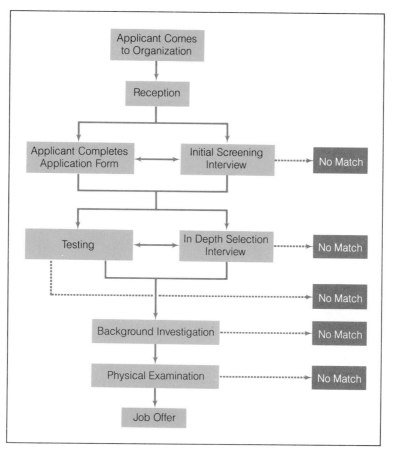

FIGURE 9–2
A Typical Selection Process.

he may go on to an in-depth interview or to testing, depending upon the job sought and the cost of testing. If he is applying for a job that requires typing, he may be given a typing test before he has an in-depth interview. However, if he is applying for a job as a lab technician, he probably will have the in-depth interview before any tests are given. If he does not meet the minimum validated test scores or is deemed unsuitable through the in-depth interview, he will likely be rejected.

Assuming everything is going well up to this point, Dickens' references and background may be investigated. If favorable feedback is received, he may be asked to take a physical exam. Based upon the results of the physical exam, he will either be given a job offer or rejected. Some firms wait to give a physical until after he has accepted the job, especially if the job has no specific physical requirements.

This process can take place in a day or over a much longer period of time. If the applicant is processed in one day, checking of references usually takes place after selection. If the process takes longer, checking of references may be done before the selection decision is made. Often one or more phases of the process are omitted, or the order is changed, depending upon the job applied for, the size of the employer, and other factors.

Disparate Treatment

One factor that should not differ during the selection process is the treatment of the individual applicant. If some applicants are required to pass through more phases of the selection process than others, the possibility of disparate treatment exists. Disparate treatment occurs when employees who are members of a protected group are treated differently from other employees. For example, one small manufacturing firm required all female applicants to take a mechanical aptitude test, but male applicants were not required to take the test. Another firm checked credit references on all racial minority applicants but did not check these references on white applicants.

It is important that the selection process be seen as a series of data-gathering activities that is similar for all applicants. It should generate as much job-related information as possible to aid in choosing the right individual to fill a job. The selection process model in Figure 9–2 shows the various data-gathering steps that can be used. The rest of this chapter examines each of these steps separately.

Can you diagram a typical selection process?

Reception

A person's first impression of the organization is made at the reception stage. The importance of making a favorable impression at this time cannot be overemphasized. The person's attitudes about the organization and even about the products or services it offers, can be influenced at this encounter. Whoever meets the applicant initially should be tactful and able to offer assistance in a courteous, friendly manner. If no jobs are available, applicants can be informed at this point. Employment possibilities must be presented honestly and clearly.

Initial Screening Interview

In some cases, before the applicant has filled out the application blank for an available job, it is appropriate to have a brief interview to see if the applicant is likely to match any of the jobs available in the organization. In other situations, the applicant may complete an application form before the short interview. This brief interview is called an *initial screening interview.*

Questions can be asked to determine if the applicant is likely to have the ability to perform available jobs. Typical questions might concern job interests, location desired, pay expectations, and availability for work. One firm that hires security guards and armored car drivers uses the screening interview to verify that an applicant meets the minimum qualifications for the job. These questions ask if the applicant has a valid driver's license, has been free of any conviction for a crime in the past five years, and has used a pistol. Because these items and others are required minimum standards, any applicant who cannot answer them according to the requirements is not given an application form to complete. The *structured interview,* in which the interviewer has a list of questions that require short answers, is the most suitable method for conducting this initial screening.

Application Forms

Application forms are a widely-used selection device. Properly prepared, like the one in Figure 9–3, the application form serves three purposes: (1) it is a record of the applicant's desire to obtain a position; (2) it provides the interviewer with a profile of the applicant that can be used in the interview; and (3) it is a basic personnel record for applicants who become employees.

EEO Considerations and Application Forms. While application forms may not usually be thought of as "tests," the Uniform Guidelines and court decisions define application forms as an employment test. Consequently, the data requested on application forms must conform to EEO guidelines and be valid predictors of job-related behavior. One review of application forms from 50 large, national corporations revealed that all but two firms had at least one "legally inappropriate" question on their forms.[3]

Another critique of forms from 94 organizations found that 73 percent of the forms had one or more illegal questions. In this review the most frequently-asked question of doubtful legality were:

- Marital status
- Height/weight
- Number and ages of dependents
- Information on spouse
- Who to contact in case of emergency, and relationship to employee[4]

This data indicates that many employers need to "clean up" their application forms because all such questionable inquiries could become bases for legal actions.

One interesting point to remember is that an employer must collect data on the race and sex of those who apply to fulfill requirements for reporting to EEOC, but the application blank cannot contain these items. As pointed out in Chapter 5, the solution picked by a growing number of employers is one in which the applicant provides EEOC reporting data on a separate form. This form, shown in Figure 5–2, is then filed separately and is not used in any other personnel selection activities.

Weighted Application Forms. One way to make the application form more job-related is by developing a weighted application blank. A job analysis is used to determine ability, skills, and behavioral characteristics needed for the job. Then weights, or numeric values, are placed on different responses to application blank items, and the responses of an applicant are scored and totalled.[5]

There are several problems associated with weighted application

FIGURE 9–3
Sample Application Form

THE C COMPANY

AN EQUAL OPPORTUNITY EMPLOYER

PLEASE PRINT ALL INFORMATION

Name _____

Present Address (Number, Street, City, State and ZIP Code)	Telephone Number	Alternate Phone Number

Relatives working for The C Company (Name, relationship and department in which they work)

Type of work preferred	Are you willing to work:			Work skills you possess
		YES	NO	
Work location preferred	Over 40 hours per week?	☐	☐	Typing ____ WPM
	Irregular shifts?	☐	☐	Shorthand ____ WPM
	Nights?	☐	☐	Keypunch ____ SPH
Would you accept any other positions?	Saturdays or Sundays?	☐	☐	License(s) _____
☐ YES ☐ NO	Holidays?	☐	☐	Other _____
	Travel?	☐	☐	
Date Available for Employment				

ADDITIONAL WORK SKILLS

_____

_____

Circle highest grade completed:

High School _____ 9 10 11 12 Graduated? ☐ YES ☐ NO
College _____ 13 14 15 16 Degree Received _____ Major _____
Graduate School _____ Other schools (Vocational, Military, etc.) _____

Have you ever been employed by The C Company before?		☐ YES ☐ NO
If Yes, Position	From To	Reason for Leaving
Department	Supervisor Name & Title	Location

IF YOU ARE NOT A U.S. CITIZEN, DOES YOUR VISA OR IMMIGRATION STATUS PERMIT LAWFUL EMPLOYMENT?	IF EMPLOYED, CAN PROOF OF CITIZENSHIP, VISA OR ALIEN REGISTRATION NUMBER BE PROVIDED?
☐ YES ☐ NO ☐ N/A	☐ YES ☐ NO ☐ N/A

List current and previous employers: (List most current first, next most current second, etc.)
May we contact your current employer? ☐ YES ☐ NO

Position	Employer		Location	
Supervisor	Telephone Number	Dates Worked From To	Pay Rate $	

Position	Employer		Location	
Supervisor	Telephone Number	Dates Worked From To	Pay Rate $	

Position	Employer		Location	
Supervisor	Telephone Number	Dates Worked From To	Pay Rate $	

Have you been convicted of a crime within the last seven years or have you been imprisoned for the conviction of a crime within the last seven years?   ☐ YES   ☐ NO   The existence of a record of convictions for criminal offenses is not considered an automatic bar to employment.

Date of conviction _____ Describe Circumstances _____

Military service? ☐ YES ☐ NO	If Yes. From To	Branch of Service	MOS/Duties
Highest Rank Obtained	Reserve status ☐ NATIONAL GUARD ☐ ACTIVE RESERVE ☐ NONE		

---

forms. One difficulty is the time and effort required to develop such a form. For many small employers, and for jobs that do not require numerous employees, the cost of developing the weights can be prohibitive. Also, the blank must be updated every few years to ensure that the factors previously identified are still valid predictors of job success. Finally, many of the items that earlier studies identified as good predictors of success cannot be asked about now because of EEO restrictions. For example, asking about family responsibilities (marital status, number of children) and age is likely to cause the employer difficulty because of the need to show the job-relatedness of those inquiries. In a survey of 437 firms, only 11 percent were found to be using a weighted application blank.[6] Thus it appears that weighted application blanks are more attractive in theory than in practice.

Resumes. One of the most common methods applicants use to provide background information is the resume. Resumes, also called vitae (or *curriculum vitae*) by some, vary in style and length. Technically, though, a resume used in place of an application form must be treated by an employer as if it were an application form for EEO purposes. Consequently, even though an applicant may provide some "illegal information" voluntarily on a resume, the employer should not use that information during the selection process. In one large firm, a clerk in the employment office uses a razor knife on resumes to cut out any information that would be illegal if the firm asked for it.

One of the biggest problems with resumes is that unlike an application form prepared by an employer, they contain only information applicants want to present. Some employers require that all who submit resumes complete an application form as well so similar information will be available on all applicants. Individuals who mail in resumes are sent a thank-you letter and a blank application form to be completed and returned. Because resumes also represent "applicant flow" for many jobs that are nationally advertised, applicant flow forms should be mailed to applicants who send in a resume so that accurate EEO data may be obtained. Some specific suggestions for constructing a resume are available in Appendix A on "Getting a Job."

Using Application Forms. Many employers use only one application form. This practice may not target the application form to specific occupational groups as much as is possible. For example, a hospital might need one form for nurses and medical technicians, another for clerical and office employees, another for managers and supervisors, and one for support persons in housekeeping and food service areas.

The information received on application forms or resumes may not always be completely accurate. This problem is discussed in greater detail later but an important point must be made here. In an attempt to correct inaccuracies, many application forms carry a statement at the bottom of the form which the applicant is required to sign. That states, in effect: "I realize that falsification of this record is grounds for dismissal if I am hired." Whether or not this phrase reduces inaccurate information on the application form is not known. However, "misrepresentation" of facts has been used by many employers to terminate someone who has been hired.

Application forms traditionally have also asked for the names of references and requested that the applicant give permission to contact them. Rather than asking for personal or general references, it may be more useful to request the names of previous supervisors on the application form.

If the applicant shows no obvious disqualifications, testing can be scheduled or the applicant can be given an in-depth interview. As mentioned earlier, the choice of moving next to the interview or to a test depends upon the nature of the job applied for, the cost of the test, and other related factors.

Can you discuss the reception and application form phases of the selection process?

SELECTION TESTING

Many people claim that, when properly used and administered, formal tests can be of great benefit in the selection process. Considerable evidence supports this claim. However, because of EEO concerns, many employers reduced or eliminated the use of tests beginning in the early 1970s. A 1983 survey revealed that 112 of 437 firms surveyed had discontinued or changed their selection process in the preceding five years. Many of the changes had centered on discontinuance of or restrictions on employment testing. Formal tests that had been eliminated include those that test mental ability (math, spelling, grammar), general intelligence (Wonderlic), clerical (typing, shorthand) personality tests, polygraphs, and dexterity tests. Nineteen firms had added tests, but these were skill tests and job knowledge tests. The same survey provided cost data on 16 firms that used employment tests. That data, shown in Figure 9–4, indicated that the cost per applicant ranged from $3 per applicant to $135 per applicant.[7]

Types of Tests

According to the Uniform Guidelines, any employment requirement is a "test." However, the focus in this section is on formal tests. There are many different tests that can be used for selection screening. Some are paper-and-pencil tests (such as a math test), others are motor skill tests, and still others use machines (polygraphs, for instance). One listing of tests contains information on over 1,000 tests.[8] Some employers purchase prepared tests, while others develop their own.

Tests also have varying degrees of sophistication. Some of them are very crude while others are prepared by staff industrial psychologists. One Texas-based corporation has seven employees trained in industrial psychology who develop, administer, and interpret tests used by the firm throughout the world. The discussion that follows is intended to highlight several types of formal tests that may be used for selection purposes.

TYPE OF ORGANIZATION	ANNUAL OPERATING COST FOR TESTING	COST PER APPLICANT	TEST DEVELOPMENT AND VALIDATION EXPENDITURES	NUMBER OF EMPLOYEES
Southern manufacturer	$ 25	$ —	$ —	1,404
Central manufacturer	100	5.00	—	—
Central transportation firm	500	—	—	650
Southern health care organization	<1,000	3.00	—	400 +
Western educational institution	1,000	—	—	845
Southern wholesaler	1,000	50.00	—	1,200
Southern local government	1,320	8.52	—	860
Northeastern health care organization	2,000	10.00	1,000	200
Northeastern local government	5,800	3.00	9,000	1,600
Western municipal government	6,500	—	—	350
Western manufacturer	21,000	135.00	—	1,119
Western health care organization	21,000	—	—	2,000
Southern municipal government	100,000	—	35,000	4,200
Central municipal government	185,000	56.85	—	2,393
Western municipal government	750,000	25.00	60,000	8,000
Southern state government agency	5,000,000	20.00	100,000	120,000
Central health care organization	—	—	56,000	650
Southern manufacturer	—	—	3,500	2,400
Central bank	—	—	11,000	477

SOURCE: "Employee Selection Procedures," *Bulletin to Management*, ASPA-BNA Survey 45 (May 5, 1983), p. 11. Reprinted by permission from *Bulletin to Management*, copyright 1984 by the Bureau of National Affairs, Inc., Washington, D.C.

General Personality and Psychological Tests

FIGURE 9–4
Selection Testing Costs.

General psychological tests attempt to measure personality characteristics. The legendary Rorschach "ink blot" test and the Thematic Apperception Test (TAT) are examples. In the TAT, an applicant is shown a picture and asked to create a story about the picture. A picture might show an executive sitting at a desk cluttered with papers, apparently gazing at a photograph of family members on the desk. Some of the most well-known personality tests include the Minnesota Multiphase Personality Inventory (MMPI) the Predictive Index, the Edwards Personal Preference Schedule, and the California Personality Inventory.

Such tests are difficult to validate as job-related for many jobs. They are the least-preferred tests from a legal standpoint in many situations. Due to their nebulous definitions of personality and the difficulties of tying specific personality characteristics to specific job requirements, general psychological and personality tests represent the shakiest type of tests used for selection purposes. After all, being an extrovert or an introvert may have little to do with successful performance of individuals who become internal accountants, welders, or shipping room clerks. Also, with such tests, it is possible for applicants to "falsify" responses. Some of the concerns with personality tests are highlighted in the special discussion of the MMPI. However, general personality tests are not the most controversial selection tests used. One much-debated area of testing, genetic screening, is discussed at the end of the chapter. Three other types—*graphoanalysis, polygraphs,* and *honesty* tests—are discussed next.

ASSESSING THE MMPI

Have you ever indulged in unusual sex practices? Does life give you a raw deal? Do you believe in the second coming of Christ? Do you like to go to parties and other affairs where there is lots of loud fun? Do you get all the sympathy you should?

Think carefully before you respond. Your answers to these and similar questions—typical of the Minnesota Multiphasic Personality Inventory (MMPI)—could cost you a job. The most-frequently used personality test in America and probably the world, the MMPI has been translated into 100 languages and taken by millions of people. Here and abroad it figures heavily in hiring and promotion of policemen, firement, airline pilots, and those who work in sensitive areas of nuclear power plants.

Recently, however, these tests have been used for many non-critical occupations. Business executives, social workers, sometimes even cashiers have been tested. And it seems that, almost universally, hiring and promotion decisions, once based on a manger's intuition, have been given over to elaborate assessment programs that often include some personality tests.

The MMPI consists of 566 statements to which the respondent answers true or false. Standards for evaluating performance on the test were developed using two groups of subjects—a group of hospitalized psychiatric patients and a group of normal people. It was found that the two groups answered questions differently, that normals and psychiatric patients showed different response patterns, and that schizophrenics, depressives, neurotics and other groups also could be differentiated by their responses.

Test advocates contend that MMPI scores give information about psychopathology. But many behavioral science researchers regard the MMPI and other personality tests with suspicion, if not outright contempt.

Many of the nation's 2,500 industrial and organizational psychologists believe personality tests are useful for predicting an applicant's performance in the work force. The consensus, however, is that personality tests are applicable in a limited number of contexts, and that their weight in the personnel selection process should be minimized.[9]

Graphoanalysis (Handwriting Analysis). This test relies heavily on a graphologist, who analyzes samples of an individual's handwriting and attempts to discern personality characteristics as they are revealed in a person's handwriting.[10] Such items as how people dot an "i," cross a "t," whether they write with a left or right slant, and size and boldness of letters are analyzed by a graphologist to reach conclusions about individuals, their personalities, and their suitability for employment. MDP Data Processing, a New York firm, uses graphoanalysis for hiring at all organizational levels, from clerk to management. Phillips Supply Company of Cincinnati has applicants complete application forms and write about ten lines telling why they want a job. These samples are then sent to a graphologist for analysis and the results are used in the final selection of an individual.[11]

The major problem with such a test is that so much depends upon the graphologist who interprets the results. Also, as with many personality tests, an employer might have difficulty identifying the relationship between a series of personality traits and job performance.

Polygraph. The polygraph, more generally and incorrectly referred to as the "lie detector," is a mechanical device that measures the galvanic skin response, the heart and pulse rate, and the breathing rate of a person. The theory behind the polygraph is that if a person answers incorrectly, the body will "reveal" the falsification through the polygraph's recording mechanisms.

The extent of polygraph usage is demonstrated by the fact that in the U.S. over 1 million people per year take polygraph examinations. About 50 percent of all retail firms, 20 percent of all corporations, and many banks use polygraph tests.[12] One drug store chain headquartered in Florida, Jack Eckerd Corporation, tests each of its 30,000 employees annually.[13] Organizations involved in security and law enforcement are also heavy users of the polygraph.

Serious questions have been raised about the usage of polygraph in employment settings, especially about its constitutionality and the invasion of the privacy of those tested. Such concerns are clearly captured in the description given in the "Personnel in Practice" by an applicant for a job at a brewery in the western U.S. (even though the situation described may be a bit extreme). This particular firm has since reduced its usage of the polygraph.

Another criticism of polygraphs is the heavy reliance placed on the examiner who interprets a person's responses. There has been little attempt to exercise control over the qualifications of these examiners.

As a result of these concerns, twelve states have passed laws banning the use of polygraph tests for employment purposes. Nineteen states have laws about licensing requirments for operators, with Illinois having the most restrictive regulations.[14] Also, several bills have been introduced in Congress to regulate or outlaw polygraph use in employment situations.

In spite of these criticisms and the difficulty of identifying the job-relatedness of some questions used in polygraph examinations, polygraphs probably will continue to be used unless further restrictive legislation is passed. It has been said that the cost/benefit analysis often used to justify polygraph usage should be modified to include the legal and public relations "costs."[15]

Honesty Tests. A third type of controversial test is one that purports to measure employee "honesty." The Reid Report and the Stanton Survey are the two most widely used of these pencil-and-paper tests. Individuals who take honesty tests answer "yes" or "no" to a list of questions. Sample questions include:[16]

■ Would you tell your boss if you know of another employee stealing from the company?
■ Is it all right to borrow company equipment to use at home if the property is always returned?
■ Have you ever told a lie?
■ Have you ever wished you were physically more attractive?

One retail chain indicated that employee theft was cut by 28 percent after the the Reid Report honesty test was put into use.[18] Nevertheless, these tests may suffer from the same weaknesses as the polygraph and graphoanalysis. An employer who uses these tests should be aware of the potential legal risks being taken, even though honesty tests have yet to be outlawed in any states.[19]

Aptitude and Proficiency Tests

Aptitude and proficiency tests are less controversial than those just discussed. Aptitude tests are used to measure an applicant's ability to perform the work for which he or she is being considered. Included are tests of "general aptitude," such as mental ability, and "specific aptitude," such as finger dexterity. *Mental aptitude* and *general intelligence* tests were used more extensively before the *Griggs* v. *Duke Power* decision in 1971.

Tests that measure *mechanical ability* and *mathematical aptitude* can be shown to be job-related much more easily than general intelligence tests. A *proficiency test* is a more specific skills-oriented test. The typing test that many firms give to secretarial applicants is a commonly-used proficiency test.

Work sample tests that require an applicant to perform part of the job that is being applied for are especially useful because of their close tie to the job. The 40-yard dashes and blocking drills used in pro football training camps are examples. Asking an applicant for a truck driver's job to actually back the truck to a loading dock is a proficiency test. If you have ever rented a trailer and tried to back your car and trailer into a driveway, you can understand why such proficiency would be important to a test for truck driver's job.

A basic requirement for the development or use of these tests is a good job analysis of what tasks are performed in the job. By knowing exactly what is done, a test using an actual work sample can be derived.

Assessment Centers and Selection. An assessment center is not a place but is a selection and development device composed of a series of evaluative exercises and test. In one assessment center, candidates go through a comprehensive interview, pencil-and-paper test, individual and group simulation, and work exercises. The candidates' performances are then evaluated by a panel of trained raters.

A number of state and local governments use the assessment center when selecting department or division heads because of the potential charges of political favoritism that could be leveled if they used a less comprehensive selection process. One major city has used the assessment center to select its director of public works, fire chief, city engineer, and employee relations administrator.

Assessment centers are especially useful in determining promotable employees and in helping to develop them. These issues are discussed in Chapter 11.

Test Usage

The most important factor to consider when choosing and using any employment test is the validity of the test. As emphasized in the chapters on equal employment opportunity regulations, unless the test measures what it is supposed to measure (validity) on a consistent basis (reliability), it should not be used. Individuals trained in testing and test interpretation should be involved in the establishment and maintenance of a testing system. Finally, the role of tests in the overall selection process must be kept in perspective.[20] Tests represent only one possible data source. Because of the problems discussed earlier, it is easy to see why some employers, especially small ones, have dropped tests. The result is that much more weight and emphasis is placed on the in-depth interview.

Can you identify two general types of tests and some concerns about their usage?

A STRUCTURED
INTERVIEW
is conducted using a set
of standardized ques-
tions that are asked all
applicants for a job.

A general selection interview is designed to probe areas of interest to the interviewer in order to determine how well the applicant will match the needs of the organization. This in-depth interview is designed to integrate all the information from application forms, tests, and reference checks so that a selection decision can be made. Because of the integration required and the desirability of face-to-face contact, the interview is the most important phase of the selection process in many situations. Conflicting information may have emerged from the tests, application forms, or references. As a result, the interviewer must obtain as much pertinent information about the applicant as possible during the limited interview time and then evaluate this information against job standards.

Equal Employment and Interviewing

The interview, like a pencil-and-paper test and an application form, is a type of predictor and must meet the standards of job-relatedness and nondiscrimination. Some court decisions and EEOC rulings have attacked the interviewing practices of some firms as being discriminatory. In one EEOC case the court ruled that by relying on questions not related to the job, interviewers violated EEOC guidelines.[21] Many experts feel that the safest and fairest type of interview to use is a structured interview, one of several types of interviews.[22]

Types of Interviews

There are three special types of interviews: *structured interviews, nondirective interviews,* and *stress interviews.* Each type is discussed next.

Structured Interview. The pupose of the **structured interview** is to generate data on applicants through the use of some standardized questions. If an interviewer asks Mary Mazzaro one question and does not ask the same question of Steve Smith, the interviewer has no similar basis for evaluating each of the applicants.

This type of interview also allows an interviewer to prepare in advance questions that are job-related and to then complete a standardized interviewee evaluation form. Completion of such a form provides documentation if anyone, including an EEO enforcement body, should question why one applicant was selected over another. Sample questions that might be asked of an applicant for a production maintenance management opening are:[23]

■ Tell me about how you trained workers for their job.
■ How can you tell how much work you and the maintenance crew will have to do during a day?
■ What effect does the production schedule of the plant have on what a mechanic ought to repair first?

- How do you know what the needs of the plant are at any given time and what mechanics ought to be doing?
- How did you or would you go about planning a preventive maintenance program in the plant?

Even though a series of patterned questions are asked, the structured interview does not have to be rigid. The predetermined questions should be asked in a logical manner, but the interviewer should avoid reading the questions and rigidly continuing down the list of questions. The applicant should be allowed adequate opportunity to clearly explain the answers given. Also, the interviewer should probe until an adequate understanding of the applicant's response in each area has been gained.

Nondirective Interview. The nondirective interview is heavily used in psychological counseling, but it is also widely used in selection. The interviewer asks general questions designed to prompt the applicant to discuss herself or himself. The interviewer then picks up on an idea in the applicant's response to one question to shape the next question. For example, if the applicant says, "One aspect of my last job that I enjoyed was my supervisor," the interviewer might ask, "What type of supervisor do you most enjoy working with?"

Difficulties with a nondirective interview include maintaining its job-relatedness and obtaining comparable data on each applicant. Some managers may indicate a preference for the nondirective interview as a way to hide a lack of preparation for the interview. Also, by not having the same data from each applicant, a manager may hire one applicant instead of another because of "general attractiveness" or "good vibes." Not restricted to physical appearance, the idea of "general attractiveness" is often a result of an interviewer's subjective perceptions and biases, which may not bear any direct relationship to an applicant's ability to perform the job. While these biases can enter into a structured interview also, they are more likely to appear in the nondirective interview.

Stress Interview. The stress interview is a special type of interview designed to create anxiety and put pressure on the applicant to see how the applicant responds. In the stress interview, the interviewer assumes an extremely aggressive and insulting posture. Those who utilize this approach often justify its use for interviews with individuals who will encounter high degrees of stress on the job, such as a consumer complaint clerk in a department store or an air traffic controller.

The stress interview is a "high risk" approach. The typical applicant is already somewhat anxious in any interview. The stress interview can easily generate a very poor image of the interviewer and the employer, thus creating resistance by applicants who might be offered jobs.

Can you discuss three types of interviews?

Interviewing Considerations

Many people think the ability to interview is an innate talent, but this contention is difficult to support. Just because someone is personable and likes to talk, there is no guarantee that the person will be a good interviewer. Interviewing skills are developed through training and through following some of the suggestions below.

Planning the Interview. Effective interviews do not just happen; they are planned. Pre-interview planning is essential to a well-conducted in-depth selection interview. The interviewer should review the application form and other data before beginning the interview. Analyzing the information on the application form on three major dimensions is recommended: (1) the information given, (2) the skills in presenting the information, and (3) insight to the applicant's thinking as gleaned from the answers given.[24]

Using a Chronology. A useful planning tool to probe an individual's past history, especially in the case of unexplained gaps in an individual's past work or school record, is a chronology. For example, when Herb Ellis applies for a job as a management trainee, the in-depth interviewer may ask Ellis, while reviewing the application form, to recall his past work experience. All the jobs Ellis has had for the last five years are arranged into a time-frame, allowing the interviewer to see any gaps in the chronology. By questioning Ellis about the dates of his employment, the interviewer may notice that two years ago there was a four-month period during which Ellis was neither working nor going to school. Careful questioning reveals that Ellis had been involved in an automobile accident and had suffered a back injury. He had not noted this fact on the application form.

Control. An important aspect of the interview is control. If the interviewer does not control the interview, the applicant usually will. Control involves knowing in advance what information must be collected, systematically collecting it, and stopping when everything needed is collected.

Having control of the interview does not mean doing a lot of talking. The interviewer should talk no more than 20–25 percent of the time in an in-depth interview. If the interviewer talks more than that, the interviewer is being interviewed.

The interviewer can lose control by the type of question he or she asks. Janet Markely, an interviewer, might ask, "Can you tell me about your part-time jobs?" The applicant then might take off on a 30-minute discussion. Control of the interview is lost if the interviewer cannot break in. Letting the applicant know what is to be accomplished during the interview and how it is to be accomplished helps establish control because the applicant understands his or her role in the interview.

Realistic Job Preview. Although the interviewer should limit the amount of time he or she spends talking, a key part of the interview is to provide information about the job for which the interviewee is applying. One approach that has been widely researched is the **Realistic Job Preview (RJP)**. An RJP is the process of providing a job applicant with an accurate picture of a job.

The purpose of an RJP is to inform job candidates of the "organizational realities" of a job so that they can more accurately evaluate their own job expectations and the realities of the job. By presenting applicants with a clear picture of the job, the organization hopes to reduce employee disenchantment or unrealistic expectations, and thereby to experience less turnover and employee dissatisfaction.[25] A review of research on RJPs found that they sometimes can have beneficial effects.[26] However, the evidence on the effects of RJPs and when it is best to use them is mixed.[27] Nevertheless, it is important for an interviewer to provide some information on the job, not just get information from the applicant.

Questioning Techniques

The questioning techniques used can and do significantly affect the type and quality of the information obtained. Some specific suggestions follow next.

Good Questions. Many questions an interviewer asks assume that the past is the best predictor of the future and it usually is. An interviewer is less likely to have difficulty when questioning the applicant's demonstrated past performance than asking vague questions about the future.

Some types of questions provide more meaningful answers than others. Good interviewing technique is dependent upon the use of open-ended questions directed toward a particular goal. An open-ended question is one that cannot be answered "yes" or "no." *Who, what, when, why, tell me, how, which* are all good ways to begin questions that will produce longer and more informative answers. "What was your attendance record on your last job?" is a better question than "Did you have a good attendance record on your last job?" because the latter question can be answered simply, "Yes."

Poor Questions. Certain kinds of questions should be avoided:

1. *Questions that rarely produce a true answer.* An example is "How did you get along with your co-workers?" This question is almost inevitably going to be answered, "Just fine."
2. *Leading questions.* A leading question is one in which the answer is obvious from the way the question is asked. For example, "You do like to talk to people, don't you?" Answer: "Of course."
3. *Illegal questions.* Questions that involve race, creed, sex, national origin, marital status, number of children, and so on are illegal. They are also just as inappropriate in the interview as they are on the application form.

A REALISTIC JOB PREVIEW (RJP) is the process of providing a job applicant with an accurate picture of a job.

4. *Obvious questions.* An obvious question is one for which the interviewer already has the answer, and the applicant knows it. Questions already answered on the application blank should be probed, not re-asked. If an interviewer asks, "What high school did you attend?" Joyce Sauer is likely to answer, "As I wrote on my application form, South High School in Caveton." Instead, ask questions that probe the information given: "What were your favorite subjects at South High, and why?"

5. *Questions that are not job-related.* All questions asked should be directly related to the job for which the applicant has applied. Some people believe discussion about the weather, sports, or politics helps a candidate relax and become at ease. However, those questions consume interview time that could be more appropriately used in other ways. Also, many times the interviewee does not relax and the interviewer may not listen to the responses because he or she is using the "chit-chat" time to review the candidate's application form or to otherwise make up for the interviewer's lack of planning and preparation.

There are certain question areas that an interviewer probably should minimize. These areas can be referred to as the "egad" factors, which are questions the interviewer asks about the applicants expectations, goals, aspirations, and desires. While the answers to an "egad" question may produce a meaningful answer, usually the applicant will respond with a prepared "pat" answer. For example, in answer to the question, "What are your aspirations:" the college graduate will often respond that he or she wants to become a company vice-president. The person settles for vice-president instead of president because of the desire not to appear egotistical. Yet it is considered "culturally acceptable" in our society to demonstrate a certain amount of ambition and the vice-presidential level appears to be appropriate.

Because the applicant is not likely to be able to answer an "egad" question in a realistic manner, the answer an interviewer receives is usually the applicant's idea of what the interviewer wants to hear. Many times the answer seems to be taken straight from advertisements and recruiting brochures; for example, "I am looking for a job that provides a challenge and an opportunity for advancement."

The answer to an "egad" question is not likely to be very predictive. The attainment of a B+ average in school, or other such information, is a fact, is verifiable, and is likely to be more predictive.

Listening Responses. The good interviewer avoids listening responses such as nodding, pausing, casual remarks, echoing, and mirroring. Listening responses are an essential part of everyday, normal conversation. While they are necessary to maintain rapport, they may unintentionally provide feedback to the applicant. Applicants may try to please the interviewer and look to the interviewer's listening responses for cues. Even though the listening responses may be subtle, they do provide information to the applicant.

While the total absence of listening responses can create stress, too much use of listening responses may constitute what is called *cultural noise.* For example, one interviewer used the casual remark, "That's nice," constantly. After every statement the applicant made, the interviewer would comment, "That's nice," while trying to think of the next question. This habit had a tendency to encourage the interviewee to talk about areas that were really not pertinent to the interview and the job at hand. As a result, the interview took much longer than necessary.

Problems in the Interview

There are a number of pitfalls that interviewers should avoid. Operating managers and supervisors most often use poor interviewing techniques because they do not interview often and have not been trained to interview. Some of the most common problems encountered in the interview are highlighted next.

Snap Judgments. Ideally, the interviewer should collect *all* the information possible on an applicant before making a judgment. Reserving judgment is much easier to recommend than to do. It is very difficult not to form an early impression. Too often, interviewers form an early impression and spend the balance of the interview looking for evidence to support it. Research on the interview confirms this and indicates that interviewers make a decision within the first four or five minutes of an interview. Decisions about high-quality applicants usually take longer.[29]

Negative Emphasis. Research studies show that unfavorable information about an applicant is the biggest factor considered in decisions about overall suitability. Unfavorable information is given roughly twice the weight of favorable information. It has been found that a single negative characteristic may bar an individual from being accepted, while no amount of positive characteristics will guarantee a candidate's acceptance.[30]

Halo Effect. Interviewers should strictly try to avoid the "halo effect," which occurs when an interviewer allows some very prominent characteristic to overshadow other evidence. The halo effect is present if an interviewer lets a candidate's accomplishments in athletics overshadow other aspects and leads the interviewer to hire the applicant because "athletes make good salespeople." "Devil's horns" (a reverse halo effect), such as an unattractive physical appearance or a low GPA, may affect an interviewer as well.

Biases. An interviewer must be able to face up to personal biases. For example, studies on the interview process have found that women are generally rated lower, by both female and male interviewers.[31] The selection of an applicant who falls below standards or the rejection of an applicant who meets standards is an indication that personal bias has influenced a selection decision. An interviewer should be able be honest and write down the reasons for selecting a particular applicant. The solution to the problem of bias lies not in claiming that a person has no biases, but in demonstrating that they can be controlled.

Cultural Noise. The interviewer must learn to recognize and handle "cultural noise." Applicants want a job; to get it they know they have to get by the interviewer. They may feel that if they divulge any of the "wrong things" about themselves, they may not get the job. Consequently, applicants may be reticent to tell an interviewer all about themselves. Instead, they may try to give the interviewer responses that are *socially* acceptable but not very revealing. These types of responses are called *cultural noise*—responses the applicant believes are socially acceptable rather than facts.

An interviewer can handle cultural noise by not encouraging it. Any support of cultural noise by the interviewer is a cue to the applicant to continue those answers. Instead, the applicant can be made aware that the interviewer is not being taken in. An interviewer can say, "The fact that you were the best tent handler in your Scout troup is interesting, but tell me about your performance on your last job."

Can you discuss six key considerations or problems in the selection interview?

The Interview Process

The following section describes procedures for the in-depth selection interview. These techniques are appropriate for most interviews; however, for highly skilled positions or professional or managerial positions, different techniques may be more appropriate.

Setting the Stage. The interviewer should set the stage for the interview by letting the applicant know what is going to happen and what is expected. For example, the interviewer might suggest: "The purpose of this interview is to determine whether there is a match between your interests and qualifications and what we have to offer. To do this, I'd like to briefly review your history from 1980 to the present, paying particular attention to your school and work activities, and then I'd like to come back and have you cover some of the areas in greater detail."

Exchange of Information. After the stage has been set, the interviewer can review the chronology presented on the application form. The interviewer can then probe important areas. The interviewer might say: "You worked for Orbus Company from January 1981 to September 1984 as a clerk. What were your responsibilites?" "How did you get the job?" "What were several reasons you had for leaving?"

The applicant's questions also must be answered and the job situation should be examined through a Realistic Job Preview or some other format. Whether hired or not, the applicant should feel that he or she has been given fair consideration and treatment.

Interviewer Believability. Interviewers represent their employer and must be believable. Glowing accounts of the company and rambling testimonials are a form of cultural noise given by interviewers. One study found that applicants see such interviewers as noncredible sources. Providing negative information about a job increased the interviewer's credibility, but, as expected, it decreased the likelihood of the applicant accepting a job offer.[32]

Close the Interview. Finally, the interviewer closes the interview. One question has proved very useful for closing an interview: "Is there anything else about you I should know before we close this interview?" Many times interviewees will use this opportunity to bring out something that may have been bothering them through the course of the interview. It also indicates that this question is the last one before the interview closes.

The Turndown. A large percentage of applicants are not hired. The manner in which they are turned down can have a personal effect on the individual and on that person's impression of the organization. Most people can perform successfully in some kind of job in some organization—it is simply a question of finding a match. The best interest of the applicant is served if the applicant is not placed in an unsuitable position. The interviewer does well to direct attention to this fact.

A standard turndown phrase can be quite beneficial if properly developed. One company uses the turndown phrase, "In my judgment, we do not have a match between your qualifications and the needs of the job for which you have applied that would use your qualifications to their best advantage."

It is generally good practice not to give reasons, beyond a turndown phrase, for not hiring someone. Considerable experience in this area has indicated that giving reasons for not hiring encourages argument or comparison of the applicant with a present employee. Reasons may be misquoted by the applicant when talking with other individuals, resulting in many other problems. In addition, such reasons may be taken as advice or counseling on the part of the interviewer. Vocational advice or counseling is inappropriate at this point. Interviewers should be trained to recognize qualifications for their own particular organization, but these qualifications may not hold for other occupations or organizations. Also, the applicant should not be encouraged to hope for a job with the company if there is no future possibility that he or she will be hired.

Such phrases as "Try back again in six months" or "We'll keep your application in our files and call you if something comes up" are not justifiable if they are untrue. Utmost care must be taken not to hold out hope where none exists. Although it might be more comfortable for the interviewer, it simply is not fair to the applicant.

Written Record of the Interview. During or immediately after the interview, a decision is made about whether or not to further consider the applicant. It is important that the interviewer make job-related notes regarding data collected during the interview so the information can be reevaluated later if necessary.

A written evaluation of interview data gives an overall view of findings, provides a check for consistency, and points out items that need further investigation. More important, the interviewer must use the information to support a final decision. Requiring written records forces the interviewer to justify the decision.

However, it is important that factual responses that are recorded be job-related. Instead of writing "Individual does not seem to have much initiative," it would be better for the interviewer to note: "Individual indicated he did not plan to finish his college degree." Also, comments about factors such as appearance, family situations, or personal biases of the interviewer are inappropriate. Because the written record represents data used in the selection process, any notes made could become used in defending a discrimination complaint. Consequently, written information on the answers in the interview should be limited to factual, job-related notations.

What Interviewers Look For. Overall, interviewers attempt to see evidence of well-roundedness, competence, and success. A survey of personnel executives found that *personality and demeanor during the interview,* affects hiring decisions the most. The second most important factor was *experience,* followed by *specific skills and qualifications.* Expansive resumes were given the lowest priority.[33]

In another job study, interviewers rated resumes portraying applicants with average grades, excellent work experience, and appropriate interest lower than resumes portraying people with poor work experience and inappropriate interests, but high scholastic standing. The information about scholastic standing in this study was so overwhelmingly important that the latter resumes received good evaluations.[34] Certain items are obviously more important to interviewers, but if they are not job-related, they must be viewed with caution.

Critique of Selection Interviewing. Despite its widespread use, the selection interview is probably one of the weakest tools for predicting an applicant's job performance. No one is sure that much of the information covered in an interview is predictive of performance on the job because few firms attempt to validate their interviews. In addition, of the information that is predictive, much of it cannot be measured reliably in an interview.[35]

Why bother then? The interview does provide some information that cannot be obtained in other ways, such as the applicant's ability to communicate and attitudes. Also, personal contact reassures both applicants and interviewers.

*Can you construct a guide for conducting a
selection interview?*

*"Excellent. Now do you have any other
references besides your mother?"*

BACKGROUND INVESTIGATION

Background investigation, as noted earlier, may take place either before or after the in-depth interview. Checking a person's background is highly recommended, considering that some of the information accumulated on the application form and in the interview may be incorrect. Background checks may require investing a little time and money, but they are generally well worth the effort.

Types of References

Background references can be put in several categories:

- Academic references
- Prior work references
- Financial references
- Personal references

PERSONNEL IN PRACTICE
LIARS 1, EMPLOYERS 0?

It may be a shock to many people's basic beliefs about the goodness and honesty of others, but many employers have found that applicants frequently misrepresent their qualifications and backgrounds.

One of the most publicized "faking" of credentials involved Janet Cooke, a *Washington Post* reporter, who claimed to have a B.A. degree from Vassar College and an M.A. from the University of Toledo. Only after she received a Pulitzer Prize for reporting did her employer discover that she had lied about her credentials, as well as made up the story for which she won the prize. However, that use is only the tip of the "resume fraud" iceberg.

Many universities report that inquiries on graduates and former students often reveal that the individual never graduated or may have never attended the university listed. Columbia University reports that five or six inquiries a week prove to be false. The vice-president of human resources for a major corporation has estimated that 20 percent of all resumes contain at least one "factual misstatement." A representative of a firm that checks academic records for companies estimates that 30–40 percent of all people lie on resumes when applying for jobs.

Along with credential fraud, another problem is the mail-order "degree mill." In order to enhance their chances of employment, individuals purchase degrees from organizations that grant unaccredited degrees for a fee. One school advertising in major publications claims that a person can receive a degree with "no exams, no studying, no classes." Another school, located in New Orleans, grants doctorate degrees for a fee of $5,000. To see the "opportunities" for yourself, read the classified ads in the *Wall Street Journal* or many other national magazines and publications.

The only way for employers to protect themselves from resume fraud and false credentials is to request verification or proof from applicants either before or after hire. If hired, the employee may be terminated for falsifying employment information.

It is unwise for employers to ignore the problem or continue to assume that "someone else has already checked." One expert in the area has said, "If you can fool your first employer, you may be able to fool all the ones that follow because they all assume the first one checked." However, "factual misstatements" may be uncovered easily when background investigations are done by employers.[36]

Personal references often are of little value; they probably should not even be required. No applicant will ask somebody to write a recommendation who is going to give a negative response. Therefore, personal references from relatives, ministers, or family friends are likely to be a weak source of selection information.

Impact of Privacy Legislation

A variety of federal and state laws has been passed to protect the privacy of personal information. The most important is the Federal Privacy Act of 1974, which applies primarily to governmental agencies and units. However, bills to extend the provisions of the privacy act to other employers have been regularly introduced. Employers should be aware of the potential impact of pending privacy legislation on their employment practices, especially on background investigations.

One proposed privacy provision would require a signed written release from a person before information could be given to someone else. As an example, many colleges will not release a person's grades and/or transcripts unless given written authorization from the individual. Also, under some legislation proposed in the past, either a copy of the information would be given to the individual, or the person would be given the right to inspect the personnel file. In some cases, a person or employer who gave information that could not be documented and that later prevented an applicant from obtaining a job has been successfully sued.[37] Other privacy provisions that would affect personnel files and records are discussed in Chapter 18. It must be emphasized that many of these provisions were not law, but merely proposals at the time this book was prepared.

Contacting References

In spite of the potential limitation imposed by privacy concerns, many employers do contact references. A study found that 97 percent of the employers who responded checked references or records.[38]

Problems in investigating applicants' backgrounds arise when managers must contact people in other organizations whom they may not know. Often people are hesitant to give a negative reference, especially in written form, for a former employee. Some employers have a policy of giving only the essential information such as dates of employment, title of the last job, and perhaps salary. Although this information can be used to verify the applicant's statements, it has little other use.

Reference Methods. Several methods of obtaining reference information are available to a potential employer. Telephoning a reference is the most widely used and preferred method. Most of the other methods are written ones. Some firms have preprinted reference forms that are sent to individuals who are acting as references for applicants. Specific or general letters of reference are requested by some employers and/or provided by applicants.[39]

Figure 9–5 provides some guidelines for defensible reference-checking and reference-giving. These guidelines emphasize that dealing with references requires reliance on factual and verifiable information.

Can you explain how and why privacy concerns affect background investigations of applicants?

1. Don't volunteer information. Respond only to specific company or institutional inquiries and requests. Before responding, telephone the inquirer to check on the validity of the request.

2. Direct all communication only to persons who have a specific interest in that information.

3. State in the message that the information you are providing is confidential and should be treated as such. Use qualifying statements such as "providing information that was requested"; "relating this information only because it was requested"; or "providing information that is to be used for professional purposes only." Sentences such as these imply that information was not presented for the purpose of hurting or damaging a person's reputation.

5. Provide only reference data that relates and pertains to the job and job performance in question.

6. Avoid vague statements such as: "He was an average student"; "She was careless at times"; "He displayed an inability to work with others."

7. Document all released information. Use specific statements such as: "Mr. ___ received a grade of C—an average grade"; "Ms. ___ made an average of two bookkeeping errors each week"; or "This spring, four members of the work team wrote letters asking not to be placed on the shift with Mr. ___."

8. Clearly label all subjective statements based on personal opinions and feelings. Say "I believe . . ." whenever making a statement that is not fact.

9. When providing a negative or potentially negative statement, add the reason or reasons why, or specify the incidents that led you to this opinion.

10. Do not answer trap questions such as "Would you rehire this person?"

11. Avoid answering questions that are asked "off the record."

FIGURE 9–5
Guidelines for Defensible References.

Medical Examinations

A medical examination may be given to all applicants who otherwise meet hiring requirements. Often this examination is one of the last steps in the employment process. A medical examination is usually given in a company medical office or by a physician approved and paid by the organization. The purpose of a medical examination is to obtain information on the health status of the applicant being considered for employment.[40] Medical information is useful in:

1. Assigning workers to jobs for which they must be physically and emotionally fit and which they must be capable of performing in a sustained and effective manner.
2. Providing data about an individual as a basis for future health guidance.
3. Safeguarding the health of present employees through the detection of contagious diseases.
4. Protecting applicants who have had health defects from undertaking work that could be detrimental to themselves or might otherwise endanger the employer's property.
5. Protecting the employer from workers' compensation claims that are not valid because the injuries or illnesses were present when the employee was hired.

Physical standards for jobs should be realistic, justifiable, and geared to the job requirements.[41] Many very good potential employees may be rejected inappropriately because of unnecessarily rigid medical standards. One of the most controversial new techniques, discussed at the end of the chapter, is genetic screening.

Physically-handicapped workers can perform quite adequately in many jobs. These individuals, if they have the ability, can be among the best workers the organization has. However, in many places, they are rejected because of their handicaps, rather than being carefully screened and placed in jobs where their handicaps will not matter.

Some firms use a preemployment health checklist that the applicant completes. Then, depending upon the responses given, a physical examination may be scheduled with a physician. With the cost of a very simple physical examination being $75 or more per person, it is easy to see the potential savings available by using a questionnaire.

Can you identify why medical examinations can be useful in selection?

PERSONNEL TODAY AND TOMMOROW

HOW ARE YOUR CHROMOSOMES?

© 1982 by NEA. Inc. Jim Berry 8-c

"Pity! You, yourself, tested-out well. Your GENES didn't make it!"

This cartoon is not as far from reality as you might image. A 1983 survey of 366 large companies found that 6 firms were using genetic tests, 17 firms had used them in the past, and 59 firms were considering using them in the future.

Employers that make use of genetic screening tests do so for several reasons. One use of genetic tests is for diagnosis of an ill worker. Also, the tests may identify links between work place health hazards and individuals with certain genetic characteristics. Third, genetic testing may be used to make workers aware of genetic problems that may occur in certain work situations with some workers. The fourth use is the most controversial: to exclude individuals from certain jobs if they have genetic conditions that increase their health risks. Because someone cannot change his or her genes, the potential for racial, sex, or some other type of information is very real. For example, sickle-cell anemia is a condition found only in Blacks. If chemicals in a particular work environment can cause health problems for individuals with sickle-cell anemia, Blacks are going to be adversely affected. Other genetic deficiencies or problems occur only in women or in certain other sub-groups in the population.

At this point genetic testing for employment-related purposes is very limited. Congressional hearings on the topic have examined many of the issues involved, but no specific laws dealing with genetic testing have been passed. And, relatively few employers are using genetic tests for employment screening. Nevertheless, in the future applicants may be tested to determine how their chromosomes and genes match up with jobs and job hazards.[42]

SUMMARY

■ Selection is a process whereby individuals and their qualifications are matched to jobs in an organization.

■ Because of governmental regulations and the need for better coordination between the personnel unit and other managers, many organizations have established a centralized employment office as part of the personnel department.

■ From the reception of an applicant, through the application and initial screening process, to testing, the in-depth selection interview, background investigation, and the physical examination, the entire process must be handled by trained, knowledgeable individuals.

■ Application forms must meet Equal Employment Opportunity guidelines and ask only for job-related information.

■ Selection tests can include general personality and psychological tests, aptitude and proficiency tests, and assessment centers. Any tests used should relate directly to the jobs for which individuals apply.

■ From the standpoints of effectiveness and equal employment compliance, the most useful interview is the structured interview, although nondirective and stress interviews can be used.

■ Sound interviewing requires planning and control. Applicants must be provided a realistic picture of the jobs for which they are applying. Also, good questioning techniques should be used to reduce problems that commonly occur.

■ Background investigations frequently involve concerns about invasion of an individual's privacy. Consequently, reference checking should be done carefully.

■ Medical examinations may be an appropriate part of the selection process for some employers.

REVIEW QUESTIONS AND EXERCISES

1. Why do many employers have a specialized employment office?

2. You are starting a new manufacturing company. What phases would you go through to select your employees?

3. Agree or disagree with the following statement: "A good application form is fundamental to a good selection process." Explain your conclusion.

4. Discuss the following statement: "We stopped giving tests altogether and rely exclusively on the interview for hiring."

5. Make two lists. On one list indicate what information you would want to obtain from the screening interview, on the other indicate what information you would want to obtain from the in-depth interview.

6. Develop a structured interview guide for a 20-minute interview with a retail sales clerk applicant. Include specific questions you would ask.

7. How would you go about investigating a new college graduate's background? Why would this information be useful to you in making a selection decision?

8. List the advantages and disadvantages of having a complete medical examination given to all new employees.

Exercises

a. Contact an employer or sign up for an interview through your placement office. Go through the interview, then make a list of good and poor interviewing techniques that you experienced in the interview.

b. Assume you are a potential employer for a management trainee job. Construct a guide for obtaining reference information on applicants that would conform to privacy concerns.

CASE
SELECTING A PROGRAMMER

Marie Pendergrass has been a data processing supervisor for two years. She is in the process of selecting a candidate for a programmer trainee position she has created. Her plan is to develop the trainee into a systems analyst within two years. Since this is a fast track, she needs a candidate whose aptitude and motivation is high.

Fourteen candidates applied for the job in the employment section of the personnel department. Six were women, eight were men. An employment specialist screened the candidates for Mary, using a carefully prepared interview format that included questions to determine job-related skills. Six candidates, three women and three men, were referred to Marie.

Marie then conducted structured, in-depth interviews and further narrowed the selection to one woman and two men. Her boss, a company vice-president, agrees with her judgment after hearing Marie's description of the candidates. However, Marie's boss feels particularly unsure of the abilities of the female candidate. From the selection interview, past job experience, and education, there is no clear indication of the candidate's ability to perform the job. The vice-president is insistent that Marie screen the candidate with a programmer aptitude test devised by a computer manufacturing firm. The test had been given four years ago, and some of the most successful current analysts had scored high on it.

Marie went to the personnel department and asked them to administer the test to the "questionable" candidate. The personnel manager informed her that the company policy had been to do no testing of any kind during the last two years. Marie explained that the request had come from a vice-president and asked that she be given a decision on her request by Friday.

Questions

1. Identify and evaluate the stages of the selection process reflected in the case.

2. If you were Marie, what would you do?

NOTES

1. *Guidebook for Developing a Reality-Based Employment System* (Milwaukee, WI: Manpower, 1983).

2. Andy Rooney, *Chicago Tribune Syndicate.*

3. R. S. Lowell and J. A. DeLoach, "Equal Employment Opportunity: Are You Overloading the Application Form?" *Personnel*, July–August 1982, pp. 40–55.

4. Carl Camden and Bill Wallace, "Job Application Forms: A Hazardous Employment Practice," *Personnel Administrator*, March 1983, pp. 31–32ff.

5. To learn more about the construction of a weighted application blank, see D. G. Lawrence, B. L. Salsburg, J. G. Dawson, and Z. D. Fasman, "Design and Use of Weighted Application Blanks," *Personnel Administrator*, March 1982, pp. 47–53ff.

6. "Employee Selection Procedures," *Bulletin to Management*, ASPA-BNA Survey 45 (May 5, 1983), p. 2.

7. *Ibid.*

8. O. K. Buros, *Eleventh Mental Measurements Yearbook* (Highland Park, NJ: Gryphon Press, 1981).

9. Brent Staples, "Personality Tests Under Scrutiny," *Chicago Sun Times*, March 1984.

10. R. J. Klimoski and Rafaeli Anat, "Inferring Personal Qualities Through Handwriting Analysis," *Journal of Occupational Psychology* 56 (September 1983), pp. 191–198.

11. Laura Rohmann, "Write You Are," *Forbes*, May 9, 1983, pp. 185–189.

12. "Lie Detector Tests Untrustworthy," *USA Today*, February 1981, p. 16.

13. Ted Gest, "When Employers Turn to Lie Detectors," *U.S. News and World Report*, April 4, 1983, p. 78.

14. John A. Belt, "The Polygraph: A Questionable Personnel Tool," *Personnel A5ministrator*, August 1983, pp. 65–69ff.

15. *Ibid.*

16. "Saint or Sinner? Score Yourself Honestly," *Omaha World Herald*, October 18, 1981, p. 7A.

17. Andrew Kahn, *et al.* "The Intimidation of Job Tests," *AFL-CIO Federationist*, January 1979, p. 3. Used with permission.

18. "Pre-Hire Tests Cut Chain's Theft By 28%," *Chain Store Age Executive*, June 1983, p. 25.

19. Diane Botnick, "Written Honesty Tests Differ in Cost, Time, and Tabulation," *Merchandising*, April 1982, pp. 114–116.

20. Mary L. Tenopyr, "The Realities of Employment Testing," *American Psychologist* 36 (1981), pp. 1120–1127.

21. Richard A. Arvey, *Fairness in Selecting Employees* (Reading, MA: Addison-Wesley, 1979), p. 165.

22. R. L. Cochran, J. Cochran, and M. Jennings, "Legal Restrictions in Interviewing and Hiring," *Journal of Accountancy*, September 1982, p. 41.

23. Robert Bloom and Erich P. Prien, "A Guide to Job-Related Employment Interviewing," *Personnel Administrator*, October 1983, pp. 81–86ff.

24. "Evaluating Employment Applications," *Personnel Journal*, January 1984, pp. 22–24.

25. Paula Popvich and John P. Wanous, "The Realistic Job Preview as a Persuasive Communication," *Academy of Management Review* 7 (1982), pp. 570–578.

26. James A. Breaugh, "Realistic Job Previews: A Critical Appraisal and Future Research Directions," *Academy of Management Review* 8 (1983), pp. 612–619.

27. Roger A. Dean and John P. Wanous, "Effects of Realistic Job Previews on Hiring Bank Tellers," *Journal of Applied Psychology* 69 (1984), pp. 61–68.

28. *Wall Street Journal*, February 17, 1984, p. 27.

29. William L. Tuller et al., "Effects of Interview Length and Applicant Quality on Interview Decision Time," *Journal of Applied Psychology* 64 (1979), pp. 669–674.

30. T. W. Dobmeyer and M. D. Dunette, "Relative Importance of Three Content Dimensions in Overall Suitability Ratings of Job Applicant Resumes," *Journal of Applied Psychology* 54 (1970), p. 69.

31. Arvey, *Fairness in Selecting Employees*, pp. 174–176.

32. Cynthia Fisher et al., "Source Credibility, Information on Favorability and Job Offer Acceptance," *Academy of Management Journal* 22 (March 1979), pp. 94–103.

33. *Management World*, June 1981, p. 23.

34. Dobmeyer and Dunette, "Content Dimensions of Resumes," p. 70.

35. For an excellent review of research on the interview, see Richard D. Arvey and James E. Campion, "The Employment Interview: A Summary and Review of Recent Research," *Personnel Psychology* 35 (1982), pp. 281–322.

36. *Forbes*, May 25, 1981, pp. 155–156; *Wall Street Journal*, October 14, 1980, p. 25; and *Kansas City Star*, May 4, 1982, p. C–1.

37. Mitchell S. Novit, "Negative References and Legal Liability," *Supervisory Management*, November 1982, pp. 14–18.

38. "Employee Selection Procedures," p. 2.

39. B. D. Wonder and Kenneth S. Kelemon, "Increasing the Value of Reference Information," *Personnel Administrator*, March 1984, pp. 98–103.

40. Charleen Freeman, "Importance of Pre-Employment Physicals," *Occupational Health Nursing*, May 1983, pp. 35–37.

41. For more details, see Michael A. Campion, "Personnel Selection for Physically Demanding Jobs: Review and Recommendations," *Personnel Psychology* 36 (1983), pp. 527–550.

42. T. H. Murray, "Warning: Screening Workers for Genetic Risk," *The Hastings Center Report*, February 1983, pp. 5–8; and J. D. Olien and T. C. Snyder, "The Implications of Genetic Testing," *Personnel Administrator*, January 1984, pp. 19–27.

SECTION CASE III

NORTHEASTERN BANK

Northeastern Bank, which is owned by a large multibank holding company, is the fourth largest bank in a moderately sized city. It employs 150 people and relies heavily on part-time employees, especially college students. Northeastern has three banking facilities in the city, the maximum allowed by state law. Its main facility has the largest number of employees and contains all major departments of the bank.

There are two branch facilities. One facility, located near rail lines and the stock yards, caters to the clients of the bank engaged in agricultural activities and is primarily oriented toward agricultural activities, such as auctions and commodities. It accounts for a substantial portion of the bank's deposits. The other facility is located in the fast-growing western section of the city. The orientation of this facility is to attract new customers and "sell" the bank's services to them.

In the state where Northeastern Bank is located, the legislature is considering a bill that would allow banks in the state to open another branch facility in the same city. The banking community has lobbied for many years to get this bill passed, and last year the bill was narrowly defeated. This year, however, because of changes in federal banking laws, the bill is given a very good chance of passage. If the bill is passed, the banks in the state will be allowed to open an additional facility 30 days after the bill is signed by the governor.

The top management at Northeastern is very excited at the prospect of opening a new facility, and they want to be prepared to move quickly after the bill is passed. Therefore, they have directed the manager of the west branch facility to train a person for the position of bank representative/night manager and to prepare two tellers to be moved to the new facility once it is opened.

Although the manager of the new bank will be chosen from the staff at the bank's main facility, top management wants the other staff members to come from the west branch. They feel that employees of the west branch facility will be better prepared for the task of opening a new branch facility. Banks are restricted in the functions they can perform at their branch facilities. For example, branch facilities can only take loan applications and forward them to their main facility. They cannot approve loans.

John Wilson has been chosen as the person to be trained as bank representative/night manager. For the past three months, Wilson has trained in this capacity and is now able to perform the duties expected of him with little supervision. He still works as a teller when the need arises because of illness or vacation, but this is not unusual, because all bank representatives at the west facility are expected to perform teller duties when the need arises.

However, in Wilson's opinion, management is using this situation as a basis for not giving him a full promotion. Management still classifies Wilson as a teller and not as a bank representative. There is a significant difference in responsibilities and salary between the two positions. Management says that they are not willing to fully promote Wilson until he assumes his duties at the new facility. If the bill is not passed and the new facility not opened, Wilson will reassume his job as a teller and be promoted to bank representative when a position opens up.

Wilson is unhappy with this situation, and has had numerous discussions with management about his predicament. Management has not yet made a decision. Wilson has decided to give management an ultimatum: either promote him fully to bank representative or he will look elsewhere for employment. His boss does not want this to happen because Wilson is an excellent employee and is already trained for the position. Furthermore, he is admired and well respected by nearly all the employees with whom he works. His leaving because of this situation would have a negative impact on other employees.

A second employee in the west branch facility, Mildred Pierce, is a part-time college student who has just been hired for a full-time job in the bookkeeping department at Northeastern. When she left the interview, Pierce thought it was going to be the perfect job. She was told the hours would be 8:30 A.M. to 4:30 P.M., four days a week, and 8 A.M. to 5 P.M., Saturdays. The duties of the job were filing checks, answer the phone, and operating a CRT. The bank provided full training and in a few months Pierce would have the opportunity to learn how to run the proof machine or move into a teller position. She was also assured of a raise from $4.10 an hour to $4.25 or more after a review in three months.

During the first week, everything went well for Pierce. She filed checks, observed the other employees on the job, and learned her way around the bank. The second week she was given her own desk and told she was on her own. The check filing was simple, but when it came to the phone and the CRT, everything went wrong. Customers asked her questions about which she had no information, and many of the CRT procedures had been changed. When she informed the supervisor of her problems, the supervisor told Pierce that she would help her "later." Later never came and Pierce ended up training herself by trial and error while upsetting quite a few customers along the way.

On the first Tuesday of the second month, Pierce came into work at 8:30 and was immediately called into her supervisor's office. She was told that everyone was expected to come in as early as possible on statement day (first Tuesday of each month) to help get the statements out on time. Because Pierce was a part-time student, it was very difficult for her to come in early. When she informed her supervisor, she was told to change her schedule if she wanted a good review. Pierce changed her schedule and began coming in early on statement day. When she went in for her review a month later, she was told that a new bank policy had gone into effect and it would be another three months before she would receive a raise, and that it would be impossible to train her for another position for a few months. Consequently, Pierce put in her two-week notice the next day.

Since Pierce quit two months ago, five other part-time employees have left and several of the bank's top management members including the personnel director, have quit.

QUESTIONS

1. Discuss problems with the selection process as Wilson and Pierce experienced it.
2. How might human resource planning have been useful to Northeastern Bank?
3. Assume you were being considered to replace the personnel director. What specific recommendations would you make to address the staffing process problems faced by the bank?

TRAINING AND DEVELOPING HUMAN RESOURCES

In any organization people must receive some training to perform jobs, and to advance to better jobs. Training programs provide employees with the opportunity to learn new skills and ideas so that the organization develops its internal talent for the future.

Training and orientation are the topics of Chapter 10. Orientation is the first organizational training an employee receives. Before a person can perform well on the job, he or she must be properly introduced, or oriented, to the organization. Determining training needs and evaluating the effectiveness of training are two other important current issues.

Part of Chapter 11 deals with some on-the-job and off-the-job methods to develop employees. Development is a broad, longer-range type of training. By developing employees, especially managers, an organization prepares itself for the future. Another part of this chapter focuses specifically on the importance of career planning for employees.

Once an employee has been trained to perform a job, a manager must review the employee's performance. This review is a vital part of the ongoing de-velopment of an employee. For a person to develop, that individual must receive feedback on what he or she is doing well and what areas need improvement.

The process of examining employee performance is called performance appraisal. Appraisals are also useful in solving some personnel problems, but the practice creates still other problems. Chapter 12 covers behavioral reactions to appraisals, common mistakes made in appraising performance, and some components of a successful appraisal process.

Orientation and Training

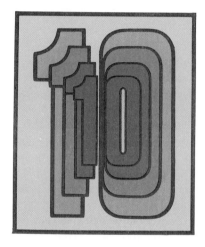

When you have read this chapter, you should be able to:

1. Describe five characteristics of an effective orientation system.
2. Explain what training is and discuss at least five learning principles that relate to training.
3. Discuss the three major phases of a training system in an organization.
4. Identify three ways to determine training needs.
5. List and discuss at least four training methods.
6. Give an example of each of the four levels of training evaluation.
7. Identify three designs used in evaluating training.

PLAYING "GAMES" ON THE JOB

Beyond the supertanker's bridge the lights of buoys and ships twinkle in the Persian Gulf. The bow of the tanker moves easily from Saudi Arabia's Ras Tanura. The captain and crew plot their course as the huge engines growl deep below the helm.

Everything in this scenario is simulated but the captain and crew, and they are trainees at the Maritime Institute of Technology in Linthicum Heights, Maryland. Here, simulation as a training method has evolved to an art form. A computer simulation shows the ship's channel and the traffic on the gulf. The "bridge" rolls and pitches like a ship at sea, and the view out the windows is a computer-driven television picture of the Persian Gulf.

In the motion picture War Games, *a fictional computer is programmed to simulate global thermonuclear war— and to wage that war. The U.S. military is not far behind the movie in its actual ability to simulate such conditions. In Orlando, Florida, at the Naval Training Equipment Center a naval tactical game can simulate battles between American and Soviet fleets. Thousands of variables, including firepower, steaming speed, and defense armaments, can be programmed at once. Simulators also help the military train personnel to operate tanks, land on aircraft carriers, and fly helicopters. Astronauts simulate an entire run-through of their mission on earth before they go into space.*

Learning from mistakes without losing lives or expensive equipment is what simulation is all about. The use of simulators in training commercial pilots is well established. Recently, nuclear power plants, oil refineries, and paper and chemical company operations have also been simulated. Simulation is both an excellent training tool and a good source of research data.

A division of the Singer Company, Link Simulation Systems, specializes in designing simulations. The 1979 malfunction at Three Mile Island in Middletown, Pennsylvania, caused a boom in Link's simulation sales. Four years later, 75 percent of the country's nuclear plants have simulators. Depending on the complexity desired, the cost of a simulator can range from $500,000 to $8 million. When Link is simulating the control rooms of power plants, it uses the same control panels that the trainee will use on the job. That way when training is over, the new operator will see the simulator's twin and can begin work immediately.

The simulator, although expensive, is an excellent alternative to procedure manuals, the other frequent training choice. Such manuals are often written for engineers or experienced operators and are hard for a new person to understand. They also do not provide a good feeling for the dynamics of process operations. Simulation may cost around $1,000 per student per week, but compared to the cost of a plant shutdown, it is minimal–and effective.[1]

"To be conscious that you are ignorant of the facts is a great first step to knowledge."
BENJAMIN DISRAELI

ORIENTATION
is the planned introduction of employees to their jobs, co-workers, and organizations.

In order to be an asset to the organization, new employees must know organizational policies and procedures and must understand how to perform their jobs. But learning does not stop after this initial introduction. Working in an organization is a continuous learning process, and learning is at the heart of training and development activities.

Whether done formally or informally, training occurs in all organizations. One study found that in companies with more than 5,000 employees, 83 percent conducted sales training; 74 percent, clerical training; and 83 percent, skills training. In companies smaller than 5,000 employees, 56 percent conducted sales training; 69 percent, clerical training; and 63 percent, skills training.[2] The expensive simulations mentioned previously usually are aimed at skills training.

Orientation is a special kind of training designed to provide the basic information an employee needs to function in the company. After first discussing orientation, this chapter turns to examine other dimensions of training.

ORIENTATION

In **orientation** an attempt is made to "install" a new employee so that he or she is sufficiently acquainted with the company to feel comfortable and learn the job. This does not mean orientation should be a mechanical process. A sensitive awareness to employees' anxieties, uncertainties, and needs is important.

Purposes of Orientation

The orientation process has several important purposes. The overall goal is to help new employees learn about their new work environments.

Create an Initial Favorable Impression. A good orientation program creates a favorable impression of the organization and its work. Just as a favorable initial impression of an individual helps to form a good relationship, a good initial impression of the company, co-worker, or supervisor can help a new employee adjust. The lack of a good orientation program may be responsible for a high turnover rate among employees during their first months on the job. One study concluded that the effectiveness of orientation had a lasting effect on absenteeism and turnover.[3]

Enhance Interpersonal Acceptance. Another purpose of orientation is to ease the employee's entry into the work group. Meeting new people can create anxiety and concern, even in informal situations such as a party. Similarly, new employees are concerned about meeting the people in their work unit. They may be thinking, "How will I get along with the people I work with?" "Will people be friendly?" As pointed out earlier, one of the characteristics of work groups is the presence of group norms acting as codes of behavior. New employees must be "instructed" or "socialized"; that is, they must be introduced to what the group expects of them. The expectations of a group of employees may not always parallel the management's formal orientation. However, if a manager does not have a well-planned formal orientation, the new employee may be oriented only by the group.

Aid Adjustment. An effective orientation program will reduce the adjustment problems of new employees by creating a sense of security, confidence, and belonging. Another purpose of orientation is to sustain or build up a new employee's self-confidence. Research suggests that new employees are afraid they will not be able to perform well and are anxious in front of the experienced employees.[4] Orientation can help minimize such problems.

Orientation Responsibilities

Orientation requires cooperation between individuals in the personnel unit and other managers and supervisors. In a very small firm without a personnel department, such as a machine shop, the new employee's supervisor or manager has the total orientation responsibility. In large organizations with personnel departments, managers, supervisors, and the personnel department should work as a team in employee orientation.

Figure 10–1 illustrates a common division of orientation responsibilities in which managers work with personnel specialists in orienting a new employee. Together they must develop an orientation process that will communicate what the employee needs to learn.

Certain types of information probably can be presented best by the immediate supervisor, while other orientation information can be explained better by the personnel unit. A supervisor may not know all the details about health insurance or benefit options, but he or she usually can present information on safety rules, allowing the personnel department to explain insurance and benefits. One study found that

FIGURE 10–1
Orientation Responsibilities.

PERSONNEL UNIT	MANAGERS
■ Places employee on payroll	■ Prepare co-workers for new employee
■ Designs formal orientation program	■ Introduce new employee to co-workers
■ Explains benefits and company organization	■ Provide overview of job setting and work rules
■ Develops orientation checklist	
■ Evaluates orientation activities	

the personnel director is more likely to have the overall responsibility for orientation than a line manager in organizations that have formal programs.[5]

ESTABLISHING AN EFFECTIVE ORIENTATION SYSTEM

A systematic approach to orientation requires attention to attitudes, behaviors, and information that new employees need. Unfortunately, orientation is often rather haphazardly conducted. The general ideas mentioned next highlight some components of an effective orientation system.

Prepare for New Employees

New employees must feel they belong and are important. Both the supervisor and the personnel unit should be prepared to receive the employee.[6] It is very uncomfortable for a new employee to arrive at work and have a manager say, "Oh, I didn't realize you were coming to work today" or "Who are you?" This depersonalization obviously does not create an atmosphere of initial acceptance and trust.

Further, co-workers should be informed that a new employee is arriving. This awareness is especially important if the new employee will be assuming certain duties that might threaten a current employee's job status and security. The manager or supervisor should prepare the current employees by discussing the new worker and the purpose for hiring that person.

Present Information New Employees Want to Know

The guiding question in the establishment of an orientation system is, "What does the new employee need to know *now?*" Often new employees receive a large amount of information they do not immediately need, and they fail to get information needed the first day of a new job.

In a large organization it is especially important that managers and personnel specialists coordinate the presentation of information to new employees. In a small organization the manager or supervisor usually determines what is to be explained. Some organizations systematize this process by developing an orientation checklist. Figure 10–2 indicates the items to be covered by the personnel department representative and the new employee's supervisor. Using a checklist, the manager and the personnel representative can insure that all necessary items have been covered. However, the presentation should not resemble a military briefing. The most important concern is that the new employee be acquainted with policies and procedures. Much of the information on retirement and insurance will be forgotten in the confusion of the first day anyway. Attempts to reduce information overload will result in better retention later.

FIGURE 10–2
Orientation Checklist.

Name of Employee _____
Starting Date _____
Department _____

Name of Employee _____
Starting Date _____
Department _____
Position _____

PERSONNEL DEPARTMENT

Prior to Orientation
____ Complete Form A and give or mail
to new employee
____ Complete Form B
____ Attach Form B to "Orientation
Checklist–Supervisor" and give to
the supervisor

Employee's First Day

*Organization and Personnel Policies and
Procedures*
____ History of XYZ Inc.
____ Organization chart
____ Purpose of the company
____ Employee classifications

Insurance Benefits
____ Group health plan
____ Disability insurance
____ Life Insurance
____ Workers' Compensation
Other Benefits
____ Holidays
____ Vacation
____ Jury and election duty
____ Death-in-the-family leave
____ Health services
____ Professional discounts
____ Appointments
End of Orientation—First Day
____ Make appointment for second day
____ Introduce employee to supervisor

Other Items
____ Job posting
____ Bulletin board—location and use
____ Safety
____ No drinking
____ Where to get supplies
____ Employee's records—updating

At the end of the employee's first two
weeks, the supervisor will ask if the employee has any questions on the above
items. After all questions have been satisfied, the supervisors will sign and date
this form and return it to the Personnel
Department.

SIGNATURE _____

DATE

SUPERVISOR

Employee's First Day

____ Introduction to Co-workers
____ Tour of department
____ Tour of company

Location of
____ Coat closet
____ Rest Room
____ Telephone for personal use and
rules concerning it

Working Hours
____ Starting and leaving
____ Lunch
____ Breaks
____ Overtime
____ Early departures
____ Time clock

Pay Policy
____ Pay period
____ Deposit system

Others Items
____ Parking
____ Dress

Employee's Second Day
____ Pension retirement plan
____ Sick leave
____ Personal leave
____ Job posting
____ Confidentiality
____ Complaints and concerns
____ Termination
____ Equal Employment Opportunity

During Employee's First Two Weeks

Emergencies
____ Medical
____ Power failure
____ Fire

ORIENTATION CONDUCTED BY

Present Three Types of Information

Three types of information usually are included in the orientation process. The first concerns the normal workday and the employee's job.

Normal Workday. The immediate supervisor or manager probably is better prepared to outline a normal day for the employee. The manager or supervisor should devote some time during the first morning solely to covering daily routine information with the new employee. This information includes such essentials as: introducing the new employee to other employees, showing the employee the work area, letting the new employee know when and where to take coffee breaks and lunch, indicating what time work begins and ends, identifying where to park and where the restrooms are, and indicating whether the custom is to "brown-bag" or not.

Nature of Organization. A second type of information is a general organizational orientation. This overview might include a brief review of the organization and its history, its structure, who the key executives are, what its purpose is, its products and/or services, how the employee's job fits into the big picture, and any other general information. If an annual report is prepared for a firm, giving an employee a copy is an effective aid in providing a general overview of an organization and its components.

Organizational Policies, Rules, and Benefits. Another important type of initial information is the policies, work rules, and benefits for employees. Typically, this information is presented by both the personnel unit and the supervisor. Employee policies about sick leave, tardiness, absenteeism, vacations, benefits, hospitalization, parking, and safety rules are important facts that every new employee should know.

Determine How to Present the Information

Managers and personnel representatives should determine the most appropriate way to present orientation information. For example, rather than telling an employee about them verbally, information on company sick leave and vacation policies may be presented on the first day in an employee handbook. The manager or personnel representative can review this information a few days later to answer any of the employee's questions.

Information Overload. One of the common failings of many orientation programs is *information overload*. This overload occurs when so many facts are presented to new employees that they ignore important details or inaccurately recall much of the information. By providing a handbook, the employee can refer to information when needed.

Employees will retain more of the orientation information if it is presented in a manner that encourages them to learn. Orientation materials, such as handbooks and information leaflets, should be made available and be reviewed periodically for updates and corrections. Some organizations have successfully used film strips, movies, slides, charts, and teaching machines. However, even when using such aids, the emphasis should be on presenting information, not just on "entertaining" the new employee.

Employees need both the formal information presented in handbooks, pamphlets, or visual aids, and the informal information presented by other people. A useful additional orientation technique is to pair the new person with a "sponsor" or "buddy" to show them around. This approach provides information and identifies a friend and contact point when one is needed. Obviously, the choice of the person is important, because a poor selection could lead to confusion or to the employee receiving inaccurate information.

Evaluation and Follow-Up

A systematic orientation program should have an evaluation and follow-up. Too often, typical orientation efforts assume that, once oriented, employees are familiar with everything they need to know about the organization forever.

A personnel representative or a manager can evaluate the effectiveness of the orientation by follow-up interviews with new employees a few weeks or months after the orientation. Employee questionnaires can also be used. Some firms even give new employees a written test on the company handbook two weeks after orientation.

Reorientation. A reorientation program in which all employees are periodically given a refresher "introduction" should be a part of follow-up. One study found that about 28 percent of firms give some kind of second orientation.[7]

Reorientation is especially important if significant changes in organizational policies or structure have occurred. For example, if one company is purchased by another, a reorientation of employees of both firms may be necessary because of changes in operating relationships and policies caused by the merger. Orientation is a never-ending process of "introducing" both old and new employees to the current state of the organization. It can be thought of as part of the lifetime education process.

Although orientation introduces or reintroduces the organization to employees, they also need information about their jobs and how to perform them. Orientation is one special type of training. The next section examines the general nature of training.

Can you explain the five characteristics of an effective orientation system?

TRAINING

Many other types of training exist besides orientation. Job skill training, supervisory training, and management development are a few of the types of training. The focus here will be on job skill training, with employee development covered in the next chapter.

Training Defined

Training can be defined either narrowly or broadly. In a limited sense, training is concerned with teaching specific and immediately usable skills. In a broad sense, training provides general information used to develop knowledge for future long-term application.

The narrow definition of training means that it explores job-related skills, while development denotes the broad scope of training. To illustrate, a person can receive *training* to improve skills on a new word-processing machine, whereas *development* may come from a management course on effective leadership. The hope is that over time the trainee will develop into a better leader. However, this distinction between training and development can be an artificial one because both focus on learning. Training in this text will be used to include both the job-related and developmental dimensions.

Training Responsibilities

One division of training responsibilities is shown in Figure 10–3. Notice that skill training, developmental training, and organization development are all included. In the division shown, the personnel unit serves as an expert source of training assistance and coordination. The personnel unit often has a more long-range view of employee careers and of the importance of developing the entire organization than do individual operating managers. This difference is especially true at lower levels in the organization.

On the other hand, managers are likely to be the best source of the technical information used in skill training and of decisions about when employees need training or retraining. Because of the close and continual interaction they have with their employees, managers determine and discuss employees' career potentials and plans. Organizational development and change efforts will fail without active managerial participation and involvement. If an organization is small,

TRAINING is a learning process whereby people acquire skills, concepts, attitudes, or knowledge to aid in the achievement of goals.

PERSONNEL UNIT	MANAGERS
■ Prepares skill training materials	■ Provide technical information
■ Coordinates training efforts	■ Monitor training needs
■ Conducts or arranges for off-the-job training	■ Conduct the on-the-job training
■ Coordinates career plans and personnel development efforts	■ Continually discuss employees' future potential and monitor employees' growth
■ Provides input and expertise for organizational development	■ Participate in organizational change efforts

FIGURE 10–3
Training Responsibilities.

managers may have to handle the activities normally performed by personnel specialists in larger organizations.

Can you explain what training is?

Importance of Training

Training has both current and future implications for job success. It is a learning process, whether its focus is orientation, initial job-skill training, developing employee potential, or retraining employees because of changes in technology or job assignments.

Training can contribute to higher production, fewer mistakes, greater job satisfaction, and lower turnover. Also, it can enable employees to cope with organizational, social, and technological change. Effective training is an investment in the human resources of an organization, with both immediate and long-range returns. Regardless of whether training is called *education* (to denote conceptual learning) or *job training* (to denote skill learning), learning has to occur for training to be successful. A basic understanding of the psychology of learning is necessary for managers to become effective trainers.

LEARNING PRINCIPLES: THE PSYCHOLOGY OF TRAINING

Learning is a psychological process that has been researched for many years. Managers can use the findings of this research to make their training efforts more effective. Some of the major learning-oriented considerations that guide personnel training efforts are presented here.

Modeling

Modeling is the most elementary way in which people learn—yet it can be among the best. Modeling is simply copying someone else's behavior. If Sam Taylor sees his boss successfully handle morale problems in a certain way, he may use that method himself. That method is *modeling*. Modeling can also work to keep people from making mistakes they see others make.

Most training programs are not adequately structured to take advantage of modeling. Passive classroom training, for example, allows little modeling, while videotapes of people showing the desired behavior do. When modeling is used, it is important to select a model who can and will provide the right kind of behavior to be modeled. An informal group leader who shares management's values is often a good choice. "Mentoring" uses modeling and other psychological processes in the assistance and sponsorship of a younger employee by an older one.[9] Merrill Lynch, Federal Express, the U.S. Army, and the IRS are all using mentors to help new management employees.[10]

Intention to Learn

Motivation, which is heavily influenced by values, attitudes, and perceptions, underlies all learning. People learn information they think is beneficial, providing that it is presented when they want to learn it. For learning to take place, *intention to learn,* even if subconscious, is necessary. It increases attention to what is being said, done, and presented. Motivation to learn is determined by the answers to questions like "How important is my job to me?" "How important is it that I learn that information?" "Will learning this help me in any way?" "What's in it for me?"

People are more susceptible to learning when the material is important to them. Some of the following goals may encourage intention to learn in certain people.

- Achievement
- Advancement
- Authority
- Co-workers' influence
- Creativity
- Curiosity
- Recognition
- Responsibility
- Status
- Comprehension
- Variety

It should be emphasized that learning is a complex psychological process that is not fully understood by practitioners or research psychologists. Often, trainers or supervisors present information and assume it has been learned. However, learning takes place only when information is received, understood, and internalized, and some change or conscious effort has been made to use the information.

Reinforcement

The notion of reinforcement is based upon the *law of effect*, which states that if a behavior is positively rewarded, it probably will be repeated. Providing positive rewards for certain behavior is called *positive reinforcement*. Learning theories that revolve around the idea of reinforcement state that people tend to repeat response patterns that give them some type of positive reward and to avoid repeating actions associated with negative consequences.

The rewards, (reinforcements) an individual receives can be either external or internal. For example, a registered nurse receives an external reward for learning how to use a new electrocardiogram machine by receiving a certificate of completition.

An internal reward appeals to the trainee's internal needs. For example, John Lange, a machinist, learned to use a new lathe in the machine shop. Although he made many mistakes at first, he was beginning to do well. One day he knew he had mastered it and was quite pleased with himself. This feeling of accomplishment is a type of internal reward.

Many training situations provide both internal and external rewards. If a new salesclerk answers her supervisor's question correctly and is complimented for giving the correct answer, she may receive both an external reward (the compliment) and an internal reward (a feeling of pride).

Behavior Modification

A comprehensive approach to training has been developed based upon the concept of reinforcement. This approach is known as behavior modification. Built upon the theories of psychologist B. F. Skinner, *behavior modification* has become increasingly popular.

Intervention Strategies. Behavior modification makes use of four means of changing behavior, labeled intervention strategies.[11] The four strategies are positive reinforcement, negative reinforcement, punishment, and extinction.

A person who receives a desired reward receives **positive reinforcement.** If an employee is on time every day during a week and, as a result, receives extra pay equivalent to one hour of normal work, the employee has received positive reinforcement of his or her good attendance by receiving a desired reward.

Negative Reinforcement occurs when an individual works to avoid an undesirable "reward." An employee who arrives at work on time every day may do so to avoid the criticism of a supervisor. Thus, the potential for criticism leads to the employee taking the desired action.

Action taken to repel a person from undesirable action is **punishment.** A grocery manager may punish a stock clerk for leaving the stock room dirty by forcing him or her to stay after work to clean it up. Behavior can also be modified through a technique known as extinction.

Extinction refers to a situation in which no response is given to an individual. Assume an employee dresses in a new style to attract the attention of her superior. The supervisor just ignores the dress. There is no reinforcement, positive or negative, and no punishment given. With no reinforcement of any kind and no clear confirmation, the likelihood of the employee extinguishing, or stopping, the new dress behavior is increased. The expectation is that unreinforced behavior will not be repeated.

Immediate Confirmation

Another learning concept closely related to reinforcement is **immediate confirmation.** This concept calls for feedback to occur as soon as possible after training.

To illustrate, a corporate purchasing department has developed a new system for reporting inventory information. The new system is much more complex than the old one and requires the use of a new form that is longer and more difficult to complete. However, it does give computerized information much more quickly and helps eliminate errors in the recording process which delay the total inventory report. The purchasing manager who trains inventory processors may not have the trainees fill out the entire inventory form when teaching them the new procedure. Instead, the manager may explain the total process, then break it into smaller segments and have each trainee complete the form a section at a time. By checking each individual's form for errors as each section is completed, the purchasing manager can give immediate feedback or confirmation before the trainees fill out the next section. This immediate confirmation corrects errors that, if made throughout the whole form, might establish a pattern to be unlearned.

Spaced Practice

Psychological research shows that, for certain kinds of tasks, several practice sessions spaced over a period of hours or days result in greater learning than the same amount of practice in one long period. For example, training a cashier to operate a new machine could be alternated with having him do a task he already knows how to do. Thus, the training is distributed instead of being concentrated into one period. For this reason some firms spread their orientation of new employees over an entire week by devoting an hour or two daily to orientation, instead of covering it all in one day.

For *memorizing* tasks, "massed" practice is usually more effective. Can you imagine trying to memorize a long poem by only learning one line per day? By the time you learned the last stanza, you would forget the first one. For *acquiring skills,* spaced practice is usually best. This incremental approach to skill acquisition minimizes the physical fatigue that deters learning.

Whole Learning

The concept of whole learning suggests that it is better to give an overall view of what a trainee will be doing than to deal immediately with the specifics. Another term for whole learning is *Gestalt learning.*

CHAPTER 10 ORIENTATION AND TRAINING

Job training instructions should be broken down into small elements after the employees have had an opportunity to see how the elements fit together. For example, in a plastics manufacturing operation it would be good to explain to trainees how the raw chemical material gets to them in the plant and what is done with the plastic moldings after they finish their part of the manufacturing process. The information is explained as an entire logical process, so that trainees can see how the various actions fit together into the "big picture." After a supervisor goes over the entire operation, he or she can break the information into its separate parts.

Active Practice

Active practice is more effective than learning by reading or by passively listening. For example, serving a tennis ball demands attention and concentration. Actual performance, rather than just reading about the process or hearing an explanation of how to do it, is necessary to learn to do it well.

Once some basic instructions have been given, active practice should be built into any learning situation. It is one of the advantages of good on-the-job training. Jill McDonald is being trained as a customer service representative. After being given some basic selling instructions and product details, Jill should be allowed to call on a customer to use the knowledge she has received. Mixing learning methods such as reading and listening with more active methods is effective.

Learning Curves and Plateaus

The rate at which people learn can be demonstrated by use of learning curves (see Figure 10–4). Different curves are characteristic of different training situations.

FIGURE 10–4
Four Common Learning Curves.

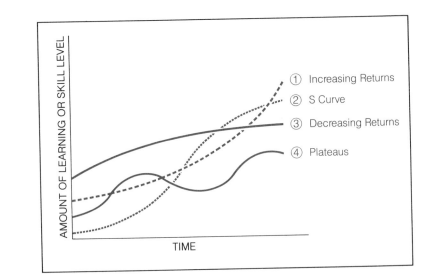

Curve 1 (decreasing returns) illustrates the most common way that learning takes place. Learning of most skills and mental tasks follows this form. The amount of learning and/or the skill level increases rapidly at first; then the *rate* of improvement slows. For example, when an employee first learns to operate a stamping machine, the rate of production increases rapidly at first, then slows as the normal rate is approached. Learning to perform most *routine* jobs follows such a curve.

Curve 2 (increasing returns) is the opposite of Curve 1. It is much less common than the decreasing return curve and occurs most often when a person is learning a completely unfamiliar task. What this curve shows is that the learner is "learning how to learn" the material. Starting a completely new job with little formal orientation or training might require a slow beginning while the important vocabulary and relationships are learned. Then the learner really begins to pick up expertise quickly.

Curve 3 (the S-shaped curve) is a combination of the decreasing return and increasing return curces. S-curves usually result when a person tries to learn an unfamiliar, difficult task that also requires insight into the basics of the job. Learning to debug computer systems is one example, especially if someone has had little previous contact with computers.

Curve 4 (the curve with plateaus) shows that as knowledge, skill, or speed is being acquired, a point is often reached when there is no apparent progress. At this point, trainees should be encouraged and advised that these temporary plateaus are expected, common, understandable, and are usually followed by new surges in learning. Encouragement is needed to prevent a feeling of despair or a desire to "give up."

Applicability of Training

Training should be as real as possible so that trainees can successfully transfer the new knowledge to their jobs. The training situation should be set up so that trainees can picture the types of situations they can expect on the job. For example, training of managers to be better interviewers should involve role-playing with "applicants" who can respond the same way that real applicants would.

The learning concepts and training ideas discussed above can be used by managers, training specialists, and personnel representatives to make their efforts more effective. Whether the training is a formal course, an orientation course, on-the-job preparation, or a supervisory development seminar, using the above learning concepts can result in better performance by trainees.

SYSTEMS APPROACH TO TRAINING

The success of any training can be gauged by the amount of learning that occurs. Too often, unplanned, uncoordinated, and haphazard training efforts significantly reduce the learning that can be expected.

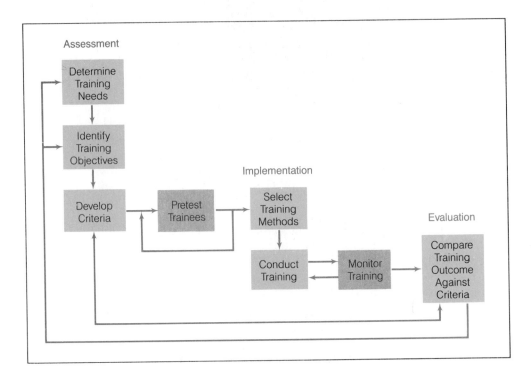

FIGURE 10–5
Model of Training System.

Training and learning will take place, especially through informal work groups, whether an organization has a coordinated training effort or not. Employees learn from other employees, but without well-designed, systematic training, what is learned may not be what is best for the company. Figure 10–5 shows the components of such a system. Notice that there are three major phases in a training system: (1) the assessment phase, (2) the implementation phase, and (3) the evaluation phase.

In the *assessment* phase, the need for training is determined and the objectives of the training effort are specified. Looking at the performance of clerks in a billing department, a manager might find that their typing abilities are weak, and that they would profit by having typing instruction. An objective of increasing the clerks' typing speed to 60 words per minute without errors might be established. The number of words per minute without errors is set as the criterion against which training success is to be measured and represents the way the objective is made specific.

In the next phase, *implementation*, the clerks would be given a typing test, and the billing supervisor and a personnel training specialist would work together to determine how to train the clerks to increase their typing speed. A programmed instruction manual might be used in conjunction with a special typing class set up at the company. Then the training is actually conducted.

The *evaluation* phase is crucial and focuses on measuring how well the training accomplished what it set out to do. Monitoring of training serves as a bridge between the implementation phase and the evaluation phase. A good method of evaluation that can also be used for planning training is **cost/benefit analysis.**

Comparing costs and benefits is easy until one has to assign an actual dollar value to some of the benefits. The best way is to measure the value of the output before and after training. Any increase represents the benefit resulting from training. However, precise measurement may not always be possible, and sometimes estimates of benefits must be made.

Can you discuss the three phases in a training system?

, COST/BENEFIT ANALYSIS is comparing what efforts will cost with the benefits received to see which is greater.

TRAINING NEEDS ASSESSMENT

All types of training are designed to help the organization accomplish its objectives. Determining organizational training needs is the diagnostic phase of setting training objectives. Just as a physician must examine a patient before prescribing medication to deal with the patient's ailments, an organization or an individual employee must be studied before a course of action can be planned to make the "patient" healthier or function better.

Training needs can be assessed in several ways:

■ Observation of job performance
■ Organization analysis
■ Surveys and interviews

Needs assessment is not an end in itself, but a way to find out where training is needed. Asking people about their problems and jobs is often a more fruitful way to proceed than asking them what they need.[12] They may or may not know what they need but they do know how they handle a particular situation.

The use of a job performance criteria in analyzing training program needs (as shown in Figure 10–6) is the most commom approach. To assess training needs through the performance appraisal process, an employee's performance inadequacies must first be determined in a formal review. Then some type of training is designed to help the employee overcome the weakness.

Pinpointing Needs: Job Performance

Appraisals of job performance can point to a number of problems that may require training to correct. Through performance appraisals many organizations have found that deficiencies in basic reading, writing, and math skills have hurt many employees. Test scores have documented that high schools, and even technical schools and colleges, are graduating students deficient in English and math. Continental Illinois Bank and Trust Company is one organization that has begun offering

FIGURE 10—6
Using Job Performance to
Analyze Training Needs.

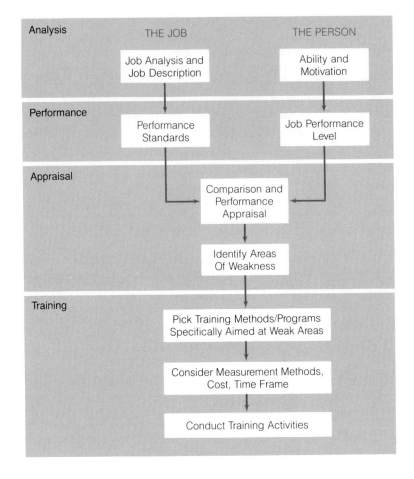

remedial English courses to those who need it. One study found that 35 percent of the companies surveyed have to provide training in areas that schools provide.[13] That these firms are willing to do so indicates the serious consequences of errors made by deficiently educated people. For example, at JLG Industries, a manufacturer of cranes and aerial lifts, one employee who did not know how to read a ruler wasted $700 worth of sheet steel in one morning through mismeasuring. JLG had also purchased electronic equipment to handle inventories and schedules, but corrections made necessary when poorly educated employees kept feeding incorrect numbers into the computer cost the company nearly $1 million.

Employees have been injured, or even killed, when they could not read warning signs. At Westinghouse Electric in California, several young workers who could not read well were fired because management was fearful of such accidents around defense equipment.

Performance Appraisal. Performance appraisal can be used for (1) determining training needs and (2) evaluating training effectiveness. Looking at performance evaluations for a department or an entire organization, it becomes apparent where additional training is necessary. For example, in one large organization employees were rated on several job dimensions, including written communication ability and job knowledge.[14] Completed performance appraisals showed that quite a number of employees had received unsatisfactory ratings on written communication. All employees achieved satisfactory scores on job knowledge, however. If a training program was given to improve written communication and the next round of performance appraisals were better on written communication, one could conclude that the training was effective.

Job Requirements. To assess training needs, it is necessary to examine job descriptions and job specifications. These items provide information on the skills and abilities necessary for employees to perform jobs. The results of job analysis—job descriptions and job specifications—provide the basis for a comparison of performance with the expectations of management.

Pinpointing Needs: Organizational Analysis

A second way of diagnosing training needs is through organizational analysis. Organizational analysis considers the organization as a system. Both internal and external factors need to be considered. For example, as part of a five-year business plan, a manufacturer of mechanical cash registers identifies the need to shift to the production of computer-based electronic equipment. As the organization implements its plans, current employees will need to be retrained so that they can do electronic instead of mechanical assembly work. The analysis of the firm's business strategies and objectives helps identify training needs before those needs become critical.

On a continuing basis, detailed analysis of personnel data can show training weaknesses. Departments or areas with high turnover, high absenteeism, low performance records, or other deficiencies can be pinpointed. After such problems are analyzed, training objectives can be developed. Specific sources of information for an organizational-level needs analysis may include:

- Grievances
- Accident records
- Observations
- Exit interviews

- Complaints from customers
- Equipment utilization figures
- Training committee observations
- Waste/scrap/quality control data

Pinpointing Needs: Surveys, Interviews, and Tests

A third way training needs may be assessed is through surveys, interviews, and tests of both managerial and nommanagerial employees.

Such tools can provide insight into what employees believe are their problems and what actions they recommend. Some surveys may be generalized to include more than one employer. A survey of top level supervisors in state and local government units in North Carolina was useful in identifying that individualized training would be more useful than general programs because the supervisors identified widely varying needs among employees.[15]

A survey can take the form of questionnaires or interviews with supervisors and employees on an individual or group basis. The purpose is to gather information on problems, as perceived by the individuals involved. Sources include:

- Questionnaires
- Job knowledge tools
- Skill tests
- Attitude surveys

- Records of critical incidents
- Data from assessment centers
- Role-playing results

Prioritizing Training Needs

Because training seldom is an unlimited budget item and there are multiple training needs in the organization, it is necessary to prioritize needs. Ideally, training needs are ranked in importance on the basis of organizational objectives, with the training that is most needed to improve the health of the organization done first. However, other considerations including the following, may enter into the decision:

- Upper management choices
- Time involved
- Trainers' abilities and motivations
- Money
- Likelihood of tangible results

An example of successful needs analysis occurred at CMDC Corporation, a middle-sized wholesaler in Denver, Colorado. The company was experiencing a very high error rate in its shipping records, which were prepared by a group of 23 clerical employees. The needs assessment consisted of checking all shipping records for one week and tabulating errors for each clerk. Five people accounted for 90 percent of the errors. These five were then observed for 4 hours each until a clear pattern of the source of the errors was identified. It turned out that these people did not understand 4 of the 25 basic shipping transactions. A 2-hour training session for those employees reduced the error rate by 95 percent.

Can you name three ways in which training needs can be identified?

Setting Training Objectives

Once training needs are determined, objectives should be set to begin meeting these needs. As Figure 10–7 suggests, training objectives can

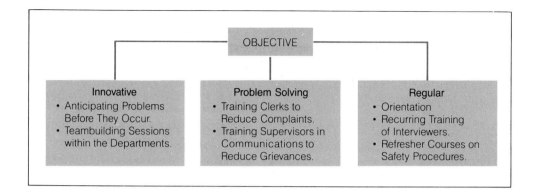

FIGURE 10–7
Types of Training Objectives.

be of three types. The most basic training objective is *regular training,* which is ongoing. Orientation is an example of regular training because it attempts to provide learning for all employees as they begin work in the organization. The second type of training objective is *problem-solving.* The emphasis is on solving a particular problem instead of presenting general information concerning problem areas. The final objective is *innovation,* or change-making, which has a longer-range focus.

TRAINING METHODS

Once needs and objectives have been determined, the actual training effort must begin. Regardless of whether the training is job-related or developmental in nature, a particular training method must be chosen. Some methods involve the use of visual aids to enhance the learning experience. The following overview of common training methods and techniques classifies methods into several major groups.

On-The-Job Training

The most common type of training at all levels in an organization is on-the-job training. (OJT) Whether or not the training is planned, people do learn from their job experiences, particularly if these experiences change over time. This type of training usually is done by the manager and/or other employees. A manager or supervisor who trains an employee must be able to teach, as well as show, the employee. The problem with OJT is that it often is haphazardly done. Trainers may have no experience in training, no time to do it, and no desire to participate. Under such conditions learners essentially are on their own and training likely will not be effective.

A special, guided form of on-the-job training is Job Instructional Training (JIT). Developed during World War II, JIT is still used widely. The JIT method is a four-step instructional process involving preparation, presentation, performance tryout, and follow-up.[16]

On-the-job training is by far the most commonly used kind of train-

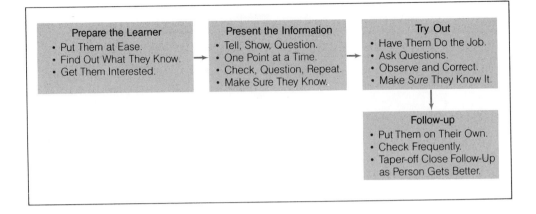

Prepare the Learner	Present the Information	Try Out
• Put Them at Ease. • Find Out What They Know. • Get Them Interested.	• Tell, Show, Question. • One Point at a Time. • Check, Question, Repeat. • Make Sure They Know.	• Have Them Do the Job. • Ask Questions. • Observe and Correct. • Make *Sure* They Know It.

Follow-up
• Put Them on Their Own.
• Check Frequently.
• Taper-off Close Follow-Up as Person Gets Better.

FIGURE 10–8

Job Instruction Training (JIT) Process.

ing. It is flexible and relevant to what the employee is doing. However, OJT has some problems as well. It can disrupt regular work, and the person doing the training may not be a very effective trainer. Unfortunately OJT can amount to no training in some circumstances, especially if the trainee simply is abandoned to learn the job.

Cooperative Training

There are three widely used cooperative training methods: internships, apprentice training, and vestibule training. Another less common cooperative method involves transferring professionals and their families to a cooperating company in another country for one to two years. This method can provide an interesting training alternative in certain situations.[17]

Internships. One type of cooperative job-experience training is an internship. An internship is a form of on-the-job training that usually combines job training with classroom instruction in trade schools, high schools, colleges, or universities.

Apprentice Training. Another form of cooperative training that involves employers, trade unions, and government agencies is apprentice training. An apprenticeship program provides for on-the-job experience by an employee under the guidance of a skilled and certified worker. Certain requirements for training, equipment, time length, and proficiency levels may be monitored by a unit of the U.S. Department of Labor. Apprentice training is used most often to train people for jobs in skilled crafts, such as carpentry, plumbing, photoengraving, typesetting, and welding. Apprenticeships usually last two to five years, depending upon the occupation. During this time the apprentice receives lower wages than the certified individual.

Vestibule Training. Vestibule training uses a duplicate work operation that is set up independently of the work site. In this setting, trainees can learn under realistic conditions but away from the pressures of the production schedule. Allowing Rose Hoffman to practice on a switchboard in a simulated setting before taking over as a telephone receptionist allows her to learn her job. Consequently, she is likely to make fewer mistakes in handling actual incoming calls. Airlines use simulators to train pilots and cabin attendants, and astronauts train in mock-up space capsules.

One caution about simulated training is that it must be realistic. The equipment should be similar to the type the trainee will actually use so the transfer of learning can be made easily.

Behaviorally-Experienced Training

Some training efforts focus on emotional and behavioral learning. Employees can learn about behavior by *role-playing*, in which individuals portray an identity in a certain simulation. *Business games, cases,* larger cases called *incidents,* and short work assignments called *in-baskets* are other behaviorally-experienced learning methods. *Sensitivity training* or *laboratory training* is an example of a method used for emotional learning.

The critical issue in any situation using these methods is that the purpose of the exercise be clear. For instance, role-playing can be perceived by employees as "fun" or "annoying." It is best that trainees understand what the exercise is attempting to teach.

Classroom and Conference Training

Training seminars, courses, and presentations can be used in both job-related and developmental training. Lectures and discussions are a major part of this training. The numerous management development courses offered by trade associations and educational institutions are examples of conference training.

Company-conducted short courses, lectures, and meetings usually consist of classroom training, while company sales meetings are a common type of conference training. This type of training frequently makes use of training techniques, such as case discussions, and media, such as films and tapes, to enchance the learning experience.

Training methods of this kind are familiar to trainees, because they have seen them in school. However, they are essentially one-way communications, and are not appropriate for motor-skill acquisition.

TRAINING MEDIA

Several aids are available to the trainer presenting training information. Some of these aids can be used in many settings and with a variety of training methods. The most common ones are programmed instruction, computer-assisted instruction, and audiovisual aids.

Programmed Instruction

Programmed instruction is a method of guided self-learning that provides immediate confirmation and step-by-step learning to trainees. The information to be learned is divided into meaningful segments. Using either a "teaching machine" or a book, small segments of information of progressively greater difficulty are presented. Trainees respond to each segment of information by answering a question or responding on a machine. The trainee receives an answer or looks up the answer. Correct responses allow the trainee to proceed to other material. If an incorrect response is given, the trainee is guided back to previous material for review.

Examination of the effectiveness of programmed instruction reveals that it reduces average training time by one-third, but it does not appear to be more or less effective in increasing retention than conventional training.[18] The logical conclusion is that managers or trainers should not expect programmed instruction to do their training better, only faster.

Computer-Assisted Instruction

Another medium, using sophisticated modern equipment, is computer-assisted instruction (CAI). It allows trainees to learn by interacting with a computer. Recent studies show that CAI leads to faster learning times. Further, when coupled with peer training (using other students as an active learning resource), learning time can be cut even more.[19]

Audiovisual Aids

Other technical training aids are audio and visual in nature, including audio and video tapes, films, closed-circuit television, and teleconferencing. These tools are especially useful if the same information, such as new product details for sales personnel in several states, must be conveyed to different groups at different times.

However, trainers must avoid becoming dazzled with the "machine gadgetry" and remember that the real emphasis is on learning and training. The effectiveness of the technologies and media need to be examined as a part of the evaluation of the training effort. When one-way communication is acceptable, these media are appropriate. They also allow presentation of information that cannot be recreated in a classroom. Demonstrations of machines, experiments, and examinations of behavior are examples. However, the methods are not flexible and they usually are designed especially for a particular training program. Such specialized designs take more time to develop and may increase overall training costs. Factors influencing the choice of a specific training method include: (1) what the training is trying to accomplish, (2) how well the material is to be learned—simple knowledge, minimum skill, or proficiency, (3) cost, (4) time, and (5) number of trainees.

Can you discuss four training methods?

To be justified, training must make an impact on the performance of the employees trained. But training does not always work, and when it does, it is not always completely effective.[20] Evaluation of training compares the post-training results to the objectives expected by managers, trainers, and trainees. Too often, training is done without any thought of measuring and evaluating how well the objectives are accomplished. Because training is both time-consuming and costly, evaluation of training should be built into any training effort.

For example, a training program designed to help minority students advance in the retail business was offered in Philadelphia. The training included such standard retailing subjects as business math and sales methods. But it went further to include coaching in dress, behavior, and language. Businesses involved in the training are evaluating its effectiveness. Several have decided it is worth doing again. Others are disappointed with the retention rate, and about 50 percent of the trainees are no longer with the companies sponsoring the training.[21]

Training should be cost-effective. If it costs $3,000 to run a training program, a firm should get at least $3,000 worth of benefits from it. However, careful measurement of both the costs and benefits may be difficult in some cases. Figure 10–9 shows some costs and benefits that may result. Some of the benefits, (such as attitude change) also are hard to quantify. However, a cost-benefit comparison remains the best way to determine if training is cost-effective.

Levels of Evaluation

The way in which training is to be evaluated is best considered before training begins in order to allow design flexibility in evaluating a program's success. Training can be evaluated at four levels, as shown in Figure 10–10.

Reaction. Reaction-level evaluation can be measured by conducting interviews or by administering questionnaires to the trainees. However,

COSTS	BENEFITS
■ Trainer's salary	■ Increase in production
■ Materials for training	■ Reduction in errors
■ Living expenses for trainer and trainees	■ Reduction in turnover
■ Cost of facilities	■ Less supervision necessary
■ Equipment	■ Ability to advance
■ Transportation	■ New skills lead to ability to do more jobs
■ Trainee's salary	■ Attitude changes
■ Lost production (opportunity cost)	
■ Preparation time	

FIGURE 10–9
Costs and Benefits for Training Evaluations.

PERSONNEL IN PRACTICE

MANVILLE TRAINS WITH STYLE

Manville Building Materials is headquartered in Denver. Like most other companies, Manville is well aware that training costs money—not only in direct outlays but in valuable selling time lost by sales staff. The company feels that the employee must leave the training with an increased ability to make up for lost opportunity or the training is not worth the cost.

A few years ago Manville felt a need to improve the sales staff's understanding of customer behavior, and management feels the company's "Social Style" training program has done the job. The program teaches employees how to "read" a customer's behavior and how to proceed. The training began with the top corporate managers. Then district sales managers were trained and a field test was conducted with several local salespeople. The test was a success; now the program is a mandatory module in the routine sales development program. Salespeople do not receive this part of their training until they have at least three years' experience so they can develop their own selling skills first.

The results of the training program are: (1) salespeople are willing to call on customers they had previously avoided, (2) salespeople and managers get along better, and (3) a spin-off program has been developed at the salespeople's insistance for their customers. Manville feels this program *is* cost-effective.[22]

the immediate reaction may measure how the people liked the training, rather than how it benefitted them.

Learning. Learning-level evaluation measures how well trainees have learned facts, ideas, concepts, theories, and attitudes. Tests on the training material are commonly used for evaluating learning and can be given both before and after training to compare scores.

FIGURE 10–10
Levels of Training Evaluation.

1.	**Reaction**	*How well did the trainees like the training?*
2.	**Learning**	*To what extent did the trainees learn the facts, principles, and approaches that were included in the training?*
3.	**Behavior**	*To what extent did their job behavior change because of the program?*
4.	**Results**	*What final results were achieved (reduction in cost, reduction in turnover, improvement in production, etc)?*

SOURCE: Ralph F. Catalnello and Donald L. Kirkpatrick, "Evaluating Training Programs—The State of the Art," *Training and Development Journal*, May 1968, pp. 2–3. Reproduced by special permission from the May, 1968 *Training and Development Journal*. Copyright 1968 by the American Society for Training and Development, Inc.

Behavior. Evaluating training at the behavior level attempts to measure the effect of training on job performance. This level is more difficult to measure than the previous ones. Interviews of trainees and their co-workers and observation of job performance are ways of evaluating training at the behavior level.

Results. The results-level evaluation of training measures the effect of training on the achievement of organizational objectives. Because results such as productivity, turnover, quality, time, sales, and costs are more concrete, this type of evaluation can be done by comparing records before and after training.[23]

The difficulty with this measurement is pinpointing whether or not training caused the changes in results. Other factors may have had a major impact as well. Correlation does not imply causation. For example, Joe Rivera, a department manager for a shoe manufacturer, has completed a supervisory training program. By comparing turnover in Joe's department before the training, some measure of results can be obtained. However, turnover is also dependent on the current economic situation, demand for shoes, and the quality of employees being hired. Therefore, when using results evaluation, Rivera's manager should be aware of all the issues involved in determining the exact effect of his training.

*Can you give an example of the four levels
of evaluating training?*

Evaluation Designs

There are many ways to evaluate what the effect of training has been. The three most common are shown in Figure 10–11.

Post-Measure. The most obvious way to evaluate training effectiveness is to determine after the training whether or not the individuals can perform the way management wants them to perform. Assume that you, as a manager, have 20 typists you feel could improve their typing speed. They are given a one-day training session and then given a typing test to measure their speed. If the typists can all type the required speed after training, was the training good? It is difficult to say; perhaps they could have done as well before training. You cannot know whether the typing speed is a result of the training or could have been achieved without training.

Pre/Post-Measure. By designing the evaluation differently, the issue of pre-test skill levels could have been considered. If you had measured the typing speed before and after training, you could have gotten a better idea of whether or not the training made any difference. However, a question remains. If there was a change in typing speed, was the training responsible for the change, or did these people just type faster because they knew they were being tested? People often perform better when they know they are being tested on the results.

FIGURE 10—11
Training Evaluation Designs.

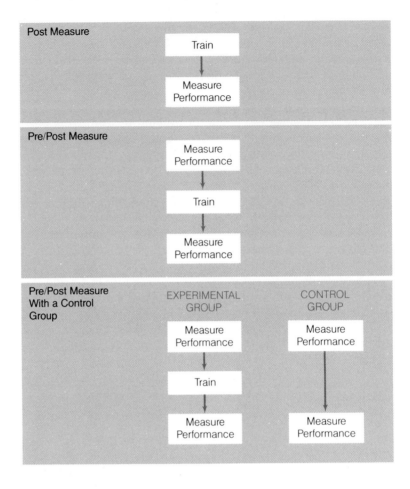

Pre/Post-Measure with Control Group. A final evaluation design can address this problem. In addition to the 20 typists who will be trained, you can test another group of typists who will not be trained to see if they do as well as those who are to be trained. This second group is called a *control group.* If, after training, the trained typists can type significantly faster than those who were not trained, you can be reasonably sure that the reason is the training. The final portion of Figure 10—11 shows the sequence for a pre/post-measure design with a control group.

There are other designs that can be used, but these three are the most commonly used. It should be noted that, where possible, the pre/post-measure or pre/post-measure with control group designs should be used because they provide more accurate measurement than the post-measurement alone.

Can you identify three training evaluation designs?

PERSONNEL TODAY AND TOMORROW

RETRAINING OF OBSOLETE WORKERS—STARTING OVER

Times change, and as they do companies must change to stay competitive. That may mean adopting new production processes, cutting costs (perhaps by cutting labor), or simply developing new ways of doing work within the old framework. Employees are affected by these changes in several ways. They may find themselves having to learn new methods, having to completely retrain for a new job in the same company, or losing a job altogether as an old industry dies.

People react in different ways to having to start over. Many fear the new and unknown. They may approach retraining only under duress. Others may gladly move toward retraining. For example, Wanda Horn found herself at age 33 in a dead-end clerical job paying $13,300 per year. She had heard of the opportunities in word processing and quit the dead-end job to retrain herself. Today she holds a responsible job paying $25,000 per year. Wanda is just one example of people who find themselves in dead-end jobs or jobs that are becoming obsolete, and who voluntarily do something about it.

Many people who were laid off (often permanently) from the steel mills and auto plants during the 1981–83 big recession faced similar problems. For those who were younger the transition was often less difficult. Many actually ended up with better jobs than they had. But others still sit and wait for a recall that will never come.

For years, IBM has had a policy that tries to minimize layoffs. The key to the successful use of such a plan is their system of retraining. IBM employees in obsolete jobs are trained for new jobs in the company. For this giant computer manufacturer with a reputation for excellence in management, the results have been beneficial.

For professionals, retraining may take many forms. For example, learning to work with microcomputers in their classes has meant a major retraining effort for faculty members at many universities. One finance professor gave his students a tough pencil-and-paper problem as a homework assignment. Some of the students knew how to work with the microcomputers and were able to arrive at a set of solutions within minutes. Other students who had not used the computer came close to rioting after spending an average of ten hours on the problem without finding an answer. The professor, realizing the computer was far superior to other methods, finally learned to use the machine and integrated it into other classes.[24]

SUMMARY

■ Training may be formal or informal.

■ Orientation is a special kind of training designed to help new employees learn about their work environment.

■ Components of an effective orientation system include: preparing; determining what information is needed and when it is needed by the employee; presenting information about the workday, the organization, and policies, rules, and benefits; and evaluation and follow-up.

■ Every manager will have to train. Yet, if learning does not occur, training cannot be effective.

■ Basic learning principles include modeling, intention, reinforcement, behavior modification, immediate confirmation, spacing practice, whole learning, active practice, plateaus, and applicability.

■ A training system should include assessment, implementation, and evaluation phases.

■ Of the many training methods OJT is the most often used and abused.

■ Training media such as programmed instruction, computer-assisted instruction, and other audiovisual aids each have advantages and disadvantages. They should be matched with training situations where they best apply because they will not all work in all situations.

■ Evaluation of training success is important because if the training does not return as much in benefits as it costs, there is no reason to train. Training can be evaluated at four levels: reaction, learning, behavior, and results.

■ A pre/post-measure with control group design is the best practical evaluation design.

REVIEW QUESTIONS AND EXERCISES

1. Identify the importance of orientation and tell how you would orient a new management trainee.

2. Differentiate between training and development. Indicate how learning is a part of each.

3. Why are learning principles so important to remember when designing training efforts? Be specific.

4. What are the three major phases in a training system? Identify the processes within each phase.

5. You are training keypunch operators. What training methods would you use?

6. You want to evaluate the training received by some keypunch operators. Give examples of how to evaluate the training at four different levels.

Exercises

a. Evaluate your personnel course at the reaction, learning, and behavior levels.

b. Design a test to measure what should have been learned about learning principles from this chapter.

CASE

THE NEW PAYROLL CLERK

Irene Kemp has just completed her first day on a new job at Key Data Processing Company (KDP). Although she had been out of the work force while raising a family, she was hired recently as a payroll clerk, primarily because of three years' experience she had 15 years ago. Quite naturally, she approached a job with more anxiety than the average person taking a new job.

That evening, Jim, her 15-year-old son, asked "How did it go today?" Irene replied, "Oh, okay I guess, although I'm not really sure." She continued describing her day to her son and related that upon arriving at work, she went to the personnel department. The personnel assistant said, "Are you starting today? Have a seat while I get some forms for you to fill out." After spending 30 minutes having various hospitalization, retirement, and other benefits explained, Irene was thoroughly confused, but managed to complete all the relevant forms. The personnel assistant then told her to go the accounting department.

After taking two wrong turns, Irene entered the accounting department and asked one of the clerks where Mrs. Schultz, the supervisor, was. "Oh, she's in a meeting and will be back in about an hour. Can I help you?" Upon learning that Irene was a new employee, Roy Harmon, the clerk, introduced Irene to the other six people in the department. Roy got Irene some coffee and began telling her "the true story" about KDP, including the fact that two supervisors had quit in other departments. He also told her how to "get along with Fran (the supervisor)."

About 10:15, Fran Schultz returned from her meeting, saw Irene and said, "Oh, I'm sorry, I forgot you were starting today. Why don't you observe what Roy is doing while I return some calls." At 10:45, Fran called Irene into her office and spent 45 minutes reviewing work rules and the job responsibilities of payroll clerks. Then Fran left for lunch after asking one of the other clerks to "let Irene tag along with you for lunch."

After returning from lunch, Fran showed Irene the forms she would work on, and where her desk was, and gave her some time cards to have the hours computed. Irene spent most of the rest of the day completing the time cards, except for a break in mid-afternoon. At 4:10, Fran checked back with Irene, noted a few errors, and explained that she would have more time to spend with Irene tomorrow. Irene then punched out at 4:30 and went home.

Irene's son Jim, with the candor of a 15-year-old, said, "Man, they sound disorganized." Later that evening, Irene told her son that she was having some doubts about staying on the job at KDP.

Questions

1. What problems can you identify with the orientation activities experienced by Irene?
2. What changes would you make in the orientation?

NOTES

1. Adapted from Henry Eason, "Games That Pay Off on the Job," *Nation's Business*, November 1983, pp. 66–67.
2. "Training: Personnel's Bread and Butter," *Training*, August 1983, p. 79.
3. J. P. Wanous, *Organizational Entry* (Reading, MA: Addison-Wesley, 1980), p. 8.
4. D. Reed-Mendenhall and C. W. Millard, "Orientation: A Training and Development Tool," *Personnel Administrator*, August 1980, p. 41.
5. "Employee Orientation Programs," *ASPA-BNA Survey* 32, *Bulletin to Management*, (August 28, 1977).
6. David F. Jones, "Developing a New Employee Orientation Program," *Personnel Journal*, March 1984, pp. 86–87.
7. "Employee Orientation Programs," p. 8.
8. Adapted from "Training Lure," *Wall Street Journal*, June 7, 1983, p. 1.
9. O. M. Hunt and C. Michael, "Mentorship: A Career Training and Development Tool," *Academy of Management Review* 8 (July 1983), p. 475.
10. "Formal Mentors Help Junior Staffers at Firms and U.S. Agencies," *Wall Street Journal*, November 15, 1983, p. 1.
11. Fred Luthans and Robert Kreitner, *Organizational Behavior Modification*, (Glenview, IL: Scott, Foresman, 1975).
12. F. Lulschak, *Human Resource Development: The Theory and Practice of Needs Assessment* (Reston, VA: Reston Publishing, 1983).
13. "Remedial Bosses," *Wall Street Journal*, January 22, 1981, p. 1.
14. R. B. McAfee, "Using Performance Appraisals to Enhance Training Programs" *Personnel Administrator*, November 1982, pp. 31–34.
15. Thomas H. Jerdee and Richard P. Calhoun, "Training Needs of First-Level Supervisors," *Personnel Administrator*, October 1976, pp. 23–24.
16. War Manpower Commission, *The Training Within Industry Report* (Washington: DC: Bureau of Training, War Manpower Commission, 1945), p. 195.
17. A. Pazy and Y. Zeira, "Training Parent-Country Professionals in Host-Country Organizations," *Academy of Management Review* 8 (April 1983), pp. 262–272.
18. Allen N. Nash, Jan P. Muczyk, and Frank L. Vettori, "The Relative Practical Effectiveness of Programmed Instruction," *Personnel Psychology* 24 (1971) pp. 397–418.
19. D. L. Dossett and P. Hulvershorn, "Increasing Technical Training Efficiency: Peer-Training via Computer-Assisted Instruction," *Journal of Applied Psychology* 62 (November 1983), pp. 552–558.
20. R. Ribler, *Training Development Guide*, (Reston VA: Reston Publishing, 1983), p. 169.
21. *Omaha World Herald*, February 6, 1981.
22. Adapted from J. B. Dorsey, "Manville Trains With Style," *Sales and Marketing Management*, August 15, 1983, p. 66.
23. D. L. Kirkpatrick, "Four Steps to Measuring Training Effectiveness," *Personnel Administrator*, November 1983, pp. 19–25.
24. S. Barber, "Faculty Training on the PC: Compute or Perish?" *Newsline* (AACSB), 14, no. 3 (February 1984), pp. 15–19.

Employee Development and Career Planning

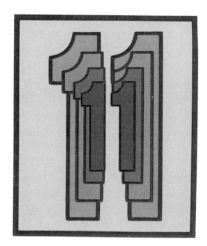

When you have read this chapter, you should be able to:

1. Define human resource development and identify two conditions for its success.
2. List and describe at least four on-the-job and off-the-job development methods.
3. Discuss specific benefits and problems associated with assessment centers.
4. Explain issues involving the development of women managers.
5. Differentiate between organization-centered and individual-centered career planning.
6. Explain how life stages and career stages parallel each other.

PERSONNEL AT WORK

A CASE OF BADLY NEEDED MANAGEMENT DEVELOPMENT

The Vice President for Manufacturing at a big company (which must remain unnamed) was becoming a liability. This man had been highly valued by top management, but he chronically blew up at his subordinates, badly undermining morale. His case was handled by Beam-Pines, Inc., a New York psychological counseling firm that specializes in changing the behavior of executives whose careers are in the trouble. In this case, Dr. Jerome Beam, the psychologist who founded the firm, taught the executive to control his temper—no matter what. The first time the man had to hold his tongue, his knuckles turned white under the strain. But he kept quiet. Little by little he changed, and he stayed with the company.

Companies that have used services like this one include large organizations like Time, Inc., and Warner Lambert; medium-sized concerns like Ponderosa, Inc. and Estee Lauder; as well as smaller companies. In another situation, a women marketing executive became an alcoholic and drew complaints from the retailers with whom she worked. She insisted she had no problem, but Beam-Pines told her she would have to change or be fired. Reluctantly she went to Alcoholics Anonymous. Today she has been promoted twice, and her employer is very pleased with her progress.

In another case, a newly hired young man had outstanding ability and was on the fast track to success. But he knew he was good. He came across to others as arrogant and his behavior created a major morale problem. When the development counselors told him how he appeared to his fellow workers, he was genuinely shocked. Gradually he changed his behavior.

Not every problem manager can be "developed," nor can every career be saved through counseling or other development activities. But Beam-Pines estimates more than 90 percent can be. The firm also is involved from time to time in situations in which a career is stymied and no further promotions are possible until some behavior changes.

This kind of career development does nothing to improve a manager's technical skills. But it does provide growth that can result in improved judgment, responsibility, and maturity—all critical areas for success in management.[1]

11

"Human behavior flows from three main sources: desire, emotion, and knowledge."
PLATO

HUMAN RESOURCE DEVELOPMENT focuses on increasing the capabilities of employees for continuing growth and advancement in the organization.

Development occurs from the experiences people encounter as they mature and is different than simple skills training. It is possible to train most people to ride a bicycle, drive a truck, operate a computer, or assemble a radio. Those skills can be taught with technical training. But how can someone be trained to demonstrate judgment, responsibility, compassion, or empathy in dealing with people? Such factors develop over time with experiences that may occur accidentally or as part of a planned program. Managers, particularly, need a variety of experiences to enhance their development. But a planned system of developmental experiences for all employees can help expand the overall level of abilities in an organization and increase its potential and flexibility.

HUMAN RESOURCE DEVELOPMENT—WHAT IS IT?

The purpose of **human resource development** is to enhance an employee's capacity to successfully handle greater responsibilities. Development usually is concerned with improvement in the intellectual or emotional abilities needed to do a better job. This improvement may be accomplished through formal or informal means. One study found that about 50 percent of the surveyed companies have formal development efforts for first-level management.[2]

An employee's development depends, to an extent, on the relationship with his or her superior. By concentrating on the individual employee's goals and potential, a manager can significantly affect an employee's development. Performance appraisal obviously plays an important role in development. Through discussions about an employee's past performance and current strengths, concrete proposals can be planned for future development. For example, a performance appraisal can determine, if employees are placed in jobs that exceed their abilities, or if they need additional training to improve performance. Then plans can be initiated to develop the required knowledge and skills. As shown in Figure 11–1, personnel specialists typically take a more guided and coordinated approach to development. Managers at all levels must be deeply involved, however, for development to succeed.

Can you define human resource development?

Conditions for Successful Employee Development

Employee development is much more than just acquiring a specific skill, such as learning to type. For instance, development might include: (1) attitudes about the greater involvement of employees, (2) im-

FIGURE 11–1
Human Resource Development Responsibilities.

PERSONNEL UNIT	MANAGERS
■ Develops and coordinates employee and management development efforts ■ Maintains management replacement charts ■ Evaluates employee development efforts for the organization ■ Administers details of development programs ■ Keeps abreast of new advances in development techniques	■ Participate in management development programs ■ Identify employees' development needs ■ Assign employees tasks designed to "stretch" them ■ Plan for their own development ■ Evaluate subordinates' development

proved abilities to communicate, and (3) better judgement on innovative decisions. Regardless of the objective, two conditions are critical for successful employee development: top management support and an understanding of the interrelated nature of development.

Top Management Support. Top management's belief in the importance of development efforts is necessary to give people the "room" they need to expand their capabilities. Top management must be willing to delegate some decision-making authority to lower-level positions in the organization to develop young managers. These efforts must be made even if some of them fail. For example, if top management is afraid or unwilling to relinquish control and authority to a younger manager for learning purposes, little management development is likely to result.

Development Interrelationships. Important relationships exist between human resource development efforts and selection, placement, compensation, and appraisal activities. Neglect of any of these important links can stymie development efforts throughout the whole system. The result may be the failure of the organization to use its human resources effectively.[3]

But development is no substitute for good selection. If a person is chosen for a job who does not have the capacity to do the work, no amount of development will change that. Likewise, improper placement of a person in the organization can seldom be rectified by development. Expecting one set of behaviors from an employee, but rewarding that person through pay raises for another set of behaviors, also will not lead to the desired development. For example, managers in one firm are expected to meet quarterly with each employee in their departments to discuss performance issues. However, one manager consistently has refused to do so. In spite of his refusal, the manager has continued to receive excellent ratings and above average salary increases. Consequently, the manager continues to ignore his developmental responsibilities.

Can you identify two key conditions for successful development?

Developmental Replacement Charts

With information from some of the interrelated sources mentioned above, replacement charts (similar to depth charts used by football teams, which show the back-up players at each position) can be drawn. The purpose of replacement charts is to ensure that the right individual is available at the right time and has had sufficient experience to handle the job. In Figure 11–2, a replacement chart for the APLO Manufacturing Company is shown.

Replacement charts are an excellent basis for determining what kind of development is need by which employees. Note that the chart spec-

FIGURE 11–2
Replacement Chart for APLO Manufacturing Company.

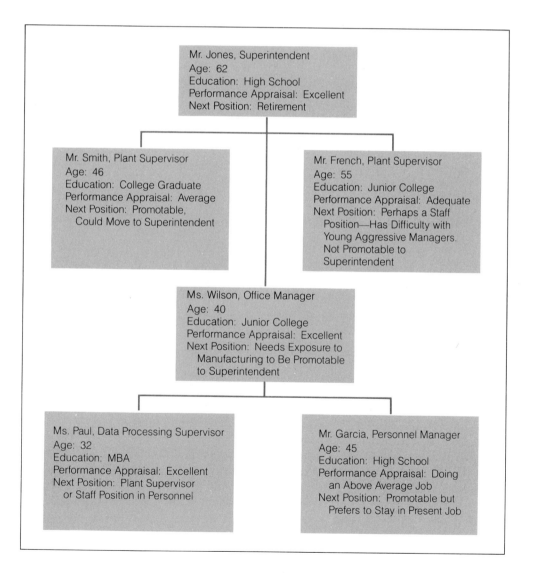

ifies the kind of development each individual needs to be promotable. Ms. Wilson needs exposure to manufacturing to be promotable to superintendent. Her job as office manager has not given her much exposure to the production side of the company. Ms. Paul needs exposure to plant operations and personnel. Mr. French needs to learn how to handle young, aggressive managers. However, Mr. French's appraiser felt French would not be promotable to superintendent, even with additional training. Such information can be used to identify "career paths" and "promotion ladders" for people.

Replacement charts indicate where weaknesses exist. If some positions are without adequate back-up, then a decision must be made either to develop someone internally to fill the position or to recruit outside. An individual must be selected, placed in the proper position, then trained, and appraised on the basis of performance. This information then becomes feedback to the entire employee development system. For jobs requiring more expertise, the development process is longer and the likelihood of having to recruit outside the compnay is greater.

A problem with replacement charts is the potential for a person to become "labelled." On such a progression chart a person who has been placed in the "mediocre performer" category because of a mismatch with a given job may become unpromotable. Replacement charts can help individuals who need assistance to become promotable, but management must be realistic in its appraisal of the reasons why they are considered promotable.

Problems in Development

Development efforts are subject to certain common mistakes and problems. Managers at all levels, especially top managers, make these same mistakes. Most of these problems result from inadequate planning and narrow thinking about coordinated employee development efforts.

Specific problems include the following:

- Sloppy needs analysis
- Trying out fad programs or training methods
- Abdicating responsibility for development to staff
- Trying to substitute training for selection
- Lack of training among those who lead the development activities
- Using only "courses" as the road to development
- Encapsulated development

Encapsulated Development. Failure to consider how employee development fits the organization can result in encapsulated development. This problem occurs when an individual learns new methods and ideas in a development course and returns to a work unit that is still bound by old attitudes and methods. The reward system and the working conditions have not changed. Although the trainee has learned new ways to handle certain situations, these methods cannot be applied because of the resistance of the *status quo* and the unchanged work situation. The new knowledge remains encapsulated in the classroom setting. Encapsulated development is an obvious waste of time and money because it is ineffective. It can be avoided if training is reinforced by the trainee's supervisor.

CHOOSING A DEVELOPMENT PROGRAM

Many employee development methods are available. Before describing several, it is important to identify some criteria for their use. The goals of the development effort can be people-oriented, job-specific (technical), or oriented toward planning and conceptual learning. Different techniques serve these different goals. Figure 11–3 shows the extent to which each method is suited to each of the three goals. A discussion of each of these methods, both on-the-job and off-the-job, follows.

On-the-Job Methods

On-the-job methods generally are directly job-related, which is advantageous to the organization and to the individuals involved. Some of the most common advantages are:

1. Effective training can be tailored to fit each trainee's background, attitudes, needs, expectations, goals, and future assignments. Off-the-job training cannot usually be tailored as well to the exact needs of each trainee.
2. The importance of learning by doing is well recognized in on-the-job training.
3. Some development programs can be very time-consuming and managers in training may be reluctant to leave the organization for the amount of time required. On-the-job training is not as time-consuming.
4. The employee's development is influenced to a large extent by the immediate supervisor and he or she is likely to accept the superior's expectations in an on-the-job training situation.
5. When an organization relies mostly on off-the-job training, supervisors do not feel a primary obligation to develop their subordinates. Consequently, development tends to be neglected. On-the-job training focuses a supervisor's attention on the subordinate's development.

These five points emphasize that on-the-job methods focus on day-to-day learning. The major difficulty with on-the-job methods is that often too many unplanned activities are grouped under the heading of *development*. It is imperative that managers plan and coordinate development efforts so that the desired learning actually occurs.

An example of a well-designed and successful management development program is Sun Chemical's General Management Development Program.[4] Sun selects MBAs with three to five years of technical experience and assigns them to a year of working on special assignments selected to give them well-rounded skills and a familiarity with the corporation. All the projects are important ones, though the company would ordinarily lack managerial resources to complete them.

FIGURE 11–3
Matching Development
Goals and Methods.

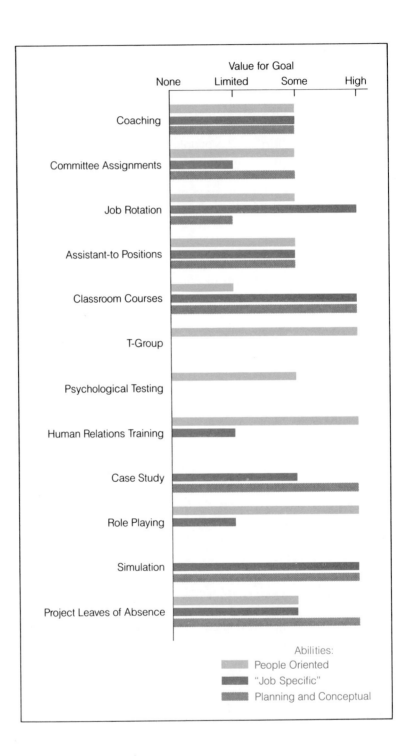

Coaching. The oldest on-the-job development technique is that of coaching, the daily instruction of subordinates by their immediate supervisors. It is a continuous process of learning by doing. For coaching to be effective, a healthy and honest relationship must exist between subordinates and their supervisors or managers. Also, managers and supervisors should have some training to be effective as coaches. A major insurance firm in the Midwest conducts formal training courses to improve managers' coaching skills.

Subordinates will benefit from coaching only if they consider it a positive development tool. At the heart of an effective coaching relationship are mutual goals and objectives, including a personal career plan for the subordinate. This plan must be followed up by regular discussion between the employee and the manager.

Unfortunately, as with other on-the-job methods, coaching can be too easy to implement without any planning at all. If someone has been good at a job or a particular part of a job, there is no guarantee that he or she will be able to teach someone else to do it well. It is often too easy to fall short in systematic guidance of the learner, even if the "coach" knows which systematic experiences are best. Sometimes doing a full day's work gets priority over learning. Also, many skills have an intellectual component that might be better learned from a book or lecture before coaching occurs.

These problems should not lead one to believe that coaching cannot work. It can, but it requires a knowledgeable coach and some planning.

Special Projects. Special projects can encompass many programs. The Sun Chemical development program is an example. Another is *conference leadership*, which usually requires that the trainee organize and chair problem-solving conferences. For instance, junior executives may be asked to plan and preside at meetings with other managers to solve problems, such as why the production department has been unable to meet a sales request on time. In so doing, the junior executives will learn more about sales and production problems and human nature, as well as how to organize a conference. Many other types of special projects can be devised, such as assignment to a task force or "think tank." The possibilities are unlimited.

Committee Assignments. Assignment of a promising employee to important comittees can be a very broadening experience. Employees who participate in committees that make important decisions and plans may gain a real grasp of personalities, issues, and processes governing an organization. Assigning employees to a safety committee may give them the safety experience needed to become supervisors. Also, they may experience the problems involved with maintaining employee safety awareness. This committee experience often helps employees emphasize safety to workers they supervise. However, caution should be exercised so that committee assignments do not become time-wasting activities.

Job Rotation. Job rotation has been discussed in the section of this book on job design. But it is much more widely used as a development technique than as a part of job design. Job rotation involves shifting an employee from one position to another similar one. For example, a promising young manager may spend three months in the plant, three months in corporate planning, and three months in purchasing. When properly handled, rotation encourages a deeper and more general view of the organization. The General Electric Company uses job rotation during a 15-month sales training program. Trainees work in at least three areas. Included are assignments in contractor sales, retail sales, credit, advertising, and product training.

In some companies, job rotation is unplanned; other companies have elaborate charts and schedules precisely planning the program for each employee. Managers should recognize that job rotation can be expensive because a substantial amount of managerial time is lost as the trainee takes time after each change of position to become reacquainted with different people and techniques in the new unit.

A disadvantage of job rotation is that it may discourage the trainee from taking a long-term perspective on the job. If a move is imminent, the employee may become more concerned with short-term problems.

"Assistant-To" Positions. The "assistant-to" position is a staff position immediately under a manager. Through this job, trainees can work with outstanding managers they may not otherwise meet. Some organizations have "junior boards of directors" or "management cabinets" to which trainees may be appointed. Assignments such as these are useful if trainees have the opportunity to deal with challenging or interesting assignments.

Can you list and describe four on-the-job methods of employee development?

Off-the-Job Techniques

Off-the-job development techniques can be effective because an individual has an opportunity to get away from the job and to concentrate solely on what is to be learned. Meeting with other people who are concerned with somewhat different problems and different organizations may provide an employee with new perspectives on old problems. A variety of methods may be used.

Classroom Courses. Many off-the-job development programs include some classroom instruction. The advantage of classroom training is that it is widely accepted because most people are familiar with it. Classroom training can be conducted by specialists who are either employed by the organization or are outside experts.

A disadvantage of classroom instruction is that lectures often result in passive listening and a lack of participation. Sometimes trainees have little opportunity to question, clarify, and discuss the lecture material. Classroom effectiveness depends upon the size of the group, the ability of the instructor, and the subject matter. Many companies encourage continuing education by paying for employees to take college courses. Some encourage employees to study for advanced degrees, such as the MBA, in the same manner. Such degrees are often earned at night school, after the employee's regular workday.

Special Programs. A widely used personnel development method is to send employees to externally-sponsored courses or short courses. These programs are offered by many colleges and universities and by professional associations such as the American Management Association and the American Society for Personnel Administration.

Some larger organizations have established training centers exclusively for their own employees. For example, the federal government has created Executive Seminar Centers in Kingspoint, New York, and in Berkley, California, and the Federal Executive Institute in Charlottesville, Virginia. Trainees in these courses are exposed to a variety of problems and learning materials. However, a common complaint about these programs is that they do not deal specifically with the realities of an individual's work place and a high percentage of the participants simply are not ready for the courses they attend. Some attend at the wrong time in their careers, while others are near retirement. Many have not had the preliminary training in management that the programs assume.

T-Group Training. T-group training has also been called sensitivity training, encounter group, and laboratory training. It is a technique for learning about one's self and others by observing and participating in a group situation. These small groups may meet for two hours or more daily for a period of a week or longer, usually off the job site. The leader attempts to keep a free format of activities and group interactions.

At first, group members tend to be frustrated and often do not understand why they are "wasting" their time. They may be openly hostile toward the leader and each other. The leader tries to encourage "openness" in the expression of feelings and reactions to other people in the group. Motives and impressions of other people are among the most common subjects discussed. The participants may gradually open up and show their true feelings.

T-group training is supposed to develop an awareness of human, group, and personal behavior. Even though people may be changed by the training, the sponsoring organization may not always benefit from the changes in the employees if they do not apply the changes to their jobs. This type of training seems to be useful in changing people, but its use in changing organizations is less clear.

Psychological Testing. Psychological pencil-and-paper tests have been used for several years to determine an employee's developmental potential. Intelligence tests, verbal and mathematical reasoning tests, and personality tests are often used. Such testing can provide useful information to employees in understanding such points as motivation, reasoning difficulties, leadership styles, interpersonal response traits, and job preferences. All such instruments, however, must meet EEO concerns.

The biggest problem with psychological testing lies in interpreting the results. An untrained manager, supervisor, or worker usually cannot accurately interpret test results. After a professional reports scores to someone in the organization, the interpretation is left essentially to untrained novices who may attach their own meanings to the results. It should also be recognized that some psychological tests are of limited validity and can be easily faked. Psychological testing is appropriate only when closely supervised by a qualified professional throughout the testing and feedback process.

Human Relations Training. Human relations training originated in the well-known Hawthorne studies. Originally the purpose of the training was to prepare supervisors to handle the "people problems" brought to them by their employees. This type of training focuses on the development of human relations skills a person needs to work well with others. Many human relations training programs are aimed at new or relatively inexperienced first-line supervisors and middle managers. Human relations programs typically have sessions on motivation, leadership, communication, and humanizing the workplace. Participation is emphasized and the prerequisites of high employee morale are carefully examined.

No one questions the importance of human relations skills in successful management. In fact, again and again they are cited as the major difference between successful and unsuccessful management.[6] The problem with such programs is the difficulty in measuring their effectiveness. The development of human relations skills is a long-range goal; tangible results are hard to identify over the span of several years. Consequently, such programs are often measured only by participants' reactions to them. As mentioned in the previous chapter, reaction-level measurement is the weakest form of evaluating the effectiveness of training.

Case Study. The case study is a classroom-oriented development technique that has been widely used. Cases provide a medium through which the trainee can study the application of management or behavioral concepts. The emphasis is on application and analysis rather than mere memorization of concepts.[7]

One common complaint about the case method is that the cases sometimes cannot be made sufficiently realistic to be useful. Also, cases may contain information inappropriate to the kinds of decisions that trainees would make in a real situation.

Role-playing. Role-playing is a development technique that requires the trainee to assume a role in a given situation and act out behavior associated with that role. Participants gain an appreciation of the many factors influencing on-the-job situations. Andrew McBride, a labor relations director, may be asked to play the role of the union vice-president in a negotiating situation to give him insight into the constraints and problems facing union bargaining representatives. Role-playing is a useful tool in some situations, but a word of caution applies: trainees are often uncomfortable in role-playing situations, and care must be taken to introduce the situation so that learning can occur.

Simulation (Business Games). Several business games or simulations are available commercially. Some are computer-interactive games in which individuals or teams draw up a set of marketing plans for an organization to determine such factors as the amount of resources to be allocated for advertising, product design, selling, and sales for effort. The participants make a decision, then the computer tells them how well they did in relation to competing individuals or teams. Other computer-based business games often have to do with labor-management

PERSONNEL IN PRACTICE

CAREER SELF-DEVELOPMENT AT HEWLETT-PACKARD

In the late 1970s, employees at Hewlett-Packard began to ask for more company assistance with individual career planning and development. The old standbys were not working: job posting proved cumbersome because too many unqualified employees applied; and, combining career planning with performance appraisal had proved difficult. A consultant discovered that an important part of getting promoted at Hewlett-Packard was "tooting your own horn," and nominating oneself for promotion. But employees usually cannot do a good job of nominating themselves for new positions if they had no idea where they want to go.

So was born Hewlett-Packard's career self-management program. Self-analysis is taught in a 14-week personal career management course. The participants are guided to make career choices based on extensive self-analysis. They also identify general goals and chart a career path. The participants then study how careers develop at Hewlett-Packard. When the program is over, managers interview subordinates to solicit their career objectives. That information then is available to upper management to use in human resource planning.

The results of the program have been impressive. Hewlett-Packard has been able to have much more flexibility in moving employees (37 percent of the employees have moved to new jobs in 6 months). Also, the whole experience has resulted in the company doing some succession planning (which few companies actually do). This planning, similar to replacement charts, is used to identify back-ups for many positions and to aid in the development of those back-ups.[8]

negotiations. In one such simulation, a player takes the role of either management or the union and the computer takes the other role. The trainee and the computer bargain on such items as wages and benefits.

Simulation, when properly done, can be a useful management development tool. However, simulation receives the same criticism as role-playing: Realism is sometimes lacking and the learning experience is diminished. Learning must be the focus, not just "playing the games."

Sabbaticals and Leaves of Absence. Sabbatical leaves are a very useful development tool. Sabbaticals have been popular for many years in the academic world, where professors take a leave to sharpen their skills and advance their education or research. Similar sorts of plans have been adopted in the business community. For example, Xerox Corporation gives some of its employees six months or more off with pay to work on "socially desirable" projects. Projects include training people in urban ghettos or providing technical assistance to overseas countries.

Paid sabbaticals can be an expensive proposition, however. Also, the nature of the learning experience is not within the control of the organization and the exact nature of the developmental experience is left somewhat to chance.

Can you list and discuss four off-the-job development methods?

Assessment Centers

Assessment centers can help identify areas in which employees need development. They also are useful for selecting managers. Typically, a potential manager spends two or three days in an assessment center going through many activities. These activities may include role-playing, pencil-and-paper tests, cases, leaderless group discussions, management games, in-basket exercises, and peer evaluations. An advantage of assessment centers is that they help identify potentially talented employees in a large organization. Supervisors may nominate people for the assessment center or employees may volunteer. The volunteering process especially helps find people who may not be recognized by their supervisors.

Operation of Center. During the exercises, the participants are observed by several specially-trained judges. For the most part, these exercises are samples of managerial situations that require the use of managerial skills and behaviors. The "center" is a set of activities rather than just a physical location.

One major company has made large-scale use of the assessment center concept. Trained observers watch the candidates' behaviors in detail and record impressions. Each assessor writes a report on each candidate which is given to the candidate's superior to use in selection and promotion decisions. The reports often identify guidelines for further development of the assessed employee.

Problems. Assessment centers are an excellent means for determining management potential. However, some managers may use the assessment center as a way to avoid difficult promotion decisions. For example, suppose a plant supervisor has personally decided that a subordinate is not a qualified candidate for promotion. Rather than stick by the decision and tell the employee, the supervisor may send the employee to the assessment center, hoping that the report will show that the employee is not qualified for promotion. Problems between the employee and the supervisor will be worse if the employee receives a positive report. However, if the report is negative, the supervisor's views are validated. Using the assessment center in this way is not recommended. Two other problems often encountered are: (1) making sure the exercises in the assessment center are valid predictors of management performance, and (2) properly selecting and training the assessors.

Validity of Centers. The validity of assessment centers for selection has been the subject of many studies. These studies have generally suggested that assessment centers predict management success much better than other methods. However, some researchers have been concerned with the very positive statistical results in these studies. They question whether the use of salary growth and advancement is appropriate to measure the success of assessment centers. It can be argued that these items may not be related to competence, effectiveness, or superior performance.

Finally, assessment centers are expensive. The actual cost varies from organization to organization, but it usually costs $600 to $6,000 for each candidate to go through a center. However, the cost of making a mistake in management selection is great, too: Some estimates far exceed $20,000 worth of legal, salary, and benefit payments to terminate a department head. Even though they are costly, many major firms, including General Electric, Union Carbide, AT&T, and IBM, have created assessment centers.

Can you discuss specific benefits and problems of assessment centers?

MANAGEMENT DEVELOPMENT: SPECIAL ISSUES

Two additional areas of special interest when dealing with management development are: (1) managerial modeling and (2) special problems of women managers. These areas will be examined to show the impact and importance of sound management development planning and implementation.

Managerial Modeling and Mentoring

There is an old adage in management development that says managers tend to manage as they were managed. Another way of saying this is that much management is learned by modeling the behavior of other managers, which is not surprising because a great deal of human behavior is learned by modeling others. Children learn by modeling parents and older children; they are quite comfortable with the process by the time they grow up.

Modeling, a very powerful management development tool, has been used successfully in industry in several ways.[9] Over 2,700 first-line supervisors at General Electric have been trained in the use of modeling to help ease the hard-core unemployed into the work world. As a supervisory development method, modeling has been used by firms such as Quaker Oats, Ford Motor Company, Xerox, Lukens Steel, Gulf Oil, and American Cyanamide.

Modeling is a very natural way for managers to develop because it probably will occur regardless of design, intent, or desire. Management development efforts can take advantage of natural human behavior by matching young or developing managers with appropriate models and then reinforcing the desirable behaviors that are exhibited.

Mentoring is a relationship between a manager at midpoint in his or her career and a young adult in the first stage of a career. Such a relationship aids the younger person by helping with the development of technical, interpersonal, and political skills. Senior adults may feel challenged and creative in being a mentor with wisdom to share.

One study identified four stages in most successful mentor relationships.[10]

■ *Initiation*—The initiation stage lasts 6 to 12 months. The young adult admires the senior manager's competence and recognizes the capacity to be a source of support and guidance. The older manager realizes the younger manager is someone with potential and is "coachable."
■ *Cultivation*—This stage lasts from two to five years. The senior manager provides challenging work, coaching, visibility, protection, and sponsorship. The young manager gains self-confidence, new attitudes, values, and styles of operation.
■ *Separation*—The third phase is marked by some turmoil, anxiety, and feeling of loss. The young manager experiences independence and autonomy while the senior manager can demonstrate his or her success at developing management talent as they move apart.
■ *Redefinition*—The relationship becomes a friendship. The senior manager continues to be a supporter and takes pride in the younger manager's accomplishments. The younger manager responds with gratitude for the early years, but is not dependent.

Management Development and the Woman Manager

Management development efforts for some groups may need a different orientation than for other groups.[11] During the last several years, an increasing number of women have been promoted into management positions. Both legal and societal pressures have encouraged the movement of women out of traditional "women's" or "pink-collar" jobs and into the mainstream of management activity.

The biggest obstacle for a women seeking advancement in management is the traditional attitude of both men and women toward masculine and feminine roles. Development of women managers seems to require an understanding of their special needs, as well as of the requirements of the business.

Rather than resort to special training for potential women managers, it would be most efficient to select those who are already qualified. However, the demand for qualified women managers sometimes precludes this solution, especially when there is need to hire and promote qualified female managers under an affirmative action plan.

As the foregoing suggests, if special training for women is necessary, it is likely to be more attitudinal in nature than ability-oriented.[12] In fact, the popularity of assertiveness training among women managers indicates that the special problems women encounter in management situations are more related to attitudes than to ability.

As with any social change, the initial introduction of women into management has been difficult for some organizations. Some male managers maintain that special training for women is "reverse discrimination." As a result, organizations should continue to take positive steps to ensure that a talented man has the opportunity to develop his managerial ability. Of course, the same treatment must also be available for talented women.

With all the difficulties they sometimes encounter, women are succeeding quite well in management. In a recent study, senior female executives with average salaries of about $92,000 attributed their successes to ambition, drive, and a willingness to take risks. They blame their failures on a male world and their lack of confidence in it.[13] The study shows clearly that women are on the way up, but that it has been lonely among the few women at the top.

CAREER PLANNING AND GUIDANCE

In the past, career guidance has been considered a service for high school or college students. However, as the employee work role becomes more complex, more employers are providing career counseling. Exxon Corporation is just one of many employers that use career planning for their managers.

Certain common career concerns are frequently expressed by employees in all organizations. These concerns include the following:

- "What do I really want to do?"
- "What do I know how to do?"
- "What career opportunities can I expect to be available?"
- "Where do I want to go?"
- "What do I need to do to get there?"
- "How can I tell how well I am doing?"
- "How do I get out of the box I am in?"

Usually, in-house career planning and guidance is limited to what the organization has to offer. However, these internal opportunities may not adequately reflect all possibilities, especially those in other organizations.

Organization-Centered vs. Individual-Centered Career Planning

The nature of career planning can be somewhat confusing because two different types exist. Career planning can be *organization-centered* and/or *individual-centered*.

Organization-centered career planning focuses on jobs and constructing career paths that provide for the logical progression of people between jobs. These paths represent "ladders" that each individual can climb to advance in certain organizational units. For example, one might enter the sales department as a sales counselor, then be promoted to account director, then sales manager, and finally to vice-president of sales.

Individual career planning, on the other hand, focuses on individuals rather than jobs. People's goals and skills are the focus of the analysis. Such analysis might consider situations both within and outside the organization that can expand an employee's capabilities. It might even include movement to another organization. The points of focus for organization- and individual-oriented career planning are compared in Figure 11–4.

Human resource planning forms the basis for successful organizational career planning. Only by forecasting the demand for people needed in various jobs in the future and the current internal supply of people and their potentials can a career system be put together for the organization.

If careful matching of organizational needs and personal goals takes place, human resource planning will consider both the organizational and individual perspectives. Unfortunately, many organizations often compile recruiting plans and career ladders, or both, without considering how current employees fit into those plans.

How Do People Choose Careers?

Studies indicate that four general individual characteristics affect how people make career choices.[14]

1. *Interests*—People tend to pursue careers that they believe match their interests.
2. *Self-Identity*—A career is an extension of a person's self-image, as well as a molder of it.
3. *Personality*—This factor includes an employee's personal orientation (whether one is realistic, enterprising, artistic, etc.) and personal needs (including affiliation, power, and achievement needs).
4. *Social Backgrounds*—Socioeconomic status and the education and occupation level of a person's parents are a few of the factors included in this category.

Less is known about exactly how and why people choose specific organizations. One factor is the opportunity for and availability of a job

ORGANIZATION CAREER PLANNING (OCP)	INDIVIDUAL CAREER PLANNING (ICP)
Future needs	Self-awareness: abilities and interests
Career ladders	Planning goals: life and work
Assessment of individual potential	Planning to achieve goals
Connecting organizational need/opportunity with individual need/desire	Alternatives, internal and external to organization
Coordination and audit of career system	Career ladders, internal and external to organization

FIGURE 11–4
Two Approaches to Career Planning.

SOURCE: Elmer Burack, "Why All the Confusion About Career Planning?" *Human Resources Management*, Summer 1977, p. 21. Graduate School of Business Administration, University of Michigan, Ann Arbor, MI 48109.

A CAREER
is the sequence of work-
related positions occu-
pied throughout a per-
son's life.

when the person is looking for work. The amount of information available about alternatives is an important factor as well. Beyond these issues, people seem to pick organizations on the basis of a "fit" between the climate of that organization as they perceive it and their own personal characteristics.[15]

Career/Life Stages

A **career** usually includes many positions, stages, and transitions, just as a person's life does. Progression from childhood through adulthood can be viewed as following a pattern. Although it is not exactly the same for everyone, there are similarities, especially for those who do not have interruptions in their careers. Women may follow different life and career stages, depending upon family and child-rearing concerns. Figure 11–5 shows the combination of life stages and career stages on one diagram.

FIGURE 11–5
Career/Life Stages.

Exploration. From approximately late adolescence to age 25 individuals feel a need to break with their parents and establish themselves. The

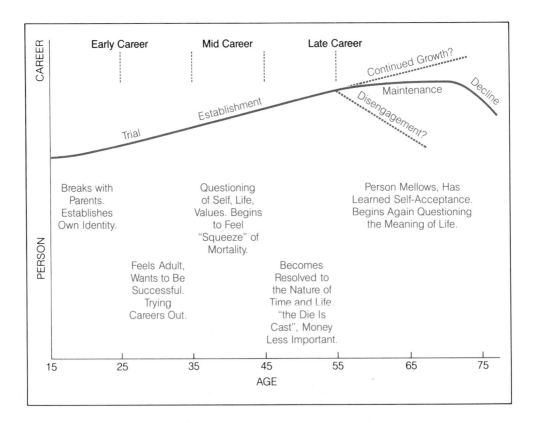

SOURCE: Adapted from Douglas T. Hall, *Careers in Organizations* (Pacific Palisades, CA: Goodyear Publishing, 1976), and R. Gould "Adult Life Stages: Growth Through Self-Tolerence" *Psychology Today* (1975).

SECTION IV TRAINING AND DEVELOPING HUMAN RESOURCES

career during this time goes through a testing period and an education process. Experiences in college or trade school, socialization, and "reality testing" are important parts of this stage.

Trial and Autonomy. As a person establishes autonomy, the principal concern becomes proving competence. Toward the end of the period, the emphasis shifts to children and the person begins asking "What is life all about?" Career growth is rapid.

Questioning. From the early forties, the questioning becomes more intense for the individual. There is an increasing awareness of a time squeeze. People may wonder "Have I made the right choice and is there still time to change?" This is the time of the infamous "mid-life crisis" when a person must resolve these difficult issues.

Maturity. This period is one of resolution. The individual is comfortable in a career, money is less of an issue, and the troubling issues of the forties have been resolved. Life settles down to become more even. The career may take one of three directions, depending upon the person and the situation.

Late Career. During this period, a person's attention may turn to personal health. Managers may concern themselves with the next generation of managers.

Retirement

Whether retirement comes at 55 or 70, for some people it can be a major shock. Of course, from the standpoint of the organization, retirement is an orderly way to phase people out at the end of their careers. Even so, some companies are experimenting with "phased retirement" through reduced workweeks or increased vacation time. The purpose of such programs is to make the break in work life more gradual for the retiree.

Some common emotional adjustments faced by the retiree include[16]:

■ *Self Management*—The person must adjust to being totally self-directed after retirement. There is no longer any supervisor or work agenda dictating what to do.

■ *Need to Belong*—When a person retires he or she is no longer a member of the work group that took so much time and formed an important social structure for so many years. What will take its place?

■ *Pride in Achievement*—Achievement reinforces self-esteem and is often centered around work. In retirement, past achievements quickly wear thin as a source of self-esteem.

■ *Territoriality*—Personal "turf," in the form of office, company, and title, are lost in retirement. They must be replaced with other sources to satisfy a person's territoriality needs.

■ *Goals*—Organizations provide many of a person's goals. That may leave some people unprepared to set their own goals when they retire.

Pre-retirement and post-retirement programs aimed at these problems can help employees make the transition to a useful retirement.

Can you explain how life stages and career stages parallel one another?

Effective Individual Career Planning

Good career planning at the individual level first requires that a person accurately know himself or herself. One must face issues such as: How hard are you really willing to work? What factors are most important to you? What trade-off between work and family or leisure are you willing to make? These questions and others must be confronted honestly before personal goals and objectvives can be realistically set. Professional counseling sometimes may be needed to help individuals make these decisions.

Supervisors and managers can help a person determine what skills and talents are necessary for success at each organizational level. Other information on occupations or careers outside the employee's current organization often must be gathered by the employee. Once this material is gathered, decisions can be made.

Individual career goal-setting is an important first step. Once goals have been set, plans must be formulated for their achievement. This planning consists of determining a series of actions that will lead to the goals. Steps may include a variety of training and development methods, such as those discussed earlier.

Career planning is still more an art than a science. However, the alternative of no career planning is not a sound one for either the organization or the individual.[17]

Can you differentiate between organization-centered and individual-centered career planning?

Career Path Development

Development of career paths is concerned with the process of logically mapping out steps that employees might follow over time. One method for accomplishing this development is to gather information on historical patterns of movement in the organization. Unfortunately, this information shows what patterns have been developed in the past, not necessarily what they should be.

A better method is to select groups of appropriate jobs or "job families" at lower levels that will prepare an employee for a higher-level job. Career paths developed from such an analysis may emphasize upward mobility within a single area or occupation, such as that shown in Figure 11–6.

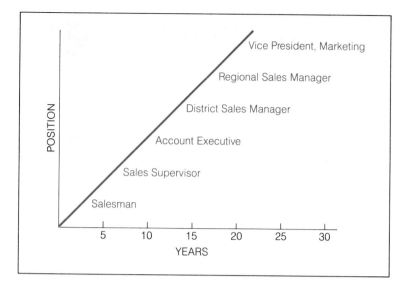

FIGURE 11–6
Career Path Within a Single Area.

Career paths, however, do not have to be linear, nor do they always have to move up the organizational structure. Lateral movement within levels should be a possibility as well.

The Dual Career Ladder. Professional and technical people, such as engineers and scientists, provide a difficult challenge for the development of career paths. Those who want to stay in their labs and at their drawing boards rather than move into management face a dilemma: Advancement frequently requires a move into management. Most of these people like the idea of the responsibility and opportunity associated with advancement, but they do not want to leave the technical puzzles and problems at which they excel.[18]

The dual career ladder is an attempt to solve this problem. A person can advance up either the management ladder or a corresponding ladder on the technical side. Unfortunately, what happens too often is that the technical ladder leads to "second class citizenship" within the organization. For that reason, a person who follows the technical ladder sometimes is viewed as being "put out to pasture" rather than following a viable career path.[19] Figure 11–7 shows a dual career path.

Emerging Careers. Recent research on career mobility has found that the time spent in various jobs in a career depends on such factors as an employee's marketability, the importance of job security, and community ties.[20] In addition, the emergence of new careers will cause an impact on career planning because many of these openings will be filled with people whose original training was in another area. For example, consider where an organization might find the following, all examples of relatively new or emerging careers:[21]

FIGURE 11-7
A Dual Career Path.

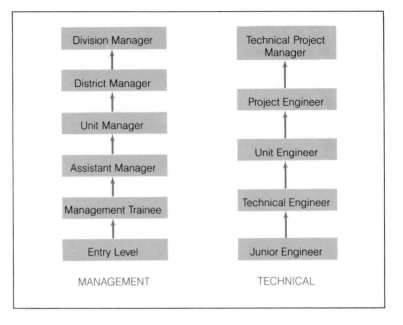

MANAGEMENT

Division Manager
District Manager
Unit Manager
Assistant Manager
Management Trainee
Entry Level

TECHNICAL

Technical Project Manager
Project Engineer
Unit Engineer
Technical Engineer
Junior Engineer

- Certified financial planner
- Computer security specialist
- Electronic data processing auditor
- Family mediator
- Health physicist
- Information broker
- Ombudsman
- Robotic engineer
- Wind prospector

- Complaints manager
- Data base manager
- Site selector specialist
- Transplant coordinator
- Strategic planner
- Sports psychologist
- Sex counselor
- Volcanologist
- Systems analysis manager

Dual-Career Marriages

The increasing number of women in the work force, and particularly in professional careers, is leading to a great increase in the number of dual-career families. The U.S. Bureau of Labor Statistics reported that 50 percent of all couples are dual-career couples.[22] This percentage is expected to increase to 86 percent by 1990. Leading areas of growth in the number of dual-career couples are the West Coast, Denver, Chicago, New York, and Washington D.C.-Baltimore area.[23]

Many recent female recruits are now progressing to senior positions and being asked to relocate. According to the U.S. Department of Labor, 27.5 percent of all managerial and administrative positions were held by women as of 1981.[24] This number should increase in the next few years due to the growing percentages of women enrolled in MBA and engineering programs. About 32 percent of all MBA students and 10 percent of all engineering students in 1981 were women.[25]

Traditionally, it has been the woman who made the sacrifice of diminishing, or even giving up, her career when her husband was required to relocate. This pattern is changing, however, as more women are holding professional positions and considering their own career ambitions to be as important as those of their husbands.[26] The dual-career couple must face the problems of outdated societal values and organizational beliefs which make the dual-career lifestyle difficult and, in some cases, impossible.

The Employee Relocation Council estimates that 1.5 million work-related moves took place in 1983. Forty percent of these, or 600,000 moves, involved dual-career couples.[27] With almost half of all transfers involving dual-career couples, it is time for organizations to begin dealing with the special concerns and problems of these couples. The trend is toward considering the wife's career as just as important as the husband's.[28] Because these couples bring in two paychecks, more people can now afford to say "no" to transfers. And, today more people are willing to risk their careers in order to live where they choose.

For these reasons, some companies are trying to reduce the amount of relocation necessary in a person's career. One study found that there is a general reduction in the number of positions considered open to transfer.[29] In one company, only people making over $80,000 get moved. In 1977, the salary cutoff for the same company was $25,000. IBM now relocates 3 percent of its people yearly, down from 5 percent a few years ago. It cites the "disruptive impact" and the problem of two-career moves (which it tries to arrange).

Some companies are using temporary transfers, particularly in cases in which the move is mainly for developmental purposes. Stress is reduced if employees and their families know they will be moved back to the same place in a year or two. Often they will choose to rent out their old house, which saves the employer a lot of moving costs. The couple also may choose commuting, if feasible, since the transfer will not be permanent.

PERSONNEL TODAY AND TOMORROW

OVERCOMING CYBERPHOBIA—YOU'LL JUST LOVE THE COMPUTER!

Whether we accept it or not, "computer-literacy" seems to be one of the buzz words of the 1980s. Lots of people have the attitude: "No problem—it's just a machine!" But many people do *not* feel that way at all. One professor estimates that 30 percent of the business people who must interact with the machine suffer from "cyberphobia"—a fear of computers. Developing people to overcome this fear is a challenge.

Symptoms include nausea, sweaty palms, and high blood pressure. Cyberphobia is caused by some bad experience with computers and is based on a fear of losing control to the machine. Some managers have even considered changing careers after their companies were computerized rather than develop their abilities to work with the machines.

Cyberphobia seems to affect occupational groups equally. Secretaries or managers, males or females, educated or uneducated—all seem to develop the fear proportionately. Obviously, those who are in the computer industry are less likely to have the problem. It is predicted that an increase in computer phobia will occur when voice input systems become available, because many more people will be in contact with computers directly and daily. But 10 to 15 years after the introduction of voice activated computers, there should be a decrease in cyberphobia as the machine becomes a routine part of our lives.

Cyberphobia can be dealt with in the short run, however, like most phobias. "Desensitization" through making people more familiar with the source of the fear in a nonthreatening situation often works. For people who have a great fear of snakes, for example, exposure to the creatures under the careful eye of someone who understands and does not fear them can help. Similar treatment can help cure a fear of the computer "snake."

Behavior modification techniques can work as well. Positive reinforcement and shaping behavior away from fearful reactions can win acceptance of the computer if given enough time. If 30 percent of the work force is really bothered by such fears, special programs can be designed for them, while general appreciation courses can help those who do not suffer from severe cases of cyberphobia.[30]

SUMMARY

- Development is different than training; it focuses on less tangible attitudes and values than training, which focuses on skills.
- Successful development requires top management support and an understanding of its relationship to other personnel activities.
- Replacement charts are like football depth charts. They form a basis

for making decisions about developing people internally versus going outside for new talent.

■ On-the-job development methods include: coaching, special projects, committee asignments, job rotation, and "assistant-to" positions.

■ Off-the-job development methods include: classroom courses, T-group training, special programs, psychological testing, human relations or project, training, case study, role-playing, simulation, and sabbatical, leaves.

■ Assessment centers provide valid mehods of assessing management talent and development needs.

■ Mentoring and modeling are two very natural ways for younger managers to acquire the skills and know-how necessary to be successful. Mentoring follows a four-stage progression in most cases.

■ Women managers have special challenges and may require special development. Many are now succeeding in management positions.

■ Career planning may focus on organizational needs or the individual's needs (or both).

■ A person chooses a career based on interests, self-image, personality, and social background.

■ A person's life follows a pattern, as does his or her career. Putting the two together provides a perspective that can be useful in understanding employee problems.

■ Retirement often requires one or more common emotional adjustments.

■ Development of career paths may be done by historically charting ways of moving up in the organization, or by identifying job families that will provide the desired experience to move up.

■ The dual career ladder is used with scientific or technical employees.

■ Dual-career marriages increasingly are becoming a consideration when relocating emplyees. Companies are having to reconsider career moves in this context.

REVIEW QUESTIONS AND EXERCISES

1. What is personnel development and why is top management support so important to it?

2. You are the head of a governmental agency. What two methods of on-the-job development would you use with a promising supervisor? What two off-the-job methods would you use? Why?

3. Why do you believe that many large companies have started assessment centers?

4. "Women managers should be treated like men when it comes to development activities. Neither group should receive special treatment or have unique activities planned for them." Discuss.

5. Discuss whether you would prefer organization-centered or individual-centered career planning.

6. Identify your anticipated career stages in conjunction with the life stages discussed in the chapter.

Exercises

a. Interview a manager about the career paths in his or her company.

b. Generate a list of options for a company in dealing with dual-career marriages when the company wishes to transfer either the husband or the wife.

CASE

DEVELOPED TODAY, GONE TOMORROW?

A large midwestern firm maintains an organizational policy of promoting individual growth. By offering generous allowances for costs associated with tuition, books, and miscellaneous expenses, employees are supported in their efforts to further their education at the college or training school level. This program is also offered to employees whose goals are graduate-level education, if their fields are ones that could be advantageous to the corporation.

The computer programming department has a high rate of participation in the educational support program. It is generally accepted that this high rate is due to the above-average aptitudes of the personnel in the department and to the high personal goals set by them. In addition, the department has its own in-house set of training courses and purchases "space" in various seminar classes. These programs are geared to making the employee significantly more valuable to the department. The managers in the programming department have been very proud of the development of their personnel and feel that education from all sources has improved departmental performance.

Recently, however, the system seemed to backfire in the programming department. Ezra Brooks, a very bright and aspiring young programmer for whom management had high hopes, quit. Ezra had found that the extensive intraorganization training, the invaluable work experience, and a newly awarded college diploma represented a fairly lucrative portfolio of credentials, which he took to a large national accounting firm. Ezra had expressed a desire to stay, but he was told that there were no anticipated openings at managerial levels in the computer area.

Ezra's manager had a dilemma. Loss of Ezra meant a ten-month setback for the project Ezra was working on. He also felt that the extensive training Ezra had received at the company's expense was little utilized compared to what Ezra would have contributed had he remained with the company. However, the manager's greatest concern was that Ezra was the first in a group of several employees who would graduate from college under company sponsorship in the near future. Ezra had shown to the remaining group that if the firm would not recognize his achievement and aspirations, other employment could be easily found.

Questions

1. As Ezra's manager, what would you do to retain him?
2. What changes would you recommend in the educational aid program?

NOTES

1. Adapted from J. Perham, "The Antisocial Executive," *Dun's Business Month,* July 1983, pp. 52–56.

2. H. Z. Levine, "Consensus," *Personnel,* November–December 1983, p. 4.

3. An excellent discussion of the interrelated nature of development can be found in R. W. Walters, "Developing Future Managers: Systems Approach," *Personnel Administrator,* August 1980, p. 47.

4. E. E. Barr, "Experiencing Success: Breaking Them In at Sun Chemical," *Business,* September–October 1980, pp. 9–14.

5. Adapted from C. Hymowitz, "Wearing Two Hats," *Wall Street Journal,* August 9, 1983, p. 1.

6. M. W. McCall, Jr., and M. W. Lombardo, "What Makes a Top Executive?" *Psychology Today,* February 1983, p. 31.

7. H. Kelley, "Case Method Training," *Training,* February 1983, p. 46.

8. Adapted from W. R. Wilhelm, "Helping Workers to Self-Manage Their Careers," *Personnel Administrator,* August 1983, pp. 83–89.

9. P. J. Decker, "The Enhancement of Behavior Modeling Training of Supervisory Skills by the Inclusion of Retention Processes," *Personnel Psychology* 29 (1982), pp. 323–33.

10. K. E. Kram, "Phases of the Mentor Relationship," *Academy of Management Journal* 26 (December 1983), pp. 608–625.

11. M. Londen, "Toward a Theory of Career Motivation," *Academy of Management Review* 8 (1983), pp. 620–630.

12. For further amplification, see Loretta M. Moore and Annette U. Richel, "Characteristics of Women in Traditional and Non-Traditional Managerial Roles," *Personnel Psychology* 33 (1980), pp. 317–333.

13. J. B. Hull, "Female Bosses Say Biggest Barriers are Insecurity and 'Being a Woman'," *Wall Street Journal,* November 2, 1982, p. 29.

14. Douglas T. Hall, *Careers in Organizations* (Pacific Palisades, CA: Goodyear Publishing, 1976), pp. 11–13.

15. S. R. Rhodes and M. Doering, "An Integrated Model of Career Change," *Academy of Management Reivew* 8 (1983), pp. 631–637.

16. L. P. Bradford, "Retirement: A Concern for Organizational Behavior," *Exchange: The Organizational Teaching Journal* 3 (1978).

17. M. M. Kennedy, "Blueprint for Career Planning," *Business Week's Guide to Careers,* Fall–Winter 1983, p. 60.

18. L. Bailyn, "Technical Careers," *Technology Review,* November–December 1982, p. 42.

19. T. Danforth and A. Alden, "Dual Career Pathing: No Better Time, No Better Reason," *Employment Relations Today,* Summer 1983, pp. 189–201.

20. J. F. Veiga, "Mobility Influences During Managerial Career Stages," *Academy of Management Journal* 26 (1983), pp. 64–85.

21. S. N. Feingold, "Tracking New Career Categories," *Personnel Administrator,* December 1983, p. 90.

22. M. K. Levenson and R. W. Hollmann, "Personnel Support Services in Corporate Relocation Programs," *Personnel Administrator,* September 1980, p. 46.

23. D. Martin, "Dual-Career Marriages are Altering American Business," *Times* (San Mateo, California), February 2, 1983.

24. N. Jaffe, *Men's Jobs for Women: Toward Occupational Equity*, Public Affairs Pamphlet #606 (Washington, D.C.: Public Affairs Committee, 1982), p. 12.

25. B. Fleming, "Relocation," *The Denver Post*, November 14, 1982, p. 17.

26. A. C. Kilpatrick, "Job Change in Dual-Career Families: Danger or Opportunity?" *Journal of Applied Family and Child Studies*, July 1982, p. 363.

27. L. Tutelian, "How to Move Your Family When You're Moving Up," *USA Today*, January 26, 1983, p. D1.

28. Kilpatrick, "Job Change," p. 364.

29. "Corporate Moves Slow," *Wall Street Journal*, July 26, 1983, p. 1.

30. Adapted from "Fearing Computers," *Management World*, July 1983, pp. 23–24.

Appraisal of Human Resources

When you have read this chapter, you should be able to:

1. Identify the three major uses of appraisals.
2. Discuss three different categories of raters.
3. Give examples of three general types of appraisal methods.
4. Explain three rater errors.
5. Describe how to construct behaviorally anchored rating scales (BARS).
6. Identify the management by objectives (MBO) process.
7. Discuss several concerns about appraisal feedback interview.
8. List the characteristics of a legal appraisal system.
9. Describe at least two characteristics of an effective appraisal system.

PERSONNEL AT WORK

DWINDLING COMPLAINTS

Several years ago, University Research Corporation of Chevy Chase, Maryland, surveyed its employees to find out what they thought of the firm's appraisal system. The complaints were voluminous. Employees described the system as arbitrary and capricious.

"When I became president in 1975," recalls Gary F. Jonas, "the number one management issue facing our corporate leadership was an unfair performance appraisal system." In revamping its approach, the company emphasized flexibility and self-evaluation. The Work Planning/ Performance Review system, as it is now called, had to be flexible, Mr. Jonas notes, "because we recognized that jobs change, tasks end, and performance expectations are often modified. The system had to accommodate our dynamic and changing work environment."

When a task is completed, or University Research is at the end of a review period, an employee completes a performance appraisal form, which assesses how well he or she did in meeting preset goals. The form includes a "work plan" outlining key subtasks and deadlines. Once the employee has written this brief self-assessment, the supervisor adds his or her brief critique and selects one of five "grades"—from "did not meet any performance expectations" to "exceeded all performance expectations." After the form is filled out, the supervisor and the staff member discuss the evaluation and develop work plans for the next review period.

Employees' complaints about performance appraisal unfairness have been virtually eliminated at University Research. "While they may not agree with the judgments of the supervisor, they do feel that the system gives them a fair shake," says Mr. Jonas. "The old system was haphazard—and worse, it was demoralizing and undermined employee performance."

The new system has done more than improve morale, he adds. It has improved the entire process of corporate planning: "The need to define responsibilities helps our managers plan for their whole division. It helps them delegate better, determine staffing needs, and be surer of their evaluations."[1]

"What a man makes out of his work is important, but what his work makes out of him is more important."

F. H. FERRIS

After an employee has been selected for a job, has been trained to do it, and has worked on it for a period of time, his or her performance should be reviewed. **Performance appraisal,** the process of deciding how well employees do their jobs, has also been called employee rating, employee evaluation, performance review, performance evaluation, and results appraisal.

USES OF APPRAISAL

Appraisal systems measure how well employees are performing their duties and meeting their job responsibilities. The ratings are most often done by immediate supervisors who follow a format provided by the personnel department. The information provided by performance appraisal is useful in three major areas: *compensation*, *placement*, and *training/development* (see Figure 12–1).

Compensation

The first and most common use of appraisal is as a basis for pay raises. Managers need performance appraisal to identify employees who are performing at or above expected levels. This approach to compensation is at the heart of the idea that raises should be given for merit rather than for seniority. Under *merit* systems, employees receive raises based on performance.

Placement

Appraisal information also is used for placement decisions. When merit is the basis for reward, the person doing the best job receives the promotion. An individual doing a poor job may be subject to discharge or demotion. Either placement decision requires an appraisal of the employee's performance.

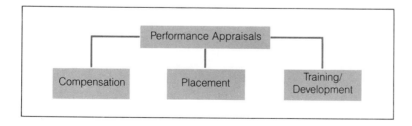

FIGURE 12–1
Uses of Performance Appraisal.

CHAPTER 12 APPRAISAL OF HUMAN RESOURCES

Training and Development

Performance appraisal information also has a training use. It identifies the weaknesses and potentials of subordinates, and can identify training needs. Performance appraisal can inform employees about their progress and tell them what skills they need to develop to become eligible for pay raises, promotions, or both.

Can you identify the three major uses of appraisal?

INFORMAL VS. SYSTEMATIC APPRAISAL

Performance appraisal may occur in two ways, informally or systematically. An *informal appraisal* is conducted whenever the supervisor or personnel manager feels it is necessary. The day-to-day working relationship of a manager and an employee provides an opportunity for the employee's performance to be judged. This judgment is communicated through conversation on the job, over coffee, or by on-the-spot examination of a particular piece of work.

A *systematic appraisal* system is used when the contact between manager and employee is formalized and a system is established to report supervisory impressions and observations on employee performance. When a formalized, or systematic, appraisal is used, the interface between the personnel unit and the appraising manager becomes more important. A personnel unit can assist the manager in seeing that appraisal is done effectively.

Appraisal Responsibilities

The appraisal process can be quite beneficial to the organization and to the individuals involved if done properly. It also can be the source of a great deal of discontent if not done equitably and well. In situations in which an employer must deal with a very strong union, performance appraisals may be conducted only on salaried, nonunion employees. The emphasis on seniority over merit is the major cause of union resistance to appraisals.

Figure 12–2 shows that the personnel unit typically designs a systematic appraisal system. The manager does the actual appraising of the employee, using the procedures developed by the personnel unit.

FIGURE 12–2
Appraisal Responsibilities.

PERSONNEL UNIT	MANAGERS
■ Designs and maintains formal system	■ Actually rate performance of employees
■ Establishes formal report system	■ Make formal reports
■ Makes sure reports are on time	■ Review appraisals with employees
■ Trains raters	

As the formal system is being developed, the manager usually provides input on how the final system will work. Only rarely does a personnel specialist actually rate a manager's employees.

Timing of Appraisals

An important characteristic of a sound appraisal system is assessing employee performance on a regular basis. Systematic appraisals typically are conducted every six months or annually. One study of 244 firms found that appraisals were most often conducted once a year, usually near the employee's anniversary date.[2]

This regular time interval is a feature of formal or systematic appraisals and distinguishes them from informal appraisals. Both employees and managers are aware that performance will be reviewed on a regular basis and necessary adjustments are planned. Nevertheless, an informal appraisal should still be conducted whenever a manager feels it is necessary or will be useful.

WHO DOES THE APPRAISING?

Performance appraisal can be done by:

- Supervisors who rate subordinates
- Subordinates who rate their superiors
- Peers who rate each other
- A combination of raters

The first method is the most common. The immediate superior has the sole responsibility for appraisal in most organizations, although it is common practice to have the appraisal reviewed and approved by the appraising superior's boss.

Supervisor Rating of Subordinates

Rating of subordinates by supervisors is based on the assumption that the manager is the most qualified person to evaluate the subordinate's performance realistically, objectively, and fairly. The "unity of command" notion—that every subordinate should have only one superior—underlies this approach.

As with any rating system, the supervisor's judgment should be objective and based on actual performance. Toward this end, many managers keep logs of what employees have done. These logs provide examples when rating time arrives. They also serve to jog the memory of managers, who cannot be expected to remember every detail of performance over a six-month or a one-year period.

A manager's appraisal of subordinates typically is reviewed by the manager's superior. This review is done to make sure the manager has done a proper job of appraisal, and to make sure the recommended salary increase is justified. (Figure 12–3 shows this review process.)

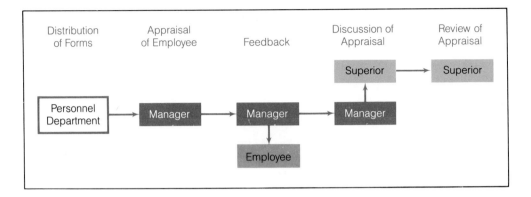

| Distribution of Forms | Appraisal of Employee | Feedback | Discussion of Appraisal | Review of Appraisal |

FIGURE 12–3
Appraisal Process.

Appraisals then remain a part of the employee's personnel file for a period of time.

A recent study has shown that managers and subordinates evaluate performance appraisal systems on different bases. Employee satisfaction with a performance appraisal system is related to:

- Experience with the system
- The appraisal discussion
- The assistance the forms provide in discussing and planning career development

Managers tend to evaluate the performance appraisal system on how well it helps them communicate employee performance to employees.[3]

Subordinate Rating of Superiors

The concept of having superiors rated by subordinates is being used in a number of organizations today. A prime example of this type of rating takes place in colleges and universities where students evaluate a professor's performance in the classroom. However, industry has also used some subordinate rating for developmental purposes. Results are used to help superiors improve themselves or to help assess managerial leadership potential.

Advantages. The are some advantages to having subordinates rate superiors. First, in situations where superior-subordinate relationships are critical, subordinates' ratings can be quite useful in identifying competent superiors. The rating of leaders by combat soldiers is an example. This type of rating program also can help make the superior more responsive to subordinates, though this advantage can quickly become a disadvantage if it leads to the superior trying only to be "nice" rather than managing the workers. Nice people without other qualifications may not be good managers in many situations.

Disadvantages. A major disadvantage is the negative reaction many superiors have to being evaluated by subordinates. The fear of reprisal may be too great for employees to give realistic ratings. The principles of "proper" superior-subordinate relations may be violated by having subordinates rate superiors, and employees may resist rating their bosses because they do not perceive it as a "proper" part of their job. If this situation is the case, the subordinates may rate the superior only on the way the superior treats them, and not on critical job requirements.

The problems and disadvantages associated with subordinates rating superiors seem to limit the usefulness of this appraisal approach. It may be useful in certain special situations, such as in a university or an engineering research department. However, the traditional nature of most organizations appears to restrict the applicability of subordinate rating except for self-improvement purposes.

Peer Ratings

The use of peer groups as raters is a third type of appraisal system. The peer technique seldom is used in open committee form. If a group of salespersons met as a committee to talk about each other's ratings, future work relationships might be impaired. Therefore, the peer rating approach is best done by summarizing individual ratings. Also, it should be noted that most of the research on peer ratings has been done on military personnel at the "management or pre-management" level (officers or officer candidates) rather than on employees in business organizations.

There are several likely reasons for the scarcity of peer ratings in industry. One is that members of peer groups in industry may not be as closely knit as peer groups in military training settings. Another reason is that peer ratings may be most useful when carried out by and for managers in order to identify leadership potential.

One study suggests that peer evaluations will work best when:

■ They are limited to people who see themselves as similar
■ Peer raters have had the chance to see the other person perform at the task
■ More objective sources of feedback are lacking[5]

One use of peer ratings occured in Levi Strauss & Company in 1984. As part of a workforce reduction of 3,6000, approximately 2000 executive, sales, and other professional employees rated fellow employees. These ratings, along with ratings from supervisors, were used to identify candidates for job-loss.

Committee of Superiors. If rating is done by a committee of superiors, more useful information may be available because more people have had a chance to know and observe the individual being rated. With more information, an organization can better pinpoint employees for promotions or future job assignments.

However, as with any personnel technique, there are some disadvantages. Having more information does not necessarily mean better information. Without objective data to make appraisals, committees may simply be pooling their collective ignorance.

Other problems arise with committee appraisals. They can be quite time-consuming, and the choice of the committee chair can be crucial in determining the efficiency of the appraising committee and the outcome. If the employee being rated thinks the committee members are hostile, that person will not benefit from the appraisal. Further, the committee members must realize the purpose of the appraisal system is to help an individual, not to "nail" the employee.

Multiple Rating System. The multiple rating system is very simple. It merely requires that several superiors separately fill out rating forms on the same subordinate. The results are then tabulated.

Such rating of subordinates by superiors is especially appealing when the preservation of organizational status is important. A young loan officer in a bank who is responsible for loan judgments may have her performance reviewed by a group of superiors comprising the bank's loan committee. This method preserves the role of judge for the superiors involved in the rating process.

Can you discuss three different categories of raters?

METHODS FOR APPRAISING PERFORMANCE

Appraisal can be conducted using a number of methods. In Figure 12–4 the various methods are categorized into four major groups.

Category Rating Methods

The simplest methods are those that require a manager to indicate how an employee rates on a form by marking a level of performance. The graphic rating scale, the checklist, and forced choice methods are common category rating methods.

Graphic Rating Scale. The graphic rating scale is the most commonly used method. Figure 12–5 shows a typical graphic rating scale form used by managers in rating office employees. The rater checks the appropriate place on the scale for each duty listed. More detail is then added by providing space for comments following each factor rated.[6]

There are some obvious drawbacks to the graphic rating scale. Often separate traits or factors are grouped together and the rater is given only one box to check. Another drawback is that the descriptive words often used in such scales may have different meanings to different ra-

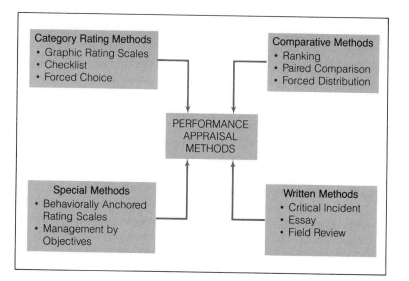

FIGURE 12–4
Performance Appraisal Methods.

Date sent _____   Return by _____

Name _____   Job title _____

Department _____   Supervisor _____

Full-time _____   Part-time _____   Date of Hire _____

Period   From _____   To _____

Reason for appraisal (check one): Discharge _____

Regular interval _____   Probationary _____   Counseling only _____

Major job duties
  Job duty 1: _____

Lowest 1	2	Satisfactory 3	4	Highest 5

  Explanation _____
  _____
  _____

  Job duty 2: _____

Lowest 1	2	Satisfactory 3	4	Highest 5

  Explanation _____
  _____
  _____

  Job duty 3: _____

Lowest 1	2	Satisfactory 3	4	Highest 5

  Explanation _____
  _____
  _____

  Job duty 4: _____

Lowest 1	2	Satisfactory 3	4	Highest 5

  Explanation _____
  _____
  _____

FIGURE 12–5
Sample Performance Appraisal Form.

ters. Factors such as *initiative* and *cooperation* are subject to many interpretations, especially when used in conjunction with words such as *outstanding*, *average*, or *poor*.

Checklist. The checklist is a simple rating method in which the manager is given a list of statements or words and asked to check statements representing the characteristics and performance of each employee. The checklist can be modified so that varying weights are assigned to the statements or words. The results can then be quantified. Usually the weights are not known by the rating supervisor, but are tabulated by someone else, such as a member of the personnel unit.

Attendance:

		Satisfactory		
Lowest				Highest
1	2	3	4	5

During rating period, number of absences _____

Comments: _____

_____

_____

_____

OVERALL:

Consider a general view of the employee's job performance during the rating period:

		Satisfactory		
Lowest				Highest
1	2	3	4	5

Explanation _____

_____

_____

_____

_____

_____

Areas of Improvement: Please identify 2 or 3 areas in which the employee needs to improve. Also note specifically how the employee can make progress toward better performance: _____

_____

_____

_____

Supervisor: _____ Date _____

Please comment on the degree to which you agree or disagree with this performance rating.

_____

_____

_____

Employee signature _____ Date _____

Director _____ Date _____

Comments _____

_____

Some difficulties with the checklist are: (1) the words or statements may have different meanings to different raters; (2) the rater cannot readily discern the rating results if a weighted checklist is used; and (3) the rater does not assign the weights to each factor. These three difficulties limit the use of the information by a rater when discussing the rating with the employee. Thus, effective developmental counseling may be difficult.

Forced Choice. The *forced choice* technique is a more complex version of the checklist. The rater is required to check two of four statements: one that the employee is "most like" and one that the employee is "least like." The items are usually a mixture of positive and negative statements. The intent is to eliminate or greatly reduce the rater's personal bias.

FIGURE 12–5
(Continued)

The difficulty of constructing and validating the statements is the major limitation of the forced choice method, especially for relatively small organizations. This method is also more difficult to explain in an appraisal interview than some other methods. An example of a forced choice item.might be as follows:

> Choose the statements which most nearly and least accurately describe the person being rated by placing M (most) and L (least) in the space to the left.
> _____ A. Seldom wastes time
> _____ B. Comfortable around others
> _____ C. Fails to plan ahead
> _____ D. Learns concepts quickly

Comparative Methods

Another group of methods requires that managers directly compare the performances of their employees against each other. For example, a keypunch operator's performance would be compared to other keypunch operators' by the computing supervisor. This group of techniques includes *ranking, paired comparisons,* and *forced distribution.*

Ranking. The ranking method is relatively simple. The rater simply lists all subordinates from highest to lowest in one listing. With ten employees, they are ranked 1 through 10—best to poorest in performance.

The primary drawback of the ranking method is that the size of the difference between individuals is not well defined. For example, there may be little difference in performance between individuals ranked second and third, but a big difference in performance between those ranked third and fourth. This drawback can be overcome to some extent by assigning points to indicate the size of the gaps existing between employees.

Ranking also means that someone must be last. It is possible that the last-ranked individual in one group would be the top employee in a different group. Further, ranking may be affected by rater bias or varying performance standards.

Exxon uses ranking as a part of its performance appraisal system. The ranking is done by the immediate supervisor *and* the next level of managers. This approach is an attempt to eliminate situations in which a manager rates all subordinates as top performers and all as comparatively good.

Paired Comparisons. The rater using the *paired comparison* method formally compares each employee with every other employee in the rating group one at a time. The number of comparisons can be calculated using the formula $\frac{n(n-1)}{2}$ where N is the number of people rated. For example, a manager with 15 subordinates would compare one person's performance to the other 14 employees. Each employee in turn would be compared in similar fashion. The manager doing the ratings would have to make 105 different comparisons on each rating factor. Use of the paired comparison method provides more information about individual employees than the straight ranking method. Obviously, the large number of comparisons that must be made is the major drawback of this method.

Forced Distribution. The *forced distribution* method (not to be confused with the forced choice technique mentioned earlier) compares subordinates and, at the same time, overcomes the drawback involved in the paired comparison method. Using the forced distribution method, a head nurse ranks subordinate nursing personnel along a scale, placing a certain percentage of employees at various performance levels. This method assumes that the widely known "bell-shaped curve" of performance exists in a given group. Figure 12–6 shows a scale used with a forced distribution.

A drawback of forced distribution is that a supervisor may resist placing any individual in the lowest (or the highest) group. Difficulties can arise when the rater must explain to the employee why he or she was placed in one grouping and others were placed in higher groupings. Further, with small groups there may be no reason to assume that bell-shaped distribution of performance really exists. Finally, in some cases the manager may feel forced to make distinctions among employees that may not exist.

Written Methods

Another group of methods requires a manager or personnel specialist to provide written appraisal information. Documentation and description are the essence of the *critical incident*, the *essay*, and the *field review* methods.

Critical Incident. The critical incident method is slightly different from the previous methods because it is more of a recording of employee

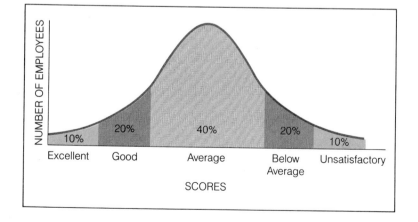

FIGURE 12–6
Forced Distribution on a Bell-Shaped Curve.

actions than an actual rating. The manager keeps a written record of the highly favorable and highly unfavorable actions in an employee's performance. When something happens (a critical incident involving an employee), the manager writes it down. A list of critical incidents is kept during the entire rating period for each employee. Because the critical incident method does not necessarily have to be a separate rating system, it can be used with other methods as documentation of the reasons why an employee was rated in a certain way.

There are several drawbacks with the critical incident method. First, what constitutes a critical incident is not defined in the same way by all supervisors. Next, producing daily or weekly written remarks about each employee's performance can take considerable time. Further, the critical incident method can result in employees becoming concerned about what the superior writes about them. Employees may begin to fear the manager's "black book."

Essays. The essay, or free-form appraisal, method requires the manager to write a short essay describing each employee's performance during the rating period. The rater usually is given a few general headings under which to categorize comments. The intent of this method is to avoid restricting the rater as other methods do.

There are some drawbacks to the essay method. First, some supervisors communicate in writing better than others do.[7] Therefore, the quality of the ratings depends on the writing ability of the rater. Also, the method can be time-consuming, and it is difficult to quantify or express numerically for administrative purposes.

Field Review. Under the field review method, the personnel unit becomes an active partner in the rating process. A member of the personnel unit interviews the manager about each employee's performance. The personnel representative then compiles the notes of each interview into a rating for each employee. Then the rating is reviewed by the supervisor for needed changes. This method assumes that the representative of the personnel unit knows enough about the job setting to help supervisors give more accurate and thorough appraisals.

The major limitation of the field review method is that the personnel representative has a large amount of control over the rating. While this control may be desirable from one viewpoint, supervisors may see this method as a challenge to their managerial authority. Some managers may also misinterpret the information given to the personnel specialist. In addition, the field review method can be very time-consuming, particularly if a supervisor has a large number of employees to be rated.

SPECIAL APPRAISAL SYSTEMS: BARS AND MBO

Two special appraisal systems that attempt to overcome some of the difficulties associated with appraisal are Behaviorally Anchored Rating Scales (BARS) and Management By Objectives (MBO). BARS seems to hold promise for situations in which many people are doing the same job, while MBO is useful for management appraisals.

Behaviorally-Anchored Rating Scales (BARS)

A BARS system (occasionally called a Behavioral Expectation Scale) is designed to overcome the problems of category methods by describing examples of good or bad behavior. These examples are "anchored," or measured, against a scale of performance levels. Figure 12–7 shows a BARS for a college professor's attitude toward students. What constitutes various levels of performance is clearly defined in the figure. Spelling out the behavior associated with each level of performance helps minimize some of the problems noted earlier.

Constructing BARS. Construction of a BARS begins by identifying the important *job dimensions* associated with the job. The dimensions are the most important performance factors in an employee's description. To continue with our college professor example, assume the major job dimensions associated with teaching are:

1. Course organization
2. Attitude toward students
3. Fair treatment
4. Competence in subject area

FIGURE 12–7
Behaviorally Anchored Rating Scale for Professor's Attitude Toward Students.

Short statements, similar to critical incidents, that describe both desirable and undesirable behaviors (anchors) are developed. Then they

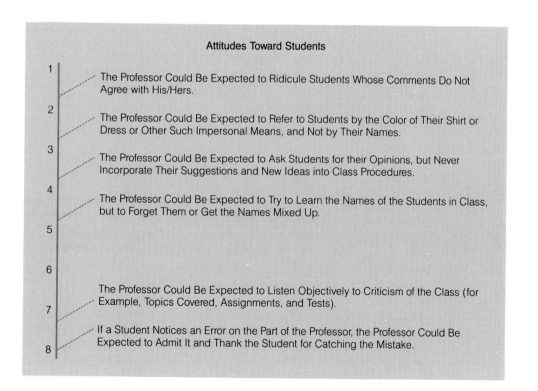

Attitudes Toward Students

1
   The Professor Could Be Expected to Ridicule Students Whose Comments Do Not Agree with His/Hers.

2
   The Professor Could Be Expected to Refer to Students by the Color of Their Shirt or Dress or Other Such Impersonal Means, and Not by Their Names.

3
   The Professor Could Be Expected to Ask Students for their Opinions, but Never Incorporate Their Suggestions and New Ideas into Class Procedures.

4
   The Professor Could Be Expected to Try to Learn the Names of the Students in Class, but to Forget Them or Get the Names Mixed Up.

5

6

   The Professor Could Be Expected to Listen Objectively to Criticism of the Class (for Example, Topics Covered, Assignments, and Tests).

7
   If a Student Notices an Error on the Part of the Professor, the Professor Could Be Expected to Admit It and Thank the Student for Catching the Mistake.

8

PERFORMANCE APPRAISAL IN THE FEDERAL GOVERNMENT

Performance appraisal systems can easily miss the mark. Instead of actually measuring performance, they may take an indirect approach by asking managers to assess knowledge, skills, or abilities. The recently passed Civil Service Reform Act requires that federal managers establish performance standards as a basis for merit pay, promotion, training, and performance improvement. Appraisal measures, too, must be specified.

Different agencies have taken different approaches to the task.

Graphic rating scales, checklists, and MBO are all used. But by far the most popular approach has been the use of "Standard/Based Job-Specific Rating Scales," which is similar to BARS. In this method, the manager establishes a precise measure of work at various points on a scale. Usually two or three points on a five-point scale are described. For example, the following standards have been developed by a unit in the Department of Defense for employee development.[8]

PERFORMANCE ELEMENT	FULLY SATISFACTORY	OUTSTANDING
a. Maintains organization's statistics on training and its benefits b. Ensures training needs are met. c. Discusses and arranges training with Training Office.	Maintains a work force of at least 80 percent fully-trained employees. Keeps abreast of training needs by continually assessing the workers' effectiveness. Plans employee training to disrupt work as little as possible.	Maintains a work force of at least 95 percent fully-trained employees. Meets top two training needs fully during the period.

are "retranslated" or assigned to one of the job dimensions. This task is usually a group project and assignment to a dimension usually requires the agreement of 60–70 percent of the group. The group then assigns each "anchor" a number, which represents how good or bad the behavior is. When numbered, these anchors are fitted to a scale. Figure 12–8 shows a flow diagram of the BARS construction process.

BARS require extensive time and effort to develop and maintain. They also require several appraisal forms to accommodate different types of jobs in an organization. In a hospital, nurses, dieticians, and admission clerks all have different jobs; separate BARS forms would need to be developed for each.

BARS represent an emerging area of research and application. How-

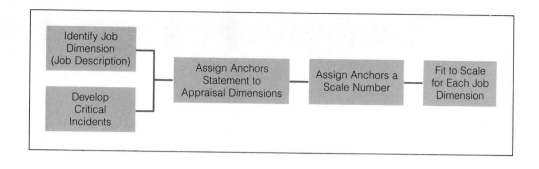

FIGURE 12–8
Flow Diagram of BARS
Construction.

ever, there are several problems and concerns that indicate that BARS may not represent the ultimate objective, job-related appraisal system.[9]

Can you describe how to construct Behaviorally-Anchored Rating Scales?

Management By Objectives

A system of "guided self-appraisal" called Management By Objectives (MBO) is useful in appraising managers' performances. Although not limited to the appraisal of managers, MBO is most often used for this purpose. Disenchantment with previously discussed approaches has increased MBO's popularity. Other names for MBO include *appraisal by results, targeting-coaching, work planning and review, performance objectives,* and *mutual goal-setting.*

MBO specifies the performance goals an individual hopes to attain within an appropriate length of time. The objectives each manager sets are derived from the overall goals and objectives of the organization, though MBO should not be a disguised means for a superior to dictate the objectives individual managers or employees set for themselves.

Key MBO ideas. Three key assumptions underlie an MBO appraisal system. First, if an employee is really involved in planning and setting the objectives, a higher level of commitment and performance may result. Instead of having the standards and ratings set by some other person, in MBO the employee plays a key role in setting the standards and determining the measurement scheme. Employee participation in determining the goals is believed to lead to greater acceptance of goals.

Second, if what an employee is to accomplish is clearly and precisely defined, the employee will do a better job of achieving the desired results. Ambiguity and confusion may arise when a superior determines the objectives for an individual and this may result in less effective performance. By having the employee set objectives, the individual gains an accurate understanding of what is expected and these expectations can be more clearly communicated.

A third key part of MBO is that performance objectives should be measurable and should define results. Vague generalities such as "initiative" or "cooperation," which are common in many superior-based appraisals, should be avoided. MBO objectives are composed of specific actions to be taken or work to be accomplished. Sample objectives for MBO might include:

- Submit completed regional sales report no later than the third working day of every month.
- Obtain orders from at least five new customers per month.
- Maintain payroll costs at 10% of sales volume.
- Have scrap loss less then 5%.
- Fill all organizational vacancies within 30 days after openings occur.

The MBO Process. Implementing a guided self-appraisal system using MBO is a four-stage process. These phases are shown in Figure 12–9 and are discussed next.

1. *Job Review and Agreement.* The employee and the superior review the job description and the key activities that comprise the employee's job. The idea is to agree on the exact make-up of the employee's job.
2. *Development of Performance Standards.* Specific standards of performance must be mutually developed. This phase specifies a satisfactory level of performance that is specific and measurable. For example, a salesperson's quota of selling five cars per month may be an appropriate performance standard because selling that number of cars can be measured and may be considered a satisfactory level of performance.
3. *Guided Objective Setting.* Objectives are established by the employee in conjunction with, and guided by, the superior. Continuing the example of the automobile salesperson, an objective might be set to challenge the employee to improve performance; the salesperson might set a new objective of selling six cars per month. Notice that the objective set may be different from the performance standard. Objectives should be set so that attainment realistically is possible.
4. *Ongoing Performance Discussions.* The employee and the superior use the objectives as bases for conitnuing discussions about the employee's performance. While a formal review session may be scheduled, the employee and the manager do not necessarily wait until the appointed time for performance discussion. Objectives are mutually modified and progress is discussed during the period.

FIGURE 12–9
MBO Process.

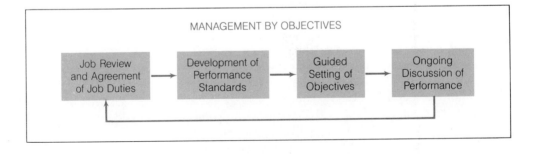

MBO Critique. No management tool is perfect. One of the most important cautions advanced is that MBO is not appropriate for all employees or all organizations. Jobs with little or no flexibility are not compatible with MBO. An assembly-line worker usually has so little job flexibility that performance standards and objectives are already determined. The MBO process seems to be most useful with managerial personnel and employees who have a fairly wide range of flexibility and self control in their jobs.

Additionally, MBO may be seen as a disguised means of managerial manipulation since it seems to require an organizational climate that is open and allows for sharing of responsibilities. When imposed upon a rigid and autocratic management system, MBO may fail. Extreme emphasis on penalties for not meeting objectives defeats the developmental and participative nature of MBO.

Can you identify the MBO process?

RATER ERRORS

There are many possible sources of error in the performance appraisal process. One of the major sources is mistakes made by the rater. There is no simple way to eliminate these errors, but making raters aware of them is helpful.

Problems of Varying Standards

When appraising employees, a manager should try to avoid using different standards and expectations for individual employees performing similar jobs. Employees become angry when they believe their boss uses different standards in appraising the performance of different individuals.

Even if an employee has actually been appraised on the same basis as other employees, the employee's perception is critical. If Joe Atista, a student, felt a professor had graded his exam harder than another student's exam, he might ask the professor for an explanation. The student's opinion might not be changed by the professor's claim that he had "graded fairly." So it is with performance appraisals in a work situation. If performance appraisal information is to be useful, the rater must use the same standards and weights for every employee and be able to defend the appraisal.

Recency Problem

The recency problem occurs in appraisal when recent occurences are given greater weight than earlier performance. Examples are giving a student a course grade based only upon performance in the last week of class or giving a drill press operator a high rating even though he made the quota only in the last two weeks of the rating period.

The recency problem is an understandable rater error because of the difficulty in remembering performance that may be seven or eight months old. Also, employees become more concerned about their performance and behavior as formal appraisal time approaches. Some employees may attempt to take advantage of the recency factor by "apple polishing" their boss shortly before an appraisal is to be completed.

Rater Bias

Another error occurs when a rater's values, beliefs, or prejudices distort the rating. If John Ennis, manager of a machine section in a tool plant, has a strong dislike of persons of certain races, this bias is likely to result in distorted appraisal information for some people. Age, religion, seniority, sex, appearance, or other arbitrary classifications may be reflected in appraisals if the appraisal process is not properly designed.[10] Having a supervisor's ratings checked by his or her superior should uncover this problem if it exists.

Rater bias is very difficult to overcome, especially if a manager is not aware of the bias or will not admit that such bias is affecting appraisals. Examination of ratings by higher level managers may help correct this problem.

Rater Patterns

Students are well aware that some professors tend to grade easier than other professors, some harder. Likewise, a manager may develop a similar "rating pattern." For example, Dolores Bressler, office manager, tends to rate all her employees as average or above average. Even the poor performers receive an average rating from Dolores. However, Jane Carr, the billing supervisor, believes that if employees are poor performers, they should be rated below average. An employee of Jane's who is rated average may well be a better performer than one rated average by Dolores.

Leniency errors are often the result of the reluctance of a superior to give a low appraisal. Appraisers generally find evaluating others difficult, especially if negative evaluations must be given. In the same way, a professor experiences more uneasiness and greater reservations when having to give a student a course grade of F rather than B. The leniency error (or any rater error, for that matter) can render an appraisal system useless. If everyone is judged *excellent* or *outstanding*, the system has done little to differentiate among employees.

Another rather common pattern is seen when appraisers rate all employees within a narrow range (as when a professor gives class grades that are nearly all Bs), regardless of actual differences in performance by the employees. This type of error is the *central tendency error*.

Making an appraiser aware that he or she has fallen into a pattern is one way to deal with the problem. Also, including precise and explicit definitions of categories on the rating form and allowing for considerable rating spread on each item are other ways to reduce the effect of rater patterns.

Halo Effect. The halo effect occurs when a manager rates an employee high or low on all items because of one characteristic. For example, if a worker has few absences, her supervisor might give the worker a high rating in all other areas of work, including quantity and quality of output, because of the employee's dependability, without really thinking about other characteristics separately. Giving a management trainee a high rating because he was a good athlete would also be an example of the halo effect.

An appraisal that shows the same rating on all characteristics may be evidence of the halo effect. Clearly specifiying the categories to be rated, rating all employees on one characteristic at a time, and training raters to recognize the problem are some means of reducing the halo effect.

Can you explain three appraisal errors?

THE APPRAISAL FEEDBACK INTERVIEW

Once appraisals have been made, it is important that they be communicated. The results should be discussed with employees so workers have a clear understanding of how they stand in the eyes of the immediate superior and the organization. In the appraisal interview, emphasis should be placed on counseling and development, not solely on telling the employee "Here is how you rate and why." Focusing on development provides an opportunity to consider the employee's performance and its potential for improvement.

Common Concern

The appraisal interview presents both an opportunity and a difficult situation.[11] It is an emotional experience for the manager and the employee because the manager must communicate both praise and constructive criticism. A major concern is how to emphasize the positive aspects of the employee's performance while still discussing ways to make needed improvements. If the interview is handled poorly, resentment and conflict may result, which probably will be reflected in future work.

Employees commonly approach an appraisal interview with some concern. They often feel that discussions about performance are very personal and important to their continued job success. At the same time, they want to know how the manager feels they have been doing.

It is fairly common for organizations to require that managers discuss appraisals with employees. One survey of 244 organizations found that approximately 90 percent of the surveyed firms required an appraisal interview.[12] Figure 12–10 summarizes hints for an effective interview.

Reactions to Performance Appraisals

The reaction of students to grades and tests (which are both forms of performance appraisal) illustrates the emotional and behavioral nature of appraisal. Students typically are very concerned about the equity of

PERSONNEL IN PRACTICE

WEYERHAUSER AND FEEDBACK

To the Weyerhauser Company of Tacoma, Washington, what is important in performance appraisal is to keep it simple. The company feels that the real reason for a performance review is to provide feedback to the employee.

Susan Ensey, a human resources department manager, feels that the review provides a mechanism "to let employees know what's expected of them. This review can improve their results as much as a strong feedback system." Weyerhauser uses an MBO approach but also considers behavioral factors.

The once-secret evaluations are no longer treated as "privileged" information. At one time, a supervisor elsewhere in the company could not even get a copy of a performance appraisal with which to judge a transferring employee. Now a copy is given to the employee and another is kept in a central personnel file.[13]

the grading process and the criteria on which they will be evaluated. Like students, employees are concerned about the fairness, consistency, and usefulness of appraisals. Managers also have these concerns.

Reactions of Managers. Managers and supervisors who must complete appraisals on their employees often resist the appraisal process. The manager may feel he or she is "put in the position of playing God." A major part of a manager's role is to assist, encourage, coach, and counsel subordinates to improve their performance. However, being a judge on one hand and a coach and counselor on the other causes internal conflict and confusion for the manager.[14]

The fact that appraisals may affect an employee's future career may cause raters to alter or bias their rating. This bias is even more likely

FIGURE 12–10
Hints for the Appraisal Interview.

DO	DON'T
■ Prepare in advance	■ "Lecture" the employee
■ Focus on performance and development	■ Mix performance appraisal and salary or promotion issues
■ Be specific about reasons for ratings	■ Concentrate only on the negative
■ Decide on specific steps to be taken for improvement	■ Do all the talking
■ Consider your role in the subordinate's performance	■ Be overly critical or "harp on" a failing
■ Reinforce the behavior you want	■ Feel it's necessary that both of you agree on everything
■ Focus on the future performance	■ Compare the employee to others

when managers know that they will have to communicate and defend their ratings to the employees, their bosses, or personnel specialists. From the manager's viewpoint, providing negative feedback to an employee in an appraisal interview can be easily avoided by making the employee's ratings positive.

Reactions such as these are attempts to avoid unpleasantness in an interpersonal situation. In the end, this avoidance helps no one. A manager owes an employee a well-considered appraisal.

Reactions of the Appraised Employee. A common reaction by employees is to view appraising as a zero-sum game (in which there must be a winner and a loser). Employees may well see the appraisal process as a threat and feel that the only way to get a higher rating is for someone else to receive a low rating. This win-lose perception is encouraged by comparative methods of rating.

Appraisals can be both zero-sum and non-zero-sum (in which both parties win and no one loses) in nature. Emphasis on the developmental and self-improvement aspects of appraisal appears to be the most effective means to reduce some of the zero-sum reactions of those involved in the appraisal process.

Another common employee reaction can be seen in the way students view tests. Because a professor prepares a test he or she feels is fair, it does not necessarily follow that the students will feel the test is fair. They simply may see it differently. Likewise, employees being appraised will not necessarily agree with the manager doing the actual appraising. In most cases, however, employees will view well-done appraisals for what they are meant to be—constructive feedback.

Can you discuss some appraisal feedback concerns?

PERFORMANCE APPRAISAL AND THE LAW

A growing number of court decisions have focused on performance appraisals, particularly in relation to equal employment opportunity concerns. The Uniform Guidelines issued by the Equal Employment Opportunity Commission (EEOC) and other federal enforcement agencies make it clear that performance appraisals must be job-related and nondiscriminatory. Further, a review of court cases filed on age discrimination charges found that employers using only "informal" methods of performance appraisal lost those cases more than half the time.[15]

Court Cases and Appraisals

It may seem somewhat odd to emphasize that performance appraisals must be job-related because appraisals are supposed to measure how well employees are doing their jobs. Yet, in numerous cases courts have ruled that performance appraisals in use by organizations were discriminatory and were not job-related. Three important cases are summarized below.

Brito v. *Zia Company.* In this case, Zia Company used appraisal scores to determine which workers would be laid off; those with low performance appraisals were laid off. However, the court found that a disproportionate number of workers in protected classes were laid off. The court stated that appraisals were "tests" and subject to validation against the job duties the workers performed. Also, the court stated that Zia's appraisals were "not administered and scored under controlled and standardized conditions.[16]

Albemarle Paper v. *Moody.* In this case, the U.S. Supreme Court again held that performance appraisals were "tests" that are subject to EEOC guidelines. One important issue in this case related to performance appraisal: *subjective supervisory ratings.*

The problem of subjective supervisory ratings in appraisal is captured in the following quote from the court decision:

There is no way of knowing precisely what criteria of job performance the supervisors were considering, whether each of the supervisors was considering the same criteria—or whether, indeed, any of the supervisors actually applied a focused and stable body of criteria of any kind.[17]

U.S. v. *City of Chicago.* In this case, the courts found that the performance appraisal systems used by the Chicago Police Department discriminated against blacks and Hispanics. Also, the exams for the positions of officer and sergeant were found to be discriminatory. The court ruled that "supervisory ratings are not a fair measurement of an employee's suitability for promotion.[18] The city was also prohibited from using tests or the appraisal system and was forced to hire minorities according to a court-established quota system until nondiscriminatory instruments were developed.

Elements of A Legal Performance Appraisal System

By investigating existing case law, the elements of a performance appraisal system that can be expected to survive court tests can be determined[19]:

1. Absence of adverse impact evidence or presence of validity evidence.
2. Formal evaluation criteria that limit a manager's absolute discretion in the appraisal process.
3. Personal knowledge and contact with the person whose work is being rated.
4. A review process that prevents one manager acting alone from controlling an employee's career.

It is clear that the courts have taken an interest in seeing that performance appraisal is both fair and nondiscriminatory. Employers must decide how to design their appraisal systems to the satisfaction of the courts, enforcement agencies, and their employees.[20]

Can you list the characteristics of a legal appraisal system?

AN EFFECTIVE PERFORMANCE APPRAISAL
SYSTEM

Regardless of which performance appraisal method is used, an understanding of what an appraisal is supposed to do is what makes or breaks the system.[21] When performance appraisal is used to develop the employee as a resource, it usually works. When management uses it as a whip or fails to understand its limitations, it fails. The key is not which form or which method is used. Performance appraisal depends upon managers who understand its purposes. In its simplest form, performance appraisal is a manager's statement: "Here are your strengths and weaknesses, and here is a way to shore up the weak areas."[22]

Training of Appraisers

Because appraisal is important and sometimes difficult, training of appraisers is valuable. Providing managers and supervisors with some insights and ideas on rating, documenting appraisals, and conducting appraisal interviews increases the value and acceptance of an appraisal program.[23] In many organizations, managers and supervisors have had little appraisal training. Training appraisers gives them confidence in their ability to make appraisals and handle appraisal interviews. Familiarity with common rating errors can improve rater performance as well.

Performance appraisal and training share many common elements.[24] It has been suggested that the training section of personnel departments may be uniquely suited to overseeing performance appraisal in large organizations.[25] It has also been suggested that rating the raters may be a way to reduce systematic bias among raters. Successful programs to do so have been developed at R. J. Reynolds, Nestle, and Florida Power and Light.[26]

Beware "The Number"

There is a nagging tendency to distill the performance appraisal system to a single number that can be used to support pay raises.[27] Systems based on this concept are geared to reducing the complexity of each indivdual's contribution to a single number. This orientation often is designed to satisfy compensation system requirements, rather than to give employees feedback or pinpoint training and development needs. In fact, a single rating is a barrier to useful performance discussions since the emphasis is on attaching a "label" to a person's performance and defending or attacking that label. Effective performance appraisal systems recognize that human behaviors and capabilities cannot be meaningfully collapsed into a single score.[28]

Can you describe at lease two characteristics of an effective performance appraisal system?

CHAPTER 12 APPRAISAL OF HUMAN RESOURCES

PERSONNEL TODAY AND TOMORROW
GRADING TEACHERS

Concern with the quality of American public education has focused in recent years on the performance of classroom teachers. Government officials and others have argued that a performance appraisal system for teachers could help identify those who are not performing up to standards. After all, the performance appraisal system has been used in business and industry for years. A report card for the teachers might be a first step in improving instruction in public schools.

Teaching, however, presents some special problems for appraisal. Performance standards obviously should be set either in terms of changes in the pupils' abilities or in terms of teacher behaviors that can be clearly linked by research to learning. Emphasizing such items as how well the teacher gets along with students or the appearance of the room is beside the point. In fact, the idea that there is a single best method of teaching may prevent an unbiased evaluation of just how good a teacher may be.

When (or if) proper criteria for teacher evaluation are identified and used, they will become targets for teaching activity. Yet, discovering those criteria is not easy. Witness one study of 60 Georgia teachers. Trained observers visited their classes for 2 years and reported on how well the teachers did on 25 abilities often measured in teacher competency tests. When the results were formulated, it became clear that not much was clear. About half of the measures had no relationship to either student achievement scores or student self-esteem (the dependent variables used in the study.) Skills such as using praise, responding to student questions, and giving students a voice in decision-making actually were negatively related to academic achievement. Use of supportive classroom techniques also was negatively related to self-esteem. This is only one study, but the mixed or negative support given to factors thought to be related to good teaching suggests that those who wish to formulate teaching appraisal standards should proceed with caution.

Steen Kellman, a professor at the University of Texas at San Antonio, describes his concerns with ranking something that may or may not be rankable. He notes that we already rank everything from football teams and restaurants to popular tunes and congressmen. And, the movie "10" dramatizes a practice of people-ranking that is probably more common than most men and women are willing to concede.

Clearly, teacher evaluation at any level is neither easy nor noncontroversial. For performance appraisal to be properly applied to this kind of endeavor will require a major advancement in the technology of appraisal, as well as common sense in the use of any resulting "measuring stick."[29]

SUMMARY

■ Appraising employee performance is useful for compensation, placement, and training/development purposes.

■ Performance appraisal can be done either informally or systematically. If done systematically, appraisals usually are done annually.

■ Appraisals can be done by superiors, subordinates, peers, or a combination of raters.

■ Superiors' ratings of subordinates are most frequently used.

■ Four types of appraisal methods are available: category ratings, comparative ratings, written appraisals, and special rating methods.

■ Category rating methods, especially graphic rating scales, are the most widely used methods. Checklists and forced choice instruments are others.

■ Ranking, paired comparison, and forced distribution are all comparative methods.

■ Written methods of appraisal include the critical incident technique, essay approach, and a field review.

■ BARS (Behaviorally Anchored Ratings Scales) and MBO (Management By Objectives) are two special methods of appraisal that are widely used.

■ Construction of a BARS requires a detailed job analysis; the rating criteria and anchors must be job-specific.

■ MBO is an approach that requires joint goal-setting between a superior and a subordinate.

■ Several performance appraisal problems are: varying standards, rater bias, rater patterns, leniency, and the halo effect.

■ The appraisal feedback interview is a vital part of any appraisal system.

■ Both managers and employees may react to appraisals by exhibiting signs of resistance.

■ Federal employment guidelines and numerous court decisions have scrutinized performance appraisals. Subjectivity and the absence of specific job-relatedness can create legal problems.

■ Training of appraisers and guarding against "number magic" are important to an effective appraisal system.

REVIEW QUESTIONS AND EXERCISES

1. What are the three major uses that can be made of appraisals?
2. Identify the advantages and disadvantages of using different rater approaches.
3. What are three methods of appraisal? Which method would you prefer as an employee? As a manager? Why?
4. Suppose you are a supervisor. What errors might you make when doing an employee's performance appraisal?
5. Describe how to prepare a BARS for a payroll clerk.
6. Identify MBO and some problems associated with it.

7. Construct a plan for a post-appraisal interview with an employee who has performed poorly.

8. Discuss the following statement: "Most performance appraisal systems in use today would not pass legal scrutiny."

9. Why is training of appraisers so vital to an effective performance appraisal system?

Exercises

a. Use the appraisal form in Figure 12–5 and appraise your performance on your current job. What problems did you have completing it? How do you think your rating would compare to an appraisal of you by your current boss?

b. Contact a local employer or your current employer and obtain a blank performance appraisal form. Then critique it in terms of its legality.

CASE

CONGRATULATIONS, AND WELCOME BACK!

Janet Janousek joined the Customer Information section of a large manufacturing company as a secretary in December 1983. Janet's transfer to Customer Information came after a previous transfer from the Market Analysis section to the Sales Department in an attempt to improve her performance.

On November 1, 1985, Janet was given a performance appraisal. The appraisal followed counseling sessions on July 3, 1985, July 30, 1985, and September 15, 1985. The November appraisal indicated that Janet appeared to be making improvements in her job performance; however, her performance again deteriorated, as noted by her performance appraisal in January, 1986.

Her supervisor felt that Janet's poor performance was related to her personal affairs, and led to a number of activities felt to be incompatible with the efficient and effective operation of the office. Such activities occurred as: spending an inordinate amount of time making personal telephone calls; appearing preoccupied with her personal problems; and frequently reporting to work in a very tired state.

The supervisor felt that Janet possessed positive attributes. Her education and skills were well-matched to her secretarial duties, and she worked quickly when the task was clearly stenographic. The supervisor also observed that Janet's poor performance may have been a result of her pregnancy.

It was clear to the supervisor that Janet's problems at work were related to her personal affairs and that she did not have the ability to adapt rapidly to "uncertain environments" in which resourcefulness and initiative were required. On March 4, 1986, Janet left the company on a maternity leave of absence. The supervisor has just received word that Janet gave birth to a 7 pound, 6 ounce baby boy, and wants to return to work in 6 weeks.

Questions

1. Describe the performance appraisal problems that exist.
2. In what ways does the fact that the employee is a woman and pregnant affect the appraisal and the supervisor's choice of action?
3. As the supervisor, what would you do?

NOTES

1. Adapted from B. S. Moskal, "Employee Ratings: Objective or Objectional?" *Industry Week*, February 8, 1982, p. 51.
2. "HRM Update," *Personnel Administrator*, June 1983, p. 16.
3. M. K. Mount, "Comparison of Managerial and Employee Satisfaction with a Performance Appraisal System," *Personnel Psychology* 36 (1983), pp. 99–109.
4. Adapted from "Reversing Performance Review," *Psychology Today*, March 1984, p. 80.
5. M. D. Mumford, "Social Comparison Theory and the Evaluation of Peer Evaluators: A Review and Some Applied Implications," *Personnel Psychology* 36 (1983), p. 879.
6. May not be reproduced without permission; Robert L. Mathis, Omaha, Nebraska.
7. S. Pinsker, "The Written About and Those Who Write," *Business*, April–June, 1983, p. 54.
8. Adapted from R. G. Pajer, "Performance Appraisal: A New Era for Federal Government Managers," *Personnel Administrator*, March 1984, pp. 82–83.
9. For a review of BARS literature, see Gary P. Latham and Kenneth N. Wexley, *Increasing Productivity Through Performance Appraisal* (Reading, MA: Addison-Wesley, 1981), pp. 51–64.
10. W. H. Mobley, "Supervisor and Employee Race and Sex Effect on Performance Appraisals," *Academy of Management Journal* 25 (1982), pp. 598–606.
11. For a review of research, see Douglas Cederblom, "The Performance Appraisal Interview: A Review, Implications, and Suggestions," *Academy of Management Review* 7 (1982), pp. 219–227.
12. B. S. Moskal, "Employee Ratings: Objective or Objectionable?" *Industry Week*, February 8, 1982, p. 51.
13. "HRM Update," p. 16
14. A. S. Grove, "Performance Appraisal: Manager as Judge and Jury," *Research Management*, November–December 1983, p. 32.
15. M. H. Schuster and C. B. Miller, "Performance Appraisal and the Age Discrimination in Employment Act," *Personnel Administrator*, March 1984, p. 57.
16. *Brito* v. *Zia Company*, 478 F2d. 1200 (1973).
17. *Albermarle Paper Co.* v. *Moody*, 74–389 (1975).
18. *U.S.* v. *City of Chicago*, 549 F2d 415 (1977) *Cert. denied* 434 US 875 (1977).
19. P. Linnenberger and T. J. Keaveny, "Performance Appraisal: Standards Used by the Courts," *Faculty Research Paper* (Univ. of Wyoming) no. 317, January 1980, p. 9.
20. H. S. Feild and W. H. Holley, "The Relationship of the Performance Appraisal System Characteristics to Verdicts in Selected Employment Discrimination Cases," *Academy of Management Journal* 25 (1982), pp. 392–406.

21. R. B. McAfee, "Using Performance Appraisals to Enhance Training Programs," *Personnel Administrator*, November 1982, p. 31.

22. P. J. McGuire, "Why Performance Appraisals Fail," *Personnel Journal* 59 (September 1980), p. 745.

23. Mark Edwards and Leonard Goldstein, "Experiential Learning Can Improve the Performance Appraisal Process," *Human Resource Management*, Spring 1982, pp. 18–23.

24. M. A. Von Glinon et al., "The Design of a Career-Oriented Human Resources System," *Academy of Management Review* 8 (1982), p. 23.

25. R. B. McAfee, "Performance Appraisal: Whose Function?" *Personnel Journal* 60 (April 1981), p. 298.

26. M. R. Edwards and J. R. Sproull, "Rating the Raters Improves Performance Appraisal," *Personnel Administrator*, August 1983, p. 82.

27. R. L. Heneman and K. N. Wexley, "The Effects of Time Delay in Rating and Amount of Information Observed on Performance Rating Accuracy," *Academy of Management Journal* 26 (1983), pp. 677–686.

28. D. B. Gehrman, "Beyond Today's Compensation and Performance Appraisal Systems," *Personnel Administrator*, March 1984, p. 22.

29. "How Do You Grade Teachers?" *Science News*, February 14, 1981, p. 119; and S. G. Kellman, "Confession of a Rank Amateur," *Newsweek*, May 24, 1982, p. 19.

"HEY, BUDDY, CAN YOU SPARE $95?"*

John Whitney, division director in a government agency, has been confronted with a thorny personnel issue. His Director of Administration, Cathy Cummings and her deputy, Ron D'Angelo are arguing over how best to handle a deteriorating situation involving one of their administrative specialists. Both are now appealing to Whitney for support and guidance. For Whitney, the situation is unusually complicated because it entails not only a personnel issue but also chain of authority and racial considerations. Moreover, if the problem is not resolved quickly it will damage the division's morale and effectiveness.

The focal point of the disagreement is Sam Crandall, a career administrative specialist with approximately 15 years of government service. Although he has considerable tenure, Crandall has not progressed as rapidly as most of his peers. In discussions with supervisors and subordinates, he likes to represent himself as the experienced "old hand," but his general performance does not always match his words. In fact, for a person with his length of service, Crandall's overall performance is below average.

In his first three years in the division, Crandall worked in the Technical Branch. During the last two years there have been disagreements—both personal and professional—between Crandall and his supervisor. In the beginning, Crandall's work generally met standards although he had a tendency to procrastinate and he generally required more supervision than other employees. Then he began to have money problems. At one point, his creditors approached his supervisor seeking help in collecting overdue debts. (The policy of the agency for which Crandall works is not to act as a collection service, but it does expect its people to be financially responsible.) In this case, Crandall was counseled about his obligations, but his supervisor did not formally document the incident because he did not want to be the one to put a "black mark" on Crandall's record.

By the third year, the disagreements between Crandall and his supervisor were becoming more frequent and severe. Crandall resented the counseling sessions and responded by arguing that his supervisor was "too young" and that he didn't understand the branch well enough to really appreciate how much work he was doing. There were also some subtle hints that Crandall felt he was being discriminated against because he was black. He was also heard to complain that he was being denied the supervisory experience he needed for promotion. Finally, at the request of both Crandall and the branch chief, John Whitney transferred Crandall to the Administrative Branch. In doing so, he made it clear that he wanted to end the friction between Crandall and his supervisor. He also told Crandall that this was his chance for a fresh start and that he would be given a chance to acquire the supervisory experience he needed and wanted.

About three months after Crandall's transfer to the Administrative Branch, problems began to surface. In one way or another, all of the problems involved Crandall. Because of his seniority, he had been made supervisor of three junior clerks. However, his professional and personal relations with his subordinates left much to be desired. All three clerks were new to the agency and were considered bright, well-motivated, and definitely well worth retaining. All were eager to learn as much as possible about their Branch responsibilities and about their new career fields. Unfortunately, Crandall did little to help them; his "management" style was simply to pass along the work that needed to be done, but he would not (or could not) provide much guidance when questions arose. When one of the clerks received an early promotion for exceptional performance, Crandall appeared to resent it and relations between the two cooled perceptibly. To make matters worse, Crandall began borrowing from his co-workers and subordinates. At first, the borrowing was limited to relatively small items, such as cigarettes and lunch money. But he rarely

*Reprinted with permission of Robert F. Colwell and Kathleen C. Brannen, PhD. Creighton University.

repaid what he borrowed. The problem came to a head when he borrowed $95 from Mike Rogers, one of his young clerks, with the understanding that it would be repaid at the end of the week. Friday came and went, and nothing happened. On Monday, Rogers asked for his money, and Crandall rebuffed him, saying, "You didn't ask for it on Friday, so I spent it. See me at the end of the month."

Crandall's action put a considerable burden on Rogers, who complained to his fellow workers but would not make a formal complaint. Instead, he and several clerks pressed Crandall to repay the money, which he finally did. When Crandall attempted to continue his borrowing habits, his subordinates resisted. Again, no one would formally complain, but it was soon an "open secret" that Crandall was trying to use his position to get loans. There were also rumors of heated closed-door sessions in which Crandall allegedly threatened unspecified reprisals if anyone complained to management.

At this point, several workers began talking about leaving the agency, and the depth of the problem (but not all the details) became apparent to management. Unfortunately, the first-echelon supervisor, Ron D'Angelo, and the Director of Administration, Cathy Cummings, disagreed on how to handle the situation. D'Angelo was sympathetic and held that Crandall's behavior was the result of a lack of prior supervisory experience. He had several informal "chats" with Crandall, but was reluctant to take formal action. Instead, he believed that the best thing to do was to simply give Crandall more time to "learn the ropes." Cummings, a strong performer with considerable administrative and supervisory experience, disagreed. She was worried about the decline in morale in administration and about Crandall's borrowing habits. (For obvious reasons, the agency discouraged borrowing from subordinates.) She thus pressured D'Angelo to formally counsel Crandall, arguing that it was necessary to develop a record of his unsatisfactory performance in case more drastic action become necessary. D'Angelo flatly refused. He did not want to put anything on paper that might damage Crandall's career. He also accused Cummings of trying to "micromanage" *his* section and threatened to take early retirement. Both sides then started coming to John Whitney for support of their opinions and actions.

For Whitney, this was almost a "no-win" situation. Two of his best managers were in open disagreement and if he directly intervened he risked alienating or, in D'Angelo's case, losing

a valued asset. Moreover, the issue had become common knowledge in the division and many of the younger workers were watching to see what action, if any, would be taken against Crandall. For his part, Crandall was sending a variety of informal signals indicating that any attempt to discipline him would be regarded as racially motivated and that he was "ready to tell it all" (whatever that meant) to the Social Actions Department. The subtle threats did not bother Whitney as much as the lack of documentation on the whole affair. Legislation of the last decade or so had provided a variety of new recourses to employees with real—or perceived—grievances, and Whitney realized that he could not fire Crandall without submitting to a lengthy review process. He also realized that his chances of success in such a process were slim at best since there was little documentation of Crandall's earlier problems upon which to base his case. Likewise, he could not transfer Crandall. His prior job in the technical branch had been filled by an extremely capable individual, and there were no other suitable openings within the agency. Transfer to another agency was also out of the question because of Crandall's prior below-average performance evaluations. (The evaluations were enough to make other agencies wary of a transfer, but were definitely not enough to justify removal for cause.) Moreover, Whitney was not inclined to pass his problems along to someone else. He also realized that further delay was unwise, failure to begin treating the problem in administration would only exacerbate a situation that was already threatening a division that had always enjoyed a deserved reputation for effectiveness and high morale. The problem was deciding exactly how and where to begin the treatment.

QUESTIONS

1. How does intervention into an individual's personal life and its relationship to performance play a part in this case?
2. To what extent have organizational deficiencies in training and career development made the problems in the agency more severe? Be specific.
3. What problems can you identify with the performance appraisal process used in the agency?
4. If you were Whitney, what steps would you take to defuse the current problems, as well as prevent future ones of a similar nature?

COMPENSATING HUMAN RESOURCES

One major reason for appraising an employee's performance is to reward those who do more work with more compensation. To provide themselves with the necessities of life, most people "sell" their services to organizations for money. Pay usually means more to people than just legal tender. It can be a reward or a status symbol. But, it is still compensation for effort. People want to be compensated fairly and are concerned about equity—fair treatment in pay.

Equitable pay can be determined in a number of ways. Effective organizations use well-designed personnel systems, such as job evaluation, to see that employees are paid fairly. Systems to evaluate the worth of jobs are discussed in Chapter 13, which also includes a discussion of the legal constraints on compensation practices.

People are not only paid in money. Incentives and executive "perks" are also forms of compensation. Different kinds of incentives can be designed to achieve a variety of results. Some incentive systems and details on executive compensation systems are discussed in Chapter 14.

Chapter 15 discusses a major expense item for firms—Employee Benefits. Benefits are varied, ranging from the company bowling team to retirement and health insurance plans. Health care cost containment has become a major concern for most employers recently. Flexible benefits are another current approach, which allows employees more benefits for the dollars spent.

Now that benefits average about 37 percent of the payroll dollar, both employees and managers are concerned that benefit programs be well-designed and that benefits be distributed equitably. Chapter 15 also provides details on this important area of personnel management.

Compensating Jobs and Work

When you have read this chapter, you should be able to:

1. Define three types of compensation.
2. Discuss three compensation considerations.
3. Identify the basic provisions of the Fair Labor Standards Act.
4. Briefly explain three federal laws that can affect compensation practices.
5. Identify three meanings of compensation.
6. Differentiate between pay secrecy and pay openness.
7. Define job evaluation and discuss four methods of performing it.
8. Outline the process of building a wage/salary administration system.

PERSONNEL AT WORK
EQUITABLE COMPENSATION

Equitable Federal Savings and Loan is headquartered in Fremont, Nebraska, a town of approximately 20–25,000 people. With assets of approximately $250 million and 85 employees, Equitable also has branches in some smaller farming communities around Fremont.

Until 1981, Equitable had been operating with a compensation system that had been devised by its accounting firm several years earlier. However, because of growth and changes within the firm, William H. DeForest, the personnel manager, felt it was time for a complete review of the firm's base compensation program. The review became even more important as Equitable, like many other savings and loans, faced earnings declines and losses due to a combination of economic factors, high interest rates, and the deregulation of the industry begun in 1980.

To begin the project DeForest contacted a professional acquaintance with expertise in compensation who had assisted other financial institutions in similar projects as a consultant. After an initial meeting with the consultant, DeForest undertook a detailed reviewed all of the firm's job descriptions. Some changes were identified in the loan operations area and revised descriptions were written by DeForest.

The next stage of the project was a comparison of Equitable's existing pay structure to that of other employers in the area and in the industry. A job evaluation committee, composed of several executives, a supervisor in the accounting area, DeForest, and the consultant, was formed. Using a job evaluation point system, the committee individually assigned points to all jobs in the organization on such factors as knowledge required, experience required, supervision given and received, interpersonal contacts, and working conditions. Then the committee met several times, compared points assigned for each job, discussed each job, and reached a point total consensus for each job.

Using all of this data the consultant constructed a recommended pay structure containing about 20 separate pay grades and the minimum and maximum pay for each range. Based upon the job evaluation points assigned, all jobs were placed into the appropriate grades. Then the pay for all employees was reviewed to determine to what extent employees were being paid below, within, or above the recommended pay ranges. With only a few exceptions, all employees' pay fell within the new ranges. A decision was made to address those situations when the next pay raises were given.

From that point on, all managers and supervisors completed performance appraisals on their employees on their anniversary dates in their jobs. Using the appraisal information employees were given pay adjustments in line with what the executives at Equitable determined to be affordable at the time. Fortunately, Equitable has continued to administer its base compensation program in a fair and effective manner during the succeeding years.

Used with permission.

"Let's do what we did in the Senate the other day. We found that all Senators have merit, and we increased their pay."

Sen. ERNEST HOLLINGS

PAY
is the basic compensation employees receive, usually as a wage or salary.

INCENTIVES
are rewards designed to encourage and reimburse employees for efforts beyond normal performance expectations.

BENEFITS
are rewards available to an employee or group of employees as a part of organizational membership.

Establishing and maintaining a pay system in a firm such as Equitable represents only one aspect involved in putting together a compensation package. As the description of the process at Equitable illustrates, some specialized activities are needed to insure that payroll expenditures are made in a sound and effective manner. This chapter discusses the compensation process and the base pay that employees receive. Because incentives and benefits are special types of compensation, they are discussed in separate chapters that follow.

TYPES OF COMPENSATION

Formal compensation can be offered using three types of rewards. **Pay** refers to the base wages and salaries employees receive. Compensation forms such as bonuses, commissions, and profit-sharing plans are **incentives** designed to encourage employees to produce results beyond normal expectations. Health insurance, vacation pay, or retirement pensions are examples of **benefits,** which represent a more indirect type of compensation.

Compensation costs are very significant expenditures in most firms. At one large hotel, employee payroll and benefits expenditures compose about 50 percent of all costs of doing business. Many retail chains have payroll expenditures that amount to 8–10 percent of sales. Although compensation costs are relatively easy to calculate, the value derived by employers and employees is much more difficult to identify.

Compensation Responsibilities

A typical division of compensation responsibilities is illustrated in Figure 13–1. Personnel specialists usually guide the overall development and administration of an organizational compensation system by conducting job evaluations and wage surveys. Also, because of the technical complexity involved, personnel specialists typically are the ones who develop the wage and salary structures and policies. On the other hand, operating managers try to match employees' efforts with rewards by using guidelines provided by the personnel unit when recommending pay rates and pay increases. Much managerial activity goes into monitoring employee attendance and productivity. Because time and/or productivity are the bases for compensation, this monitoring is a vital part of any manager's job.

Can you define three types of compensation?

CHAPTER 13 COMPENSATING JOBS AND WORK

FIGURE 13–1
Compensation Responsibilities.

PERSONNEL UNIT	MANAGERS
■ Develops and administers compensation system ■ Conducts job evaluation and wage survey ■ Develops wage/salary structures and policies	■ Attempt to match performance and rewards ■ Recommend pay rates and pay increases, based upon guidelines from personnel unit ■ Monitor attendance and productivity for compensation purposes

WAGES
are pay directly calculated on the amount of time worked.

SALARY
is compensation that is consistent from period to period and is not directly related to the number of hours worked.

COMPENSATION CONSIDERATIONS

Planning, implementation, and maintenance of a coordinated compensation system requires that several factors be considered. These factors are grouped into the following areas:

- Compensation bases
- Unions and compensation
- External forces

- Behavioral aspects
- Legal considerations
- Administration

Compensation Bases

Several forms of compensation are available to managers and employees in an overall remuneration program. There are three bases for compensation: *time, productivity,* and a *combination* of time and productivity.

Time. Employees may be paid for the amount of time they are on the job. The two pay classes in many organizations are identified according to the way pay is distributed and the nature of the jobs. The classifications are: (1) *hourly* and (2) *salaried.*

The most common means of payment based on time is *hourly* pay; employees paid hourly are said to receive wages. **Wages** are pay directly calculated on the amount of time worked. Hourly employees are paid overtime in most cases because they are not exempt from the overtime provisions of the Fair Labor Standards Act (discussed later in this chapter.) To compute this type of pay, the number of hours an individual works is multiplied by the wage rate to determine gross pay, with overtime usually being computed at 1½ times the regular rate of pay.

Salary is another means of paying people for the time worked. Being on salary typically has carried higher status for employees than being paid wages. Salary is payment that is consistent from period to period and is not directly related to the number of hours worked by the individual.

A fairly recent development is for some manufacturing and clerical personnel traditionally paid on an hourly basis to be paid on a salary. Several corporations have used an all-salaried approach in some plants with success. The reason for this switch is to create a sense of loyalty and organizational commitment among employees. Putting blue-collar workers on salary is a drastic change from historical patterns of pay.

Productivity. Another basis for compensation is to tie pay to productivity. Commissions set as a percentage of sales are a common example of pay based on productivity. Another productivity-based means is a "piece-rate" system. An employee who works in an electronics plant packaging radios is paid on the basis of how many she packages. If the employee is paid 50 cents for each radio packaged and is expected to package 80 radios a day, she will earn $40 per day. Employees who want to earn more can produce more units or work at a faster pace.

A productivity-based pay system should be developed with caution so that quality, as well as quantity, is encouraged. For example, paying the radio packager only on the basis of quantity might lead to some radios being carelessly packed, thus sacrificing quality. Another possible drawback to a piece-rate system is that a productivity compensation rate must be determined for each specific job. These rates can be determined through motion and time studies.

Other methods of piece-rate pay have been developed at various times. "Modified" piece-rate plans offer workers the opportunity to receive higher pay for units produced above a quota. For example, since the radio packager's standard is to package 80 radios per day, the employee might be paid 10¢ extra for each radio packaged above the standard.

Combination Methods. Employees also can be paid by combining time methods with productivity methods. The base pay plus commission arrangements for sales representatives are familiar combinations used by many firms. Sally Jones is a sales representative for a consumer products company that manufactures cosmetics. She is paid $1,000 a month plus 1 percent of the dollar value of all merchandise she sells. Combining a salary with a productivity reward is a way of motivating Jones to sell more, while also recognizing that some continuity of income is necessary. Executive level managers typically receive a salary plus some type of bonus plan for sales, production, or profitability. These combination systems will be examined in more detail in the next chapter on incentives.

Compensation and Task Structure

The type of task done should be matched with the type of compensation appropriate for it. Individuals paid on an hourly basis, such as production workers or clerical workers, typically have more routine and shorter job cycles than do white-collar professionals do. If the task is such that individual productivity can be determined, a piece-rate or incentive type of system can be utilized.

Unions and Compensation

A major variable affecting the compensation systems used by an employer is whether or not any of the employees are represented by a labor union. In nonunion firms employers have significantly more flexibility in determining pay levels and pay policies. Unionized employees typically have their pay set according to the terms of a collective bargaining contract between their employers and the unions that represent the employees.

According to the U.S. Bureau of Labor Statistics, employers having unionized employees generally have higher wage levels than nonunion employers. The strength and extent of unionization in an industry and in a firm also affect wage levels. Firms in heavily unionized industries with highly unionized workforces generally have higher wage levels.

Unionized employees frequently have pay rates tied to a negotiated contract containing *cost of living adjustment* (COLA) provisions. The COLA provisions frequently are tied to general economic indicators such as the Consumer Price Index (CPI) or Personal Consumption Expenditures (PCE) data, so that as those indicators rise, the pay of employees rises also.

Another factor present in many unionized situations is the emphasis placed on *seniority* as a basis for making compensation decisions. Specific pay rates for specific jobs are established in many union contracts, and pay increases are based on how long an employee has worked on a job in the organization.

All of these factors together significantly affect the way compensation is administered in a unionized work force. Because of the higher wage levels and restrictions on management discretion that occur when unions represent employees, most employers resist unionization efforts.

External Forces

Employers also must consider several other external factors that affect the compensation offered to employees. One of the most obvious is what the employer can afford to pay. For example, as seen in the introductory description of Equitable Federal Savings and Loan, the economic difficulties faced by Equitable and other savings and loans in the early 1980s limited their ability to compensate their employees.

Another concern is the compensation offered by competing employers, especially those in the same industry and/or the same geographic area. For example, a number of midwestern meat packers have had to close down or request pay reductions from their employees in order to compete with lower-cost competition. Likewise, airlines such as Eastern and TWA have had to obtain pay concessions from their employees in order to compete with cost-cutting airlines like People Express and New York Air.

Wage rates vary from one city to another and from one region to another. As would be expected, wage rates vary by city size, with wages being higher, in larger cities, although other factors may alter this relationship.[1] Large employers with multiple locations throughout the U.S. and in other countries also must address whether or not to offer "area differentials" based on varying standards of living.

The supply of qualified employees is another consideration faced by employers. Plentiful supply or restricted availability of certain skills may force changes in compensation practices. One example of the impact of the labor market is the current shortage of labor in some computer-related specialities. Hiring bonuses and higher pay than what would normally be given are common devices used by employers trying to attract and retain computer-oriented employees.

In addition to all of these external forces, employers must comply with several laws that specifically focus on compensation. The major ones are highlighted next.

Can you discuss three compensation considerations?

LEGAL CONSTRAINTS ON PAY SYSTEMS

Another consideration that managers must face when designing base pay systems is the myriad of governmental constraints on pay practices. Minimum wage standards and hours of work are two important areas that are addressed by the laws discussed next.

Fair Labor Standards Act of 1938

The major law affecting compensation is the Fair Labor Standards Act of 1938 (FLSA) and its amendments. This act has three major objectives: (1) to establish a minimum-wage floor, (2) to encourage limits on the number of weekly hours employees work through overtime provisions, and (3) to discourage oppressive use of child labor. The first two objectives are the most relevant to this chapter.

Minimum Wage. The FLSA sets a minimum wage to be paid to a broad spectrum of employees. In 1966, the FLSA was amended to update the act and to include more employees and industries. Currently, most organizations and employees are covered, with the exception of state and local governmental entities. The basic minimum wage, beginning January 1, 1981, was set at $3.35 per hour.

Overtime. The FLSA also contains overtime pay requirements. Still in effect under the 1938 version are provisions setting overtime pay at 1½ times the regular pay rate for all hours in excess of 40 hours per week, except for employees who are exempt from coverage under the law.

The workweek is defined as a consecutive period of 168 hours (24 hours *x* 7 days) and does not have to be a calendar week. Hospitals are allowed to use a 14-day period instead of a 7-day week as long as overtime is paid for hours worked beyond 80-hours in a 14-day period. Overtime provisions do not apply to farm workers, who also have a lower minimum wage schedule. No daily number of hours requiring overtime is set, except for special provisions relating to hospitals and other specially-designated organizations. Thus, if a manufacturing firm has a 4-day/10-hour schedule, no overtime pay is required by the act.

Exempt and Nonexempt Status. Under the FLSA employees are classified as exempt or nonexempt. **Exempt employees** are those who hold positions identified as *executive, administrative, professional,* or *outside sales* according to the FLSA.[2] Employers are not required to pay overtime to these employees.

Three major factors are considered in determining whether or not an individual holds an exempt position. They are:

■ Discretionary authority for independent action
■ Percentage of time spent performing routine, manual, or clerical work
■ Earnings level

Figure 13–2 shows the impact of these factors on each type of exemption. Under provisions of the FLSA, jobs can be categorized in three groupings:

■ Hourly
■ Salaried nonexempt
■ Salaried exempt

Hourly jobs are those that typically require employers to pay overtime and comply with the FLSA. Each salaried position must be identified as *salaried exempt* or *salaried nonexempt.* Employees in positions classified as salaried nonexempt are covered by the overtime provisions of the FLSA, and therefore must be paid overtime. Typical salaried nonexempt positions would include secretarial, clerical, or salaried blue-collar positions. Figure 13–3 illustrates calculations of overtime for a salaried nonexempt employee.

Individuals holding salaried-exempt positions are exempt from the FLSA overtime provisions and are not required by law to receive overtime payment. Salaried-exempt positions include executive, administrative, professional, and outside sales positions.

Enforcement. Compliance with the provisions of the FLSA is enforced by the Wage and Hour Division, a part of the U.S. Department of Labor. To meet its requirements, employers are required to keep accurate time records and maintain these records for several years. Inspectors from the Wage and Hour Division investigate complaints based upon industries in which violations are common, such as the restaurant industry, or in response to employee complaints. If individuals believe they have not received the overtime payments due them, they may file complaints with the Wage and Hour Division and be protected from reprisal by their employers. Penalties for wage and hour violations often include awards of back pay for affected current and former employees up to two years. One small service station had to pay over $5,000 because the employer had not paid overtime to two employees who were labeled as "night managers," but spent most of their time pumping gas and doing minor auto repair jobs. The experience of Hudson Oil shows that violations can be costly.

EXEMPTION CATEGORY	A DISCRETIONARY AUTHORITY	B % OF TIME	C EARNINGS LEVELS
Executive	1. Primary duty is managing 2. Regularly directs work of at least two others 3. Authority to hire/fire or recommend these	1. Must spend 20% or less time doing clerical, manual, routine work (less than 40% retail or service establishments)	1. Paid salary at $155/wk or 250/wk if meets AI–A2
Administrative	1. Responsible nonmanual or office work related to management policies 2. Regularly exercises discretion and independent judgment and makes important decisions 3. Regularly assists executives and works under general supervision	1. Must spend 20% or less time doing clerical, manual, routine work (less than 40% retail or service establishments)	1. Paid salary at $155/wk or 250/wk if meets A1–A2
Professional	1. Performs work requiring knowledge of an advanced field *or* creative and original artistic work *or* works as teacher in educational system 2. Must do work that is predominantly intellectual and varied.	1. Must spend less than 20% of time doing nonprofessional work	1. Paid salary at least $170/wk or $250/wk if meets A1
Outside Sales	1. Customarily works away from employer site *and* 2. Sells tangible or intangible items *or* 3. Obtains orders or contracts for services	1. Must spend 20% or less time doing work other than outside selling	1. No salary test

Note: Different salary levels exist for Puerto Rico, Virgin Islands, and America Samoa. For more details see *Executive, Administrative, Professional, and Outside Sales Exemptions Under the Fair Labor Standards Act,* WH Publication no. 1363 (Washington DC: U.S. Department of Labor, Employment Standards Administration, Wage and Hour Division, 1980).

Equal Pay Act of 1963

Another piece of legislation that was passed as a major amendment to the FLSA in 1963 is the Equal Pay Act. The original act and subsequent amendments focus on wage discrimination on the basis of sex. The act applies to both men and women and prohibits paying different wages to men and women performing substantially the same jobs. Except for differences justifiable on the basis of merit (better performance) or seniority (longer service), similar pay must be given for jobs requiring equal skills, equal effort, equal responsibility, or jobs done under similar working conditions.

FIGURE 13–2

Wage/Hour Status Under Fair Labor Standards Act.

PERSONNEL IN PRACTICE

PAY UP, HUDSON OIL!

Kansas City–based Hudson Oil and its subsidiaries had to make a large back pay settlement as a result of violations of federal wage and hour laws. Over 30,000 present and past employees of Hudson Oil split approximately $9–10 million in back pay. Employees who worked for Hudson Oil between 1974 and 1981 were affected. The repayment is the largest one ever required both in terms of dollars and of the number of individuals affected.

Hudson Oil and its subsidiaries were found guilty of violating the Fair Labor Standards Act of 1938. The firm had not kept adequate records of employee hours worked and had not paid employees minimum wages and overtime as required by the act.[3]

Most of the equal pay cases decided in court have been situations in which women were paid less than men for doing similar work, even though different job titles were used. For example, a manufacturing company employed both male and female analytical chemists in the quality control department. Because the firm was paying the female a lower salary, an attempt was made to change the title of the male chemist and slightly alter his duties. However, the court decided that when equal pay provisions are violated, compliance must be achieved by raising the pay of the lower-paid employee.[4]

The more difficult issue to be addressed is *comparable worth,* which concerns jobs that are dissimilar, but may be comparable in terms of required knowledge, skills, and abilities. Comparable worth was discussed in detail in Chapters 4 and 5.

Can you identify the basic provisions of the Fair Labor Standards Act?

Walsh-Healey Act of 1936

Many of the provisions of the Walsh-Healey Act of 1936 were incorporated into the FLSA passed two years later. However, the Walsh-

FIGURE 13–3
Computing Salaried Nonexempt Overtime Pay.

Helen Gibson, a keypunch operator, receives $180/week.
$180 ÷ 40 hrs per week = $4.50/hour
Assume she works 44 hours; she is due 4 hours of overtime
Overtime rate (1½ × $4.50) = $6.75
Total pay = 40 hours × $4.50 = $180
4 hours × $6.75 = 27
Helen's gross pay for the week $207

Healey Act requires companies with *federal supply contracts* exceeding $10,000 to pay a prevailing minimum wage. This act applies only to those working directly on the contract or who substantially affect its performance. For example, if a company has a contract to supply shoes to the Army, those employees directly involved in making and supplying the shoes have to be paid a minimum wage. Executive, administrative, and maintenance employees are not covered by the act.

A difference between the Walsh-Healey Act and the FLSA is that the Walsh-Healey provisions require overtime payment for hours over eight per day or 40 per week, but the FLSA requires overtime pay only for those over 40 per week and includes no clause about the number of daily hours. As Figure 13–4 shows, an employee working on a federal contract with a 4-day/10-hour schedule would have to be paid overtime for two hours per day under the Walsh-Healey Act, even though the weekly hours would be kept to 40 hours.

Periodic efforts are made to change the Walsh-Healey Act and bring it more in line with the FLSA. The primary change that is proposed is to remove the provision requiring overtime for employees who work more than 8 hours in a day even though they do not exceed 40 hours in a week. The different requirements force many firms to set up separate or supplemental record-keeping systems to identify who does and does not work on a supply contract. Costs associated with the separate system ultimately are added to the prices paid by the government under supply contracts. Estimates have been made that changing the Walsh-Healey Act would save considerable time and money for affected employers.

Davis-Bacon Act of 1931

Another act that has been attacked as causing higher costs on government projects is the Davis-Bacon Act of 1931. Still in force with many of the original dollar levels intact, the Davis-Bacon Act of 1931 affects compensation paid by firms engaged in federal construction projects valued in excess of $2,000. It deals only with *federal construction projects* and does not contain specific minimum wage provisions. However, it does require that the prevailing wage rate be paid on all federal construction projects.

FIGURE 13–4
Wage Calculations.

Employee: David Tomeski Regular Pay Rate: $5.00		Hours Worked: 10 hrs/day, Monday-Thursday = 40/week	
FAIR LABOR STANDARDS ACT		**WALSH–HEALEY ACT**	
Regular Pay: 40 hrs/week × $5.00		Regular Pay: 8 hrs/day × 4 days = 32 hrs	
Total Pay:	$200.00 (no overtime due)		× $5.00 $160.00
		Overtime Pay: 2 hrs/day × 4 days = 8 hrs (5.00 × 1½)	× $7.50 $60.00
		Total Pay:	$220.00

GARNISHMENT
is a court action in
which a portion of an
employee's wages is set
aside to pay a debt
owed a creditor.

Prevailing Wage Determination. Until 1984, the prevailing wage was determined by the U.S. Department of Labor by using a 30 percent rule: If there was no clear majority of workers paid one wage, then a wage was set for each job at a rate equal to the highest 30 percent of the workers surveyed in each category. Using this rule, the prevailing wage frequently was the average union rate for the local area where the construction was being done. Thus, if the average rate for carpenters in a city is $17 per hour, the carpenters building a new post office in the city were paid at least $17 per hour, whether or not they were union members.

It has been estimated that by using the 30 percent formula, the cost of federal construction projects was increased by over $600 million per year. Even the official agency charged with auditing federal government expenditures, the General Accounting Office, agreed that the prevailing wage provisions needed review and revision.[5]

As a result of these concerns, the Reagan administration proposed changing to a 50 percent rule, so that the approved rates are those paid to at least half the workers. Additional changes were made in the ways prevailing wages are calculated and some restrictions were placed on the use of "semiskilled workers." In spite of legal challenges to these changes by unions, the Supreme Court upheld the revisions.[6] While many states also have had their own versions of the Davis-Bacon provisions, many of them are being dropped.

Garnishment Laws

A **garnishment** of an employee's wages occurs when a creditor obtains a court order that directs an employer to submit a part of the employee's pay to the creditor for debts owed by the employee. Regulations passed as a part of the Consumer Credit Protection Act established limitations on the amount of wages that can be garnished and restricted the right of employers to discharge employees whose pay is subjected to a single garnishment order.[7] All 50 states also have laws that apply to wage garnishments.

State Laws

Modified versions of federal compensation laws have been enacted by many states and municipal governmental bodies. These laws tend to cover workers included in intrastate commerce not covered by federal law. If a state has a higher minimum wage than that set under the Fair Labor Standards Act, the higher figure becomes the required minimum wage.

Many states once had laws that limited the number of hours women could work. However, these laws generally have been held to be discriminatory in a variety of court cases. Consequently, most states have dropped such laws.

*Can you briefly explain three federal laws
that can affect compensation practices?*

People work to gain rewards for their efforts. Because an employee's motivation is closely related to the rewards given, the behavioral dimensions of compensation cannot be ignored by managers. When people work they expect to receive fair value (equity) for their labor. This perception of fair value is at the heart of equity theory (described in Chapter 3) and has a significant impact on the satisfaction and performance of employees. In one study, an increase in job satisfaction was linked to high job rewards and low job costs.[8] By exchanging their labor and talents for rewards, employees are induced to continue contributing to the organization.

Meaning of Compensation to Employees

The compensation employees receive is often a prime reason for working. However, it usually has several meanings to employees.

Economic. The economic meaning is the most obvious because pay serves as a way of obtaining the necessities and luxuries people need and want. For most people, employment in an organization is the way to obtain economic resources that can be exchanged for such items as food, rent or house payments, a car, clothes, furniture, vacations, and countless other goods and services. The economic allure of compensation is summed up in the following statement from an anonymous employee: "Some people are rich and some are poor—rich is better!"

Psychosocial. A second meaning of compensation is psychosocial in nature. Pay and other types of compensation provide a symbolic means of "keeping score" and a sense of achievement. If Ed Schwinn receives a raise, he may see his change in compensation as recognition of his efforts and he may derive a sense of achievement from his work. This internal satisfaction may mean more to him than what he can buy with the additional money. Conversely, the absence of adequate compensation may cause him to become discouraged or dissatisfied. Research on pay indicates that the satisfaction of psychological and social needs, such as the needs for status and recognition, are affected by the pay a person receives.[9]

Status is the social ranking of a person in relation to others. The fact that compensation acts as a status symbol is well known. As confirmed by research, people compare their base pay to determine how they "rank" in the social structure. As a measure of status, compensation gives highly rewarded individuals high social standing and importance. Because compensation can symbolize such rewards as status, pay and other forms of compensation often remain important even though the basic material needs of an employee are satisfied.[10] For example, an executive who is provided a luxury company car, such as a Mercedes Benz or a Cadillac, may consider the type of car important as a status symbol, even though a less expensive car of a different make would fulfill the executive's basic transportation needs.

This status ranking also can occur within work groups. A division manager might compare her pay to that of other employees in the division and with other division managers. She may be satisfied with her pay when comparing it to the other division managers. Or, she may feel that, based on pay, there are higher-status and lower-status division managers.

Growth. Compensation is also a means to measure growth. From the viewpoint of the organization, people are compensated for performance. Therefore, compensation can be used as one measure of how well employees have grown in their performance and capabilities.[11] Based upon expectancy theory, increased compensation can serve as a goal for which people will strive if they see that greater effort brings more compensation.[12] However, the amount and type of compensation that serves to motivate one employee to produce more may not motivate another employee.

Can you identify three meanings of compensation?

Pay Secrecy

Because comparison is such a critical part of how employees view compensation, some advocate the need to "open up" pay systems by providing more pay information to employees. Pay information that is typically kept secret in "closed" systems includes how much others make, what raises others have received, and the pay grades and ranges in the organization.

Closed Pay Systems. One reason for secret or closed pay systems is the fear that open pay systems will create discontent, petty complaining, and tension. If an accountant knows for sure that he is paid less than another accountant, he may become dissatisfied and feel he is receiving "inequitable" treatment. Also, a closed pay system does not force managers to explain and justify pay differences.

Open Pay Systems. A growing number of companies are opening up their pay systems to some degree. Information that some firms supply to employees includes compensation policies, a general description of the basis for the compensation system, and where an individual's pay is within a salary grade. The Bechtel Group tells workers their own salary grades and the ranges (minimum- to- maximum) of the grades. At two banks, BankAmerica and Seattle First National Bank, use of a policy of salary openness is said to improve morale and to address employee concerns about equity.[13] By being given pay information, employees have the information needed to make more accurate equity comparisons.

An open pay system requires that managers be able to explain satisfactorily any pay differences that exist. Consider this situation: You and a co-worker have the same education and length of service, but you feel you work harder than he does. When raises are awarded you both get exactly the same raise. Because you feel undercompensated, your manager must be able to explain why you are paid the same.

An open pay system provides the basis for discussion and accurate comparison. Research on pay secrecy has revealed that in some situations, open policies on pay are related to high motivation and performance. In other settings, open policies on pay have caused low satisfaction, low motivation, and conflict between managers and their employees.[14]

Policies that prohibit discussion of individual pay are likely to be violated anyway. Co-workers do share pay information and may feel that an open pay system recognizes this fact. Also, by having the pay system explained in the open, employers can avoid distortions and other misinformation carried by the "grapevine."

A situation in which pay openness might be appropriate involves certain types of sales representatives. Many sales representatives do have objective performance measures (such as amount of sales or number of customers contacted), they work independently, and their pay can be tied fairly closely to sales efforts. Therefore, each month sales representatives can be shown what the level of sales (and therefore commissions) of everyone in the sales group has been.

*Can you differentiate between pay secrecy
and pay openness?*

WAGE AND SALARY ADMINISTRATION is the group of activities involved in the development, implementation, and maintenance of a base pay system.

WAGE AND SALARY ADMINISTRATION

The development, implementation, and ongoing maintenance of a base pay system usually is described as **wage and salary administration.** The purpose of wage and salary administration is to provide pay that is both competitive and equitable. Underlying the activities administered are pay policies that set the overall direction of pay within the organization.

Pay Policies

Organizations must develop policies as general guidelines to govern the pay system. Uniform policies are needed for coordination, consistency, and fairness in compensating employees.

One of the policy decisions that must be made is the comparative level of pay the organization tries to maintain. Specifically, if Arrow Stores has a policy such as "paying the going rate" or "paying above area averages for similar jobs," the policy reflects Arrow's philosophy as an employer.

Another decision involves specific company policies about the relationship between pay expenditures and such factors as productivity, sales, or number of customers. In the retail industry it is common to have a policy of maintaining payroll expenditures at 8–10 percent of gross sales volume.

One policy area that has already been discussed concerns the degree of openness or secrecy on pay matters that the organization tends to allow. The example cited earlier of an all-salaried work force used by some manufacturing firms reflects another pay policy decision.

Development of a Pay System

Once pay policies have been addressed, the actual development of a pay system begins. As Figure 13–5 shows, the development of a wage and salary system assumes that accurate job descriptions are available. The job descriptions then are used in two activities: *job evaluation* and *wage/salary surveys*. These activities are designed to insure that the pay system is both internally equitable and externally competitive.[15] Then the data compiled in those two activities are used to design pay structures, including pay grades and minimum-to-maximum pay ranges. After the pay structures have been developed, individual jobs must be placed in the appropriate pay grades and employee's pay adjusted based upon length of service and performance. Finally, the pay system must be monitored and updated as needed.

Continuous Example. To aid you in understanding the development of a wage and salary system, a continuous example will be followed through all the stages involved. Assume that Danbo Manufacturing Company is a small manufacturing firm with a nonunion work force located in Arkansas. It has approximately 300 employees, including 30 clerical/office employees and 20 supervisory and management personnel. More details on Danbo will be developed through examples given in each section.

FIGURE 13–5
Development of a Pay System.

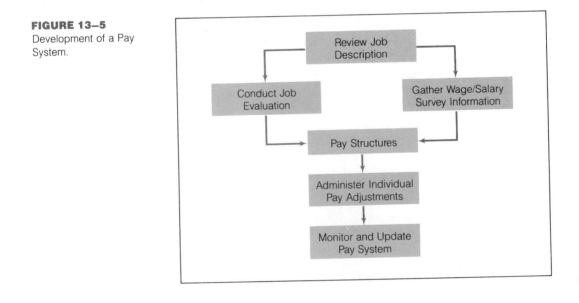

JOB EVALUATION
is the systematic deter-
mination of the relative
worth of jobs within an
organization.

Job evaluation flows from the job analysis process and uses job descriptions as its base. When doing job evaluation, the job description of
every job in an organization is examined by comparing:

- Relative importance of the job,
- Relative skills needed to perform the job
- Difficulty of one job compared to other jobs[16]

The principal aim of **job evaluation** is to provide an equitable basis
for determining the relative worth of jobs. Systematic evaluation of
jobs is an attempt to reduce favoritism and ultimately leads to the
"pricing" of jobs. Although job evaluation uses a systematic approach,
managers should be aware that job evaluation can never be totally objective. Subjective judgments cannot be avoided, and managers and
personnel specialists should make sure the "objectivity" of the job evaluation system is not overemphasized. Using a job evaluation committee in which several evaluators rate jobs can help improve the reliability of the evaluation.

One study reported that union leaders viewed job evaluations with
some distrust.[17] Managers of unionized employees must be aware of
this concern, regardless of the job evaluation methods used.

There are several methods used to determine internal job worth
through job evaluation. All methods have the same general objective,
but each method differs in its complexity and means of measurement.
Regardless of the methods used, the intent is to develop a usable, measurable, and realistic system to determine compensation in an organization.

Market Pricing

Although considered a job evaluation method, market pricing does not
attempt to assess the relative internal worth of a job. Instead, it simply
assumes that the pay set by other employers is an accurate reflection
of a job's worth. One difficulty with this approach is the assumption
that jobs are the same in another organization. Direct market pricing
also does not adequately consider the impact of economic conditions,
employer size, and other variables.

To illustrate, assume one of the major employers in the same area as
Danbo, a company with a highly unionized work force. Because clerical
pay is based on the pay scale in the unionized part of the company, a
beginning secretary is paid $1,500 per month; consequently, the firm
always has a waiting list of extremely experienced and qualified persons available. However, a Danbo manager who is hiring a secretary
would have extreme difficulty justifying such an expenditure. As a result, the manager might hire someone for considerably less money.
This example illustrates that basing pay scales on market pricing alone
has some definite pitfalls. Consequently, more complex methods have
been developed.

Ranking Method

The ranking method is one of the simplest methods used. Managers and personnel specialists using the ranking method place jobs in order ranging from highest to lowest in value. The entire job is considered rather than the individual components. Variations on straight ranking can be used. Alternation ranking and paired comparison ranking are two common variations.

Advantages and Disadvantages. Ranking methods are extremely subjective and managers may have difficulty explaining why one job is ranked higher than another to employees, especially since these rankings will ultimately affect the pay received by individuals on those jobs. When there is a large number of jobs, the ranking method also can be awkward and unwieldy. Consider a personnel specialist in Danbo who must rank all 85 jobs from file clerk to president. This method would be almost impossible to use in a way that could be justified. Therefore, the job ranking method is limited in use and is more appropriate to a small organization having relatively few jobs.

Classification Method

The classification method of job evaluation was developed under the old U.S. Civil Service System and was widely copied by state and local governmental entities. A number of classes, or GS (Government Service) grades, are defined. Then the various jobs in the organization are put into grades according to common factors found in jobs, such as degree of responsibility, abilities or skills, knowledge, duties, volume of work, and experienced needed. The grades are then ranked into an overall system.

Steps in Classification. Several steps are needed to classify jobs. Based upon information taken from job descriptions and job specifications, jobs are separated into types (such as sales jobs, manufacturing jobs and clerical jobs at Danbo). Next, several job factors are used to grade or classify the jobs. Once the jobs are classified, descriptions of job classes are formulated by writing statements such as: "Jobs falling in this classification have the following characteristics." Finally, individual jobs are placed in the appropriate classifications.

Advantages and Disadvantages. One of the major reasons that the job classification method is widely used in government and other organizations is that it is a system employees and managers can understand. Also, this method provides some flexibility in the classification of a wide variety of jobs.

The major difficulty with the classification method is the subjective judgments needed to develop the grade descriptions and to accurately place jobs in them. With a wide variety of jobs and generally-written grade descriptions, some jobs may appear to fall into two or three different grades. Thus, some subjective judgments must be made.

Another problem with the classification method is that it relies heavily on job titles and duties and assumes they are similar from one organization to another. For example, a production supervisor in one department may have different job responsibilities than a production supervisor in a smaller department or a different type of work area. If both are evaluated using a classification system, some inappropriate grading of responsibilities may result. For these reasons a number of federal, state, and local governmental entities are shifting to the use of a point system or a factor comparison system.[18]

Point Method

The point method is the most widely used job evaluation method.[19] It breaks down jobs into various identifiable components and places weights or points on these components. The components are developed from a job analysis by identifying factors that are common to the jobs under study. Then the relative weights, or points, are assigned to each degree of the component.

The point method is more sophisticated than the ranking and classification methods. Because the different job components carry different weights, each is assigned a numerical value. The values of the various components then are added for each job and compared to other jobs.

The individual using the point chart in Figure 13–6 looks at a job description and identifies the degree to which each element is necessary to perform the job satisfactorily. To minimize bias, this determination is often made by a group of people familiar with the job. Once point totals have been determined for all jobs, the jobs are grouped together into pay grades.

Advantages and Disadvantages. The major reason the point method has grown in popularity is because it is a relatively simple system to use. It considers the components of a job rather than the total job, and it is a much more comprehensive system than either the ranking or classification method. Once points have been determined and a job evaluation point manual has been developed, the method can be used easily by people who are not specialists. A definite advantage is that the system can be understood by managers and employees.

Another reason for the widespread use of the point method is that it does not consider current pay for a job. It evaluates the components of a job and determines total points before the current wage structure is considered. In this way, a realistic assessment of relative worth can be made instead of just relying on past patterns of worth.

One major drawback to the point method is the time needed to develop a point system. For this reason, manuals and systems developed by management consultants or other organizations often are used by employers. Another disadvantage is that even though the point system does attempt to be objective, managers must still make subjective judgments to determine how many points should be allotted for each element. Human error through misinterpretation or misjudgment is definitely possible. Even though the point system is not perfect, research

FIGURE 13–6
Point Method Charts.

CLERICAL GROUP					
Skill	1st Degree	2nd Degree	3rd Degree	4th Degree	5th Degree
1. Education	14	28	42	56	
2. Experience	22	44	66	88	110
3. Initiative & ingenuity	14	28	42	56	
4. Contacts with others	14	28	42	56	
Responsibility					
5. Supervision received	10	20	35	50	
6. Latitude & depth	20	40	70	100	
7. Work of others	5	10	15	20	
8. Trust imposed	10	20	35	50	70
9. Performance	7	14	21	28	35
Other					
10. Work environment	10	25	45		
11. Mental or visual demand	10	20	35		
12. Physical effort	28				

The specific degrees and points for Education, Trust Imposed, and Work Environment are as follows:

Education Education is the basic *prerequisite* knowledge that is essential to satisfactorily perform the job. This knowledge may have been acquired through formal schooling such as grammar school, high school, college, night school, correspondence courses, company education programs, or through equivalent experience in allied fields. Analyze the minimum *requirements of the job and not the formal education of individuals performing it.*

1st Degree—Requires knowledge usually equivalent to a two-year high school education. Requires ability to read, write, and follow simple written or oral instructions, use simple arithmetic processes involving counting, adding, subtracting, dividing and multiplying whole numbers. May require basic typing ability.

2nd Degree—Requires knowledge equivalent to a four-year high school education in order to perform work requiring advanced arithmetic processes involving adding, subtracting, dividing, and multiplying of decimals and fractions; maintain or prepare routine correspondence, records, and reports. May require knowledge of advanced typing and/or basic knowledge of shorthand, bookkeeping, drafting, etc.

3rd Degree—Requires knowledge equivalent to four-year high school education plus some specialized knowledge in a particular field such as advanced stenographic, secretarial or business training, elementary accounting or a general knowledge of blueprint reading or engineering practices.

4th Degree—Requires knowledge equivalent to two years of college education in order to understand and perform work requiring general engineering or accounting theory. Must be able to originate and compile statistics and interpretive reports, and prepare correspondence of a difficult or technical nature.

studies have found that the point method of job evaluation is highly reliable.[20] Because it quantifies job elements, it is probably better than the two previous systems discussed.

Responsibility for Trust Imposed This factor appraises the extent to which the job requires responsibility for safeguarding confidential information and the effect of such disclosure on the Company's relations with employees, customers or competitors.

1st Degree Negligible. Little or no confidential data involved.

2nd Degree Some access to confidential information but where responsibility is limited or where the full import is not apparent.

3rd Degree Occasional access to confidential information where the full import is apparent and where disclosure may have an adverse effect on the Company's external or internal affairs.

4th Degree Regularly works with and has access to confidential data which if disclosed could seriously affect the Company's internal or external affairs or undermine its competitive position.

5th Degree Full and complete access to reports, policies, records and plans of Company-wide programs, including financial cost and engineering data. Requires the utmost discretion and integrity to safeguard the Company's interests.

Work Environment This factor appraises the physical surroundings and the degree to which noise is present at the work location. Consider the extent of distraction and commotion caused by the sounds.

1st Degree Normal office conditions. Noise limited to the usual sounds of typewriters and other equipment.

2nd Degree More than average noise due to the intermittent operation by several employees of adding machines, calculators, typewriters, or duplicating machines.

3rd Degree Considerable noise generated by constant machine operation such as is present in the Data Processing section.

SOURCE: *Wage and Salary Administration: A Guide to Current Policies and Practices.* (Chicago: Dartnell Corp., 1969), pp. 135–141. Used with permission. Revision published every three years.

FIGURE 13–6
(Continued)

Factor Comparison

The factor comparison method, which is very quantitative and complex, involves determining the key jobs, called benchmark jobs, in an organization. A **benchmark job** is one performed by many individuals or having special significance to the organization. For example, one key job in Danbo Manufacturing might be that of an assembly worker. The factor comparison method is actually a combination of the ranking and point methods.

To develop this method, as shown in Figure 13–7, benchmark jobs are categorized according to levels of responsibility, physical demands, skills required, knowledge demands, and working conditions. All benchmark jobs then are ranked factor by factor against each other. Then the individual doing the evaluation compares these positions in terms of the above factors and ranks them according to the importance of the factors in each job. Monetary values then are assigned to each one of the factors and compared with the existing market monetary scales for the benchmark jobs. Finally, evaluations of all other jobs in the organization are made by comparing them to the benchmark jobs. The results of this process are demonstrated in Figure 13–7. A market pay rate of $5.20 has been assigned to the clerk-typist position, based

Benchmark Jobs	Responsibility	Physical Demands	Skills Required	Knowledge Required	Working Conditions	Market Pay
Clerk-Typist	8 ($.50)	5 (1.00)	1 (3.00)	8 (.30)	6 (.40)	$5.20
Secretary	7 ( )	8 ( )	4 ( )	7 ( )	8 ( )	$6.00
Payroll Clerk	6 ( )	6 ( )	7 ( )	5 ( )	7 ( )	$6.15
Design Engineer	2 ( )	9 ( )	9 ( )	19 ( )	10 ( )	$12.70
Computer Operator	4 ( )	10 ( )	6 ( )	4 ( )	9 ( )	$5.80
Production Supervisor	1 ( )	7 ( )	5 ( )	2 ( )	5 ( )	$9.30
Warehouse Worker	9 ( )	1 ( )	10 ( )	10 ( )	3 ( )	$6.50
Custodian	10 ( )	4 ( )	8 ( )	9 ( )	4 ( )	$4.50
Assembly Worker	5 ( )	2 ( )	3 ( )	6 ( )	1 ( )	$7.10
Machine Operator	3 ( )	3 (	2 ( )	3 ( )	2 ( )	$6.90

Note: Rank of 1 is highest

FIGURE 13–7
Sample Factor Comparison Chart, Danbo Manufacturing Corporation.

on the rankings for each job factor. To see the complexity of this method, try to complete the chart.

Hay Plan. A special type of factor comparison method used by a consulting firm, Hay and Associates, has received widespread application. However, it should be noted that the Hay Plan is most often used with exempt employees. The Hay Plan uses three factors: *know-how*, *problem-solving*, and *accountability*, and numerically measures the degree to which each of these three elements is required in each job.[21]

Advantages and Disadvantages. One of the major advantages of the factor comparison method is that it is tied specifically to one organization. Each organization must develop its own key jobs and its own factors. For this reason, buying a packaged system may not be appropriate. The factor comparison method does establish quantitative weights, as the point method does, but it requires the evaluator to make a specific comparative identification of the weights assigned. Finally, factor comparison not only tells which jobs are worth more, but it also indicates how much more, so the factor values can be more easily converted to the monetary wages.

The major disadvantages of the factor comparison method are its difficulty and complexity. It is not an easy system to explain to employees and it is time-consuming to establish and develop. Also, a factor comparison system may not be appropriate for an organization with many similar types of jobs. For example, some organizations have had difficulty using the Hay Plan with nonexempt employees, primarily because many clerical jobs differ very little in accountability. Managers attempting to use the method should consult a specialist or one of the more detailed compensation books or manuals that discuss the factor comparison method.

Can you define job evaluation and discuss four methods of doing it?

A WAGE/SALARY
SURVEY
is a means of gathering
data on existing com-
pensation rates for
workers performing
similar jobs in other
organizations.

Once internal equity is determined through job evaluation, a key part of building a total pay system is available. Another part of the process is data obtained through a wage/salary survey on the pay other organizations provide for similar jobs.

Wage/Salary Survey

A **wage/salary survey** is a means of gathering data on existing compensation rates for workers performing similar jobs in other organizations. An employer may use wage/salary surveys conducted by other organizations or may decide to conduct its own survey.

Using Prepared Wage/Salary Surveys. Many different wage/salary surveys are available from a variety of sources. National surveys on many jobs and industries are available through the U.S. Department of Labor, the Bureau of Labor Statistics, or through national trade associations. In many communities employers participate in a wage survey sponsored by the Chamber of Commerce to provide information to new employers interested in locating in the community.

When using surveys from other sources, it is important to use them properly. Some questions that should be addressed are[22]:

1. Is the survey a realistic sample of employers, or is it dominated by a few large employers?
2. Is the data provided by other personnel specialists, not individual operating managers?
3. How old is the information?
4. How sound and experienced is the organization that prepared the survey?

Developing a Wage/Salary Survey. If needed wage information is not already available, the organization can undertake its own wage survey. Employers with comparable positions should be selected.[23] Also, employers considered to be "representative" should be surveyed. If the organization conducting the survey is not unionized, the wage survey probably should examine unionized as well as nonunionized companies. Developing wages competitive with union wages may deter employees from joining a union.

Another decision the manager must make is the positions to be surveyed. Not all jobs in all organizations can be surveyed, and not all jobs in all organizations will be the same. An accounting clerk in a city government office might perform a different job than an accounting clerk in a credit billing firm. Therefore, managers should select jobs that can be easily compared, have common job elements, and represent a broad range of jobs. Generally, it is advisable to provide brief job descriptions for jobs surveyed in order to insure more accurate matches.

The next phase of the wage survey is for managers to decide what

PAY GRADES
are used to group individual jobs having approximately the same job worth together.

compensation information is needed for various jobs. Information such as starting pay, base pay, overtime rate, vacation and holiday pay and policies, and bonuses all can be included in a survey. However, requesting too much information may discourage survey returns.

The results of the wage survey may have to be made available to those participating in the survey in order to gain their cooperation. Most surveys specify confidentiality, and data are summarized to provide anonymity. Different job levels often are included and the wages are presented both in overall terms and on a city-by-city basis to reflect regional differences in pay. The problems that can be caused by using incorrect survey data are illustrated by the situation faced by city employees in Santa Clara, California.

Pay Structure

Once wage/salary survey data are gathered, the pay structure for the organization can be developed. One means of tying wage survey information to job evaluation data is to plot a *"wage curve"* or *"scattergram."* This plotting is done to establish pay grades, which are used to group together individual jobs having approximately the same job worth.

Pay grades are determined by first making a graph that charts job evaluation points to wage/salary survey rates for all jobs. Usage of wage/salary survey data puts more emphasis on external market conditions. In this way the distribution of pay for surveyed jobs can be shown and a trend line using the "least squares regression method" can be drawn to plot a "market line." This line shows the relationship between job value, or points, and wage/salary survey rates. An example is shown in Figure 13–8.

Once the market line is graphed, several decisions must be made:

■ How wide are the pay ranges to be?
■ How many pay grades are needed?
■ How much overlap between grades is desired?

Calculating Pay Ranges. Using the market line as a starting point (see Figure 13–8), maximum and minimum pay levels can be determined by making the market line the midpoint line of the firm's new pay structure. By calculating values that are the same percentage above and below the midpoint value, the minimums and maximums can be determined. For example, if the market line (midpoint line) is at a point of $5, going up and down 10 percent establishes a minimum and maximum of $4.50–5.50.

General guidelines for constructing a pay structure are that a smaller range (minimum-to-maximum) be used for lower-level jobs than higher level jobs, primarily because employees in lower-level jobs tend to stay in them for shorter periods of time and have greater promotion possibilities than do upper-level employees.[25] At Danbo Manufacturing a clerk-typist might advance to the position of secretary or word-processing operator. However, a design engineer likely would have fewer possibilities for future upward movement in the organization. At the lower end of a pay structure, the pay range may be 20 percent (minimum-to-maximum), whereas upper-level ranges may be as high as 100 percent

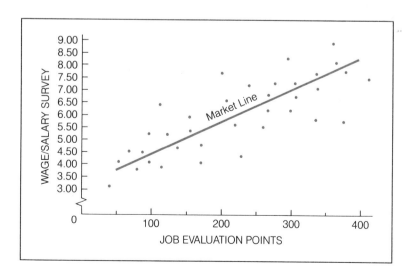

FIGURE 13–8
Pay Scattergram.

FIGURE 13–9

Example of Priced Labor
Grades

GRADE	POINT RANGE	HOURLY PAY RANGE
1	100 and under	3.57–4.46
2	101–135	4.11–5.13
3	136–170	4.73–5.91
4	171–205	5.44–6.80
5	206–240	6.26–7.82
6	241–275	7.20–9.00
7	276–310	8.28–10.35
8	311–345	9.52–11.90
9	over 345	

*Note: 15% between grade minimums, with a 25% grade spread.

(minimum-to-maximum). To make administration of a pay system easier in small firms such as Danbo, the same percentage range sometimes is used at all levels.

Establishing Pay Grades. There are no set rules to be used when establishing pay grades. However, some overall suggestions have been made. Generally, 11 to 17 grades are used in small companies such as Danbo Manufacturing.[26] Having overlap between grades, such as those do in Figure 13–9, allows an experienced employee in a lower grade to be paid more than a less experienced employee in a job in the next pay grade. Overlap between three adjacent grades is recommended, but more than that is not.[27]

By using pay grades, an organization can develop a coordinated pay system. The intent is to avoid having to determine a separate pay rate for each position in the organization. A firm using a point method of job evaluation would group jobs having about the same number of points into one pay grade. As discussed previously, the factor compensation method uses monetary values. An organization using that method can easily establish and price pay grades. A vital part of the classification method is developing grades, and the ranking method can be converted to pay grades by grouping several ranks together. Figure 13–9 shows the pay grades determined through a typical point system.

Individual Pay

Once rate ranges for pay grades are determined, the specific pay for individuals can be determined. Each of the dots in Figure 13–10 represents an individual employee's current pay in relation to the pay grades that have been developed. Setting a range for each pay grade provides flexibility by allowing individuals to progress within a grade instead of having to be moved to a new grade each time they receive a raise. Also, a pay range allows some flexibility to reward the better

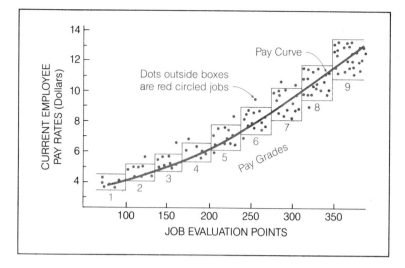

FIGURE 13–10
Pay Structure Depicted
Graphically.

performing employees, while maintaining the integrity of the pay system.

"Red Circle" Rate. A job whose pay rate is out of grade or range is identified as a *red circle rate*. A red-circled job is noted on the graph in figure 13–10. For example, assume Isaac Washington's current pay is $5.18 per hour, but the pay grade price is between $5.44 and $6.80. Isaac's job would be red-circled and attempts would be made over a period of time to bring Isaac's rate into grade.

A pay rate more than the determined pay rate is also red-circled. An attempt should be made to bring these rates into grade also. Occasionally managers may have to deviate from the priced grades to hire scarce skills or to consider competitive market shortages of particular job skills. If skilled people such as welders are in short supply, the worth of a job may be evaluated at $6–10 an hour, but the going rate for welders in the community may be $12 an hour. In order to fill the position, the firm must pay $12 an hour.

Pay Compression. One major problem many employers face during the 1980s is **pay compression.** Such compression occurs for a number of reasons, but the major one is that labor market pay levels increase more rapidly than an employer's pay adjustments. To illustrate, at Danbo Manufacturing because of a shortage in the labor market, the firm has been forced to hire new machine operators at $7 per hour but several operators who have been with the firm for five years are making only $7.10 per hour.

Pay compression is a difficult problem. The major ways to deal with it are through wider pay grades and more grade overlaps. Another strategy is to have a policy of maintaining a 15–20 percent differential, for example, if the compression occurs between supervisors' pay and the pay of those supervised.[28] Compression between supervisors and those they supervise is a common compression problem.[29]

PAY COMPRESSION occurs when pay differences between individuals become small.

Many universities face pay compression in the hiring of faculty in such high-demand areas as the business disciplines. Unlike history departments, which face an overabundance of potential candidates, accounting and other areas in business schools must continue to increase the pay offered to new recruits. However, funding approved by university regents and/or state legislators has not grown as fast as the pay being offered to new recruits. Consequently, existing faculty members with several years' experience actually may end up being paid less than new faculty members with less experience.

Pay Increases. One pay policy decision is how pay increases are to be distributed. Seniority, or time with the company, time on a particular job, merit (performance), or some combination of time and merit can be used as yardsticks. Similarly, many employers have policies that indicate the minimum time persons must be employed before they are eligible for pay increases. If across-the-board or cost-of-living increases are to be given, this policy should be specified. Also, how often these or other automatic increases are given (once a year, for instance) should be identified.

One common pay raise practice is the use of a so-called *standard raise* or *cost-of-living raise.* The theory underlying this approach is that giving employees a standard percentage increase enables them to maintain the same real wages in a period of economic inflation. Unfortunately, some employers give across-the-board raises and call them *merit raises.* If all employees get a pay increase, the frequent reaction is to view this raise as a cost-of-living adjustment that has very little tie to merit and good performance. For this reason, employers giving a basic percentage increase to all employees should avoid using the term *merit* in awarding it. The merit or performance part should be identified as that amount above the standard raise.

Many employers profess to have a merit pay system that is based on performance, as indicated by performance appraisal ratings. However, reliance on performance appraisal information for making pay adjustments assumes that the appraisals are done well, especially for employees whose work cannot be easily measured. Some system for integrating appraisals and pay changes must be developed and applied equally.

In a true merit system, no pay raises are given except for increases in performance.[30] Giving pay increases to people because they have 10 to 15 years' experience, even though they are mediocre employees, helps defeat a merit approach. Also, unless the merit portion of a pay increase is fairly significant, employees may feel it is not worth the extra effort.[31] Giving an outstanding industrial designer making $30,000 a year the "standard raise" of 8 percent plus 1 percent for merit means only $300 for merit versus $2400 for "hanging around another year."

Monitoring and Updating Pay Systems

An organization changing from an informal and uncoordinated pay system to a formalized pay structure should try to make the transition as smoothly as possible. The behavioral reactions of employees definitely must be considered. Clear communication to employees, a description of the new pay system, and an explanation of the need for change are all important parts of the transition. Whether or not the system is new, changes in the pay system should be phased in gradually. Attempts to institute radical and immediate changes in pay are likely to cause strong employee reactions.

Can you outline the process of building a wage/salary administration system?

PERSONNEL TODAY AND TOMORROW
TAKING THEIR LUMPS

Most employees who receive pay increases, either for merit or seniority, have their base pay adjusted after which the amount of their regular monthly or weekly paycheck increases. For example, an employee who made $1200 per month, and received a 6 percent increase, would get a paycheck for $1,272 per month. However, some employers have adopted a different approach—lump-sum increases (LSI).

In an LSI plan an employee receives a one-time payment of the pay increase per year. In our example, the employee would receive a check for $720 (before taxes are deducted). However, some firms place a limit on how much of a merit increase can be taken as a lump-sum payment. One of the first companies to use the LSI, Union Mutual Insurance Company, allows eligible employees to take up to 30 percent of their annual salary as a lump-sum. Other firms split the lump-sum into two checks, each representing one-half the year's pay raise. Firms that use the LSI often limit eligibility for the plan to employees with longer service who are not in high turnover groups. Also, some firms treat the lump-sum payment as an advance, which must be repaid if the employee leaves the firm before the year is finished.

As with any plan, there are advantages and disadvantages. The major advantage of an LSI plan is that it heightens employee awareness of what their performance "merited." A lump-sum check also gives employees some flexibility in their spending patterns so that they can buy big-ticket items without having to take out a loan. In addition, the firm can slow down the increase of base pay, so that the compounding effect of succeeding raises is reduced. One disadvantage is the administrative tracking that must occur, including the establishment of a system to handle income tax and Social Security deductions from the lump-sum check. Also, workers who take a lump-sum payment may become discouraged because their base pay has not changed. To some extent, this problem can be reduced by splitting the merit increase to include some in the base pay and some in the lump-sum payment.

One survey found that 47 firms, many of which were insurance companies, were using lump-sum plans. However, companies like Westinghouse, Timex, and B. F. Goodrich also have used lump-sum plans. Some experts have speculated that LSI plans will grow in popularity in the future, so that more workers can "take their lumps."[32]

SUMMARY

■ Compensation provided by an organization can come through pay (base wages and salaries), incentives (performance-based rewards), and benefits (indirect compensaton).

■ Determination of compensation can be based on time, productivity, or a combination of the two, and should be matched to the tasks performed.

■ A variety of forces external to the organization, including unions and economic factors, affect the types and amount of compensation provided to employees.

■ The Fair Labor Standards Act, as amended, is the law that affects pay systems most. It requires most firms to pay a minimum wage and to meet the overtime provisions of the act, including appropriately classifying employees as exempt or nonexempt.

■ Other laws have been passed that place restrictions on employers who have federal supply contracts, federal construction contracts, or who garnish employees' pay.

■ Regardless of whether compensation is seen by employees principally in terms of economic, psychosocial, and/or growth factors, managers should be concerned with providing adequate rewards in exchange for employees' inputs.

■ Differing degrees of pay secrecy or pay openness can be practiced.

■ Administration of a wage/salary system requires the development of pay policies that deal with how the organization is to compare with the pay offered by other employers.

■ To ensure internal equity, job evaluation is necessary. Job evaluation is concerned with determining the relative worth of jobs, and it can be done through the use of market pricing or through the use of ranking, classification, point, or factor comparison methods.

■ Once the job evaluation process has been completed, wage/salary survey data must be collected and the pay structure developed. To have an effective pay system, changes will have to be expected and made on a continuing basis.

REVIEW QUESTIONS AND EXERCISES

1. People can be paid in three basic ways. What are they?
2. Give an example of the basic uses for determining compensation and how each might be affected by external factors.
3. What factors should be considered to determine if an employee who worked over 40 hours in a week would be due overtime?
4. In what ways are the following laws different:
(a) Walsh-Healey Act
(b) Davis-Bacon Act
5. What did compensation mean to you on your most recent job? Why?
6. Discuss how pay secrecy and pay openness relate to equity.
7. Considering all methods, why do you believe the point method is the most widely used job evaluation method?

8. You have been named compensation manager for a hospital. How would you establish a pay system?

Exercises

a. Contact a local firm and interview the owner or manager in charge to determine what he or she does and does not know about the overtime requirements of the Fair Labor Standards Act. What misinformation did the individual have? What potential violations of the Fair Labor Standards Act do you think you discovered?

b. Obtain a copy of a local wage/salary survey. Then examine its information on one job. What type of information is included? Why do you think it is included?

CASE
SCIENTIFIC TURMOIL

Joan is the director of scientific computing at a large utility company. The people she supervises are all college graduates with backgrounds in science, engineering, or math. These people do systems work and computer programming that is more problem-oriented than other programmers in the company, and the people in Joan's department are quite close-knit.

Joan hired Fred into the group from the engineering department. Fred, who had worked for the company for seven years, learned the programming easily and was doing quite well. One year later Bob was hired into the group by Joan. Bob and Fred both assimilated in the group quickly.

About a month later, Joan's problems began. Information was quite freely shared by members of the group, especially job-related information such as salary. When Fred learned that Bob was making more money than he was, he was quite upset. Bob was doing the same kind of work and had less experience at his new job. He also had less total working time with the company—only four years.

When Fred voiced his concern to his boss, he was told that the company had specific guidelines for raises and wide salary ranges for each job level. Bob was just on the high side of his old job's salary range and thus received a hefty raise when he was promoted to this new job.

Fred was not pleased with the setup because he had received a raise just before Bob came and knew that it would be a year before he would get another one. In Fred's mind, he was not more qualified, more experienced, and had better knowledge of the company; if nothing else, he certainly had more seniority than Bob. Fred's discontent was apparent in his work, and although Joan could not really prove it, Fred caused serious delays in projects. Also, new errors seemed to be cropping up in the computer programs that came out of Joan's section.

Questions

1. What role does equity play in this case?
2. Should companies demand that individuals not reveal their salaries? Why or why not?
3. Comment on the salary system and weaknesses you see in it.
4. As the director, how would you handle Fred?

NOTES

1. Joseph F. Quinn and Karen McCormick, "Wage Rates and City Size," *Industrial Relations* 20 (Spring 1981), pp. 193–199.

2. For more details see *Executive, Administrative, Professional and Outside Sales Exemptions Under the Fair Labor Standards Act*, WH Publication #1363 (Washington DC: U.S. Dept. of Labor, Employment Standards Administration, Wage and Hour Division, 1980).

3. *Omaha World Herald*, October 16, 1983, p. 5–8.

4. *Marshall v. Hodag Chemical Corporation* (U.S. D.C. N.Ill., 1978) 23 WH Cases 882.

5. Report to the U.S. Congress by the Comptroller General of the United States, *The Davis-Bacon Act Should be Repealed*, (Washington, D.C.: General Accounting Office, HRD 79–18, April 1979).

6. *Building & Construction Trades Department, AFL-CIO v. Donovan*, 1984.

7. Consumer Credit Protection Act, Public Law 90–321, May 29, 1968.

8. C. E. Rusbalt and D. A. Farnell, "A Longitudinal Test of the Investment Model . . .," *Journal of Applied Psychology* 68 (1983), pp. 429–438.

9. Gene Milbourn, Jr., "The Relationships of Money and Motivation," *Compensation Review*, Second Quarter 1980, pp. 33–44.

10. Edward E. Lawler, III, *Pay and Organization Development* (Reading, MA: Addison-Wesley, 1981), p. 23.

11. See R. E. Kopelman and Leon Reinharth, "The Effect of Merit Pay Practices on White-Collar Performance," *Compensation Review*, Fourth Quarter 1982, pp. 30–40.

12. For a detailed discussion, see Marc J. Wallace and Charles H. Fay, *Compensation Theory and Practice* (Boston: Kent, 1983), pp. 73–87.

13. *Wall Street Journal*, June 8, 1982, p. 1.

14. Julio D. Burroughs, "Pay Secrecy and Performance: The Psychological Research," *Compensation Review*, Third Quarter 1982, pp. 44–54.

15. John D. McMillan and Valerie C. Williams, "The Elements of Effective Salary Administration Programs," *Personnel Journal* 61 (November 1982), pp. 832–838.

16. D. P. Schwab and Robert Grams, *A Survey of Job Evaluation Practices Among Compensation Specialists* (Phoenix: American Compensation Association, 1984).

17. Harold D. Jones, "Union Views on Job Evaluation," *Personnel Journal* 58 (February 1979), pp. 80–89.

18. Stephen McConomy and Bill Ganschinietz, "Trends in Job Evaluation Practices of State Personnel Systems . . ." *Public Personnel Management*, Spring 1983, pp. 1–12.

19. *Job Evaluation Policies and Procedures*, PPF Survey no. 113 (Washington, DC: Bureau of National Affairs, June 1976), p. 4.

20. D. Doverspike, A. M. Carlisi, G. V. Barrett, and R. A. Alexander, "Generalizability Analysis of a Point-Method Evaluation Instrument," *Journal of Applied Psychology* 68 (1983), pp. 476–483.

21. Angela M. Bowey, ed., *Handbook of Salary and Wage Systems*, 2nd ed., (Aldershot, Hants., England: Gower, 1982), Chapter 16.

22. "Hiring at the Right Price," *Personnel Journal* 59 (December 1980), p. 968.

23. Barbara L. Fielder, "Conducting a Wage and Salary Survey," *Personnel Journal* 61 (December 1982), pp. 879–880.

24. Adapted from *Omaha Sunday World Herald*, December 18, 1983, p. 5–R.

25. E. J. Brennan, "Everything You Need to Know About Salary Ranges," *Personnel Journal*, March 1984, pp. 10–16.

26. Warren E. Scott, *Dartnell's Corporate Guide to Sound Compensation Practices* (Chicago: Dartnell Corp., 1980), p. 190.

27. Richard I. Henderson, *Compensation Management*, 4th ed. (Reston, VA: Reston Publishing, 1985), pp. 290–292.

28. *Ibid.*, p. 436.

29. L. Priefert, T. J. Bergmann, and F. S. Hills, "Pay Compression: Causes, Results, and Possible Solutions," *Compensation Review*, Second Quarter 1983, pp. 17–26.

30. For a discussion of issues involved with merit pay, see *Merit Pay: Fitting the Pieces Together*, (Chicago: Commerce Clearing House, 1982).

31. R. E. Kopelman, "Linking Pay to Performance as a Proven Management Tool," *Personnel Administrator*, October 1983, pp. 60–68.

32. D. M. Gluckman, "Lump-Sum Merit Increases, *Compensation Review*, First Quarter 1983, pp. 66–72,and *Compensation* BNA Policy and Practice Series, (Washington DC: The Bureau of National Affairs), Sec. 313, pp. 405–408.

Incentives and Executive Compensation

When you have read this chapter, you should be able to:

1. Define an incentive and list four guidelines for an incentive program.
2. Discuss three types of individual incentives and some problems with them.
3. Describe the nature of a Scanlon Plan and an Employee Stock Ownership Plan (ESOP).
4. Identify three components of executive compensation.

PERSONNEL AT WORK
INCENTIVE MANAGEMENT AT LINCOLN ELECTRIC

A company 90 years old using an incentive system it started in 1907 may serve as an example of the future. Cleveland-based Lincoln Electric Company has been using incentive compensation effectively with its employees, most of whom are production workers manufacturing the firm's major products, arc welding equipment and induction motors.

The management practices used with the 2,500 employees at Lincoln are somewhat unique. Most workers are paid on a piece-rate basis, which means that there is no base pay. If a worker is sick, he or she receives no pay, and if a defective machine is produced, the worker must fix it on his or her own time. Turnover averages a low 6 percent a year. There have been no layoffs since 1951, and employees with at least two years service are guaranteed at least 30 hours per week of work. Employees have averaged as much as $45,000 each yearly, which includes a year-end bonus that often doubles employees' base pay. The bonuses are given for teamwork and reliability, and employees who make productivity-improving suggestions receive bonus points in return. Overtime is mandatory when orders are backed up. Furthermore, employees own over 70 percent of the company's stock, which they must sell back at book value when they leave.

At the heart of the management system at Lincoln is employee self-motivation. There is no seniority system at Lincoln, and all employees compete on merit for the few jobs that are not paid by piece work. However, some people have not been able to handle the productivity pressure. One disgusted ex-employee referred to Lincoln as a "sweatshop," and another said that it was both physically and mentally tough on workers. It is also an intensely competitive environment. Nevertheless, Lincoln Electric has continued to grow and prosper using its "incentive management system."[1]

"Incentive is the driving force which can improve one's fated course."

A. L. ROMANOFF

Not all firms make use of incentives to the extent that Lincoln Electric does; however, many companies do use a variety of means to tie compensation directly to productivity. The use of incentives at Lincoln Electric illustrates why many organizations feel it is important to provide compensation beyond base pay. Consequently, special compensation arrangements are made to provide a direct tie between performance and additional compensation through the use of *incentive systems*. Those managers at the top of the organization often receive additional rewards through *executive compensation* plans. These two types of direct compensation are discussed in this chapter.

AN INCENTIVE
is additional compensa-
tion directly related to
performance.

The main purpose of incentives is to tie employees' rewards closely to their achievements. This tie is done by providing more compensation for better performance. Whether or not an individual will strive for increased productivity and receive the additional rewards that follow from the increased performance depends upon the individual. Some people may prefer some extra time off, for example, rather than more money.

Incentive Defined

An **incentive** provides additional compensation for those employees who perform well. It attempts to tie additional comepnsation as directly as possible to employee productivity.

Incentive Program Guidelines

Incentive systems can be very complex and take many forms. Managers should consider the following general guidelines when establishing and maintaining incentive systems.

Tie to Performance. Incentive systems should be tied as much as possible to performance. If an incentive is actually to spur increased performance and effort, employees must see a direct relationship between their efforts and their rewards.[2] Further, both workers and managers must see the rewards as equitable and desirable. If a *group* incentive system is to be used, it clearly should reflect employees' efforts as a group of individuals.

Recognize Individual Differences. Incentive plans should provide for individual differences. Recognition of the complex view of personnel management (as outlined in Chapter 3) means that a variety of incentive systems may have to be developed to appeal to various organizational groups and individuals.[3] Not everybody will want the same type of incentive rewards.

Recognize Organizational Factors. The incentive system chosen should be consistent with the climate and constraints of an organization. For example, it is inconsistent to devise an incentive plan requiring a high degree of employee participation for an organization that adheres to traditional procedures and rules. The incentive plan also should be compatible with organizational resources and be developed in close consultation with the firm's financial officers to determine how much incentive compensation an organization can afford.

Continue to Monitor. An incentive system should consistently reflect current technological and organizational conditions. Offering an incentive for clothing sales clerks to sell outdated merchandise would be more appropriate than offering incentives to sell only current fashion items that are already in high demand. Incentive systems should be

	Performance Measure	Tie Pay to Performance	Produce Negative Side Effects	Encourage Cooperation	Employee Acceptance
Salary					
Individual plan	Productivity	4	1	1	4
	Cost-effectiveness	3	1	1	4
	Superiors' rating	3	1	1	3
Group plan	Productivity	3	1	2	4
	Cost-effectiveness	3	1	2	4
	Superiors' rating	2	1	2	3
Organizational plan	Productivity	2	1	3	4
	Cost-effectiveness	2	1	2	4
Bonus					
Individual plan	Productivity	5	3	1	2
	Cost-effectiveness	4	2	1	2
	Superiors' rating	4	2	1	2
Group plan	Productivity	4	1	3	3
	Cost-effectiveness	3	1	3	3
	Superiors' rating	3	1	3	3
Organizational plan	Productivity	3	1	3	4
	Cost-effectiveness	3	1	3	4
	Profit	2	1	3	3

SOURCE: Edward E. Lawler, III, *Pay and Organization Development* (Reading, MA: Addison-Wesley 1981), p. 94.

FIGURE 14–1
Ratings of Various Pay Incentive Plans on a Scale of 1 to 5, 1-low and 5-high.

reviewed continually to determine whether they are operating as designed. Follow-up, through an attitude survey or other means, will determine if the incentive system is actually encouraging employees to perform better. If it is not, then managers should seriously consider changing the system.

Types of Incentives

Organizations often use a combination of incentive systems. As Figure 14–1 shows, salary reward and bonus incentive plans can be set up as *individual, group,* or *organizational* in nature. Performance can be measured using productivity, cost-effective, and superior's ratings. The remaining columns indicate that differing combinations of plan type and performance measures result in varying behavioral consequences. A discussion of each type follows.

Can you define an incentive and list four guidelines for an incentive program?

INDIVIDUAL INCENTIVES

Though there are types of individual incentive systems, they all attempt to relate individual effort to individual reward. For a sales clerk who works on a salary-plus-commission basis, the commission portion represents the individual incentive compensation.

Individual incentive systems may have to be tailored to individual desires; thus, if a worker wants additional time off instead of additional take-home pay, an effective incentive system will have to provide that option. Expectancy motivation indicates that incentives are most effective when employees clearly can see that their extra work leads to increased rewards. It is important to provide extra compensation to employees as a reward for extra effort.

An individual incentive system may also be used as a means of measuring individual capabilities and initiative. Those employees who have special abilities and exert more effort can be identified for promotions or transfers to other more demanding and rewarding jobs. Two basic types of individual incentives are piece-rate systems and bonuses.

Piece-Rate Systems

The most basic individual incentive system is the piece-rate system. Under the straight piecework system, wages are determined by multiplying the number of units produced (such as garments sewn or customers contacted) by the piece-rate for one unit. The rate for each piece does not change regardless of the number of pieces produced. Because the cost is the same for each unit, the wage payment for each employee is easy to figure, and labor costs may be accurately predicted.

Differential Piece-Rate

A specialized type of piece-rate system, the *differential piece-rate* system, pays employees at one piece-rate if they produce less than a standard output, and at a higher piece-rate if they produce more than the standard. Developed by Frederick W. Taylor in the late 1800s, this system is designed to stimulate employees to achieve or exceed established standards of production. Managers often determine the quotas or standards by using thorough time and motion studies. For example, assume that the standard quota for a worker is set at 300 units per day and the standard rate is 14 cents per unit. For all units over the standard, however, the employee receives 20 cents per unit. Under this system, the worker who produces 400 units in one day would get $62 in wages (300 × 14¢; + (100 × 20¢). There are many other possible combinations of straight and differential piece-rate systems. The specific system used by a company depends upon many situational factors.

Despite its incentive value, the piecework system is difficult to use. One reason is that standards for many types of jobs are difficult and costly to determine.

In some instances, the cost of determining and maintaining the standards may be greater than the benefits derived from piecework. Jobs in which individuals have little control over output or in which high standards of quality are necessary also may be unsuited to piecework. Though the system still is widely used in certain industries, such as the garment industry, it is seldom used in white-collar, office, and cler-

ical jobs, in which an individual employee's performance often is affected by factors beyond the employee's control. For example, paying
a bank teller on a piece-rate basis for each customer transaction handled would be inappropriate. The teller does not control whether the
customer chooses one line or another and probably is not responsible
for that customer choosing to make a deposit or withdrawal.

Commissions

An individual incentive system that is widely used in sales jobs is the
commission. A commission is compensation that is computed as a percentage of sales in units or dollars. Commissions are integrated into
the pay given to sales workers in two common ways: straight commission and bonuses.

Straight Commission. In the straight commission system, a sales representative receives either a set amount or a percentage of the value of
the sales made. Adam Markson is a sales representative working for a
consumer products company. He receives no compensation if no sales
are made, but for all sales made in his territory Adam receives a percentage of the total amount of the sales. The advantage of this system
is that the sales representative must sell to earn. However, it has the
disadvantage of providing no security for the sales staff, even though
the product or service sold might be one that requires a long lead time
before purchasing decisions are made. One sales representative with a
telecommunications firm spent five months working with a large corporation to sell a $1 million phone and communication system, for
which he received a sizeable commission. However, during that five
months, he received no income; he was paid only when the sale was
closed and the equipment installed.

For that reason some employers use a **draw** system, in which the
sales representative can draw advance payments against future comis-
sions. The amount drawn then is deducted from future commission
checks. From the employer's side, one of the risks in a draw system is
that future commissions may not be large enough to repay the draw,
especially for a new or marginally successful salesperson. In addition,
arrangements must be made for repayment of drawn amounts if an
individual leaves the firm before earning the drawn amount in commission.

According to a national survey, about 21 percent of all sales representatives are paid through commissions only. The most frequently
used form of sales compensation is the *salary plus commission* approach.
Over half of the sales representatives surveyed are covered by this approach.[4]

Salary-Plus-Commission. The salary-plus-commission method of compensation is an attempt to combine the stability of a salary with the
performance emphasis of a commission. A common split is 80 percent
salary to 20 percent commission, although that split varies by industry
and with other variables.

National Linen Service, based in Atlanta, has 64 plants located from Florida to California in the Sunbelt states, providing linens and uniforms to a wide range of businesses. Each day the 1,250 National Linen route drivers pick up soiled linens and uniforms and replace them with clean ones. However, the route drivers, called *route sales representatives,* also are encouraged to look for new business and possible customers while making their route deliveries.

In the past, National Linen had used short sales contests to generate additional sales. During the contests, commissions were raised. These contests generated new business during a contest, but then the route sales representatives stopped selling until a new contest was announced.

To overcome these problems, a ten-month incentive program was developed using a bowling theme called "Strike It Rich." During the program drivers received their normal commissions for new accounts. In addition, each month sales representatives were awarded points for making new sales. Depending upon the average weekly dollar amount of

new account sales, a driver received a Spare (2236 points), a Strike (4472 points), or a Super Strike (6708 points). Those who held onto new accounts also generated additional superstrikes, strikes, and spares. Sales managers and route supervisors accumulated points based upon the results of their sales representatives.

All points earned could be converted into a gift certificate that could be used to purchase items from a merchandise award catalog. Each Super Strike earned allowed a driver to enter a Grand Slam drawing for the grand prize of a new car or ten consolation certificates valued at $1,000 each.

From the company standpoint, the most important result of the program was that sales increased by 35 percent—even more than management expected. Also, sales held fairly steady at the new level after the program ended and the route sales representatives were more aware of their selling responsibilities. In sum, the company and its route sales representatives did "strike it rich" through the use of a special incentive program.[5]

Special Incentive Programs. Another type of incentive is a special incentive program. Although special incentive programs can be developed for groups and for entire organizations, they focus on rewarding only high-performing individuals. Giving the salesperson who sells the most new cars a trip to Las Vegas is one example of a special incentive program. Sales contests, productivity contests, and other incentive schemes can be conducted so that individual employees receive extra compensation.

Special incentive programs are used widely in sales-related jobs. A national survey of 313 firms found that 64 percent of the surveyed firms used merchandise, travel, cash, or other incentives besides. Cash, merchandise, travel, and combinations of those were the most frequently used rewards. The main reasons for using the awards, according to those surveyed, were to achieve immediate sales gains and to focus attention on specific products.[6]

Bonuses

The bonus form of individual incentive compensation often is used at the executive or upper-management levels of an organization, although it can be used at lower levels too. Because of the broad nature of executive responsibilities, the bonuses for many executives are based on corporate or divisional performance. Many bonuses are similar to profit-sharing plans except that the bonus incentives are usually limited to upper-level managers instead of being shared with many employees. Executive bonus plans will be discussed in greater detail later in this chapter.

One method of determining an employee's annual bonus is to compute it as a percentage of the individual's base salary. Though technically this type of bonus is individual, it comes very close to being a group or organization-wide system. Since it is based on the profits of the division, the total performance of the division and its employees must be considered. A logical extension of this thinking is to offer group or organization-wide incentive systems.

Problems with Individual Incentives

There are a number of problems that must be faced with individual incentives. One major concern is to *keep the system current.* A bonus payment to a sales clerk on the basis of the dollar value of the sales may require changes to compensate for inflation or changes in the product line.

Another concern is that *employee competition* for incentives may produce undesirable results. Paying sales clerks in a retail store a commission may result in some clerks "fighting" over customers. Some sales clerks may be reluctant to work in departments that sell lesser-valued items if their commissions are figured on the basis of total sales. For example, clerks in a department store may concentrate on selling major appliances without giving adequate attention to the small household appliances. Ostracism and coercion of high performers also has been known to occur.

Any incentive system requires a *climate of trust and cooperation* between employees and managers. Figure 14–2 illustrates that the factors of trust and objectivity are related. As the amount of trust between employees and managers increases, the criteria used for determining

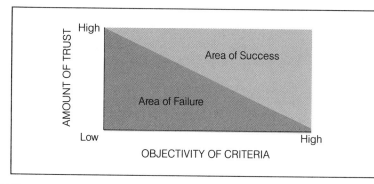

FIGURE 14–2
Factors Affecting Performance Rewards: Trust and Objectivity of Performance Criteria.

SOURCE: E. E. Lawler, III, "Using Pay to Motivate Job Performance," *Pay and Organizational Effectiveness: A Psychological View,* (NY: McGraw-Hill, 1971), pp. 157–59, 162–75.

rewards tied to performance can become less objective. In some situations trust may be so low that even use of highly objective measures may be unwise. However, if workers have a high level of trust and good working relationships with their superiors, they may accept more subjective performance measures.

In addition, if the workers believe that the incentive system is just a management scheme designed to make them work harder and that they will not adequately share in the gains, the individual incentive system will not be effective. A former sales representative with a major computer firm told of another sales person who spent months to secure a $2 million contract with a new customer and received a commission of $4,000. The former sales representative said, "You now have to excel and overachieve simply to make a living."[7]

Another problem is that an incentive system sometimes leads to overemphasis on one dimension of a job: If you are not careful, you may get more of what you emphasize than you wanted. An employee in a mattress factory who receives incentive compensation based on the number of units produced may turn out many mattresses but they may be of lower quality than they would be without the incentive system. A department store manager who is rewarded only for keeping costs down may not make some really necessary expenditures. Such problems have often occurred in Russia under its economic planning system.

Finally, individual incentive systems may be resisted by unions. Many unions are built on the concepts of security, seniority, and group solidarity instead of individual productivity. Incentive systems may favor only the most highly motivated, competent workers and may actually depress the average workers' earnings. For this and other reasons, group or organizational incentive systems often are used.

*Can you discuss three types of individual
incentives and some problems associated
with them?*

GROUP AND
ORGANIZATIONAL INCENTIVE SYSTEMS

A group or organizational incentive system provides rewards to all employees in a work unit, department, division, or organization. These incentives are designed to promote cooperation and a coordinated effort within the group or organization.

Group Incentives

A group incentive system may be useful in overcoming some of the problems associated with individual incentives. However, it may not lead to higher productivity than individual incentive systems because individual effort is not as directly tied to rewards. One critical factor in the group incentive system is the size of the group. If it becomes too large, employees may feel their individual effort will have little or no effect on the total performance of the group and the resulting reward.

Small-group incentive plans are a direct result of the growing number of complex jobs requiring interdependent effort. Small-group plans may encourage teamwork in groups of as many as 40 employees; however, there is nothing to encourage cooperation *between* groups. Groups, like individuals, may restrict output, resist revision of standards, and seek to gain at the expense of other groups.

Compensating different employee groups with separate incentives may cause them to overemphasize certain efforts to the detriment of the overall organizational good. For example, conflict often arises between the marketing and production branches of organizations because marketing's incentive compensation is based upon what is sold, while production's incentive compensation is based upon keeping unit production costs as low as possible. Marketing representatives may want to tailor products to customers' needs to increase their sales, but production managers want long production runs to lower costs. The overall company good may take second place. To deal with problems such as these, organizational incentive systems have been developed.

Organizational Incentives

An organization-wide incentive system compensates all employees in the organization based upon how well the organization as a whole does during the year. At Eastman Kodak Company in 1984, 93,000 employees shared $254.3 million in "wage dividends." Individual amounts were determined partly by employees' lengths of service; the average distributed to each participant was $2,730.[8]

The basic concept behind organization-wide incentive plans is that overall efficiency depends on organization or plantwide cooperation. The purpose of these plans is to produce teamwork.[9] For example, the conflict between marketing and production can be overcome by using an incentive that emphasizes organizational profit and productivity. To be effective an incentive program should include everyone from hourly paid employees to managers and executives. Common organizational incentive systems include Scanlon plans and various profit-sharing plans.

Scanlon Plan. A unique type of organization-wide incentive plan is the Scanlon plan. Since its development in 1927, the Scanlon plan has been implemented in many companies, especially smaller industrial ones.

The basic concept underlying the Scanlon plan is that efficiency depends on teamwork and plantwide cooperation. The plan has two main features: (1) a system of departmental committees and a plant-screening committee to evaluate all cost-saving suggestions, and (2) a direct incentive to all employees to improve efficiency.

The system is activated through the establishment of employee committees. The committees receive and review cost-saving ideas. Suggestions beyond the level of authority of departmental committees are passed to the plant committee for review. Savings that result from suggestions are passed on to members of the organization, as in the quality circle approach discussed in Chapter 6.

Incentive rewards are paid to employees on the basis of improvements in pre-established ratios. Ratios of "labor costs to total sales value" or "total production" or "total hours to total production" are most commonly used.[10] Savings due to differences between actual and expected ratios are placed in a bonus fund. A predetermined percentage of this fund then is split between employees and the company.

The Scanlon plan is not a true profit-sharing plan because employees receive incentive compensation for reducing labor costs, regardless of whether or not the organization ultimately makes a profit. Where the Scanlon plan has been implemented, some firms have experienced an increase in productivity and a decrease in labor costs. Also, employee attitudes have become more favorable, and cooperation between management and workers has increased.

Profit Sharing. As its name implies, a profit-sharing program distributes a portion of the profits of the organization to the employees. Typically, the percentage of the profits to be set aside for distribution to employees is agreed upon by the end of the year before profits are distributed.

Profit-sharing plans often distribute a substantial amount of extra compensation to employees. Southland Corporation, the holding company for 7-Eleven Stores, has 50,000 employees at 7,000 work locations. Under its profit-sharing plan the company shares 10 percent of its profits before taxes. Employees participating in the plan defer part of their pay and Southland matches part of it based upon an employee's length of service.[11]

The major objectives of profit-sharing plans are to make employees more profit-conscious, to encourage cooperation and teamwork, and to involve employees in the success and growth of the organization. In some profit-sharing plans, employees receive their portion of the profits at the end of the year; in others, the profits are deferred, placed in a fund, and made available to employees upon retirement or upon leaving the organization.

Unions used to be skeptical of profit-sharing plans. However, in recent years, organized labor has supported profit-sharing plans in which employees' pay increases are tied to improved company performance. These plans, some of which are labeled *gain-sharing* plans, have been used by Eastern Airlines, Wheeling-Pittsburgh Steel, and other firms.[12]

Employee Stock Ownership Plan (ESOP)

A common type of profit sharing is the **employee stock ownership plan (ESOP).** An ESOP is designed to give employees some ownership of the company for which they work, thereby increasing their commitment, loyalty, and effort. ESOPs have also been used by employees to buy out firms that might otherwise have been closed. Because it leads to favorable income tax treatment for the firm, employee ownership of the company, through grants of stock to the employees, is encouraged.

Establishing an ESOP. An ESOP is established when a company uses its stock as collateral to borrow capital from a financial institution. Once the loan repayment begins through the use of company profits, a certain amount of stock is released and allocated to an Employee Stock Ownership Trust (ESOT). Employees are assigned shares of stock in the trust based upon their length of service and pay levels. Upon retirement, death, or separation from the company, employees or their beneficiaries can sell the stock back to the trust or on the open market, if the stock is publicly traded.[13]

Advantages and Disadvantages. There are several advantages to an ESOP. The major one is that the firm receives highly favorable tax treatment of the earnings that are earmarked for use in the ESOP. Secondly, an ESOP gives employees a "piece of the action" so that they can share in the growth and profitability of their employer.[14]

However, that sharing also can be a disadvantage because employees have "all of their eggs in one basket." Both their base wages/salaries and their retirement benefits are dependent upon the performance of the firm. If the stock has not increased in value because the company has not prospered, the employee may become disenchanted with this form of compensation. In particular, setting up an ESOP to save a firm that would have otherwise gone bankrupt does not guarantee that the firm will survive. In spite of some disadvantages, ESOPs have grown in popularity. The examples of Denver Yellow Cab and People Express illustrate why ESOPs have grown in usage.

PAYSOPs. A special type of ESOP is a **PAYSOP,** a payroll-based stock ownership plan. In a PAYSOP, stock of a firm is placed into a trust. The amount is not tied to company earnings but to the firm's payroll, and up to 3.25 percent of the payroll over a five-year period can be directly credited against the federal income owed by the firm. Employees receive allocations, in proportion to their pay, of up to $100,000

ESOP FABLE

Through an Employee Stock Ownership Plan (ESOP) a group of employees was able to purchase Denver Yellow Cab in 1979. Before that date the company had a driver turnover rate of 200–300 percent a year and absentee ownership. Worried about their job security, a group of union cab drivers bought the company for $2 million. By contributing $200,000 from their union strike fund and borrowing from a bank, the drivers established an ESOP. Ownership shares are computed on the basis of the number of hours worked. Part-time and full-time employees who work at least five days a month can participate. A rotating board of directors sets policy for a four-person executive team that replaced the top manager in the firm. However, not all employees have joined, and shop workers and dispatchers have their own unions.

By 1984, the bank loan was repaid and ESOP members started receiving dividends. The turnover rate dropped below 20 percent, the safety record improved, maintenance costs decreased, and drivers took better care of "their" equip-ment. Several Yellow Cab drivers who talked with a reporter in 1983, said, "We're going to buy our building and modernize our dispatching system as soon as we pay off the bank loan." The emphasis was placed on "we."

A different reason for an ESOP is illustrated by People Express Airline. Operating mainly in the eastern U.S., People Express has 3,000 full- and part-time workers. An individual must buy 100 shares of stock in order to work for the company. If an employee cannot afford the stock, an interest-free loan, which is repaid through payroll deductions, is arranged. The purpose of the ESOP is to generate capital to buy new equipment and planes for the airline. Also, because the employees are not unionized, People Express has flexibility in making work assignments. Pilots take reservations between flights and other employees are cross-trained as flight attendants, ticket counter workers, and baggage handlers. This flexibility means lower costs, allowing People Express to offer lower fares than its competition on many routes.[15]

each year. They do not pay any tax on the PAYSOP allocations until the funds are removed upon retirement, death, or separation from the firm.[16] Because it is based on payroll rather than capital investments and assets, a PAYSOP is appropriate for many firms, especially service-oriented firms that may not have large capital asset needs.[17]

Can you describe the nature of a Scanlon Plan and an Employee Stock Ownership Plan?

Many firms, especially large ones, administer executive compensation somewhat differently than compensation for lower-level employees. Such administration often includes incentives, as well other forms of compensation. An executive typically is someone in the top two levels of an organization, such as president or corporate vice-president. Two objectives influence executive compensation:

1. Tying the overall performance of the organization over a period of time to the compensation paid executives
2. Insuring that the total compensation given key executives is competitive with the compensation packages in other firms that might employ them.

At the heart of most executive compensation plans is the idea that executives should be rewarded if the organization grows in profitability and value over a period of years. Because many executives are in high tax brackets, their compensation often is provided in ways that offer significant tax savings. Therefore, their total compensation package is more significant than their base pay.

Executive Compensation Components

There are four components in most executive compensation packages. Base *pay* and *benefits* offered to executives are the two components that are similar to the compensation provided other employees. However, the other two components, *bonuses* and *stock options*, accentuate the idea of executive compensation as a package.

Performance-based supplemental compensation in the form of executive bonuses and stock options attempt to tie executive compensation to the long-term growth and success of the organization. As would be expected, this supplemental compensation is prevalent in the private sector, but rarely used in the public sector and other nonprofit organizations. The final component of an executive compensation package is composed of a wide range of special benefits and amenities known as *perquisites*, often referred to as *"perks."* As shown in Figure 14–3, a survey of 275 firms found that the average top executive's compensation package is put together as follows: 48 percent salary, 37 percent supplemental compensation (bonuses, stock options, incentives, etc.), 14 percent benefits, and 1 percent perks.

Each component is discussed in this chapter, but it is important to indicate how executive compensation is determined. The president of a family-owned company told a consultant, "My compensation will be whatever I want it to be and that the company can afford." That approach may be widespread in private companies, but in publicly-owned firms (those that trade their stock on the open market) executive compensation oversight and review responsibilities commonly are handled by a compensation committee.

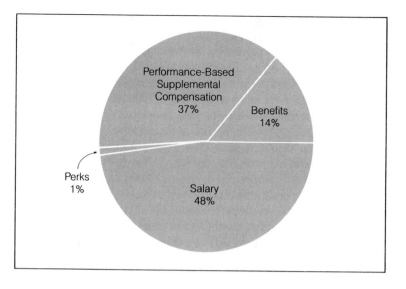

FIGURE 14–3
Executive Compensation
Components.

SOURCE: Percentages from *U.S. News & World Report*, October 17, 1983, pp. 72–74.

Compensation Committee. A **compensation committee** usually is a subgroup of the board of directors that is composed of directors who are not officers of the firm. Compensation committees generally make recommendations for approval by the board of directors on overall pay policies, salaries for the top officers, supplemental compensation such as stock options and bonuses, and additional perquisites for executives. A survey of 122 companies found that about 40 percent of the compensation committees also become involved in top management succession planning.[18]

A COMPENSATION COMMITTEE usually is a subgroup of the board of directors composed of outside directors.

Executive Pay

Salaries of executives vary by type of job, size of company, region, and industry. Top executives in the New York City area and in California have higher average cash compensation (approximately $150,000 per year), than executives in the southeastern and southwestern U.S. ($116,500-$126,400 per year). On average, salaries make up about half of top executives' total compensation.[19] One study of executive cash compensation (which includes salary and cash bonuses) found that what an executive earns depends more on the company and the job held than it does on the executive's qualifications. Job complexity and the company's ability to pay were much more important than the experience and education of the executive.[20]

Performance-Based Supplemental Compensation

It is common for executive compensation to be tied to performance of the company as a whole or to the performance of a unit for which an executive has responsibility. The most common supplemental methods are bonuses and stock options.

Executive Bonus Plans. Because executive performance is difficult to determine, bonus compensation for executives must reflect some kind of performance measure if it is to be meaningful. As an example, Pier 1, a retail chain with over 250 stores based in Fort Worth, Texas, ties annual bonuses for managers to store profitability. The bonuses have amounted to as much as 35 percent of a store manager's base salary.[21]

Bonuses for executives can be determined in several ways. One simple way is to use a discretionary system, whereby bonuses are awarded based upon the judgments of the chief executive officer and the board of directors. However, the absence of formal, measurable targets is a major drawback of this approach. Another way is to tie bonuses to specific measures, such as return on investment, earnings per share, or net profits before tax. More complex systems create bonus pools and thresholds above which bonuses are computed.[22] Whatever method is used, it is important to describe it so that executives trying to earn bonuses understand the plan; otherwise the incentive effect will be diminished.[23]

Stock Options. Another way to provide incentive compensation to executives is through the use of stock options. A **stock option** gives an employee the right to buy stock in a company, usually at an advantageous price. Many different types of stock options have been used, depending upon the tax laws in effect. It is beyond the scope of this text to list and discuss the different types. However, one type, the *incentive stock option*, is highlighted to illustrate how stock options work.

With the incentive stock option (ISO), an executive is granted an option to buy stock. On that date, the option price must be at the fair market value of the stock, and the option can be effective for up to 10 years. The executive then exercises the option at some future date. All options must be exercised in the order in which they were granted. When the executive sells the stock, the difference between the grant price and the sale price is taxed at the capital gains rate. Tax regulations require the executive to hold the stock at least two years after the grant date and at least one year after the option is exercised. The stock shares that are purchased are provided by the company through treasury stock, the purchase of the stock on the open market at the time the option is granted, or the issuance of new stock.[24]

Created by the Economic Recovery Tax Act of 1981, ISOs have grown in popularity since then. Within a year after the passage of the Act, 61 percent of the 100 largest firms and 54 percent of the smaller corporations surveyed had created ISOs.[25] The popularity of ISOs undoubtedly will continue to grow unless changes are made in the tax laws.

One advantage of an ISO is that it provides an executive the opportunity to benefit from the long-term growth of the firm. The president of one company whose stock was selling at a depressed price of $4 a share, has received stock options at that price on 10,000 shares. Over

PERSONNEL IN PRACTICE

"THE MILLIONAIRES"

Is any executive worth $1 million? In 1983–84 top executives with NCR, Ford Motor Company, E-Systems, Exxon, Apple Computer, General Motors (GM), Sears Roebuck, and other firms received over $1 million in salary and bonuses in one year. For instance, by exercising stock options received over a ten-year period and through a salary and bonus plan, William S. Anderson, Chairman of NCR, received $13.2 million in one year. Chairman Philip Caldwell, Ford's Chairman, made $1.4 million in salary and bonuses in 1983, compared to $445,833 in 1982. At General Motors in 1983, Chairman Roger Smith received $1 million; nearly 6,000 other executives received bonuses averaging $31,289 per person. In answer to critics, executives point out that while these amounts may seem large, they should be compared to the $45 million a year received by Beatle Paul McCartney, $2.2 million received by Tom Brokaw of NBC News, and the $3.9 million over three years received by football player Herschel Walker. Also, the huge payments often represent the exercising of stock options given over several years as an incentive to guide a firm to long-term growth.

Nonetheless, such large payments have led to cries of outrage by politicians, union leaders, and others. Moreover, the huge payments for GM and Ford executives came shortly before these companies were to start contract negotiations with the United Auto Workers (UAW) union which represented many of the companies' employees. During those negotiations GM and Ford asked the union to limit wage and benefit increases. As a result, UAW President Owen Bieber said, "If these executives who are providing so well for themselves think for one minute that they can convince workers to do without an up-front raise this summer, they'd better think again."

Even well-known management writer Peter Drucker has expressed concern about the size of the payments and suggested that either voluntary or mandatory limitations be placed on executive compensation by corporate boards. In several cases, an executive's compensation increased at a rate that exceeded the growth in profitability of a firm. For example, in 1983 the chief executive for Mobil received a 36 percent pay increase, even though Mobil's earnings dropped 43 percent. Undoubtedly, executives will continue to receive large payments, and critics will continue to suggest steps to limit executive compensation.[26]

time, if the stock price increases to $25 a share, the executive stands to gain $210,000 for making a $40,000 investment when he exercised his option, and the gain is taxed at the lower capital gains rates.

Another advantage is that the executive is tied to the company with "golden handcuffs." Because all options must be exercised within 90

PERQUISITES ("perks") are special benefits for executives that are usually non-cash items.

days after leaving the company, an executive who leaves may forfeit gains based upon the future growth of the former employer.

Criticism of Performance-Based Supplements. The major criticism of executive compensation is the disparities between the total compensation received and corporate performance. Although supplements such as bonuses and stock options are supposed to be tied to the performance of the firm, several studies have found that executive compensation is not closely related to performance. For example, over a 10-year period, the bonuses of senior executives in 400 companies were increased by 12 percent in real dollars. Long-term incentives tied to earnings added 25 percent to total compensation. Yet, the shareholders' value of the stock declined in real dollars by 2 percent.[27]

Another criticism is that executive compensation does not provide long-term rewards. Instead, performance within a given year leads to

FIGURE 14–4
Special Benefits and Perks for Executives.

FIRMS	SHARE OF FIRMS GIVING TO EXECUTIVES
Industrial Companies	
Executive physical exams	88%
Executive parking	73%
Stock options	66%
Assigned company car	62%
Liability insurance	60%
Country club membership	47%
Luncheon club membership	45%
Special vacation policy	41%
Financial counseling	36%
Deferred compensation	35%
Assigned chauffeur	29%
Executive dining room	22%
Banks	
Assigned company car	89%
Executive parking	79%
Executive physical exams	79%
Luncheon club membership	75%
Country club membership	68%
Liability insurance	64%
Executive dining room	57%
Assigned chauffeur	50%
Stock options	46%
Special vacation policy	43%
Deferred compensation	18%
Financial counseling	14%

SOURCE: Reprinted from *U.S. News & World Report* issue of Oct. 17, 1983, p. 74. Copyright, 1983, U.S. News & World Report Inc.

large rewards even though corporate performance over time may be mediocre. This difference is especially true if the yearly measures used are carefully chosen. Even earnings per share can be manipulated by selling assets, liquidating inventories, or reducing research and development expenditures. All of these actions may make company performance look better, thus giving executives bigger bonuses, but the actions may impair the long-term growth of the firm.[28] Reaction to the large bonuses received by General Motors and Ford executives illustrates some of the problems with large supplements. For these reasons, stock options, especially incentive stock-options, provide a better tie to performance over time than do bonuses.

Executive Benefits and Perquisites

In addition to the regular benefits received by other employees, executives often have special benefits and perquisites available to them. **Perquisites** ("perks") are special benefits for executives that are usually non-cash items. Figure 14–4 lists some that are available.

Perks and special executive benefits are useful in tying executives to firms and demonstrating their importance to the company. It is the "status enhancement" value of perks that is important to many executives. Visible symbols of status allow executives to be seen as "very important people (VIPs)" inside and outside their companies. In addition, perks can provide substantial tax savings to executives with high salaries because many perks are not taxed as income.[29]

Can you identify the components of an executive compensation package?

PERSONNEL TODAY AND TOMORROW
THE GOLDEN PARACHUTE

One special type of benefit available to some executives is known as a "golden parachute." A golden parachute provides protection and security to executives who may be affected if their firms are acquired by another firm. Typically, employment contracts are written so that special compensation is given to executives if they are negatively affected in a merger of acquisition. For example, the chief executive officer of Federal-Mogul Corporation is guaranteed five years worth of salary if termination occurs for any reason besides retirement, death, or disability or if he resigns within 12 months after a demotion. Essex Chemical Corporation provides golden parachute protection for the top five officers and Phillips Petroleum Company provides protection for the top six officers.

A survey found that, if used, just 50 percent of the parachute packages offered by large companies could cost the companies $1–5 million. With all of the mergers, acquisitions, tender offers, and corporate buyouts that occur each year, it is no surprise that top executives insist on protection. Having a golden parachute is one of the privileges of being an executive which is likely to continue to be important in future years.[30]

SUMMARY

■ An incentive is additional compensation that is related to performance.

■ An effective incentive program should tie incentives to performance, recognize individual differences, recognize organizational factors, and be continually monitored.

■ There are three types of incentive systems: individual, group, and organization-wide.

■ Individual incentives include piece-rate systems, commissions, special incentive programs, and bonuses.

■ To overcome some of the problems associated with individual incentives, group and organizational incentive systems are used.

■ One organizational incentive system is the Scanlon plan. The Scanlon plan provides rewards to employees based upon cost savings and is built on cooperation and participation.

■ Profit-sharing plans set aside a portion of the profits earned by organizations for distribution to employees.

■ An Employee Stock Ownership Plan (ESOP) is a stock bonus plan in which employees gain ownership in the firm for which they work. A PAYSOP is a special type of profit-sharing stock plan based on payroll expenditures.

■ Executive compensation must be viewed as a total package composed of pay, performance-based supplemental compensation, and special benefits or perquisites.

■ A compensation committee, which is a subgroup of the board of directors, has authority to review executive compensation plans.

■ Performance-based supplemental compensation plans often represent a significant portion of an executive's compensation package. Executive bonus plans and stock options are the two most common plans. An incentive option is a special type of stock option that has wide usage.

■ Many different special benefits and perks, all of which provide additional non-cash compensation, are available to executives.

REVIEW QUESTIONS AND EXERCISES

1. Identify what an incentive is and list some key guidelines that should be followed when establishing an incentive system.

2. Give several examples of individual incentives that you have received or that have been used in an organization in which you are employed. What problems did you observe with those you mentioned?

3. Why do you think that increased emphasis on productivity in the U.S. has led to greater interest in Scanlon plans and Employee Stock Ownership Plans?

4. Why are performance-based supplements and special benefits and perks important in an executive compensation package?

Exercises

a. Contact a local firm or sales representative and find out what individual incentive, bonus, and special programs are used for people in sales jobs. Be sure to ask about special contests, trips, and awards that have been given. Then prepare a written or oral report for presentation to your instructor.

b. Organize a debate of the following statement: "Many executives receive too much compensation. It is absurd for anyone to make $800,000 to $1 million in a year, when total compensation is figured." Take either the positive or negative side, research the issue, and conduct the debate in class.

CASE

HOW CAN WE GET THEM TO WORK "ON CALL"?

Sara Richards has been a nuclear medicine technologist at University General Hospital for five years. The only aspect of Sarah's job that she has found dissatisfying is having to "take call"; that is, to be available to come in and work on short notice. She receives no compensation for her waiting time even though it limits what she can do. Two months ago Sarah accidentally discovered a difference in compensation practices between her department and the other departments of radiology.

The policy for taking call in Sarah's department states that the technologist will be on call for one-week periods, either by telephone or electronic pager; the technologist is not paid for the time spent being on call, but is compensated by receiving time-and-a-half for the hours actually worked when called in. The on-call policy for the other departments states that the technologist will be on call for one-week periods and will receive 18 hours' straight pay for being on call and time-and-a-half for hours actually spent at the hospital if called in.

Sarah and the other technologists decided that the discrepancy between the two policies should be brought to the attention of the nuclear medicine administration liaison, John Kifer. When Kifer told Dr. Benson, head of the radiology department that the technologists were very unhappy and that they might refuse to take call, Dr. Benson said that the department could not afford to pay them for on-call time.

The technologists are frustrated and disappointed by the response to their complaints. They feel that the "benefits" that accrue to others in the radiology area are not being fairly distributed. They now feel that they have exhausted all their options and can see no other alternative but to stop taking call in an effort to force a decision. Although Sarah realizes the complications in refusing to take calls, she can see no other alternative. As of February 23, the technologists have decided that there will be no call list and the pagers will be left at work.

Questions

1. How might individual incentives be used in this situation?
2. Why might a group incentive system be a possible alternative?
3. What would you do as the hospital administrator if the technologists refuse to take calls?

NOTES

1. Adapted from William Baldwin, "This Is the Answer," *Forbes*, July 5, 1982, pp. 50–52, and Maryann Mrowca, "Ohio Firm Relies on Incentive-Pay System to Motivate Workers and Maintain Profits", *Wall Street Journal*, August 12, 1983, p. 19.
2. Cheryl B. Robbins, "Design Effective Incentive Plans," *Personnel Administrator*, May 1983, pp. 8–10.
3. A review of research can be found in Paul Tolchinsky and Donald C. King, "Do Goals Mediate the Effects of Incentives on Performance?" *Academy of Management Review* 5 (October 1980), pp. 455–457.
4. John A. Byrne, "Motivating Willy Loman," *Forbes*, January 30, 1984, p. 91.
5. Adapted from Reg Manhood, "National Linen Service Drives Home a Message," *Sales and Marketing Management*, April 2, 1984, pp. 107–110.
6. Al Urbanski, "Good Times or Bad, Motivators Rage On," *Sales & Marketing Management*, April, 1984, pp. 107–110.
7. John A. Byrne, "Motivating Willy Loman," p. 91.
8. "Kodak Workers To Receive Bonus," *Omaha World Herald*, March 18, 1984, p. C3.
9. K. Dow Scott and Timothy Coller, "The Team That Works Together Earns Together," *Personnel Journal*, March 1984, pp. 59–67.
10. Linda S. Tyler and Bob Fisher, "The Scanlon Concept: A Philosophy As Much As a System," *Personnel Administrator*, July 1983, pp. 33–37.
11. John V. Hoerr, "Why Labor and Management Are Both Buying Profit Sharing," *Business Week*, January 10, 1983, p. 84.
12. "Profit Sharing Design Fits Company/Worker Needs," *Employee Benefit Plan Review*, December 1982, pp. 24–26 ff.
13. For more explanation, see John J. Miller, "ESOPS, TRASOPS, and PAYSOPs: A Guide for the Perplexed Manager," *Management Review*, September 1983, pp. 40–45.
14. Randy G. Swad, "Stock Ownership Plan: A New Employee Benefit," *Personnel Journal* 60 (June 1981), pp. 453–455.
15. Adapted from Polly T. Taplin, "ESOPs Meet the Needs of a Variety of Companies," *Employee Benefit Plan Review*, June 1983, pp. 10–14, and Lucien Rhodes, "That Daring Young Man and His Flying Machines," *INC.*, January 1984, pp. 42–52.
16. Frederick W. Rumack and Robert E. Wallace, "The PAYSOP: A Gift from ERTA," *Personnel Administrator*, January 1983, pp. 66–69.
17. Howard V. Sontag and Gary G. Quintiere, "PAYSOPs: ERTA's Revised TRASOPs," *Compensation Review*, Second Quarter 1982, pp. 14–27.
18. *Compensation*, no. 909, sec. 313 (Washington, DC: Bureau of National Affairs, 1984), pp. 155–156.
19. "What Executives Are Getting Paid These Days," *U.S. News & World Report*, October 17, 1983, pp. 72–74.
20. N. C. Agarwal, "Determinants of Executive Compensation," *Industrial Relations* 20 (1981), pp. 36–45.

21. R. H. Bork, "Coming of Age," *Forbes*, January 30, 1984, p. 96.

22. For a description of various plans and their advantages and disadvantages, see *Management Incentive Plans* (Chicago: A. S. Hansen, n.d.).

23. Lawrence Wangler, "Simplicity Improves Understanding of Executive Compensation," *Personnel Administrator*, June 1983, pp. 90–93.

24. A discussion of ISOs can be found in Stephen H. Wolfe, "Investment Strategies for the Incentive Stock Options Created By the 1981 Tax Act," Compensation Review, First Quarter 1982, pp. 10–20.

25. "Most Large Companies Pay Executive Bonuses and Offer Long-Term Incentives," *Employee Benefit Plan Review*, January 1983, p. 79.

26. Adapted from Stephen Koepp, "Those Million-Dollar Salaries," *Time*, May 7, 1984, pp. 84–85, and *Business Week*, May 7, 1984, pp. 89–92.

27. Luis J. Brindisi, "Why Executive Compensation Programs Go Wrong," *Wall Street Journal*, June 14, 1982, p. 18.

28. "Executive Compensation: Looking to the Long Term Again," *Business Week*, May 9, 1983.

29. Karen M. Evans, "The Power of Perquisites," *Personnel Administrator*, May 1984, pp. 45–52.

30. John D. McMillan and Gregory S. Reisinger, "Takeover Protection for Executives: The Golden Parachute," *Compensation Review*, First Quarter 1983, pp. 34–43; and "Look Out Below," *Forbes*, February 13, 1984, p. 8.

Employee Benefits

When you have read this chapter, you should be able to:

1. Define a benefit and highlight why benefits are important to both employees and employers.
2. Explain two security benefits.
3. Identify three retirement policy issues, including some Social Security changes and concerns.
4. List and define at least eight pension-related terms.
5. Differentiate among an IRA, 401(k) plan, and Keogh plan.
6. Concisely describe three benefits related to time off.
7. Explain why health-care cost management has become important and list some methods of achieving it.
8. Identify four types of financial and other benefits offered.
9. Discuss benefit communication and flexible benefits as benefit administration considerations.

PERSONNEL AT WORK

ST. PAUL GOES FLEXIBLE

The St. Paul Companies, Inc., a large and diversified insurance firm with 8,700 regular salaried employees, implemented a flexible benefit program beginning in July 1983. St. Paul had made the decision to consider flexible benefits in late 1981.

"While the benefit program in existence was adequate," observed Carol L. Beatty, Compensation Administrator, "it was not tailored to meet the needs of our current employee population. Also, we were interested in something that would make our benefits more visible and more valuable to our employees. The company felt it could offer a better health care program with flexible benefits. Certain tax advantages also made flexible benefits attractive."

The choices available under the "Flex" program include several health plans, dental coverage, long-term disability coverage, optional life insurance for the employee and dependents, the option of purchasing additional vacation days, two reimbursement accounts (one for medical and dental expenses, one for legal services and work-related dependent care), and a 401(k) plan called Voluntary Tax Deferred Savings.

Employees can pay for these options with "Flex dollars" (pretax dollars) which come partly from the company and partly from their salaries. A flex-dollar limit represents the upper limit an employee can spend on a pre tax basis. Any benefits purchased in excess of this limit must be bought with after-tax dollars. However, the pre-tax limit is more than sufficient for most employees.

The formula for the company flex dollars contribution contains two variables: a flat dollar amount based on medical/dental costs and a percentage amount based on long term disability, which is tied to salary. The flat dollar rate is determined by where the employee lives. "We divided the country into four rating zones and varied the medical premium based on area." The same is true for salary reduction—a flat dollar rate and a percentage based on salary.

While the flex formula was devised to allow employees sufficient funds to use the reserve accounts, flex dollars can be used in other ways as well. Contributions to 401(k) up to 5% of an employee's salary are allowed from flex dollars. Employees can also buy up to five additional days vacation.

The implementation of the St. Paul Flexible Compensation Program included the development of a suitable design, an administrative system that would interface with existing systems, and a communications pro-

gram that would enable employees to get the most value from the program. Three teams worked simultaneously for almost 1½ years to produce a program that would meet corporate goals and the budget and time constraints set by top management. The key to success seemed to lie in the great amount of advanced planning done in all areas. Furthermore, the goals in each area were reasonable considering the accepted constraints. Developing an enrollment system that could accommodate the Flex selections and then interface with the existing payroll and profit-sharing systems presented one of the biggest challenges. For instance, because of the complexity of the recordkeeping system and the need to fulfill IRS regulations, it was necessary to place some limitations on employees' ability to change Flex choices during the year.

Beatty said, "Our graphics department created several sketches for a series of newsletters and posters that would run over a ten-week period. The one chosen for the kickoff of our employee benefits enrollment program was a sketch of a mime juggling, with all sorts of things up in the air. That was pretty much how we felt at the time—employees were juggling all those decisions." Beatty felt that all the selections would fall neatly into place by the end of the enrollment process and this prophecy seemed to hold true for most employees. All employees received a personalized enrollment form along with a workbook containing instructions and a sample form. In addition, at employee meetings a slide-and-tape presentation was followed by a question-and-answer session in all locations. The audiovisual program urged employees to think through their decisions and make their selections by using a cafeteria analogy. Individual consultations were held at the employee's request. The result was that every eligible employee was enrolled and received the first flex-produced paycheck on time.

When preliminary statistics were collected there were no major surprises, according to Beatty. The percentage of people who waived medical coverage increased from 18 percent to 21 percent. "This was probably because employees felt they could obtain adquate insurance through a spouse's plan and use the Flex dollars in another way. About 10 percent chose the higher deductibles, which is well in line with other companies' experiences."

The company now is several years into the program and it continues to be a success. Only efforts by the Internal Revenue Service to institute tax regulations that would make employees count the value of flexible benefits as taxable income have caused a continuing concern. But from the perspective of both the employees and the company, St. Paul's flexible benefits program is a winner.[1]

A BENEFIT
is additional compensa-
tion given to employees
as a reward for organi-
zational membership.

*"Companies are recognizing that they sim-
ply cannot afford to continue to pile on benefits year after year, as they have for the
past two decades."*
THOMAS E. WOOD

The innovative effort of the St. Paul Companies to better manage
benefits programs illustrates both the importance and the creativity required in this area. Unlike incentive programs, benefits are available to
all employees as long as they are members of the organization, regardless of differences in individual performance. For example, if an accountant is performing poorly but is still employed, he or she is entitled to medical insurance and other benefits. Only when the employee
resigns or is terminated does the individual lose benefits.

BENEFITS OVERVIEW

A **benefit** is additional compensation given to employees as a reward
for organizational membership. The benefits given to employees by an
employer represent *indirect compensation*, which is, tangible benefits in
a form other than money. The employees get the *value* of the money
without actually receiving money. That is why benefits generally are
not taxed as income to employees, in spite of repeated attempts by the
U.S. Internal Revenue Service to do so. For this reason, benefits represent a somewhat more valuable reward to employees than an equivalent cash payment. For example, Marlene Boetcher, who is employed
by Larle Corporation, is in a 25 percent income tax bracket. For her to
pay the $300 tuition for some graduate classes at a local university,
Marlene would have to earn $400 [$400 − (25% tax × $400) = $300
net pay after taxes]. However, if Larle as her employer provides a tuition plan and pays the $300, Marlene does not claim that amount as
income. So, benefits represent a very desirable form of compensation
to employees, especially if a wide range of benefits is available.

Benefit Costs

Although benefits are generally not considered a part of an individual's
compensation for tax purposes, they do represent a significant expenditure from an employer's point of view. The U.S. Chamber of Commerce surveys a large number of industries on a regular basis to determine the extent of benefit payments. In a recent survey, benefits
represented an average of 36.6 percent of total payroll. As a result, the
average employee receives $7,582 worth of benefits per year. However,
the amount of benefits varied significantly in different fields. An employee in the department store industry averaged over $100 per week
less in benefits than an employee in the chemical manufacturing industry.[2]

PAYMENTS	PERCENTAGE
Legally required payments (Employer's share only)	9.0%
Pension, insurance, and other agreed upon payments (Employer's share only)	13.6%
Paid rest periods	2.3%
Paid leave	9.4%
Profit-sharing payments, bonuses, etc.	2.3%
Total	36.6%

Reprinted with the permission of the Chamber of Commerce of the United States of America from *Employee Benefits, 1983.*

FIGURE 15–1
Average Benefit Payments 1983.

Figure 15–1 shows some details from the Chamber of Commerce survey. The largest benefit costs were associated with pension and insurance benefits. The average U.S. employee received 13.6 cents in pension and insurance benefits for every dollar of base pay. Within this area health insurance represented the greatest expense, and that expense has grown significantly in the past decade. The second most costly area was payments for time-off related benefits. Vacation pay represented the greatest expenditure in this segment, while holiday pay and paid sick leave followed vacation pay as costs. Nine percent of total benefits costs reported were legally required payments. These include social security, unemployment compensation, and worker's compensation. Finally, profit-sharing and paid rest periods each represented 2.3 percent of payroll. The profit sharing area includes profit-sharing plan payments, contributions to employee thrift plans, service awards, suggestion system awards, Christmas bonuses, and employee tuition aid expenditures.

Can you define a benefit and highlight why benefits are important to employees and employers?

Types of Benefits

There are many different types of benefits provided employees, as shown in Figure 15–2. For ease of classification, they are grouped into several types and a discussion of each of the following types is discussed.

■ Required security
■ Voluntary security
■ Retirement-related benefits
■ Time off-related benefits
■ Insurance and financial services
■ Social, recreational, and other benefits

WORKERS' COMPEN-SATION provides benefits to a person injured on the job.

There are several benefits that provide protection and/or security to employees. Some of the benefits are required by federal and state laws. Others are given voluntarily by management or are made available through provisions in labor/management contracts.

Workers' compensation, unemployment compensation, and *retirement-related* benefits are the most important of the required security benefits. Retirement benefits, including Social Security and pensions, are discussed in a separate section later in this chapter.

Workers' Compensation

Starting with the Federal Employee's Compensation Act of 1908 and laws enacted by California, New Jersey, Washington, and Wisconsin in 1911, workers' compensation laws have spread to all the remaining states. Workers' compensation costs are borne entirely by the employer on the theory that industrial accidents should be considered one of the costs of production.

Workers' compensation provides two types of payments to injured workers or to a killed worker's next of kin. Payment can be either in *cash paid directly to the worker* or it can be a *reimbursement for medical expenses, pain, and suffering.*

Workers' compensation plans originally provided only for physical injury. They have been expanded in many areas to cover emotional impairments that may have resulted from a physical injury. Also, emotional illnesses caused by job-related strain, stress, anxiety, or pressure may be covered. In one situation in Rhode Island, an employee became drunk at an office Christmas party and then fell and injured himself. Because the party was sponsored by the employer and employees were "expected" to attend, a court ruled that the company had to pay the costs as a workers' compensation claim.

Employers pay premiums for workers' compensation through participation in a private insurance fund or in a state-oriented compensation plan. Employer compensation rates often are related to job risk and safety records. The amount of compensation paid to employees depends upon the nature and severity of injury and varies from state to state, but it generally is equal to about two-thirds of the employee's regular earnings.

Compulsory vs. Elective plans. Workers' compensation laws may be either compulsory or elective. As of the writing of this text, all states but Texas, New Jersey, and South Carolina had compulsory laws for private employees. Every employer subject to *compulsory* law must comply with its provisions for compensation of work injuries. Under an *elective* law, employers have the option of accepting or rejecting the act. With an elective law, if an employer has rejected the act, an employee injured on the job may be unable to get compensation unless he or she sues for damages. In most states employees cannot be fired for filing workers' compensation claims.[3]

FIGURE 15–2
Examples of Different Benefits.

REQUIRED SECURITY	VOLUNTARY SECURITY	RETIREMENT RELATED	TIME OFF-RELATED	INSURANCE	FINANCIAL	SOCIAL & RECREATIONAL
1. Workers' compensation	1. Severance pay	1. Social Security	1. Birthdays	1. Medical	1. Credit union	1. Tennis courts
2. Unemployment compensation	2. Supplemental unemployment benefits	2. Pension fund	2. Vacation time	2. Dental	2. Cash profit-sharing	2. Bowling league
3. Old age, survivors' and disability insurance	3. Leave of absence	3. Early retirement	3. Company-subsidized travel	3. Survivor benefits	3. Company-provided housing or car	3. Company newsletter
4. State disability insurance		4. Preretirement counseling	4. Holidays	4. Accidental dismemberment insurance	4. Legal services	4. Professional memberships
5. Medicare hospital benefits		5. Retirement gratuity	5. Sick pay	5. Travel accident insurance	5. Purchase discounts	5. Retirement gratuity
		6. Retirement annuity plan	6. Military reserve time off	6. HMO fees	6. Stock plans	6. Counseling
		7. Disability retirement benefits	7. Election day	7. Group insurance rates	7. Financial conseling	7. Company-sponsored events
			8. Social-service sabbatical	8. Disability insurance	8. Moving expenses	8. Child care services
				9. Life insurance	9. Tuition assistance	9. Cafeteria
				10. Cancer insurance	10. Relocation mortgage differential	10. Season tickets
				11. Auto insurance		11. Service award jewelry

Criticisms of Workers' Compensation Laws. Because of the wide variation in state benefits, organized labor and other groups have pushed for the federal government to provide more control and more standardized benefits. Employers have resisted these efforts because many of the standardized provisions would raise benefit levels and employer costs. Several special workers' compensation laws have been passed at the federal level to focus on longshoremen, coal miners, and federal employees. However, costs of these programs have increased dramatically and numerous examples of abuse have been cited.[4] In addition, varying levels of benefits and costs by states provide some advantages for states with low benefit levels in attracting new industry because of lower payroll tax costs.[5]

Unemployment Compensation

Another legally-required benefit is unemployment compensation, which was established as part of the Social Security Act of 1935. Each state operates its own unemployment compensation system, and the provisions differ significantly from state to state.

Employers finance this benefit by paying up to 3.5 percent tax on the first $7,000 (or more, depending upon the state) annual earnings of each employee; this is paid to state and federal unemployment compensation funds.[6] If an employee is out of work and is actively looking for employment, he or she normally receives up to 26 weeks of pay, at the rate of 50 to 80 percent of normal pay.

Most employees are eligible. However, workers fired for misconduct or those who are not actively seeking work are generally ineligible. One problem is that some employees take advantage of the situation. In 1980, there were over 175,000 cases of fraud and abuse, involving $52.8 million in overpayments. For example, an unemployed Ohio woman listed her canary as a dependent to receive more money. She was caught when a state investigator called the school to check on the "dependent child."[7]

Criticisms of Unemployment Insurance. Proposed changes in unemployment insurance laws have been introduced in bills at both state and federal levels. One reason is the abuses, which have been estimated to cost over $50 million a year.[8] Another reason for the proposed changes is that many state unemployment funds are exhausted during economic slowdowns. In one economic dip the federal government had to loan 26 states about $14 billion to cover deficits in state unemployment funds.[9]

A major revision involving standardization of the laws has been suggested. Many state laws allow union workers who are on strike against an employer to collect unemployment benefits, a provision bitterly opposed by many employers. However, as long as the current laws stand, it is important for employers to be knowledgeable about them and to take action to reduce their unemployment insurance costs by keeping accurate records and sound follow-up.[10]

Supplemental Unemployment Benefits (SUB). Supplemental Unemployment Benefits (SUB) are closely related to unemployment compensation, but they are not required by law. First obtained by the United Steel Workers in 1955, a SUB program is a benefit provision negotiated by a union with an employer as part of the collective bargaining process. The provision requires company contributions to a fund which supplements the unemployment compensation available to employees from federal and/or state sources, or both. However, employers do not have unlimited financial responsibilities to SUB programs; during the early 1980s the SUB funds for employees at U.S. Steel, General Motors, and Firestone were underfunded because of the large number of workers laid off; thus, workers found that their SUB benefits were cut or eliminated.[11]

SUB programs, common to the automobile, rubber, and some metals industries, attempt to guarantee employees who are laid off or temporarily unemployed an amount close to the normal take-home pay for a limited amount of time. For example, one SUB plan provides laid-off employees 90 percent of their take-home pay for 26 weeks. The SUB payment is added to normal unemployment compensation to reach the 90 percent figure. Figure 15–3 shows a sample calculation for an SUB plan.

Severance Pay

Severance pay is a security benefit offered by some employers. Employees who lose their jobs permanently may receive a lump-sum payment if they are terminated by the employer. For example, if a plant closes because it is outmoded and no longer economically profitable to operate, the employees who lose their jobs receive a lump-sum payment based on their years of service because their employment with that company is permanently severed. Severance pay provisions often appear in union/management agreements and usually provide larger payments for employees with longer service.

A 1984 survey found that about three-fourths of the responding employers have severance pay plans. About a third of the firms pay one week of severance pay for each year of company service. The other firms have more varied methods of determining the amounts to be paid to severed employees. Most firms apply their policies to all employees, rather than differentiating by employee level.[12]

Can you explain at least two security benefits?

Normal pay at $5/hr and 40/hrs week	=	$200/wk
90% of normal pay	=	$180/wk
State unemployment compensation	=	− $ 82/wk
SUB pay		$ 98/wk

FIGURE 15–3
Sample Supplemental Unemployment Benefit Calculation.

A widespread package of benefits offered by most employers is one that attempts to provide income for employees when they retire. Few people have independent reserves to use when they retire. However, financial resources represent only one facet of the broader issue of retirement policies.

Retirement Policies

As a result of a 1978 amendment to the Age Discrimination in Employment Act, employers can no longer force employees to retire before age 70. Federal government workers cannot be forced to retire at any age, and several bills have been introduced in Congress to extend that prohibition to the private sector. Employers have developed different policies to comply with these regulations, but common policies used are the following:

- Normal retirement at age 65; mandatory at age 70
- Mandatory at age 70
- Normal retirement at 65; voluntary thereafter, with no mandatory age

"Normal retirement" is the age at which employees can retire and collect full pension benefits. One key issue that must be addressed by employers is whether or not individuals past age 65 who continue working receive the full benefit package, especially pension credits.[13] As changes in Social Security increase the age for full benefits past 65, these policies likely will be modified.

One author has forecast that the concept of retirement will become obsolete by the 21st century due to the number of significant social changes occurring, the aging of the workforce, and changes in technologies.[14] Nevertheless, in the short run some firms have special policies to encourage workers to retire early or to continue working part-time.

Early Retirement. Provisions for early retirement currently are included in many pension plans. Early retirement provides an opportunity for people to get away from a long-term job. Individuals who have spent 25 or 30 years working for the same employer may wish to use their talents in other areas.

From the employer's viewpoint, early retirement buy-out programs can be a way to cut back a work force and reduce costs. For example, Bank of America offered early retirement to salaried employees with at least 25 years of service. Over 3,000 employees were eligible and about one-third of them took advantage of the program, which offered special incentives for early retirees. In addition to normal pension benefits, BankAmerica Corporation also provided an employee the equivalent of a year's pay in monthly payments over two years or until age 65. Through the program and attrition, Bank of America targeted a work force reduction of at least 5 percent. Many other employers have offered such programs, including Beatrice Foods, Tektronix Corporation, Mutual of Omaha, and Eastman Kodak.[15]

Phased-in and part-time retirements represent another approach to retirement. However, some employers offer other less traditional options. According to one survey, almost 25 percent of employers offer older employees part-time work through reduced hours and reduced pay. Flex-time and job sharing each are practiced by about 15 to 17 percent of the employers. And, about one-third of the employers allow workers, especially executives, to be paid for doing consulting work with their old firms.[16]

A vital part of retirement is an awareness of the special needs and anxieties of managers and workers as they approach retirement. These problems may be dealt with through a preretirement counseling program.

Preretirement Counseling

Preretirement counseling is aimed at easing employees' anxieties and preparing them for retirement and the benefits associated with it. The biological changes of aging may be a cause for concern, but suddenly having no job as a basis for one's life can cause even more anxiety.

Preretirement counseling should not begin just before retirement; it should be a systematic process of gradual preparation. A good approach is to begin preretirement counseling several years before employees actually retire and to increase counseling opportunities as retirement approaches. The extent of counseling depends upon how complete a program the organization can afford.[17] If an organization cannot afford a preretirement program, managers can encourage preretirees to check with state and federal agencies which may offer preretirement assistance and information. Associations such as the American Association of Retired Persons also are available.

Establishment of preretirement counseling indicates that an employer recognizes that retirement involves a mental and financial adjustment for which employees should be prepared. Good preretirement planning is multifaceted, with two of the most important dimensions focusing on employees' psychological adjustments and their financial planning.

Psychological Adjustment. Preretirement counseling recognizes that retirement involves an adjustment for which employees should be prepared. One aim of preretirement counseling is to make employees aware of the psychological changes caused by retirement. Employees should be encouraged to think about how they are going to use their time, the types of activities in which they will be involved, and employment and housing opportunities for older persons.

Financial Planning. Another aim of such a program is to encourage people to begin their financial planning before they retire. Employees need to be aware of the amount of resources they will have, where these resources come from, their health and insurance benefits, and related assistance available through governmental and private sources. Social Security benefits and pensions represent the most significant financial resources available to many retirees.

Can you discuss several retirement policy issues?

Social Security

The Social Security Act of 1935, with its later amendments, established a system providing old age, survivor's, disability, and retirement benefits. Administered by the U.S. government through the Social Security Administration, this program provides benefits to previously employed individuals. Both employees and employers share in the cost of Social Security by paying a tax on the employees' wages or salaries. The tax rates as of the writing of this book are noted in Figure 15–4.

Coverage. In order to receive benefits under Social Security, an individual must have engaged in some form of employment covered by the act. This act includes most private enterprises, most types of self-employment including farming, active military service, employment in some nonprofit organizations, and most government agencies. Amendments to the Social Security Act 1984 brought all federal government employees hired starting in 1984 into coverage under the act. A phased-in limitation was placed on "double dippers," who are individuals who receive both federal civil service pensions and other pensions.

Social Security Changes. Because the Social Security system affects a large number of individuals and is governmentally-operated, it is a very politically sensitive program, and increases in Social Security are often voted by Congress. Since a few years ago, Social Security payments have been tied to the cost of living (through the Consumer Price Index). This action, plus the increasing number of persons covered by the Social Security system, has raised concerns about the availability of

FIGURE 15–4
Social Security Tax Schedule.

SOCIAL SECURITY CONTRIBUTION PERCENTAGES AND MAXIMUM EARNING LEVELS

	Both Employees and Employers	Ceiling
1985	7.05	$39,600
1986	7.15	*
1987	7.15	*
1988	7.51	*
1989	7.51	*
1990	7.65	*

*Automatic escalator each year based on cost of living increases.

SECTION V COMPENSATING HUMAN RESOURCES

future funds from which to pay benefits. Aging of the population and the increased longevity of many people also may place severe strains on the system.

Social Security Amendments Act of 1983. To confront problems such as these, the Social Security Amendments Act of 1983 was passed to make some major changes in the costs and benefits of Social Security. The tax rate on both employers and employees was raised to the levels shown in Figure 15–4. The normal retirement age for workers who attain age 65 by the year 2002 will be increased in two-month increments per year from age 65 to 67 (for all employees born in 1960 and later). Similar phase-in schedules for spouses and widows or widowers will increase the minimum age for full coverage from 62 to 65. A more conservative approach to figuring cost of living increases in benefits also was passed. In addition, individuals with higher incomes for the first time will have a portion of their Social Security payments included in gross income for taxation purposes.[18]

It has been forecast that these changes will put the Social Security system on a sounder fiscal basis. However, critics are skeptical and future debates and political activity probably will continue as a greater percentage of the U.S. population becomes eligible for Social Security benefits.

Can you identify some personnel concerns affected by Social Security?

Pensions

A second group of retirement benefits are provided through private pension plans established and funded by employers and employees. Pensions are considered rewards for long service and are not incentives to work more efficiently or effectively. They are deferred wages and are perceived as a reward earned by employees, not as a gift given by an employer. The number of people covered by private pension plans is expected to grow as the work force expands.

Employee Retirement Income Security Act. Because pensions are so complex, employees often do not bother to learn about the provisions of their pensions and the advantages of various plans. Widespread criticism of pension plans led to the passage in 1974 of the Employee Retirement Income Security Act (ERISA). The purpose of this law, and subsequent amendments to it, is to regulate private pension plans in order to assure that employees who put money into pensions plans or depend upon a pension for retirement funds, actually will receive the money when they retire.

ERISA is a technically-worded and complex act that also established a federal agency to administer its provisions. Because of the requirements and the complexity of the law, a significant number of firms, especially smaller companies, have terminated their pension plans. ERISA probably has had the effect of limiting the number of new plans introduced because compliance is seen as too costly. The most signifi-

An UNFUNDED PLAN pays pension benefits out of current income to the organization.

The FUNDED PLAN provides pension benefits over a long period from funds accumulated ahead of time.

An UNINSURED PLAN is one in which the benefits at retirement are determined by the employer based upon calculations that consider the employee's age, years worked, and other factors.

An INSURED PLAN is one administered through an insurance company, which guarantees the payment of benefits through the purchase of individual insurance contracts which buy retirement annuity policies.

A CONTRIBUTORY PLAN is one in which the money for pension benefits is contributed by both employees and employers.

A NONCONTRIBUTORY PLAN is one in which the employer provides all the funds.

A DEFINED CONTRIBUTION PLAN is one in which the employer's *contribution* rate is fixed and the employees' retirement benefits depend upon the contributions and employees' earning levels.

cant difficulty in complying with ERISA seems to be the voluminous paperwork involved in the record-keeping and reporting requirements.

The complexity of the law has resulted in much confusion by employers, banks, insurance companies, and other fiduciaries. However, ERISA has provided increased security to employees through regulation of pension plans. Employees who contribute to a pension plan can have more confidence that they will receive their benefits upon retirement. A brief presentation of some of the basic terms and types of pension requirements follows.

Pension Funding. Funds for paying pension benefits can be accumulated in two basic ways: funded and unfunded. An **unfunded plan** pays pension benefits out of current income to the organization.

Therefore, an unfunded plan relies on present income or sales dollars to generate the money necessary to pay pensions. Obviously, the unfunded plan depends very much on the economic conditions of the organization. Employees and former employees may be left without adequate pension benefits if the firm's current revenues are insufficient to pay these benefits.

A **funded plan** provides pension benefits from money saved previously in a fund. By amassing funds and interest prior to actual need, employers can insure employees that their pension benefits will actually be available. For this reason, the funded plan is preferred and is more widely used.

Pension Insurance. Funds from a pension plan are accumulated in a trust fund that is either an insured or uninsured plan. An **insured plan** is one administered through an insurance company, which guarantees the payment of the benefits through the purchase of individual insurance contract or other financial institutions who purchase retirement annuity policies. These plans are considered to be more stable and financially sound than uninsured plans. An **uninsured plan** is one in which retirement benefits are determined by the employer based on calculations that consider the employee's age, years worked, and other factors.

Pension Contributions. Pension plans can be either contributory or noncontributory. In a **contributory plan** money for pension benefits is paid in by both employees and employers.

However, an employer provides all of the funds in a **noncontributory plan.** As would be expected, the noncontributory plan is preferred by employees and labor unions.

Pension Benefits. Pension plans can pay benefits based upon one of two types of plans. A **defined contribution plan** is one in which the employee *contribution rate* is fixed and employees' retirement benefits depend upon the contributions and employees' earning levels. Profit-sharing plans, employee stock ownership plans (ESOPs), thrift plans, and the like often are defined contribution plans. Because these plans depend upon contributions that can vary according to profitability or other factors, employees have less security and predictability with their retirement benefits.

A **defined benefit plan** is one in which an employer's contributions are determined by actuarial calculations which consider the *benefits* to be received by employees after retirement and the *methods* used to determine such benefits. The amount of an individual employee's benefits is determined by considering a person's length of service with the organization and the person's average earnings over a five-year period. A defined benefit plan provides greater assurance of benefits and greater predictability in the amount of retirement benefits that will be available to an employee upon retirement.

Portability. Another feature of some employee pensions is **portability**. In a portable plan, employees can move their pension benefits from one employer to another. For example, a plan that is portable within the paper industry will allow workers to move from one paper company to another without losing pension benefits. A commonly used portable pension system in colleges and universities is the Teacher Insurance Annuity Association (TIAA) system. Under this system, any faculty or staff member who accumulates pension benefits at one university can transfer these benefits to another university within the TIAA system.

If individuals are not in a portable system, they must take a *lump-sum settlement* of the money they contributed to the plan plus accumulated interest on their contributions when they leave. Unless their pensions are vested, they also do not receive the employer's contribution.

Vesting Rights. Certain rights, including *vesting*, are attached to employee pension plans. **Vesting** is the right of employees to receive benefits from their pension plans. Typically, vesting allows employees to be assured of receiving a certain pension, providing that they have worked a minimum number of years. If an employee resigns or is terminated before he or she is vested (that is, before an individual has been employed for the required time), no pension rights accrue to the person except to receive the funds he or she has contributed. If employees stay the allotted time, they retain their pension rights and receive benefits from both the funds contributed by the employer and their own funds.

There are several methods of vesting. The major ones are

■ *Gradual Vesting*—An employee vests 25 percent after 5 years, 50 percent after 10 years, and is fully vested at 15 years.
■ *Ten-Year-Period*—An employee vests 100 percent after 10 years, but has no vesting until 10 years service has accrued.
■ *Rule of 45*—An employee must be 50 percent vested when the employee's age plus length of service equals 45. The employee then vests 10 percent each year after that until 100 percent vesting occurs.

Can you list and define at least eight pension-related terms?

A DEFINED BENEFIT PLAN
is one in which the retirement *benefits* to be paid to employees and the methods of determining those benefits is set so that the employer's contributions can be statistically determined.

PORTABILITY
allows employees to move their pension benefit rights from one employer to another.

VESTING
is the right of employees to receive benefits from their pension plans.

Discrimination in Pension Plans

The pension area is like many others in the personnel area—it is constantly changing. The more recent changes are highlighted in this section and are concerned with making pension plans nondiscriminatory.

Unisex Pension Concern. Pension plans that require women to contribute greater amounts because they live longer, as a group, have been
found to be illegal by the U.S. Supreme Court. The *Arizona Governing
Committee* v. *Norris* ruling forced pension plan administrators to use
"unisex" mortality tables that do not reflect that women as a group
generally live longer.[19] To bring legislation in line with this decision,
the Retirement Equity Act was passed in 1984.

Retirement Equity Act of 1984. This 1984 amendment to ERISA and the
Internal Revenue Code, liberalized pension regulations that affect
women, guaranteed access to benefits, prohibited pension-related penalties during absences from work such as maternity leave, and lowered
the vesting age. The act provided for these workers to receive pension
credits beginning at age 18, instead of age 22 as set previously by ER-
ISA. Also, employers must enroll workers in pension plans at age 21,
instead of age 25 as set previously. In addition, workers can leave jobs
for five years without sacrificing pension credits and the pension rights
of homemakers whose working spouses die before retirement are guaranteed.

Individual Considerations

The pension area is made more complex by the availability of options
that employees can choose. Three options are Individual Retirement
Accounts (IRAs), 401 (k) plans, and Keogh plans.

Individual Retirement Account (IRA). An **individual retirement account
(IRA)** allows an employee to set aside funds in a special account which
are tax-deferred until the employee retires. Many workers have taken
advantage of the IRAs offered by financial institutions, insurance companies, and brokerage firms. Working individuals can set aside up to
$2,000 (or 100 percent of total compensation if less than $2,000) per
year until age 70½. For workers who have nonworking spouses, a limit
of $2,250 is set. By being able to deduct the amount of their IRA con-
tributions from yearly income, individuals can defer paying taxes on
that portion of their income until they begin withdrawal of the funds
sometime after age 59½. Except for unusual situations, individuals
who withdraw IRA funds before age 59½ must pay a 10 percent penalty and any tax due. The major advantages of an IRA are the ability
to accumulate extra retirement funds and the shifting of taxable income
to later years, when total income, and therefore taxable income, is
likely to be lower.

401(k) Plan. The 401(k) plan gets its name from Section 401(k) of the
federal tax code. A **401(k) plan** allows employees to choose whether to

receive cash or have employer contributions from profit-sharing and stock-bonus plans placed into tax-deferred accounts. Because of the deferral feature, 401(k) plans also are called *salary reduction plans*. In these plans employees can elect to have their current pay reduced by a certain percentage and that amount paid into a 401(k) plan. According to one attorney, the major advantages of 401k plans are:[20]

A KEOGH PLAN (H.R.10 PLAN) allows self-employed individuals to establish an individualized pension plan.

■ Employees get some flexibility in financial planning
■ Employers provide more in retirement benefits
■ Contributions are made with pretax dollars
■ A higher contribution limit exists for these plans than for IRAs ($30,000 or 25 percent of pay, whichever is less).

The 401k plans are especially popular for higher-paid executives, although they must be offered to most employees and cannot be limited just to executives. The complexity of the rules governing 401k plans is their major drawback.

Keogh Plan. A Keogh plan is a special type of retirement plan. Also called H.R.10 plans, a **Keogh plan** allows self-employed individuals to establish individualized pension plans. Individuals who are self-employed can set aside a percentage of their self-employed income into a pension account. Keogh plans can either be deferred contributions or defined benefits in nature. Because of the complexity and special regulations covering Keogh plans, it is not unusual that advice from tax specialists must be obtained by self-employed individuals.

Can you differentiate among three individualized retirement-benefit plans?

TIME OFF-RELATED BENEFITS

Employers provide an employee with time off with pay in a variety of circumstances. Figure 15–5 shows the results of a survey on the various types of leaves made available by employers. Paid holidays and vacations are the most well-known. However, leaves are given for a number of other purposes. Some of the more common ones are discussed next.

Holiday Pay

Most, if not all, employers provide pay for such established holidays as Labor Day, Memorial Day, Christmas, New Year's Day and the Fourth of July. Other holidays are offered to some employees through selected laws or union contracts. According to one survey, the average number of holidays given is ten days per year. Almost half of the employers surveyed had "floating holidays" which can be selected by employees at their discretion or selected by management or management/union agreements.[21]

	PERCENT OF COMPANIES							
	All Companies	By Industry			By Size		Union Status†	
		Mfg.	Nonmfg.	Nonbus.	Large	Small	Union	Nonunion
PLANT/SERVICE	(203)	(109)	(41)	(53)	(89)	(114)	(89)	(114)
Paid jury duty leave	95%	94%	98%	96%	98%	93%	94%	96%
Paid funeral leave	94	94	95	92	98	90	91	96
Short-term military leave	91	87	98	92	94	88	89	92
Paid sick leave	69	50	93	92	83	59	60	77
Maternity leave	83	74	95	92	85	82	81	85
Paid personal leave	46	39	46	60	54	39	37	53
Paternity leave	39	32	39	53	42	37	38	39
Adoption leave	22	12	32	36	33	14	19	25
Unpaid leaves of absence	97	96	93	100	99	95	97	97
OFFICE/CLERICAL	(251)	(114)	(75)	(62)	(99)	(152)	(18)	(233)
Paid jury duty leave	97%	96%	97%	97%	99%	95%	100%	97%
Paid funeral leave	94	94	95	94	97	92	94	94
Short-term military leave	93	94	92	92	97	90	100	92
Paid sick leave	93	88	99	95	95	91	100	92
Maternity leave	88	81	95	94	87	89	89	88
Paid personal leave	50	42	57	55	57	45	56	49
Paternity leave	43	37	44	52	44	41	50	42
Adoption leave	24	16	28	32	33	17	39	22
Unpaid leaves of absence	96	95	93	100	97	95	100	95
MANAGEMENT/EXEMPT	(249)	(113)	(74)	(62)	(98)	(151)		
Paid jury duty leave	96%	96%	97%	97%	98%	95%		
Paid funeral leave	93	93	95	92	97	91		
Short-term military leave	92	91	92	92	96	89		
Paid sick leave	91	85	96	95	94	89		
Maternity leave	87	80	93	94	87	87		
Paid personal leave	46	39	53	52	54	41		
Paternity leave	40	33	42	50	43	38		
Adoption leave	23	16	27	31	33	17		
Unpaid leaves of absence	94	92	93	100	97	93		

Note: Percentages are based on the number of companies responding for each employee group.
†Firms classified as "nonunion" indicated that less than a majority of their employees are covered by union contracts.
SOURCE: *Policies on Leave from Work*, Personnel Policies Forum no. 136, (Washington DC: Bureau of National Affairs, June 1983), p. 3. Reprinted by permission from Personnel Policies Forum, copyright 1983 by The Bureau of National Affairs, Inc., Washington, D.C.

FIGURE 15—5
Provisions for Paid and Unpaid Leave by Employee Group.

To control abuse, employers commonly require that employees must work the last scheduled day before the holiday and the first scheduled work day after a holiday to be eligible for holiday pay. Some employers pay time and a half to hourly employees who must work holidays. Exempt employees can take "comp time" (compensatory time off) by taking a different day off.

Vacation Pay

Paid vacations are a very common benefit. Employees often have graduated vacation time scales based on length of service. Some firms also allow employees to accumulate unused vacation. To prevent abuse, policies similar to holiday pay that require employees to work the day before and the day after vacations sometimes are used.

Leaves of Absence

Leaves are given for a variety of reasons. Some, such as *military leave*, *election leave*, and *jury leave*, are required by various state and federal laws. All of these leaves add to employer costs, although employers commonly pay only the difference between the employee's regular pay and the military, election, or jury pay. However, some firms are more supportive. For example, Greg Schumann is in the Army National Guard. During the two-week summer camp, his employer grants him time off without penalty, and pays him his regular pay, while he also receives his military pay. Federal law prohibits taking discriminatory action against military reservists.

Funeral or bereavement leave is another common leave offered. This leave is usually up to three days for immediate family members, as specifically defined in many employers' policy manuals and employee handbooks.[22] Some policies also give unpaid time off for the death of more distant relatives or friends.

Child-related Leaves. In the past ten years employer policies regarding child-related leaves have become more flexible. As a result of the Pregnancy Discrimination Act of 1978, *maternity leave* must be treated in the same manner as any other medical condition or disability that would require a leave. Therefore, pregnant women may work as long as their physicians allow, in most situations, just as an employee with a heart condition would be allowed to do. Also, women who leave to give birth must be offered an opportunity to return to work, although not necessarily in the same job. A maximum length of leave time for all medical leaves is set by some employers.

Some firms offer *paternity leave* for male workers. It is most frequently done through the use of paid annual leave, paid sick leave, or unpaid paternity leave. However, few employers offer specifically-designated paid paternity leave and a relatively low percentage of men take it.[23] For employees who adopt children, Honeywell Corporation subsidizes adoption costs up to $1,000 per child. When questioned about the benefit, a Honeywell vice president said, "Since Honeywell provides medical coverage to employees who have children through childbirth, we decided it would make sense to also help our employees who have children through adoption."[24]

Sick Leave. Another common type of pay is given for time not worked. Many employers allow their employees to miss a limited number of days because of illness without losing pay. Some employers allow employees to accumulate unused sick leave, which may be used in case of catastrophic illnesses. Others contain provisions whereby employees receive pay for unused sick leave.

The change from emphasizing sick pay to rewarding people who do not use it has led to the term *well-pay*. Well-pay rewards employees who stay well, unlike sick pay, which pays people who are sick. One organization found that when it stopped designating a specific number of sick leave days and implemented a plan that combined sick leave, vacations, and holidays into a total of days that could be taken off with pay, absenteeism dropped, time off was better scheduled, and employee acceptance of the sick leave policy improved.[25] Programs such as this illustrate the growing efforts employers have made to manage and control health-related benefits.

Can you concisely describe three time off-related benefits?

INSURANCE-RELATED BENEFITS

Another major group of benefits provided by employers is composed of various types of insurance coverage. Medical, disability, dental, life, legal, and auto insurance are all offered by employers.

Health-Related Benefits

Costs for health care in the U.S. have risen dramatically in the past two decades. In 1960, about $26 billion was spent on health care, representing 5.4 percent of the nation's gross national product. By 1983, the total bill for health care increased 14 times to $362 billion, or about 11 percent of the gross national product.[27] The costs of providing health care benefits to employees have risen just as severely, with employers paying over $100 billion a year. The three largest automobile companies spend over $3 billion a year for medical insurance. These benefits amount to about $3000 per worker, or $2000 per retired worker, and the costs add over $400 to the price of each car![28] Cost increases of 20 percent per year have not been uncommon for smaller employers.

Health Care Cost Management

Faced with the prospects of continuing cost increases for health-care benefits, many employers have begun aggressive efforts to manage and control their health care costs. Instead of offering health insurance to employees and paying all or most of the premiums, employers are using a variety of strategies to contain costs.[29] Some of the common methods are highlighted next.

Self Funding. **Self-Funding** occurs when an employer sets aside funds to pay health claims itself in lieu of insurance coverage. Basically, the employer earmarks a certain amount (i.e., $800,000) to cover normal medical insurance benefits. The exact figure is based upon an analysis of previous health benefit usage patterns. Instead of buying health insurance plans from a firm such as Blue Cross and Blue Shield or Aetna, the employer sets aside funds and then buys an *excess policy*. The employer agrees to pay up to the normal amount (i.e., $800,000) of employees' health care costs. The excess policy then provides coverage for all expenses beyond that level. Just as the premium for your car insurance is much lower if you choose a $1,000 deductible rather than a $100 deductible, the employer pays significantly less for the excess coverage than it would for a total coverage package.

Furthermore, the employer earns interest on the funds that are set aside because these funds are paid out throughout the year as employees use their health benefits rather than at the beginning of the year to pay an insurance premium. Employers can either process the claims themselves or contract with an outside service to administer them. Some large insurance firms even provide this claims administration service for a percentage fee of the value of the claims. Many other special options also are available.

Employers using self-funding have reported cost savings of up to 25 percent in the first year, and continuing savings of 6 percent or more over the traditional medical insurance approach.[30] To benefit from self-funding, an employer generally must have an employee base of at least 100 employees so that sufficient spreading of costs over the employee pool can occur. The growing use of self-funding reflects its popularity as a health care cost managment strategy.

Preferred Provider Organization (PPO). Another cost containment strategy used by employers is the establishment of a **Preferred Provider Organization (PPO)**. A PPO is a health care provider that contracts with an employer or an employer group to provide health care services to employees at a competitive rate. The operation of a PPO is described in the experiences of Stouffer Corporation.

SELF-FUNDING occurs when an employer sets aside funds to pay health claims in excess of the amount provided by funding in lieu of insurance coverage.

A PREFERRED PROVIDER ORGANIZATION (PPO) is a health care provider that contracts with an employer or an employer group to provide health care services to employees at competitive rates.

A HEALTH MAINTENANCE ORGANIZATION (HMO) is a form of health care which provides services for a fixed period on a prepaid basis.

By encouraging employees to use lower-cost providers, employers can reduce their benefit outlays. For a hospital or group of doctors, the advantage of being a PPO is the assurance of a continuing source of patients, even though employees have the freedom to go to other providers if they want to pay the difference in costs. The major features of PPOs are:[32]

- A limited group of physicians and hospitals is utilized.
- Fee schedules are negotiated in advance.
- Utilization controls or claims reviews are required.
- Consumers choose their own providers.
- Claims payments are rapid.
- Benefit levels are flexible.

Health Maintenance Organization. A unique form of health care is available through a **Health Maintenance Organization (HMO)**, an organized form of health care providing services for a fixed period on a prepaid basis. Unlike other health-care benefits, the HMO emphasizes prevention as well as correction. An employer contracts with an HMO, which has doctors and medical personnel on its staff, to provide complete medical care, except for hospitalization. The employer pays a flat rate per enrolled employee or per family. The covered individuals may then go to the HMO for health care as often as they need. Supplemental policies for hospitalization also are used.

Some employers offer this benefit because HMOs encourage broader health care services at a reasonable cost to employees. This form of health care represents an alternative to traditional health insurance systems. One review found that almost 300 HMOs were in operation, and about 11 million individuals were covered by HMOs. Also, HMOs were established in 38 states, with California having the greatest number of plans and enrolled members. The prevalence of HMOs is partly due to a federal law that required employers with at least 25 employees to offer an HMO as an option to traditional health insurance, if an HMO exists in the area.[33]

Other efforts to contain health-care costs include preventive health and physical fitness programs communication and education efforts to make employees more knowledgeable about health-care costs, and cost-sharing options. Several of these strategies are highlighted at the end of this chapter.

Dental Insurance. As an insurance benefit, dental insurance is highly desired by a growing number of employees. A study of 141 companies found that 85 percent of the companies provided dental benefits. Of the plans surveyed, 79 percent also provided orthodontic coverage, which is usually more costly.[34]

> *Can you explain why health-care cost management has become important and discuss some methods of controlling costs?*

Other Insurance Benefits

Besides health-related insurance, employers also provide other types of insurance. It is common for employers to provide *life insurance* for employees. This insurance is bought as a group policy, and the employer pays the premiums, but the level of coverage is usually low and is tied to an employee's base pay. A typical level of coverage is 1½ or two times an employee's annual salary. However, some executives may get more as part of an executive compensation package.

Another insurance benefit that frequently is tied to employee pay levels is *long-term disability insurance*. This insurance provides continuing income protection for employees if they should become disabled and unable to work.

Legal Insurance. As society becomes more complex, more people need legal assistance. However, attorney fees have increased to the point that many who become involved with wills, contracts, divorces, and other situations cannot afford legal advice. An insurance plan that pays a portion of legal fees saves the employees money because the legal fees are paid with pretax dollars, not out of the employees' take-home pay.

Auto Insurance. Group auto insurance plans represent another new benefit for some employees. At Transnational Motors in Grand Rapids, Michigan, employees have 40 percent of their total auto insurance premium paid by the company. At group rates, employees also save money because the premiums are less than they would be on an individual basis. If some state and federal insurance regulations are changed, rapid growth of such plans will be possible. Several large insurance firms such as Aetna and Prudential have started experimental plans.[35]

In summary, a variety of group insurance benefits is offered by employers: automobile insurance, dental insurance, health and disability insurance, legal insurance, prescription drug insurance, and eye-care insurance. These benefits present major advantages to employees because many employers pay some or all of the costs. In addition, cheaper insurance rates are available through group programs.

FINANCIAL AND OTHER BENEFITS

A wide range of financial benefits has been provided by employers. From the point of view of the employer, offering unique benefits can be useful in attracting and retaining employees. Workers like receiving special benefits because they are not taxed as income. To provide a perspective on the variety of benefits offered, *financial, educational, child-care, social and recreational,* and *miscellaneous* benefits are highlighted next.

Financial Benefits

Financial benefits can include a wide variety of items. A *credit union* provides savings and lending services for employees. *Purchase discounts* allow employees to buy goods or services from their employers at reduced rates. For example, a furniture manufacturer may allow employees to buy furniture at wholesale cost plus 10 percent. Or, a bank may offer the use of a safety deposit box and free checking to its employees.

Employee *thrift, saving,* or *stock investment plans* may be made available. Some employers match a portion of the employee's contribution. These plans are especially attractive to executive and managerial personnel. To illustrate, in a stock purchase plan the corporation provides matching funds equal to the amount invested by the employee to purchase stock. In this way, employees can benefit from the future growth of the corporation. Also, it is hoped that employees will develop a greater loyalty and interest in the company and its success.

Financial planning and counseling is a benefit that is especially valuable to executives. They may need information on investments, tax shelters, and comprehensive financial counseling because of their higher compensation.

Numerous other financial-related benefits are offered. The use of a company car, company expense accounts, and help in buying or selling a house when transferred are other common financial-related benefits.

Educational Benefits

Another benefit used by employees comes in the form of *tuition aid plans*. These plans pay for some or all of the costs associated with formal education courses and degree programs. The extent of these plans is revealed by statistics from the Association of American Colleges, which show that 13 percent of U.S. adults are continuing their schooling, and 40 percent of that group of students are in the middle to upper income levels. Approximately one-fourth of these students have tuition and fees paid by their employers.[36] Some employers also provide educational benefits for dependents of employees through scholarship competitions. Eastman Kodak, for example, spends over $2 million per year for continuing education support of Kodak employees and dependents.[37]

A key caveat is that the courses must be job-related; otherwise the costs of courses can be treated as a taxable benefit. However, most courses that are paid for by employers are job-related. Many employers also pay for required books and laboratory materials. Some employers pay for schooling on a proportion schedule, depending upon the grade received by employees; others simply require a passing grade of C or above.

Child-Care As a Benefit

Inflation, life-style changes, women's liberation, and other trends have led to a dramatic increase in the number of mothers of preschool children who work. As more and more mothers of preschool children in this country enter the labor market and more households have two paycheck earners, the need for child care is increasing. Employers and labor representatives have recognized child care as a major employee concern and are offering benefits to address this concern.

In 1960, only about 20 percent of mothers who had both a husband and preschool children were in the labor force, but by 1983, over half of all women with children under age six were in the labor force. Finding reliable child care has been a problem for many working parents. One study found that working parents use an average of four different child care arrangements simultaneously because no one arrangement is consistently reliable.[38]

Management and labor representatives are aware of the link between unsatisfactory child care arrangements and employee absenteeism. A growing number of employers have helped solve their own absenteeism problems and their employees' child care problems by sponsoring or supporting reliable child care services. Wang Laboratories, Xerox, Stride Rite, Measures, Hewlett-Packard, Polaroid, and many other companies provide day care in their own centers or help locate and pay for outside services.

The value of child care as a benefit is seen in the results of a study that compared a company that offers child day-care to a similar one that does not. Absenteeism decreased slightly and turnover was lower in the company offering day-care compared to the company that did not offer day-care.[39]

For companies considering a child care benefit, it is clear that good needs assessment is important. The number of employees eligible to use the service and the number willing to use it are not the same. One of the major reasons child care centers have been closed is that too few employees were using them for them to meet their costs. Nevertheless, many employers will probably be considering addition of this benefit.

Social and Recreational Benefits

Some benefits and services are social and recreational in nature, such as bowling leagues, picnics, parties, employer-sponsored athletic teams, organizationally-owned and provided recreational lodges, and other sponsored activities and interest groups. Dances, banquets, and other social events provide an opportunity for employees to become better acquainted and strengthen interpersonal relationships. The employer should retain control of all events associated with the organization because of possible legal responsibility.

Strong emphasis on numerous social and recreation programs is designed to encourage employee happiness and team spirit. Employees *may* appreciate this type of benefit, but managers should not necessarily expect increased job productivity or job satisfaction as a result.

Other Benefits

Other benefits too numerous to detail here are made available by various employers. Food services, counseling services, paid professional memberships, and organizationally-provided uniforms are just a few. Some of the unique benefits now being offered by companies include: "free ice cream" days offered by an ice cream producer, free computers given by a computer company after a year's service, and an employee vegetable garden which was developed by one company from a vacant lot.[40]

Can you identify and briefly explain at least four types of financial and other benefits offered by employers?

BENEFIT ADMINISTRATION

With the myriad of benefits and regulations, it is easy to see why many organizations must have coordinated efforts to administer benefit programs. Figure 15–6 shows how benefit administration responsibilities can be split between personnel specialists and other managers. Notice that the greatest role is played by personnel specialists, but managers are responsible for being knowledgeable in a general way about benefits. Good communication with employees about their benefits also is important.

PERSONNEL UNIT	MANAGERS
■ Develops and administers benefit systems	■ Answer simple questions on benefits
■ Answers employee's technical questions on benefits	■ Maintain liaison with personnel specialists on benefits
■ Assists employees in claiming benefits	■ Maintain good communications with employees near retirement
■ Coordinates special preretirement programs	

FIGURE 15–6
Benefit Responsibilities.

Communication of Benefits

Some employers have instituted special benefit communication systems to address employee ignorance about the value of the benefits provided. Holding periodic meetings, preparing special literature, and using in-house employee publications to heighten awareness of benefits are among the methods used. Many employers also give employees an annual "Personal Statement of Benefits" that translates benefits into dollars and cents.

A unique approach to generating awareness of benefits was used at a 288-bed hospital, Mercy Medical Center, in Coon Rapids, Minnesota. An "Employee Benefits Fair" was held in four separate sessions, which were scheduled to allow all employees to attend, regardless of their shifts. Booths were set up in three adjoining classrooms at the hospital. In addition to having booths staffed by members of the hospital's Human Resources Department, health and dental insurance providers also were represented. Free snacks, carnival music, balloons, and clowns were used to create the appropriate atmosphere. About two-thirds of the employees attended and a follow-up survey found that employees felt they were more knowledgeable about their benefits after attending the fair.[41]

Flexible Benefit System

A flexible, or "cafeteria-style," approach to benefits represents a major step in the evolution of employee benefits. It recognizes that individual situations differ because of age, family status, and life-style. By allowing each employee to select an individual combination of benefits within some overall limits, the organization makes a variety of "dishes," or benefits available. Sometimes employees may even be given the option of contributing some of the benefits to a "benefits fund" that can be used to pay medical deductions, etc.

In addition to the St. Paul Companies (discussed at the beginning of this chapter), American Can, TRW, Educational Testing Service, and a growing number of other employers offer some flexibility in their benefit plans. In 1980, only eight employers offered flexible benefit plans. By the end of 1984, it was estimated that over 400 such plans were in use, and these plans covered over one million employees.[42]

Advantages. The flexible benefits approach has several advantages. One is that this scheme takes into consideration the complex view of human beings. Because employees in an organization have different desires and needs, they can *tailor benefit packages* to fit their individual life situations. A survey of employees in three companies who have had flexible benefits found that employees were very satisfied with their programs. Over 70 percent of the surveyed TRW employees indicated that their benefits better fit their needs and 82 percent said they preferred the flexible benefits system. Similar ratings of approval were found at American Can and Educational Testing Services.[43]

Another advantage of the variable-benefit approach is heightened *employee awareness* of the cost and the value of benefits. By having to determine the benefits they will receive, employees know what they receive and what the trade-offs are.

Another advantage is that employers with flexible benefit plans can recruit and hire employees more easily because of the *attractiveness* of flexible plans. Also, the employer is better able to control costs.[44]

Disadvantages. The flexible approach to benefits is not without some drawbacks. The major problem is the *complexity* of keeping track of what each individual chooses, especially if there is a large number of employees. Sophisticated computer software is now available to manage these complexities. As more benefits are made available, employees may not be able to understand the options because the benefit structure and its provisions can often become quite complicated.

Another problem is that an *inappropriate benefit package* may be chosen by employees. A young construction worker might not choose disability benefits; however, if he or she is injured, the family may suffer financial hardship. Part of this problem can be overcome by requiring employees to select a core set of benefits (life, health, and disability insurance) and by offering options on other benefits. Also, because many insurance plans are based on a group rate, the employer may face higher rates if insufficient numbers of employees select an insurance option.

An additional problem is the *tax treatment* of flexible benefit plans. In 1984, the Internal Revenue Service (IRS) provided a ruling which defined and limited flexible benefits options. Some abuses have been eliminated but many options still remain its efforts to tax employees for the value of their flexible benefits. The IRS feels that giving individuals choices is similar to paying them and then allowing them to spend their money at a "company benefit store." As would be expected, employers with flexible benefit systems disagree with the IRS and have lobbied to have Congress limit the efforts of the IRS. If the IRS position ultimately stands, flexible benefit plans probably will become less popular.[45] Time and politics will determine if flexible benefit plans continue to grow in popularity.

*Can you discuss benefit communication
and flexible benefits as two benefit administration considerations?*

PERSONNEL TODAY AND TOMORROW

TRY NOT TO GET SICK

Employers have changed the focus of their health care benefits in the last few years because of rising costs. Instead of encouraging employees to use their health care benefits, employers increasingly tell employees, "Try not to get sick." To "encourage" employees to follow this advice, a multifaceted approach is being used.

One approach to health-care insurance is to have employees pay part of the premiums. *Copayment* requires employees to pay a monthly amount as part of the premium costs. However, if you work in an organization in which you must pay part of the cost for your health insurance, your employer still is in the minority. Changes in federal tax regulations that would limit the amount of health insurance costs that employers can deduct as business expenses may force more organizations to adopt employee copayment schemes.

Comprehensive Coverage. Many employers traditionally have provided what is called *first dollar* coverage, which means that all expenses, from the first dollar of health care costs, are paid by the employee's insurance, with the exception of costs associated with hospitalized illnesses covered by major medical plans. It is common for a small deductible amount to be paid by employees for illnesses covered under major medical plans, but most basic coverage plans have not had an employee-paid deductible. Experts say that by having first-dollar coverage in the basic plan, employees run to the doctor for the smallest illnesses, which results in overuse of the health care benefits.

Consequently, employers increasingly are providing health care insurance that is comprehensive, which means that employees pay a deductible on all medical care costs. Many employers also are raising the deductible from $50 to $100 to $200 or more. For example, a California telecommunications equipment firm, Plantronics, had a first-dollar coverage plan for its 1,500 employees. However, Plantronics changed to a comprehensive plan in which employees do not receive first-dollar coverage for hospital expenses. This and other changes resulted in a 13 percent reduction of medical benefit costs in one year. In 1984, Ford Motor Company began requiring its salaried employees and white collar retirees to pay up to $750 a year for medical services that were previously free.

Education. Plantronics and many other employers have set up specialized educational programs to make employees aware of health care costs. Blue Cross and Blue Shield of Indiana has established a "Health Promotion Service," through which it promotes good employee health practices. Employee wellness programs, discussed in the next chapter, illustrate this part of the education efforts. Other firms have used newsletters to show how overuse of health benefits affect individual employees.

Abbot Laboratories has included puzzles and quizzes on health care costs in its employee newspaper. Quaker Oats has two education programs, one that focuses on employee health awareness and one that is a consumer education program on how best to use health care services. Offered to 6,000 employees, the programs have given employees material to read at home, after which they complete a programmed workbook. Zenith Corporation has published and discussed "11 Commandments" to help employees become better health care users. In summary, educating employees that health care benefits represent costs that can be controlled is a growing part of benefit administration.[46]

SUMMARY

■ Benefits provide additional compensation to employees as a reward for organizational membership.

■ Because benefits generally are not taxed, they are highly desired by employees. As a result, the average employee now receives an amount equal to over 36 percent of his or her pay in benefit compensation.

■ Workers' compensation, unemployment compensation, and severance pay are three prominent security-oriented benefits.

■ Organizations that provide retirement-related benefits should develop policies on early retirement, offer preretirement counseling, and plan how to integrate Social Security benefits into employees' benefit plans.

■ The pension area is a complex area governed by the Employee Retirement Income Security Act (ERISA). There are a number of key terms that must be learned in order to understand ERISA.

■ Individual Retirement Accounts, 401(k) plans, and Keogh plans are important individual options available for supplementing retirement benefits.

■ Holiday pay, vacation pay, and various leaves of absence are means of providing time off-related benefits to employees.

■ Health care benefits are the most costly insurance-related benefits. Employers have become more aggressive in managing their health care costs through the use of self-funding, Preferred Provider Organizations, and Health Maintenance Organizations.

■ Numerous insurance, financial, and other benefits are provided by employers. Some of them are legal and auto insurance, financial planning, tuition aid, and child care.

■ Because of the variety of benefit options available and the costs involved, a major benefit administration activity is benefit communications.

■ Flexible benefit systems have grown in popularity , but they present some disadvantages.

REVIEW QUESTIONS AND EXERCISES

1. Why have benefits grown in importance to employees? To employers?

2. Why are workers' compensation, unemployment compensation, and severance pay appropriately classified as security-oriented benefits?

3. Take a position on the following statement and explain your reasoning: "Forced retirement and early retirement probably will be considered an obsolete idea by the year 2000."

4. Define the following terms:

  a. Unfunded plan   d. Defined benefit plan

  b. Insured plan   e. Portability

  c. Contributory plan   f. Vesting

5. What differences exist among an IRA, a 401(k) plan, and a Keogh plan?

6. Why do you believe some experts have forecast that time off-related benefits will expand in the future?

7. Discuss the following controversial statement: "Health-care costs are out of control in the U.S. in the 1980s, and it is up to employers to put pressure on the medical system to reduce costs."

8. What types of financial and other benefits would you most prefer? Why?

9. Relate your answers in Question 8 to the concepts of benefit communication and flexible benefits.

Exercise

JDR Inc. is a New York–based company which is locating a new plant in Arkansas. This new plant, which will be operated as a profit center, will have 300 employees (250 nonexempt and 50 exempt). It has been determined that wages at the plant will average $6 per hour and benefits will equal 30 percent of the hourly wages. As the new personnel manager you are to determine the benefits package. The costs of various benefits are as follows. Develop your benefit package.[47]

Social Security	7.15%
Unemployment Insurance	4.4%
Workers' Compensation	1%
Pension	11%
One Holiday	2.4 Cents
Rest Periods	3.6 Cents
Sick Leave 1 Day/Month	1.2 Cents
One-Day Vacation	2.4 Cents
Family Dental Care	9.8 Cents
Drug Insurance Program	4.9 Cents
Life Insurance (3 × Salary)	4.9 Cents
Hospitalization 120 Days + Major Medical	27.9 Cents
Christmas Bonus	2.2 Cents
Long-Term Disability Salary Contributions	1.1 Cents
Vision Care Insurance	2.4 Cents

Group Auto Insurance .... 4.9 Cents
Funeral Payment .... .9 Cent
Employee Meals Furnished Free .... .1 Cent
One Employer/Family Party .... 1.2 Cents
100% College Tuition Waiver .... 1.1 Cents
Discounts on Company-Produced Goods .... .8 Cent
Recreational Program .... .3 Cent
Prepaid Legal Services .... .7 Cent
Employee Thrift Plan .... 1.5 Cents
Credit Union Facilities .... .2 Cent
Child Care Center .... 2.2 Cents

CASE:
BENEFITTING CONNIE

Connie Carlingson has been an inbound sales agent for a telemarketing firm in Arizona for four years. The firm employs 240 people who take reservations for a national hotel chain when customers call a toll-free telephone number. Approximately two years ago Connie voluntarily moved to a night shift position.

Shortly after her move she began complaining to the night shift manager that her immediate supervisor was picking on her. In particular, Connie alleged that her supervisor was constantly nagging her about taking breaks that were too long. She also said that the supervisor was deliberately scheduling her breaks at different times than when her close friend had hers. Eventually, Connie's complaining led the night manager to talk to the supervisor and those complaints seemed to subside. However, a new problem with Connie has recently developed.

During her four years of employment Connie has regularly used sick leave. The company policy provides for employees to receive sick leave only as it is accrued, which means that an employee earns one day of sick leave for each month of employment. Because Connie has consistently taken at least one day of sick leave each month, she almost never has accumulated any carry-over sick leave time. Therefore, she has been forced to request unpaid medical leaves of absence whenever she has had the flu or some other health problem. Always in the past these leaves have been granted to Connie without too many questions being asked.

Recently Connie requested a medical leave for the sixth time this year. When the supervisor and night manager brought Connie's request to the attention of the director of the reservations center, the director granted Connie's request but told her that her medical leaves were becoming excessive and the company would no longer grant leaves of absence to her for any reasons. Connie became very upset when she heard this and told the director, "Now, I'm not a complainer, but it's not fair."

Questions

1. What problems exist with the benefits program offered by the employer, as described in the case?

2. What can be done to deal with Connie and to prevent similar problems from arising with other employees in the future?

NOTES

1. Used with permission of Carol Beatty, Compensation Administrator, St. Paul Companies, St. Paul, Minnesota.

2. James R. Morris, *Employee Benefits, 1983,* (Washington, D.C.: Chamber of Commerce of the United States, 1984).

3. *U.S. News & World Report,* January 9, 1984, p. 71.

4. "Cutting Costs, Abuses in Disability Insurance," *U.S. News & World Report,* May 28, 1984, pp. 80–81.

5. Eugene Carlson, "States' Widely Varying Laws on Disability Costs Irk Firms," *Wall Street Journal,* October 11, 1983, p. 37.

6. BNA Policy and Practice Series, (Washington, DC: Bureau of National Affairs, 1983), Sec. 356, pp. 31–33.

7. "The Great Ripoff in Unemployment Pay," *U.S. News & World Report,* March 16, 1981, pp. 63–64.

8. *Ibid.*

9. "More Woes for States Over Jobless Benefits," *U.S. News & World Report,* April 2, 1984, pp. 73–74.

10. Bonnie DeClark, "Cutting Unemployment Costs," *Personnel Journal* 62, (November 1983), pp. 868–870.

11. Seymour LaRock and Mary Popa, "Future of Supplemental Unemployment Benefits," *Employee Benefit Plan Review,* February 1983, pp. 8–12ff.

12. "Severance Pay Plans for Employees," *Resource,* January 1984, p. 2.

13. "Fringe Cuts for Post-65ers?" *Dun's Business Month,* October 1983, pp. 95–96.

14. Caroline Bird, "Retirement Will Become Obsolete . . ." *Personnel Administrator,* December 1983, pp. 106–111.

15. "BankAmerica To Reduce Costs with Early Retirement," *Employee Benefit Plan Review,* March 1984, p. 88.

16. Nicholas J. Bentell, "Managing the Older Worker," *Personnel Administrator* August 1983, pp. 31–40.

17. For details on the planning and control of a program see Diane F. Roth, "Why Sponsor a Preretirement Program?", *Personnel Journal* 62 (September 1983), pp. 720–724.

18. For more details see "Social Security," *Hansen Reviews,* August 24, 1983, pp. 1–8.

19. *Arizona Governing Committee v. Norris,* 103 S.Ct., 3492, 32 FEP Cases 233 (1983).

20. "Advantages, Disadvantages of Sec. 401(k) Plans," *Employee Benefit Plan Review,* September 1983, pp. 25–28.

21. *Paid Holidays and/or Vacation Policies,* Personnel Policies Forum no. 130 (Washington, DC: Bureau of National Affairs, November, 1980), p. 1

22. *Policies on Leave from Work,* Personnel Policies Forum no. 136 (Washington, DC: Bureau of National Affairs, June 1983), pp. 5–6.

23. Nancy Norman and James T. Tedeschi, "Paternity Leave: The Unpopular Benefit Option," *Personnel Administrator,* February 1984, pp. 39–43.

24. *Forbes*, February 16, 1981, p. 116.

25. B. H. Harvey, J. A. Schultze, and J. F. Rogers, "Rewarding Employees for Not Using Sick Leave," *Personnel Administrator*, May 1983, pp. 55–69.

26. Adapted from "Campbell Soup Announces Child-Adoption Benefits," *Employee Benefit Plan Review*, August 1983, pp. 28–31.

27. *Forbes*, November 7, 1983, p. 38.

28. Barry Stavro, "Sick Call," *Forbes*, October 24, 1983, p. 116.

29. Gary T. McIlroy, "Health Care Cost Containment in the 1980s," *Compensation Review*, Fourth Quarter 1983, pp. 15–31.

30. For a review of self-funding see Ronald Bryan, "A Primer on Self-Funding Health Care Benefits," *Personnel Administrator*, April 1983, pp. 61–64.

31. Adapted from "Pioneers Provide Preliminary PPO Program Profiles," *Employee Benefit Plan Review*, December 1983, pp. 54ff.

32. Melanie E. Frishman, "What Makes Preferred Provider Group Preferred?" *Employee Benefit Plan Review*, October 1983, pp. 32–34ff.

33. *Employee Benefit Plan Review*, May 1983, p. 98.

34. *Employee Benefit Plan Review*, June 1983, p. 29.

35. Robert Ricklefs, "Some Employers Help Pay Auto Insurance; Experts Suggest Benefit Could Catch On," *Wall Street Journal*, January 13, 1981.

36. *CPA Client Bulletin*, April 1984, p. 2

37. *Training and Development Journal*, June 1983, p. 10.

38. Oscar Oranti and Carol Buchham, "Day Care: Still Waiting Its Turn as a Standard Benefit," *Management Review*, May 1983, pp. 57–61.

39. Stewart A. Youngblood and Kimberly Chambers-Cook, "Child Care Assistance Can Improve Employee Attitudes and Behaviors," *Personnel Administrator*, February 1984, pp. 45–47ff.

40. *Modern Office Procedures*, May 1983, p. 20.

41. Stephen N. Gerberding, "Communicate Your Benefits Program Through an Employee Fair," *Personnel Administrator*, May 1983, pp. 51–53.

42. "Flexible Benefits Become the Wave of the Present. . . ." *Employee Benefit Plan Review*, March 1984, pp. 22–24.

43. "Employees Satisfied with Flexible Benefit Programs," *Employee Benefit Plan Review*, September 1983, pp. 29–32.

44. Nancy Gore, "Flexible Fringe Benefits Allow Employees to Select Tailored Plans," *Business & Industry*, March 1984, pp. 78–81.

45. Joann S. Lublin, "IRS Promotes Uproar by Attacking Corporate Reimbursement Plans," *Wall Street Journal*, March 20, 1984, p. 31.

46. Sources used included *Employee Benefit Plan Review*, December 1983, pp. 12–13; *Resource*, August 1983, p. 12; *Personnel Journal* (January 1984), p. 43; *Personnel Administrator*, March 1984, p. 16; and *Employee Benefit Plan Review*, March 1984, pp. 26–32.

47. Daniel R. Hoyt, Ph.D., Associate Professor.

SECTION CASE V

COMPENSATING OSCAR

Osmax Memorial Hospital (OMH) is located in the northeastern U.S. and employs over 2,000 people in over 400 separate jobs. The job with the most positions—almost 300 employees—is "Staff Registered Nurse." However, there are several jobs with only one employee. The jobs are classified as:

■ Professionals—Registered Nurses, Physicians, and Pharmacists
■ Technicians—Therapists, Laboratory Technicians, and Dieticians
■ Administrators—Department Heads, Supervisors, and Specialists in Accounting and Personnel
■ Support—Engineers, Security, Janitors, and Cooks

The hospital environment is highly competitive. OMH has a shortage of registered nurses, and has an average of 35 to 50 positions open at all times. The same shortages are evident at other hospitals in the area. Shortages also occur within other hospital jobs, especially in one-of-a-kind technical positions. Not only do area hospitals crave the services of these "healers," but facilities across the nation vie for the area's labor supply. Hospitals in Florida have been known to beckon experienced troops from the chills of northern winters with posters and advertisements showing palm trees and sunny beaches.

In an effort to keep desirable help and discourage less competent employees, OMH uses a merit pay system developed for it by an international consultant firm specializing in compensation. The plan was very expensive to develop, but Fred Richards, OMH's salary administrator, is pleased with its day-to-day workings. Since the system was introduced six years ago there have been fewer disagreements between employees and the hospital over the worth of the positions held by the employees.

For years, the hospital participated in semi-annual market surveys of compensation conducted by the Northern Hospital Personnel Association. The surveys provided the hospital with average compensation rates (but not ranges) for large groups of hospital jobs. The surveys are still used by other large hospitals and by hospitals not large enough to have a formal pay system. However, the surveys are neither precise nor formal and OMH no longer participates in this program.

Richards believes the merit pay system has helped keep the unions from organizing OMH employees. He claims that his problems with equity of compensation from department to department have ceased, and adds that the system has shielded the hospital from complaints about comparable pay and wage and hour lawsuits.

Oscar Renta is a Respiratory Equipment Technician. This is one of four jobs in the Respiratory Therapy Department. There are 50 employees in the department, ranging from lowest to highest jobs as follows:

■ Respiratory Equipment Technicians
■ Non-Certified Respiratory Therapists
■ Certified Respiratory Therapists
■ Registered Respiratory Therapists

The hourly wages for these jobs range from $4.25 to $9. Oscar has worked at OMH for two years, one of them as a Respiratory Equipment Technician, landing the job the summer after completing high school. He received two weeks of training at the hospital and is expected to keep up-to-date on the equipment used in the hospital. Renta loves his work and takes personal pride in keeping the machines working at peak efficiency. He knows that both his work and the equipment help the respiratory therapy patients recuperate.

In spite of his love for his work and a promotion one year ago to Non-Certified Respiratory Therapist, Renta has become disgruntled. In discussing his disaffection with his supervisor, Mike Maxey, Renta says:

You guys didn't teach me everything I know, you know. When I started here two years ago, I brought plenty of knowledge about equipment with me. I just found out that a girl I went to high school with is starting out here next week as a Certified Respiratory Therapist. You know what she told me? She'll get more pay to start than I get after two years here! What gives? Why is she so special?

Maxey asked Renta to calm down. He explained that the new employee completed two more years of school to gain that certification. With the type of patient she would be dealing with and because of the medication and treatments required, education and training are required for this job. "Let's call the personnel department," Maxey said, "and see what's gone into the decision to pay a starting employee in that job more than a veteran employee in your job."

Maxey and Renta discovered the following: In a formal system such as OMH has, set criteria determine the points for a job and points determine the salary range. OMH and Richards disclose the point structures of its job when asked to, but do not routinely disclose them at any other time. When a position opens, the hospital publishes the starting salary range only. Several employees at OMH were aware of the point system, but were concerned only with their current wage, not with the range or the points associated with the wage.

In this particular case, Renta's job had been assigned 273 points. The job's wage range this year is $5 to $7.08/hour, with most employees earning the mean. The Certified Therapist job had 333 points. This translates to a $5.80 to $8.33 hourly wage range; however, the job is "red-tagged" because of severe shortages of qualified people. Because of the red-tagging, the job pays at the 368-point level with an hourly range of $6.20 to $8.96.

The time had come for Renta's annual performance appraisal and merit pay increase. All he wanted out of life at this time was a raise. He didn't know what kind of an increase to expect, but he understood from reading the newspaper that the cost of living had increased about 12 percent in the past year, and that the

hospital had given all nonexempt employees a 6 percent increase for inflation in June.

A month later, Renta had an appointment with Maxey for his performance appraisal session.

"Let's review what's happened here, Oscar," said Maxey, after completing the appraisal discussion. "Last year at this time you were appraised as meeting all standards, so you got a 5 percent merit pay increase on top of the cost-of-living increase. This year, you've surely met all the standards, and you've even exceeded some of them. Now, I'm not supposed to give you an 'exceeding all standards' rating for that, but I have because that's the only way I can pay you enough to survive inflation. What the heck, I've got to pay the certified therapists more than their job is worth. I won't discuss this with any of the other techs or therapists, and you have to promise to improve your performance even more in the next 12 months."

QUESTIONS

1. Evaluate the wage and salary administration system in use at OMH as a general approach to compensation management. What is your opinion of the following specific features of the system:

    a. Disclosing points and salary ranges to those who ask.

    b. Paying an experienced employee below a new employee in a higher grade job.

    c. What is your evaluation of "red-tagging" the Certified Respiratory Therapist job and the consequences of doing so versus not doing so?

2. What mistakes does Maxey make in dealing with Renta and the salary system?

3. Is it realistic to expect Renta to "keep the secret" of what Maxey did? Why or why not?

4. If you were Richards, how would you go about dealing with Renta's problem and Maxey's efforts to distort the system?

ORGANIZATIONAL MAINTENANCE

Healthy and safe employees are likely to be more productive than those who are affected by unhealthy or unsafe occurrences. Every year organizations lose money because of illnesses, accidents, and injuries on the job. A part of personnel management is to provide employees with working environments that are safe and to insure that employees with health problems receive help.

Traditionally, safety received only minor attention in many organizations. The Occupational Safety and Health Act of 1970 has changed this outlook and added a new dimension to personnel management responsibilities. The regulations contained in the act are complex and sometimes compliance is difficult. Managers must also maintain an atmosphere of safety consciousness in the organization through continuous communication. Suggestions on dealing with the problem of health and safety and some details of the Occupational Safety and Health Act are included in Chapter 16.

Coordination of personnel efforts requires policies and rules. However, if not well designed and enforced, policies and rules can be sources of irritation and targets of criticism. Chapter 17 discusses personnel coordination as it is affected by policies, rules, and formal personnel communication.

Chapter 18 considers Personnel research and HRIS (Human Resources Information Systems). Basic research helps define problems that might exist in an organization. It also provides information to aid in solving those problems.

Personnel record keeping has been a major function for a long time but recently, with the advent of computers, it has also become an opportunity for more information for making decisions. HRIS and privacy concerns are discussed.

Personnel Health and Safety

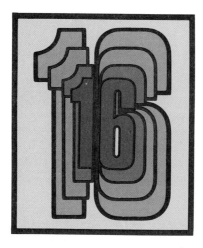

When you have read this chapter, you should be able to:

1. Define health and safety and explain their importance in an organization.
2. Discuss three factors that affect health and safety in organizations.
3. Explain the impact of four health problems in organizations.
4. Identify how organizations respond to employee alcoholism, drug abuse, and other health problems.
5. Identify the basic provisions of the Occupational Safety and Health Act of 1970.
6. Describe OSHA record-keeping and inspection requirements, and five types of OSHA citations.
7. Discuss both positive and negative problems with OSHA.
8. Identify and briefly explain the basic components of a systems approach to safety.

PERSONNEL AT WORK
THE LIVING AND THE DEAD—THE DIAL PAINTERS

Ottawa, Illinois, was once the home of a plant run by Luminous Processes, Inc., where the dials of watches were painted with radium to make them glow in the dark. This plant received worldwide publicity when ominous findings about employee illnesses began to appear. Nearly 700 dial painters (mostly women) have been studied extensively. Most are still living and some worked with radium as recently as 1975.

During the 1930s, headline writers labeled these women "the living dead." More than 30 cases of cancer caused by ingested radium at the plant have become textbook examples of workplace hazards. The radium was ingested during the early days because dial painters licked their brushes to form a fine point. The breast cancer rate among the dial painters who went to work after the brush-licking was stopped is still twice as high as would be expected.

More recently, however, the exposure to low levels of radiation externally is of interest to many industries and the dial painters provide a laboratory group to study. When Ottawa's "radioactive women" die, their bodies are taken for a radioactivity analysis by scientists from Argonne National Laboratory before they are buried. This subject is politically sensitive because the establishment of a strong link between low-level radiation and cancer could force many employers, including the government, to spend more money for workers' protections.

The Ottawa women have also raised questions about how much protection should be provided by an employer. Many say that precautions were nonexistent at the plant and that workers were constantly contaminated with radiation. Company officials told them the radium was safe to handle, the women say. Some even painted their fingernails with the stuff; others took it home and painted light switches so they would glow in the dark. Their skin and hair were in contact with the material daily and they regularly wiped paint on their work smocks. One woman tells of getting up at night and looking in the mirror to see her hair glowing. Other former workers say that management deliberately misled inspectors who visited the plant two or three times per year in the 1970s. "When the company found out the inspectors were coming they'd tell us to clean everything up. But that wasn't the way we worked. They didn't want the real conditions to show," one woman claims. Investigators have tracked down information on the 64 workers who have died since the 1960s. Of those, 28 died of cancer—well over double the expected rate for the group.

Not everyone sees management's health and safety practices as the villain. Dorothy Griffith supervised dial painters for 45 years until 1971. The company warned workers to be careful, she says. Her own health problems at age 75 are limited to "just a few of those little tumors everybody gets between their toes."[1]

"The preservation of health is a duty. Few men seem conscious that there is such a thing as physical mortality."

HERBERT SPENCER

HEALTH
refers to a general state of physical, mental, and emotional well-being.

SAFETY
refers to protection of the physical health of people.

Organizations are obligated to provide employees with a safe and healthful environment. Requiring them to work with unsafe equipment or in areas where hazards are not controlled is a highly questionable practice. Managers also must ensure that employees are safety-conscious and maintain good health. Both managers and personnel specialists are involved in health and safety in an organization. This chapter looks at ways in which organizations can maintain safe working environments for employees.

HEALTH AND SAFETY DEFINED

The terms *health* and *safety* are closely related. Although they are often used in the same context, a distinction should be made.

Health is a broader and somewhat more nebulous term than safety. A healthy person is one who is free of illness, injury, or mental and emotional problems that impair normal human activity. However, the question of exactly what is healthy or normal behavior is open to interpretation. Health maintenance or management refers to maintaining the overall well-being of an individual.

Typically, **safety** concerns physical well-being instead of mental or emotional well-being. The main purpose of effective safety programs in organizations is to prevent work-related injuries and accidents.

The focus of health and safety policies is the safe interaction of people and the working environment. Because many employers' efforts in the past were inadequate, the federal Occupational Safety and Health Act of 1970 was passed. This act has had a tremendous impact on the workplace, so that any person interested in personnel management must develop a clear knowledge of the act's provisions and implications.

Can you define health and safety?

Health and Safety Responsibilities

As Figure 16–1 indicates, the primary health and safety responsibilities in an organization usually fall on supervisors and managers. A personnel specialist or safety specialist can help investigate accidents, produce safety program materials, and conduct formal safety training. However, department supervisors and managers play key roles in maintaining safe working conditions and a healthy work force. A supervisor in a ball bearing plant has several health and safety responsibilities. Examples are: reminding an employee to wear safety glasses; checking on the cleanliness of the work area; observing employees to see if any

FIGURE 16–1
Health and Safety Inter-
face.

PERSONNEL UNIT	MANAGERS
■ Coordinates health and safety programs	■ Monitor health and safety of employees daily
■ Develops safety reporting system	■ Coach employees to be safety-conscious
■ Provides accident investigation expertise	■ Investigate accidents
■ Provides technical expertise on accident research and prevention	■ Observe health and safety behavior of employees daily

of them have alcohol, drug, or emotional problems that may affect their work behavior; and recommending equipment changes (such as screens, railings, or other safety devices) to specialists in the organization.

A personnel safety specialist in the same plant has other safety responsibilities: maintaining government-required health and safety records; coordinating a safety training class for new employees; assisting the supervisor in investigating an accident in which an employee was injured; and developing a plantwide safety communication program and informational materials. The interface between the supervisor and the personnel specialist is crucial to a coordinated health and safety maintenance effort.

NATURE OF HEALTH AND SAFETY

Every year employers lose an astounding amount of money and resources because of accidents. A Bureau of Labor Statistics survey for a recent one-year period provides some rather startling statistics:[2]

■ Job-related injuries and illnesses average 7.6 per 100 workers
■ Work-related fatalities numbered 3,100, with approximately 30 percent being the result of truck and car accidents. This figure represented a decrease of one thousand fatalities from the year before.
■ About 4.9 million work-related injuries and illnesses occurred
■ Average number of work days lost per injury was 17 days
■ Work injuries caused 2.14 million lost work days.

With problems of this magnitude, health and safety must be a prime concern in the management of human resources. Knowledge about factors affecting employee health and safety is critical.

Worker Attitudes and Accidents

Because health and safety are concerned with the well-being of individuals, employees' attitudes about safety must be considered in planning health and safety programs. Employees' attitudes toward their working conditions, accidents, and jobs should be analyzed when an organization's health and safety activities are examined. Many more problems are caused by careless employees than by machines or employer negligence.[3]

At one time, it was thought that workers who were dissatisfied with their jobs would have a higher accident rate. However, this assumption has been questioned in recent years. One study of accident proneness found that younger and less-experienced employees were involved in more injuries and accidents. This same study suggested that there were some differences in personality and emotional characteristics between people who had no accidents and those who had repeated accidents.[4] Another study found that biorhythm cycles were not significantly related to the occurrence of accidents.[5] These results suggest that while employees' personalities, attitudes, and individual characteristics may have an effect on accidents, a cause-and-effect relationship is very difficult to establish.

Worker Boredom and Monotony. Employees doing the same job repeatedly each day can become bored. They either begin to pay less attention to their tasks or they develop bad habits that can cause accidents and injuries. One way to deal with worker boredom is to relieve the monotony by redesigning the job. Elements of job design such as job scope and job depth were discussed previously.

Engineering Approach to Health and Safety Some accidents can be prevented by designing machines, equipment, and work areas so that workers who daydream periodically or who perform mechanical jobs cannot injure themselves or others. This engineering approach tries to prevent accidents by constructing the working environment so that it is very difficult for employees to injure themselves. Providing safety equipment and guards on machinery and installing emergency switches are equipment changes often made to prevent accidents. To prevent a punch-press operator from mashing her finger, a safety guard is attached to a machine so her hand cannot accidentally slip into the machine. Actions such as providing safety rails; keeping aisles clear; and providing adequate ventilation, lighting, or heating and air conditioning can all help make the work environment safer.

Ergonomics. A specialized field which has been developed to better design the work environment is ergonomics. Ergonomics comes from the word *ergon* meaning *work* and the suffix *-omics* meaning *management of.* An ergonomist studies the physiological, psychological, and enginerring design aspects of a job. Other aspects such as fatigue factors, lighting, tools, equipment layout, and placement of controls are also considered. Human factors engineering is a related field.

Behavioral/Human Approach

Engineers approach safety from the perspective of redesigning the machinery or the work area. Industrial psychologists see safety differently. Their approach emphasizes the proper selection of people for their jobs and the training of employees to use safety methods, reduce fatigue, and be aware of hazards.

Can you discuss some factors that may affect health and safety?

HEALTH

Employee health problems are inevitable in all organizations. These problems can range from an illness, such as a cold, to serious injuries on the job or elsewhere. Some employees have emotional problems; others have drinking or drug problems. All these difficulties may affect organizational operations and individual employee productivity.

There are four major health problem areas that have direct relevance to personnel management: physical illness, emotional illness, alcoholism, and drug abuse. As depicted in Figure 16–2, resolution of problems in all these areas is necessary for the development of healthy individuals.

Physical Health and Illness

Physical illnesses and problems may reduce an employee's ability to perform a job. Organizations help employees who have physical illnesses and health problems by providing hospitalization and health insurance. However, sound health programs focus on preventing employees from getting sick as well as helping employees to get well.

Some organizations have staff medical professionals, such as doctors or nurses, to treat minor illnesses and job-related injuries. If a claims clerk at a large insurance company comes to work feeling rather weak because he has a cold, the company doctor can prescribe some medication to help the clerk feel better. Many larger companies provide on-site medical assistance because the Occupational Safety and Health Act requires certain first-aid treatment and health services to be available "in near proximity" to work stations.

FIGURE 16–2
Major Health Problems.

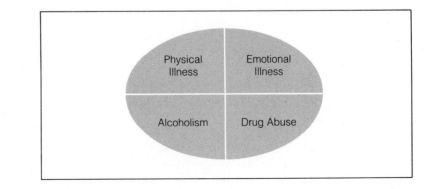

Health Concerns and the Work Environment. Many people have heard of the health problems developed by asbestos workers, coal miners, and some chemical workers. Cancer, black lung disease, and radiation poisoning are among the many health concerns of employers and employees. For example, it has been estimated that over 150,000 U.S. workers in 56 different occupations are exposed to mercury on the job.[7]

Other health problems can be caused by a work environment that exposes workers to excessive noise or harmful lighting. One example of new health problems that are developing because of new technology involves employees who work at computer video display terminals. Terminal operators studied have complained of dizziness and eye problems.[8]

Managers and personnel specialists must exhibit a heightened awareness of health problems; they must not just concentrate on safety problems. The engineering approach is likely to be used even more in the future to reduce the exposure of workers to health-damaging substances and environments. In cases of potentially hazardous jobs and environments, employers should continually monitor employee health through physical examinations.

Physical Exams. Employers may sponsor in-depth general physical examinations yearly or on a regular basis. Organizations providing this service are investing in the physical health of employees who may not see a doctor regularly because of work schedules, personal reluctance, or lack of money. Regardless of the type of physical exam given, organizations who offer them to employees believe that the employer benefits financially and organizationally when healthier employees are on the job.

Physical Fitness. Another way in which some employers help employees maintain good physical health is by providing physical fitness programs. Some programs offer lunch-hour exercise classes or stop-smoking clinics while others use complete gymnasiums provided by employers. Internorth, Texaco, IBM, Pepsi Co, Kimberly Clark, Merrill Lynch, and many smaller employers have fitness programs.

Pinpointing potential health problems and dealing with them early allows an employer to have the continued service of a valuable employee. Sometimes physical health and hygiene problems are caused by emotional or mental health factors.

Employee "wellness" programs focus on keeping people from getting sick instead of repairing health damage after it has occurred. The "Personnel Today and Tomorrow" feature at the end of this chapter expands on corporate wellness programs.

Stress

The pressures of modern life, coupled with the demands of a job, can lead to emotional health concerns that are collectively labelled *stress*. The evidence of stress can be seen everywhere, from the 35-year-old executive who dies of a sudden heart attack to the dependable older worker who unexpectedly commits suicide. One indicator of stress is *hypertension* (high blood pressure). According to data provided by the Blue Cross and Blue Shield Association, 17 million U.S. workers suffer from hypertension, resulting in $20 billion of lost wages and productivity every year.[9] Other problems such as alcoholism and drug abuse may result from severe emotional strain as employees turn to them to help reduce stress.

Stress is not necessarily more prevalent now than it has been before, but medical experts increasingly are identifying it as the source of physical problems and it is getting more attention. There is a better understanding now of how the body reacts to stress. When the brain perceives danger, it triggers certain chemicals in a "fight-or-flight" response that heightens the hearbeat and sharpens reflexes. This reaction allows for peak physical responses to dangerous situations.

But if this reaction is left "on" for longer periods of time, it can damage the body it was designed to protect. If the system remains on, it triggers intense physical and psychological reactions again and again. Then the body begins to deteriorate as common stress symptoms appear: anxiety, headaches, sweaty palms, the need to urinate frequently, deep sighing, and impatience.[10]

Consider Fred Williamson, a 46-year-old vice president who firmly believed that when his boss gave him a job to do he wanted results, not problems. Fred's stoic, self-contained posture had over the years taken its toll. He developed high blood pressure and an ulcer. Eventually, he sought solace in an intimate relationship with a woman who had been a longtime friend. But he soon felt guilty and ended the affair. The breakup left him crushed. He says, "I became distant from my family and friends. I stopped eating and lost 25 pounds. Everything bothered me. I'd be in the middle of a conversation and forget what I was talking about." Fred finally got some help from counseling.

Until recently, most corporations reasoned that if their managers could not handle stress, they were not tough enough for the job. But now many companies offer counseling programs aimed at stress reduction.[11]

It should be noted that not all stress is unpleasant. To be alive means to respond to the stimulation of achievement and the excitement of a challenge to be met. In fact, there is evidence that people *need* a certain amount of stimulation and that monotony can bring on some of the same problems as overwork. What is usually meant by the term *stress* is excessive stress, or distress.

What is Stressful? Individual differences determine what any given person will find stressful. Those who have a hard time adjusting to change are more susceptible. Other factors, including biochemistry, physical strength, psychological makeup, values, and habits, affect individual reactions. Other major contributors to stress have been found to be[12]:

■ Lack of control
■ Inability to predict
■ Inaccurate perceptions of events
■ Intense responsibility

Stress: A Survey. A survey done for the *Wall Street Journal* uncovered several interesting facts about stress and business.[13] The poll found that 49 percent of the surveyed small business proprietors saw stress as a problem, compared with 33 percent in medium-sized companies and 19 percent of those in big companies. Of executives who do complain of stress, a large percentage are young, suggesting that as people grow older they may learn to handle stress better (or perhaps people who do not handle stress well do not grow older).

Executives in the survey attributed more stress to certain industries. Commodity trading, advertising, and investment banking were considered by many to be stressful industries. At large and medium-sized companies employees were cited by executives as the biggest cause of stress. At smaller firms, financial problems were the main source.

Strategies used by executives to cope with stress included physical exercise (golf, tennis, hunting or fishing, aerobics, and running), a change of scene, reading, and hobbies. When asked to give advice to young executives on how to deal with stress, most of the respondents suggested learning not to worry about it: "Do your best and don't worry, ignore it, and avoid it."[14]

Management of Stress When an emotional problem (stress-related or otherwise) becomes so severe that it disrupts an employee's ability to function normally, the employee should be directed to appropriate professionals for help. Because emotional problems are very difficult to

STRESS AT GULF OIL

During late 1983 and early 1984, Texas oilman T. Boone Pickens waged a bitter takeover battle for Gulf Oil Corporation. The battle lasted months before Gulf was finally acquired by another firm.

The proxy contest and corporate takeover attempt was the largest in corporate history, and involved excessive workloads as armies of investment bankers, lawyers and public relations consultants descended on the company. Only a small percentage of the company's emloyees were directly involved in the day-to-day activities of the proxy fight, but all Gulf employees, from top management downward, became involved, even if it meant picking up the duties of a co-worker involved in the fight.

Company officials acknowledged that the situation placed unprecedented pressure on every employee in the firm. "Intense emotions, round-the-clock hours, and an all out fight" is how one executive at the company's Pittsburgh headquarters characterized the atmosphere that enveloped the company.

The ability of individuals to cope with the changing events varied widely. The intense atmosphere, countless tasks, and unrelenting hours caused a high degree of stress for those involved. During the proxy fight, much of the stress was the adrenaline-pumping type which kept up morale and pushed employees to volunteer to work late nights and weekends, even holidays. It was a "campaign" which resulted in a tremendous coming together of people working for the same case. An intense loyalty and identification with their company emerged among employees.

Once the company was taken over, a high stress level remained, but the cause changed to uncertainty about jobs. Some employees complained of classic symptoms of stress such as decreased energy levels or sleeping problems, resulting largely from anxiety about the future.

Throughout the period, management recognized the high stress level of the situation and the need for increased communication with employees. Frequent desk-top information sheets and videotapes on the progress of the situation were prepared and distributed. A "hotline" was set up during the most intense period of the proxy fight so that employees could follow events on a daily basis. Stress management seminars were provided throughout the company following the merger to provide employees with better skills to cope with the pressures that had been created.[15]

diagnose, supervisors and managers should not become deeply involved. If a quality control inspector is emotionally upset because of his marital difficulties, his supervisor should not get personally involved trying to solve the employee's problems. Even though most supervisors and managers are concerned about employees' problems, they should realize that appropriate professionals are better qualified to help troubled employees.

Alcoholism

Alcoholism is a costly health problem. It has been estimated by a U.S. governmental agency that problem drinkers on payrolls cost American industry approximately $20 billion a year in lost production, mishandling of resources, sick pay, absenteeism, and other costs; and up to 10 percent of the American work force suffers from various degress of alcoholism.

Alcoholism Assistance Programs. Because of the problems and costs involved, a growing number of organizations are sponsoring programs to deal with alcoholic managers and workers. Usually these programs are supported enthusiastically by unions. Some health insurance programs consider alcoholism as a disease and help to pay for treatment of drinking problems. By dealing with alcoholism, employers are able to retain otherwise good workers who are disabled by drinking problems. Insurance companies have been very active in providing comprehensive programs to help treat alcoholism. The Kemper, Equitable, Traveler's, and Prudential insurance companies have employee programs that classify alcoholism as a disease that can be treated. The director of an alcoholism assistance program for Union Pacific Railroad reports that more than 2,500 employees have used the program. The success rate has been about 86 percent.[16]

The United States is not the only country with alcohol-related problems. The Soviet Union recently cracked down on its twin (and related) productivity problems: absenteeism and alcoholism. Now anyone found drunk on the job can be fired and has to pay for damaged goods and lost production.[17]

One process for handling problem drinkers is shown in Figure 16–3. Managers and supervisors should encourage employees with drinking problems to seek specialized treatment. This treatment can be made available through a company program, a cooperative program between an employer and a union, a private agency, state or local health and social service agencies, or voluntary organizations such as Alcoholics Anonymous.

Assisting employees who have drinking problems is part of good personnel management. Although some alcoholic employees may resist treatment at first, alcohol rehabilitation programs generally have had an excellent success rate. Instead of immediately firing an employee with a drinking problem, many employers create a confrontation that leads to the alcoholic admitting there is a problem, after which he or she can be directed to a treatment program.[18]

Drug Abuse

The impact of drug abuse is evident throughout society. The problems cover the full range, from the use of legal drugs, such as barbituates and tranquilizers, to the use of minor drugs, such as marijuana, to the

FIGURE 16–3
Policy on Problem Drink-
ing.

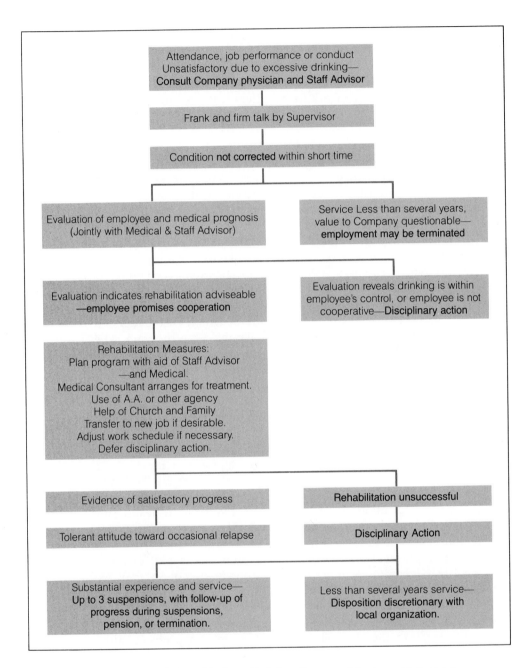

SOURCE: Adapted from August Ralston, "Employee Alcoholism: Response of the Largest Industrials,"
The Personnel Administrator. August 1977, p. 52. Reprinted with permission.

overuse of illegal hard drugs, such as heroin. Some firms have found employees selling drugs to other employees at work. One computer firm discovered a drug ring grossing $10,000 a week that involved over ten employees. In a firm in California some employees were observed drying cocaine in a microwave oven in the company cafeteria![19]

Dealing with Employee Drug Problems. Employers have responded to their employees' drug-related problems by establishing programs to treat drug and other substance abuse through employee assistance programs. Managers faced with a problem of employee drug abuse should be aware of drug-induced changes in an employee's behavior. Possible tip-offs to drug abuse are: excessive absenteeism, increased tardiness, decreasing job performance, and unexplained personality and behavior changes. However, a supervisor or manager can do little other than inform the company physician or counseling specialist about the problem and direct the employee to appropriate professionals.

Policies on drug abuse are needed in many organizations. Improving selection procedures to screen out persons who abuse drugs offers a possible solution. Some firms utilize urine tests as a part of their selection process, but this screening is very imprecise and may discriminate against persons who once had a drug problem but have overcome it. Obviously, smoking marijuana occasionally is a different matter from being hooked on heroin. To address drug problems, organizations should: (1) develop an awareness of drug problems, and (2) develop policies and responses to cope with drug abuse.

More companies are doing just that because of increasing evidence of the link between drug abuse and accidents or shoddy work. Consider these actual cases:[20]

■ A forklift operator smokes a joint at lunch and then runs his forklift loaded with cargo into a door.
■ A Wall Street trader cannot remember an $18 million trade because his cocaine habit has affected his memory.
■ A construction worker falls 8 stories to his death; an autopsy shows he used pot on the job.

The cost of such drug abuse clearly is very high and companies are beginning to react in a number of ways.[21]

■ Blue Cross and Blue Shield in Boston fired 21 employees after an undercover operation showed they were using drugs at work.
■ Burns International fired 21 unarmed guards at a California nuclear plant after they failed or refused to take urine tests.
■ Shell Oil conducts random drug searches on workers going on-and off-duty aboard drilling rigs.
■ The National Transportation Safety Board investigated 7 train accidents involving either alcohol or drugs in an 11-month period.

Other companies, although alarmed by the consequences of substance abuse, do not want to create an investigative atmosphere. For these

firms, instituting employee assistance programs and quick confrontation of abuse problems are more appropriate actions.

Employee Assistance Programs. One method that organizations are using
to respond to employees' emotional, physical, and personal problems
is an **employee assistance program (EAP)**. In such a program, an employer establishes a liaison relationship with a social service counseling
agency. Employees who have problems may then contact the agency,
either voluntarily or by employer referral, for assistance with a broad
range of problems. Counseling costs are paid for by the employer in
total or up to a preestablished limit.

EAPs are attempts to help employees with their most difficult problems. Some personnel managers feel that EAPs make their other personnel programs more effective. For example, in one large company
the Vice-President of Personnel found that much of his department's
time was being taken up in dealing with such problems as employee
anxiety reactions, suicide attempts, alcohol- and drug-related absences,
and family disturbances. Further, the medical department was not able
to provide accurate information on whether or not affected employees
could successfully return to work. The vice-president decided an EAP
might save a great deal of time and money.

It is no secret that most companies have employees with health and
personal problems. Common problems are: *personal crises* (such as marriage, family, or legal problems), *alcoholism and drug abuse*, and *emotional illness*.

Part of the reason for the sudden increased interest in EAPs is the
increase in the incidence of these problems in the working population.
Slightly less than half the companies responding to one survey offer
in-house counseling for alcoholism or personal crises. About a third
provide in-house counseling for emotional illness. In one large corporation, over 14,000 employees used the EAP in a three-year period.[22]
Such a response rate indicates that firms that provide EAPs are truly
answering the health needs of their employees.

*Can you identify how organizations re-
spond to employee alcoholism, drug abuse,
and other health problems?*

OCCUPATIONAL SAFETY AND HEALTH ACT

The Occupational Safety and Health Act, which became effective in
1971, was passed "to assure so far as possible every working man or
woman in the Nation safe and healthful working conditions and to
preserve our human resources."[23] Every employer engaged in commerce who has one or more employees is covered by the act. Farmers
having fewer than ten employees are exempt from the act. Covered
under other health and safety acts are employers in specific industries
such as coal mining. Federal, state, and local government employees
are covered by separate provisions or statutes.

Basic Provisions

The act established the Occupational Safety and Health Administration, known as OSHA. The act also established the National Institute of Occupational Safety and Health (NIOSH) as a supporting body to do research and develop standards.

Enforcement Standards. To implement the act, specific standards were established concerning equipment and working environment regulations. OSHA often uses national standards developed by engineering and quality control groups. Employers are required to meet the provisions and standards under OSHA. Figure 16–4 gives examples of some specific OSHA standards.

"General Duty" Clause. Section 5a(1) of the act is known as the "general duty" clause. This section requires that in areas in which no standards have been adopted, the employer has a *general duty* to provide safe and healthy working conditions. Employers who know of, or who should

§1910.151 Medical services and first aid.

(a) The employer shall ensure the ready availability of medical personnel for advice and consultation on matters of plant health.

(b) In the absence of an infirmary, clinic, or hospital in near proximity to the workplace which is used for the treatment of all injured employees, a person

♦ ♦ ♦ ♦ ♦ ♦ ♦ ♦ ♦ ♦ ♦ ♦

§ 1910.157 Portable fire extinguishers.

(a) *General requirements*—(1) *Operable condition.* Portable extinguishers shall be maintained in a fully charged and operable condition, and kept in their designated places at all times when they are not being used.

(2) *Location.* Extinguishers shall be conspicuously located where they will be readily accessible and immediately available in the event of fire. They shall be located along normal paths of travel.

(3) *Marking of location.* Extinguishers shall not be obstructed or obscured from view. In large rooms, and in certain locations where visual obstruction cannot

or persons shall be adequately trained to render first aid. First aid supplies approved by the consulting physician shall be readily available.

(c) Where the eyes or body of any person may be exposed to injurious corrosive materials, suitable facilities for quick drenching or flushing of the eyes and body shall be provided within the work area for immediate emergency use.

♦ ♦ ♦ ♦ ♦ ♦ ♦ ♦ ♦ ♦ ♦ ♦

be completely avoided, means shall be provided to indicate the location and intended use of extinguishers conspicuously.

(4) *Marking of extinguishers.* If extinguishers intended for different classes of fire are grouped, their intended use shall be marked conspicuously to insure choice of the proper extinguisher at the time of a fire.

...

(9) *Temperature range.* Extinguishers shall be suitable for use within a temperature range of at least plus 40° to 120° Fahrenheit.

FIGURE 16–4
Sample OSHA Standards.

SOURCE: General Industry Standards, USDOL Pamphlet OSHA No. 2206, Nov. 7, 1978, OSHA Safety & Health STDS (29CFR1910).

reasonably know of, unsafe or unhealthy conditions can be cited for violating this clause. The existence of standard practices or of a trade association code, which is not included in OSHA standards, often is used as the basis for citations under the "general duty" clause.

Employers are responsible for knowing about and informing their employees of safety and health standards established by OSHA and for putting up OSHA posters in prominent places. In addition, they are required to enforce the use of personal protective equipment and to provide safety communications to employees so they are aware of safety considerations. Employees who report safety violations to OSHA cannot be punished or discharged.

Worker's Right to Refuse. Both union and nonunion workers have refused to work when the work was unsafe. Although such actions may appear to be illegal, in many cases they are not.

Two important Supreme Court cases have shed light on this issue. In *Whirlpool* v. *Marshall* (1980) a major victory for employees and unions was won. The U.S. Supreme Court unanimously ruled that workers have the right to walk off a job if they believe it is hazardous without fear of reprisal by the employer. Court argued that "employees have the right not to perform an assigned task because of a reasonable apprehension of health or serious injury coupled with a reasonable belief that no less drastic alternative is available."[24] The requirements for employees to refuse unsafe work were clarified in the *Gateway Coal* v. *the United Mine Workers* case.[25] Current legal conditions for refusing work because of safety concerns are:[26]

1. The employee's fear is objectively reasonable.
2. The employee tried to get the dangerous condition corrected.
3. Using normal procedures to solve the problem has not worked.

Can you discuss the basic provisions of OSHA?

Record-keeping Requirements

OSHA established a standard national system for recording occupational injuries, accidents, and fatalities. Employers are generally required to maintain an annual detailed record of the various types of accidents for inspection by OSHA representatives and for submission to the agency.

Summary Log. Employers who have good safety records in the previous year and who have less than ten employees are not required to keep detailed records. Figure 16–5 shows the OSHA summary log that employers must complete. The portion to the right of the dotted line must be posted for employee review during February of every year.

Criticism of OSHA's record-keeping requirements resulted in significant changes in 1977. Many small employers having less than ten employees were exempted from having to complete the summary records.

FIGURE 16–5
Log and Summary of Occupational Injuries and Illnesses.

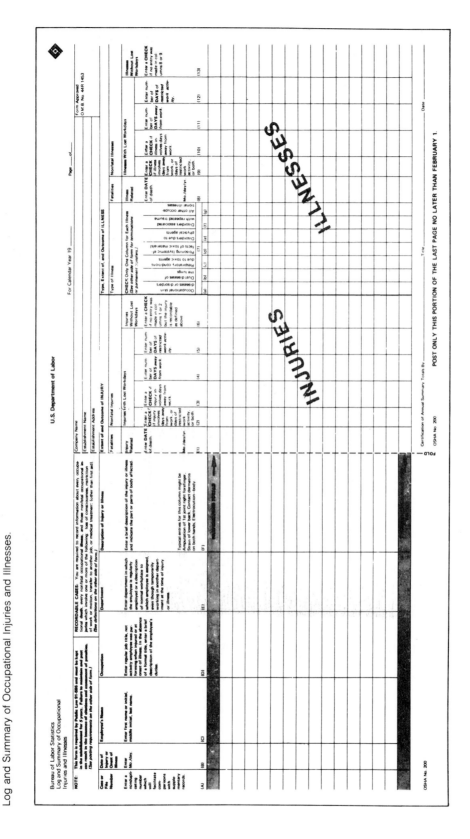

Only those small firms meeting the following conditions must complete OSHA Form 200, the basic reporting document:

1. Firms having frequent hospitalization injuries or illnesses
2. Firms having work-related deaths
3. Firms included in OSHA's annual labor statistics survey

Accident Frequency Rate. Accident frequency and severity rates also must be calculated. OSHA regulations require organizations to calculate injury frequency rates per 100 full-time employees on an annual basis. The accident frequency rate is figured as follows:

$$\frac{N}{EH} \times 200,000$$

where N = number of occupational injuries and illnesses
    EH = total hours worked by all employees during reference year
200,000 = base for 100 full-time equivalent workers (working 40 hours per week, 50 weeks per year)

Accident severity rates are computed by figuring the number of lost-time cases, the number of lost workdays, and the number of deaths. These figures are then related to total work hours per 100 full-time employees, and compared to industry-wide rates and other employers' rates.

Reporting Injuries/Illnesses. There are several types of injuries or illnesses defined by the act:

1. *Injury or illness-related deaths*
2. *Lost-time or disability injuries:* Disabling or job-related injuries that cause an employee to miss his or her regularly scheduled work on the day following the accident
3. *Medical care injuries:* Injuries requiring treatment by a physician but that do not cause an employee to miss a regularly scheduled work turn.
4. *Minor injuries:* Injuries that require first-aid treatment and do not cause an employee to miss the next regularly scheduled work turn.

The record-keeping requirements under OSHA are summarized in Figure 16–6. Notice that only minor injuries do not have to be recorded for OSHA. Managers may attempt to avoid reporting lost-time or medical care injuries. For example, if several managers are trained in first-aid, some injuries can be treated on the work site. In one questionable situation an employee's back injuries were treated with heat packs by the plant personnel manager to avoid counting the accident as a medical care injury.

Employers sometimes try moving injured employees to other jobs to avoid counting an injury as a lost-time injury. For example, if a seamstress in a clothing factory injured her hand on the job so that she could not operate her sewing machine her employer might ask her to

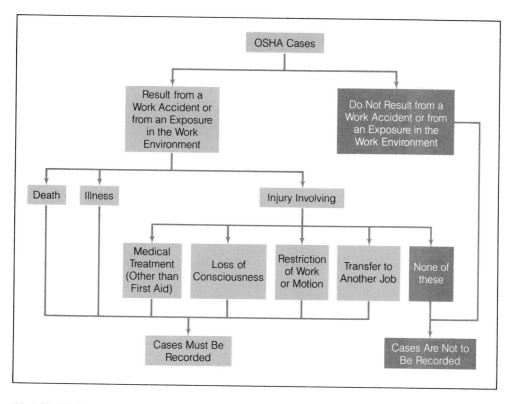

SOURCE: U.S. Department of Labor, Bureau of Labor Statistics, *What Every Employee Needs to Know About OSHA Record Keeping.* Washington DC: Government Printing Office, November 1978), p. 3.

FIGURE 16–6
Guide to Recordability of Cases Under the Occupational Safety and Health Act.

carry thread to other operators and perform other "make-work" jobs so that she did not miss work, and the injury would not have to be reported. Current regulations attempt to control this kind of subterfuge by requiring employees to perform the same type of job they performed before being injured.

There are several major reasons why employers try to make injuries appear less severe for reporting purposes. An abnormal number of lost-time or medical care injuries are warning flags to OSHA representatives and may lead to intensive investigations. Also, an employer's workers' compensation and liability insurance rates may be affected by increased injuries and accidents.

Inspection Requirements

The act provides for on-the-spot inspection by OSHA agents, known as *compliance officers* or *inspectors.* Under the original act, an employer could not refuse entry to an OSHA inspector. Further, the original act prohibited a compliance officer from giving prior notification of an inspection. This provision was included to permit inspection of normal operations, instead of allowing an employer to "tidy up." This so-called *no-knock provision* was challenged in numerous court suits. Finally, in 1978, the U.S. Supreme Court ruled on the issue.

Marshall v. Barlow's Inc.[27] In this case, an Idaho plumbing and air conditioning firm, Barlow's, refused entry to an OSHA inspector. The employer argued that the no-knock provision violated the Fourth Amendment of the U.S. Constitution, which deals with "unreasonable search and seizure." The government argued that the no-knock provision was necessary for enforcement of the act and that the Fourth Amendment did not apply to a business situation in which employees and customers have access to the firm.

The Supreme Court rejected the government's arguments and held that safety inspectors must produce a search warrant if an employer refuses to allow an inspector into the plant voluntarily. However, the Court ruled that an inspector does not have to prove probable cause to obtain a search warrant. A warrant can be obtained if a search is part of a general enforcement plan.

Although this decision was initially viewed as a victory for employers, later analysis of the decision revealed that the Supreme Court took a middle-of-the-road position. Inspectors no longer must be admitted through the no-knock provision. However, warrants are relatively easy to obtain because of the "general enforcement plan" aspects of the decision. An employer can refuse admittance, but the process of obtaining a warrant for OSHA is not extremely restrictive.

A number of cases have been filed challenging the use of *ex parte* search warrants. This type of warrant can be obtained by OSHA without notice to the employer, and the employer cannot argue against the warrant being the granting. Some lower federal courts have ruled against the use of the *ex parte* warrant while other courts have allowed them. Until a definite ruling is made by the U.S. Supreme Court, these warrants will continue to be used.

Conduct of Inspection. When the compliance officer arrives, the manager should request to see the inspector's credentials. After entering, the OSHA officer typically requests a meeting with the top representative or manager in the organization. The officer also may request that a union representative, an employee, and a company representative be present as the inspection is conducted. The OSHA inspector checks organizational records to see if they are being maintained and how many accidents have occurred. Following this review of the safety records, the inspector conducts an on-the-spot inspection and may use a wide variety of equipment to test compliance with the standards. After the inspection, the compliance officer can issue citations for violations of standards and provisions of the act.

Safety Consultation. OSHA, in conjunction with state and local governments, has established a safety consultation service. An employer can contact the state agency and have an authorized safety consultant conduct an advisory inspection. The consultant cannot issue citations or penalties and generally is prohibited from providing OSHA with any information obtained during the consultation visit. Such a visit provides an employer with an opportunity to receive a report useful in preventing future difficulties when OSHA does conduct an inspection.

Can you describe key OSHA record-keeping and inspection requirements?

Citations and Violations

The type of notices of violations and citations issued depends on the severity and extent of a violation and the employer's knowledge of possible violations. There are basically five types, ranging from minimal to severe.

De minimis. A *de minimis* condition is one that does not have a direct and immediate relationship to the employees' safety or health. A citation is not issued but it is mentioned to the employer. Lack of doors on toilet stalls is an example of a *de minimis* violation.

Other-Than-Serious. This type of violation is one that could have an impact on employees' health or safety but probably would not cause death or serious harm. Having loose ropes in a work area on which people could trip and hurt themselves might be classified as a nonserious violation.

Serious. A serious violation is issued if there is great probability the condition could cause death or serious physical harm and the employer should know of the condition. Examples are the absence of a protective screen on a lathe (which could easily allow an employee to mangle a hand) or the lack of a blade guard on an electric saw.

Willful and Repeated. This type of violation is somewhat different from the others. Willful and repeated violation citations are issued to employers who have been previously cited for violations. If an employer knows about a safety violation or has been warned for a violation and does not correct the problem, a second citation is issued. The penalty for a willful and repeated violation can be as high as $10,000. If death results from a willful violation, a jail term of six months can be imposed on responsible executive's or managers.

Imminent Danger. An imminent danger citation is a notice that is posted by an inspector if there is reasonable certainty the condition will cause death or serious physical harm if it is not corrected immediately. Imminent danger situations are handled on the highest priority basis. They are reviewed by a regional OSHA director and the condition must be corrected immediately. If the condition is serious enough and the employer does not cooperate, a representative of OSHA may go to a federal judge and obtain an injunction to close the company until the condition is corrected. The absence of any guard railings to prevent an employee from falling three stories into heavy machinery could be classified as an imminent danger violation.

Penalties. In place of a rather rigid fine system, OSHA inspectors now use a regulated penalty calculation process. This process, which is somewhat complex, considers the probability of occurrences and the severity of possible injury. Then a penalty is calculated.

One significant change OSHA has made is that fines are levied only if more than ten violations (except *de minimis* conditions) are found. Thus, a machine shop owner who has had eight "other-than-serious" violations is not penalized if unsafe conditions are corrected by the next inspection.

Can you list the five types of OSHA citations?

Effects of OSHA

OSHA has had a significant impact on companies by making employers and employees more aware of safety and health considerations. However, the answer to the question "Has the act been effective?" is not yet certain. Although the effect on injury rates is still somewhat unclear, it does appear that OSHA regulations have been able to reduce the number of accidents and injuries in some cases. Some studies have shown that OSHA has had a positive impact; others have shown that OSHA has had no impact. Still other studies suggest that, at best, OSHA could only hope to affect 25 percent of all accidents anyway.[28]

Criticisms of OSHA

Most employers agree with the act's intent to provide healthy and safe working conditions for all employees. However, criticism of OSHA has emerged for several reasons.

Vague Standards. One reason is that some standards are vague, especially the "general duty" clause, and it is difficult to know whether or not one is complying. In one case a standard required that a plant having a certain number of workers have qualified medical personnel "in near proximity" to the work area. This standard has been the subject of several OSHA violations and cases; but what is "near proximity?" Is it in the work area? In the plant? Is it a hospital ten minutes away?

Highly Technical Rules. Secondly, the rules are often very complicated and technical. Thus, small-business owners and managers who do not have a safety specialist on staff find the standards very difficult to read and understand. The presence of many very minor standards also hurts OSHA's credibility. To counter such criticism, OSHA has revoked about 900 minor or confusing standards.

Need for Safety Counseling. A third major criticism is that the OSHA inspector cannot serve as a safety counselor. With the establishment of the consultation program, however, this criticism has lost some of its strength. OSHA officials also can now meet employers who are designing and building new facilities to review blueprints and plans. This review enables the employers to design the facilities correctly in order to comply with OSHA regulations.

Costs of Compliance. A fourth concern is that the cost of correcting violations may be prohibitive for many employers. Requiring a small company to make major structural changes in a building may not be financially possible. The cost of compliance may not be realistic given the cost of the violation. Saunders, Inc., a 60-employee foundry in Wichita, Kansas, went out of business rather than pay the $500,000 needed to comply with OSHA regulations involving extensive electrical work. Although OSHA was willing to negotiate, the owner refused to participate; so he closed the business and sold all the machines.[29]

In one case, the U.S. Supreme Court indicated that OSHA regulations limiting the exposure of workers to cotton dust do not have to meet a cost/benefit test. The decision in the case indicated that congressional intent of the act establishing OSHA was to provide maximum worker protection. Use of a cost/benefit approach would lead to less protection because of high costs, which would violate the law.[30] As a result of this decision, some efforts have been made to amend the act to include cost/benefit considerations. However, such efforts have been strongly resisted by the AFL-CIO and other labor organizations.

Probability of Inspection. With so many worksites to inspect, many employers have only a relatively small probability of being inspected. Labor unions and others have criticized OSHA and Congress for not providing enough inspectors. One interesting study revealed that because the probability of being inspected and fined is so low, many employers pay little attention to OSHA enforcement efforts.[31]

In summary, it can be said that OSHA has had a significant impact on organizations. However, not all the results have been of a positive nature. Some changes in the law and enforcement efforts are likely. As changes are made, continuing compliance with OSHA should be a major focus for any organization, and safety programs should be approached systematically.

Can you discuss some positive and negative aspects associated with OSHA?

A SYSTEMS APPROACH TO SAFETY

Effective safety management considers the type of safety problems, accidents, employees, and technology in the organizational setting. Furthermore, the systems approach to safety recognizes the importance of the human element in safety. Simply attempting to engineer machines, without dealing with the behavioral reactions of employees and without trying to encourage safe behavior, compartmentalizes the safety effort. Several basic components are involved in a systematic approach to safety.

Organizational Commitment

Any comprehensive and systematic approach to safety begins with organizational commitment to a comprehensive safety effort. This effort should be coordinated from the top to involve all members of the organization and be reflected in their actions and work. One study of five plants that won safety awards found that "active management involvement in occupational safety makes the major difference between success and failure."[32] If the president of a small electrical manufacturing firm does not wear a hard hat in the manufacturing shop, he can hardly expect to enforce a requirement that all employees wear hard hats in the shop. Unfortunately, sincere support by top management is often missing from many safety programs.

Coordinated Safety Efforts

Once a commitment is made to organizational safety, planning efforts must be coordinated, with duties assigned to supervisors, managers, safety specialists, and personnel specialists. Naturally, the types of duties vary according to the size of the firm and the industry. For this reason, it is impossible to suggest a single proper mixture of responsibilities. The focus of any systematic approach to safety is the continued diligence of workers, managers, and other personnel.[33] Employees who are not reminded of safety violations, who are not encouraged to be safety-conscious, or who violate company safety rules and policies are not likely to be safe employees.

Safety Committees. Involvement of workers in safety frequently is done through the use of safety committees. These committees are often composed of workers of different levels and from a variety of departments. At least one member of the committee is usually from the personnel unit. A safety committee generally has a regularly scheduled meeting, has specific responsibilities for conducting safety reviews, and makes recommendations for changes necessary to avoid future accidents.[34]

The safety emphasis must be consistenly made and enforced. Properly coordinated efforts between personnel units and managers will aid in developing safety-conscious and safety-motivated employees.

Employee Safety Motivation Encouraging employees to continually keep safety standards in mind while performing their jobs is difficult. Often, employees think safety measures are bothersome and unnecessary until an accident or injury occurs. For example, a requirement that employees wear safety glasses in a laboratory may be necessary most of the time. However, if the glasses are awkward, employees may resist using them, even when they know they should have protection. Some employees may have worked for years without them and think this new requirement is a nuisance.

Safety Discipline. Enforcement of safety rules and disciplining of violators is important if safety efforts are to be meaningful. Frequent reinforcement of the need for safe behavior and feedback on positive safety

PERSONNEL IN PRACTICE

HEALTH AND SAFETY AT ST. REGIS

A $2 million annual investment reflects the commitment to employee health and safety at St. Regis Corporation. As a large paper industry firm, St. Regis has highly diversified operations. Included in the annual expenditures are $50,000 for analyzing air samples and $110,000 for monitoring noise levels. The Corporate Director of Safety and Environmental Health, Alan J. Kaplan, says, "The company has the highest commitment to providing whatever controls are required to protect employees. We have better monitoring equipment than the government has to test the working environment. The company also responds very promptly whenever we suspect a potential health hazard."

One area of company concern is noise control. St. Regis has a hearing conservation program in which workers at all locations are tested every two or three years for changes in their hearing levels. It's called "audiometric testing." Half of the St. Regis work force may be checked on an annual basis in the future, because the Occupational Safety and Health Administration also is concerned with work environments in which noise levels are more than 85 decibels (formerly the accepted level was 90 decibels). "Eighty-five," says Kaplan, "is about the intensity of sound made by a home food processor. Ninety decibels requires the human voice to be raised to almost a shout to be heard."

Just to be on the safe side, St. Regis insists that employees who work in confined spaces (cleaning tanks, for instance) get annual physical checkups. Many employees must wear personal protective equipment, including coveralls, aprons, chaps, sleeves, boots, or gloves, in special situations.

At the most basic level St. Regis programs also involve "spreading the word" about the industrial dangers of contact lenses. There's also a company-specified correct and an incorrect way to wear ear plugs in potentially noisy areas.

St. Regis has a wide range of safety procedures for everything from tree-falling and bucking to natural disasters (what to do in case of earthquakes, hurricanes, tornadoes, and floods), but Kaplan is in the process of developing some new ones, including one to upgrade the role of supervisory safety people.

"St. Regis is a safer place to work than our industry on the whole," Kaplan says. "Ninety-three percent of St. Regis' accidents are not the result of unsafe working conditions, but rather because of unsafe actions on the part of employees. In other words, only 1 percent are due to mechanical hazards, compared to 15 percent for the industry as a whole." But that does not stop the company from continuing to protect employees from head to toe, from hearing to wearing apparel, in any area where it sees a potentially hazardous safety or environmental health problem.[35]

practices have been found to be extremely effective in improving worker safety. Further, the use of behavior modification techniques, including feedback and incentives, has been found to reduce the rate, frequency, severity, and costs of accidents.[36]

Consistent enforcement has been used by employers as a defense against OSHA citations. In one situation a utility foreman was electrocuted while operating an overhead crane. However, the company was exonerated because it had consistently enforced safety rules and penalized violators. The employee who was killed violated a safety rule for grounding equipment even though the company had given him regular safety training, had posted signs prominently, and had warned all employees about grounding equipment. The OSHA district director ruled that the employee's action was an isolated incident, and management was not to blame.

Safety Incentives. Some firms have used safety contests and given incentives to employees for safe work behavior.[37] Jewelry, clocks, watches, and even vacation trips have been given as a reward to employees for good safety records. Safe driving awards for drivers in a trucking firm have been quite successful in generating safety consciousness. Belt buckles and lapel pins are especially popular with the drivers.[38]

Safety Training and Communications. One way to encourage employee safety is to involve all employees at various times in safety training sessions and committee meetings. Another means is to have employee safety meetings frequently. In addition to safety training, continuous communication programs to develop safety consciousness are necessary. Posting safety policies and rules is part of this effort. Contests, incentives, and posters are all ways employers can heighten safety awareness.

One common way to communicate safety ideas is through safety films and videotapes. Viewing possible unsafe situations and the accidents that can result is good exposure to the need for safety. Changing safety posters, continually updating company bulletin boards, and attractively posting company safety information in high-traffic areas are also recommended. Merely sending safety memos is a very inadequate approach to the problem.

Safety Inspection. It is not necessary to wait for an OSHA inspector to inspect the work area for safety hazards. Such inspections may be done by a safety committee or by the safety coordinator. They should be done on a regular basis because OSHA may inspect firms with above-average lost workday rates more frequently.

In investigating the *scene* of an accident, an attempt is made to determine the physical and environmental conditions that contributed to the accident. Poor lighting, poor ventilation, and wet floors are all possible considerations at the scene. Investigation at the scene of the accident should be done as soon as possible after the accident so that conditions have not significantly changed. One way to obtain an accurate view of an accident scene is to photograph or videotape the scene.

The second phase of the investigation is the *interview*. The injured employee, his or her supervisor, and witnesses to the accident should be interviewed. The interviewer attempts to determine what happened and how the accident was caused. These interviews may also generate some suggestions on how to prevent similar accidents in the future.

The third phase of any good accident investigation is the *accident investigation report*, such as the one in Figure 16–7. This report provides the data necessary to fill out the forms and records required by OSHA. One of the more humorous accident reports encountered is included as a "Personnel in Practice".

As a part of an investigation, recommendations should be made on how the accident could have been prevented and what changes could prevent further accidents. Identifying why an accident occurred is useful, but identifying steps to prevent it from occurring again is the important part of a systematic safety program.

FIGURE 16–7
OSHA form.

OSHA No. 101

Form approved

Case or File No. _ _ _ _ _ _

OMB No. 44R 1453

Supplementary Record of Occupational Injuries and Illnesses

EMPLOYER

  1. Name _

  2. Mail address _
             (No. and street)   (City or town)   (State)

  3. Location, if different from mail address _ _ _ _ _ _ _ _ _ _ _ _ _ _ _

INJURED OR ILL EMPLOYEE

  4. Name _ _ _ _ _ _ _ _ _ _ _ _ _ _ _ _ Social Security No. _ _ _ _ _ _ _
         (First name) (Middle name) (Last name)

  5. Home address _
          (No. and street)   (City or town)   (State)

  6. Age _ _ _ _   7. Sex: Male_ _ _ _ Female_ _ _ _ (Check one)

  8. Occupation _
         (Enter regular job title, *not* the specific activity he was performing at time of injury.)

  9. Department _
         (Enter name of department or division in which the injured person is regularly employed,
         even though he may have been temporarily working in another department at the time of
         injury.)

THE ACCIDENT OR EXPOSURE TO OCCUPATIONAL ILLNESS

 10. Place of accident or exposure_ _ _ _ _ _ _ _ _ _ _ _ _ _ _ _ _ _ _
             (No. and street)   (City or town)   (State)

     If accident or exposure occurred on employer's premises, give address of plant or establishment in which it occurred. Do not indicate department or division within the plant or establishment. If accident occurred outside employer's premises at an identifiable address, give that address. If it occurred on a public highway or at any other place which cannot be identified by number and street, please provide place references locating the place of injury as accurately as possible.

 11. Was place of accident or exposure on employer's premises? _ _ _ (Yes or No)

 12. What was the employee doing when injured? _ _ _ _ _ _ _ _ _ _ _ _
                   (Be specific. If he was using tools or equipment

_ _
or handling material, name them and tell what he was doing with them.)

 13. How did the accident occur? _ _ _ _ _ _ _ _ _ _ _ _ _ _ _ _ _ _
             (Describe fully the events which resulted in the injury or occupational illness. Tell what

_ _
happened and how it happened. Name any objects or substances involved and tell how they were involved. Give

_ _
full details on all factors which led or contributed to the accident. Use separate sheet for additional space.)

OCCUPATIONAL INJURY OR OCCUPATIONAL ILLNESS

 14. Describe the injury or illness in detail and inciate the part of body affected. _ _ _ _
(e.g.: amputation of right index finger)

_ _
at second joint; fracture of ribs; lead poisoning; dermatitis of left hand, etc.)

 15. Name the object or substance which directly injured the employee. (For example, the machine or thing he struck against or which struck him; the vapor or poison he inhaled or swallowed; the chemical or radiation which irritated his skin; or in cases of strains, hernias, etc., the thing he was lifting, pulling, etc.)

_ _

 16. Date of injury or initial diagnosis of occupational illness _ _ _ _ _ _ _
                               (Date)

 17. Did employee die? _ _ _ _ _ (Yes or No)

 18. Name and address of physician _ _ _ _ _ _ _ _ _ _ _ _ _ _ _ _ _

 19. If hospitalized, name and address of hospital _ _ _ _ _ _ _ _ _ _ _

_ _

  Date of report _ _ _ _ _ Prepared by _ _ _ _ _ _ _ _ _ _ _ _ _

  Official position _ _ _ _ _ _ _ _ _

Accident Research. Closely related to accident investigation is accident research to determine ways to prevent accidents. Employing safety engineers or ergonomists, or having outside experts evaluate the safety of working conditions, is useful. If a large number of the same type of accident seem to be occurring in an organizational unit, a safety education training program may be necessary to emphasize the importance of working safely. For example, a publishing con.pany reported a greater-than-average number of back injuries caused by employees lifting boxes. Safety training on the proper way to lift heavy objects was then initiated to prevent back injuries.

Evaluation of Safety Efforts

Organizations need to monitor their safety efforts. Just as a firm's accounting records are audited, periodic audits of a firm's safety efforts should also be made. Accident and injury statistics should be compared to previous accident patterns to determine if any significant changes have occurred. This analysis should be designed to measure progress in safety management. A manager at a hospital might measure its safety efforts by comparing the hospital's accident rate to hospital industry figures and to the rates at other hospitals of the same size in the area.

Another part of safety evaluation is updating safety materials and safety training aids. The accident investigation procedures and accident reporting methods should also be evaluated continually to see that these are actually generating ideas useful in reducing accidents. Safety policies and regulations should be reviewed to be sure they comply with both existing and new standards set up by OSHA, state, and professional agencies.

A systematic safety program requires constant effort to maintain safe working environments. Managers and specialists should continually work to insure progress in developing a safe and healthful environment for all workers.

Can you identify and briefly explain the
major components of a safety system?

PERSONNEL TODAY AND TOMORROW
CORPORATE WELLNESS PROGRAMS—SHAPE UP!

It has been said that every person retains the inalienable right to eat, drink, or smoke himself or herself to death. But companies are becoming more concerned about the "wellness" of their employees—not because they have suddenly developed a bigger social conscience, but because in one recent year business spent $65 billion in group life and health insurance premiums. Much of that money goes to finance care after emergencies like heart attacks that are, at least to some degree, preventable.

Almost half of all worker deaths are from cardiovascular diseases (such as heart attacks or strokes). Both employees and employers would benefit from better conditioning of employee hearts.

But can employers impose health programs? And would they be accepted or make any difference? Two examples might give some guidance. In Belgium 19,400 factory workers (men between the ages of 40 and 59) were divided into two groups. Men in Group A were given counseling in smoking reduction, exercise, cholesterol intake, and control of weight and blood pressure. Group B got no such counseling, After 5 years Group A showed a death rate 17.5 percent lower than Group B and a heart attack rate 24.5 percent lower.

An ongoing experiment in Mankato, Minnesota, is scheduled to run through 1989. It aims to reduce heart disease in that city through counseling and publicity. Progress is measured by randomly choosing 500 adults each year to check their cholestrol levels, blood pressure, and other health indicators. Classes in exercise, eating patterns, and smoking withdrawal are offered, and the school system has a physical education curriculum that promotes cardiovascular fitness.

Two companies in Mankato have tried putting some muscle in the program. First National Bank of Mankato imposed a ban on employee smoking during office hours. It also sponsored exercise programs. Hubbard Milling is working toward eliminating smoking at work. This firm also caters "health" lunches, requires managers to take annual physical exams, and subsidizes exercise programs and weight-loss counseling.

A company cannot totally prohibit smoking, some argue, because it is a violation of smokers' rights. Others feel it is clearly within the company rights to protect the health of nonsmoking employees. If the Mankato experiment proves to be a success, it will undoubtedly encourage more companies to enter "wellness" programs. They may not be compulsory, but as with many programs, management support will provide "persuasive encouragement" to improve heath.[40]

SUMMARY

■ Health is a general state of physical, mental, and emotional well-being.
■ Safety is protection of a person's physical health.
■ Accidents and industrial health concerns are a major problem.
■ Worker attitudes play a major role in accidents and accident prevention.
■ Accident prevention can be approached from an engineering or behavioral perspective, but *both* should be considered.
■ Stress is a major concern today because of its relationship to physical distresses. However, not all stress is bad.
■ People find that situations which they cannot control, accurately predict, accurately perceive, or in which they cannot escape intense responsibility are very stressful.
■ Alcoholism affects about 10 percent of the American work force.
■ Alcoholism and drug abuse are extremely expensive to industry and many employers are reacting by getting tough or by increasing use of EAPs.
■ OSHA is designed to help improve the accident-prevention and health situation in business and industry.
■ The act requires record keeping, reporting of injuries, and possible inspection of work sites.
■ OSHA has not been very popular and criticisms range from charges of vague standards to a lack of effectiveness.
■ A good safety program that considers accident prevention from a systems perspective includes: organizational commitment, coordination, employee motivation, accident investigation, accident research, and evaluation of safety efforts.

REVIEW QUESTIONS AND EXERCISES

1. Differentiate between health and safety as personnel activities. Then identify some factors that affect health and safety.
2. Discuss the following statement by a supervisor: "I feel it is my duty to get involved with my employees and their personal problems to show that I truly care about them."
3. Why should a firm be concerned about alcohol and drug usage by employees?
4. Describe the Occupational Safety and Health Act and some of its key provisions about standards, record keeping, and inspection requirements.
5. Discuss the following comment: "OSHA should be abolished because it just serves to harass small businesses."
6. Why is a systems approach to safety important?

Exercises

a. Do a safety inspection in a cooperating organization by identifying conditions that you think could violate OSHA regulations.

b. Organize a debate between advocates of stern disciplinary action vs. the employee assistance plan approach to drug and alcohol problems.

CASE
"WHAT'S HAPPENED TO BOB?"

"What's happened to Bob?" was the question asked Jack Otto, production supervisor, by one of his manufacturing workers, Clyde Fisher. Otto had been wondering the same thing for several weeks about Bob Hill, another of his welders.

Otto is a 54-year-old production supervisor who has been with Store Fixture Manufacturing Company (SFM) for 20 years. He is well liked and respected by his peers and subordinates and is very competent at the technical aspects of his supervisory job.

Hill, 40 years old, has been a generally competent and productive welder at SFM for 10 years who has been popular with his coworkers. Although he periodically "blows up" at them, he always apologizes afterwards. His absenteeism rate has been higher than average for the last several years, with most absenteeism on Mondays. Also, it is not uncommon for Hill to be 10 to 15 minutes late at least once a week. But, because of a shortage of experienced welders and because Hill often cuts his lunch hour short to make up his tardiness time, Otto and other managers at SFM have decided to live with Hill's attendance problems as long as they don't become extensive.

It is not uncommon for many company employees to stop for a beer after work. Fisher told Otto that Hill has been staying at the neighborhood bar for several hours after work most nights. Fisher also said he had heard rumors that Hill was having personal problems at home.

Otto doesn't like to pry into the lives of his workers, but he knows that he can't ignore the situation much longer, especially with others beginning to talk about Hill's problems:

Questions

1. Identify some ways that the company and Jack Otto have contributed to the existing problem with Bob Hill.
2. What actions, if any, should Jack Otto take?

NOTES

1. Adapted from Bill Richards, "The Dial Painters," *Wall Street Journal*, September 19, 1983, p. 1.
2. Bureau of Labor Statistics, press release, Nov. 14, 1984.
3. Janet Macan, "Number of Occupational Deaths Remains Unchanged," *Monthly Labor Review*, May 1983, pp. 42–44.

4. John B. Miner and Mary G. Miner, *Personnel and Industrial Relations*, 3rd ed. (New York: Macmillan, 1977), pp. 433–438.

5. Davis W. Carvey and Roger G. Nibler, "Biorhythmic Cycles and the Incidence of Industrial Accidents," *Personnel Psychology* 30 (Autumn 1977), pp. 447–454.

6. Adapted from "RX for Blue Cross," *Modern Office Technology*, November, 1983, p. 150.

7. U.S. Department of Labor, Occupational Safety and Health Administration, *Mercury*, OSHA Pamphlet No. 2234.

8. "Modern Offices Spawn New Aches, Pains," *Omaha World Herald*, January 15, 1984, p. 14A.

9. "High Blood Pressure," *Personnel Journal* 59 (November 1980), p. 884.

10. M. Waldholz, "Stress Increasingly Seen as a Problem, With Executives More Vulnerable," *Wall Street Journal*, September 28, 1982, p. 26.

11. "Executive Stress Gets Corporate Attention," *Omaha World Herald*, February 12, 1984, p. 12-K.

12. P. Goldberg, *Executive Health* (New York: McGraw-Hill, 1982), pp. 30–35.

13. R. Ricklefs, "Many Executives Complain of Stress, but Few Want Less-Pressured Jobs, *Wall Street Journal*, September 29, 1983, p. 27.

14. For example, see Paul J. Rosch, "Coping with Stress on the Job," *Nation's Business*, February 1984, p. 65.

15. Used with permission of Susan LeBon, Gulf Oil Co.

16. Robert McMorris, "Workers and U.P. Benefit from Program to Aid Those Detailed by Drinking," *Omaha World Herald*, February 28, 1980.

17. "Getting Everyone on the Wagon," *Time*, August 22, 1983, p. 39.

18. R. S. Greenberger, "Sobering Methods," *Wall Street Journal*, January 18, 1983, p. 1.

19. "Drugs on the Job: The Quiet Problem" *Newsweek*, September 15, 1980, pp. 83–84.

20. "Taking Drugs on the Job," *Newsweek*, August 22, 1982, p. 52.

21. C. W. English, "Getting Tough on Worker Abuse of Drugs, Alcohol," *U.S. News & World Report*, December 5, 1983, p. 85.

22. Luis R. Gomez-Mejia and David B. Balkin, "Classifying Work-Related and Personal Problems of Troubled Employees," *Personnel Administrator*, November 1980, pp. 27–32.

23. U.S. Department of Labor, Occupational Safety and Health Administration, *All About OSHA*, OSHA Pamphlet no. 2056 (Washington, DC: Government Printing Office), p. 3.

24. *Whirlpool* v. *Marshall*, 78-1870 (1980).

25. *Gateway Coal Co.* v. *the United Mine Workers of America*, 94 S.Ct. 641.

26. J. J. Hoover, "Workers Have New Rights to Health and Safety," *Personnel Administrator*, April 1983, p. 47–51.

27. *Marshall* v. *Barlow's, Inc.*, 76–1143 (1978).

28. B. G. Gricar and H. D. Hopkins, "How Does Your Company Respond to OSHA?" *Personnel Administrator*, April 1983, p. 53–54.

29. Sanford L. Jacobs, "Rather Than Dicker with OSHA, 'Model' Foundry Closes Up Shop," *Wall Street Journal*, September 15, 1980, p. 31.

30. *American Textile Manufacturing Institute, Inc., et al.*, v. *Donovan, et al.*, 101 S.Ct. 2478, 69 LEd 2d 185 (1981).

31. John M. Gleason and Darold T. Barnum, "Effectiveness of OSHA Sanctions in Influencing Employee Behavior: Single and Multi-period Decision Models," *Accident Analysis and Prevention* 10 (1978), pp. 35–49.

32. "NIOSH: Management is the Key," *National Safety News*, September 1979, p. 41.

33. J. M. Kushnir and U. R. Kastury, "How to Self-Police for Regulatory Compliance," *Management Review*, July 1982, pp. 47–51.

34. U.S. Department of Labor, Occupational Safety and Health Administration, *Planning for Safety on Jobsite* (Washington, DC: Government Printing Office, 1982).

35. Adapted from "Safe and Fit for Productivity," *Reach*, p. 22.

36. R. S. Hayes, R. C. Pine, and H. G. Fitch, "Reducing Accident Rates with Organizational Behavior Modification," *Academy of Management Journal* 25 (June 1982), pp. 406–416.

37. Carol Carin, "Prizes Help Promote Safety," *Business Insurance* 17 (1983), p. 47.

38. Edward D. Dionne, "Motivating Workers with Incentives," *National Safety News*, January 1980, pp. 75–79.

39. R. J. Griffiths, Toronto Star, from *National Lampoon*.

40. Adapted from K. McMamus, "Forced Wellness?" *Forbes*, November 7, 1983, pp. 246–248.

Personnel Coordination

When you have read this chapter, you should be able to:

1. Identify the nature and purpose of personnel policies.
2. Diagram the three stages in the life cycle of a rule.
3. Explain the nature of progressive discipline.
4. Identify and describe at least four different guidelines for developing effective personnel policies and rules.
5. List and briefly explain at least four types of formal personnel communications.

PERSONNEL AT WORK

BETTER COORDINATION THROUGH COMMUNICATION AT THE BANK

An assistant vice-president at Hartford's Connecticut Bank and Trust Company took time recently to explain unique changes the bank had made in its formal communication system. Several years ago, an attitude survey pinpointed some problem areas in the bank which has over 3,500 employees. Forty percent or more of the employees were unsatisfied with the company's communication processes; other complaints seemed to be tied to the same problem, if indirectly. For example, employees were unhappy with their pay even though the bank paid somewhat higher salaries than its competitors.

The president took a personal interest in the problem and assumed responsibility for solving it. He formed and chaired a committee to address the issue. The personnel policy area soon emerged as a major example of the problem. Few people felt that personnel policies were coordinated and administered uniformly from department to department. The policies themselves were not uniform and up-to-date. The personnel director soon produced a new policy manual to replace the inadequate older model. Training then was scheduled for supervisors to update their knowledge of the policies in the new manual.

The committee made five major changes designed to improve communication and reduce confusion. First, changes were made about the issuance of policy and procedure memos. The committee found that eight different staff departments were regularly sending memos directly to the employees (not to supervisors) telling them how to do their jobs. New rules specified that written communication of a policy nature had to go to supervisors. For written messages that did not deal with policy or procedures, the question was asked, "Can the newsletter communicate this? Is a memo necessary?"

Next, a "communications officer" was appointed to help the division heads, who were made completely responsible for the information going to and from their staffs. Then a checklist was developed to help the communications officer reduce the quantity and improve the quality of memos.

A "bounce-back" policy was also adopted. People were informed that it was the bank's policy for employees to receive instructions only from their boss, and that memos must be clear. "Underground" memos that did not meet these criteria were "bounced back" to a division communications officer, who suggested improvements and returned them to the producing division. Finally, each manager was made completely accountable for communication both in and out of his or her area.

The change in communication patterns improved coordination of efforts and the number of memos that were sent dropped by 57 percent. When the bank readministered the attitude survey a year later, all pertinent measures had improved.[1]

"Good communication will attack the problems as they arise; excellent coordination will anticipate them and prevent their occurrence."

HAROLD KOONTZ and
CYRIL O'DONNELL

Coordination can be defined as "a state of harmonious adjustment or functioning." Where personnel activities are concerned, coordination (or harmonious functioning) is critical. For example, how would an employee feel if he or she discovered that in another department someone with the same service gets three weeks' vacation instead of the two weeks he or she receives? How would people react to each supervisor maintaining his or her own pay system? How would you feel if you got fired for something everyone else did all the time in the rest of the company?

To avoid this kind of confusion, personnel activities must be coordinated through the organization. Coordination is accomplished through a number of "coordinating mechanisms": They are:

- Policies
- Procedures
- Rules
- Discipline
- Formal communication

The first three mechanisms require people to think or act in a certain way. Discipline enforces these required behaviors, and formal communication provides information on the other coordination mechanisms and creates a receptive climate for their implementation.

The coordination responsibilities of the personnel unit and line managers are shown in Figure 17–1. The personnel unit helps to achieve organizational objectives as well as its own objectives. For example, if the organization has a policy of nondiscrimination in its hiring practices and an objective of having as many minority individuals in the

PERSONNEL UNIT	MANAGERS
■ Designs formal mechanisms for coordinating personnel policies	■ Help in developing personnel policies and rules
■ Provides advice in development of company-wide personnel policies and rules	■ Review policies and rules with employees
■ Provides information on proper disciplinary procedures	■ Enforce employees' observation of rules through discipline
■ May help explain personnel rules and policies to managers	■ Serve as first source of explanation of rules and policies for employees

FIGURE 17–1
Personnel Coordination
Responsibilities.

work force as would be indicated by their proportion in the general population, the personnel unit must design its selection, training, and other programs to help accomplish these objectives. Both within the personnel unit and in activities between the unit and others in the organization, coordination is necessary to achieve the objective.

Because managers are the main users and enforcers of rules and policies, they should receive some training and explanation in how to use personnel policies and rules effectively. While it is not necessary for the personnel unit to always support other managers, it is critical that any conflict between the two entities be resolved so that employees receive a fair and coordinated response.

POLICIES AND PERSONNEL

Personnel policies may come from many different sources. Policies may even be imposed, in effect, from outside the organization. For example, competition for skilled labor may lead to the creation of a policy to pay higher-than-average wages for certain types of employees. In the same way, government regulations have led to EEO-related policies in organizations.

Long-term objectives of the organization may help dictate personnel policy, too. For example, an objective of doubling organizational size and output in ten years may help shape personnel policies regarding management development and recruiting practices. Whatever the source of personnel policies, they serve to guide the actions of organizational members.

Nature of Policies and Procedures

Where there is a choice among actions, policies act as guides to choosing the appropriate actions. **Policies** are general in nature, while procedures and rules are situation-specific. The important role of policies in guiding organizational decision making requires that they be reviewed regularly because obsolete policies can result in poor decisions and poor coordination. Policy proliferation also must be carefully monitored. Failure to review, add to, or delete policies as situations change may lead to problems. For example, some employers in the past had policies stating that an employee who had alcohol or drug problems should be fired. However, because of social changes and the practices of other employers, many organizations have changed their personnel policies regarding "troubled employees"—those with alcohol, drug, or emotional problems. Figure 17–2 shows a policy statement and the supporting procedures for dealing with troubled employees.

Procedures are customary methods of handling activities and are more specific than policies. For example, policy may grant that employees will be given a vacation. Procedures will establish a specific method for authorizing vacation time without disrupting work.

PERSONNEL IN PRACTICE

DRESS CODE POLICIES

Dress codes are much more widespread than people think. A recent survey showed that about 60 percent of firms had an informal, unwritten dress code. Thirty percent had a formal policy on dress and only 10 percent had none at all.

The policies (written or unwritten) favored suits or sports coats for men. For women, dresses, suits, or skirts with blazers were the rule. Nearly as many employers said skirts and blouses or pantsuits were fine. Very casual clothing was unacceptable.

Hairstyles were often included in the dress policies. Beards and moustaches are acceptable. When a hairstyle was considered to be unacceptable, most procedures called for the supervisor to talk with the employee.

One-third of the companies send an improperly dressed employee home (with no pay loss) to change clothes. Another third simply sent employees home for the day.[2]

Nature of Rules

Rules are similar to procedures in that they guide action and they typically allow no discretion in their application. They may be part of a procedure, but seldom constitute the entire procedure. A rule reflects a management decision that action be taken—or not taken—in a given situation.

RULES
are specific guidelines that regulate and restrict the behavior of individuals.

POLICY

The company recognizes that a wide range of human problems which are not directly associated with job functions can affect an employee's work performance. These problems include physical illness, mental or emotional upset, alcoholism, drug abuse, and other concerns. The company has several medical programs which address themselves to these problems with the intent of identifying them at the earliest possible moment and recommending appropriate treatment on an individual and confidential basis.

PROCEDURES

1. The initiation of any action with respect to an employee is contingent upon unsatisfactory job performance resulting from apparent medical or behavioral abnormalities. Judgments regarding unsatisfactory work performance remain the prerogative of cognizant supervision, which has the responsibility of seeking medical assistance through the Medical Department.
2. In the event an employee refuses to undergo diagnosis and treatment, the Employee Relations Division shall be notified.

SOURCE: Bureau of National Affairs, "Counseling Policies and Programs for Employees with Problems," *ASPA-BNA Survey*, No. 34, BNA Policy and Practice Series, March 23, 1978, p. 9. Used with permission.

FIGURE 17–2
Employee Assistance Program for the Troubled Employee in a Large Northern Manufacturing Firm.

Rules are coordination mechanisms. They provide more specific behavioral guidelines than policies. For example, one welding company has a policy stating that management intends to provide the highest quality welding service in the area. One of the rules that helps realize that policy is that a welder with fewer than five years of welding experience will not be hired. This rule constrains personnel selection decisions.

Finally, the need for rules leads to the need to enforce these rules. Discipline is a necessary part of every manager's job. Often personnel specialists become involved in either interpreting disciplinary procedures or, in some instances, doing some of the disciplining. Therefore, another coordinating mechanism to be considered is "progressive" discipline.

Can you identify the nature and purpose of personnel policies?

RULES AND DISCIPLINE

Rules serve several purposes in organizations. They are coordination devices as discussed above, but they also maintain stability and serve as handy decision guides so that routine decisions do not have to be made again and again. However, rules can pose problems as well. They can block new ways of doing work, become excuses rather than reasons, and add to the red tape in organizations.

Life Cycle of Rules

Policies and rules are enacted to solve certain needs. Because those needs can change, occasional audits and changes are important. It may be useful to think about rules as having a "life cycle." Figure 17–3 shows the life cycle of a rule.

In Stage I, the rule-making process is set in motion because of a need to limit behavior or coordinate activities. In Stage II, the rule is accepted and obeyed because it is seen as fulfilling an organizational need. In Stage III, the rule is rejected because situations have changed or it is no longer helpful in getting the job done. People start to deviate from the behaviors prescribed by the rule. This deviation may be accompanied by a reduction in the enforcement of the rule. Before a rule reaches this point in its life cycle, it should be changed to fit the current situation, as shown in Rule #1A in Figure 17–3.

Enforcement problems can result if policies and rules are completely unacceptable to employees. If a rule is not enforced, it will not be useful. For example, simply having a plantwide rule that prohibits smoking is insufficient. One factory has had a no-smoking rule for years, but the rule has not been enforced because the superintendent is a pack-a-day man. Other workers who feel they are in a safe area sneak a smoke when they can because they see the rule violated in the office. To be effective, rules must be enforced or changed.

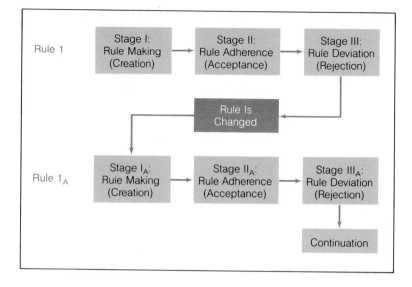

SOURCE: Adapted from J. H. Jackson and S. W. Adams, "The Life Cycle of a Rule," *Academy of Management Review 4* (1979), pp. 269–273.

When writing a rule for distribution to employees the rule should be stated in an appropriate manner. The tone should not be threatening or patronizing. Care should be taken not to allow proliferation of rules. It is impossible to make a rule to cover every situation; therefore, a certain amount of reliance on people's good judgment is inevitable.

Can you diagram the stages in the life cycle of a rule?

Nature of Discipline

Discipline is a form of training that enforces organizational rules. It can be approached in two basic ways: *preventive* and *punitive*. Although these may sound like conflicting approaches, they are related. The goal of preventive discipline is to heighten employees' awareness of organizational policies and rules. Knowledge of disciplinary actions may prevent violations. The emphasis on preventive discipline is similar to the emphasis on preventing accidents.

Counseling by a supervisor in the work unit can have positive effects. Many times people simply need to be made aware of a rule, and counseling can provide that awareness. The best discipline is self-discipline. Developing an awareness of acceptable behavior through counseling is better than the punitive approach.[3]

The punitive approach is used when violations of rules or discipline problems occur. The hope is that, after punishment, employees will not repeat the undesired behavior. Most organizations use both these approaches to emphasize that rules must be followed. Certain offenses typically carry more severe penalties than others, as can be seen in Figure 17–4.

FIGURE 17–4
Offenses and Penalty
Patterns.

PROBLEM	TYPICAL HANDLING		
	Warnings	Suspension	Discharge
Attendance	X	XX	XXX
Intoxication at work		XX	XXX
Fighting		O	XXX
Failure to use safety devices	X	O	XXX
Sleeping on the job	X		XXX
Possession of weapons			XXX
Theft			XXX
Falsifying employment application			XXX
Outside criminal activities			XXX

Note: O means this step may be omitted

Employee Theft as an Example. Employee theft is a growing concern, especially for retailers. It has been estimated that employee theft costs firms considerably more than $20 million a year.[4] As shown in Figure 17–4, theft most frequently leads to immediate discharge. Some interesting research has indicated that employee theft is related to job satisfaction, motivation, and alienation. Employees who have higher job satisfaction, are more motivated, and are less alienated have more negative attitudes toward employee theft.[5] Consequently, it may be realistic to see employee theft as symptomatic of broader personnel problems, not just as a disciplinary situation.

Equity, or fairness, must be considered in designing discipline systems to enforce rules. Few problems arise if employees understand the policies and rules, see them as fair, and if discipline is carried out with the appropriate degree of severity. The "progressive" nature of good discipline gives employees a chance to correct their ways. In this sense, discipline can be seen as training, because for each failure to learn, the penalty is more severe. Progressive discipline is used for less serious violations. Major violations (such as theft or striking a manager) are usually grounds for immediate discharge.

Progressive Discipline

Progressive discipline is best viewed as the training or shaping of behavior in order to modify unacceptable behavior. This shaping may or may not include punishment. As noted earlier, discipline is certainly not limited to punishment.

The concept of progressive discipline holds that attempts to modify behavior should become more severe as the employee continues to exhibit improper behavior. Figure 17–5 shows steps in a typical progressive discipline system. In this system, an employee is given an opportunity to correct deficiencies before being dismissed. This opportunity should include at least steps 1, 2, and 4 in Figure 17–5. These steps

FIGURE 17–5
Progressive Discipline.

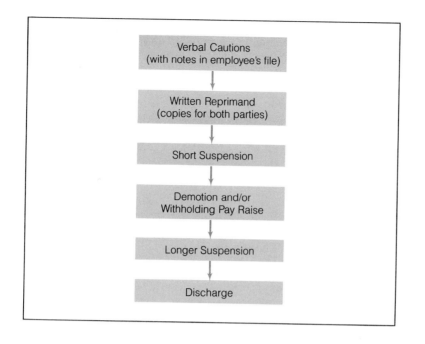

ensure that both the nature and seriousness of the problem have been communicated to the employee. The manager is responsible for seeing that the discipline is appropriate.

Defensible Dismissal

Special note must be made of the last step in the progressive discipline procedure—discharge or dismissal. While dismissing an employee is never a pleasant prospect, sometimes it must be done. However, to be defensible termination as the final point in a progressive discipline procedure must be carried out properly.

In one way, unionized organizations have an advantage over nonunionized organizations. A unionized organization almost always has a series of disciplinary steps written into its labor contract. These steps are agreed upon as fair by both union and management. Elements of the progressive discipline model described here are the basis of most union contract agreements on discipline and are widely accepted by management professionals as an appropriate route to dismissal.

Nonunion organizations may design a dismissal procedure in keeping with the models developed by unionized firms. They may use a procedure that is generally accepted as equitable, or they may act in some other fashion. Unfortunately, many public and private organizations fail to develop an equitable system until a dismissal has been made and they are forced to consider it. Many firms do not have a formal discipline procedure at all.

A progressive discipline procedure is not designed to make it difficult to dismiss an employee who is not doing the job. Rather, it is designed to force the manager to document the efforts made to work with the employee on the problem. When there is not a third party to represent the employee, such as a union, this process also helps ensure that the employee is not a victim of arbitrary action on the part of a particular manager.

Outplacement. Some companies have gone so far as to make rehabilitation programs available to fired managers to help them deal with termination and find another job. "Outplacement" assistance often includes career counseling, resume preparation, and training in interviewing techniques. PepsiCo, Union Carbide, and many other employers make use of outplacement firms.[6]

Dismissal procedures are under legal attack in some quarters as a result of challenges to the concept of "employment at will." For a contemporary discussion of this issue, see "Personnel Today and Tomorrow" at the end of this chapter.

Can you explain the nature and importance of progressive discipline?

EFFECTIVE PERSONNEL POLICIES AND RULES

The following guidelines suggest that well-designed personnel policies and rules should be consistent, reasonable, necessary, applicable, understandable, and distributed and communicated. A discussion of each characteristic follows.

Consistent

Rules should be consistent with organizational policies, and policies should be consistent with organizational goals.[7] The principal intent of policies is to provide written guidelines and to specify actions. If some policies and rules are enforced and others are not, then all tend to lose their effectiveness.

Reasonable

Ideally, employees should be able to see policies as being fair and realistic. Policies and rules that are so inflexible that individuals are penalized unfairly should be reevaluated. Apex Corporation has a policy that anyone promoted to vice-president must have a college degree. This policy might be seen as unfair and unreasonable for someone who began working for the company 20 years ago and satisfactorily performs the job. Adding a provision stating that "only in exceptional cases can experience substitute for formal education" might lead to the rule being perceived as more reasonable and fair.

A rule forbidding workers to use the company telephone for personal calls may be unreasonable if emergency phone calls are occasionally necessary. Limiting the amount of time the telephone can be used for personal business and the number of calls might be more reasonable. Figure 17–6 contains a list most people would agree is unreasonable.

FIGURE 17–6
Policy Change Memorandum.

Memorandum

To: All Personnel

Subject: New Sick Leave Policy

It has been brought to my attention that the attendance record of this department is a disgrace to our gracious benefactor, who, at your own request, has given you your job. Due to lack of consideration for your jobs with so fine a department, as shown by such absenteeism, it has become necessary for us to revise some of our policies. The following changes are in effect immediately.

1. SICKNESS:
   No excuse . . . We will no longer accept your doctor's statement as proof, as we believe that if you are able to go to the doctor, you are able to come to work.

2. DEATH:
   (Other than your own) . . . This is no excuse. There is nothing you can do for them, and we are sure that someone else with a lesser position can attend to the arrangements. However, if the funeral can be held in the late afternoon, we will be glad to let you off one hour early, provided that your share of the work is ahead enough to keep the job going in your absence.

3. LEAVE OF ABSENCE:
   (For an operation) . . . We are no longer allowing this practice. We wish to discourage any thoughts that you may need an operation, as we believe that as long as you are an employee here you will need all of whatever you have and you should not, under any circumstances, consider having anything removed. We hired you as you are and to have anything removed would certainly make you less than we bargained for.

4. DEATH:
   (Your own) . . . This will be accepted as an excuse, but we would like two weeks notice as we feel it is your duty to train someone else for your job.

   ALSO, entirely too much time is being spent in the restroom. In the future, we will follow the practice of going in alphabetical order. For instance, those whose names begin with "A" will go from 8:00–8:15, "B" will go from 8:15 to 8:30, and so on. If you are unable to go at your time, it will be necessary to wait until the next day when your turn comes again.

Policies and rules should not be so inflexible that necessary exceptions are excluded. A company policy requiring all sales representatives to limit air travel to coach class may need exceptions. For example, an employee may need to fly to another city to confer with a client at a time when no seats are available in coach class. Requiring the employee to pay the difference in fare would be unreasonable and unfair.

Some of the most ticklish company policies and rules involve employee behavior. Dress codes are frequently attacked, and organizations that have them should be able to justify them to the satisfaction of both employees and outside sources that might question them. No-smoking policies also can generate considerable heat. Generally, rules should not be written so that a great amount of time is required to enforce them.

Necessary

Personnel policies and rules should have some value; to this end, managers should confirm the intent and necessity of proposed rules and eliminate obsolete ones. Policies and rules should be reviewed whenever there is a major organizational change. Unfortunately, this review is not always done, and outdated rules are still on the books in many organizations.

Applicable

Because personnel policies are general guidelines for action, they should be applicable to a large group of employees. If this applicability is not so, then the appropriate areas must be identified. For instance, if a sick leave policy is applicable only to nonexempt employees, it should be specified in the company handbook. Policies and rules that apply only to one unit or type of job should be developed as part of specific guidelines for that unit or job.

FUNNY BUSINESS **By Roger Bollen**

© 1974 Newspaper Enterprise Association, Inc.

Understandable

Personnel policies and rules should be written so that employees can clearly understand them. One way to determine if policies and rules are understandable is to ask a cross-section of employees with various positions, education levels, and job responsibilities to explain the intent and meaning of a rule. If the answers are extremely varied, the rule should be rewritten.

To illustrate, at Environmental Products one policy stated: "Employees will remain in the company's employ as long as their work merits it." Another policy said, "If a layoff is necessary, merit rating is the basis for deciding who remains." Conversations with a number of different employees showed a variety of interpretations of what would be done if a layoff occurred. Some thought that merit would be considered only when a decision had to be made between two people with equal seniority. The office workers thought the rule applied only to workers in the plant. Supervisors had another interpretation. The personnel manager decided that clarification was needed.

Distributed and Communicated

Personnel policies must be distributed and communicated to employees to be effective. Employee handbooks can be creatively designed to explain detailed policies and rules so that people can refer to a handbook at times when no one is available to answer a question. Supervisors and managers can maintain discipline by reminding their employees about policies and rules. Some of the major methods used to formally communicate with employees are highlighted below.

Can you define at least four guidelines for
effective policies and rules?

COORDINATION THROUGH
FORMAL COMMUNICATION

Formal communication helps in coordination because it is the basis for understanding. To be effective, formal communication must allow information to flow both up and down the organization.[9] Personnel information can be formally communicated in several ways. Some are: employee handbooks, suggestion systems, employee communication committees, an organizational ombudsman, and various types of publications, such as newspapers and magazines.

Employee Handbook

Providing personnel information though a handbook gives employees a reference source for company policies and rules. The main purpose of an employee handbook is to help employees have all necessary information together in one place for reference. Figure 17–7 indicates some items contained in a typical handbook.

Readability. A common problem with employee handbooks is that the specialists who prepare them may not write on the same level as those who will read them. A study of 50 company handbooks found that the average level of most handbooks was the third year of college which is much higher than the typical reading level in a company.[11] One solution is to test the readability of the handbook on a sample of employees before it is published.

Use. Another important factor to be considered in preparing an employee handbook is its method of use. Simply giving an employee a

FIGURE 17–7

Employee Handbook Table of Contents.

CHAPTER 17 PERSONNEL COORDINATION

handbook and saying, "Here's all the information you need to know," is not sufficient. In one study employee handbooks ranked third behind a supervisor and "the grapevine" as a source of information.[12]

Some organizations distribute handbooks as part of their orientation process. One company periodically gives all employees a written test on the company handbook. Questions consistently missed become the focus of personnel communication efforts. These tests are also used to update the handbook.

Management should take a close look at employee handbooks because some courts considering employment-at-will have viewed them as "implied contracts." This concept suggests that anything in the handbook can be subject to negotiation before it can be changed. In keeping with this "contract approach," some even recommend that employees sign a receipt when they receive the handbook stating that it is a "statement of policy and the company reserves the right to change the policies at any time."[13]

Suggestion Systems

A suggestion system is a formal way to move communication upward through the organization. In addition, giving the employees the opportunity to suggest changes or ways in which operations could be improved may develop loyalty and commitment to the organization. Often an employee in the work unit knows more about how waste can be eliminated or how hazards can be controlled than do managers, who are not as close to the job.

Making Suggestion Systems Work. A suggestion system should be publicized, and good suggestions should be put to use. The suggestions should be collected often and evaluated by a suggestion committee, usually composed both of managers and nonmanagers. Suggestions selected by this committee are then passed on to upper management.

Employees submitting useful suggestions should receive rewards, such as a flat amount, as a savings bond, or a percentage of the savings resulting from the suggestion. For example, a computer programmer working in a hospital noticed that the hospital was throwing away all the old computer printouts of patient rosters. She suggested that these printouts be sold to a paper recycling firm. Her suggestion was accepted and she now gets 5 percent of the $1,500 the hospital receives annually for the paper. General Electric's Space Division offers "suggestion dollars" certificates that can be cashed in for $2 apiece whether or not the suggestion is adopted. There is no limit to the number of certificates an employee can acquire.[14]

The oldest continuously operating suggestion system in the United States is at Eastman Kodak Corporation. It began in 1898 with a $2 award to a man who pointed out the advantages of washing windows in the production department.[15] In one recent year Kodak received over 80,000 suggestions from 24,000 employees, and 28,000 were adopted. Almost $2.8 million was paid out. Four awards of $50,000 were made and the average award was $90.43.[16]

Feedback. A good suggestion system provides prompt feedback to all employees submitting suggestions. If employees are not told why their suggestions are accepted or rejected, much of the underlying momentum will be lost. The major reason suggestion programs fail is the inattention of management to feedback.

Suggestions seldom appear as fully developed plans. They are usually "ideas" that need some work on the part of management to succeed. Figure 17–8 summarizes some important dos and don'ts of suggestions systems.

Employee Communication Committees

Some firms have established formal communication committees composed primarily of nonmanagerial employees. General Electric has made effective use of an *employee sounding board* at its large Maryland appliance complex. According to a GE spokesperson, current personnel practices and work activities are the most frequent subjects discussed by the group.[17]

An approach somewhat similar is in use at Norton Company, an industrial manufacturing firm in Massachusetts. In this firm, 21 in-plant "employee counselors" assist first-line supervisors by providing information to other workers on company personnel policies and practices. These communication counselors also provide some employee assistance counseling on personal job-related problems. The personnel director for Norton Company comments: "The In-Plant Counselor Program is eroding many barriers to effective communication that have existed and is helping build a solid relationship between Norton Company and its employees."[18]

Both these programs illustrate the advantage of involving nonmanagerial employees in formal personnel communications. Other formats are in use in other firms; all are designed to enhance personnel coordination.

Organizational Ombudsman

The ombudsman, a concept originating in Sweden, is a person outside the normal chain of command who serves as a "public defender" or problem solver for management and employees. For example, Xerox

DO	DON'T
■ Commit management to answer every suggestion	■ Reject a suggestion because it is not "polished"
■ Publicize the program	■ Allow the suggestions to get "lost" in the system
■ Reward successful suggestions	
■ Respond to *all* signed suggestions	■ Fail to institute a suggestion system simply because it isn't a "sophisticated" system
■ Use locked boxes and printed forms, and pick up routinely	

FIGURE 17–8
Dos and Don'ts of Suggestion Systems

Corporation uses an ombudsman to resolve complaints from employees that cannot be settled through the employee's supervisor or the personnel department. The ombudsman reviews the employee's information and complaint. After the problems are discussed with other individuals, such as the employee's supervisor or a representative of the personnel department, the ombudsman recommends a solution to the problem. Making such an individual available gives employees the opportunity to talk freely about complaints and frustrations. Some of these complaints may not otherwise surface until they become serious problems.

The concept has been slow to gain acceptance in the United States, although General Electric and Boeing Vertol Company also have tried using ombudsmen. A major problem has been finding an appropriate niche in the organizational structure for such a person. Some managers and supervisors may resent the ombudsman's privilege of hearing and deciding on their employees' problems.

An ombudsman must have exceptional human-relations skills and training in behavioral sciences or counseling in order to improve communications and create a more open atmosphere. The ombudsman concept should not be a short-term program or gimmick. Establishing such a position indicates that the organization is aware of the long-range effect of good personnel relations on organizational effectiveness.

Use of an ombudsman can provide a good source of information that can be used to revise policies and procedures. It is one way in which management can check to see if current policies are working properly. If complaints indicate, for example, that a job posting system is required or that the performance appraisal system is not working, changes can then be made.

The "Open Door" Policy

The so-called open door policy whereby a manager announces that his or her "door is open anytime you have questions or problems" is sometimes used as a substitute for better personnel practices. Usually it is a poor substitute. Some companies use it as an excuse not to communicate with employees more formally. Others use it as a substitute for a formal grievance procedure. Still others may take its use (or more likely its lack of use) as a sign that all is well in the company.

The problem with an open door policy relates to the power and status differences between managers and their subordinates. Often, subordinates may not feel free to discuss their concerns with their manager (especially if the manager is the problem). Further, if the manager disagrees with the employee, there is no place to appeal that decision. An open door policy may make a manager feel better, but it does little to address employees' communication problems.

Employee Publications

Organizations also communicate with employees through internal publications, sometimes called *house organs*. These publications include newspapers, company magazines, or organizational newsletters. Such publications frequently contain feature stories on employees and their families, including news of promotions, retirements, and awards, and news about the organization and its operations.

Some very elaborate publications in larger companies require a full-time public relations staff. In small organizations, a secretary in the personnel department may prepare a mimeographed newsletter. Ex-Cell O Corporation effectively used a company house organ to foster a "family" spirit throughout the organization after a recent merger. The marriage of the two major and complex organizations was made easier by educating all employees, new and old, about both organizations.[19]

Honesty Is the Key. The publication should be an honest attempt to communicate information employees need to know. It should not be solely a public relations tool to build the image of the company. Bad news, as well as good news, should be reported objectively in readable style. Cartoons, drawings, and photographs improve the graphic appearance of publications and draw employee interest.

An airline publication has a question-and-answer section in which employees can anonymously submit tough questions to management. Management's answers are printed with the questions in every issue. Because every effort is made to give completely honest answers to these questions, this section has been very useful. The same idea fizzled in another large company because the questions were answered with "the company line" and employees soon lost interest in the less-than-candid replies.

A column in Sun Company's publication, *SUN NEWS*, illustrates the importance of openness and honesty. Robert Finucane's column raises questions about such topics as nepotism, indecisive middle managers, and sluggish elevator service. Among his biggest fans is the chairman of Sun Company who notes that "Bob doesn't get nasty or mean."[20] But it is clear that the column does not hesitate to chastise either side when it is wrong. Such reporting in a company publication makes it more than simply a management "mouthpiece."

Evaluate the Mission. Attention also should be paid as to whether the newsletter is doing what management wants it to do. Two cases illustrate this point.[21] In a large pharmaceutical company, one entire division considers itself neglected by corporate management, partially because the company's monthly newsletter fails to give this division the coverage it gives to other divisions. In another organization with six plants, the company paper printed personal news about employees from all the plants. The objective was to provide the feeling of "one big happy family," even though the plants were far apart. A study showed that the workers did not care about people in other plants and simply were not interested in the newspaper. The solution was six separate newspapers, though this expansion increased the costs and time involved.

It has been suggested that the publisher of a newsletter and the manager in charge must know:

1. What the publication is trying to achieve
2. Exactly who is the audience being reached
3. How the publication can involve the audience in its purposes
4. Whether the cost of the whole process is worth the benefit[22]

Other formal communication methods include bulletin boards, posters, movies, and slides. Organizational communication is much broader than the forms of formal personnel communication discussed in this chapter, but the formal techniques covered here can play a part in improving the coordination of personnel activities.

Can you list and briefly explain four forms of formal personnel communication?

PERSONNEL TODAY AND TOMORROW
EMPLOYMENT-AT-WILL—FREEDOM TO FIRE?

Many executives consider the right to fire at will as a necessary basis of management authority. In fact, the *employment-at-will* doctrine was based on the ideas of freedom and mutuality of contract. The employee had a right to quit whenever he or she wanted to and the employer retained a similar right to determine how long to continue employment relations.

Today, however, there is a growing tendency for the courts to find exceptions to this general rule. For example, American Airlines, Blue Shield and Blue Cross of Michigan, McGraw-Hill and many other companies have found that some courts consider employee handbooks to be implied employment contracts. *Formal* written employment contracts, of course, are just that—contracts. Baseball, basketball, and football pros have them; so do movie stars and recording artists. But most employees do not.

If a company's personnel department issues a publication such as a handbook setting forth a discharge policy, that provision may be enforced by a court. For example, a McGraw-Hill employee felt he was unjustly fired after eight years of service. He argued that the company's personnel policies protected him against dismissal except for "just and sufficient cause." The court agreed and said that the handbook in which the statement was made constituted a contract between employee and employer.

In this developing area of law, it is hard to know how far the courts will go. California, Michigan, and West Virginia courts appear to be sympathetic to employees, while in Indiana, Illinois, Alabama, Texas, and Georgia, management has won "at-will" cases. Federal and state laws have long prohibited dismissing someone because they are of a particular race, sex, religion, national origin, or age. Collective bargaining agreements and civil service regulations also offer employees some protection from firing. Further, in some states an employer is prevented by law from discharging an employee for filing a workers' compensation claim or from firing an employee in order to cheat him or her out of a pension. Other laws protect so-called whistleblowers (those who point out organizational wrongdoing).

But in the United States there is no law that says a manager must retain *any* subordinate who is demonstrably incompetent, lazy, uncooperative, or abusive. In fact, U.S. managers are more free to dismiss employees than managers in most other Western democracies.

However, courts now seem to be saying that management has the responsibility to show that discharge is appropriate. Management must live by "promises" that have been made in the past and show that the motives for the discharge are not morally or socially unacceptable. Some legal counsels are calling the trend "the white male's anti-discrimination law." An American Airlines executive says companies will have to be aware that when they "fire managers and other unorganized employees, they had better document the reasons pretty thoroughly because they might end up in court."

To fire someone and have a documentable reason, managers should consider the following procedure:

1. Check whether the company's personnel policies allow freedom to proceed.
2. Check if any oral or written statements have been made to the employee that might be construed as an implied employment contract.
3. If there are none, ask oneself if the employee could argue convincingly that the real reason for the firing was retaliation.
4. If so, see an attorney first.
5. If not: Fire away.[23]

SUMMARY

■ Good coordination is especially important if personnel activities are to promote uniform fair treatment.

■ Policies, procedures, rules, discipline, and formal communications are some methods used to achieve personnel coordination.

■ Polices are general guidelines to action.

■ Procedures are customary methods of handling activities.

■ Rules specify action to be taken in a situation and appear to have a life cycle. Many outlive their original purpose and should be periodically reviewed.

■ Discipline should be seen as a method of training. Progressive discipline uses increasingly severe penalties in an attempt to reshape undesirable behavior.

- Effective policies and rules must be consistent, reasonable, necessary, applicable, understandable, and communicated.
- Employee handbooks are often referred to as a source of information for employees.
- Suggestion systems can be a good source of new ideas if they are handled properly.
- The organizational ombudsman is a person with access to employees and managers who can cut across normal communication lines.
- An open-door policy is often used as a poor substitute for more formal personnel practices.
- A variety of employee publications can be used to enhance formal personnel communication efforts.

REVIEW QUESTIONS AND EXERCISES

1. What is the intent of personnel coordination activities?

2. Discuss the following statement: "Rules are always the basis for increased red tape in an organization."

3. Why might a progressive discipline procedure be seen as a logical extension of a policy of giving employees fair and equitable treatment while employed?

4. You have been assigned the task of writing a personnel policy manual. What general guidelines for writing policies would you use?

5. If you had to establish a formal means of communicating personnel policies in a community college, what means would you use? Why?

Exercises

a. Obtain a copy of an employee handbook from some organization and critique it. What policies or rules violate any of the guidelines listed in the chapter? How should they be changed?

b. Contact a local employer that has a suggestion system. Find out how many suggestions are submitted each month, how they are evaluated, what feedback is given to the suggesting employees, and what awards are used for accepted suggestions. Also, ask what problems have been experienced.

CASE

"IT'S TIME TO TRAVEL"

Eastern Valley State College is a regional state college with approximately 6,000 students. The Department of Business has seven faculty members. The faculty policy manual contains the following statement: "Faculty members are expected to maintain their professional competence and the college affirms a policy of supporting faculty in this regard."

One of the main ways faculty maintain currentness in their professional fields is by attending professional meetings. When hired, Professor Hargraves was told that the college pays for a faculty member to attend one professional meeting each academic year. Because of his teaching responsibilities, Professor Hargraves waited until April 2 to apply to attend the Southern Business Meeting. He was told by his department chairman that the department was low on travel funds because another faculty member had attended two meetings to present research papers. Therefore, the department chairman denied Professor Hargraves' request. Professor Hargraves was naturally upset, especially since there had been no written notice provided the faculty about the travel fund situation. Professor Hargraves returned to his office very disgruntled and started preparing his resume to use in applying for a job at another college.

Questions

1. Evaluate pros and cons of the policy statement about professional competence and the formal communication system relating to it.
2. Discuss the apparent inequity present in applying the policy and how the policy could be rewritten and better implemented.

NOTES

1. Adapted from J. L. Digaetani, "A Systems Solution to Communication Problems," *Business Horizons*, October 1983, pp. 2–6.
2. Adapted from "Companies Without Dress Codes Are in the Minority," *Resource*, March 1983, p. 8.
3. Alan W. Bryant, "Replacing Punitive Discipline with a Positive Approach," *Personnel Administrator*, February 1984, pp. 79–87.
4. *The Professional Report*, August 1983, p. 28.
5. Joe A. Cox and M. Ray Perryman, "An Empirical Investigation of the Relationship Between Employee Theft Perceptions and Other Additional Variables," *Academy of Management Proceedings, 1979*, pp. 236–240.
6. C. W. English, "New Growth Industry: Help for Fired Workers," *U.S. News & World Report*, August 1, 1983, pp. 63–64.
7. Stuart P. Bloom, "Policy and Procedure Statements that Communicate," *Personnel Journal* 62 (September 1983), pp. 711–716.
8. Adapted from "Companies Refuse to Hire, Promote Those Who Smoke," *Resource*, August 1983, p. 2.
9. K. P. Shapiro, "Good Communications Require Planning, Goals, and Continuity," *Business Insurance*, April 5, 1982, p. 28.
10. Lane Tracy, "Remarks," *Personnel Journal* 61 (December 1982), p. 883.
11. Debra L. Heflich, "Developing Readable Employee Handbook," *Personnel Administrator*, March 1983, pp. 80–84.
12. S. Friedman, "Where Employees Go for Information," *Administrative Management*, September 1981, pp. 72–73.
13. "Labor Lawyer Cites Danger of Employee Handbooks," *Editor and Publisher*, July 23, 1983, p. 17.

14. "Idea Spur," *Personnel Administrator*, June 1979, p. 48.

15. A. W. Bergerson, "Employee Suggestion Plan Still Going Strong at Kodak," *Supervisory Management*, May 1977, pp. 32–33.

16. "Kodak Employees Awarded $2.8 Million," *Omaha World Herald*, April 2, 1981, p. 30.

17. Douglas G. Curley, "Employee Sounding Boards: Answering the Participants' Needs," *Personnel Administrator*, May 1978, pp. 69–73.

18. P. B. Marshall, "Employee Counselors: Opening New Lines of Communication," *Personnel Administrator*, November 1978, pp. 44–48.

19. H. Dundas, "The Voluntary Approach to Employee Communication," *Public Relations Journal*, July 1982, pp. 32–33.

20. Erick Larson, "Corporate Grapevine Produces Ripe Fruit for Robert Finucane," *Wall Street Journal*, March 9, 1981, p. 1.

21. Jim Mann, "Is Your House Organ a Vital Organ?", *Personnel Journal* 56 (September 1977), pp. 461–462.

22. E. Howard, "More than a Bulletin Board," *Public Relations Journal*, July 1982, p. 34.

23. J. W. Whittlesey, "A View from Management," *ILR Report*, Fall 1982, p. 16; D. W. Ewing, "Your Right to Fire," *Harvard Business Review*, March–April 1983, pp. 32–43; "A Fight Over Freedom to Fire," *Business Week*, September 20, 1982, p. 116.

Human Resource Research and Information Systems

When you have read this chapter, you should be able to:

1. Identify four methods for researching personnel problems.
2. Define and briefly compare the concepts of a personnel audit and human resource accounting.
3. Describe several absenteeism control strategies.
4. Discuss turnover concerns and control strategies.
5. Explain the importance of personnel recordkeeping.
6. Discuss the importance of a Human Resources Information System (HRIS).
7. List cautions to be observed in assuring the privacy of personnel records.

PERSONNEL AT WORK

STEMMING TURNOVER IN RETAIL EDP DEPARTMENTS

The national average for personnel turnover in data processing is about 30 percent annually. In the retailing industry, it has historically been much worse. It took that industry some time and research to discover what would keep these highly mobile and difficult-to-replace people around.

Norman Weiser, vice-president at Federated Department Stores, says, "Retailers felt they were competing for EDP people with other retailers." They now recognize that they are in competition with banks and manufacturing companies for data processors and have to pay competitive wages. But companies found that it takes more than just money to keep turnover in line. For example, at Allied Stores, Lenore Shaw has discovered the role of the corporate training program in retaining employees. The company's philosophy is to hire people with no data processing background and train them to its system and standards. "In three to six months they become productive and eventually they fill the lower and intermediate spots on our staff," she says. The company's research showed that people trained this way tend to remain with the company.

Another company's research found that offering EDP training to their own employees has not worked. JoAnne Teasdale, director of systems and programming for The Gap, says that company-trained employees make satisfactory systems analysts because they know the user's side. "But these people have been hard to keep because once they get a taste of data processing, they don't want to be typecast as retail-only people and they move on to other fields."

Questionnaire research has shown that EDP personnel feel they are under a constant deluge of assignments. Norman Weiser of Federated Stores works around that problem by setting benchmarks so that people will feel accomplishment in a reasonable period of time. JoAnne Teasdale dealt with the problem by setting up a buffer team to handle 75 to 80 percent of the emergencies that cause the feeling of being swamped.

Personnel research, both formal and informal, has helped managers to improve the turnover situation in retail EDP. Retailing once was second choice or worse for trained EDP people, but as retailers have changed reward systems, adopted more advanced systems, and learned what it takes to keep these people, the situation has improved.[1]

Emerging slowly is the belief that personnel research . . . may point the way . . . to a better industrial system or to a wiser, juster utilization of the present system.

R. M. YERKES (1922)

By studying personnel activities, managers can determine the quality and extent of employee performance and the need for new personnel practices and systems. Research on personnel management activities provides an understanding of what works, what does not work, and what needs to be done.

Such research is ongoing and requires that good records be kept. In addition, the government has imposed recordkeeping requirements on most business organizations. Auditing of personnel activities is a type of research that relies upon personnel records. These audits are not always well received, but it is a sign of a healthy organization when management allows and encourages detailed analyses of personnel activities.

Increased numbers of personnel records have resulted in a "personnel data base" in many companies that can be a source of good information for making personnel decisions. However, for that data to be usable it should be part of a *Human Resources Information System* (HRIS).

The research and records responsibilities of the personnel unit and operating managers are shown in Figure 18–1. The personnel unit usually guides the design and collection of data, while managers provide assistance and necessary information. This chapter examines personnel record-keeping and research activities and their importance in ongoing personnel management operations.

PERSONNEL RESEARCH

Conducting research is often crucial to solving personnel problems because it is difficult to make good decisions without accurate information. Many managers are intimidated by the word "research" and its

PERSONNEL UNIT	MANAGERS
■ Designs human resources information system	■ Have access to human resources information system as needed
■ Keeps required records	
■ Provides expertise to design and evaluate data gathering	■ Provide information on people in the work units
■ Provides overview of organization climate	■ Assist in gathering data on organizational climate
■ Evaluates turnover and absenteeism throughout the organization	■ Control absenteeism and turnover in own work unit
■ Conducts personnel audit	■ Cooperate in personnel audit

FIGURE 18–1
Personnel Research and Records Responsibilities.

PERSONNEL
RESEARCH
analyzes past and pres-
ent personnel practices
through the use of col-
lected data and records.

academic implication. However, much research is quite simple and straightforward. For example, managers in a state education agency completed an attitude survey on job satisfaction in their unit. This survey pointed out problem areas that would otherwise not have been discovered, such as dissatisfaction with supervision and promotion policies.

Personnel research often is necessary to answer questions about such factors as absence records, safety problems, grievances, wage and salary rates, training executives, recruiting methods, and the validity of selection techniques. There are many ways to research the status of personnel management in an organization. Some of the most important ones follow.

Employee Questionnaires

One type of research makes use of questionnaires that give employees an opportunity to voice their opinions about specific personnel management activities. For example, questionnaires may be sent to employees to collect ideas for revising a performance appraisal system. Or employees may be asked to evaluate specific organizational communication methods, such as the employee handbook or the company suggestion system. Possible questionnaire items might include the following:

1. How would you describe the benefits in the organization?
Excellent __ Good __ Average __ Fair __ Poor __
2. How do you feel about the company policy of "buying back" sick leave?
Like it __ Dislike it __ Don't know __
Explain why?
3. Would you use a company tuition reimbursement plan at local educational institutions?
Yes __ No __ Not sure __
4. Would you be in favor of a flexible workweek schedule?
Yes __ Undecided __ No __

Questionnaires can be distributed and collected by supervisors, distributed with employee paychecks, or mailed to employees' homes. More accurate information usually is obtained if employees can return completed questionnaires anonymously. For example, Linda Stice, a manager in a large insurance company, was considered to be a very tough supervisor and her section consistently had more grievances than the others. When the personnel department designed a survey to pinpoint problems in the company, Linda was instructed to distribute and collect the questionnaires. The employees felt sure Linda would look at their answers before returning the forms to the personnel department; consequently, they did not answer the questions honestly. For such reasons, many companies use outside consultants to conduct attitude surveys.

Attitude Surveys. Attitude surveys focus on feelings and motives in order to pinpoint the employees' underlying opinions about their working environments. These surveys can be used as a starting point for improving productivity.[3] One source suggests three basic purposes for conducting attitude surveys: (1) for use as a base in comparing results to other survey results, (2) as a measurement of the effect of change before and after an organizational change occurs, and (3) to determine the nature and extent of employee feelings regarding specific organizational issues and the organization in general.[4]

Surveys serve as a sounding board for employees' feelings about their jobs, supervisors, co-workers, organizational policies and practices, and the organization in general. Many prepared attitude surveys are available. One should be careful, however, to check published reliability and validity statistics before using a prepared survey. Only surveys that are accepted as valid and reliable can really measure attitudes accurately. Often a "research" survey that is self-developed by a manager is poorly structured, asks questions in a confusing manner, or "leads" employees to respond in a manner that will give the manager the "desired results."

Surveys can be used for many purposes. One use can be to determine if employees are satisfied with their benefit programs. Some companies survey employees before granting new benefits to see if they are desired by employees.[5]

ORGANIZATIONAL CLIMATE is a composite view of the characteristics of an organization as seen by employees.

Organizational Climate Surveys. One useful survey is the measurement of **organizational climate,** which attempts to determine how employees feel about the organization or specific aspects of it. For instance, in one company employees liked the work they did, but problems with the company's structure and policies hampered their job performance and satisfaction. In this particular case, employee satisfaction with work differed from their satisfaction with the company. The value of an organizational climate study is that it can be used to diagnose the current state of an organization and indicate where changes are needed.

It is important to remember that the climate of an organization varies from one unit to another. At a hospital, the climate of the housekeeping unit might be different from the climate of the intensive care unit. When researching organizational climate, the results should be identified both by subunits and as a whole to provide an accurate organizational picture. Dimensions of organizational climate commonly measured include:[6]

1. Structure—Feelings about rules, procedures, and constraints
2. Responsibility—Feelings about the individual's decision-making freedom
3. Reward—Degree to which employees perceive fairness in pay and other rewards
4. Risk—Sense of challenge and desire to take risks
5. Team spirit—Feeling of group friendliness and identification with the organization
6. Standards—Emphasis on goal attainment and achievement of performance standards.

Organizational climate may be measured and the results used as a diagnostic tool for managers or consultants. For example, a large bank used organizational climate research to measure employees' feelings in one unit of the bank and to recommend changes based upon the results. Climate surveys are used as research devices to intervene in an organization and provide a basis for making changes. They are typically conducted by external consultants, in which case it is often the role of the personnel department to recommend a consultant and to translate the consultant's recommendations into action.

Good advice for any employee survey, based upon experience with such exercises, includes:[7]

■ *Survey everyone*—While sampling is statistically accurate, employees usually want to feel included in the process
■ *Provide plenty of notice and explanation*—Without both, people will not respond; let them know the importance of the survey
■ *Use instruments for which norms are available*—If 30 percent of your computer operators say they are looking for jobs, is that good or bad? No one knows without norms with which to compare the information
■ *Follow up with recommendations and action*—Employees become very cynical if they participate in a survey and do not get any feedback. Not seeing problem areas changed creates similar difficulties.

Research Interviews

A research interview is an alternative to the opinion survey and may focus on a wide variety of problems. One widely used type of interview is the exit interview.

Exit Interview. In an exit interview people who are leaving the organization are interviewed and asked to identify problems that caused them to resign. This information can be used to correct problems so that others will not leave. Personnel specialists rather than supervisors usually conduct exit interviews, and a skillful interviewer can gain useful information.

One problem with the exit interview is that resigning employees may be reluctant to divulge their real reasons for leaving because they do not want to "burn any bridges." They may also fear that candid responses will hinder their chances of receiving favorable references. The major reason an employee usually gives for leaving a job is an offer of more pay elsewhere. While this reason is acceptable, the pay increase not be the only factor involved. Former employees may be more willing to provide information on a questionnaire mailed to their homes or in telephone conversations conducted sometime after they leave the organization.

Experiments

Experiments provide useful data through tests undertaken to discover or demonstrate a premise. They allow the recording of events under conditions that can be carefully controlled. Two formats for setting up experiments are: (1) measuring conditions before and after a change is made, and (2) having some employees perform a job in a new way while others perform the same job in the old way, and comparing the results. People trained in experimental design and statistics are usually needed to conduct such studies and interpret the results.

Research Using Other Organizations

Personnel specialists can gain new insights from managers and specialists in other organizations by participating in professional personnel groups. The most prominent professional organizations are the American Society for Personnel Administration (ASPA) and the International Personnel Management Association (IPMA). These organizations publish professional journals and newsletters, conduct annual meetings and conferences, and provide many other services, often through local chapters. ASPA is composed primarily of private sector personnel administrators, whereas members of IPMA are primarily personnel managers from local, state, and federal government agencies.

Private management consulting firms and local colleges and universities also provide assistance in personnel research. These outside researchers may be more knowledgeable and unbiased than people inside the organization. Consultants skilled in questionnaire design and

A PERSONNEL AUDIT
is a formal research ef-
fort to evaluate the cur-
rent state of personnel
management in an orga-
nization.

data analysis can provide expert advice on personnel research. Appendix C contains a list of organizations and agencies having information useful to personnel specialists and other managers.

National or Area Surveys. Surveys by other organizations can provide some perspectives on a company's internal research. Some professional organizations, such as the Bureau of National Affairs and the Conference Board, sponsor surveys on personnel practices in different communities, states, and regions. The results are distributed to participating organizations. An organization also may conduct its own comparative outside surveys, such as wage surveys.

Current Literature. Professional personnel journals and publications provide a useful communication link between managers, personnel specialists, researchers, and other practitioners. Appendix B at the back of the book contains a list of journals that often publish personnel management information. Such publications help to keep personnel professionals current about changes in the field and about what other companies are doing.

Importance of Personnel Research

Personnel management decisions can be improved through personnel research because better information leads to better solutions. Good personnel management comes through analyzing problems and applying experience and knowledge to particular situations. A manager who just "supposes" that a certain result may occur is not likely to be effective. In some organizations personnel research is formalized through a personnel audit. Such an audit provides an overall look at personnel activities and helps identify areas that need improvement.

Can you identify four methods for researching personnel problems?

PERSONNEL AUDIT

A **personnel audit,** similar in purpose to a financial audit, examines, verifies, and evaluates the current status of personnel management in an organization. The research sources mentioned earlier, such as questionnaires and interviews, can be used in personnel audits. These sources can tell top executives, personnel specialists, and managers how well the organization is managing its human resources. Through the development and use of statistical reports and research data, personnel audits attempt to evaluate how well personnel activities have been performed. A formal comprehensive audit can examine many areas (See Figure 18–2).

A personnel audit begins with management determining the objectives it wants to achieve in the personnel area.[8] The audit then compares the actual state of personnel activities to the objectives.

Human Resource Accounting

Human resource accounting is similar in principle to preparation of an accounting statement. Just as financial accounting reflects the cost of capital assets such as machinery and buildings, **human resource accounting** which is done either once a year or at regular intervals attempts to place a value on organizational human resources by formulating a human resource "balance sheet." This instrument demonstrates that human resources are an asset instead of an expense, and should therefore be computed as part of the total worth of an organization.

People as "Investments." Human resource accounting shows the investment the organization makes in its people and how the value of these people changes over time; the acquisition cost of employees is com-

HUMAN RESOURCE ACCOUNTING is a specialized personnel audit that continually attempts to quantify the value of organizational human resources.

FIGURE 18–2
Personnel Audit Checklist.

PERSONNEL AUDIT CHECKLIST

Score **Work Analysis**
____ Current job descriptions (at least 80% of jobs)
____ Job specifications/qualifications
____ Job design considerations

Staffing
____ Human resource planning procedures and forecasts
____ Use of internal recruiting sources
____ Use of external recruiting media
____ EEO compliance recruitment
____ Legal application blank
____ Validation of testing procedures
____ Privacy concerns and reference checking
____ Affirmative action plan
____ Employment of women/minorities/handicapped
____ Training of interviewers (including supervisors)

Training and Development
____ Orientation of new employees
____ Job skill training programs
____ Career planning programs
____ Management development programs

Appraisal
____ Job-related appraisal
____ Appraisal feedback training for managers

____ Internal equity of appraisal program
____ Tie between appraisals and compensation

Compensation
____ Formal wage and salary system
____ Consistency with external wage/salary survey
____ Incentive program
____ Employee recognition program
____ Benefit programs
____ Retirement plan and counseling

Maintenance
____ Safety compliance/investigation
____ Discipline policies and procedures
____ Turnover/absenteeism analysis and control
____ Personnel records/employee privacy protection
____ Employee-related activities and programs
____ Exit interview procedures
____ Staffing and budgetary requirements

Union
____ Formal grievance procedure
____ Union problem prevention training
____ Collective bargaining procedures

Scoring: Where you think your personnel department is going a *very good* job, give yourself a score of 3. For an *adequate* job (one that needs some improvement) score 2. If you are *weak* in an area (and need major improvement) score 1. Score a minus 1 (-1) where the activity is basically nonexistent. Typically, a small company's personnel department should score at least 90 if it is to be effective. How much work do you have to do?

SOURCE: Robert L. Mathis and Gary Cameron, "Auditing Personnel Practices in Smaller-Sized Organizations: A Realistic Approach," *Personnel Administrator,* April 1981, 606 N. Washington St., Alexandria VA 22314, $32 per year.)

pared to the replacement cost. The value of employees is increased by training and experience over a period of time. Upjohn, a large pharmaceutical manufacturer, has used human resource accounting to estimate that an employee represents a $2.34 million investment over a 30-year period when all relevant costs are considered.[9]

The importance of human resource accounting is illustrated by the effect of a major change in human resources on the stock market. If a change occurs in a company's top management or key personnel, the price of that company's stock may go up or down. The board of directors of a large food company, for example, decided to remove the president, vice president, and controller. When this news reached the stock market, the price of the company's stock soared because the market viewed this action as a major improvement in the company's operations. That illustrated the value placed on the top management team—in this case, it was low.

To summarize, human resource accounting is a sophisticated way to measure the effectiveness of personnel management activities and the use of people in an organization. It is presented here as an illustration of a way in which attempts have been made to measure the effectiveness of personnel activities.

Can you define the concepts of a personnel audit and human resource accounting?

ABSENTEEISM AND TURNOVER

Absenteeism and turnover are major concerns in most organizations.[10] These two personnel problems are universally studied by managers because of their impact on organizational operations. Many employers regularly collect turnover and absenteeism data. If a manager needs 12 people to work in a unit to get the work done, and four of the 12 are absent most of the time, the unit's work will probably not get done. Research on the reasons for absenteeism should be done by using organizational records.

Absenteeism

Employees can be absent from work for several reasons. Illness, death in the family, or other personal reasons are unavoidable and understandable; however, excessive absences may cause organizational coordination problems.[11] Many employers have sick-leave policies that allow employees to take paid absences a certain number of days per year. Employees who miss fewer days are reimbursed with sick pay.

A formula for computing absenteeism rates, suggested by the U.S. Department of Labor, is as follows:

$$\frac{\text{Number of person-days lost through job absence during period}}{(\text{Average number of employees}) \times (\text{Number of work days})} \times 100$$

The rate can be computed based on the number of hours instead of days. Absenteeism often varies in the range of 2 to 12 percent per month.

Organizations have noted that consistently there are more absences on Fridays and Mondays than on other days. One reason for this pattern is that some employees stretch the weekend to three or four days. Other causes for absenteeism can be suggested. For instance, a relationship has been found between absenteeism and job satisfaction. Employees with higher job satisfaction will probably be absent less often than those who are dissatisfied with their jobs.

Absenteeism Control

Controlling or reducing absenteeism must begin with continuous monitoring of absenteeism statistics in work units.[12] This monitoring helps managers pinpoint employees who are frequently absent and departments with excessive absenteeism. Offering rewards for good attendance, giving bonuses for missing fewer than a certain number of days, and "buying back" unused sick leave are all methods of reducing absenteeism. If absenteeism is excessive, the problem employees can be dismissed.

Organizational policies on absenteeism should be clearly stated in an employee handbook and stressed by supervisors and managers. Counseling and discussing the matter with employees may correct some of the problems that make people reluctant to come to work and may suggest positive actions to be taken. Absenteeism control options fall into three categories: (1) discipline, (2) positive reinforcement, or (3) a combination of discipline and reinforcement.

Disciplinary Approach. Scott, a large paper company, used the disciplinary approach in its Mobile, Alabama, plant to good effect. People who were absent were first given an oral warning, but subsequent absences brought written warnings, suspension, and finally dismissal. In five years under this system, 70 workers were fired and the absenteeism rate dropped from 7 percent to around 4 percent.[13]

Positive Reinforcement. Positive reinforcement includes such methods as giving employees cash, recognition, time off, and other rewards for meeting attendance standards. In one firm, employees with perfect attendance records were given the "right" to participate in a lottery with a cash reward. The program reduced absenteeism markedly.

Combination Approaches. Combination approaches ideally reward desired behavior and punish undesired behavior. At a Detroit architectural engineering firm each employee gets a time-off "account," against which vacations, holidays, and sick days are drawn. If employees run out of days in their accounts, they are not paid for the days missed. However, they can accrue sick time yearly.

Can you discuss several absenteeism strategies?

TURNOVER
is the process in which
employees leave the or-
ganization and have to
be replaced.

Turnover is the process in which employees leave an organization and have to be replaced. It can be a very costly problem. One firm had a turnover rate of over 120 percent per year. It cost the company $1.5 million a year in lost productivity, increased training time, increased personnel selection time, lost work efficiency, and other indirect costs.

The turnover rate for an organization can be computed using the following formula from the U.S. Department of Labor (*separations* are people who left the organizations).

$$\frac{\text{Number of employee separations during the month}}{\text{Total number of employees at midmonth}} \times 100$$

Common turnover figures range from 2 percent to 35 percent per year. It is important to note that turnover rates vary among industries. Supply and demand is a factor, as in the case of Silicon Valley engineers, who have a turnover rate of more than 30 percent per year.[14] Tradition can also be a factor in an industry's turnover rate. For example, in the publishing industry turnover has always been high. One editor-in-chief says it is because "the field looks more glamorous than it is—lots of failures and disappointments, lots of clever people moving on.[15]

Organizations that require little skill for entry-level employees are likely to have a higher turnover rate among those employees than among managerial personnel.[16] As a result, it is important that turnover rates be computed by work units. For instance, one organization had a company-wide turnover rate that was not severe—but 80 percent of the turnover occurred within one department. This imbalance indicated that some action was needed to resolve problems in that unit.

Turnover often is classified as *voluntary* or *involuntary* and/or *avoidable* and *unavoidable*. Involuntary turnover occurs when an employee is fired. Voluntary turnover occurs when an employee leaves by his or her own choice, and can be caused by many factors. The obvious ones are those that cause job dissatisfaction. Some less obvious causes of turnover can include absenteeism, ability, performance, and the competition for expected job openings.[17] The *Monthly Labor Review* reports turnover data monthly by industry, which can be quite useful for comparative purposes.

Turnover Control

Turnover can be "controlled" in several ways. Because it is related to job satisfaction, matching an employee's expectations of rewards and satisfaction to what is actually provided by the job may help reduce turnover problems. A good way to eliminate turnover is to *improve selection* and the matching of applicants to jobs. By fine-tuning the selection process, and hiring people who are more likely to stay, managers can decrease the chances that employees will leave.

Good *employee orientation* will also help reduce turnover. Employees who are properly inducted into the company and are well-trained tend to be less likely to leave. If people receive some basic information about the company and the job to be performed, they can determine early whether or not they want to stay. Another reason for turnover is that individuals believe there is no opportunity for career advancement.[18] Consequently, career planning and internal promotion can help an organization keep career personnel.

In addition, a fair and equitable *pay system* can help prevent turnover. An employee who is underpaid relative to employees in other jobs with similar skills may leave if there is an inviting alternative job available. An awareness of employee problems and dissatisfaction may provide a manager with opportunities to resolve them before they become so severe that employees leave. Turnover problems can often be pinpointed by researching personnel records.

Can you discuss turnover concerns and control strategies?

PERSONNEL RECORDS

The only function of many early personnel departments was record keeping. It should be apparent by this point in the book that the contemporary personnel department has many more activities today. However, the need for keeping personnel records has taken on much greater importance because of increased government demands and such new sophisticated personnel activities as human resources forecasting.

Personnel-related records and data provide an excellent source of information for auditing or assessing the effectiveness of a personnel department, or any unit. They also provide the basis for researching the possible causes of problems in organizations. Figure 18–3 shows some of the personnel records and data that may be available to organizations.

Personnel records also serve as important documentation in certain cases. For example, a new employee stated on the application form that he had a driver's license; he then was hired to drive a delivery truck. Examination later revealed the new employee did not have a driver's license, and he was fired for falsifying the application. Without the record of the falsified application, proving that he had lied would have been difficult because he claimed he had never said he had a driver's license.

Records and the Government

Federal, state, and local laws require that numerous records be kept on employees. The requirements are so varied that it is difficult to identify exactly what should be kept and for how long. Each specific case must be dealt with separately. Generally, records relating to wages, basic employment, work schedules, job evaluations, merit and seniority systems, and affirmative action programs should be kept by all employers who are subject to provisions of the Fair Labor Standards Act. The most commonly required retention time for such records is three years.

FIGURE 18–3
Examples of Personnel
Records and Data
Sources.

PERSONNEL RECORDS AND DATA SOURCES	
Accident Records	Termination Records
Employment Requisition Records	Job Specifications
Personnel Inventories	Job Descriptions
Applicant Records	Salary Increase Records
Interview Records	Training Records
Turnover Records	Personal History Records
Transfer Records	Affirmative Action Records
Payroll Records	Medical Records
Work Schedule Records	Insurance Records
Test Score Records	Other Benefit Records
Performance Records	Committee Meeting Records
Grievance Records	Retired Employee Records
Arbitration Awards	Personal Interest Records
Occupational Health Records	Attitude/Morale Data
Job Bidding Records	Open Jobs Records
Exit Interview Records	Labor Market Data
Employee Expense Records	

A HUMAN RE-
SOURCE INFORMA-
TION SYSTEM (HRIS)
is an integrated comput-
erized system designed
to provide information
to be used in making
personnel decisions.

In addition, other records may be required on issues relating to EEO, OSHA, or the Age Discrimination Act. Such record-keeping requirements have not been accepted easily by managers who must adapt to the additional paperwork. Even though personnel records must be kept, many managers feel that they can be a source of major trouble by allowing the past actions of management to be questioned.

The major problem presented by personnel record keeping is the inability to retrieve needed information without major difficulties. For example, better personnel decisions can be made if good information is available on such matters as the nature, causes, and severity of accidents; the reasons for absenteeism; the availability of experience; and the distribution of performance appraisals. But for many organizations such information is not readily available. There probably is a point beyond which it costs more to keep records than can be gained by doing so. A solution to the problems associated with record keeping and with getting useful information from the records is a well-designed human resource information system.

*Can you explain the importance of person-
nel record keeping?*

Human Resource Information Systems

A **human resource information system** (HRIS) uses a computer, its attendant hardware and software, and a data base. Figure 18–4 shows a very simple model of a personnel information system.

Most of the records and data sources listed can be stated in numerical terms. These numbers can then be combined or manipulated in the

HRIS to provide the type of information necessary for planning, controlling, making decisions, or preparing reports.

The computer has simplified the task of analyzing vast amounts of data. It can be an invaluable aid in personnel management, from payroll processing to record retention. But the computer is only a machine. If it is given bad information, it returns in kind ("garbage in, garbage out"). Extracting useful information from raw data requires knowledgeable approaches and common sense.

It was natural when computer technology became available to use it to keep personnel records. Today's micro- and mini-computers have

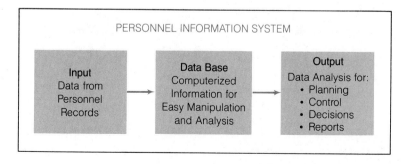

FIGURE 18—4
A Simple Model of a Personnel Information System.

been developed to the point that they can be very useful in personnel record keeping. Personnel software for minicomputers is now readily available; consequently, smaller companies with less capital and smaller employee populations are bringing computers into the personnel department.

Biographical and historical data are still the items of major concern, but many companies now are calculating the cost of hires, transfers, promotions, and benefits. Lonza, Inc., for example, found that with its HRIS it could project the amount of money needed from its parent company to cover across-the-board raises and individual salary increases, given certain performance levels. Resort International's Casino Hotel in Atlantic City is checking labor costs by job classification to identify target labor-hours per function. This data will provide hotel management a basis from which to control costs. Norden Systems (a defense subsidiary of United Technologies) can track sources of new hires and calculate how much it costs to hire new employees from each source.[20]

HRIS Design

In order to design an HRIS properly, experts say to start from the standpoint of the data. A manager should ask what information is available, and what information will be needed about people in the company? To what uses will the information be put? In what format should the output be presented to fit with other company records? The answers to these questions help pinpoint the necessary hardware and software.

An HRIS manager must clearly understand the record-keeping and reporting requirements before designing the system. Each employer's problems are unique and there are no standard outputs. Each has to be tailored to the organization. However, some common reports are:

■ *Personnel Profile*—Name, sex, race, age, marital status, address and phone number, service dates
■ *Career Profile*—Performance appraisal, job title changes, job classification changes, salary changes, promotions, transfers, career paths
■ *Skill Profile*—Education, training, certificates, licenses, degrees, skills, hobbies, requested training, interests
■ *Benefits Profile*—Insurance coverage, disability provisions, pension, profit sharing, vacation, holidays, sick leave.[21] In addition to such basic reports, an HRIS can be put to many other uses. Each company's usage is limited only by its data and imagination, as Figure 18–5 shows.

Retrieval Systems

Using the computer as the sole component in an HRIS can present some problems when it comes to retrieving the information stored in it. The first problem is putting the contents of a large number of paper personnel files into the machine in the first place. Another concern is the potential for erasing the data base memory.[22]

A computer-assisted retrieval system (CAR), which allows the automatic locating and displaying of documents from microfilm, is one solution to the latter problem. Because it is used in conjunction with a computer, data can be manipulated and hard copies made, but a backup source of data is retained in the form of microfilm.[23]

Training People to Use HRIS

Overcoming people's resistance to using the HRIS takes some training. Even though much of the new software is extremely easy to use, some training is necessary. One trainer notes, "No matter how easy the product is to learn, or how well the documentation is written, some people won't read the manuals. And in order to learn to use the computer, you must be away from your work environment and in a classroom setting".[24]

Such training, as well as the design of the HRIS, is usually under the direction of a Human Resources Data Administrator. Although this new position was almost nonexistent five years ago, nearly 80 percent of major corporations now have one.[25] Top management has realized: (1) that an HRIS does not run itself, and (2) that taking full advantage of the system requires both personnel and computer expertise.[26]

Can you discuss the importance of an HRIS?

FIGURE 18–5
HRIS Uses.

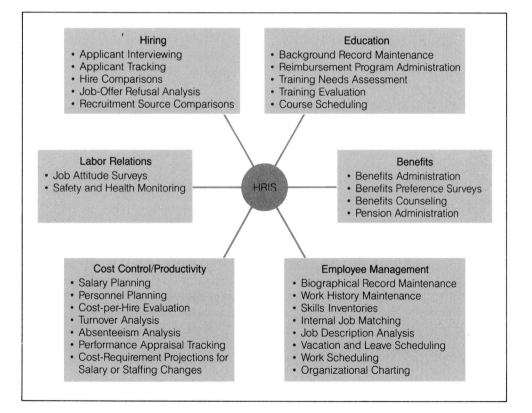

As a result of concerns regarding the protection of individuals' privacy rights, the Privacy Act of 1974 was passed. It includes provisions affecting personnel records systems. This law applies to federal agencies and companies supplying services to the federal government, but similar state laws have also been passed.

Five principles serve to guide the development of policies on the privacy of personnel data bases:

1. Employees should know of the existence of the HRIS.
2. Employees should be able to find out what is in their records and how that information is used.
3. Employees should be able to prevent unauthorized uses of their own data.
4. Employees should have a means of correcting errors in their data.
5. Any organization creating, maintaining, using, or disseminating records of identifiable personal data must assure the reliability of the data for their intended use and must take precautions to prevent misuse.[27]

Pioneering companies in the privacy area include Bank of America, IBM, Aetna Life, Cummins Engine, Avis, TRW, General Electric, Atlantic Richfield, AT&T, Control Data, Prudential, and General Motors. These companies have conducted information audits of their current practices and have eliminated much unnecessary or objectionable information on employees. United Technologies, General Tire and Rubber, and Chase Manhattan Bank have recently adopted policies limiting data that are kept and access to that data. One estimate is that over 450 companies now have privacy policies on their books; several years ago the number would have been closed to 50.[28]

A survey done by Sentry Insurance found that while most employees do not view their employers as engaged in improper collection of personal information, they do favor a new system of rules to handle sensitive information that is collected. Further, they want decisions on promotions, job assignments, and discipline made on the basis of information that can be examined if a dispute arises. In the survey, both employees and the public viewed fair information practices as a matter of good personnel management.[29]

Another study found that employees have rather limited knowledge about what types of information their company keeps on file. Further, they are more concerned about disclosure of personal information to parties outside the firm than they are about how the information is used inside the firm.[30] These findings may require rethinking and reorganizing of many existing record-keeping systems in personnel units, in line with Figure 18–6; doing so can minimize problems later.[31]

The records kept on employees provide excellent sources for doing research inside the organization. Personnel research, as was suggested earlier, provides management with the information it uses to make adjustments in its policies and procedures, if any are needed.

Can you explain how privacy concerns affect personnel record keeping?

FIGURE 18–6

Guidelines for the Privacy Protection of Personnel Records

1. Develop Policies about Personnel Records

Policies should be developed that cover the gathering, use, disclosure, and retention of records covering employment, personnel and payroll, security, medical, and insurance matters. The policies should:

a. limit the collection, use, and retention of such records

b. set up procedures to ensure the accuracy, timeliness, and completeness of information collected, maintained, and disclosed

c. allow current employees, former employees, and applicants to see, copy, correct, and amend records maintained about them

d. limit internal use of and access to records

e. limit external disclosure of information in records

f. restrict use of arrest and conviction records except to the extent necessary to comply with governmental regulations, and maintain such records separately from other personnel files

g. restrict use of military discharge records if other than honorable

h. notify applicants and employees about sources used for information and record-gathering purposes

i. designate records of employees, former employees, and applicants that the employer will allow to be reviewed and copied, and will not allow to be reviewed and copied

j. notify employee, former employees, and retirees about any fees for copying and mailing records and documents

k. explain to them any records kept separately from personnel files, such as medical and benefits information

2. Disclosure Statement

A disclosure statement should be developed for distribution to employees, former employees, and job applicants that includes the following:

a. the type and number of records maintained on all workers—past, present, and prospective

b. the usage, disclosure, and retention period for each record

3. Review Files Regularly

An employer should review all current personnel files individually to ensure that outdated, unnecessary, and potentially damaging documentation is removed and destroyed.

4. Designate File Custodian

An employer should designate a file custodian either within its personnel department or to some other officer of the organization.

5. Restrict Separate Files

As much as possible, an employer should restrict, if not eliminate, the maintenance of any separate employee files by managers.

6. Base Decisions on File Information

All decisions to transfer, promote, or discipline employees should be made solely on the basis of information maintained in the personnel department's master employee file.

7. Train Managers

All managers should be trained on how to structure and draft effective, liability-free documentation for employees' personnel files.

SOURCE: Mary P. Carlton, "Workers Privacy: A Call for Voluntary Action," p. 19. Reprinted by special permission from the July 1980 issue of *ABA Banking Journal*. Copyright 1980 by the American Bankers Association.

PERSONNEL TODAY AND TOMORROW

YOUR "PRIVATE" COMPANY TELEPHONE

Privacy issues are not always clear-cut. Telephone usage is becoming more an issue at some companies as the cost goes up. One story is that one manager at Citibank wheeled a big computer into a branch office and posted a notice saying the computer would monitor all telephone conversations. The computer box was empty, but the hoax worked. Personal calls almost ceased and the number of long distance calls dropped significantly until the people discovered the trick—two weeks later.

Computerized call accounting systems are currently very hot items. These systems have been developed so that they are much more accurate and inexpensive than their predecessors. Typically, when such a system is installed, phone usage drops dramatically—as much as 40 percent in some cases. Once a company starts keeping a log of calls, it becomes clear that not all calls are business-related.

Besides calling out-of-town relatives and friends, employees have used company phones to call well-publicized recordings featuring jokes, pornographic comments, and even messages to make people relax (called *dial-a-trance*). Phone records have revealed personal secrets too. A call-tracking system at a New York financial services company showed a series of long-distance calls from one executive office phone to the home phone of another executive. A little examination showed that the first executive was having a love affair with the second executive's wife. The first executive was fired.

Companies concede that keeping phone records may threaten an employee's privacy. But they argue that employers are paying for the phones and have a right to know how they are being used (or misused). In their view, a telephone in a company facility is there for company business and the company has every right to keep track of its use, just as the use of company cars is tracked! What do you think?[32]

SUMMARY

■ Research on personnel activities answers questions with facts, not guesswork.

■ Such information can be gathered from several sources: questionnaires, attitude surveys, climate surveys, exit interviews, experiments, and by comparison with other organizations.

■ Personnel audits can be used to gather information on the state of personnel matters in an organization.

■ Absenteeism is a big problem for some companies. Controlling absenteeism requires information and management commitment.

■ Turnover varies from industry to industry, but in any industry, it is very costly. Orientation, career planning, and equitable pay systems may be useful control activities.

■ Personnel records provide an excellent source of information *if* they are in a form that can be used easily.

■ An HRIS (Human Resource Information System) utilizes a computer to make records more useful to management as a source of information.

■ An HRIS can be designed for almost any personnel matter. Design of a specific program has to be tailored to the company, but a number of flexible software packages are now available.

■ Privacy in HRIS and other record-keeping methods has become a problem. However, some employers have taken the lead in the last few years in developing policies to prevent abuses of personal privacy in company records.

REVIEW QUESTIONS AND EXERCISES

1. You are a personnel director for Consolidated Widgets. What means would you use to conduct personnel research on turnover and absenteeism problems in your firm?

2. A personnel audit and a human resource accounting system are somewhat different. Differentiate between them.

3. If you were a manager in a retail firm in which high absenteeism occurred, what would you do to reduce it?

4. Why should you be concerned about turnover problems?

5. "Personnel record keeping is a necessary but mundane part of personnel management." Discuss.

6. What are the components of a Human Resource Information System?

7. Discuss the following statement: "Privacy concerns will have a significant impact on personnel record-keeping systems."

Exercises

a. Using Figure 18–4, identify the basic personnel reports you feel a company should have.

b. Check with your college or university registration and records office to see to what extent it conforms to the American Bankers Association privacy recommendations in Figure 18–6.

CASE

SURVEYING SUPERVISION

Lorna Jacobs, a 33-year-old with a degree in medical technology, manages the clinical laboratory department of a 200-bed hospital. Nine years ago she began her employment in the department as a medical technologist; she became section supervisor after three years of service. Two years later, Jacobs was named Laboratory Manager, a position she has held for the last four years.

The laboratory in this hospital operates 24 hours a day, seven days a week. The staff totals 52 and consists of medical technologists, phlebotomists, and clerical personnel. The supervisory staff of the department is comprised of 5 section supervisors, all of whom are medical technologists who report directly to Jacobs.

Recently, the hospital conducted an employee attitude survey. One problem area identified in the survey process involves the supervision in the laboratory. In reviewing and discussing the results with Jacobs, the personnel director indicates that the results show the supervisors in the laboratory are dissatisfied with Jacobs and with their own roles. One complaint of the supervisors is the lack of understanding of what is expected of them as supervisors. They feel they are given very little latitude in solving problems and fulfilling their responsibilities, particularly in the realm of personnel administration.

In addition, the results indicate that Jacobs is seen as harsh and insensitive toward the personal needs and concerns of the entire laboratory staff. She allows for no participation in decision making, nor does she explain the reasoning behind a decision. Because she is perceived in this way, employees indicated that they were reluctant to present ideas or suggestions to either their supervisor or Jacobs.

Jacobs questions whether or not the current state of affairs is a result of the way the department has evolved during the past six years. Supervisors were nonexistent in the laboratory before Jacobs became the chemistry section supervisor. At the time when supervisors were first utilized, their main responsibility was to oversee the daily operations within the assigned areas. They had no responsibility to handle any aspect of personnel administration. When Jacobs was promoted to laboratory manager, she found herself doing all the hiring, counseling, and evaluating of the entire staff in addition to handling her other managerial duties. She realized the inefficiencies of the system and proceeded to prepare the supervisory staff for additional responsibilities.

As none of the supervisors had any experience in personnel administration, Jacobs had them attend training sessions conducted by the hospital. This training was reinforced through group and individual counseling conducted by Jacobs. All of the laboratory supervisors were eventually assigned the responsibility for personnel administration in their respective areas. To emphasize this expanded role of the supervisors, Jacobs ceased handling the problems and requests of the staff members as she had previously done; instead, the employees were instructed to take these concerns directly to their supervisor. In analyzing this process, Jacobs remembered that three of the supervisors now employed have been hired since these changes occurred, and each one was hired having no prior supervisory experience.

In looking at the current situation, Jacobs considers other factors that could be contributing to the problem identified in the employee survey. The five supervisors frequently come to meetings unprepared to discuss the announced agenda items. Consequently, decisions often are made *in* the meetings, with the majority of the input provided by Lorna. The supervisors leave these meetings and report back to their employees with "Jacobs' decision." Similarly, the supervisors frequently request advice from Jacobs on how to handle various employee requests or problems. After the advice is given, the supervisor goes back to the employee and reports on how "Jacobs says" the situation is to be handled.

Jacobs has thought about her own behavior and recognizes that it also could be contributing to her problems. She has minimized personal contact with the majority of the laboratory staff by communicating through the supervisors. In addition, she has not pursued her intention of developing performance standards for the supervisory positions. Jacobs also feels she has lessened the accountability of the supervisors by being too specific and directive when counseling a supervisor.

Jacobs believes that the department cannot effectively accomplish its objectives without competent supervision. She recognizes the detrimental nature of the current situation in developing and producing competent supervisors. Faced with the history and facts presented, Jacobs must evaluate the information and design a plan for resolving the problems in the department.

Questions

1. How useful and accurate do you believe the attitude survey results to be?
2. In what ways can attitude surveys be used as "action research" devices?
3. What changes in managerial behavior would you suggest to Lorna Jacobs? Why?

NOTES

1. Adapted from "EDP Department Turnover," *Chain Store Executive*, January 1982, pp. 7–8.
2. G. A. Kesselman, "The Attitude Survey: Does It Have a Bearing on Productivity?" *Advanced Management Journal*, Winter 1984, p. 18–24.
3. Rene V. Dawis and William Weitzel, "Worker Attitudes and Expectations," *ASPA Handbook of Personnel and Industrial Relations*, eds. Dale Yoder and Herbert G. Heneman Jr. (Washington, DC: Bureau of National Affairs, 1979), pp. 6–40.
4. J. B. Wetzel, "Employee Surveys," *Business Insurance*, July 11, 1983, p. 19.
5. Adapted from Kesselman, "The Attitude Survey," p. 22.
6. For example, see P. K. Tyaqi, "Perceived Organizational Climate and the Process of Salesperson Motivation," *Journal of Marketing Research*, May 1982, pp. 240–254.
7. M. R. Cooper, "Traditional Employee Attitude Surveys Don't Work," *Management Review*, August 1982, pp. 56–57.

8. Robert L. Mathis and Gary Cameron, "Auditing Personnel Practices in Smaller-sized Organizations: A Realistic Approach," *Personnel Administrator*, April 1981, pp. 45–49.

9. Charles R. Day, Jr., "Solving the Mystery of Productivity Measurement," *Industry Week*, January 26, 1981, p. 66.

10. R. T. Keller, "The Role of Performance and Absenteeism in the Prediction of Turnover," *Academy of Management Journal* 27 (1984), p. 176.

11. S. A. Stumpf and K. Hartman, "Individual Exploration to Organizational Commitment or Withdrawal," *Academy of Management Journal* 27 (1984), pp. 308–329.

12. P. J. Lightkep, "Solving Attendance Problems," *Personnel Journal* 61 (July 1982), p. 496.

13. T. H. Stone, "Absence Control: Is Your Company a Candidate?" *Personnel Administrator*, September 1980, p. 81.

14. T. J. Murray, "Silicon Valley Faces Up to the People Crunch," *Dun's Review*, July 1981, p. 60.

15. S. Dong, "Publishing's Revolving Door," *Publisher's Weekly*, December 19, 1980, p. 27.

16. R. T. Mowday, C. S. Koberg, and A. W. McArthur, "The Psychology of the Withdrawal Process," *Academy of Management Journal*, 27 (March 1984), pp. 79–94.

17. S. A. Stumpf and P. K. Dawky, "Predicting Voluntary and Involuntary Turnover Using Absenteeism and Performance Indices," *Academy of Management Journal* 24 (March 1981), p. 148; and G. F. Dreher and T. W. Dougherty "Turnover and Competition for Expected Job Openings: An Exploratory Analysis," *Academy of Management Journal* 23 (December 1980), pp. 766–771.

18. E. F. Jackofsky, "Turnover and Job Performance: An Integration Process Model," *Academy of Management*, 9 (January 1984), pp. 74–83.

19. Adapted from W. E. Blundell, "Equal Employment Records: To Know Them Is to Love Them," *Wall Street Journal*, March 19, 1984, p. 24.

20. J. Kelleher, "New Help for Personnel," *Business Computer Systems*, February 1984, p. 93.

21. V. R. Ceriello, "The Human Resources Management System," *Personnel Journal* 61 (October 1982), p. 767.

22. L. S. Lee, "Micrographic Solutions for Personnel Systems," *Journal of Systems Management*, August 1983, p. 15.

23. G. Meyer, "Curing Personnel Department 'Technemia' " *Personnel Administrator*, September 1983, p. 26.

24. C. Zarley, "Training People to Use Their Computers," *Personal Computing*, January 1984, p. 127.

25. "Data Keepers," *Wall Street Journal*, January 25, 1981, p. 1.

26. A. J. Walker, "The Newest Job in Personnel: Human Resources Data Administrator," *Personnel Journal* 61 (December 1982), pp. 924–928.

27. "The Meaning of Privacy," *Personnel Journal* 61 (December 1982), p. 929.

28. "Respecting Employee Privacy," *Business Week*, January 11, 1982, p. 130.

29. A. F. Westen, "What Should Be Done About Employee Privacy?" *Personnel Administrator*, March 1980, pp. 27–30.

30. R. W. Woodman et al., "A Survey of Employee Perceptions of Information Privacy in Organizations," *Academy of Management Journal* 25 (September 1982), p. 660.

31. For an excellent summary of the legal issues involved in privacy, see D. Jan Duffy, "Employee Privacy: A New Challenge for Personnel," *EEO Today*, Autumn 1982, pp. 253–265.

32. Adapted from C. Ricci, "Personal Use of Company Phones is Target of Cost-Cutting Efforts," *Wall Street Journal*, April 11, 1984, p. 29.

OSHA—NUISANCE OR NECESSITY?

The Chemco Corporation is composed of ten autonomous divisions and corporate headquarters. This case focuses on the Rural plant, which manufactures chemical solvents.

The Rural plant is housed in a five-story building erected in 1924. The top two floors are not used because the floors are too dangerous, and the second and third stories have places where the floor has rotted.

The third floor holds the laboratory and the marketing department. The second floor holds the rack shop, office, some warehousing, and some chemical compound production lines. The first floor contains the warehousing for heavier materials and the rest of the manufacturing lines. The rack shop is a support unit that makes racks for drying chemicals. The plant is nonunion.

The plant manager is Joe Allen, who has been with the Chemco Corporation for 20 years—all at the Rural plant. He has done almost everything at the plant. He started as foreman in the manufacturing unit, supervised the rack shop and the warehouse, and also sold the compounds. He has not, however, worked in the office or laboratory. The employees like Allen, although they are a bit afraid of him. He has wide latitude to run the plant as he sees fit; the Rural plant is both geographically isolated and far from Chemco's headquarters in New York City.

Because the Rural plant consistently makes more money for Chemco than its budgets and forecasts call for, corporate headquarters leaves Allen alone. Turnover and absenteeism are also lower than expected. The plant safety and health record is considered to be "average" for a Chemco operation. All in all, the Chemco Corporation and Joe Allen are satisfied with the operation of the Rural plant.

The local OSHA inspector, George Hlavecek, comes to the Rural plant fairly regularly. In April, Hlavecek came to the Rural plant when Allen was at a meeting at Chemco Corporation headquarters. Hlavecek determined that part of the chemical-compound manufacturing process was producing toxic gases. As was his right, he shut down the plant that day. Allen promptly

flew back and modified the gas filters himself. Hlavecek inspected the filters the next day, passed them, and the Rural plant resumed operation.

In May, Hlavecek came back and shut down the plant again, this time when Allen was at another meeting. Once again the filters were cleaned and modified. By now, Allen was beginning to become upset with these unannounced inspections and subsequent shutdowns.

The following month, the OSHA inspector again appeared at the Rural plant. Joe Allen succeeded in convincing him that he should come back the next day.

The rest of the day at the Rural plant was a "red alert." No work was done and the whole plant was cleaned up. Bottles in the laboratory that leaked toxic chemicals were secured. Handguards were put on the processing machines (they weren't used otherwise). Machines for which there were no handguards were covered up and moved to look as if they were out of service. The gas filters were cleaned. Dust masks were issued to the employees. The following day, Hlavecek came back, toured the plant with Allen, and passed the operation.

In August, Hlavecek again appeared at the Rural plant. Allen stalled him for 45 minutes when he asked to make the inspection. Finally, the inspector and a foreman inspected the plant but the foreman took Hlavecek to the warehouse first to give the rest of the plant time to clean up. It didn't help. The inspector issued four warnings and gave the Rural plant 24 hours to comply or he would initiate action to have the plant closed permanently. By now Allen was quite angry; the constant inspections, modifications, and procedural changes were beginning to result in declining output and rising expenses. He became angrier still when he heard that the OSHA inspector had referred to the plant, within earshot of the employees, as a "deathtrap," a "sweatshop," and an "accident waiting to happen." Allen now became convinced that OSHA was "out to get him" and his operation.

The next day, Allen contacted the office of

Representative Smith, his congressman. He informed Smith's office that he was being harassed by OSHA with constant inspections and shutdowns, and that the OSHA inspector was out to make an example of him and his operation. He further informed the congressman that the OSHA inspector had handeled himself in an unprofessional manner in conducting his inspection. From that point, things moved swiftly. Smith contacted the head of OSHA directly, indicating that if things didn't change, he would request that the House Subcommittee on Occupational Safety and Health hold hearings on the matter. The OSHA Administrator promised him that action would be taken. The following week, Hlavecek was transferred to the OSHA regional office in St. Louis, halfway across the country.

About this time, Arthur Jackson, manager of the health and safety division of Chemco's corporate personnel department in New York, received word (from the media) about the Rural plant's recent experience with OSHA. He thereupon decided to visit the Rural plant and make his own inspection. The day he arrived, Allen was ill. However, even though he had never been to the Rural plant before, Jackson went ahead and inspected it anyway. He found numerous OSHA violations and several violations of Chemco's own safety and health regulations.

QUESTIONS

1. Evaluate the charge of harassment leveled at OSHA and how that charge was received in Washington, D.C.
2. What responsibilities have been neglected by corporate headquarters and Arthur Jackson? Why did the neglect occur?
3. Discuss Joe Allen's approach to safety and contrast it with a systems approach to safety.
4. If you were Arthur Jackson, corporate safety director, what would you recommend be done at the Rural plant?

ORGANIZATION/UNION RELATIONSHIPS

Some organizations formally interact with their employees through unions. To understand the basis of this relationship, the history of the labor movement and labor legislation must be studied. Chapter 19 provides a useful synopsis of the evolution of unionism and labor legislation in the United States. The process of unionization in an organization is one that is often misunderstood, but an understanding of the steps in the process is an important part of a manager's knowledge.

If an organization is unionized, a labor contract is the basis for the relationship between an employer and a union. The process of reaching a contract agreement is known as collective bargaining, an important part of labor/management relations. The bargaining process and typical issues in collective bargaining are discussed in Chapter 20.

Grievance procedures and arbitration are methods union members use to solve problems with the organization. In Chap-

ter 20, the daily administration of a labor agreement through the grievance procedure is discussed. If grievances cannot be settled, than an arbitrator may be selected to decide what must be done. An analysis of some common problems arbitrators face and the relationship between a manager's behavior and grievance rates are also discussed in Chapter 20. Grievances are also an important source of information for analyzing personnel activities.

Nature of Union-Management Relations

When you have read this chapter, you should be able to:

1. Compare and contrast the philosophies of U.S. and European unions.
2. Describe two current and future trends in unionism.
3. Describe the general structure of unions.
4. Trace the evolution of labor unions in the United States from 1800 to 1935.
5. Explain the acts which make up the National Labor Code.
6. Identify and discuss the stages in the unionization process.

PERSONNEL AT WORK
JOBS FOR LIFE

The United Auto Workers union in its negotiations with Ford and General Motors has moved in a direction considered "radical" for American manufacturing. The union has been negotiating guaranteed jobs for its members. The union has argued that to be more productive, like Japanese auto workers, its members need job security like the Japanese have. Besides, the union knows that preserving jobs may be the best it can do considering auto industry trends. They see more automation leading to fewer jobs in the long run.

Two programs have been developed. One is called "Guaranteed Income Stream" and assures veteran laid-off workers jobs with one of the company's U.S. plants, or 50–75 percent of their last weekly paycheck until they can retire. But as good as the plan sounds, it is not popular with GM workers in California for whom it was designed. About 700 workers laid off in California were offered jobs in Oklahoma City. But many did not want to go. Some said GM should look instead for volunteers; others pled hardship. Still others complained that it was too far to move. One veteran who chose to move said, "It's better than sitting around doing nothing waiting for a job that might never be there." But he was in the minority.

In Chicago, a Ford assembly plant was to be the site of a program that would assure 80 percent of the work force immunity from layoffs. To get that concession from management the union had to agree to the following: mandatory Saturday overtime when necessary, recall of workers based on performance rather than seniority, and tougher absenteeism measures. When asked to vote on the plan, the workers rejected it. One employee didn't like the recall procedure change. He said, "I've got a good work record now, but I don't know what it'll be a couple years from now." Another worker did not like required weekend overtime. "Nobody tells me I have to work on Saturday," he said.

Union officials had been solidly behind the two proposals. One official said, "What can you do to please everybody? We thought we were helping those people."[1]

19

"Because the union's objectives are frequently incompatible with those of management, it's not surprising that traditional labor-management relations have been characterized by a high degree of conflict."

ROBERT ALLEN AND
TIMOTHY KEAVENY

A UNION
is a formal association of workers that promotes the welfare of its members.

Some people contend that a **union,** as a formal association of workers that promotes the welfare of its members, represents an "outside force" caused by management neglect. Others argue that the union is an internal force because it is made up of employees in an organization. Regardless of the internal/external issue, it is an undeniable fact that the existence of a union or of unionization pressure presents an additional challenge for managers and personnel specialists.

Figure 19–1 shows a typical set of responsibilities for the personnel unit and operating managers in dealing with unions. This pattern may vary in different organizations. In some organizations, the personnel unit does not become involved at all with labor relations because the operating management handles them. In other organizations, the personnel unit is almost completely in charge of labor relations. The division of responsibilities shown in Figure 19–1 is a midpoint between these extremes.

This chapter takes a broad look at some of the trends and philosophies associated with unionism. The evolution and history of unions, current trends, union structures, and unionism in the public sector are all discussed. Specific information on how unions become employee representatives is presented also.

When employees choose a union to represent them, formal collective bargaining between management and union representatives over certain issues must occur. Once these issues are resolved into a labor contract, management and union representatives must work together to manage the contract and prevent grievances. Grievances are formal complaints filed by workers with management. Collective bargaining and grievance procedures are two of the important interfaces that occur between management and labor unions once a union has gained recognition as a legal representative of employee interests. Both areas are examined in the next chapter.

PERSONNEL UNIT	MANAGERS
■ Deals with union organizing attempts at the company level	■ Provide conditions conducive to a positive relationship with employees
■ Monitors "climate" for unionization and union relationships	■ Avoid unfair labor practices during organizing efforts
■ Helps negotiate labor agreements	■ Administer the labor agreement on daily basis
■ Provides detailed knowledge of labor legislation as may be necessary	■ Resolve grievances and problems between management and employees/union members

FIGURE 19–1
Union Relations Responsibilities.

CHAPTER 19   NATURE OF UNION-MANAGEMENT RELATIONS

Most of the concepts underlying unionism in the United States have come from philosophies and ideas about organized labor that originated in Western Europe, especially England. The Industrial Revolution encouraged both employers and employees to seek personal advancement through collective action because individual effort was inadequate. However, unionism in the United States has developed its own philosophy and concepts.

Unionism in the U.S.

Unionism in the United States has followed a somewhat different pattern than unionism in other countries. In such countries as Italy, England, and Japan, the union movement has been at the forefront of nationwide political trends. For the most part, this politicalization has not been the case in the United States. Perhaps the reason is that workers in the U.S. tend to identify with the American free enterprise system. Further, there is a lesser degree of class consciousness and conflict between the working class and the management class in the United States than in many other countries. Ownership of private property by both management and union members is a further mediating influence in the United States.

Job-Centered Emphasis. The primary emphasis of unionism in the United States has been the collective pursuit of "bread-and-butter" issues: higher wages, shorter working hours, job security, and good working conditions. To help protect workers' security, large unions in the United States have become politically active, although such activity has traditionally been oriented more toward workplace issues than toward broad social concerns. However, since the mid-1960s unions have taken positions on economic issues, on full employment, and on some social issues as well.

A good example of a job-centered emphasis is the current attempt of hospital unions to improve health and safety for hospital workers. Hospitals use almost twice as many chemicals as manufacturers do and many of the chemicals are hazardous. In addition, there are other hazards, such as disposing of contaminated needles and linen. In fact, hospital workers are 41 percent more likely to need time off for a serious accident or injury than the average worker. Health workers unions have made some progress toward better conditions. Some hospitals have agreed to form safety committees, and Oregon nurses have won the right to be transferred away from assignments and equipment they feel are hazardous.[2]

Unions as a Countervailing Force. Perhaps the most beneficial view of unions is to see them as a countervailing force to help keep management "honest" and to make management consider the impact of its policies upon its employees. However, a rather delicate balance exists between management power and union power in an organization. It is very easy for this balance to be tipped one way or the other.

Through their respective representatives management and unions spend a great deal of time and effort disagreeing with each other. This disagreement is to be expected because of the nature of their built-in adversary roles. Yet, it is naive to suppose that either position or group is right all the time; neither is it correct to assume that there are many serious disagreements that lead to strikes. Figure 19–2 indicates that time lost to work stoppages because of strikes of lockouts has constituted a relatively small percentage of total work time. The U.S. figures are considerably lower than those of many other countries.

Unionism in Europe

Unions in a number of European countries have a somewhat different emphasis. They tend to be very ideological and political because they see themselves representing the working class. In several European countries political parties and trade unions work together; in Great Britain, one of the major political parties actually is named the Labour Party. One writer notes that European unions:

. . . embarked upon a course of advancing the entire working class by transforming the total society, in contrast to the emphasis of the American movement on the immediate specifics of wages, hours, and working conditions for its members only.[3]

The degree of union involvement in some European countries is demonstrated by statistics indicating that almost all wage earners in Austria, Belgium, and Sweden are covered by collective bargaining agreements.

Codetermination. Another facet of foreign unions that has not been widely adopted in the United States is the notion of worker involve-

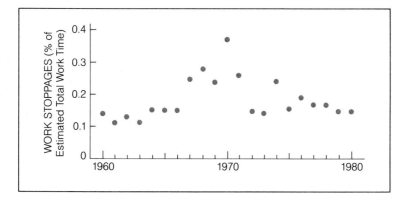

FIGURE 19–2
Work Stoppages in the U.S.

SOURCE: U.S. Department of Labor, Bureau of Labor Statistics, *Handbook of Labor Statistics, 1980* (Washington, DC: Government Printing Office, December 1980), p. 415, as updated.

CODETERMINATION is a practice whereby union or worker representatives are given positions on a company's board of directors.

ment in managerial decision making. **Codetermination** occurs when union or worker representatives are given positions on a company's board of directors.

Different countries have different forms of codetermination. For example, in West Germany workers are represented on the board of directors and exercise some veto power over certain proposals by management. However, worker representatives usually cannot outvote management and stockholder representatives. Codetermination is also a key part of labor relations in Sweden.

Unionism in Japan

In Japan company unions rather than national unions are predominate, especially in firms having over 500 employees. During the spring of every year employees use wall posters and signs to press for wage increases, but strikes are rare.[4] This activity is called the People's Spring Offensive and includes other social groups as well as labor unions.

Many Japanese employers provide lifetime employment and emphasize paternalism and seniority. Companies often provide housing, vacations, and medical coverage for employees.

In the past, Japanese workers rarely changed employers. However, some shifts began in the late 1970s as a result of a slowdown in the Japanese economy. Layoffs of unneeded workers have occurred and a growing number of highly educated, younger workers are pushing for advancement. Such changes are expected to continue and probably will significantly change the labor/management scene in Japan during the late 1980s.

Merging Concepts of Unionism

As a result of widespread international trade and the growing number of international firms, cross-fertilization of unionism concepts between the United States and other countries is on the increase. International labor organizations may be labor's response to the multinational corporation. Already, automobile workers' unions in Europe and the United States are discussing cooperative efforts. However, it is unlikely that a true labor party will be formed in the United States or that the labor unions in Europe and Japan will become less politically oriented. Some interchange and adaptations will occur, but the European and American unions probably will retain distinctly different characteristics.

Union/Management Cooperation

The practice of worker participation through codetermination is not common in the U.S. However, in return for wage freezes and financial assistance, the president of the United Auto Workers has been made a member of the board of directors of Chrysler Corporation. Such a highly visible step toward codetermination may be repeated in the future in individual situations. However, a number of U.S. unions have opposed codetermination as a goal of labor and it is unlikely that it will become widespread.[6]

Labor/Management Committees

An example of union/management cooperation that has been successful in the U.S. is labor/management committees. These committees have been used to attract industries to communities such as Evansville, Indiana, and Scranton, Pennsylvania whose economic bases are changing. Jointly supported programs dealing with employee absenteeism, vandalism, and alcoholism problems also have been developed between individual companies and unions.

Can you compare and contrast U.S. and foreign unionism?

CHAPTER 19   NATURE OF UNION-MANAGEMENT RELATIONS

Reliable statistics on union membership in the United States are very difficult to obtain. Some unions tend to exaggerate membership reports to gain respect. Other unions have been known to report fewer members than they actually have for financial reasons, such as trying to avoid making higher payments to the labor federation to which they belong.

Membership Trends

Figures available from the Bureau of Labor Statistics showed that membership in labor unions and public and professional employee associations headquartered in the United States, excluding Canadian members, was 19.0 million in 1984. It is revealing that the number of union members as a percent of the total work force has declined from 24.7 percent in 1970 to 19.0 percent in 1984. Figure 19–3 shows this decline on the chart. What this decline indicates is that labor unions are not adding members as fast as new employees are being added to the work force.

Part of the reason for the slowdown in membership growth is the shifting character of the U.S. work force. The highly unionized manufacturing industries, such as the automobile and steel industries, are those that have been hardest hit by layoffs and work-force reductions, causing union membership to shrink. At the same time, the number of traditionally nonunionized white-collar and women workers has been increasing. As a result, the overall figure showing approximately 20 percent of the work force to be unionized is somewhat misleading. Certain industries are quite heavily unionized, whereas others are hardly unionized at all.

Two recent developments have caused union concern and seem to

FIGURE 19–3
Union Membership as a Proportion of the Labor Force, 1970–1984

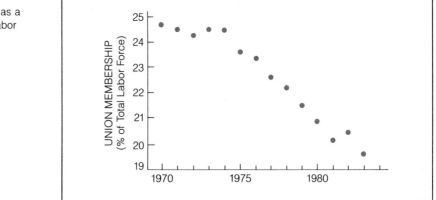

SOURCE: U.S. Department of Labor, Bureau of Labor Statistics.

give management more weapons to use in dealing with undesirable union situations. These are the use of bankruptcy and plant closures.

Bankruptcy. A 1984 decision by the Supreme Court involving a New Jersey building materials company named Bildisco ruled that companies can declare bankruptcy and immediately ignore their labor contracts. It also set broad standards whereby federal judges can decide if dismantling of the labor agreement was justified.

Continental Airlines declared bankruptcy and then continued to operate in reorganization, having gotten out of a very expensive union contract. Unions argued that this tactic took away their ability to negotiate with employers. Employers, on the other hand, felt that it was necessary for their survival in deregulated industries which permit open competition and often engage in price-cutting wars.[7]

Congress finally decided the issue in 1984 when it passed a new bankruptcy law. The law basically represents a compromise between the positions of employers and labor unions. Under the law an employer must petition the courts for a hearing on proposed changes in a labor contract and must provide financial data to the union. The court can then allow an employer to reject a labor contract if the court finds that the union rejected the proposal without good cause and evidence clearly supports the employer's plea for relief.

Plant Closings. During the 1970s, unions sometimes successfully kept companies from moving their plant locations. But when Otis Elevator Company wanted to move its research and development function from New Jersey to Connecticut, the Supreme Court decided that an employer could close a business for economic reasons without bargaining with employees over the decision. Later rulings by the National Labor Relations Board (NLRB) have expanded the law so that companies are now relatively free to move. Unions contend that such decisions will lead to a wave of plant closings to escape unions' influence, but management feels such steps are only fair because they are management rights and unrelated to labor costs.[8]

White-Collar Unionism

White-collar unionization efforts are increasing for several reasons. One is that advances in technology have boosted the number of white-collar workers in the work force. With the proportion of employees in white-collar jobs relative to manufacturing jobs on the increase, unions have had to focus on white-collar areas in order to obtain new members.

Further, union leaders feel there is a growing realization among white-collar workers and professionals that their employment problems are not too different from those of manufacturing workers in the areas of pay, job security, and grievances. Also, professionals in areas such as nursing, teaching, and engineering are seen as potential union members. For example, because of increases won by the Teamsters

Union for other employees at Honeywell Corporation in Minneapolis, over 1,000 engineers and technicians signed cards requesting a union representation election.[9]

However, studies of professionals show a quite different mentality and set of preferences than those held by blue-collar union members. For example, one study found that professionals define fairness in pay differently than blue-collar workers. The professionals saw fairness as pay based on individual performance, while the blue-collar workers always have preferred pay based on equality and seniority.[10]

Unionism in the Public Sector

Unions have been somewhat successful in finding members in the public sector. An increasing number of local, state, and federal government employees have joined unions. Figure 19–4 shows that government union memberships, especially at the local and federal levels, grew slightly during the late 1970s and then leveled off.

State and Local Government Unionism. Unionism of state and local government employees presents some unique problems and challenges. First, many unionized local government employees are in exclusive and critical service areas. Police officers, firefighters, and sanitation workers all provide essential services in most cities. Allowing these workers to strike endangers public health and safety. Consequently, over 30 states have laws prohibiting public employee work stoppages. These laws also identify a variety of ways to resolve negotiation impasses including arbitration.

FIGURE 19–4
Governmental Union
Membership.

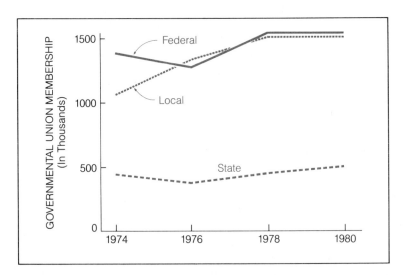

SOURCE: U.S. Department of Labor, Bureau of Labor Statistics, *Handbook of Labor Statistics, 1980* (Washington, DC: Government Printing Office, December 1980), pp. 407–408, as updated.

The impact of public employee wage increases on taxes is another concern. As taxpayers, the general public is increasingly critical of state and local government tax expenditures. Thus wage demands by public employees are often met with distrust and become political issues. In one metropolitan school district, voters approved a spending lid of 7 percent on funding. Yet, a state court ordered a 16 percent increase in teaching salaries. The only course of action for the school board was to cut school programs such as junior high athletics, art programs, and the like, so that the salary hike could be put in effect.

Another problem is that state and local government unions often face widely varying laws and hiring policies from city to city and state to state. The existence of civil service and so-called merit systems makes the public sector vastly different from the private sector. State and local laws not federal labor laws, take precedence, so unique legal situations often occur. Also, lack of experience with unions and the collective bargaining process among local and state officials hampers union/management relations. Consider a farmer and a dentist serving on a county board; their limited knowledge of union-related activites and processes might easily stand in the way of arriving at effective union/management decisions.

Unionism and the Federal Government. Although unions in the federal government hold the same basic philosophy as unions in the private sector, they do differ somewhat. Through past executive orders and laws, realistic methods of labor/management relations that consider the special circumstances present in the federal government have been established. The Office of Personnel Management has considerable control over personnel policies and regulations. For example, because of limitations on collective bargaining, federal government unions cannot bargain over wages. Allowing federal employees to organize and join unions definitely presents new problems and challenges for personnel administration in the federal government.

Can you describe the current state of U.S. unionization?

Future Trends in Unionism

During the 1980s unions will face some interesting challenges. Several of the most likely ones are noted below:

Public Opinion and Unions. Numerous polls of public opinion have revealed that unions are increasingly being viewed in a negative light. Since 1980, an important number of labor-backed congressional candidates have lost elections. Such results reduce labor's political power. Consequently, many programs that were formerly backed by labor face modification or repeal. Labor unions have been seen as a major reason for inflation and the decline in productivity. In addition, wage increases tied to cost-of-living clauses in labor contracts that are not given equally to nonunionized workers have created resentment rather than a desire to join a union among many Americans. Unions will have to respond to such views effectively if they are to improve their public image.

Shifting Economic Factors. Another challenge for unions is halting the decline in the proportion of their membership in the work force. As mentioned earlier, shifts in the U.S. work force are causing an increase in workers in groups that traditionally resist unionization. Women, white-collar workers, and professionals have been reluctant to join unions. Yet, because of their growth, these groups represent the market segment with the greatest potential for union membership.

Geographic shifts in population and industries also represent a challenge for unions. The greatest economic growth is occurring in the so-called Sun Belt states located in the Southwest, South, and West. Social and cultural values in those areas have traditionally been rather anti-union. Yet, as facilities are closed in northern and eastern states, union jobs are being reduced. Consequently, unions must follow the jobs to the new areas to maintain membership and grow.

Emerging Issues in Unionism. In the future, unions will be facing a number of issues that they have not yet had to confront seriously. One is the concern about foreign imports displacing American jobs and workers. It is no coincidence that the growth in Japanese automobile sales in the U.S. has been accompanied by an increase in the number of members of the United Auto Workers who have been laid off or lost their jobs. Similar job displacements have occurred in the electronics and textile industries. Unions have tried to attack such problems by working with management to increase productivity, lobbying with government officials to push for import restrictions, and talking with foreign firms to attract foreign-owned industrial facilities to the U.S.

Foreign competition seems to be having the indirect effect of reducing the strength of certain unions. It has forced management in the auto and steel industries to replace expensive labor with machines. The long-term effect of this trend has been to reduce the strength of the UAW and United Steel Workers (USW) as their members retire or move to other industries.

A number of other issues also must be confronted. Management's increasing sophistication and use of special tactics to keep workers satisfied has resulted in drastic changes in the labor scene, like the drop from 78 percent to 52 percent in the unionized share of coal production.[11] A more pervasive issue is the "generation gap": union members are often younger and more educated than the national leaders of the labor movement. These members do not want to "do as they are told" and may view union leaders as "out of step" with them. This generation gap can only be resolved by a transition in leaders, a process which takes time and is often resisted by older union leaders.

The advent of robotics and increased computerization are accelerating the movement of labor out of blue-collar jobs and into white-collar jobs. Because unions may soon be forced to change to survive, it is helpful to look at how today's unions are structured.

Can you describe some future trends U.S. unions face?

UNION STRUCTURE

Unions have developed complex organizational structures with multiple levels of leadership. As Figure 19–5 illustrates, the American Federation of Labor and the Congress of Industrial Organizations (AFL-CIO) is composed of a number of individual unions.

The AFL-CIO is a rather loose confederation of national unions, each of which is semiautonomous. The AFL-CIO represents nearly two-thirds of the national unions in this country. Approximately one-third of the nationals, however, are not affiliated with the AFL-CIO. For example, the United Mine Workers and the International Brotherhood of Longshoremen are not members of the AFL-CIO.

Union Hierarchy

The national or international unions are autonomous from the federation though they often are affiliated with it. They have their own boards, collect dues, have specialized publications, and separate constitutions and bylaws. Such national/international unions as the United Steel Workers (USW) or the American Federation of State, County, and Municipal Employees (AFSCME) determine broad union policy and

FIGURE 19-5

Structure of the AFL-CIO.

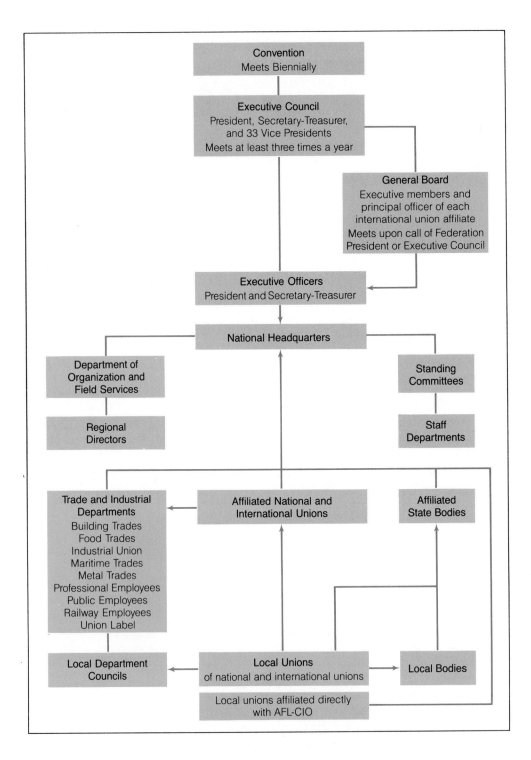

SOURCE: U.S. Department of Labor, Bureau of Labor Statistics, *Directory of National Unions and Employee Associations, 1977.* (Washington, DC: Government Printing Office, 1977), p. 2.

provide services to local union units. They also help maintain financial records, provide a base from which additional organization drives may take place, and control the money for strike funds.

Intermediate union organizational units coordinate the activities of a number of local unions. All the local unions in a state, or in several states, may be grouped together with some type of joint governing board. Such organizations may be citywide, statewide, or multistate-wide.

Local Unions

Local unions may be centered around a particular employer organization or around a particular geographical location. For example, the Communication Workers of America local in Dallas, Texas, might include all the nonexempt Southwestern Bell telephone company employees in Dallas. (Nonexempt employees are subject to the overtime provisions of federal wage and hour laws).

The policy-making process of the local union is generally democratic in form. Members vote on suggestions by either the membership or the officers. Normally, secret ballots are used. Officers in local unions are elected by the membership and are subject to removal if they do not perform satisfactorily. For this reason, local union officers tend to be very concerned with the effect of their actions on the membership. Then tend to react to situations as politicians would react because they, too, are concerned about obtaining votes.

Business Agents and Union Stewards. Some unions have *business agents,* who are full-time union officials and are usually elected. The agent may run the local headquarters, help negotiate contracts with management, and may become involved in any attempts to unionize employees in other firms. *Union stewards* are usually elected by the local union membership and represent the lowest elected level in the local union. They usually negotiate grievances with the supervisors and generally represent the workers at the work site.

*Can you describe how unions in the U.S.
are typically structured?*

EVOLUTION OF U.S. UNIONS

It has been suggested that the labor movement in the United States arose when when craftsmen in similar occupations banded together voluntarily to protect their jobs.[13] Voluntary union membership is based on *job consciousness:* jobs are a scarce resource and union members must protect them. Under this line of reasoning, the union's chief concern is *job control.* A union is expected to control the jobs under the union's jurisdiction, such as plumbing, electrical work, or carpentry. Job control has been one of the cornerstones of American unionism.

As early as 1794, shoemakers in the United States organized into a union, picketed, and conducted strikes. However, in the early days, unions in the United States received very little support from the courts. In 1806, when the shoemakers' union struck for higher wages, a Philadelphia court found union members guilty of engaging in a *criminal conspiracy* to raise wages.

Commonwealth v. Hunt

In 1842 a very important legal landmark, the case of *Commonwealth v. Hunt*, was decided. The Massachusetts Supreme Court ruled that: "For a union to be guilty of conspiracy, either its objective or the means used to reach it must be criminal or unlawful."[14] As a result of this decision, unions were no longer seen as illegal conspiracies in the eyes of the courts, and the conspiracy idea lost favor.

Post–Civil War Period

The end of the Civil War in 1865 was followed by rapid industrial expansion and a growth of giant business trusts. The 1870s were characterized by industrial unrest, low wages, long hours, and considerable unemployment. In 1877, great railroad strikes spread through the major U.S. railroad lines in protest against the practices of railroad management. Eight years later, a group of workers formed the Knights of Labor.

Knights of Labor. The goals of the Knights of Labor were: (1) to establish one large union embracing all workers and (2) to establish a cooperative economic system to replace capitalism. They emphasized "political reform" and the establishment of "work cooperatives." However, after their peak in 1885, the Knights soon faded from the labor scene.

American Federation of Labor. In 1886, the American Federation of Labor (AFL) was formed as a federation of independent national unions. Its basic principle was to organize *skilled craft workers*, like carpenters and plumbers, to bargain for such "bread-and-butter" issues as wages and working conditions. Samuel Gompers was the AFL's chief spokesman and served as president until his death in 1924.

At first, the AFL grew very slowly. Six years after its formation, its total membership amounted to only 250,000. However, it managed to survive in the face of adversity while other labor groups withered and died.

While *craft unions* (made up of skilled craftsmen) survived and the AFL grew, the Civil War gave factories a big boost. Factory mass-production methods, which used semiskilled or unskilled workers, were necessary to supply the armies. Though factories provided a potential area of expansion for unions, they were very hard to organize. Unions found they could not control entry to factory jobs because most of the jobs were filled by semiskilled workers who had no tradition of unionism. This difference ultimately led to the founding of the Congress for Industrial Organization (CIO) in 1938. Unionism outside the skilled crafts remained very uncertain, with the consequence that *industrial unions* were formed much later than *craft unions*.

Early Labor Legislation. The right to organize workers and engage in collective bargaining is of little value if workers are not free to exercise it. As historical evidence shows, management has used practices calculated to prevent workers from using this right, and the federal government has taken action to both hamper unions and protect them.

Sherman and Clayton Acts. The passage of the Sherman Antitrust Act in 1890 forbade monopolies and efforts to illegally restrain trade. Later, as a result of a 1908 Supreme Court case *(Loewe* v. *Lawlor),* union boycott efforts were classed as attempts to restrain trade.

In 1914 the Clayton Act, which limited the use of injunctions in labor disputes, was passed. However, it had little effect on the labor movement in the United States because the courts interpreted the Clayton Act to mean that the *activities* of a union determined whether or not it was in violation of the law. As a result, union strength declined throughout the 1920s.

Railway Labor Act. The Railway Labor Act (1926) was significant because it represented a shift in governmental regulation of unions. As a result of a joint effort of railroad management and unions to reduce the possibilities of transportation strikes, this act gave railroad employees "the right to organize and bargain collectively through representatives of their own choosing." In 1936, airlines and their employees were added to those covered by this act. Both these industries are still covered by this act instead of by others passed later.

The act set up a rather complex series of steps to prevent work stoppages. Although a detailed explanation is beyond the scope of this book, it should be noted that many labor experts today feel that the airline and railroad industries should be covered under the same laws as all other industries. Because times have changed, they argue that the Railway Labor Act should be eliminated.[15]

Norris-LaGuardia Act. In 1932 Congress passed the Norris-LaGuardia Act, which guaranteed workers some rights to organize and restricted the issuance of court injunctions in labor disputes. The Norris-LaGuardia Act substantially freed union activity from court interference and made the infamous *"yellow dog" contract* illegal. Under this type of contract, signed by the worker as a condition of employment, the employee agreed not to join a union upon penalty of discharge. It was called a yellow dog contract because, according to union sympathizers, only a "yellow dog" would take a job under such conditions.

In 1933 the National Industry Recovery Act (NIRA) was passed. It contained, among other clauses, provisions extending the policies of the Railway Labor Act for railroad employees into interstate commerce. Also, the act set up election machinery permitting employees to choose collective bargaining representatives. However, the NIRA was declared unconstitutional in 1935, and it was replaced by the Wagner Act.

Can you sketch U.S. labor history from
1800 to 1932?

The progress made by unions through the early 1930s provided the basis for the development and passage of several acts: (1) the *Wagner Act*, (2) The *Taft-Hartley Act*, and (3) the *Landrum-Griffin Act*. These later acts have the most direct and continuing impact on employers and unions today and form "the National Labor Code."

Each of the acts in the Code was enacted to protect some entity in the union/management relationship. Figure 19–6 shows each of the segments of the code and which entity received the greatest protection. The nature of this protection will become clearer as each of the acts is discussed.

The Wagner Act (National Labor Relations Act)

The Wagner Act has been called the Magna Carta of labor and was, by anyone's standards, pro-union. It encouraged union growth in three ways:

1. It established the right to organize, unhampered by management interference.
2. It provided definitions of unfair labor practices on the part of management.
3. It set up the National Labor Relations Board to see that the rules were followed.

The NLRB, although set up as an impartial umpire of the organizing process, changes its emphasis depending upon which political party is in power to appoint members.[16]

The act established the principle that employees should be protected in their rights to form a union and to bargain collectively. To protect union rights, the act made it an unfair labor practice for an employer to do any of the following:[17]

1. Interfere with, restrain, or coerce employees in the exercise of their rights to organize, bargain collectively, and engage in other concerted activities for their mutual aid or protection
2. Dominate or interfere with the formation or administration of any labor organization or contribute financial or other support to it
3. Encourage or discourage membership in any labor organization by discrimination with regard to hiring or tenure or conditions of employment, subject to an exception for valid union security agreement
4. Discharge or otherwise discriminate against an employee because he or she filed charges or gave testimony under the act
5. Refuse to bargain collectively with representatives of the employees

The effect of the act was to dramatically increase union membership during the period from 1935 to 1947. It increased approximately fourfold to 14 million members during those 12 years.

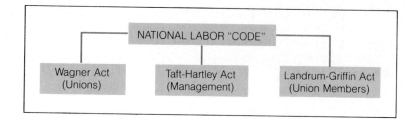

FIGURE 19–6
National Labor Code.

The Taft-Hartley Act (Labor Management Relations Act)

When World War II ended, the pent-up demand for goods was frustrated by numerous strikes—about three times as many as before the war. These conditions led to the passage of the *Taft-Hartley Act* in 1947.

The Taft-Hartley Act was an attempt to balance the collective bargaining equation. It was designed to offset the pro-union Wagner Act by limiting union tactics and was considered to be *pro-management*. It provided the second part of the National Labor Code.

The new law amended or qualified in some respect all of the Wagner Act's major provisions and an entirely new code of conduct for unions was established. The Taft-Hartley Act forbade a series of unfair labor practices by unions. It became unlawful for a *union* to:[18]

1. Restrain or coerce employees in the exercise of their rights under the act; restrain or coerce any employer in the selection of his bargaining or grievance representative
2. Cause or attempt to cause an employer to discriminate against an employee on account of membership or nonmembership in a labor organization, subject to an exception for a valid union shop agreement
3. Refuse to bargain collectively in good faith with an employer if the union has been designated as bargaining agent by a majority of the employees
4. Induce or encourage employees to stop work for the object of forcing an employer or self-employed person to join a union or forcing an employer or other person to stop doing business with any other person (boycott provisions)
5. Induce or encourage employees to stop work for the object of forcing an employer to assign particular work to members of a union instead of to members of another union (jurisdictional strike)
6. Charge an excessive or discriminatory fee as a condition to becoming a member of the union
7. Cause or attempt to cause an employer to pay for services that are not performed or are not to be performed (featherbedding)

"Right to Work." One specific provision (Section 14b) in the Taft-Hartley Act deserves special explanation. The so-called right-to-work provision outlaws the closed shop, except in construction-related occupations and allows states to pass right-to-work laws. A **closed shop** requires individuals to join a union before they can be hired.

A CLOSED SHOP requires individuals to join a union before they can be hired.

The act did allow the *union shop*, which requires that an employee join the union, usually 30–60 days after being hired. Right-to-work laws are state laws that prohibit both the closed shop and the union shop. They were so named because they allow a person the "right to work" without having to join a union. Approximately 20 states have enacted these laws (see Figure 19–7).

The Landrum-Griffin Act (Labor/Management Reporting and Disclosure Act)

In 1959, the third segment of the National Labor Code, the Landrum-Griffin Act, was passed as a result of a congressional committee's findings on union corruption. The major union investigated was the Teamsters Union headed by Dave Beck and James Hoffa. This law was aimed at protecting individual union members. Among the provisions of the Landrum-Griffin Act are:[19]

1. Every labor organization is required to have a constitution and by-laws containing certain minimum standards and safeguards.
2. Reports on the union's policies and procedures, as well as an annual financial report, must be filed with the Secretary of Labor and must be disclosed to the union's members.
3. Union members must have a bill of rights to protect their rights within the union.
4. Standards are established for union trusteeship and union elections.
5. Reports on trusteeships must be made to the Secretary of Labor.
6. A fiduciary relationship is imposed upon union officers.
7. Union leaders are required to file reports with the Secretary of Labor on conflict-of-interest transactions.
8. The Secretary of Labor is made a watchdog of union conduct. He is a custodian of reports from unions and their officers and he is given the power to investigate and prosecute violations of many of the provisions of the act.

Union Member Rights. A union is a democratic institution in which union members vote on and elect officers and approve labor contracts. The Landrum-Griffin Act was passed to ensure that the federal government protects those democratic rights. Some of the important rights guaranteed to individual union members are:

1. Right to nominate and vote on officers
2. Right to attend and participate in union meetings
3. Right to have pension funds properly managed

In a few instances, union officers have attempted to maintain their jobs by physically harassing or attacking individuals who try to oust them from office. An extreme example occurred in the early 1970s when the president of the United Mine Workers ordered the person running against him murdered. In other cases, union officials have "milked" pension fund monies for their own use. Such instances are not typical of most unions, but illustrate the need for individual union members to be protected.

FIGURE 19–7
Right-to-Work States.

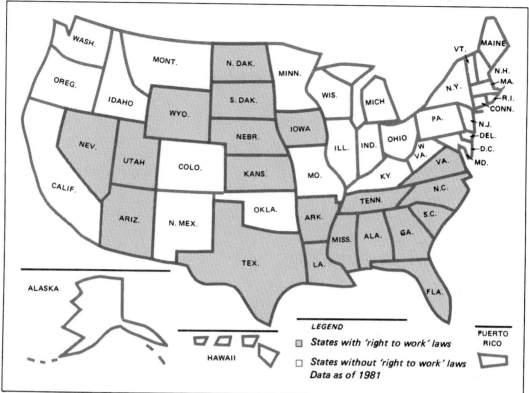

LEGEND
☐ States with 'right to work' laws
☐ States without 'right to work' laws
Data as of 1981

Union employees can strike a union just as they can strike any other employer. That happened when the Washington, D.C., headquarters of the American Federation of Government Workers was struck by 120 workers demanding fair negotiating practices. The pickets chanted, "Practice what you preach." Ultimately the strike was settled.[20]

As society changes, the National Labor Code will continue to evolve. The collective bargaining relationship may need to be revised again. Proposed extensions of the National Labor Code include: compulsory arbitration; extended injunction powers for the President in national emergency situations; and some kinds of extension of the price-wage control system to include management/union agreements. The important point is that this legal foundation of labor/management relations *does* change with time.

Can you explain the acts of the National Labor Code?

THE ORGANIZING PROCESS

The following overview of the organizing process is designed to familiarize you with how unions become employee representatives. Figure 19–8 shows the stages in a typical unionization effort. The first stage is handbilling.

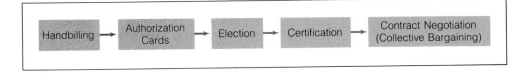

FIGURE 19-8
Typical Unionization Process.

Handbilling

This stage serves the same purpose as advertising does for a product: it creates interest in "buying" the union. Brochures, leaflets, or circulars are all types of handbills. These items can be passed out to employees as they leave work, mailed to their homes, or even attached to their vehicles. Their purpose is to convince employees to sign authorization cards.

Authorization Card

This card, which is signed by an employee, indicates the employee's desire to vote on having a union. It does not necessarily mean that the employee is in favor of a union, but that he or she would like to have the opportunity to vote on having one. One reason employees who do not want a union might sign an authorization card is to attract management's attention to the fact that employees are disgruntled.

Candidates Favoring Unionization. One study found that employees who were dissatisfied with wages and benefits, job security, and supervisory treatment tended to vote for union representation. However, the type of work done did not seem to be as great a factor in unionization as working conditions.[21]

A listing by the United Steel Workers of key factors leading to success in organizing white-collar workers reads like a checklist of "management don'ts." Important areas of employee discontent that can lead to unionization include:[22]

1. A lack of communication between employees and management
2. Management's ignorance of workers' problems
3. Lower salary scales than most other employers in the same geographical areas
4. Salary inequities in which people doing identical work receive different rates of pay.
5. Inequities in promotions in relation to seniority
6. The absence of medical and surgical insurance, sick leave, or noncontributory pension plans.
7. Poor working conditions
8. Overtime work without compensation
9. Constant pressure and harassment for work completion
10. Management that treats employees as if the employees were unintelligent.

Representation Election

An election to determine if a union will represent the employees is supervised by the NLRB or another legal body. If two unions are attempting to represent employees, the employees will have three choices: union A, union B, or no.

An employer can choose not to contest an election and have a *consent election*. However, employers usually do contest an election and attempt to provide employees with information to convince them not to vote for a union. The unfair practices identified in both the Wagner Act and the Taft-Hartley Act place restrictions on the actions of both an employer and the union in this process.

Do's and Don'ts. A number of tactics are used by management representatives to try to defeat a unionization effort. Such tactics often begin when handbills appear or when authorization cards are being distributed. Figure 19–9 contains a list of some of the more common tactics that management can and cannot use. A tactic to avoid was the one

FIGURE 19–9

Management Dos &
Don'ts in the Unionization
Process.

DO	DON'T
■ Tell employees about current wages and benefits and how they compare to other firms	■ Promise employees pay increases or promotions if they vote against the union
■ Tell employees you will use all legal means to oppose unionization	■ Threaten employees with termination or discriminate when disciplining employees
■ Tell employees the disadvantages of having a union (especially cost of dues, assessments, and requirements of membership)	■ Threaten to close down or move the company if a union is voted in
■ Show employees articles about unions and negative experiences others have had elsewhere	■ Spy on or have someone spy on union meetings
■ Explain the unionization process to your employees accurately	■ Make a speech to employees or groups at work within 24 hours of the election (before that, it is allowed)
■ Forbid distribution of union literature during work hours in work areas	■ Ask employees how they plan to vote or if they have signed authorization cards
■ Enforce disciplinary policies and rules in a consistent and fair manner	■ Urge employees to persuade others to vote against the union (such a vote must be initiated solely by the employee)

taken by the owner-manager of a small manufacturing firm who fired a worker for poor job performance who was soliciting authorization cards from other employees at lunch. The worker's poor performance was not adequately documented and the company was asked why the worker's performance became so poor so quickly. The result was that the employee was reinstated and a representation election was ordered. However the company won the election 28 to 3. If hasty action had not been taken by management, the entire matter would have died down much sooner and no election would have been held.

Some firms have experts who specialize in helping management combat unionization efforts. But, as one writer points out, the most important actions in reducing unionization threats are listening to employees and responding to their real concerns.[24]

Election Process. Assuming an election is held, the union only needs to receive the votes of a *majority of those voting* in the election. For example, if a group of 200 employees is the identified unit and only 50 people vote, only 26 employees would need to vote "yes" in order for a union to be named as the representative of all 200. If either side believes that unfair labor practices have been used by the other side, the election results can be appealed to the NLRB. If the NLRB finds that unfair practices were used, it can order a new election. Assuming that no unfair practices have been used and the union obtains a majority in the election, the union then petitions the NLRB for certification.

Certification

Official certification of a union as the legal representative for employees is given by the NLRB, or the relevant body, after reviewing the results of the election. Once certified, the union attempts to negotiate a contract with the employer. The employer *must* bargain, as it is an unfair labor practice to refuse to bargain with a certified union.

Contract Negotiation (Collective Bargaining)

Negotiation of a labor contract is one of the most important methods used by unions to obtain their major goals. A general discussion of collective bargaining is contained in the next chapter.

When a union is certified and a contract is negotiated, problems in the relationship are not necessarily over. For example, J. P. Stevens, a textile manufacturer, and the Textile Workers Union fought a bitter battle for many years; ultimately, the union was certified and gained a contract. During the long fight the company had nurtured anti-union sentiment in its plant managers. Now a time had come to learn to live with the union, and it was a bitter pill for some to swallow.[25]

Decertification

DECERTIFICATION is a process whereby a union is removed as the representative of a group of employees.

Employees who have a union and no longer wish to be represented by it can utilize the election process called **decertification**. The decertification process is very similar to the unionization process and requires that employees attempting to oust a union obtain decertification authorization cards signed by at least 30 percent of the employees in the bargaining unit. Then an election is called, and if a majority of those voting in the election vote to remove the union, the decertification effort succeeds. One caution, however, is that management may not assist the decertification effort in any way by providing assistance or funding.

Can you identify and discuss how a union becomes a representative of employees?

PERSONNEL TODAY AND TOMORROW

"YOU-JUST-CAN'T-WIN DEPT."—FIRM SUES WORKERS FOR FAILING TO STRIKE

An Ohio nursing home sued a union because the union *didn't* go on strike. When the Service Employees International Union contract with Colonial Manor Nursing Home near Youngstown, Ohio, expired in May, both sides decided to keep negotiating. But talks bogged down, and the union rejected a management offer. In late June, the union's members authorized a strike. The union gave Colonial Manor a 10-day notice of a strike, as required by federal law.

The nursing home responded by recruiting, interviewing, and training people to fill the 47 jobs it expected to be vacant on July 12, the day it believed the strike would begin. Colonial Manor, a subsidiary of Health Enterprises, Inc., says this effort cost $15,000.

"We had everybody there on July 12," but the union workers "never went on strike. They all came to work," says Bertyl Johnson, Colonial Manor's vice-president and general counsel. "We had to meet payroll for two staffs for a couple of days."

So the company struck back in the county court, asking $3 million in punitive damages in addition to actual costs. Johnson concedes he isn't aware of any precedent for the action. But he says, "When you think you have a wrong committed against you, you're entitled to go to court. They told us they were going to strike and they didn't."

Kenneth Lewis, the union local's president, says a company official told him "He'd sue me, but I thought he was kidding. Our lawyer thought it was hilarious; he never heard of such a thing."

The union claims it made it clear that it was willing to keep negotiating despite the strike threat. "The threat of a strike is a bargaining tool," Lewis says. "It's more meaningful than a strike itself, once the employer finds out the membership is dead serious."

Meanwhile, the union's members are still working at Colonial Manor, even though neither the labor dispute nor the lawsuit has been resolved. A tentative contract agreement unraveled. Now union president Lewis sounds a little like he might be unleashing the strike-threat weapon again. "I was delighted when I thought we could settle this thing without a strike," he says. "Now I'm a little dismayed and angry."[26]

SUMMARY

■ Unionism in the U.S. has developed in a different way than unionism in Europe or Japan. American unions have traditionally had a job-centered emphasis.

■ Unions can be viewed as countervailing forces to management. They have a variety of weapons at their disposal including five different kinds of strikes.

■ Union membership as a percent of the work force is down from around 25 percent in 1970 to around 19 percent.

■ The use of bankruptcy and moving the work site away from unfavorable union situations are tactics that have recently been upheld by the Supreme Court.

■ The major area of union growth is among white-collar groups and government employees.

■ Foreign competition, automation, and losing touch with a younger, more educated membership are three important union concerns.

■ The union hierarchy is built around local unions.

■ Labor history in the U.S. survived many ups and downs but enjoyed its greatest growth from 1935 to 1947.

■ The "National Labor" Code is composed of three laws that provide the legal basis for our labor relations today. The three laws are the Wagner Act, Taft-Hartley Act, and Landrum-Griffin Act.

■ The Wagner Act was designed to help the unions and workers. Taft-Hartley restores some powers to management, and Landrum-Griffin was designed to protect individual union members.

■ The process of organizing usually includes handbilling, collecting of authorization cards, a representation election, NLRB certification, and collective bargaining.

■ The process can be reversed through decertification.

REVIEW QUESTIONS AND EXERCISES

1. Discuss: "Unions in the United States and Europe are and always will be distinctly different."

2. Unionism in the United States is undergoing some changes. What are some of the current trends and changes?

3. What is the meaning of a "confederation" of unions? What are the levels within a union confederation?

4. List five key events that occurred in U.S. labor history before 1935.

5. Identify the three parts of the National Labor Code and the key elements of each act.

6. An employee has just brought you a union leaflet that urges the employee to sign an authorization card. What events would you expect to occur from that point?

Exercises

a. Organize a debate in class. Have one person take the position that "unions are no longer needed in the U.S." Have another take the position that "unions are more crucial today than ever before."

b. Interview a personnel manager in a unionized and one in a nonunionized company about working with a union. Contrast their responses.

One of the most interesting cases in the history of the National Labor Relations Board involved a union election in Puerto Rico. The General Cigar Company (GCC) filed an unfair labor practices charge against the International Association of Machinists and Aerospace Workers (IAM). The final election results were 255 for the IAM, 222 for no union and 6 challenged votes, but the company asked the NLRB to void the election for several reasons:

1. An IAM supporter persuaded some other workers to smell the contents of a bottle of magic potion bought from a local "bujera" (witch or sorceress) and then told them they could not vote against the union without repercussions.

2. A publicly acknowledged witch was paid $150 by the wife of another employee to work for the union.

3. A male midget was hired by another pro-union employee to persuade employees to vote for the IAM.

4. The weather before and after the election was clear and sunny. However, during the election a torrential rainstorm hit.

The GCC also charged the IAM with threatening and bribing employees to vote pro-union. The IAM called the charges ludicrous and said the complaints showed the need for a union to protect employees from management.[27]

Questions

1. If you were on the NLRB, what specific laws would you need to consider?

2. Do any of these charges make any difference to employees?

3. Would you rule for GCC or the IAM? Why?

NOTES

1. Adapted from D. D. Buss, "Lifetime Job Guarantees in Auto Contracts Arouse Second Thoughts Among Auto Workers," *Wall Street Journal*, April 18, 1983, p. 27.

2. J. S. Lublin, "As Job Hazards Increase, Hospital Unions Push Employers, U.S. for Better Protection," *Wall Street Journal*, August 5, 1983, p. 21.

3. Everett M. Kassalow, "The Development of Western Movements: Some Comparative Considerations," in *Labor: Readings on Major Issues*, ed. Richard Lester (New York: Random House, 1965), p. 74.

4. Robert C. Wood, "Japan's Multitier Wage System," *Forbes*, August 18, 1980, p. 57.

5. Adapted from D. D. Buss, "Japanese-Owned Auto Plants in the U.S. Present Tough Challenge for UAW," *Wall Street Journal*, March 23, 1983, p. 27.

6. Kenneth A. Kovach, Ben F. Sands, and William W. Brooks, "Is Codetermination a Workable Idea for U.S. Labor-Management Relations?" *MSU Business Topics,* Winter 1980, pp. 49–55.

7. L. M. Apcar, "Unions Press Congress to Reverse Decision by High Court on Bankrupt Firm's Pacts," *Wall Street Journal,* March 21, 1984, p. 31.

8. J. S. Lublin, "NLRB Rules Employers Needn't Bargain with Unions Before Moving Operations," *Wall Street Journal,* April 11, 1984, p. 16.

9. Kathryn Christensen, "White Collar Blues . . . ," *Wall Street Journal,* June 23, 1980, p. 1.

10. F. S. Hills and T. Bergmann, "Professional Employees: Unionization Attitudes and Reward Preferences," *Personnel Administrator,* July 1982, pp. 50–73.

11. S. Carey, "UMW Organizing Bids are Blunted by Aggressive Nonunion Operators," *Wall Street Journal,* August 3, 1983, p. 25.

12. Adapted from "Backtrack for Hard Hats," *Forbes,* March 12, 1984, p. 64.

13. S. Perlman, *A History of Trade Unionism in the United States* (New York: Macmillan, 1929).

14. *Commonwealth of Massachusetts* v. *Hunt,* Massachusetts, 4 Metcalf 3(1842).

15. For more details on the act, see R. E. Allen and T. J. Keaveny, *Contemporary Labor Relations* (Reading, MA: Addison-Wesley, 1983), pp. 332–333.

16. "The NLRB: Headed Right—Maybe," *Dun's Business Month,* December 1983, pp. 54–61.

17. Reprinted by permission from *Primer of Labor Relations,* 17th ed., copyright 1969 by The Bureau of National Affairs, Inc., Washington, D.C. 20037.

18. Reprinted by permission from *Primer of Labor Relations,* 17th ed., copyright 1969 by The Bureau of National Affairs, Inc., Washington, D.C. 20037.

19. Reprinted by permission from *Primer of Labor Relations,* 17th ed., copyright 1969 by The Bureau of National Affairs, Inc., Washington, D.C. 20037.

20. "Now Strikes by Union's Own Workers," *U.S. News & World Report,* November 28, 1983, p. 16.

21. Jeanne M. Brett, "Why Employees Want Unions," *Organizational Dynamics,* Spring 1980, pp. 47–59.

22. "White-Collar Unionization," *Generation,* September–October 1970, pp. 20–21.

23. Adapted from A. Hershman and M. Rozen, "Corporate Big Brother Is Watching You," *Dun's Business Month,* January 1984, pp. 36–39.

24. Woodruff Imberman, "Union Avoidance Campaigns: You Need More Than Hocus-Pocus," *Management Review,* September 1980, pp. 45–49.

25. "An Uneasy Peace Reigns at J. P. Stevens," *Business Week,* February 22, 1982, p. 116.

26. Robert S. Greenberger," You Just Can't Win Dept.: Firm Sues Workers for Failure to Strike," *Wall Street Journal,* September 21, 1983, p. 31. Reprinted by permission of *Wall Street Journal,* © Dow Jones & Company, Inc. 1983. All Rights Reserved.

27. Adapted from information in *Business Week,* October 19, 1968, p. 132.

Collective Bargaining and Union/Management Relations

When you have read this chapter, you should be able to:

1. Define collective bargaining and identify some bargaining relationships and structures.
2. Identify and describe a typical collective bargaining process.
3. Differentiate between a grievance and a complaint.
4. Describe the importance and extent of grievance procedures.
5. Explain the basic steps in a grievance procedure.
6. Discuss arbitration as the final phase of a grievance procedure.
7. Contrast the legalistic and behavioral approaches to grievance resolution.

PERSONNEL AT WORK
COORDINATED BARGAINING—REST IN PEACE?

The American steel industry, outmoded and bloated with huge wage bills, is not currently competing well with foreign steel producers. It has had some success pleading for protection in Washington, D.C. but the industry cannot count on that for the long-term resolution of its problems. It is slowly beginning to restructure itself, and this restructuring may bring about one of the most radical transformations in U.S. labor relations history. It seems inevitable that the industry-wide bargaining structure used in the steel industry will be broken into a company-by-company approach that may make steel producers more competitive in terms of labor costs—but once again liable for strikes.

After World War II the United Steelworkers negotiated agreements with U.S. Steel Corporation (nicknamed "Big Steel") that were then extended to other companies. These pattern-setting contracts were consistently met or exceeded by other large steel producers in order to stay competitive. Eventually, most firms decided it would make sense to join with "Big Steel" in coordinated industry-wide bargaining. But U.S. Steel still controlled the bargaining within the group and prevented its competitors from winning a better deal from the union. Both sides got what they wanted—the union got a uniform wage across the industry, and the companies were not faced with wage competition. The result was that average hourly employment costs in the steel industry in 1984 reached $22 per hour—fully 33 percent higher than the average for all U.S. manufacturers. (This was after a 10 percent cut in wages and benefits the previous year.)

The steel companies in the coordinated bargaining arrangement were: U.S. Steel, Bethlehem, LTV, Jones & Laughlin, Republic, National, Inland, and Armco. However, coordinated bargaining has been unable to adjust wages for production of different types of steel, which have come under heavy competitive pressure from more efficient "minimills." Workers in rod-and-wire, bar, and welded-tube mills are paid the same basic wage as workers in the high-volume flat-rolled-steel mills. The union has refused to negotiate a lower wage rate where it was necessary for competition. Having wage tiers was felt to be contrary to the union's principle of equal pay for equal work.

The union is trying to prevent companies from forcing locals to undercut each other's wage agreements by a policy of "no more wage concessions", but the companies have the fall-back position of using the bankruptcy laws. The union may have to change its policy if thousands of jobs are threatened by the failure of a major company such as Republic Steel.

It is unclear who will take the lead in dropping out of the coordinations committee. But one fact is clear: Union/management relations in the steel industry will face a period of testing and adjustment.[1]

"Collective bargaining should be more than a fistfight, more than rulemaking. It must be more than merely adversarial. And there is ample evidence that it can be."

D. QUINN MILLS

COLLECTIVE
BARGAINING
is the process whereby
representatives of man-
agement and workers
negotiate over wages,
hours, and conditions of
employment.

Union/management relations come into focus in an organization following a successful unionization attempt. The final stage of the unionization process is the negotiation and signing of a contractual agreement between a union and an employer. This chapter discusses the
process of contract negotiation through collective bargaining, which
can be done on an industry-wide basis, as in the steel industry, or on
a one-firm–one-union basis. Then it examines one of the most important areas of day-to-day union/management relations—grievances.

COLLECTIVE BARGAINING

In the United States, collective bargaining is somewhat different than
in other countries, due to the different philosophical and political origins of the collective bargaining systems.[2] Different legal frameworks
for collective bargaining also exist in different countries.

Collective bargaining is intended to be a mutual give-and-take between representatives of two organizations for the mutual benefit of
both. Although the power relationship in collective bargaining also involves conflict, the threat of conflict seems necessary to maintain the
relationship. Perhaps the most important aspect of collective bargaining, however, is that it is ongoing. It is not a relationship that ends
immediately after agreement is reached.

Can you define collective bargaining?

Types of Bargaining Relationships

One of the important factors determining the relationship between
union and management is the attitude of management toward unions.
This attitude plays a major role in determining the strategic approach
used by management. Collective bargaining should be more than just
rulemaking. The collective bargaining process must move beyond confrontation and into a more constructive mode.[3]

Management/union relationships in collective bargaining can follow
one of several patterns. Figure 20–1 shows the relationship as a continuum, ranging from conflict to collusion. On the left side of the continuum, management and union see each other as enemies. On the right
end of the continuum, the two entities join together illegally. There are
a number of positions in between, and a discussion of the six strategies
follows.[4]

Conflict. In the conflict strategy, management takes a totally uncom-
promising view. An attitude of "busting the union" may underlie the

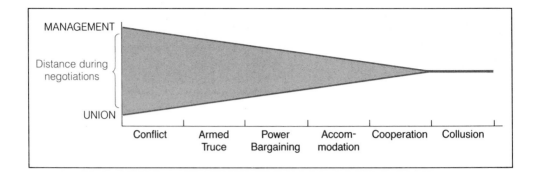

FIGURE 20–1
Collective Bargaining Relationship Continuum.

use of the conflict strategy. To paraphrase a saying from an old western movie, management takes the approach that "the only good union is a dead union!"

Armed Truce. Management representatives who practise the armed-truce strategy take the position that they are well aware of the vital interests of the company, while the union is poles away and always will be. The armed-truce approach does not mean that forcing head-on conflict is in the best interests of either party; it recognizes that the union is not likely to disappear. Many union/management relationships, especially in smaller businesses, have not progressed beyond this stage.

Power Bargaining. Managers engaged in a power bargaining relationship can accept the union; many even pride themselves on the sense of "realism" which forces them to acknowledge the union's power. Managerial philosophy here assumes that management's task is to increase its power and then use it whenever possible to offset the power of the union.

Accommodation. Accommodation involves learning to adjust to each other and attempting to minimize conflict, to conciliate whenever necessary, and to tolerate each other. This strategy in no way suggests that management goes out of its way to help organized labor. However, it does recognize that the need to reduce confrontation is helpful in dealing with common problems that are often caused by external forces, such as imports and governmental regulations. One labor expert has suggested accommodation will be needed in many new areas during the 1980s.[5]

Cooperation. The cooperation strategy involves full acceptance of the union as an active partner in a formal plan; its occurrence is relatively rare. In cooperation, management supports both the right to and the desirability of union participation in certain areas of decision making. The two parties jointly resolve personnel and production problems as they occur. Labor/management committees and codetermination are examples of cooperation.[6]

Collusion. The collusion form, which is relatively rare in American labor history, has been deemed illegal. In the collusion strategy, union and management engage in labor price fixing designed to inflate wages and profits at the expense of the general public.

Bargaining Structures

Bargaining structures come in many forms. The *one-employer–one-union* structure is the simplest. A more complex model is the *multi-union bargaining* structure. This structure is common in the construction industry, where one employer may face several different building trade unions representing a number of different crafts.

Another variation, *multi-employer bargaining,* was developed in the coal mining and garment industries. This structure has been used extensively in the steel industry, which uses a two-tier system: a "master contract" supplemented by a local contract dealing with individual company and/or plant issues.

Also, a bargaining structure may change over time as unions attempt to stay up-to-date with changes in organizational or industry structure or technology. Such changes are similar to those that often occur in corporate organizations in response to similar pressures.

Can you identify some possible bargaining relationships and structures?

PROCESS OF COLLECTIVE BARGAINING

The collective bargaining process is composed of a number of stages.[7] Over time, each union and management situation develops slight modifications that are necessary for effective bargaining to occur. The process shown in Figure 20–2 is a typical one.

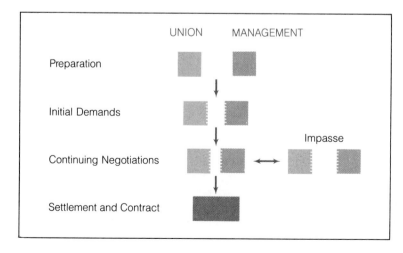

FIGURE 20–2
Typical Collective Bargaining Process.

Preparation

Especially after a bitter organizing campaign, it may take a union months to win an initial contract.[8] Both labor and management representatives spend extensive time preparing for negotiations. Employer and industry data about wages, benefits, working conditions, management and union rights, productivity, and absenteeism often are gathered. Once the data are analyzed, each side identifies what its priorities are and what strategies and tactics it will use to obtain what it wants. Each party tries to allow itself some flexibility in order to trade off less important demands for more critical ones.

Initial Demands

Typical bargaining includes an initial presentation of expectations (called *demands*) by both sides. The amount of rancor or calmness exhibited will set the tone for the future negotiations between the parties. Union and management representatives who have been part of previous negotiations may adopt a pattern that has evolved over time. In negotiations for the first contract between an employer and a union, the process can become much more difficult. Management representatives have to adjust to dealing with a union and employees who are leaders in the union must adjust to their new roles.

Continuing Negotiations

After opening positions have been taken, each side attempts to determine what the other side values highly and to reach the best bargain possible. For example, the union may be asking for dental benefits to be paid by the company as part of a package that also includes wage demands and retirement benefits. However, the union may be most interested in the wages and retirement benefits and willing to trade the dental payments for more wages. Management, however, has to determine what the union wants more and decide exactly what the company must give up.

Bargaining Behavior. Collective bargaining is not just a logical and rational process. The behavior of the negotiators is critical. Four behavior subprocesses are often present in collective bargaining.[10]

Distributive bargaining occurs when there is conflict over an issue and one party must win and the other lose. If a union wants a dues *check-off*, through which employee union dues are deducted from paychecks by the employer, and the employer does not want a check-off, only one side can win. Either there will or will not be a check-off.

Interactive bargaining occurs when both management and union face a common problem and must work together for a solution. If a steel company and the United Steelworkers union are concerned about employee absenteeism and discipline problems caused by worker alcoholism, the parties in an interactive bargaining process might negotiate a joint program that identifies how alcoholism-caused discipline problems are to be handled and requires both parties to provide some funds to pay for alcoholism treatment activities.

Attitudinal structuring occurs when each side attempts to affect the tone or "climate" of the negotiations. The climate created and the attitudes of the other party often determine which of the six bargaining strategies identified earlier in this chapter is adopted during negotiations.

Intraorganizational bargaining occurs when disagreements exist *within* labor or management. If some union members feel that dental insurance should be included in a union proposal and other union members feel that higher retirement benefits are more important than dental insurance, some consensus about dental insurance would have to be reached within the union membership. The union negotiation team must have this consensus to take to the bargaining table.

"Good Faith." Provisions in federal labor law suggest that employers' and employees' bargaining representatives are obligated to bargain in "good faith." *Good faith* means that the parties agree to bargain and that they send negotiators who are in a position to make decisions, rather than someone who does not have the authority to commit either group to a decision. Good faith also means that the decisions are not changed after they are made and the meetings between the parties are not scheduled at absurdly inconvenient hours. In addition, it means agreeing to have a written contract and not using blatantly anti-union

or anti-management propaganda during the bargaining process. The specifics of the collective bargaining "good faith" relationship are defined by a series of NLRB rulings and court rulings.

Settlement and Contract Agreement

After an initial agreement has been made, the two sides usually return to their respective constituencies to determine if what they have informally agreed on is acceptable. A particularly crucial stage is **ratification.** In this stage, the union negotiating team explains the agreement to the union members and presents it for a vote. If approval is voted, this agreement is then formalized into a contract. Typical subjects for inclusion in a formal labor agreement, or contract, are shown in Figure 20–3.

Notice that a wide range of issues are covered in the contract. The primary areas covered are wages, benefits, working conditions, work rules, and other necessary legal conditions. It is important for the contract to be clearly and precisely written. Unclear or imprecise wording often leads to misunderstandings that result in grievances or other problems. It may even be advisable to do a readability test on the contract to ensure that it is understandable as well as legally accurate.[11]

Bargaining issues may change somewhat in the years ahead. Competitive wages, insurance, and retirement pay are all becoming standard. Contracts in the future may deal with skill utilization, participation, employment security, and preventive health and safety.[12]

Bargaining Impasse

Regardless of the structure of the bargaining process, labor and management do not always reach agreement on the issues.[13] In such cases, a deadlock may lead to strikes by the union or a lockout by management. During a *strike,* union members stop work and often picket the employer by carrying placards and signs. One union tactic that is used to bring pressure on an employer during a strike is to persuade other unions to honor the picket line. At a trucking company in the South,

FIGURE 20–3
Typical Items in a Labor Agreement, or "Contract."

1. Purpose of agreement	11. Separation allowance
2. Nondiscrimination clause	12. Seniority
3. Management rights	13. Bulletin boards
4. Recognition of the union	14. Pension and insurance
5. Wages	15. Grievance procedure
6. Incentives	16. No-strike or lockout clause
7. Hours of work	17. Definitions
8. Vacations	18. Terms of the contract (dates)
9. Sick leave	19. Appendices
10. Leaves of absence	

some warehouse workers went on strike and set up a picket line that a truck drivers' union honored. Consequently, the employer could no longer ship goods, even if members of management agreed to load them. In a *lockout*, management shuts down company operations to prevent union members from working. This action also may avoid possible damage or sabotage to company facilities and employees who continue to work.

Types of Strikes. There are several types of strikes. Workers' rights vary depending on the type. For example, in an economic strike an employer is free to replace the striking workers. But during unfair-labor-practice strikes, workers who want their jobs back at the end of the strike must be reinstated. The types of strikes include the following:

■ *Economic Strikes*—These strikes occur when the parties fail to reach agreement during collective bargaining.
■ *Unfair-Labor-Practice Strikes*—Union members strike over what they feel are illegal employer actions, such as refusal to bargain.
■ *Wildcat Strikes*—These occur during the life of the collective bargaining agreement without approval of union leadership. Strikers can be discharged or disciplined.
■ *Jurisdictional Strikes*—These strikes occur when a union tries, by striking, to force an employer to assign work to its members instead of to another union.
■ *Sympathy Strikes*—The union strikes to express its support for another union involved in a dispute, even though the first union has no disagreement with the employer.

However, both strikes and lockouts are relatively rare occurrences. Efforts to forestall such drastic actions on the part of either party can take the form of conciliation/mediation or arbitration. The Taft-Hartley Act created the Federal Mediation and Conciliation Service which provides mediation in impasse situations with no costs charged to either management or union.

Conciliation, or Mediation. Conciliation, or mediation, efforts occur when an outside individual attempts to help two deadlocked parties continue negotiations and arrive at a solution. The mediator does not attempt to impose an external solution upon the parties but merely tries to keep them talking and may suggest compromise situations.

Arbitration. An arbitrator is an impartial individual whose job is to determine the relative merits of each argument and then make a decision, called an *award*. Contract arbitration is very rare except in parts of the public sector, such as police and fire departments. Most arbitration is grievance arbitration. Mediation and arbitration are different in that the mediator "suggests" solutions and the arbitrator has the power to impose solutions.

Can you describe a typical collective bargaining process?

Complexity of Collective Bargaining

Collective bargaining is a subject with so many ramifications that it is a separate technical area of study at many universities. This brief discussion of collective bargaining presents some of the more important issues involved.

Collective bargaining may or may not be handled by the personnel department, and exactly what the personnel unit does handle varies from employer to employer. However, one study found that many managers felt that collective bargaining activities should be handled by operating managers rather than by personnel executives. Collective bargaining promises to become more complex as issues change and as union officials get seats on company boards of directors—a small but growing trend.[15]

Two-Tiered Bargaining

A relatively recent phenomenon is two-tiered bargaining. It occurs when management needs to cut labor costs but current union members are unwilling to take cuts in their wages and benefits. The parties agree, for example, to cut wages or benefits for newly hired employees. Those hired after the agreement is signed obviously have no vote in the union at the time the decision is made. "Grandfathering", which means leaving current employees unaffected by the cuts, is sometimes the easiest way for management to gain the needed concessions.

CONTRACT "MANAGEMENT" AND GRIEVANCES

Once a collective bargaining contract is signed, that contract becomes the main governing document in union-management relations. The typical contract details what management can and cannot do and what the responsibilities of the union are.

The day-to-day administration of a contract most often focuses on employee and employer rights. When a unionized employee feels his or her rights under the contract have been violated, that employee can file a grievance. The distinction between a grievance and a complaint is important.

A **grievance** is a specific, formal notice of dissatisfaction expressed through an identified procedure. A complaint, on the other hand, is merely an indication of employee dissatisfaction which has not taken the formal grievance settlement route. Management should be concerned with both grievances and complaints because many complaints can become grievances and because complaints are good indicators of potential problems within the work force.

Alert management knows that an unsettled dissatisfaction, whether real or imaginary, expressed or unexpressed, is a potential source of trouble. Hidden dissatisfaction grows and soon arouses an emotional state that may be completely out of proportion to the original complaint. Before long, workers' attitudes can be seriously affected. Therefore, it is important that complaints and grievances be handled properly.

Can you differentiate between a complaint and a grievance?

Grievance Responsibilities

Figure 20–4 shows a possible division of responsibilities between the personnel unit and managers. These responsibilities vary considerably from one organization to another, but the personnel unit usually has the more general responsibility. Managers must accept the grievance procedure as a possible constraint on some of their decisions.

In an organization in which a union exists, grievances might occur over any of several matters: interpretation of the contract, disputes not covered in the contract, and the grievances of individual employees. In nonunionized companies, complaints also tend to relate to a variety of individual concerns, such as wages, benefits, working conditions, and equity.

FIGURE 20-4
Grievance Responsibilities.

PERSONNEL UNIT	MANAGERS
■ Assists in designing the grievance procedure	■ Operate within the grievance procedure
■ Monitors trends in grievance rates for the organization	■ Attempt to resolve grievances where possible as "person closest to the problem"
■ May assist preparation of grievance cases for arbitration	■ Document grievance cases at own level for the grievance procedure
■ May have responsibility for settling grievances	■ Have responsibility for grievance prevention

Importance of a Grievance Procedure

Grievance procedures are important for effective employee-employer relations. The chance of a union successfully organizing a company's employees is much greater if a firm has no formal procedure to hear employee grievances. Without a grievance procedure, management may not know about employee discontent in important areas, and therefore may be vulnerable to organizing attempts.

Union organizers often conduct a careful examination before attempting to organize any company. A survey often reveals more about the feelings of a company's employees than many managers are aware of through daily relationships with these people. Such information does not always automatically come to the attention of management. A great deal of it is dismissed at lower levels, and it never gets to levels where decisions can be made to rectify problems. For these reasons, a formal grievance procedure can be a very valuable management communication tool because it provides workers a fair hearing for their problems.

Grievances and Job Security

Because many American workers are concerned with the protection of their jobs, formal grievances often concern job security problems. Suppose that Paula Goldberg filed a grievance when an employee with a lower job classification was promoted instead of her. Paula claimed that the contract stipulated seniority would be the first consideration in promotion. Paula really is not concerned about the meaning and intent of the contract. She knows employees in higher job classifications are less likely to be laid off during slack periods. The basis for her grievance is her own long-term security. A person's need for security is a recognized behavioral fact, and formal grievance procedures can help reduce fears about security.

Individual Grievances and the Union

Individual union members do not always feel their best interests are properly served by the union. Workers and unions may not agree on the interpretation of a contract clause. For example, Craig Hensley feels strongly that his suspension for drinking was not sufficiently represented by the union because the shop steward is a teetotaler. What is Craig to do?

If the individual does not feel the union has properly and vigorously pursued the grievance, he or she may have recourse to the federal court system. Such cases attempt to pinpoint individual rights inside the bargaining unit, and also to determine what those rights are if a person has been denied due process through the grievance procedure. In fact, an individual can pursue a grievance against an employer on his or her own if a union does not back the claim.[16]

Extent of Grievance Procedures

Grievance procedures are almost always included in labor/management contracts. One review found that 99 percent of contracts in all industries contained grievance procedures.[17] However, the pattern is significantly different when examining organizations where employees are not unionized.

NonUnion Grievance Procedures. Managers commonly insist they have an "open door" policy—if anything is bothering employees, all they have to do is come to management and talk. However, employees are often skeptical of this approach, feeling that their complaint would probably be viewed as an unnecessary "rocking of the boat." An open-door policy is not sufficient as a grievance procedure. Ideally, grievance procedures should not be necessary. A "super manager" should be able to maintain open channels of communication and quickly spot and rectify any troubles that might become grievances. However, "super managers" who have this degree of communication ability are very rare.

During the 1980s it is likely that an increasing number of employers will adopt formal "employee due process procedures," as they are often called in nonunion settings. One expert estimated that only a few hundred firms out of 20,000 U.S. companies have such procedures.[18] One reason some firms have "due process" procedures is the belief that an appeals mechanism helps maintain a nonunionized work force. An electronics manufacturer in Oregon, TEKTRONIX, has voluntarily instituted such a process for its 20,000 employees. The procedure has five steps and each grievance is formally reviewed by higher level management at each step. However, the first step takes care of almost 90 percent of the employee grievances filed. McDonald's Corporation uses an ombudsman as a part of its "due process" procedures.[19]

Can you describe the importance and extent of a grievance procedure?

GRIEVANCE PROCEDURE

Grievance procedures are usually designed so that a grievance can be settled as close to the problem as possible. First-line supervisors are usually closest to the problem; however, the supervisor is concerned with many other matters besides one employee's grievance and may even be the subject of an employee's grievance.

Supervisory involvement presents some very real problems in solving a grievance at this level. For example, William Dunn is 27 years old and a lathe operator at Baker's Machine Shop. On Monday morning, his foreman, Joe Bass, approached him, told him that his production was lower than his quota, and advised him to catch up. Dunn reported that there was a part on his lathe needing repair. Bass suggested that because the mechanics were busy, Dunn should repair it himself to maintain his production. Dunn refused and a heated argument ensured, which resulted in Bass ordering Dunn home for the day.

This illustration shows the ease with which an encounter between an employee and a supervisor can lead to a breakdown in the relationship. This breakdown, or failure to communicate effectively, could be costly to Dunn if he lost his job, a day's wages, or his pride. It could be costly to Bass, who represents management, and to the owner of Baker's Machine Shop if production was delayed or halted. Grievance procedures can resolve such conflicts.

However, Baker's Machine Shop had a contract with the International Brotherhood of Lathe Operators, of which Dunn was a member. Further, the contract specifically stated that company plant mechanics were to repair all manufacturing equipment. It appears there is a clear violation of the union contract. What is Dunn's next step? He may begin to use the appeals machinery provided for him in the contract. The actual grievance procedure is different in each organization. It depends on what the employer and the union have agreed upon and what is written into the labor contract.

Steps in a Grievance Procedure

A **grievance procedure** is a formal channel of communication used to resolve formal complaints (grievances). As Figure 20–5 shows, several basic steps exist in most grievance procedures. The grievance can be settled at any stage.

1. The employee discusses the grievance with the immediate supervisor.
2. The employee then discusses the grievance with the union steward and the supervisor.
3. The union chief steward discusses it with the supervisor's manager.
4. The union grievance committee discusses the grievance with the unit plant manager or the employer's industrial relations department.
5. The representative of the national union discusses it with the company general manager.
6. The final step may be reference to an impartial umpire or arbitrator for ultimate disposition of the grievance.

Employee and Supervisor. In our example, Dunn has already discussed his grievance with the foreman. The first step should eliminate the ma-

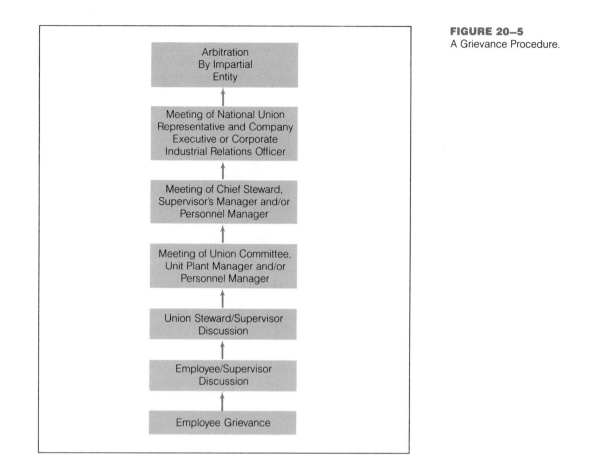

FIGURE 20–5
A Grievance Procedure.

jority of gripes and complaints employees may view as legitimate grievances.

Supervisors are generally responsible for understanding the contract so that they can administer it fairly on a day-to-day basis. They must be accessible to employees for grievance investigation and must gather all the pertinent facts and carefully investigate the causes, symptoms, and results.

Union Steward and Supervisor. The second step involves the union steward. The main task here is to present the grievance of a union members such as Dunn to management. However, the responsibility rests not only with the individual steward but also, to a large degree, with the union membership as a whole. The effect of this grievance on the relationship between union and management must be determined. One industry study found that the steward's need for dominance is related to the number of grievances filed.[20]

Assume the grievance remains unsettled after the second step. The steward takes it to the chief steward who contacts the supervisor's boss and/or the unit's personnel manager. In most grievance procedures, the grievance is documented and, until it is settled, much of the communication between management and the union is in writing. This written communication is important because it provides a record of each step in the procedure and constitutes a history for review at each subsequent step. If the department manager (who is Bass's boss) backs Bass against the chief steward, the grievance goes to the next step.

Union Grievance Committee and Unit Manager. Pressure tends to build with each successive step because grievances that are not precedent-setting or difficult are screened out earlier in the process. The fourth step involves the local union management grievance committee. In our case, the grievance committee of the union convinces the plant manager that Bass violated the contract and Dunn should be brought back to work and paid for the time he missed. The plant manager gave in partly because he thought the company had a weak case and partly because, if the grievance continued past him, it would probably go to arbitration, and he did not feel the issue was worth the cost. Although in Dunn's case a grievance committee was used, not all grievance procedures use committees. This step may be omitted in many procedures.

National Representatives and Arbitrators. If the grievance had remained unsettled, national representatives for both sides would have met to try to resolve the conflict. An arbitrator would have been selected and asked to make a decision on the matter. The manner of selecting an arbitrator varies but usually involves each party eliminating names from a list of potential arbitrator candidates until only one name remains. Most contracts call for union and management to share equally in the cost of arbitration.

Can you explain the steps in a grievance procedure?

GRIEVANCE ARBITRATION

Grievance arbitration is a means of settling disputes arising from different interpretations of a contract. This dispute resolution is not to be confused with contract arbitration, which is arbitration to determine how a contract will be written. Grievance arbitration is a deeply ingrained part of the collective bargaining system, although it was not always so. In earlier times, arbitration was not considered a useful part of the process of settling labor disputes.

However, in 1957, a court decision that established the right of unions to sue for specific performance arbitration awards gave arbitration new strength. Later court cases added more powers to the arbitration process. It was ruled that a company had to arbitrate all issues not specifically excluded in the contract. Courts were directed not to rule on the appropiateness of an arbitration award unless misinformation, fraud, or negligence was involved.

Arbitration is very flexible. It can be applicable to almost any kind of controversy except those involving criminal matters. Voluntary arbitration may be used in the negotiation of agreements or in interpretation of clauses in existing agreements, or both. However, because labor and management, for the most part, agree that disputes over negotiations of a new contract should not be arbitrated, arbitration plays its most important part in labor relations as a final point in the grievance procedure.

Grievance arbitration presents several problems. It has been criticized as being too costly, too legalistic, and too time-consuming. In addition, many feel there are too few acceptable arbitrators.

One alternative to arbitration, using mediation to settle grievances, has been tested successfully in the coal mining industry. The vast majority of grievances were settled by the process. It was faster (taking only about one-third the time) and cheaper (about a quarter of the cost) than arbitration, and both management and the union liked it at least as well as arbitration.[21]

Can you discuss grievance arbitration?

Arbitration and the Contract

The grievance procedure is the union member's most tangible contact with collective bargaining. The procedure set up in the contract is likely to have a visible, direct, immediate, and personal influence on the union member.

A very common issue in arbitration is the wording of the contract clause that accurately expresses each party's intent relative to arbitration. It is important to spell out the types of disputes that may be taken to arbitration. Most collective bargaining contracts suggest that either party may start arbitration proceedings. Others, however, state that only the union can initiate arbitration proceedings. Still others permit arbitration only when both parties agree.

Preventive Arbitration

Labor and management sometimes tend to ignore potential problem areas in a relationship until it is too late. The result can be an explosive dispute that does a great degree of harm. However, preventive arbitration can minimize this sort of difficulty. The use of this sort of arbitration is sometimes advocated to settle disputes in nonunion office situations.[22]

It is the duty of a preventive arbitrator to meet periodically (at least monthly) with union and management representatives to discuss areas of potential trouble between the parties. Although the use of a preventive arbitrator is not a panacea for resolving difficulties in labor management relations, it can be a potentially useful tool. The plan calls for adherence by both parties to the arbitrator's recommendations during a 60-day period. During that time, the problem is to be solved calmly and coolly.

COMPULSORY OVERTIME—BONANZA OR HEADACHE?

One grievance many unemployed workers have a hard time understanding is mandatory overtime. Overtime pay at time and a half is attractive to many workers. But others feel it is not worth the extra work. As a result, many grievances have been filed over manadatory overtime.

For example, at Chrysler's Twinsburg plant outside Cleveland, employees at one point had been working so much overtime they would explode over minor matters at foremen, other workers, their wives, and even their dogs.

"You get on edge," Virgil Archer says. "Sometimes I ask my wife what day it is." In 1983, workers got so angry about the long hours that they shut the plant down, costing Chrysler $90 million. These Chrysler workers were working 60 hours a week one year and laid off the next.

Because they often work extra hours, office workers do not always understand the overtime complaints of those in manufacturing. But office work is usually more interesting than running a stamping press. And office workers can sit down, take time for coffee and, if necessary, slip out to the dentist.

Many union leaders hate compulsory overtime—but many companies fire those who refuse it. Companies are hesitant to hire workers who might have to be laid off again when business slows down, so when times are booming the tendency is to turn to mandatory overtime rather than hire more workers. Yet employees who have been working long overtime hours talk of feeling guilty about keeping others from working. Dorothy Gleason, a Chrysler employee, says, "It makes you feel bad that you are working overtime and others are desperate because they aren't working at all."[23]

LEGALISTIC VS. BEHAVIORAL GRIEVANCE RESOLUTION

The inclusion of a union in a formal grievance procedure sometimes leads management to conclude that the proper way to handle grievances is to abide by the "letter of the law." This approach means management does no more nor less than what is called for in the contract. Such an approach can be labeled the *legalistic approach* to the resolution of grievances. A much more realistic approach, the *behavioral approach*, recognizes that a grievance may be a symptom of an underlying problem that management should investigate and rectify.

The difference is apparent in the following example. At Acme Bolt Company, a union has recently been voted in to represent the employees. One of the first actions the union took was to insist on having a formal grievance procedure recorded in the contract. One of the clauses in the grievance procedure states that a grievance cannot be reopened once it has been resolved to the satisfaction of both management and the union.

Ed Dysart, a custodian for the Acme Bolt Company, filed a grievance about the danger involved in working around some of the machinery. Dysart felt that he could not safely get close enough to clean around the machines. As a result, the workplace was not very clean. Dysart's grievance was that his performance was being hurt by the situation and had resulted in a warning for poor work from his supervisor. The grievance was resolved at the second level in the grievance procedure when it was discussed with the union steward and the supervisor. The union "traded" Dysart's case for another involving an employee who had taken extra days of leave for a funeral. The union felt that the second case was more important to the employees at large than Dysart's. Consequently, the union dropped Dysart's grievance.

Dysart, feeling that the situation has not improved, has *again* filed a grievance. Management is rejecting it, however, under the contract clause that says a second grievance cannot be filed on the same issue. Management's *legalistic* approach in this case is hiding a very real problem: the employee is concerned about safety. Management has a duty to provide safe working conditions for its employees; if it fails to recognize that there is a problem here, the federal government can become involved through the Occupational Safety and Health Administration.

Management should consider a grievance a behavioral expression of some underlying problem. This statement does not mean that every grievance is symptomatic of something radically wrong. Employees do file grievances over petty matters as well as important concerns, and management must be able to differentiate between the two. However, to ignore a repeated problem and take a legalistic approach to grievance resolution is to miss much of what the grievance procedure can do for management.[24]

Grievances and Leader Behavior

In a classic study done at International Harvester Company, two researchers discovered a relationship between the number of grievances filed and the leadership behavior of the supervisors involved. The two dimensions of leadership used in this study (consideration and structure) can be defined as follows:

1. *Consideration* includes behavior that indicates mutual trust, respect, and certain warmth and rapport between the supervisor and the work group. This dimension appears to emphasize a deeper concern for group members' needs and includes such behavior as allowing subordinates participation in decision making and encouraging two-way communication.

2. *Structure*, on the other hand, includes behavior in which the supervisor organizes and defines group activities in direct relation to the groups. The supervisor defines the role expected of each member. The leader assigns tasks, plans ahead, establishes ways of getting things done, and pushes for production. This dimension seems to emphasize overt attempts to achieve organizational goals.[25]

Figure 20–6 depicts the relationship between leader behavior and grievance rates. The curves show that as the leader's behavior becomes more structured, the grievance rate tends to increase; as the leader's behavior becomes more considerate, the grievance rate drops substantially.

Different combinations of consideration and structure relate to the grievance rate. Some supervisors score high on both dimensions, and some supervisors score low on both dimensions. Figure 20–7 shows the relationship between structure, consideration, and grievances; notice that for high-consideration supervisors (those represented by the lowest of the three lines), the amount of structure used can be increased without substantially increasing the rate of grievances. However, *the reverse is not true.* For supervisors low in consideration (the top line), reducing structure did not reduce their grievance rate very much. For those supervisors who were average or medium on consideration (middle line), grievances were lowest where structure was the lowest and increased as structure increased. Apparently, high consideration can compensate for high structure, but low structure will not offset low consideration.[26]

In summary, this study found that a supervisor's leadership behavior can affect the number of grievances received from the work unit. High-structure supervisors receive more grievances, and high-consideration supervisors receive fewer grievances.

FIGURE 20–6
Grievance Rates and
Leader Behavior.

Can you discuss the legalistic and behavioral approaches to grievance resolution?

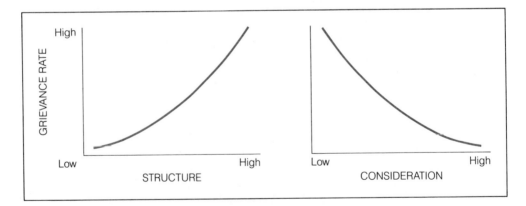

SOURCE: E. A. Fleishman and E. F. Harris, "Patterns of Leadership Behavior Related to Employee Grievances and Turnover," *Personnel Psychology* 15 (Spring 1962) pp. 43–56. Used with permission.

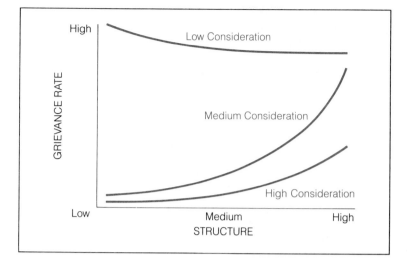

FIGURE 20-7
Combined Effect of Structure and Consideration on Grievance Rates.

SOURCE: E. A. Fleishman and E. F. Harris, "Patterns of Leadership Behavior Related to Employee Grievances and Turnover," *Personnel Psychology* 15 (Spring 1962), pp. 43–56. Used with permission.

PERSONNEL TODAY AND TOMORROW

GIVE-BACK BARGAINING—ONE STEP FORWARD, TWO STEPS BACK

It has been called "a fundamental shift in power to employers from unions," and a "transfer of billions of dollars in income from workers to employers." Give-back, or concessionary, bargaining probably got its start in the mid-1970s when New York municipal workers found that they had to take pay and benefit cuts, as well as loosen up on work rules.

Recession and foreign competition led to a wave of concessionary bargaining in the early 1980s. Unions agreed to concessions in the auto, airline, rubber, meat-processing, steel, and trucking industries, among others. When the unions refused to grant concessions, companies simply shut down. Checker Motors (maker of Checker Taxicabs) announced a shutdown when its workers failed to agree to concessions. GM sold its Clark, New Jersey, ball bearing plant to the workers. The company was going to close it if no purchaser was found.

The plant closings that often result from the failure of concessionary bargaining have produced some surprises too. The Singer Company closed a plant in Elizabeth, New Jersey, and workers filed a class action suit saying Singer had reneged on an agreement to invest $2 million in the plant in return for concessions made earlier. Singer eventually settled the suit for $3.5 million.

Even when concessions are made, it is not always clear how they should be handled. The United Steelworkers granted U.S. steelmakers a $1 billion concession in wages. The steelmakers later argued that the concessions included vacation pay and supplemental unemployment benefits too since they were all tied together. The union did not think so, although both sides admitted that these benefits had not even been discussed when they were bargaining. One negotiator noted, "We had no track record of any kind with concession agreements."

Even the concessions some unions have made have not brought U.S. wages in line with those of other countries. In 1983, the average hourly pay of U.S. production workers was $12.31. But the disparity between U.S. and other nations' pay levels seems most pronounced at the managerial level. In the auto industry, for example, the pay a top blue-collar worker receives is 1/36th that of a top executive. In Japan it is only 1/7th. That difference is not likely to be lost on American auto workers when they go to the bargaining table.[27]

SUMMARY

■ Collective bargaining occurs when management negotiates with representatives of the workers over wages, hours, and working conditions.

■ Different collective bargaining relationships exist. Conflict, armed truce, power bargaining, accommodation, cooperation, and collusion are recognized as special relationships.

■ The bargaining process includes preparation, initial demands, negotiations, and settlement.

■ Two-tiered bargaining is a recent phenomenon in which the union bargains one agreement for workers currently employed and another for workers yet to be hired.

■ Once an agreement, or contract, is signed between labor and management it becomes the document governing what each party can and cannot do.

■ Grievances are expressions of dissatisfaction or differences in interpretations about the contract by workers. Grievances follow a formal path to resolution.

■ A formal grievance procedure is usually specified in a union contract, but it should exist in any organization to provide a system for handling such problems.

■ A grievance procedure begins with the first level supervisor—and ends (if it is not resolved along the way) with arbitration.

■ Approaching grievances from the standpoint of fixing underlying problems is a good practice for management to follow.

■ Certain leadership behaviors have been found to be related to grievances. Those who are consistently high in consideration are less likely to incur grievances.

REVIEW QUESTIONS AND EXERCISES

1. What is collective bargaining? What are three bargaining strategies that can be used?

2. Briefly describe a typical collective bargaining process.

3. Give an example of a grievance and one of a complaint.

4. Identify the basic steps in a grievance procedure.

5. What is grievance arbitration, and how is it useful in resolving grievances.

6. Identify and compare the legalistic and behavioral approaches to resolving grievances.

7. Discuss the statement: "A leader's behavior can affect the number of grievances."

Exercises

a. Obtain a copy of a union contract and examine its provisions for union security.

b. Check the local newspaper for a negotiation that is currently underway or about to begin. List management's and the union's initial positions, then follow the negotiations to completion. How did the demands change?

CASE

THE WILSON COUNTY HOSPITAL

The Wilson County Hospital has recently seen its nurses organized after a long and bitter struggle that included dismissals and forced rehiring of some of the organizers. The nurses' union has been designated the official bargaining agent for the nurses at Wilson County Hospital by the NLRB after an election. The nurses contended all along that the only reason they needed to organize was to force the hospital administration to listen to important complaints. The complaints were primarily about poor working conditions and inappropriate patient care brought on by lack of proper facilities. The administration long ignored the nurses' pleas, claiming that limited funding precluded any action on the facilities and working conditions.

The nurses have asked for a 7 percent cost-of-living increase in salary for each of the next 3 years. The hospital has steadfastly refused to offer any kind of pay increase, claiming that it simply does not have the money available to pay higher salaries. Further, since it has no money available, the hospital administration has declined to bargain with the nurses' union about salary issues. Vernon Cohn, the hospital administrator, was quoted as saying, "Hell, it makes no difference what they want to talk about. There's nothing I can do. We have no money for salaries; therefore there's no sense in talking about it. I will not meet with the nurses to discuss salary."

Wilma Jones, the president of the local union, was reinstated in her job with the hospital after having been fired prior to the election. The NLRB found that Jones had been fired for her organizing activities. In addition to a cost-of-living adjustment, Jones feels very strongly that the nurses have several valid ideas on improving conditions and facilities for patient care (if only management would listen). Some method for presenting these ideas is needed because many of the nurses feel even more concerned about these issues than about salary increases.

Questions

1. Discuss the hospital administrator's refusal to bargain from both a behavioral viewpoint and a legal viewpoint.

2. If you were chairman of the Board of Directors for the hospital, what actions would you suggest to address the problems presented in the case?

NOTES

1. Adapted from "The Beginning of the End for Industry-wide Wage?" *Business Week*, March 5, 1984, p. 78.

2. C. M. Rehmus, "Arbitrators in China," *ILR Report*, Fall 1983, p. 28.

3. D. Q. Mills, "Reforming the U.S. System of Collective Bargaining, *Monthly Labor Review*, March 1983, p. 22.

4. The six strategies are adapted from R. E. Allen and T. J. Keaveny, *Contemporary Labor Relations* (Reading, MA: Addison-Wesley, 1983), p. 126.

5. Harry R. Gudenberg, "New Areas of Accommodation," *Labor Law Journal* 33 (August 1980), p. 462

6. R. D. Leone and M. F. Eleey, "The Origins and Operations of Area Labor-Management Committees," *Monthly Labor Review*, May 1983, pp. 37–41.

7. A realistic explanation of a detailed collective bargaining process can be found in Gary K. Himes, "Contract Negotiations—What Goes On?" *Supervision*, June 1980, pp. 12–16.

8. D. R. Whitehead, "Meet the Teamsters' New 'Miss Dynamite'," *Business Week*, October 3, 1983, p. 108.

9. Adapted from C. W. English, "Behind Those New Wrinkles in Contracts," *U.S. News & World Report*, January 30, 1984, p. 80.

10. Richard E. Walton and Robert B. McKersie, *A Behavioral Theory of Labor Negotiations* (New York: McGraw-Hill, 1965).

11. Samuel C. Walker, "The Dynamics of Clear Contract Language," *Personnel Journal* 60 (January 1981), pp. 39–41.

12. J. D. Levy, "Global View," *ILR Report*, Spring 1983, p. 4.

13. R. B. McKersie and J. A. Klein, "The Industrial Relations Dimensions of Productivity: A Summary," *ILR Report*, Fall 1983, pp. 9–14.

14. Adapted from C. W. English, "Strike No Longer a Scare Word to Companies", *U.S. News and World Report*, October 3, 1983, pp. 72–73.

15. C. W. English, "Companies Learn to Live with Unions in Board Rooms," *U.S. News & World Report*, January 30, 1984, p. 63.

16. "Newsline," *Business Week*, April 2, 1984, p. 83.

17. "Basic Patterns: Grievances and Arbitration," in *Collective Bargaining Negotiations and Contracts* (Washington, DC: The Bureau of National Affairs, 1979), p. 51–1.

18. Lawrence Ingrassia, "Nonunion Workers are Gaining Status, But So Far the Talk Outweighs the Action," *Wall Street Journal*, July 24, 1980, p. 36.

19. "The Antiunion Grievance Ploy," *Business Week*, February 12, 1979, pp. 117–120.

20. Dan R. Dalton and Willian B. Todor, "Manifest Needs of Stewards: Propensity to File a Grievance," *Journal of Applied Psychology* 64 (June 1979), pp. 654–659.

21. S. B. Goldberg and J. M. Brett, "An Experiment in the Mediation of Grievances," *Monthly Labor Review*, March 1983, pp. 37–41.

22. Robert Coulson, "An Informal Way to Settle Office Disputes," *Modern Office Procedures*, June 1980, pp. 182–186.

23. Adapted from G. Stricharchuk and R. E. Winter, "Worked Up," *Wall Street Journal*, January 20, 1984, p. 1.

24. M. P. Rowe and M. Baker, "Are You Hearing Enough Employee Concerns?" *Harvard Business Review*, May–June 1984, pp. 127–135.

25. E. A. Fleishman and E. F. Harris, "Patterns of Leadership Behavior Related to Employees' Grievances and Turnover," *Personnel Psychology* 15 (Spring 1962), pp. 43–56.

26. *Ibid*.

27. Adapted from "Did Steelworkers Give Up More Than They Thought?" *Business Week*, August 15, 1983, pp. 28–29; and A. I. Malabre, Jr., "Persistent Pay Gap," *Wall Street Journal*, April 18, 1984, p. 1.

SECTION CASE VII

HI-TECH PLASTICS COMPANY

In union/management relations, collective bargaining is essentially a power relationship. It is through the implied and actual use of power that parties are compelled to resolve their conflicts. This was the situation when the management of Hi-Tech Plastics Company sat down with the Amalgamated Plastics Workers to negotiate a new contract.

Allen Springer, the 35-year-old president and owner of Hi-Tech, was surprised at the list of demands presented by the APW business agent, Tony Mattson. But Springer was completely taken aback by the union's tenacity. Throughout the six-hour session the union team refused to budge from their initial positions. It was not the first time the APW had caught Springer off guard; the organizing drive that brought the union into Hi-Tech had also come unexpectedly.

Allen Springer took the reins of this Midwest company following the untimely death of his father, the founder of the company. At that time, Detroit automakers needed plastic body parts, trim pieces, and fasteners to meet government-mandated high mileage standards. Allen took full advantage of this demand and shifted his company's output from consumer to industrial lines. Under this strategy, sales volume almost tripled and the employee roster doubled to its present size of 105 employees (Measured against the industry leaders, however, Hi-Tech is still a small firm).

In the third year of Springer's presidency, a recession caused major setbacks in the auto industry; Hi-Tech's revenues declined and unsold inventory stacked up. In the midst of this bad news, Allen Springer was hit with another blow—his workers were signing cards and pressing for union certification.

Following the successful drive, the union represented 65 Hi-Tech employees. The first contract was easily drafted, and included a 6 percent wage hike in a one-year pact, but the renewal negotiations were more militant. Battle lines formed on three union demands.

1. *A three-year agreement, with a 30 percent wage boost the first year of the contract and 13 percent for each of the following two years.*

Because contract negotiations were time-consuming and expensive, Springer wanted the contract to run longer than the one-year term of the first contract, but not at the proposed wage increases. He offered what he believed was a generous 8 percent wage hike.

But Tony Mattson claimed that stingy wage hikes over the preceding five years had cut severely into the union members' standard of living. A 30 percent increase, he stated, was just bridging the gap between past wage increases and the inflation rate, as measured by the Consumer Price Index.

2. *A dental health plan.* On this point the talks became heated. Mattson pounded on the table, jumped to his feet, and shouted, "How can management claim to care about their workers while ignoring their health?"

3. *Reinstate service pins.* From the time Hi-Tech opened its doors, the elder Springer had acknowledged employee loyalty with 24-carat gold service pins for 5, 10, 15, and 20 years of uninterrupted employment. But in the face of declining income, and with gold prices at almost $500 per ounce, Allen Springer had halted the practice. The union was quick to respond with a grievance calling for the pins to be brought back. At contract negotiation time the issue was still unresolved, but the APW members were adamant—give us our pins, they said, or submit the entire issue to binding arbitration.

Aside from the specific demands, what troubled Springer the most was the apparent willingness of the members to strike if their demands were not met. Throughout the session the power of a strike was implied. Several times Mattson hinted that the rank-and-file members had already voted for a strike if their demands were not met to the letter.

During a break in the negotiations, Mattson confided to Springer that, although he was personally against a strike, the members were prepared. His manner was in sharp contrast to the shouting and table pounding during the bargaining. Now he was speaking in low, even tones. "The local has already rented office space across the street from the plant for strike headquarters," he said. "The central labor union is giving advice and the other labor unions have pledged their support. I'm afraid they mean business."

This information disturbed Springer. If the union employees went on a picket line, he would be left with only clerical personnel, a sales staff, and six production supervisors.

As Springer reflected on the demands and the strike threat, he was at least grateful that this was only the first bargaining session with two more to go, and that the present contract had 15 more days before it expired. He had 3 days to prepare for the next bargaining meeting.

QUESTIONS

1. What information does Springer need to prepare for the next session? How would the information be useful?

2. What past practices of poor labor relations practices can you identify?

3. What strategy or strategies would you suggest Springer use? Should he "take a strike" or try to avert it? Why?

4. What could be done to develop more effective labor relations on a long-term basis?

PERSONNEL AND THE FUTURE

In order to keep abreast of progress and change, managers must anticipate the impact of future changes on personnel activities.

The workforce of the future will be different than that faced by organizations today. Social, economic, demographic, and many other trends are likely to change the way human resources are managed in the future.

The last chapter looks at personnel management in the future and examines some forces that will significantly affect it. Also, there is a brief discussion of personnel as a career specialization and the continuing need for people knowledgeable in the management of personnel activities.

Personnel in the Future

When you have read this chapter, you should be able to:

1. Give examples of several changes that will affect work organizations in the future.
2. Identify at least one possible future change in each of the seven personnel interfaces.
3. Discuss personnel as a career field.

PERSONNEL AT WORK
NAISBITT VIEWS THE FUTURE

Futurist John Naisbitt, author of the best-seller Megatrends, *has iden-tified some trends that he expects to have an impact on the management of human resources in the future. Some of his thoughts follow:*

There are the beginnings of a job revolution in America, a basic re-structuring of the work environment from top-down to bottom-up.

Whenever pressing economic trends converge with changing personal values, you get a change in a society. That's why we can start to look for some revolutionary changes in the workplace. A whole new attitude toward American workers is on the way. And it could result in a revitalization of the spirit of work and America's sagging productivity.

Over the last two decades, personal values have been changing radically; there's a growing demand for more satisfaction from life. Workers feel it, too. Their psychic pain is reflected in their low productivity. They are sick of being treated like machines in the service of increased productivity. Workers refuse to produce and even deliberately sabotage the products they make.

They are no longer content with the traditional remedies offered up by labor unions, such as more pay, four-day weeks, better health benefits. What they really want, like everybody else, is deep human satisfaction from their work.

But industry had no compelling need to give it to them—until now. These dropping productivity figures will finally force industry, in economic depression, to give more than token attention to the mental health of workers. The workplace is in for a good shaking up. And the American worker is about to be saved by one of the most unlikely forces in society—call if humanization, "the human potential movement," participatory management. Call it whatever, it is about to converge with economic necessity to rescue the American worker from a deadened existence. For one thing, American industry is beginning to eye the way Japanese companies are run.

When the Japanese use their techniques on American workers, the changes are astounding. The Japanese Matsushita Company several years ago took over a Motorola plant near Chicago and began to produce Quasar TV sets. The company retained 1000 on-line workers but dismissed half of the 600 supervisors and managers. Within two years, production doubled and the reject rate of sets dropped from 60 percent to 4 percent. Moreover, through good quality control, the company reduced its annual warranty costs from $14 million or $2 million.

Our workers are not stupid or lazy. They, like everybody else, want a chance for more personal satisfaction. And they are about to get it— even if the trigger is such an eyeglazing event as lower productivity figures. U.S. industry leaders may not understand such a trend as changing personal values, but they do understand dropping productivity. Because of how economically interlaced the U.S. is with the rest of the world, the only weapon it has against inflation that is in its full control is productivity improvement. As Peter Drucker says in his book, *Managing in Turbulent Times*, productivity improvement will be management's most important task for the '80s. And in this regard, creative management will be more important than creative technology.[1]

"The future has a habit of suddenly and dramatically becoming the present."

R. BABSON

The management of human resources is much more complex now than it has been in the past because of changes in the external environments faced by organizations. As Naisbitt indicates, future trends will affect the way work and workers interact.

Organizations are in a continuous state of flux and must always be so if they are to remain in balance with a changing environment. As a result, an ongoing state of change must characterize such organizational factors as structure, functions, work load, and types of jobs, as well as employees and their qualifications, capacities, and behaviors. Developments within the organization may necessitate promotions, transfers, demotions, layoffs, or other actions affecting personnel. Think, for example, of the many reorganizations caused by the widespread adoption of computers as management tools.

FORCES OF CHANGE

Is continual change necessary? Can an astute manager avoid it? Certainly, not everything needs changing all the time, but forces affecting the management of people in an organization dictate that change inevitably *does* and *will* take place. Some of the forces dictating change include:

1. Changing product life-cycles and changes in the demand for products and services
2. Material shortages or surpluses and changing sources and forms of energy
3. Competition, both domestic and international
4. Technological advances, especially in computer-related equipment
5. Changing values and expectations of individuals in society
6. New knowledge of human behavior and ways of organizing work
7. Varying levels of economic uncertainty that affect employees
8. Increasing government involvement in the employer-employee relationship
9. Shifts by unions in strategies and priorities
10. Increasing complexity of organizational life

Because an organization is comprised of people, changes in work and in ideas about what a job should be draw attention to the management of people in work situations. Increasing concern about the "quality of life" at work is an indicator of changing attitudes. Interest in flexible scheduling and job-sharing reflects changing views about work's relationship to life-styles and the composition of the work force.

Work Force Composition

One trend affecting personnel management is the shifting character of the work force. More and more occupations require entry-level educational qualifications, and people without high school diplomas are increasingly hard-pressed to find jobs. The importance placed on education and the expansion of available educational opportunities have resulted in a more educated labor force. One forecast is that by 1990, 80 percent of the U.S. work force will be composed of highly educated information workers.[2]

While the need for more educated workers is increasing, the fastest growing segments of the U.S. population are minority groups whose education levels traditionally have lagged behind those of white workers. Hispanics, Blacks, and Asians represent growing percentages of the total U.S. work force. Yet, whereas about 50 percent of white males in 1980 had college degrees, only 18 percent of Blacks and 15 percent of Hispanics had graduated from college. Similar disparities existed between minority-group and white females.[3]

In addition, the "aging" of the United States population means an ever-increasing number of older persons will be working. Some of these changes have already resulted in new laws to restrict or eliminate mandatory retirement provisions.

Women in the Work Force. The influx of women into the work force represents another major social change that has had a great impact on personnel management. It has been estimated that the number of women in the work force will have increased by 21 million from 1960 to 1985, when the female work force is expected to reach 51 million. Women are expected to represent 47 percent of the U.S. work force by 1996. Further, almost half of all working women are single, separated, divorced, or widowed, so they are "primary" income-earners, not "secondary" income-providers.[4]

Employee Expectations

Instead of attempting to force employees to conform to a "corporate mold," future managers may well have to make more allowances for individual differences in people. Consider the problem caused by employers hiring more highly educated workers. Workers with more education may not be as willing to "mark time" in their jobs and wait patiently for promotions. Organizations that do not change their internal systems to accommodate this impatience may see their turnover rates balloon.

While some turnover is inevitable and even desirable, too much is an indication of problems. How much is too much? The answer is: "It depends." Some determining factors include the type of industry, historical trends, other employment opportunities in the community or geographical area, and the unemployment rate for the region. An efficient organization will plan for, anticipate, and "manage" turnover through human resource planning and other managerial activities.

Life-Style Changes

Other important changes in the composition of the work force are the result of changing life-style patterns. Many of today's younger employees have different life-styles than employees in the same age group only ten years ago, and thus bring different values to their jobs.

Mobility Changes. In the last decade, there has been a growing reluctance on the part of managers to accept relocation as a precondition of moving up in the organization. This trend has forced many organizations to change their development policies and practices. Employers have had to consider the costs of moving employees. The average cost of relocating one employee within the U.S. runs to more than $40,000.[5]

Dual Careers. The presence of working spouses also hampers employer-initiated relocation efforts. Close to half the work force now are women and many of them are not willing to leave their jobs if their husband is transferred. Men married to career women who are being considered for transfer face the same problems. Rather than risk dislocations, some couples have chosen to have a "commuter marriage."

A number of firms help working spouses, most frequently women, find jobs if a transfer occurs. In a survey conducted for General Mills, 22 percent of the responding companies offered job-hunting assistance for the working spouse of a transferred employee and 59 percent expected to adopt such a practice by 1986.[6]

Environmental Changes

The social changes just described are one kind of environmental change. But the most direct environmental change for most organizations since 1960 has been the increasing involvement of government in organizational operations. Federal and state governments have established agencies and enacted statutes that dictate the wages that must be paid, certify the safety of working conditions, monitor the quality of air surrounding many plants, provide minimum standards for hiring, and demand to see extensive records in order to scrutinize how organizations operate. This environmental change has forced managers to change personnel-related selection, record keeping, promotion, benefits, safety, and compensation practices.

Governmental Regulation. Today, managers of organizations are confronted with an expanding and often bewildering array of governmental rules and restrictions that have a tremendous impact on the management of human resources. Government regulation of personnel activities has occurred for many years, and EEOC, OSHA, and ERISA are acronyms familiar to many managers. A brief comment on equal employment opportunities illustrates continuing changes affecting personnel management activities.

The Equal Employment Opportunity Commission (EEOC) can require employers to alter their hiring and promotion practices to assure that certain groups of people are provided equal chances for employment. With good reason, increasing emphasis has been placed on providing equal opportunities for women. The increasing concern about equal opportunities for women and the continuing concern for equal opportunities for racial minorities have had, and will have, a significant effect on organizations in years to come.

The EEOC has used its enforcement powers to such an extent that some EEOC officers now require organizations to report information such as how many of their employees are of American Indian-descent, including the tribal affiliation of each person claiming at least one-sixteenth Indian descent. Affirmative action programs and the related problem of "reverse discrimination" are destined to receive increasing attention in personnel management, and may generate resistance from non-protected male workers.

Governmental regulations currently have an important impact on personnel management, and these pressures will continue to markedly affect the personnel field in the future. More organization time, money, and effort will have to be allocated to comply with government regulations.

Can you give examples of several changes that will affect work organizations in the future?

PERSONNEL MANAGEMENT IN THE FUTURE: POSSIBLE CHANGES

This book has stressed the concept of "interfaces" between the personnel unit and other managers. The days when personnel activities can be ignored or relegated to one part of the organization are gone. All managers will have to understand the basic issues and problems associated with personnel management if the organization is to be effective. A brief summary of each of these critical activities follows.

Work

A good working relationship between people and their jobs does not just happen. It requires analysis of the job to be done and proper design of the work people do. Job analysis, job descriptions, and job specifications will grow in importance for employers to comply with EEO regulations and make validation of employment activities easier.

Job Redesign. During the mid- and late-1980s great emphasis on job redesign is likely to occur. The many forms of job redesign reflect a consensus about ways to improve productivity. Also, the need to appeal to a more varied work force will lead to greater use of flextime, job sharing, and other alternative work arrangements. The view of the future even encompasses situations in which employees will "punch in" by turning on a computer terminal at home, as the description of telecommuting at the end of the chapter indicates.

Expressivism. Concern about the quality of work life (QWL) will lead to greater involvement of workers in their jobs. Two writers have suggested that people increasingly will seek to satisfy expressive values. *Expressivism* occurs when individuals take their survival and maintenance of their standard of living for granted, so that personal growth and self-development become the primary motives for working.[7] The need for expressivism may force managers and administrators to restructure work so that workers can find expression of their needs for creativity, autonomy, and entreprenuership in their jobs. Although this view may sound like the organization humanism approach of an earlier era (see Chapter 3), growth in jobs that require information-processing and that are performed by technologically-educated employees may indeed force more diversity in work situations. Figure 21–1 indicates the wide range of new and emerging jobs.

Productivity. Changes in work and jobs often flow from a desire to improve productivity. A survey of top executives revealed that productivity improvement was the number one area that they thought should receive increased attention by personnel professionals. Effective employee communication was their area of concern, an indication that the needs outlined in the previous section about expressivism may be high on managers' lists too.[8]

Staffing

Human resource planning, affirmative action, and structured interviews were terms seldom used 25 years ago. Yet, these concepts form the cornerstone of modern staffing practices. They affect personnel managers, as well as production, marketing, and finance managers. All these managers have to staff their jobs with people in a way that is compatible with current legal and social expectations.

A number of interesting trends appear to be developing. Increased use of a "work sample" approach through content validation will lead to a resurgence in testing for selection purposes. Growing emphasis will be placed on using structured interviews and training all who interview in effective and legal interviewing techniques. Shortages of skilled professionals such as engineers and computer specialists will intensify and complicate recruiting efforts. Privacy protection regulations to outlaw polygraph (lie detector) testing and restrict background investigations will be passed unless employers "voluntarily" change their practices.

The importance of human resource planning in preparing an organization for the future likely will continue to grow. Only by anticipating the future and developing specific human resource plans can employers be prepared to staff their changing organizations.

The significance of staffing is seen in the results of a survey of over 1,000 chief executive officers of small businesses. When asked what problems weigh the most heavily on their businesses, the most frequently cited problem was finding competent help. Of the responding CEOs, 39 percent indicated that finding competent help is of major

FIGURE 21–1
Emerging Jobs for the
21st Century

PROFESSIONAL		
Cable TV auditor	Gene splicing worker	Professional ethnicist
Certified alcohol counselor	Geneticist	Robot engineer
Certified financial planner	Genetic counselor	Robotic scientist
Child advocate	Geriatric nurse	Security engineer
Communications specialist	Health physicist	Selenologist
Computer designer	Hibernation specialist	Sex therapist
Data base designer	Image consultant	Software writer
Data base engineer	Information broker	Solar designer
Divorce mediator	Marine geologist	Space colonist
EDP auditor	Mineral economist	Space botanist
Energy auditor	Molecular biologist	Sports psychologist
Engineering geologist	Neutrino astronomer	Strategic planner
Environmental engineer	Ombudsman	Thanatologist
Ethicist	Oncology nutritionist	Theoretical chemist
Family mediator	Phobia therapist	Underwater archeologist
Forecaster	Planetary engineer	Volcanologist
Forensic scientist	Planetary scientist	Wind prospector
Fusion engineer		

SKILLED		
Asteroid miner	Exotic welder	Medicine aid technician
Bioconversion technologist	Fiber optic technician	Nuclear fuel technician
Biomedical technician	Hazardous waste technician	Nuclear reactor technician
Computer service technician	Hibernation technician	Rehabilitation housing technician
Cryogenic technician	Laser technician	Telecommunications technician
Cyborg technician	Lunar miner	Underwater culture technician
Dialysis technician	Materials utilization technician	

SOURCE: *Work in the 21st Century*, ed. Catherine D. Bower, (Alexandria, VA: American Society for Personnel Administration, 1984), pp. 108–109. Reprinted from the December, 1983 issue of *Personnel Administrator*, copyright 1983, the American Society for Personnel Administration, 606 North Washington Street. Alexandria, VA 22314, $30 per year.

concern and 35 percent indicated that it was of some concern.[9] Some have even turned to "employee leasing" (see Personnel in Practice).

Training and Development

Training needs assessment, training evaluation, and career planning have grown in importance. However, training costs—like all other costs—are increasing, and management has a right to know whether or not it is receiving a dollar's worth of benefit for a dollar spent in this area. Further, as women and minorities with special training needs become more predominant in a broader range of jobs, there will be a greater need for specialized types of training and development.

A special concern is the retraining of employees who are "technologically obsolete." For example, a shortage of word processing specialists is forcing firms to retrain clerk-typists and secretaries to operate the more sophisticated word processing equipment. The significance of training and retraining has been highlighted by Glenn Watts, president of the Communications Workers of America, who says, "The normal life cycle of many jobs is on an irreversible decline. In the past, it was possible to train for a job and expect the job requirement to remain relatively stable for at least five to ten years. Today, jobs and the skills and knowledge required to perform them are evolving much more rapidly. A much broader range of abilities is thus needed to keep pace with the ever-present changes."[11]

The other option is dismissal of employees who are no longer needed, combined with the closing of unneeded facilities. Layoffs and closings by such firms as Chrysler, Goodyear, U.S. Steel, and others have generated pressure for "outplacement." Through outplacement, firms assist their former employees to locate new jobs and/or to be retrained into new job skills. Continuing economic readjustments are likely to increase outplacement activities during the 1980s. One forecast is that over 1 million workers in such industries as steel, automobile, textiles, rubber, and railroads will never get their old jobs back. Also, legislation to regulate plant closings has been introduced in the past and is likely to constitute a continuing governmental attempt to force employers to assist affected employees.

The need for better management training and development will probably continue unabated. Through increased managerial development activities, organizations contribute both to their long-term effectiveness and to a more flexible organizational climate.

Appraisal

Performance appraisal typically has been done very poorly in most organizations. Yet, as the cost of keeping poor employees continues to grow, performance appraisal increasingly will be important, because the cost associated with unrecognized excellence and potential is at least as great. Well-designed, properly-implemented appraisal systems, perhaps more than any other personnel activities, require the cooperative efforts of the personnel unit and operating managers.

Training managers to provide sound appraisals of job performance rather than of personality traits continues to be a major concern. The American Society for Personnel Administration Foundation surveyed its local chapter leaders and found that managerial performance appraisal was the number one issue needing research in the early 1980s. With the removal of automatic retirement at age 65, employers must develop legally defensible performance appraisals to use when making decisions about when individual older workers are no longer performing satisfactorily. In addition, more effective ways to tie performance appraisals to pay are necessary if true "pay for performance" systems are to be instituted.[12]

Compensation

Compensation adminstration is becoming increasingly complex. The Employee Retirement Income Security Act (ERISA) has greatly changed pension benefit plans, and the expanding unionization of white-collar jobs will make the tie between productivity and compensation even more complex. New ideas and a professional approach to compensation and benefits are vital if equity is to be achieved in this area. A particular challenge to existing compensation practices is the issue of pay equity (comparable worth) between men and women doing dissimilar jobs.

The rapid increase in benefit costs, especially for health-related benefits, will continue to be a major issue. At the same time, employee and union pressure for new and improved benefit options is likely. One trend to watch is the use of benefit systems that offer employees more flexibility in using their benefit dollars. Preretirement counseling and retirement-related benefits also will become more prominent concers because of the aging of the U.S. work force.

In addition, organizations must develop and refine their basic wage and salary systems. Firms such as Scott Paper and others have been experimented with new ideas such as holding employee base pay steady but giving "merit raises" as lump sum bonuses. Such efforts are likely to be attempted by a broad range of organizations.

Public sector compensation systems are likely to change and become more similar to those in the private sector. The old system, first established in the federal government, is being dropped by a growing number of governmental entities in favor of more sophisticated and realistic pay practices.

Maintenance

Largely because of OSHA requirements, but also because of increasing management awareness of its social responsibility to the public and employees, personnel health and safety will continue to grow in importance. Further, personnel policies and rules must be updated if organizations are to remain viable and competitive, especially in light of challenges to the right to terminate employees through employment-at-will cases.

OSHA requirements are likely to continue to change as a result of the many criticism leveled at them. Less emphasis will be placed on small businesses and other firms with good safety and health records. In a broader health focus, assisting troubled employees through employee assistance programs (EAP) will be seen as a way to retain otherwise satisfactory employees. Also, employee wellness programs to promote good health and exercise are likely to become more widespread.

Improved personnel communications and coordination systems will be needed to tap employee talents and improve productivity. Suggestion systems, used in conjunction with quality circle plans, represent an appealing strategy for a growing number of employers.

Privacy legislation, proposed or adopted, should have an impact on personnel record-keeping systems. At the same time, the development and usage of computerized human resource information systems will enable firms to do a better job of human resource planning and personnel research.

Union Relations

Finally, the interface with labor organizations increasingly will become important in some organizations. In others a rethinking and reformulation of existing relationships may be necessary for the industries to grow and remain viable. The construction industry is an example of an industry in which this reexamination appears to be occurring, as more nonunion construction firms get contracts. Cooperative efforts between labor and management are likely in the steel and automobile industries and others hard hit by foreign competition.

Public sector and white-collar unions will continue to be fast-growing segments of the labor movement. Some employees who previously saw unions as villians are "seeing the light" and joining unions. School teachers, university professors, firefighters, police officers, and nurses are just a few of the professionals who have experienced the increased appeal of unions.

Managers in a variety of organizations will have to adjust to negotiating with newly unionized employees. At the same time, established unions and their leaders will be facing internal challenges from younger workers. New bargaining strategies, such as the inclusion of no-strike clauses and compulsory arbitration in contracts, will have to be considered by both employers and unions.

Nonunion employers probably will try to fend off unions by continuing to use sophisticated tactics and consultants. Adoption of employee "due process" and formal grievance systems will be another technique used by nonunion employers to counteract workers' desires for representation.

Unions typically have had the effect of causing organizations to be more professional and careful about their personnel policies and practices. Especially in certain white-collar and professional occupations, a major reanalysis of personnel management activities will be required if predicted changes in unionization occur.

To the Year 2000

Throughout this book it has been stressed that personnel management is a series of activities that must be performed in organizations. Coordination between personnel specialists and other managers is vital. The areas just discussed illustrate some challenges managers and personnel specialists are going to face in the future. But there are many others.

A group of experts identified changes that are expected to affect personnel management by the year 2000. Forecasted changes on which most of the experts agreed are the following:

Social and Technical Changes.
■ Life span is expected to increase.
■ People will be more vigorous and remain so even in later years.
■ Increased immigration, especially from the Southern Hemisphere, may offset the shortage of native-born youth.
■ About 75 percent of adult women will have some connection with the labor force.
■ Among married people, 70–75 percent will be in two-income families.
■ Women will continue to enter occupations that once were considered to be male preserves.
■ Education of the young will improve.
■ There will be an emphasis on continuing education and skills upgrading.
■ The technological structure of our society will become increasingly complex.
■ Government regulations will be an area of considerable tension and dispute.

Effect of Social and Technical Changes on the Workplace.
■ A large number of physically vigorous older people will want to continue working.
■ It will be necessary to make downgrading in the work force a socially acceptable practice to accommodate those who are losing competence.

■ A larger percentage of older people in the work force will block the rise of younger people and require more lateral transfers.

■ Employers will be under pressure to do more entry-skill training of younger people because of the inadequacy of public education.

■ More training and retraining will be done because of the pace of technological change.

■ Pressure for more employee participation in job matters will continue.

■ The high cost of doing business will lead to increased pressure for more productivity.

Changes in Personnel Administration.

■ The scope of personnel (human resources) departments will run the gamut from records administration to participation in strategic planning.

■ The degree to which personnel professionals are involved with strategic-planning will determine their position in the corporate hierarchy.

■ Outplacement will become a routine procedure.

■ Management development will acquire increasing importance due to the need to keep managers up-to-date and to motivate managers who won't reach the top.

■ In labor/management relations, attention will go toward developing a more collaborative atmosphere.

■ Counseling programs will become more common and more extensive.[13]

Can you identify one possible change in each of the seven personnel interfaces?

PERSONNEL AS A CAREER SPECIALIZATION

Emphasis on personnel management as a set of activities does not ignore the fact that effective personnel management requires professional personnel specialists. As personnel activities become more and more important, the demands placed on individuals who make personnel their career specialty will increase. Projections made by the U.S. Bureau of Labor Statistics indicate that personnel jobs will grow at least as fast as the average of all other occupations in the U.S.[14] However, the significance and impact of these jobs are likely to increase.

There are five levels of personnel jobs: *clerical, specialist, technical, managerial,* and *executive.*[15] Examples of each are noted below:

■ Clericals—Personnel clerks, personnel secretary
■ Specialists—Interviewer, benefits counselor
■ Technical—Job analyst, trainer
■ Managerial—Employment manager, personnel manager
■ Executive—Vice-president of human resources, personnel director

STRICTLY BUSINESS   McFeatters

"I'm looking for a job as personnel manager."

The qualifications needed for each level vary significantly, as would be expected. For the clerical and specialist levels, a high school diploma or its equivalent and clerical skills such as typing and bookkeeping usually are needed. Beginning at the technical level, a college degree is a common requirement. Experience requirements also are added as someone progresses to managerial and executive levels.

Career Preparation

Several steps appear to be helpful in preparing someone for a career in the personnel field. Education is a must.

Educational Preparation. The breadth of personnel issues to be faced means that future personnel professionals will need to be well-educated in a broad range of business and other topics. Knowledge of three specific areas has been suggested, with special emphasis in the fields noted:[16]

1. General Education—English, mathematics, psychology, and social sciences
2. Business Core—Accounting, finance, computers, marketing, economics, business law statistics
3. Personnel Management—Personnel management, labor law, human behavior, wage and salary administration, collective bargaining, industrial psychology

It is especially useful for those planning a career in personnel to take elective courses that have direct relevance to preparation for a personnel career.

Courses having the greatest relevance for entry-level personnel jobs are shown in Figure 21–2. As would be expected, courses that focus on personnel management and specialties within it are the most preferred. A survey of corporate personnel executives found that business administration was by far the most preferred area for academic preparation for entry-level personnel jobs.[17]

A graduate degree (M.B.A., M.A., or M.S.) in personnel/industrial

FIGURE 21–2

Rating of College Courses for Entry-Level Personnel/Human Resource Management Positions.

COURSE TITLE	MANUFACTURING MEAN	NONMANUFACTURING MEAN
Personnel Management	1.37 (1)	1.37 (1)
Employee Selection	1.60 (2)	1.45 (2)
Compensation Administration	1.60 (2)	1.67 (5)
Equal Employment/Affirmative Action	1.70 (4)	1.67 (5)
Managerial Principles and Practices	1.70 (4)	1.57 (4)
Employee Training and Development	1.71 (6)	1.53 (3)
Industrial Relations	1.71 (6)	1.80 (8)
Listening	1.72 (8)	1.92 (11)
Interpersonal Relations	1.73 (9)	1.88 (10)
Labor Law	1.86 (10)	2.10 (13)
Organizational Change and Development	1.89 (11)	1.76 (7)
English Composition	1.93 (12)	1.96 (12)
Manpower Planning	1.93 (12)	1.82 (9)
Public Speaking	2.10 (14)	2.10 (13)
Labor Economics	2.25 (15)	2.26 (17)
Group Dynamics	2.27 (16)	2.39 (19)
Psychology	2.23 (17)	2.25 (16)
Statistical Analysis	2.35 (18)	2.20 (15)
Benefits	2.38 (19)	2.45 (21)
Women and Management	2.50 (20)	2.73 (27)
Computer Science	2.51 (21)	2.43 (20)
Health and Safety	2.56 (22)	2.82 (29)
Quantitative Methods	2.67 (23)	2.35 (18)
Economics	2.68 (24)	2.56 (23)
Small Group Analysis	2.70 (25)	2.86 (30)
Sociology	2.76 (26)	2.65 (24)
Financial Management	2.77 (27)	2.71 (26)
Psychological Measurements	2.82 (28)	2.55 (22)
Accounting Principles	2.85 (29)	2.66 (25)
Managerial Accounting	2.86 (30)	3.00 (31)
Research Methodology	2.87 (31)	2.73 (27)
Production Management	2.99 (32)	3.33 (33)
Marketing Principles	3.14 (33)	3.10 (32)

( ) Indicates count rank
NOTE: Rating Scale 1 = Critical. 2 = Important. 3 = Helpful. 4 = Not Necessary

SOURCE: T. J. Bergmann and M. J. Close, "Preparing for Entry-Level Human Resource Management Positions," Reprinted from the April 1984 issue of *Personnel Administrator*, p. 98, copyright 1984, The American Society for Personnel Administration, 606 North Washington Street, Alexandria, VA 22314, $32 per year.

relations represents additional educational preparation. Over 80 percent of the respondents to a survey of personnel professionals indicated that a master's degree is important.[18] Because of this perceived importance and the projected growth in personnel-related jobs, it is likely that more specialized master's degree programs in personnel will be developed at colleges and universities.

Accreditation and Involvement. Through the efforts and support of the American Society for Personnel Administration (ASPA), the Personnel Accreditation Institute has established an accreditation program for personnel professionals. This program allows individuals who take and pass the accreditation examination to become fully accredited after they have gained several years of work experience. Details on the accreditation program appear in the accompanying Personnel in Practice section.

In addition, ASPA, through its over 300 regular chapters, has established student personnel chapters at over 160 colleges and universities. More information on both these activities is available from ASPA. Involvement in professional organizations such as the International Personnel Management Association (IPMA) and others listed in Appendix C, can be valuable also. Student and community groups in which an individual can demonstrate leadership are additional ways to prepare for a career in personnel.

Experience. Results of a survey indicate that present employees in an organization are more likely to have an advantage in obtaining an entry-level personnel job than individuals from outside. In summarizing the study, the researchers state:

It is also apparent that while many firms recruit from outside to fill entry-level Human Resource Management positions, many place a premium on experience.[19]

This observation illustrates the fact that personnel as a career field is not as easily entered without experience as some other fields, such as sales or finance. While this pattern may not be as true in large metropolitan areas such as New York City or Houston, in smaller communities it is often the case.

Consideration should be given to obtaining some experience through part-time jobs, summer internships, or other means to overcome a lack of experience. The "I need experience, but how can I get it?" dilemma must be dealt with by using nontraditional strategies. Some firms will not put anyone directly into a managerial job in personnel above trainee level until the person has "gotten to know the territory" by working in sales, manufacturing, or some other operating area. Individuals hoping for a career in personnel also must decide if they want to be personnel specialists (in the training or benefits areas, for example) or generalists who deal with a broad range of personnel activities.

Personnel Salaries

The growth in personnel professional salaries is a reflection of two factors: (1) the importance of personnel activities to the organizations, and (2) the increase in education and professionalism of personnel practitioners. Figure 21–3 identifies the median salary levels of some personnel jobs.

Type of Organization. According to one survey, top personnel jobs in manufacturing organizations generally were paid more than those in nonmanufacturing organizations. However, pay levels of specialists and technicians did not vary between organizational types. Utilities, petroleum companies, and communication firms paid the most for personnel jobs, whereas hospitals and educational institutions tended to be the lowest-paying employers.[20] Also, as would be expected, personnel practitioners in small organizations made less than their counterparts in large organizations.

Other Bases for Differences. Personnel salary levels often vary by geographic area, with individuals in large metropolitan areas being more highly paid. Regional variations indicate that a top personnel executive in New York averages 41 percent higher pay than does a similar executive in the Mountain states, such as Colorado or Utah. Having some international personnel responsibilities also appears to lead to higher personnel salaries at managerial and executive levels.

The educational level of a personnel professional also affects salary. Of particular interest is the finding that personnel professionals with M.B.A. degrees make about 12 percent more than those with a B.A. or B.S. degree, and 60 percent more than those without a college degree. Finally, there is a direct relationship between experience and pay, especially at managerial and executive level positions.[21]

Can you discuss personnel as a career field?

JOB TITLE	MEDIAN YEARLY SALARY
Testing Specialist	$17,514
Employment Interviewer	18,000
Personnel Information Systems Specialist	21,000
Professional and Managerial Recruiter	24,700
Safety Specialist	25,410
Employment Manager	26,135
Training Manager	29,450
Compensation and Benefits Manager	30,847
Labor Relations Manager	38,341
Top Personnel Executive	42,780

FIGURE 21–3
Typical Personnel Salaries.

SOURCE: Adapted from data in Steven Langer, "The Personnel/Industrial Relations Function," *Personnel Journal* 62 (July 1983), pp. 540–543.

PERSONNEL IN PRACTICE

PERSONNEL ACCREDITATION

One of the characteristics of a learned profession is some type of program for certifying professional knowledge and competence. The CPA title used by accountants and the CLU designation used in the insurance industry are two examples. Because personnel as a profession is much younger and less defined, certification is not as widely used. Nevertheless, a program that certifies professional competence in personnel is available through the Personnel Accreditation Institute (PAI), which is affiliated with the American Society for Personnel Administration (ASPA). Started in 1972, over 6000 personnel professionals have become accredited through the PAI program. Although some changes and refinements in the program have been necessary, PAI's current accreditation program has met with growing acceptance.

Basically, the program is two-tier in nature: It offers basic accreditation and senior accreditation. Different designations are used for each, as the chart that follows indicates.

Special provisions are available for college students. Degree candidates and recent college graduates may take either of the basic level

Used with permission from the Personnel Accreditation Institute, ASPA, 606 North Washington Street, Alexandria, VA, 22314.

examinations (specialist or generalist) even though they currently do not meet the work experience requirements. If they pass the examination, they will receive a letter certifying examination results. Then they will have three years in which to complete the specific experience requirements to earn accreditation. Full accreditation will be granted as soon as they submit evidence of meeting the work experience requirements. In addition, all accredited individuals must demonstrate that they have continued their professional learning and competence by meeting reaccreditation requirements every three years.

Other professional associations in specialized areas of personnel have also developed accreditation or certification programs. Compensation and training professionals can become accredited or certified through programs offered by the American Compensation Association (ACA) and the American Society for Training and Development (ASTD), respectively. Addresses for all of these entities are available in Appendix C. If you plan to make personnel your career field, you should take advantage of the programs available because professional personnel accreditation is likely to become more significant in the future.

LEVELS OF ACCREDITATION FOR PERSONNEL PROFESSIONALS

BASIC ACCREDITATION
PROFESSIONAL IN HUMAN RESOURCES(PHR)

Specific Requirements:

Practitioners: Four years of professional experience in the field in the last six years. A B.B.A., B.S., or B.A. in personnel management or social sciences may be substituted for experience, allowing two years for a bachelor's degree and three years for a master's degree. The minimum experience requirement is one year of recent full-time professional practice in the field.

Educators: Three academic years of full-time teaching at the undergraduate level or two years at the graduate level at an accredited college or university. Two current years of teaching in the personnel or human resources field.

Consultants or Researchers (academe, business, government, etc.): Four years of consulting or significant and recorded research related to the field of personnel or human resources. Minimum of one current full-time year of consulting or research in the field.

Combination: Practical experience, teaching, research and/or consulting may be combined. A minimum of one year of recent experience or two recent academic years of teaching in the field of personnel and human resources.

Examination:

Successful completion of the basic examination of the body of knowledge in the field of personnel and human resources.

SENIOR ACCREDITATION
SENIOR PROFESSIONAL IN HUMAN RESOURCES (SPHR)—SPECIALIST

FUNCTIONAL AREAS:
1. Employment, Placement, and Personnel Planning
2. Training and Development
3. Compensation and Benefits
4. Health, Safety, and Security
5. Employee and Labor Relations
6. Personnel Research

Specific Requirements:

Practitioners: Eight years of experience in the field. College degrees may be substituted for experience (see PHR). Minimum experience is five years. Recent three years must include policy-developing responsibility. Recent position must encompass the full scope of the functional area in which accreditation is sought.

Educators, Researchers, or Consultants: Eight years of experience equivalent to that specified for practitioners.

Combination: Eight years of combined practical experience, teaching, research, and/or consulting. Minimum of five years of experience in the functional area in which accreditation is sought. Recent position must encompass the full scope of senior responsibilities in the functional area in which accreditation is sought.

Examination:

Successful completion of an examination at the senior level in one, or possibly two, functional areas. The examination also includes some items from the basic body of knowledge across the personnel and human resources field.

SENIOR ACCREDITATION
SENIOR PROFESSIONAL IN HUMAN RESOURCES (SPHR)—GENERALIST

Policy level senior experience in four of the six functional areas plus an examination covering all functional areas and management practices.

Generalists are typically practitioners, although some consultants may qualify.

Specific Requirements:

Eight years of experience in the field. College degrees may be substituted for experience (see PHR). Minimum of five years of experience in the field. Three years of recent experience with policy-developing responsibility spanning at least four functional areas. Candidates with specialist and generalist policy influencing experience may qualify with at least two years in each of four functional areas in the last six years.

Examination:

Successful completion of an examination at the senior level demonstrating broad-based knowledge across the personnel and human resource field.

A major perspective of this book is that, to a certain extent, all managers are personnel managers. All managers, including personnel professionals, must expand their knowledge of activities that focus on the management of human resources. In addition to a basic familiarity with the many ideas and issues contained in this text, managers and personnel professionals must continually develop their knowledge of general management and human behavior.

In the future, personnel management will play an increasingly important role in the destiny of organizations. This book has attempted to capture the essence and challenge of personnel management today, so that the readers will be better prepared for the organizations of tomorrow.

PERSONNEL TODAY AND TOMORROW
"TOUGH DAY AT THE TERMINAL?"

Kathy Tunheim goes to work at 4 A.M., but never leaves homes. While her husband and new baby are still sleeping, Tunheim goes into her home's office, turns on her computer terminal, and starts her workday. As a manager of public relations for Honeywell Corporation, she can get in five hours work before the baby wakes up. In that five hours, she will access a computer in Honeywell's office and send her work in for review by her boss. Also, she will send messages to people working for her in Boston, Phoenix, and Minneapolis.

Another Honeywell worker, Joan Orke, was out of the work force for five years because of arithritis problems. However, she is now working through "telecommuting," the process of going to work through the use of electronic computing and telecommunications equipment. Orke says she can get up at 8 A.M. and be "at work" by 8:15 A.M.

Honeywell is not the only employer using telecommuting. According to estimates, in 1984 over 50,000 people were telecommuting, and the number is growing. Many of the early telecommuters worked in the computer industry, but firms in other industries have begun using telecommuting. Blue Cross and Blue Shield of South Carolina, Federal Reserve Bank of Atlanta, Mountain Bell, and Allstate Insurance are among those using telecommuting.

The advantages of telecommuting are numerous. Better usage of time, more flexibility in time spent with families, and the reduction or elimination of the cost of physically commuting frequently are cited. In addition, telecommuting allows handicapped individuals who might not otherwise be able to hold a job to work at home. However, not all the news about telecommuting is positive.

Some telecommuters report that they miss the social interactions associated with work in an office. The difficulties associated with setting up work and restructuring jobs to be suitable for telecommuting have discouraged some buyers from trying it. Labor unions are adamantly opposed to telecommuting because of fears that workers will be exploited. June McMahon of the Service Employees Internal Union (which represents over 50,000 clerical workers) says, "Trying to enforce things like the minimum wage and occupational safety and health laws in people's homes is just useless." She adds: "From a union's point of view, we feel these workers are outside the realm of being able to be organized."

In spite of these problems, telecommuting is forecast to spread to as much as 10 percent of the total work force by the year 2000. If that prediction comes true, it is quite possible that current and future workers will complain about a "tough day at the terminal" even though they never left home.[22]

SUMMARY

■ Organizations face change as an inevitable process.

■ Changes in the composition of the work force, employee expectations, life-styles, the environment, and governmental regulations all will affect work organizations.

■ Management of the personnel interfaces in the future will reflect changes in personnel practices and activities.

■ Personnel jobs can be grouped into five levels: clerical, specialist, technical, managerial, and executive.

■ Preparation for a career in personnel includes both broad and specialized education, accreditation and involvement, and experience.

■ Salaries in the personnel field differ by job level and type, industry and size, geographic region, educational background, and experience.

REVIEW QUESTIONS AND EXERCISES

1. What forces will be shaping personnel in the future? What will be their effects?

2. List each of the personnel interfaces and then identify two specific changes you anticipate in personnel activities in each interface.

3. Would personnel be a possible career field for you? Why or why not? Would you prefer to be a specialist or a generalist? Why?

Exercise

a. Read *Megatrends* by John Naisbitt. Then, from the changes he predicts, list those that you believe will most affect the future management of human resources.

b. Interview a personnel professional about his or her experiences and preparation for personnel as a career specialization. Ask specifically what areas of preparation were the least valuable and which were the most valuable.

CASE
MERICA, INC.

Joan Martin stood up and walked out of her supervisor's office without a departing comment. She had just been told that her position was eliminated as a result of their operating company's merger with a new acquisition and the subsequent restructuring of the profit center. Martin knew discussing the matter further was pointless because the decision was probably irrevocable and, besides, her supervisor did not control the situation.

He said to her, "The boys from New York are calling the shots. You know how these things work. Two plus two equals three, not four. Each company had to cut x-number of engineers from every one of the district locations." Also, he told her that he figured she would have an easier time getting a job than the other engineers because she was a woman, and there was a shortage of women engineers. He also promised to write her a good reference letter and told her she would be getting three months' severance pay.

Until this morning, Martin worked for Merica, Inc., a widely diversified, international energy conglomerate with sales over $5 billion. The corporation operates in a dynamic environment and offers a diverse product line. Departmentation is by product, function, and location, with a total employment of just over 20,000.

During the '70s, the Merica Corporation had developed a large centralized corporate staff offering a full range of services to each profit center. A staff of over 1,200 provided financial and strategic planning, engineering, tax, legal, risk management, organizational development, and public relations services. In response to the softening in demand and falling prices for energy products, the executive committee embarked upon a twofold strategic and structural change in the organization. They agreed to a major decentralization of corporate staff personnel and responsibilities. In addition, the focus of the executive committee and their reduced staff was directed toward the development and coordination of long-range strategic planning.

Concurrent with these changes, the corporation acquired Spartan Oil, a gas exploration and production company. Spartan's former Chief

Executive Officer, who became president of the new profit center, set out to combine all operations within a 6 week time frame. Top managers from both sides formed task forces to direct the various processes of formulating objectives, identifying staff changes, and physically combining the work environments.

Managers at both companies were required to rank their employees into five categories according to job performance. Each category had to contain 20 percent of the total number of employees composing each major job description. Those employees like Martin who fell into the lower 20 percent were immediately terminated. Those in the 20–40 percent range were placed on six-month probation and faced competition for a limited number of permanent positions. Great emphasis was placed upon monitoring overhead expenses and minimizing future expenditures.

Martin returned to her desk both angry and befuddled at the immediacy of her termination. In the past, when "staff adjustments" had been made, the corporation had always provided a "safety pool" for those whose positions were eliminated. Employees in the pool retained their salaries and were provided training and counseling for eventual placement either inside or outside the corporation. She is now trying to decide what her next steps will be.

Questions

1. In what ways does the case illustrate the changes facing people in organizations in the future?
2. Discuss how environmental changes forced Merica to change its management practices. What is your opinion of the soundness of those changes?
3. If you were Joan Martin, what would you do? Why?

NOTES

1. John B. Naisbitt, "Opinions and Trends: The New Economic and Political Order of the 1980s," *Aide,* Winter 1980, p. 15.
2. John M. Roach, ed., "How 1990s Demographics Will Affect Employer Practices," *Management Review,* August 1983, p. 54.
3. Eleanor H. Norton, "Minority Workers of Tomorrow. . . ." in *Work in the 21st Century,* Ed., Catherine D. Bower (Alexandria, VA: American Society for Personnel Administration, 1984), pp. 65–76.
4. M. F. Paysor, "Wooing the Pink Collar Work Force," *Personnel Journal,* January 1984, pp. 48–53.
5. Arlene A. Johnson, "Relocation: Getting More for the Dollars You Spend," *Personnel Administrator,* April 1984, pp. 29–ff.
6. Maria Sekas, "Dual-Career Couples—A Corporate Challenge," *Personnel Administrator,* April 1984, pp. 37–45.
7. Daniel Yankelovich and John Immerwahr, "The Emergence of Expressivism . . . ," *Personnel Administrator,* December 1983, pp. 34–39.
8. R. Foltz, K. Rosenberg, and J. Foehrenback, "Senior Management Views

the Human Resource Function," *Personnel Administrator*, September 1982, pp. 1–12.

9. *Nation's Business*, March 1984, p. 31.

10. Adapted from james Drummond, "Employee Leasing Firm Offers Service to Bosses," *Houston Chronicle*, May 10, 1984.

11. Glenn Watts, "Training and Retraining Workers . . ." in *Work in the 21st Century*, ed. Catherine D. Bower (Alexandria, VA: The American Society for Personnel Administration, 1984), p. 100.

12. Douglas B. Gehrman, "Beyond Today's Compensation and Performance Appraisal Systems," *Personnel Administrator*, March 1984, pp. 21–33.

13. From *Human Resources Management News* (formerly *Industrial Relations News*), quoted in *National Report for Training and Development*, December 17, 1982, pp 1–3.

14. Nicholas Basta, "Human Resource Managers," *Business Week's Guide to Careers*, 1983 Spring Edition, p. 11.

15. William J. Traynor, *Opportunities in Personnel Management* (Lincolnwood, IL: National Textbook, 1983).

16. Adapted from Daniel R. Hoyt and J. D. Lewis, "Planning for a Career in Human Resource Management," *Personnel Administrator*, October 1980, pp. 53–54.

17. T. J. Bergmann and M. J. Close, "Preparing for Entry-Level Human Resource Management Positions," *Personnel Administrator*, April 1984, pp. 95–99.

18. "Higher Education for Personnel Managers," *Personnel Journal* 60 (March 1981), p. 154.

19. Bergmann and Close, "Preparing for Entry-Level. . . ," p. 98.

20. Steven Langer, "The Personnel/Industrial Relations Function," *Personnel Journal* 62 (July 1983), pp. 540–543.

21. *Ibid*.

22. Mike Lewis, "If You Worked Here, You'd Be Home Now," *Nation's Business*, April 1984, pp. 50–52; and Ann Lallande, "Probing the Telecommuting Debate," *Business Computer Systems*, April 1984, pp. 102–113.

THE MIDVALE PLANT (A): THE REORGANIZED PERSONNEL DEPARTMENT

The Midvale Plant of the Abacus Corporation* is located in a suburb of Metro City, some 15 miles from the corporate main office and major manufacturing facilities in the central city. The plant was established as the principal source of small coil windings and subassemblies for the company's radio and television production. In its first 15 years of operation, the plant experienced a slow, steady growth to a size of 300 employees, 25 of whom were management or supervisory personnel. Many technical and managerial services were provided by home-office personnel, whom the Midvale people referred to as "city folk" located at "the city."

The plant manager at Midvale, George Whitfield, had 25 years with the corporation and had been on his present job for 11 years. He was interested primarily in the production work at the plant, constantly strove for increased output, and displayed very little interest in personnel administration. He left routine personnel matters in the plant to the supervisors and his secretary, Patricia Martin.

The employee group at Midvale consisted primarily of production workers, a majority of whom were female. The plant was not highly regarded by employees in the company because many of them felt that Midvale was a "dumping ground" and that anyone assigned to it probably had little future with the company. Until two years ago employees at the plant had resisted all attempts to be organized by labor unions. About that time, however, the morale of most departments was not good, and a majority of the employees felt a need for some form of union representation. One of the unions that represented employees in the main plant became interested in the group at Midvale and determined to organize them. The union-organizing campaign met little resistance, and a short time later the union won recognition from the company as the bargaining agent for Midvale production employees. The union-relations and collective-bargaining activities were carried on by management representatives from the central manufacturing office.

Plant Growth and Reorganization

The Midvale plant started to grow rapidly. In three years' time, production at the plant almost doubled. The number of production employees grew to 650; the management group increased to 60 personnel, over half of whom were female supervisors and managers. This growth necessitated the expansion of manufacturing facilities, which formerly occupied a one-story building. An adjoining two-story warehouse was taken over by the Midvale plant, and several new production units were installed in it. Once the decision to expand was made, major changes occurred frequently in every department and unit. Many times the employees found that their workbenches or desks had been moved or their supervisors had been changed before adequate explanations were made to them. Situations of this kind often had to be handled by the union as complaints or grievances discussed with the plant manager.

As a result of rapid growth and many personnel changes in the plant, a complete reorganization of line and staff functions took place. The parent Abacus Corporation sent several new managerial people to Midvale from other manufacturing plants. George Whitfield, who previously had had four departments and the office manager reporting to him, was relieved of all other responsibility and was given responsibility for supervision of the assembly department. He moved his office from the attractive quarters in the front of the plant to a small room in the warehouse building where the assembly department was relocated. Two of the men who assumed departmental supervisory jobs in the new organization were brought in from other company plants.

A new plant manager and experienced manufacturing executive, Oliver Hawk, was transferred from the company's main office to Midvale. After participating in the reorganization of

*All names and places are fictitious.

other Abacus plants, Hawk had become a strong proponent of decentralization in management and organization. He insisted on the transfer of accounting, production control, labor relations, and personnel functions from the home office to the Midvale plant. In addition, he appointed one of his former assistants to the position of plant controller with responsibility for certain records, bookkeeping, and cost and payroll activities. Some of these functions, especially payroll and employee records, had been handled by the office manager, whose responsibilities after the reorganization were reduced to office services, the purchase of supplies, and supervision of the stenographic pool.

In spite of these changes and rapid growth, the work in the plant continued to go quite well. Production and financial results improved each year even though the changes taking place had created many problems.

Personnel Management

Before the reorganization, the personnel work in the plant, consisting primarily of such concerns as hiring, general wage and salary administration, and union relations was theoretically provided by the industrial-relations section in the home office. Actually, the department heads at Midvale hired most of their workers personally, even though the paperwork and formal procedures required services from the employment office in "the city." Over the years the majority of the work concerning routine salary and wage administration, employee benefits, vacations, incidental absences, and so forth, had been handled by Patricia Martin, George Whitfield's secretary, who acted as an unofficial chief clerk. Everyone at Midvale had come to look to her for answers to routine personnel questions, and she had accepted these responsibilities willingly. She took a great deal of pride in being "busy," and she derived pleasure from telling her associates that she did not know "what they would do without her." With Martin assuming authority and responsibility in routine personnel matters, supervisors usually did not try to answer questions from their employees that concerned personnel policies, but instead referred them to Martin. Few of Martin's rulings, procedures, and practices were in writing, and she stated frequently that she preferred to keep most personnel policies "flexible, and juggle them around in my head as needed." Martin was well liked by the union stewards at Midvale, and most union grievances were minor and quickly settled.

At the time of the reorganization, Hawk decided that a full-time personnel supervisor was

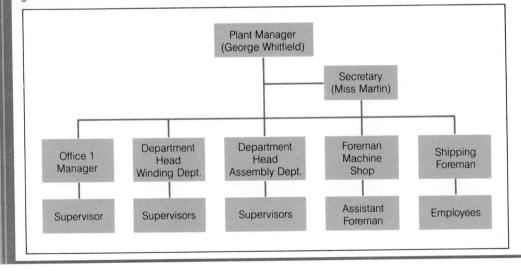

FIGURE 2
The Midvale Plant Organization Chart After Reorganization

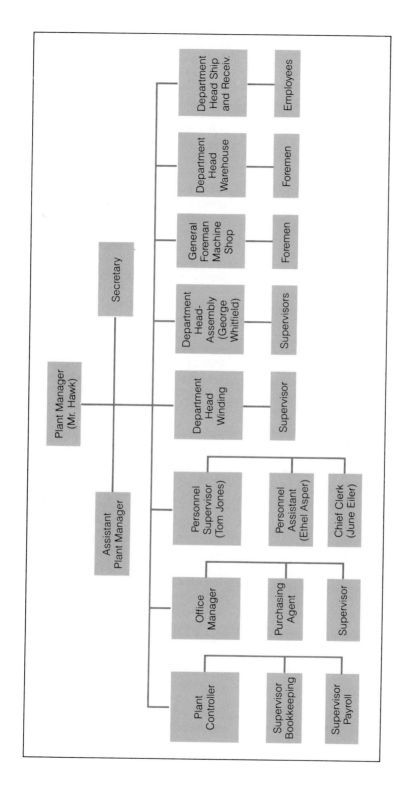

needed in the plant. A young man named Tom Jones, a college-educated junior executive having several years' experience with the parent company, was appointed to this new post. Most department heads and supervisors at Midvale welcomed this appointment because they believed that Jones would handle all their problems in much the same way that Martin previously had done, and with more expertise.

Jones was given wide latitude in setting up the personnel department. A general description of his authority, provided by Hawk, was as follows:

To be responsible for labor-relations activities and to represent the company in bargaining with the union. To be responsible for the hiring, placement, and induction of employees in the plant. To be responsible for wage and salary administration. To be responsible for liaison with the benefit department in the home office on all plant matters. To be responsible for employee activities, leaves of absence, disability, incidental absence, and so on, and to act in a staff capacity.

In setting up the new department, Jones appointed a personnel assistant, Ethel Asper, and delegated most of the responsibility related to the employment of workers to her. In addition, Patricia Martin was assigned to the personnel office and given the title of chief clerk. In terms of her salary, this was not a demotion, but neither was it a promotion. Martin did not look on it too kindly, and she appeared to be envious of the new personnel assistant. Deciding to retire a few months earlier than necessary, Martin left the company shortly after Tom Jones arrived to assume his responsibilities. He promptly appointed June Eiler to the chief clerk's job. Eiler was entirely unfamiliar with the work that had been handled by Miss Martin.

Organizational Relations

The majority of the managers and supervisors in the plant had been trained under George Whitfield and believed that technical and production aspects of their jobs were more important than personnel and human-relations problems. One department head, Alice Jeffries, was quoted as having said, "I hope this new fellow Jones doesn't hold a lot of meetings and keep my people off the job." However, the newer

supervisors and department heads who had transferred into Midvale had worked in plants that had personnel supervisors. They seemed to be more accustomed to the new organization and the services available from a personnel department.

After assuming his job as personnel supervisor, Tom Jones found that the new chief clerk, June Eiler, was being consulted on routine personnel matters as Martin had been. He was disturbed by a telephone call from George Whitfield, who said, "Tom, I know that you are new on this job, but you'll have to do something about vacation plans. One of our women on the assembly line was told by Miss Martin that she could take her vacation in May, and now your new chief clerk says she has to wait until July. You'll probably have to talk to her.

"And there's another thing. A month ago we started to hire a young fellow named Jorgenson for benchwork, filing, polishing, and miscellaneous work. Miss Martin and I thought we had him hired, but the employment office over at the city stopped it, saying we can't hire anyone who's not a high school graduate. Why in hell does a filer have to be a high school graduate? Now this applicant isn't a relative or a friend or anything special, but I have a supervisor who's going to be very unhappy until we get that young guy on the payroll. You're going to have to do something about these problems and get them handled the way Miss Martin used to do."

Tom tried to interrupt and answer but Whitfield went right on talking. "And I think you ought to know that the union reps are stirring up a fuss about some of the things going on around here. The stewards in my department are concerned that you haven't met with them and talked about union problems, grievances, and negotiations. They think you've got the company bigshot attitude and that personnel problems are going to be hard to settle around here without Miss Martin."

During the telephone conversation Tom Jones tried to explain several new policies designed by the home office to upgrade Abacus plant personnel. For example, the company management had decided that for an indefinite period of time only high school graduates were to be employed for all jobs other than custodial work. Jones was not successful in convincing

Whitfield of the merits of this policy. Upon completing the call, Jones decided to make a list of matters pertaining to plant personnel relationships that he should discuss with Oliver Hawk.

QUESTIONS

1. Evaluate Patricia Martin's role in Personnel before the reorganization?
2. Evaluate the responsibility and authority statement provided by Oliver Hawk.
3. Why did so many managers view the Personnel Department skeptically?
4. What alternatives are now open to Tom Jones to improve his situation with:
  a. Company supervisors
  b. Higher managers
  c. The union and employees
5. Outline a strategy for Jones to make the Personnel Department more viable.

THE MIDVALE PLANT(B): THE RESIGNATION OF "MARY POPPINS"

The Situation

Howard Howlett, controller of the Midvale plant, was concerned about his scheduled appointment with Mary Priesmeyer, supervisor of the general ledger section. Because of her slight resemblance to actress Julie Andrews and her occasional use of a large black umbrella, she was affectionately nicknamed "Mary Poppins" by everyone in the department. For more than five years Priesmeyer had supervised the general accounting functions and had become an informal troubleshooter and problem solver for anyone with accounting problems.

A warning had come when Bill Nolan, an acquaintance and a partner in a local public accounting firm, had called and told Howlett that he had interviewed Priesmeyer and his firm wanted to make her a job offer. Howlett knew that he should have done something about it immediately, but he had been busy and had procrastinated. And now. Preismeyer, who had always been pleasantly informal, had made an appointment with him through his secretary.

Other problems also seemed to plague the department. In the eight years since Oliver Hawk had been Midvale's plant manager, the dollar volume of production had doubled, and employees in the plant now numbered about a thousand. Howlett's division had increased in size by at least 50 percent. The office manager and his staff were placed in the controller's division, and soon after that change, George Whitfield, the assembly department manager who had previously been plant manager, suffered a mild heart attack. He was offered and accepted the position of office manager (see Figure 3). With only three years until his retirement, George had acquired considerable office know-how. His reorganization of procedures for purchasing supplies was commendable, and he bragged about saving the company "thousands of dollars in buying paper towels and paper clips." However, Whitfield was openly critical of many of the newer supervisors, and the supervisors in his filing and steno sections had said that they "were afraid" of him. One of the employees had been quoted as saying,

"Old George thinks that he and Mary Poppins have a monopoly on the brains in this department!"

Recently George Whitfield had complained specifically and had been openly resentful of the appointment of the new assistant controller, Gloria Hawkins, a young black woman transferred to Midvale by the corporate headquarters. Whitfield let it be known that he still reported directly to the controller, Howlett, and not to the new assistant controller. Hawkins learned of this attitude and acquiesced to it but with some personal distress. She had attended the business school of a large midwestern university where she had specialized in accounting and computer science and was awarded the B.S.B.A. degree. In five years with the Midvale plant's parent company, Abacus Corporation, she had helped install several accounting information centers and computer programs in branch plants. She had worked in an Ohio branch plant as a supervisor in the plant's accounting department for one year, and she was given a major promotion to become assistant controller at Midvale.

Most of the people in the controller's office at Midvale accepted Hawkins as being competent in her position. She was the only black employee in the department except for one of the payroll clerks. In four months' time, Hawkins had taken over responsibility for several important reports and was making progress on transferring additional accounts to the computer. When questioned directly, even George Whitfield admitted to Howlett that Hawkins knew accounting systems, and that she was efficiently contributing to the work of the department. But he also said, "Howard, she's only 29 years old. The boys at headquarters have her on a 'fast track.' You know, I know, and everyone else knows that she's here because she's black and female, and the company has been under pressure to do something about the so-called affirmative action program. But, damn it, it's not fair to others who really deserve promotions!"

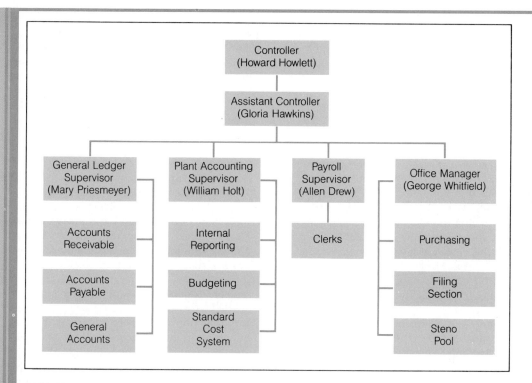

```
                          Controller
                       (Howard Howlett)
                               |
                       Assistant Controller
                       (Gloria Hawkins)
                               |
      ┌──────────────┬─────────┴──────────┬──────────────────┐
  General Ledger   Plant Accounting     Payroll          Office Manager
  Supervisor       Supervisor           Supervisor       (George Whitfield)
  (Mary Priesmeyer) (William Holt)      (Allen Drew)

  Accounts          Internal            Clerks            Purchasing
  Receivable        Reporting

  Accounts          Budgeting                             Filing
  Payable                                                 Section

  General           Standard                              Steno
  Accounts          Cost                                  Pool
                    System
```

FIGURE 3
Controller's Division of the
Midvale Plant of the Aba-
cus Corporation.

The Interview with "Mary Poppins"

At the apointed time, Mary Priesmeyer sat down across the desk from Howard Howlett and said, "I really don't know how to begin, Howard. I guess I'll just tell you quickly and easily that, after 11 years with Abacus, I want to leave the company. I'm going to take a job with another firm."

"I hate to hear you say that, Mary," said Howlett. "But I had some warning a couple of weeks ago when Bill Nolan told me that his public accounting firm was going to make you an offer. I've thought about it a lot lately. Do you really want to go into public accounting?"

"Well, I've decided that I ought to try it," replied Priesmeyer. "This should be a better opportunity for me. You know that I've taken almost every evening course the local university offers in accounting. I have my B.A. degree, and Mr. Nolan thinks I could qualify to take the CPA exam in about two years. I've enjoyed the years of experience I've had here at Midvale. You know that I've worked on almost every job in the department, and you've given me the opportunity to get into every aspect of plant accounting. I'm only 38 years old, and at this point I think I might have a better future elsewhere."

"But listen, Mary. Don't you know that you are well respected in our company? Something might turn up for you, and isn't there the possibility that you will marry again?" asked Priesmeyer.

Priesmeyer responded, "I've thought it over very carefully. There is some risk involved, but I now believe I will have a better opportunity if I get some public accounting experience and try for a CPA. I don't see any possibility of a promotion here. It's no secret that I was disappointed that I lost out on the assistant controller's job. Even being a woman with 11 years of service didn't get me anywhere!

"And as for marriage," continued Priesmeyer, "I think my interest in that died with my husband in Vietnam; but that's another rather private story. Besides, who would want to marry a plain-looking woman with two kids to raise?"

"Don't talk that way, Mary. You are a very attractive person. Why else would we all call you 'Mary Poppins'? And, by the way, how are the children?" queried Howlett.

"They're just great," said Priesmeyer. "Since my father passed on, my mother has been with us. She is in good health and does everything for the kids that I can't do. Little Tommy is the only man in the house, but we get along fine. I want you to know that I wouldn't have considered this change if my mother were not available to help at home. And I still would not consider leaving Abacus if a part of the change was not the possibility of noticeably greater earnings. With rather small resources, Mom and I are still definitely planning on a college education and a good life for the kids."

"I just don't know what I can do to keep you here, Mary. I just looked up your salary, and I think I could get you a 10-percent raise immediately if that would help," said Howlett. (It passed through his mind that Gloria Hawkins had been assigned to the assistant controller's job at a salary some $5,000 higher than Priesmeyer's) "I'm inclined to agree with you that your move to the accounting firm may be an unusual opportunity, but I'm wondering if the appointment of Gloria Hawkins as assistant controller is an appropriate reason for making such a decision."

"Well, Howard, I certainly respect Gloria. She's really very competent. But Bill Nolan tells me that there are opportunities for women in public accounting. Maybe Gloria's appointment has just shown me that I could benefit from being a woman too if I get a chance in the right company. Believe me, I have worked hard at 'not coveting' my neighbor's success. This plan for a job change has helped me get some perspective."

"Thank you, Mary, for being so frank," said Howlett. "Tell me, do you think there are any other serious problems of this kind in the department?"

"Well," replied Priesmeyer, "if we are speaking in confidence, I might as well tell you about a rumor that's being widely circulated. Another person who felt he should have received the assistant controller's job and didn't get it is Bill Holt. He is acting like a gentleman, especially in his contacts with Gloria. But he thinks he should have had the job, and unfortunately, he thinks it should be a man's position. He talks about being the wrong sex and color.

"I don't know how many years ago you brought Bill into the department to install the standard costs system, and he has done a fine job in plant accounting. Several years ago he took some of the accounting courses I've taken. He mentioned the other day that he's looking around for a job in industrial engineering or systems analysis, and it may or may not be in this plant."

"Your comments are appreciated, Mary," said Howlett. "Actually, Bill has a good chance for promotion somewhere in Abacus, but he's only been in this department for six years. I should have talked to him, though. Well, I certainly want the best of everything for our 'Mary Poppins.' All I ask is that you help us get organized to operate without you. How soon does Bill Nolan want you?"

"Right away, so he says," replied Priesmeyer. "But I know that I can stay and help you for two or three weeks if you need me."

"Good. Let's get together with Gloria and plan for your successor. If you have any other ideas about the department that I should know, please let me have them," said Howlett as he closed the interview.

The Conversation with Gloria Hawkins

Before going home that evening, Howlett told Gloria Hawkins that Mary Priesmeyer was leaving the company. Hawkins's only comment was, "I'm sorry she's leaving us. She's a good accountant, but we can replace her."

Howlett pondered whether he should discuss with Hawkins the substance of his conversation with Priesmeyer, and what, if any, actions he should take in regard to the situation in his division.

QUESTIONS

1. Compare the qualifications of Mary Priesmeyer and Gloria Hawkins. Why is it hard to tell if race is an issue?
2. Should length of service play a role in such decisions? Why or why not?
3. Does William Holt have a legitimate concern? Why or why not?
4. Is reverse discrimination a legitimate concern here? How should the company answer that issue?
5. What action should Howard Howlett take about:
    a. Approaching Gloria Hawkins. Outline his approach
    b. William Holt. Outline his approach
    c. Informing higher management about the ramifications of this issue

SOURCE: Hilgert/Schoen/Towle: CASES AND POLICIES IN PERSONNEL/HUMAN RESOURCES MANAGEMENT, Fourth Edition, Copyright © 1982 by Houghton Mifflin Company. Used with permission.

"Getting A Job"

Questions asked by students in personnel management classes often reflect their concerns about getting a job. This appendix, prepared with the assistance of a senior student, provides an overview of some of the activities involved in getting a job.* Throughout this section, specific tips and suggestions are made. No attempt has been made to direct you to specific references, as similar points are made in many sources. Instead, you should consult the suggested list of readings that conclude this appendix for more information on specific ideas highlighted in the following discussion.

Know Thyself

Before you can tell anyone what your skills, knowledge and abilities are, you have to understand them yourself. Prior to writing your resume, you should sit down and identify your strengths. There are four primary areas that you need to explore: the skills you possess; activities that interest you; your personal attributes; and past job and activity results.

Your Skills. In defining your skills, you should make a list of what you do well. Keep the list basic and do not leave out the obvious; reading and writing well do count. Now go back and check off those skills that you are willing to use in your work. For example, if you are good at research, would you be willing to take a job that required you to spend time sorting through information to prepare a report? Next get specific. Pick 10 or 12 of the skills that you have checked and define them in more detail. Describe how you

have applied or could apply these skills in either work or non-work activities. Finally, pick out the skills that are most valuable to you, write them down, and set that list aside. The next step is to identify your areas of interest.

Your Interests. What do you like to do? What would you like to do if you had the chance? What kind of people do you like? These items do not have to be work-related because this listing is meant to identify activities that give you pleasure. Be honest and do not include items just to make your list "look better." Now narrow the list down to the 10–12 interests you would like to have included in your job. Then, put this list with your list of skills and move on to an exploration of your personal attributes.

Your Attributes. "I am _____." Now fill in the blank. This is how you identify your attributes. You try to identify who are you, not just the you that people think you are, or the you that you let other people see. The "you" that must be identified here is how you see yourself. Are you hard-working, temperamental, creative, energetic, honest, shy? If so, put all of them down, but be honest with yourself. If you think you are intelligent, then write it down. Be careful not to list "labels" you've been given by others if you do not think they are true.

The next step is the same as in the first two areas: narrowing your list down. You should identify your 5 strongest and most positive attributes. Now put this list (you guessed) with the others and move on to the final area: your results.

*The authors acknowledge the assistance provided by Steven Howell.

Your Results. What important accomplishments have you had? What have you done of which you are proud? Did you work part-time while you were in school? Did you write a paper or build something? Did you organize and lead some project? If the results are there, then write them down. You may need to use your list of skills and interests to get started. Do not leave any area out. Work, school, military service, community service, hobbies, are all areas from which you may show the results of your activities.

Now you should identify the 10 accomplishments you consider to be most relevant to the type of work you want to do in the future. By writing them down and putting that list with the other three, you now have the foundation for your resume and you are about ready to prepare it. There is just one more bit of background work to do: Find out about your job.

Research the Employer

By now you have a good idea of what you want to do, but you must identify what a future employer will expect you to do. The best way to find out is to ask. Contact some organizations in the area that employ people in the fields or jobs in which you would like to work. Talk to a wide range of people, including supervisors or managers, and individuals who are working in those areas. Also, you should talk to the career counselors and professors at your college or university and read books and articles about your field of interest. Make a special effort to find out what kinds of tasks you will be expected to perform and what types of responsibilities you will have. You may think you know all there is to know about the job you want, but you might be wrong. If you are wrong, then your resume also may be wrong (and useless). While you are asking all of these questions, do not forget to find out what kind of a person most employers are interested in hiring.

Then, take the information you have gathered and compare it with the lists you have already prepared. The items that match should go on your resume.

The Resume

Preparation of a resume starts you on the road to employment. A resume is a summary of your academic accomplishments, your work experiences, and your expectations for employment. It is the first "picture" that most employers will have of you. Because those doing the hiring do not have the time to try to understand what you are trying to say in your resume, you must ensure that your resume shows them, simply and precisely, what contribution you would be to their operations.

As with everything else in life, there are hard and fast rules governing the preparation of a resume—except for the exceptions.

Rule #1: Your resume should be concise; many experts recommend no more than one page. Two pages at the absolute maximum.

Rule #2: Your name, address, and phone number are printed at the top, 1½ inches down, and they are centered on the page.

Rule #3: Your resume should be typed using a high-quality, electric typewriter. If you do not have one, find one. If you cannot find one, hire someone who has one to type your resume.

Rule #4: NO MISTAKES! Have two or three people critique it. If there is an error, retype it. A sloppy resume will lose you jobs.

Rule #5: Use action verbs. "Supervised 5-member work crew" looks and sounds much better than "I was in charge of the supervision of the day-to-day workings of a 5-person crew."

Rule #6: Keep your resume simple and uncluttered. If your resume is direct and to the point and the sections are separated with plenty of white space, it stands a much better chance of being read seriously.

Rule #7: No personal data. Your personal description, any references to your age, sex, national origin, religion, marital status, or a photograph have no place on or with your resume. In addition, requests for information in these areas are not legal and should be tactfully denied. No exceptions.

Rule #8: No references. You should have a

separate sheet listing your references. The last line of your resume should read: "References available upon request." No exceptions.

By now you must be thinking that if you follow these rules, your resume will look just like everyone else's. While this may be possible it is not very probable. A man came to the Career Planning Office on a college campus a few years ago with a copy of his resume requesting assistance. He had three graduate degrees (two were Ph.D.'s) and a very handsome work record. However, he was having difficulty tying down any job offers, or even getting any interviews. The first recommendation he received was to completely rework his resume. His original "resume" amounted to nothing more than a listing of the companies he had worked for, when he worked for them, and a list of his degrees. It appeared as though it had been typed on a manual machine. There was no listing of job titles or duties performed. In all, it presented a very poor image of the man. Chances are it was not even read by a majority of the people to whom it had been submitted. He broke many of the rules listed above.

A resume can follow several forms: chronological, functional, targeted, the resume alternative, or the creative resume. The choice of form depends upon the specific situation, but for the majority of newly graduated college students the chronological or functional formats are the most appropriate. Examples of both are shown in Figure A–1 and A–2. While the spacing between sections depends upon the individual resume, some specific guidelines for preparing your resume are as follows:

First, below your name and address, along the left margin (one inch from the left edge of the paper), type the word "OBJECTIVE:" followed by a one-or two-sentence description of what job (or career field) for which you are applying. It should be single-spaced and no more than three lines.

The next area presented is your educational background. The word "EDUCATION:" should appear along the left margin, followed by the degree or degrees you earned, your major, the school you attended (if more than

one list them in chronological order starting from the most recent, one to a line) and the year of your graduation. For people with more experience, education probably should follow the skills section discussed next.

The center sections of your resume are where you tell the employer what you will bring to her/his company. You should get your preparatory lists from before. Can the skills required by the employer for this job be grouped into two or three major categories? If so, then group your skills and accomplishments under these categories and list them from most important to less important (the *least important* does not belong in your resume). If not, then list your skills under the heading "CAPABILITIES:" and your accomplishments under "ACHIEVEMENTS:". Start with the items that best match the requirements listed by your outside sources. In either case, remember Rule #5: Use action verbs. These sections can be single- or double-spaced, depending on the room you have. The word "I" should not appear anywhere on your resume.

The last two sections of your resume should be your WORK HISTORY and REFERENCES. As with the other sections, these headings should appear in capital letters at the left margin. Start the work history section with your most recent job and go back in time for four or five jobs. If you had a job more than five years ago but it is extremely relevant to this job, include it also. Start with the dates that you worked at that job. Next list the job title and the name of the company or organization for which you worked. If you performed any duties that are relevant to the job you are applying for, list them on separate lines. The reference section was covered by Rule # 8. If employers want your references, they can ask for them later.

You should always remember that your resume is your "paper picture." Taking the time to insure that it looks good, and experimenting with layout and spacing may force you to revise your draft resume. A third draft will almost always be better than a first.

Now you are ready to use your "perfect" resume. The cover letter transmitting the resume may be as important as the resume itself.

The Cover Letter

Whenever you send your resume to a company, you should include a cover letter. The cover letter is your personalized introduction to the company and is just as important as your resume. Sending a resume without a cover letter is like sending a piece of junk mail and will almost guarantee that your resume will not be read.

The letter should be addressed to a specific person, by name and position. In general, it is better if you send your letter and resume to the director or supervisor of the department or section for which you would expect to be working. Personnel departments receive countless resumes every week and many of them can become "lost in the shuffle." In addition, it is usually the department head that has the final decision on whether or not you get the job.

Rules for the preparation of the cover letter are similar to those for the resume. Use a high-quality, electric typewriter and quality (20-lb.) bond paper. You should include the date at the top, along the right margin and the complete address of the recipient along the left margin. As with any standard business letter, never, never, never send a generic cover letter with the name and address of the individual filled in at the top. This innocent shortcut only succeeds in giving the impression that the recipient is just another name on your list.

The body of the letter should be about half a page long. It should point out two or three facts from the resume and expand upon them. The letter should state your reason for sending it, but it should contain something more than "I think I would like to work for your company."

You should always include some personal comment directed specifically to the individual and the company. For example, you might mention a problem that you are aware they are having, and a possible solution that you have. Or, if the individual's name appeared in a newsarticle and that is where you got the idea to contact him or her, say that.

You should always close your cover letter with the suggestion of a meeting but do not just say "I would like to talk to you about this further." Include a time frame. If the company is out of town, you should tell the individual when you will be in that area. In any case, give a date when you will be in contact with her or him again. A statement like "I will be interviewing in your area on May 14 and 15 and would appreciate the opportunity to speak with you further on this subject. I will call the week before I am there to set up a time that is convenient for you" is a very good closing for a cover letter. Then end your letter with an appropriate closing and your signature. Also, it is a good idea to include your address and telephone number above the date, in case the letter and resume are separated.

The Application

Some college graduates will not be required to complete an application form when they apply for a job. Most college placement offices supply the companies who will be interviewing their graduates with data sheets that contain all of the relevant information on the candidate. Nevertheless, many graduates will be required at some time to complete a standard application form for a job. The most frequent concern voiced by students is how to handle one problem: illegal questions.

As was mentioned in the text of this book, many of the job application forms in use today contain questions that, by law, do not have to be completed by the applicant. These questions are ones that concern race, sex, age, national origin, religion, and mental and physical limitations not relevant to the performance of the job. In addition, application forms should not ask questions concerning arrests, as people are not judged guilty of a crime solely on the basis of arrests. Questions concerning criminal convictions should be asked only insofar as they pertain to the performance of the job. Questions concerning credit ratings or current financial situation may not be asked unless they have a direct relationship to the job (i.e., if the job will place you in a situation of being unsupervised and around sums of money). Questions about any political or ideological affiliations may not be asked. It is also illegal to ask questions about physical descriptions unless they can be shown to be *Bona Fide* Occupational Qualifications (BFOQ). Also questions concerning marital status and family may not be asked.

As a general rule, it is best if you, as the applicant, leave blank any of these illegal questions on application forms. If the employers are asking questions for the purpose of maintaining EEO compliance records, they should have a separate form or obtain appropriate information after you have been hired.

The Interview

You have submitted your resume, contacted the company, and been invited in for an interview, or you have made an appointment with one of the recruiters who will be visiting your campus. Either way, there are four areas of knowledge that may help you have a better interview: preparation for the interview; behavior during the interview; your rights in the interview; and following up on the interview.

Preparation for the Interview

Once you know that you have an interview, you need to begin preparing for it. As with your resume, a little preparation can set you far above the other applicants in the race for the job. First, find out all the information you can about the company with which you will be interviewing. Questions include: What do they do? What are their markets? Who are their competitors? How are they doing financially? Most of this information is available from the company itself, especially if the company is large enough and publicly-traded. Quite often you will be able to find articles concerning the company in newspapers and magazines. If nothing else, you can call and ask questions of someone working for the company. In addition, you should also try to gather as much information concerning the

job for which you are applying. Find out what the duties are for that position, what the salary range is (if possible), why the position is open, and what happened to the last person who had the job.

As the day of the interview draws near, you need to begin preparing yourself for the interview. The appropriate clothing often is a vested suit for men and a skirted suited for woman. Your clothing makes a statement about yourself and it should say what you want it to say (for a detailed discussion of the proper clothing, see *Dress For Success* or *The Woman's Dress For Success Book* both by John T. Molloy). Your personal appearance—whether your hair is neatly groomed, whether you are clean-shaven (men) or tastefully made-up (women)—is also critical. You should make sure you look as sharp and crisp as you can before arriving for the interview.

Behavior During the Interview

On the day of the interview, it is vital for you to arrive on time. If necessary, give yourself a half-hour head start, just in case. By arriving at the site of the interview 10 minutes or so before your appointment, you give yourself time to relax. Arriving just in the nick of time, out of breath and flushed, is almost as bad as arriving late. Also, it is generally recommended that you curb your desire for a cigarette and spit out your gum before you walk in the door.

When the person with whom you will be interviewing comes to get you (being called into an office usually is not done), stand, smile, and extend your hand. At that point, the interview has just begun and you can lose the job before the first question is even asked. You should exude confidence and your handshake should be firm, but not a crusher. Also you may wish to take along a small note card with questions you want to ask printed on it.

During the interview you should sit in an erect but comfortable manner. As much as possible, try to avoid any unnecessary body movement such as drumming your fingers, swinging your legs, or squirming in your seat. All of these actions will be distracting to the interviewer and may be the first and major fact that is remembered about you. You should maintain eye contact with the interviewer, but not to the point that you are staring. When asked a question, answer it in an even voice at a conversational level. Above all, remember that an interview is a two-way experience. The interviewer is checking you out and you are checking out the company.

It is important for you to assert yourself during the interview. If the company does offer you a position, you want to be sure that it will suit you as much as you will suit it. By asking questions, you can put the information you gathered prior to the interview to use. Avoid emphasizing questions about benefit plans for employees. Instead focus on questions concerning the job. You should try to answer all questions precisely, but if you feel that the wrong impression has been given from your response, do not hesitate to add to your answer. Never forget that you too have rights in the interviewing process.

Your Rights

At some point in the interview, a question may be asked of you that you do not feel is job-related and that may be illegal. However, you should not let yourself be intimidated. If the interviewer asks if you have ever been arrested, you can decline to answer. You should explain that you have never been convicted of any crime and that you have never missed any work time as a result of an involvement with the authorities (provided that it is true). You can, of course, answer any question that you wish, but remember, the interviewer is not legally authorized to ask those types of questions and he or she should know that. However, the interview is not the time to try to correct any illegal practices on the part of the interviewer.

Following up the Interview

At the close of the interview, you should be sure to thank the interviewer for her or his time and shake hands once again. When you return home, make a note or two about the facts discussed during the interview. Then, a day or two after the interview, write a brief thank-you note. The note should thank the interviewer once again for the time spent and should mention something of importance that was brought up in the interview, especially if it was favorable for you.

In summary, remember that you are an equal partner in any interview and you have rights. Prepare in advance for the interview. Focus on your positive attributes during the interview and know your rights. Then, follow the interview up with a brief thank-you note. The tips in this appendix should help you to get many more second interviews and job offers. Good luck.

SUGGESTED READINGS

Allen, Jeffrey G. *How to Turn an Interview Into a Job.* New York: Simon & Schuster, 1983.

Chapman, Elwood N. *From Campus to Career Success.* Chicago: Science Research Associates, 1978.

German, Richard and Arnold, Peter. *Bernard Haldane Associates' Job and Career Building.* Berkeley, CA: Ten Speed Press, 1980.

Irish, Richard K. *Go Hire Yourself an Employer.* Garden City, NY: Anchor Press/Doubleday, 1978.

Jackson, Tom. *Guerrilla Tactics in the Job Market.* New York: Bantam Books, 1978.

———. *The Perfect Resume.* Garden City, NY: Anchor Press/Doubleday, 1981.

Komar, John J. *The Interview Game: Winning Strategies for the Job Seeker.* Piscataway, NJ: New Century Publishers, 1979.

Molloy, John T. *Dress for Success.* New York: Warner Books, 1976.

———. *The Woman's Dress for Success Book.* New York: Warner Books, 1978.

Roffwarg, Steven M., ed. *AMBA's MBA Employment Guide,* 1984 ed. New York: Association of MBA Executives, 1983.

DEBRA JAMES
5421 Dodge Avenue
Omaha, Nebraska 68104
(402) 221-9908

* OBJECTIVE

Entry-level management track position in marketing/sales.
Desire opportunity for training and professional growth.

* EDUCATION

University of Nebraska at Omaha
Bachelor of Science in Business Administration, May, 1982
Specialization in Marketing   Cumulative GPA: 3.4 (4.00)

Participated in two special research projects with Small Business
Administration: 1) to assist Boardwalk Shopping Center, Omaha,
to become more visible to the public and increase sales, 2) to
study the feasibility of opening an interior designer showcase in
the Omaha area.

* EXPERIENCE

Shepler's Western Wear, Omaha, Nebraska, 7/80–present (part-time).
Salesperson. Average twenty-five hours per week involving customer
contact. Formulated a marketing research proposal relating to
different lines of western clothing not currently in stock.

University of Nebraska at Omaha, 5/79–7/80 (part-time). Student
Programming Organization (SPO), Student Director. Planned and
implemented 10 educational and cultural programs. Selected
programs for presentation, negotiated contracts with booking agents,
managed ticket sales based on budgeted expenses.

The Tree, Affiliate of J.L. Brandeis, Inc., Omaha, Nebraska,
10/76–8/78 (full-time). Sales Associate. Originated, planned and
supervised new fashion show presentations. Identified, selected,
and assisted in training of part-time sales force. Suggested
several advertising campaigns that were implemented.

* ACTIVITIES

President, Phi Chi Theta, professional women's business fraternity,
    Spring, 1982: Vice President, Fall, 1981
Student Orientation Leader (3 semesters)
Member, American Marketing Association
Member, UNO Moving Company, modern dance group

* REFERENCES

Available upon request

William Smith
2020 Jackson Blvd.
Omaha, NE 68111
(402) 664-9496

EDUCATION:

B.S. Journalism, University of Nebraska at Omaha, 1982

WRITING:

* Wrote articles for the sports section of college newspaper.

* Had three articles published in Omaha Sun Newspaper.

* Served as assistant editor of the sports section of college newspaper.

* Editor of high school student newspaper.

SPORTS:

* Played collegiate basketball four years.

* Captain and starting center for UNO's defending North Central Conference champion basketball team.

* Voted most improved player by teammates as a junior and chosen to All-Conference tournament team during senior year.

* Nominated to the NCC All-Academic squad.

* Coached high school basketball players at summer clinic.

COMMUNICATION/RADIO/VIDEO:

* Announced live broadcasts of football games on college radio.

* Wrote and delivered nightly sports news for radio on football weekends.

* Assisted in developing basketball training via video.

* Delivered sports promotional spots on local college radio station.

WORK HISTORY:

1979-80   KVNO, Campus Radio, University of Nebraska at Omaha. Reporter.

Summer 1979   Smietrews Restaurant, Omaha, Nebraska. Night Manager.

Summer 1976-
1977   Mutual of Omaha, Omaha, Nebraska. Pressman.

REFERENCES:

* Available upon request

The Current Literature in Personnel Management

Students are expected to be familiar with the professional literature in their fields of study. The professional journals are the most immediate and direct communication link between the researcher and the practicing manager. Two groups of publications are listed below:

A. *Research-oriented journals.* These journals contain articles that report on original research. Normally these journals contain rather sophisticated writing and quantitative verifications of the author's findings.

Academy of Management Journal
Academy of Management Review
Administrative Science Quarterly
American Journal of Sociology
American Psychologist
American Sociological Review
Behavioral Science
British Journal of Industrial Relations
Decision Sciences
Human Organization
Human Relations
Industrial & Labor Relations Review
Industrial Relations
Interfaces
Journal of Abnormal Psychology
Journal of Applied Behavioral Science
Journal of Applied Psychology
Journal of Business
Journal of Business Communications
Journal of Business Research
Journal of Communications
Journal of Experimental Social Psychology
Journal of Counseling Psychology
Journal of Industrial Relations
Journal of Management
Journal of Management Studies

Journal of Personality and Social Psychology
Journal of Social Psychology
Journal of Social Issues
Journal of Vocational Behavior
Management Science
Occupational Psychology
Organizational Behavior and Human Performance
Pacific Sociological Review
Personnel Psychology
Psychological Monographs
Psychological Review
Social Forces
Social Science Research
Sociometry

B. *Management-oriented journals.* These journals generally cover a wide range of subjects. Articles in these publications normally are aimed at the practitioner and are written to interpret, summarize, or discuss past, present, and future research and administrative applications. Not all the articles in these publications are management-oriented.

Administrative Management
Advanced Management Journal
American Journal of Small Business
Arbitration Journal
Australian Journal of Management
Business
Business and Society Review
Business Horizons
Business Management
Business Quarterly
California Management Review
Canadian Manager
Columbia Journal of World Business

Compensation Review
Dun's Business Month
Employee Benefit Plan Review
Employee Benefits Journal
Employee Law Journal
Employment Relations Today
Forbes
Fortune
Harvard Business Review
Hospital & Health Services Administration
Human Behavior
Human Resource Management
Human Resource Planning
Industry Week
Labor Law Journal
Long-Range Planning
Manage
Management Advisor
Management Planning
Management Review
Management World
Michigan State University Business Topics
Monthly Labor Review
National Productivity Review
Nation's Business
Organizational Dynamics
Pension World
Personnel
Personnel Administrator
Personnel Journal
Personnel Management
Public Administration Review

Public Opinion Quarterly
Public Personnel Management
Psychology Today
Research Management
Sloan Management Review
Supervision
Supervisory Management
Training
Training and Development Journal
Working Woman

In addition, in this group are area business publications such as Arkansas Business, Arizona Business Review, or the Atlantic Economic Review.

Abstracts & Indices. For assistance in locating articles, students should check some of the following indices and abstracts that often contain subject matter of interest:

Applied Science and Technology Index
Business Periodicals
Dissertation Abstracts
Employees Relation Index
Index to Legal Periodicals
Index to Social Sciences and Humanities
Management Abtracts
Management Contents
Personnel Management Abtracts
Psychological Abstracts
Reader's Guide to Periodical Literature
Sociological Abstracts

Important Organizations in Personnel Management

Administrative Management Society
2360 Maryland Rd.
Willow Grove, PA 19090
(215) 659-4300

AFL-CIO
815 16th St. NW
Washington, DC 20006

American Arbitration Association
140 W. 51st St.
New York, NY 10020
(212) 484-4800

American Compensation Association
P.O. Box 1176
Scottsdale, AZ 85252
(602) 951-9191

American Management Associations
135 W. 50th St.
New York, NY 10020
(212) 586-8100

American Society for Hospital Personnel Administration
840 N. Lakeshore Dr.
Chicago, IL 60611
(312) 280-6428

American Society for Industrial Security
1655 N. Fort Meyer Dr., Suite 1200
Arlington, VA 22209
(703) 522-5800

American Society for Personnel Administration
606 N. Washington
Alexandria, VA 22314
(703) 548-3440

American Society for Public Administration
1120 "G" St. NW, Suite 500
Washington, DC 20005
(205) 393-7878

American Society for Training and Development
600 Maryland Ave. SW, Suite 305
Washington, DC 20024
(202) 484-2390

American Society of Pension Actuaries
1700 K St. NW, Suite 404
Washington, DC 20006
(202) 737-4360

American Society of Safety Engineers
850 Busse Highway
Park Ridge, IL 60068
(312) 692-4121

Association of Executive Search Consultants, Inc.
151 Railroad Ave.
Greenwich, CT 06830
(203) 661-6606

Association for Fitness in Business
1312 Washington Blvd.
Stamford, CT 06902
(203) 359-2188

Bureau of Industrial Relations
University of Michigan
Ann Arbor, Michigan 48104

Bureau of Labor Statistics (BLS)
Department of Labor
3rd Street & Constitution Ave. NW
Washington, DC 20210

Bureau of National Affairs (BNA)
1231 25th Street, NW
Washington, DC 20037

Canadian Public Personnel Management Association
220 Laurier Ave. West, Suite 720
Ottowa, Ontario
Canada K1P 5Z9
(613) 233-1742

Department of Labor
3rd Street & Constitution Ave. NW
Washington, DC 20210

Employee Benefit & Research Institute
2121 K St. NW, Suite 860
Washington, DC 20037
(202) 659-0670

Employee Relocation Council
1627 K St. NW
Washington, DC 20006
(202) 857-0857

Employment Management Association
20 William St.
Wellesley, MA 02181
(617) 235-8878

Equal Employment Opportunity Commission
(EEOC)
2401 E. Street, NW
Washington, DC 20506

Human Resource Systems Professionals, Inc.
3051 Adeline St., 2nd Floor
Berkeley, CA 94703
(415) 548-1364

Human Resources Planning Society
P.O. Box 2553
Grand Central Station
New York, NY 10163
(212) 837-0630

Industrial Relations Research Association
7226 Social Science Bldg.
Madison, WI 53706
(608) 262-2762

Internal Revenue Service (IRS)
111 Constitution Ave., NW
Washington, DC 20224

International Association for Personnel
Women
211 E. 43rd St., Suite 1601
New York, NY 10017
(212) 867-4194

International Foundation of Employee Benefit
Plans
18700 Blue Mound Rd.
Brookfield, WI 53005
(414) 786-6700

International Personnel Management Association
1850 K St. NW, Suite 870
Washington, DC 20006
(202) 833-5860

International Society of Pre-Retirement Planners
3500 Clayton Rd., Suite B
Concord, CA 94519
(415) 676-0397

Labor Management Mediation Service
1620 I St. NW, Suite 616
Washington, DC 20006

National Association for the Advancement of
Colored People (NAACP)
1790 Broadway
New York, NY 10019

National Association of Manufacturers (NAM)
1776 F St. NW
Washington, DC 20006

National Association of Personnel Consultants
1432 Duke St.
Alexandria, VA 22314
(703) 684-0180

National Association of Temporary Services
1001 Connecticut Ave., NW, Suite 932
Washington, DC 20036

National Employee Services & Recreation Association
2400 S. Downing Ave.
Westchester, IL 60153
(312) 562-8130

National Public Employer Labor
Relations Association
55 E. Monroe St.
Chicago, IL 60603
(312) 782-1752

Occupational Safety and Health Administration (OSHA)
200 Constitution Ave., NW
Washington, DC 20210

Office of Federal Contract Compliance Programs (OFCCP)
200 Constitution Ave., NW
Washington, DC 20210

Pension Benefit Guaranty Corporation
P.O. Box 7119
Washington, DC 20044

Profit Sharing Council of America
200 N. Wacker Drive, Suite 722
Chicago, IL 60606
(312) 372-3411

U.S. Chamber of Commerce
1615 H St., NW
Washington, DC 20062

Glossary

Adverse Impact occurs when there is a substantially different rate in hiring, promotion, or other employment decisions which works to the disadvantage of members of protected groups.

Affirmative Action refers to efforts by employers to identify problem areas in the employment of protected group members, and goals and steps to overcome those problems.

Arbitration process whereby an impartial entity determines the relative merit of different viewpoints and makes a decision called an "award".

Authority is the right to use resources to accomplish goals.

Benefits are rewards available to an employee or group of employees as a part of organizational membership.

Bonafide Occupational Qualification (BFOQ) is a legitimate reason why an employer can exclude persons on otherwise-illegal bases of consideration.

Career is the sequence of work-related positions occupied throughout a person's life.

Centralization is the extent to which decision-making authority/responsibility is concentrated.

Chronology is a structured review of activities during a period of time.

Closed Shop requires individuals to join a union before they can be hired.

Codetermination is a practice whereby union or worker representatives are given positions on a company's board of directors.

Collective Bargaining is the process whereby representatives of management and workers negotiate over wages, hours, and conditions of employment.

Commission is compensation that is computed as a percentage of sales in units or dollars.

Comparable Worth is the concept that jobs requiring comparable knowledge, skills, and abilities should be paid similarly.

Conciliation is a process in which an outside entity attempts to help two deadlock parties continue negotiation and arrive at a solution (also called *mediation*).

Compensation Committee usually is a subgroup of the board of directors composed of outside directors.

Consideration refers to behavior indicating trust, warmth, friendship, and mutual respect between the leader and the group members.

Contributory Plan is one in which the money for pension benefits is contributed by both employees and employers.

Cost/Benefit Analysis is comparing what efforts will cost with the benefits received to see which is greater.

Decentralization is the extent to which decision-making authority/responsibility is dispersed downward.

Decertification is a process whereby a union is removed as the representative of a group of employees.

Defined Benefit Plan is one in which the retirement benefits to be paid to the employees and the method of determining those benefits is set so that the employer's contributions can be statistically determined.

Defined Contribution Plan is one in which the employer's contribution rate is set and the employees' retirement benefits depend upon the contributions and employees' earning levels.

Discrimination (EEOC definition) is the use of any test that adversely affects hiring, promotion, transfer or any other employment or membership opportunity of classes unless the test has been validated and is job related, and/or an employer can demonstrate that alternative hiring, transfer, or promotion procedures are unavailable.

Draw is an amount advanced to an employee and repaid from future commissions earned by the employee.

Duty is a work segment performed by an individual composed of a number of tasks.

Employee-Assistance Program provides counseling and other help to employees having emotional, physical, or other personal problems.

Employee Stock Ownership Plan (ESOP) is a stock bonus plan whereby employees gain ownership in the firm for which they work.

Equity is the perceived fairness of what the person does (inputs) compared with what the person receives (outcomes).

Exempt Employees are those who are not required to be paid overtime under the Fair Standards Act.

Expatriate is a person working in a country who is not a national citizen of that country.

Extinction is the absence of a response to a situation.

Flex-Time refers to variations in starting and quitting times, but assumes that a number of hours (usually eight) is worked each day.

Four-fifths (4/5th) Rule states that discrimination generally occurs if the selection rate for a protected group is less than 80 percent of the selection rate of the majority group.

401(k) Plan allows employees to receive cash or to have employer contributions from profit-sharing and stock-bonus plans placed into a tax-deferred account.

Funded Method provides pension benefits over a long period from funds accumulated ahead of time.

Garnishment is a court action in which a portion of an employee's wages is set aside to pay a debt owed a creditor.

Grievance is a specific, formal notice of dissatisfaction expressed through an identified procedure.

Grievance Procedure is a formal channel of communication used to resolve formal complaints (grievances).

Health refers to a general state of physical, mental, and emotional well-being.

Health Maintenance Organization (HMO) is a form of health care which provides services for a fixed period on a prepaid basis.

Human Resource Accounting is a specialized personnel audit that continually attempts to quantify the value of organizational human resources.

Human Resource Development focuses on increasing the capabilities of employees for continuing growth and advancement in the organization.

Human Resource Information System (HRIS) is an integrated computerized system designed to provide information to be used in making personnel decisions.

Human Resource Planning consists of analyzing and identifying the need for and the availability of the human resources required for an organization to meet its objectives.

Immediate Confirmation indicates that people learn best if reinforcement is given as soon as possible after training.

Incentives are rewards designed to encourage and reimburse employees for efforts beyond normal performance expectations.

Individual Retirement Account (IRA) allows an employee to set aside in a special account funds which are tax-deferred until the employee retires.

Initiating Structure refers to task-oriented efforts on the part of the leader to get the job done.

Insured Plan is one administered through insurance companies or similar institutions which buy retirement annuity policies.

Interfaces are areas of contact between the personnel unit and other managers in an organization that occur in personnel activities.

Job is a grouping of similar positions.

Job Analysis is a systematic investigation of the tasks, duties, and responsibilities required in a job, and the necessary skills, knowledge, and abilities someone needs to perform the job adequately.

Job Depth is the amount of planning and control responsibilities in a job.

Job Description is a summary of the tasks, duties, and responsibilities in a job.

Job Design refers to a conscious effort to organize tasks, duties, and responsibilities into a unit of work to achieve an objective.

Job Enlargement is the concept of broadening the scope of a job by expanding the number of different tasks to be performed.

Job Enrichment is increasing the depth of a job by adding employee responsibility, planning, organizing, controlling, and evaluating the job.

Job Evaluation is the systematic determination of the relative worth of jobs within an organization.

Job Rotation is the process of shifting a person from job to job.

Job Scope refers to the number and variety of tasks performed by a job holder.

Job Specifications list the skills, knowledge, and abilities an individual needs to do the job satisfactorily.

Keogh Plan (H.R.10 Plan) allows self-employed individuals to establish an individualized pension plan.

Matrix Organization is an organization in which both a project-team organization and a functional organization exist at the same time.

Motivation is derived from the word "motive" and is an emotion or desire operating on a person's will and causing that person to act.

Negative Reinforcement is action taken to repel the person from the undesired action.

Noncontributory Plan is one in which the employer provides all the funds.

Norms are expected standards of behavior, usually unwritten and often unspoken, that are generally understood by all members of a group.

Open System is a living entity which takes energy from its environment processes it, and returns output to the environment.

Organization is a goal-oriented system of coordinated relationships between people, tasks, resources, and managerial activities.

Organization Development is a value-based process of self-assessment and planned change, involving specific strategies as.

Organization Structure is the formally-designed framework of authority and task relationships.

Organizational Climate is a composite view of the characteristics of an organization as seen by employees.

Orientation is the planned introduction of employees to their jobs, their co-workers, and their organizations.

Pay is the basic compensation employees receive, usually as a wage or salary.

Pay Grades are used to group individual jobs having approximately the same job worth together.

Pay Compression occurs when pay differences between individuals become small.

PAYSOP is a payroll-based stock ownership plan.

Performance Appraisal is the process of determining how well employees do their jobs compared to a set of standards, and communicating that information to the employees.

Perquisites ("perks") are special benefits for executives that are usually non-cash items.

Personnel Audit is a formal research effort to evaluate the current state of personnel management in an organization.

Personnel Generalist is someone who has responsibility for performing a varied range of personnel activities.

Personnel Management is a set of activities focusing on the effective use of human resources in an organization.

Personnel Research analyzes past and present personnel practices through the use of collected data and records.

Personnel Specialists is someone who has in-depth knowledge and expertise in a limited area of personnel.

Policies are general guidelines that regulate organizational actions.

Portability allows employees to move their pension benefits rights from one employer to another.

Position is a collection of tasks performed by one person.

Positive Reinforcement occurs when a person receives a desired reward.

Preferred Provider Organization (PPO) is a health care provider that contracts with an employer or an employer group to provide health care services to employees at competitive rates.

Procedures are customary methods of handling activities.

Protected-Group Member is an individual who falls within a group identified for protection under equal employment laws.

Punishment is action taken to repel the person from undesired action.

Quality Circles are small groups of employees that meet on a regular basis to discuss ways to improve productivity and to cut costs.

Ratification occurs when union members vote to accept the terms of a negotiated labor agreement.

Realistic Job Preview (RJP) is the process of providing a job applicant with an accurate picture of a job.

Recruiting is the process of generating a pool of qualified applicants for organizational jobs.

Red Circle Rate is a job whose current occupant's pay is out of grade or range.

Reliability refers to the consistency with which a test measures an item.

Responsibilities are obligations to perform certain tasks and duties.

Reverse Discrimination may exist when a person is denied an opportunity because of preferences given to protected-group individuals who may be less qualified.

Rules are specific guidelines that regulate and restrict the behavior of individuals.

Safety refers to protection of the physical health of people.

Salary is compensation that is consistent from period to period and is not directly related to the number of hours worked.

Selection is the process of picking individuals who have relevant qualifications to fill jobs in an organization.

Self-actualization is the striving of an individual to reach the highest level of potential.

Self-funding occurs when an employer sets aside funds to pay health claims in excess of the amount provided by funding in lieu of insurance coverage.

Sexual Harassment refers to actions that are sexually-directed, unwanted, and subject the worker to adverse employment conditions.

Status is the relative social ranking an individual has in a group or organization.

Stock Option gives an employee the right to buy stock in the company, usually at the fixed price for a period of time.

Structured Interview is conducted using a set of standardized questions that are asked all applicants for a job.

Task is a distinct identifiable work activity composed of motions.

Technology consists of types and patterns of activity, equipment, materials, and knowledge or experience used to perform tasks.

Title VII is that portion of the 1964 Civil Right Act prohibiting discrimination in employment.

Training is a learning process whereby people acquire skills, concepts, attitudes, or knowledge to aid in the achievements of goals.

Turnover is the process in which employees leave the organization and have to be replaced.

Unfunded Plan pays pension benefits out of current income to the organization.

Uninsured Plan is one in which the benefits at retirement are determined by the employer based upon calculations that consider the age of the employee, years worked, and other factors.

Union is a formal association of workers that promotes the welfare of its members.

Validity means that a "test" actually predicts what it says it predicts.

Vesting is the right of employees to receive benefits from their pension plans.

Wage and Salary Administration is the group of activities involved in the development, implementation, and maintenance of a base pay system.

Wage/Salary Survey is a means of gathering data on existing compensation rates for workers performing similar jobs in other organizations.

Wages are pay directly calculated on the amount of time worked.

Work Group is a collection of individuals brought together to perform organizational work.

Workers' Compensation provides benefits to a person injured on the job.

Name Index

Friedman, S., 141, 524
Frishman, Melanie E., 462
Fulghum, Judy B., 140
Fulk, J., 78
Fullerton, H. N., 233

Gannon, M. J., 205
Ganschinietz, Bill, 403
Gehrman, D. B., 366, 636
Gerberding, Stephen N., 462
Gest, Ted, 269
Gleason, John M., 499
Gluckman, D. M., 404
Goldberg, P., 499
Goldberg, S. B., 607
Goldstein, Leonard, 366
Gomez-Mejia, Luis R., 499
Gore, Nancy, 462
Gorlin Co., H., 177
Gould, R., 326
Grams, Robert, 403
Greenberger, R. S., 499, 581
Greenlaw, Paul S., 140, 141
Gricar, B. G., 499
Griffin, R. W., 177
Griffiths, I. D., 177
Griffiths, R. J., 500
Grove, A. S., 365
Gudenberg, Harry R., 607
Guest, R. H., 177
Guyan, Janet, 78
Gyllenhammer, P. G., 177

Hackman, J. R., 155, 177
Hall, Douglas T., 326, 335
Harris, E. F., 602, 603, 607
Hartman, K., 548
Harvey, B. H., 462
Hayes, R. S., 500
Heflich, Debra E., 524
Hellriegel, D., 78
Henderson, Richard I., 205, 427
Heneman, H. L., 366
Heneman Jr., H. G., 6, 22, 205, 547
Henson, Bob, 52
Hersey, P. S., 70, 78
Hershman, A., 581
Herzberg, F., 62, 78
Hills, F. S., 404, 581
Himes, Gary K., 607
Hitt, M. A., 52, 178
Hodes, Bernard S., 233
Hoerr, John V., 427
Holland, W., 78
Holley, W. H., 365
Hollmann, R. W., 335
Hollon, Charles J., 141

Holmes, W., 52
Hoover, J. J., 499
Hopkins, H. D., 499
House, Robert, 69, 78
Howard, Cecil G., 53
Howard, E., 524
Hoyt, Daniel R., 462, 636
Hull, J. B., 335
Hulvershorn, P., 306
Hunt, O. M., 306
Hymowitz, C., 335

Imberman, Woodruff, 581
Immerwahr, John, 636
Ingrassia, Lawrence, 607

Jackofsky, E. F., 548
Jackson, J. H., 507
Jacobs, Bruce A., 53, 205
Jacobs, Sanford L., 206, 499
Jaffe, N, 336
Jennings, M., 269
Jerdee, Thomas H., 306
Johnson, Arlene A., 636
Johnson, C. M., 178
Johnson, Ronald D., 107
Jones, A. P., 205
Jones, David F., 306
Jones, Harold D., 403

Kahn, Andrew, 269
Kassalow, Everett M., 580
Kastury, U. R., 500
Keaveny, T. J., 365, 581, 607
Kelemon, Kenneth S., 270
Kelleher, J., 548
Keller, R. T., 78, 141, 548
Kellman, S. G., 366
Kelly, Charles M., 140
Kelly, H., 335
Kennedy, M. M., 335
Kesselman, G. A., 547
Kilkpatrick, James J., 141
Kilpatrick, A. C., 336
King, Donald C., 426
Kirkpatrick, Donald L., 300, 306
Kleiman, L. S., 233
Klein, H., 178
Klein, J. A., 607
Klimoski, R. J., 269
Klinger, Donald, 52
Knapp, C. L., 233
Koberg, C. S., 548
Koepp, Stephen, 427
Kohl, John P., 140, 141
Kopelman, R. E., 403, 404
Kovach, Kenneth A., 581

Kram, K. E., 335
Kreitner, Robert, 306
Kruchko, John G., 141
Krupp, N. B., 53
Kushnir, J. M., 500

Lacy, W. B., 177
Lallande, Ann, 636
Langer, Steven, 629, 636
Lanier, A. D., 53
LaRock, Seymour, 461
Larson, Erick, 524
Latham, Gary P., 365
Lawler III, Edward E., 63, 78, 403, 408, 413
Lawrence, D. G., 269
Lawrence, Paul R., 52
LeBon, Susan, 499
Lee, L. S., 548
Leone, R. D., 607
Lester, Richard, 580
Levenson, M. K., 335
Levine, E. L., 205
Levine, H. Z., 335
Levitan, S. A., 178
Levy, J. D., 607
Lewis, J. D., 462, 636
Lewis, Mike, 636
Lifchey, Raymond, 141
Lightkep, P. J., 548
Linnenberger, P., 365
Lombardo, M. W., 335
London, M., 78, 335
Lowell, R. S., 269
Lubbock, James E, 233
Lublin, Joann S., 462, 580, 581
Lulschak, F., 306
Luthans, Fred, 306

MacArthur, A. W., 548
Mahoney, Thomas A., 140
Malabre Jr., A. I., 607
Manaktala, V. K., 206
Manhood, Reg, 426
Mann, Jim, 524
Marino, Kenneth E., 140
Markowitz, J., 205
Marshall, P. B., 524
Martin, D., 336
Maslow, A. H., 61, 78
Mathis, Robert L., 52, 178, 233, 365, 533, 547
Matusewitch, Eric, 141
Mauro, Tony, 141
Mausner, B., 78
McAfee, R. B., 306, 366
McCall, M. W., 335
McConomy, Stephen, 403

McCormick, E. J., 205
McCormick, Karen, 403
McDonough, Wallace, 52
McGregor, Douglas, 61, 78
McGuire, P. J., 366
McIlory, Gary T., 462
McIntyre, D. A., 177
McKersie, Robert B., 607
McMamus, K., 500
McMillan, John D., 403, 427
McMorris, Robert, 499
Merritt-Haston, Ronni, 140
Messer, Richard J., 24, 25, 37
Meyer, G., 548
Michael, C., 306
Middlemist, R. D., 52
Milbourn Jr., Gene, 403
Millard, C. W., 306
Miller, C. B., 365
Miller, John J., 427
Mills, D. Q., 607
Miner, John B., 499
Miner, Mary G., 499
Mitchell, T., 78
Mobley, W. H., 365
Moore, Loretta M., 335
Morris, James R., 433, 461
Morrison, Malcolm H., 233
Moskal, B. S., 365
Mount, M. K., 365
Mowday, R. T., 548
Mrowca, Maryann, 426
Muczyk, Jan P., 306
Mumford, M. D., 365
Murray, T. H., 270
Murray, T. J., 548

Nagel, Thomas, 141
Naisbitt, John B., 636
Nash, Allen N., 306
Nelson, Susan, 53
Newman, J., 53
Nibler, Roger G., 499
Nold, Jon M., 141
Nollen, Stanley D., 163
Norman, Nancy, 140, 461
Norton, Eleanor H., 636
Novit, Mitchell S., 270

Oldham, G. R., 155, 177
Olien, J. D., 270
Oranti, O. A., 22, 462
Orphen, C., 177
Ottemann, Robert, 205
Ouchi, W. G., 178

Pajer, R. G., 365
Pasmore, W. A., 169
Pati, Gopal C., 140
Paul, R. J., 107
Paysor, M. R., 636
Pazy, A., 306
Perham, J., 335
Perlman, S., 581
Perryman, M. Ray, 524
Phillips, Lawrence C., 53
Piker, F., 52
Pine, R. C., 500
Pingpank, Jeffrey C., 140
Pinsker, S., 365
Popa, Mary, 461
Popvich, Paula, 270
Porter, Lyman W., 63, 78
Powell, Gary N., 140
Priefert, L., 404
Prien, Erich P., 269
Prock, Don, 52

Quinn, Joseph F., 403
Quintiere, Gary G., 427

Rahim, Afzalur, 53
Ralston, August, 478
Reed-Mendenhall, D., 306
Rehfuss, John, 52
Rehmus, C. M., 606
Reinharth, Leon, 403
Reisinger, Gregory S., 427
Rhodes, Lucien, 427
Rhodes, S. R., 335
Ribler, R., 306
Ricci, C., 548
Richards, Bill, 498
Richel, Annette U., 335
Ricklefs, Robert, 462, 499
Roach, John M, 636
Robbins, Cheryl B., 426
Robertson, David E., 107
Rocsh, Paul, 499
Rogers, J. F., 461
Rohmann, Laura, 269
Rooney, Andy, 240, 269
Rosen, Benson, 140
Rosenberg, K., 636
Rosow, J. M., 177
Roth, Diane F., 461
Rowe, M. P. 607
Rozen, M., 581
Rumack, Frederick W., 427
Rusbalt, C. E., 403
Rynes, Sara, 140

Salsburg, B. L., 269
Sands, Ben F., 581

Schein, Edgar, 78
Schneider, B., 205
Schultze, J. A. 462
Schuster, M. H., 365
Schwab, D. P., 403
Scott, K. Dow, 426
Scott, Warren E., 404
Searle, Bruce A., 53
Sekas, M. H., 22, 636
Shapiro, K. P., 524
Shepard, J. M., 177
Siegel, Gilbert B., 52
Slocum, J., 78
Snyder, T. C., 270
Snyder, Robert A., 141
Snyderman, B., 78
Sontag, Howard V., 427
Sproull, J. R., 366
Stahl, O. Glen, 52
Staples, Brent, 269
Stavro, Barry, 462
Stillabower, Linda M., 53
Stone, T. H., 548
Stoops, Rick, 233
Stricharchuk, G., 607
Stumpf, S. A., 548
Stutzman, T. M., 205
Swad, Randy G., 426
Swanson, Stephen C., 141
Syrtt, M., 178

Taplin, Polly T., 427
Teague, Burton W., 53
Tedeschi, James T., 140, 461
Tenopyr, Mary L., 269
Thomas, Clarence, 140
Thompson, D. E., 205
Thompson, T. A., 205
Tiffin, J., 205
Todor, William B., 607
Tolchin, Martin, 52
Tolchin, Susan, 52
Tolchinsky, Paul, 426
Tracy, Lane, 524
Traynor, William J., 636
Tschetter, John, 233
Tuller, William L., 270
Tung, Rosalie, 53
Tutelian, L., 336
Twardy, Edward, 52
Tyaqi, P. K., 547
Tyler, Linda S., 427

Urbanski, Al, 426

Vecchio, R., 78
Veiga, J. F., 335

Vettori, Frank L., 306
Von Glinon, M. A., 366
Vroom, Victor H., 63, 78

Waldholz, M., 499
Walker, A. J., 548
Walker, C. R., 177
Walker, James W., 214, 233
Walker, Samuel C., 607
Wallace, Bill, 269
Wallace, Marc J., 403
Wallace, Robert E., 427
Walters, R. W., 335
Walton, Richard E., 607
Wangler, Lawrence, 427

Wanous, John P., 270, 306
Watts, Glenn, 636
Weiss, W. H., 205
Weitzel, William, 547
Wendler, E. R., 78
Wesman, Elizabeth C., 140
Westen, A. F., 548
Wetzul, J. B., 547
Wexley, Kenneth N., 140, 365, 366
White, H. C., 34, 52
Whitehead, D. R., 607
Whittlesey, J. W., 524
Wilhelm, W. R., 335
Williams, Mary, 148, 177
Williams, Valerie C., 403
Winter, R. E., 607

Wofford, J. C., 78
Wolfe, M. N., 34, 52
Wolfe, Stephen H., 427
Wonder, B. D., 270
Wood, Robert C., 580
Woodman, R. W., 78, 548

Yankelovich, Daniel, 636
Yoder, Dale, 205, 547
Young, J. P., 264
Youngblood, Stewart A., 462

Zarley, C., 548
Zeira, Y., 306

Subject Index